**Books are to be returned on or before
the last date below.**

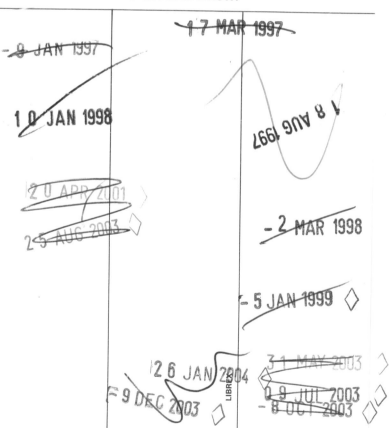

RESEARCH FRAME SYNERGIES

ADVANCES IN CONSUMER RESEARCH, Volume XXIII

Kim P. Corfman and John G. Lynch, Jr., Editors

International Standard Book Number (ISBN): 0-915552-36-1

International Standard Serial Number (ISSN): 0098-9258

Kim P. Corfman and John G. Lynch, Jr., Editors

Advances in Consumer Research, Volume 23

(Provo, UT: Association for Consumer Research, 1996)

Preface

The twenty-third Annual Conference of the Association for Consumer Research was held at the Minneapolis Hilton and Towers in Minneapolis, Minnesota on October 19-22, 1995. This volume is made up of papers that were presented at those meetings.

Forty-two members of the Association served as the Program Committee for the 1995 conference. Following ACR custom, these scholars reviewed the special session proposals. They also gave generously of their time and their ideas for improving the conference experience and taking advantage of the attractions of our host city of Minneapolis. Most of our "innovations" that were actually new—rather than copied from the innovations of recent past co-chairs—came directly from the members of the Program Committee. Another 228 members of the Association served as reviewers for papers in the competitive paper and working paper tracks, with some of these serving further as session chairs and discussion leaders. We are indebted to all of the committed and conscientious scholars whose reviews determined what was to be presented at the conference.

The members of ACR submitted 155 competitive and working papers, and 77 special session proposals for review. Of these, 107 and 42, respectively, were accepted for presentation in Minneapolis and inclusion in this volume. Approximately 600 people attended the conference. We thank all the consumer researchers who submitted papers and proposals, and who presented their work at the conference. ACR remains a vibrant and developing community of scholars, and this volume reflects the current state of the field.

ACR President Don Lehmann chose the conference theme of "Research Frame Synergies". We encouraged papers and sessions that focussed on some common substantive consumption phenomenon or context, bringing together scholars who have worked in disparate methodological and theoretical domains. We were pleased by the number of sessions at the conference that reflected this sort of disciplinary cross-fertilization. Many of the most stimulating and heavily attended sessions at the conference had this quality. We thank Joan Z. Bernstein of the Federal Trade Commission and William Schultz of the Food and Drug Administration for contributing to the interdisciplinary flavor of conference by agreeing to address the ACR membership at our Saturday lunch. They spoke about consumer protection initiatives at their respective agencies and the roles ACR members could play in conducting research to inform those initiatives. Their papers in this volume provide more guidance about where we can make meaningful contributions to current public policy initiatives at the FTC and FDA.

We also want to thank a number of other people whose behind the scenes work made the conference possible. Keith Hunt is a human repository of ACR history and procedures, and plain wisdom. We could not have done our jobs without his help. We also benefitted greatly from the advice of those who co-chaired the last several conferences. We copied some of their innovations and their collective experience kept us from starting at the very bottom of the experience curve. Jeff Inman wrote and ran the program that helps match reviewers and papers for the competitive and working paper tracks. Jim Muncy and Steve Barnett handled the process of converting hundreds of diskettes into the volume you are now reading. Akshay Rao and Barbara Loken were Arrangements Co-Chairs. They selflessly and diligently researched restaurants and nightclubs to advise us on where to spend our evenings, evaluated potential special event sites, handled arrangements for our great field observation at the Mall of America, helped set up our inaugural working paper poster session, and recruited Minneapolis business leaders to participate in the conference. We also want to thank Julie Ritter and Jenny Ryan for excellent secretarial support, and doctoral students at the University of Florida and at New York University—especially Stacy Wood—who helped in many ways.

Finally, we want to thank ACR President Don Lehmann for his faith in us in asking us to serve as co-chairs. We had a great time working with each other and with all of the colleagues mentioned above whose collective work and cooperation made the conference happen.

Kim P. Corfman, New York University
John G. Lynch, Jr., University of Florida
1995 ACR Conference Co-chairs / Proceedings Editors

Margaret C. Campbell

Ziv Carmon

Jeff T. Casey

Goutam Chakraborty

Murali Chandrashekaran

Subimal Chatterjee

Cindy Clark

Cathy Cole

Leslie Cole

Larry D. Compeau

Joseph A. Cote

Eloise Coupey

Deborah Ann Cours

Elizabeth H. Creyer

Mary T. Curren

Pratibha A. Dabholkar

Peter Dacin

John Deighton

Albert J. Della Bitta

Ravi Dhar

Alan S. Dick

Cornelia Droge

Julie A. Edell

Dogan Eroglu

Pete Fader

Corinne Faure

Lawrence F. Felck

Fred Feinberg

Marla Felcher

Leslie Fine

Robert J. Fisher

Susan M. Fournier

Karen Russo France

Meryl P. Gardner

Hubert Gatignon

Charles Gengler

Elisabeth Gilster

Peter Golder

Ronald C. Goodstein

Stephen Gould

Donald H. Granbois

Kent Grayson

Eric Greenleaf

Michael Guiry

Bruce Hardie

Bari A. Harlam

William D. Harris

Manoj Hastak

Curtis P. Haugtvedt

William J. Havlena

Susan E. Heckler

Deborah D. Heisley

Paul M. Herr

Ron Hill

Elizabeth C. Hirschman

Jacqueline C. Hitchon

Susan L. Holak

Stephen Holden

Douglas B. Holt

Daniel J. Howard

Wayne D. Hoyer

Cynthia D. Huffman

Eva M. Hyatt

Julie Irwin

Shailendra P. Jain

David Jamison

Gita Venkataramani Johar

Richard D. Johnson

Joseph M. Jones

Annamma Joy

Lynn R. Kahle

Harold H. Kassarjian

James J. Kellaris

Kevin Lane Keller

Punam Anand Keller

Tina Kiesler

Amna Kirmani

Jill G. Klein

Noreen M. Klein

Susan Shultz Kleine

Robert E. Kleine III

Aradhna Krishna

H. Shanker Krishnan

Kathleen T. Lacher

France Leclerc

Angela Lee

Moonkyu Lee

Roxanne Lefkoff-Hagius

Katherine N. Lemon

Donald R. Lichtenstein

Therese A. Louie

Mary Frances Luce

Karen A. Machleit

Gerry Macintosh

Scott B. MacKenzie

Carole Macklin

Jayashree Mahajan

Durairaj Maheswaran

Ken C. Manning

Howard Marmorstein

Mary C. Martin

Charlotte H. Mason

Leigh McAlister

John A. McCarty

Ann L. McGill

Kim McKeage

Edward F. McQuarrie

Geeta Menon

Satya Menon

Joan Meyers-Levy

David Mick

Paul W. Miniard

Sanjay Mishra

Deborah Mitchell

Andrew Mitchell

John Mittelstaedt

Todd A. Mooradian

Elizabeth S. Moore-Shay

Maureen Morrin

Vicki Morwitz

David L. Mothersbaugh

Carol M. Motley

James A. Muncy

Amitabh R. Mungalé

A.V. Muthukrishnan

Sunder Narayanan

Prakash Nedungadi

Steve Nowlis

Suzanne O'Curry

Thomas O'Guinn

T.J. Olney

Julie Ozanne

Thomas J. Page

Yigang Pan

Greta Eleen Pennell

Michel T. Pham

Carol Pluzinski

Manuel C. Pontes

Drazen Prelec

Lydia Price

William J. Qualls

Priya Raghubir

S. Ramaswami

S. Ratneshwar

Srinivas Reddy

Peter H. Reingen

Dennis W. Rook

Bill Ross

John R. Rossiter

Martin S. Roth

Julie Ruth

Arti Sahni

John Sailors

Mohanbir Sawhney

Robert Schindler

Bernd H. Schmitt

Wendy Schneier

Jonathan Schroeder

David W. Schumann

Sankar Sen

Stewart Shapiro

L.J. Shrum

Surendra N. Singh

Atanu Sinha

Jackie Snell

Michael R. Solomon

Mark T. Spence

Susan Spiggle

Richard A. Spreng

Douglas M. Stayman

Joel Steckel

Debra Stephens

Michal Strahilevitz

Saroja Subrahmanyan

Alka Subramanian

Suresh Subramanian

Harish Sujan

Fareena Sultan

Patriya S. Tansuhaj

Nader Tavassoli

Kimberly A. Taylor

Kelly Tepper

Rajiv Vaidyanathan

Alladi Venkatesh

Robert W. Veryzer, Jr.

Madhubalan Viswanathan

Beth A. Walker

Wanda H. Wallace

Michaela Wanke

Brian Wansink

Luk Warlop

Klaus Wertenbroch

Patricia M. West

Elizabeth J. Wilson

Cecelia Wittmayer

Robert B. Woodruff

David B. Wooten

Newell D. Wright

Richard Yalch

Rami Zwick

Table of Contents and Conference Program

ASSOCIATION FOR CONSUMER RESEARCH ANNUAL CONFERENCE

OCTOBER 19-22, 1995
MINNEAPOLIS, MINNESOTA

THURSDAY, OCTOBER 19

ACR BOARD OF DIRECTORS MEETING
11:00 a.m. - 5:00 p.m.

REGISTRATION
4:00 - 7:30 p.m.

RECEPTION
5:30 - 7:30 p.m.

FRIDAY, OCTOBER 20

REGISTRATION
8:00 - 11:50 a.m.

SESSION ROOMS AVAILABLE FOR ROUNDTABLES
7:00 - 8:20 a.m.

SCP EXECUTIVE COMMITTEE MEETING
7:00 - 8:30 a.m.

NEWCOMERS' WELCOME BREAKFAST
7:30 - 8:30 a.m.

1.1   Special Session: The Dynamics of Preference

Chair: Christina L. Brown, New York University
Discussion Leader: Drazen Prelec, Massachusetts Institute of Technology

Hedonic Planning vs. Local Maximization: Do Consumers Avoid Repeated Consumption of Favorite
Pleasures in Order to Protect Future Tastes?
          Barbara Kahn, The University of Pennsylvania
          Rebecca K. Ratner, Princeton University
          Daniel Kahneman, Princeton University

The Effects of Time on the Valuation and Perceived Attractiveness of One's Current and Former Possessions
          Michal Strahilevitz, University of Illinois at Urbana-Champaign
          George Loewenstein, Carnegie Mellon University
          Daniel Kahneman, Princeton University

Consumption Vocabulary and Preference Formation
          Patricia M. West, The University of Texas at Austin
          Christina L. Brown, New York University
          Stephen J. Hoch, The University of Chicago

1.2   Special Session: Will You Still Love Me Tomorrow: Dynamic Developments in Service Quality and
**   Customer Retention**

Chair: Katherine N. Lemon, Duke University
Discussion Leader: Donald Lehmann, Columbia University

The Quality Double Whammy: The Rich Stay Rich and The Poor Stay Poor
          William Boulding, Duke University
          Ajay Kalra, Carnegie Mellon University
          Richard Staelin, Duke University

A Bayesian Model of Quality and Customer Retention
          Roland Rust, Vanderbilt University
          Jeffrey Inman, University of Wisconsin-Madison
          Anthony Zahorik, Burke Institute

A Longitudinal Test of the Investment Model: Towards a Conceptual Framework for Understanding Customer
Retention and Disadoption
          Tiffany Barnett, Duke University
          Katherine N. Lemon, Duke University

1.6 *Competitive Paper Session*: **Qualitative Investigations of Consumer Experience**

Chair: Howard Marmorstein, University of Miami
Discussion Leader: Edward McQuarrie, Santa Clara University

1.7 *Competitive Paper Session*: **Effects of Advertising on Emotions, Attitudes, Evaluations, and Intentions**

Chair: Michael J. Barone, Florida International University
Discussion Leader: Luk Warlop, Katholic University of Leuven

FRIDAY, OCTOBER 20

SESSION 2
10:20 - 11:50 a.m.

2.1 *Special Session*: **Imposed School Dress Codes: Implications for Consumer Behavior and Consumer Behavior Implications for Understanding the Long-Term Effects of Dress Codes**

Chair: Marian Friestad, University of Oregon
Discussion Leader
and Organizer: Terence A. Shimp, University of South Carolina

Idols of the Tribe: Imposed Dress Codes and the Reformation of Group Identity among School-Aged Children
David Jamison, University of Florida

You Are What You Wear: The Meaning of Brand Names to Children
Deborah Roedder John, University of Minnesota

Sociological Perspectives on Imposed Dress Codes: Consumption as Attempted Suppression of Class and Wealth Symbolism
Melanie Wallendorf, University of Arizona
David Crockett, University of Arizona

2.2   *Special Session*: **Inferences about Pricing and Promotion**

Chair: Joel E. Urbany, University of Notre Dame
Discussion Leaders: Peter Dickson, University of Wisconsin-Madison
                             Mark Heckman, Marsh Supermarkets, Inc.

Special Session Summary

Carl F. Mela, University of Notre Dame
Joel E. Urbany, University of Notre Dame

Consumer Inferences about Retail Promotions
Jeffrey Inman, University of Wisconsin-Madison
Carl F. Mela, University of Notre Dame
K. Patrick Meline, University of Wisconsin-Madison
Joel E. Urbany, University of Notre Dame

The Manufacturer-Retailer-Consumer Triad: Differing Perceptions Regarding Price Promotions
Aradhna Krishna, Columbia University
Bari Harlam, University of Rhode Island
Page Moreau, Columbia University

"Schemer Schema" Influences on Consumers' Perceptions of Fair Pricing
Margaret C. Campbell, University of California-Los Angeles

2.3   *Special Session*: **When You're Happy and You Know It...: Self-Referencing, Memory, and Affect**

Chairs: Gita Venkataramani Johar, Columbia University
                             Geeta Menon, New York University
Discussion Leader: Mita Sujan, Pennsylvania State University

Special Session Summary

Gita Venkataramani Johar, Columbia University
Geeta Menon, New York University

The Effect of Self-Referencing on Persuasion and Recall
Joan Meyers-Levy, University of Chicago
Laura A. Peracchio, University of Wisconsin-Milwaukee

Valence Of Personal Vs. Product Experiences: What Do You Remember When You're Feeling Blue?
Geeta Menon, New York University

Feelings as Information: The Impact of Moods on Judgment and Processing Strategies
Norbert Schwarz, University of Michigan

2.4 *Special Session*: **The Changing American Family: Causes, Consequences and Considerations for Consumer Research**

Chairs: Aric Rindfleisch, University of Wisconsin-Madison
                     James E. Burroughs, University of Wisconsin-Madison
Discussion Leader: Donald H. Granbois, Indiana University

2.5 *Special Session*: **Understanding Consumer Response to Cause-Related Marketing**

Chairs: Ida E. Berger, Queen's University
                     M. Peggy Cunningham, Queen's University
Discussion Leader: Minette Drumwright, University of Texas-Austin

2.6 *Competitive Paper Session*: **Cross-Cultural Differences in Markets and Consumers**

Chair: John Mittelstaedt, University of Wyoming
Discussion Leader: Corinne Faure, Virginia Polytechnic Institute and State University

2.7   *Competitive Paper Session*: **Qualitative Investigations of Symbolic Consumption**

Chair: Charles Gengler, Rutgers University-Camden
Discussion Leader: Susan Spiggle, University of Connecticut

FRIDAY, OCTOBER 20

LUNCHEON
12:00 - 2:00 p.m.

ACR BUSINESS MEETING

PRESENTATION OF AWARDS

PRESIDENTIAL ADDRESS
Donald R. Lehmann,
"Knowledge and the Conventions of
Consumer Research: A Study in Inconsistency"

3.3 *Special Session*: Cognitive Aging in Consumer Contexts

Chair: Carolyn Yoon, University of Toronto
Discussion Leader: Catherine Cole, University of Iowa

Special Session Summary

Circadian Arousal and Cognitive Functioning
Cynthia P. May, University of Arizona
Lynn Hasher, Duke University

Age Differences in Consumers' Processing Strategies and Implications for Persuasion
Carolyn Yoon, University of Toronto
Lynn Hasher, Duke University

Are Aging Consumers More Vulnerable to the Belief Enhancing Effects of Repetition?
Sharmistha Law, University of Toronto
Fergus I. M. Craik, University of Toronto

3.4 *Special Session*: **Who Am I and Who Do You Think I Am? The Role of Role in Consumers' Responses to Advertising, Sales, and Service Interactions**

Chairs: Jennifer Aaker, University of California-Los Angeles
Margaret C. Campbell, University of California-Los Angeles
Discussion Leader: Peter Wright, Stanford University

Special Session Summary

Why Did She Do Thaty?': The Important Influence of Situational Role on Perceptions of Others' Behavior
Margaret C. Campbell, University of California-Los Angeles

This Bud is NOT for You: The Processing and Effects of Target and Non-Target Marketing
Jennifer Aaker, University of California-Los Angeles
Anne Brumbaugh, Duke University
Sonya Grier, Northwestern University

The Self-Conscious Consumer: Effects of Anticipation and Actual Evaluation of the Consumer by the Service Provider
Aimee Drolet, Stanford University
Punam Anand Keller, University of North Carolina
Ann L. McGill, Northwestern University

3.5 *Special Session*: **Let's Talk Shop: Multiple Interpretive Perspectives on Studying Consumer Shopping Behavior**

Chair: Michelle Nelson, University of Illinois at Urbana-Champaign
Discussion Leader: Nancy Ridgway, University of Colorado

Special Session Summary

3.6   *Competitive Paper Session*: Consuming the Internet

Chair: Allan D. Shocker, University of Minnesota / Hong Kong University of Science and Technology
Discussion Leader: Michael Guiry, Fairleigh Dickinson University

3.7   *Competitive Paper Session*: Environmental Behavior Across Cultures

Chair: Dogan Eroglu, Georgia State University
Discussion Leader: Therese Louie, University of Washington

3.8   1996 ACR Program Committee Meeting

Chairs: Merrie L. Brucks, University of Arizona
                   Deborah J. MacInnis, University of Southern California

---

FRIDAY, OCTOBER 20

SESSION 4
4:00 - 5:30 p.m.

4.9   Working Paper Session

1. *The Role of Affect in Buyer-Seller Dyads: Its Relationship to Shared Values and Trust*
    Carolyn Y. Nicholson, Clarkson University
    Larry D. Compeau, Clarkson University
    Rajesh Sethi, Clarkson University

2. *The Role of Prior Affect and Sensory Cues on Consumers' Affective and Cognitive Responses and Overall Perceptions of Quality*
    Larry D. Compeau, Clarkson University
    Kent B. Monroe, University of Illinois at Urbana-Champaign

3. *Using the Sorting Task to Examine Product Representations in Consumer Research*
    Madhubalan Viswanathan, University of Illinois at Urbana-Champaign
    Michael Johnson, University of Michigan
    Seymour Sudman, University of Illinois at Urbana-Champaign

4. *Separating the Different Forms of Familiarity-Generated Affect for Marketing Stimuli*
    Marc Vanhuele, Groupe HEC

5. *Attitude Accessibility, Priming Typical and Less Typical Products, and Attitude-Behavior Correspondence*
    Joann Peck, University of Minnesota
    Barbara Loken, University of Minnesota

6. *Memory Based Comparisons of Brand Attributes: The Effects of Task, Information Format, and Information Mode*
    Madhubalan Viswanathan, University of Illinois at Urbana-Champaign
    Sunder Narayanan, University of Illinois at Urbana-Champaign

7. *Concept Mapping as a Research Tool: Uncovering Consumers' Knowledge Structure Associations*
    Christopher Joiner, University of Minnesota

8. *Relational Processing, But Type A or Type B?*
    Karen Finlay, University of Guelph

9. *How Much Will I Spend? Factors Affecting Consumers' Estimates of Future Expense*
    Geeta Menon, New York University
    Priya Raghubir, Hong Kong University of Science and Technology
    Norbert Schwarz, University of Michigan

10. *The Inter-Stimulus Interval: Can You Have Too Much of a Good Thing?*
    G. Douglas Olsen, University of Calgary

11. *The Many Faces of Credit Card Consumption: An Exercise in Scale Development*
    Arti Sahni, University of San Diego

12. *Gift Giving at Childbirth: All Fathers Are Not Created Equal*
    Kathleen A. O'Donnell, San Francisco State University

FRIDAY, OCTOBER 20

JCR Editorial Board Meeting
5:30 - 7:00 p.m.

Reception
5:30 - 7:30 p.m.

SATURDAY, OCTOBER 21

Session Rooms Available for Roundtables
7:00 - 8:05 a.m.

JCP Editorial Board Meeting
7:00 - 8:15 a.m.

Registration
8:00 - 11:30 a.m.

SATURDAY, OCTOBER 21

SESSION 5
8:15 - 9:45 a.m.

5.1 *Special Session*: Community Matters: Research on Consumer Experiences of Communal Relationships in a Postmodern World

Chairs: Craig J. Thompson, University of Wisconsin
Douglas B. Holt, Pennsylvania State University
Discussion Leader: David Mick, University of Wisconsin-Madison

5.2 *Special Session*: Building Brand Equity Through Packaging: A Multi-Methodological Perspective

Chair: Robert Underwood, Virginia Polytechnic Institute and State University
Discussion Leader: Stephen J. Hoch, University of Chicago

6.1   *Special Session*: **Does Economics Have Anything to Say About Consumer Behavior?**

Chair: Russell S. Winer, University of California-Berkeley
Discussion Leader: Kent Nakamoto, University of Colorado

Special Session Summary
        Russell S. Winer, University of California-Berkeley

Learning From Each Other
        Sridhar Moorthy, University of Rochester

The Effect of Brand Experience on Extension Choice Probabilities: An Empirical Analysis
        Byung-do Kim, Carnegie Mellon University
        Mary Sullivan, University of Chicago

The Role of Inference in Context Effects
        Drazen Prelec, Massachusetts Institute of Technology
        Birger Wernerfelt, Massachusetts Institute of Technology
        Florian Zettelmeyer, Massachusetts Institute of Technology

Discounting and its Impact on Durables Buying Decisions
        Russell S. Winer, University of California-Berkeley

6.2   *Special Session*: **Communities of Consumption: A Central Metaphor for Diverse Research**

Chair: Christine Wright-Isak, Young & Rubicam Advertising
Discussion Leader: Barbara Stern, Rutgers University

Special Session Summary
        Christine Wright-Isak, Young & Rubicam Advertising

Brand Community and the Sociology of Brands
        Albert Muniz, Jr., University of Illinois at Urbana-Champaign
        Thomas C. O'Guinn, University of Illinois at Urbana-Champaign

The Community of Brands: Social Constructions of Meaning
        Arthur J. Kover, Fordham University

Triangulating Methods to Study Community Phenomena: Discovering the Whole is Greater than the Sum of its Members
        Christine Wright-Isak, Young & Rubicam Advertising

6.5   *Special Session*: **New Insights into Variety Seeking**

Chairs: Michal Strahilevitz, University of Illinois at Urbana-Champaign
                     Daniel Read, University of Illinois at Urbana-Champaign
Discussion Leader: Leigh McAlister, University of Texas-Austin

Special Session Summary

Variety for Sale: Mass Customization or Mass Confusion?
        Cynthia Huffman, University of Pennsylvania
        Barbara Kahn, University of Pennsylvania

Variety Seeking in Charitable Giving
        Michal Strahilevitz, University of Illinois at Urbana-Champaign

Choice Bracketing as a Cause of Situational Differences in Variety Seeking
        Daniel Read, University of Illinois at Urbana-Champaign
        George Loewenstein, Carnegie-Mellon University

6.6   *Competitive Paper Session*: **Consumer Memory**

Chair: Susan M. Broniarczyk, University of Texas-Austin
Discussion Leader: Carol Pluzinski, New York University

6.7   *Competitive Paper Session*: **Influencing Brand Equity**

Chair: Maureen Morrin, Boston University
Discussion Leader: Paul M. Herr, University of Colorado-Denver

```
SATURDAY, OCTOBER 21

LUNCHEON
11:45 a.m. - 2:15 p.m.


ACR Fellow Address
Elizabeth Hirschman
"On Being A Female Fellow: My Life As an Oxymoron"


Guest Speakers


Joan Z. Bernstein
Director, Federal Trade Commission
Bureau of Consumer Protection


William B. Schultz
Deputy Commissioner for Policy,
Food and Drug Administration
```

```
SATURDAY, OCTOBER 21

SESSION 7
2:15 - 3:45 p.m.
```

7.1 *Special Session*: **Something's Missing: Modern Cognitive Approaches to Decision Making with Incomplete Information**

Chair: Julie R. Irwin, New York University
Discussion Leader: Robert Meyer, University of Pennsylvania

Special Session Summary

Image Theory and the First Phase: How are Consideration Sets Formed When Information is Missing?
        Joydeep Srivastava, University of California-Berkeley
        Gillian Naylor, University of Arizona
        Lee Roy Beach, University of Arizona

When is Constructive Processing Necessary? Familiarity and Reasoning in Judgment and Choice
        Eloise Coupey, Virginia Polytechnic Institute and State University
        Julie R. Irwin, New York University
        John W. Payne, Duke University

Inference Generation and Correction: Cognitive Capacity and the Use of Relevant Cues
        Gita V. Johar, Columbia University
        Carolyn G. Simmons, Lehigh University

7.2   *Presidential Session*: **Another Cup of Coffee: The View from Different Frames (Double Session)**

Chair: Donald R. Lehmann, Columbia University
Discussion Leader: Jay Russo, Cornell University

7.3   *Special Session*: **Consuming Experiences and Experiencing Consumption: It's Not What You Consume, But How You Consume It**

Chair: Ruth Ann Smith, Virginia Polytechnic Institute and State University
Discussion Leader: Marsha Richins, University of Missouri

7.4 *Special Session*: **Panel Discussion on Information Gaps in Public Policy: Things I Have Been Told But Don't Quite Believe—Can Consumer Researchers Help?**

Chair: Joel B. Cohen, University of Florida

Special Session Summary

Panel Discussion and Audience Question and Answer
    Joan Z. Bernstein, Director, Federal Trade Commission, Bureau of Consumer Protection
    William B. Schultz, Deputy Commissioner for Policy, Food and Drug Administration
    Andrew J. Strenio, Jr., Hunton & Williams
    Joel B. Cohen, University of Florida
    William L. Wilkie, University of Notre Dame

7.5 *Special Session*: **ACR/JCR Robert Ferber Awards**

    Brian Sternthal, Editor, *Journal of Consumer Research*

Goal-Oriented Experiences and the Development of Knowledge
    Cynthia Huffman, University of Pennsylvania
    Michael J. Houston, University of Minnesota

Atraesando Fronteras/Border Crossings: A Critical Ethnographic Exploration of the Consumer Acculturation of Mexican Immigrants
    Lisa Peñaloza, University of Colorado

Toward a Reconciliation of Advertising Effects on Price Elasticity
    Anusree Mitra, American University
    John G. Lynch, Jr., University of Florida

7.6 *Competitive Paper Session*: **Self-Concept Formation and Expression**

Chair: Tina Kiesler, Rutgers University
Discussion Leader: Thomas O'Guinn, University of Illinois at Urbana-Champaign

Constellations, Configurations, and Consumption: Exploring Patterns of Consumer Behavior Amongst U.K. Shoppers
    Margaret K. Hogg, University College Salford
    Paul C.N. Michell, University of Manchester

7.7 *Competitive Paper Session*: Affect, Mood, and Emotion

Chair: Hans Baumgartner, Pennsylvania State University
Discussion Leader: Ronald C. Goodstein, University of California-Los Angeles

---

SATURDAY, OCTOBER 21

SESSION 8
4:00 - 5:30 p.m.

8.1 *Special Session*: Customers in Organizational Context: How Organizations' Decisions Incorporate Customer Information

Chair: Prakash Nedungadi, Indiana University
Discussion Leader: Ajay K. Kohli, University of Texas-Austin

Special Session Summary

Engineering Customer Experiences
Lewis P. Carbone, Carbone and Company, Ltd.

When the Manager Becomes the Measure: The Use of Personal Information in the Development of Managers' Understanding of Consumers
Christine Moorman, University of Wisconsin-Madison

Foundations of a Customer Orientation: The Content of Managers' Knowledge About Customers
Prakash Nedungadi, Indiana University
Beverly B. Tyler, Indiana University

8.2 *Presidential Session*: Another Cup of Coffee: The View from Different Frames (Continuation of Double Session, abstracts under 7.2)

Chair: Donald R. Lehmann, Columbia University
Discussion Leader: Jay Russo, Cornell University

Insights from Scanner Panel Data
Randy Bucklin, University of California-Los Angeles
Sunil Gupta, Columbia University

Loyalty and Brand Recall: Good 'til the Last Name Drops
   Eric J. Johnson, University of Pennsylvania
   Wes Hutchinson, University of Pennsylvania

Interpersonal Relationship Perspective on Loyalty
   Susan Fournier, Harvard University
   Julie Yao, Harvard University

Game Theory Perspective on Loyalty
   Jagmohan S. Raju, University of Pennsylvania

Loyalty as Portrayed in Ads and Media
   William D. Wells, University of Minnesota

Social Customs Influence on Coffee Usage and Brand Loyalty
   Christine Wright-Isak, Young & Rubicam Advertising

8.3   *Special Session*: Consumers "R" Us: Exploring the World of Children's Consumer Behavior

Chairs: Leslie Cole, Tulane University
                     Greta Eleen Pennell, Rutgers University
Discussion Leader: Carole Macklin, University of Cincinnati

Understanding the Purchase Influence Attempts of Young Children: Moving from Self-Accounts to a Scale Based on Social Power Theory
   Laura A. Williams, Louisiana State University
   Alvin C. Burns, Louisiana State University

Why Some Girls are Harmed by the Presence of Beautiful Models in Ads and Others Benefit: Investigating the Convoluted Role of Motives for Comparison
   Mary Martin, University of North Carolina at Charlotte
   James W. Gentry, University of Nebraska-Lincoln
   Patricia F. Kennedy, University of Nebraska-Lincoln

Measuring Materialism in Children
   Greta Eleen Pennell, Rutgers University
   Leslie Cole, Tulane University

8.4   *Special Session*: Magic and Consumer Behavior

Chair: Cele Otnes, University of Illinois at Urbana-Champaign
Discussion Leader: John F. Sherry, Jr., Northwestern University

Natural Magic: Packaging the Transformative Power of Nature
   Eric J. Arnould, University of South Florida
   Linda L. Price, University of South Florida

The Magic of the Maker: Witchcraft and Cosmetics in American History
   Linda M. Scott, University of Illinois at Urbana-Champaign

The Transformative Power of Products
   Cele Otnes, University of Illinois at Urbana-Champaign

8.5 *Special Session*: **Meet the Editors**

Chair: Harold H. Kassarjian, University of California-Los Angeles

Dipankar Chakravarti, *Journal of Consumer Psychology*
Brian Sternthal, *Journal of Consumer Research*
TBA, *Journal of Marketing*
Russell S. Winer, *Journal of Marketing Research*
Robert J. Meyer, *Marketing Letters*
Wes Hutchinson, *Marketing Science*

8.6 *Competitive Paper Session*: **Sociological Analysis**

Chair: L. J. Shrum, Rutgers University
Discussion Leader: Paul Anderson, Pennsylvania State University

8.7 *Competitive Paper Session*: **Country of Origin Effects**

Chair: Deepak Sirdeshmukh, Case Western Reserve University
Discussion Leader: Durairaj Maheswaran, New York University

SUNDAY, OCTOBER 22

Session Rooms Available for Roundtables
7:00 - 8:20 a.m.

JCR Policy Board Meeting
8:00 a.m. - 3:00 p.m.

SESSION 9
8:30 - 10:00 a.m.

9.1 *Special Session*: **Real Things: The Social and Symbolic Value of Genuine Products and Brands**

Chair: Kent Grayson, London Business School
Discussion Leader: Barbara B. Stern, Rutgers University

Special Session Summary

Seeing Double? Consumers' Perceptions of Similarity Between Original Products and Knockoffs
        Charlotte Mason, University of North Carolina-Chapel Hill
        Roxanne Lefkoff-Hagius, University of Maryland
        Yih Hwai Lee, University of North Carolina-Chapel Hill

The Genuine Article: Product Authenticity and its Value to Consumers
        Kent Grayson, London Business School
        David Shulman, Northwestern University

To Thine Own Self Be True: The Meaning of Sincerity In Brands and Its Impact on Consumer Attitudes
        Jennifer Aaker, University of California-Los Angeles
        Aimee Drolet, Stanford University

9.2 *Special Session*: **New Perspectives on Brand Differentiation**

Chairs: Alex Chernev, Duke University
                Ziv Carmon, Duke University
Discussion Leader: Ziv Carmon, Duke University

Special Session Summary

Consumer Response to Differentiation and Defensive Imitation
        Gregory S. Carpenter, Northwestern University
        Donald R. Lehmann, Columbia University
        Kent Nakamoto, University of Colorado
        Suzanne Walchli, Babson College

Differentiation through Similarity: The Effect of Attribute Similarity on Brand Choice
        Alex Chernev, Duke University

Differentiation in Multiattribute Space: An Alternative Explanation of the Asymmetric Dominance Effect
        Dan Ariely, Duke University
        Thomas Wallsten, University of North Carolina-Chapel Hill

9.3 *Special Session*: **Capturing The Dynamics Of Consumption Emotions Experienced During Extended Service Encounters**

Chairs: Laurette Dubé, McGill University
Michael S. Morgan, Cornell University
Discussion Leader: Douglas M. Stayman, Cornell University

Special Session Summary

Using Participant Observation to Unravel Emotional Moments of Extended Service Encounters
Eric J. Arnould, University of South Florida
Linda L. Price, University of South Florida
Angela Hausman, University of South Florida

Dynamic Modeling of Hedonic Consumption Experience
Jehoshua Eliashberg, University of Pennsylvania
Mohanbir S. Sawhney, Northwestern University

Gender Differences in Retrospective Judgments of Consumption Emotions in Extended Service Transactions
Laurette Dubé, Université de Montreal
Michael S. Morgan, Cornell University

9.4 *Special Session*: **A Forum On Health-Related Consumer Behavior**

Chairs: Meryl P. Gardner, University of Delaware
William D. Harris, Quinnipiac College
Discussion Leader: Stephen J. Hoch, University of Chicago

Special Session Summary

A Model of Consumer Health-Related Behavior: Conceptual Development and Empirical Test
William D. Harris, Quinnipiac College
Meryl P. Gardner, University of Delaware

An Investigation of the Effects of the Nutritional Labeling and Education Act on Consumer Behavior
Christine Moorman, University of Wisconsin

Message Framing and Cancer-related Consumer Behavior
Peter Salovey, Yale University
Alexander Rothman, University of Minnesota

9.5 *Competitive Paper Session*: **Product Perception and Preference**

Chair: Amitabh Mungalé, Rutgers University
Discussion Leader: Jackie Snell, San Jose State University

9.6   *Competitive Paper Session*: Health and Safety Issues

Chair: Elisabeth Gilster, University of Arizona
Discussion Leader: Alan Andreasen, Georgetown University

9.7   *Competitive Paper Session*: Social Influence

Chair: Wendy Schneier, Boston University
Discussion Leader: Peter Reingen, Arizona State University

SUNDAY, OCTOBER 22

SESSION 10
10:20 - 11:50 a.m.

10.1   *Special Session*: The Necessity of Metaphorical Reasoning and its Effect on Knowledge Representation and Decision Making

Chair: George S. Babbes, University of California at Berkeley
Discussion Leader: William D. Wells, University of Minnesota

Special Session Summary

10.7 *Competitive Paper Session*: **Music and Shopping**

Chair: Karen Machleit, University of Cincinnati
Discussion Leader: Richard Yalch, University of Washington

Knowledge Generalization and the Conventions of Consumer Research: A Study in Inconsistency

Donald R. Lehmann, Columbia University

Alas that it should come to this. Lunch is over and there is no graceful way to exit. Perhaps I should proclaim that here is a second dessert. It doesn't get any better than that, does it?

First, some background. In terms of important career goals, I considered running for President; after all I own a house in New Hampshire. However, I was first eligible in the inauspicious year of 1984. Also, having received two-thirds of the votes cast when running as the only candidate on the ballot for one of three seats on a local school board (which suggests one-third of the voters knew who I was), the karma seemed wrong.

I considered a career in athletics, possibly as an Olympian (Atlanta '96 is less than a year away), but the pie eating contest isn't even a demonstration event and my role model is Rudy. Coaching also seemed out of the question, having been fired twice by the same high school as a football coach (fool me twice, ...?).

Thus I realized my true calling: an academic. Unfortunately, while academics like to talk, we don't always have much to say.

In thinking what to say today, I made extensive use of my research on delay in decision making: I delayed. Next I thought about incorporating the delightful personal touches that my predecessors have included. Unfortunately I'm not artistically talented, being better suited to moving or chainsawing a piano than playing one, and I suspect you aren't interested in my prized collection of old Converse Chuck Taylor sneakers.

Eventually I decided to talk about consumer research from the perspective of meta-analysis, that is the goal of accumulating knowledge. In keeping with the spirit of this talk which questions many of our conventions, I present no references. I do want to acknowledge the tremendous debt we all owe to those who have preceded us. I specifically acknowledge my Purdue professors and my colleagues at Columbia. What I know is a reflection of their inspiration.

I begin by making several observations about the field, offer a brief explanation for them, and then make some suggestions, hopefully in time for a break before the next sessions begin. Incidentally, there are three reasons I use regular overheads here rather than color slides. First, slides require more money and effort and I'm cheap and lazy. Second, I'm tired of the escalating competition in education in terms of fancy presentations. I view this as a prisoner's dilemma with no real benefit to students and certainly a cost to me. In the words of Poe's Bartleby the Scribner, "I Prefer not." And finally I suspect that if I turn the lights down, some of you might take the opportunity to depart gracefully or nod off and we wouldn't want that, now would we?

I make these observations about consumer research from the perspective of someone who was trained as a quantitative researcher, works in a business school, is proud to have been associated with MSI, and perhaps most important is a major proponent of meta-analysis as both a technique and, more important here, a way of thinking about research. This frame that I bring to the discussion is neither right nor wrong (though my tastes lean to calling it right) but rather may explain certain emphases and omissions.

The basic logic behind this talk is:
PREMISES:

1. The purpose of academic research is to produce generalizations.
2. Meta-Analysis is the process of generalizing across different studies/results by establishing a base result (i.e., average) and systematic differences.

CONCLUSION:

The purpose of academic research is to prepare for (and occasionally perform) meta-analysis.

While generally thought of as a technique for summarizing of quantitative results, the basic thought process of meta-analysis applies to qualitative work as well. Any single study, no matter how well executed, has an infinite number of covariates that could potentially explain the results. By contrast, generalizations can emerge only from a collection of studies. Taking this point of view, a number of observations seem to follow:

1. THEORY, TYRANNY, AND EMPIRICAL GENERALIZATION

In the "it would be nice to have" category for advancing knowledge, two things seem particularly desirable. The first is the identification of a repeatable phenomenon, A.K.A. an empirical regularity. That is, part of knowledge development involves establishing patterns that are likely to recur in the future. The limitation to much case and qualitative work is that it focuses on the particular situation in detail (which is good) without much concern for what other situations are similar or where the same patterns might recur (which is bad if your goal is general knowledge).

The second major desideratum is an explanation for what happened (note how anyone with a dictionary can use big words). While understanding why something occurs (the causal mechanism) is desirable, a simple descriptive story often provides value. Notice that rather than the value laden term theory (as in, don't submit a paper without it), I use the term "story." For all the homage we pay to the concept of theory, theory is basically a story that describes how, and where possible why, a phenomenon works. The current operational definition of a theory seems to be a story someone else managed to get published.

The appropriate goal of academic research is to develop empirically supported theory (stories). I prefer theory that is as specific and as quantitative as possible (i.e., a formula). Debates about which comes first, data or theory, are basically silly, having ended with Adam and Eve or maybe Socrates and Plato or chickens and eggs. Similarly debates about the inherent superiority of theory or data are akin to arguing whether the skin or the mind is more important; without one, the other cannot function. We should get on with the task of improving both rather than belabor the inadequacies of either. Most important, it is foolish to require theory before a result can be examined. Most humans construct theory to explain the world and rejecting data with no strong prior theory holds back progress (e.g., without Brahe, Kepler would have produced no laws). Theory is the appropriate end goal but not the only means.

2. OVERJUSTIFICATION (A.K.A. BIBLIOGRAPHIC OVERKILL)

Have you noticed the gradual increase in the length of literature reviews and bibliographies? Now it is important to place research in a context and for review articles the literature review is obviously crucial. However, it is not important, useful, or an efficient use of journal pages for every paper to completely review the field, especially when the review essentially lists past work with no original insights. Given access to computerized literature searches, there is even less need for extensive literature reviews now than there once was.

It has been rumored that some pad bibliographies and literature reviews to (a) appeal to the egos of cited authors who might be reviewers or (b) subtly suggest who the reviewers should be. This is not a good way to advance knowledge and may not even be effective at increasing the acceptance probability for a paper. Long bibliographies make missed cites that much more painful and increase the chance of mis-interpreting someone else's work, which quickly alienates many reviewers.

Ask yourself questions like, "Does it make sense for a 30-page empirical paper to have 15 pages of literature review?" or "Do you really read these (unless you plan to use them to help you write your own literature review)?" Or, in a slightly different vein, "Why do job talks spend so much time on the literature and so little on what the dissertation will do?" Since at some level what is done must stand on its own, shouldn't what was done, and not a preamble, be the focal point (both in emphasis and length) of a paper?

3. DERIVATIVE INCREMENTALISM

Most papers are remarkably unremarkable; that is, they fit neatly into established paradigms. In some ways this is related to the over-emphasis on literature reviews. Having spent considerable effort mastering (or at least citing) the literature, it becomes more difficult to think creatively. As Pope suggests, "Behold the bookful blockhead, ignorantly read, with loads of learned lumber in his head."

Near-replications increase certainty about results, and form inputs to meta-analysis, which makes meta-analysts like me happy. Further, many/most researchers are better suited to, and make a real contribution to knowledge by, engaging in this type of work.

Still, two thoughts emerge. First, why do we insist on presenting these incremental papers as though they were earth shattering? You don't have to be wildly creative nor apologize for not being so to contribute to knowledge.

Second, why not encourage more "discontinuous innovation" in our work? We owe a lot to those less timid souls who take a chance and view the world differently. "Far better it is to dare mighty things, to win glorious triumphs, even though checkered by failure, than to take rank with those poor spirits who neither enjoy much nor suffer much, because they live in grey twilight that knows not victory or defeat." (T. Roosevelt)

4. UNREALISM (OR LIFE IN NEVER-NEVER LAND)

Consumer research, or at least ACR, began with an applied focus. The purpose was to focus attention on the behavior of consumers in economic settings in a way that would be more relevant to practitioners and public policy makers than the more abstract work of, say, economists and psychologists. Yet a lot of research seems remarkably sterile/removed from real consumers.

I'm not opposed to student samples; they are useful for many purposes. What isn't very appealing, however, is observing behavior in situations that bear no relevance to the world consumers face. As part of your investigation of a theory, a study on real subjects or using existing data is helpful. Sure it's messy but since the goal is generalization, triangulation by different methods is a plus, not a weakness.

Now this lack of realism is not confined to experimental researchers. Economic modelers are famous for this. Markets of 1 or 2 producers, 1 or 2 consumers, perfect information, etc. tend to exist only in our journals, usually accompanied by such comforting phrases as "without loss of generality, we assume ..." and "it is easily shown that...." Ever wonder why, if it is so easy to show, that they don't bother to show it? There is a procedure for showing a result holds for any number of competitors called proof by induction where you show (a) it is true for a monopoly and (b) given it is true for K firms, then it is true for K+1 firms. How often have you seen it used? Or why are fixed and variable costs considered important in operations research but assumed to be zero in so many models? The answer is mathematical tractability (a.k.a., convenience).

There was a time a generation ago when closed form solutions were needed. Given current computer power, however, it is quite feasible to numerically analyze complex functions that incorporate more realistic assumptions and then to describe the solutions with a simple formula or graph. That this approach has not been more widely adopted is a nice example of resistance to innovation.

5. HYPOTHESOSIS

H0: Construct A, also known as _____, will, when combined with B, produce result C under condition D. However, if B is combined with E or condition D' occurs, then result F will appear unless it is Tuesday.

Our field suffers from a suffocation of hypotheses. To a reader of our work, it would appear that nothing is ever uncovered that is not hypothesized. Brian Sternthal and Alice Tybout have made the case for why it doesn't matter when a hypothesis arises as long as you rule out alternative explanations. I agree. However, I want to go further and ask why we need so many formal hypotheses.

Hypotheses are implicit in what we measure and analyze. It is certainly instructive to briefly communicate why you think certain constructs are worthy of study. Still the fact you measured them eloquently communicates that you (or some outside party like a reviewer) thought they might have an impact. Why is this not adequate? Further, since often the expected relations can be communicated by a flowchart or series of equations, why repeat each link as a hypothesis?

Many of our hypotheses are basically checks on whether subjects are paying attention. For example:

H1: A positive reaction to _____ will increase attitude toward _____.
H2: As price increases, sales will decrease.

While there are situations where H1 and H2 may not obtain (e.g., when attitudes are strongly held or price is a major signal of quality), in most situations these results "better" obtain. Why give them the same stature as interesting hypotheses? Perhaps a category of manipulation check hypotheses should be created, especially for mathematical model based simulations where the assumptions clearly drive the conclusions.

Finally, avoid the tendency to create hypotheses where the null effect is zero. This is disingenuous at best and essentially dishonest, can *only* be true due to limited statistical power (no effect is ever exactly zero), and is contrary to the goal of cumulative learning.

6. POLYSYLLABIC SLOBBERING: AN IVORY TOWER OF BABEL

A number of research approaches are discussed and debated including positivist, post-positivism, and post modern (which sounds like an oxymoron to me; is it really the future and if so, how do we know what it is?). All provide different views (or frames) on a phenomenon and are inherently both useful and incomplete. Yet the debate that has dragged on for several years seems intent on establishing the general superiority of a method by criticizing others. The debate reminds me of stories about people living in glass houses. Since at best we can establish method superiority for a given purpose, the debate seems off-base, a bit self-serving, and quite tiresome. The phrases "give it a rest" or "give it up" seem appropriate here.

As a discipline matures, it is natural for various sub-areas to form. Specialized language plays an important role in communicating among members of sub-areas. Unfortunately, that same language makes conversations across sub-areas difficult, especially since much of it either is not used in ordinary conversation (e.g., hermeneutic) or is used in ways at variance with its normal English (or other language) meaning (e.g., counter factual reasoning). Reading our work you might never guess hierarchical regression is the same as nested model testing. These language barriers work against generalizing knowledge. While the first ACR I attended in 1970 had behavioral researchers and quantitative modelers happily attending the same session and talking with each other, recent conferences often resemble a collection of mini-conferences except for cocktail parties and less-than-welcome lunch speeches like this one.

Of course barriers can be surmounted if people want to surmount them. Sadly, however, many people do not. The comfort of being in a sub-group is reinforced by the knowing smiles of approval when the particular paradigms/passwords (e.g., collinearity, demand effects, Stackelberg competition) are uttered. Why go to another track's session when all your friends, role models, mentors, etc. are in your own area's session? It will be uncomfortable and frustrating; while you know your group's passwords, you probably won't know theirs. Further you will probably marvel at either how trivial or how sloppy their work seems (without, of course, casting the same level of scrutiny on your own). Thus if you venture outside your area, Skinner's operant conditioning and Bentham's pursuit of pleasure will drive you home.

Why bother venturing outside the comfortable world of your own? There is no incentive if you are satisfied with being one of many fish in a small pond and incremental change. On the other hand, if you want to make major contributions/innovations, you have to. And even if you don't, for the sake of your area consider discussing your work in such a way that outsiders can at least comprehend what you are doing. Try the following test: could you explain what you are doing to neighbors who are plumbers, your mother, or to a high school class?

7. CONTINGENCIES VS. CROSSOVER INTERACTIONS

Finding the boundaries in which a theory or result holds is an important goal of research. For example, where does the average price elasticity of Tellis' meta-analysis (-1.76) provide a good estimate and where does it not? Trying a theory out in disparate areas of application both makes sense and is more likely to lead to different results (i.e., what is true for paper towels is more likely to be true for paper napkins than for oil well drilling equipment).

Now of course there is a certain excitement in finding a cross-over interaction or a category where the price elasticity is positive. However, to enhance general knowledge, finding an unexplored domain where the theory (or parameter) applies is every bit as useful as finding one where the result is reversed. Adding information about the new domain is far more important for knowledge development than whether the result matches or contradicts past patterns. Perhaps we should worry more about the domain extension rather than finding contradictions per se.

8. STATISTICAL STERILITY

The use of classical statistics, as typically practiced, has provided welcome rigor to our thinking. On the other hand, the blind use of cookbook statistics has produced a rigor mortis in our thought process.

Basically we approach problems with some notion about a phenomenon. That notion (which some call theory) is drawn from past experience, analogies, and formal learning. We then, subject to all the biases and imperfections in human judgment, alter the notion or our behavior to the extent that current information requires us to do so. This learning is essentially Bayesian, requiring gradual updates, or in a stickier form, related to control charts where at some level of discrepancy between current evidence and theory we dramatically alter our theory.

Now contrast this process of adaptive learning with the cookbook use of classical statistics. In standard statistics (i.e., those t, F, and χ^2 values that appear in computer programs), we test the "null hypothesis" of nothing. That is, we examine the straw man of no effect or no relation.

First, statistical significance is pretty arbitrary. Why is a p-value of .09 so much different than one of .11? (Hint: they are not generally statistically distinguishable.) Answer: because we arbitrarily set .10 (or .05 or .01) as a cut-off. As a consequence, we struggle to get "significant results" by hook (e.g., increasing the sample size or hyping the manipulation/signal or the attention payed to it) or by crook (e.g., only discussing hypotheses that lead to significant results.)

Second, consider the goal of empirical generalization. The primary substantive result is the impact of a variable (i.e., the mean difference due to a treatment or the size of a regression coefficient). If we want to weight results based on their reliability, then standard errors are needed. All the p-values, F ratios, and log-likelihood ratios provide is an indirect measure of standard error. Yet many articles report p-values, etc. and never directly present the size of the effect. Besides being frustrating to meta-analysts, this works against knowledge accumulation. (As an aside, the term "effect size" is unfortunate since it often refers to the explanatory power of a variable which depends on both the effect consistency and the average size of the effect.)

In summary, the real issue is not if or whether or when something has an effect (everything does, even if a very small one), but rather how much effect it has in different circumstances. Focus statistical reasoning on this issue, recognizing past results are important information for current estimation. The best estimate for the effect in your study is some combination of what your data shows and what has been found in the past. If you must have a null hypothesis, then it should be based on past research and you should, for the sake of establishing generalization, hope to fail to reject it.

9. SOPHISTICATED ≠ COMPLICATED

We often mask simple results in our complicated calculations and confuse complication with sophistication. As an example, reconsider the figure used to highlight a 3-way interaction (Observation 7). While an ANOVA might find a significant interaction, examining the means could tell a different story. Seven of the eight conditions produce a mean of about 8 and are not (for reasonable sample sizes) statistically different. Only in the low, low, A cell is the mean different. Doesn't it make more sense to report this even if it isn't standard output or very elegant?

As another example, consider LISREL. Now it is an elegant and useful tool in the hands of a skilled user but likely to cause harm in the hands of a novice. For example, if we want to generalize, we may prefer to measure a construct the same way across studies. Yet as a one-step procedure that creates measures of constructs simultaneously with estimating structural relations among the constructs, the LISREL measure weights, and hence the operationalization of the construct, will differ across studies even if the same measures are used. Why not just use indexes that are simple averages and at the same time avoid capitalizing on chance variation?

Finally, consider the goals of (a) communicating to a broad audience and (b) providing input to meta-analyses. In general, simpler is better.

10. MEASURE VS. MANIPULATION

A fascinating tradition involves the choice to use an experimental manipulation of a construct to represent the construct instead of the measure of the construct. When a measure is taken (often for use in a manipulation check), why not use the measure of the construct directly in the analysis?

Other than tradition, the implicit reason has to do with error. Basically the true value of the construct depends on (a) the manipulation, (b) other influences on the construct (e.g., personal characteristics), and (c) a random component (e1). Similarly the measured value depends on (a) the true value and (b) a random component including measurement error (e2). Using the manipulated (generally binary) level assumes that the impact of other variables and the random component e1 is smaller than e2. For constructs such as involvement and mood and relatively weak manipulations such as "you may get your chosen snack" or a happy vs. sad story, one suspects personal factors play a large role. Assuming that the measured value has greater error associated with it seems a bit of a stretch, especially when multiple measures are used. Even if you can't draw the typical 2 x 2 plot as easily, consider using the measured value.

11. SOCIAL APPROVAL / TENURE

Most of us like peer approval and if we want tenure, actually need it. This leads to the dreaded research strategy whereby you (a) develop a strategy to be an expert in some often-obscure area and (b) network yourself. Now focusing some of your efforts makes sense and being nice to people,

especially smart ones, is both common sense and a way to learn something. Carrying these to extreme, however, is both unproductive (leading to derivative, non-interesting work) and unappealing. Can you think of many businesses that make strategies and don't alter them for seven years?

Two questions arise. First, does game playing really contribute to general knowledge? Second, having been positively rewarded for one type of behavior for seven years, are you likely to change to different behavior even if you know intellectually it is superior? And if you change will it involve burn-out rather than increased commitment to scholarship?

I was fortunate to get in this business when tenure was easier to obtain but I still think I would rather be a roofer or run a chain saw than endure a seven-year mental and social makeover.

A PARSIMONIOUS EXPLANATION

I have observed some empirical regularities, but not offered an explanation. My story (theory) of the reason is complex but with a simple focal element: insecurity. Basically we tend to consider ourselves inferior to natural scientists or real psychologists or economists. We seize on their trappings without questioning and hide from practitioners in stilted prose.

SUGGESTIONS

What suggestions do I have? Here are my top ten:

1. *Consider yourself first a student of consumer behavior and only secondarily an information processor or scanner data modeler.* Work on disseminating as well as creating knowledge in your own sub-area.

2. *Stop feeling inferior.* Business schools exist because various "classic" disciplines such as economics, sociology, and psychology failed to see the opportunity that business in general and consumer behavior in particular provided for studying something that is both impactful and provides an important lens into the behavior of people in general. We aren't going to win many Nobel prizes but neither are most doctors or economists. The input quality in marketing Ph.D. programs has been high for 20 years which means we are up to competing on raw I.Q. points.

3. *Give back to the other disciplines.* There is no need to continually defer to other disciplines. Neither is it helpful to stand by and knowingly criticize them (i.e., "look at the ridiculous assumptions economists make about consumers"). Why let economists eventually incorporate our results? Wouldn't it be more interesting to incorporate them ourselves, in essence exporting finished product rather than just raw material in the form of assumptions?

4. *Recognize we're not curing cancer.* I firmly believe market economies benefit consumers and by understanding them we can increase the benefits. However, we're not providing dramatic life-saving new drugs or procedures. We chose to work in this area, many in business schools, because the combination of intellectual stimulation and monetary reward appealed to us. It does no good to feel bad about the choice; either change the choice or accept the trade-offs.

5. *Recognize even our best work is inevitably wrong.* In spite of constant reminders from reviewers, we often behave as though our work should somehow be correct. Philosophical

discussions about what is truth aside, in an active field subsequent work will alter, modify, or even invalidate the best that has gone before. Notice how few citations go back more than 15 years. Basically, 100 years ago they didn't know you were coming and 100 years from now they won't know you were here. This doesn't mean you should take your work less seriously; since you chose to work on it, it must be the most important thing in the world to you at the time and should be treated accordingly. It does suggest you might be less sensitive to criticism and less strident in your criticism of others. "Whoever thinks a faultless piece to see, thinks what ne'er was, nor is, nor e'er shall be." (A. Pope)

6. *Make the literature review an appendix.* I found during my time at MSI that literature reviews are one of the reasons practitioners don't like to read academic papers. They are also one of the reasons I and many of you don't like reading them, especially when they are bloated with references to please reviewers.

    One view of a paper is a conversation with a reader. Thought of this way a paper would have four sections:

    1. An introduction that basically states what you are interested in.
    2. What you did, basically an abstract of the method section in plain English.
    3. What you found, restricted to means, cross-tabs, correlations, and OLS regression or ANOVA generated mean differences plus graphs.
    4. What next, describing future research.

    Appendices would then be presented for:

    1. The traditional literature review.
    2. Details on the method.
    3. More extensive analyses.
    4. Detailed limitations and directions for future research.

    Notice this would make papers shorter and more accessible to members of other sub-areas of consumer behavior as well as practitioners and government employees, potentially leading to a more important role in policy making. (Notice how when questions are asked in the public arena about consumers, lawyers and economists are prominent, while marketers and consumer behavior researchers are rarely involved.)

7. *Structure your work so it aids future generalization studies.* Meta-analysis suffers from a preponderance of studies of a single type and a large fraction of empty cells. To contribute to knowledge development, fill the empty cells (which means method and paradigm pluralism is a virtue, not something to be wiped out by the stronger group). Put differently, exact replication isn't of much value but Ehrenberg's notion of differentiated replication/extension is. And whatever you do, report results so that they can be incorporated in a subsequent meta-analysis.

8. *Don't test the null hypothesis of zero effect and report the size of the effect as the primary result.* You don't believe there is no effect, though in some cases you may hope some are small enough to be ignored. The magnitude of effects are useful for accumulating knowledge; p-values are for juries deciding guilt and innocence.

9. *Recognize your contribution to the field will be hard to track.* Maximizing citations or awards may be mildly satisfying but chances are your biggest contributions may go unlauded. While awards may reflect short run impact, long run impact typically occurs through people and the subtle impact we have on them.

10. *Do what you want.* The advice you just received was at best free and at worst gratuitous. Research should be fun. Remember "Fanaticism consists in redoubling your efforts when you have forgotten your aim." (G. Santayana)

I see my time is up. Thanks to those of you who stayed for your patience. I wish you and ACR well.

The following figures were prepared by Dr. Lehmann and were presented as slides during his Presidential Address. They are being published in the Proceedings as a supplement to his Address.

KNOWLEDGE GENERALIZATION AND THE

CONVENTIONS OF CONSUMER RESEARCH:

A STUDY IN INCONSISTENCY

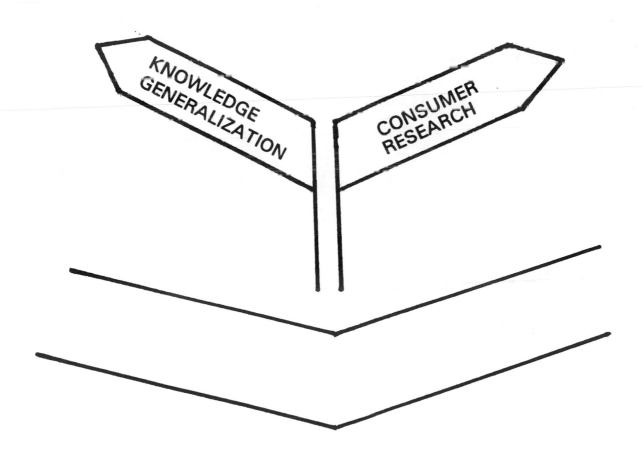

UNDERLYING LOGIC

PREMISES:

1. The purpose of academic research is to produce generalizations.

2. Meta-Analysis is the process of generalizing across different studies/results.

CONCLUSION:

The purpose of academic research is to prepare for (and occasionally perform) meta-analysis.

GOALS OF META-ANALYSIS

1. Establish the base level (e.g., overall average)

2. Assess systematic differences

3. Establish the range of the results

4. Use past results to make predictions for other situations.

OBSERVATION 1: THEORY, TYRANNY, AND

EMPIRICAL GENERALIZATION

OR

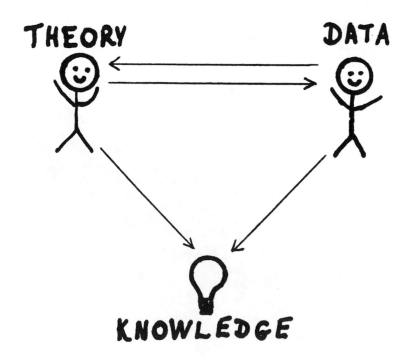

OBSERVATION 2: OVERJUSTIFICATION
(A.K.A. BIBLIOGRAPHIC OVERKILL)

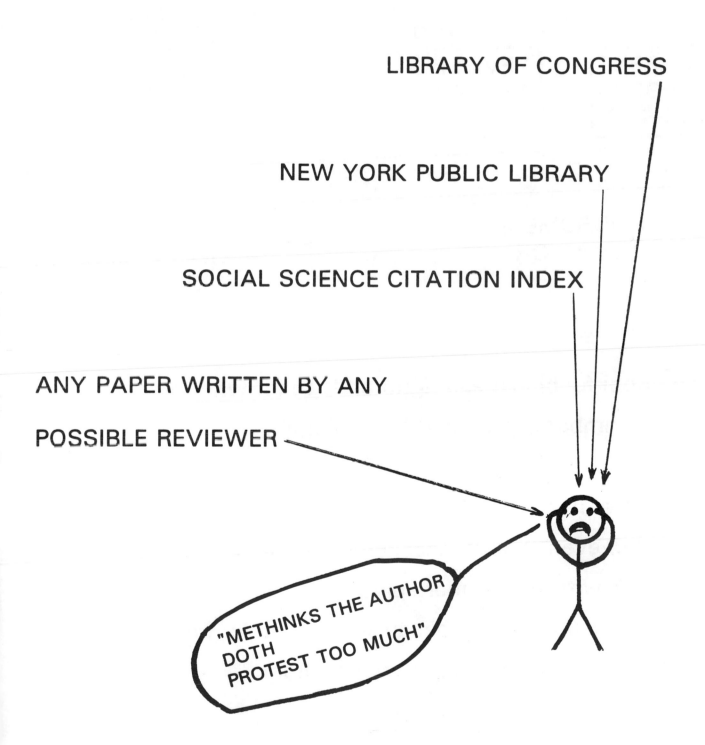

OBSERVATION 3:

DERIVATIVE INCREMENTALIZATION

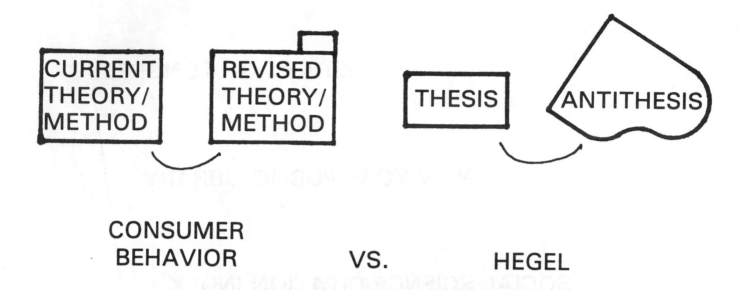

CONSUMER
BEHAVIOR   VS.   HEGEL

"The bookful blockhead, ignorantly read, with loads of learned lumber in his head." (A. Pope)

"Far better it is to dare mighty things, to win glorious triumphs, even though checkered by failure, than to take rank with those poor spirits who neither enjoy much nor suffer much, because they live in grey twilight that knows not victory or defeat."
(T. Roosevelt)

OBSERVATION 4: UNREALISM

(OR LIFE IN NEVER-NEVER LAND)

ONE
CONSUMER

STUDENT
SAMPLES

ONE
PRODUCER

SINGLE
STIMULUS

PERFECT
INFORMATION

ATTENTIVE
RESPONDENTS

OBSERVATION 5: HYPOTHESOSIS

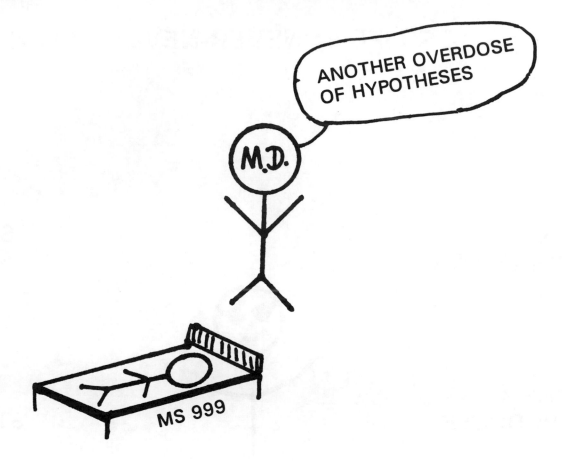

H_0: Construct A, also known as _____, will, when combined with B, produce result C under condition D. However, if B is combined with E or condition D' occurs, then result F will appear unless it is Tuesday.

OBSERVATION 6:

POLYSYLLABIC SLOBBERING –

AN IVORY TOWER OF BABEL

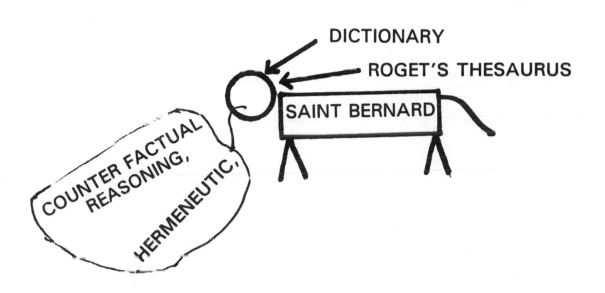

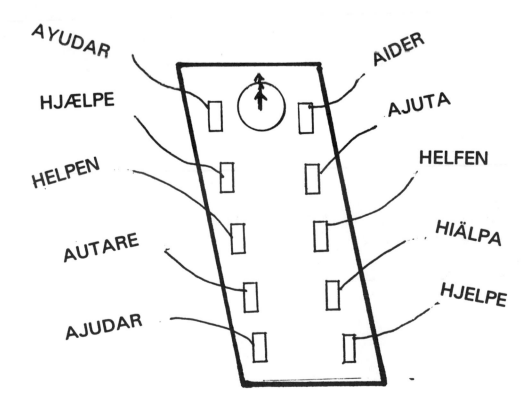

OBSERVATION 7: CONTINGENCIES VS.

(CROSSOVER) INTERACTIONS

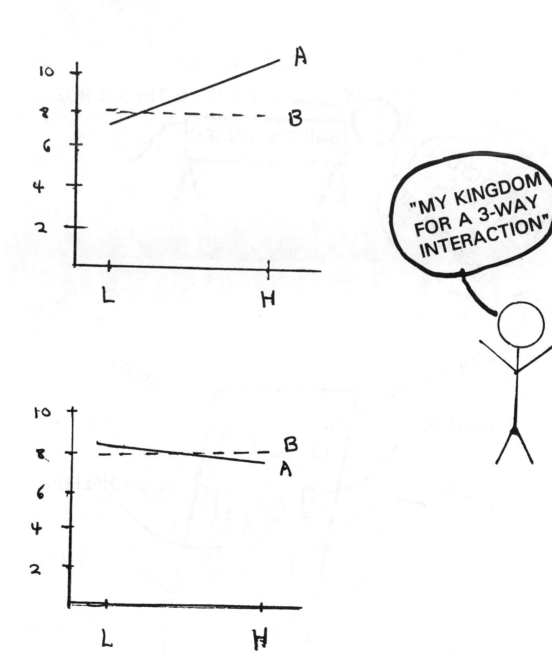

OBSERVATION 8: STATISTICAL STERILITY

OBSERVATION 9:

SOPHISTICATED ≠ COMPLICATED

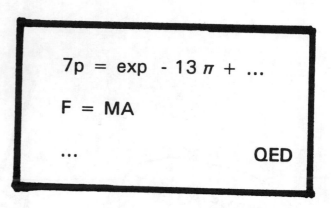

$7p = \exp - 13\pi + \ldots$

$F = MA$

$\ldots$ QED

<u>O R</u>

OBSERVATION 10:

MEASURE VS. MANIPULATION

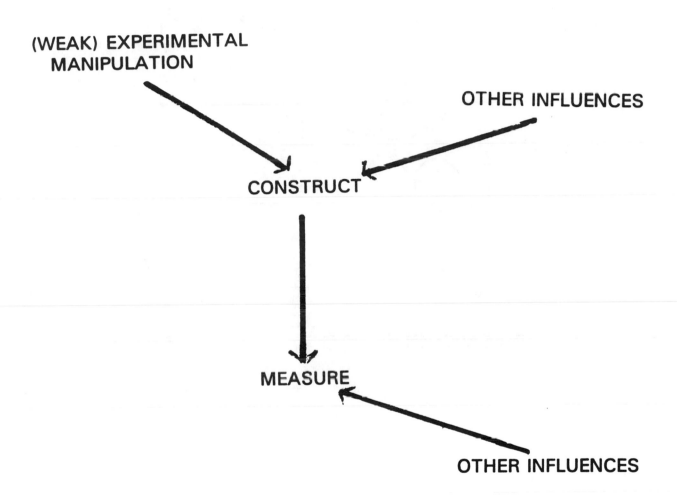

OBSERVATION 11:

SOCIAL APPROVAL / TENURE

RESEARCHER   FAUST

TEN SUGGESTIONS

1. Consider yourself first a student of consumer behavior and only secondarily an information processor or scanner data modeler.

2. Stop feeling inferior.

3. Give back to the other disciplines.

4. Recognize we're not curing cancer.

5. Recognize even our best work in inevitably wrong.

6. Make the literature review an appendix.

7. Structure your work so it aids future generalization studies.

8. Don't test the null hypothesis of zero effect; report effect sizes as the primary result.

9. Recognize your contribution to the field will be hard to track.

10. Do what you want.

"Fanaticism consists in redoubling your efforts
when you have forgotten your aim."

(G. Santayana)

THAT'S ALL, FOLKS

On Being a Female Fellow: My Life as an Oxymoron

Elizabeth C. Hirschman, Rutgers University

It is a very weighty task talking to you today as number 17 in a line of ACR Fellows. I feel a tremendous intellectual burden pressing down on me from the combined talent and giftedness of my 16 predecessors, all of them highly productive, extremely creative contributors to our field.

In my search for an appropriate topic, I found myself casting about for a point-of-view somehow unaddressed by those who had come before me—a vantage point not yet surveyed. I thought there might be three possibilities—three characteristics that set me apart from those who had preceded me. First, as a confessed substance abuser, I thought perhaps I could discuss my philosophy of better living through chemistry. However, upon reflection, I realized that I had already talked about that subject and that, given the identity of some recent fellows, I was not likely to be the first controlled substance consumer to address you.

Then I considered describing my history of emotional volatility. After all, I have never been a *normal* person and perhaps recounting my struggles with emotional highs and lows would give encouragement to those similarly afflicted. However, once again upon reflection—and considering the behaviors of some prior recipients—I realized that I would probably not be the first crazy person to address you.

And so I turned to a third characteristic that I believed did truly set me apart from previous fellows. Unless one of them has really been keeping something "in the closet," I am the first *woman* to become an ACR Fellow—a wondrous distinction, indeed: a female fellow. It had a sort of oxymoronic quality to it, kind of like "jumbo shrimp," "military intelligence," and "Protestant sexuality"—two concepts that just don't seem to belong together and yet are forced upon one another in an ungainly pairing.

Upon reflection, I realized that metaphorically my entire life could be viewed as one long, awkward struggle to marry together the two concepts implied by the terms "female" and "ACR Fellow," for example, "woman" and "scientist," "mother" and "researcher," "wife" and "professor."

Origins

The origins of this oxymoronic—and existential—journey can be found in a long-ago time, called the 1950's and a far-away place, called Kingsport, Tennessee—a very different time and a very different place than the world as we now know it.

Kingsport, Tennessee in the 1950's was much like the rest of the United States in the 1950's, only more so. The dads went to work in a suit and tie, while the moms stayed home and kept house wearing shirtwaist dresses and comfortable shoes. The kids went to school and belonged to Girl Scouts and Boy Scouts. Our family very much conformed to this pattern. My Dad, John Caldwell, who died this past July, was a research scientist at the Eastman-Kodak Corporation. During the course of his career he generated over 300 chemical patents—a feat matched by few other scientists in the country. He was certainly a brilliant and creative researcher.

My Mom, Virginia, was also a chemist who had graduated as valedictorian of her college class and been elected to Phi Beta Kappa. She was very attractive and had excellent managerial skills. But she was a woman, and it was the 1950's, and so she was a *mom*. She took care of me and my brother, cooked the meals, cleaned the house, made the beds, went to the grocery store, attended the PTA meetings, led the Girl Scout troop and took us to the Presbyterian church every Sunday. Just like all the other moms.

Around the age of 9 or 10, after almost a decade of careful participant observation, I discerned that there were basically two career paths in life and which one you took was determined by whether you were born a girl or a boy. If you were a girl, you got to grow up to be like your mom; you got to wash clothes, make meals, vacuum floors, change diapers and go on Girl Scout camping trips. If you were a boy, you could be President of the United States, an astronaut, a Supreme Court justice, a scientist, a policeman, a fireman, a doctor, a lawyer or an Indian chief.

Girls and boys were groomed for these two career paths from birth onward. Girls were taught to be polite, wait their turn and be considerate of others' feelings. Girls were encouraged to make good grades in school, so that they could go to a good college, meet a man, who would be a good provider, marry him and then devote themselves to caring for his children—preferably sons.

Boys were taught to play hard, be strong, and learn to get ahead. They made good grades in order to get into a good college so that they could graduate and get a good job, doing something that was challenging, personally meaningful and paid a good salary.

Early Philosophical Musings

By about the age of 11, I realized that women in the U.S. were encased in what has been termed the patriarchal tradition. Women's lives were in all ways subordinate to those of men. Their task was to serve as caretakers for their husbands and sons who carried out the real business of life. Trapped in a female body, women were at best excellent caretakers for those whose gender entitled them to *act* upon the world. This was very much the state of things, as I grew up in the 1950's.

However, things were not as bleak as they seemed, for as I entered my second decade, two entities were about to rebel—Beth Caldwell and the rest of the culture. My rebellion began very slowly and cautiously. I always tried—overtly at least—to be a good girl, to do the right thing, to behave in the right way. However, I did not always succeed. Quite hyperactive as a child, I once returned home from school in the fifth grade and proudly told my mother, "Mom, they gave me a whole row all by myself." At the age of 13, I resigned from the Presbyterian church—our family religion for at least ten generations—over the doctrine of Predestination. In brief, Predestination holds that all people are born either Elect, that is Good or Saved, or Non-elect, that is Bad or Damned. We Presbyterians, of course, knew that we were among the Elect—we were white, well-to-do, and respectable. We were successful, we were American, and we ran the country.

However, by age 13 I was beginning to have doubts about Predestination and the whole culture in which it was embedded. Where were the places for Negroes, for Catholics, for Latinos, for poor people and especially for *women*? I was as smart as most of the boys I went to school with, and I was easily as ambitious. Why couldn't I have a life!? I did not want to cook, clean, and iron shirts for a living. I wanted to *do* something.

Fortunately, for small, skinny Beth Caldwell in Kingsport, Tennessee, the non-white, non-male majority of the culture was asking the same question. The decades of the 1960's and the 1970's saw enormous upheaval in the accreted layers of white Anglo Saxon male privilege that had encrusted the country since its founding. All kinds of previously invisible folk came trudging forward bearing their grievances on placards. We stood there—in front of the Lincoln Memorial, surrounding the Pentagon, marching down Christopher Street in New York City—and said, collectively, as Blacks, as women, as gays, as Hispanics: We want a Life! Life with a capital "L."

And in many ways we have been able to fashion one, although many types of compromises have been made along the way. I passed the late 1960's and early 1970's at the University—the "in" place to be during that time period. My time there was well-spent, although as I look back on it now I see that many of the most valuable lessons were not learned in the classroom.

Good Beth/Bad Beth

In college I continued my Good Girl/Bad Girl pattern. From Sunday afternoon until Friday afternoon, I was a very good girl. I always studied hard, made good grades and remained consistently on the Dean's list. However, from Friday afternoon until Sunday morning I was Bad Beth. I was on what would later be titled Experiential or Hedonic Consumption Time—this was akin to Miller Time, but was usually produced by imbibing wine and inhaling marijuana, rather than drinking beer. My left-wing politics flourished during this period. I was a hippie; I lived in a communal house, wore bell-bottom jeans, tie-dyed t-shirts, buffalo sandals, belonged to the SDS and engaged in several demonstrations, marches, and other forms of political protest.

It was a rather schizophrenic existence. Good Beth followed the rules and worked slavishly for high grades and other traditional forms of achievement. Bad Beth broke the rules, challenged their underlying authority and basically misbehaved in every possible way.

A vignette about a bad drug experience during this time period will provide a somewhat metaphoric illustration. One night a group of us were dabbling around with acid. I had a nightmarish trip in which my mind and body separated. My mind floated up to the ceiling, which seemed to be about 10 or 12 feet high, while my body remained sitting on the floor eating a box of vanilla wafers. What was so terrifying about this experience is that my body really enjoyed eating the entire box of cookies, which tasted indescribably delicious, while my mind hovered above it, in constant fear of falling, unable to connect-up to my physical being. Finally, I came "down," literally and figuratively, and re-integrated myself.

Keeping my mind and body integrated has proved to be the central challenge of my adult life on two levels. The first, most essential basis for this dualism arose very early in my childhood when I realized that I had my father's creative scientific "male" head stuck atop my mother's female body. My head had always told me I wanted to be one thing—a researcher, a scientist, which was culturally reserved for males. My body told me I wanted to have children and be a mother, which was culturally—and biologi-cally—given to women. For the first 30 years of my life I resolved this by letting my head predominate over my body. I masqueraded as a consumer researcher who just happened to be running around in a female body.

Raymond Arrives

Two events acted to moderate this dualism. The first was that I moved "up North" for a brief time after undergraduate school and, while there, I met and married the only poor, Jewish boy in all of New York City, Raymond Hirschman.

Alice and Carol Appear

When Ray and I got married I made it clear that I didn't want to get trapped into doing all those things that women and wives were supposed to do. I didn't want to cook, I didn't want to clean, and I didn't want to have children. Shortly after we married, I entered graduate school with the intention of getting my Ph.D. and settling down to a nice small college and a career in teaching. It was an enormous step for me to seek a career at all; the notion of my actually pursuing *research* seemed completely beyond the realm of possibility. And then two miraculous events occurred right in the middle of my Ph.D. program. Their names were Alice Tybout and Carol Scott. Like angels from some female-inhabited heaven, they appeared in the field and began conducting and presenting and publishing *research*. *Women* were doing *research*, in *my* field. And they were doing it very well.

This was for me, and I am sure for many other women, a watershed event. It opened up a psychological door, it breached a sociological barrier that hitherto had remained tightly shut to us. Now I could see myself doing this thing that only men did—research. Alice and Carol's pioneering efforts were central to my—and other women's—progress (and even *presence*) in the field. If Alice and Carol had not come along *when* they did and *how* they did, in all honesty I can say, Beth Hirschman would not be standing here before you today.

Jerry Shows Up

A third very important figure for me during this critical early part of my career was an errant sociologist I encountered at the AMA doctoral consortium, Jerry Zaltman. Jerry, as many of you know, is not only a highly gifted scholar, but also an iconoclast and an intellectual rebel. Perhaps because of this, Jerry has—in addition to producing many scholarly contributions to the field—also been the foremost male promoter of women as researchers.

Over the course of his career, Jerry served on the dissertation committees of both Alice Tybout and Carol Scott, and also those of Melanie Wallendorf, Robin Higle-Coulter, Meera Venkatramen, Debbie MacInnis, and Christine Moorman. And most importantly for people like Linda Price and *me*, Jerry has served as mentor, guide, friend, constructive critic and adviser. It was through contact with Jerry that my interest in the cultural and subcultural aspects of consumer behavior were both encouraged and strengthened.

Melanie

Coincident with meeting Jerry, I also met my first female ally in the field, Melanie Wallendorf. I was fortunate the year I was at the University of Pittsburgh to serve on Melanie's dissertation committee. Melanie's topic was sociological in content, having to do with the communication of information across groups, and being associated with it, and with her, served to further strengthen my interest in the cultural dimensions of consumption.

Morris Moves In

After a year in Pittsburgh, Ray and I moved to New York City. Ray was working at Young and Rubicam and I was at NYU. Shortly afterwards, at the 1979 ACR Conference, I presented a paper that would change my life. It was a simple, typical conference paper titled "Attributes of Attributes and Layers of Meaning." In it I was critical of the work of another young assistant professor whom I had never met, but whose ideas I thought were just completely off-base. And so, with all the fervor of misdirected youth, I trounced him soundly. At the conclusion of my talk, which I felt had gone brilliantly, a young, somewhat forlorn-looking man approached me and extended his hand in a gesture of friendship. "Hi!" he said, "My name is Morris Holbrook and I'm really sorry you don't like my work." I remember thinking to myself, "Uh, oh. I'm in big trouble now." (Actually, to be ethnographically accurate, what I really thought was, "Uh, oh, this guy is going to beat the shit out of me for sure!").

Remarkably, instead of being violently angry, Morris invited me to attend his session on consumption aesthetics the following day. I did. It was interesting. We hit it off; we even learned that we lived next door to each other on Riverside Drive. It was the start of a long and lasting friendship that still, quite happily, endures.

After organizing the Symbolic Consumer Behavior Conference in 1980, Morris and I began collaborating on two papers designed to address a second type of mind-body dualism which both of us were experiencing. The basic problem was that neither of us acted in ways consistent with the then-prevailing view of consumer behavior as logical, rule-guided information processing. We were weird. In contrast, I believe that, for example, Jim Bettman, whom I admire, like and respect very much, *does* act in a logical, rational fashion. I think if you opened up Jim's head, you would find a very efficient, highly intelligent, rational, orderly place. Everything would be neat, clean and organized.

In contrast, if you opened up my or Morris' head, you would find a jumble of randomly occurring, enormously digressive and contradictory thoughts. Morris' head would be more upscale and sophisticated than mine, but we would have the same topical categories. For example, under "Drama," Morris would have plays by Tina Howe and Shakespeare, whereas I would have 15 years of "The Young and the Restless," my soap opera, stashed away. Under "Good Things to Eat," Morris would have cabernet, escargot and arrugula, while I would have salsa and chips, chocolate, and buttered popcorn. Under "Emotions," Morris would have complex, elaborate feelings such as anomie, ecstasy and existential angst; I would have "really happy," "really sad" and "bored." All of these various categories would be tied together in a hodge-podge of neuron wirings that mixed fantasy and fact, myth with musings and big thoughts, e.g., "What does life mean?" with little thoughts, e.g., "Is it time to eat yet?"

We decided to formalize our disjointed thinking and published two papers describing it in the *Journal of Consumer Research* and the *Journal of Marketing*. Remarkably, upon publishing these models of our hopelessly disorganized and emotionally over-wrought minds, some sparks of self-recognition arose from others in the field who experienced a similar level of mental chaos. Thus inspired, Morris and I have gone on to collaborate on several other papers and books over the past 15 years. It's been a lot of fun and, hey, we actually got tenure.

Baby Time

In 1983 a different kind of mind-body struggle arose for me. I had hit 30 and my proverbial biological clock was going "Ding, Dong!, Wake Up!, it's time to make a baby!" And following my usual careful, cautious and conservative path of rational decision making, I made an immediate 180° swing from declaring "I never want children" to "If I don't get pregnant right now, I'll kill myself!"....

[I told some people about my decision, and then some bad things happened to me....]

The following month I did become pregnant and nine months and four days later, Alix Hirschman was born. As her mother and an objective social scientist I can attest that she was, and is, a real cutie. At age one she posed as cover girl for the 1984 ACR Conference Proceedings, as drawn by that Picasso of consumer research, Morris Holbrook.

.... Neither my research nor my teaching fell apart. Around 1985, Ray and I decided that the first baby had turned out so well, it was time to make another one. This time I made doubly sure to cover all bases professionally. I published two papers in *JCR* and the "Humanistic Inquiry" piece in *JMR*. I served as Treasurer of ACR and on the AMA Marketing Thought Task Force headed by Kent Monroe. In addition, I headed the AMA's Academic Division as Vice President of the Educators' Council. I continued to teach my full course load and earned high teaching ratings. So, when Annie Hirschman was born in May 1986, I felt confident that I had fulfilled my professional duties responsibly.

Three days after I returned home from the hospital after giving birth, I was told to come into New York City.... I loaded 8-day old Annie and myself into my car, drove to the train station, unloaded all our paraphernalia from the car and onto the train and rode into Grand Central Station. Upon arriving there I hailed a cab and clutching Annie to me, we hurtled downtown.... [and then some more bad things happened to me]....

I gathered up Annie and all of our baby stuff, hailed the cab, caught the train, got back in the car, and went home. By the time I arrived there, I had decided that I was tired of struggling... over being female and being a professor. I could *do it*, I had *done it*. I was tired of awaiting... recognition and approval. And so I began looking around for a happier place to be me. A year and a half later, I received a very generous, cordial offer from Rutgers University and I happily, gratefully accepted it.

My Glorious Coauthors

Life at Rutgers over these past seven years has been happy and productive. I returned to a behavior pattern that I had all but abandoned—working with really gifted coauthors. I had noticed some super bright and talented young people on the horizon over the past few years while I was at NYU, but they were at other schools and I was too distracted fighting the gender wars to approach them. Now I had both the time and the motivation.

I began with Barbara Stern, who fortunately was right up the road at Rutgers-Newark. Barbara is a remarkable pioneer in her own right. Over the past decade, she has carved out an excellent career for herself—and research path for the rest of us—by applying the methods of literary criticism to advertising and consumer behavior. She also was one of the first researchers in our field to bring a feminist perspective to bear on important research issues. Through my collaborations with Barbara, I've been able to soak up some of her large knowledge about literary genres and formal analysis.

A second, very stimulating intellectual partnership has been forged with Craig Thompson. From Craig I've gained a great reverence for the works of Michael Foucault and found true happiness working with a fellow phenomenologist. Craig, as you may know, also comes from Eastern Tennessee and I figure the karma on our working together has to be pretty powerful. The odds against two existentialists both emerging from the Appalachian mountains and actually discovering one another must be long indeed.

Even more recently I've been working with our field's second Lit-Crit pioneer, Linda Scott, and an advertising research veteran, Bill Wells, on the cultural meaning of product categories. Linda has taught me an enormous amount about discourse theory, reader-response theory and rhetoric, while Bill has kept both of us honest about the pragmatics of doing grounded research.

I've also teamed up with fellow bleeding-heart liberal, commie-pinko, left-winger, Ron Hill, in our never-ending battle to overcome social injustice, wherever it may rear its ugly head. Thus far, we have tackled the Great Depression and are now moving onward to even more depressing topics.

Finally, true to my sociological roots in Pittsburgh, I've cajoled Clinton Sanders to join me in a series of collaborations on human-animal research projects. One of our central findings is that animals have much to teach us about human virtue.

Girl Babies Are the Hope of the World

Working with all these extremely gifted and talented people has not only been very stimulating, it's also been highly productive. I re-discovered something I had already learned from working with Morris Holbrook. That is if you pick the right coauthors, *they* will do all the work and *you* will get half the credit. What a deal! I soon found I had excess time on my hands. What to do? So, I went and had another baby! Yes, little Shannon Hirschman was born March 15, 1994.

The birth of Shannon, my third child, was a wonderfully happy event. But I was also very happy about two other births that occurred during the early 1990's. I had known Alice Tybout and Carol Scott by that time for many years. I had enormous personal affection and professional respect for both of them. And over the course of time I had known them, the thought had often occurred to me that both of them would make great moms. But as the years passed, I began to despair that this would never happen for them. And I felt guilty, because in many ways I believed that Carol and Alice, because they were *the* female pioneers, had to pay the highest price for being first. Their professional sacrifices had eased the way for all the rest of us women who had followed in their wake.

And so, I was filled with great joy when, first, Carol and then Alice had babies, both girls. What a miracle! Next to those babies' parents, I was the happiest person on the planet.

It's been a long journey from Kingsport, Tennessee, to this place. The world has changed enormously since I was a little girl, and mostly, I believe, it's changed for the better. It is a place now where little girls—my little girls, Alice and Carol's little girls, your little girls, can grow up to become pretty much anyone they want to be—a U.S. Senator, a University President, a Supreme Court Justice, an astronaut, a firefighter, a police officer, a doctor, a lawyer, or an Indian chief. And if they are really fortunate, they just might grow up to be an ACR fellow.

Thank you!

The Dynamics of Preference
Christina L. Brown, New York University

The economic approach to preference assumes that preferences are independent of transient endowments, and that tastes are stable over time. The three papers in this session looked at consumer preference formation dynamically to demonstrate whether the adaptation and development of preferences over time, which we call "preference dynamics," generate any exceptions to these assumptions. The topic of preference dynamics is of interest to consumer behavior researchers because: (1) it addresses the age old question of whether or not individual preferences are meaningful and stable; (2) it sheds light on issues associated with consumer learning and expertise development; and (3) it examines issues associated with "hedonic consumption." Drazen Prelec was the discussant. The papers identified several key conceptual and methodological issues to stimulate additional research in this area:

How does past experience or ownership of a product impact current utility?

The paper by *Michal Strahilevitz, George Loewenstein, and Daniel Kahneman* focused on the effects of previous ownership on present utility. The paper demonstrated a potential violation of the economic assumption of independence by showing that although previous ownership does not affect attractiveness of a product, it does affect willingness to trade or sell, thus implying that previous ownership caused subjects to value a product at a level greater than the utility (attractiveness) it provides. Reported results showed that items never possessed may be valued less than items previously possessed. Furthermore, the findings indicated that the value placed on a current possession will increase as a function of the amount of time that has elapsed since the object was acquired. Among the theoretical issues addressed was the notion of simultaneous multiple reference points which may include both what we currently have and what we have had in the past.

To what extent are consumers able to predict the impact of current consumption on future utility?

Utility gained from consuming a good should diminish as the rate of consumption increases. The paper by *Barbara Kahn, Rebecca Ratner, and Daniel Kahneman* concerned whether people actually act as though they understand this—that their current consumption behavior affects future utility. In an experiment involving repeated consumption of favorite popular songs over time, subjects not only demonstrated an implicit understanding of diminishing returns by avoiding overexposure to favorites, but overcompensated by decreasing consumption too much (i.e., before experienced utility began to decrease). This is contrary to Herrnstein's principle of melioration, which suggests that people tend to be myopic by choosing their favorite to consume immediately, without taking into account that the utility of a good diminishes as the rate of consumption increases. Thus consumers acted appropriately but were not well calibrated in predicting their own future responses.

What affects whether consumers' preferences develop to a meaningful, predictable state or remain unfocused and unpredictable? How might the development of consumer preferences over time be modeled?

Fischhoff (1991) has suggested that consumers often do not have well-developed preference functions except for the most basic and frequently-encountered products. The paper by *Patricia M. West, Christina L. Brown, and Stephen J. Hoch*, examined prerequisites for the development of meaningfully consistent preferences. They proposed that consumers have difficulty learning their own preferences without the aid of a skeletal category structure, or "consumption vocabulary." They demonstrated how a rudimentary vocabulary of product attributes can encourage learning by providing such a structure. The "vocabulary" effect was tested in an experiment in which subjects provided with a vocabulary 1) exhibited better-defined and more consistent preferences than control subjects; 2) showed improved cue discovery, by becoming more consistent with regard to "implicit" attributes visible in the stimuli but omitted from the provided vocabulary; and 3) showed learning—i.e., increases in consistency over time. Repeated exposures allowed the degree of preference formation to be tracked dynamically over the course of the experiment through a novel moving-window model estimation procedure.

Will You Still Love Me Tomorrow: Dynamic Developments in Service Quality and Customer Retention

Katherine N. Lemon, Duke University

This special session addressed two questions: (1) How do customers update their perceptions of service quality over time? And, (2), given that customers do change their perceptions of a service over time, how do on-going service relationships (between customers and providers) develop, deteriorate, and, ultimately, end over time? In this session, we sought to bring together divergent research approaches to discuss dynamic models of service relationships, and to work toward a research agenda for service quality and customer retention issues. The three papers address both of these areas. Each incorporates the dynamic nature of the decision process—whether the customer is assumed to be updating his or her perceptions of the service, or making the decision to continue or disadopt the service. In addition, each of the three papers finds that the traditional, utility maximization model does not fully capture the complexities of the process at hand: past experiences "cloud" perceptions of current experience; consumers take "sunk costs" into effect when evaluating the merits of a service; consumers do not act in a truly "Bayesian-like" fashion when updating service quality perceptions. The three papers direct us to a much richer formulation of models for understanding the formation and updating of service quality perceptions and the customer's decision to continue or disadopt.

In the first paper, "The Quality Double Whammy: The Rich Stay Rich and the Poor Stay Poor," Boulding, Kalra and Staelin investigate the effects of prior expectations on customers' cumulative perceptions of quality. Consumers have been found to exhibit a confirmatory bias in evaluating new data (e.g., Hoch and Ha, 1986). This paradigm suggests that individuals are more likely to select and attend to information that confirms their prior beliefs than information which disconfirms them. Therefore, when evaluating new information about a service (e.g., a new service encounter) the authors find that prior expectations get "double-counted" as customers update perceptions of quality. Unlike previous Bayesian-like models, it appears that individuals form "biased" perceptions of the new experience based upon their prior expectations. The results suggest that customers' prior perceptions influence not only their *overall* assessments of quality, but also their perceptions of each *specific* transaction. This double-whammy effect provides insight into why many durable good and service firms find it hard to change customers' perceptions of their quality even after making, by objective standards, significant quality improvements. Thus the model provides a formal explanation for why customers' perceptions are slow to change over time.

The second paper, "A Bayesian Model of Quality and Customer Retention," by Rust, Inman and Zahorik, also examines the process by which customers update their perceptions of service quality. Using a Bayesian framework, the authors derived several propositions regarding the way that consumers form their perceptions of quality, satisfaction and probability of choice and then dynamically update them over time. In contrast to Boulding, Kalra and Staelin, the empirical results suggest that consumers appear to behave in a manner that is largely consistent with the Bayesian framework. On average, they update their perceptions of quality over time and are not overly sensitive to any one particular outcome occasion. Specifically, the results suggest that consumers are sensitive not only to the average performance of a product or service, but also to its variability around this mean. In addition, the

authors found that consumers are more likely to rechoose a brand or a service if the brand or service performs as expected, *i.e.*, consumers appear to interpret "meeting expectations" as a favorable outcome. Finally, under certain conditions, the probability of choice is not adversely affected by an outcome that is slightly less than expected. This research adds to our knowledge in the important area of how consumers dynamically update their quality perceptions and their preferences.

Although these first two papers appear to suggest opposing findings, they are actually quite complementary. Boulding, Kalra and Staelin's findings suggest that customer perceptions are very difficult to change when customer attitudes are well formed; therefore, customers do not appear "bayesian." Rust, Inman and Zahorik's results suggest that customers act most like bayesians when they have little or no experience with the product or service category. Results from both papers suggest that the most important time to establish quality perceptions in the minds of customers is at the time when customers have little prior experience with the category.

In the third paper, "The Effect of Cumulative Investment and usage Disconfirmation on Customer Disadoption Decisions," Barnett and Lemon examine specific factors that may impact the inexperienced customer's perceptions and behavioral intentions. The authors hypothesize that *customer usage disconfirmation, i.e.,* whether actual usage of the service is more or less than expected usage of the service, should have a significant impact on customer satisfaction, commitment and likelihood to drop the service. In addition, the customer's perceived total costs or *cumulative invest ment* in the service should also impact these measures. The results suggest that providing a cumulative investment "reminder" can moderate the impact of usage disconfirmation on customer perceptions of the service and future behavioral intentions. Specifically, this interaction suggests that if customers are reminded of their overall investment, and actual use of the service is greater than expected use (positive usage disconfirmation), they will be more satisfied, more committed to the service, and less likely to drop the service (compared to the no reminder condition). Alternatively, if customer actual use is less than expected (negative usage disconfirmation), and the cumulative investment reminder is present, customers will be less satisfied, less committed to the service and more likely to drop.

The discussion leader, Don Lehman, tied the three papers together and offered some insightful directions for future research. The discussion focused upon understanding the factors which come into play when consumers update perceptions of service quality, and/or when consumers decide to end relationships with service providers. Additional reserach is warranted to explore the variables that account for heterogeneity in consumers' updating processes. The key managerial insight provided by this session is an understanding of how marketing mix variables can be utilized to (a) improve customer perceptions of service quality, and (b) retain the customer for the long term.

Views from Across the Bridge: Industry Perspectives on Brand Equity Management
Akshay R. Rao, University of Minnesota

The term brand equity has come to be associated with some positive element of a brand name. In this session, a variety of brand equity management issues that practitioners face were highlighted. Four premier Minneapolis/St. Paul based Fortune 100 firms were represented in this set of presentations. The four presentations are summarized next.

1. "A Rose By Another Name: The Transformation of IDS into American Express Financial Advisors".

Mr. Peter Lefferts, American Express Financial Advisors spoke first. In his comments, he described how American Express Financial Advisors Inc. (formerly "IDS Financial Services") undertook a significant corporate transformation. This very successful company changed its name just as it completed its 100th year as IDS. Despite the fact that current customers were uncomfortable with the American Express name, a significant proportion of prospective customers felt that the American Express name added credibility, and thus the decision was made to change the name. Mr. Lefferts indicated that, based on the available evidence, the name change had been a successful strategic move.

2. "Is it a bird, is it a plane...? Measurement Issues in Brand Equity Research."

Ms. Vivian Milroy, General Mills focussed her talk on measurement issues. She noted that the only thing clear about brand equity is that the meaning of the term is not at all clear. Instead of accepting this complexity, definitions and measurements have been oversimplified. Tests of new product ideas have focuses on breadth of appeal instead of differentiated imagery associated with the new product. When testing offerings against the competition, reliance has been placed on blind comparisons, ignoring the impact of imagery on consumer preference. When analyzing the impact of market spending, the focus has been on short term volume gains rather than the long term impact on the health of the brand. Even when tracking attitude change, there has been a failure to recognize changes in the consumer's definitions of attributes such as "convenience", thus ignoring the possibility that changes in preference occur even though brand image has stayed constant. Ms. Milroy suggested that measurement should focus as much, if not more, on what the brand could be, rather than what it currently is.

3. "What's In a Nom: Managing Global Brand Families at 3M."

Mr. Douglas Rowen, 3M was the third speaker and addressed issues and challenges related to managing a global family of brands which span 60,000 products in over 150 countries. 3M's brand family covers more than 20 major industries from consumer products to electronics and health care products. With more than 50% of sales coming from outside the United States, maximizing the benefit of a global brand family is an increasingly complex task. Issues range from adjusting for local differences, global measurement and communication vehicles, and trademark selection.

4. "Dough in the doughboy: Leveraging Equity in Visual Symbols at Pillsbury-Grand Metropolitan"

Mr. Steve Zuber, Pillsbury-Grand Metropolitan was the final speaker and emphasized that the core of Grand Metropolitan's food business is the Pillsbury company, comprising four major American brands: Pillsbury, Green Giant, Haagen Dazs and Burger King.

All these brands have substantial volume and profitability, and the attempt has been to build them into global "megabrands". In the case of Pillsbury, the most enduring symbol of the brand is the doughboy, followed by the Green Giant and the Little Sprout. His presentation focussed on how Pillsbury has attempted to use evidence that these are more than animated characters, but in fact are useful vehicles for establishing Pillsbury brands with new consumers worldwide.

Finally, Deborah Roedder John summarized the comments of the speakers, identified emergent themes, and lead a discussion that included several interesting and provocative questions from the audience.

SPECIAL SESSION SUMMARY
The Meaning of Gifts and Greetings
Russell W. Belk, University of Utah

Giving presents is a talent; to know what a person wants, to know when and how to get it, to give it lovingly and well. Unless a character possesses this talent there is no moment more annihilating to ease than that in which a present is received and given (Pamela Glenconner, *Edward Wyndhan Tennant: A Memoir*, 1919; npn, chapter 5).

Gift-giving is attracting a growing amount of attention in both consumer research (e.g., Otnes and Beltramini forthcoming) and other disciplines (e.g., Carrier 1994; Derrida 1992; Hendry 1995; Miller 1993; Schmidt 1995; Waits 1993). Nevertheless, numerous questions remain intriguingly unanswered involving the basic meanings of gifts and gift-giving rituals. For gift-giving does not accord well with assumptions of self-interested rationality. It is known to be a highly symbolic, highly emotional, interpersonal medium that helps us say things that we find difficult or impossible to say in words. At the same time, it appears that few of us speak this symbolic language well and miscommunication, disappointment, and failure are frequent. Since this language and attendant rituals are culture-specific, we will need to frame our research cross-culturally. The papers in this session explored the symbolic role of greeting card exchange, cross-cultural differences in the role of mothers in family gift-giving, and reciprocal Christmas gifts from young children.

The presentation by Greta Pennell (dressed in her Pip the Elf costume) turned prior work on its head by using participant observation as Santa's helper and a content analysis of children's letters to Santa Claus to find that children actively participate in a reciprocal gift economy with this commercial deity, rather than simply act as greedy recipients of Santa's largesse. Pennell's findings take the perspective of the child into consideration and demonstrate that far from being a passive recipients of gifts, even very young children engage in a number of distinct types of reciprocity with Santa.

A cross-cultural and familial examination of gift giving among Anglo-Celtic, Sino-Vietnamese, and Israeli mothers was presented by Constance Hill and Celia Romm. These cultures were chosen to exemplify different points on the power distance and individualism/ collectivism cultural continua suggested by Hofstede (1980). The study examined the implication of these differences for that chief keeper of gift-giving rituals: the mother. Meaningful differences in gift motivations, selections, presentation rituals, and recipient reactions were detected in their depth interview data, as will be seen in the paper.

The third paper by Kimberly Dodson and me examined the role of birthday cards in interpersonal relationships. While there is a small amount of literature addressing birthday celebrations (e.g., Chudacoff 1989; Linton and Linton 1952; Mooney and Brabandt 1987; Otnes and McGrath 1994; Shamgar-Handleman and Handleman 1991) or examining selected effects of greeting cards (see the paper), a comprehensive examination of the intended and actual messages communicated by these cards has been missing. Focusing on both card givers and recipients, the study detected a "mine field" of miscommunication possibilities.

Following the presentations, Cele Otnes led a lively discussion that focused on cross-cultural differences in gift-giving and the difficulties of such cross-cultural work, on gender differences in card-giving and the research possibilities introduced by personal-

ized greeting card machines, and on the materialism versus altruism revealed by children's requests to Santa Claus. The only disappointment in an otherwise stimulating and enriching session was when "Pip" stepped out to find a toilet and was told by hotel personnel that they had no toilets for elves.

REFERENCES

Carrier, James (1994), *Gifts and Commodities*, London: Routledge.

Chudacoff, Howard P. (1989), *How Old Are You?*, Princeton, NJ: Princeton University Press.

Derrida, Jacques (1992), *Given Time: I. Counterfeit Money*, Peggy Knauf, trans., Chicago: University of Chicago Press.

Hendry, Joy (1995), *Wrapping Culture*, Oxford: Clarendon Press.

Hofstede, Geert (1980), *Culture's Consequences*, Beverly Hills, CA: Sage.

Linton, Ralph and Adelin Linton (1952), *The Lore of Birthdays*, New York: Henry Schuman.

Miller, Daniel, ed. (1994), *Unwrapping Christmas*, Oxford: Clarendon Press.

Mooney, Linda A. and Sarah Brabant (1987), "Birthday Cards, Love, and Communication," *Sociology and Social Research*, 72 (October), 106-109.

Otnes, Cele and Richard Beltramini, eds. (forthcoming), *Gift-Giving: An Interdisciplinary Anthology*, Bowling Green, OH: Bowling Green University Popular Press.

Otnes, Cele and Mary Ann McGrath (1994), "Ritual Socialization and the Children's Birthday Party: The Early Emergence of Gender Differences," *Journal of Ritual Studies*, 8 (Winter), 73-93.

Schmidt, Leigh Eric (1995), *Consumer Rites*, Princeton, NJ: Princeton University Press.

Shamgar-Handelman, Lee and Don Handelman (1991), "Celebrations of Bureaucracy: Birthday Parties in Israeli Kindergartens," *Ethnology*, 30 (October), 293-312.

Waits, William B. (1993), *The Modern Christmas in America: A Cultural History of Gift Giving*, New York: New York University Press.

The Birthday Card Minefield

Kimberly J. Dodson, University of Utah
Russell W. Belk, University of Utah

ABSTRACT

Why do we give birthday cards? What are their intended meanings? How do their received meanings compare to those intended? To investigate these questions MBA students selected three birthday cards for an older, younger, and same age recipient whom they described. They then conducted depth interviews with the recipients and compared their reactions to those the cards were meant to evoke. Results show that birthday card exchange is riddled with "landmines" that may cause mild to catastrophic miscommunication. We analyze gender, age, and relationship characteristics associated with these problems and discuss how birthday card selection may aid or interfere with bonding and ego consolidation.

INTRODUCTION

Americans will buy nearly seven and a half billion greeting cards of all brands this year at the rate of eight million cards a day (Hirshey, 1995). We are driving this demand with our messy, complicated lives. Greeting card developers provide us cards appropriate for an increasing variety of occasions and personal circumstances (Hirshey, 1995). Market research helps the industry provide cards for new occasions and recipient groups from former in-laws to gay lovers, and greeting cards are considered good indicators of social change and cultural attitudes (Brabant and Mooney, 1989; Demos and Jache, 1981; Hirshey, 1995; McGough, 1986; Mooney and Brabant, 1987).

Birthdays are an important North American ritual occasion in which people of all ages, ethnicities, and genders are celebrated as "special" individuals (Demos and Jache, 1981; Mooney and Brabant, 1987). The birthday card has become critical in these rituals and transforms communication into a gift. It has been suggested that the card's price is a sign value mediating the relationship signified by the exchange (Schrift, 1994). Previous studies have considered birthday cards as indicators of societal attitudes toward aging (Demos and Jache, 1981; Dillon and Jones, 1981; Huyck and Duchon, 1986; Schrift, 1994), communication of love (Mooney and Brabant, 1987), and gender-based expressiveness (Brabant and Mooney, 1989). However, there has been limited examination of the expectations held by givers and receivers of birthday cards and the complex role that birthday cards play as a vehicle through which to judge the quality or depth of interpersonal relationships.

This paper presents themes that emerged from personal journals and depth interviews. These themes suggest that birthday cards carry very distinctive messages and that both givers and receivers have well-defined expectations that may not be mutually recognized. As a result, the practice of giving a birthday card is a more problematic communication than it might seem. In many ways, the consequences of unsuccessful birthday card selection may be greater than those of not having exchanged a card at all. This paper utilizes a "minefield" metaphor to discuss the social risks and relationship dangers associated with giving and receiving birthday cards. The "birthday card minefield" must be negotiated for the giver to successfully select and deliver a card to the receiver. If the card reaches its destination and conveys the message hoped for by the sender and desired by the receiver, then the "mission" is a success. Unspoken expectations act as landmines that threaten to maim a relationship when they are inadvertently trod upon. Giving birthday cards to those with different personal characteristics, generations, or genders often involves crossing an especially dangerous field that threatens to create a card-giving cataclysm.

METHODOLOGY: BIRTHDAY JOURNALS, CARDS, AND INTERVIEWS

Qualitative data focusing on birthdays were obtained from slightly more than 100 depth interviews and personal birthday journals. MBA students at a Western university were asked to create personal journals reflecting their beliefs and memories associated with birthdays. In addition to the journal, each student selected three birthday cards: one card chosen for someone a generation younger than the student, the second card selected for a peer or spouse, and the final card targeted for someone at least a generation older than the student. As part of a larger study of birthdays, the personal journals included descriptions of these cards, the people for whom they were chosen, and the rationale for each particular selection.

The students subsequently completed two depth interviews: one interview with someone younger than themselves and one interview with someone older than themselves (often, but not always, the recipients intended for the cards selected earlier). These informants were shown the three birthday cards selected by the interviewer and asked to describe how they would feel if they were to receive each card. They were then asked to describe someone to whom they would send each card. A total of 98 cards were available for content analysis. The cards tended to be either humorous or sentimental, either directed to a particular person (e.g. Mother, Father, Sister, Nephew) or generic (no specific role identified), and almost always designed specifically as birthday cards. Analysis was facilitated by a qualitative data retrieval program.

THE BIRTHDAY CARD MINEFIELD: WHY SEND A CARD?

A seemingly simple card can present a complex image for both the giver and receiver based on its particular style, genre, and content. The nuanced nature of this complexity is important when considering the emotional and sentimental value often attached to a card (Brabant and Mooney, 1989). Because sending a greeting card is an act of communication that does not require an immediate response, it is considered an excellent mode for transmitting messages difficult to deliver face-to-face (Huyck and Duchon, 1986).

For some informants, giving a card provides an avenue for communicating sentiments that would be too difficult for them to speak. For these people the printed message of the card is a tool for eloquently saying that which they feel they cannot say, or can only say more clumsily. In the words of one such person:

> I prefer cards that can say what I can't say, because they come up with the words so well.
> (55-year-old female)

Card givers often add a handwritten note to the card expressing personal sentiments specific for the intended recipient (Brabant and Mooney, 1989). These notes and letters expound on the feelings associated with the card and contribute a personalizing element to its message. Writing words on a page is often easier and "safer" than speaking those same words, and cards encourage the writing of thoughts that might otherwise go undocumented.

EXHIBIT 1

To My Wife
I may not be
the neatest, handsomest
richest husband
in the
world...

... but I sure am
the luckiest !

Happy Birthday

Renée

Through a letter or card I am able to tell people my feelings and express myself easier. So that is one reason I like birthdays, because I can tell that person about my love for them. The card is probably most important.
(25-year-old female)

Only a limited number of cards selected by the informants explicitly spoke of "love" within their text. Mooney and Brabant (1987) found similar results. But many cards were perceived as expressing love and emotion, even if they did not do so literally in the text. The very act of sending or presenting a card is sometimes seen as an expression of some level of love. When describing the card in Exhibit 1, one man said:

It shows that you consider yourself lucky to have your wife and that you love your wife a lot. I think it is very important to tell your wife that you love her and this does that. The picture is cute, too.
(56-year-old-male, Exhibit 1)

Studies have shown that humorous birthday cards provide a means for expressing and diffusing anxieties about changes linked to age (Demos and Jache, 1981; Huyck and Duchon, 1986). Humor can also be used to minimize the anxiety associated with expressing emotion within relationships (Huyck and Duchon, 1986). In these cases, the remembrance of the occasion with a card is perceived to convey emotion without having to confront it directly. This was frequently seen in the exchange of cards between men.

The reason for the card is that, although close, we have never been able to express how much we care about each other. The humor couches the sentiment to make it more comfortable for both of us.
(27-year-old-male, Exhibit 2)

Cards and Price

The purchase of a birthday card to commemorate the event or identify the giver of a gift is so prevalent that many in our sample did so without question. In the younger generations (those below the age of 50) some do not even consider the acquisition of a card as a monetary expenditure.

But now-a-days I just send them a card or make a phone call so I don't spend money.
(25-year-old female)

Informants sometimes equated the quality of the card with its price, and placing limits on the card selection due to price constraints was thought to minimize the value of the message and the sentiments expressed. For these individuals, it was important that a high quality medium be chosen as the carrier of their message. Because the card is often seen to reflect the giver's sincerity in acknowledging a relationship with the recipient, the quality of the card was seen to add value to the expressed relationship.

I just pick out the card. No I shouldn't say that because I know that when you look at the rack the cheap cards are way down at the bottom and the expensive ones are at the top. I start looking at the top and work my way down. Even if I like the message in a cheap card, I usually won't get it, I'll look for something that's a little more expensive.
(46-year-old female)

However, consumers in the older generation recognize that the price of cards has substantially increased over time. They are not as desensitized to price as are younger people, and acknowledge that buying a card truly is an expenditure of money.

It is that they have gotten so expensive. I hate it that I go to the store and I'm going, "Oh my gosh! $2.50! $1.95!" It's just like

EXHIBIT 2

...to a relatively
booger - free adult!

Happy Birthday!

I'm getting them a present . . .The card is gift enough.
(54-year-old female)

In some cases, the cost can be a deterrent for the purchase of a card altogether. This avoids the pitfall of the "birthday card minefield" by never entering into it, although it is uncommon.

THE BIRTHDAY CARD MINEFIELD: THE GIVER

The process of birthday card exchange begins when the giver decides to select and present a card to an individual celebrating his or her birthday. Careful to recognize the inherent value of this process, most informants place importance on the card itself, as well as on the methods of card selection and purchase.

Personalization Emphasis

There is a general acknowledgment of the importance of selecting a card that best "fits" the individual who will receive it. Rather than pick just any card, considerable conscious thought is usually put into matching characteristics of the card and the recipient. Taking the time to evaluate the card's match with intended recipient allows people to appropriate mass-produced cards in order to send an "individualized" message. In this way, the selection of a birthday card seems related to the importance of "appropriateness" in the perfect gift (Belk, forthcoming).

What kind of cards do I usually buy? I usually buy humorous ones. Stuff that seems to fit the person and whether you think they can handle it. . .So I guess a lot of times I buy the kind that I guess that person would pick out, that fits their personality. (33-year-old male)

In addition to the effort expended in finding the perfect card, many respondents spend time writing a personal message in the card. The act of adding a personal note provides the means for further personalizing a rather generic medium of communication.

A certain amount of anxiety does exist in the card selection process, as givers feel pressured to acknowledge unique characteristics of recipients in order to find the best card both for expressing the desired message and for avoiding offense. If the giver does not know the recipient very well, this can be problematic. Rather than having the ability to reflect on the recipient, the giver must instead project his or her tentative beliefs about that individual into the process to compensate for their limited understanding of this person. With less familiarity with the recipient there is therefore less personalization of the card and more generic or stereotypical cards selected because they are safer.

I would send this . . .because I would be comfortable sending anybody a Garfield card. No matter what their age because he is a popular character and most people of all ages like him . .
.
(46-year-old female)

Mood of the Giver

The giver generally seeks a card that best meets the desires of the recipient and appeals to this person's personality and tastes. It is not only the recipient's characteristics, however, that affect the card decision. Often the giver's mood is also an important consideration in the ultimate selection. Women of all ages in the sample indicated that their personal mood at the time of shopping influenced card selection.

Gender Expectations

In selecting cards appropriate for family, friends, and acquaintances, givers of cards utilize very consistent selection criteria based on gender expectations. These criteria act as guides to help in narrowing the focus for potential cards, and generally involve the differentiation between humorous and sentimental cards; humor is seen as best for men and sentimental expressions as best for women. The notion that men should receive humorous cards while women

EXHIBIT 3

It's been a long time, but the stork still remembers you...

...he never forgets the ones he drops !!

---

are "unable to handle them" is a common theme throughout the interviews, and one that is validated directly by some of the informants. The concern over women's inability to understand or appreciate humor is a strong deterrent to selecting humorous cards for women. Even if the giver herself enjoys the card and doesn't find it offensive, she might hesitate about sending such a card to a female friend.

Informant:	Ooh! This one's dangerous! Ooooh! That's kind of a funny thought. For friends you might like but don't really like.
Interviewer:	Would you give it to one of your friends?
Informant:	Male friends. Women don't take kindly to that kind of thing.

(46-year-old female, Exhibit 3)

Socialization to the idea of gender-specific card content was already evident among the younger informants interviewed.

Interviewer:	Who might receive this type of card? [Exhibit 4]
Informant:	A sentimental person, usually a girl.
Interviewer:	How would you feel if you received this card? [Exhibit 3]
Informant:	It's funny, and I wouldn't mind getting a card like this.
Interviewer:	Who might receive a card like this?
Informant:	Guys that like joking around.

(13-year-old male, Exhibits 3 & 4)

Safety Net

Many respondents expressed a preference for humorous cards, but realize that the message conveyed through this type of card can be more easily misunderstood. To avoid the dangers of being misunderstood and also enjoy the fun of giving a humorous card, some people attempt to develop a "safety net" for themselves by

giving more than one card. The use of more than one card can also provide the giver with the opportunity to convey more than one type of message to the recipient. In many ways this could be likened to a "public" and "private" card, so that a person has a humorous card to display to friends and family, and one that is more private and personal.

> My husband gave me two cards. One was nice, kind of a little humorous. He saved the really naughty one for the next day.
> (48-year-old female)

THE BIRTHDAY CARD MINEFIELD: THE RECEIVER

The actual card recipient is the person who ultimately determines the success or failure of the birthday card experience. Although the giver of the card can try to ascertain the expectations of the recipient, there is never complete knowledge about what a particular recipient desires. Just as the giver of the card enters into the process of selecting and giving a birthday card with certain assumptions, so too does the potential recipient of the card.

The card needs to be "Me"

It is very important to a recipient of a birthday card that it "be 'Me'". In saying this, the recipient is communicating a desire that the card appeal to him or her at a very personal level. The overall impression of the card should result in the recipient feeling that he or she was at the forefront of the giver's mind when the card was selected. Adding a handwritten note to a card is a very effective means of personalizing the card so that it immediately becomes unique to that person.

Informant:	To me, it is the personal things that are added to it, it's the little notes that let you know they didn't just buy a card and sign it to get their job done for your birthday.
Interviewer:	What do you think of this card?

EXHIBIT 4

*May you have a
happy day and
a beautiful year.*

HAPPY BIRTHDAY

Informant: It looks silly. It doesn't have any applicability to me; it is a generic birthday card you
could give to anybody.
(15-year-old female)

Cards are remembered and saved

To aid in the ability to remember specific birthdays and the
recognition by family and friends of the event through cards, some
recipients keep the cards they have received, much as they would
memorabilia for a scrapbook. This is supported by the findings of
a 1986 Greeting Card Association survey which reported that nine
out of ten people have at least one or two cards that they keep
because they like them so much (Meer, 1986). In our study, aside
from one man who talked about keeping the cards that his children
had made, all of those who talked about "stashing" their cards
someplace were women. These women varied in age from 13 to 73-
years-old, with representation among all age groups. For some
women, saving cards provides a means of remembering people and
documenting their lives.

...So I put them in my basket or my file folder, and I probably
never look at them again, but I know they're there. Family
ones are the ones I'll always save. It's kind of neat if you save
some of the early ones. I have appreciated that I saved some
cards from my grandparents.
... You have their handwriting and that's kind of nice. Their
signature.
(54-year-old female)

Recipients place great value on the cards that they receive,
especially as they grow older. Therefore, the giver of the card
should recognize the statement that he or she is making through the
card and realize that for some, the card will be a timeless reminder
of the relationship they share. A lifetime of interpersonal memories
can be stored in a box containing birthday cards, and givers would

ideally hope to be remembered as the one who sent the "perfect"
card that year.

THE BIRTHDAY CARD MINEFIELD:
LANDMINES

The successful delivery of a birthday card message is dependent on the careful alignment of the efforts of the giver with the
expectations of the recipient. The giver and the receiver both enter
the birthday card exchange laden with preconceived notions, sub-
conscious beliefs, and hoped-for results. The inability to successfully realize all of the underlying messages leads to "landmines."
Landmines are often tripped by personal, generational, and gender
differences, and a differing perspective on any one of these levels
can quickly lead to a failed birthday card mission.

Personalization

The first landmine is based on an oversight of the importance
of personalization to the recipient. Many people value cards that are
seemingly chosen just for them and include a handwritten note, and
yet they themselves may not attend to these things when giving
cards to others. The desire to be recognized as a unique individual
and remembered on or near one's birthday is critical, and often a
generic card that has been signed but not personalized does not
fulfill this wish.

Several of my siblings are card senders and never miss my
birthday. While this may sound good on its face, the cards
usually don't have any personal message in them and I
discount them heavily. It is better to get a card with no
inscription than no card at all, but it is best to get a handwritten
message in the card. The commercial content of the card does
not mean very much to me ...Getting a card with no personal
message is about the same as the computer generated cards I
used to get from my dentist wishing me Happy Birthday and
reminding me that I was due for a check-up. No message, no

EXHIBIT 5

I have an idea
where we can spend
your birthday.

---

meaning.
(28-year-old female)

Generational

Aside from demanding different content and style for a "child" card as compared to an "adult" card, there is seldom recognition of any differences by age and generation that might affect the success of card exchange. Of all of the landmines, this is one of the most interesting, because it highlights the difficulties of trying to cross boundaries (those created by generations). In most of these situations, the giver of the card approaches the birthday card selection with the desire to find a personalized card and appeal to the uniqueness of the individual, and the recipient enters open-mindedly and ready to have his or her expectations met. Unfortunately, somewhere in-between the message is lost and the end result is uncomfortable. Some of the older people consider the difficulty in communicating cross-generationally as simply a by-product of an age-graded society:

> Whether you like it or not, there is no way that one generation can know what another generation is doing or likes or does. You can be aware of it, but you are who you are.
> (54-year-old female)

Making a more explicit claim, another woman explained why she is frustrated with characteristics she deems indicative of "today's generation."

> I think that is typical of today's generation, I do . . .Well, they're not direct, they like to say I love you but they, um, they do love you and you can feel that but they're just not saying it like we were.
> (63-year-old female)

In many instances, this inability to understand and communicate between generations arises when the older generation is unable to understand the humor or sentiments expressed in cards preferred by the younger one. A classic example of mis-interpreting what would seem to be a rather obvious card is found when a 76-year-old man tried to understand a risqué card.

Interviewer:	How do you like these cards? Who would you send them to?
Informant:	Well, I think they're all right nice. Yeah, I think they're real pretty. The first one I really don't know what it is. Looks like a couple of people wrestling . . .
Interviewer:	. . . actually, it is a woman with her legs wrapped around a man
Informant:	Well why would she want to do that? She might hurt him. I wouldn't send that to anybody.

(76-year-old male, Exhibit 5)

As difficult as it might be for some members of the older generation to understand the humor and subtleties of cards, those in this group are distinctive in their willingness to accept almost any type of card as a symbol of being remembered.

The lack of complete communication goes from young to old as well, as younger people repeatedly expressed their anger and disappointment with "grandparents" because they are unable to understand what youth really want in a card. With younger recipients, the tolerance for child-like cards was much lower.

Gender

The final potential landmine is one which involves gender issues. As discussed earlier, givers of cards have clearly defined beliefs regarding what is appropriate for a particular gender. Unfortunately, this can lead the giver astray, as numerous women mentioned that they like humorous cards (despite the giver stereotype evidenced in our data that women like to receive sentimental cards) and some men commented that they would not be completely opposed to receiving a card with some heartfelt sentiment (even if veiled by humor) from family and close friends rather than always getting generic humorous cards. Just as women too like to laugh, men like to hear that they are loved and are important in someone's life.

Unfortunately, however, stepping outside of the accepted "stereotypical" cards for a particular gender can be detrimental. One of the greatest problems confounding the gender issue is the belief that males and females approach birthday cards differently.

Girls always seem to like cards. Boys always wonder what to do with them.
(54-year-old male)

THE BIRTHDAY CARD MINEFIELD: CONCLUSIONS

This analysis of the role of birthday cards and the issues surrounding the giving and receiving of them is beneficial in helping to better understand birthday card communication and the ritual significance of birthdays in a highly individualistic society. Many of us take for granted the importance of giving a card to recognize a birthday, and more often than not, we are not aware of the difficult journey we embark on in order to select the "right" card. The exchange of birthday cards has the potential to be a tool for social solidarity in that it helps connect people and generations, confront various gender issues, and provide a medium through which people can communicate feelings and sentiment that they find difficult to express in person. Unfortunately, every purchase of a card holds with it the threat of failure because of poor recognition of unspoken expectations or the inability to meet the personal desires of the recipient. Those receiving birthday cards are not necessarily forgiving, and those giving the card are often venturing into a potentially disastrous situation without being adequately prepared. In order to successfully negotiate this minefield and for the act of giving cards to have a desired outcome, the personalization, generational, and gender issues must be carefully considered and sensitively approached.

REFERENCES

Belk, R. (forthcoming), "The Perfect Gift," in *Gift Giving: An Interdisciplinary Anthology*, Cele Otnes and Richard Beltramini, eds., Bowling Green, Ohio: Bowling Green University Popular Press.

Brabant, S. and L. Mooney (1989), "Him, Her, or Either: Sex of Person Addressed and Interpersonal Communication," *Sex Roles*, 20: 47-58.

Demos, V. and A. Jache (1981), "When You Care Enough: An Analysis of Attitudes Toward Aging in Humorous Birthday Cards," *The Gerontologist*, 21: 209-215.

Dillon, K. and B. Jones (1981), "Attitudes Toward Aging Portrayed by Birthday Cards,"*International Journal of Aging and Human Development*, 13: 79-84.

Hirshey, G. (1995), "Happy [ ] Day to You," *The New York Times Magazine*, July 2, 21-27.

Huyck, H. and J. Duchon (1986), "Over the Miles: Coping, Communicating, and Commiserating through Age-Theme Greeting Cards," *Humor and Aging*. Eds. Lucille Nahemow, Kathleen A. McCluskey-Fawcett and Paul McGhee. Orlando: Academic Press, Inc.

McGough, R. (1986), "Pansies are Green," *Forbes*, February 10, 89-92.

Meer, J. (1986), "What A Card," *Psychology Today*, January, 16.

Mooney, L. and S. Brabant (1988), "Birthday Cards, Love, and Communication," *Sociology and Social Research*, 72: 106-109.

Schrift, M. (1994), "Icons of Femininity in Studio Cards: Women, Communication and Identity," *Journal of Popular Culture*, 28 (Summer), 111-122.

The Role of Mothers as Gift Givers: A Comparison Across Three Cultures

Constance Hill, University of Wollongong
Celia T. Romm, University of Wollongong

ABSTRACT

The major research objective was to use the four elements in our gift-giving model, i.e. motivation, selection, presentation, and reaction, to compare and contrast the role of mothers in the Anglo-Celtic, Sino-Vietnamese, and Israeli cultures. A particular emphasis was placed on the why, when, where, and how mothers in these three cultures exchange gifts with their children. The data was collected through a series of in-depth interviews with 60 mothers, i.e. 20 mothers from each culture. The results indicate that even though mothers in all three cultures play a central role in family gift giving, there are significant differences in the way in which this role is played in each culture. These cultural differences are highlighted in relation to two behavioural dimensions, i.e. power distance and individualism/ collectivism, previously identified by Hofstede (1980).

INTRODUCTION

Much of the gift giving research to date has focused on the family with the role of mother as major gift giver being stressed. Women have been described as prime initiators and agents who do most of the shopping, decorating and gift-wrapping. Only recently has the role of mother as gift giver been explored across cultures (Hill and Romm 1995).

The major objective of this research is to explore the role of mothers in family gift giving across three cultures. The underlying assumption here is that family gift giving is one of the main ways in which consumer socialisation occurs. It is through this process that parents shape their children's present and future behaviour as consumers. Understanding gift giving in the family context is a key for understanding consumer behaviour and, consequently, for designing effective marketing strategies within and across cultures.

The theoretical model on which this study is based derives from the works of Belk (1979) and Sherry (1983) on gift-giving behaviour. The model assumes that family gift-giving is a continual process that consists of four interactive elements, namely: (1) motivation, (2) selection, (3) presentation, and (4) reaction. It also assumes that these four elements do not take place in fixed periods of time but rather, once activated, continue to play a direct or indirect role throughout the entire family gift-giving process. In this study, we use the four elements to compare and contrast the role of mothers as gift givers in Anglo-Celtic, Sino-Vietnamese, and Israeli cultures.

LITERATURE REVIEW

Tribal cultures were the first context in which gift-giving practices were studied (Levi-Strauss 1949; Malinowski 1922, 1926; Mauss 1954). In the 1960s, psychologists and sociologists began to study gift giving (Blau 1964, Gouldner 1960, Sahlins 1965, Schwartz 1967). By the late 1970s, the study of gift-giving behaviour began to be explored by consumer researchers (Belk 1979, Sherry 1983).

Family Gift Giving. Luschen (1972) was the first to explore family gift giving. His findings revealed that regardless of the change in family structure to isolated nuclear units, gift giving remains important as a means of promoting and strengthening family ties. Later, Caplow (1982) came to the same conclusion. More recently, Cheal's (1988) findings mainly supported these previous studies.

The Role of Mothers in Family Gift Giving. In accordance with Mead's (1934) role theory, the role of mothers in family gift giving is defined here as the expected patterns of behaviour that the mother learns and internalises through the socialisation process and expresses during gift exchange. Principal researchers to consider the significance of the mothers' gift-giving role include Caplow (1982), DiLeonardo (1987), Cheal (1988), and Fischer and Arnold (1990). Still, these studies did not fully explore why, when, where, or how mothers exchange gifts within the family.

Family Gift Giving Across Cultures. Most research on family gift giving has focussed on the West. Only recently have researchers started to consider the importance of extending this research to non-Western cultures. Belk (1984) proposed that gift giving serves different purposes across cultures, relating these differences to the extent to which the culture emphasises the individual. In collectivistic cultures, individuals evaluate themselves and others on group-based characteristics, e.g. ancestral background and national, historical achievements. In such cultures, e.g. Chinese societies, the purpose of gift giving is to reinforce a group-based self-concept. In contrast, in individualistic cultures, individuals assess themselves and others on personal characteristics, e.g. age, occupation, and education. In such cultures, e.g. Australia, the purpose of gift giving is to reinforce an individual-based self-concept.

The Gift-Giving Process. Even though Belk (1979) was the first consumer researcher to consider gift-giving, his emphasis was on givers, gifts, recipients, and situational conditions rather than on the gift-giving process. Sherry (1983) was the first consumer researcher to consider the actual gift-giving process, emphasising the temporal aspects of gift giving which correspond to the consumer decision-making model (Engel, Kollat and Blackwell 1968). In Sherry's conceptualisation, gift giving is a process which starts by the giver being motivated to give a gift, continues through the selection and exchange, and culminates with the recipient's response. Both Belk and Sherry recognised gift exchange is essentially a communication process.

The theoretical framework for this research builds on Sherry's (1983) work in which gift-giving behaviour is conceptualised as a process consisting of the following four elements: (1) motivation [M], (2) selection [S], (3) presentation [P], and (4) reaction [R]. Our model assumes that even though the gift-giving process can be described in terms of these four elements, it is more complex. Thus, over a period of time, each family member goes through the process more than once. Also, the assumption is made that when family members go through the process, it is in a simultaneous and complementary way, with each family member simultaneously initiating and responding to the gift-giving behaviour of the others. Figure 1 presents the basic components of our simultaneous complementary family gift-giving model. The term 'parent' in the figure refers in this instance to mothers.

The motivation element [M] is defined here as the trigger for the gift-giving process. The motive for gift giving can be a special occasion or an ad hoc situation impelling one family member to give a gift to another. To operationalise the motivation element, the following issues are addressed: (1) how mothers explain what they try to achieve by giving a gift, i.e. justification; (2) how mothers explain the significance of a gift, i.e. significance; and (3) how mothers explain the timing for giving a gift, i.e. timing.

FIGURE 1
The Simultaneous Complementary Family Gift-Giving Process

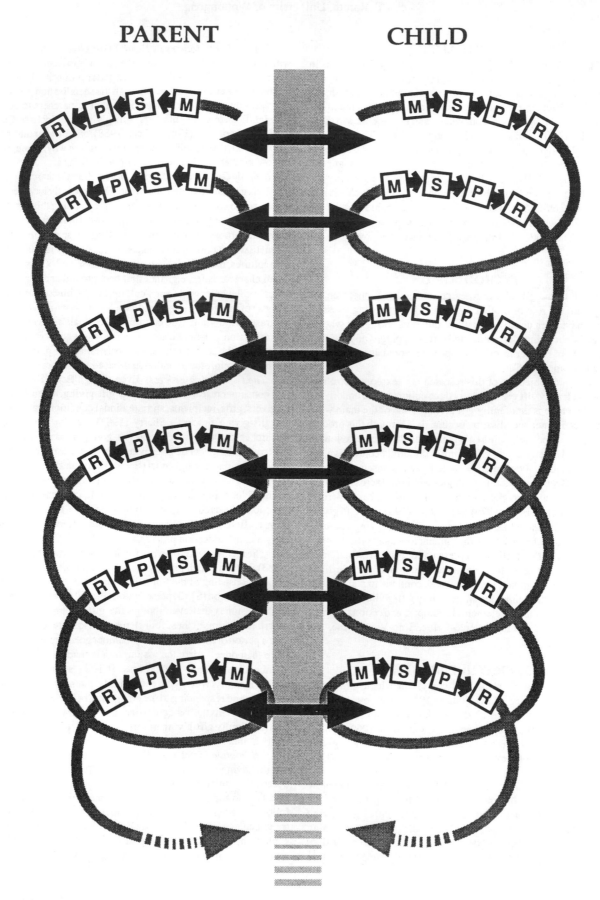

The selection element [S] is defined here as an internal and external search and evaluation process whereby the giver decides on a suitable gift for the recipient. To operationalise the selection element, the following issues are addressed: (1) how mothers explain their involvement during gift selection, i.e. involvement; (2) how mothers explain the family influences on them during gift selection, i.e. family influences; (3) how mothers explain the advertising and point-of-sale influences on them during gift selection, i.e. promotional influences; and (4) how mothers explain the necessary attributes of gifts, i.e. gift attributes.

The presentation element [P] is defined here as the point in time when the actual gift exchange takes place. To operationalise the presentation element, the following issues are addressed: (1) how mothers explain what they are trying to say through gift presentation, i.e. presentation messages; (2) how mothers explain what they are trying to say through gift allocation, i.e. allocation messages; and (3) how mothers explain the recipient's understanding of what they are trying to say through the presentation and allocation of gifts, i.e. understanding of messages.

The reaction element [R] is defined here as the direct or indirect manner in which the recipient responds to the gift. To operationalise the reaction element, the following issues are addressed: (1) how mothers explain whether they achieve what they originally intended by giving a gift, i.e. achievement; (2) how mothers explain the feedback from the recipient about the gift, i.e. feedback; and (3) how mothers explain what the recipient does with the gift, i.e. usage.

METHODOLOGY

An inductive, qualitative approach was used in which an attempt was made to explain the phenomena's significance as described from the respondents' perspective. Thus, in-depth interviews were required.

Sample. The sample consisted of 60 mothers, 20 from each cultural group: Anglo-Celtic, Sino-Vietnamese, and Israeli. The Anglo-Celtic mothers, who were born in Australia, and the Sino-Vietnamese mothers, who were born in Vietnam, were all interviewed in Sydney, Australia. The Israeli mothers, who were born in Israel of first-generation European parents, were interviewed in Beer Sheva and Tel Aviv, Israel. These cultural groups were selected because they represent different positions on a continuum ranging from extreme individualism (Anglo-Celtic), mid-range (Israeli) and extreme collectivism (Sino-Vietnamese) as indicated by Hofstede (1980). An attempt was made to keep all variables constant to highlight cultural differences. Thus, the study focussed on mothers who were all homemakers, drawn from middle-class nuclear families in which both biological parents were living together with their children. Within this type of family structure, the mothers all had children of adolescent age, i.e. between the ages of 12 to 21, who lived at home and attended high school, university, or trade school. All the mothers had received at least a high school education.

Research Instrument. The research instrument was a semi-structured interview. During the interviews, the mothers were asked to discuss issues that involved the four gift-giving elements, i.e. motivation, selection, presentation, and reaction. See Table 1 for the interview agenda.

Data Collection and Analysis. Separate interviews, lasting about 2 hours, were conducted by the authors in the mothers' homes. The interviews were tape recorded and transcribed verbatim. To gain access, the study relied on snowball sampling. During the interviews, probing and cross-checking were used continually to assess data validity. The Ethnograph served as an augmenting tool to data analysis.

FINDINGS

Motivation Element

The mothers in all three cultures indicated they were motivated to give gifts that benefit their children. But, differences between the three cultures are worth noting.

Justification. Firstly, the Anglo-Celtic mothers indicated they give gifts to gain short-term benefits for their children, i.e. enhanced self-concept, and for themselves, i.e. their children's love. Secondly, the Sino-Vietnamese mothers indicated they give gifts to gain long-term benefits for their children, i.e. enhanced education and finances. There was no mention of gifts being given to benefit the Sino-Vietnamese mothers themselves. Thirdly, the Israeli mothers indicated they give gifts to gain long-term benefits for their children, i.e. enhanced education, and short-term benefits for themselves, i.e. the children's love.

Significance. Firstly, the Anglo-Celtic mothers indicated that birthday gifts are the most significant because they are very personal and commemorate the individual. Secondly, the Sino-Vietnamese mothers indicated gifts that provide insurance for their children's future, i.e. lucky money, gold jewellery, and academic aids, are the most significant. Thirdly, the Israeli mothers indicated that they only regard a gift as significant if the recipient, i.e. the child, regards it as such.

Timing. Firstly, the Anglo-Celtic mothers indicated they primarily time their gifts to coincide with special occasions, e.g. Christmas and birthdays. Also, they prefer not to give gifts to reward their children's academic endeavours. Secondly, the Sino-Vietnamese mothers indicated that while they always give lucky money at Chinese New Year and sometimes birthday gifts, they rarely give Christmas gifts because of its religious connotation. However, they prefer to give gifts as the need arises or to reward their children's academic progress rather than wait for special gift-giving occasions. Thirdly, the Israeli mothers indicated they primarily give personal gifts on their children's birthdays and gifts for the entire family on other occasions. Also, they all said that gifts are not given at other times of the year as rewards.

Selection Element

The mothers in all three cultures indicated they are the dominant family member during gift selection. But, differences between the three cultures are worth noting.

Involvement. Firstly, the Anglo-Celtic mothers indicated that they spend more time selecting gifts for their children than the fathers. However, most Anglo-Celtic mothers said they enjoy the task and, thus, put a lot of time and effort into it. Secondly, the Sino-Vietnamese mothers indicated that even though they are the main family member responsible for selecting tangible gifts, they do not enjoy the task. For this reason, when gifts are selected, they make the decision as quickly as possible. Thirdly, the Israeli mothers indicated that while they primarily select their children's gifts, they do not spend a lot of time doing so.

Family Influences. Firstly, the Anglo-Celtic mothers indicated their children are the main source of influence in the family. Secondly, the Sino-Vietnamese mothers indicated that even though they are guided by what their children want, they always make the final decision. At those times, the Sino-Vietnamese mothers do not give gifts that they regard as useless or too expensive. Thirdly, the Israeli mothers indicated that while they usually make the gift decisions alone, their children accompany them to the stores when a correct size is needed. At those times, the children do influence the gift decisions.

Promotional Influences. Firstly, the Anglo-Celtic mothers

TABLE 1
Interview Agenda

MOTHERS' GIFTS TO CHILDREN

1. GIFT-GIVING MOTIVATION

Justification: Why do you buy gifts for your children? (short-term vs. long-term goals)

Significance: What makes a gift important? (prestige, money, practical)

Timing: When are gifts usually given in your family? (birthdays, holidays, rewards)

2. GIFT-GIVING SELECTION

Involvement: Describe how you select gifts for your family. (time and effort)

Family Influences: Does anyone else in the family influence your decisions? (bartering with children, husband's power of veto, single or joint gift selection)

Promotional Influences: Are you influenced by brand names? (sales merchandise, point-of-sale material, sales staff, newspapers)

Gift Attributes: What is the most important thing for you when buying a gift? (price, quality, convenience)

3. GIFT-GIVING PRESENTATION

Presentation Messages: What do you want your children to learn from the gifts that you give them? (immediate versus delayed self-gratification)

Allocation Messages: How many gifts are given to the members of the family on any given occasion? (single or multiple) Are there any family members who get more gifts or more expensive gifts? (eldest child, mother)

Understanding of messages: Do you think that the family members understand what you are trying to tell them through gifts?

4. GIFT GIVING REACTION

Achievement: Do you think that you achieved what you wanted to achieve through gift giving? (always vs. not always)

Feedback: How do your children respond to your gifts? (more expressive vs. less expressive)

Usage: What do the children do with the gifts? (often private vs. often shared)

---

indicated they are mainly influenced by letterbox leaflets. However, the Anglo-Celtic mothers believed they are indirectly influenced by television advertising since it often directly influences their children's gift requests. Also, because most gift decisions are made before the Anglo-Celtic mothers go to the shops, they did not regard point-of-sale material or sales staff as a significant influence. Secondly, the Sino-Vietnamese mothers indicated they preferred to use their own judgment when selecting gifts rather than allow sales staff or promotions to influence them. Thirdly, the Israeli mothers indicated that while they are influenced by newspaper advertisements that promote merchandise at reduced prices, they are never influenced by television advertising. Also, the Israeli mothers said that sales staff rarely influence them since they often shop in self-serve stores.

Gift Attributes. Firstly, the Anglo-Celtic mothers indicated that they tend to give name brand items to their children as gifts because they are superior quality. Also, the Anglo-Celtic mothers preferred not to give money gifts, considering them impersonal and lacking in thought and effort. Secondly, the Sino-Vietnamese mothers indicated that they want their gifts to be useful. For this reason, the Sino-Vietnamese mothers said they prefer to give money to their children rather than tangible gifts since money can

be saved for the future. However, when tangible gifts are given, price is an important consideration. Consequently, gifts of good quality are often bought on sale. Thirdly, the Israeli mothers indicated that they try to give their children useful gifts that are the best 'quality' within their price range. For this reason, they often buy gifts on sale. Also, the Israeli mothers frequently give money to their children, particularly adolescents, instead of tangible gifts so the children can make their own gift selections.

Presentation Element

The mothers in all three cultures indicated they try to express love to the children during gift presentation. But, differences between the three cultures are worth noting.

Presentation Message. Firstly, the Anglo-Celtic mothers indicated that when they present gifts to their children, they are trying to communicate the fact that they have invested a large amount of time and effort and sometimes made sacrifices to respond to their children's requests. Secondly, the Sino-Vietnamese mothers indicated that when they present tangible gifts to their children, they are trying to communicate that rewards can be expected for academic achievement. When money gifts are presented, however, the Sino-Vietnamese mothers are trying to communicate the need to save for the future. Thirdly, the Israeli mothers indicated that when they present gifts to their children, they are trying to communicate a general feeling of well being.

Allocation Message. Firstly, the Anglo-Celtic mothers indicated that a number of gifts are allocated to each child on special occasions. At those times, they try to communicate impartiality, especially at Christmas when comparisons are made. Secondly, the Sino-Vietnamese mothers indicated that it is not the usual practice for the children to receive multiple gifts or gifts of the same economic value. Instead, gifts are given as the need arises. Also, the older children generally receive a greater amount of lucky money than the younger children since their needs are greater. Thirdly, the Israeli mothers indicated that their children tend to be allocated only one gift per occasion. Since gifts are also allocated according to their children's individual needs, the gifts vary in economic value.

Understanding of Messages. Firstly, the Anglo-Celtic mothers indicated that they are reasonably satisfied that their gift messages are understood and accepted by their children. Secondly, the Sino-Vietnamese mothers indicated that they are satisfied that their children understand and accept their gift messages. They mentioned the fact that the children are diligent students and careful with their money as proof that they do, indeed, get the intended message. Thirdly, the Israeli mothers indicated that they do not believe their children fully understand their gift messages.

Reaction Element

The mothers in all three cultures indicated their daughters are more expressive than their sons when gifts are exchanged. But, differences between the three cultures are worth noting.

Achievement. Firstly, the Anglo-Celtic mothers indicated that their objectives are usually achieved since their children are generally satisfied with their gifts. Secondly, the Sino-Vietnamese mothers indicated that their objectives tend to be achieved since their children are generally satisfied with their gifts and able to put them to good use. Thirdly, the Israeli mothers indicated that while their children are able to put their gifts to good use, they are not necessarily satisfied with them. Thus, the objectives of the Israeli mothers are not altogether achieved.

Feedback. Firstly, the Anglo-Celtic mothers indicated that even though their daughters and sons tend to gain the same amount of satisfaction from their gifts, the feedback from the daughters is more expressive than the sons. Secondly, the Sino-Vietnamese mothers indicated that even though their daughters and sons give positive feedback about their gifts, they are not inclined to express their feelings openly. Thirdly, the Israeli mothers indicated that their daughters and sons tend to be indifferent about their gifts. When their children do express themselves, however, they are more inclined to give negative rather than positive feedback.

Usage. Firstly, the Anglo-Celtic mothers indicated their children tend to use their gifts separately. Secondly, the Sino-Vietnamese mothers indicated their children tend to share their tangible gifts with their siblings. However, when their children receive money, the older children save most of it in their personal bank accounts and the younger children give it back to their parents for safe keeping. Thirdly, the Israeli mothers indicated their children tend to use their gifts privately since their gifts are given separately and, thus, pertain to each person's individual preferences.

DISCUSSION

As mentioned before, this study placed a particular emphasis on why, when, where, and how mothers in the three cultures

exchange gifts with other family members. As our findings indicate, the role mothers play during family gift giving is essentially the same across cultures. The mothers invest more time, energy, and thought than other family members in all aspects of the gift-giving process. Thus, they are more involved in the selection, purchase, wrapping, and presentation of gifts. The mothers also play a central role in shaping the gift-giving behaviour of other family members by overt and subtle messages. Further, the mothers in all three cultures seem to define their identity to a large extent around their role as gift givers, considering it to be a fundamental component of their motherhood. While these findings agree with previous research (Caplow 1982, DiLeonardo 1987, Cheal 1988, and Fischer and Arnold 1990), our contribution is in demonstrating that the central gift-giving role of mothers is universal across cultures.

Even though mothers play the central role in family gift giving across cultures, a closer analysis reveals there are distinct cultural differences in their gift-giving behaviour. Table 2 summarises these major differences.

As Table 2 indicates, the three cultures differ on each of the four gift-giving elements: (1) motivation, (2) selection, (3) presentation, and (4) reaction. The typical gift-giving behaviour of the Anglo-Celtic mother is characterised by an emphasis on short-term goals, prestigious name brand items which are regarded as "quality", and an intense influence on the mother by the children of all ages. The typical gift-giving behaviour of the Sino-Vietnamese mother is characterised by an emphasis on long-term goals, money and practical gifts that are usually obtained at reduced prices, and an intense influence on all family members by the mother. Finally, the typical gift-giving behaviour of the Israeli mother is characterised by an emphasis on both long-term and short-term goals, money and gift items that are usually obtained at reduced prices, and a moderate influence on the mother by the children, depending on their age.

Hofstede's (1980) research was used in this study to offer possible explanations for the unique patterns reflected in the gift-giving behaviour of mothers in the three cultures. Even though Hofstede's research focused on organisations, our study assumes his findings are applicable to group behaviour in other contexts, i.e. the family. In particular, two of Hofstede's dimensions seem especially applicable to our study: power distance and individualism/collectivism.

Hofstede (1980) uses the term power distance as a measure of the extent to which a society accepts the unequal distribution of power. A high power-distance society accepts wide differences in power. Its members show a great deal of respect for those in authority. Title, rank, and status carry a significant weight. In contrast, a low power-distance society plays down inequities. While superiors still have authority, they are not feared or revered.

Hofstede (1980) uses the term "*individualism*" to refer to a loosely-knit social framework in which people are chiefly supposed to look after their own interests. Its opposite is the term "*collectivism*" which refers to a tight social framework in which people expect others in the group to which they belong, e.g. the family, to nurture and protect them. In exchange for this security, they feel they owe absolute allegiance to the group.

Table 3 presents the Hofstede (1980) data for the two cultural dimensions relevant to our study, i.e. power distance and individualism/collectivism. Australia represents our Anglo-Celtic group, Israel represents our Israeli group, and Taiwan represents our Sino-Vietnamese group. While Hofstede's study did not include China or any Overseas Chinese group, Taiwan was included to represent a Chinese culture. For this reason, our Sino-Vietnamese group, as a Chinese culture, is represented here by the data for Taiwan.

TABLE 2
Major Differences Between Gift-Giving Behaviour of Anglo-Celtic, Sino-Vietnamese, and Israeli Mothers

	Anglo-Celtic Mothers	Sino-Vietnamese Mothers	Israeli Mothers
GIFT-GIVING ELEMENTS:			
1. MOTIVATION			
Justification	Short-term goals	Long-term goals	Long-term/short-term goals
Significance	Prestige gifts	Practical gifts	Importance to
	Birthday gifts	Lucky Money	recipient
Timing	Special occasions, e.g. birthdays, Christmas	Chinese New Year and academic reward	Birthdays and general needs
2. SELECTION			
Involvement	High-Priority Social and psychological risks	Low Priority Financial Risks	Low Priority
Family Influences	Children	Mother	Mother dominant with younger children and influenced by older children
Promotional Influences	Status Symbols	Sale Items	Sale Items
Gift Attributes	Quality Money unsuitable	Price Money suitable	Price Money suitable
3. PRESENTATION			
Presentation Messages	Immediate self-gratification	Delayed self-gratification	Immediate self-gratification
Allocation Messages	Multiple gifts Mothers favoured	Single gifts Eldest child favoured	Single gifts
Understanding of Messages	Always	Not always	Never
4. REACTION			
Achievement	Often	Most of the time	Never
Feedback	More expressive	Less expressive	Least expressive
Usage	Often private	Often shared	Never shared

As Table 3 indicates, the three cultures significantly differ on the power-distance dimension. While Taiwan (Sino-Vietnamese) is reasonably high on this dimension (58), Australia (Anglo-Celtic) is moderate (36), and Israel (Israeli) is extremely low (13). The different positions of the three cultures on the power-distance dimension can explain the nature of the negotiation process that takes place between mothers and their children prior to and during gift selection. Thus, the Sino-Vietnamese mothers, who are members of a high power-distance culture, report they make all gift selections alone, frequently ignoring their children's preferences. The Anglo-Celtic mothers, who are members of a moderate power-distance culture, report that even though they are generally influenced by their children's preferences, they still reserve the right to 'surprise' them with gifts the children did not specifically request. It is only the Israeli mothers, who are members of a very low power-distance culture, who go so far as to say that with their older children they prefer to give money, expecting them to make their own gift selections.

As Table 3 also indicates, the three cultures differ significantly on the individualism-collectivism dimension. While Australia (Anglo-Celtic) is extremely high on individualism (90), Israel (Israeli) is moderate (54), and Taiwan (Sino-Vietnamese) is extremely low (17). The different positions of the cultures on the individualism-collectivism dimension can explain the way in which mothers in the cultures justify why they buy gifts for their children. The Anglo-Celtic mothers, as members of a highly individualistic culture, report they buy gifts to satisfy the selfish needs of their children rather than to strengthen the children's long-term relationship within the family. The Sino-Vietnamese mothers, as members of a culture that is very low on individualism (highly collectivistic), mention that gifts and money are given to bolster the children's long-term family relationship. Finally, the Israeli mothers as members of a culture in the middle of the individualistic-collectivistic continuum, indicate gift items and money are sometimes given to strengthen the children's long-term family relationship (educationally-related gifts) and sometimes to satisfy the children's immediate desires.

IMPLICATIONS FOR FURTHER RESEARCH

Since this study was exploratory, the sample was not intended to be statistically significant. Instead, the data was intended to be used as a basis for identifying major patterns of gift-giving behaviour

TABLE 3
The Hofstede Data for the Three Cultures

	AUSTRALIA (Anglo-Celtic)	TAIWAN (Sino-Vietnamese)	ISRAEL (Israeli)
Individualism	90	17	54
Power Distance	33	58	13

[Based on Hofstede (1980)]

characteristic of mothers in the three cultures. Consequently, the conclusions drawn from this research should not be seen as necessarily representing the general population from which the sample was drawn. Thus, our study's design leaves ample scope for further research in several directions.

Firstly, further research could go beyond the nuclear, middle-class family to consider other family types and social classes. Also, cultures other than the three that were explored could be considered. In future, other cultures that represent extreme high, extreme low, and medium on Hofstede's (1980) two dimensions could be investigated. For instance, considerations could be the U.S. for extremely high on individualism, Pakistan for extremely low on individualism, and Japan for medium on individualism. This would help establish if our study's findings are idiosyncratic to the three cultures selected or reflect their ranking on the Hofstede dimensions. Another possibility could be to extend the study into cultures that are not necessarily at the extremes or the middle of the Hofstede continuum. Finally, even though we looked at three cultures which happened to be different on the power-distance and Individualism-collectivism dimensions, further research could explore if cultures which differ on other dimensions in Hofstede's model also exhibit distinct gift-giving behaviour patterns.

Secondly, further research could also be extended to include family members other than mothers. Various family gift-giving roles could be explored in isolation as in this study or in an interactive way, looking at the entire family within and across cultures.

Finally, Belk (1979) highlighted the need to link gift giving with the general body of consumer behaviour literature. He also indicated gift giving is one of the most important ways in which parents socialise their children as consumers. Our findings suggest there is indeed a link between mothers' gift-giving behaviour and children's perceptions and behaviour as consumers. Thus, future extensions of our research should look at how gift-giving behaviour of different family members, particularly mothers, affects and shapes children's consumer behaviour across cultures.

REFERENCES

Belk, Russell W. (1979), "Gift-Giving Behavior", in *Research in Marketing,* Vol 2., Jagdish Sheth (ed.), Greenwich CT: JAI, 95-126.

Belk, Russell W. (1984), "Cultural and Historical Differences in Concepts of Self and Their Effects on Attitudes Towards Having and Giving", *Advances in Consumer Research*, Vol. 11, 753-760.

Blau, Peter M. (1964), *Exchange and Power in Social Life*, New York: Wiley.

Caplow, Theodore (1982), "Christmas Gifts and Kin Networks", *American Sociological Review*, Vol. 47, Issue 3 (June), 383-392.

Cheal, David (1988), *The Gift Economy*, London: Routledge.

DiLeonardo, Micaela (1987), "The Female World of Cards and Holidays: Women, "Families and the Work of Kinship", *Signs,* 12 (Spring), 440-453.

Engel, J.F., Kollat D.T., and Blackwell, R.D. (1968), *Consumer Behavior* (First Edition), Holt, Rinehart & Winston, New York.

Fischer, Eileen and Arnold, Stephen J. (1990), "More than a Labor of Love: Gender Roles and Christmas Gift Shopping", *Journal of Consumer Research*, Vol. 17 (December), 333-45.

Gouldner, Alvin W. (1960), "The Norm of Reciprocity: A Preliminary Study", *American Sociological Review*, Vol. 25, 161-178.

Hill, Constance and Romm, Celia T. (1995), "Gift-giving Family Styles: A Cross-Cultural Study with Consumer Socialisation Implications", *Academy of Marketing Science, American World Marketing Conference, (*July 6-10), Melbourne, Vic., Australia.

Hofstede, Geert (1980), *Culture's Consequences: International Differences in Work-Related Values,* Beverly Hills, CA: Sage.

Levi-Strauss, Claude (1969), *The Elementary Structures of Kinship,* London: Eyre & Spottiswoode. (Original French publication: *Les Structures Elementaires de la Parente* (1949), Paris: Presses Universitaires de France).

Luschen, Gunther (1972), "Family Interaction with Kin and the Function of the Ritual", *Journal of Comparative Family Studies,* Vol. 3, 84-98.

Malinowski, B. (1922), *Argonauts of the Western Pacific,* London: Routledge & Kegan Paul.

Malinowski, B. (1926), *Crime and Custom in Savage Society,* London: Kegan Paul, Trench, Trubner.

Mauss, Marcel (1954), *The Gift: Forms and Functions of Exchange in Archaic Societies,* English Translation by Ian Cunnison, London: Cohen and West. (Original French publication: *Essai sur le Don: Forme et Raison de l'Echange dans les Societes archaiques* (1925) in Annee Sociologique, nouv. serie I: 30-186).

Mead, G. H. (1934), *Mind, Self and Society*, Chicago: Chicago University Press.

Sahlins, Marshall D. (1965), "On the Sociology of Primitive Exchange", in *The Relevance of Models for Social Anthropology,* Michael Banton (ed.), ASA Monographs, London: Tavistock, 139-236.

Schwartz, Barry (1967), "The Social Psychology of The Gift", *American Journal of Sociology*, 73(1), 1-11.

Sherry, John F. (1983), "Gift-Giving in Anthropological Perspective", *Journal of Consumer Research*, Vol. 10 (2), 157-168.

Answering Recall Questions: Implications For Consumer Judgment And Choice

Barbara Bickart, Rutgers University–Camden

Over the past several years, there has been a growing body of research examining how people answer survey questions (see Sudman, Bradburn, and Schwarz 1995 for a review). Within this body of research, there have been two distinct areas of attention. One area focuses on how people recall past experiences in order to construct behavioral frequency reports (e.g. Blair and Burton 1987; Menon 1993), while another focuses on how respondents construct subjective judgments, such as assessments of customer satisfaction or overall brand evaluations (e.g. Bickart 1993). In this session, we attempted to bring together these areas of research by examining the relationship between event recall and subjective judgments in a survey context.

Many consumer surveys require that the respondent recall a specific experience or series of experiences from memory. For example, in order to answer a behavioral frequency question, respondents must recall either specific occurrences of the behavior, a rate-of-occurrence, or some other non-numeric impression of how frequently the behavior occurs (e.g. Menon 1993). Likewise, implicit in an evaluation of customer satisfaction is the notion that consumers will base their judgment on previous experiences with the service provider. Consumers may recall a specific experience or an abstraction based on multiple experiences in order to answer such a question. The three papers in this session all presented experimental research that examined how people use recalled experiences to construct either a behavioral frequency judgment or a subjective assessment of customer satisfaction. In addition, the papers examined characteristics of the behavior itself, the individual, or the judgment context that affect how the recalled experiences were used in forming these judgments.

We began the session by examining how characteristics of a behavior might affect the strategy used to estimate its frequency. Frederick Conrad presented the results of two experiments (conducted with Norman Brown) that examined how the abstractness of a category and the distinctiveness of its members affect the strategies and accuracy for frequency estimates. In the first study, carried out as a telephone survey, two broad classes of estimation strategies were identified based on verbal protocols: those using numerical information (enumerating remembered episodes and applying knowledge about rate of occurrence) and those based on non-numerical information (general impressions and memory assessment). Respondents shifted strategies as the nature of the events in question shifted: low frequency distinctive events were enumerated; high frequency, non-distinct events promoted the use of general impressions; regularly occurring events led respondents to use their knowledge about rate of occurrence. Response times corroborate the interpretation of the protocols. A second study focused on the accuracy of different estimation strategies when the abstractness of the target objects varies. Enumeration led to underestimation regardless of category level and non-numerical strategies led to underestimation for superordinate categories. However, non-numerical strategies led to overestimation for basic level categories. While non-numerical strategies make it hard for subjects to fix an upper bound on their estimates, they do provide fairly accurate order information.

While the Conrad and Brown paper focused on how people recall multiple events to construct a frequency estimate, in the second paper, Barbara Bickart showed how the way in which a specific event is recalled can affect a subsequent satisfaction

judgment. In an initial study, students recalled either a positive or a negative consumer experience prior to evaluating their satisfaction with the service provider. When subjects were asked to recall a positive experience, they evaluated the service provider more favorably when asked to describe *how* (versus why) the experience occurred, while when subjects recalled a negative experience, they evaluated the service provider more favorably when asked to describe *why* (versus how) the experience occurred. Subjects' reported mood mediated these effects. In a second study, focusing only on negative experiences, the respondent's ability and motivation to think about an experience moderated the effects of the question type manipulation (how versus why). Specifically, the question type manipulation only affected the evaluations of subjects who were high in need for cognition. These results suggest that when a consumer experience is recalled, associated emotions or feelings can also come to mind and can affect subsequent satisfaction judgments.

Michaela Wanke then discussed her research (conducted with Claudia Gerke) examining the factors that determine *how* accessible information related to specific experiences is likely to be used to construct a subsequent judgment. Her findings suggest that recalled experiences are not always used as a direct input to judgment. Of key importance is the perceived diagnosticity of the recalled information. Using an innovative research design, she was able to manipulate subjects' perceptions of the number of positive or negative experiences recalled (e.g. whether they recalled few or many experiences), while holding constant the actual number of experiences recalled. When subjects believed they had recalled many experiences, assimilation effects occurred, presumably because the accessible information was perceived to be diagnostic to a consumer satisfaction judgment. When subjects believed they had recalled only a few experiences, contrast effects occurred. In this case, the accessible information was perceived to be nondiagnostic. Thus, contextual factors affected the perceived diagnosticity of recalled information, and consequently, the way it is used to form a subsequent judgment.

Eric Johnson served as the discussion leader for the session. Eric began by comparing research on answering survey questions to behavioral decision research on preference judgments. He noted several distinctions between these research contexts. First, while preference judgments focus on "looking forward", survey judgments focus on "looking back". As a consequence, research on preference judgments tends to be stimulus-based and research on answering survey questions tends to be memory-based. Second, research on preference judgments typically uses a comparison to a normative standard—this is usually not the case in research on the survey judgment process.

The general discussion focused on two issues raised by Eric. First, we discussed the methodological problems associated with identifying the theoretical underpinnings of these kinds of effects, particularly with regard to understanding the relationship between the nature of the memory representation of an experience (for example, its "graininess") and a subsequent recall strategy. New methodological approaches may be required in order to advance theory development in this area.

Further, Eric asked how important these kinds of effects are in the real world of survey measurement. For example, he suggested it would be interesting to examine the connections between context effects on satisfaction judgments and subsequent consumer behavior. Members of the audience raised two related issues. First, a number of people were curious about the extent to which the manipulations in the studies reported here parallel actual survey design, particularly in the satisfaction domain. Second, the research reported here is consistent with the idea that answers to survey questions are often constructed on the spot. Thus, we discussed the implications of this research for evaluating the validity of survey responses. Given these and related findings, we may need to rethink traditional conceptions of response validity.

REFERENCES

Bickart, Barbara A. (1993), "Carryover and Backfire Effects in Marketing Research," *Journal of Marketing Research*, 30, (February), 52-62.

Blair, Edward A. and Scot Burton (1987), "Cognitive Processes Used by Survey Respondents to Answer Behavioral Frequency Questions," *Journal of Consumer Research*, 14, 280-288.

Menon, Geeta (1993), "The Effects of Accessibility of Information in Memory on Judgments of Behavioral Frequencies," *Journal of Consumer Research*, 20 (December), 431-440.

Sudman, Seymour, Norman M. Bradburn, and Norbert Schwarz (1996), *Thinking About Answers: The Application of Cognitive Processes to Survey Methodology*. San Francisco: Jossey-Bass Publishers.

Gifts: What Do You Buy the Person Who Has ~~Everything?~~ *Nothing?*

Daniel R. Horne, Providence College
Shay Sayre, California State University, Fullerton
David A. Horne, California State University, Long Beach

ABSTRACT

This paper reports the results of a preliminary investigation into the receiving of gifts by those who have lost all or most of their possessions in a natural disaster. While it is possible that no social imperative exists for the giving of gifts in this type of situation, our findings showed this behavior to be quite common. Additionally, gifts tended to come from sources outside traditional gift giving circles. These and other finding from a small sample of victims lead to the suggestion of topics for future research.

INTRODUCTION

In a recent work on the classification of gift givers and recipients, Otnes, Lowrey and Kim (1993) discuss the effort which may be required during the gift selection process. They showed marked differences in purchasing strategies used for an "easy" recipient as compared to a "difficult" recipient. Some of the characteristics which help determine these classifications involve an understanding of the recipient's preferences, a compatibility of tastes, and the perception of a current needs inventory of the intended recipient. In this last case, the recipient who already "has everything" is classified as one for whom selecting a gift is "difficult." Is the converse true? That is, is it easy to purchase gifts for those who have nothing?

In a research project investigating consumption behavior of those who survive disasters or catastrophic losses, we examined some of the interpersonal behavior of the loss survivors with their kinship and social networks. A frequent theme was the outpouring of assistance, both in terms of emotional support and outright gifts (c.f., Barton 1970). This work looks at this gift giving situation and explores how it may differ from extant theory developed to explain the gift giving process. Findings of a small, preliminary study are presented and directions for future research are suggested.

BACKGROUND

Unfortunately, disasters in the United States extract a major economic toll. In the U.S., the insurance industry defines a catastrophic loss as one totaling more than $5,000,000 and/or more than 1000 claims filed for a single event. Using that criteria, there were $23 billion in catastrophic losses in 1992 (a record because of Hurricane Andrew) and $5.3 billion in 1993 in the United States (Scism 1994). Since the losses from uninsured victims of recognized catastrophes and claims from smaller scale events are excluded, the actual loss is much higher. Thousands of devastated households comprise these sobering figures.

Disaster research has been recognized as a multi-faceted issue that can best be undertaken by concentrating on respondents who have personally gone through some portion of the mass trauma. The principal lines of inquiry have been on individual and societal recovery and mental rejuvenation. For views of this topic see Green (1986), and Lystad (1985). However, while previous research has concentrated on mental recovery aspects, these disasters create an interesting, and heretofore unexplored, setting in which to study victims as consumers. The post-disaster behavior of impacted individuals provides an opportunity to investigate several specific issues, including repurchase priorities, family decision making,

alteration in the importance of possessions (Sayre 1994), and the receipt of gifts, to name a few possibilities.

When an individual or a family experiences a catastrophic loss, members of kinship and social networks, as well as community-based and national relief organizations, seek to mitigate the damage and disruption to the extent possible (Barton 1970; Quarantelli and Dynes 1986). Zelizer (1979) notes that this type of mutual assistance behavior was more common in the past, before the shift from personal aid to that provided by impersonal systems such as the government or insurance companies. Still, assistance from friends, family, and acquaintances is very common and it is noteworthy that individuals or groups outside of these intimate networks may also attempt to reach out to those perceived to be in need (Barton 1970). Support, in this manner, may take the form of a gift presented to the afflicted party. However, the rationale theorized to justify gift relationships may not fully account for behavior in this context.

A variety of frameworks have been proposed to examine gift giving (c.f., Belk and Coon 1993; Cheal 1988; Mauss 1990/1950). While these often use differing terminology, there are many concepts held in common which attempt to provide a foundation for gift giving behavior. Some of the motivations for this behavior include social obligation (Belk 1976; Mauss 1990/1950), the need to reciprocate for a previous gift or induce future reciprocation (Belk and Coon 1993; Camerer 1988; Levi-Strauss 1964), the need to communicate information about the giver-recipient relationship through the symbolic messages associated with the gift (Belk and Coon 1993; Cheal 1988, Otnes, Lowrey and Kim 1993; Wolfinbarger 1990), and truly selfless, altruistic designs (Belk and Coon 1993). Gift giving under the conditions described may be the square peg that does not neatly fit into the above round holes.

In the case of gifts to those who have suffered a loss, it is doubtful whether a social imperative exists, except within certain religious sects, such as the Mennonite community. A large number of disasters, natural and otherwise, occur every year. Yet, while the number is significant and probably perceived to occur at even higher than actual levels due to availability and vividness (Tversky and Kahneman 1973), the probability of an individual being thus affected or that an individual will personally know an affected survivor will be very small. When someone suffers a catastrophic loss, those who wish to provide assistance generally have no direct experience to help them decide between alternative forms of aid. Further, the type of social obligation which would suggest social punishments for those who give no support (Blau 1964) is not found.

While this lack of experience creates difficulties in the selection process, potential givers may still attempt to give gifts which symbolically reaffirm the importance of existing relationships, although the actual form of gift may vary from a traditional gift to one of emotional support. The strengthening of relationships is critical at this time of major emotional stress. However, traditional gift or emotional support, giving the gift with the highest level of utility for the recipient requires that the giver predicts the preferences of someone whose current position is very different from their own (Waldfogel 1993) or any position in which they have ever been. The level of uncertainty, thus, increases the risk of giving an in-kind gift for those for whom moral support is not an available option. At the same time, the benefits of less traditional, albeit more flexible, gift alternatives, such as money or near money (e.g., gift certificates), increase.

Yet gifts of money have long been problematic and are considered inappropriate or too impersonal for many gift giving situations (Carrier 1995; Webley, Lea and Portalska 1983; Zelizer 1994). In the first place, gift givers do not like to appear as though they are placing a dollar value on the relationship (Cheal 1987). Further, part of the evaluation of the gift by the recipient involves the effort and the thought that went into the selection (Belk and Coon 1993). In any event, the symbolic component of the gift is outweighed by consideration of societal norms and/or is subject to misinterpretation. An additional problem is a potential limitation on the strength of the memory trace that cash gifts create. For some time after the presentation of a gift, the giver and the occasion are associated in the mind of the recipient (Sherry, McGraph and Levy 1992). Tangible gifts have a lasting nature which may continue to reinforce the communications originally intended by the giver (Cheal 1988). Gifts of cash may be earmarked for specific use (Zelizer 1994), or it may instead become mingled with general household funds and spent on everyday necessities, thus leaving few memories.

Some exceptions to this restriction in gift giving have been marked, most notably downward, inter-generational transfers, such as from grandparent to grandchild (Douglas and Isherwood 1979; Waldfogel 1993), and as wedding gifts in certain cultures and sub-cultures (Cheal 1988). Recently, however, this general proscription has come into question both theoretically (Waldfogel 1993) and from some limited survey evidence of attitudes towards gifts (Athay 1993). The rapid growth in near cash gifts, such as gift certificates (Horne and Kelly forthcoming), provides support for the idea that, under certain circumstances, gifts of cash or given monetary values are not viewed with disfavor but may actually be highly prized. A catastrophic loss will likely lead to a suspension of traditional gift giving norms, such as the prohibition of money gifts to equals (Zelizer 1994), which will increase the likelihood of gift presentations of this nature.

The theoretic justifications involving reciprocation and true altruism are much harder to untangle. It is very difficult to rule out desire for future reciprocation as a motivating factor. While this seems awkward, givers may, consciously or not, wish to ingratiate themselves in order to gain later tangible rewards, prestige, or even power (Batson 1991; Belk and Coon 1993; Mauss 1990/1950). If this is the case, however, then the concept of true altruism is precluded.

Belk and Coon's (1993) discussion of agapic or selfless love in the exchange of gifts in dating relationships opens the door in consumer research to the idea that all gifts may not be exclusively based on the self interest of the giver. Recently, investigations of altruism (c.f., Batson 1990; 1991), have provided evidence that some motivational component for helping behavior is ultimately the increased welfare of those receiving aid. This altruistic component, although not based on the notion of romantic love as described by Belk and Coon (1993), might help provide understanding of gifts in this context. Research in this area may need to consider work dealing with charitable donations (e.g., Weyant 1984), although that typically involves donations from an individual or collective to an organization or possibly an unknown individual (cf., Griffin et al. 1992). Medical donations of organs and tissues have been studied extensively (Pessemier, Bemmaor and Hanssens 1977; Shanteau, Harris and VandenBos 1992) and might also provide insights.

RESEARCH DESIGN AND STUDY

Researching the consumer behavior of disaster victims is different from the usual consumer study. First, in order to elicit any sort of cooperation with disaster victims, the researcher must establish genuine empathy for the subject. Second, gaining access to victims is greatly enhanced if the researchers have some form of insider status with the group or at least attain sanction as an outsider. Disaster victims quickly become suspicious of the motives of anyone they do not recognize asking questions as tales of scam artists and con-men abound (Valente 1995). Further, if fatalities have occurred, this provides an ominous backdrop against which interviews must be conducted.

The problem of access to disaster victims merits elaboration. Every disaster victim quickly receives literally hundreds of solicitations, most of which receive only a cursory consideration. A request from an unknown source to cooperate in a research project would in all likelihood be ignored. Unfortunately, one of the authors suffered a complete loss of home and most personal possessions in a recent natural disaster. After the disaster, the author helped organize a group of homeowners in the disaster area. At one of their regular meetings, a request was made for assistance with a personal research project. More than enough victims volunteered. This access was critical and most likely would not have been afforded to an outsider.

The specific nature of the research subject requires a data collection methodology that is empathic yet allows for extensive elaboration and disclosure by the respondents. The more typical exploratory research techniques were considered inappropriate. For example, focus group members might be reluctant to openly share feelings after a disaster with someone they might directly or indirectly know, and disaster victims are geographically concentrated.

A hybrid of photoelicitation (Heisley and Levy 1991), which we call video-elicitation, whereby victims would respond to the videotaped comments of other victims was devised to overcome the shortcomings of the more common exploratory techniques. Empathy could be established through the depicted victims. If the victims appeared genuine and their comments plausible, then the respondents could identify with them and share their own behavior. Thus, video-elicitation would jog their memories about different aspects of the event and simultaneously be sensitive to their privacy needs.

However, we did not feel it would be possible to discuss the act of receiving gifts in this exploratory video. Since there was little previous research on this specific subject, there were no indications as to the prevalence of gift giving to disaster victims. The need to appear sensitive to the respondents caused us to wonder what would be the effect of someone on a video discussing their gifts and how much they appreciated their family and friends thinking of them when a particular subject being interviewed had not received anything. However, the gift issue was extremely interesting and we wanted to include some form of inquiry. It was decided to use written questions about gift receiving on a separate form that would be completed after the video process. In that manner, a person not receiving gifts would not have to disclose that possibly embarrassing fact in such an open manner.

Eighteen interviews were conducted. All the respondents had suffered complete losses of their homes, though a few managed to save a handful or so of personal items. After the tape was finished and the discussion had ended, the respondents completed a short questionnaire about themselves, about the gifts they received, and about the interview they just went through. As a follow-up, post-interview discussions were held with several of the respondents a week or so after their interview to clarify some of the responses.

This last step was useful in probing for more specific information about the gifts that the victims had received.

RESULTS AND DISCUSSION

The respondents were equally divided between men and women. Their ages ranged from the 30's to over 70 and their profiles quite closely matched the entire victim population for this particular disaster, which had middle to upper-middle class demographics.

All subjects, with one exception, received gifts after they suffered the loss. The gifts included household and personal items, some quite mundane (e.g., a broom); gifts of services (e.g., lodging for the displaced family); gifts of food (e.g., a basket of snack foods such as crackers and cheese); clothing; and gifts of cash and gift certificates. These last two categories made up the majority of the gifts presented, accounting for nearly 40% of the gifts reported. Approximately 30% of the gifts were household items and slightly less than 25% of the gifts were personal items such as clothing.

It is interesting that several of the respondents noted that friends had thrown showers on their behalf. Some of these recipients seemed especially grateful for not only the gift received but also for the concept of having a shower, as many had expressed intense sorrow over the loss of treasured possessions such as wedding gifts (cf., Sayre 1994). Further, these showers involved not only traditional shower gifts (i.e., kitchen items) but work items as well. One subject, an artist, was given a shower in which she received equipment, tools and supplies to help her return to work. Four subjects also noted that they had "registered" at local retailers, for example, Crate and Barrel.

Two findings provide indications of the lack of social imperative for gift giving under these conditions. These are the number of gifts and from whom the gifts were received. First, the number of gifts received seems quite small with the average being just over 2.5 for each individual. This may be related to the fact that the gifts tended to come from outside kinship networks. In several cases all gifts received were from individuals or cooperatives outside traditional gift giving circles. For instance, one recipient received three separate gifts, all from colleagues or co-workers with whom he had previously never engaged in any gift exchanges. One gift was a substantial amount of money ($2,500) which was collected by office personnel at his firm's home office in Japan, a place he visited only two or three times a year. While it is reported that giving gifts to those who suffer losses is common in Japan (c.f., Hulme 1995), collections were raised for this victim by co-workers in the U.S. as well.

It is certainly plausible to think that aid to victims from kinship and close social networks comes by way of emotional support rather than tangible gifts. Those outside this intimate circle may strongly feel the need to provide support, yet may feel ill at ease in attempting to understand and deal with the emotional aspects of the trauma or may lack "permission" to fulfill such a role (Otnes, Lowrey and Kim 1993). These individuals might be termed "compensators" by Otnes, Lowrey and Kim (1993) because of their desire to utilize the gift to "make it up to you" and "as one of consolation rather than of apology" (pg. 235). However, the very lack of social intimacy which makes providing emotional support so difficult would make it less likely that aid of any sort would be given. Lack of intimacy might also decrease the effectiveness of the symbolic component of any gift presented.

The significant proportion of cash and near cash gifts received is an indication of the difficulty givers had in selecting gifts for these recipients. In general, cash type gifts are more often presented in situations where the level of knowledge of the specific wants and needs of the recipient are less well known (Cheal 1988; Zelizer 1994). Gifts of cash and near cash serve to lessen the level of uncertainty and anxiety felt by the givers, while, at the same time, increasing stress due to the skirting of societal norms. Anecdotal evidence from our sample supports this idea. Recipients who received cash reported that, upon presentation, givers were "almost apologizing" and used terms like "we wanted to do something but we didn't know what to do, but please accept this (money)." Two members of the sample were actually informed by co-workers that meetings were held to discuss possible group responses to the situation and these groups were in a "quandary" over what to do for the victim. In both cases, collections were taken and the proceeds presented to the victims. These subjects were asked about the disposition of these cash gifts. One respondent said that the money was simply put into the checking account with other household funds, while the other stated that the money had been mentally "set aside" in a fund designated for the purchase of replacements for an art collection that had been lost in the fire. In a thank you note this victim expressly informed his benefactors of this intention. This specific earmarking likely leads to a stronger and/or more positive memory trace of the gift and the occasion.

Additionally, respondents were asked to describe their feelings when they were presented with gifts. By far, the majority of adjectives utilized by the recipients dealt with feelings of gratitude. Nearly half of the responses (49%) were items such as "grateful" and "touched." Less prevalently, in large part due to the occasion for the gift, some listed "happy" (13%). More interesting, however, were the less positive responses that were noted. Several of the respondents listed "embarrassed" (13%) as their reaction to the gift. "Humbled" was noted in 11% of the responses. Less common, but still noteworthy, is that two of the respondents listed "obligated," indicating that, even if they were intended, perceptions of pure altruism did not exist (Levi-Strauss 1964). Finally, two respondents listed "humiliated," which is reminiscent of early gift theory which suggested the use of gifts as a form of domination (c.f., Mauss 1967; Veblen 1934).

A final question dealt with the idea of what should be given to people in like circumstances. The questions asked that if they were advising others what to give survivors of a different disaster what would be appropriate gifts. Five different categories of gifts were listed and subjects were asked to indicate their responses on a 5-point scale anchored by Very Appropriate (1) and Very Inappropriate (5). The most appropriate gifts were felt to be gifts of in-kind. These were gifts of food and beverages (mean=1.89) and gifts of household goods (mean=1.94). Gifts of near cash products were thought to be slightly less appropriate on average with store gift certificates having a mean response of 2.06 and mall or credit card gift certificates having a mean of 2.33. The final category, "Contributions in the victim's name to a general victims' fund" was felt to be neutral (mean 3.00).

CONCLUSIONS AND DIRECTIONS FOR FUTURE RESEARCH

The purpose of this paper was to present findings of an exploratory investigation into the gift receiving behavior of individuals who have lost most or all of their possessions in a disaster. Several issues arise which warrant further consideration and research. First, a complete understanding of the social dynamics of gifts given to victims will not be forthcoming until we look not just at tangible gifts but at all forms of succor. Although at the beginning of the research project we implicitly defined gifts as only traditional objects (i.e., things wrapped up, tied with ribbon and presented in fairly formal or structured manner), victims reported to us that aid from those closest to them tended to come more from an outpouring of needed emotional support as well as help with the many tasks which lay before them. Future work should include a more encompassing view of a gift following Carrier's (1995) definition, which includes labor and ideas with more traditional presents. Unfortunately, this definition may violate the conditions put forth by Sherry (1983), which includes a prestation component. Thus Carrier would describe a spouse going to the store to buy milk as a gift whereas Sherry would not. In this particular situation, those outside the traditional gift circle may have utilized gifts as their best means of communicating their sympathy, as they would possess limited access to provide differing forms of support. Future work should establish the level of intimacy between the parties involved and examine whether this pattern holds.

In addition, the lack of information or knowledge about the needs and desires of the victim makes the selection of gifts a difficult task. Recent work which examine gifts of cash (Athay 1993; Waldfogel 1993; Zelizer 1994) and the rapid growth of near cash gift certificates would suggest that under these conditions givers and recipients would benefit from not giving in-kind gifts but rather cash or the equivalent. The finding that several members of this sample received money or near money, and their comments about their feelings, may indicate that under these conditions knowledge of needs is low. It might also suggest that, given high levels of stress, traditional mores do not apply. Further work on the contexts in which gifts of money are acceptable or even preferred will be important in establishing a more complete understanding of the entire gift giving process.

Finally, the needs and the objectives of the givers should be examined. Creative projective techniques, such as the video-elicitation method discussed above, could prove beneficial in making certain that all sides of this gift giving process are covered.

REFERENCES

Athay, Sherri (1993), "Giving and Getting" *American Demographics*, 15 (December), 46-52.
Barton, A.H. (1970), *Communities in a Disaster. A sociological analysis of collective stress situations*, Garden City, NY Doubleday Anchor Books.
Batson, C. Daniel (1990), "How Social an Animal," *American Psychologist*, 45 (March), 336-346.
_____ (1991), *The Altruism Question*, Hillsdale, NJ: Erlbaum Associates.
Belk, Russell W. (1976), "It's the Thought that Counts: A Signed Diagraph Analysis of Gift-Giving," *Journal of Consumer Research*, 3 (December), 155-162
_____ and Gregory S. Coon (1993), "Gift Giving as Agapic Love: An Alternative to the Exchange Paradigm Based on Dating Experiences," *Journal of Consumer Research*, 20 (December), 393-417.
Blau, Peter M. (1964), *Exchange and Power in Social Life*, New York: John Wiley and Sons.
Carrier, James G. (1995), *Gifts and Commodities*, New York: Routledge.
Cheal, David (1987), "'Showing Them You Love Them': Gift Giving and the Dialectic of Intimacy," *Sociological Review*, 35 (1), 150-169.
_____ (1988), *The Gift Economy*, New York: Routledge.
Douglas, Mary, and Baron Isherwood (1979), *The World Of Goods*, New York: Basic Books, Inc.

Green, B. L. (1986), "Conceptual and Methodological Issues in Assessing the Psychological Impact of Disasters," in *Disasters and Mental Health: Selected Contemporary Perspectives and Innovations in Services to Disaster Victims*, (Eds.) B. J. Sowder and M. Lystad, Washington, DC: American Psychiatric Press, 191-208.
Griffin, Mitch, Barry J Babin, Jill S. Attaway and William R. Darden (1992), "Hey You, Can Ya Spare Some Change? The Case of Empathy and Personal Distress as Reactions to Charitable Appeals," in *Advances in Consumer Research*, (Eds.) McAlister and Rothschild, Provo, UT: Association for Consumer Research, 508-514.
Heisley, Deborah D. and Sidney J. Levy (1991), "Autodriving: A Photoelicitation Technique," *Journal of Consumer Research*, 18 (December), 257-272.
Horne, Daniel R., and J. Patrick Kelly (forthcoming), "Gift Certificates and Customer Value: Some Preliminary Findings," *Proceedings of the 8th International Conference on Research in the Distributive Trades*.
Hulme, David (1995), "Quake Stirs Corporate Soul," *Tokyo Business Today*, 63 (May) 30-32.
Levi-Strauss, Claude (1964), "The Principle of Reciprocity," in *Sociological Theory*, 2nd edition, eds. L. Coser and B. Rosenberg, New York: Macmillan, 74-84.
Lystad, Mary H. (1985), "Human Responses to Mass Emergencies: A Review of Mental Health Research," *Emotional First Aid*, 2, 5-18.
Mauss, Marcel (1990/1950), *The Gift: Forms and Functions of Exchange in Archaic Societies*, translated by W. D Halls, New York: W.W. Norton and Company.
Otnes, Cele, Tina M. Lowrey and Young Chan Kim (1993), "Gift Selection for Easy and Difficult Recipients: A Social Roles Interpretation," *Journal of Consumer Research*, 20 (September), 229-244.
Pessemier, Edgar A., Albert C. Bemmaor and Dominique M. Hanssens (1977), "Willingness to Supply Human Body Parts: Some Empirical Results," *Journal of Consumer Research*, 4 (December), 131-140.
Quarantelli, E.L. and Russell Dynes (1986), "Community Responses to Disasters," in *Disasters and Mental Health: Selected Contemporary Perspectives and Innovations in Services to Disaster Victims*, (Eds.) B. J. Sowder and M. Lystad, Washington, DC: American Psychiatric Press, 191-208.
Sayre, Shay (1994), "Possessions and Identity in Crisis: Meaning and Change for Victims of the Oakland Firestorm," in *Advances in Consumer Research*, vol. 21, (eds.) Chris T. Allen and Deborah Roedder John, Provo, UT: Association for Consumer Research, 109-114.
Scism, Leslie (1994), "Insurers' Losses on Catastrophes Reach $7 Billion," *Wall Street Journal*, March 29, A2.
Shanteau, James, Richard J. Harris and Gary R. VandenBos (1992), "Psychological and Behavioral Factors in Organ Donation," *Hospital and Community Psychiatry*, 43 (March) 211-212.
Sherry, John F., Jr. (1983), "Gift Giving in Anthropological Perspective," *Journal of Consumer Research*, 10 (September), 157-168.
_____ , Mary Ann McGrath and Sidney Levy (1992), "The Disposition of the Gift and Many Unhappy Returns," *Journal of Retailing*, 68 (Spring), 40-65.

Tversky, Amos, and Kahneman, Daniel (1973), "Availability: A heuristic for judging frequency and probability," *Cognitive Psychology,* 5, 207-232.

Valente, Judith (1995), "They Steal from the Devastated," *Parade Magazine,* June 4, 4-5.

Veblen, Thorstein (1934), *Theory of the Leisure Class,* New York: Modern Library.

Weyant, James M. (1984), "Applying Social Psychology to Induce Charitable Donations," *Journal of Applied Social Psychology,* 14 (Sept./Oct.), 441-447.

Waldfogel, Joel (1993), "The Deadweight Loss of Christmas," *American Economic Review,* 83 (December), 1328-1336.

Webley, P., S.E.G. Lea and R. Portalska (1983), "The Unacceptability Of Money As A Gift," *Journal of Economic Psychology,* 4, 223-238.

Wolfinbarger, Mary F. (1990), "Motivations and Symbolism in Gift-Giving Behavior," in *Advances in Consumer Research,* Vol. 17. eds. Goldberg, Gorn, Pollay, Provo, UT: Association for Consumer Research, 699-706.

Zelizer, Viviana (1979), *Morals & Markets,* New York: Columbia University Press.

_____ (1994), *The Social Meaning of Money,* New York: Basic Books.

Exploring Nostalgia Imagery Through the Use of Consumer Collages

William J. Havlena, Fordham University
Susan L. Holak, City University of New York-College of Staten Island

ABSTRACT

Collages created by small groups were analyzed to explore the nature and structure of nostalgia. Images in the collages relate to both personal and cultural history and memories. The collages are discussed using a four-way classification of nostalgia based on two dimensions—private versus collective and direct versus indirect experience—that yields four distinct classes: personal nostalgia, interpersonal nostalgia, cultural nostalgia, and virtual nostalgia. Consumption associations are prevalent in the collages, with food and entertainment images predominating.

INTRODUCTION

The meaning of nostalgia has been studied by researchers using a variety of qualitative research methods. Davis (1979) utilized depth interviews with a small number of informants to develop insights and hypotheses concerning the nature and function of nostalgia in individuals' lives. Verbal descriptions of nostalgic experiences have been used to identify common themes and subjects for nostalgic reflection (Holak and Havlena 1992). Stern (1992) has compared historical and personal forms of nostalgia in advertising to their literary antecedents in the historical romance and sentimental novel.

This paper presents the results of an examination of nostalgic meaning using visual images as stimuli for consumer reflection and elicitation of nostalgia. Subjects were directed to create collages of nostalgic imagery and then to explain their reasons for the inclusion and arrangement of the collage components.

Collage construction has been used as a projective technique in psychiatric evaluation and therapy (cf., Carter, Nelson, and Duncombe 1983, Froehlich and Nelson 1986). For example, the use of collages based on magazine images has been discussed as an alternative to the classic Thematic Apperception Test for multicultural assessment and treatment (Landgarten 1993). Its application to consumer research is an alternative to the use of TAT-type pictures, autodriving, and psychodrawing (Gordon and Langmaid 1988, Heisley and Levy 1991, Rook 1991, Rook and Levy 1983). While collages have been used in the design of advertising (Rickard 1994), their use in basic consumer research has been limited. This method provides a combination of visual and verbal information about the perception and meaning of nostalgia that includes a broad array of consumer-oriented imagery.

METHOD

The research was conducted with groups of individuals assigned to create collages representative of nostalgia. Using groups had the effect of reducing the sample size and the impact of individual differences, but it stimulated a significant amount of interaction within the groups concerning the meaning of nostalgia and representative images for individual members of the groups, perhaps increasing creativity and interest in the task. In other contexts individual collages may be more appropriate.

The subjects for the research were twenty graduate students of business at a private Eastern university. All were enrolled in upper-level marketing courses. They were not provided with any prior information about nostalgia or its use in marketing.

The subjects were assigned to groups of four students and were instructed to create collages that would portray or represent nostalgia. They were told to use images or words from a set of ten magazines supplied by the researcher—*Esquire, Good Housekeeping, Life, People, Redbook, Sports Illustrated, The Inside Collector, Traditional Home, Vanity Fair*, and *Victoria*—and to arrange them in a collage so that the most important or meaningful materials were positioned at the center of the collage, with the less relevant images placed toward the edges. Thus, both individuals and stimuli were sampled. The stimuli were selected to provide a reasonably broad array of images within the limited time available to the subjects for the task.

The groups were told that they would be observed and video-taped during the task, which would last about thirty minutes. They were also advised that they would be asked to explain their collages at the end of the task.

Five groups completed the task. The groups were run in two sessions, with three groups working simultaneously in the first session and two groups in the second session. The groups were physically separated during the collage task and were unaware of the activities of the other group(s) until after the collages were completed. After completing the collages, but prior to describing them, members of the groups were asked to complete a brief questionnaire designed to measure nostalgia-proneness.

Each group described its collage in front of the researchers and the members of the other group(s) in the session. The researchers prompted group members for more information during and after the initial description of each collage. Notes were taken on the verbal information and the presentations were videotaped. Following all the presentations in each session, the purpose of the task was discussed with the groups.

RESULTS

Task

The groups tended to approach the task by dividing the magazines among the members, with each person browsing through a magazine and then passing it along to another member of the group. Questions about whether to include an item were usually resolved by polling the group. In most cases, groups reached or tried to achieve consensus regarding the inclusion of images. In general, the groups began the task by considering nostalgia as individuals and then discussed the images collectively. The groups noted repeatedly during their presentations that images were included even if they evoked nostalgia for only one member of the group.

Typically, once a set of images had been culled from the magazines the members of the group entered into a discussion of the arrangement of the items within the collage. In most cases, the discussion first centered on the general approach and then moved on to the consideration of individual objects. As will be noted later, the approaches and rules for the placement of images differed markedly across the groups.

Discussion occurred in the group settings concerning the nature of nostalgia. For example, the inherent nostalgic character of black-and-white (as opposed to color) images was discussed within the groups. In addition, as images were collected, group members offered spontaneous recollections of nostalgic associations with the images, often appearing to forget the initial motivation for the task and to be enjoying the experience itself.

Advances in Consumer Research
Volume 23, © 1996

FIGURE 1
Consumer Collage #1

There was some initial discussion about the nature of the study in one group, with a few members of the group guessing that the task might be a group dynamics exercise. Other groups did not openly discuss the purpose of the task.

Collages

The consumer collages are presented in Figures 1 through 5. The visual images will be discussed in terms of content, using verbal information provided by the subjects during construction and explication of the collages to aid in the interpretation.

IMAGERY OF NOSTALGIA

Certain image characteristics appear to convey nostalgia. Several subjects mentioned that black-and-white photographs seemed more nostalgic than color images. Here, the feeling of age was the primary determinant and was not linked to any emotional reaction or attachment to the subject of the image. The participants also noted explicitly that age was a criterion for an image to represent nostalgia. One group limited nostalgia to objects that were between twenty and forty years old or were associated with that period, although these products might still be available or

people might still be alive. The relevance of childhood as a period for nostalgic memory was described by one woman in talking about the inclusion of the word "Forever" in her collage (Figure 3):

I put that in, I think, because a lot of the things that we remember as a child just keep going on for us forever, at least in our lifetime they are meaningful to us.

This sentiment was mirrored in the comments of another group, which viewed something as nostalgic only if it had touched their lives individually. Images were included only if they had personal meaning to at least one member of the group. This view of nostalgia is reflective of the definition offered by Davis (1979) in considering only direct, personal memories.

Another group viewed nostalgia more broadly and included references to more distant periods of American history, such as the Civil War and the women's suffrage movement (Figure 1). One woman justified their inclusion thusly:

I just remember a lot from history books in social studies in grade school, in middle school....it just seemed to be a focal

FIGURE 2
Consumer Collage #2

point...just the women in the long dresses, its just so distinctive....but it's off to the side because, you're right, I wasn't there.

Although Davis (1979) maintains that personal experience is necessary in defining a relevant past for nostalgia, the collages seem to suggest that relevant past may also include situations and events outside the subject's personal experience. These phenomena are associated with the individual's past through learning or communication and then become available for nostalgic reflection. Instead, what may differ in these cases is the character of the nostalgia, rather than its presence or absence. For the subject quoted above, the costumes and demeanor of the women in the suffrage movement evoke nostalgia, but it is mixed with memories of learning about the subject in school.

CLASSES OF NOSTALGIA

Many of the images presented in the collages clearly refer to personal memories. For example, one of the subjects explained the inclusion of a large picture of a ham (Figure 4) in this way:

Those Easter Sunday dinners or, you know, dinners with your grandparents....always preparing big hams and turkeys...

Clearly, this image evokes a strong response involving personal memories for this woman. However, the images in the collages did not always hold personal meaning, but were sometimes chosen because of cultural or historical relevance.

One way to describe the images of nostalgia reflected in the collages is to classify them into four categories based on the degree to which they reflect individual or collective experience and the extent of direct experience with the object of nostalgia (Havlena and Holak 1995). The first class, *personal nostalgia*, is evidenced in the reference to holiday dinners with family. It reflects direct experience with the object of nostalgia where the meaning is unique to the individual. This is similar to what Baker and Kennedy (1994) term "real nostalgia." However, many of the collage images did not fit into this category. The other three classes of nostalgia—*interpersonal nostalgia*, *cultural nostalgia*, and *virtual nostalgia*—were implied by group members in describing and defending their collages.

FIGURE 3
Consumer Collage #3

Cultural nostalgia, while rooted in direct personal experience, is based on shared symbols, so that the resulting feeling of nostalgia reflects the individual's connection to other members of the culture. Interpersonal nostalgia results from indirect experience obtained through direct interpersonal contact and is essentially individual, rather than collective, in its focus. Through the recollections of family members or close friends one can almost feel personally connected to the experience. Davis (1979) refers to this as intergenerational nostalgia. Virtual nostalgia, dealing with indirect, collective experience, may involve one's own cultural history or may reflect a longing for a different cultural environment. The basis of virtual nostalgia is in nonpersonal communication, whereas interpersonal nostalgia is rooted in personal relationships with others who communicate their own nostalgia.

Interpersonal and virtual nostalgia are reflected in these collages through the presence of images related to American history. All the collages contain photographs of one or more members of the Kennedy family. Their presence was explained using references to both interpersonal and virtual nostalgia. One subject invoked interpersonal nostalgia as justification for the inclusion:

We were indirectly affected [by the Kennedy assassination] I think, because our parents and anyone older than us whenever they see that it just totally attracts their attention and really moves them....everybody remembers where they were when Kennedy got shot....and so it kind of affects you, too.

Clearly, for these young students, their indirect knowledge of the event through the recollections of parents and elders resulted in the experience of interpersonal nostalgia. For their parents and elders, however, the experience, with its collective emphasis, resembles cultural nostalgia—"*everybody* remembers where they were."

Other subjects noted the importance of the event and its effect on them, although they had not been alive at the time. This is illustrated by one subject's reference to virtual nostalgia, in this case for an historical event:

Basically...it was very important in history...it has been romanticized in every type of media—in literature, in movies, in print, in books, in articles, there are clubs; I am sure that the Internet has its share now of conspiracy clubs...but it has just always, I mean, any age group knows about the Kennedys.

FIGURE 4
Consumer Collage #4

In all these collages virtual nostalgia was essentially historical in character, involving U.S. history. Images of other cultures (such as an ancestral homeland), either in the present or in the past, and of fantasy or fictional settings did not appear.

The difference between direct and indirect experience is highlighted by the subjects' reference to the presence of Princess Diana in one collage (Figure 1):

Princess Di, my God...we remembered...it was a big deal when she first got married...Now, especially in the news with all her unfortunate marital situations, you always go back to the time...Oh, when they first got married...Was she better off before she met him?

In contrast to the images of the Kennedy family, the picture of Princess Diana evokes vivid memories for the subjects related to their own past.

The clear distinction between personal and other classes of nostalgia was evident in the way some groups structured their collages. One group started the discussion of their collage by noting that the center of the collage contained images that related directly and were important to them personally, while the perimeter con-

tained images that were related to society as a whole. They went on to describe the difficulty they experienced in positioning items that were both directly related to them and to the larger society as a whole—items that evoked cultural nostalgia.

PEOPLE AND NOSTALGIA

Images involving people associated with memories of time in school were common. Three of the five collages included a photo of a cheerleader. One of the women mentioned that, although she had not been a cheerleader herself, the image was closely linked with her own memories of high school. Three of the collages also contained a photo of a young boy looking up at a blackboard containing a long arithmetic problem. Subjects mentioned that the photo stirred reminiscences of similar experiences as well as memories of washing the blackboards and of scraping chalk in elementary school. Another woman discussed the nostalgic memories of her own past evoked by a photo of a candy striper reading at a hospital bedside (Figure 4). In all these cases, the nostalgia was of a personal nature, although the subsequent discussion of the subject revealed its cultural components as various members of the groups discovered the similarities in their experiences.

FIGURE 5
Consumer Collage #5

Relationships figured prominently in the images. One group even mentioned explicitly that the collage was structured around a black-and-white photo of an older couple standing side by side, smiling, with glasses of wine in their hands (Figure 5). They imagined the couple reflecting on their own pleasant memories and experiencing their own nostalgia. Another photo of an older couple was positioned near the first. A second group included a photo of a young child with an adult, apparently the boy's father (Figure 4). The links to childhood and to the relationship with one's parents were cited by members of the group.

PRODUCTS, ADVERTISING, AND NOSTALGIA

Certain products, generally associated with childhood, were present in all the collages. Food products, both branded and nonbranded, were present in every collage. One woman referred to the presence of orange juice during her childhood (Figure 1):

Minute Maid, frozen Tropicana—always, as a child, my mom...we had the frozen orange juice thing—never could figure out why frozen orange juice, but...it always was the case.

Another woman talked about a photograph of freshly baked bread (Figure 5):

That, actually, my mother baked bread every Saturday and the house just smelled of bread and that just brings it all back to me.

In some cases, individual brands were associated with family rituals or with holidays. Several subjects reported nostalgic associations with Jell-O:

Janet [another subject] and I bonded on that one, cause my mom always used to make Jell-O molds...always, every big holiday, Thanksgiving...get out that mold, do the layers...you know how you make that design with Jell-O—but no more.

Aunt Jemima appeared in all the collages, in one case positioned directly at the center (Figure 3), and was mentioned by almost all the subjects as a vivid memory from childhood. Other brands were used by several groups as well—Coca-Cola, Planter's peanuts, and Life cereal (with frequent references to Mikey and

"Mikey likes it"). Chocolate—in the form of Nestle's Toll House cookies (paired with milk, of course), M&M's, and Hershey's candy bars—was viewed as nostalgic, as was Campbell's soup. These were cited as comfortable symbols of home during childhood. Personal memories were mentioned in connection with all the food items.

One group included a photo of a young boy eating a slice of process cheese (Figure 4). A member of the group included it because it reminded him of an ad from his own past. During the presentation other group members corrected him about the subject of the original ad—it was an advertisement for bologna, not for cheese—but the nostalgic association survived the change of product category, being driven instead by the overall look of the ad.

Some clothing items were also included in the collages. One group incorporated a photo of Buster Brown shoes, mentioning that they all could remember wearing them as kids. Another included a photo of No Nonsense pantyhose (Figure 1), since one member associated it with her teen years when she used to dress up. Compared to food, clothing was more often described in terms of the individual and was less likely to evoke references to family or social interaction.

Grooming and personal care products were also used in the collages. Ivory soap was included by one group because of personal associations, as well as the explicit intergenerational appeal in the ad itself (Figure 4). Other images included a baby playing with a toy boat in a bathtub, toothbrushes, and hairbrushes, all associated with childhood and adolescence. One collage contained a set of directions for tying a men's necktie, a learning experience that was considered to be a rite of passage for young men (Figure 1).

Products in other categories also appeared. Another group used a Marlboro advertisement, citing personal or family use of the brand in the past (Figure 1). Nostalgic associations with brands used or chosen by others in the family sometimes surfaced in unexpected ways. One man talked about his inclusion of Shell and Texaco signs in the collage (Figure 3):

Actually, I can remember as a kid looking at those signs for hours on end when there were gas shortages back in 1973...you know, when you had odd or even license plate numbers you would get gas.

In this case, the collective experience of the gas shortage during the 1970s resulted in personal nostalgic memories for this individual.

A photo of a rotary dial telephone appeared in more than one collage. In addition to memories of the "old-fashioned" design, several subjects mentioned the importance of the telephone in their teen years and the memories that the photo evoked.

Toys associated with the subjects' childhood figured prominently in the collages. Barbie, Raggedy Ann and Andy, building toys, and teddy bears were all present. In one case, a current toy reminded a subject of a slightly different toy she played with as a child (Figure 4):

We realize too that these aren't Lego's, but they reminded us of Lego's...we couldn't find the Lego's.

ENTERTAINMENT AND NOSTALGIA

Baseball appeared in various forms in four of the five collages, positioned centrally in two of them. The groups noted the importance of baseball in their own pasts and in American popular cultural history, although the prominence of the image may also reflect the current sense of loss created by the baseball players' strike.

Photos of celebrities and entertainment figures, such as movie stars and musicians, were conspicuous in the collages. Characters, both human and cartoon (Disney and otherwise), from the subjects' childhood were used repeatedly. Images from the comics, television, and the movies included Superman, King Kong, *Star Trek*, *Bonanza*, and *The Andy Griffith Show*. Several subjects in one group discussed their memories of watching *The Ten Commandments* with Charlton Heston on television every year at Easter.

DISCUSSION

Consumer collages may prove to be a useful method for researching imagery and its meaning. The nostalgia collages discussed in this paper offer insights into consumers' understanding of the structure and subjects of nostalgic experience. They contain examples of all four classes of nostalgia and the subsequent discussion of the collages by their creators confirms the existence of all four classes in consumers' minds.

Obviously, the content of the collages will be constrained by the images contained in the materials used by the subjects. Publications such as *Car and Driver*, *Popular Mechanics*, or the *National Enquirer* might have provided images not available in the magazines used in this study. However, the range of images in the materials provided here was reasonably broad. Clearly, some subjects present in the magazines—such as sports cars, designer clothing, laundry detergent, and basketball—do not appear in the collages, while other images appear repeatedly across the collages. It is necessary for the researcher to ensure that a wide variety of images are presented for selection.

The twenty subjects who participated in this study were all American-born graduate students between the ages of 23 and 42. Future research could compare the imagery and meaning of nostalgia for other groups in the population. For example, does the imagery of nostalgia differ markedly for older consumers or do many of the same images manifest themselves? Although the images may be similar, the meanings may differ across groups.

Finally, the imagery contained in the collages may provide marketers with insights concerning the positioning of and associations with their own nostalgic brands. While psychological and sociological analysis of nostalgia as a phenomenon has concentrated on personal nostalgia, marketing has often used cultural nostalgia—such as the release of *The Brady Bunch Movie*—and virtual nostalgia—such as Disney's unsuccessful attempt to locate an American history theme park near Washington, D.C. The collages and the explanations attached to them may clarify the extent to which brands evoke personal nostalgia as opposed to cultural nostalgia. New ideas for evoking virtual nostalgia may be suggested. As such, the collages can aid in developing products or messages that may prove more satisfying to consumers in terms of creating nostalgic associations.

REFERENCES

Baker, Stacey Menzel and Patricia F. Kennedy (1994), "Death By Nostalgia: A Diagnosis of Context-Specific Cases," in Chris T. Allen and Deborah Roedder John (eds.), *Advances in Consumer Research*, Vol. 21, Provo, UT: Association for Consumer Research, 169-174.

Carter, Barbara A., David L. Nelson, and Linda W. Duncombe (1983), "The Effect of Psychological Type on the Mood and Meaning of Two Collage Activities," *American Journal of Occupational Therapy*, 37 (October), 688-693.

Davis, Fred (1979), *Yearning for Yesterday: A Sociology of Nostalgia*, New York: Free Press.

Froehlich, Jeanette and David L. Nelson (1986), "Affective Meanings of Life Review Through Activities and Discussion," *American Journal of Occupational Therapy*, 40 (January), 27-33.

Gordon, Wendy and Roy Langmaid (1988), *Qualitative Market Research*, Hants, England: Gower.

Havlena, William J. and Susan L. Holak (1995), "Nostalgia and Nostalgia-Proneness: An Alternative Classification and Measurement Instrument," unpublished working paper.

Holak, Susan L. and William J. Havlena (1992), "Nostalgia: An Exploratory Study of Themes and Emotions in the Nostalgic Experience," in John F. Sherry, Jr. and Brian Sternthal (eds.), *Advances in Consumer Research*, Vol. 19, Provo, UT: Association for Consumer Research, 380-387.

Heisley, Deborah D. and Sidney J. Levy (1991), "Autodriving: A Photoelicitation Technique," *Journal of Consumer Research*, 18 (December), 257-272.

Landgarten, Helen B. (1993), *Magazine Photo Collage: A Multicultural Assessment and Treatment Technique*, New York: Brunner/Mazel.

Rickard, Leah (1994), "Focus Groups Go to Collage," *Advertising Age*, November 14, 39.

Rook, Dennis W. (1991), "I Was Observed (In *Absentia*) and Autodriven by the Consumer Behavior Odyssey," in Russell W. Belk (ed.), *Highways and Buyways: Naturalistic Research from the Consumer Behavior Odyssey*, Provo, UT: Association for Consumer Research, 48-58.

Rook, Dennis W. and Sidney J. Levy (1983), "Psychosocial Themes in Consumer Grooming Rituals," in Richard P. Bagozzi and Alice M. Tybout (eds.), *Advances in Consumer Research*, Vol. 10, Provo, UT: Association for Consumer Research, 329-333b.

Stern, Barbara B. (1992), "Nostalgia in Advertising Text: Romancing the Past," in John F. Sherry, Jr. and Brian Sternthal (eds.), *Advances in Consumer Research*, Vol. 19, Provo, UT: Association for Consumer Research, 388-389.

Consumption Behaviour in the Sex 'n' Shopping Novels of Judith Krantz:
A Post-structuralist Perspective
Stephen Brown, University of Ulster

ABSTRACT

Literary analysis is emerging as a major focus of contemporary marketing and consumer research. This paper aims to contribute to this growing body of scholarship by examining consumption behaviour in two best-selling "sex 'n' shopping" novels, *Scruples* and *Scruples Two* by Judith Krantz. Although the sex 'n' shopping sub-genre is renowned for its brand name-dropping and celebration of conspicuous consumption, the analysis reveals that the two Scruples novels offer contrasting visions of consumer behaviour. In appropriately post-structuralist fashion, the underpinning binary oppositions - sacred/profane and male/female - are transposed and self-cancelling in the course of both books.

INTRODUCTION

Although they were revolutionary statements at the time, few contemporary commentators would disagree with Stern's (1989a, p.322) contention that, "literary criticism...may provide an additional way of learning about consumers", or Belk's (1986, p.27) ringing declaration that, "art can be a useful way of generating knowledge...art has much to contribute to consumer behaviour...art may be seen to provide an attractive alternative to more traditional 'scientific' means of consumer research". Indeed, as a consequence of the latter-day "interpretive turn" (Sherry 1991; Hirschman and Holbrook 1992), the analysis of artistic artifacts in general and works of literature in particular has become a firmly established, if not exactly mainstream, approach to marketing and consumer research (see Holbrook and Hirschman 1993).

This growing interest in literary analysis is made manifest in a variety of ways, but for the purposes of explication these can be divided into two main categories: "marketing in literature" and "literature in marketing". The former involves the study of marketing and consumption phenomena as portrayed in various works of literature. Examples include Friedman's (1985) analysis of brand names in post-war popular fiction; Belk (1987) and Spiggle's (1986) explications of consumption behaviour in diverse comic books; and Holbrook and Hirschman's (1993) meditations on Homer's *Odyssey*, Virgil's *Aeneid*, Goethe's *Faust* and Joyce's *Ulysses* amongst others. The latter category, by contrast, applies the tools and techniques of literary criticism to marketing artifacts, advertising in particular. Analyses of allegory, prosody, rhetoric and resonance in effective marketing communication have been undertaken (Stern 1988, 1989b; McQuarrie and Mick 1992), as have explorations of the many and varied schools of literary criticism - psychoanalytical, reader-response, marxist, new criticism, feminist and so on (e.g. Stern 1989a, 1993; Scott 1994).

Pathbreaking though the "marketing in literature" and "literature in marketing" perspectives have proved to be, there remains ample scope for additional investigation. The exponents of the marketing in literature school, for example, have only explicated a minute fraction of the literary canon and, more importantly perhaps, have tended to employ a comparatively limited number of methodological and critical approaches (content analysis, structuralism and abduction in the main). Devotees of literature in marketing, on the other hand, have been assiduous in their application of the manifold schools of literary criticism, but they have tended to concentrate on a single aspect of the marketing mix, namely advertising and promotion. There are, admittedly, a number of important exceptions to these statements, nevertheless it is arguable

that the "marketing in literature" perspective could be enhanced by a greater diversity of critical approaches and that the "literature in marketing" perspective would be enriched by applications outside the advertising arena.

The present paper aims to extend the overall scope of literary analysis by examining consumption behaviour in the Scruples novels of Judith Krantz. It contributes to the literature in marketing perspective by moving beyond advertising to the study of retail stores, albeit a fictional (if verisimilous) retailing organisation, and adds to the marketing in literature perspective by adopting a critical posture predicated on post-structuralist literary theory. In addition, it addresses an aspect of popular culture - romantic fiction - which possesses considerable, though largely unexplored, research potential (however, see Stern 1991; Scott 1993; Stern and Holbrook 1994). As the generic term for the sub-genre amply testifies, "sex 'n' shopping" novels are likely to contain much of intrinsic interest to marketing and consumer researchers.

The paper to follow commences with a discussion of romantic fiction and the latter-day advent of the "sex 'n' shopping" novel; continues with a plot summary of *Scruples* and *Scruples Two*; culminates in a post-structuralist reading of some of the novels' key themes, particularly those that pertain to extant investigations in the "marketing in literature" and "literature in marketing" traditions; and concludes with a very brief outline of some broader research issues.

ROMANTIC FICTION AND THE SEX 'N' SHOPPING NOVEL

Although the term "romance" has been applied to all manner of literary endeavours, from medieval tales of questing and heroic knights to novels which begin on dark and stormy nights in deserted gothic mansions (see Radford 1986), it is usually associated with the, "kind of love story found next to the candy bars in supermarket checkout lanes [with] titles like *Always Love* or *Pagan Adversary*" (Elam 1992, p.5). Written by, for and about women, such works of romantic fiction are enormously popular. Sales figures in the industry are notoriously suspect, but it is estimated that 250 million copies of "trademark romances" (Harlequin, Silhouette and Mills and Boon are the best known imprints) are sold each year and the market for second-hand volumes is reputed to be equally brisk (Dubino 1993).

Despite their undoubted popularity, works of romantic fiction are rarely short-listed for literary awards or are the recipients of critical acclaim (Berger 1992). On the contrary, they are routinely dismissed as mass produced fantasies that are atrociously written, mindlessly consumed and concocted according to the same tired and tiresome recipe. Albeit a commonplace, such disparagement is not simply a reflection of literary critics' traditional hostility toward the popular - the "if it sells it must be devoid of merit" school of thought. Nor is it merely a manifestation of misguided male commentators, such as the much-maligned Margolies (1982), who are quick to condemn "the things women enjoy, from soap opera to melodrama to romance fiction, as superficial and over-emotional trash, while football and detective fiction are elevated to semi-mystical heights" (Moore 1991, p.86). The disdain, in fact, is also attributable to first generation of radical feminist writers who regarded romantic fiction as sugar-coated instantiations of oppressive patriarchal ideology. The phallocentricity in the novels' basic premise, that the attainment of connubial bliss is the principal aspiration of contemporary womankind, was not only inaccurate, outmoded and simplistic, but it also served to reinforce the very structures of androcentric subordination that the women's movement sought to overthrow. As Germaine Greer (1971, p.188) pointed out in *The Female Eunuch*, romantic fiction "is the opiate of the supermenial...[which]...sanctions drudgery, physical incompetence and prostitution".

If the first generation of feminist critics regarded romantic fiction as politically regressive, the second generation has adopted a much more positive stance. As a result of the pioneering investigations by Tania Modelski (1982) and Janice Radway (1987), which respectively comprised a comprehensive re-assessment of "mass produced fantasies" and an empirical study of the reading habits of 49 married women, the emancipatory function of romantic fiction is now frequently acknowledged, albeit not universally acclaimed (see Thurston 1987; Cohn 1988; McCafferty 1994). Radway in particular revealed that for many women romances provide a form of existential and emotional succour, an escape from the daily round, a period of respite, of self-indulgence, of personal development that is denied to them in their principal familial duties as wife, mother, quartermaster and, increasingly, breadwinner. As such, romantic fiction possesses subversive potential - not least because men find it threatening (e.g. *Playboy* 1988) - and reading it encourages women to repudiate the self-abnegating role traditionally expected of them (Elam 1992). True, for many feminist commentators romantic novels continue to reproduce patriarchal relationships, but is now widely accepted that in their own small way romances are making a meaningful contribution to the grail of female emancipation (Pearce and Stacey 1995).

Alongside this change in critical temper, the nature of the books themselves has been radically transformed. Although the style, structure and settings of the novels remain decidedly conventional, contemporary romantic fiction tends to be much more sexually explicit than before (traditional trademark romances of the Mills and Boon or Silhouette variety were - and are - exceptionally chaste). Exemplified by the best-selling works of Jackie Collins, Shirley Conran and Julie Burchill, and variously referred to by the disparaging epithets "sex 'n' shopping" novels, "humping and hoarding" romances or the "shopping and fucking" sub-genre, they are invariably characterised by strong, aggressive, self-made female protagonists who seek sexual, economic and social independence, though not necessarily in that particular order of priority. On the contrary, sexual gratification is often treated as secondary to successful personal development, the attainment of career objectives and, above all, revelling in the material rewards of their hard-earned endeavours. As Lewallen (1988, p.89) emphasises, "expensive commodities and designer names drip through the pages as indicators of the heroines' increasing wealth and success".

The origins of the "sex 'n' shopping" novel have been traced back to Flaubert's *Madame Bovary*, the "bodice-ripper" sub-genre, of which Winsor's *Forever Amber* is a prime example and the latter-day era of female sexual emancipation epitomised by Jong's *Fear of Flying* and Susann's *Valley of the Dolls* (de Botton 1994). It is generally accepted, however, that the works of Judith Krantz comprise the apotheosis of this particular literary form. According to Cadogan's (1994, p.304) recent history of the romantic fiction genre, "the dismissive 'shopping and fucking' (S and F) tag has probably been tied on Judith Krantz's novels more than those of any other romantic block-busting best-sellers". Born in Manhattan, educated at Wellesley College and married to a Hollywood movie and television producer, Krantz began her literary career as a fashion editor and contributor to various women's magazines. Her first book, *Scruples*, was published in 1978, to considerable popular if not critical acclaim, and she has since written seven further works of romantic fiction, most of which became No.1 best-sellers and were made into television mini-series. While all of her novels, portraying the glamorous, hyper-affluent lifestyle that Krantz knows at first hand, have proved extremely popular (career sales to date have been calculated at more than 50 million copies), perhaps her most celebrated creation is Scruples, the self-proclaimed "best fashion store in the world". Scruples, in fact, is turning into something of a literary mini-series in itself, since no less than three of Krantz's (1978, 1992, 1994) eight novels feature the characters associated with the fictional boutique. However, as the third and most recent of these volumes, *Lovers*, does not deal directly with the trials and tribulations of the retail store, the present investigation is confined to *Scruples* and *Scruples Two*.

PLOT SUMMARY

The protagonist of *Scruples* is Whilhelmina Hunnenwell Winthrop Ikehorn Orsini, or Billy for short. Born into the impoverished wing of a rich Boston family, Billy is a grotesquely over-weight and unloved child who fails to get into college and is sent to Paris for a year. This ugly duckling, however, returns to the United States as a beautiful and sophisticated swan having lost weight, learnt French, had a doomed love affair with an impoverished aristocrat and, most importantly of all, having developed an acute fashion sense. She enrols in secretarial college in New York, joins the firm of Ikehorn Enterprises, has an affair with and then marries its fabulously wealthy septuagenarian founder, Ellis Ikehorn, and after his death inherits his entire fortune. As an extremely affluent young widow, she indulges in an orgy of compulsive consumption, but due to Rodeo Drive's inability to satisfy her needs, she decides to establish her own speciality clothing store, the eponymous Scruples. Although it is the last word in retailing luxury, the store is unsuccessful and is only rescued by the appointment of marketing authority, Spider Elliott, and haute couture specialist Valentine O'Neill. Between them, they completely re-organise, re-arrange, re-stock, re-position and, eventually, re-launch the new, improved Scruples to enormous acclaim, instant success and unparalleled profitability. Secure in her position as a fashion retailing superstar, Billy is invited by one of her regular customers to the Cannes film festival. There she meets, is charmed by, falls in love with and subsequently marries a dynamic, wheeler-dealing, somewhat unscrupulous film producer, Vito Orsini. She assists with the making of his next film, *Mirrors*, which wins the Oscar for best picture, despite the studio's attempt at sabotage. The book ends on Oscars night with Billy pregnant, Vito triumphant and Spider and Valentine in love.

Scruples Two opens on Oscars night with Billy pregnant, Vito triumphant and Spider and Valentine in love, but the euphoria does not last for long. Billy quickly realizes that she takes second place to Vito's career and discovers that he has a sixteen year-old daughter from a previous marriage, Gigi Orsini. Outraged at Vito's neglect of his offspring and traumatised by a miscarriage, she initiates divorce proceedings, takes Gigi under her wing and is emotionally devastated by an accidental fire which kills Valentine O'Neill and completely destroys the original store. Shattered by the death of his wife, Spider Elliott buys a yacht and sets off to sail around the world. Billy closes down the entire Scruples operation, flees to Paris where she has a passionate fling with a sculptor, only to retreat to New York after his abrupt termination of the relationship. There she catches up with the progress of her step-daughter, Gigi Orsini, who has developed a passion for collecting antique lingerie and shares an apartment with Sasha Nevsky, an avid catalogue shopper and self-styled "Great Slut of Babylon". Not the most reticent of individuals, Sasha suggests to Billy that they develop a Scruples mail order catalogue featuring Gigi's antique creations. Outraged at the very thought of debasing Scruples' good name, Billy flies in high dudgeon to Los Angeles, and calls to see Spider Elliott, recently returned from his travels. Spider recognises the potential of the catalogue shopping concept and persuades Billy that it might just work. After the development of an appropriate format, Sasha and Gigi relocate to Los Angeles and the book ends with Spider and Billy in love and, needless to say, the Scruples Two catalogue a triumphant success.

DECONSTRUCTING SCRUPLES

As the foregoing synopsis indicates, the Scruples novels are suffused with designer labels, brand names, marketing institutions and consumption activities-cum-pathologies. It is impossible to do justice to the books' content in the present paper, but it is possible to offer a partial post-structuralist interrogation of the texts. Post-structuralism, as several leading exponents of the "literature in marketing" perspective have shown, differs from its more familiar predecessor in so far as it eschews the notion of deep, stable, unique, universal structures of underlying meaning (Scott 1992; Stern 1993). On the contrary, it maintains that the meaning of any textual artifact (and, according to post-structuralists, almost anything can be considered a "text" whether it be a haircut, holiday, motion picture or work of literature) is extremely difficult if not impossible to tie down. Meaning is contingent, unstable, temporary, suspended, deferred and very much dependent on both the specific use context and the interpretive preconceptions brought to the text by individual readers (Brown 1995).

There are a number of schools of post-structuralist thought and several methodological procedures associated with the movement (Selden and Widdowson 1993). Perhaps the best known of these is the deconstructive technique of Jacques Derrida (Broadbent 1991). Although it has entered popular parlance as a chic synonym for "subversion", "investigation" or "analysis", and although it is a methodology that eschews its methodological status, deconstruction is a procedure for interrogating texts which seeks to expose their inconsistencies, contradictions, unrecognised assumptions and implicit conceptual hierarchies. To show, as Norris (1991, p.35) aptly puts it, that a text "cannot mean what is says...or say what it means". In theory, deconstruction involves the identification of binary oppositions, or polar antitheses, within the text (as per the structuralist orthodoxy), demonstrating that each pole is inherent in and dependent upon the other, and ultimately that neither is privileged or preferable. In practice, however, deconstructive readings of a Derridian kind invariably seize upon a small, seemingly inconsequential, aspect of the narrative in question and show how it reflects, infects and unlocks the entire textual edifice (Norris 1991).

With regard to the Scruples novels, the deconstructive key is inscribed in the four movies that are "made" in the course of the overall narrative. Apart from the obvious parallelism between both books - two movies are made in the first and two in the second - and a noteworthy inclination towards inversion in their respective "performances" at the box office (a moderate failure and massive success in *Scruples* versus a massive failure and moderate success in *Scruples Two*), every single film involves some sort of transposition or reversal whether it be in time, space, actor and/or character. The same is true of the Scruples novels themselves in that they are mirror images - complete opposites - of one another. What is celebrated in *Scruples* is disdained in *Scruples Two*, what is condemned in the former is lauded in the latter and issues that are

overlooked in the first novel are central to the sequel. The books, in effect, cancel each other out. Like most works of literature, according to the notorious post-structuralist critic Paul de Man, the Scruples novels *self-deconstruct*.

When the books are examined in detail, a host of intriguing binary oppositions can be discerned. These include up/down, in/out, production/marketing, past/present and fake/real, all of which effectively transpose and erase themselves in the course of both novels. For the purposes of the present paper, however, discussion will be confined to two dichotomies that have been identified in previous investigations of "marketing in literature" and "literature in marketing": namely, sacred/profane and male/female.

Sacred/Profane

In what is perhaps the nearest published equivalent to the present study, Elizabeth Hirschman (1991) has conducted a literary analysis of Charles Dickens' *A Christmas Carol*. The fundamental underpinning structure consisted of a sacred/secular (or profane) duality, which was made manifest in the characters, settings, possessions, and overall consumption activities portrayed in the book (and which, according to Hirschman, is evident in numerous other works of popular culture). This sacred/profane antithesis is equally apparent in the Scruples novels, though it is somewhat less pronounced than in Dickens' much-loved masterpiece. Indeed, such is the extent of the mendaciousness, covetousness, maliciousness, deceitfulness, selfishness, lasciviousness and gross moral turpitude portrayed in Krantz's best-sellers, and so pervasive is obscenity and blasphemy, that a casual reader might reasonably conclude that the books are paeans to profanity rather than celebrations of the sacred. As is well known, however, one of the key premises of structuralism and post-structuralism is that textual signs derive meaning from what they are not. Hence, the unremitting inventory of the seven deadly sins, only serves to throw the sacred side of the Scruples novels into particularly sharp relief.

This sacredness is made apparent in many small acts of kindness, generosity and nobility perpetrated by the principal characters - for example, Aunt Cornelia's early concern for her unloved and unlovable niece, Billy's devotion to Ellis Ikehorn after his incapacitation and her self-appointed role as Gigi Orsini's godmother - but it is most clearly marked in the personal achievements of the protagonists. Virtually every figure in the books is an embodiment of the American Dream and a monument to the adage that it is necessary to suffer in order to succeed. Whether it be Billy Ikehorn, Vito Orsini, Valentine O'Neill, Maggie McGregor, Gigi Orsini or whomever, each and every one emerged from a poor, dysfunctional or in some way underprivileged background and attained the pinnacle of personal accomplishment, financial well-being and social status by dint of sheer hard work and a determination to make it regardless of the odds, obstacles or setbacks. They thus *earned the right* to indulge in various forms of conspicuous consumption - dressing in the most elegant outfits, dining in the most exclusive restaurants, disporting the most extravagant displays of jewellery, driving the most expensive automobiles, staying in the very best suites in the very best hotels, or purchasing apartments, aeroplanes, vineyards or retail stores on the merest whim.

Despite the overall pervasiveness of the Protestant work ethic, a clear distinction is discernible between the two novels. If the first is dominated by profanity with only a smattering of the sacred, the second is primarily sacred in ethos with only a slight leavening of profanity. The spirituality of *Scruples Two* is evident not simply in the novel's comparative lack of eroticism and obscenity (there are only seven descriptions of sexual encounters, as opposed to twelve in *Scruples*, and the total number of swear words falls by approximately 40%), but it is apparent in several other forms, such as Billy's eradication of the entire Scruples retailing empire - at the very height of its success - as a penance for causing the death of Valentine O'Neill and her subsequent symbolic plunge into the painstaking resurrection of a beautiful but neglected Parisian mansion. The sacred is equally evident in characters' widespread sense of guilt concerning past moral misdemeanours. Thus, the promiscuity, covetousness and narcissism that is celebrated in *Scruples*, is regretted, disavowed and overcome in the sequel. In the opening pages of *Scruples Two*, for example, Billy expresses her distaste for the rich, idle women that patronise her store; indulges in a diatribe about the moral bankruptcy of the movie-making community; denounces the dreadful implications of the impossible pursuit of physical perfection by means of plastic surgery; is treated to a severe tongue-lashing concerning her own self-indulgent, super-affluent lifestyle; and purports to be profoundly shocked by Vito's abandonment of his off-spring (even though she expressly eschews the encumbrances of parenthood in the first novel). Indeed, it is arguable that the defining moment of the entire narrative occurs when Billy *resists* the temptation to spend a fortune in an exclusive Parisian jewellers, even though she is at an emotional and spiritual nadir after the break-up of her affair with sculptor, Sam Jamison.

More important perhaps than penance, guilt and abstinence, it is arguable that the dominant refrain of *Scruples Two* is the old adage that worldly success does not bring spiritual contentment. Enormous wealth, professional acclaim, physical perfection and every conceivable manifestation of "the good life" are no guarantee of happiness, equanimity or personal fulfilment. Quite the reverse. The most ecstatic section of the second novel occurs when Billy is posing as a penniless, albeit emotionally sated, schoolteacher in Paris. This stands in marked contrast to the most joyous moments in *Scruples*, when she was frantically working for the material rewards that accompany the production of a successful motion picture. At the very end of the second novel, moreover, Billy states that all her worldly possessions are less fulfilling than the pleasure she obtains from hard work, honest toil and the creation of something (the mail order catalogue) that is likely to enhance the daily lives of millions of people (see Hirschman 1990).

Male/Female

In addition to their exemplification of the sacred/profane duality, as identified by the leading exponent of the "marketing in literature" approach, the Scruples novels illustrate a polar opposition that inheres in the work of a prominent advocate of "literature in marketing". In a series of publications, Barbara Stern has demonstrated how the male/female dichotomy is inscribed in various advertising campaigns (e.g. Stern 1991, 1993), and, more importantly from the perspective of the present paper, she has drawn upon the conventions of romantic fiction in her analysis of an advertisement for Paco Rabanne (Stern and Holbrook 1994). Apart from its apparent lack of focus on the heroine, the advertisement provided a classic illustration of the various elements of formula romances - courtship, consumption, love, fantasy, matrimony and sexual decorum - though this interpretation is predicated to some extent on the gender of the reader.

Even when allowances are made for gender induced distortions, it is difficult to avoid the conclusion that the Scruples novels do *not* offer a conventional portrayal of romantic love. As noted earlier, the entire sex 'n' shopping sub-genre is distinguished by its abandonment of the traditional Harlequin or Mills and Boon style heroine - passive, flighty, loving and subordinate to the aggressive, pagan, domineering, often brutal, qualities of the heroic male. In actual fact, *Scruples* comprises a complete reversal of the arche-

typal romantic fiction schema, in that the female protagonist is endowed with the "standard" male characteristics. She is tall, dark, handsome, temperamental, unpredictable, impetuous, driven and totally indifferent to wedded bliss, parenthood and pleasures of procreation. "To a stranger who might have seen her for the first time at that moment, and assessed her height, her proud walk, her strong throat, her imperious head, she would have looked as autocratic and as strong as a young Amazon queen" (p.26). Endowed, moreover, with a voracious sexual appetite (cf the succession of nurses during Ellis Ikehorn's incapacitation), the heroine is more than capable of treating men as sexual playthings and readily disposable commodities (see Hirschman and Stern 1994).

If, as her name implies, Billy is a female embodiment of the masculine qualities of the romantic hero, Spider Elliott exemplifies the traditional romantic heroine. Although he is a man among men, a rampant heterosexual in the notoriously homosexual milieu of high fashion and glamour photography, he is endowed with numerous ostensibly "feminine" characteristics. He is intuitive, creative, sensitive, artistic, trusting, empathetic, caring, desperate for romantic fulfilment and determined to find the one true love of his life. This quest ultimately proves successful when he marries Valentine O'Neill, though it is noteworthy that she is described as "boyish" and, indeed, that her first sexual encounter is with Alan Wilton, a leading fashion designer and closet homosexual. Be that as it may, the feminine side of Spider's nature figures prominently in the narrative. "He had a passion for everything and anything that was part of the female element in the world...[and possessed a]...very special knack for moving through a woman's mind, trading easily in her idiom, speaking directly to her, cutting across the barriers of masculinity and femininity" (pp.14, 84).

Set against this usurpation of romantic fiction conventions, *Scruples* continues to adhere to one particularly important aspect of the genre - its preoccupation with consumption. As the foregoing plot summary indicates, the entire narrative is suffused with the celebration of consumption behaviour. It reeks of luxury, affluence, profligacy, pampered self-indulgence and, indeed, aspiration. The book contains numerous detailed descriptions of complete outfits, interior designs, social mores and fashion advice for, presumably, the super-rich aspirants among the readership. So much so, that one reviewer, the renowned feminist writer and critic Angela Carter (1982, p.153) concluded that, "the final effect of the novel is of being sealed inside a luxury shopping mall whilst being softly pelted with scented sex technique manuals". True, the negative consequences of unbridled consumption are referred to at length and in no uncertain terms. Nevertheless, compared to the eschewal of excess, the consuming rectitude, the abandonment of wasteful extravagance that is exhibited in *Scruples Two*, it is undeniable that the first novel is an extended, occasionally ecstatic, encomium to the hedonistic joys of irresponsible, irrepressible, unrestrained consumption behaviour.

Ironically, the distaste for conspicuous consumption that typifies *Scruples Two* is unconventional in itself, in so far as the entire book represents a reversion to romantic fiction norms. Whereas the first book comprised an innovative break from the traditional formula, the sequel regresses to the mean. It is a relatively traditional, comparatively chaste, very orthodox work of romantic fiction. The novel is replete with references to flower arranging, cookery, gardening, courtship, parenthood, sensible clothing, school choice and teenage emotional trauma, topics which simply do not feature in the first book. Billy, moreover, becomes preoccupied with "traditional" female concerns of finding true love, familial responsibilities, monogamous relationships and her soft, gentle, generous, vulnerable side is on display throughout. Spider Elliott, by contrast, is transformed into a "real man" by dint of his stoic forbearance after the death of Valentine and his abandonment of the effete world of fashion retailing for the archetypal "masculine" aspiration to circumnavigate the globe (on his return, Billy even refers to his "pagan" qualities). Indeed, the book actually concludes with that most cliched of romantic fiction cliches - Spider proposing to Billy on bended knee in a secret garden. This, needless to say, is swiftly followed by the sort of culminating embrace that is known in the romantic fiction industry as "the big clinch" (Jones 1986).

CONCLUSION

In recent years, a number of prominent marketing and consumer researchers have argued that meaningful insights can be obtained by means of literary analysis. This paper has attempted to further the "marketing in literature" and "literature in marketing" research traditions by exploring the consumption behaviours in two best-selling sex 'n' shopping novels of Judith Krantz. Although it comprises a small portion of a more extensive research programme, which deals with Scruples' explication of compulsive consumption, materialism, gift-giving, hedonic consumption, acculturation and theories of retail change (not to mention a straightforward content analysis of brand name citation), the paper highlighted the marked differences between the two novels. A historicist interpretation of these differences might seek to explain them in terms of the contrasting socio-economic climates in which the books were written (late '70s versus early '90s), but the present paper argues that they represent an instantiation of post-structuralist literary theory. Two previously established binary oppositions - sacred/profane and male/female - were identified in the novels, as was their inversion, erasure and ultimate self-deconstruction.

REFERENCES

Belk, R.W. (1986), "Art versus science as ways of generating knowledge about materialism", in *Perspectives on Methodology in Consumer Research*, eds. D. Brinberg and R.J. Lutz, New York: Springer-Verlag, 3-36.

_____ (1987), "Material values in the comics: a content analysis of comic books featuring themes of wealth", *Journal of Consumer Research*, 14 (June), 26-42.

Berger, A.A. (1992), *Popular Culture Genres: Theories and Texts*, Newbury Park: Sage.

Broadbent, G. (1991), *Deconstruction: A Student Guide*, London: Academy Editions.

Brown, S. (1995), *Postmodern Marketing*, London: Routledge.

Cadogan, M. (1994), *And Then Their Hearts Stood Still: An Exuberant Look at Romantic Fiction Past and Present*, London: Macmillan.

Carter, A. (1982), *Nothing Sacred: Selected Writings*, London: Virago.

Cohn, J. (1988), *Romance and the Erotics of Property: Mass-market Fiction for Women*, Durham: Duke University Press.

De Botton, A. (1994), *The Romantic Movement: Sex, Shopping and the Novel*, London: Macmillan.

Dubino, J. (1993), "The Cinderella complex: romance fiction, patriarchy and capitalism", *Journal of Popular Culture*, 27 (3), 103-118.

Elam, D. (1992), *Romancing the Postmodern*, London: Routledge.

Friedman, M. (1985), "The changing language of a consumer society: brand name usage in popular American novels in the post-war era", *Journal of Consumer Research*, 11 (March), 927-938.

Greer, G. (1971), *The Female Eunuch*, London: Paladin.

Hirschman, E.C. (1990), "Secular immortality and the American ideology of affluence", *Journal of Consumer Research*, 17 (June), 31-42.

_____ (1991) "Secular and sacred consumption imagery in Charles Dickens' 'A Christmas Carol'", reprinted in *The Semiotics of Consumption*, M.B. Holbrook and E.C. Hirschman (1993), Berlin: de Gruyter, 286-295.

_____ and M.B. Holbrook (1992) *Postmodern Consumer Research*, Newbury Park: Sage.

_____ and B.B. Stern (1994) "Women as commodities: prostitution as depicted in 'The Blue Angel', 'Pretty Baby' and 'Pretty Woman'", in *Advances in Consumer Research Vol. 21*, eds. C.T. Allen and D.R. John, Provo: Association for Consumer Research, 576-581.

Holbrook, M.B. and E.C. Hirschman (1993), *The Semiotics of Consumption: Interpreting Symbolic Consumer Behaviour in Popular Culture and Works of Art*, Berlin: de Gruyter.

Jones, A.R. (1986), "Mills and Boon meets feminism", in *The Progress of Romance: The Politics of Popular Fiction*, ed. J. Radford, London: Routledge and Kegan Paul, 195-218.

Krantz, J. (1978), *Scruples*, London: Warner Books.

_____ (1992), *Scruples Two*, London: Bantam Books.

_____ (1994), *Lovers*, London: Bantam Press.

Lewallan, A. (1988), "Lace: pornography for women", in *The Female Gaze: Women as Viewers of Popular Culture*, eds. L. Gamman and M. Marshment, London: The Women's Press, 86-101.

Margolies, D. (1982), "Mills and Boon: guilt without sex", *Red Letters*, 14, 5-13.

McCafferty, K. (1994), "Palimpsest of desire: the re-emergence of the American captivity narrative as pulp romance", *Journal of Popular Culture*, 27 (4), 43-56.

McQuarrie, E.F. and D.G. Mick (1992), "On resonance: a critical pluralistic inquiry into advertising rhetoric", *Journal of Consumer Research*, 19 (September), 180-197.

Modelski, T. (1982), *Loving With a Vengence: Mass-produced Fantasies for Women*, Hamden: Archon Books.

Moore, S. (1991), *Looking for Trouble: On Shopping, Gender and the Cinema*, London: Serpent's Tail.

Norris, C. (1991), *Deconstruction: Theory and Practice*, London: Routledge.

Pearce, L. and J. Stacey (1995), *Romance Revisited*, London: Lawrence and Wishart.

Playboy (1990), "A man's guide to heaving-bosom women's fiction", *Playboy*, May, 72-75, 178.

Radway, J. (1987), *Reading the Romance: Women, Patriarchy and Popular Literature*, London: Verso.

Radford, J. (1986), *The Progress of Romance: The Politics of Popular Fiction*, London: Routledge and Kegan Paul.

Scott, L.M. (1992), "Playing with pictures: postmodernism, poststructuralism and advertising visuals", in *Advances in Consumer Research Vol. 19*, eds. J.F. Sherry and B. Sternthal, Provo: Association for Consumer Research, 596-612.

_____ (1993), "Spectacular vernacular: literacy and commercial culture in the postmodern age", *International Journal of Research in Marketing*, 10 (3), 251-275.

_____ (1994), "The bridge from text to mind: adapting reader-response theory to consumer research", *Journal of Consumer Research*, 21 (December), 461-480.

Selden, R. and P. Widdowson (1993), *A Reader's Guide to Contemporary Literary Theory*, Hemel Hempstead: Harvester Wheatsheaf.

Sherry, J.F. (1991) "Postmodern alternatives: the interpretive turn in consumer research", in *Handbook of Consumer Research*, eds. T.S. Robertson and H.H. Kassarjain, Englewood Cliffs: Prentice Hall, 548-591.

Spiggle, S. (1986), "Measuring social values: a content analysis of Sunday comics and underground comix", *Journal of Consumer Research*, 13 (June), pp. 100-113.

Stern, B.B. (1988), "Medieval allegory: roots of advertising strategy for the mass market", *Journal of Marketing*, 52 (July), 84-94.

_____ (1989a), "Literary criticism and consumer research: overview and illustrative analysis", *Journal of Consumer Research*, 16 (December), 322-334.

_____ (1989b), "Literary explication: a methodology for consumer research", in *Interpretive Consumer Research*, ed. E.C. Hirschman, Provo: Association for Consumer Research, 48-59.

_____ (1991), "Two pornographies: a feminist view of sex in advertising", in *Advances in Consumer Research Vol. 18*, eds. R.H. Holman and M.R. Solomon, Provo: Association for Consumer Research, 384-391.

_____ (1993), "Feminist literary criticism and the deconstruction of ads: a postmodern view of advertising and consumer responses", *Journal of Consumer Research*, 19 (March), 556-566.

_____ and M.B. Holbrook (1994), "Gender and genre in the interpretation of advertising text", in *Gender Issues and Consumer Behaviour*, ed. J.A. Costa, Thousand Oaks: Sage, 11-41.

Thurston, C. (1987), *The Romance Revolution: Erotic Novels for Women and the Quest for a New Sexual Identity*, Urbana: University of Illinois Press.

The Evolution and Antecedents of Transformational Advertising: A Conceptual Model

Vanitha Swaminathan, University of Georgia
George M. Zinkhan, University of Georgia
Srinivas K. Reddy, University of Georgia

ABSTRACT

Transformational advertising provides a key concept for explaining consumers' reactions to advertising. The Product Life Cycle literature suggests that advertising evolves as product-markets develop. The consumer learning perspective suggests that consumers also evolve as markets mature. This suggests that consumers' information needs change with the passage of time. The antecedents of transformational advertising are identified, and an overall model is created to predict the likelihood of transformational advertising. Among the proposed predictor variables are consumer factors (e.g., involvement, conspicuousness) and market factors (e.g., product homogeneity, technological stability). The framework presented here furthers our understanding of the relationship between consumer behavior and advertising trends.

INTRODUCTION

The metaphors of advertising as "brain surgery" and the advertiser as "mirror maker" have now become clichés (Fox 1984; Pollay 1986). Advertising has been accused of shaping mass tastes and reinforcing materialistic values in society (thus practicing brain surgery on the populace). The use of emotion to sell mundane objects (e.g., toothpaste and detergent) creates an artificial world where "...socks, tires, cameras, instantaneous hot water heaters...[become] symbols and proofs of excellence..., substitutes for joy and passion and wisdom" (Lewis 1922, p.95).

The use of emotion and imagery has an economic function; advertisers employ emotion to link advertising experiences and feelings to the actual experience of using the advertised product (Puto and Wells 1984). In some instances, emotional desires dominate utilitarian ones for guiding product choices (Hirschman and Holbrook 1982). The main focus of this paper is emotion in advertising (that is, transformational advertising).

Transformational advertising provides a key concept for explaining consumers' reactions to commercial messages. The purpose of this paper is to create an overall model for explaining the incidence and use of transformational advertising. As such, some predictors of this model are managerial in nature, while others are more closely linked to traditional consumer behavior variables. The ultimate goal of the paper is to understand how markets evolve, with a special emphasis on understanding how advertising messages evolve in a consumer market. Some of the key consumer behavior concepts that are incorporated into the model include: consumer learning, elasticity of demand, level of risk, involvement, and product conspicuousness. Strategic variables include product homogeneity, market concentration, and technological stability. Consumer and strategic variables are integrated to explain the criterion variable "likelihood of transformational advertising". We are interested in creating a model to understand the conditions that are conducive to the appearance of transformational advertising in the marketplace.

Informational and Transformational Advertising

In keeping with the Puto-Wells (1984) conceptualization, an informational advertisement is defined as one that provides consumers with factual, relevant brand data. An ad is informational if the consumer perceives the data as important and verifiable. An ad for a book-club membership that contains price information (e.g., Buy one get one free) is an informational ad. A transformational ad is one that associates the experience of using the product with a unique set of psychological characteristics that consumers do not typically associate with the brand. For example, an ad for a long-distance company that encourages consumers to "Reach out and touch someone" transforms the experience of making long-distance calls by linking it to emotions; this ad may be viewed as transformational.

The terms informational and transformational advertising do not mean to suggest that an informational ad is purely informational and a transformational ad is purely transformational. Instead according to Puto and Wells (1984), it is possible to classify an ad as 'primarily informational' or 'primarily transformational' or neither. Elements of both informational and transformational advertising may exist in each ad. It is in this sense that the terms informational and transformational advertising appear throughout this paper.

Familiarity and Information Search Behavior

Much of the literature relating to information-search behavior is relevant to our explanation of why one form of advertising (e.g., informational or transformational) is likely to be more prevalent than another. Advertising is one form of mass communication that consumers use as a source of information in the adoption process (Berning and Jacoby 1974). Punj and Staelin's (1983) work suggests two factors that account for increased information search: usable prior knowledge that is inversely related to search and prior memory structure that facilitates search by helping one organize the information more effectively. Empirical and theoretical findings on search and familiarity (Alba and Hutchinson 1987; Brucks 1985; Srinivasan and Ratchford 1990) suggest that there are two distinct processes that are at work. Knowledge may limit search by allowing responses to become routine. Knowledge may also increase search by allowing consumers to have a richer understanding of what they are evaluating. One possible explanation for the differences in findings could be that experienced consumers increase search when there is relevant new information present in the environment, but limit their search in the absence of new information. As product categories mature, and the amount of usable prior knowledge increases in consumers' minds, it is possible that buyers seek less external information than consumers at the introductory stages of product categories.

In a related stream of research, Howard (1977) suggests that consumers engage in 'Extensive Problem Solving'(EPS) when faced with a radically new product class. A characteristic of EPS is substantial information requirements. Consumers require information to group a brand in the correct class of product classes, to distinguish it from the other classes, to relate values to criteria for brand choice, to determine the salience of each criterion and to locate a new brand on the various choice criteria.

Advertising and communication at the introduction stage has to provide information in clear and concrete terms. In the introductory stages of a product category, benefit-oriented information may be viewed as informational by consumers who are novices in a specific product category (Maheswaran and Sternthal 1990). As the product category becomes established, information needs decline as the consumer engages in Limited Problem Solving (LPS). Here, the communication objective is to differentiate a brand from its competition. In the example for Kodak cameras, the entry of

Advances in Consumer Research
Volume 23, © 1996

'me-too' products with the Kodak brand name resulted in shifting emphasis of advertising from educating consumers to building brand awareness. The communication had to focus on building brand identification and brand preference. Transformational advertising is used in order to build brand image.

The transition to routinized response behavior (RRB) occurs when consumers are familiar with nearly all the brands and brand choice is a simplified process. Under RRB, consumers become highly selective with respect to attention and search. Use of transformational elements (e.g., the spokesperson, the music) serve as attention-getting devices. Transformational advertising also helps to maintain brand distinctiveness by creating favorable attitude about the brand.

The Product Life Cycle

The change in consumer requirements and needs is simultaneous with a set of changes in the product-market scenario. These changes are embodied in the Product Life Cycle (PLC). The PLC summarizes the product-market realities in different stages (introduction, growth, maturity, and decline) as a product evolves over time. Howard (1983) has linked the changes in consumer requirements to changes in supplier behavior. He has suggested that 'customer driven firms' change their strategy to match consumer requirements at different stages in the PLC. The consumer learning perspective and the PLC literature (Porter 1985) suggests that advertising changes its basic nature moving from communicating information on the product (informational advertising) in the early stages of the PLC to building brand image through emotion, feeling and mood (transformational advertising) in the later stages. Indeed, this change from informational to transformational advertising is a typical pattern in many consumer product industries. The PLC concept suggests that transformational advertising evolves over time and gives us an opportunity to identify the processes that cause this change. Transformational advertising is comparable to other psychological descriptors applied in advertising (such as, mood, emotion, feeling and image advertising). Although the role of emotional advertising in creating brand affect is a focus area, scant research exists in the area of identifying the antecedents of such advertising.

Evolution of Advertising over the PLC

A new PLC commences when a substantial change in technology, customer function or customer group occurs that is outside the scope of all or most of the current suppliers (Day 1981). Managers change advertising messages over the Product Life Cycle in response to changing objectives in each stage of the life cycle. In the introduction stage, for example, the need to create primary demand for the new product puts emphasis on communicating product features. Here, informational advertising is likely to dominate.

When the motor car was mass marketed in the early twentieth century, the manufacturers made attempts to persuade a reluctant public to abandon the horse for the motor car. Advertising itself was at a nascent stage in this era, and manufacturers attempted to *inform* the public of the various features that made the motor car superior to the horse-drawn carriage. At the time, the then prevalent alternate modes of transportation, the horse and rail transport, were organized and powerful. Manufacturers had to overcome consumer resistance by a relatively long period of informational advertising.

A characteristic of the growth phase is the emergence of competition with numerous close substitutes. This calls for a differentiation strategy. Advertising stresses functional benefits that differentiate a brand from competition and remains mainly informational with some transformational elements. From 1900

onwards, motor car ads highlighted the merits of one or other of the alternative motive powers. Considerations of reliability, simplicity and comfort were main selling points. The use of motor-cars for racing made it a symbol of masculine prowess. While advertising in this period was mainly informational, it contained elements of transformational advertising such as speed, competitive prestige and excitement. By 1920, Ford's Model-T was the market leader (Goodrum and Dalrymple 1990). Ford's competitors engaged in efforts to differentiate themselves from the Model-T through advertising that appealed to consumers with specific levels of income or social class. This saw the introduction of transformational advertising for cars.

The automobile example illustrates what happens as a product moves through the growth stage into maturity stage. Lewis (1922) declares in his novel *Babbit (p.74)* "In the city of Zenith, in the barbarous twentieth century, a family's motor indicated its social rank as precisely as the grades of peerage determined the rank of the English family." Advertising themes stressed two aspects: (a) a planned obsolescence that involved making the car customer dissatisfied with their cars and (b) automobile symbolism.

The maturity phase of the Product Life Cycle involves intense competition, and oligopolies evolve. Consumers understand basic issues; therefore, marketers seek to differentiate the product by using advertising messages. Transformational advertising is one effective differentiation strategy. The evolution of advertising messages outlined in the motor car industry provides evidence of this. By the 1950s, cars had become personal expressions of the owner seen as mistresses, workhorses, weapons, plumes or bait for sexual conquest (Goodrum and Dalrymple 1990). While car advertising today contains elements of informational and transformational advertising, the use of transformational appeals is more common today than in the early days of car advertising.

The evolution of ad messages as described in the motor car example is typical of patterns found in many consumer product industries. We now attempt to analyze some of the evolutionary processes that underlie the change in messages from informational to transformational.

A MODEL OF TRANSFORMATIONAL ADVERTISING

Figure 1 illustrates the factors that influence the use of transformational advertising. The criterion variable in the model is the "likelihood of transformational advertising". That is, how likely are advertisers to use transformational advertising in a product category. Some of the predictor variables have been chosen using the Product Life cycle literature. The predictors used are descriptive of the maturity stage of the life cycle. We therefore, present the model as a cross-sectional study that enables us to predict the use of transformational advertising across several product categories, depending on the product-market realities at a point in time. The level of analysis suggested is a product category. That is, we analyze the likelihood of transformational advertising being used in a product category at any point in time. Product and consumer variables include newness of the product, level of risk, product conspicuousness, product involvement and service (versus product). Market related factors or market dynamism factors include product homogeneity, price elasticity of demand, and technological stability. Some predictors of transformational advertising may include factors that are inherent characteristics of the product and some characteristics are dynamic over time. Propositions are presented in the next section.

FIGURE 1
A Model of Transformational Advertising

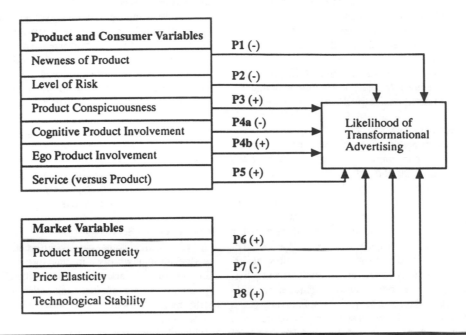

PRODUCT AND CONSUMER VARIABLES

Newness of the Product

In the case of new products, advertising has to focus on educating consumers and tends to be informational. As discussed in a preceding section, information requirements of consumers at various stages of the product life cycle vary, creating a need for varying the message content of advertising over the PLC.

In the introduction stage, consumers search for information to acquire knowledge including 'scripts'. Concept acquisition is the search process for criteria for identifying and evaluating a radically new product category (Cohen and Basu 1987). As a category becomes well formed in consumers' minds, the decision-making becomes a heuristic process. The consumers' information needs decline as they move from Extensive Problem Solving to Limited Problem Solving and to Routinized Response Behavior. The advertising has to vary to suit the information requirements of the consumer, moving from being informational in the early stages of the Product Life Cycle to being transformational in the later stages. In the Kodak example, for instance, the early ads focused on information needs of consumers. In recent times, the 'Kodak moment' ad signifies use of transformational advertising to maintain brand distinctiveness and to create favorable brand attitude. The preceding discussion of the newness of the product category suggests that the age of the product category or the time elapsed since introduction could be an indicator of whether a category is new or old. Therefore, we propose the following:

P1: Transformational (Informational) advertising is more likely to be used later (earlier) in the product life cycle rather than earlier (later). (Note: All propositions are illustrated in Fig 1.)

Level of Risk

Individuals encounter risk when a decision, action or behavior leads to different possible outcomes (Bem 1980). When an individual's action produces social and economic consequences

they cannot estimate with certainty, the individual encounters risk (Zinkhan and Karande 1991). Most of the risk literature (Bauer 1960; Jacoby and Kaplan 1972) deals with five different types of risk: financial, performance, physical, psychological and social risk. Risk relates to either situations and problems (Dowling 1986) or persons' attitude to risk (Zinkhan and Karande 1991). Here, we will focus on risks that consumers associate with product categories.

Jacoby and Kaplan (1972) measure the risk involved in product categories and identify components of risk involved. Financial risk and social risk are the prime components of risk involved in purchasing a foreign sports car. Bauer (1960) suggests that information search is an important risk-handling strategy. This suggests that advertisers will emphasize informational elements in high risk product categories.

Product category risk is high in the introduction stages of the life cycle. For new products, the uncertainty associated with outcomes leads to high risk. The consumer seeks out information from a wide variety of sources including advertising (Aaker and Myers 1975). Berning and Jacoby (1974) suggest that the circumstance of reduced information affects perceived risk, which in turn, increases the information search of consumers. The need for information points to the use of informational advertising in the early stages of the life cycle (when the risk associated with the product category is high).

As product-markets evolve, brand familiarity is high, and consumers encounter established purchase alternatives. Berning and Jacoby (1974) have found that under conditions of high brand familiarity, perceived risk declines, information requirements decline, thereby suggesting that the information content in advertising may tend to decline over the PLC.

The decline in perceived risk in the later stages of the PLC creates what is analogous to the low elaboration likelihood suggested by Petty and Cacioppo (1985). Although elaboration likelihood is a situational variable, the situation of low elaboration likelihood outlined is similar to the consumer in the later stages of the PLC. This research suggests that consumers under low elaboration likelihood (due to the lower perceived risk in the later stages of the PLC), use a peripheral information processing route. In these conditions, transformational elements such as music in the ad, use of spokesperson, emotional elements are likely to be more persuasive. This suggests the use of transformational advertising under low risk conditions as encountered later in the PLC.

P2: The higher (lower) the level of risk involved in purchasing a product, the lower (higher) the likelihood of transformational (informational) advertising.

Product Conspicuousness

Product conspicuousness refers to the intended communication role played by certain consumption decisions (Belk, Bahn and Mayer 1982). Communicating through consumption choices involves decoding information about others based on their consumption behavior. From this perspective, it appears that people see possessions as a part of or an extension of themselves. A number of studies have focused on the product categories where there is a high congruence between self-image and images of the owned or desired products. These products such as automobiles, health, grooming and cleaning products, beer, leisure products and activities, clothing and accessories, food products, cigarettes are 'conspicuous' products (Belk, Bahn and Mayer 1982). For conspicuous products, the high congruence between self-images and images of owned or desired products provides opportunities for the use of transformational advertising. Transformational advertising for conspicuous products such as clothing or automobiles bestows meaning through imagery, emotion and feeling.

P3: Transformational (informational) advertising is more likely to be used with more (less) conspicuous products.

Product Involvement

Krugman (1965) defines involvement as the number of conscious, bridging experiences, connections or references per minute that the viewer makes between his own life and the stimulus. We use this definition to suggest that some products are higher involvement (e.g., perfumes, automobiles) while others are low involvement (e.g., detergent, household cleaners).

Involvement can be person-related, stimulus-related or situation-related (Zaichkowsky 1994). Involvement results from an interaction between person, stimulus, and situation. Nonetheless, there is a long tradition in marketing and consumer behavior literature to classify products as inherently high or low involvement. The literature on involvement makes a distinction between cognitive involvement and affective or ego involvement (Greenwald and Leavitt 1984; Park and Young, 1984). A large body of research explains the persuasiveness of informational cues (substantive features in advertising) under conditions of high cognitive involvement (Petty and Cacioppo 1984; Chaiken 1980). *Ego-involvement (affective involvement)* refers to the relationship between the issue and object and the domain of one's ego. *Issue-involvement (cognitive involvement)* refers to the degree to which an issue is personally relevant. Cognitive involvement refers to the extent to which a product may have important consequences for consumers or the need to form an informed opinion when consumers may expect to discuss or defend their opinions or engage in behavior congruent with their expressed opinions (Chaiken 1980).

Just as certain consumption situations or product classes can be classified as ego-involvement and cognitive-involvement we suggest that it is also possible to distinguish between ego-involvement products and cognitive-involvement products. Ego-involvement, by its nature, contributes to use of transformational advertising while cognitive involvement might contribute to use of informational advertising.

Advertising for high ego-involvement products tends to be transformational as ego-involvement products are used as symbols. Ads for such products are organized in meaningful ways to portray self-concept, actual or ideal. Emotion and images are quite prominent in perfume advertising. For high cognitive involvement products, consumers require information to arrive at decisions. Therefore, the following two-part proposition is proposed:

P4a: Transformational advertising (informational advertising) is less (more) likely to be used for high cognitive involvement products.

P4b: Transformational advertising (informational advertising) is more (less) likely to be used for high ego-involvement products.

Product versus Service

Characteristics that chiefly differentiate services from products include intangibility, simultaneity of production and consumption, heterogeneity and perishability. Intangibility is a fundamental difference between products and services. Because services are performances, consumers cannot see, feel, taste or touch services in the same manner in which consumers of goods can sense products (Zeithaml, Parasuraman and Berry 1985). Because intangibility causes problems of communicating features and benefits, service firms tend to concentrate on building brand image. Examples of service advertisers focusing on corporate image include banks, financial services firms (e.g., Merrill Lynch, American Express) and airlines (British Airways). Service advertising may tend to use more transformational advertising to give life to intangible service features. Zinkhan, Johnson and Zinkhan (1992) have found that of the three ad types (i.e., product, retail and service), service ads made the heaviest use of transformational advertising, while product ads use transformational ads the least. The authors suggest that converting an intangible service into a meaningful association may increase consumer understanding of service offering.

P5: Transformational advertising is more likely to be used with services than with products.

MARKET CHARACTERISTICS

In dynamic markets, there is continuous product innovation, continuous entry and exit of competitors, product differentiation among competitors and price competition. Any of these activities in isolation or combination is likely to create an environment where a consumer is faced with new information about the product category. In such situations, the extent of usable prior knowledge decreases, so consumers are forced to seek information. In such situations, informational advertising is likely to be more successful. Product homogeneity, price elasticity and technological stability are each discussed in the following section as factors influencing market dynamism.

Product Homogeneity

Product homogeneity refers to the extent to which consumers perceive products as closely related substitutes of one another. In markets where such feature neutralization occurs, there is more transformational advertising. Ogilvy (1964) states that the greater the similarity between the brands (e.g., as in the case with cigarettes or whiskey), the less part that reason plays in brand selection. Organizations that build the most sharply defined personality get the largest share of the market at the highest profit. This need for product differentiation suggests that transformational advertising builds brand distinctiveness when no real product differentiation exists.

Product homogeneity is a result of competitive processes over the life cycle. At the introduction stage, the pioneering activities of firms attract competition. In this stage, where the population of firms is new, competition is likely to be indirect and diffuse because the abundance of resources (Brittain and Wholey 1988). With the entry of firms in the growth stage, competition intensifies and causes feature neutralization. In the maturity stage, there is likely to be a high level of product homogeneity.

Heath, Mccarthy and Mothersbaugh (1994) investigate the role of competition as a moderator on the effect of substantive features (or the use of informational advertising). The results suggest that when brands are relatively homogenous, the influence of non-substantive features was significant. Non-substantive features including spokesperson character, music in the ad contribute to transformational advertising. Aaker and Myers (1975) propose that as long as a brand, regardless of the complexity of the product involved, has what amount to closely competing substitutes, the possibilities of distinguishing on purely functional grounds is reduced. This also suggests that increased product homogeneity increases use of transformational advertising.

> P6: The higher (lower) the product homogeneity in the market, the higher the likelihood of transformational (informational) advertising.

Price Elasticity of Demand

Price elasticity indicates how sensitive to price consumers in a particular market are. This is important because markets with a highly elastic demand are driven by price rather than imagery. This suggests the use of informational advertising in highly price elastic markets where advertising mainly stresses price positioning.

Tellis (1988) suggests that under assumptions of rational and reasonably informed consumers, price elasticity should be negative. Nonetheless, price elasticity varies from product category to product category. Pharmaceutical products, for example, exhibit less price sensitivity or less negative price elasticity because they are high risk products, often purchased in an emergency or on a prescription.

Tellis (1988) found evidence that price elasticity increases over the life cycle. In markets where the price sensitivity is relatively high so as to become the primary decision-making variable, advertising remains primarily functional or informational. Comparative informational advertising (which stresses the price) is likely to dominate.

> P7: The higher the price elasticity of demand, the lower(higher) the likelihood of transformational (informational) advertising.

Technological Stability

Most research on how technology evolves in an industry has grown out of the PLC concept. Early in the product life cycle, product innovation is largely driven by technology. Later in the life cycle, innovations are more process driven (e.g., resulting from refinements in the distribution process). After a certain stage in the life cycle, the technology stabilizes and a dominant design emerges. Growing scale makes mass production feasible, re-inforced by the growing product standardization. Technological diffusion eliminates product differences and compels process innovations by firms

to remain cost competitive. In some industries with undifferentiated products, a dominant design emerges quickly. In others, technology is the differentiating tool.

The role of technology in advertising is relevant as it influences the ability of firms to differentiate products. In technologically turbulent markets, advertising tends to be highly informational stressing technical features or superiority of products. In a market that is technologically stable, transformational advertising is more likely. From the consumers' perspective, in markets where the technology is changing rapidly, there is new information about the technological innovations in the product that may be required to re-evaluate consumers' buying decisions. Here, informational advertising may be required to match the consumers' search for new information relevant to the technological changes. This leads to the proposition that:

> P8: A technologically stable environment increases the likelihood of transformational advertising.

THE MODEL

The proposed model is presented in Figure 1. The propositions summarize the conditions that influence the use or likelihood of transformational advertising. The predictor variables are broadly sub-divided as product characteristics and market characteristics. The model could be tested through a cross-sectional study with product category serving as the unit of analysis.

Proposed Method of Testing

Content analysis of print and TV ads could be used to test the proposed model. The dependent variable "likelihood of transformational advertising" can be coded using the Puto and Wells (1984) scale as a basis. It is recognized that the Puto and Wells (1984) scale is a preliminary scale. Some refinement of the scale may be required in order to make it reliable and valid.

Coders can be trained to rate commercials as informational, transformational or neither. In a similar study, Zinkhan, Johnson, and Zinkhan (1992) used a similar procedure where by coding a large number of ads within a product category, it was possible to estimate the percentage of ads within that category that use transformational advertising. A percentage measure could serve as input to measurement of the dependent variable "likelihood of transformational advertising".

Technological stability could be measured by studying the number of technological innovations in a year in a product category and comparing across categories. Judges could be trained to classify a product offering as being either 'mainly product' or 'mainly service'. The chronological age of the product category could be used as a surrogate measure for the newness of the product category.

A consumer survey would be required to measure product conspicuousness, product involvement and level of risk. We make a distinction between cognitive involvement and ego involvement products. The former could be operationalized through a modified version of Buchanan's (1964) measure of product interest. A measure of ego-involvement could be obtained with Slama and Tashchian's (1987) Enduring Involvement scale. A suitable scale for product conspicuousness is not readily available. Prior studies on conspicuousness (Hong and Zinkhan 1995; Dolich 1969) have manipulated conspicuousness as a variable but have not directly proposed a scale to measure it. A suitable scale to measure this construct across product categories could be adapted from the product interest scale proposed by Dolich (1969). Risk can be measured along the lines of the scale proposed by Jacoby and

Kaplan (1972). In all instances, the output from the consumer surveys would provide product category scores, thus preserving the product category as the unit of analysis.

DISCUSSION AND SUMMARY

Transformational advertising plays an important role in creating brand differentiation. When manufacturing parity among competitors has been reached, or when features and benefits of the product offering are well understood by consumers, benefit-based (informational) advertising emphasizes category promotion rather than brand promotion. In such situations, organizations may use transformational advertising as a means to attaining a competitive edge. Advertising thus creates value in products by the nature of emotional associations that are conveyed. Products become representative of goals attained or desired role performances. The role of transformational advertising in creating brand equity is also a potential area for future research.

As consumer behavior researchers, we are beginning to realize that it is important to understand consumer trends over a period of time. For example, there is a group of published studies that examine how consumer values (e.g., materialism) change through the decades. In this paper, we create a framework to explain how advertising styles evolve, depending upon certain consumer characteristics and certain market characteristics. At present, there is an unresolved issue about the relationship between consumer values and advertising trends. It may be that advertising reflects consumer values (as advertisers and their agencies follow the marketing concept). However, it may also be the case that advertising trends lead or lag changes in consumer tastes and behavior. At present, there is an unresolved issue about the relationship between consumer values and advertising trends (Zinkhan and Shermohamed 1986). However, it may be that advertising bears no relationship whatsoever to consumer behavior. The model developed in this paper provides a useful framework for thinking about these important issues in consumer behavior research. Advertising is, perhaps, the most salient aspect of marketing management (as perceived by consumers); and it is important to understand how advertising styles and methods evolve and change over time.

REFERENCES

Aaker, David A. and John G. Myers (1975), *Advertising Management*. Englewood Cliffs, NJ: Prentice-Hall Inc.

Alba, Joseph and J. Wesley Hutchinson (1987), "Dimensions of Consumer Expertise," *Journal of Consumer Research*, 13 (March), 411-454.

Bauer, Raymond, A. (1960), "Consumer Behavior as Risk Taking," reprinted *in Risk Taking, and Information Handling in Consumer Behavior*, ed. Donald F. Cox,, Boston: Harvard University Press, 23-33.

Belk, Russell W., Kenneth D. Bahn, Robert N. Mayer (1982), " Developmental Recognition of Consumption Symbolism," *Journal of Consumer Research*, 9 (June), 4-16.

Bem, Daryl (1980), " The Concept of Risk in the Study of Human Behavior," in *Risk and Chance*, Jack Dowie and Paul Lefrere II, eds., Milton Keynes, England: The Open University Press, 1-15.

Berning, Carol A. Kohn and Jacob Jacoby (1974), " Patterns of Information Acquisition in New Product Purchases," *Journal of Consumer Research*, 1 (September), 18-22.

Bettman, James and C. Whan Park (1980), "Effects of Prior Knowledge and Experience and Phases of the Choice Process on Consumer Decision Processes: A Protocol Analysis," *Journal of Consumer Research*, 7 (December), 234-248.

Brittain, J. Wand Douglas R. Wholey (1988), "Competition Co-existence in Organizational Communities: Population Dynamics in Electronics Components Manufacturing," in *Ecological Models of Organizations*, Cambridge, MA: Ballinger.

Brucks, Merrie (1985), "The Effects of Product Class Knowledge on Information Search Behavior," *Journal of Consumer Research*, 12 (June), 1-16.

Buchanan, Dodds I. (1964), " How Interest In the Product Affects Recall: Print Ads vs. Commercials," *Journal of Advertising Research*, 4 (1), 9-15.

Chaiken, Shelley (1980), "Heurisitc versus Systematic Information Processing and the Use of Sourcevs. Message Cues in Persuasion," *Journal of Personality and Social Psychology*, 39 (5), 752-765.

Cohen, Joel and Kunal Basu (1987), " Alternative Models of Categorization: Toward a Contingent Processing Framework," *Journal of Consumer Research*, 13 (March), 455-472.

Day, George S. (1981), " The Product Life Cycle: Analysis and Applications Issues," *Journal of Marketing*, 45 (Fall), 60-68.

Dolich, Ira J. (1969), " Congruence Relationships Between Self Images and Product Brands," *Journal of Marketing Research*, 6 (February), 80-84.

Dowling, Grahame R (1986)," Perceived Risk: The Concept and its Measurement," *Psychology and Marketing*, 3(3), 193-210.

Fox, Stephen (1984), *The Mirror Makers*, New York: William Morrow and Company.

Goodrum, Charles and Helen Darlymple (1990). *Advertising in America, The First 200 Years*. New York: Henry N.Abrams.

Greenwald, Anthony G. and Clark Leavitt (1984), " Audience Involvement in Advertising: Four Levels," *Journal of Consumer Research*, 11 (June), 581-592.

Heath, Timothy B., Michael S. Mccarthy, Michael, David L. Mothersbaugh (1994), " Spokesperson Fame and Vividness Effects in the Context of Issue-Relevant Thinking: The Moderating Role of Competitive Setting," *Journal of Consumer Research*, 20 (March), 520-534.

Hirschman, Elizabeth and Morris B. Holbrook (1982), "Hedonic Consumption: Emerging Concepts, Methods, and Propositions," *Journal of Marketing*, 46 (Summer), 92-101.

Hong, J.W., and George M. Zinkhan (1995) "Self Concept and Advertising Effectiveness: The Influence of Congruency and Response Mode," *Psychology & Marketing*, 12(1), 53-77.

Howard, John A. (1977), *Consumer Behaviour: Application of Theory*: New York: McGraw-Hill.

Howard, John A.(1983), "Marketing Theory of the Firm," *Journal of Marketing*, 47 (Fall), 90-100.

Jacoby, Jacob and Leon B. Kaplan (1972), " The Components of Perceived Risk," *Advances in Consumer Research*, M. Venkatesan, ed., 392-393.

Krugman, Herbert E. (1965), "The Impact of Television Advertising: Learning Without Involvement," *Public Opinion Quarterly*, 29 (Fall), 349-356.

Lewis, Sinclair (1922), *Babbit*, New York: Harcourt, Brace and Company, Inc.

Maheswaran, Durairaj and Brian Sternthal (1990), "The Effects of Knowledge, Motivation, and Type of Message on Ad Processing and Product Judgments," *Journal of Consumer Research*, 17 (June), 66-73.

Ogilvy, David (1964), *Confessions of an Advertising Man,* NewYork: Atheneum.

Park, Whan C. and S. Mark Young, "The Effects of Involvement and Executional Factors of a Television Commercial on Brand Attitude Formation," Report #84-100, *Marketing Science Institute*, Cambridge, MA.

Petty, Richard E. and John T. Cacioppo (1984), "Source Factors and the Elaboration Likelihood Model of Persuasion," *Advances in Consumer Research,* 11, 668-675.

Pollay, Richard W. (1986), "The Distorted Mirror: Reflections on the Unintended Consequences of Advertising," *Journal of Marketing,* 50 (April), 18-36.

Porter, Michael E. (1985), *Competitive Advantage,* New York: The Free Press.

Punj, Girish N. And Richard Staelin (1983), " A Model of Consumer Information Search Behavior for New Automobiles," *Journal of Consumer Research*, 9 (March), 366-380.

Puto, Christopher P., and William D. Wells (1984) "Informational and Transformational Advertising: The Differential Effects of Time", in Thomas C. Kinnear ed., Provo, UT: *Advances in Consumer Research,* Association of Consumer Research, 638-643.

Slama, Mark E. amd Armen Tashchian (1987), "Validating the S-O-R Paradigm for Consumer Involvement with a Convenience Good," *Journal of the Academy of Marketing Science,* 15 (Spring), 36-45.

Srinivasan, Narasimhan and Brian T. Ratchford (1991), "An Empirical Test of a Model of External Search for Automobiles," *Journal of Consumer Research*, 18 (September), 233-242.

Tellis, Gerald J. (1988) " The Price Elasticity of Selective Demand: A Meta-Analysis of Sales Response Models", Report # 88-105, *Marketing Science Institute,* Cambridge, MA.

Zaichkowsky, Judith Lynne (1994), " The Personal Involvement Inventory : Reduction, Revision and Application To Advertising," *Journal of Advertising,* 23 (4), 59-70.

Zeithaml, Valerie A., Parasuraman A., and Leonard L. Berry (1985), "Problems and Strategies in Services Marketing," *Journal of Marketing,* 49 (Spring), 33-46.

Zinkhan, George M. and Kiran W. Karande (1991), " Cultural and Gender differences in Risk-Taking Behaviour Among American and Spanish Decision Makers," *Journal of Social Psychology,* 131 (5), 741-742.

Zinkhan, George M., Madeline Johnson and Christian F. Zinkhan (1992), "Differences Between Product and Services Television Commercials," *Journal of Services Marketing,* 6 (Summer), 59-66.

Zinkhan, George M. and Ali Shermohamed (1986), "Is Other-directedness on the Increase? An Empirical Test of Riesman's Theory of Social Character," *Journal of Consumer Research,* 13 (1), 127-130.

Headline-Visual Consistency in Print Advertisements: Effects on Processing and Evaluation

Edwin R. Stafford, Utah State University
Beth A. Walker, Arizona State University
Vincent J. Blasko, Arizona State University[1]

INTRODUCTION

Increased use of unusual visual-verbal combinations in print ads (cf. McQuarrie and Mick 1992) reflects a growing recognition that the level of consistency between the picture and the words influences an ad's effects. An inconsistency exists when the ad's headline and visual deviate from the reader's expectations. While advertisements may feature unrelated, irrelevant, or extremely inconsistent verbal-visual information (Heckler and Childers 1992), the verbal-visual meanings in an ad often reflect a moderate level of inconsistency (Blasko and Mokwa 1986). Unlike an extreme inconsistency which cannot be resolved (Meyers-Levy and Tybout 1989), a moderate inconsistency encourages the reader to uncover the underlying connection between the picture and the words that makes the advertisement understandable. Rhetorical figures (e.g., resonance, irony), for example, are used by advertisers to present the consumer with a moderate inconsistency (McQuarrie and Mick 1992). Consider a dairy association ad picturing healthy adults drinking milk accompanied by the headline, "Everybody Knows that Milk's for Babies." This ad employs irony by using "babies" to refer to adults (literal opposites) (Corbett 1990). Resolution of the inconsistency between "babies" and the picture invokes the interpretation that adults, like babies, need milk.

Research on ad headline-visual consistency has been limited and has produced conflicting results. Researchers have typically examined two extreme forms of verbal-visual combinations — a complete match or complete mismatch of verbal-visual information. Isolating memory for brand information as the dependent variable, inconsistent advertisements have been found to be both more effective (Houston, Childers and Heckler 1987) and less effective (Edell and Staelin 1983) than consistent verbal-visual combinations. Moderate verbal-visual inconsistencies have not been explicitly examined.

This study examines the effect of the degree of consistency between the headline and visual in print ads on processing and evaluation. Particular interest centers on the relative effects of moderately inconsistent headline-visual combinations that employ irony by combining a headline and visual that convey opposite meanings (Corbett 1990). "Opposites" represent a moderate form of inconsistency because they have strong implicit associations and can be readily related to one another (cf. Colombo and Williams 1990). Drawing on the information processing (Mandler 1984) and psychology of aesthetics (Berlyne 1971) literatures, we posit that the process of decoding and interpreting a text is intrinsically rewarding. Further, successful interpretation should create liking for the ad. We propose that the process of resolving a moderate inconsistency within a print ad is most rewarding and may result in more positive ad and, consequently, brand evaluations and purchase intentions when compared to consistent and extremely inconsistent headline-visual combinations. Extending previous work, this study uses ad-related processing, ad and brand evaluation, and purchase intention as dependent measures.

RESEARCH ON VERBAL-VISUAL CONSISTENCY: AN OVERVIEW

Communications and psychology research suggests that consistent verbal and visual information produces better memory and is more easily understood than inconsistent information. Incongruent visual and verbal information is less easily interpretable and reduces memory and learning for text material as compared to consistent visual and verbal material (Bock and Milz 1977; Peeck 1974; Stein, et al. 1987). Although the finding that consumers process visual and verbal information differently has been well established in marketing (cf. Childers and Houston 1984; Lutz and Lutz 1977), research on verbal-visual consistency in print advertisements is limited and the findings are conflicting. Comparing consistent (framed), inconsistent (unframed), and verbal-only print advertisements, Edell and Staelin (1983) found that consistent ads outperformed inconsistent and verbal-only messages in terms of brand-item recall. Evoking a "distraction" explanation, the authors explained that the inconsistent visual impeded comprehension, memory, and evaluation processes by distracting the consumer from thinking about the advertised brand. In contrast, Houston, Childers and Heckler's (1987) study of advertisements containing congruent and incongruent verbal and visual information revealed an advantage for inconsistent verbal-visual combinations. Suggesting that deviations from expectations stimulated elaborative processing which improves memory, the authors found that inconsistent ad information was more memorable than consistent information.

The conflicting findings may be resolved by considering the degree of verbal-visual inconsistency used across investigations. Most studies of verbal and visual information have used an extreme operationalization of inconsistency — verbal information that conflicted with the visual depiction. Here, "inconsistent" information was less effective than consistent verbal-visual information. The inconsistency in the ads used by Houston, Childers and Heckler (1987), however, was more moderate. The authors noted that the verbal information was different from, but not in "sharp contrast" to (p. 68), the visual information. These ads were more effective than their consistent ads. While research has implied either a positive or negative linear relationship between verbal-visual consistency and ad effectiveness, a nonmonotonic relationship may exist. Ads featuring moderate levels of verbal-visual inconsistency may be more effective than either consistent or extremely inconsistent ads.

Evidence suggesting that individuals appreciate moderate levels of discrepancy stems from the psychology (Berlyne 1971) and advertising (McQuarrie and Mick 1992) literatures. Blasko and Mokwa (1986) proposed that ads with headlines and visuals conveying opposite meanings may be particularly effective. Since "opposites" have strong implicit associations and can be readily related to one another (cf. Colombo and Williams 1990), these ads may be easily understood. Further, because the moderate inconsistency between the headline and visual may be perceived as clever, the ad evaluation may be enhanced.

Examining "resonance" in advertising, McQuarrie and Mick (1992) also provide evidence for the success of moderately inconsistent headline-visual combinations. In addition to conveying

[1] The authors wish to thank Peter Reingen and Michael Hutt for their helpful comments and advice.

multiple meanings, by definition, resonant ads contain moderately inconsistent information that deviates from expectations and normal usage, but are nonetheless understandable because the headline and visual are relevant to each other. An ad picturing men's ties arranged to form a bouquet that was described by the caption, "Forget-Me-Knots," illustrates the resonance concept. The researchers found that, compared to consistent verbal-visual combinations, resonant ads generated more positive ad and brand attitudes as well as better unaided recall of ad headlines. Finally, moderate inconsistencies have been studied in the context of understanding the evaluations of new products. Meyers-Levy and Tybout (1989) found that new products that were moderately inconsistent with consumers' existing product category schema received more positive brand evaluations than new brands that were either schema consistent or extremely inconsistent with expectations.

A SCHEMA CONSISTENCY APPROACH TO UNDERSTANDING AD EFFECTS

Mandler (1984) provides a framework for understanding headline-visual consistency effects. Mandler posits that it is the extent to which an object deviates from expectations and the ability of an individual to resolve the inconsistency that influences processing and evaluation. Mandler theorizes that, under conditions of schema consistency, expectations are met, and processing is automatic, not effortful (Sujan 1985). Consequently, a consumer produces fewer thoughts as compared to processing an inconsistency. In addition, the absence of effortful processing reduces the extremity of the evaluation (Meyers-Levy and Tybout 1989). For example, when a print ad for an arthritis foundation features a young girl in a wheel chair accompanied by the headline, "This Little Girl has Arthritis," the reader will extend minimal effort since the headline and visual convey equivalent messages.

More central to Mandler's framework is the relative consequences of moderate and extreme inconsistencies. Inconsistencies stimulate elaborative processing as individuals attempt to integrate the headline and the visual. However, the extent of the inconsistency and the ability of the individual to resolve the inconsistency influence the nature of processing and the valence of evaluation. According to Mandler (1984), moderate inconsistencies can be resolved. For example, an arthritis foundation ad depicting a young girl in a wheel chair followed by the headline "This Little Old Lady has Arthritis," the headline (old lady) and visual (young girl) may be considered moderately inconsistent. While the particular headline-visual combination is unexpected, the inconsistency can be resolved without requiring a fundamental change in the consumer's cognitive structure. Berlyne (1971) suggests that the very process of successfully resolving an inconsistency is rewarding, which may bolster a consumer's evaluation of the advertisement and brand. This is in line with McQuarrie and Mick (1992) who suggest that consumers perceive moderate inconsistencies in ads as clever and enjoy deciphering their meaning.

Extremely inconsistent headline-visual combinations are difficult to reconcile. An arthritis foundation ad featuring a young girl in a wheel chair accompanied by the headline "Tennis Elbow can be an Early Sign of Arthritis" may be considered extremely inconsistent. The connection between the girl and tennis elbow is simply impossible to find. While extreme inconsistencies may heighten attention and stimulate processing, the inability to resolve the inconsistency generates confusion and frustration, which may result in more negative evaluations of the advertisement. This relationship between inconsistency, processing, and evaluation is supported in the aesthetics literature (Berlyne 1971).

In sum, Mandler and Berlyne predict an inverted U-shaped nonmonotonic relationship between schema inconsistency and evaluation. Objects that are moderately inconsistent with expectations are evaluated more favorably than those that are consistent or extremely inconsistent with expectations. Further, the process of inconsistency resolution is proposed to underlie the effects of consistency on evaluation. In advertisements, the picture establishes an expectation for the verbal material that follows (Houston, Childers and Heckler 1987). The level of consistency, then, is determined by the degree of discrepancy between the schema elicited by the picture and the meaning conveyed in the headline.

Though the level of inconsistency is central to understanding an ad's effects, operationalization of moderate and extreme inconsistency is less apparent (Meyers-Levy and Tybout 1989), and this has led to considerable debate in the verbal-visual processing literature. Mandler (1984) suggests that levels of consistency are determined by the ease with which the inconsistency is resolved. Drawing from Heckler and Childers' (1992) framework, we identify *relevancy* and *expectancy* as determinants of the degree of inconsistency. Relevancy refers to the extent to which the headline and visual contribute to (or detract from) communicating a unified message. Expectancy is defined as the degree to which the headline fits the pattern of structure evoked by the visual portion of the advertisement. We posit that a consistent headline-visual combination is both expected and relevant. A moderately inconsistent message is relevant, but not expected. Because the headline and visual are relevant to each other, a moderate inconsistency can be resolved with relative ease (Meyers-Levy and Tybout 1989). An extremely inconsistent headline-visual combination is neither expected or relevant. In contrast to moderate inconsistencies, extreme inconsistencies cannot be resolved because they diverge dramatically from a consumer's established patterns of thought.

HYPOTHESES

Based on Mandler's (1984) framework, we advance the following hypotheses:

H1: Moderately inconsistent advertisements will lead to more favorable ad evaluations than consistent or extremely inconsistent ads.

Hypothesis 1 reflects Mandler's central premise that objects that are moderately incongruent will be more favorably evaluated than objects that are congruent or extremely incongruent with expectations. Specifically, the experience of successfully resolving the inconsistency should create liking for the ad. Mandler further proposes that the process of resolving the inconsistency underlies the effect of schema inconsistency on evaluation. Not only should this process affect the number and type of thoughts generated, but it may also affect ad-related beliefs formed as the result of the headline-visual inconsistency (e.g., this ad is confusing, irritating, interesting). Because the effect of inconsistency on evaluation is influenced by the extent of elaboration and the ability of the consumer to resolve the inconsistency, we propose the following four hypotheses:

H2: As compared to consistent advertisements, moderate and extremely inconsistent advertisements will result in more (a) references to the headline-visual combination and (b) ad-related thoughts.

H3: As compared to extremely inconsistent and consistent advertisements, moderately inconsistent ads will (a) generate more positive references to the headline-visual combination, (b) generate more positive ad-related thoughts, and (c) be perceived as more interesting.

H4: As compared to moderately inconsistent and consistent advertisements, extremely inconsistent advertisements will (a) generate more negative references to the head-line-visual combination, (b) generate more confusion ad-related thoughts, (c) be perceived as the most irritating, and (d) be perceived as the least comprehensible.

H5: Cognitive responses that reflect the resolution process will mediate the relationship between ad type and ad evaluation.

Finally, consistent with recent work on the relationship between ad evaluations (A_{ad}), brand evaluations (A_{brand}), and purchase intentions (PI) (cf. Miniard, Bhatla and Rose 1990; Mittal 1990), the following hypothesis is suggested:

H6: Through their impact on ad evaluations, moderately inconsistent advertisements will lead to (a) more positive brand evaluations and (b) greater purchase intentions than consistent or extremely inconsistent advertisements.

METHOD

A 3 (headline-visual consistency) by 2 (product class) between-subjects experiment was designed to examine how verbal-visual consistency affects processing, ad and brand evaluation, and purchase intention. Product was manipulated to assess the generalizability of the findings.

Stimuli

Six full-page black and white advertisements were developed by combining ad type (consistent; moderately inconsistent; extremely inconsistent) with product class (mountain bike and a zoo). These product classes were both relevant and familiar to the subject population. The constant portion of each ad contained a brand name (Klein Mountain Bike; St. Louis Zoo) and logo in the lower right corner and a visual of either a cyclist covered with mud racing a bike on a mountain trail or of a growling lion. Each visual was accompanied by a headline that either conveyed a consistent ("Taking the Dirty Off-Roads"; "Come See the Lions"), moderately inconsistent ("Good Clean Fun"; "Come See the Little Kitties"), or extremely inconsistent ("Tire Repair Made Easy"; "Come See the East African Elephants") message for the bike and zoo ads, respectively. Following studies of advertising rhetoric (e.g., McQuarrie and Mick 1992), we employed irony to manipulate the moderate level of inconsistency. Irony employs contradiction by using a word to convey a meaning opposite to the literal meaning of another word (Corbett 1990). We assumed that this type of contradiction, while unexpected, is resolvable (cf. Williams and Lilly 1985).

Pretests

A pretest was conducted using 115 subjects to determine if the six headlines by themselves produced differences on the dependent measures. Subjects reviewed one of six headlines for ten seconds and then completed the measures of cognitive response, ad-related beliefs, and ad and brand evaluations that were used in the main experiment. Pair-wise comparisons of the subjects' responses who were randomly assigned to one of the six headline conditions revealed no differences between headlines on most of the measures. Three exceptions included ad interestingness ($F[2,113]=5.71$, $p<.004$) (where extremely inconsistent headlines were perceived as less interesting than consistent and moderately inconsistent head-

lines), level of irritation ($F[2,113]=3.57$, $p<.031$) (where consistent headlines were perceived as more irritating than moderate and extremely inconsistent headlines), and positive ad-related thoughts ($F[2,113]=4.03$, $p<.020$) (where moderately inconsistent headlines generated more positive thoughts than extremely inconsistent but not consistent headlines). However, in each case the pattern of means in the headline-only conditions differed from the results in the main experiment, suggesting that the headline-visual combination and not the headline alone, produced the effects in the main experiment.

A second pretest (n=105) using seven-point scales measured the relevancy (extremely irrelevant-extremely relevant; extremely unrelated-very closely related; correlation=.75) and expectancy (extremely unexpected-extremely expected; extremely surprising-extremely predictable; correlation=.86) for each headline-visual combination. Subjects were randomly assigned to one of six headline-visual combinations. We expected that consistent headline-visual combinations would be both expected and relevant, moderately inconsistent ads would be unexpected and relevant, and extremely inconsistent headline-visual combinations would be both unexpected and irrelevant. As predicted, the main effect of headline-visual consistency on relevancy was significant ($F[2,101]=36.83$, $p<.001$). Extremely inconsistent headline-visual combinations were significantly less relevant to each other ($\bar{x}=3.18$, where 1 is extremely irrelevant) than the consistent and moderately inconsistent conditions ($\bar{x}=5.67$ and $\bar{x}=5.53$, respectively). The impact of consistency on expectancy was also significant ($F[2,101]=21.40$, $p<.001$). As expected, consistent headline-visual combinations were significantly more expected ($\bar{x}=4.70$, where 1 is extremely unexpected) than the moderate ($\bar{x}=3.69$) and extremely inconsistent ($\bar{x}=2.59$) conditions.

Experimental Procedure

Undergraduate students (n=109) were randomly assigned to one of the six treatment conditions. Subjects viewed the ad for 10 seconds and at their own pace completed a thought-listing task, 7-point bipolar scales measuring manipulation effectiveness, and the dependent variables.

Measures

Cognitive Responses. Following exposure to a test ad, written protocols were collected by asking subjects to report any and all thoughts, no matter how simple, complex, relevant, or irrelevant. Consistent with Buckholz and Smith (1991), three judges blind to the experimental conditions each coded two-thirds of the thoughts in terms of their content (product-related; ad-related; combination-related; other) and valence (positive; negative; neutral; confusion). Combination thoughts included references to the relationship between the headline and the visual of the ad (i.e., "The caption did not really fit the picture," "It said 'Come see the Elephants' at the zoo but it showed a lion"). Confusion-related thoughts included statements that indicated difficulty in understanding the advertisement or product (i.e., "It is hard to understand," "I had to read it a couple of times to get the meaning"). All thoughts were coded by two judges. Interjudge reliability was 82.5% for content of thought and 84.8% for valence of thought. Disagreements were resolved by discussion.

Ad-related Beliefs. Beliefs about the ad that reflected subjects' ability to resolve inconsistencies were also assessed. By averaging subjects' responses to 7-point bipolar scales, ad interestingness (interesting-uninteresting; provocative-not provocative; intrigued-bored; alpha=.83), ease of comprehension (easy to understand-difficult to understand; not at all confusing-very confusing; correlation=.79), and the level of irritation generated by the ad (irritating-not irritating; annoying-not annoying; correlation=.78) were measured. Factor analysis confirmed the constructs as three distinct factors.

Evaluations. Subjects' responses to two sets of three 7-point bipolar scales (good-bad; favorable-not favorable; positive-negative) were averaged to provide measures of ad (A_{ad}) and brand (A_{brand}) evaluation. The coefficient alpha scores for A_{ad} and A_{brand} were .90 and .94, respectively. The average of two 7-point bipolar scales (likely-unlikely; probable-not probable) served as the measure for the purchase intention (PI) (correlation=.96).

Manipulation Checks. Subjects were asked to rate the extent to which the visual and headline conveyed the same or similar meanings (same-different; similar-dissimilar; correlation=.72) (cf. Houston, Childers and Heckler 1987) and the extent to which the headline and visual conveyed opposite meanings (opposite-not opposite; contradictory-not contradictory; correlation=.88).

RESULTS

A 3 X 2 between-subjects ANOVA revealed no differences across product class on the dependent measures. Collapsing across product class, quadratic trend analysis was used to test the nonmonotonic relationships proposed in hypotheses 1, 3, and 6. The remaining hypotheses were tested using one-way between-subjects ANOVA.

Manipulation Checks

The main effect of headline-visual consistency on similarity was significant (F[2,105]=22.90, p<.001). Planned contrasts revealed significant differences between all treatment conditions. As expected, the headline and the visual in the consistent advertisements were rated as significantly more similar in meaning ($\bar{x}$=2.65, where 1 is similar) than the moderate ($\bar{x}$=4.42) and extremely inconsistent advertisements ($\bar{x}$=5.44). The main effect of headline-visual consistency on the opposite meaning conveyed in the headline and visual was also significant (F[2,105]=30.82, p<.001). As expected, the headline and the visual in the moderately inconsistent ads were perceived as conveying more opposite meanings ($\bar{x}$=2.03, where 1 is opposite) than the extremely inconsistent ($\bar{x}$=3.60) or consistent advertisements ($\bar{x}$=5.29). Together with the pretest results, these findings provide strong evidence that each of the ads conveyed the intended level of headline-visual inconsistency.

Tests of Hypotheses

Table 1 summarizes the analysis of variance findings. Hypothesis 1 proposed that ad evaluations would be more positive for moderately inconsistent advertisements than for consistent and extremely inconsistent ads. The results of the quadratic trend analysis revealed the expected inverted U-shaped main effect of headline-visual consistency on ad evaluation (F[1,103]=20.33, p<.001). Planned contrasts indicated that moderately inconsistent ads were evaluated significantly more favorably than the consistent or extremely inconsistent advertisements. The evaluations of consistent and extremely inconsistent ads were not significantly different. Hypothesis 1 was supported.

Since inconsistent conditions stimulate more elaborative processing than consistent conditions, hypothesis 2 posited that moderate and extremely inconsistent ads would generate more combination thoughts and more ad-related thoughts. ANOVA using combination thoughts as the dependent measure revealed a main effect of headline-visual consistency (F[2,105]=11.60, p<.001). As predicted, planned contrasts revealed that significantly more combination thoughts were generated for the moderate and extremely

inconsistent than for the consistent ads. ANOVA also revealed a main effect of ad type (F[2,105]=3.85, p<.024) on the number of ad-related thoughts. As expected, planned contrasts indicated that significantly more ad-related thoughts were generated for the moderate and extremely inconsistent than for the consistent ads. Hypothesis 2 was supported.

Hypothesis 3 proposed that if moderate but not extreme inconsistencies can be resolved and the resolution process itself produces positive affect, as compared to consistent and extremely inconsistent advertisements, moderately inconsistent ads will generate more positive combination thoughts, more positive ad-related thoughts, and be perceived as more interesting. ANOVA results showed main effects of ad type on the number of positive combination thoughts [F(2,105)=7.00, p<.001], on the number of positive ad-related thoughts [F(2,105)=4.87, p<.010], and on perceived interestingness (F[2,105]=3.58, p<.031). As hypothesized, planned contrasts indicated that moderately inconsistent ads generated significantly more positive combination thoughts than either the consistent or extremely inconsistent conditions. Also, planned contrasts indicated that moderately inconsistent ads produced significantly more positive ad-related thoughts than the consistent ads but, contrary to expectations, not the extremely inconsistent ads. In addition, moderately inconsistent ads were perceived as more interesting than consistent but not extremely inconsistent advertisements. Hypothesis 3 was partially supported.

Because extreme inconsistencies cannot be resolved, hypothesis 4 suggested that, as compared to consistent and moderately inconsistent ads, extremely inconsistent ads will generate more confusion-related combination thoughts, more confusion-related thoughts overall, be perceived as most irritating and the least comprehensible. ANOVA results supported the main effects of ad type on confusion-related combination thoughts [F(2,105)=4.80, p<.010], on confusion related thoughts (F[2,105]=17.91, p<.001), perceived irritation (F[2,105]=5.87, p<.004), and ease of comprehension (F[2,105]=39.27, p<.001). As expected, extremely inconsistent ads generated more confusion-related combination thoughts and more confusion ad-related thoughts overall than either the consistent or moderately inconsistent ads. In addition, extremely inconsistent ads were perceived as more irritating than moderately inconsistent but not consistent advertisements. Finally, extremely inconsistent ads were perceived as less understandable than consistent and moderately inconsistent ads. Interestingly, planned contrasts also revealed that moderately inconsistent ads were perceived to be significantly easier to understand than consistent advertisements. Hypothesis 4 received partial support.

Hypothesis 5 was proposed to more directly test the mediation effects of the underlying cognitive processes on ad evaluation. Because references to the particular headline-visual combination may be the best measure of the underlying processes, an index of cognitive responses was formed (positive combination-related thoughts minus confusion-related combination thoughts) to capture both the positive and negative indicators of the inconsistency resolution process. Using the index as a covariate, the results of a quadratic trend analysis suggested that the cognitive response index partially mediated the effect of ad type on ad evaluation. Although the index had a significant effect on ad evaluation [F(1,102)=4.09, p<.045], the nonmonotonic impact of ad type on ad evaluation, while reduced, remained significant [F(1,102)=6.63, p<.002]. Hypothesis 5 was partially supported.

Hypothesis 6 addressed the relationship between level of consistency, brand evaluation (A_{brand}), and purchase intention (PI). As expected, quadratic trend analysis revealed a significant nonmonotonic relationship between ad type, A_{brand}

TABLE
ANOVA Summary of Dependent Measures

Dependent Measures	Sum of Squares	df	F	sig	Consistent	Moderately Inconsistent	Extremely Inconsistent
A$_{ad}$ (where 1 = most favorable)	41.41	1[a]	20.33	.001	3.70	2.67[b]	4.21
Number of Combination Thoughts	3.67	2	11.60	.001	0.00[b]	0.39	0.38
Number of Ad-Related Thoughts	22.81	2	3.85	.024	2.39[b]	3.36	3.35
Number of Positive Combination Thoughts	0.667	2	7.00	.001	0.00	0.167[b]	0.00
Number of Positive Ad-Related Thoughts	8.39	2	4.87	.010	0.45[c]	1.08[c]	0.56
Perceived Interestingness (where 1 = most interesting)	15.83	2	3.58	.031	4.31[c]	3.38[c]	3.98
Number of Confusion-Related Combination Thoughts	0.322	2	4.80	.010	0.00	0.00	0.18[b]
Number of Confusion-Related Thoughts	22.67	2	17.97	.001	0.13	0.19	1.15[b]
Perceived Irritation (where 1 = most irritating)	31.21	2	5.87	.004	5.05	5.89[c]	4.57[c]
Perceived Ease of Comprehensibility (where 1 = most favorable)	162.07	2	39.27	.001	2.50[b]	1.54[b]	4.53[b]
A$_{brand}$ (where 1 = most favorable)	31.23	1[a]	19.49	.001	3.41	2.24[b]	3.33
PI (where 1 = most favorable)	19.13	1[a]	6.68	.011	3.35	2.64[c]	3.67[c]

[a]Degrees of freedom reflect quadratic trend analysis.
[b]Scheffe contrasts indicate the mean is significantly different from the others at p < .05 level.
[c]Scheffe contrasts indicate the pair of means are significantly different from each other at p < .05 level.

(F[1,103]=19.49, p<.001) and PI (F[1,104]=6.68, p<.011). As shown in table 1, moderately inconsistent advertisements resulted in (1) more positive brand evaluations than consistent and extremely inconsistent advertisements, and (2) greater purchase intentions than extremely inconsistent but not consistent advertisements.

Using A_{ad} as a covariate, quadratic trend tests were run to assess the mediating role of A_{ad} on the relationship between ad type on A_{brand} and PI. The results of the analyses indicated that (1) A_{ad} partially mediated the effect of ad type on A_{brand} (F[1,102]=24.51, p<.001), but the nonmonotonic relationship of ad type on A_{brand}, while reduced, remained significant (F[1,102]=6.06, p<.015), and (2), together, A_{ad} (F[1,100]=16.97, p<.001) and A_{brand} (F[1,100]=11.47, p<.001) completely mediated the nonmonotonic relationship between ad type and PI (F[1,100]=.28, n.s.). Hypothesis 6 was partially supported.

DISCUSSION AND IMPLICATIONS

Consistent with Mandler's model, a quadratic trend test revealed a nonmonotonic relationship between the level of headline-visual consistency, ad and brand evaluation, and purchase intention. Moderate levels of headline-visual inconsistency produced more positive ad and brand evaluations than ads with consistent and extremely inconsistent headline-visual combinations. Moreover, the moderately inconsistent headline-visual combination generated greater purchase intentions than the extremely inconsistent headline-visual combination.

Analyzing consumers' cognitive responses revealed that inconsistencies stimulate elaborative processing, as compared to consistent headline-visual combinations, moderate and extremely inconsistent ads generated more combination thoughts and a greater number of ad-related thoughts. In a study of product-related processing, Sujan (1985) reported a similar result. In line with our results, consistent information was processed automatically and without extensive elaboration. In addition, Mandler asserts that the absence of elaboration reduces the extremity of affect. In support, we found that ad evaluations for consistent advertisements were less extreme than the evaluations in both inconsistent conditions.

While inconsistencies may stimulate elaborative processing, the consumer's ability to resolve the inconsistency influences the nature of the processing and subsequent valence of evaluation. Because moderate headline-visual inconsistencies can be resolved and the resolution process itself is rewarding, subjects produced more positive combination thoughts and more positive ad-related thoughts than consistent or extremely inconsistent headline-visual combinations. Further, moderately inconsistent ads were perceived as more interesting than consistent ads, providing additional evidence that consumers enjoy deciphering moderately inconsistent messages. Because the meanings of the headline and visual in the extremely inconsistent advertisements cannot be resolved, subjects in the inconsistent ad conditions generated thoughts reflecting confusion and frustration.

In line with related research, we found that extremely inconsistent verbal-visual combinations were less comprehensible than more consistent combinations (e.g., Heckler and Childers 1992). However, we also found that moderately inconsistent headline-visual combinations were more easily comprehended than consistent combinations. This finding may conflict with Heckler and Childers' finding that expected-relevant information (our consistent condition) was easier to understand than unexpected-relevant information (our moderately inconsistent condition). However, literary theory suggests that the use of opposites (i.e., irony) enhances learning and comprehension (Williams and Lilly 1985). Further, opposites are more easily recalled and comprehended than

synonyms (Colombo and Williams 1990), and research on inference formation (Kardes 1988) asserts that a consumer's active participation in interpreting an ad with incomplete information results in better recall than when complete information is provided. Recall is often used as an indicator of comprehension (cf. Houston, Childers and Heckler 1987). Moderate inconsistencies invite the consumer to uncover the underlying headline-visual connection that makes the ad comprehensible. Consistent combinations provide the connections for the reader. Finally, the results of the covariance analysis provided partial support that the resolution process mediated the effect of ad type on ad evaluation. Further, the same nonmonotonic pattern of results of ad type on ad evaluation was found for brand evaluation and purchase intentions.

Inconsistency results from the structural relationship among elements (i.e., the headline, visual, and copy) within an ad. The manipulation of inconsistency, however, is not possible without also potentially changing the content of the ad. By using extensive pretesting and manipulation and confound checks, we attempted to control for this possibility. Alternative explanations due to content changes, however, can never be ruled out entirely (McQuarrie and Mick 1992). Moreover, to enhance internal validity, ad copy was omitted. The inclusion of ad copy may alter the processing of headline-visual inconsistencies. However, since only a fifth of those who note an ad in a magazine actually read the copy (Pollay and Mainprize 1984), ad copy may have limited impact on results. Our respondents' cognitive responses revealed that none of our test ads were perceived as unrealistic. Finally, the laboratory setting differs dramatically from the natural viewing context. Future investigations should extend this research by combining multiple methodologies (e.g., McQuarrie and Mick 1992).

REFERENCES

Berlyne, Daniel E. (1971), *Aesthetics and Psychobiology,* New York: Appleton-Century-Crofts.

Blasko, Vincent J. and Michael P. Mokwa (1986), "Creativity in Advertising: A Janusian Perspective," *Journal of Advertising,* 15 (December), 43-50, 72.

Bock, Michael and Bernhard Milz (1977), "Pictorial Context and the Recall of Pronoun Sentences," *Psychological Research,* 39 (1), 203-220.

Buckholz, Laura M. and Robert E. Smith (1991), "The Role of Consumer Involvement in Determining Cognitive Response to Broadcast Advertising," *Journal of Advertising,* 20 (1), 4-17.

Childers, Terry L. and Michael J. Houston (1984), "Conditions for a Picture Superiority Effect on Consumer Memory," *Journal of Consumer Research,* 11 (September), 531-563.

Colombo, Lucia and John Williams (1990), "Effects of Work and Sentence-Level Contexts Upon Word Recognition," *Memory & Cognition* 18(2), 153-163.

Corbett, Edward P. J. (1990), *Classical Rhetoric for the Modern Student,* New York: Oxford University Press.

Edell, Julie A. and Richard Staelin (1983), "The Information Processing of Pictures in Print Advertisements," *Journal of Consumer Research* 10 (June), 45-61.

Heckler, Susan E. and Terry L. Childers (1992), "The Role of Expectancy and Relevancy for Verbal and Visual Information: What is Incongruency?" *Journal of Consumer Research,* 18 (March), 475-492.

Houston, Michael J., Terry L. Childers, and Susan E. Heckler (1987), "Picture-Word Consistency and the Elaborative Processing of Advertisements," *Journal of Marketing Research,* 26 (November), 359-69.

Kardes, Frank R. (1988), "Spontaneous Inference Processes in Advertising: The Effects of Conclusion Omission and Involvement on Persuasion," *Journal of Consumer Research*, 15 (September), 225-33.

Lutz, Kathy A. and Richard J. Lutz (1977), "Effects of Interactive Imagery on Learning: Application to Advertising," *Journal of Applied Psychology*, 62 (August), 493-498.

Mandler, George (1984), *Mind and Body*, New York: W. W. Norton & Company.

McQuarrie, Edward F. and David Glen Mick (1992), "On Resonance: A Critical Pluralistic Inquiry into Advertising Rhetoric," *Journal of Consumer Research*, 19 (September), 180-197.

Meyers-Levy, Joan and Alice M. Tybout (1989), "Schema Congruity as a Basis for Product Evaluation," *Journal of Consumer Research*, 16 (June), 39-54.

Miniard, Paul W., Sunil Bhatla, and Randall L. Rose (1990), "On the Formation and Relationship of Ad and Brand Attitudes: An Experimental and Causal Analysis," *Journal of Marketing Research*, 27 (August), 290-303.

Mittal, Banwari (1990), "The Relative Roles of Brand Beliefs and Attitude Toward the Ad as Mediators of Brand Attitude: A Second Look," *Journal of Marketing Research*, 27 (May), 209-219.

Peeck, J. (1974), "Retention of Pictorial and Verbal Content of A Text with Illustrations," *Journal of Education Psychology*, 66 (6), 880-888.

Pollay, Richard W. and Steve Mainprize (1984), "Headlining of Visuals in Print Advertising: A Typology of Tactical Techniques," in *Proceedings: American Academy of Advertising*, Donald R. Glover, ed. Denver: American Academy of Advertising, 24-28.

Stein, Barry S., Karla F. Brock, Donny R. Ballard, and Nancy J. Vye (1987), "Constraints on Effective Pictorial and Verbal Elaboration," *Memory & Cognition*, 15 (4), 281-290.

Sujan, Mita (1985), "Consumer Knowledge: Effects of Evaluation Strategies Mediating Consumer Judgements," *Journal of Consumer Research*, 12 (June), 31-46.

Williams, Richard N. and John Paul Lilly (1985), "The Effects of Oppositional Meaning in Incidental Learning: An Empirical Demonstration in the Dialectic," *Journal of Mind and Behavior*, 6 (Summer), 419-434.

Assessing Emotional Reactions to TV Ads: A Replication and Extension with a Brief Adjective Checklist

Haim Mano, University of Missouri - St. Louis

ABSTRACT

This study examines the replicability of a brief checklist (yes/no) version of a 11-point scales' questionnaire for assessing emotional reactions to TV advertisements. By applying two different methodological paradigms, classification and dimensionality, the analyses revealed that, as with the longer form questionnaire, the structure of feelings experienced during exposure to TV ads can be described by affect's two primary dimensions, Pleasantness and Arousal. Based on this structure, a simple method designed to assess the emotional intensity of TV ads is offered. The method is tested by comparing emotional reactions to first-time and previously seen ads. The results suggest that, overall, previously-seen ads were liked more than first-time seen ads.

Television advertisements are filled with emotional messages that can evoke a broad spectrum of emotional experiences. Many TV ads contain affective stimuli as background features (e.g., pleasant music, "touching" stories) and, in many, affect is the ad's main message (e.g., fun, threat). Because of their ease of replicability and the various degrees of intensity of emotional responses they can evoke, TV ads also have practical advantages for examining the structure and intensity of affect. Indeed, since TV ads are unanticipated external stimulations intentionally targeted at altering the viewer's emotional state, watching them can allow mood induction(s) by exposing subjects—over a relatively short period of time—to a number of diverse emotional stimuli of controlled nature and varied intensity.

STUDY OBJECTIVES

The present study has four objectives. First, to propose and examine the validity and suitability of a simple checklist (yes/no) questionnaire for assessing the emotional impact of TV ads and other mood evoking stimuli. The examined checklist questionnaire is based on an instrument developed by Mano (1991) that used 11-point items. A short adjective checklist offers two advantages that facilitate the judgmental processes required for reporting one's emotional state: (i) a relatively small number of adjectives and (ii) the fast and easy response mode (simple check) without the need to quantify the extent to which a particular emotion was felt during exposure to the stimulus. In contrast to longer and multi-point items, these may be critical considerations particularly since TV ads usually last no more than 30 seconds and many times invoke only limited-intensity and short-lived emotional reactions. (For another approach that uses a simple graphic tool for assessing emotional reactions see the Affect Grid; Russell Weiss and Mendelsohn 1989).

The second goal, and part of the questionnaire's validity examination, is to further assess the evidence on the convergence and complementarity of the two paradigms of the structure of affect, dimensionality and classification. Replicating and extending Mano (1991), the paradigms will be contrasted by applying three alternative structure-probing methods: (1) multidimensional scaling of correlations (MDS), intended to reveal the items' primary underlying spatial dimensions, (2) factor analysis, aimed at classifying and dimensionally describing the items, and (3) cluster analysis, aimed at dividing items into clusters of similar groups. The three-method approach allows to contrast the paradigms and examine various

aspects of affect's structure emphasized by each. A central question of psychometric concern of this study is the structural invariance of the factorial and other dimensional solutions under different response formats. In particular, there are two major differences between a multipoint (like the one used by Mano 1991) and a checklist (yes/no) format. First, responding to whether a particular feeling was experienced is not conceptually identical to rating the strength of that feeling. And, second, restriction of response range in the yes/no format strongly attenuates inter-item correlations which in turn could have had a profound effect on the results of correlation-based methods used here (MDS and factor analysis).

The third objective is to apply the proposed instrument for assessing the emotional intensity of different TV ads. Finally, the fourth objective is to examine whether and how prior familiarity with an ad can influence emotional responses to it. Despite theoretical and empirical implications for advertising, past research has not addressed the relationships between ad-familiarity and affect. Zajonc (1968) suggested that repeated exposure leads to liking. The question could therefore be raised as to what aspects of the emotional spectrum are influenced by repeated experience. In particular, since liking involves positive hedonic tone, it is expected that previously seen ads would lead to an increase of the Pleasantness dimension.

DIMENSIONALITY AND CLASSIFICATION OF EMOTIONS

Research on the relationships among emotions usually endorses one of two paradigms, dimensionality or classification. The dimensional view describes emotions in terms of a minimal number of basic dimensions. A substantial body of research suggested Pleasantness and Arousal (Russell 1980) or the 45-degree rotation of Positive and Negative Affectivity (Watson and Tellegen 1985) as affect's primary dimensions (Figure 1).

To date, a number of studies have found that these two dimensions and their combinations underly emotional reactions to TV ads (e.g., Batra and Holbrook 1990, Edell and Burke 1987, Holbrook and Batra 1987, Mano 1991, Olney Holbrook and Batra 1991) and product consumptions (Mano and Oliver 1993).

The parsimony and generality of few dimensions, however, is challenged by those advocating for comprehensive classifications of emotions (e.g., Clore Ortony and Foss 1987). The need to cover a broad spectrum of emotions stems from the multitude of emotional stimuli found in TV ads. As a result, a unique feature of past research has been the large number of items used to assess the structure and intensity of ad-evoked emotional reactions (e.g., Batra and Holbrook 1990, Batra and Ray 1986, Holbrook and Batra 1987).

In attempting to compare and contrast the classification and dimensional paradigms, however, it is important not to view them as antithetical but as complementary (Mano 1991; Russell 1980). Some of the contrasts between the paradigms could be reconciled if differences between their respective methodologies were taken into account. Procedurally, dimensionality relies on the primary dimensions revealed in MDS analyses of judgments of similarity or on the principal components found in factor analysis of emotional items. Classification, on the other hand, examines the results and interpretability of full factorial solutions (i.e., all factors with

Advances in Consumer Research
Volume 23, © 1996

FIGURE 1
The Affect Circumplex

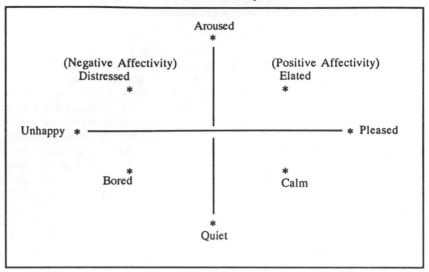

eigenvalue>1) or cluster-analytic techniques. In order to contrast the paradigms, Mano (1991) applied dimensional and cluster analytic methods on emotions elicited during lecture attendance and by exposure to TV ads. The results suggested a convergent and complementary understanding of the paradigms. Classification solutions identified Good Mood, Bad Mood, Arousal, Quietness, Elation, Distress, Calmness, and Boredom as interpretable groups of emotions while the two-dimensional solutions parsimoniously described the relationships among these groups as depicted in Figure 1.

METHOD

Subjects-Judges. Eighteen subjects (7 females, 11 males) were recruited by announcements posted in a midwestern university campus. They were run individually and paid $7.50 for participating in a session that lasted about 50 minutes.

Advertisements. Forty one national and local ads (the same ones used in Mano, 1991) were used as the affect inducing stimuli. Some of the ads lacked strong emotional content and were informational. Most ads lasted 30 seconds. To enhance generalizability, the ads were randomly assigned to two series of 21 (Tape 1) and 20 (Tape 2) presented to two different groups of judges.

Instrument. After seeing each ad, subjects were presented with a list of the emotion describing adjectives used by Mano (1991) and asked to indicate (by placing an X) whether they experienced that particular emotion while watching the ad. Three or four items represented each region in the circumplex (Arousal: Astonished, Surprised, Aroused; Elation: Elated, Active, Excited; Pleasantness: Pleased, Satisfied, Happy, In Good Mood; Calmness: Calm, At rest, Relaxed; Quietness: Quiet, Still, Quiescent; Boredom: Sleepy, Sluggish, Drowsy; Unhappiness: Unhappy, Sad, Blue, In Bad Mood; Distress: Anxious, Fearful, Nervous).

Procedure. Nine subjects (Group 1) viewed and responded to Tape 1 and the other 9 (Group 2) to Tape 2. After viewing each ad, the subject paused the VCR and responded. The tapes were professionally edited to include a short 10-seconds blank (blue) screen between ads. The data were gathered on a booklet in which each page corresponded to an ad with the Product/Ad name at the top. The twenty six adjectives were presented in random order

(same for all ads) and subjects were requested to place an X near any of the adjectives that best described their feelings after watching the ad. Subjects were then prompted to add in writing any additional emotions felt while watching that ad not mentioned in the list (places were provided for four additional traits).

Ad Familiarity. At the bottom of each page, subjects indicated whether they had seen the ad in the past.

RESULTS

The basic units of analysis were the responses to the 41 ads made by the judges. Responses were coded as 1 (if the trait was marked) or 0. The data consisted of 189 sets of responses for Group 1 (9 subjects X 21 ads) and 180 (9 X 20) for Group 2. Each set contained the 26 original and any other items noted by the subject. Content analysis of the additional items revealed that Bored/Boring was mentioned in 4.6% of the responses (across all ads and subjects) and was added as the 27th item. Of the 27 items, subjects marked, on average, 4.87 items per ad.

For purposes of structural analysis, combining assessments for the same ads and across the same subjects introduces some degree of dependence. To detect this dependence, the robustness of the MDS, factor, and cluster analyses between groups was first assessed (the dichotomous response format does not allow for within-subject standardization of responses aimed at eliminating between-subjects variability). As the results showed, there was considerable factorial invariance and a particularly strong cluster and dimensional-scaling invariance between the two Groups thus allowing for across-group aggregations.

MDS. For Group 1, the stress coefficients of the MDS of the item correlation matrix, for dimensions 1 to 4, were .49, .18, .11, and .08 (explaining 43%, 84%, 90% and 94% of item variance); for Group 2, .52, .25, 0.17 and .12 (33%, 70%, 77% and 83%). Based on stress reduction and interpretability, both two-dimensional solutions were considered appropriate. The emerged dimensions in both maps were Pleasantness and Arousal. The two maps were very similar: the Pleasantness coordinates correlated .92 and the Arousal coordinates .94. The canonical coefficient between the two sets of coordinates was .97. Given this high resemblance, the combined data sets were subjected to MDS. The stress coefficients for the first

FIGURE 2
Two-dimensional scaling solution of the 27 adjectives

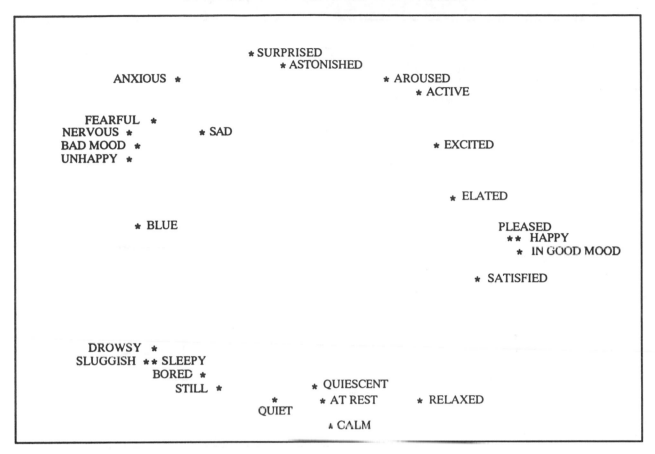

four dimensions were 0.50, .19, .13, and .09 (40%, 83%, 89%, and 93% of the variance). The two-dimensional solution (Figure 2) deemed appropriate in terms of stress reduction and interpretability, with Pleasantness and Arousal emerging as the underlying dimensions. One of this solution's most salient features is its high visual similarity with the theoretical model in Figure 1.

Factor Analysis. Separate factor analyses for Groups 1 and 2 revealed moderately high factorial invariance across groups. In the combined data set, seven factors with eigens>1 were revealed, accounting for 56% of the variance; the respective eigenvalues were 2.82, 2.58, 2.53, 2.18, 1.84, 1.73, 1.34. Items and loadings contributing to each factor were: Sleepy .80, Bored .76, Sluggish 0.72, Drowsy .59 (interpreted as Boredom); Excited .82, Active .72, Elated .64, Aroused .58 (Elation); Nervous .77, Anxious .72, Fearful .62 (Distress); Quiet .69, Calm .67, Still .64, At rest .58 (Calm-Quiet); Blue .76, Sad .73 (Sad); Astonished 0.76, Surprised .72 (Surprised); and Quiescent .74. The following items did not load above .5 on any of the factors: Relaxed, Satisfied, Pleased, Happy, Unhappy, In good mood, and In bad mood.

A number of observations regarding the theoretical appeal of the seven-factor solution are pertinent. First, all factors were monopolar. Second, the first two pairs of factors (Bored-Elated, Distressed-Calm) contained conceptually opposed items which, in the MDS solution, were diametrically opposed. Third, all items loading above .5 in a factor appear in spatial contiguity in the two-dimensional scaling solution. Fourth, items conceptually related to

Pleasantness-Unpleasantness were not included in any factor. Finally, the seventh factor (Quiescent) contained only one item with>.5 loading, indicative that this may not be a meaningful factor. Taken together these results suggest that a lower order factor solution may be theoretically more justifiable. Eigenvalue reduction in the seven-factor solution, however, was rather smooth and therefore it is not clear how to reduce the number of factors.

Given the predominance of two dimensions in the MDS solution, it is theoretically appealing to examine the congruence between the two primary factors and the two-dimensional solution. To that goal, the varimax-rotation constrained-to-two-factors analysis of the data was conducted. The resulting factorial configuration was very similar to the two-dimensional solution presented in Figure 2 (the canonical correlation between the MDS and factor-analytic sets of coordinates was .996).

Taken together, the results indicate that the two-dimensional and the two-factor solutions were very similar. Also, the positions of the 27 adjectives in both solutions corresponded with the configuration suggested by the theoretical model presented in Figure 1.

At this point it is also noteworthy that the canonical correlations between the coordinates of the MDS and two-factor solutions in this study and the corresponding MDS and two factor solutions in Mano (1991) were extremely high ranging from .976 to .985.

Cluster Analysis. The category-sort task is commonly used for revealing typologies of semantic structures. In it, subjects sort terms according to their perceived similarity into non-overlapping

FIGURE 3
Hierarchical clustering of the feelings experienced watching the 41 TV ads

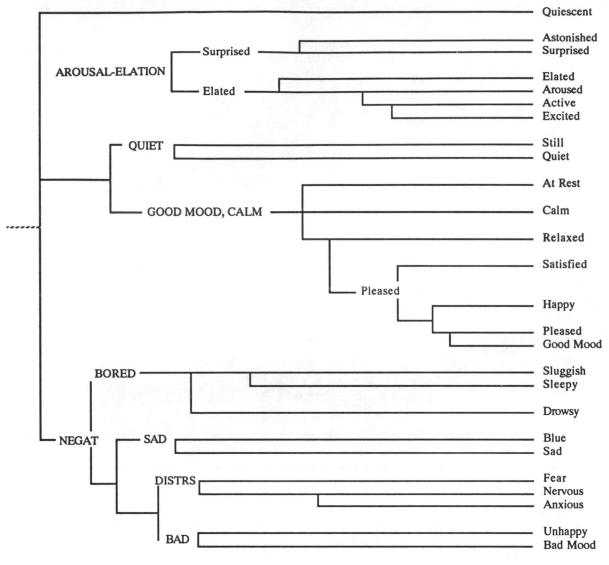

groups and the across-subjects co-occurrence matrix is submitted to a cluster analytic method. The adjective checklist used here allows to treat responses to a particular ad as sorted into two groups (checked and non-checked). By counting (across ads and subjects) the number of times each pair of items co-occurred, a matrix of item co-occurrences can be derived whereby a higher value of a matrix entry reflects a higher degree of item co-occurrence. Note that (a) co-occurrence matrices are different from the across ads and subjects inter-correlation matrices used in MDS and factor analyses, and (b) they do not merely yield the structure of semantic meanings but, rather, the structure of the affective experiences associated with the affective stimuli.

The across-ads-and-subjects co-occurrence matrices of Groups 1 and 2 were first separately submitted to Johnson's (1967) hierarchical cluster analysis. The two hierarchical structures were very similar and, therefore, the two populations were pooled and their matrix re-submitted to the analysis. The results of the combined matrix are presented in Figure 3.

Figure 3 suggests that all items contained in the revealed clusters were adjacent on the two-dimensional-factorial circumplex. Moreover, the various same-branch clusters were also on contiguous regions of the circumplex. Thus, the hierarchical cluster analysis revealed that the examined emotions can also be aptly described in terms of the circumplex.

Synthesis. Taken together, these results suggest the suitability of the brief checklist format for assessing the emotional impact of TV ads or other emotional stimuli. In particular, the findings allow the aggregation of the items into eight scales: Arousal (Astonished, Surprised, Aroused); Elation (Elated, Active, Excited); Pleasantness (Pleased, Satisfied, Happy); Calmness (Calm, At rest, Relaxed); Quietness (Quiet, Still, Quiescent); Boredom (Sleepy, Sluggish, Drowsy); Unpleasantness (Unhappy, Sad, Blue); and Distress (Anxious, Fearful, Nervous). The two-dimensional scaling solution of the correlations among the eight scales is presented in Figure 4 (stress=.039); as seen, the solution highly resembles the circular configuration of Figure 1. Thus, aggregation of the items into the

FIGURE 4
Two-dimensional scaling solution of the octant scales

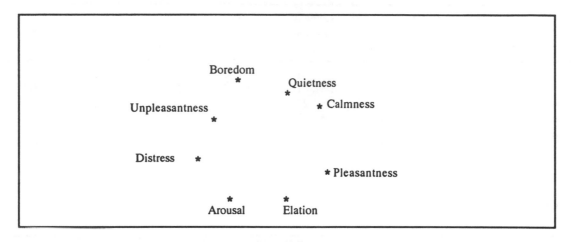

eight scales further reinforces the generalizability of the circumplexial model of affect.

APPLICATIONS AND IMPLICATIONS

Assessing Emotional Impact

Item aggregation into the eight-scale profile can be applied to assess different aspects of TV ads (or other emotion eliciting stimuli). These include across-ads or within-ad comparison and assessment of salient emotional features. To this goal, consider in Table 1 the emotional tone of some of the ads and all the ads used in the study. Such descriptions on the scales can form the basis for classifying the ads by any relevant a-priori criteria (e.g., elating, calm, sad and distressing, etc.). Furthermore, correlations between stimuli based on the eight scales can provide a measure of emotional similarity of the stimuli; subsequently, intercorrelations of ads can be used as the basis for ad-hoc segmentation or other forms of cluster analysis.

Based on the responses given to an ad across the eight scales (i.e., total number of items checked per ad), we can also assess how ads differ in their total emotional impact, an index that can capture the overall emotional intensity of an ad. For example, the lowest average number of responses for an ad was 3.33 (s.d.=1.73), while the highest was 7.00 (s.d.=2.45).

Table 1 also shows the total number of responses on the scales for all the ads used in this study. Although the 41 ads may not consist a representative sample, they generally reflect many of the typical themes found in TV ads. The most salient feature of the aggregation of the 41 ads is their strong emphasis on Pleasantness. It appears that advertisers prefer to create and show pleasant ads more often than any other type of ads.

Familiarity Effects. Based on subjects' report that they had seen the ad before, familiar and first-time seen ads were compared on each of the 27 items (Table 1). Of the 369 observations, 130 were previously seen ads. Across subjects and ads, significant familiarity differences were revealed for the four following items: Satisfied, noted for 48% of the 130 previously seen ads versus 34% for the 239 unfamiliar ads (p=.008); Happy (55% vs. 39%, p=.005); In Good Mood (60 % vs. 45%, p=.006); Bored (1% vs. 7%, p=.009). The first three items belong to the domain of Pleasantness, suggesting that prior familiarity with an ad can enhance its positive hedonic tone and emotional appeal. Familiar ads were also judged less boring than unfamiliar ads. This result stands in some contrast with the common notion that boredom is more likely to be associated with familiar stimuli and that novel stimuli would be more interesting. It seems that, in general, prior familiarity with an ad renders it more pleasing and less boring than a first-time seen ad. These findings suggest that prior familiarity with an ad enhanced its likeability.

Two issues are noteworthy about this relationship. First, since subjects stated ad recognition and not familiarity (i.e., the extent of their prior exposure), these results could be strictly interpreted as suggesting a link between likeability and recognition. Nonetheless, since most TV ads are shown and viewed many times, the link may actually be between repeated exposure and likeability. Clearly, the links between emotional reactions and the extent of prior exposure to an ad, likeability, and subsequent ad-wearout require further research.

The second issue concerns the predominance of pleasantness in the ads and the earlier suggestion that advertisers prefer to show pleasant ads. This statement should now be qualified by the positive relationship between prior exposure and likeability: if previously seen ads are liked more, then ad likeability could also be stemming from ad familiarity. To examine this issue closer, the scores on the eight scales were compared for the previously seen and the first-time seen ads (Table 1). These comparisons revealed significant differences only for the Pleasantness scale: previously seen ads were perceived as more pleasant than first-time-seen ads; (1.59 out of the possible 3 vs. 1.23; t(367)=2.88, p<.005). Thus, at least some of the likeability of previously seen ads should be attributed to subjects' familiarity with them. Nonetheless, it should also be pointed out that for the first time seen ads too, the scale of Pleasantness had the highest score (1.23), thus reinforcing the notion that, overall, advertisers prefer to show pleasant ads.

LIMITATIONS

Some of the limitations of the present research should be noted. First, despite the convergence of the two-factorial solutions with previous research, the disadvantages of dichotomous data should be acknowledged. In particular, attenuation of correlations induced by a yes/no (as opposed to a multi-chotomous) format precludes effective estimation of scale reliability. Also, attenuated

TABLE 1
Responses on the Octant-Scales

Scale	Running Shoes	Cancer Society	Air Line	Standard. Greeting *Cards*		Score Canned Soup	All 41 Ads	Not Seen Before	Seen Before
Arousal	8	14	8	1	3	2	227	.62	.60
Elation	20	3	4	5	7	0	239	.62	.71
Pleasantness	18	3	6	25	25	9	500	1.23	1.59+
Calmness	2	4	5	5	7	12	215	.57	.61
Quietness	0	2	7	1	2	2	74	.23	.15
Bored	0	0	4	0	0	2	90	.28	.18
Unpleasantness	0	14	1	3	1	0	85	.78	.76
Distress	0	9	8	0	0	1	137	.41	.29

+ indicates that the difference in the standardized scores between first-time and previously seen ads is statistically significant, $p < .005$

correlations raise the issue whether factor analyses should be applied to such data. For example, the gradual descent in eigenvalues in the full (seven) factor solution should be mostly attributed to correlation attenuation. Or, consider, that while Pleasantness typically emerges as the primary factor in full factorial solutions of emotional adjectives, the present full factor solution did not include Pleasantness as a distinct factor; or, that in the full factorial solution, the item Quiescent emerged as a unique factor. Taken together, these findings suggest that caution should be applied when attenuated correlations are subjected to factorial analyses.

A second issue concerns whether the intensity of some emotional experiences are adequately captured by the yes/no response. For example, some emotions may have been checked but experienced at a relatively weak level by one subject, whereas, another subject, may have had a strong emotion associated with only one of the adjectives. Perhaps, in addition to intensity, the suggested scales also measure an ad's emotional diversity.

A third, and related, limitation is that the validity of any solution ultimately depends on the validity of the items; (for example, "tired", "sleepy" and "quiescent" may not be considered appropriate exemplars of affective adjectives). Thus, a specific sample of items and their semantic similarity could "drive" the two dimensional configuration (Clore Ortony and Foss 1987). Nonetheless, it should be noted that even when using much larger batteries of traits, Pleasantness and Arousal (or Positive and Negative Affectivity) still emerge as the primary dimensions of emotions (e.g., Holbrook & Batra 1987, Watson and Tellegen 1985).

Fourth, given the self-report and correlational nature of the present data, it is not clear whether increased liking for previously seen ads is driven only by familiarity or by some simple inferential process. Future research should experimentally control ad familiarity and incorporate samples of ads representative of TV programs. For example, the stimuli could consist of all prime time ads shown by a TV station during one evening combined with new (unfamiliar) ads and/or ads from other parts of the country.

Finally, the possible differences between emotional reactions invoked *while* versus *after* watching an ad need to be highlighted. Even though subjects were requested to report their feelings while watching the ad, the reports were made after seeing the ad. This raises the issue of whether the items captured the summative mood effects ("after") or, rather, reactions to some of the ad's emotional

elements ("while"). It is possible that summative mood effects may contain fewer checked items than emotions experienced while watching the ads, thus resulting in smaller correlations (or fewer co-occurrences) between items under the "after" scenario.

CONCLUSION
The present study suggests that the proposed checklist questionnaire is suitable for assessing the structure and intensity of emotions elicited by TV ads. Two central findings of this study are (1) the high degree of structural convergence revealed across methods and (2) the strong agreement that the circumplex of affect is the basic structure of the examined emotional experiences. As seen, factorial solutions and cluster analyses identified interpretable groups of emotions while, at the same time, the two-dimensional solutions parsimoniously described the relationships among the items in these groups as well as the interrelationships among the groups. Finally, an application of the proposed tool suggested that previously seen ads are, overall, liked more than first-time seen ads.

REFERENCES
Batra, Rajeev and Morris B. Holbrook (1990), "Developing a typology of affective responses to advertising: A test of validity and reliability," *Psychology and Marketing*, 47 (1), 11-25.

Batra, Rajeev and Michael L. Ray (1986), "Affective response mediating acceptance of advertising," *Journal of Consumer Research*, 13, 234-249.

Clore, G.L., Ortony, A., and Foss, M.A. (1987), "The psychological foundations of the affective lexicon," *Journal of Personality and Social Psychology*, 14, 421-433.

Edell, Julie A. and Marian C. Burke (1987), "The power of feelings in understanding advertising effects," *Journal of Consumer Research*, 14, 421-433.

Holbrook, Morris B. and Rajeev Batra (1987), "Assessing the role of emotions as mediators of consumer responses to advertising," *Journal of Consumer Research*, 14, 404-420.

Johnson, S.C. (1967), "Hierarchical clustering schemes," *Psychometrica*, 42, 241-254.

Mano, Haim (1991), "The structure and intensity of emotional experiences: Method and context convergence," *Multivariate Behavioral Research*, 26 (3), 389-411.

Mano, Haim and Richard L. Oliver (1993), "Assessing the Dimensionality and Structure of the Consumption Experience: Evaluation, Feeling, and Sartisfaction," *Journal of Consumer Research*, 20 (December), 451-466.

Olney, Thomas J., Morris B. Holbrook, and Rajeev Batra (1991), "Consumer Responses to Advertising: The Effects of Ad Content, Emotions, and Attitude toward the Ad on Viewing Time," *Journal of Consumer Research*, 17 (March), 440-453.

Russell, James A. (1980), "A circumplex model of affect," *Journal of Personality and Social Psychology*, 36, 1152-1168.

Russell, James A., Anna Weiss and Gerald A. Mendelsohn (1989), "Affect grid: A single-item scale of pleasure and arousal," *Journal of Personality and Social Psychology*, 57, (3) 493-502.

Watson, David and Auke Tellegen (1985), "Toward a consensual structure of mood," *Psychological Bulletin*, 98, 219-235.

Zajonc, Robert B. (1968), "Attitudinal effects of mere exposure," *Journal of Personality and Social Psychology Monograph Supplement*, 9 (2), 1-27.

Anticipating the Future: The Role of Consumption Visions in Consumer Behavior

Diane M. Phillips, Pennsylvania State University

ABSTRACT

People can imagine themselves performing a variety of different behaviors (Rook 1988). One broad category of behaviors concerns those related to consuming products. "Consumption visions" are self-constructed mental simulations of future consumption situations. Consumers can imagine themselves, for example, carrying a new briefcase to work or driving a new car around town. Because consumption visions depict the self enacting detailed product-related behaviors, consumption visions may be particularly motivating. Specifically, consumption visions may help to motivate consumers to enact those behaviors they imagine in the consumption vision. This paper examines the antecedents and consequences of consumption visions as well as the extent to which consumption visions may mediate the effects of advertising variables on consumer behavior.

WHAT ARE CONSUMPTION VISIONS?

When consumers construct consumption visions, they imagine themselves playing the major role in a tentative future consumption situation. A consumption vision consists of a series of vivid mental images of product-related behaviors and their consequences, which allows consumers to more accurately anticipate actual consequences of product use (Walker and Olson 1994; Phillips, Olson and Baumgartner 1995). Consumption visions are not merely self-relevant images of the future, they are visions of the self behaving within an imagined scenario and experiencing the outcomes of those behaviors. Consider the individual who is contemplating the purchase of a new car. This individual may imagine driving to work, washing and waxing the new car, and showing it off to friends. For this consumer, each of these images of the self consuming the product are components of the consumption vision.

Constructing consumption visions may have certain decision-making and behavioral implications. By envisioning oneself performing a particular behavior and picturing the various steps involved in the consumption of a product — by "tasting" it, by "feeling" it — the consumer may better predict the consequences of actual consumption of the product. In this way, consumption visions make the imagined scenario more "tangible" and can help the consumer make better, more informed decisions. Specifically, consumption visions may make it easier for consumers who engage in *imagined* consumption to anticipate that *actual* consumption will occur. This is because when people imagine a future scenario, they are more likely to predict that the scenario will actually occur (Carroll 1978, Anderson 1983, Shedler and Manis 1986). Envisioning oneself as the main character in a future behavioral scenario may have particularly strong behavioral implications. Indeed, when the self is the main character in an imagined scenario, behavioral intentions (Anderson 1983, Sherman and Anderson 1987, McGill and Anand 1989) and enactment of the imagined behaviors (Gregory, Cialdini and Carpenter 1982, Markus and Nurius 1986, Sherman and Anderson 1987, Markus and Ruvolo 1989, Cross and Markus 1990) are increased. One explanation for this influence of self-as-main-character visions of the future on decision-making and behavior is that these visions act as self-relevant goals that need to be attained (Markus and Nurius 1986, Emmons 1986, Emmons and King 1988, Markus and Ruvolo 1989, Cross and Markus 1990). Thus, consumption visions may energize consumers to work to engage in actual consumption of the product.

The phenomenon of imagining the future should be of particular interest to consumer researchers (Bettman 1993, Walker and Olson 1994, Phillips, et al. 1995). Consumers who construct consumption visions may become more committed to achieving actual consumption and may thus demonstrate predictable increases in traditional marketing-related variables such as attitudes and intentions. Further, consumption vision construction may be facilitated in an advertising context by including certain advertising variables within the ad itself. As such, the focus of this study will be an investigation of advertising variables that may be manipulated to facilitate consumption vision construction, the marketing-related consequences of construction, and the extent to which a consumption vision acts as a mediator between these antecedents and consequences.

THE ROLE OF CONSUMPTION VISIONS

Antecedents of Consumption Visions

Three advertising variables are expected to influence the construction of a consumption vision (Lutz and Lutz 1978): an explicit invitation to construct the consumption vision, the degree of verbal detail in the ad, and the degree of visual detail in the ad.

Invitation to Create a Consumption Vision. One way to get consumers to form consumption visions is to simply ask them to do so. An invitation could be viewed as an explicit instruction to imagine the self doing something. One invitation could be, "imagine yourself behind the wheel of a Lexus." Such an invitation to imagine the self engaging in a specific consumption situation should greatly facilitate consumption vision construction. This is supported by one study which found a positive impact on product judgments for only those subjects who were given instructions to use "the power of your imagination to envision" the product (McGill and Anand 1989). Indeed, compared to subjects who were not given such explicit instructions, subjects who did receive these instructions imagined more complex "consumption visions" and more detailed product attributes (McGill and Anand 1989). This suggests that when advertising copy explicitly invites consumers to imagine themselves performing a variety of product-related behaviors within a consumption vision, consumers may be more likely to construct consumption visions. Based upon this conjecture, the following hypothesis was generated.

H1: An explicit invitation in an ad to imagine the self in a future consumption situation will positively influence the extent to which a consumption vision is constructed.

The direct approach to facilitating consumption vision construction may be an invitation. There may also be indirect ways to facilitate consumption vision construction: verbal detail and visual detail in the advertisement itself.

Degree of Verbal Detail. One indirect way to encourage consumers to form consumption visions would be to include detailed verbal descriptions of what to expect during actual consumption of the product. Indeed, detailed verbal descriptions facilitate the extent to which individuals construct future scenarios (Carroll 1978). One study had subjects read a two-page, single-spaced account of a future scenario (Gregory, et al. 1982) while another encouraged subjects to close their eyes and imagine for 2-

Advances in Consumer Research
Volume 23, © 1996

3 minutes the different steps involved in successfully completing the imagined task within the scenario (Sherman and Anderson 1987). One underlying mechanism by which concrete and detailed messages exert their influence is purported to be the greater imagability of detailed messages. That is, descriptions that use concrete language and specific details are easier to imagine and elaborate (Taylor and Thompson 1982, McGill and Anand 1989). Another explanation is that verbal detail in the message could trigger greater comprehension of the ad via the increased ability to make personal, self-relevant embellishments of the message or product (Mick 1992). Construction of detailed consumption visions should thus be facilitated by fairly detailed verbal descriptions of the consumption experience. Thus, in order to induce consumption vision construction, print ads must use a high degree of verbal detail. In that regard,

H2: Detailed verbal descriptions will positively influence the extent to which a consumption vision is constructed.

Degree of Visual Detail. Another indirect means by which consumption vision construction can be facilitated in an advertising context is with a pictorial depiction of the consumption experience. A detailed visual representation, or a product-relevant picture, in the advertisement should help consumers anticipate what actual consumption may be like (Mitchell and Olson 1981, Miniard, Bhatla, Lord, Dickson, and Unnava 1991). Just as a detailed verbal description of the consumption situation should facilitate the extent to which a detailed consumption vision is created, a visual representation of the situation should also help consumers imagine or picture themselves acting within the consumption context. Consumption visions are expected to consist of two principal components: the self and the consumption situation. If the situation is presented visually in the advertisement, one half of the foundation for the consumption vision is established. All the individual must do is imagine himself or herself in that situation. Depending on a consumer's ability or preference, a consumer may differentially process the visual and verbal components in an advertisement (Childers, Houston, and Heckler 1985). Previous research also suggests that the addition of a picture in an advertisement may help individuals learn about the product itself (Mitchell 1986) as well as see connections between the product and the self (Debevec and Romeo 1992). As such,

H3: Advertisements that are high in visual detail will positively influence the extent to which a consumption vision is constructed.

In summary, it is expected that three factors will positively influence the extent to which consumers construct a consumption vision: an explicit invitation to create a consumption vision, the degree of verbal detail in the ad, and the degree of visual detail in the ad. What are the likely consequences of consumption vision construction?

Consequences of Consumption Visions

As a consequence of constructing consumption visions, consumers may be more likely to have more positive attitudes toward the particular advertisement, more positive attitudes toward enacting the target behavior, and higher behavioral intentions.

Attitude Toward the Ad. Partial support for the importance of consumption vision construction on attitudes and intentions is provided in one study where it was found that verbal and visual advertising elements both independently influenced attitude to-

ward the ad (Aad) and product beliefs which in turn influenced attitude toward the brand (Mitchell 1986). This study also found that positively valenced pictures had a positive impact on Aad (Mitchell 1986). Although Mitchell (1986) doesn't explicitly discuss how mental imagery impacts the extent to which these effects (Aad and Abrand) occur, the present study specifies the underlying process as a consequence of consumption vision construction. In a related vein, ads that evoke autobiographical memories enhance ad evaluations (Sujan, Bettman, and Baumgartner 1993). Although consumption visions are mental images of the future, not the past, it is likely that consumption vision construction may also lead to more positive ad evaluations. Accordingly,

H4: The extent to which consumption visions are constructed will positively influence attitude toward the advertisement.

Attitude Toward the Act and Behavioral Intentions. If the consumption vision is positive, it is likely that the consumer will develop more positive attitudes toward enacting the behavior (Aact) and intentions toward engaging in that behavior (BI). Detailed consumption visions should make the product seem "closer" to the individual. By vicariously experiencing an interaction with a particular product, the consumer may be more certain about the probable outcomes of product use. Indeed, it has been found that when individuals self-reference (Debevec and Romeo 1992) or create self-as-main-character visions (Anderson 1983), they are more likely to have positive attitudes and intentions. Further, individuals believe they are more likely to perform a behavior after they have imagined performing that behavior (Carroll 1978, Anderson 1983). Finally, individuals will be more motivated to enact goal-directed behaviors after they have imagined a possible future (Markus and Nurius 1986, Markus and Ruvolo 1989, Cross and Markus 1990). Accordingly,

H5: The extent to which consumption visions are constructed will positively influence attitudes toward enacting product related behaviors.

H6: The extent to which consumption visions are constructed will positively influence behavioral intentions.

The hypotheses mentioned above were empirically examined and the results of these tests are described in the next section.

METHOD

Subjects

One hundred and twenty nine students from a large university participated in this study in partial fulfillment of a course requirement. Five subjects were deleted because of incomplete data, leaving 124 (76 men and 48 women) usable responses.

Experimental Stimuli and Manipulations

A 2 (invitation vs. no invitation) X 2 (verbal detail vs. no verbal detail) X 2 (visual detail vs. no visual detail) between-subjects design was used to test the hypotheses. Subjects looked at print ads which encouraged them to form consumption visions about taking a tropical vacation to Aruba. This consumption vision was chosen for several reasons. First, it was unlikely that many subjects had experience with taking a trip to Aruba and would therefore be unlikely to have pre-existing consumption visions about Aruba. Second, a consumption vision was chosen that might be somewhat difficult for some individuals to construct. Since a vacation to

Aruba is very costly, it was believed that very few college students would spontaneously construct this consumption vision. In order to be more credible and realistic, all ads started with "Aruba..." and concluded with the statement, "Call your travel agent today."

Invitation to Create A Consumption Vision. In the invitation conditions, the advertising copy explicitly invited readers to construct a consumption vision by using statements such as "take a moment and imagine yourself..." and "picture yourself..." throughout the ad. In the no invitation condition, no such invitations were used.

Degree of Verbal Detail. Verbal detail was manipulated by the use of concrete, detailed verbal embellishments of the attributes of Aruba (e.g., "pristine beaches that sparkle and shine" and "gentle breezes that caress and embrace," etc.). Thus, in the verbal detail conditions, the advertising copy used concrete, detailed language describing the benefits of each attribute. Conversely, the copy in the no verbal detail conditions simply listed the attributes of Aruba with no verbal embellishments (e.g., "...turquoise waters, pristine beaches, warm sunshine, gentle breezes and relaxing atmosphere").

Degree of Visual Detail. The visual detail component of consumption vision construction was operationalized by including a color picture for visual detail conditions and no picture for the no visual detail conditions. The color picture was a visual depiction of many of the attributes mentioned in the advertising copy. It consisted of a bright, sunny beach scene with turquoise water, white sand, palm trees, etc.

Procedure and Dependent Measures

Upon entering the room, subjects were greeted and given some general instructions about the study. Then, subjects were asked to examine the magazine advertisement as if they were considering taking a trip to Aruba after graduation. After the time was up (90 seconds), subjects were instructed to complete the questionnaire and then wait quietly for further instructions. The first item in the questionnaire was an open-ended thought listing that asked subjects to describe what they thought about while they examined the ad.[1] All subsequent items on the questionnaire were forced choice scales.

Consumption Vision Scale (CVS). The extent to which subjects constructed consumption visions was assessed via the CVS. The CVS consisted of four bi-polar scales developed to capture self-reports of consumption vision construction. The first two questions were designed to check the extent to which subjects imagined, visualized, or pictured a detailed consumption experience, "How

---

[1]A content analysis of the thought listings was performed. The written thought listings were coded by two coders who were blind to the experimental condition of each subject. A thought was considered a consumption vision if it mentioned the self engaging in a specific consumption situation. The total number of distinct thoughts, or "snapshots," was noted. Inter-coder reliability was 74% and disagreements were resolved by discussion. As a measure of the extent to which subjects formed consumption visions, this measure did not produce any significant results. This may be due to the fact that although some subjects may have formed consumption visions, they may not have written down statements that were considered by the coders to be consumption vision "thoughts." For example, subjects may have written, "white, sandy beaches" but may have also imagined themselves walking along those beaches; it was impossible to tell. A better measure would have been to interview each subject to determine what specifically they may have imagined while viewing the ad.

much did the advertisement bring to mind concrete images or mental pictures?" and "When thinking about the trip to Aruba, how vivid or detailed was the image that came to your mind?" The endpoints were: very much-not at all and very vivid-not at all vivid, respectively. The last two questions were designed to assess the extent to which subjects could see themselves as the main character in the consumption vision, "When thinking about the trip to Aruba, how easy was it to see yourself taking such a trip?" and "While reading the advertisement for Aruba, to what extent were you able to 'transport' yourself into the ad?" The endpoints were labeled: very easy-not at all easy and very much-not at all, respectively. Results of a factor analysis suggest that one underlying factor can account for 77% of the variance in the responses. Because of this, the results of these four scales were combined to form one CVS rating (Cronbach alpha=0.90).

Attitude Toward the Act. This question asked subjects to complete a 9-point, four-item scale that described their "feelings toward taking a trip to Aruba" with endpoints labeled unpleasant-pleasant, favorable-unfavorable, good-bad, and negative-positive. These ratings were summed to create an overall Aact measure (Cronbach alpha=0.96).

Attitude Toward the Ad. Next, "feelings toward the advertisement for Aruba" were assessed using the same 9-point, four-item scale. These ratings were summed to create an overall Aad measure (Cronbach alpha=0.97).

Behavioral Intentions. Subjects then completed six, 9-point scales to assess their intentions toward taking a trip to Aruba after graduation. Each scale started with "After graduation..." and ended with a statement such as: "...I intend to take a trip to Aruba" or "...I plan to take a trip to Aruba." The end points for all six scales were labeled: definitely yes-definitely no. These ratings were summed to create an overall BI measure (Cronbach alpha=0.96).

RESULTS

Several subjects created very detailed consumption visions about taking a tropical vacation to Aruba. Examples of different consumption visions are as follows:

I pictured myself relaxing in a comfortable atmosphere. Maybe catching a tan. Swimming in unpolluted water. Trying out a jet ski. I pictured how beautiful and romantic the island appeared. I pictured perfect weather and a great time.

I was wishing that I was there. Picturing myself swimming in clear water with palm trees blowing in the wind. Then I pictured myself lying on the beach with a pina colada in one hand and my boyfriend lying next to me underneath a palm tree.

I immediately pictured the beach and could feel myself lying in the sun. I didn't picture myself meeting anyone though. I was just relaxing by myself, getting away from everything.

The first phase of the data analysis was conducted to examine the antecedents of consumption vision construction. The independent variables were invitation, verbal detail, and visual detail while the dependent variable was the extent to which people formed consumption visions. The second phase of the data analysis attempted to examine the consequences of consumption vision construction. Using the same three independent variables, the dependent variables were Aad, Aact and BI.

Antecedents of Consumption Visions

CVS. The CVS was used to assess the extent to which individuals constructed consumption visions.[2] Overall, individuals report higher CVS ratings with ads using verbal detail (mean rating=6.25, on a 7-point scale) than ads with no verbal detail (mean rating=5.40). This trend was supported by an ANOVA which produced a significant overall model ($F(7,116)=2.45$, $p<0.05$) and a main effect of verbal detail ($F(1,116)=5.44$, $p<0.05$).

Hypothesis 2 is thus supported. In addition, individuals report higher CVS ratings for ads with a picture (mean rating=6.35) than with no picture (mean rating=5.34). The ANOVA also produced a main effect of visual detail ($F(1,116)=8.10$, $p<0.01$). Hypothesis 3 is also supported. The analysis produced no significant effects for invitation or for any interactions. Thus, the extent to which individuals construct consumption visions is facilitated by a detailed verbal description and a detailed visual representation.

Consequences of Consumption Visions

Hypothesis 4 predicted that Aad would be positively associated with the extent to which people constructed consumption visions. This hypothesis was supported with a significant correlation between Aad and CVS ($r=0.70$, $p<0.0001$). Hypothesis 5 predicted that Aact would be positively associated with the extent to which people constructed consumption visions. Again, this prediction was supported by a significant correlation between Aact and CVS ($r=0.61$, $p<0.0001$). Similarly, hypothesis 6 predicted that BI would be positively associated with the extent to which people constructed consumption visions. Once again, this prediction is supported by a significant correlation between BI and CVS ($r=0.46$, $p<0.0001$).

A series of three ANOVAs was then conducted on the overall model relating invitation, verbal detail and visual detail to Aad, Aact and BI. With Aad as the dependent variable, the previous relationships were supported with a significant overall model ($F(7,115)=4.25$, $p<0.0005$) and significant effects for verbal detail ($F(1,115)=4.53$, $p<0.05$) and visual detail ($F(1,115)=24.14$, $p<0.0001$). No significant effects were found for invitation. For Aact, the analysis revealed a marginally significant overall ANOVA model ($F(7, 116)=1.94$, $p<0.10$) and a significant effect for visual detail ($F(1,116)=10.16$, $p<0.002$). This analysis did not produce any significant effects for verbal detail or invitation. Finally, for BI, the overall ANOVA model did not reach significance, but visual detail again exerted a significant influence on BI ($F(1,116)=5.48$, $p<0.05$). Once again, this analysis did not produce any significant effects for verbal detail or invitation.

Mediational Analysis

The final analysis examined the extent to which consumption visions mediated the influence of the three advertising variables on the consequences of consumption vision construction (Baron and

***

[2]One concern about encouraging the construction of a consumption vision about Aruba was that some students may have had direct experience with taking trips to tropical islands. It was reasonable to assume that students who had taken trips to tropical islands in the past may have had an easier time creating a consumption vision about Aruba. Although 50.8% of the subjects reported that they had taken a vacation trip "like the one described in the ad," this concern was dispelled after an examination of correlations between these previous vacation trips and the creation of detailed consumption visions ($r=0.04$), Aact ($r=0.10$), and BI ($r=0.11$).

Kenny 1986). When conducting the three step test of mediation as proposed by Baron and Kenny (1986), first regress the mediator on the independent variables, then regress the dependent variable on the independent variables, and finally, regress the dependent variable on both the mediator and the independent variables. For mediation to be present, the independent variables must significantly influence the mediator, the dependent variable must be significantly influenced by the independent variables, and the significant effects of the independent variables on the dependent variable must be significantly reduced when the mediator is introduced in the last step. Separate analyses were performed for Aad, Aact, and BI. The first step found that for all three dependent variables, the extent to which consumers form consumption visions, as measured by CVS, was significantly influenced by verbal detail ($t=2.371$, $p<0.02$) and visual detail ($t=2.883$, $p<0.005$).

In analyzing the mediational impact of Aad, it was found that Aad was significantly influenced by verbal detail ($t=2.172$, $p<0.05$) and visual detail ($t=5.010$, $p<0.0001$). When Aad was regressed on the independent variables and the mediator, the following relationships were found: Aad was significantly influenced by CVS ($t=9.781$, $p<0.0001$) and visual detail ($t=4.090$, $p<0.0001$), but not impacted by invitation and verbal detail. Thus, evidence for partial mediation of the influence of consumption visions was found for verbal detail and visual detail on Aad.

Aact was significantly influenced by visual detail ($t=3.277$, $p<0.002$). And, when Aad was regressed on the independent variables and the mediator, Aact was significantly influenced only by CVS ($t=7.972$, $p<0.0001$), providing evidence for the mediational role of consumption visions for visual detail on Aact.

Lastly, BI was significantly influenced by visual detail ($t=2.398$, $p<0.02$). In the final step, BI was significantly influenced only by CVS ($t=5.096$, $p<0.0001$). This analysis suggests that the impact of visual detail on BI is mediated by consumption vision construction.

DISCUSSION

This study represents an important first step in understanding both the antecedents and the consequences of consumption vision construction. Two primary advertising variables were found to exert an influence on the extent to which consumption visions were constructed: verbal detail and visual detail. That is, consumers are likely to form consumption visions when an advertisement depicts product attributes either verbally with concrete and detailed language or visually with a picture. The inclusion of an invitation to imagine the self did not seem to have an effect on consumption vision construction. The effect of the invitation manipulation may have been attenuated because subjects were asked to examine the ad as if they were planning to take a trip to Aruba after graduation. These instructions may have thus automatically implicated the self in any subsequent processing of the ad. Consequences of consumption vision construction are also important for making recommendations to marketing and advertising managers. The results presented in this analysis predict that marketing managers should see positive increases in Aad, Aact and BI when consumers construct consumption visions.

Of particular interest, however, is the mediational nature of consumption visions. Consumption visions mediated the impact of visual detail on Aact and BI, while evidence for partial mediation was found for verbal detail and visual detail on Aad. Consumption visions thus represent a fascinating motivational construct in consumer behavior. By depicting the self engaging in pleasurable consumption-related activities, consumption visions motivate consumers to try to engage in real, as opposed to imagined, consumption.

Limitations

Perhaps the most obvious limitation of this study stems from the nature of the consumption vision that was prompted. First, a tropical vacation to Aruba is a very high involvement, hedonic consumption experience. Perhaps consumption visions would work differently with more utilitarian consumption purchases such as a new refrigerator. A related issue in need of further research is the construction of negative consumption visions. Oyserman and Markus (1990) discuss evidence that suggests that negative consumption visions may exert a particularly strong impact on decision-making and behaviors that are designed to avoid these vivid visions of the future self. Fear appeals in advertising may be particularly impactful if they include elements that encourage consumption vision construction.

This study only tangentially addresses the complexity of consumption visions. The CVS attempts to assess the extent to which a consumption vision was formed, but it does not assess the complexity, or the number of scenes imagined, in the vision. The scale measures consumption visions along only two dimensions: the extent to which the self is incorporated in the vision and the extent to which the imagined consumption is "vivid and detailed." A more comprehensive measurement tool needs to be developed to capture the complexity dimension of consumption visions. Further, to more accurately represent the construct of interest, subsequent revisions of the scale should explicitly refer to any consumption vision construction while viewing the ad.

Future Directions

One area for future research is a focus on the lasting effects of consumption vision construction. Are consumption visions "lost" once actual consumption takes place, or do these consumption visions simply get updated with new information that can be stored for later use? Similarly, once a detailed consumption vision is constructed, how easy will it be to imagine alternative scenarios? It is possible that consumption vision construction may block the construction of alternative consumption visions. If this is the case, extensive effort may need to be expended in order to help individuals construct new consumption visions. It may also be possible, however, to encourage consumers to construct consumption visions which contain certain key elements (such as your product) or that emphasize certain key attributes as choice criteria (on which your product fares particularly well). Thus, development of an advertising program that reaches consumers at the point when they are just forming consumption visions may help consumers to construct consumption visions in which a certain product plays a critical role.

A second research question should be an identification of circumstances in which an advertiser might want to discourage the construction of consumption visions. An examination of the pattern of means for consumption vision construction indicates that consumers are the least likely to construct consumption visions in the no invitation/no verbal detail/no visual detail condition. One example of a situation in which consumption vision construction should not be used is organ donation. Indeed, a detailed advertising appeal (complete with picture) that issued an invitation to "imagine yourself" donating is likely to backfire.

Another avenue for further research is a simple one: how many consumption visions do individuals naturally construct and under what circumstances do individuals construct them? Individual differences (Strathman, Gleicher, Boninger, and Edwards 1994) may predispose some consumers to rely more on consumption visions in consumer decision making. A related question is how individuals "see" themselves performing the particular prod-uct-related behaviors in the consumption vision (Phillips et al. 1995). Individuals could "see" themselves as if they were actually performing the behaviors, for example, they may envision looking down and seeing a tropical drink in one hand. Another possibility is that they "see" themselves from the viewpoint of an outside observer who is watching the action from a distance. Extensive interviews and a detailed analysis of consumer thought protocols will likely shed some light on these questions.

The results of this study demonstrate that marketers can use certain advertising tools to help consumers construct consumption visions. These consumption visions, in turn, result in more positive attitudes and intentions which may energize consumers toward actual consumption. Although the domain of consumption vision construction is relatively new to consumer research (Phillips et al. 1995), its study has the potential to reveal many fascinating insights into the ways in which consumers imagine the future. Hopefully, this study will provide a "first step" into this uncharted territory for many future consumer researchers.

REFERENCES

Anderson, Craig A. (1983), "Imagination and Expectation: The Effect of Imagining Behavioral Scripts on Personal Intentions," *Journal of Personality and Social Psychology*, 45 (2), 293-305.

Bettman, James R. (1993), "The Decision Maker Who Came In From the Cold," in *Advances in Consumer Research*, Vol. 20, eds., Leigh McAlister and Michael L. Rothschild, Provo, UT: Association for Consumer Research, 7-11.

Baron, Reuben M. and David A. Kenny (1986), "The Moderator-Mediator Variable Distinction in Social Psychological Research: Conceptual, Strategic, and Statistical Considerations," *Journal of Personality and Social Psychology*, 51 (6), 1173-1182.

Carroll, John S. (1978), "The Effect of Imagining an Event on Expectations for the Event: An Interpretation in Terms of the Availability Heuristic," *Journal of Experimental Social Psychology*, 14, 88-96.

Childers, Terry L., Michael J. Houston, and Susan E. Heckler (1985), "Measurement of Individual Differences in Visual Versus Verbal Information Processing," *Journal of Consumer Research*, 12 (September), 125-134.

Cross, Susan E. and Hazel Rose Markus (1990), "The Willful Self," *Personality and Social Psychology Bulletin*, 16 (4), 726-742.

Debevec, Kathleen and Jean B. Romeo (1992), "Self-Referent Processing in Perceptions of Verbal and Visual Commercial Information," *Journal of Consumer Psychology*, 1 (1), 83-102.

Emmons, Robert A. (1986), "Personal Strivings: An Approach to Personality and Subjective Well-Being," *Journal of Personality and Social Psychology*, 51 (5), 1058-1068.

Emmons, Robert A. and Laura A. King (1988), "Conflict Among Personal Strivings: Immediate and Long-Term Implications for Psychological and Physical Well-Being," *Journal of Personality and Social Psychology*, 54 (6), 1040-1048.

Gregory, W. Larry, Robert B. Cialdini, and Kathleen M. Carpenter (1982), "Self-Relevant Scenarios as Mediators of Likelihood Estimates and Compliance: Does Imagining Make It So?," *Journal of Personality and Social Psychology*, 43 (1), 89-99.

Lutz, Kathy A. and Richard J. Lutz (1978), "Imagery-Eliciting Strategies: Review and Implications of Research," in *Advances in Consumer Research*, Vol. 5, ed., H. Keith Hunt, Provo, UT: Association for Consumer Research, 611-620.

Markus, Hazel and Paula Nurius (1986), "Possible Selves," *American Psychologist*, 41 (9), 954-969.

Markus, Hazel and Ann Ruvolo (1989), "Possible Selves: Personalized Representations of Goals," in *Goal Concepts in Personality and Social Psychology*, ed., Lawrence A. Pervin. Hillsdale, NJ: Lawrence Erlbaum Associates, 211-241.

McGill, Ann L. and Punam Anand (1989), "The Effect of Vivid Attributes on the Evaluation of Alternatives: The Role of Differential Attention and Cognitive Elaboration," *Journal of Consumer Research*, 16 (September), 188-196.

Mick, David Glen (1992), "Levels of Subjective Comprehension in Advertising Processing and Their Relations to Ad Perceptions, Attitudes and Memory," *Journal of Consumer Research*, 18 (March), 411-424.

Miniard, Paul W., Sunil Bhatla, Kenneth R. Lord, Peter R. Dickson, and H. Rao Unnava (1991), "Picture-based Persuasion Processes and the Moderating Role of Involvement," *Journal of Consumer Research*, 18 (June), 92-107.

Mitchell, Andrew A. (1986), "The Effect of Verbal and Visual Components of Advertisements on Brand Attitudes and Attitude Toward the Advertisement," *Journal of Consumer Research*, 13 (June), 12-24.

Mitchell, Andrew A. and Jerry C. Olson (1981), "Are Product Attribute Beliefs the Only Mediator of Advertising Effects on Brand Attitudes?" *Journal of Marketing Research*, 18 (August), 318-332.

Oyserman, Daphna and Hazel Rose Markus (1990), "Possible Selves and Delinquency," *Journal of Personality and Social Psychology*, 59 (1), 112-125.

Phillips, Diane M., Jerry C. Olson, and Hans Baumgartner (1995), "Consumption Visions in Consumer Decision Making," in *Advances in Consumer Research*, Vol. 22, eds., Frank Kardes and Mita Sujan, Provo, UT: Association for Consumer Research, 280-284.

Rook, Dennis W. (1988), "Researching Consumer Fantasy," *Research in Consumer Behavior*, 3, 247-270.

Shedler, Jonathan and Melvin Manis (1986), "Can the Availability Heuristic Explain Vividness Effects?," *Journal of Personality and Social Psychology*, 51 (1), 26-36.

Sherman, Roberta Trattner and Craig A. Anderson (1987), "Decreasing Premature Termination From Psychotherapy," *Journal of Social and Clinical Psychology*, 5 (3), 298-312.

Strathman, Alan, Faith Gleicher, David S. Boninger, and C. Scott Edwards (1994), "The Consideration of Future Consequences: Weighing Immediate and Distant Outcomes of Behavior," *Journal of Personality and Social Psychology*, 66 (4), 742-752.

Sujan, Mita, James R. Bettman, and Hans Baumgartner (1993), "Influencing Consumer Judgments Using Autobiographical Memories: A Self-Referencing Perspective," *Journal of Marketing Research*, 30 (November), 422-436.

Taylor, Shelley E. and Suzanne C. Thompson (1982), "Stalking the Elusive 'Vividness' Effect," *Psychological Review*, 89 (2), 155-181.

Walker, Beth A. and Jerry C. Olson (1994), "The Activated Self in Consumer Behavior: A Cognitive Structure Perspective," *working paper*, The Pennsylvania State University, University Park, PA 16802.

Implications of Imposed Dress Codes for Consumer Behavior, and Consumer Behavior Implications for Understanding the Effects of Dress Codes

Terence A. Shimp, University of South Carolina

Unlike the limited selections available to older baby boomers and pre-boomers, elementary and secondary school children today dress in a vast array of clothing fads and fashions. Baseball caps, team jackets, the west-coast grunge look, gang colors, preppy styles, expensive sneakers, boots, and t-shirts emblazoned with slogans are just some of the items that provide school children a means of self-expression and enable social groups to distinguish insiders from outsiders. In one sense, this panoply of clothing options represents the best of democratic ideals, with each individual given the freedom to express him or herself subject to limits imposed by norms of decency, cleanliness, and safety.

There is, however, a potential downside to this opportunity for full self-expression. School officials contend that the way students dress can lead to disruptive behaviors, inordinate competition among students for informal "best-dressed awards," disciplinary problems, and violence stemming from gang-related clothing symbolism and more general incidents of thievery. Strict dress codes have been implemented or are under consideration throughout the country–supposedly to accomplish such goals as reducing gang violence and recruitment activities, minimizing fashion competition and discrimination, and enhancing the quality of the educational experience by creating a stronger sense of educational purpose and removing disrupters such as violence and other miscreant behaviors.

The imposition of strict dress codes, including, at the extreme, mandated uniforms, might be viewed as abridging school children's constitutional right to freedom of speech. Nevertheless, in the desire to improve student behavior in the classroom and to curtail disruptive and violent behaviors, many school districts have either imposed dress codes or are contemplating the imposition of such codes. For example, the New London school district in Connecticut banned the wearing of baseball hats. The Long Beach, CA school district now requires all students from kindergarten through eighth grade to wear uniforms. Chicago is contemplating a uniform dress code policy for its 400,000 plus public school students. California recently passed legislation that allows public schools to require students to wear uniforms so as, according to the governor, to rid schools of gang colors and symbols.

The participants in this session brought a variety of theoretical and disciplinary perspectives to bear in analyzing the rationale for, the likely success of, and the individual-level and social implications of mandated dress codes. David Jamison, University of Florida, confronted the issue from an anthropological perspective. The guiding hypothesis for his presentation was that the use of dress is not just a broad-based status indicator, but, rather, is a way of measuring and interpreting the nuances of group identity. Based on field work conducted in a middle school in Florida where a dress code had recently been imposed, he posited that brand idolatry was pervasive among these students, who identified their beliefs and feelings through a series of essays about their views on the imposed uniform policy and on clothes in general. A consistent pattern of brand veneration and a propensity to relate the possession of brand name clothing to personal/group characteristics such as "coolness" or "in-ness" was inherent in the essays. These findings reflect a desire among students to possess branded clothing as a way to establish or support personal identity and group belongingness. The rationalization for school uniform policies was conceptualized as an attempt by school administrators to eliminate or reduce boundaries within the student body that have formed as a result of the possession, or inability to possess, the requisite "totems," that is, branded clothing. Anthropological theory on the use of symbols in maintaining social boundaries was also discussed.

Deborah Roedder John, University of Minnesota, examined the meaning of brand names to children. Several guiding questions directed her presentation: How do children view movements to restrict their freedom to express themselves through clothing? In particular, what do brand names mean to children and adolescents in their development as social beings? Do children and adolescents use brand names as part of the social tapestry? The presentation examined the meaning of brand names for children of different ages and overviewed an ongoing study of brand name meanings to children ranging in age from 8 to 16 years. The study examined well-known brand names, such as Nike and Levi, and the effect these names have on children's product impressions and impressions of peers who own such items. It was posited that the imposition of dress codes might lead to other types of signals, such as language or hairstyles, to supplant branded items as the indicators of social status and belonging.

Melanie Wallendorf and David Crockett, University of Arizona, scrutinized the implementation of dress codes from a sociological perspective. Primary attention focused on the likely impact of dress codes on symbolic expressions of race, class, and gender. The authors questioned whose interest is asserted through the implementation of dress codes. They hypothesized that the greater the potential for class, or wealth-based conflict, the greater the felt need among school officials and some parents to blur class distinctions, and, in turn, the stricter dress codes will be. Wallendorf and Crockett questioned whether even the strictest dress code can completely mask class distinctions and predicted the likely redirection and reemergence of symbolic expressions of class in schools implementing dress codes. They further asserted that students will use dress code exemptions, variable items, and boundary challenges to reestablish class, wealth and group identities. They also addressed the potential benefits of dress codes and posited that the greatest benefit is reaped by the coalition of teachers, administrators, and parents. School dress codes serve to reassert authority over a population that often questions authority. The codes also serve to reestablish a sense of community by refocusing group identification away from unsanctioned groups onto sanctioned groups. Also, adherents of disciplinarianism benefit from dress codes. Parents and taxpayers, frustrated with the rise (or perceived rise) in violence, can point to dress codes as a symbolic demonstration of a more disciplined (and thus better) learning environment. Finally, local school administrators and school boards, often frustrated in attempts to discipline undesirables, believe they have a new weapon at their disposal.

Terry Shimp, University of South Carolina, analyzed nation-wide articles in magazines and newspapers and classified into seven issue categories the prevailing arguments in favor of or in opposition to the imposition of dress codes: (1) School-Related Behaviors–uniforms will sharpen kids' focus on learning and declare that street behaviors and attitudes are unacceptable in school; (2) Parent-Child Relations–uniforms will reduce parent tension by cutting arguments with teenagers over what to wear to school; (3) Crime & Violence Implications–uniforms will reduce violence by decreasing gang influence and assuaging pressure on kids to steal, sell drugs, or skip school to earn spending money so they can dress "right"; (4) Social Impact Implications–uniforms unify students, rather than dividing them by social class or other demarcations; an opposing view is that uniforms do *not* stop competition and fighting; kids will compete over sunglasses and shoes if not jeans, jerseys, and jackets; (5) Economic Impact Implications–proponents argue that uniforms will reduce clothing expenses; opponents assert that less-privileged families will be unable to afford uniforms; (6) Child-Development Implications–uniforms teach kids that there is more to a person than clothing; an opposing view is that uniforms encourage conformity and therefore undermine cornerstones of American education such as creativity and independent thinking; and (7) Freedom & Dignity Implications–uniforms lessen kids' individuality or interfere with students' rights to exercise free expression.

The school dress-code issue is an area ripe for consumer research. Whereas consumer researchers traditionally have studied fully volitional behavior, the present issue is one of *constrained consumer behavior*. Moreover, whereas most consumer research involves theorizing and testing of the antecedents of consumer behaviors, the focus of the dress-code issue is more a matter of the *consequences* of that behavior. For example, what implications will dress codes hold for considerations such as child safety, family relations, and the quality of the learning environment? Is it probable that imposed dress codes will *not* accomplish the salutary objectives that school officials and politicians have in mind? Presently there is virtually no scholarly research on this topic. Public policy is being directed by opinions and emotions. Consumer researchers have as much, or more, to contribute to the understanding of the issues surrounding the imposition of dress codes as any other group of social scientists. Quasi experimentation and ethnographic field studies would seem especially appropriate methodologies for examining the tough issues involved. Regardless of methodology, researchers must be especially mindful to carefully conceptualize the putative causes and effects for example, exactly what is a dress code? What behavior(s) reflect effectiveness, or lack thereof, of dress codes? Great care also must be taken to rule out potential confounds that covary with the imposition of dress-code policies–such as intensified disciplinary action, curriculum changes, and physical-plant improvements.

Inferences about Pricing and Promotion

Carl F. Mela, University of Notre Dame
Joel E. Urbany, University of Notre Dame

SESSION OVERVIEW

This session was organized with the objective of exploring consumer beliefs about persuasion attempts which come in the form of price changes, price promotions, and displays. The concept of schemer schema (or more generally, persuasion knowledge) has emerged in the literature as a potentially important moderator of marketer influence attempts. Little attention has been given to the notion that consumer beliefs or inferences about marketer promotion behavior may determine how they respond. The four papers summarized below addressed several dimensions of such beliefs.

SUMMARY OF INDIVIDUAL PAPERS

Consumer Beliefs about Retail Prices and Promotions
Carl F. Mela, University of Notre Dame
Joel E. Urbany, University of Notre Dame

In twelve in-depth interviews of consumers, Mela and Urbany find that only a small proportion had extensive knowledge of prices and promotion behavior across several categories, but that nearly all interviewed were knowledgeable about prices and promotions in one or two categories. Further, these expectations were multi-dimensional, suggesting the possibility that in any given product category, enough consumers will be knowledgeable about price promotions that they have perceptions of brand promotion behavior over time.

Additionally, Mela and Urbany examined whether their respondents offered explanations for seller promotion behavior, finding significant heterogeneity within the sample. Those respondents who did offer explanations varied between inferences about the brands or products (object perception: e.g., "The brand which promotes more is not selling well.") and inferences about motives of the seller (nonobject perception: e.g., "The retailer needs to generate traffic."). The authors conclude that enough consumers appear to attend to brand promotions over time and think about possible explanations of promotion behavior that longer term patterns of price promotions may indeed influence consumer brand beliefs, an issue which continues to be controversial in the literature.

Consumer Beliefs about In-Store Displays
J. Jeffrey Inman, University of Wisconsin-Madison
K. Patrick Meline, University of Wisconsin-Madison

Product displays are an important tool at the point-of-purchase which can serve to remind customers, stimulate impulse purchases, and enhance store atmosphere. However, recent research on persuasion knowledge suggests that customers may hold beliefs about marketer tactics which can adversely impact display performance. A basic assumption of this model is that consumers must be cued to the fact that they are being persuaded before persuasion knowledge is utilized. Inman and Meline examine consumer beliefs about marketer tactics involving point-of-purchase materials.

Their preliminary studies revealed significant variance in consumers' conception of what constituted a "display" and several dimensions describing consumer beliefs about displays (e.g., display as information, display as high/low quality, display as decoration). The authors are currently fielding a survey which measures the beliefs identified in the exploratory research. These data will be linked to store-level panel data and information about the store environment at the point of purchase to allow an assessment of the relative impact of beliefs on purchase behavior.

The Manufacturer-Retailer-Consumer Triad: Differing Perceptions Regarding Price Promotions
Aradhna Krishna, Columbia University
Bari Harlam, University of Rhode Island
Page Moreau, Columbia University

Krishna et al. noted that while scanner data provide marketers with some insight into consumers' reactions to promotions, the conclusions drawn are based solely on actual purchase data. Little information regarding consumers' perceptions of both the retailers' and the manufacturers' intentions can be gleaned from these data sources. Their study provides unique insight into consumers' beliefs about promotion behavior, as well as "second-order" perceptions: one party's perception of another's schema (e.g., what retailers think that consumers think). In their ongoing study, Krishna et al. ask parallel questions of three groups: consumers, retailers, and manufacturers. Preliminary results show substantial differences between retailer/manufacturer estimates of consumer beliefs and what consumers actually report. For example, consumers disagreed that "a product on end-aisle display has a good price cut," while both retail and manufacturer respondents expected that consumers would overwhelmingly agree. Similarly, the sellers predicted that consumers would tend to believe the retailer was primarily responsible for determining which products go on sale in the store, while consumers actually believed it was both manufacturer and retailer. These preliminary results suggest that retailers and manufacturers could increase promotional effectiveness by improving their understanding of consumer beliefs about such tactics.

"Schemer Schema" Influences on Consumers' Perceptions of Fair Pricing
Margaret C. Campbell, UCLA

Campbell's work focuses on factors which influence consumer judgments of fairness in evaluating seller price changes. She reviewed the dual entitlement theory of Kahneman, Knetsch, and Thaler as well as other perspectives, all of which suggest that the fairness of another's actions is judged by considering her/his intentions. This is particularly relevant in a pricing context, as consumer beliefs about a firm's motives in raising its price may substantially influence consumer response to that price. Results from several experiments were reviewed, suggesting that apparent seller intentions play an important role in perceived fairness. The research supports the idea that consumers think about why marketers take particular actions and that the perceived reasons influence response to those actions.

DISCUSSION LEADERS
Peter R. Dickson, University of Wisconsin-Madison
Mark Heckman, Marsh Supermarkets (in abstentia)

Peter and Mark's comments encouraged taking a broader view of the issues under study. For example, Mark (who relayed his comments through Peter) indicated that increases in store size have consumers adjusting their in-store traffic patterns such that they may skip certain aisles, but attend increasingly to end-of-aisle displays. Such basic trends in consumer shopping behavior may have important implications for the issues discussed by the session participants. In addition, the study of price fairness might be fruitfully expanded to consider not just apparent seller intent in a particular instance, but also more generally consumer evaluation of such behavior with an understanding of the market mechanism whereby excess profits earned attract other firms who enter and drive prices down. Further, Peter discussed a model of market prices which is in constant disequilibrium, where both buyer and seller beliefs about each others' behavior change over time in response the ebb and flow of the market price distribution. Understanding consumer inferences about seller promotion behavior may be facilitated by recognizing the longer term dynamics of those perceptions.

When You're Happy and You Know It ...: Self-Referencing, Memory, and Affect

Gita Venkataramani Johar, Columbia University
Geeta Menon, New York University

INTRODUCTION

Literature on self-referent encoding suggests that information about oneself is elaborated upon and is therefore accessible in memory. Activating such information about oneself can affect the manner in which people make judgments about a related stimulus object such as a product. This finding is explained by the affect transfer process where affect associated with the product memory is transferred to the product evaluation.

Two research questions that emerge from this literature are: (a) Does self-referencing *always* enhance persuasion?, and (b) If not, is it because retrieved product memories are not always positive? These issues are important to consumer behavior because self-referencing cues are often used in advertising.

SUMMARY OF PAPERS

The first paper by Joan Meyers-Levy and Laura Peracchio was entitled "Moderators of the Impact of Self-Referencing on Persuasion." They examined how self-referencing affects persuasion and whether the motivation to process the ad moderates these effects. Self-referencing was manipulated using wording of the ad copy and the perspective from which the ad photo was shot. Results indicated that moderate levels of self-referencing enhanced persuasion, while extreme levels undermined it. Further, such self-referencing effects only emerged when the ad had an unfavorable outcome which motivated subjects to attend to the ad. No self-referencing effects were observed under low motivation conditions when the ad had a favorable outcome. Recall of ad material showed the same pattern of results. Diminished recall under extreme self-referencing conditions was attributed to interference from excessive thoughts about the self.

Another possible explanation for diminished persuasion under high levels of self-referencing is the valence of the retrieved information about the self. This was the focus of the second paper. Geeta Menon and Gita Venkataramani Johar presented this paper which was entitled "Valence of Personal vs. Product Experiences: What do you remember when you're feeling blue?" This research investigated the accessibility of positive versus negative experiences in memory. Past research on the retrieval of personal experiences has demonstrated that positive experiences are more accessible in memory than negative ones. Experiment 1 replicated these findings for *person* memory but showed that both positive and negative *product* experiences were accessible. The authors suggested that one reason for observing the positivity bias in person memory is mood congruence. Subjects may have been in a positive mood at the time of retrieval. Mood congruency may not be present for product memory because mood may not be strongly linked to product experiences in memory. Experiment 2 tested this proposition and established that manipulating mood at the time of retrieval influenced the valence of recalled personal experiences, but not that of product experiences.

Finally, Norbert Schwarz summarized a comprehensive research program that investigated the informative functions of affective states in his presentation entitled "Feelings as Information: The Impact of Moods on Judgment and Processing Strategies." This presentation explored the use of one's affective state as a heuristic on the basis of which people arrive at different kinds of judgments. Traditional models that trace the impact of mood to mood-congruent recall of valenced information in memory were contrasted with those that view affective states as informational input to judgments. Schwarz presented findings from a series of research studies which showed that the impact of mood on processing strategy and judgments was eliminated when its informational value for the judgment was discredited via misattribution for the mood. Schwarz discussed implications of these findings for product evaluation and advertising strategies.

DISCUSSION

Mita Sujan set off the discussion by presenting her view of research on self-referencing and affect. She suggested that self-referencing can vary along dimensions such as extent, valence and content. She also pointed out that affect can serve many functions including informational ones.

The ensuing discussion focused on both theoretical and methodological issues. Some of these issues were: the outcome favorableness manipulation used to motivate ad processing in the first paper; an editing explanation for the lack of mood congruence in the second paper; the differences in the valence of recalled product experiences between the two experiments reported in the second paper; the relevance of the "affect as information" heuristic to consumer behavior; and ideas for future research on self-referencing and affect.

The Changing American Family: Causes, Consequences, and Considerations for Consumer Research

Aric Rindfleisch, University of Wisconsin-Madison
James E. Burroughs, University of Wisconsin-Madison

SESSION OVERVIEW

This session explored the causes, consequences, and consumer implications of the changing structure of the American family. The main objective of this session was to highlight and draw research attention to the consumer behavior implications of the changing family. The session contained three presentations and a question and answer session moderated by the discussion leader. The papers presented in the session represented a breadth of theoretical and methodological domains. Despite this considerable amount of theoretical and methodological diversity, the three papers are tied together by their examination of one or more of three central themes: (1) an outline of these changes and their causal influences; (2) methods for measuring and modeling these changes, and (3) the implications of these changes for consumer research. A brief summary of each of the three presentations as well as key comments from the discussion period is contained in the following section.

SUMMARY OF INDIVIDUAL PAPERS

"The Changing American Family: Characteristics and Research Challenges"
Robert E. Wilkes, Texas Tech University

Wilkes led off this session by documenting many of the recent changes in American family life, including the growth of single-parent households, delayed marriage and parenthood, and the rise in cohabitating partners. He noted that this movement away from the traditional nuclear family has rendered much of the extant research on the American family either outdated or of restricted generalizability. Wilkes also suggested that because of these changes, consumer researchers should consider using the term "close relationships" in place of the term "family" when describing and explaining household living arrangements. Wilkes observed that the changing American family poses particular challenges to consumer researchers interested in such topics as family decision making. The complexity of contemporary family life has made family decision making much more problematic to explain. In order to get a better grasp of the impact of family diversity on decision making, Wilkes suggested that consumer researchers adopt grounded theoretical and qualitative methodological approaches.

"The Life Cycle Revisited: An Empirical Test of a New Modernized Household Life Cycle Model"
Charles M. Schaninger, SUNY-Albany
Dong H. Lee, SUNY-Albany

This paper conceptually and empirically developed three versions of a modernized household life cycle model following the recommendations of Schaninger and Danko (1993). Schaninger and Lee provide a comparative test of full nest and childless couple submodels, as well as overall tests of each model's ability to capture attitudinal and consumption differences. The reduced form of their new model outperformed the Gilly-Enis model in capturing attitudinal and consumption patterns of non-traditional full nest catego-

ries. The full form of their model results in an improved explanation of the attitudinal and consumption differences among newlyweds, delayed marriage/childless couples, empty nest, and older couples. In terms of consumption differences, Schaninger and Lee found that couples who forego or delay progression through traditional life cycle stages tended to display more modern sex roles and less traditional values, consume healthier and more gourmet-oriented foods and beverages, and (except for delayed empty nest couples) acquire a greater number of durable assets more suited to their nontraditional lifestyles.

"Family Disruption and Consumer Attitudes and Behavior"
Aric Rindfleisch, University of Wisconsin-Madison
James E. Burroughs, University of Wisconsin-Madison
Frank Denton, University of Wisconsin-Madison

In this final paper, Rindfleisch, Burroughs, and Denton presented the results of a survey which examines the relationship between family disruption and the presence of materialistic attitudes and compulsive consumption among two hundred young adults raised in intact versus disrupted family structures. In addition to examining the direct effects of family disruption, they also explored the degree to which the relationships between family disruption and materialism and compulsive consumption is mediated by both the amount of resources available in the family and the degree of family stress. Considering the documented reduction in financial well being experienced by disrupted families, they also examined the degree to which the impact of family disruption on family resources and stressors is moderated by socioeconomic status. Their findings indicated that: (1) compared to persons raised in intact families, young adults from disrupted families exhibit higher levels of materialism and compulsive consumption; (2) the impact of family disruption on compulsive consumption is mediated by family resources and stressors, and (3) the impact of family disruption on family resources is moderated by socioeconomic status.

"Discussion Leader Comments"
Donald H. Granbois, Indiana University

Granbois commented on the importance of this area of research and noted that all three papers offer valuable and interesting perspectives on the changing American family, and represent the growth of research interest in this topic. He also commented that this research area is implicitly based on the normative assumption that the changing American family produces undesirable effects. Granbois suggested that this normative assumption should be brought more explicitly to the surface and needs to be carefully considered. For example, he noted that parental divorce often leads to stronger ties among siblings. Granbois also recommended that researchers in this area should consider the question of "what difference do these changes make?" and focus their research efforts on the impact that the changing American family has on individual consumers themselves.

The session was chaired by Aric Rindfleisch and Jim Burroughs.

REFERENCES

Schaninger, Charles M. and William D. Danko (1993), "A Conceptual and Empirical Comparison of Alternative Household Life Cycle Models," *Journal of Consumer Research*, 19 (March), 580-594.

Family Disruption and Consumer Attitudes and Behavior: An Exploratory Investigation

Aric Rindfleisch, Univesity of Wisconsin-Madison
James E. Burroughs, Univesity of Wisconsin-Madison
Frank Denton, University of Wisconsin-Madison

ABSTRACT

Despite the rapid and dramatic changes in the structure of the American family over the past 25 years, consumer researchers have largely neglected how these alternative family forms influence consumer behavior. As a preliminary inquiry into this area, we present an exploratory study which examines the relationship between family disruption and the presence of materialistic attitudes and compulsive consumption behavior among young adults reared in intact versus disrupted family forms. The specific family measures used to investigate these relationships include: (1) whether a family disruption had occurred, (2) respondent's age at initial disruption, and (3) the number of total disruptions. Considering the well documented reduction in financial resources experienced by disrupted families, we also controlled for differences in household income. Although we found no evidence of a relationship between family structure and materialism or compulsive consumption, we did discover significant relationships between these dependent measures and both age at initial disruption and the number of total disruptions. No statistical support was found for the attenuating effects of household income.

INTRODUCTION

The consumption activities of the American family has long been of interest to consumer researchers. Family-related issues have been a major topic of investigation in such diverse areas of research as consumer socialization (e.g., Carlson and Grossbart 1988; Churchill and Moschis 1979), the family life cycle (e.g., Murphy and Staples 1979; Schaninger and Danko 1993) and family decision making (e.g., Corfman and Lehmann 1987; Rubin, Riney, and Molina 1990). The findings from these research streams, while enhancing our knowledge of family influences on consumer decision making, are limited by their use of the intact two-parent family household as the unit of analysis. Over the past 25 years, this traditional family structure has become increasingly less representative of the types of families and households in which most Americans live. Currently, married couples with children represent only 37% of all families and 26% of all households in the United States (Ahlburg and De Vita 1992). Moreover, demographic estimates indicate that fewer than half of all children will spend their entire childhood in a two-parent family (Bumpass 1984; Cherlin 1992).

Since most of the extant family-related research focuses almost exclusively on the traditional two-parent family (Ahuja and Stinson 1993), we know very little about consumption among members of non-traditional family structures. This study represents an initial effort to explore this gap in our knowledge about the consumption patterns of alternative family structures by investigating the relationship between family disruption and the presence of materialistic attitudes and compulsive consumption behavior among a young adults. Considering recent criticism of the rather static and superficial family structure measures typically used by family researchers (Martinson and Wu 1992; Wu and Martinson 1993), we examine the consumption-related effects of multiple facets of family disruption, including family structure (intact vs. disrupted), age at initial family disruption, and number of total disruptions. In addition, since family disruption is often associated with decreases in financial resources (McLanahan 1985; McLanahan and Booth

1989), we examine the influence of household income on the relationship between family disruption and materialism and compulsive consumption.

LITERATURE REVIEW

Research in Consumer Behavior

Although both Nicosia and Mayer (1976) and Kerkhoff (1976) called for consumer researchers to study the consumption-related implications of the changing American family 20 years ago, very little research has been done on this topic over the past two decades. As noted in a recent literature review by Ahuja and Stinson (1993), only a handful of studies have examined the marketing or consumer research implications of alternative family structures. Two studies which merit special attention are Kourilsky and Murray's (1981) examination of the use of economic reasoning models in family budget decisions and Wilkes' (1995) recent study of expenditures among single-parent families. Kourilsky and Murray (1981) find that, compared to children living in intact two-parent families, children who live in single-parent families are more likely to assume adult-like purchasing responsibilities. Using data from the Bureau of Labor Statistics' Consumer Expenditure Survey, Wilkes (1995) observes that "two-parent families outspent one-parent families in absolute dollars in virtually every reported product category" (p. 272). After adjusting for income differences, Wilkes notes that the proportion of one-parent families' income spent on health care, reading, and education is substantially less than the spending on these categories in two-parent families.

Research in Family Sociology

In contrast to the scant attention paid to the changing American family by consumer researchers, a wealth of insightful research on this topic can be found in the family sociology literature. Family sociology researchers have conducted a number of empirical studies demonstrating that the well-being and attainment of children who have experienced one or more family disruptions (e.g., divorce, separation, remarriage) is, on average, lower than that of children raised exclusively in two-parent households. Over the past decade, family sociologists have compiled an impressive array of research suggesting that family disruption is associated with a wide variety of undesirable behaviors and outcomes for children in disrupted families. Compared to children living in intact two-parent families, children from single-parent families are more likely to drop out of school, to have lower incomes, to engage in delinquent behavior, to be involved in a teenage pregnancy, and to suffer from drug and alcohol abuse (Amato 1993; Cherlin 1992; Flewelling and Bauman 1990; McLanahan and Booth 1989; Wu and Martinson 1993).

Unfortunately, much of the family sociology literature suffers from a lack of adequate theory development and is controversial in regards to its concepts and methods (Amato 1993; Demo 1993; Flewelling and Bauman 1990; McLanahan and Booth 1989; Wu and Martinson 1993). One source of incisive criticism is the way in which most of these researchers attempt to measure family structure (Wu and Martinson 1993). In specific, family sociologists typically assess family structure by asking subjects to identify the type of family (i.e., intact two parent, single mother, etc.) they lived in at age 14. Under this approach, any deviation from a intact, two-biological-parent unit is generally classified as a disrupted family (Flewelling and Bauman 1990). Although this measurement technique has some advantages (e.g., easy recall for the subject and a quick assessment for the researcher), it suffers from a number of limitations (Martinson and Wu 1992; Wu and Martinson 1993). Perhaps its most significant shortcoming is the fact that, by focusing on family structure at a given point in time, it confounds both the age at which a disruption occurs as well as the number of total disruptions experienced by a subject. As noted in the following sections, there is reason to believe that both age at initial disruption and number of total disruptions may be more refined indicators of the dynamics being played out within a disrupted family setting.

Age at Initial Disruption: In addition to the significant loss of economic resources which is normally associated with single-parent families (Cherlin 1992), children in disrupted families often experience the loss of other forms of parental support, including adult supervision, practical help, emotional support, and guidance (Amato 1993; Cherlin 1992; Thompson, Hanson, and McLanahan 1992). Family sociologists suggests that a family breakup is particularly harmful to individuals who experience disruption as young children since, on average, they will spend a longer period of time under conditions of diminished resources.

Although the association between age at time of disruption and child well-being has received mixed support from family researchers (Amato 1993), there is a substantial amount of developmental research which suggests that it is particularly difficult for young children to adjust to the reduction in family resources associated with traumatic life changes (Craig 1993). For example, in their study of the impact of the Great Depression on the lives of children, Elder (1974) found that boys who were younger during this era were more adversely impacted by the social changes it created in their family patterns. According to Erickson's (1982) theory of psychosocial development, the family unit represents the most significant set of relations for young children between the ages of one and six (i.e., Erickson's early childhood and play age stages). Finally, as Moschis (1987) notes, the frequency of children's consumption-oriented interactions with and economic dependence on their parents declines with age.

Number of Family Disruptions: Family researchers have widely observed that children who are subject to one or more family disruptions experience a number of particularly stressful events, including parental conflict, movement to a new home, loss of friends and relatives, and changes of adult caregivers (Amato 1993; McLanahan and Booth 1989; Martinson and Wu 1992; Wu and Martinson 1993). According to Amato (1993), the instability and change associated with family disruption often results in emotional and behavioral problems that are sometimes severe and long-lasting. Furthermore, family researchers have found that each successive parental transition places a child at an increased risk to encounter such stressors (Kurdek and Fine 1993). In support of this contention, Rutter (1983) discovered that children who experience chronic stress react more adversely to a stressful event than children who experience only a single stressful event. More recently, Wu and Martinson (1993) found that the number of family disruptions was positively related to the risk of teenage pregnancy.

HYPOTHESIZED RELATIONSHIPS

This study empirically examines the relationship between family disruption and young adults' consumption attitudes and behaviors. In specific, we selected materialistic attitudes and compulsive consumption behavior as appropriate constructs for investigation since both are generally regarded as undesirable by-products of our consumer culture (Belk 1985; Faber and O'Guinn 1992; Hirschman 1992; O'Guinn and Faber 1989; Richins and Dawson 1992). We examine both of these constructs across three conceptually distinct measures of family disruption: (1) family structure (intact vs. disrupted), (2) age since initial disruption, and (3) number of family disruptions.

Materialism

Materialism is defined as a "set of centrally held beliefs about the importance of possessions in one's life" (Richins and Dawson 1992, p. 308). These beliefs are manifested by the extent to which material possessions represent a primary source of an individual's satisfaction or dissatisfaction with his or her life. Though not inherently negative, a strongly held materialistic attitude is generally regarded to be harmful to an individual's well-being.

Belk (1985) identifies three ways in which excessive levels of materialism can result in harm to the individual: possessiveness, nongenerosity, and envy. Possessiveness refers to a condition in which an individual becomes obsessed with the ownership or control of material objects. Nongenerosity, defined as an unwillingness to give or share possessions with others, may result in difficulties in interpersonal exchanges and relationships. Envy refers to a general displeasure or ill will towards the good fortune of another. Envy has been shown to lead to highly aggressive and socially dysfunctional behavior toward others. Relatedly, Richins and Dawson (1992) find that material values are associated with low self-esteem, dissatisfaction with one's life, and a desire for higher income.

The antecedents of materialism may be traced, at least in part, to an individual's childhood. Material objects constitute an integral part of our culture's reward system and underlie some of our earliest experiences with interpersonal relationships, e.g., buying a child a new toy as a reward for getting good grades (Belk 1985). As noted by Isaacs (1935), the use of material rewards as behavioral modifiers may inadvertently lead children to associate them with parental love or as surrogates for more developed social exchanges. Furthermore, it seems reasonable to conclude that materialistic tendencies may be most acute in those situations where other, more positive reinforcers such as parental guidance and adequate material support are lacking.

The characterization of persons with strong materialistic orientations (e.g., low self esteem, unsatisfying personal relationships, and dissatisfaction with financial resources) bears a strong resemblance to the characteristics that family researchers have discovered among children growing up in disrupted families. For example, as An, Haveman and Wolfe (1993) observe, young adults who face stressful life changes during childhood or early youth often experience feelings of insecurity which they try to assuage by claiming "possession" of persons or objects they can control. Moreover, the breakdowns in communication that accompany divorce appear to have an impact on children's consumer socialization. Children from households characterized by infrequent communication with parents are less likely to perform socially desirable consumption activities and are more materialistic than children raised in families characterized by frequent and open consumption oriented communication (Moore and Moschis 1981). Finally, as noted earlier, children of disrupted families typically have less parental contact and communication. Due in part to this decreased parental contact and supervision, young adults raised in broken families are likely to be exposed to a higher amount of unmediated materialistic advertising messages (Churchill and Moschis 1979). In sum, we offer the following hypotheses regarding materialistic attitudes among children of disrupted families:

H1a: Young adults from disrupted families will be more materialistic than young adults from intact families.

H1b: The materialistic attitudes of young adults from disrupted families will be inversely related to their age at the time of initial disruption.

H1c: The materialistic attitudes of young adults will be positively related to the number of family disruptions they have experienced.

Compulsive Consumption

Compulsive consumption is defined as "a response to an uncontrollable drive or desire to obtain, use, or experience a feeling, substance or activity that leads the individual to repetitively engage in behavior that will ultimately cause harm to the individual and/or others" (O'Guinn and Faber 1989, p. 147). As noted by Hirschman (1992), compulsive consumption appears to be intimately related to family composition, as many consumers with compulsive personalities appear to have been raised in families characterized by the emotional conflict associated with parental divorce or separation. Hirschman concludes her general theoretical treatise on compulsive consumption by pointing out that "Addicted consumers appear to have in common an emotional vacancy that they are compelled to fill with something" (p. 178). Likewise, O'Guinn and Faber (1989) observe that compulsive buyers often appear to be more interested in attaining positive interpersonal interactions and increased self-esteem from their purchases rather than economic or utilitarian value. Psychologists have found that children's capacity to delay gratification is positively correlated with the presence of a father in the home (Rook 1987).

Thus, it appears that the development of compulsive consumption may also be rooted in childhood experiences. Children who grow up in an environment characterized by uncertainty and frequent disruption may develop a behavioral predisposition to "take what they can while they can" (Walls and Smith 1970). Moreover, children of disrupted families may often lack the requisite parental guidance needed to teach them the benefits of deferred gratification (Bandura and Mischel (1965). Considering the pain and turmoil typically associated with the disruption of a family, it is difficult to ignore the possible relationship between family disruption and compulsive consumption. Family researchers have collected a sizable and impressive amount of empirical evidence that demonstrates that children from single-parent households have a higher propensity to engage in other compulsive activities, such as drug and alcohol abuse, compared to children raised in two-parent households (Cherlin 1992; Flewelling and Bauman 1990; Fuchs 1983; McLanahan and Booth 1989). Thus, we offer the following hypotheses regarding compulsive consumption behaviors among children of disrupted families:

H2a: Young adults from disrupted families will exhibit greater compulsive consumption tendencies than young adults from intact families.

H2b: The compulsive consumption behaviors of young adults from disrupted families will be inversely related to their age at the time of initial disruption.

H2c: The compulsive consumption behaviors of young adults will be positively related to the number of family disruptions they have experienced.

The Attenuating Effects of Household Income

Many of the adverse effects of disrupted family structures upon children and young adults appear to be at least partially attributable to the tremendous gap in parental resources (especially financial support) that exists between intact two-parent families and alternative family forms (Cherlin 1992; McLanahan 1985; McLanahan and Booth 1989; Thompson, Hanson, and McLanahan 1992). Family researchers have estimated that the vast difference in average household income between intact and disrupted families explains, on average, about half the relationship between family disruption and decreased child well-being (Cherlin 1992; McLanahan 1985). However, individual studies which have controlled for this difference in economic resources have produced a wide variety of empirical results, with some studies finding no effects due to income (Cherian 1989) and others concluding that many of the adverse consequences associated with disrupted family structures essentially disappear when family income and other measures of parental resources are statistically controlled (Crockett, Eggebeen, and Hawkins 1993; Thompson, Hanson, and McLanahan 1992). However, most empirical studies have found that household income has the potential to alleviate at least some of the problems associated with family disruption (e.g., helping to assure adequate physical resources, providing an opportunity to hire professional counseling, etc; see Amato 1993 for a review). This leads to our study's final hypothesis:

H3: The relationships between family disruption and materialism and compulsive consumption suggested in both H1 and H2 will be attenuated when differences in household income are statistically controlled.

METHOD

Pretesting

Based on our hypothesized relationships, measures were adopted from previous research or generated for this study. A pretest was administered to 71 undergraduate students in introductory marketing courses at a large midwestern university to purify the measures and refine the survey instrument. Since all measures demonstrated adequate reliability and validity, the final questionnaire reflected only minor format changes.

Subjects and Procedures

The subjects for this study consisted of undergraduate students enrolled in marketing courses at a large midwestern university. In order to avoid possible confounds due to differences in cultural backgrounds or generational influences, all subjects had to be both born within the U.S. and 22 years old or younger. To help ensure maximum confidentiality and encourage candid and honest responses, subjects were given approximately one week to complete the survey at home and then submit it in a centrally-located collection box. This technique was considered preferable to a classroom-administered survey considering the highly sensitive and personal nature of the family-background questions. As an incentive to participate, each student received a nominal amount of extra credit from his or her instructor. On average, the survey took about 15 minutes to complete. Of 170 distributed questionnaires, 143 usable surveys were collected (an 84% response rate). Of our 143 subjects, 84 (59%) were female and 132 (92%) were white; the mean age of our subjects was 21.

Measurement

The survey instrument contained multi-item measures of materialism, compulsive consumption, three single-item measures

TABLE 1
T-tests of Mean Differences Between Intact vs. Disrupted Families

Measure	Family Type		t-value	p-value
	Intact	Disrupted		
Material Values	3.13 (.65)	3.29 (.54)	1.38	.09
Centrality	3.30 (.72)	3.44 (.68)	1.01	.16
Happiness	3.08 (.95)	3.35 (.77)	1.67	.05
Success	2.97 (.80)	3.06 (.65)	.61	.27
Compulsive Buying	1.96 (.57)	2.04 (.60)	.61	.27

Note: Standard deviations are listed in parentheses.

of family disruption and a standard set of demographic variables including gender, race and annual household income. Materialism was measured using Richins and Dawson's (1992) Material Values scale (with its three dimensions of centrality, happiness and success), while compulsive consumption was assessed via Faber and O'Guinn's (1992) Clinical Screener for Compulsive Buying. Both measures were assessed via five-point scales and demonstrated adequate levels of reliability; the Material Values scale had an overall coefficient alpha of .86 (with alphas of .77, .82 and .79 for the centrality, happiness and success dimensions, respectively), while the Clinical Screener for Compulsive Buying had an alpha of .69.

As noted earlier, we employed multiple measures of family disruption. Specifically, we assessed family disruption by asking respondents: (1) whether they have always lived with their biological mother and father, (2) their age when their initial family disruption occurred, and (3) the number of total family disruptions they had experienced before their 18th birthday. These measures demonstrated moderate but significant intercorrelations (see Appendix), indicating that the three measures tap conceptually distinct yet related aspects of respondents' family life experience. For coding purposes, subjects from intact families were coded as a "1" while those from disrupted families were coded as a "0." Therefore, since all 111 subjects from intact families have (by definition) never experienced a family disruption, we find a highly negative correlation (-.74) between family structure and number of disruptions. Household income was assessed by asking subjects to estimate their average *annual* household income over the past five years.

RESULTS

To evaluate these three sets of hypotheses, we conducted t-tests of the differences in sample means, and full and partial correlation analysis. These multiple methods helped assess the relationship between the three measures of family disruption and material values (both overall and across its three dimensions of centrality, happiness and success) and compulsive consumption. Since all of our hypotheses are directional in nature, we employ one-tailed significance test criterion and designate p<.05 as our level of statistical significance.

Both the intact and disrupted groups are large enough to permit statistical inferences. Of our total sample, 32 respondents (22%) had experienced a family disruption. In other words, 78% of our sample have spent their entire lives living with both of their biological parents. This percentage is above the national average of 61% of children living with both biological parents (Kurdek and Fine 1993), as well as the standard demographic estimate that half of all today's children will experience parental disruption (Bumpass 1984; Cherlin 1992). It appears that this is primarily a by-product of the selective nature of our sampling frame (i.e., college students at a major residential university). In general, most sample characteristics are fairly equally distributed among individuals from both family structures. The most glaring distinction between these two groups is the large difference in average household income levels between intact (mean=$56,700) and disrupted families (mean=$38,900). This large income differential is consistent with the well-documented relationship between family structure and household income described in the marriage and family literature (Amato 1993; Cherlin 1992; McLanahan and Booth 1989). The only other notable difference between the two groups is the large percentage (75%) of subjects from disrupted families who were female. This female bias is in line with family research findings which suggest that boys who live in female-headed households generally have more academic-related difficulties than girls (McLanahan and Booth 1989). Consequently, the large number of females in our disrupted family sample may simply be an indicant of their superior academic adjustment compared to their male counterparts.

H1a and H2a were first evaluated via t-tests of the mean differences in material values and compulsive buying between young adults of intact and disrupted families. As reported in Table 1, although respondents from disrupted families demonstrate slightly higher levels of both material values and compulsive buying tendencies, the differences are not statistically significant (mean differences of .16 and .08; and p-values of .09 and .27, respectively). Therefore, both H1a and H2a are not supported. Since family structure (intact vs. disrupted) does not appear to be statistically related to our constructs of interest, the remaining analyses focus on our two remaining measures of family disruption (number of total disruptions and age at initial disruption).

TABLE 2
Full and Partial Correlation Analysis of Age
at Initial Disruption and Number of Total Disruptions

	Age at Initial Disruption (n=32)				
	Material Values				Compulsive Buying
	Overall	Centrality	Happiness	Success	
Correlation	-.32[b]	-.43[a]	-.05	-.23	-.35[b]
Partial correlation	-.32[b]	-.43[a]	-.05	-.22	-.35[b]

	Number of Total Disruptions (n=143)				
	Material Values				Compulsive Buying
	Overall	Centrality	Happiness	Success	
Correlation	.17[b]	.16[b]	.20[a]	.05	.15[b]
Partial correlation	.19[b]	.23[a]	.15[b]	.09	.15[b]

[a]Statistically significant at $p<.01$.
[b]Statistically significant at $p<.05$.

To test the remaining hypotheses, we calculated a set of full and partial correlation coefficients between both material values and compulsive buying, and our two remaining measures of family disruption. These correlations are reported in Table 2. The full correlations examined H1b, H1c, H2b, and H2c, while the partial correlations tested the attenuating effect of household income as expressed in H3, by extracting the common effects of income from these relationships (Kachigan 1991). As hypothesized in H1b and H2b, the age at initial family disruption is significantly and negatively correlated with both material values (overall, $r=-.32$; centrality, $r=-.43$) and compulsive buying ($r=-.35$). Likewise, as suggested in H1c and H2c, the number of total family disruptions is also significantly correlated with both material values (overall, $r=.17$; centrality, $r=.16$; happiness, $r=.20$) and compulsive buying ($r=.15$). In sum, these findings are consistent with our hypothesized relationships, and thus H1b, H1c, H2b and H2c are supported.

As seen by the partial correlation coefficients reported in Table 2, household income did *not* appear to attenuate the relationship between family disruption and either materialism or compulsive consumption. Overall, compared to the full correlation coefficients, the partial correlation analysis actually revealed a slight increase in the correlation between overall material values and number of total disruptions (produced by a small decrease in the correlation for the happiness dimension, offset by a slightly larger increase in correlation for the centrality dimension). Acknowledging the relatively high levels of household income among our respondents from disrupted family backgrounds, we believed that the attenuating effects of household income deserved closer inspection. In specific, we examined the differences in average material values and compulsive buying tendencies among respondents with annual household incomes near or below the U.S. poverty level ($16,000) compared to subjects with incomes above this cut point. These tests revealed no significant differences in either compulsive buying ($p=.19$ with means of 4.04 and 3.91 for the higher and lower income groups, respectively) or material values ($p=.49$ with an identical mean score of 2.84 for both groups). These tests of mean differences further support the contention that income does not attenuate the relationship between family disruption and either

materialism or compulsive consumption. Therefore, H3 is not supported.

DISCUSSION

These initial findings provide exploratory evidence that family disruption is related to the *presence* of undesirable consumer attitudes and behaviors among young adults. A key finding is the large amount of variation in explanatory ability among our three measures of family disruption. Our dichotomous measure of family structure (intact vs. disrupted) was unable to detect significant differences, while both of the more dynamic measures of age at initial disruption and total number of disruptions performed fairly well. This suggests that since divorce is a complex and messy event, such dichotomous measures should be used in conjunction with more specific measures of family disruption. This measurement issue is currently being debated by family researchers, who have made the call for more refined measurement techniques in this area of research (Martinson and Wu 1992; Wu and Martinson 1993).

The relationships uncovered between family disruption (age at initial disruption and number of total disruptions) and materialism and compulsive consumption appear to be consistent with the prior work of both consumer and family researchers. For example, Richins and Dawson (1992) suggest that people with high material values desire higher levels of income and financial security and place lower emphasis on personal relations. As noted earlier, our disrupted sample had substantially lower average household incomes, which may encourage them to place a higher degree of importance on financial concerns. Family researchers have noted that persons in disrupted families often have much greater difficulty forming emotional attachments (Cherlin 1992; McLanahan and Booth 1989). The high correlation between the centrality dimension of the Material Values scale and age at initial disruption is particularly noteworthy, as it indicates that these young adults may have used material objects as surrogates for absentee parents.

At first glance, the lack of support for the attenuating effects of household income appears to contradict the bulk of family research, which usually finds that socioeconomic status explains a

APPENDIX
Correlation Matrix of Key Measures

	(1)	(2)	(3)	(4)	(5)	(6)	(7)	(8)	(9)
Material Values:									
Overall (1)	1.0								
Centrality (2)	.82	1.0							
Happiness (3)	.72	.29	1.0						
Success (4)	.87	.64	.45	1.0					
Compulsive buying (5)	.37	.44	.26	.19	1.0				
Family structure (6)	.10	.08	.13	.05	.05	1.0			
Number of disruptions(7)	.17	.16	.20	.05	.15	-.74	1.0		
Age at initial disruption (8)[a]	-.32	-.43	-.05	-.23	-.35	na[b]	-.41	1.0	
Household Income (9)	.04	.15	-.18	.10	-.03	.42	-.02	-.34	1.0

[a]Age at initial disruption contains only 32 cases since only 32 respondents reported a family disruption. The sample size for all other reported measures in 143 cases.

[b]The correlation coefficient between family structure (6) and age at initial disruption (8) could not be computed due to the lack of variance in family structure (i.e., all disrupted) among the 32 respondents who experienced a family disruption.

---

substantial portion of the relationship between family structure and children's behavior and outcomes (Amato 1993; McLanahan 1985). However, most of these studies have investigated behavioral phenomena that are known to be highly influenced by income and social status, such as high school completion, teenage pregnancy and criminal behavior. This raises the issue of whether there is truly an inherent connection between household income and materialistic attitudes and compulsive buying. Consumer research has not established any strong linkages between financial resources and materialism or compulsive consumption. Both Belk (1985) and Wernimont and Fitzpatrick (1972) find no relationship between socioeconomic status and materialism. Likewise, research by both Hirschman (1992) and Faber and O'Guinn (1992) suggests that compulsive consumption is a phenomenon which afflicts persons of all socioeconomic strata.

Overall, our results are generally in line with the findings of family researchers, who typically note small but significant effects of the negative impact of family disruption upon children and young adults (Amato 1993; Flewelling and Bauman 1990). This study provides preliminary evidence of the effects of family disruption upon the consumption attitudes and behaviors of young adults. Given the importance of the consumption-related aspects of family life, this exploratory investigation offers a contribution to both consumer behavior research by introducing this area, and to family research by extending this stream to include consumption phenomena.

Study Limitations and Future Research Issues

While these findings suggest the presence of such a relationship, they do not indicate the mechanism by which this relationship arises. For example, was this relationship present prior to the family disruption itself? Furthermore, if these relationships are truly the products of disruption, is family breakup the causal force, or are the effects of disruption mediated by concomitant factors? While these empirical questions can be resolved only by future research, we believe that our initial results provide a number of interesting findings about the nature of the relationship between family disruption and both materialism and compulsive consumption among the young adults in our sample.

Since this study represents an exploratory investigation into an area of research largely unexplored in our field, it naturally entails

a number of limitations, many of which point to important and interesting issues for future research. First, as noted earlier, our respondents represent a very homogeneous, relatively affluent and highly educated sample. In specific, our sampling frame effectively screens out many of those who likely demonstrate the most severe effects of family disruption. Therefore, we believe that our study represents a conservative test of these hypotheses and that the differences between young adults of intact vs. disrupted families may be much greater in a more heterogeneous population. Considering these limitations, we recommend that future research attempt to replicate this study with a more heterogeneous sample.

A second sample-related issue is the relatively small number (n=32) of individuals from disrupted families. This small sample limits both the measurement of family disruption and the analysis of the sample itself. Collection of a larger sample would allow for finer distinctions between individuals from various family backgrounds. For example, family researchers have commented on the distinction between single-parent families due to divorce and single-parent families created by the death of a parent. In particular, widowed mothers typically have greater access to both financial and emotional support than their divorced counterparts (Cherlin 1992). Moreover, both family and consumer researchers have noted that socialization dynamics differ among boys and girls (Cherlin 1992; Moschis 1987). Thus, a larger sample would permit examination of differences in behaviors and attitudes among these different subgroups and would provide greater confidence in our findings.

We also acknowledge the shortcomings of our attempts to measure family disruption. In specific, our assessments of age at initial disruption and total number of family disruptions represent only indirect measures of differences in family processes that affect children's development (Kurdek and Fine 1993). As noted by Amato (1993), family disruption often leads to an increase in family stressors and a decrease in family resources. In order to properly assess the importance of these mediating processes, future research should attempt to directly measure both the key resources and stressors that characterize disrupted families (see Amato 1993 and Cherlin 1992 for more information about resources and stressors in disrupted families).

A final limitation centers on our attempt to control for differences in economic resources. While we found a significant income gap between these two groups, household income did not mediate any of the relationships between our measures of family disruption and materialism and compulsive consumption. Perhaps the effect of economic resources may be non-linear, so a difference of $10,000 may have greater impact on family making $15,000, than on a family earning $50,000. Since most of our respondents from disrupted families were financially privileged, our sample may not provide a fair assessment of the effects of household income by excluding those persons most likely to be adversely impacted by a reduction in financial resources. The household income measure also does not distinguish between the socioeconomic determinants and the consequences of the events leading to family disruption (Thompson, Hanson and McLanahan 1992). Consequently, if this clear income difference was a cause of family disruption, rather than a consequence, it may be quite important, while not readily apparent in this study. Therefore, although we found no direct relation between income and materialism and compulsive consumption, there may be important indirect effects between income and these attitudes and behaviors. Future research could help clarify the relationship between financial resources and consumption attitudes and behaviors by employing longitudinal studies which track a family's financial resources over time.

CONCLUSION

This initial research effort represents an exploratory investigation of the potential impacts of family disruption on consumption attitudes and behaviors, and has empirically uncovered a linkage between family disruption and the presence of a higher degree of socially undesirable attitudes and behavior among young adults. In addition to the relevance of these findings for the research community, this area of research presents consumer researchers with an opportunity to enhance the lives of the individuals most severely impacted by family disruption, namely the children of disruption. For example, a better understanding of the development of undesirable consumption attitudes and behaviors within various family structures would allow researchers to help businesses and government agencies develop public policy to assist children in learning more socially conscious consumption patterns. However, these findings must remain cautionary since a causal relationship is not fully apparent. Clearly, much work needs to be done in order to sort out the specific factors related to family disruption which underlie this relationship, as well as the processes by which they operate.

REFERENCES

Ahlburg, Dennis A. and Carol J. De Vita (1992), "New Realities of the American Family," *Population Bulletin*, 47 (August).

Ahuja, Roshan and Kandi Stinson (1993), "Female Headed Single Parent Families: An Exploratory Study of Children's Age in Family Decision Making," *Advances in Consumer Research*, Vol. 20, Leigh McAlister and Michael L. Rothschild, eds. Provo: UT, Association for Consumer Research, 469-474.

Amato, Paul R. (1993), "Children's Adjustment to Divorce: Theories, Hypotheses, and Empirical Support," *Journal of Marriage and the Family*, 55 (February), 23-38.

An, Chong-Bum, Robert Haveman, and Barbara Wolfe (1993), "Teen Out-of-Wedlock Births and Welfare Receipt: The Role of Childhood Events and Economic Circumstances," *Review of Economics and Statistics*, 75 (May), 195-208

Bandura, Albert and Walter Mischel (1965), "Modification of Self-Imposed Delay of Reward Through Exposure to Life Symbolic Models," *Journal of Personality and Social Psychology*, (2), 698-705.

Belk, Russell W. (1985), "Materialism: Trait Aspects of Living in the Material World," *Journal of Consumer Research*, 12 (December), 265-280.

Bumpass, Larry L. (1984), "Children and Marital Disruption: A Replication and Update," *Demography*, 21 (February), 71-82.

Carlson, Les and Sanford Grossbart (1988), "Parental Style and Consumer Socialization," *Journal of Consumer Research*, 15 (June), 77-94.

Cherian, Varghese I. (1989), "Academic Achievement of Children of Divorced Parents," *Psychological Reports*, 64, 355-358.

Cherlin, Andrew (1992), *Marriage, Divorce, Remarriage*, Revised edition. Cambridge, MA: Harvard University Press.

Churchill, Gilbert A., Jr. and George P. Moschis (1979), "Television and Interpersonal Influences on Adolescent Consumer Learning," *Journal of Consumer Research*, 6 (June), 23-35.

Corfman, Kim P. and Donald R. Lehmann (1987), "Models of Cooperative Group Decision-Making and Relative Influence: An Experimental Investigation of Family Purchase Decisions," *Journal of Consumer Research*, 14 (June), 1-13.

Craig, Grace J. (1993), *Human Development*, 6th ed. New York: McGraw Hill.

Crockett, Lisa J., David J. Eggebeen, and Alan J. Hawkins (1993), "Father's Presence and Young Children's Behavioral and Cognitive Adjustment," *Journal of Family Issues*, 14 (September), 355-377.

Elder, Glen H. (1974), *Children of the Great Depression: Social Change in Life Experience*. Chicago: University of Chicago Press.

Erickson, Eric H. (1982), *The Life Cycle Completed: A Review*. New York: Norton.

Faber, Ronald J. and Thomas C. O'Guinn (1992), "A Clinical Screener for Compulsive Buying," *Journal of Consumer Research*, 19 (December), 459-469.

Flewelling, Robert L. and Karl E. Bauman (1990), "Family Structure as a Predictor of Initial Substance Use and Sexual Intercourse in Early Adolescence," *Journal of Marriage and the Family*, 52 (February), 171-181.

Fuchs, Victor R. (1983), *How We Live: An Economic Perspective on Americans from Birth through Death*. Cambridge, MA: Harvard University Press.

Hirschman, Elizabeth C. (1992), "The Consciousness of Addiction: Toward a General Theory of Compulsive Consumption," *Journal of Consumer Research*, 19 (September), 155-179.

Isaacs, Susan (1935), "Property and Possessiveness," *British Journal of Medical Psychology*, 15 (1), 67-78.

Kachigan, Sam Kash (1991), *Multivariate Statistical Analysis: A Conceptual Overview*, 2nd ed. New York: Radius Press.

Kerckhoff, Alan C. (1976), "Patterns of Marriage and Family Formation and Dissolution," *Journal of Consumer Research*, 2 (March), 261-275.

Kourilsky, Marilyn and Trudy Murray (1981), "The Use of Economic Reasoning to Increase Satisfaction with Family Decision Making, *Journal of Consumer Research*, 8 (September), 183-188.

Kurdek, Lawrence A. and Mark A. Fine (1993), "The Relation Between Family Structure and Young Adolescent's Appraisals of Family Climate and Parenting Behavior," *Journal of Family Issues*, 14 (June), 279-290.

McLanahan, Sara S. (1985), "Family Structure and the Reproduction of Poverty," *American Journal of Sociology*, 90 (4), 873-901.

_____ and Karen Booth (1989), "Mother-only Families: Problems, Prospects and Politics," *Journal of Marriage and the Family*, 51 (August), 557-580.

Martinson, Brian C. and Lawrence L. Wu (1992), "Parent Histories: Patterns of Change in Early Life," *Journal of Family Issues*, 13 (September), 351-377.

Moore, Roy L. and George P. Moschis (1981), "The Effects of Family Communication and Mass Media Use on Adolescent Consumer Learning," *Journal of Communication*, 31 (Fall), 42-51.

Moschis, George P. (1987), *Consumer Socialization: A Life-Cycle Perspective*. Lexington, MA: Lexington Books.

Murphy, Patrick E. and William A. Staples (1979), "A Modernized Family Life Cycle," *Journal of Consumer Research*, 6 (June), 12-22.

Nicosia, Francesco M. and Robert N. Mayer (1976), "Toward a Sociology of Consumption," *Journal of Consumer Research*, 3 (September), 65-75.

O'Guinn, Thomas C. and Ronald J. Faber (1989), "Compulsive Buying: A Phenomenological Exploration," *Journal of Consumer Research*, 16 (September), 147-157.

Richins, Marsha L. and Scott Dawson (1992), "A Consumer Values Orientation for Materialism and Its Measurement: Scale Development and Validation," *Journal of Consumer Research*, 19 (December), 303-316.

Rook, Dennis (1987), "The Buying Impulse," *Journal of Consumer Research*, 14 (September), 189-199.

Rubin, Rose M., Bobye J. Riney, and David J. Molina (1990), "Expenditure Pattern Differentials Between One-Earner and Dual-Earner Households: 1972-1973 and 1984," *Journal of Consumer Research*, 17 (June), 43-52.

Rutter, Michael (1983), "Stress, Coping and Development: Some Issues and Some Questions," in *Stress, Coping and Development in Children*, N. Garmezy and M. Rutter, eds. New York: McGraw Hill, p. 1-42.

Schaninger, Charles M. and William D. Danko (1993), "A Conceptual and Empirical Comparison of Alternative Household Life Cycle Models," *Journal of Consumer Research*, 19 (March), 580-594.

Thompson, Elizabeth, Thomas Hanson, and Sara S. McLanahan (1992), "Family Structures and Child Well-Being: Economic Resources vs. Parent Socialization," NSFH Working Paper No. 29, University of Wisconsin-Madison Center for Demography and Ecology, Madison, WI 53706.

Walls, Richard T. and Tennie S. Smith (1970), "Development of Preferences for Delayed Reinforcement in Disadvantaged Children," *Journal of Educational Psychology*, 61 (2), 118-123.

Wernimont, Paul F. and Susan Fitzpatrick (1972), "The Meaning of Money," *Journal of Applied Psychology*, 56 (3), 218-226.

Wilkes, Robert E. (1995), "Redefining Family in American: Characteristics and Expenditures of Single-Parent Families," in *Marketing Theory and Applications*, Vol. 6, David Stewart and Naufel Vilcassim, eds. Chicago: American Marketing Association, 270-276.

Wu, Lawrence L. and Brian C. Martinson (1993), "Family Structure and the Risk of Premarital Births," *American Sociological Review*, 58 (April), 210-232.

Understanding Consumer Responses To Cause-Related Marketing

Ida E. Berger, Queen's University
M. Peggy Cunningham, Queen's University

Cause-related marketing (CRM) involves the affiliation of corporate 'for-profit' marketing activities with the fund raising requirements of 'not-for-profit' organizations. Typically cause-related marketing campaigns try to induce the consumer to buy a specific good or service by promising, in return, to donate to a specific cause. However, many variations of this basic format have been derived. For example, money is not the only form of donation. Firms have provided business expertise and seconded corporate personnel to help run a charity or fund raising event.

Although the growth of CRM campaigns has been phenomenal, little is known about how consumers respond to or assess these marketing tactics or how different campaign characteristics influence these assessments. Even a cursory examination of current practice raises a number of questions. In particular, is cause-related marketing a new type of marketing or just another promotional technique? What features characterize strong versus weak cause claims in the eyes of consumers? What attributions do consumers make about CRM appeals? Do consumers view these marketing practices as a form of charity and a manifestation of corporate social responsibility or only as exploitive techniques for increasing business profits? What types of product/cause pairings work together most effectively. How do CRM campaigns affect attitudes and purchase intentions? More generally, how do consumers process the information in CRM appeals and what theories can be brought to bear to address these questions?

The goal of this special topic session was to address these questions. Increasing knowledge of consumer responses to CRM appeals is important for marketers designing persuasive campaigns as well as for causes seeking to maximize their fund raising potential. The session was designed to help researchers share their learning as well as to see different methodologies and theoretical bases applied to related research questions.

Following a brief introduction to the topic by Peggy Cunningham, Pam Ellen presented an overview of a program of research in which she and colleagues Lois Mohr and Deborah Webb are exploring the effects of type of offer and degree of consumer/corporate participation in giving on consumer evaluations. They use an attribution theory framework to understand why certain types of offers, or certain types of consumer/corporate relationships are preferred. Their results show that more positive evaluations are related to attributions of genuine altruism and that donations of products, particularly products unrelated to a marketers business, are preferred to cash.

Next, Michal Strahilevitz described a series of experiments in which she examined the interaction between type of charitable contribution, the nature of the product and the magnitude of the contribution to determine the effectiveness of CRM campaigns. She reported that cause claims are more effective when paired with 'decadent luxuries' explaining that cause associations offset the guilt associated with consuming decadent products.

Peggy Cunningham and Ida Berger presented the results of a study (conducted with Robert Kozinets) in which they treated "cause strength" as an independent variable. Contrasting dual process models (e.g. ELM) with a motivation, opportunity and ability framework (McInnis, Moorman and Jaworski 1991) they traced how consumers process CRM appeals. Their experiment manipulated cause strength, brand involvement and brand argument strength in order to examine the extent to which causes act as peripheral cues, processing motivators, arguments or biasing mechanisms. They reported that cause executions increase processing motivation and thereby persuasion, raising issues regarding the dynamic nature of involvement.

Minette Drumwright, the discussion leader for the session, raised important questions for future consideration including: (1) whether or not the phenomenon needed reconceptualization, (2) how many consumers would respond to cause claims, (3) whether or not the effects of causes were due to their novelty and whether this effect would wear-out, (4) do cause claims affect stakeholders other than a firm's customers, (5) what strategies are appropriate for cause-product alliances, (6) will cause claims have deleterious effects on either the firm or society, and (7) what motivates managers to utilize CRM programs?

The session generated provocative discussion and raised other issues including the possibility that "altruism" might be an individual difference variable suitable for segmenting markets.

Is Relationship Marketing Culturally Bound: A Look at GuanXi in China

Lee C. Simmons, University of Texas at Arlington
James M. Munch, University of Texas at Arlington

ABSTRACT

Many companies currently emphasize the importance of a relationship marketing orientation. In addition, globalization of markets continues to become more prevalent. It is within this context that researchers have tried to develop frameworks for understanding "relationship." In this paper we argue that understanding how business works in the United States does not necessarily help to understand the meaning of relationship cross culturally. To demonstrate our position we examine the concept of guanxi which defines "relationship" in China.

Sheth and Parvatiyar (1993) suggest that the United States is undergoing a paradigm shift towards a relationship orientation and away from a transactions orientation. This shift is changing the structure of the market and the way people think about it. In transaction-based markets, competition is viewed as the sole driver of value creation. Independence of market actors is the mechanism that creates an efficient system. In relationship-oriented markets, firms begin to integrate suppliers, lateral relationships, buyers, and internal partnerships (Morgan and Hunt 1994). These relational partners examine each others ideas, goals and abilities in search of overlaps and synergies.

RELATIONSHIP MARKETING IN CHINA: GUANXI

Although it is undergoing a change from a centrally planned to a market driven system, China (as well as many Third World countries) continues to function as a transactional market. Competition and independent market transactions operate within constraints set forth by the government. Historically, Chinese companies have been able to sell all that they are able to manufacture. However, as China becomes more market driven, there are concerns about market supply and demand. Successful market transactions are relying more heavily on business relationships. Compared to U.S. industry however, China's relationship orientation among businesses, managers and government is unique.

The Chinese system of relationships is referred to as guanxi or guanxi wang. If you ask someone who speaks Chinese what guanxi means they will tell you it means relationships. This is true only in a limited sense. If the characters for guanxi are translated directly they mean "joined chain". Wang means net or large interconnected web. The character for wang even looks like a web or net. Thus, when Chinese use the expression "guanxi wang" they mean an interconnected web of relationships. In his book *Chinese Negotiating Style*, Lucien Pye describes guanxi;

"Coupled with the Chinese concern about face is their concept of guanxi-a word for which there is no English equivalent. It can be described as a special relationship individuals have with each other in which each can make unlimited demands on the other. Guanxi, which is closely linked psychologically to the Chinese sense of dependency and of face, rules that if there is some kind of a bond between two people-whether as close as blood relation or as distant as being classmates or coprovincials, or even having grandparents who were friends-then each can tax the other and expect automatic special consideration (p. 101)."

In China, guanxi may define both personal and business friendships. Although personal friendships may exist without guanxi, business friendships are difficult for Chinese people to express in the absence of a guanxi relationship. It is both the way they understand and define a relationship. Pye (1968) refers to interpersonal relationships as "...a powerful web that holds a person in place and gives him a basic orientation in life." Such relationships are fragile. Almost no other culture gives such high importance to maintaining interpersonal relationships. The Chinese believe that success depends more on your guanxi and less on personal effort. Existence in society is defined by relationships with others; one cannot change the environment but must harmonize with it (Brunner, Chen, Sun, and Zhou 1989).

Obligation and China's Shame Culture

Another dimension of guanxi is obligation. Obligations are more important than emotional attachments in the guanxi relationship. For example, if a Chinese person is asked to describe his relationships he is able to talk at great length about their obligations, complexities, gradations and value while seemingly oblivious to emotional attachments in those relationships. They are also able to describe relationships in emotional terms, and may do so in a completely unemotional manner.

Pye points out that frequently the weaker person in a guanxi relationship has more power as the stronger feels obligation and the weaker has less to give. Face is the reason that the weaker person has more power in a guanxi relationship. As Brunner and You (1988) explain, "... persons of subordinate positions can take advantage of the fact that superiors must maintain their "face" at their high level." In other words, those in high position have more face to maintain and must expend more effort to maintain it. It must be remembered that China is not a "guilt culture" as the West rather they are a "shame culture" and someone would find themselves extremely uncomfortable if shamed without giving a request to someone in their guanxi relationship. The difference between a guilt culture and a shame culture is the locus of control (Hofstede 1991). In a guilt culture the locus is internal. What someone feels about their actions and them self is of all importance. Therefore, it is important for society to inculcate the "proper" ideas of what is right and wrong in childhood so the adult will feel guilty if something is done that it against societies rules. In a shame culture the locus is external and the child is taught that what other people think about your actions is the most important. The child is taught that if you bring shame on yourself it reflects to your family and society will not believe you worthy of decent treatment. As a consequence the family who was supposed to inculcate values is also not worthy of decent treatment. If you do something honorable then not only are you of high worth but so is your family. In a shame culture law isn't as important as not shaming your family. If everyone behaves this way, as they would in a shame culture, laws are more difficult to enforce. Particularly if these laws don't make sense in a culture or if there is no public perception of their need or efficacy. This could be part of the reason that intellectual property laws are so difficult to enforce and find consensus for in China and Asia.

How Trust is Kept by Face

Trust and subsequently commitment are key elements of guanxi relationships. Partners must work at preserving these relationships by cooperating with exchange partners. In addition, the partners must also have a commitment to the system that provides for these alliances. This is similar to US businessmen who have a commitment to the system in which they work. Trust develops when one party has confidence in an exchange partner's reliability and integrity. Partners are willing to rely on others in the "joined chain net". Face and need keep them honest. If he does not keep his commitments then his "face will have dirt on it".

The concept of face is more than what Westerners understand. It includes what you think of yourself, how you work with others, what others think of you, what kinds and levels of relationships you have. Simply put, face is the process by which one gains and maintains status as well as moral reputation (Brunner and You 1988). When you "put gold" on someone's face it enhances one's status and reputation. When you "throw dirt on their face" these aspects are negatively affected.

Giving face can also be thought of as flattery and Westerners are not accustomed to seeing flattery in a positive light. Although people in the United States are happy to receive and give it, flattery does not have the same meaning in the US as in China. In China flattery means enhancing one's reputation. For example, it is making sure that you show by your actions that someone is high in your estimation. Unexpectedly, the first author gained gold on his face from an assistant by paying for a short cab ride during a rainstorm in Shanghai. Ever after, she appreciated that he thought enough of her to even offer. Things went much more smoothly in encounters with her from that point forward.

The most classic Chinese examples of giving face occur with respect to dinner meetings and gift giving. At dinner let the important person sit next to you, give him a toast (gang bei, which literally translates to "touch cup" or "cheers"), never refuse a toast (only take a small sip). When toasting first, toast his company's future then toast your (joint) venture's future, then toast his health and his family.

Some additional ways to show respect for Chinese people during dinner meetings include: waiting for them to start especially if they are late (being late shows your high position); giving them the important seat (usually the one facing south or the center seat); letting them sit first; having a picture taken with you holding their hand; and most importantly, never use their given name when speaking. Always use their both their name and title.

Giving gifts is also important. Small personal business use gifts or souvenirs are best (they prefer 24 karat gold). Give everyone in the group the same gift, save the big gift for the head man and present it in private. There are some notable exceptions. For example, never give a clock as the word is a homonym for the end of something such as life or the relationship and is seen as a negative superstition.

Giving face frequently and in the right manner enhances guanxi. Never forget that a guanxi relationship means a lifetime commitment. Partners expect you to remember them and possibly do small favors for them when you are in China. Although this is a big obligation remember that partners are under the same obligation to you and you can use it to further your interests.

The Language of Friendship and Negotiation

The Chinese are masters at developing friendships and creating an environment for negotiation. They socialize while eating and drinking, but a major goal of this socialization is relationship building. Excellent foods of some rarity or expense, are used to honor guests. It is important that the host himself, serve the choicest morsels to key guests. Such meals are used to "size up" others and for them to do the same of you. Both host and guest must be assured that they are of the same social level, that they can be trusted and that each is the kind of person he wants in his chain of relationships. These meals are not for the granting of favors or power they are only to gather impressions of each other to see who gets into the guanxi wang, the group that you will pull from to form the virtual organizations needed to get something accomplished. It is very difficult to remove someone from your guanxi wang after all of the people have become interconnected so they must be careful who is admitted.

People have different groups for different kinds of things. As new people in any one chain get to know each other they will go through the person who is the power center directly rather than come through you as a broker. If this happens you lose much power. You are left out of the loop and the person requesting something no longer owes anything for the favor you may have brokered from someone else. During these meals much must be considered before making someone your partner and when you add someone to your guanxi wang you commit yourself to long-term interdependence. There is much thrust and parry at these "events", it goes on even when Westerners have a meal with Chinese business associates. If the Westerner does not see it the Chinese will think that the Westerner does not understand their cultural imperatives and be less interested in doing business with the Westerner.

Chinese are consummate negotiators because they must do it every day in every aspect of their lives. It is one of the top things on their mind at all times. The jockeying and maneuvering that most Americans find only in office politics is used by the Chinese to hone their skills in every aspect of their life, including their home life.

There is obviously a learning curve in the power brokering process. Early in one's career, the "Chuppy" (authors' term for Chinese yuppie) must make friends and do many favors to build his network (guanxi wang) and become part of other networks. The Chinese tend to see the manipulation of human relationships as the natural and normal approach for accomplishing most things in life (Pye 1968).

In summary, while relationship marketing in the United States is defined by firms' interdependencies and synergies, the meaning of relationship in China is defined by guanxi. Key dimensions of guanxi include a sense of personal obligation with unemotional ties, trust, and face. Chinese history suggests that guanxi has been the dominant form of friendship, negotiation, and transactional governance in China for centuries (Davies, Leung, Luk, and Wong 1995). We now examine the GuanXi Wang, the Chinese network of joined relationships.

GUANXI WANG

Guanxi wang is a form of strategic alliances among individuals. It is more than an exchange of information, it is also exchange and access to resources. Not only do people exchange what they have, they also exchange what other partners have. In order to meet their obligations people do things for those they don't know because someone in their guanxi wang used some of their available guanxi capital in that asking. Although guanxi is referred to as simple influence peddling (Wall 1990), guanxi is both how the Chinese do business and how their relationships work. Guanxi is not only an appropriate activity, but also is a part of Chinese culture.

One current type of U.S. strategic alliance formation is the trend toward "virtual organizations"— pulling people together as needed for a project. Chinese are the masters of these virtual organizations. These interrelationships have been around for cen-

FIGURE

Supplier Partnerships

Relational exchanges between manufacturers and their goods suppliers.
JIT procurement and TQM such as ISO 9000. (Frazier, Spekman & O'Neal, 1988; O'Neal 1989)

Relational exchanges involving service providers. Advertising or market research agencies and their respective clients. (Beltramini & Pitta, 1991, Moorman, Zaltman & Deshpande, 1992)

In a society with nearly all businesses owned by the government, the only way to work is together. If the managers and those in charge of supplies do not have a relationship then very few goods get shipped. By getting the supplier into his guanxi wang, the manager will get what he needs. In China even electricity is in short supply.

Lateral Partnerships

Relationships between firms and their competitors, such as technology, co-marketing or global strategic alliances. (Nueno & Oosterveld, 1988; Bucklin & Sengupta, 1993; Ohmae, 1989)

Relational alliances between firms and non-profit organizations and public purpose partnerships. (Steckel & Simons, 1992)

Partnerships between firms and governmental enterprises for joint research or development. (Comer, O'Keefe & Chilenskas, 1980)

Within China there are few large scale co-marketing alliances, although there are technology and strategic competitors as they see it as losing power and having to give up perks that come with the guanxi type relationships. Working together is complicated since "face" must be considered. There must be agreement on all aspects of any project before it can advance. Alliances with non-profit organizations are usually for the avoidance of taxes.

Buyer Partnerships

Buyer Partnerships between firms and their ultimate customers. (Services Marketing, Berry, 1983).

Exchanges between the firm and intermediate customers Working partnerships in channels of distribution. (Anderson & Narus, 1990).

Whether a manager is dealing with an ultimate or intermediate customer, the receiving organization must keep the supplier happy through guanxi and by giving him face. The receiver must ensure that the supplier wants to send him the goods not only for the company, but also for his personal aggrandizement.

Internal Partnerships

Internal Partnerships between functional departments such as that between marketers and engineering. (Ruekert & Walker, 1987)

Relationships between a firm and its employees, such as internal marketing. (Arndt, 1983)

Exchanges between business units, subsidiaries, divisions or strategic business units. (Porter, 1987)

In China the difference between business units and functional departments is not always clear. They work together because those involved feel a need to maintain and give face to each other and because of obligations in their guanxi relationships. Employees will use the goods they can sell directly from their company to others to build their own guanxi.

---

turies and the forms are well established. As these relationships are formed and added to over one's life they become very formal. Even social relationships take on a formal air. Husbands and wives must act toward each other in specific ways defined by the relationship. Personal relationships become more formally structured, the formal and business relationships take on some friendlier aspects.

UNITED STATES AND CHINESE RELATIONSHIP MARKETING COMPARED

If we conceptualize relationships in China being a chain, or web, and relationships in the US as being channel-driven, we begin to appreciate how important the meaning of "relationship" is to

cross cultural business success. In a recent paper on global relationship marketing Morgan and Hunt (1994) present four dimensions of relationships among businesses in the United States. We now compare these differences. More detailed cites are provided in the Figure.

Supplier Relationships

In the US efficiency is a major focus of the business. We are concerned with eliminating waste of all kinds; time, materials, equipment, and workers. To this end the relationship becomes a close one so that the partners understand each others business and the problems they must overcome together. The needs and the decision making structure of each partner must be understood. This necessitates close and lasting relationships.

In China there is an entirely different definition of "relationship" between a firm and its suppliers. Firms are generally required by the government to work with certain suppliers. Only if a manager has sufficient power will he be able to convince his governmental controllers to let him work with a supplier whose manager is already in his guanxi wang. It is more likely that he will develop a guanxi relationship with the manager of a firm with which he is working than to start with such a relationship. There is no reason for commitment or close cooperation in new forced relationships.

Nonetheless, when firms are thrust together they must learn to trust each other and to commit to a relationship. Eventually they will feel obligated to give each other face and to cooperate within the guanxi wang. Interpersonal loyalties will develop, but not necessarily loyalties to the system. When a Taiwanese executive secretary was shown this article, she could not believe that business is done any other way than through guanxi type connections. Her quite innocent question was, "What benefit is there for US companies to work together if it is just the companies (who benefit) and not the managers?"

Lateral Relationships

Morgan and Hunt (1994) consider lateral relationships in the US a form of symbiotic or helpful marketing exchange. Competitors work together to use their unique skills to form a more potent partnership in the market. Only by linking can some high tech products be brought to the market. The cost has simply gotten too high for one company working alone. There must be a mutual benefit. Engineers and marketers must work together. Companies do worry about knowledge loss. Does the alliance move in a different area than they want to be involved? Not every company can be everywhere. Co marketing shares resources allowing entry into many markets at once with new or advanced products.

Chinese managers use the contacts that have come to them through lateral relationships to build their guanxi wang. Sometimes they form these alliances because of who may already be in their net, or who may be in the net of a friend. For the Chinese manager self goals come first. They have worked to build their personal power and they have no interest in giving up any of what they have so carefully developed. Partnerships with nonprofits are usually for the purpose of avoiding taxes. Since the government takes care of nearly everyone in the country, there is less imperative for companies to work with charities. Interestingly, in a shame culture if you don't donate money or time to help the handicapped there is no shame attached unless that person is a part of your family. Public image of the company is far less important than in the US.

Whether owned by the government or not, R&D is typically budgeted for and conducted internally. In this way no one gets access to information and the manager's power and prestige improves. Only when the government requires a firm to engage in R&D with another firm or when a manager cannot get sufficient funds to do it themselves will they develop an outside relationship. Even then it is a personal relationship, because how else can they trust each other?

Managers do not use their contacts to help the company or any alliances unless the company or alliances helps them personally in some way. It isn't that the manager is particularly selfish or greedy, it is the way the system works. This is how the manager in China gets to the top, by building power, not by making the company he works for richer.

Buyer Partnerships

In the US retaining customers by working with them to ensure their satisfaction is cheaper than continually prospecting for new customers. Also, the profit increases each year a customer stays. Customers that receive satisfactory service and commitment from a supplier will value the relationship and retain that partnership. Conversely, suppliers will better understand buyers' needs. They depend on each other and need the relationship.

Managers in China view buyer partnerships as a micro issue. Most markets have too many customers and too few goods. Because prices, until recently, were set by the government firms don't focus on customer satisfaction. There is always someone else that will purchase. Storing goods is not a cost when they own the factory and warehouse and the cost is already sunk. Instead it is the customer who must keep the seller happy in order to ensure delivery of goods. Naturally, having the customer wanting to keep you happy only makes your guanxi stronger.

Obviously there are some notable exceptions to the idea of a seller's market. These are generally in the areas of handicrafts, textiles and some building materials. These companies will use guanxi to get someone to purchase from them. For example, a friend of the first author is a manager in a large architectural firm that designs textile factories. She is frequently given free food, presents, and trips to "view" a firms wares in the hope that they will be specified in the architectural drawings. The relationship remains person to person for the benefit of the joined partners. Company to company gain is incidental.

Internal Partnerships

Traditionally employees in the US had job stability and enjoyed a long term partnership with their firm. More recently this perspective has changed as firms continue to downsize, merge, and so on. Employee-employer trust has declined dramatically.

Within the firm most interpersonal interaction is horizontal, informal, and moderately effective. Departments depend on each other to attain the firm's ultimate goals. The company is the product so the political paradigm must be maintained throughout the organization. Business units must work together to form and implement corporate strategy. Without trust and strong internal relationships effective strategies are neither formed nor implemented.

Most Chinese companies are controlled by the government and realize that their employees and managers are not committed to the firm. Employees are guaranteed lifetime employment and pay. Only recently has this begun to change. Companies are laying off workers, but the government still gives them their base pay each month. If they start their own business or work for another entrepreneur they give up their base salary and benefits, hospitalization and retirement. If they do start their own business or find a job with a foreign or entrepreneur firm they will need their guanxi connections all the more. Whether the employees and managers keep their lifetime job or move into/with some entrepreneur effort they are more committed to increasing their guanxi wang. Guanxi will usually go with them wherever they are. They can use it to improve their lot in life through these relationships. By helping their bosses they are the ones recommended for higher positions. The bosses realize that someone who they have helped move up will in turn help them later.

DISCUSSION

As firms race toward globalization of markets notions of business to business relationships, and relationship marketing, are becoming strategic criteria for both domestic and international business success. However, such a focus presumes that the meaning of relationship cross culturally is both consistent and well understood. The purpose of this paper is to help illustrate that "relationship" in China versus the United States is dramatically different.

Unlike the United States, Chinese relationships function under a guanxi system. Although there are different types of guanxi (Davies et. al 1995) in a business setting guanxi may best be thought of as a network of relationships established and fostered for self-gain.

A fundamental tenant of guanxi is obligation. Since China is a shame culture and the locus of control is not within you, but resides with others outside of you, failure to oblige brings shame on you and your family. "Getting dirt on one's face" is the result of not fulfilling these obligations. Renewing one's guanxi after having lost it is not an insignificant task.

Although US businessmen may consider themselves consummate negotiators, the Chinese are truly the masters at developing friendships and creating an environment for negotiation. Group decision making has been the norm for centuries. One interesting reason for this negotiation style is that no one wants to take complete credit (or blame) for the negotiation outcome. A successful outcome puts "gold" on everyone's face while a failure spreads the "dirt" around.

Business alliances in China are structured as GuanXi Wang—joined-chain networks. Unlike the United States they are not customer or channel driven, but are the result of personal relationships. Market forces such as supply and demand are relegated to secondary status.

Over three decades ago Hall's (1960) seminal work highlighted our shortsightedness regarding cross cultural business dealings. Unfortunately, it appears that we continue to suffer from cross cultural myopia when we assume a common cross cultural understanding of "relationship."

REFERENCES

Anderson, J. and Narus, J. (1990), "A Model of Distributor Firm and Manufacturer Firm Working Partnerships", *Journal of Marketing* Vol. 54 (January).

Arndt, J. (1983), "The Political Economy Paradigm: Foundation for Theory Building in Marketing", *Journal of Marketing* Vol. 54 (Fall).

Beltramini, R. and Pitta, D. (1991), "Underlying Dimensions and Communications Strategies of the Advertising Agency-Client Relationship", *International Journal of Advertising* Vol. 10.

Berry, L. (1983), "Relationship Marketing" in *Emerging Perspectives on Services Marketing*, Berry, L., Shostack, G. L. and Upah, R. Eds Chicago: American Marketing Association

Bucklin, L. and Sengupta, S. (1983), "Organizing Successful Co-Marketing Alliances", *Journal of Marketing* Vol. 57 (April).

Brunner, James A. and You, Wang, (1988) "Chinese Negotiating and the Concept of Face", *Journal of International Consumer Marketing* Vol. 1(1).

_____ , Chen, J., Sun, C., and Zhou, N. (1989), "The Role of Guanxi in Negotiations in the Pacific Basin", *Journal of Global Marketing* Vol. 3(2).

Comer, J., O'Keefe, R. and Chilenskas, A. (1980), "Technology Transfer from Government Laboratories to Industrial Markets", *Industrial Marketing Management* Vol. 9.

Davies, H., Leung, T. K. P., Luk, S. T. K., and Wong, Y. (1995), "The Benefits of "Guanxi", *Industrial Marketing Management* 24.

Frazier, G., Spekman, R. and O'Neal, C. (1988), "Just-In-Time Exchange Relationships in Industrial Markets", *Journal of Marketing* Vol. 52 (October).

Hall, E. T. (1960), "The Silent Language in Overseas Business", *Harvard Business Review* Vol. 38 (May-June).

Hofstede, G. (1991), *Cultures and Organizations*, Software of the Mind McGraw-Hill.

Morgan, R., and Hunt, S. (1994), "The Commitment-Trust Theory of Relationship Marketing", *Journal of Marketing* Vol. 58 (July).

Moorman, C., Zaltman, G. and Deshpande, R. (1992), "Relationships Between Providers and Users of Market Research: The Dynamics of Trust Within and Between Organizations", *Journal of Marketing Research* Vol. 29 (August).

O'Neal, C. (1989), "JIT Procurement and Relationship Marketing", *Industrial Marketing Management* Vol. 18.

Nueno, P. and Oosterveld, J. (1988), "Managing Technology Alliances", *Long Range Planning* Vol. 21.

Ohmae, K. (1989), "The Global Logic of Strategic Alliances", *Harvard Business Review* (May-June).

Porter, M. (1987), "From Competitive Advantage to Corporate Strategy", *Harvard Business Review* (May-June).

Pye, L. (1992), *Chinese negotiating Style Commercial Approaches and Cultural Principles*, New York: Quorum Books.

_____ (1968), *The Spirit of Chinese Politics a Psychocultural Study of the Authority Crisis in Political Development*, Cambridge MA: The M.I.T. Press

Sheth, J., and Parvatiyar, A. (1993), "The Evolution of Relationship Marketing", Emory Business School Paper at the Sixth Conference on: Historical Thought in Marketing (May).

Ruekert, R., and Walker, O. (1987), "Marketing's Interaction With Other Functional Units: A Conceptual Framework and Empirical Evidence", *Journal of Marketing* Vol. 51 (January).

Steckel, R. and Simons R. (1992), *Doing Best by Doing Good*, New York: Dutton Books.

Wall, J. (1990), "Managers in the People's Republic of China", *Academy of Management Executive*, Vol. 4 No. 2.

Private Labels and Consumer Benefits: The Brazilian Experience

Suzana de M. Fontenelle, University of Houston/EAESP-FGV
Inês Pereira, EAESP-FGV

ABSTRACT

Grocery products commercialized under private labels provide benefits to consumers in more developed countries. With the emergence of private labels in supermarkets, consumers can buy, essentially, good quality products at prices that are lower than the prices charged by the leading brands. These benefits are particularly relevant when considering less developed countries where consumers with lower levels of income, generally, comprise the majority of the population.

The purpose of this paper is to examine whether the benefits derived from the purchase of private labels in more developed countries can be extended to the context of less developed countries.

A historic overview of the evolution of private labels in Brazilian supermarkets is presented and an exploratory study is conducted with Brazilian supermarket managers. Research propositions are examined and directions for future research are suggested.

INTRODUCTION

The growth of the food retailing industry has been sustained by its expansion into international markets and private labels (PLs) have increasingly become an important part of retailers' growth strategy. Private labels share of food retailers' sales is rising steadily in supermarket chains across Europe. In the United States, the share of private label products' in the total supermarket sales of packaged groceries have increased from 15.3% in 1988 to 19.7% in 1993 (The Economist 1995, Retailing Survey p.11). However, little is known about the evolution of PLs in less developed countries (Pereira 1991).

Research has shown that, in general, the quality of the products commercialized under PLs is equivalent to the quality of products commercialized with the manufacturers' brands (MBs). Although PL products are similar to the goods commercialized with MBs, they are, commonly, sold at lower prices (Richardson, Dick, and Jain 1994; Swan 1974). Thus, PLs provide benefits to consumers, who can buy, essentially, the same products at lower prices. These benefits are particularly relevant when considering less developed countries (LDCs), where low income segments, generally, comprise the majority of the population.

PLs studies on the evolution of PLs have indicated that, historically, the emergence of PLs coincide with the attainment of higher levels of economic concentration in the retail sector (Borden 1967; Chernatony 1989; McGoldrick 1987). Work by the Boston Consulting Group shows that the share of PLs in overall food sales is directly proportional to market concentration (The Economist 1995). Other studies have examined the characteristics of the marketing mix for PLs, and their consumers' profiles, mainly, in the United States and in the UK (Jain 1985, Stern 1970 and Shawn 1974).

How have PLs evolved in less developed countries? Has the evolution of PLs in LDCs departed from the experience of their European and American counterparts? Have consumers in LDC's benefited from the lower prices offered by PLs?

The purpose of this paper is to address these research questions in the context of Brazilian supermarkets. The paper is organized as follows: first, a literature review on the evolution of PLs in more developed countries is presented (specifically, the evolution of PLs in the United States and in the UK). Next, research propositions are presented. The research propositions are examined in the following fashion: (a) the presentation of a historic overview of the evolution of PLs in Brazilian supermarkets; (b) in depth interviews with supermarket managers. Results are presented and directions for future research are suggested.

As the largest economy is Latin America and an important member of Mercosul[1], Brazil is a priority for American and European investments (Smith and Hinchberger 1994). The peculiarities in the evolution of retailing systems in LDCs have received insufficient attention in the literature (Jain 1985). This exploratory study about the Brazilian experience may contribute to reduce this gap in the consumer behavior literature.

LITERATURE REVIEW

Private Labels and Retail Economic Concentration

The evolution of PLs needs to be examined in the context of the power relationships in the food retailing industry. PLs evolved as a result of a more balanced relationship between manufacturers and retailers. Over the years, power shifted into the hands of retailers at the expense of manufacturers' clout.

With the rise of national advertising, manufacturers' brands (MBs) became widely recognized by consumers who elected their preferred brands and became loyal to them. Over time, manufacturers could exercise greater influence over the final demand for their products and secured a better bargaining position when dealing with retailers (Grant 1987). Retailers saw their margins drastically reduced, and their power to determine the prices to consumers depreciated (Borden 1967).

In the food retailing industry, supermarket chains were no longer able to compete, solely, on the basis of price. A way found by retailers to beat competition was through the establishment of PLs (Chernatony 1989).

PLs constitute an example of how supermarket chains started to incorporate functions traditionally held by manufacturers, such as: product distribution, packaging, advertising, and product development (PLs). PLs enable supermarket chains to face manufacturers' dominance over the final demand for products (Grant 1987). The two main advantages derived from the adoption of PLs by retailers are: bigger margins, and increased store loyalty.

The evolution of PLs parallels greater levels of concentration in the food retailing industry. In the UK where the food retailing industry is highly concentrated[2], it is estimated that the market share of PLs in 1965 was 10%; 26% in 1985, and 30% in 1995 (Chernatony 1989; The Economist 1995).

Evolution models of channels of distribution in the marketing literature suggest that trends observed in more developed countries (MDCs) will be repeated in other areas in earlier stages of economic development. The underlying premise of these models is that the marketing systems observed in MDCs provide a model for low

---

[1]Mercosul is the recently created common market comprising of : Argentina, Brazil, Paraguay and Uruguay.

[2]The top five food retailers in Britain have 60% of market participation (The Economist, 1995)..

income countries to emulate (Findlay and Paddison 1990). The rise of PLs in less developed countries would, then, mirror the evolution pattern of PLs in more developed countries.

The Marketing Mix of Private Labels

The quality of the products commercialized under PLs tends to be perceived by consumers as similar to the quality of products commercialized under MBs (McGoldrick 1985). According to Chernatony (1989), PLs have increased in quality in the last twenty years because retailers, looking to increase store loyalty and the attractiveness of their stores have been working with producers and making sure of the quality of the products (Shutte and Cook 1966). However, better quality has not translated into higher prices.

PLs are usually described in the literature as cheaper than their comparable MBs, with price differences ranging from 10% to 30% (Gelb 1980, Bond 1984, Bellizzi 1981). PLs lower prices can be sustained because: (a) retailers pay lower prices to producers[3]; (b) the increasing concentration of the food retailing industry enabled retailers to buy in large quantities and to bargain for better deals with producers (McGoldrick 1985 and Mason 1968); (c) the promotion of PLs tend to be less costly than the promotion of MBs and promotions of PLs tend to concentrate in store displays and in greater shelf space for PLs (Chernatony 1989).

The distribution of PLs is regarded as advantageous to retailers because: (a) supermarket chains are able to purchase the products at lower prices than the ones charged for comparable products commercialized under MBs; (b) PLs have lower costs of distribution compared to MBs; (c) profit margins are higher; (c) PLs attract customers to the store because they offer quality products at competitive prices (Uncles and Ellis 1989).

The Consumer of PLs

Research on the profile of PL consumers has presented 'level of income' as negatively related to the purchase of PLs. Conversely, 'level of education' has been positively associated with the purchase of PLs. Research has also pointed to the importance of 'price' for PL consumers and their store loyalty (for a summary of these studies see Table 1). The brief overview presented here on the growth of PLs and their basic characteristics fosters the conclusion that the emergence of PLs can be best understood as a result of, basically, three factors: (1) the concentration of the food retailing industry over the years promoted a shift in the power relationships between retailers and manufacturers which, in turn facilitated the appearance of PLs; (2) the ability of retailers to offer quality products at lower prices (3) price as a determinant for consumer brand choice, and consumers' loyalty to stores that are able to offer quality products at lower prices under their own PLs.

The following propositions reflect these conjectures:

P1: PLs emerge as a result of high levels of concentration in the food retailing sector in more developed countries (MDCs). Economic concentration combined with the modernization of the food retailing sector enable food retailers to face the competition from MBs. These characteristics of the evolution of PLs are expected to hold in the context of LDCs.

P2: In MDCs, the products commercialized under PLs have lower prices but equivalent quality standards relative to

their MBs counterparts. PLs are also characterized by lower distribution costs and low promotion costs. These characteristics of PLs are expected to hold in the context of LDCs.

P3: In MDCs, consumers of PLs are price sensitive, educated, and with lower levels of income. Consumers of PLs in LDCs are expected to have the same profile.

P4: Given that PLs offer quality products at lower prices, PLs provide benefits to consumers, who can buy, essentially, the same products at lower prices. These benefits are particularly relevant to consumers in developed countries (LDCs), where low income segments, generally, make up the majority of the population.

In order to investigate the first research proposition a historic overview of the development of the food retailing industry in Brazil is presented. In order to examine the remaining propositions, the results of an exploratory research, conducted with supermarket professionals, are presented .

Food Retailing and Supermarkets in Brazil

When supermarkets first appeared in Brazil in the mid fifties, the Brazilian economy was characterized by increasing industrial and urban development. Supermarkets were located in highly populated areas and catered to consumer segments with upper levels of income (Cyrillo 1987).

In its first years, supermarkets had a very modest contribution to retail sales in general. According to Cyrillo (1987) several factors contributed to this state of affairs: (a) supermarkets were not officially recognized and no special credit lines were available for investments in this sector; (b) other retailers did not view supermarkets as an interesting investment opportunity; (c) consumer buying habits were attuned with small independent stores (mom-and-pop stores, for example); (d) small independent stores had cost advantages due to lower rental costs, and lower maintenance and equipment costs; (e) until 1968, retailers were required to pay the IVC (Tax over sales and consignments) and constant increases in the IVC had stimulated tax evasion, a practice that could not be followed by supermarkets where payment was mechanically registered during the act of purchase and in the presence of the consumer; (e) the cost advantages derived from a decrease in labor costs in American supermarkets, were not observed in the Brazilian context which was characterized by a large labor supply at low wages.

Thus, supermarkets did not offer low prices to consumers and, consequently, did not obtain neither large sales volumes, nor high turnovers. Therefore, they did not have the necessary conditions to order large quantities from suppliers and to bargain for discounts.

Between 1968-1973 Brazil experienced a period of tremendous economic expansion, which came to be called 'The Brazilian miracle'. Income redistribution favored certain middle class consumer segments which stimulated growth in the retail sector. It was during this period that supermarkets began to offer more sophisticated services and personalized products to cater to the upper-middle/upper segments.

Supermarkets were favored by tax legislation which substituted the IVC[4] by the ICM (Tax over the circulation of goods), which was levied only over the added value of each stage of the commercialization process. With the ICM the operations over the transfer of goods within one same firm were no longer taxed, which decreased supermarket costs and increased their competitiveness.

Another incentive to the supermarket industry was the creation of credit lines for supermarkets, in 1971. However, only large

---

[3]Producers are able to charge lower prices to retailers because they utilize the firm's idle capacity in the production directed to PLs, and therefore, do not incur in additional costs of production.

TABLE 1
The Consumer of Private Labels—A Summary of the Literature

Articles	Product Category	Socio-Economic Profile			Buying Habits	
		Income	*Education*		*Price Sensibility*	*Store Loyalty*
Frank & Boyd Jr. (1965)	*Food products*	Negative *relationship*	Positive relationship		—	—
Myers (1967)	*Grocery products*	Weak *relationship*	Positive *relationship*		Positive relationship	—
Rao (1969)	*Coffee*	—	—		—	—
Coe (1971)	*Food products*	Negative relationship	—		Positive relationship	—
Burger & Schott (1972)	*Jams & Compotes*	—	—		Positive relationship	—
Rothe & Lamont (1973)	*Appliances*	Negative relationship	Negative relationship		Positive relationship	—
Bellizzi et al (1981)	*Food products*	—	—		Positive relationship	Weak relationship
Cunningham et al.	*Canned products*	Weak *relationship*	Positive *relationship*		Positve relationship	—
Uncles & Ellis (1989)	*Coffee*	—	—		—	Weak relationship

firms had access to credit due to the strict credit requirements. According to Cyrillo (1987) this was a deliberate governmental policy to stimulate the concentration of the food retailing industry as an attempt to increase its efficiency.

In fact, the growth of supermarket chains, encouraged by the government, facilitated the purchase of larger volumes, which in turn, had positive effects on the efficiency of the industry: on one hand, it diluted the fixed costs into a greater volume of operations, and on the other, it increased the bargaining power of the chains with suppliers. Only then supermarkets were able to start offering competitive prices.

The level of concentration of the food retailing industry in the 70's is illustrated in Table 2. The share of the 'modern' sector of the food retailing industry (represented by supermarkets) in the overall sales of the sector, jumped from 29.3% in 1970 to 70.5% in 1978.

However, the gains in efficiency enjoyed by supermarkets in the seventies were translated into benefits to the higher income

segments, which constituted the patronage of supermarkets at that time. Consumers with higher levels of income became the main beneficiaries of the lower prices offered by supermarkets (see Table 3).

Private Labels in Brazilian Supermarkets

Private labels first appeared in Brazil in the 70's. The supermarket chain 'Pão de Açúcar' was the pioneer in the introduction of private labels back in 1971. The chain introduced several private labels, none of them carrying the name of the store. In 1989, 'Pão de Açúcar' had 22 (different) private labels and began to reduce this number, and ended up keeping only four.

Several chains followed 'Pão de Açúcar's' path and created their private labels. For example, the 'Eldorado' chain started in the mid seventies and commercializes 28 items with 3 brands associated with the store name. Other chains also commercialize products under private labels: 'Paes Mendonça' (1974), 'Disco' (1977), 'Bompreço' (1978), and others.

The historic overview, presented above, illustrates the context in which the appearance of private labels in Brazilian supermarkets took place. In summary: the emergence of private labels in

---

[4]Tax over sales and consignments

TABLE 2
The Share of Retailers According to Number of Stores (NS) and Sales (S)

Year		Modern Sector	Traditional Sector
1970	(NS)	2.2	93.7
	(S)	19.3	70.7
1972	(NS)	3.3	96.7
	(S)	41.4	58.6
1974	(NS)	5.5	94.5
	(S)	58.0	42.0
1976/7	(NS)	6.0	94.0
	(S)	70.5	29.5
1977/8	(NS)	6.2	93.8
	(S)	67.7	32.3

Source: A.C. Nielsen 1977/78

TABLE 3
Consumer Buying Habits According to Income Levels (%)
(São Paulo, 1973)

Place of Purchase	Low	Medium	High
Supermarkets	9	29	51
Small independent stores	42	17	5
Street Markets	26	24	18
Bakeries	8	10	6
Butcher	10	2	1
Peddlers	3	1	1
Other	2	7	7

Source: *FIPE - USP*

Brazilian supermarkets coincides with the increasing level of concentration within the food retailing industry and increasing competition, as it is suggested in the first research proposition (P1).

An exploratory study was conducted to investigate the remaining research propositions. The methodology used in the exploratory study is presented in the next section.

METHODOLOGY

In depth interviews administered to professionals of four supermarket chains in the city of São Paulo. The convenience sample of supermarkets includes four of the seven supermarkets with the highest revenues in the country (see Table 4 for the profile of the supermarket chains included in the exploratory study).

Pão de Açúcar supermarket chain pioneered PLs in Brazil in the early 70's and, Paes Mendonça and Eldorado which have been working with PLs for more than 15 years. The French supermarket chain, Carrefour, although recently new to the Brazilian market has accumulated international experience with PLs.

Six professionals were interviewed: three PL managers and three merchandise managers. The supermarket managers were asked about: the price of PLs; quality of PLs; the profile of consumers of PLs (the questionnaire is presented in the Appendix). The results of the interviews are presented next.

RESULTS

When asked about the price differences between PLs and MBs all respondents indicated that PLs were cheaper than their comparable MBs. In the Eldorado chain, PLs tend to be 10%-15% cheaper than comparable MBs that are market leaders. In the Paes Mendonça chain, the price difference between PLs and the market leaders is between 5%-10%.

PLs in Pão de Açúcar are, on average, 10% cheaper but the price difference can be as much as 30% for certain products. Price differences between PLs and MBs vary according to inventory turnover. For those products with high turnover the price difference is smaller.

Carrefour PLs are 10% cheaper than the market leader. The 10% limitation is explained as a function of consumers' perceptions of the relationship between price and quality. At Carrefour they believe that if the price difference was greater than 10%, consumers would tend to think less of the quality of PLs.

TABLE 4
The Profile of Pão de Açúcar, Carrefour, Paes Mendonça and Eldorado

	Pão de Açúcar	Carrefour	Paes Mendonça	Eldorado
Ranking by Revenues	1	2	4	7
Number of stores	512	19	86	6
Number of check-outs	4758	1430	1750	405
Total sales area (m^2)	533	179	206	88

Fonte: A.C. Nielsen 1989/90

When asked about the specifications given to manufacturers for the production of PLs, respondents from Paes Mendonça, Eldorado and Carrefour indicated that the products commercialized under their PLs are exactly the same products commercialized under MBs. These supermarkets chains choose those manufacturers that produce the same products to the supermarkets' PLs as they do for their own brands. The chains, however, contract specialized services for the packaging and the labelling of their PLs.

At Pão de Açúcar, some of the PL products are equivalent to the MBs but, in some instances different product specifications are determined by the laboratory responsible for product development. The idea behind different product specifications is to increase the differentiation between PLs and MBs so that the consumers who prefer the PL products will remain loyal to the store.

Respondents were also asked about the quality control of PLs. Quality control was mentioned as an important factor to the success of their PLs. Carrefour contracted the services of a firm specialized in quality control which verifies, whether the contracted manufacturer actually has the potential to yield the products with the quality desired by Carrefour. Once a contract is signed between Carrefour and the manufacturer, periodic visits are made to ensure the desired quality.

At the Pão de Açúcar chain, reports from the laboratory responsible for product development, and quality control, are used in the decision making process of choosing a manufacturer for the PLs. A group of specialists from Pão de Açúcar observes the production process and once the products are delivered to Pão de Açúcar, product samples are taken for analysis.

Paes Mendonça and Eldorado have product specifications and quality control contract agreements with manufacturers. Once the products are delivered, there is an examination of the products.

When asked about how PLs were promoted, all respondents indicated 'displays' as the most utilized promotion tool for PLs. PLs are also promoted in the supermarket's features.

The use of advertising is not recommended to promote PLs. Although respondents agree that advertising exerts a positive influence on consumers' perceptions of MBs, the use of advertising would lead to an increase in costs and, consequently, increase the price of PLs. Moreover, according to the manager from Paes Mendonça, the use of advertising could lead to large increases in sales, forcing supermarkets to extend their contracts with the manufacturers of PLs. These longer contracts are viewed as undesirable because they would be riskier to supermarkets.

Respondents indicated that PLs have lower costs of distribution when compared to MBs. Lower distribution costs are possible because: purchases can be programmed, inventory can be kept at lower levels, and there is more efficient use of transportation.

When asked about the profile of the consumers of PLs, the respondents from Eldorado and Paes Mendonça described the consumer of PLs as 'very attentive to prices'; price sensitive consumers. The manager from Paes Mendonça believes that the consumer of PLs makes most of his/her shopping at Paes Mendonça

and who has a positive image of the chain and of the brands controlled by it.

The respondents from Carrefour and Pão de Açúcar described the consumer of PLs as someone who likes to try 'innovations'. He/she tends to trust his/her own capacity of judging the quality of a product. This consumer is usually: young, well educated and a considerable level of income.

Conversely, the consumer of MBs, according to respondents, is described as someone with lower levels of income, who tends to decide on the basis of emotion. His/her purchase decision is based on the brand name of the product. These consumers tend to trust the leading brands and, consequently, tend to purchase them.

Analysis of the Propositions

Based on the information contained in: (a) the overview of the evolution of supermarkets and their PLs in Brazil; (b) the in depth interviews with supermarket managers; an analysis of the research propositions is presented.

The overview of the evolution of PLs in Brazilian supermarkets substantiates the proposition that: the relationship between the concentration of the food retailing industry and the emergence of PLs in supermarkets in MDCs is also observed in the Brazilian context (P1).

In regard to the characteristics of PLs (P2), private labels in Brazilian supermarkets seem to possess similar characteristics to their counterparts in MDCs. Brazilian PLs are cheaper than MBs and maintain the quality level of MBs.

Consumers of PLs in MDCs were described as: price sensitive, loyal to their usual store, educated and with relatively lower levels of income. It was expected that all these characteristics would hold for the consumer of PLs in Brazil, except for the income variable (P3). The information obtained in the interviews confirm this supposition.

The benefits from the lower prices offered by PLs in Brazil are enjoyed by consumers with higher levels of income versus those consumers with lower income levels (P4).

The level of concentration in the food retailing industry in Brazil presents itself as a paradox: the economic concentration of supermarkets in Brazil provided the conditions for the appearance of PLs; private labels offer good quality products at lower prices and, apparently, provide benefits to consumers. However, the consumers of PLs in Brazil are the ones with higher income levels; the ones who shop at supermarkets. Consumers with low levels of income are not able to enjoy the benefits of PLs (P4).

CONCLUSIONS AND DIRECTIONS FOR FUTURE RESEARCH

The economic concentration of the food retailing industry in Brazil provided gains in productivity which reflected in benefits to consumers. However, given that Brazilian supermarkets cater, primarily, to consumers with higher income levels, it is questionable that the economic concentration of the food retailing industry

APPENDIX I

1. What are there price differences between manufacturers' brands and your private label (s)?

2. What specifications do you give the manufacturer in regard to the products commercialized as your private label(s)?

3. Is there any quality control in regard to your private label(s)?

4. What kind of promotions do you use?

( ) larger shelf space   ( ) displays   ( ) proximity to leader brands on the shelf

( ) posters   ( ) features   ( ) TV, radio ads   ( ) other

5. Is the cost of promoting private labels higher than the cost of promoting a manufacturer brand?

6. How do you decide on the manufacturer for your private label(s)?

7. Does the supermarket offer any special concessions to the manufacturer (larger shelf space, joint promotions, etc.)?

8. Is there a difference between the profiles of private label buyers and buyers of manufacturer brands?

---

has brought significant benefits to all consumer segments. These benefits, although they exist, are enjoyed by the higher income segments and not, by the most impoverished.

In summary, this study suggests that private labels in Brazilian supermarkets have several characteristics that are similar to private labels in supermarkets of more developed countries: (1) the emergence of private labels in Brazilian supermarkets is associated with the economic concentration of the food retailing industry; (2) private labels in Brazilian supermarkets offer quality products at lower prices when compared to MBs; (3) benefits derived from private labels are enjoyed by consumers described as: price sensitive, loyal to their usual store and educated.

However, the evolution of private labels in Brazil presents a paradox to consumers: although private labels offer good quality products at lower prices, these benefits are not enjoyed by poor but, on the contrary, these benefits are enjoyed by the more affluent consumers. Further research can address the public policy implications of extending the benefits derived from private labels to other segments of society.

There are indications that consumers may still associate private labels with cheap, lower quality products. Previous research from Richardson, Dickson and Jain (1994) suggested that the promotion of private labels should concentrate not only on the price differences between PLs and MBs but also, on the development of a brand image associated with quality . Further research is needed to address these issues. For example, the extent to which these perceptions of PLs can be extended to different contexts needs to be evaluated.

This exploratory study needs to be extended not only to a greater number of supermarket chains, but also, to the consumers of private labels. Consumers' perceptions of private labels need to be addressed. The incorporation of research on the cognitive processes underlying attributional decisions (Hilton 1988; Wells and Gavanski 1989) may offer fruitful grounds for a better understanding of why consumers choose PLs over leading brands.

Further research in consumer behavior in developing countries can also be advanced. The focus on the Brazilian experience, although valuable, does not provide a comprehensive view of the diversity of consumer behavior and retail environments in LDCs.

REFERENCES

Bartels, Robert (1976), *The History of Marketing Thought*, Grid Publishing Inc., Columbus, Ohio.

Bellizzi, Joseph A. et al (1981), "Consumer Perceptions of National, Private and Generic Brands, *Journal of Retailing*, 57 (4), 56-70.

Bresser Pereira, Luis Carlos (1973), "Tendências e Paradoxos do Varejo no Brasil," *Revista de Administração* de Empresas, 13 (3), 136-140.

Bond, C. (1984), "Own Labels vs. The Brands," *Marketing*, 8:24-26.

Borden, Neil H. (1967), "Os Efeitos Econômicos da Propaganda," *Revista de Administração de Empresas*, 24 (7), 149-185.

Burger, P. C. and Schott, B. (1972), "Can Private Brand Buyers Be Identified?", *Journal of Marketing Research*, (May), 219-222.

Chernatony, Leslie (1989), "The Impact of the Changed Balance of Power from Manufacturer to Retailer in the UK Packaged groceries market," in *Retail in Marketing Channels*, ed. Luca Pellegrini and Reddy K. Srinivas, London: Routledge, 258-273.

Cunningham, Isabella C. M. et al (1982), "Generic Brands vs National Brands and Store Brands", *Journal of Advertising Research*, 22 (5), 25-32.

Cyrillo, Denise C. O. (1987), *O Papel dos Supermercados no Varejo de Alimentos*, Instituto de Pesquisas Econômicas, Série Ensaios Econômicos (n. 68), São Paulo.

Findlay, Allan M. and Ronan Paddison (1990), "Retailing in Less-Developed Countries: An Introduction," in *Retailing Environments in Developing Countries*, Allan M. Findlay, Ronan Paddison and John A. Dawson, eds., Routledge: London, 261-271.

Frank, Ronald E. and Harper H. Boyd Jr. (1965), "Are Private Brand-Prone Grocery Customers Really Different?", *Journal of Advertising Research*, 5 (4), 27-35.

Grant, Robert M. (1987), "Manufacturer-Retailer Relations: The Shifting Balance of Power," in Business Strategy and Retailing," ed. Gerry Johnson, Chichester: John Wiley & Sons, p.43-58.

Gelb, Betsy D. (1980), "No-Name Products: A Step Toward No-Name Retailing?" *Business Horizons* 23:9.

Hilton, D.J. (1988), "Logic and Causal Atrribution," in *Contemporary Science and Natural Explanation: Commonsense Conceptions of Causality*, ed. D.J. Hilton, New York: New York University Press.

Jain, Subhash C. (1985), *Marketing Planning and Strategy,* 2nd. ed., Cincinnati: South-Western Publishing Co.

Mason, J. Barry and Mayer M. Lehman (1978), *Modern Retailing - Theory and Practice*, Business Publications: Texas.

McGoldrick, Peter J. (1985), "Prodotti Senza Marca: Perche Fanno Paura," *Il Marketing*, 18: 24.

Myers, John G. (1967), "Determinants of Private Brand Attitude," *Journal of Marketing Research*, 4 (Feb), 73-74.

Pereira, Inês (1991), "Marcas de Supermercado - Um Estudo Exploratório", Master Thesis, Fundação Getúlio Vargas, São Paulo.

Rao, Tanniru R. (1969), "Are Some Consumers More Prone to Purchase Private Brands?", *Journal of Marketing Research*, 6 (Nov), 447-450.

Richardson, Paul S., Alan S. Dick and Arun K. Jain (1994), "Extrinsic and Intrinsic Cue Effects on Perceptions of Store Brand Quality," *Journal of Marketing*, 58 (October), p.28-36.

Rothe, James T. and Lawrence M. Lamont (1973), "Purchase Behavior and Brnad Choice Determinants for National and Private Brands Major Appliances," *Journal of Retailing*, 49 (Fall), 19-33.

Schutte, Thomas F. and Vltor J. Cook (1966, "Branding Policies and Practices," in *Science, Technology and Marketing*, ed. Raymond Haas, AMA, p.197-213.

Smith, Gery and Bill Hincheberger (1994), "Brazil: Is the Recovery for Real?," *Business Week*, October 3, p.20-22.

Stern, Louis W. (1970), "The New World of Private Brands,", in *Retail in Marketing Channels*, ed. Luca Pellegrini and Reddy K. Srinivas, London: Routledge, 138-141.

Uncles, Mark D. and Katrina Ellis (1989), "Own Labels: Beliefs and Reality," in *Retail in Marketing Channels*, ed. Luca Pellegrini and Reddy K. Srinivas, London: Routledge, 274-286.

Well, G.L. and I. Gavanski (1989), "Mental Stimulaton of Causality," *Journal of Personality and Social Psychology*, 56, 161-169.

Reconceptualizing Individualism-Collectivism in Consumer Behavior

Gary D. Gregory, University of Texas at Arlington
James M. Munch, University of Texas at Arlington

ABSTRACT

Research investigating the effects of individualism-collectivism in advertising communications has achieved only limited success due to: (1) the tendency of researchers to explain or predict cross-cultural preferences using Hofstede's (1980) country-level ratings of individualism-collectivism; and, (2) the operationalization of the individualism-collectivism construct as a dichotomous trade-off between personal and ingroup goals.

In the research reported here we show that individualism-collectivism is not necessarily dichotomous at the individual level, and that individual (collective) behavior may occur without being in conflict with collective (individual) values. Additionally, our findings suggest that when individual-level values are considered in a consumer-related context, the mix of important individualist and collectivist values do not vary together and are not necessarily opposed. Implications for future research in cultural values in consumer behavior are offered.

INTRODUCTION

Cultural values play an important role in the perception and use of marketing communications. Studies examining message content indicate that one very important dimension of culture to consider when developing advertising and promotional messages is that of individualism-collectivism (Han, 1990; Kale, 1991; Zandpour, 1994). Past research also suggests that advertising themes that are consistent with cultural values of the intended audience are more desirable than ads that reflect values that are inconsistent (Belk, Bryce and Pollay, 1985; Munson & McIntyre, 1978).

In addition to examining behavioral differences among cultural groups, researchers can also expect to find individual differences within a single cultural group. In the United States, for example, there exists a number of ethnic groups and geographic regions that vary in their degree of individualism and collectivism (Hecht, Anderson, & Ribeau, 1989). Numerous past studies (primarily in social psychology) have made great strides in examining and measuring similarities and differences in social behavior (e.g., both between and within individualistic and collectivistic cultures) (Hui & Triandis, 1986; Triandis, McCusker & Hui, 1990). However, marketing efforts to extend these measurements when examining similarities and differences in advertising content and behavioral responses have achieved only limited success.

The shortcomings of these studies are due, in part, to the context in which the behavior is being measured. Although previously validated measurements have been very successful in measuring normative behavior relative to *social* context at the cultural level, they may be unable to detect behavioral differences in a *consumer* context at the individual level. Two major problems associated with past research efforts includes: (1) the tendency of researchers to explain or predict cross-cultural preferences using Hofstede's (1980) hypothesized country-level ratings of individualism-collectivism; and, (2) the operationalization of the individualism-collectivism construct based on a dichotomous trade-off between personal and ingroup goals.

Recent research suggests that individualism-collectivism, as a dichotomy, is insufficient in explaining behavior at the individual level because it fails to consider values that serve goals that are collective (e.g., social justice, equality, and preservation of the environment), but do not serve a specific ingroup (Schwartz, 1990). Conversely, there are values that serve goals that are individual (e.g., hedonism, self enhancement, and stimulation) that may not be in direct conflict with ingroup goals. Applied to consumer behavior, this suggests that individuals may behave in an individualistic (collectivistic) manner without necessarily conflicting with ingroup (personal) goals. Currently, researchers who detect nuances in individualism-collectivism [text obscured by handwriting] ... cessfu ... espec ... in this ... orient: ... the cul ... intenti ...

DIST[...]

[Several lines partially obscured by handwritten annotations]

relates ... Individ ... such a: ... 1992); ... values ... etal nor ... An ... may fee ... ingroup (e.g., family, tribe, religious group). Ingroups for collectivist societies include tightly knit groups (e.g., family or tribe). Ingroups for individualist societies are loosely knit groups (e.g., coworkers or social class) (Triandis et al., 1990). In addition to subordinating personal goals to ingroup goals, individuals in a collectivistic society tend to participate more in ingroup activities, be more concerned with ingroup interests, and feel compelled to conform to ingroup opinions (Hui & Triandis, 1986). According to Triandis (1994) analysis of this construct at the cultural level should involve the study of desirable behaviors for members in society (norms), proscribed behavior of individuals relative to one another (roles), and the goals and principles that motivate individuals (values). This, of course, is based on the assumption that individuals in an individualistic (collectivistic) society have a set of norms, roles and values that are distinctively individualistic (collectivistic) in nature, and that are either individually (personally) or collectively (communally) driven. Thus, the individualism-collectivism construct, as mapped by Triandis, Hofstede and others, has been treated as a dichotomy, that revolves around the conflict between personal goals and ingroup goals.

Prior research examining individualism versus collectivism at the individual level has identified persons who display individualistic tendencies (i.e., emphasize personal goals over ingroup goals) as *idiocentrics*; and persons who display collectivist tendencies (i.e., emphasize ingroup goals over personal goals) as *allocentrics* (Triandis et al., 1990). Cultural groups contain individuals that display both idiocentric and/or allocentric tendencies, depending on the behavioral context. This should be even more evident when the individualism-collectivism dimension is extended to consumer-related behavior. For example, idiocentrics may behave in a manner that allows their private self to realize achievement (i.e., purchasing a 'well-deserved' clothing item for their personal self). On the other hand, their public self may purchase certain 'status oriented' products as an outward demonstration of their success according to social standards (resulting in compliance to a loosely-knit ingroup). The purchase of the same clothing item can be interpreted very differently if an allocentric's private self fulfills their sense of belonging (i.e., purchasing the clothing item to fulfill their personal goal of security). Likewise, their public self may be motivated to comply to local customs by purchasing items that conform to social expectations. These examples illustrate that individuals' behavior (whether individualistic or collectivistic in nature) depends largely on the examination of a mediating variable of interest that attempts to connect individual behavior to culture-level phenomenon - in this case, values. That is, people do not always behave in a strict individualistic or collectivistic manner, but rather exercise individualistic and collectivistic behavior depending on their motivational goals associated with a purchase. Furthermore, it is very likely that individuals may engage in purchase behavior based on their individualistic values (e.g., achievement, self-gratification, pleasure seeking) without necessarily opposing their ingroup goals. Although past research at the individual level (allocentrism-idiocentrism) has been very successful in identifying parallel variations in individualism-collectivism, there still exists limitations in its application due to the assumption of dichotomous tradeoffs between personal and ingroup goals.

THE LIMITATIONS OF INDIVIDUALISM-COLLECTIVISM IN EXPLAINING INDIVIDUAL-LEVEL CONSUMER BEHAVIOR

Most previous studies on cultural values in marketing communications are conducted cross-culturally, investigating similarities and differences in advertising messages between and among individualistic and collectivistic cultures (McCarty & Hattwick, 1992; Mueller, 1987; Alden, Hoyer, & Lee, 1993; Han, 1990).

McCarty & Hattwick (1992) investigated core values (e.g., individualism-collectivism, masculinity-femininity, time orientation, etc.) contained within advertisements in the U.S. and Mexico. The authors found that Hofstede's (1980) individualism-collectivism dimension was the most important dimension to consider in international advertising, with nearly one third of the ads within the U.S. and Mexico containing the individualism-collectivism dimension. However, their results indicate that for the U.S., only 61% of these ads are consistent with an individualistic orientation, and 38% are inconsistent (or are collectivistic in nature). The results for Mexico are even worse, with only 53% of the ads consistent with a collectivistic orientation and 47% inconsistent (or individualistic in nature). If individualism-collectivism, as a cultural index, is an important dimension to consider in developing marketing communications, then why are so many advertisements shown in these two countries inconsistent with Hofstede's country individualism index [rating of 91 for the U.S. and 30 for Mexico]? One explanation could be that Hofstede's country-level indices were based on work-related values and are poor indicators of individual-level consumer behavior.

Mueller (1987) used content analysis to focus on the cultural values represented within ad copy in an individualistic society (U.S.) and a collectivistic society (Japan). The research findings suggested that advertising in the U.S. and Japan generally tends to reflect the prevalent values of those cultures. However, specific values not traditionally known to be indigenous to these cultures were also found (e.g., individual/independence and status appeal in Japan; and, group consensus in the U.S.). Two explanations were

offered for the existence of foreign (or inconsistent) cultural values in advertising messages: 1) culture in foreign markets is evolving and conforming to those values of the country from which the product originates; and, 2) advertising reflects indigenous cultural values *only* as long as it is profitable. A third potential explanation may be that: *individualistic/collectivistic values depicted in advertisements differ from indigenous values due to the absence of a dichotomous tradeoff between personal vs. ingroup goals.* Consumers can behave in a collectivistic manner (i.e., favoring values that promote ingroup goals), while also having strong beliefs, attitudes or purchase intentions for a product that is advertised using an individualistic appeal. To have favorable attitudes towards a product that promotes self gratification, for example, is not necessarily in direct conflict with conformity to ingroup goals.

Alden, Hoyer & Lee (1993) examined how specific content of humorous advertising varies among individualistic and collectivistic cultures. The authors base their ad comparison on the dichotomous tradeoff between personal and ingroup goals (as suggested by Hofstede and Triandis) — where individualistic cultures tend to be characterized by smaller less demanding ingroups and collectivistic cultures tend to involve larger more demanding groups. Two important unresolved issues exist with respect to Alden et al.'s use of the normative dimension individualism-collectivism. First, the individualism-collectivism construct, as a dichotomy, is insufficient because it fails to consider values that may serve *both* personal and ingroups goals. This may be especially true for behavior in a consumer-related context. Second, although Alden et al.'s intention was to show a correlation between Hofstede's country individualism index and the depiction of indigenous values in advertisements, the conceptual meaning of such a comparison is unclear. That is, even if the individualism-collectivism construct were dichotomous and there was a significant correlation between Hofstede's index and the depiction of indigenous values in ads, does Alden et al.'s operationalization of individualism-collectivism (e.g., the number of individuals or characters playing major roles in ads) necessarily depict conformity to either personal or ingroup goals?

Han (1990) provides compelling evidence that at the country level, individualistic advertisements are more effective in the U.S. and collectivistic advertisements are more effective in Korea. Further analysis shows that this pattern varied across involvement levels and individualistic versus collectivistic product categories. The author went on to investigate the individualism-collectivism construct at the individual level, by employing a personality factor, idiocentrism-allocentrism, that attempts to replicate this cultural level difference. However, the overall results indicate that both idiocentric subjects (individualistic in nature) and allocentric subjects (collectivistic in nature) reacted equally favorably to individualistic and collectivistic ads. These results suggest that either there were no significant within-culture differences in product attitudes, or that the idiocentric-allocentric scale used (Greenwald et al.'s, (1986) Ego Task Orientation Scale) was unable to detect differences in attitudes pertaining to consumer behavior.

In sum, past research on cultural values in marketing suggests that cultural-level indices of individualism-collectivism are at best, only general measures of country-level phenomenon, and may have possible limitations when applied to individual-level consumer behavior. Before researchers can successfully extend this dimension to individual-level behavior, it may be helpful to explore a mediating construct that bridges the gap between individualism-collectivism at the cultural level, and 'individualistic' and 'collectivistic' tendencies at the individual level.

TABLE 1
Individual and Collective Values: Defined by Motivational Concern[a]

Individual Types

Hedonism: Pleasure or sensuous gratification (comfortable life, pleasure [Broader Enjoyment includes, as well: cheerful, happiness])

Achievement: Personal success through demonstrated competence according to social standards (sense of accomplishment, successful, ambitious, capable)

Self-direction: Independent thought and action — choosing, creating, exploring (creativity, independent, imaginative, intellectual, logical)

Social power: Status and prestige, control or dominance over people and resources (authority, social power, wealth, preserving my public image)

Stimulation: Excitement, novelty and challenge (a varied life, an exciting life, daring).

Collective Types

Prosocial: Preservation and enhancement of the welfare of others (equality, world at peace, social justice [universal subset]; forgiving, helpful, loving, honest [interpersonal subset])

Restrictive conformity: Restraint of actions, impulses and inclinations likely to harm others or violate social expectations (obedient, clean, politeness, self-discipline)

Security: Safety, harmony, and stability of society, of those with whom one identifies, and of self (family security, national security, social order, sense of belonging)

Tradition: Respect, commitment, and acceptance of the customs and ideas that traditional culture or religion impose (respect for tradition, accepting my portion in life, devout)

Both

Maturity: Appreciation, understanding, and acceptance of oneself, of others, and of the surrounding world (broadminded, world of beauty, wisdom, mature love)

[a] Taken from: Schwartz, S. H. (1990), "Individualism-Collectivism: Critique and Proposed Refinements," *Journal of Cross-Cultural Psychology*, 21 (2), 139-157.

BRIDGING THE GAP

Schwartz (1990, 1994) suggests that to attain a better understanding of cultural and individual differences, researchers should focus on the measurement of values that are based on motivational goals associated with personal needs, social motives, and social institutional demands. The author defines values as 'people's conceptions of the goals that serve as guiding principles in their lives' (Schwartz, 1990, 142). Realizing the need to develop a more precise, parallel measurement of individualism-collectivism at the individual level, Schwartz theoretically derived a set of ten values that are classified according to the basic principles served by the individualism-collectivism dimension (See Table 1).

Each of these values are classified according to whose interests are best served. The values in Table 1 (several of which were adopted from the Rokeach (1973) value survey) represent both the individual and collective interests of an individual, and can serve as guiding principles when making any number of consumption-related decisions. More importantly, these values do not assume that individuals must necessarily make tradeoffs between personal and collective interests. People can use these guiding principles (values) in their lives in a variety of purchase situations for their self-interest (collective-interest) without necessarily conflicting with their collective-interest (self-interest). Schwartz has provided a meaningful interpretation of individualism-collectivism at the individual level that does not operate on the assumption of a dichotomous trade-off between personal goals and collective goals. His list of universal values represent a more fine-tuned approach to measuring differences in behavior between cultural groups based on individual or collective motivational types.

Extension of Individualism-Collectivism Values to Consumer Behavior

Compared to values reflecting universal life goals, one's motivational values provide an alternative, more finely tuned approach to understanding cultural and individual differences in behavior (Schwartz, 1990). When extended to consumer decision making, motivational value types may provide better insight to measuring differences in behavior among different cultures at the individual level.

According to Schwartz (1994), much can be gained from alternative operationalizations that embed values in concrete and varied everyday situations (i.e., such as consumption decisions).

Carman (1978) for example, has developed a general model that integrates interest, time-use activities, roles and lifestyle values as a determinant of consumer behavior. And Beatty, Kahle, Homer & Misra (1985) provide an alternative List of Values (LOV) that has proved to be helpful in understanding important consumption-related decisions. Based on this perspective we sought to explore the robustness of Schwartz's universal value types by adapting five individualistic and four collectivist values to consumer behavior. Schwartz's tenth value item was omitted since it captures dimensions of both individualism and collectivism. The consumer behavior-oriented value items were modeled after typical multiattribute items used in marketing (Lutz and Bettman 1977; Peter and Olson 1994). Three items were developed for each value type. The items measured respondents' product belief, favorability (evaluation), and purchase intention scores for each of the value types. Two examples of these items include:

Individualist Values (e.g., Hedonism)

1. How likely is it that the products you own are a reflection of pleasure seeking and self gratification?
   Extremely unlikely 1 2 3 4 5 6 7 8 9 Extremely likely

2. Please indicate the favorability of products that are a reflection of pleasure seeking and self gratification.
   Very bad -3 -2 -1 0 +1 +2 +3 Very good

3. How likely is it that the primary reason you purchase goods for yourself is pleasure seeking and self gratification?
   Extremely unlikely 1 2 3 4 5 6 7 8 9 Extremely likely

Collectivist Values (e.g., Tradition)

25. How likely is it that the products you own reflect tradition, and acceptance of the customs that your culture or religion impose?
    Extremely unlikely 1 2 3 4 5 6 7 8 9 Extremely likely

26. Please indicate the favorability of products that reflect tradition, and acceptance of the customs that your culture or religion impose.
    Very bad -3 -2 -1 0 +1 +2 +3 Very good

27. How likely is it that the primary reason you purchase goods is to reflect tradition, and acceptance of the customs that your culture or religion impose?
    Extremely unlikely 1 2 3 4 5 6 7 8 9 Extremely likely

* A complete item listing is available from the authors.

METHODOLOGY

In order to examine whether or not the individualism-collectivism construct is dichotomous, we need to look at the relationship between an individual's overall value orientation and their responses to the underlying value types of the individualism-collectivism construct. If individualism-collectivism is dichotomous, then we expect that there will be no differences in an individual's overall value orientation and their responses to specific underlying dimensions. That is, idiocentrics should consider individual value types significantly more important than allocentrics, and conversely, allocentrics should consider collective value types signifi-

cantly more important than idiocentrics. One method to test these relationships is to treat individualism-collectivism as a dichotomous construct and compare the underlying value structure for allocentrics and idiocentrics. Additionally, it is important that we identify which of the nine specific underlying value types, if any, are considered more important and which are considered equally important for allocentrics and idiocentrics in a consumer-related context.

Sample

Data were obtained from 112 undergraduate business students. The sample consisted of 48 males and 64 females who attend a large southwestern state university.

Instruments

Allocentric/Idiocentric Measure. A 16-item adaptation of Triandis et al.'s (1990) individualism-collectivism scale was chosen for this study to measure subject's allocentric and idiocentric tendencies. These attitude items were used in previous studies to measure individual-level differences both across and within cultures. Subjects were asked to consider each of the 16 items, and to indicate, using a nine-point Likert scale, their degree of agreement or disagreement with the statements. We then summed the response to these 16 items and divided by the total number of items to produce a mean allocentric-idiocentric score.

Consumer Value Scale. A 27-item instrument was developed using Schwartz's (1990) Individual and Collective value types. This instrument consists of items representing nine values (five individual values and four collective values). The subjects responded to three items for each value type. One item represented each of the consumer behavior components: product beliefs, favorability (evaluation), and purchase intention. The items were scaled ranging from *extremely unlikely* (1) to *extremely likely* (9) for product belief and purchase intention items, and from *very bad* (-3) to *very good* (+3) for favorability (evaluation).

RESULTS

Overall Individualist vs. Collectivist Value Orientation

In order to identify the latent dimensions or constructs represented in Triandis et al.'s Allocentrism/Idiocentrism items, common factor analysis with oblique rotation was performed. Additionally, the variables were allowed to be correlated for subsequent testing as to whether or not the individualism-collectivism construct is dichotomous. Initial analysis revealed three factors with Eigenvalues greater than 1. When compared to previous research by Triandis et al. (1990), which also investigated U.S. allocentrics and U.S. idiocentrics, the results replicated fairly closely previous work. Although Triandis et al. used principal components factor analysis producing a four factor solution (two individualist and two collectivist factors), our findings produced factors that are conceptually identical (e.g., two individualist and one collectivist factor, with nearly identical variable loadings). If individualism and collectivism traits are dichotomous and are opposed to one another, then the individualist and collectivist factors capturing each dimension should be negatively correlated and significant. However, additional analysis revealed that for the three factors produced in the common factor solution, each of the bivariate correlations were small, positive and not significant. These results indicate that although the individualism-collectivism scale captures fairly unique cultural dimensions, these dimensions are not necessarily dichotomous and appear to be orthogonal.

TABLE 2

Mean Value Ratings for Moderate Individualists and Collectivists by Underlying Motivational Value Types [a]

	Moderate Individualist (N=52)			Moderate Collectivist (N=60)		
	Product Beliefs	Favorability (Evaluation)	Purchase Intentions	Product Beliefs	Favorability (Evaluation)	Purchase Intentions
Individualist values						
Overall	6.33*	1.48	5.64	5.89	1.48	5.06
Subtypes						
Hedonism	6.98	2.08	7.02*	6.60	1.90	6.40
Achievement	6.30*	1.29	4.62	5.47	1.08	4.07
Self-direction	7.15	2.00	6.38	6.70	1.85	5.80
Stimulation	5.31	0.92	5.30	5.30	1.10	4.92
Social Power	5.92	1.10	4.87	5.34	1.10	4.13
Collectivist values						
Overall	5.50	1.17	4.80	5.88	1.55	5.64**
Subtypes						
Security	5.94	1.52	5.19	6.30	1.70	5.68
Prosocial (universal)	4.38	0.46	3.88	4.72	0.97	4.80**
Restrictive conformity	6.33	1.92	5.75	6.22	1.90	6.32
Tradition	5.31	0.77	4.38	6.28*	1.65**	5.77**

[a]   Mean values based on *extremely unlikely* (1), to *extremely likely* (9) for product belief and purchase intention, and *very bad* (-3) to *very good* (+3) for favorability (evaluation)

*   Significantly greater (p<.05) between-group difference

**   Significantly greater (p<.01) between-group difference

The Relationship Between Overall Value Orientation and Underlying Dimensions

According to Schwartz (1990), in order to further assess the adequacy of the individualism-collectivism dichotomy at the individual level, we need to look at the relationship between an individual's overall value orientation and their responses to a more fine-tuned set of motivational type values that represent the underlying dimensions of individualism-collectivism. If individualism-collectivism is sufficient as a dichotomy, then one would expect to see no differences in an individual's overall value orientation and their responses to specific underlying dimensions.

Additionally, to explore how individualism-collectivism relates to values relevant to consumer behavior, we classified subjects according to the allocentric-idiocentric scale administered. Using the mean scores from this scale we then conducted a median split (Median=5.67). Consistent with Triandis et al. (1990), the use of U.S. student subjects resulted in a restricted range of idiocentric-allocentric scores, with idiocentrics ranging from 3.33 - 5.60 (μ=4.96), and allocentrics ranging from 5.67 - 8.13 (μ=6.28). Student subjects were classified as "moderate individualists" versus "moderate collectivists." Since there were seven subjects that fell on the median of 5.67, and since these scores were above the midpoint (5) on the scale, these subjects were included in the "moderate collectivist" group. Next, we compared the importance of the overall value types (individual and collective) for each of the two groups (allocentric-idiocentric). Finally, we compared the importance of the nine specific motivational value types relative to product beliefs, favorability (evaluation), and purchase intention for two groups. See Table 2 for comparisons.

Our results indicate that overall individualistic values are more important for product beliefs of the moderate individualist than for the moderate collectivist group. Similarly, overall collectivist values more favorably affect purchase intentions of the moderate collectivists compared to moderate individualists. Examination of group differences on the five subtypes of individualist values reveals that moderate individualists gave higher priority to hedonism for purchase intentions and to achievement for product beliefs. Considering the group differences on the four collectivist values reveals that moderate collectivists gave higher priority to universal prosocial values for purchase intentions while rating the tradition value higher on product beliefs, favorability, and purchase intentions.

Overall results generally support the notion that allocentrics and idiocentrics differ on the cultural value orientation individualism-collectivism. However, a closer look at the underlying dimensions of this construct suggests that certain motivational values are more important for allocentric and idiocentric consumers. More specifically, the results indicate that these differences (or similarities) vary as a function of product beliefs, favorability (evaluation) and purchase intentions. This issue will be addressed in more detail in the discussion section.

DISCUSSION

Research efforts based on comparisons between cultural groups at the country level should consider the limitations associated with extending culture-level correlations to individual-level behavior. Hofstede's culture-level measurements are based on the sums of individual characteristics and may have limitations when extended to individual behavior (e.g., beliefs, evaluations and intentions). Many refer to this phenomenon as an ecological fallacy. The reverse ecological fallacy is also true; where individual-level differences are extended to country-level comparisons. The existence of ecological and reverse ecological fallacies provides evidence that researchers should separate the levels of analysis and interpret results according to the appropriate level under investigation.

Hofstede's (1980) work on individualism-collectivism was originally conceived as a dichotomous construct at the country level. Numerous studies (including those mentioned in this paper) in many respects support the notion of country (or culture) level differences based on the dichotomous tradeoff between personal and ingroup goals. However, when examining individual-level behavior, researchers should heed caution to the assumption that individualist and collectivist values are opposed to one another. Recent evidence suggests that in order to better understand how differences between individuals' beliefs, evaluations and intentions are related to individual differences in value priorities, that researchers examine the individual-level value types that underlie the individualism-collectivism construct (Schwartz, 1994). This suggests that although culture-level values shape and form individual's beliefs, attitudes and behaviors, they may not determine them.

Schwartz (1990) offers several speculative hypotheses about the types of values likely to discriminate between individuals in societies that have both individualist and collectivist tendencies. Value types thought to be more important for collectivists include tradition, restrictive conformity, and prosocial values. Self-direction, stimulation and social power are hypothesized to be more important for individualists. Between-group differences for the remaining set of values are believed to be minimal. Comparing the findings (Table 2) to these hypotheses reveals several interesting differences between Schwartz's motivational values that serve as guiding life principles and our motivational values as they pertain to consumer behavior.

Individualists

Individualists are expected to rate self-direction, stimulation, and social power more highly. Our data does not support the hypothesis for any of these values. Interestingly however, hedonism and achievement are two values rated more highly by the moderate individualist group. Hedonism is shown to affect purchase intentions. The idea of pleasure and sensation seeking is not new to the marketing literature (Holbrook and Hirschman 1982; Celsi, Rose, and Leigh 1993). Sense of achievement value ratings manifest themselves on product beliefs. Consumers' need for achievement and the interrelationship between consumers' self-images and their possessions is an important consumer research topic (Sirgy, 1992).

Collectivists

Consistent with Schwartz's view, tradition appears to be a key value for collectivists in consumer behavior. Group means for product beliefs, evaluations, and purchase intentions are significantly higher for the moderate collectivist group when compared to the moderate individualist group. Additionally, there were no differences between the two groups on security. Although individuals may link their destiny to groups (i.e., family, friends, coworkers), the importance of security values is equally the same in any case. Contrary to Schwartz's speculation, group differences do not emerge on restrictive conformity values. Apparently, the notions of violating social expectations and inclinations to harm others (i.e., restrictive conformity) does not easily manifest itself in consumer decision making situations. Interestingly, one consumer decision making value that rated more highly by collectivists on purchase intention is the universal subset of prosocial values. This value may be described as consuming so as to preserve and enhance

the welfare of others, even for those individuals outside the collective ingroup. This finding supports Schwartz's belief that the individualism-collectivism dichotomy fails to consider collectivist values that foster the goals of collectives other than the ingroup (e.g., universal prosocial values).

DIRECTIONS FOR FUTURE RESEARCH

As business firms move towards globalization of markets, understanding cross-cultural values will become an increasingly important issue. One basic goal of this paper is to illustrate the limitations in applying country-level value orientations to individual-level consumer behavior. In doing so, our results support Schwartz's earlier findings that the individualism-collectivism construct may not be dichotomous at the individual level. A second goal of this paper is to show that the set of motivational value types that individuals find important in consumer decision making situations may differ significantly from value orientations based on a more general social context. Whereas most international marketing decisions are based on country-level similarities and/or differences, the consideration of cross-cultural consumer preferences requires a more fine-tuned approach to identifying differences at the individual level.

Future research should extend our efforts by considering specific areas of consumption, additional populations, and additional methods of measuring values to increase our understanding of the link between values and consumer behavior both at the cultural and the individual level. Additionally, multimethod probes that include surveys, personal interviews, direct observation, and experiments are needed to provide further validation of the link between cultural values and individual consumer behavior. Based on our premise that societal values (i.e., as reflected within advertising appeals) may not always reflect individual-level consumer behavior, further research is necessary to determine similarities and/or differences in specific motivational value types and the degree to which common norms, tastes, and values justify a globalized or customized approach to marketing communications.

REFERENCES

Alden, D. L., W. D. Hoyer and C. Lee (1993), "Identifying Global and Culture-Specific Dimensions of Humor in Advertising: A Multinational Analysis," *Journal of Marketing*, 57 (April), 64-75.

Beatty, S. E., L. Kahle, P. Homer, S. Misra (1985), "Alternative Measurement Approaches to Consumer Values: The List of Values and the Rokeach Value Survey," *Psychology & Marketing*, 2 (3), 181-200.

Belk, R. W., W. J. Bryce and R. W. Pollay (1985), "Advertising Themes and Cultural Values: A Comparison of U.S. and Japanese Advertising," In K.C. Mun and T.C. Chan (eds.), *Proceedings of the Inaugural Meeting of the Southeast Asia Region*, Hong Kong: Academy of International Business, 11-20.

Carman, J. M. (1978), "Values and Consumption Patterns: A Closed Loop," In H. K. Hunt (Ed.), *Advances in Consumer Research*. Ann Arbor: Association for Consumer Research, 5, 403-407.

Celsi, Richard L., Randall L. Rose, and Thomas W. Leigh (1993), "An Exploration of High-Risk Leisure Consumption through Skydiving," *Journal of Consumer Research* 20, (June), 1-23.

Greenwald, A. G., S. J. Breckler and E. C. Wiggins (1986), "Public, Private, and Collective Self-Evaluation: Measurement of Individualistic Differences," Unpublished Manuscript.

Han, S. (1990), *Individualism and Collectivism: Its Implications for Cross-Cultural Advertising*, Unpublished doctoral dissertation, University of Illinois, Department of Advertising.

Hecht, M., P. A. Anderson and S. A. Ribeau (1989), "The Cultural Dimensions of Nonverbal

Communication," in *Handbook of International and Intercultural Communication*, eds. M. K. Asante and W. B. Gudykunst, Newbury Park, CA: Sage, 163-185.

Hofstede, G. (1980), *Culture's Consequences: International Differences in Work-Related Values*. Sage Publications: Beverly Hills, CA.

Holbrook, Morris B. and Elizabeth C. Hirschman (1982), "The Experimental Aspects of Consumption: Consumer Fantasies, Feelings, and Fun," *Journal of Consumer Research* 9, (September), 132-140.

Hui, C. H. and H. C. Triandis (1986), "Individualism-Collectivism: A Study of Cross-Cultural Researchers," *Journal of Cross-Cultural Psychology*, 17, 225-248.

Kale, S. H. (1991), "Culture-specific Marketing Communications: An Analytical Approach," *International Marketing Review*, 8 (2), 18-30.

Lutz, R. and J. R. Bettman (1977), "Multiattribute Models in Marketing: A Bicentennial Review," in *Consumer and Industrial Buying Behavior*, eds. A. G. Woodside, J. N. Sheth and P. D. Bennett, New York: Elsevier-North Holland Publishing, 137-150.

McCarty, J. and P. Hattwick (1992), "Cultural Value Orientations: A Comparison of Magazine Advertisements from the United States and Mexico," in *Advances in Consumer Research*, 19, eds. John F. Sherry, Jr. and Brian Sternthal, Provo, Utah: Association for Consumer Research, 34-38.

Mueller, B. (1987), "Reflections of Culture: An Analysis of Japanese and American Advertising Appeals," *Journal of Advertising Research*, 27 (June/July), 51-59.

Munson, J. M. and S. H. McIntyre (1978), "Personal Values: A Cross Cultural Assessment of Self Values and Values Attributed to a Distant Cultural Stereotype," in *Advances in Consumer Research*, 6, ed. Keith Hunt. Ann Arbor, Michigan: Association for Consumer Research, 160-166.

Peter, J. P. and J. C. Olson (1994), *Understanding Consumer Behavior*, Richard D. Irwin: Homewood, IL.

Rokeach, M. (1973), *The Nature of Human Values*, New york: Free Press.

Schwartz, S. H. (1990), "Individualism-Collectivism: Critique and Proposed Refinements," *Journal of Cross-Cultural Psychology*, 21 (2), 139-157.

Schwartz, S. H. (1994), "Beyond Individualism/Collectivism: New Cultural Dimensions of Values," in *Individualism and Collectivism: Theory, Method, and Applications*, 18, eds. U. Kim, H. C. Triandis, Ç. Kagitçibasi, S. Choi, and G. Yoon: Sage Publications, 85-119.

Sirgy, M. Joseph (1992), "Self-Concept in Consumer Behavior: A Critical Review," *Journal of Consumer Research*, 9 (December), 287-300.

Triandis, H. C., C. McCusker, and C. H. Hui (1990), "Multimethod Probes of Individualism and Collectivism. *Journal of Personality and Social Psychology*, 59 (5): 1006-1020.

Triandis, H. C. (1994), "Theoretical and Methodological Approaches to the Study of Collectivism and Individualism," in *Individualism and Collectivism: Theory, Method, and Applications*, 18, eds. U. Kim, H. C. Triandis, Ç. Kagitçibasi, S. Choi, and G. Yoon: Sage Publications, 41-51.

Zandpour, F., V. Campos, J. Catalano, C. Chang, Y. Cho, R. Hoobyar, S. Jiang, M. Lin, S. Madrid, H. Scheideler, S. Osborn (1994), "Global Reach and Local Touch: Achieving Cultural Fitness in TV Advertising," *Journal of Advertising Research*, (Sept/Oct), 35-63.

Le Fromage as Life: French Attitudes and Behavior Toward Cheese

Scott D. Roberts, University of Texas at Brownsville
Kathleen S. Micken, Old Dominion University

ABSTRACT

Anthropologists study food preparation and eating rituals as one means of understanding a culture. Yet the study of eating and drinking behavior has not attracted as much attention from consumer behavior researchers, especially in the cross-cultural arena. This study is an attempt to explore the cultural meaning of one particular food, cheese, in one particular country, France. The study assesses whether cheese might serve as an appropriate metaphor for French culture. The study also investigates the structure of French attitudes toward cheese.

INTRODUCTION

"No one can bring together a country that has 365 kinds of cheese" (attributed to Charles de Gaulle, 1953).

Not only do the French consume many different varieties of cheese, they consume it in larger quantities than any other society (INSEE 1991, Toy 1994).

"Are we to be condemned to eat standardized, aseptic, industrialized cheeses?"
Le Figaro

When the European Commission (EC, now the Economic Union or EU) proposed restrictions on bacteria levels in cheese and other dairy products, "the French rose up to a man to defend their traditional raw-milk cheeses from the supposed threat from those over-interfering Eurocrats in Brussels" (*The Economist* 1992, 60). The EC, in seeking increased standardization across more than a dozen cultures that were to make up the future of Europe, failed to fully appreciate local cultural practices. More specifically, they failed to note the strong emotional and historical tie the French feel with the land and its products (Mennell 1985).

The uproar by the French over outsiders governing their beloved food has only weak parallels in the U.S. For example, when Coca-Cola introduced "new" Coke, a group calling themselves "Old Cola Drinkers of America" formed and protested that the company had violated a trust by "smoothing" the product out, ostensibly to gain wider product appeal among younger market segments (*Marketing News* 1985). But this protest was notable only because Americans so rarely consider their highly processed diet at all. While these and other protests about food controls are real, they lack the raw-nerve quality that characterizes the French relationship with its cheeses.

As an American living and teaching in Lyon, France, during the 1992-93 school year, the first author found French foodways in general, and French "cheeseways" in particular both fascinating and baffling. A well-provisioned French hypermarket may stock as many as 130 varieties of cheese, while the much smaller cheese specialty shops frequently carry about 100 (Bicard 1992). The hypermarket may devote up to 30 meters (100 feet) of shelf-front to packaged cheeses and 30 additional meters to "a' la coupe" or deli-style cheese cut to order.

To the unitiniated, many of these cheeses don't even resemble "cheese." To those raised in the U.S. without the benefit of experiential parental example, the cultural category (McCracken 1986) of cheese is of a solid or grated substance, usually orange and always wrapped in plastic, and is served at just-out-of refrigerator temperatures. This hyperreal version of cheese, a sanitized, perfect, "realer-than-real" (Belk 1995) version bears little resemblance to the original, unadulterated, closer-to-nature, and cruder product (Baudrillard 1981; Coffe 1992). The cheeses of France may be sold bottled in oils, rolled in ashes, covered with mold, filled with seasonings, surrounded by rinds or waxes, or even in various stages of decay (timed perfectly for the occasion of eating). Cheese is nearly always eaten at room temperature.

The purpose of this paper is to explore the phenomenon known as *le fromage* (French cheese). What is it about the French and their cheese? Can cheese be considered a metaphor for France the way others have characterized, say, the Turkish and their coffeehouses (Gannon 1994), or the Japanese and their rice (Ohnukey-Tierney 1993), or the Chinese and their *Quanxi* exchange networks (Mei-hui Yang 1994)? Do we learn from their passion for curded milk products something about the French consumer?

LITERATURE AND HYPOTHESES

Food and Culture

Anthropologists and other social scientists have long considered food an integral part of understanding cultures (Levi-Strauss 1969). For example, food clearly has social facilitating qualities, particularly when served in ceremonial or ritual fashion (Wallendorf and Arnould 1991). Food can also be used to signal status differentiations or separate groups such as children from adults (Levy 1981). A chronic shortage of food may actually destroy a formerly cohesive culture, as happened with the African Ik tribe, described by Turnbull (1972).

Gannon and his associates (Gannon 1994) recently published an entire book devoted to understanding seventeen countries through extensive analysis of a single item or activity said to serve as a metaphor for each culture. For example, they "unpack" the Italian opera into five major subthemes (e.g., pageantry, chorus and soloists, the family meal) which together are supposed to metaphorically align with characteristics of Italian society. Similar metaphors explored include the traditional British house, American football, the Spanish bullfight, the Russian ballet, and French wine (Gannon 1994).

Studies such as these, which seek to identify and understand variations across cultures have investigated phenomena that span the gamut from advertising (c.f. Hong, Muderrisoglu, and Zinkhan 1987) to values (c.f. Schwartz and Bilsky 1987). Food consumption behavior, however, "has not attracted much systematic attention by consumer behavior researchers" (Steenkamp 1993, p. 401). Askegaard (1993) reports on a research program to "outline regional cultural borders within Europe" with the goal of "establishing theoretical models of cultural aspects of specific eating and drinking patterns in different societies" (p. 410). While the research reported here is not part of that program, it is consistent with its theme and is consistent with Steenkamp's (1993) call for research to investigate the social and cultural influences on food preferences. Specifically, this study investigates five hypotheses about the French and cheese. The main hypothesis has already been discussed, that the French share similar attitudes and behaviors toward cheese. From this hypothesis flow four sub-hypotheses which address the structure of that attitude. We propose that the shared French attitude will reflect four dimensions: the role of cheese in national identity, the role of cheese in French xenophobia, the importance of knowledge about cheese and cheese consumption rituals, and the role of cheese in French attitudes toward the land. Each of the four sub-hypotheses is discussed next.

Cheese and the French National Identity

A government official once opined that French cuisine is an official branch of French culture (Blythman 1992). The extent of the French devotion to gastronomy is perhaps best exemplified by the decision in the early 1990s to bring top chefs into the classroom of elementary (*primaire*) schools to educate young French palates. This move was occasioned by the finding that France had the third largest expenditure on fast food of all European countries and the belief of "sixty-three percent of French people... that their culinary heritage was under 'threat' from high consumption by French children of 'over-processed junk food'" (Blythman 1992, p. 625). Knowing that 50 million Frenchmen can't be wrong, the Ministries of Education and of Culture established a national education program to rectify the situation. One of the ministers, Jacques Lang, characterized the decision this way, "The struggle for quality is something important for a country which wants to preserve its traditions... traditions which are important for the economy, agriculture, gastronomy, and many other elements of culture" (quoted in Blythman 1992, p. 626). The goal of the lessons is not only to develop a sense of the taste, touch, and smell of food, but also to develop an understanding of the components of quality. By the end of the program, "parents and educators hope that their children will be able to tell the difference between a hand-made croissant from a local craft baker and its factory-produced counterpart from the nearest hypermarché, and appreciate the characteristics of a ripe Brie de Meaux when compared with the refrigerated and pasteurised equivalent" (Blythman 1992, p. 626).

Thus, the first sub-hypothesis is that part of the French national identity is connected to their cuisine, and, in particular to their cheeses.

Cheese and French Xenophobia

The French are very proactive in their efforts to protect French culture against incursions from foreign ways. The 1994 law which would have fined advertisers, broadcast journalists and the like for using English words and which would have placed a quota on the number of non-French songs a radio station could play (*The Economist* 1994) is but one example. The rationale for a society's desire to maintain control of the sources of information is the desire to keep secure its own interpretation of the world (Douglas and Isherwood 1979). A danger arises when an alien worldview challenges the existing order. If that which is strange, which is foreign, can be avoided, it cannot damage an existing meaning system.

With regard to cheese, we expect this almost xenophobic pro-French attitude to be expressed as a strong preference for French cheeses. We expect this attitude to be something more than simply a preference for cheese made the old fashioned way from raw milk and being free of industrial processing. Indeed, the British similarly make desirable raw milk farmhouse cheese (Hallgarten and Collister 1992). Yet we expect that the French will prefer their own cheese simply because the cheese is French.

Cheese and the Importance of Food Knowledge

Berger and Luckmann (1967) introduced the idea that meaning is a social construction. Douglas and Isherwood (1979) continue the theme by suggesting that meaning is "fixed," or made more permanent, via rituals. Public rituals are seen as establishing a collaborative commitment to the meaning. All societies and cultures have their rituals for reinforcing that which is important. For the French, many of these rituals involve food.

Not only must one have a trained palate and be able to recognize and enjoy good quality, but the enjoyment must be undertaken in prescribed ways. The reader may be familiar with the British tea ritual which places importance on the "correct preparation, the correct trimmings, and the correct side dishes" which accompany the tea (Repplier 1932, p. 21-22). For the British, however, not all foods are accorded such ritualistic status. For the French, on the other hand, food and dining more often take on the aspects of ritual and show. Zeldin (1982) quotes chef Paul Bocuse as saying that a meal is like an opera; each person has a part to play, and it must be properly executed.

Thus, the third sub-hypothesis is that the French attitude toward cheese includes strong agreement that it is a person's "duty" to be educated about cheese and to understand the proper ways of consuming cheese.

Cheese and French Ties with the Land

As noted earlier, the French have strong emotional and historical ties to the land and its products (Mennell 1985). These associations are made manifest in both usual and unusual ways. When the second author was on holiday in France, she couldn't help noticing the numerous Parisian restaurants with cages of small animals used as decorations. Upon phoning a French acquaintance for a restaurant recommendation, several choices were accompanied with a comment such as, "You can't miss this one, they have sheep tied up out front." When questioned about the use of live animals to "decorate" urban restaurants, the acquaintance offered the explanation that the French still revere their agricultural roots. As *The Economist* reported,

[a]lthough 80% of Frenchmen live in towns, they regard themselves as a predominantly agricultural nation, partly because many were born in the countryside. In 1945 farmers accounted for over one-third of the working population. These links leave the urban population a soft touch for France's farm lobbyists. Many think that it is not merely the welfare of a few farmers that is at stake [in the GATT negotiations], but a part of France's identity (1993, p. 47-48).

With this knowledge, the fourth sub-hypothesis is that we expect to find this agrarian mind-set reflected in attitudes toward cheese.

METHOD

This project began as an exploration of French "foodways" (Levy 1981). Students in a senior marketing research class—nine French students and two Francophone Africans who had been educated in France—began by writing a very detailed description of how their families eat the dinner meal. This assignment produced frequent references to stereotypical French foods such as bread, wine and cheese. Since cheese stood out as an important component for the French eating experience, students were then consulted as to the idiosyncrasies surrounding its consumption. A long list of possible *a priori* themes for exploration while seeking to learn more about *le fromage* resulted. The students next conducted depth interviews with three informants whom they identified as having a strong opinions and/or preferences regarding cheese. Students were trained in the technique and given a protocol to follow. (For specific information about this phase of the research, contact the first author.)

After these interviews were transcribed and analyzed, the conclusions provided a basis for a survey instrument which listed twenty attitude and twenty behavior statements dealing with cheese. Respondents were asked to indicate the extent of their agreement with each statement by checking one of the five Likert scale boxes

TABLE 1
Description of Respondents

Age		Income		Profession	
18 - 29	28.2%	Lower Group	34.8%	Working Class	15.0%
30 - 49	46.2%	Middle Group	34.4%	Pink Collar	24.1%
50 & Over	25.6%	Upper Group	19.4%	Self-employed	13.4%
Mean* = 40.6; Std dev = 15.1				Professional	41.9%

Marital Status		Gender		Education of Head of Household	
Married	57.1%	Male	48.4%	Less than BAC	37.2%
Not married	42.9%	Female	51.6%	BAC	62.8%

Rural/Urban
On a scale of 0 to 50, respondents were asked to indicate the nature of the area in which they resided, with 0 = most rural and 50 = most urban. The mean response was 32.3; the standard deviation was 15.6.

* Actual age was recorded; mean and standard deviation are calculated from that data, not the groups reported here.

(from "completely agree" to "uncertain" to "completely disagree") which followed each statement. A sample attitude question is, "Without her cheeses, France would just be another country." (An astonishing 55 percent of respondents either agreed or completely agreed, perhaps giving some indication just how important cheese is to this sample of French respondents). A sample behavior question is, "I probably spend too much money for cheese" (to which 53 percent disagreed or completely disagreed). Additionally, the survey requested data on education, age, income and other demographic variables. The instrument was translated into French and backtranslated twice.

The students were trained in survey administration techniques and given 30 surveys each to administer. They were told they could give the survey to a maximum of three acquaintances, with no one from the same family being allowed to fill it out. They were instructed to get roughly ten each from lower, middle and upper class respondents, roughly half from rural respondents, and other instructions to avoid an upscale, urban skew in the data set. Three hundred eighty-three surveys were collected. Data were entered into a French version of the Microsoft Works spreadsheet program and later transferred to the American version. Incomplete surveys and data transfer problems resulted in a final usable sample size of 316.

Data generated from the two pre-survey studies are not analyzed here. The description of pre-survey work is given to provide the reader with a larger sense of how the survey "came to be," as there were no preexisting, pre-validated scales to choose from.

RESULTS

Description of Respondents
Data were first analyzed by looking at a description of survey respondents (Table 1). Inspection of the distribution of respondents across categories of age, income, geographical location (a rural-urban continuum), education, profession, and marital status indicates that there seem to be no biases toward any particular group. Further, when correlations among demographic variables are examined (Table 2), the result is consistent with expectations about the relationships among income, education, marital status, and age. For example, the statistically significant correlations (α=.05) indicate that income is positively correlated with education and with more professional occupations. Education is also positively correlated with occupation. Because older French people are not as

likely to have obtained a university degree, the correlation between age and education is negative. The correlation between marital status and age also is negative, indicating that older respondents are more likely to be married. Correlations between continuous variables are Pearson correlation coefficients; for ordinal variables they are Spearman correlation coefficients. These results, which were all in the direction one would expect, suggest that there are no anomalies in the data set which might be attributed to the demographic composition of the sample.

Assessment of Differences in Cheese Attitudes and Behaviors Among Respondents
Analysis next turned to an investigation of the main hypothesis, that there would be few differences in overall French attitudes and behaviors toward cheese. The hypothesis was tested by comparing mean ratings on each of the attitude and behavior measures across the demographic variables. If there are few differences, we would have evidence for the pervasive nature of these attitudes and behaviors across all French citizens, and thus for the appropriateness of cheese as a national metaphor for France.

T-tests were conducted to assess the differences between the responses provided by men and women, between respondents whose head of the household had attained the *Baccalauréat* (BAC) degree (a thirteenth year of pre-college courses that is required for advancement to a university or higher technical school) and those whose head of the household had not, between respondents who were married and those who were not, and between rural and urban dwellers. One-way analysis of variance with Scheffe comparisons were conducted to assess differences among respondents of various income groups (lower, middle, and upper), age ranges (29 years old and younger, 30 to 49 years old, and 50 years and up), and among occupations (working class occupations, "pink collar" occupations, self-employed professionals, and professionals). These results are reported in Table 3. (For the specific statistical results contact the second author.) Except for age comparisons, there are few differences in mean ratings across the demographic variables. Obviously, some variation is to be expected, but the differences which were statistically significant are consistent with what we know about French culture and society and do not negate the overall hypothesis.

Differences between rural and urban respondents were present for three measures. Rural respondents expressed more disagreement that the hypermarket could provide all the cheeses they might

TABLE 2

Correlations Among Demographic Variables

	Age	Gender	Marital Status	HH Head Educ.	Job Category	Income
Gender	.0566* (.319)					
Marital Status	-.3891* (.000)	-.1198* (.036)				
HH Head Education	-.1315 (.018)	-.1425 (.012)	-.0322 (.306)			
Job Category	.0637 (.157)	.0849 (.091)	-.0820 (.099)	.2676 (.000)		
Income	-.0303 (.316)	.0544 (.196)	-.2087 (.000)	.4199 (.000)	.4817 (.000)	
Rural/ Urban	-.0582* (.307)	.0200* (.727)	.0076* (.894)	.1239 (.025)	-.0019 (.488)	.0092 (.443)

* Pearson Correlation Coefficients
The remainder are Spearman Correlation Coefficients

---

want, and expressed more agreement that the "average Frenchman eats different cheese than the bourgeoisie," and that "a person who doesn't like cheese cannot truly be considered French." These attitudes are consistent with the more conservative rural ethic.

Differences between married and non-married respondents were also present for three measures. Married respondents expressed more agreement with statements about not being able to appreciate cheese without wine and about buying cheese at a specialty cheese retailer, perhaps reflecting the higher income of married respondents. Married respondents also expressed more agreement that they were the person in the family who was the primary purchaser of cheese. This result makes sense since married respondents also tended to be female (57 percent of married respondents were female while 45 percent of not married repondents were female).

Gender differences were reflected in responses to five measures. Consistent with the statement above, females tended to be the primary purchasers of cheese for the household. They also expressed more agreement with statements about the texture of cheese being important and about the importance of cheese and cheese rituals. This latter result is consistent with mothers being charged with the duty to maintain family and cultural rituals.

Differences based on the education level of the head of the household were reflected in responses to five measures. Respondents living in a household headed by an individual with a BAC degree or higher expressed more disagreement with the statement that people tended to eat the cheese they preferred without regard to price. Those living in a household headed by an individual *not* having attained the BAC degree, however, expressed more agreement with two relatively xenophobic statements: "I would not under any circumstances put foreign cheese on my cheese plate," and "The EC should not regulate French cheese." They were also proud of their knowledge about French cheeses, saying that people would ask their advice about cheese and that they liked to try new cheeses.

Income differences were reflected in only one statement, "I always serve cheese on a plate." Here the upper income group expressed more agreement than the lower income group, but there was no difference in mean rating between the lower and middle or the middle and upper income groups.

Differences among respondents based on occupation were reflected in ratings on four measures. Professionals expressed more agreement than "pink collar" workers that the texture of cheese was important (there were no other differences among the occupation groups). They also expressed more disagreement than self-employed professionals that they would eat the cheese they want without regard to price. Self-employed professionals, on the other hand, expressed more agreement than pink collar workers that they could "describe in detail ten different kinds of cheeses," though there was no differences in comparisons among any other paired groups for this statement. Self-employed professionals also expressed more agreement than any of the other three occupation groups that they would "always serve cheese on a plate." There was no statistically significant difference in mean ratings for the other three occupation groups. The results of these comparisons seem to suggest that the self-employed professionals, perhaps having newly acquired wealth, have adopted more bourgeois attitudes.

Age differences, however, were much more pronounced. For this analysis, respondents were grouped into three age categories: those 29 years old and under (those whose education was affected by the 1968 Paris riots[1]), those 50 years old and over (people who would have had some recollection of World War II), and those in the

---

[1]"Probably the most momentus event in recent French education history was the crisis of 1968, when violent university student demonstrations led to the decentralization of higher education, an increase in the number of institutions, and the concentration of power in councils controlled by students and faculty" (Encyclopedia Americana 1991, p. 659).

TABLE 3

Demographic Categories of Respondents Expressing Higher Mean Rating on Attitude and Behavior Measures
(α=.05)

	T-Tests				One-way ANOVA		
	Rural/ Urban	Marital Status	Gender	HH Head Educ	Income	Job Category	Age
Avg. Frenchman eats different cheese than the bourgeoisie	R						
One not liking cheese isn't truly French	R						O > Y O > M
The hypermarket has all the cheeses I want*	R						
Cannot appreciate cheese w/o wine		M					M > Y O > Y
I am primary purchaser of cheese for my HH		M	F				M > Y O > Y
Buy from a specialty cheese retailer		M					M > Y O > Y
Cheese texture is important			F			4 > 2	
Life not be appreciated w/o cheese			F				
Never put foreign cheese on my cheese plate			F	No BAC			O > M
I always serve cheese on a plate			F		Up > Low		O > M O > Y
EC shouldn't regulate French cheese				No BAC			
People eat cheese they prefer w/o regard to the price/cost*				BAC		4 > 3	
People often ask my advice about cheese				No BAC			O > Y
I like to discover new cheeses				No BAC			
It's a duty to educate others about all aspects of cheese.					Up > Mid Up > Low		O > Y
I can describe in detail 10 kinds of cheese						3 > 2	O > Y
Bread is essential for enjoying cheese							O > M
W/o cheeses, France be just another country							M > Y O > Y
Can know a personUs social class by observing the cheese he eats							M > Y O > Y
Always use fork & knife to eat cheese							M > Y O > Y
I probably spend too much money for cheese							M > Y O > Y
Cheese is near the top of my shipping list							M > Y O > Y
I could train someone to have a sophisticated knowledge about cheese							O > Y
I serve more kinds of cheese to impress others							O > Y

* Reverse Scored items

R = Rural respondents; **M** = Married Respondents; **F** = Female Respondents; **No BAC** = Respondents whose head of household did not have the baccalauréat degree; **BAC** = Respondents whose head of household did have the baccalauréat degree; **Up** = Upper Income Group; **Mid** = Middle Income Group; **Low** = Lower Income Group; **4** = Professionals; **3** = Self-employed Professionals; **2** = Pink Collar Workers; **O** = Older Respondents (age 50 and up); **M** = Middle Age Respondents (age 30-49); **Y** = Younger Respondents (18-29).

TABLE 4
Four Factor Solution

Item	F 1	F 2	F 3	F4
I could train someone to have a sophisticated knowledge about cheese	.804			
I can describe in detail 10 kinds of cheese	.748			
People often ask my advice about cheese	.675			
Cheese is near the top of my shopping list	.625			
Serve more kinds of cheese to impress others	.549		.369	
I eat more cheese than most other people	.528			
Duty to educate others about cheese	.513		.359	
Always use fork & knife to eat cheese	.395			.351
Buy from a specialty cheese retailer	.392	.316		
I probably spend too much money for cheese	.371			
Farm cheese is best		.567		
Life not be appreciated w/o cheese	.391	.564		
Cannot appreciate cheese w/o wine		.546		
W/o cheeses, France be just another country		.544	.406	
Crime to allow people to call Vache Qui Ri (ultra-pasturized cheese food for kids] cheese		.517		
EC shouldn't regulate French cheese		.478		
Bread is essential for enjoying cheese		.452		
People eat cheese they prefer w/o regard to the price/cost*		-.383	.310	
Can know a person's social class by observing the cheese he eats			.625	
Avg. Frenchman eats different cheese than the bourgeoisie			.603	
Can judge one's values by observing the cheese he consumes			.561	.422
Cheese is a symbol of French culture		.393	.498	
Never put foreign cheese on my cheese plate				.754
Never put processed cheese on cheese plate		.476		.526
One not liking cheese isn't truly French			.402	.441
I always serve cheese on a plate	.370			.405

* Reverse Scored items

NOTE: Only loadings of .3 or higher are printed

---

middle. Statistically significant differences in mean ratings were found for seventeen of the forty measures. In every instance, older respondents expressed more agreement with the statements than did the middle or younger groups, expressing more traditional opinions about cheese, cheese rituals, and France. These results are consistent with the differences in food consumption patterns of the younger French, discussed earlier, which led the French Education Minister to institute palate education programs in the schools. Specifically, the older group expressed more agreement that "without her cheeses, France would be just another country," that they would never put foreign cheese on their cheese plate, that they serve cheese on a plate, and always eat cheese with a fork and knife. This older group also believed that both bread and wine were essential accompaniments to eating cheese. The older group agreed that they were more knowledgeable about cheese and could help train another's palate. Consistent with these responses, they also agreed

that offering more cheeses on the cheese plate was one way to impress someone.

Taken as a set, there are statistically significant differences in mean ratings for demographic variables on twenty-four of the forty measures. Age differences alone, however, account for eleven of those measures. The differences accounted for by any one demographic variable, however, are few (except for age). Hence, we conclude that there is support for the main hypothesis of similarity of the French fondness and regard for cheese.

Assessment of Factors Reflecting Attitudes Toward Cheese

Having developed evidence to support the main hypothesis, the analysis next focused on the structure of the attitudes toward cheese, as reflected in the four sub-hypotheses about national identity, xenophobia, cheese knowledge and rituals, and French agricultural roots. The attitude and behavior measures were factor

TABLE 5

Five Factor Solution

Item	F 1	F 2	F 3	F 4	F 5
I could train someone to have a sophisticated knowledge about cheese	.806				
I can describe in detail 10 kinds of cheese	.747				
People often ask my advice about cheese	.678				
Cheese is near the top of my shopping list	.629				
I eat more cheese than most other people	.532				
Serve more kinds of cheese to impress others	.518		.363		
Duty to educate others about cheese	.489		.405		
Always use fork & knife to eat cheese	.422				
Buy from a specialty cheese retailer	.395	.321			
I probably spend too much money for cheese	.366				
Crime to allow people to call Vache Qui Ri (ultra-pasturized cheese food for kids] cheese		.689			
Cannot appreciate cheese w/o wine		.551			
Farm cheese is best		.528			
People eat cheese they prefer w/o regard to the price/cost*		-.433			
Bread is essential for enjoying cheese		.432			
Cheese is a symbol of French culture			.733		
W/o cheeses, France be just another country			.654		
EC shouldn't regulate French cheese			.553		
Life not be appreciated w/o cheese	.368	.388	.487		
Never put foreign cheese on my cheese plate				.796	
One not liking cheese isn't truly French			.303	.561	
Never put processed cheese on cheese plate		.449		.538	
I always serve cheese on a plate	.370			.415	
Avg. Frenchman eats different cheese than the bourgeoisie					.779
Can know a person's social class by observing the cheese he eats					.708
Can judge one's values by observing the cheese he consumes				.419	.498

* Reverse Scored items

analyzed. Because both varimax and oblique rotations failed to converge when all variables were submitted for analysis, a 40-by-40 matrix of the correlations among the variables was inspected. Variables which did not correlate with other measures at .30 or better (Tabachnick and Fidell 1989) were eliminated from the analysis, leaving a set of 26 variables. Factor analysis with varimax rotation was now successful.

The four-factor solution. Because of the four *a priori* sub-hypotheses, factor analysis was initially constrained to producing four factors (see Table 4). The factors account for 42 percent of the variation in the data. Inspection of the measures which load on each factor suggest that three of the factors (one, two, and four) are consistent with the hypotheses.

The *first factor* represents the cheese connoisseur who is knowledgeable about cheese and about the rituals surrounding the consumption of cheese. Items such as being able to describe in detail ten kinds of cheese, of playing an educational role with others with regard to cheese, and of eating cheese only with a knife and fork load on this factor.

The *second factor* seems to represent the importance of cheese to the French national lifestyle. Measures loading on this factor include the idea that farm cheese is best, that life could not be completely appreciated without cheese, and that without her cheeses France would be just another country. Two items from other factors load here as well. One is that cheese is a symbol of France; the other addresses an unwillingness to place processed cheese on the same plate with "real" cheese. If cheese represents French national identity, the purity of the symbol is important.

The *fourth factor* seems to represent the xenophobic side of attitudes toward cheese. Measures which load high on the fourth factor include not putting foreign cheese on one's plate, of never, under any circumstances, putting "industrial" cheese (processed cheese) on one's cheese plate, and the idea that a person who doesn't like cheese can't truly be considered French.

The *third factor*, however, is not consistent with our hypotheses. It reflects class and status associations with cheese, as items such as being able to determine a person's social class and values from the kinds of cheese one consumes load on this factor. Two other measures cross-load here as well. The first indicates that a person offers a wide selection of cheeses to impress others; the second is a measure of eating the cheese one likes without regard to its price.

While this third factor is not one which we hypothesized, the finding is quite consistent with Bourdieu's (1985) contention that food consumption reflects the social stratification within a society. He suggests that a society's food practices are based on social class, with the stratification being maintained via knowledge, aesthetic sensibility and by values. Douglas and Isherwood (1979) make much the same point when they suggest that elites (members of the top consumption class) reserve certain knowledge and information to themselves as a means of retaining their superior power and position. Hence, they would agree with Bourdieu that taste in food is an outward expression of the values of the social class to which one belongs.

Though the four-factor solution is appealing, twelve items do cross-load at .30 or higher. Certainly the actual structure of attitudes is not as distinctly delineated as it might appear to be from various attitude models (e.g. Fishbein's Attitude Toward the Act model). Further, the research here is not an attempt to develop a scale with orthogonal dimensions or sub-scales. Still, it would be preferable to have a "cleaner" solution. The scree plot suggests one alternative. The four- and five-factor solutions are on the same "longitudinal" line, suggesting that either solution might be acceptable. The five-factor solution also increases the variance explained to 47 percent. It also results in one-third fewer measures with cross-loadings of .30 or higher.

The five-factor solution. In the five-factor solution (see Table 5), the *first factor* to emerge is the same as before, reflecting a connoisseur's knowledge about cheese. This time, however, only three measures (instead of four) have cross-loadings of .30 or better. The *second factor* contains items which address the proper ways to eat cheese (with bread, that cheese cannot be enjoyed without wine, and the like). This factor addresses what Douglas and Isherwood (1979) would refer to as the rituals which help to solidify meaning. No measures from this factor cross-load at .30 or higher.

The *third factor* contains measures which focus on the connection between cheese and French national identity. One improvement over the four-factor solution is that the measure, "cheese is a symbol of France," has now moved to this factor, where one would expect to find it.

The *fourth factor* is the xenophobia factor. As before it is comprised of items which reflect a dislike, if not actually a fear, of strange and/or foreign cheeses. Except for one item, all measures in this factor cross-load at .30 or higher on one other factor. Though analytically messy, these cross-loadings make interpretative sense.

The *fifth factor* is the class factor. As noted above, the connection between class and food consumption patterns has been well established.

In neither the four nor the five factor solution did the expected connection between cheese and the French predilection for thinking of themselves as an agricultural nation emerge as a separate factor. This result may be explained by there being very few items which measured the idea. As Nunnally (1978) has demonstrated, factor analysis is sensitive to the number of items in the analysis which measure a given construct. Thus it is perhaps not surprising that the agricultural mind-set statements ("farm cheese is best," for example) loaded on other factors.

DISCUSSION AND CONCLUSION

This study is one attempt to advance the understanding of other cultures and is consistent with the tradition articulated by Holbrook and Hirschman (1982) that the study of consumption need not be restricted to tangible goods; experiences can also be consumed. The study is also consistent with Steenkamp's (1993) call for research into the social and cultural factors which shape perceptions of food. This study has demonstrated that for the French, because of the strong ties between gastronomy and national identity, food is an important cultural element. Hence, attitudes and behaviors with regard to cheese seems to be quite consistent across the citizenry, even though older French individuals seem to hold the strongest opinions. When these attitudes and behaviors are perceived to be disintegrating, as evidenced by preferences for pre-packaged fast food, the entire nation reacts with a program to train proper French palates.

Additionally, this study has demonstrated that within the structure of the attitude toward cheese one may find themes of the ties between cheese and national identity, between cheese and the French xenophobic zeal for stamping out that which is not purely French, and between cheese and the French obsession with knowing about food and the proper food consumption rituals. Finally, the study provided unexpected, but not inconsistent, evidence for the use of cheese in social stratification.

The obvious limitation of the study is that it is only a picture of attitudes at one point in time and is based on measures which have not been validated. The research by Askegaard (1993) and colleagues which seeks to develop models of the cultural aspects of specific eating and drinking patterns in different societies would help establish the validity of this study.

As Steenkamp has noted, "[w]hat we eat, how it is prepared, the rules and meanings which permeate every aspect of food consumption practices ... are all sociocultural matters" (1993, p. 405). For the French, food seems to be an especially important cultural category, perhaps even a cultural metaphor. While wine is perhaps more often associated with France (Gannon 1994), for the French themselves, cheese is just as important. As one respondent in the study said, loosely translated, "wine provides for enjoyment in life (*savoir vivre*), but cheese is life (*la vie*)."

REFERENCES

Askegaard, Søren (1993), "A European Regional Analysis of Selected Food Consumption Statements," in *European Advances in Consumer Research*, W.F. van Raaij and G.J. Bamossey, eds., Vol. 1, Provo, UT: Association for Consumer Research, 410-415.

Baudrillard, Jean (1981), *Simulacre et Simulations*, Paris: Galilee.

Belk, Russell W. (199?), "Hyperreality and Globalization: Culture in the Age of Ronald McDonald," *Journal of International Consumer Marketing*, 8 (3 & 4).

Berger, Peter L. and Thomas Luckmann (1967), *The Social Construction of Reality, Harmondsworth*, UK: Penguin.

Bicard, Daniel (1992), "*Fromages: l'Incontournable Merchandising*," LSA, No. 1301, April 23, 77-98.

Blythman, Joanna (1992), "Educating the Palate," in *The Good Food Guide*, T. Jaine, ed., London: Which? Books, 625-627.

Bourdieu, Pierre (1985), *Distinction: A Social Critique of the Judgment of Taste*, London: Routledge & Kegan paul.

Coffe, Jean-Pierre (1992), *Au Secours le Goût*, Paris: Presses Pocket.

Douglas, Mary and Baron Isherwood (1979), *The World of Goods*, London: Allen Lane.

Economist (1994), "Comedia Française," July 9, 54.

Economist (1993), "French Farmers Against the World," September 11, 47-48.

Economist (1992), "Runny, Smelly, and Safe," June 27, 60.

Encyclopedia Americana (1991), Volume 9, Danbury, CT: Grolier, 659.

Fazio, Russell H., Martha C. Powell, and Carol J. Williams (1989), "The Role of Attitude Accessibility in the Attitude-to-Behavior Process," *Journal of Consumer Research*, 16 (December), 280-288.

Gannon, Martin J. (1994), *Understanding Global Cultures: Metaphorical Journeys Through 17 Countries*, Thousand Oaks, CA: Sage.

Hallgarten, Elaine and Linda Collister (1992), *The Gourmet's Guide to London*, London: Vermillion.

Hirschman, Elizabeth C. and Morris B. Holbrook (1986), "Expanding the Ontology and Methodology of Research on the Consumption Experience," in *Perspectives on Methodology in Consumer Research*, ed. D. Brinberg and R. J. Lutz, New York: Springer, 213-251.

Hong, J. W., A. Muderrisoglu, and G. M. Zinkhan (1987), "Cultural Differences and Advertising Expression: A Comparative Content Analysis of Japanese and U.S. Advertising, " *Journal of Advertising*, 16, 55-69.

Institut Nationale de Statistiques et Etudes Economiques (1991), *Milk Products Production and Consumption Annual Report*.

Levi-Strauss, Claude (1969), *The Raw and the Cooked: Introduction to a Science of Mythology*, New York: Harper and Row.

Levy, Sidney J. (1981), "Interpreting Consumer Mythology: A Structural Approach to Consumer Behavior," *Journal of Marketing*, 45 (Summer), 49-61.

McCracken, Grant (1986), "Culture and Consumption: A Theoretical Account of the Structure and Movement of Cultural Meaning of Consumer Goods," *Journal of Consumer Research*, 13 (1), 71-84.

Mei-hui Yang, Mayfair (1994), *Gifts, Favors, and Banquets: The Art of Social Relationships in China*, Ithaca, NY: Cornell University Press.

Mennell, Stephen (1985), *All Manners of Food: Eating and Taste in England and France from the Middle Ages to the Present*, New York: Basil Blackwell.

Nunnally, Jum C. (1978), *Psychometric Theory*, New York: McGraw Hill.

Ohnuki-Tierney, Emiko (1993), *Rice as Self: Japanese Identities Through Time*, Princeton, NJ: Princeton University Press.

Repplier, Agnes (1932), *To Think of Tea!* Boston: Houghton Mifflin.

Schwartz, Shalom and Wolfgang Bilsky (1987), "Towards a Universal Psychological Structure of Human Values," *Journal of Personality and Social Psychology*, 53, 550-562.

Steenkamp, J. (1993), "Food Consumption Behavior," in *European Advances in Consumer Research*, W.F. van Raaij and G.J. Bamossey, eds., Vol. 1, Provo, UT: Association for Consumer Research, 401-409.

Tabachnick, Barbara and Linda S. Fidell (1989), *Using Multivariate Statistics*, Second Edition, New York: Harper & Row, Publishers.

Toy, Stewart (1994), "Vive le Camembert - Mold and All," *Business Week*, October 17, 18 E-4, 18 E-8.

Turnbull, Colin M. (1972), *The Mountain People*, New York: Touchstone.

Wallendorf, Melanie and Eric J. Arnould (1991), "'We Gather Together': Consumption Rituals of Thanksgiving Day," *Journal of Consumer Research*, 18 (June), 13-31.

Zeldin, Theodore (1982), *The French*, New York: Pantheon.

Fictional Materialism

William D. Wells, University of Minnesota
Cheri L. Anderson, University of Minnesota

ABSTRACT

Richins (1994) found that materialism, as measured by Richins and Dawson's (1992) Materialism scale, mediates the meanings of consumers' prized possessions. The present study tested, confirmed and extended that finding by observing and analyzing the possessions and behaviors of 71 fictional characters in well-known TV comedies and dramas. This outcome shows that television stories, and presumably other popular narratives, can supplement and complement more standard research data.

INTRODUCTION

In "Special Possessions and the Expression of Material Values," Marsha L. Richins (1994) administered the Richins and Dawson (1992) Materialism scale to a large sample of real consumers. She divided her respondents into upper and lower quartiles, and analyzed the public and private meanings of high materialists' and low materialists' most prized possessions.

The present study followed this pattern with three notable exceptions: (1) The "consumers" were fictional characters in prime time television comedies and dramas. (2) The Materialism scale was administered by proxy. (3) Judges identified the "consumers'" prized possessions.

METHOD

Richins (1994) mailed questionnaires to "random samples of 400 households in a small northeastern city and 300 households in a more rural area of the northeast." She received replies from "144 urban and 119 rural respondents, yielding response rates of 36.0 percent and 39.6 percent, respectively" (Richins 1994, 524). In an early part of her questionnaire she asked, "Many people have a few possessions that they care a lot about or that are especially important to them. In the spaces below list your most important possessions and explain why each is important to you"(104). A later part of the questionnaire included the Richins and Dawson (1992) Materialism scale.

Our procedure was somewhat different. We started with the 74 ongoing characters in the 19 highest Nielsen-rated prime time television comedies and dramas. For each character, we asked panels of at least four judges who were blind to the purpose of the investigation, "What are this person's most valued possessions?" and "What are the reasons he or she values them?" We asked *different* panels of at least four judges who also were blind to the purpose of the investigation to complete the Richins and Dawson (1992) Materialism scale as they thought each character would answer it. When we checked interjudge reliability, we found that, for three of the characters, agreement was not high enough to yield a stable estimate. We dropped those three characters, leaving 71 for this analysis.

Richins (1994) asked judges to sort her respondents' most valued possessions along a series of dimensions: social visibility, estimated market value, type of possession and private meaning. She also asked judges to decide, for each possession, whether people who own that possession are "likely to be materialistic or not materialistic" (530). On the basis of their Materialism scale scores, she divided her respondents into quartiles. She then compared the most valued possessions of the "high materialists"—the top quartile—with the most valued possessions of the "low materialists"—the bottom quartile—on all the rated and judged dimensions. We followed those procedures as closely as possible.

FINDINGS

Materialism Scale Statistics

Richins did not report the mean and standard deviation of the Materialism scores from her (1994) respondents. However, Richins and Dawson (1992) reported means ranging from 46 to 48 and standard deviations ranging from eight to ten from their scale-validation samples. In the present study, the 71 TV characters averaged 54 on the Materialism scale, with a standard deviation of 14. Thus, the TV characters appear to be slightly more materialistic, and more varied in materialism, than Richins and Dawson's (1992) samples of real persons. We will comment on those statistics later.

Richins (1994) reported Materialism scale alphas of .84 and .86 from her two samples. Richins and Dawson (1992) reported alphas of .80 to .88. In the present study, the Materialism scale's alpha was .98—significantly higher. We will comment on that statistic later.

Hypotheses

From previous research, Richins (1994) developed, tested and confirmed four sets of hypotheses concerning differences between high materialists and low materialists:

H1: Consumers with different levels of materialism will value different types of possessions. Compared to the possessions valued by consumers low in materialism, possessions valued by high-materialism consumers (a) tend to be publicly (rather than privately) consumed, (b) are more expensive, and (c) are less likely to be associated with important others.

H2: The private meanings of possessions valued by high-materialism consumers (as compared to those valued by low materialism consumers) are (a) less likely to concern the possession's role in representing or facilitating interpersonal ties and (b) more likely to relate to the financial worth of the possession.

H3: The public meanings of possessions value by high-materialism consumers (as compared to those valued by low-materialism consumers) are more likely to refer to success or prestige.

H4: The possessions valued by those low in materialism and those high in materialism will be consistent with socially constructed stereotypes of nonmaterialistic and materialistic consumers, respectively (Richins 1994, 523-524).

Using our fictional respondents and their "most valued" possessions (see Table 1), we retested these relationships.

Social Visibility

In the original investigation, judges sorted possessions along a "social visibility" continuum that ran from (1) used in private, through (2) displayed in the home and (3) displayed on the person, to (4) used in a public place. As expected, she found that high materialists' most valued possessions were significantly (p.<.05)

TABLE 1
Some of the Possessions Valued by Low and High Materialists in the TV Stories

Valued by Low Materialists	Valued by High Materialists
High school diploma	Fancy car
Encyclopedia	Corvette
Cooking stuff	BMW
Health food	Designer suits
Guitar	Father's credit card
Police memorabilia	Flashy jewelry
Books	Country club membership
Birds	Celebrity's Chrysler
Award for achievement	Cosmetics
Work product	Hair

TABLE 2
Social Visibility of Low Materialists' and High Materialists' Most Valued Possessions

	Original Investigation (from Richins 1944, Table 2)		Fictional Replication	
	Low (131) %	High (138) %	Low (43) %	High (59) %
Used in private	19	12	30	5
Displayed in home	50	41	35	24
Displayed on person	8	15	14	34
Used in public	23	31	21	37

Read: In the original investigation, 19% of the 131 possessions valued by low materialists were classified as "used in private," 50% were classified as "displayed in the home" etc.

Note: Possessions that could not be classified are omitted from both sets of data.

more visible than low materialists' most valued possessions. Our data showed exactly the same pattern (p.<.01, Table 2). If anything, the relationship in the TV data is a little stronger.

Estimated Market Value
In the original investigation, judges estimated the possessions' market value. The high materialists' most valued possessions were significantly (p.<.01) more expensive than the low materialists' most valued possessions. Again, the fictional data replicated the pattern (p.<.01, Table 3).

Type of Possession
In the original investigation, judges classified possessions into types: sentimental objects, practical objects, aesthetic objects, financial assets, extensions of the self, and possessions used for: transportation, recreation, and personal appearance (Richins 1994, Table 2).

In Richins' study, high materialists were significantly less likely to value sentimental and recreational possessions, and significantly more likely to value transportation, personal appearance and financial possessions. Expected differences for extensions of the self, practical objects and aesthetic objects were not statistically significant.

In the fictional replication (Table 4) high materialists were significantly more likely to value transportation (p.<.01) and personal appearance (p.<.00) possessions. As in the original study, high materialists did not differ significantly from low materialists in valuing extensions of the self. The remaining categories contained too few entries to permit firm conclusions. Thus, the fictional replication confirmed most, but not all, of Richins' findings about high materialists' and low materialists' valuation of various types of possessions. Failures to confirm were traceable to low numbers of observations. They were not statistically significant contradictions.

TABLE 3
Estimated Market Value of Low Materialists' and High Materialists'
Most Valued Possessions

	Original Investigation (from Richins 1944, Table 2)		Fictional Replication	
	Low (117) %	High (109) %	Low (33) %	High (54) %
Estimated Market Value				
Zero	6	4	21	4
<$100	10	3	32	30
$100-1000	40	20	21	22
$1000-50,000	26	47	16	28
>$50,000	18	27	11	17

Read: In the original investigation, six percent of the possessions valued by low materialists had no market value, 10 percent were valued at less than $100, etc.

Note: Possessions whose market value could not be estimated are omitted from both sets of data.

TABLE 4
Types of Possessions Valued by Low Materialists and High Materialists

	Original Investigation (from Richins 1944, Table 2)		Fictional Replication	
	Low (117) %	High (109) %	Low (47) %	High (61) %
Sentimental	28	11	9	3
Recreational	27	11	6	13
Financial assets	15	25	9	6
Transportation	12	25	2	13
Personal appearance	0	10	7	25
Practical	7	8	17	8
Aesthetic	4	6	11	8
Extensions of self	4	2	30	21
Other	3	2	11	2

Read: Of the 117 possessions valued by low materialists in the original investigation, 28% were "sentimental" possessions, 27% were "recreational," etc.

Private Meanings

Richins (1994) asked respondents to explain why their possessions were important. We asked judges who were blind to the TV characters' imputed Materialism scores and blind to the purpose of the experiment, "What are this person's most valued possessions?" and "What are the reasons he or she values them?"

Two of Richins' findings reemerged: In the replication, high materialists were significantly more likely to value possessions for financial and appearance-related reasons (both at p.<.01, Table 5). Two of Richins' findings did not reemerge. We did not find significant differences in valuing possessions for their personal connotations, or for their "utilitarian" functions. One of Richins' predictions, supported but not significant in the original, was supported and significant (p.<.001) in the replication. High materialists were less likely than low materialists to value possessions for identity reasons (Table 5).

Thus, even though imagining the motives of fictional characters is at best uncertain, the fictional replication confirmed several of Richins' (1994) predictions about "private meanings."

TABLE 5
Private Meanings of Low Materialists' and High Materialists' Most Valued Possessions

	Original Investigation (from Richins 1944, Table 3)		Fictional Replication	
	Low (204) %	High (190) %	Low (47) %	High (61) %
Financial aspects	3	12	0	13
Enjoyment	32	19	11	5
Interpersonalties	24	8	4	2
Appearance related	1	26	0	41
Identity	11	8	70	30
Other	5	19	0	6

Read: Of the 204 reasons low materialists gave for valuing their possessions, 3% were "financial," 32% were "enjoyment," etc. In the replication, "appearance" and "identity" were statistically significant (p.<.00 and p.<.01 respectively).

TABLE 6
Judged Materialism of Possessions and Measured Materialism of Possessions' Owners

	Original Investigation (from Richins 1944, Table 7)		Fictional Replication	
	Materialism of Possession's Owner		Materialism of Possession's Owner	
Materialism of Possessions	Low %	High %	Low %	High %
Low	85	31	90	36
High	15	69	10	64

Read: In the original investigation, among 48 low-materialism respondents, 85% of the valued possessions were judged to be "low materialism" possessions, and 15% were judged to be "high materialism" possessions.

Note: Multiple possessions by individual owners are included in this table. Possessions classified as "can't determine" are omitted.

"Materialistic" and "Nonmaterialistic" Possessions

Richins (1992) listed her respondents' possessions on cards, and asked 30 judges to separate the cards into "whether you think the person who mentioned the item is likely to be materialistic or not materialistic." She also permitted "can't determine" (530). Considering only those possessions for which her judges showed at least 60% agreement, she found a significant (p.<.001) positive relationship between position on the Materialism scale and ownership of stereotypically "materialistic" possessions. This relationship reappeared in the fictional replication (Table 6).

Extension

One way to enhance the construct validity of an instrument like the Materialism scale is to contrast the personality characteristics of those who score high on it with the personality characteristics of those who score low on it. In the present study, sets of (at least four) judges who were blind to imputed Materialism scale scores and to the purpose of the investigation rated the TV characters on a 41-item adjective check list. Considering only those traits that more than half the judges checked for a given character, the adjectives showed some diagnostic differences (Table 7).

TABLE 7
Traits Attributed to Low-Materialism and High Materialism TV Characters in the Fictional Replication

	Low Materialism Characters (18) %	High Materialism Characters (19) %
Hard-working	77	26
Good-natured	72	26
Calm	72	0
Broad-minded	61	5
Cooperative	55	0
Curious	55	10
Imaginative	55	16
Warm	50	10
Impulsive	22	58
Emotional	16	57
Insecure	11	42
Irresponsible	0	37

Read: 77% of the 18 low-materialism TV characters were rated "hard-working" by more than half the judges, 72% were rated "good-natured," etc. All differences between high-materialism characters and low-materialism characters are statistically significant (p. <.05).

Table 7 shows that the low-materialism TV characters were rated more hard-working, good-natured, calm, broad-minded, co-operative, curious, imaginative and warm—and less impulsive, emotional, insecure, and irresponsible—than their high materialism counterparts. These findings enrich the construct validity of the Materialism scale, and are congruent with descriptions of materialists in other investigations (Belk 1985, McKeage 1922, Micken 1992, Williams and Bryce 1992).

Factor Analysis of the Materialism Scale

In the course of developing their Materialism scale, Richins and Dawson (1992) factor-analyzed the scale items. They identified three subscales—Centrality, Success and Happiness—that tap into separate facets of the overall dimension.

When we factor-analyzed the TV data, the eigenvalues implied a two-factor solution (Table 8). In a varimax rotation, the first factor merged Centrality and Success, and accounted for 77% of the variance. The second factor, Happiness, accounted for 7% of the variance. None of the succeeding factors accounted for more than 3% of the variance.

When we forced a three-factor solution, the first factor was predominantly Success, with two low-loading Centrality items. The second factor was entirely Happiness. The third factor included the remaining Centrality statements (Table 8). As would be expected from the factor analysis, raw score (not factor score) correlations among Success, Centrality and Happiness were high and positive: Success—Centrality, .93; Success—Happiness, .83; Happiness—Centrality, .78.

One possible interpretation of this outcome is that judges' ratings of TV characters are less fine-grained than self-revelations by real persons. It seems reasonable to assume that judges form and use overall impressions, while self evaluators are more responsive to separate nuances of individual scale items. In the present study,

the Materialism scale's alpha of .98, noted earlier, supports this interpretation.

However, it is also possible that conceptually distinct facets of Materialism are positively (and maybe highly) correlated, even in self-evaluations. The alphas of .84 and .86 reported by Richins (1994) and the alphas of .80 and .88 reported by Richins and Dawson (1992) support that conclusion. If that conclusion is correct, future users of the Materialism scale will find that differences among subscales are small and relatively unreliable.

Scale Parameters

The New England adults in Richins and Dawson's (1992) standardization samples averaged 46 to 48 on the Materialism scale. The TV characters averaged 54. Fifty-four is significantly (p.<.001) higher than the standardization means, and more in line with the 58 that McKeage (1992) obtained from two samples of New England college students.

McKeage (1992) concluded that his respondents were "a bit more materialistic" (141) than Richins and Dawson's (1992) adults. There is, however, another possible explanation. In Richins and Dawson's (1992) surveys, response rates were 31 to 43 percent. If, among those who received Richins and Dawson's questionnaires in the mail, the low materialists (like the low materialists in the TV stories) were more hard-working, good-natured, cooperative and curious—and less insecure and irresponsible—than the high materialists, they would be more likely to respond to the researchers' request for assistance. If this speculation is correct, low materialists were over-represented, and high materialists were under-represented, in Richins and Dawson's (1992) standardization samples and in Richins' (1994) study of possessions. We do not know whether this explanation is correct. It is only a speculation.

TABLE 8
Factor Analysis of the Materialism Scale
(Data from the Fictional Replication)

Item (abbreviated)	Two Factor Solution		Three Factor Solution		
	One	Two	One	Two	Three
Buy only things I need	87	37	59	33	67
Try to keep my life simple	85	35	51	33	71
Like a lot of luxury	85	41	64	36	59
Buying gives me pleasure	83	36	48	34	71
Spend on things not practical	83	21	33	22	85
Things say how well I'm doing	82	34	83	25	36
Own things that impress people	80	49	74	42	43
Less emphasis on material things	79	48	68	42	48
Achievements include possessions	77	54	71	48	43
No attention to others' possessions	76	53	63	48	49
Objects not a sign of success	76	57	67	51	45
Admire people who have expensive	72	59	66	53	41
Things not important to me	70	47	60	42	42
Bothers me I can't afford	22	88	19	87	19
Have all I need to enjoy life	33	85	39	82	15
Be happier if could afford more	49	80	43	77	33
Life better if I owned more	49	76	45	72	31
Happier if I had nicer things	49	74	24	75	49

DISCUSSION AND COMMENT

We set out to extend the notion that television stories (and presumably other fictional narratives such as novels, movies, and theatrical productions) are useful sites for research on consumer behavior. An earlier "fictional replication" (Wells and Gale 1994) had shown that analysis of TV stories can complement and supplement a real-life ethnographic investigation (Otnes, Lowrey and Kim 1993). The present study focused on a measured individual difference variable—materialism, and the correlations between it and the public and private meanings of possessions.

The earlier "replication" supported many of the ethnographic findings. It was conducted by independent investigators using sharply different methods. It therefore furnished strong convergent validation (Campbell and Fiske 1959).

The earlier "replication" also extended the ethnographic findings. Because the TV narratives provided a large and diverse sample of "respondents" and situations, they yielded some findings—supported by other research (Belk and Coon 1995; Sherry 1983; Sherry, McGrath and Levy 1992)—that did not appear in the original investigation.

The present "replication" also supported many of its model's conclusions. Again, because it was conducted by independent investigators using sharply different methods, it provides strong conceptual confirmation.

The present "replication" was also an extension. Adjective check list ratings of the TV characters added meaning to the distinction between high and low materialists. Factor analysis of the Materialism scale raised cautions for future users of that instrument. An assumption that high and low materialists in real life are similar to high and low materialists in the TV stories provided a possible explanation for the comparatively low Materialism scores among Richins and Dawson's (1992) and Richins' (1994) mail questionnaire respondents. These findings and speculations seem important enough to merit further investigation.

What's going on here? An explanation that appeals to us is that writers, directors and producers of successful TV comedies and dramas, and the actors who play popular TV characters, are accurate observers human nature. If this explanation is correct, their insights (and the insights in novels, plays, biographies and cinema) may tell us something useful about the real behavior of real consumers.

Of course fictional narratives are not mirrors (Cantor 1992, Feuer 1992, Vande Berg and Streckfuss 1992). Instead, they extract, abbreviate and amplify relationships that also occur in real behavior.

In this respect, fictional narratives resemble surveys and experiments. Surveys and experiments are not natural segments of everyday life. They extract, abbreviate and amplify relationships that carry over into real behavior. The trick is to understand what they mean, and to make valid extrapolations from them.

At this point we know very little about how to make valid extrapolations from fictional narratives. However, "fictional replications" of an ethnographic study (Otnes et al. 1993) and a psychometric study (Richins 1994) encourage further exploration. In both "replications," imaginary behavior of fictional characters complemented and supplemented real behavior of real consumers.

In both "replications," fictional data from fictional narratives supported and extended real data from empirical investigations.

This experience suggests that fictional narratives can enrich our understanding of the real behavior of real consumers. In some sense art imitates life. The trick will be to use that imitation to build bridges between the wisdom resident in the humanities and the empirical data of the social sciences.

REFERENCES

Belk, Russell W. (1985), "Materialism: Trait Aspects of Living in the Material World," *Journal of Consumer Research*, 12 (December), 265-280.

_____ and Gregory S. Coon (1993), "Gift Giving as Agapic Love: An Alternative to the Exchange Paradigm Based on Dating Experiences," *Journal of Consumer Research*, 20 (December), 393-417.

Campbell, Donald T. and Donald W. Fiske (1959), "Convergent and Discriminant Validation by the Multitrait-Multimethod Matrix," *Psychological Bulletin*, 56 (2), 81-105.

Cantor, Muriel G. (1992), "*Prime-Time Television: Content and Control*, Beverley Hills, CA and London: Sage Publications.

Feuer, Jane (1992), "Genre Study and Television," in *Channels of Discourse, Reassembled*, Robert E. Allen ed., Chapel Hill NC: University of North Carolina Press.

McKeage, Kim K. R. (1992), "Materialism and Self Indulgence: Theories of Materialism in Self-Giving," in *Meaning, Measure and Morality of Materialism*, Floyd Rudmin and Marsha Richins eds., Provo, UT: Association for Consumer Research, 140-148.

Micken, Kathleen S. (1992), "Materialism Research: Suggestions for New Directions," in *Meaning, Measure and Morality of Materialism*, Floyd Rudmin and Marsha Richins eds., Provo, UT: Association for Consumer Research, 121-125.

Otnes, Cele, Tina M. Lowrey and Young Chan Kim (1993), "Gift Selection for Easy and Difficult Recipients: A Social Roles Interpretation," *Journal of Consumer Research*, 20 (September), 229-244.

Richins, Marsha L. (1994), "Special Possessions and the Expression of Material Values," *Journal of Consumer Research*, 21 (December), 522-533.

_____ and Scott Dawson (1992), "A Consumer Values Orientation for Materialism and Its Measurement: Scale Development and Validation," *Journal of Consumer Research*, 19 (December), 303-316.

Sherry, John F., Jr. (1983), "Gift Giving in Anthropological Perspective," *Journal of Consumer Research*, 20 (September), 157-168.

_____, Mary Ann McGrath and Sidney J. Levy (1992), "The Disposition of the Gift and Many Unhappy Returns," *Journal of Retailing*, 68 (Spring), 40-65.

Vande Berg, Leah R. and Diane Streckfuss (1992), "Prime-time Portrayal of Women and the World of Work: A Demographic Profile," *Journal of Broadcasting and Electronic Media* 36 (Spring), 195-208.

Williams, John, and Wendy Brice (1992), "Materialism and Care for Others," in *Meaning, Measure and Morality of Materialism*, Floyd Rudmin and Marsha Richins eds., Provo, UT: Association for Consumer Research, 149-154.

Wells, William D. and Kendra L. Gale (1994), "Fictional Subjects in Consumer Research," in Frank Kardes and Mita Sujan eds., *Advances in Consumer Research* Vol. 21, Provo, UT: Association for Consumer Research.

Reframing Ikea: Commodity-Signs, Consumer Creativity and The Social/Self Dialectic

Mark Ritson, Lancaster University
Richard Elliott, University of Oxford
Sue Eccles, University of Oxford

ABSTRACT

The use of consumption-based meanings in the construction of both self and group constructs is examined using phenomenological interviews as the basis for existential phenomenological and hermeneutic analysis. The study concentrates on a particular subculture, a lesbian group in the UK, and their use of meanings associated with Ikea, the Scandinavian furnishings store. The results suggest that a double reframing of consumption meanings takes place. First, the subculture alters the symbolic meaning of Ikea to create group identity. Second, that altered symbol is again reframed by each individual member in creating the self-construct.

Symbolic Construction and Existential Consumption

'Consumer goods, in their anticipation, choice, purchase and possession, are an important source of meanings with which we construct our lives' (McCracken 1988). This essentially semiotic perspective (Mick 1986) maintains that consumer goods like all other elements in the culturally constituted world are signs, in this case 'commodity signs' (Baudrillard 1988), which are interpreted to produce signified meanings. These meanings, derived from consumption-based activity, form an important existential source of meaning in the individual's construction of their subjective view of reality (Lyddon and Alford 1993).

Several studies have shown how consumption meanings are used within the context of consumers' lives either as the 'raw material for one person's attempts to make sense of the world' (Buttle 1991), 'the means by which they negotiate their lives' (Mick and Buhl 1992) or a resource for 'existential consumption' (Elliott and Ritson 1995).

Consumption and the Construction of Self

The role possessions play in determining the self-concept has been conceptualised in the 'extended self' construct (Belk 1988), although the motivational factors that underpin this use of consumption-based activity vary widely (Dittmar 1992). One important consideration is the ability of individuals to 'twist' or 'divert' consumption-based meanings in order to achieve congruence with self image. Both Mick and Buhl (1992) and Elliott, Eccles and Hodgson (1993) show how consumers could re-negotiate intended meanings subjectively according to their own self-constructs. This behaviour is theorised by both McCracken (1986) and Tharp and Scott (1990) who claim: 'Individuals will embroider on the cultural canvas, using personal experiences, the opinions of local experts, the prejudices of friends and so on to form subjective meanings'. This 'new existentialism' (Laermans 1993) demonstrates the ability of consumers to re-signify commodity-signs in personalised, unintended directions (de Certau 1984).

Consumption and Constructing the Group Concept

Just as products act as signs interpreted by their owner in the process of self-construction, simultaneously that same product signifies a potentially different set of meanings externally to others. As Dittmar (1992) declares: 'It is through their symbolic meanings that material objects can communicate aspects of their owner's identity to self and to others', creating elaborate communicative systems of socially shared meanings(Douglas and Isherwood 1979). This social meaning derives from the commodity-sign (Baudrillard 1988) and the semiotic potential of goods as a key way of expressing and defining group membership and group values through shared consumption symbols.

In order for any object to function as a symbol, there must be a shared reality among consumers (Hirschman 1981) which leads to 'styles of consumption' and the creation of specific social identities for subcultural groups (Bauman 1988).

The creation and maintenance of subcultures is in part dependent on the ability of the group to differentiate themselves from the hegemonic ideology of the cultural whole and to maintain their subcultural identity (Hall 1977) through a shared use and interpretation of consumption-based symbols, often based on an overt 'relocation of symbolic meaning' (Hebdidge 1979).

This relocation occurs because subcultures can, just like consumers, engage in symbolic self-construction and re-negotiate the signified meanings of commodity-signs. Indeed the 'symbolic repossession of cultural meaning is the most potent form of maintaining subcultural identity' (Hebdidge 1979) with subcultures waging 'semiotic guerrilla warfare' (Eco 1972) against the dominant cultural ideology. This process occurs by taking the two constituent elements of hegemonic culture; the object and its meaning (the sign) and 'relocating' (Clarke 1976) or 'repossessing' (Hebdidge 1979) them in order to defy hegemonic forces, oppose the dominant semiotic system and maintain subcultural identity. Because these newly appropriated signs are common only to the subculture, their apparent 'secrecy' lends added identity to the subcultural group (Hebdidge 1979).

Thus group identity derives from both the creation and maintenance of these re-appropriated, re-signified sociological meanings.

The Social/Self Dialectic

Definitions of the social and the selfish dimensions of consumption-based meaning vary: 'self/social worlds' (Dittmar 1992), 'symbols/signs' (Solomon 1983), 'intra/inter-personal' semiotic discourse (Mick 1986), 'self-definition/ collective definition' (McCracken 1990) or 'psychological/ sociological' (Hirschman 1981), but the basic social/self dialectic remains constant. But what is the relationship between the creation of both self and social worlds from the same consumption-based meanings? Richins' (1994) study of 'public' and 'private' meanings gives several examples of how group-constructed, shared consumption meanings can 'shift' towards individuals' self-concepts over time.

This social/self dialectic, implicitly recognised by Richins (1994), has also been addressed from a hermeneutic perspective. A hermeneutic approach posits that 'a person's understanding of his/her life experiences always reflects broader cultural viewpoints' (Thompson, Polio and Locander 1994). Any expression of personal meaning (e.g. in creating the self-construct) represents only an adaptation of existing group-constructed, cultural meaning (Packer 1985). Thus the social/self dialectic is addressed through the concept of 'Wiskungsgeschichte' (Gadamer 1976) or continuing representations:

'The original...and the reproduction are representations and representations represent something only in so far as they are again represented' (Weinsheimer 1985). Thus any new, personalised self-meanings, no matter how idiosyncratic, derive from a representation of an existing group-constructed meaning. This dialectic is explored through the study of a group of lesbians in the UK who developed the identity of 'Dikea'.

Methodology

The 'Dikea' group were featured briefly in a UK television report on the 'London Gay Pride Festival'. The group were approached and three of its members agreed to take part in individual phenomenological interviews (Thompson, Locander and Polio 1989) which were conducted by one of the authors in the informants' respective homes. All three informants lived in the London area, in rented or owned property. Two expressed a liking for Ikea furniture and furnishings and explained that it was quite usual for lesbians to visit, buy from or meet up at the local Ikea store. Although moderate incomes limited their purchasing power at Ikea, both had some Ikea items in their respective homes. The third informant had little knowledge about Ikea having visited her local store only once. The interviews themselves lasted two to four hours and all commenced with the informant being asked to explain her own involvement in, and perception of the Dikea group. From there, ensuing questions were based on each informant's own direction of dialogue, and further explored individual comments and experiences.

Phenomenological interviews were conducted because of their ability to record both personalised accounts of lived experience (Kvale 1983) and subcultural influences (Mick and Buhl 1992). Interpretive methodologies (particularly phenomenology) have been proposed as more appropriate for studying the rich multi-dimensionality of consumption meaning than conventional quantitative techniques (Richins 1994).

After the interviews had been completed, two forms of interpretation were conducted. First a hermeneutic methodology was adopted and 'symbolic metaphors' were interpreted from the interview transcripts. These symbolic metaphors offer a unique opportunity to study the social/self dialectic because of their ability to analyse both 'personal' and 'sociocultural meanings' and thus represent the individual's perception of self in respect to the social group (Thompson et al. 1994). Furthermore, because this method of interpretation highlights thematic differences rather then similarities in the data, symbolic metaphors representing each respondent presented a means of exploring each informant's self-construct differences in relation to each other.

However, in order to explore the relationship between each of the informant's differing self-constructs and the shared social-construction of the group, a second interpretive methodology was also needed. Existential-phenomenology (Valle and Halling 1989) was used to re-interpret the transcripts a second time. This methodology was chosen because it develops commonly shared experiential themes (O'Guinn and Faber 1989) and serves to 'unravel the structures, logic, and inter-relationships...in the phenomenon under inspection' (Valle and Halling 1989). Thus because existential-phenomenology identifies 'global themes' which 'seek to describe common patterns of experience' (Thompson et al. 1994), it was possible to use this method to isolate experiential markers of shared experience or 'common features that structure person-world interaction' (Valle and Halling 1989). It was then possible to perform a variant of triangulation (Wallendorf, Belk and Heisley 1988) between these 'common features' of group experience and the individual 'symbolic metaphors' of each differing self-construct, derived from hermeneutic analysis, thus exploring the social/self dialectic of symbolic consumption. This triangulation was possible only because both methodologies rely on the interpretation of the same raw data, the phenomenological interview. However, in

moving from the self to the social level of meaning analogies and contrasting interpretations focusing in subjective difference with that focusing on shared themes, we are not claiming to triangulate on any underlying essential truth, but are presenting two perspectives on meaning and behaviour which, taken together, build a rich multi-dimensional picture which helps to reflect the ambiguities of the individual in a post-modern world.

Lesbian Subculture and the Dikea Group Identity

Although lesbians may be considered a group of women who merely share the same sexual preference, the more commonly accepted definition of contemporary lesbianism is one of identity and community, and not simply sexual acts (Gibbs 1994). The lesbian community offers a distinct example of the features that Hebdidge (1979) associates with subcultures and 'the expressive forms and rituals of these subordinate groups' through their adoption of dress codes (such as Doc Marten's boots), political beliefs and behaviours, and their orchestrated celebrations of identity such as 'lesbian weddings'. Whilst often rejecting heterosexual mores and norms, it has become apparent recently that lesbians have intruded into mainstream culture and have taken hegemonic images, identities and fashions and subverted them for their own lifestyle and culture (Hamer and Budge 1994). Despite this subversion of 'straight' culture, the lesbian subculture also maintains its identity through overtly gay events. The most notable examples of this form of 'subcultural ritual' (Hebdidge 1979) are the 'Gay Pride Festivals' which take place annually in many major cities throughout the world, including New York and London. They feature a march around the city limits with all the participants converging on a central city location. The Pride Festivals represent an opportunity for the gay community to demonstrate their subcultural identity to both themselves and the general public. Amanda (all names are fictional), one of the informants, comments:

'That was the whole idea of it being a day where you can be obvious and you can be 'out and proud', so it's a day of having an identity and being able to walk around in the street.'

The March represents a semiotic carnival of expression and symbolic meaning for the gay community but within that larger subculture, many small subcultural entities emerge, each displaying their identity with appropriate symbolic cues. Amanda notes this nebulous subcultural mass:

'The day itself is just people all in one place with the same orientation which is important, and then within that, it's like you have a group identity within the larger identity of the March.'

The 'group identity' which Amanda and 12 of her lesbian friends chose was that of 'Dikea'. The group dressed in identical uniforms of hard hats and overalls imprinted with a large logo of 'Dikea' on the back, in the style of Ikea, the Scandinavian furnishings store, thus connecting this image with that of a 'Dyke' (slang for lesbian). Several members of the group had come up with this idea together and all the informants showed a overt consciousness of this subcultural re-signification of the meanings of Ikea. Becky explains:

'...it was about picking something for Pride. Using a name and twisting it for our own means to get a response...Putting the D in front of the Ikea and making it our own I suppose.'

Amanda suggests that this kind of 'semiotic guerrilla warfare' (Eco 1972) in order to create group identity, is not only a conscious process but common in the subcultural world:

'I don't think straight people mock or lift slogans and logos like Dyke, with the Nike logo. I've seen that and Faagan Dyke [Haagen Dazs], but I've never seen any smaller groups lift things. I don't know if straight culture would pick up on it...what can they do with Ikea? Because the marketing is aimed at straight people, then they've got no need to manipulate it, and make it specifically have reference to them.'

Clearly the group are implicitly aware of the subcultural agenda which motivates this 'practical existentialism' (Willis 1990).

Self-Constructs and the Dikea Group Identity

This paper now concentrates on this subcultural identity in relation to the subjective experiences and interpretations that three members of the group (Amanda, Becky and Cathy) encounter. Each informant's 'symbolic metaphors' are identified and linked to each of their subjective interpretations of the group's activity. This is illustrated by relating each different 'symbolic metaphor' to three shared 'global themes' of group experience; the meaning of Dikea to the respondent, the interpretation of the reactions of the spectators to the group and finally the individual's own interpretation of their feelings on the day. The relationship between each respondent and Ikea is also explored. Due to space restrictions, only brief examples can be given of the phenomenological data used to form the interpretation presented here, which is itself only one of many possible interpretations.

Amanda

Amanda was outgoing and relaxed throughout the interview and was constantly engaged in laughter. Her fellow informants had identified her as the most creative and humorous member of the group and she acknowledges both these elements in her descriptions of her involvement in group activities:

'I've written little pantomimes; I like dressing up; basically, if I can make a costume for it I will.'

'I mean, for me, a lot of it is getting everybody together to have fun. It's also quite funny that I can persuade people to do this. I think that's quite funny...it's about having fun really and getting everybody together.'

Amanda's 'symbolic metaphor' relates to her creativity and humour being combined into a search for fun. This metaphor is apparent in Amanda's interpretation of the Dikea concept:

'I wanted to keep it [the message] clear so that everybody looks the same, which I think is quite important for me, that they all look identical...I think the beauty of it is that the joke is on the back. Because I'm not in it for personal limelight, I think it's funny if I walk past someone and they get the joke...'

Amanda cements this personal interpretation of the group's identity by continually referring to the humorous nature of the day and the 'hook' of the Dikea image. She speculates on where that hook comes from:

'I think purely the joke, the play on words and because the logo is written in the same writing, it's using the same colours, the frame of the word is the same shape.'

Amanda extends this interpretation, still based on her symbolic metaphor of fun, to the reaction of the spectators:

'I thought it was funny to me, and funny to us doing it but I hadn't considered that other people would find it entertaining.'

'[a large] amount of people did talk to us, and I think they just wanted to tell us that they had got the joke, it was quite important for them to say, you know, "Oh I've got the joke"'

Similarly this symbolic metaphor also influences her recollection of her own feelings on the day of the March:

'Well the first time we did it, it was great because of the unexpected amusement from other people. The second time it was still great ... because we knew that people would be coming up to us, so we had one-liners...'

Finally Amanda describes how, for her, the symbolic meanings of Dikea emerged from its two elements combined:

'they [the spectators] had got the words, the reference to 'Dyke' and to the shop as well. I think probably they knew we were homosexual ... because they were at Pride...so I think it was more about the shop.'

Amanda explains the link with the Ikea shop further:

'If you go round Ikea then it's stuffed with homosexuals buying things, so there's a lot of people just cruising around. I've got a mortgage and I've got a sofa from Ikea, so it makes you feel quite normal to know you are spending money on the same things as straight people.'

Furthermore this subcultural joke appears to now constitute one of Hebdidge's (1979) 'secret meanings':

'I mean, I'd choose Ikea over another shop; I think I'd do that anyway but now it's like secret, I can go to Ikea and I know about the Dikea's'

Becky

In contrast to Amanda and, to a lesser extent, the other members of the group Becky sees herself as very different:

'Well, I think they're more artistic than I am. Like Amanda for example likes to involve herself in dressing-up and having a laugh.'

'I don't find [creative] things like that particularly easy. It just doesn't come naturally to me. It's like an effort to do. I could never be as creative as Amanda. I'd say I was quite different. I'm more sort of... they're very outgoing, I'm outgoing in a different way...in a practical way, in the way I communicate with other people and that sort of thing.'

This perceived practicality, particularly in relation to communication, leads Becky to see herself as very different from the others in the group and forms her symbolic metaphor of self. This practical communicative aspect of her self is reflected continually in her responses and is clear in each of the three global themes of experience. First she describes the meaning of Dikea:

'It was about er..., because you make stuff up yourself it's like a do-it-yourself kit so it's about taking control. Women taking control for themselves and, you know, dressing up...and presenting an image of strength and independence'

For Becky the meaning of Dikea was tied up in the communication of practical images of control, strength and independence. Furthermore she extends this interpretation by arguing:

'...a recognition of the name Dikea, you know, as I said before a lot of gay people use Ikea for furnishings and it would be recognised in that way by putting a D in front of it because [of] lesbians taking control'

Again, in re-appropriating the commodity sign for the purposes of the subculture, the practical message of control is conveyed. This symbolic metaphor of practicality again emerges in Becky's representations of the reactions of the spectators:

'I thought it was very positive. Erm... it was all "great", "good idea", "we like Ikea - we go there"'.

'People were cheering and saying things like "That's a good idea, that's really funny"'

Becky continually refers to the positive reaction of the crowd in appreciating the group's efforts because, again, this ties in with her symbolic metaphor: the practical message of Dikea has achieved what it was designed to *do*, it has been understood and appreciated. This interpretation also guides her own explanation of her positive experiences of the day:

'Well, we were being recognised for the efforts we put in, it was a success. We didn't just dress up and just march, we dressed up and got patted on the back so to speak...We felt quite proud actually. Quite pleased. We were proud.'

The pride that Becky feels and the 'pat on the back' from the crowd are important because they both relate to the fact that she has achieved something; something has been done and it has been a success. Her positive reaction relates to the success of her practical efforts. That practicality also influences her interpretation of Ikea as the source of the Dikea symbol based not on the experience of shopping there but on the practical quality of its products:

'I've always liked it, it's one of the better stores. It has a lot of wood, it's very ecologically sound and it's quite tasteful.'

'I don't feel any different towards it [Ikea since Dikea] at all. If we were going to get some new bookcases or stuff like that it would probably be a place of preference.'

Cathy

When asked to compare herself to the group, Cathy's first response was indicative: *'Have you got all night?'* In the course of the interviews she distinguished herself from the others on the basis of appearance, income, vocation, house, hairstyle, social circle and education. This example is typical:

'It's very difficult for me to talk about lesbian culture because I can't say what everybody else does, but there is a general picture of happily married, buy a house, get a cat, go to the garden centre at the weekends and sort of live nice. I don't live

with a partner, I don't have a car so I can't drive to Ikea and if I bought something what would I do with it? I probably earn quite a lot more money than many other people in the group.'

Her symbolic metaphor relates to her incompatibility from the group-norm in almost every aspect except her sexuality. This lack of similarity means Cathy's symbolic metaphor is a need for shared subcultural identity. This need resonates clearly in this explanation of what Dikea means to her and the 'levels on which it existed':

'It exists because once you've put on a set of clothes the same as everyone else it's like a team sport. I play football sometimes - I just remember the extraordinary buzz again, because I hate football...[but] it was the most extraordinary thing winning a football match, and we had our uniforms on again, you know our strip. Very much like a team spirit and you only come together for that one event....'

That same 'extraordinary buzz' from the shared identity of the Dikea uniforms which is stimulated by her symbolic metaphor is also reflected in her interpretation of the crowd's reaction:

'[Dikea was] a gay joke. It would have been a joke anyway but not for straight people, you wouldn't have the same feeling of contact. There was a definite feeling of contact with other people... a sort of group identity, a gay identity.'

Similarly when questioned on the 'buzz' Cathy got from the March, her symbolic metaphor again becomes clear:

'Well, it was definitely to do with being in a collective....It was the fact there were so many of us and we stood out because of the white, blue and yellow...and even though we didn't know each other very well, this sort of group identity drew us together.'

Cathy's interpretation of Ikea's role in the Dikea symbol also differs from her co-informants in her total rejection of the store or its products:

'Well it's like...I'm saying I don't go to Ikea. I don't know what Ikea is like. I only went there once for the newspapers.'

Discussion

Clearly the three informants, and the group they belong to, have utilised commodity-based meanings to construct a concept of self and social world (Dittmar 1992). The meanings derived from Ikea, subculturally shared by the group and subjectively interpreted by each respondent were a source of existential meaning (Elliott and Ritson 1995). The different sources of the Ikea meanings, derived from store (Amanda), product (Becky) and consumer (Cathy), suggest that meaning does indeed flow between the different elements of consumption (McCracken 1986) and that within any group, shared group symbolism can be derived from very different semiotic sources and that those differences of source may contribute to the differing personalised interpretations of that symbol.

By utilizing two analytic approaches to the same data, it has been possible to identify both similarities and differences in the subjective interpretations these women construct of the same subcultural behaviour. In particular, the post-structuralist attention to difference which is the focus of recent developments in discourse analysis (Elliott et al. 1995) has been captured through the concept of symbolic metaphor, which promises to be of increasing importance in interpretive research. For, as Thompson et al. (1994) point out, the conventional use of interpretive themes in qualitative analysis focuses in identifying similarities across individuals and thus runs the risk of missing key aspects of difference.

The social/self dialectic discussed here promises insight into the costs versus the benefits of consumption symbolism. Whilst it is clear that the adoption of shared consumption symbolism enables a subcultural group to construct and maintain their group identity and so to derive significant benefits, it is possible that at the same time, the individual is experiencing considerable emotional tension. By surrendering aspects of the self to the social group by the purchase and display of shared consumption imagery, the individual may experience painful threats to their self-identity which may be in conflict with their adopted symbols. Because consumption is a major cultural form in post-modernity (Firat and Venkatesh 1993), important existential questions as to the meaning of the social and the self can be explored through the study of symbolic consumption located in its cultural context.

REFERENCES

Baudrillard, Jean (1988), *Simulations*, New York: Semiotext(e).
Bauman, Zygmunt (1988), *Freedom*, Milton Keynes: Open University Press.
Belk, Russell (1988), "Possessions and the Extended Self," *Journal of Consumer Research*, 15, 139-168.
Buttle, Francis (1991), "What Do People Do With Advertising," *International Journal of Advertising*, 10, 95-110.
Clarke, J.(1976), "Style," in *Resistance Through Rituals*, ed. Stuart Hall et al., U.K.: Hutchinson.
de Certeau, Michel (1984), *The Practice of Everyday Life*, Berkley: University of California Press.
Dittmar, Helga (1992), *The Social Psychology of Material Possessions: To Have is to Be*, London: Harvester Wheatsheaf.
Douglas, Mary and Baron C. Isherwood,(1979), *The World of Goods*, New York: Norton.
Eco, Umberto (1972), "Towards a Semiotic Enquiry into the Television Message," paper presented at University of Birmingham, U.K.
Elliott, Richard, Susan Eccles and Michelle Hodgson, (1993), "Recoding Gender Representations: Women, Cleaning Products and Advertising's 'New Man',"*International Journal of Research in Marketing*, 10, 1-14.
_____, Abbey Jones, Andrew Bendfield and Matt Barlow (1995), "Overt Sexuality in Advertising: A Discourse Analysis of Gender Responses," Journal of Consumer Policy.
_____ and Mark Ritson (1995), "Practising Existential Consumption: The Lived Meaning of Sexuality in Advertising," *Advances in Consumer Research*, 22.
Firat, A Fuat and Alladi Venkatesh (1993), "The Making of Post-modern Consumption," in *Consumption and Marketing: Macro Dimensions*, ed. Russell W. Belk and Nikhilesh Dholakia, Belmont, CA: Wadsworth.
Gadamer, Hans-Georg (1976), *Philosophical Hermeneutics*, Berkeley: University of California Press.
Gibbs, Liz(1994), *Daring to Dissent*, London: Cassell.
Hall, Stuart (1977), "Culture, Media and the 'Ideological Effect'," in *Mass Communication and Society*, eds. J.Curran et al., UK:Arnold.
Hamer, D. and B. Budge (1994), *The Good, The Bad and the Gorgeous*, London: Pandora.

Hebdidge, Richard (1979), *Subculture: The Meaning of Style*, London: Routledge.
Hirschman, Elizabeth (1981), "Comprehending Symbolic Consumption: Three Theoretical Issues," in *Symbolic Consumer Research*, ed. Elizabeth Hirschman and Michael Holbrook, Ann Arbor, Mi: Association for Consumer Research.
Kvale, S.(1983), "The Qualitative Research Interview," *Journal of Phenomenological Psychology*, 14, 171-196.
Laermans, Rudi (1993), "Bringing the Consumer Back In," *Theory, Culture and Society*, 10, 153-161.
Lyddon, W.J. and D.J. Alford (1993), "Constructivist Assessment: A Developmental-Epistemic Perspective," in Greg Neimeyer (ed.), *Constructivist Assessment: A Casebook*, 1-30. Beverly Hills: Sage.
McCracken, Grant (1986), "Culture and Consumption: A Theoretical Account of the Structure and Movement of the Cultural Meaning of Consumer Goods," *Journal of Consumer Research, 3*, 71-84.
_____ (1988), *The Long Interview*, Newbury Park: Sage.
Mick, David G.(1986), "Consumer Research and Semiotics: Exploring the Morphology of Signs, Symbols and Significance," *Journal of Consumer Research*, 13, 196-213.
_____ and Claus Buhl (1992), "A Meaning Based Model of Advertising," *Journal of Consumer Research, 19*, 317-338.
O'Guinn, Thomas C. and Ronald J. Faber (1989), "Compulsive Buying: A Phenomenological Exploration," *Journal of Consumer Research*, 16, 147-157.
Packer, Martin J.(1985), "Hermeneutic Enquiry and the Study of Human Conduct," *American Psychologist*, 40(10), 1081-1093.
Richins, Marsha (1994), "Valuing Things: The Public and Private Meanings of Possessions," *Journal of Consumer Research*, 21, 504-521.
Tharp, Marye and Linda M. Scott (1990), "The Role of Marketing Processes in Creating Cultural Meaning," *Journal of Macro-Marketing*, Fall, 47-60.
Thompson, Craig, William B. Locander and Howard R. Polio (1989), "Putting Consumer Research Back into Consumer Research: The Philosophy and Method of Existential Phenomenology," *Journal of Consumer Research*, 16, 133-146.
_____, Howard R. Polio and William Locander (1994), "The Spoken and the Unspoken: A Hermeneutic Approach to Understanding the Cultural Viewpoints that Underlie Consumer's Expressed Meanings." *Journal of Consumer Research*, 21, 432-452.
Valle, Ronald S. and Steen Halling (1989), *Existential Phenomenological Perspectives in Psychology*, New York: Plenum.
Wallendorf, Melanie, Russell Belk and D. Heisley (1988), "Deep Meanings in Possessions: The Paper," *Advances in Consumer Research*, 15, 528-530.
Weinsheimer, Joel (1985), *Gadamer's Hermeneutics*, London: Yale University Press.

Kids as Collectors: A Phenomenological Study of First and Fifth Graders

Stacey Menzel Baker, University of Nebraska-Lincoln
James W. Gentry, University of Nebraska-Lincoln[1]

ABSTRACT

This paper presents the results of interviews with 79 children, 72 of whom had a collection (or collections) of one kind or another. We observed that the type of collections which children pursue depends upon the ease of entry (i.e., cost) into a collecting domain, gender norms, and current fads started by movies or cartoons. The primary objective of this study was to explore the motives underlying children's collecting behaviors using a phenomenological philosophy. We suggest that children are motivated to collect because they (1) enjoy the process of collecting as it allows them to escape boredom and sometimes reality, (2) learn or satisfy curiosity about their collecting domain, (3) satiate a passion for the objects which are desired, (4) want to differentiate themselves from others, and (5) desire to associate with others, especially family and friends. Although one of the above motives was illustrated in each of the interviews, the text suggests that children often have multiple motives for collecting.

INTRODUCTION

According to recent statistics, child consumers had an estimated $9 billion income in 1989, but influenced purchases of over $132 billion (greater than the GNP of Taiwan) (McNeal 1992). This influence came in three primary areas: items for themselves (e.g., snacks or hobby supplies), items for the home (e.g., stereos), and items for the family (e.g., food). As these figures suggest, children have a substantial amount of spending power, which is particularly significant because almost all of their income and influence goes toward discretionary purchases. In fact, children between the ages of 2 and 12 influence purchases of over $16.9 billion for play items per year and influence 40 percent of sales for "hobby items" (McNeal 1992). Many of the hobby-related purchases are likely to be items which will be added to children's collections.

Collecting is prevalent in consumer cultures; in fact, Schiffer, Downing, and McCarthy (1981) found that just over 60 percent of the households which they surveyed had at least one collection, with the average of 2.6 per household. The motivations energizing collecting behaviors have received a considerable amount of attention in the popular press as well as in the academic literature. However, most of the recent reports have focused on adults and have failed to consider child consumers and their motivations for collecting. Rheims (1961) suggests:

> If a child collects, he is very rarely a connoisseur, being chiefly interested in quantity and not caring for aesthetic considerations. But with age and the acquisition of a sense of value, often derived from stamp collecting, a child shows in miniature the psychological pressures that urge its parents to collect....as in the case of adults, more attention should be paid to the motives that oblige people to find an emotional outlet in art [or any other form of] collecting (p. 22).

[1]The authors would like to thank Pat Kennedy, Mary Martin, and the members of the marketing course including Tamera Andreasen, Lynnette Boltz, Matt Christiansen, Sarah Curry, Spencer Ebeler, Jan Hallowell, Stacey Hansen, Denise Heil, Jan Hejl, Lance Lehman, Stacey Nelson, Laura Paeglis, Bee Ling Phuar, and Geok Hwa Wee who provided invaluable assistance with the interviews.

The objective of this paper is to explore the motives of collecting for children in the first and fifth grades. First, the current literature on motivations for collecting will be reviewed. Next, the research approach will be explained. After a discussion of the types of collections which we encountered in this study, the motives underlying children's collecting behavior are explored. The paper concludes by suggesting that the motives with which the collecting process is approached and the task effects of the process aid children in their developmental process and in their search for identity.

MOTIVATIONS FOR COLLECTING

Perusing the literature in consumer research, developmental psychology, and social psychology as well as articles and books in the popular press makes it obvious that a variety of motivations for collecting have been offered. In a true Freudian fashion, Muensterberger (1994) suggests that adult collecting is the result of unresolved childhood fantasies. Even, if this view of the motives underlying adults' collecting behaviors is accepted, the motivations for children's collecting behaviors are still uncertain.

In one of the most comprehensive explorations of collecting in consumer research, Belk et al. (1991) suggest that two basic motivations can be used to explain collecting: legitimization and self-extension. Legitimization motives are characterized by collectors behaving within boundaries which the social world will accept. The authors suggest that this process begins in childhood as children learn that behavior which is done for "rational" purposes (e.g., creating, investing, building history) is not considered to be self-indulgent if one labels it as "collecting." Self-extension motives are characterized by a desire to enhance or improve the self. In fact, Belk (1988) suggested that completing the collection may symbolically complete the self.

In another study of collectors, Formanek (1991) found that respondents were motivated by investment, obsession, preservation, and legitimization of the personal and social self. She found that across all kinds of motivations, the one thing all collectors have in common is their passion for the items which they collect.

RESEARCH APPROACH

Regardless of the manner in which motivations are labeled, the energized state results in the collector working toward his/her goal of acquiring more items for the collection. In this paper, we seek to delve into the meaning of the motivations which children have for collecting activities. This research question was approached using a phenomenological philosophy which allows one to explore the meaning of a phenomenon as an informant consciously perceives it (Moustakas 1994).

Approximately 90 first and fifth grade students were interviewed about their consumption experiences with advertising and collecting. Because of time constraints, the topic of collecting was broached in only 79 of these interviews. Because we wanted to investigate what collecting experiences mean to young children, we chose to look at children in the first and fifth grades. Our rationale was that children at age 6 (first grade) would just be starting to accumulate their own things and would be in the earliest stage it seemed possible to have a conversation. By age 11 (fifth grade), children are becoming more independent and make or help make more marketplace decisions. In addition, because of matura-

TABLE 1
Types of Children's Collections

First Grade

Female(24)   Males(16)

Rocks (5)   Nothing (3)
Trolls (3)   Sports Cards (2)
Nothing (3)   Rocks (2)
Dolls (2)   Jurassic Park "stuff" (2)
Sea Shells (2)   Fossils
Calico Kittens   Dinosaurs
Cats (real ones)   Baseballs and Footballs
Garfield "things"   Pencils
Bows (from packages)   Bullet shells
Stickers   Live bugs
Glass   Maps
Bears   Money
Jewelry   Trolls
Erasers
Cars

Fifth Grade

Female(20)   Males(19)

Stuffed Animals (7)   Sports Cards (11)
  Bears (4)   Rocks (2)
  Bunnies (2)   Baseball equipment
Books (2)   Dinosaurs
Clowns   Live frogs
Rocks   Cars
Horses (glass and plastic)   Trains
Dinosaurs   Pencils
Sea shells
Plaster scenes
Stickers
Pencils
Precious Moments
Little boxes
Nothing

---

tion, they are more independent in their decision making than first graders.

The textural descriptions which are presented in this paper were obtained through interviews which were conducted by the authors as well as by members of an undergraduate directed-study course in marketing. The students who participated in the project were given course credit for reading materials on qualitative research, interviewing children, and collecting (e.g., Belk et al. 1988); attending training sessions on interviewing children; conducting interviews with first and fifth grade students; transcribing the interviews verbatim; and beginning to pick themes from the text. They received feedback at each level of the project.

The perceptions of the children were our primary interest in the interviews as we explored why children believe they collect objects to add to a collection. Thus, the grand tour question sought to determine "what is it about collecting that children like?" This was determined by asking them to tell us stories about when they acquired new items for their collections and by asking "what makes new items special?," "how do you feel when you collect things?," and "what do you think about when you collect?"

The children talked with the interviewers about collecting for between 5 and 25 minutes; the variability of time was mainly due to varying levels of involvement with collecting, but the child's attention span also was an important factor in the length of the interview. As an incentive to participate, the children received two movie passes. Parental permission was obtained for all informants.

TYPES OF COLLECTIONS

Of the 79 children who were interviewed about collecting, only 7 did not consider themselves to be collectors or said that they did not have a collection of any kind. Of those that responded to our collecting questions, only two had to be given a hint as to what a collection was (both were in the first grade). The interviewers told these two respondents that a collection was a group of "special things."

Table 1 illustrates the favorite types of collections which our informants said they looked for and enjoyed getting (by themselves or through gifts which they had solicited). In some cases the children had multiple collections, but we asked them to focus on their one (or sometimes two) favorite collection(s).

These lists of items which children collect offer insight into children's collecting behaviors. A number of children noted the care they put into maintaining their collections. Some like Sarah (1st) enjoy naming every item; she collects stuffed kittens "because when I get a new one I get to name it." Others spent time cleaning their collectibles. Brayha (1st) said her rocks were:

like clothes...everyday when I get them I like wash them and then I put them on my dresser and then when they get dirty I wash them again.

Stephanie (5th) would put a little note by each of the special rocks she had. She said:

One time when we were playing on the playground we stuffed our pockets full of rocks but my friends dumped theirs out. I didn't. I took them home and washed them and put them in my collection.

Other children keep lists of all their items, and several had special cases or shelves for them. For example, Lukas (5th) collects rocks:

For my birthday I got this rock case, this big rock case my dad made, and I shelve all these glazed shells and stuff and it has a purple light, you know white light you just turn on the knob and it can be purple or you can turn it off, and turn on the white one or both.

It is obvious that these children put a great deal of effort into building a collection (e.g., searching for rocks or bugs or putting sports cards in order).

Ease of entry is an important component of the type of collection children pursue, as evidenced by the prominence of items that can be picked up without cost (e.g., rocks) and received as a small gift (e.g., trolls for first grade females and Jurassic Park "stuff" for first grade males). The items collected by the older children were generally of a greater cost. Gender norms seem to affect what is collected. Fifth grade females are likely to collect stuffed animals (35%) and males are likely to collect sports cards (58%). The list also illustrates the timeless collections including rocks and stuffed animals; however the influence of movies, cartoons, and advertising is also apparent as the current fads include dinosaurs and Jurassic Park "things" as well as Garfield "stuff" and trolls. Perhaps, when this generation reaches adulthood, these fad items will be among their desires, as Pez dispensers are now for adults who lived through that fad. Or, perhaps not.

CHILDREN'S COLLECTING MOTIVES

Although first and fifth grade children do not have the words to articulate their feelings to the degree that adults do, children are able to express the goals they have in their collecting and enjoy talking about it. However, they are more likely to do things rather than to ponder why they do them. For several of the younger informants, the notion of collecting is quite different than the operational definition evolving from adults. For example, Jamie (1st grade) said that she does not collect anything. When probed with "Nothing?", she said, "At our school, we collect paper; white paper only. We have this box that we only put white paper in." When asked what he collects, Nathan (1st) said, "Money." He was proud of having $16.37.

First graders also displayed vivid imaginations about what collecting means. Shea (1st) collected treasure maps which led him to find eggs and "inside are gold coins." When asked how he would feel if someone hurt his card collection, Stuart (1st) said he would be mad because it "might wreck a pro basketball player." Older children had both more traditional collections and more traditional perspectives of what collecting entails. Further, they were able in many cases to take a more active role in the acquisition of their collections due to their access to more resources. As noted earlier, most first grade collections were either picked up (e.g., rocks) or were generated from gifts.

Although children have different definitions for collecting, they seem to have some expectations as to what collecting will provide to them. Our text illustrates that children have multiple motives for collecting. The motives discovered in our text help us to understand the meaning of children's collecting experiences.

Collecting as Doing

Collecting was seen by many informants as something to do. Many said they collected because collecting is "fun" and because they enjoy doing it. Not only is collecting enjoyable for children, but it also helps them to relieve their boredom. Tony (5th) talks about why baseball cards are a good thing for him to collect:

I don't know, because it's something to do when I get bored and like when I go do my travel I stop at like a Quick shop and get a few packs and look at them because I always get bored when I travel.

Similarly, Corey (5th) said that "collecting makes me feel good, because it gives me something to do like organize cars and stuff like that when there is nothing else to do." Mary (1st) collects rocks because "sometimes I get bored and it keeps me from making myself mad. It just makes me think about something else. Like when I'm picking up rocks it is hard for me to think of something else."

Besides using collecting as an escape from boredom, children also use collecting as something to do to escape from reality. For example, Stacey (5th), whose parents were "busy and worked all the time," seemed to be comforted by her book collecting. Patrick (5th) seemed to have an unhappy family life. He lives with his father and step-mother, but he does not get along with her. His own mother apparently has substance abuse problems and when he stays with her in the trailer, he sleeps with other kids on a mattress on the floor and he always comes home in rags. Patrick collects rocks, "I feel sort of happy when I'm getting hold of this stuff, just by picking something off the ground and brushing it." For Patrick, collecting seems to one activity in his life which he can completely control. Thus, collecting seems to be something he is able to do to put order into his life.

Some children suggested they collected just because they enjoyed looking at their things; most of these children were female. For example, Stacy (5th) said, "I just kind of looked at them [stuffed animals] and I thought they looked cute and everything so I started collecting them. Similarly, Molly (1st) said she collected bows [from packages] "because I think they are pretty...and they make me feel good" and Tessa (1st) said she collected erasers because "they're fun to look at."

First graders were much more likely to acquire collections which served a functional purpose (n=7) than fifth graders (n=2). When asked why he collects dinosaurs, Cole (1st) said "cause you can play with them." Similarly, Aly (1st) said that "collecting trolls was good because I like to use them and play with them." One of the two fifth graders who mentioned "using" their collections was Stacy (5th) who said:

Because I really like to read and stuff and you can't read if you don't have a lot of books, like if you have one or two books then you'd probably finish them right away, if you really liked to read then you'd have nothing else to read unless you went out and bought something.

The only other fifth grader who mentioned "using" his collections was Will, who noted differences between the sacred and the profane aspects of his pencil collection when, after noting that he used his pencils in his drawing, he said that his favorite pencils are ones "not yet used." In addition, Will was one of the few children who mentioned that it was possible to have "too many" pencils. He said that he would not always collect pencils "cause then I would collect too many and they'd never get used."

Besides the current activity associated with the collection, many informants saw their collection as a source of money in the future. That is, they saw collecting as a way of "doing" something to save for the future. Sex and age differences were noted in this "collecting as investment" perspective. Eleven of the 19 fifth grade males mentioned expectations concerning their collection growing in value, but only 3 of the 20 fifth grade females did and only 3 of the 40 first graders. Trevor, a fifth grade male said he collects baseball cards "because, like most of the cards are going to be high in price someday." Similarly, Jeremy (5th) said:

I collect race car cards, and I collect like um...old stuff. I have a lot of old stuff. Because sometimes it will be worth a lot...it'll be worth a lot of money...I have some car cards that are worth a lot of money now because the person died who drove it.

This "investor" motivation was mostly present in the children (primarily males) who collected sports cards. These children seemed to care more about what the card was worth rather than having any "special feelings" for the card. For instance, one fifth grade boy [Jason] told us that he had taken some of his cards to school and they had been stolen. When asked how he felt, he responded:

Well, that I lost some money..we cause I know they're, I know they're worth a lot if you have like a really good card.

It is not clear whether the children picked sports cards to collect because they wanted to invest in something or whether once they began collecting, they became caught up in using price guides and became socialized to collect cards for investment reasons. Whatever the explanation, the collectors of sports cards (usually males) reflect a greater concern for future fiscal eventualities that is not reflected as frequently by collectors of other types of objects.

Collecting to Learn or to Satisfy Curiosity

Several of the children, boys in particular, talked about how they used baseball cards to learn about players, teams, and also to learn how to read statistics. We found clear evidence of curiosity, at least as conceptualized by Loewenstein's (1994) information gap model. When asked why he collected baseball cards, one first grade boy [Jeff] said, "so I can see I can know

and I can learn about them."Another boy explained his collecting of baseball cards this way:

Well I started when I was like 4 years old cause my friend he's like 3 years older than me...he had a whole bunch of baseball cards and I didn't even know what they were and I looked at one and I said 'hey these are really neat. I like these.' And then I started watching a little baseball and a little football and that really got me in...And I kind of started because I just wanted to know who was on certain teams and if they weren't, if they were, how good they were. [Andy, 5th]

When asked why live frogs were a good thing to collect, T.J. (5th) said, "Because I always find something new every time I look...it makes me more interested." Consistent with Loewenstein's (1994) review of the curiosity literature, T.J.'s curiosity appears to be increasing as his knowledge increases.

Several of the children talked about how they learn about their collections. They often mentioned talking to friends or reading books; however they also often mentioned catalogs, magazines, and stores as important sources of information. Stuart [1st] said that friends were good sources of information because "sometimes they help me to know how to collect." Sherry (5th) said she tries to find out new information by reading. She said, "I read books about some of them, like my dinosaurs I get books out of the library." When asked why stores were good sources of information, Kierra [5th] said, "because you can see them before you buy them, and you can see if you want them."

Collecting to Satisfy a Passion

As in Formanek (1991) who interviewed adult collectors, one motive for most children in collecting was to find something that they like. However, the intense passion for collecting evident in adult collectors (Baker and Mittelstaedt 1995; Smith and Lee 1994) was not as clearly evident among our pre-adolescent informants. Many informants indicated that collecting was "fun," but none discussed having physical reactions (e.g., sweaty palms) as they moved toward possible acquisitions, as noted in Baker and Mittelstaedt (1995).

Similar to adults, the interviews with children show evidence of high enduring involvement both in the frequent maintenance activities observed (discussed earlier in the paper) and the description of their "learning" activities. For example, Kierra (5th) described her search for information about horses (she collects plastic and glass horses):

I find information about horses in like catalogs, magazines, and stores when we go there. I can remember like, look at a horse and remember when I got it and who gave it to me, stuff like that. I've read that book [her best friend had given her *The Love of Horses*] about ten times already. I like to go to the library and check out books on how to keep horses and train them. I spend a lot of time thinking about horses, I mean really like them, I want to be a horse trainer when I grow up.

Kierra's search for knowledge goes beyond the items collected to her passion for the objects which her collectibles symbolize. This was a common response for why they collect the items they do: they like the item they symbolize (cats, horses, athletes, rabbits, or events such as vacations). Jessica (5th) collects bears because "I just like bears and it is one of my favorite animals." Rosanne (1st) collects stuffed animals because she loves her real cat. Angie (5th) collects wooden rabbits "because I have always had my heart set on getting a rabbit."

Collecting to Be Unique

Fifth grade informants appreciate collecting because it makes them unique. None of the first graders talked about this value of collecting. For example, Jeremy (5th) said it was good to collect race cars because "You have stuff that maybe nobody else does" and Mark (5th) said he collects cards because "it makes me feel good about myself that I got some baseball cards that some other people don't have." Similarly, Maria (5th) said she collected bears "because it's a collection that many people don't have" and Laura (5th), who collects pencils, said:

Well, because not very many people are interested and you can just sort of keep it private and not show it to the world. I mean like, if you have expensive baseball cards, you want to like show it to everybody. If you have a special collection that not very many people collect, you can just think about it yourself and you don't need anybody else involved.

In some instances, this uniqueness aspect of collecting was seen as negative by several informants, all of them female. Ashley (1st) said, "Barney at school has stamps. It makes him feel happy and us feel kind of bad cause we didn't have all of them." Stacey (5th) noted that "some people who collect kind of brag about this collection and I don't like it when they start to brag." The norm against uniqueness among females also was reflected in the social sharing aspects of collecting. When asked why it is good to collect teddy bears, Jamie (5th) and Jessica (5th) said because "a lot of people have them" and "we have something in common." Stephanie (1st) and Shelly (1st) collect Barbies because their friends do and they can invite them over to play. These comments suggest that reasons for collecting reflect the gender socialization process taking placing even at the grade school level. It seems that these females are being socialized to believe that it is better not to stand out from the crowd.

Collecting to Associate with Others

A priori, we had expected the role of family to be central to the collecting process, especially in a modeling sense. There was modeling evident; for example, a few of the children mentioned that their collections were started because of their parents' or grandparents' influence or interest. Tony (5th) told one of the interviewers he started his collection of sports cards because:

my Grandpa had some cards and I just started to like them and I just kept adding them and adding them to my collection when I started them....cause I saw them at his house and then I started to collect them.

Similarly, Synneve (1st) collects kittens, as her mother is a veterinarian who is teaching her about cats. Jeremy (5th) collects race cars, as his whole family (even his grandmother) is heavily involved in car racing. For the most part, though, children's interests do not coincide with their parents' and, while they may collect items similar to what their parents did at a similar stage in life, they do not share many collecting interests.

The involvement of adults in the collections results in longer term expectations for collecting. Josh (5th) was given his first pack of baseball cards by his grandma, and he expects to collect forever, "because eventually I will give most of my collection to my grand children." Jeremy (5th), whose whole family follows car racing closely, also expects to collect race cars forever. Perhaps, Jeremy thinks that we will truly "belong" in his family if he continues to show interest in race cars.

The major role played by family in the collecting by the child is in its facilitation, by easing the child's entry into the process. Parents were mentioned more than three times as frequently as friends and siblings (52 versus 17) in discussions of how the collections were started. Most mentions were of gifts which started the collection or of continuing additions on birthdays and other holidays. Even in the case of an easy access collections (bugs), T.J. (5th) noted the role which his father played, "When I was little, my dad would always pick up rocks and I would look under them and pick up the bugs underneath them." The facilitating role played by parents diminishes as the child gains access to resources. For example, Leon (5th) noted that "my mom used to buy me cards; now I buy them myself." In those cases in which financial barriers still existed for fifth graders, collecting activity resembled that of first graders. For example, Dan (5th) used to collect baseball cards, but he ran out of money. Now he collects "junk that no one else wants and rocks."

Friends were also important motivators for children's collecting behaviors. For example, modeling of friends' collecting behaviors was evident. When asked why he started collecting rocks, Patrick P. (5th) said, "Well, one of my best friends started collecting. He had some really neat rocks so I thought if I could get some neat rocks like him." Trevor (5th) said he started collecting, "because everyone else was doing it, so I thought I might." Time spent with friends often revolves around mutual interests in collecting even though they may have different types of collections. Patrick P. (5th) said his friends didn't help him with his collection, "but they sure like to look at it."

Many children, especially the first graders, compared their material possessions to those of others. They suggested that collecting was a way of getting "more" of something than others have. Courtney (1st) said, "I try to get the most jewelry" and Chelsea (1st) said collecting rocks was an important thing for her to do "because every time I find a new rock I get more rocks in my collection." Thus, for many first graders having "more is better" and the desire to get "more" motivates their collecting.

CONCLUSION

We have found that people enjoy talking about their collections; children are no exception. For children, collecting seems to be a natural part of life. One fifth grade girl explained this, "All people collect, some just don't know it." The perceptions of the children reveal that they have multiple motives for building and creating their collections. Children collect because collecting gives them something to do with their free time while showing themselves and others what they are capable of accomplishing. They also seek possessions which interest them and help them grow as a person (e.g., by helping them learn more), thus, enhancing their self-identity. Acquiring objects for which they have a special passion is a common motive. Children also seek items for their collection to show that they are unique; however, they also often collect because of the influence or encouragement of others either to be like those people or to show others that they have "more" than them.

Although child collectors, especially first graders, have different definitions of collecting than adults, they seem to have just as much fun in the collecting process. One question that remains is whether they are able to achieve the flow that has been observed in some adults' collecting (e.g., Baker and Mittelstaedt 1995; Smith and Lee 1994). It may be that children do not achieve flow because they focus too much on their selves and what collecting will get them (i.e., the collection), instead of focusing on the task of collecting itself.

REFERENCES

Baker, Stacey Menzel and Robert A. Mittelstaedt (1995), "The Meaning of the Search, Evaluation, and Selection of 'Yesterday's Cast-offs': A Phenomenological Study into the Acquisition of the Collection," in *Enhancing Knowledge Development in Marketing*, Barbara B. Stern and George M. Zinkhan (Eds.), 152.

Belk, Russell W. (1988), "Possessions and the Extended Self," *Journal of Consumer Research*, 15(September), 139-168.

Belk, Russell W., Melanie Walendorf, John F. Sherry, Jr., and Morris B. Holbrook (1991), "Collecting in a Consumer Culture," in *Highways and Buyways*, Russell W. Belk (Ed.), Provo, UT: Association for Consumer Research, 178-211.

Belk, Russell W., Melanie Walendorf, John Sherry, Morris Holbrook, and Scott Roberts (1988), "Collectors and Collecting," in *Advances in Consumer Research*, Michael Houston (Ed.), 15, 548-553.

Formanek, Ruth (1991), "Why They Collect: Collectors Reveal Their Motivations," *Journal of Social Behavior and Personality*, 6(6), 275-286.

Loewenstein, George (1994), "The Psychology of Curiosity: A Review and Reinterpretation," *Psychological Bulletin*, 116 (1), 75-98.

McNeal, James U. (1992), "The Littlest Shoppers," *American Demographics*, February, 48-53.

Moustakas, Clark (1994), *Phenomenological Research Methods*, Thousand Oaks, CA: Sage Publications.

Rheims, Maurice (1961), *The Strange Life of Objects: 35 Centuries of Art Collecting and Collectors*, New York: Atheneum Publications.

Schiffer, Michael B., Theodore E. Downing, and Michael McCarthy (1981), "Waste Note, Want Not: An Ethnoarchaeological Study of Reuse in Tucson, Arizona," in *Modern Material Culture: The Archaeology of Us*, Michael Gould and Michael B. Schiffer (Eds.), New York: Academic Press.

Smith, Ruth Ann and Renee Lee (1994), "Going with the Flow: Collecting as an Optimal Consumer Experience," paper presented at Annual Conference of the Association for Consumer Research, Boston, MA.

SPECIAL SESSION SUMMARY
Customer Value — A Framework For Analysis and Research

Morris B. Holbrook, Columbia University[1]

ABSTRACT

This paper introduces a special topic session that brings together scholars from diverse areas to address the nature and types of Customer Value. Specifically, the author proposes a framework to distinguish among eight key types of Customer Value that appear to deserve consideration in the analysis of consumer behavior. These eight types refer to different aspects of consumption that have attracted the attention of various scholars in the field. Accordingly, distinguished researchers in these areas of inquiry discuss whether and how their concerns fit into the proposed framework, offering further insights into the applicability of the Typology of Customer Value across a broad range of research topics. In sum, consistent with the thematic focus of the conference on research-frame synergies, the session provides a systematic consideration of the proposed framework and a critical evaluation of its usefulness as an integrative scheme.

THE FRAMEWORK

If we view Marketing as a process that leads toward *exchanges* and if we define an exchange as a transaction between two parties in which each party trades something of value in return for something of greater value (Kotler 1991), it follows immediately that *Customer Value* provides the foundation for all marketing activity and deserves the attention of every consumer researcher.

For about a decade, I have wrestled with issues concerning the general *nature* and *types* of Customer Value (Holbrook and Corfman 1985; Holbrook 1986, 1994a, 1994b). In this connection, a crucial point — one that sounds amazingly simple when articulated, but one that appears to have eluded most of those who have commented on various aspects of Customer Value — is that one can understand a given type of value *only* by considering its relationship to *other* types of value. One cannot understand Quality without considering Beauty or Beauty without considering Fun or Fun without considering Ethics. In short, we can understand one type of value only by comparing it with other types of value to which it is closely related. Thus, we can understand Quality only by comparison with Beauty, Convenience, and Reputation; we can understand Beauty only by comparison with Quality, Fun, and Ecstasy.

Based on a rather extensive but neglected literature found in the philosophical field of Axiology or the Theory of Value, we have previously proposed a conceptual framework to address (1) the *nature* and (2) the *types* of Customer Value. The first attempt in this direction appeared in a chapter by Holbrook and Corfman (1985). The theme of value was revisited by Holbrook (1986) and has subsequently been elaborated in a "learned" treatise (Holbrook 1994b) and in a more "user friendly" version (Holbrook 1994a). Here, I shall briefly review my conclusions on the nature and types of Customer Value to provide a general framework as the basis for more specific issues addressed by various contributors to the special topic session.

The Nature of Customer Value

I define *Customer Value* as an *interactive relativistic preference experience*.

---

[1]The author gratefully acknowledges the support of the Columbia Business School's Faculty Research Fund.

(1) Interactive. By *interactive*, I mean that — in contrast to the position advocated by extreme subjectivists or extreme objectivists — Customer Value entails an interaction between some subject (a consumer) and some object (a product). Essentially, this interactionist position maintains that value depends on the characteristics of some physical or mental object but cannot occur without the involvement of some subject who appreciates it (Frondizi 1971; Morris 1964; Pepper 1958).

(2) Relativistic. By *relativistic*, I mean that Customer Value is (a) comparative (among objects), (b) personal (across people), and (c) situational (specific to the context). (a) It is *comparative* in that one must make utility comparisons among objects rather than among people (Frondizi 1971; Hilliard 1950; Lewis 1946); in other words, I can legitimately claim that I like Susan Sarandon better than Madonna, but *not* that I like Ms. Sarandon more than *you* do. (b) It is *personal* in the sense that it varies from one individual to another (Bond 1983; Parker 1957; Von Wright 1963); colloquially, we say that "One (hu)man's meat is another (hu)man's poison." (c) Further, value is *situational* in that it depends on the context in which the evaluative judgment occurs (Morris 1964; Taylor 1961); hence, the standards on which evaluative judgments hinge tend to be context-dependent, changing from one situation to the next, as when our preference for tea varies from hot Earl Grey (in the winter) to iced orange pekoe (in the summer) and possibly to warm herbal (before bed).

(3) Preference. By *preference*, I simply mean that consumer researchers have found a variety of names by which to refer to the general concept of an evaluative judgment (Perry 1954). These include "predisposition" (positive-negative), "attitude" (favorable-unfavorable), "opinion" (pro-con), "directional behavior" (approach-avoidance), "valence" (plus-minus), "judgment" (good-bad), or "evaluation" (liking-disliking). All these refer to value (singular) as opposed to value*s* (plural), where the latter term represents the *standards* or *criteria* on which the former depends. It must be emphasized that our focus on value (singular) is quite different from that which deals with various types of value*s* (VALS, LOV, AIO, and other types of psychographically oriented lifestyle research).

(4) Experience. Finally, by *experience*, I mean that Customer Value resides *not* in the purchase but *rather* in the consumption experience(s) derived therefrom (Holbrook and Hirschman 1982); this claim is inherent in the concept of an interactive relativistic preference and has received support from any number of philosophically inclined thinkers (Abbott 1955; Baylis 1958; in addition to those already cited).

The Dimensions of Customer Value

The *framework* that provides the basis for the proposed session reflects *three key dimensions* of value: (1) Extrinsic versus Intrinsic, (2) Self- versus Other-Oriented, and (3) Active versus Reactive.

(1) Extrinsic Versus Intrinsic Value. *Extrinsic* value pertains to a means-ends relationship wherein consumption is prized for its functional, utilitarian, or banausic instrumentality in accomplishing some further purpose. By contrast, *intrinsic* value occurs when some consumption experience is appreciated as an end in itself — for its own sake — as self-justifying, ludic, or autotelic. (Besides those already referenced, see Brandt 1967; Brightman 1962; Deci 1975; Frankena 1962, 1967; Lee 1957; Nozick 1982; Olson 1967; Osborne 1933; Rokeach 1973.)

TABLE 1
A Typology of Customer Value

		Extrinsic	Intrinsic
Self-Oriented	Active	EFFICIENCY (O/I, Convenience)	PLAY (Fun)
	Reactive	EXCELLENCE (Quality)	AESTHETICS (Beauty)
Other-Oriented	Active	STATUS (Success, Impression Management)	ETHICS (Justice, Virtue, Morality)
	Reactive	ESTEEM (Reputation, Materialism, Possessions)	SPIRITUALITY (Faith, Ecstasy, Sacredness)

(2) Self- Versus Other-Oriented Value. Value is *self-oriented* when I prize a product or experience selfishly or prudently for *my own* sake, for how *I* react to it, or for the effect it has on *me*. Conversely, *other-oriented* value looks beyond the self to some other(s) (family, friends, neighbors, colleagues) or some Other (Country, Planet, Universe, Mother Nature, Cosmos, Deity) where something is valued for *their* sake, for how *they* react to it, or for the effect it has on *them*. (See also Buber 1923; Fromm 1941, Kahle 1983; Koestler 1978; Lamont 1951; Parsons 1951; Riesman 1950; Siegel 1981; Von Wright 1983, and especially Mukerjee 1964.)

(3) Active Versus Reactive Value. Value is *active* when it entails some physical or mental manipulation of some tangible or intangible object — that is, when it involves things *done by* an individual. Conversely, *reactive* value results from apprehending, appreciating, or otherwise responding to some object — that is, from things *done to* an individual. In the first, *I* act upon *it*; in the second, *it* acts upon *me*. (See also Hall 1961; Harré and Secord 1973; Mead 1938; Mehrabian and Russell 1974; Morris 1956, 1964; Osgood, Suci, and Tannenbaum 1957).

The Types of Customer Value

By treating each of the dimensions just described as a dichotomy and combining these three dichotomies into a 2x2x2 cross-classification, we may produce the eight-celled Typology of Customer Value that appears in Table 1. Each cell of this taxonomy represents a logically distinct type of value (with examples shown parenthetically). Collectively, these various types of value provide the structural basis for the issues of concern to this special topic session.

TOPICS FOR CONTRIBUTING PARTICIPANTS

The Typology of Customer Value just described suggests an outline for organizing the presentations in the special topic session. Their order follows the structure suggested by the typology — first, from top left (EFFICIENCY) to bottom left (ESTEEM); then, from top right (PLAY) to bottom right (SPIRITUALITY). A brief summary of each focus follows — with a tentative title (in quotes)

and with the name(s) of the participant(s) (shown parenthetically) indicated for each area covered.

"Efficiency and Convenience in the Use of Time" (Bernd Schmitt and France Leclerc)

From the perspective of the present framework, *efficiency* results from the active use of a product to achieve some self-oriented purpose — as measured, for example, by the ratio of outputs to inputs or *O/I* (Bond 1983; Diesing 1962; Hilliard 1950; Lamont 1955). When the key input of interest is *time*, we typically call this O/I ratio *convenience*. Implications concerning the consumption of temporal resources figure prominently in the work by Bernd Schmitt, France Leclerc, and their colleagues on waiting time and on decisions regarding the use of time.

"Excellence, Quality, and Satisfaction" (Rich Oliver)

As conceived here, efficiency differs from *excellence* in that the latter entails an inherently reactive response in which one admires some object for its capacity to serve as the means to a self-oriented end in the performance of some function. Such a utilitarian emphasis on the appreciation of instrumentality relates closely to the concept of *satisfaction* based on a comparison of performance with expectations and appears to constitute the essence of what we mean by *quality* (Abbott 1955; Bond 1983; Juran 1988; Pettijohn 1986; Steenkamp 1989; Tuchman 1980; Zeithaml 1988). Rich Oliver has recently edited a book on *Service Quality* (with Roland Rust) and is well-known for his seminal contributions to the area of Customer Satisfaction studies.

"Status, Symbols, Impression Management, and Success" (Mike Solomon)

As employed here, the term *status* designates the active use of one's own consumption behavior toward the other-oriented end of achieving a favorable response from someone else (Nozick 1981; Perry 1954). A conspicuous example of this push toward *success* occurs when one uses one's wearing apparel as a set of *symbols* and purposely dresses with an eye to the role of clothing and accessories in *impression management*. Mike Solomon has employed insights from symbolic interactionism and other disciplinary orientations to elucidate the role of symbolic consumption and to emphasize the importance of product constellations as aspects of symbolically oriented consumer behavior.

"Esteem, Possessions, Conspicuous Consumption, and Materialism" (Marsha Richins)

The reactive counterpart to status involves the *esteem* that may result from a somewhat passive ownership of *possessions* appreciated as a means to building one's *reputation* with others (Bond 1983; Duesenberry 1949; Scitovsky 1976; Veblen 1899). Such Veblenesque examples of *conspicuous consumption* represent one facet of *materialism* frequently taken as a signal aspect of our Consumer Society. Marsha Richins has written on the undesirable social consequences of such acquisitive preoccupations and has done extensive empirical work on developing indices of materialism.

"Play, Leisure, and Fun" (John Deighton)

As a self-oriented experience — actively pursued and enjoyed for its own sake — *play* leads to having *fun* and characterizes the familiar distinction often made between work and *leisure* (Berlyne 1969; Huizinga 1938; Santayana 1896; Stephenson 1967). John Deighton has studied numerous aspects of play and performance as manifest and metaphorical components of consumer behavior; in this connection, he also co-chaired a special topic session on play at last year's ACR conference.

"Aesthetics, Fashion, Beauty, and Product Design" (Janet Wagner)

On the reactive side of play, *aesthetics* refers to a self-oriented appreciation of some object where this experience is valued as an end in itself, for example as a potential source of *beauty* (Beardsley 1967; Budd 1983; Bullough 1912; Coleman 1966; Hampshire 1982; Hilliard 1950; Hospers 1967; Iseminger 1981; Lee 1957; Lewis 1946; McGregor 1974; Olscamp 1965; Perry 1854; Rader 1979, p. 331). Clearly, *fashion* is often prized for the aesthetic merits of its *product design* — that is, on the grounds of *beauty*. As at ACR 1994, Janet Wagner has frequently focused on the aesthetic aspects of product design in general and on the connection between beauty and fashion in particular.

"Ethics, Justice, Virtue, and Morality" (Craig Smith)

The active and other-oriented pursuit of *ethics* aims at *justice, virtue, and/or morality* sought for its own sake as an end in itself (Alicke 1983; Lewis 1946; Morris 1956; Nozick 1981; Parker 1957; Pepper 1958; Von Wright 1963, 1983). Thus, deontological value entails the concept of duty or obligation to others (Bond 1983; Hilliard 1950; Perry 1954), while we imply a connection between ethics and intrinsic motivation when we say colloquially that "virtue is its own reward" (Frankena 1973; Parker 1957). Craig Smith has literally "written the books" on *Morality in the Market Place* and on *Ethics in Marketing* (with John Quelch); he is therefore uniquely well-situated to comment on these issues as they relate to Customer Value.

"Spirituality, Faith, Ecstasy, and Sacredness" (John Sherry)

As a more reactive counterpart to ethics (faith versus works), *spirituality* entails an adoption, appreciation, admiration, or adoration of the Other in which a self-motivated *faith* may propel one toward a state of *ecstasy* involving a disappearance of the Self-Other dichotomy and a profound experience of *sacredness* (Frondizi 1971; Mukerjee 1964; Parker 1957; Perry 1954; Pepper 1958).

Generally, we think of spirituality as attached to religious experience involving the Deity, some broad view of the Cosmos, or some profound concept of an otherwise inaccessible Inner Self. However, one should note that an ecstatic disappearance of the self-other dichotomy may also occur when one becomes so involved in the "flow" of a consumption experience that one loses all sense of one's own selfhood in the rapture of the consuming moment. These and other aspects of sacred consumption have served as a unifying theme in many of the important studies by John Sherry and his colleagues.

CONCLUSION

This summary overview has suggested that the nature and types of Customer Value can best be understood by placing them in a context that juxtaposes their differences and similarities so as to shed light on their underlying structure. Toward this end, I have proposed a Typology of Customer Value to provide a general framework that serves to integrate contributions on specific topics by a group of acknowledged experts in each of the various areas under consideration. These individual contributions permit a critical evaluation of the typology and an assessment of its applicability across diverse issues of interest to consumer researchers.

REFERENCES

Abbott, Lawrence (1955), *Quality and Competition*, New York, NY: Columbia University Press.

Alicke, Mark (1983), "Philosophical Investigations of Values," in *Social Values and Social Change*, ed. Lynn R. Kahle, New York, NY: Praeger, 3-23.

Baylis, C. A. (1958), "Grading, Values, and Choice," *Mind*, 67, 485-501.

Beardsley, Monroe C. (1967), "History of Aesthetics," in *Encyclopedia of Philosophy*, Vol. 1., ed. Paul Edwards, New York, NY: Macmillan and Free Press, 18-35.

Berlyne, Daniel E. (1969), "Laughter, Humor, and Play," in *The Handbook of Social Psychology*, Vol. 3, ed. Gardner Lindzey and Elliot Aronson, Reading, MA: Addison-Wesley Publishing Company, 795-852.

Bond, E. J. (1983), *Reason and Value*, Cambridge, UK: Cambridge University Press.

Brandt, Richard B. (1967), "Personal Values and the Justification of Institutions," in *Human Values and Economic Policy*, ed. Sidney Hook, New York, NY: New York University Press, 22-40.

Brightman, Edgar S. (1962), "Axiology," in *Dictionary of Philosophy*, ed. Dagobert D. Runes, Totowa, NJ: Littlefield Adams & Co., 32-33.

Buber, Martin (1923), *I and Thou*, New York, NY: Charles Scribner's Sons.

Budd, Malcolm (1983), "Belief and Sincerity in Poetry," in *Pleasure, Preference and Value: Studies in Philosophical Aesthetics*, ed. Eva Schaper, New York, NY: Cambridge University Press, 137-157.

Bullough, Edward (1912), "'Psychical Distance' as a Factor in Art and an Aesthetic Principle," *British Journal of Psychology*, 5, 87-98.

Coleman, Francis J. (1966), "A Phenomenology of Aesthetic Reasoning," *Journal of Aesthetics and Art Criticism*, 25, 197-203.

Deci, Edward L. (1975), *Intrinsic Motivation*, New York, NY: Plenum Press.

Diesing, Paul (1962), *Reason in Society: Five Types of Decisions and Their Social Conditions*, Urbana, IL: University of Illinois Press.

Duesenberry, James S. (1949), *Income, Saving and the Theory of Consumer Behavior*, Cambridge, MA: Harvard University Press.

Frankena, William (1962), "Value," in *Dictionary of Philosophy*, ed. Dagobert D. Runes, Totowa, NJ: Littlefield, Adams & Co., 330-331.

Frankena, William (1967), "Value and Valuation," in *The Encyclopedia of Philosophy*, Vol. 8, ed. Paul Edwards, New York, NY: The Macmillan Company, 229-232.

Frankena, William K. (1973), *Ethics*, Second Edition, Englewood Cliffs, NJ: Prentice-Hall.

Frondizi, Risieri (1971), *What Is Value? An Introduction to Axiology*, Second Edition, La Salle, IL: Open Court Publishing Company.

Fromm, E. (1941), *Escape from Freedom*, Oxford, UK: Farrar.

Hall, Everett W. (1961), *Our Knowledge of Fact and Value*, Chapel Hill, NC: The University of North Carolina Press.

Hampshire, Stuart (1982), *Thought and Action*, Second Edition, Notre Dame, IN: University of Notre Dame Press.

Harré, R. and P. F. Secord (1973), *The Explanation of Social Behavior*, Totowa, NJ: Littlefield, Adams & Co.

Hilliard, A. L. (1950), *The Forms of Value: The Extension of Hedonistic Axiology*, New York, NY: Columbia University Press.

Holbrook, Morris B. (1986), "Emotion in the Consumption Experience: Toward a New Model of the Human Consumer," in *The Role of Affect in Consumer Behavior: Emerging Theories and Applications*, ed. Robert A. Peterson, Wayne D. Hoyer, and William R. Wilson, Lexington, MA: D. C. Heath and Company, 17-52.

Holbrook, Morris B. (1994a), "Axiology, Aesthetics, and Apparel: Some Reflections on the Old School Tie," in *Aesthetics of Textiles and Clothing: Advancing Multi-Disciplinary Perspectives*, ITAA Special Publication #7, ed. Marilyn Revell DeLong and Ann Marie Fiore, Monument, CO 80132-1360: International Textile and Apparel Association, 131-141.

Holbrook, Morris B. (1994b), "The Nature of Customer Value: An Axiology of Services in the Consumption Experience," in *Service Quality: New Directions in Theory and Practice*, ed. Roland T. Rust and Richard L. Oliver, Thousand Oaks, CA: Sage Publications, 21-71.

Holbrook, Morris B. and Kim P. Corfman (1985), "Quality and Value in the Consumption Experience: Phaedrus Rides Again," in *Perceived Quality: How Consumers View Stores and Merchandise*, Lexington, MA: D. C. Heath and Company.

Holbrook, Morris B. and Elizabeth C. Hirschman (1982), "The Experiential Aspects of Consumption: Consumer Fantasies, Feelings, and Fun," *Journal of Consumer Research*, 9 (September), 132-140.

Hospers, John (1967), "Problems of Aesthetics," in *The Encyclopedia of Philosophy*, Vol. 1, ed. Paul Edwards, New York, NY: Macmillan and Free Press, 35-56.

Huizinga, Johan (1938), *Homo Ludens*, New York, NY: Harper & Row.

Iseminger, Gary (1981), "Aesthetic Appreciation," *Journal of Aesthetics and Art Criticism*, 39, 398-397.

Juran, J. M. (1988), *Juran on Planning for Quality*, New York, NY: The Free Press.

Kahle, Lynn R. (1983), "Dialectical Tensions in the Theory of Social Values," in *Social Values and Social Change*, ed. Lynn R. Kahle, New York, NY: Praeger, 275-283.

Koestler, Arthur (1978), *Janus: A Summing Up*, New York, NY: Vintage Books.

Kotler, Philip J. (1991), *Marketing Management*, Seventh Edition, Englewood Cliffs, NJ: Prentice-Hall.

Lamont, W. D. (1955), *The Value Judgment*, Westport, CT: Greenwood Press.

Lee, Harold N. (1957), "The Meaning of 'Intrinsic Value,'" in *The Language of Value*, ed. Ray Lepley, New York, NY: Columbia University Press, 178-196.

Lewis, C. I. (1946), *An Analysis of Knowledge and Valuation*, La Salle, IL: Open Court.

McGregor, Robert (1974), "Art and the Aesthetic," *Journal of Aesthetics and Art Criticism*, 32, 549-559.

Mead, George H. (1938), *The Philosophy of the Act*, ed. Charles W. Morris, Chicago, IL: University of Chicago Press.

Mehrabian, Albert and James A. Russell (1974), *An Approach to Environmental Psychology*, Cambridge, MA: The M.I.T. Press.

Morris, Charles (1956), *Varieties of Human Value*, Chicago, IL: The University of Chicago Press.

Morris, Charles (1964), *Signification and Significance*, Cambridge, MA: The M.I.T. Press.

Mukerjee, Radhakamal (1964), *The Dimensions of Values*, London, UK: George Allen & Unwin.

Nozick, Robert (1981), *Philosophical Explanation*, Cambridge, MA: Harvard University Press.

Olscamp, Paul J. (1965), "Some Remarks about the Nature of Aesthetic Perception and Appreciation," *Journal of Aesthetics and Art Criticism*, 24, 251-258.

Olson, Robert G. (1967), "The Good," in *The Encyclopedia of Philosophy*, Vol. 3, ed. Paul Edwards, New York, NY: The Macmillan Company, 367-370.

Osborne, Harold (1933), *Foundations of the Philosophy of Value*, Cambridge, UK: Cambridge University Press.

Osgood, Charles E., George J. Suci, and Percy H. Tannenbaum (1957), *The Measurement of Meaning*, Urbana, IL: University of Illinois Press.

Parker, Dewitt H. (1957), *The Philosophy of Value*, Ann Arbor, MI: The University of Michigan Press.

Parsons, Talcott (1951), *The Social System*, Glencoe, IL: The Free Press.

Pepper, Stephen C. (1958), *The Sources of Value*, Berkeley, CA: University of California Press.

Perry, Ralph Barton (1954), *Realms of Value*, Cambridge, MA: Harvard University Press.

Pettijohn, Caryl L. (1986), "Achieving Quality in the Development Process," *AT&T Technical Journal*, 65 (March/April), 85-93.

Rader, Melvin, ed. (1979), *A Modern Book of Esthetics*, Fifth Edition, New York, NY: Holt, Rinehart and Winston.

Riesman, David (1950), *The Lonely Crowd*, New Haven, CT: Yale University Press.

Rokeach, Milton (1973), *The Nature of Human Values*, New York, NY: The Free Press.

Santayana, George (1896), *The Sense of Beauty*, New York, NY: Dover Publications.

Scitovsky, Tibor (1976), *The Joyless Economy*, New York, NY: Oxford University Press.

Siegel, Eli (1981), *Self and World*, New York, NY: Definition Press.

Steenkamp, Jan-Benedict E. M. (1989), *Product Quality: An Investigation into the Concept and How It is Perceived by Consumers*, Assen / Maastricht, The Netherlands: Van Gorcum.

Stephenson, William (1967), *The Play Theory of Mass Communication*, Chicago, IL: University of Chicago Press.

Taylor, Paul W. (1961), *Normative Discourse*, Englewood Cliffs, NJ: Prentice-Hall.

Tuchman, Barbara W. (1980), "The Decline of Quality," *The New York Times Magazine*, (November 2), 38-41, 104.

Veblen, Thorstein (1899, ed. 1967), *The Theory of the Leisure Class*, Harmondsworth, UK: Penguin Books.

Von Wright, Georg Henrik (1963), *The Varieties of Goodness*, London, UK / New York, NY: Routledge & Kegan Paul / The Humanities Press.

Von Wright, Georg Henrik (1983), *Practical Reason*, Ithaca, NY: Cornell University Press.

Zeithaml, Valerie A. (1988), "Consumer Perceptions of Price, Quality, and Value: A Means-End Model and Synthesis of Evidence," *Journal of Marketing*, 52 (July), 2-22.

Varieties of Value in the Consumption Satisfaction Response

Richard L. Oliver, Vanderbilt University

ABSTRACT

The relation between value and the quality component of value embedded in the Holbrook typology is investigated with reference to the satisfaction response. Specifically, the temporal primacy of each of these concepts is explored. It is concluded that quality provides both value and satisfaction to consumers and that consumption value enhances satisfaction. Quality as a self-oriented reaction to extrinsic experience, as posited by Holbrook, is affirmed.

INTRODUCTION

A reasonable assumption is that consumers derive a number of valued outcomes from consumption. Generally, these valued outcomes can be summed up within the economist's notion of *utility*. Utility is a convenient overarching concept that permits discussion of consumer goals without the necessity of greater formal specification, although a number of "utility encoding" schemes have been proposed (e.g., Edwards and Barron 1994; Schoemaker and Hershey 1992). These efforts, however, bear an unmistakable resemblance to multiattribute models commonly used to describe consumer preferences for, or affective leanings toward a product or service (Vodopivec 1992; Warshaw and Dröge 1986). Moreover, although utility is frequently represented in axiomatic terms, there exists no semantic definition of utility receiving widespread acceptance. For example, early writers described utility as revealed preference, usefulness, and even satisfaction; more recent works refer to utility as hedonic quality or "pleasure" (Kahneman and Varey 1991).

Another ubiquitous goal of consumption is *value*. Most would agree that consumers derive some form of value from consumption. Yet value, like utility, is subject to numerous interpretations. For example, *Roget's International Thesaurus*, 3rd edition, lists six separate subcategories of value. Barring one specific to color quality (e.g., vividness), the remaining categories include *meaning*, *usefulness, importance, excellence*, and *worth*. Moreover, each of these subcategories are sets of a greater representation of terms that are related in various ways. Understandably, it would be of "value" to pin down those value-related terms that are more aligned with consumption outcomes.

THE HOLBROOK TYPOLOGY

Holbrook (1994; Holbrook and Corfman 1985) has made a major effort to describe value in the consumption experience. He distinguishes eight separate categories of consumer value based on a three dimensional paradigm. Shown in Table 1 are the eight categories as defined by the three dimensions.

In his paradigm, Holbrook intends that there are eight fundamental valued outcomes in consumption. In much the same way that certain human emotions have been described as fundamental, these outcomes, taken collectively, are thought to comprise the core of value in consumption. The dimensions on which they are based define the consumer's essential criteria for forming value judgments. In order, the dimensions include: (a) whether the outcomes are judged with reference to the self or others, (b) whether the outcomes are actively accomplished ("done by" the consumer) or are reactions to the accomplishments of others ("done to" the consumer), and (c) whether the outcomes are valued for their relation to another goal (extrinsic) or are valued as an end in themselves (intrinsic). Holbrook elaborates extensively on the nature of the consumption experiences in each of the eight cells.

In an apparent enigma, satisfaction, another oft-cited goal of consumption, does not appear in the Holbrook typology. This raises a number of interesting questions. Namely: (1) Is satisfaction value — are they the same concept? (2) Is satisfaction one of the values in the Holbrook typology? (3) Is it an additional value defined by another dimension not considered? (4) Is satisfaction a related, but conceptually distinct, concept? (5) If so, is satisfaction an antecedent of value — do consumers receive value from satisfaction? (6) Alternatively, is it a consequent — do consumers receive satisfaction from value in consumption? These issues are intriguing but cannot be pursued until some consensus is achieved on what satisfaction and value are. Discussion proceeds by defining both value and satisfaction as described in the consumer behavior literature.

DEFINITIONS OF VALUE

Placing the Holbrook typology on hold for the present, one might ask how consumer researchers operationalized value in prior works. Before answering this query, a very subtle distinction between consumption value and personal value requires elaboration. Specifically, it must be acknowledged that the value derived from consumption does not share a one-to-one overlap with values desired by individuals in general (cf. Corfman, Lehmann, and Narayanan 1991; Pitts and Woodside 1984). Personal values reflect desirable end states in life sought by all individuals. For example, the Kahle (1984) List of Values includes accomplishment, belongingness, enjoyment, excitement, fulfillment, fun, security, self-respect, and warm relationships. Note that some of these, such as enjoyment and security can be obtained through consumption while others, such as self-fulfillment, are not easily achieved in this manner. While means-end chain analysis provides a way of linking consumption to values (e.g., Gutman 1991), it does so indirectly. Thus, for parsimony, the consumption value focus taken here will not rely heavily on the personal values literature. Readers are directed to Kahle's work and the other cited sources for further insight.

Zeithaml (1988) provides a comprehensive perspective on value as couched in a web of consumption concepts. Using qualitative analysis, she finds that four themes define the concept of value *from a consumer's experience*. These are: (1) low price, (2) getting what is wanted, (3) quality compared to price, and (4) what is received for what is sacrificed. Generally, these themes are echoed in the trade literature surveyed in the Zeithaml article.

Based on additional reasoning, Zeithaml models value as a function of five variables. She hypothesizes that value is a positive function of: (a) quality, (b) other extrinsic attributes such as functionality, (c) intrinsic attributes such as pleasure, and (d) "high-level abstractions" including personal values. Additionally, value is posited to be a negative function of perceived sacrifice, defined in terms of both monetary outlays and non-monetary costs including time and effort. In effect, value is a positive function of what is received and a negative function of what is sacrificed. Thus, the value "equation" appears as follows:

$$Value = f(Receipts/Sacrifices).$$

VALUE AS A POSTPURCHASE COMPARISON

Under the preceding interpretation, value can be viewed as a specific type of comparative postpurchase operation. For example, in the now familiar expectancy disconfirmation model of satisfaction (e.g., Oliver 1980), consumers are believed to compare their

TABLE 1

The Holbrook Value Typology

Self/Other Orientation	Active/Reactive Orientation	Extrinsic Orientation	Intrinsic Orientation
Self	Active	(1) Efficiency	(2) Play
	Reactive	(3) Excellence	(4) Aesthetics
Others	Active	(5) Status	(6) Ethics
	Reactive	(7) Esteem	(8) Spirituality

TABLE 2

The Comparative Operators in Consumption

Performance Comparator	Resulting Cognition
Predictive expectations	Expectancy disconfirmation
Needs	Need fulfillment
Excellence	Quality
Fairness	Equity/Inequity
Counterfactual alternatives	Regret
Sacrifice	Value
<Nothing>	Unappraised cognition

outcomes to predictive expectations or other prepurchase standards, such as norms (Cadotte, Woodruff, and Jenkins 1987). Additionally, they may use other comparative options of a different conceptual nature, including sacrifice, as shown in Table 2 (see Oliver 1997).

Thus, within this framework, value takes its place among other comparative operations in postpurchase judgments. In effect, it competes with these options in the determination of the fulfillment response which most know as satisfaction (Oliver 1997). This perspective would describe the case of value as an *antecedent of satisfaction*, a perspective implicit in the Zeithaml review.

If this is so, then the eight dimensions of the Holbrook paradigm are encased in the "receipts" numerator of the value equation. Specifically, quality or excellence (cell 3 in Table 1), other extrinsic attributes (cells 1, 5, and 7), intrinsic attributes (cells 2 and 4), and higher level values (cells 6 and 8) become outcomes which are later compared to the sacrifices and costs incurred to achieve these outcomes. What results is one component of the satisfaction response.

Satisfaction as an Antecedent of Value

In a contrasting perspective, satisfaction would be one of the precursors to value. That is, some of the value derived from consumption would be satisfaction-based. The more satisfaction received, the greater the value received in consumption. Where, then, is satisfaction in the Holbrook typology? More specifically, what is satisfaction?

CONSUMER SATISFACTION

Based on previous distinctions presented in Oliver (1993b) on the difference between satisfaction and quality, satisfaction was described as an *experiential judgment* of outcomes compared to a set of goals or standards resulting in a sense of fulfillment, including over- or underfulfillment. As such, it could incorporate all of Holbrook's eight cells, but is more representative of those specific to a self orientation. While satisfaction can derive from the mediating responses of others, more generally it is an individualistic judgment of the fulfillingness of particular outcomes.

Thus, for satisfaction to be an input to consumption value, it must provide one of the outcomes in the Holbrook typology or provide an outcome not accounted for in his paradigm. Inspection of the Holbrook outcomes suggests that this is not the case. Satisfaction is not efficiency, excellence, status, esteem, play, aesthetics, ethics, nor spirituality. Rather, these outcomes would provide a sense of satisfaction to the recipient. If satisfaction is a component of value, then what is the missing dimension on which it is defined?

Lastly, to dispel the notion that satisfaction and value are isomorphic, it is only necessary to consider the possibility that satisfaction can exist in the absence of value and that value can exist in the absence of satisfaction, an exercise useful in distinguishing satisfaction from quality (see Oliver 1993b). Limiting the definition of value to receipts relative to sacrifices, it is evident that satisfaction and value can be found to diverge.

For example, if cost is sufficiently low and even zero as in a free good, an adequate level of receipts can provide immense value. The consumer, however, may judge satisfaction on another comparator, such as "what might have been" (regret) or simply on his/her needs. In short, dissatisfaction can be unrelated to high value in a consumption experience. An unneeded or unliked gift of great value would provide a common example. How many expensive silk ties are really all that satisfying to the recipient?

Similarly, satisfaction may exist in the presence of poor value. A makeshift emergency automobile repair using baling wire and duct tape may be truly satisfying if it enables a motorist to reach the nearest service station. The road mechanic may charge an exorbitant price, and poor value, for this "service." The motorist's needs, however, were fulfilled nonetheless.

Some would say that this latter example illustrates the efficiency component (cell 1) of the value typology where the out-

TABLE 3

The Role of Value in Satisfaction

Engagement	Cognitive Dimension	Affective Dimension
Active engagement	Cognitive comparison to inputs	Affect through engagement
Passive engagement	Comparison to pre-existing standards	Affect through observation

TABLE 4

Definitions of Quality

Connotations of:	Terms used:
Attainment	Innate excellence Superiority Highest achievement Uncompromising standards
Desirability	Preference Value Worth Affordable excellence
Usefulness	Fitness for use Capacity to satisfy wants Possessing desired characteristics

comes received were more related to safety and personal well-being than to the elements of the physical repair itself. The author is in some agreement on this point. What this example illustrates is the interplay between satisfaction and value. Value can be satisfying; alternatively satisfaction provides a sense of *personal* value. This may explain the basis for the conundrum of the primacy of satisfaction or value. At the same time that consumption value enhances satisfaction, satisfaction may be a valued outcome for many consumers. The extent to which satisfaction is a personal value awaits further research.

How Value and Satisfaction Coexist

To show how consumption value enhances satisfaction, the self-oriented cells of Table 1 can be redefined to reflect current satisfaction theory. See Table 3.

Table 3 shows how the self-oriented elements (cells 1 through 4) of the Holbrook typology map onto the three dimensions of the satisfaction response as shown in a number of studies. Satisfaction is now believed to have both a cognitive and an affective dimension (Oliver 1993a). Generally, cognition gives rise to the affect in consumption (Ortony, Clore, and Collins 1988), but it can also be shown that both appraised and unappraised affect play into the satisfaction response (Oliver 1989, 1997).

Additionally, the satisfaction response is known to vary by arousal. It has already been proposed that satisfaction can also be distinguished by the extent of engagement, where engagement is active or passive (Oliver 1989). When outcomes are compared to efforts or activities of the consumer, active engagement occurs. When outcomes are compared to preexisting standards, including expectations or desires, passive engagement is more evident.

Satisfaction based on purely affective content has not been extensively studied. Nonetheless it can assumed that it differs in terms of the nature of affective versus cognitive experience. Purely affective experience is evaluated along hedonistic lines (Hirschman and Holbrook 1982). Engaged affect assumes the consumer's actions generate the affect, whereas passive affect involves only the quiescent observation of pleasing stimuli.

WHAT ABOUT QUALITY?

Having explored the satisfaction-value relationship, it is now time to address quality as a factor in this process. How is quality or "excellence" related to value? Excellence may be, for most, a desired value in consumption. As Holbrook notes, it is also a component of value in broader terms. His framework presumes that the value of consumption increases as quality increases. At the same time, it is proposed here that satisfaction increases both because of increases in quality and because of increases in value. What, then is quality?

As derived from Tables 1 and 3, the perception of quality is a somewhat disengaged cognitive assessment of excellence. In Holbrook's terms, it is a reaction to the extrinsic cues of excellence. In this sense, the cues were preexistent. Hence, one can react to these value cues prior to consumption and without exposure, as in the "quality" of the crown jewels. Alternatively, one can experience quality through exposure.

Other Variants of Quality

Oliver (1997) provides a summary of quality definitions from a number of sources (e.g., Garvin 1984; Steenkamp 1990). See Table 4.

Here, attainment refers to the achievement of a high level standard of unspecified dimensions. Desirability refers to a more personal level of attractiveness to the consumer, again of unspecified dimensions. Finally, usefulness refers to the ability of the product or service to "serve" the consumer's needs, which, similarly are left unspecified.

Note, also, that the list includes the term "value," which has been described here as encompassing the concept of quality. Other

TABLE 5
Conceptual Differences Between Quality and Satisfaction

Comparison Dimension	Quality	Satisfaction
Experience dependency	None required; can be externally or vicariously mediated	Required
Attributes/dimensions	Specific to characteristics defining quality for the product/service	Potentially all attributes or dimensions of the product/service
Expectation/standard	Ideals, "excellence"	Predictions, norms, needs, etc.
Cognitive/affective	Primarily cognitive	Cognitive *and* affective
Conceptual antecedents	External cues (e.g., price, reputation, various communication sources)	Conceptual determinants (e.g., equity, regret, affect, dissonance, attribution, etc.)
Temporal focus (short- vs. long-term)	Primarily long-term (overall or summary)	Primarily short-term (transaction or encounter-specific)

terms, such as the possession of desired characteristics, access the level of attribute or feature possession, and can be viewed as more in line with a product cue interpretation of quality. Thus, these terms are useful in defining quality from a conceptual standpoint, but do not individually exhaust the many meanings offered in the literature. This illustrates the tautological nature of the various representations of quality in Table 3. Each of these phrases can be used as proxies for quality itself.

There is a more important point to be made here. While these and other definitions can be found in the literature, they are incomplete representations of the quality concept because they do not specify the comparison referent. For example, the list in Table 3 categorizes quality into dimensions of attainment, desirability, and usefulness. What, exactly, has been attained? What is it about the product/service performance that is desirable? And, for what is this performance useful? In a partial answer to these questions, the standards that have been offered in the literature are explored next.

The Comparison Referent

Some of the definitions in Table 4 hint at a comparison referent. For example, "affordable excellence" implies that excellence is achieved at a reasonable (to the consumer) cost and, hence, represents value. Similarly, even the word "superiority" implies that something must be inferior. Presumably, the superiority/inferiority referent is the set of competitive offerings available to the consumer. Generally, quality can only exist if something else is available to provide at least one other basis for comparison.

Ideals as a standard. Perhaps the earliest notion of a comparative standard in marketing is that of an ideal point. Originally developed in the context of predictive models of attitude, the "ideal" product is one which possesses ideal levels of all of its relevant features. Generally, ideals will provide the ultimate criterion against which all competitive brands must strive. More realistically, however, quality derives from the finest of what is available in the marketplace, that is the "best brand" (Cadotte et al. 1987).

Excellence as a standard. In the original version of SERVQUAL, Parasuraman, Zeithaml, and Berry (1988) measured expectations in terms of what companies *should* do to be perceived as high quality service deliverers. Use of should or desired levels of expectations was thought to access the correct referent for quality judgments at the time of their study. However, problems with the

directive of what companies should do (e.g., should do for what purpose?) led the authors to reformulate the manner in which expectations were measured.

Recognizing that, even though consumers can only perceive real world offerings, they also have the capacity to *imagine* better offerings, Parasuraman, Berry, and Zeithaml (1991) later proposed assessing performance against standards of *excellent* companies. Here, excellent companies could be either real ("best brand") or imagined (a better best brand or, perhaps, ideal). Thus, excellence as a criterion allows for the possibility that consumers can experience "true" quality, that provided by a truly excellent firm. The ideal referent, in contrast, is one step removed in a theoretically unattainable direction. Excellence, then, is what quality provides the consumer.

The Role of Quality in Satisfaction and Value

Quality vs. satisfaction. In attempting to distinguish quality from satisfaction, a number of differences have been previously drawn in Oliver (1993b). These differences occur at rather fundamental levels pertaining to: (a) whether or not the concept requires experience with the product or service, (b) the dimensions consumers use to form quality versus satisfaction judgments, (c) the nature of the expectations or standards used for these judgments, (d) the degree of cognitive vs. affective content, (e) the existence of other conceptual antecedents which might impact each of the concepts, and (f) the primary temporal focus. See Table 5.

Generally, quality is an externally mediated perception that a product or service possesses excellent levels of the key quality dimensions which define quality for that product/service (e.g., the four "Cs" of a fine diamond). It is an enduring cognitive representation which may be instilled and maintained by external cues including advertising and reputation. In contrast, satisfaction is a purely experiential sensation of an affective or cognitive nature that the product or service has fulfilled particular goals as defined by the consumer. These goals can be functional, aesthetic, conceptual, or imaginal. Typically, the satisfaction response does not persist, decaying into a consumer's attitudinal response (Oliver 1980). Thus, quality is unique from satisfaction. It is both an input to one's satisfaction as well as a stable marker of brand identification.

Quality vs. value. As presented in Table 1, quality is one of the components of value in consumption. Consumers derive value from quality; it enhances their consumption experience and, in economic terms, gives them added utility. Thus, quality is a precursor to both value and satisfaction. What remains, then, is the relation between value and satisfaction.

Value vs. satisfaction. The earlier sections of this paper reflect the author's position on the primacy of value and satisfaction. Value is one of the comparative operations consumers apply in the satisfaction response. In agreement with Zeithaml, quality is an input to value. Value, then, becomes a superordinate concept subsuming quality. The receipt of value provides additional satisfaction — satisfaction deriving first from quality and then from value.

It should not be overlooked that the value and satisfaction provided by quality derive from other desired purchase outcomes which, by their nature, define the essence of quality. As typically found in studies investigating the meaning of quality to consumers (e.g., Gutman and Alden 1985), quality brings reliability, durability, status, self-confidence, and ease of decision-making. For these reasons, quality is value, thereby being a "valued quality" in consumption.

SUMMARY

In more elementary terms, *consumption* value is a judgment of receipts compared to sacrifices. This form of value takes on greater meaning when the receipts numerator is expanded to include the many types of valued consumption outcomes, including excellence, as presented in the Holbrook typology. Value, then, becomes an input to the satisfaction response which is impacted by quality directly and indirectly through value. Consumers may derive subsequent *personal* value from satisfaction, although more conclusive evidence on this latter point awaits investigation.

REFERENCES

Cadotte, Ernest R., Robert B. Woodruff, and Roger L. Jenkins (1987), "Expectations and Norms in Models of Consumer Satisfaction," *Journal of Marketing Research*, 24 (August), 305-314.

Corfman, Kim P., Donald R. Lehmann and Sunder Narayanan (1991), "Values, Utility, and Ownership: Modeling the Relationships for Consumer Durables," *Journal of Retailing*, 67 (Summer), 184-204.

Edwards, Ward and F. Hutton Barron (1994), "SMARTS and SMARTER: Improved Simple Methods for Multiattribute Utility Measurement," *Organizational Behavior and Human Decision Processes*, 60 (December), 306-325.

Garvin, David A. (1984), "What Does `Product Quality' Really Mean?," *Sloan Management Review*, 26 (Fall), 25-43.

Gutman, Jonathan (1991), "Exploring the Nature of Linkages Between Consequences and Values," *Journal of Business Research*, 22 (March), 143-148.

Gutman, Jonathan and Scott D. Alden (1985), "Adolescents' Cognitive Structures of Retail Stores and Fashion Consumption: A Means-End Chain Analysis of Quality," in *Perceived Quality: How Consumers View Stores and Merchandise*, Jacob Jacoby and Jerry C. Olson, eds. Lexington, MA: Lexington Books, 99-114.

Hirschman, Elizabeth C. and Morris B. Holbrook (1982), "Hedonic Consumption: Emerging Concepts, Methods and Propositions," *Journal of Marketing*, 46 (Summer), 92-101.

Holbrook, Morris B. (1994), "The Nature of Customer Value: An Axiology of Services in the Consumption Experience," in *Service Quality: New Directions in Theory and Practice*, Roland T. Rust and Richard L. Oliver, eds. Thousand Oaks, CA: Sage Publications, 21-71.

Holbrook, Morris B. and Kim P. Corfman (1985), "Quality and Value in the Consumption Experience: Phaedrus Rides Again," in *Perceived Quality: How Consumers View Stores and Merchandise*, Jacob Jacoby and Jerry C. Olson, eds. Lexington, MA: Lexington Books, 31-57.

Kahle, Lynn R. (1984), *Attitudes and Social Adaptation: A Person-Situation Interaction Approach*, Oxford, U.K.: Pergamon.

Kahneman, Daniel and Carol Varey (1991), "Notes on the Psychology of Utility," in *Interpersonal Comparisons of Well-Being*, Jon Elster and John E. Roemer, eds. Cambridge: Cambridge University Press, 127-159.

Oliver, Richard L. (1980), "A Cognitive Model of the Antecedents and Consequences of Satisfaction Decisions," *Journal of Marketing Research*, 17 (November), 460-469.

Oliver, Richard L. (1989), "Processing of the Satisfaction Response in Consumption: A Suggested Framework and Research Propositions," *Journal of Consumer Satisfaction, Dissatisfaction and Complaining Behavior*, 2, 1-16.

Oliver, Richard L. (1993a), "Cognitive, Affective, and Attribute Bases of the Satisfaction Response," *Journal of Consumer Research*, 20 (December), 418-430.

Oliver, Richard L. (1993b), "A Conceptual Model of Service Quality and Service Satisfaction: Compatible Goals, Different Concepts," in *Advances in Services Marketing and Management: Research and Practice*, Vol. 2, Teresa A. Swartz, David E. Bowen, and Stephen W. Brown, eds. Greenwich, CT: JAI Press, 65-85.

Oliver, Richard L. (1997), *Satisfaction: A Behavioral Perspective on the Consumer*, New York: McGraw-Hill.

Ortony, Andrew, Gerald L. Clore, and Allan Collins (1988), *The Cognitive Structure of Emotions*, Cambridge: Cambridge University Press.

Parasuraman, A., Leonard L. Berry, and Valarie A. Zeithaml (1991), "Refinement and Reassessment of the SERVQUAL Scale," *Journal of Retailing*, 67 (Winter), 420-450.

Parasuraman, A., Valarie A. Zeithaml, and Leonard L. Berry (1988), "SERVQUAL: A Multiple-Item Scale for Measuring Consumer Perceptions of Service Quality," *Journal of Retailing*, 64 (Spring), 12-40.

Pitts, Robert E., Jr. and Arch G. Woodside, eds. (1984), *Personal Values and Consumer Psychology*, Lexington, MA: Lexington Books.

Schoemaker, Paul J. H. and John C. Hershey (1992), "Utility Measurement: Signal, Noise, and Bias," *Organizational Behavior and Human Decision Processes*, 52 (August), 397-424.

Steenkamp, Jan-Benedict E. M. (1990), "Conceptual Model of the Quality Perception Process," *Journal of Business Research*, 21 (December), 309-333.

Vodopivec, Blaz (1992), "A Need Theory Perspective on the Parallelism of Attitude and Utility," *Journal of Economic Psychology*, 13 (March), 19-37.

Warshaw, Paul R. and Cornelia Dröge (1986), "Economic Utility Versus the Attitudinal Perspective of Consumer Choice," *Journal of Economic Psychology*, 7 (March), 37-60.

Zeithaml, Valarie A. (1988), "Consumer Perceptions of Price, Quality, and Value: A Means-End Model and Synthesis of Evidence," *Journal of Marketing*, 52 (July), 2-22.

Ethics and the Typology of Customer Value

N. Craig Smith, Georgetown University

ABSTRACT

The typology of customer value (Holbrook 1994a, 1994b) posits that ethics (including justice, virtue, and morality) is one of eight kinds of value that may be obtained in the consumption experience. This paper examines ethics as a customer value and its relationship to the other of types customer value and to the framework as a whole. The merits of the typology of customer value are highlighted and the role of ethics within the framework carefully delineated. In particular, the distinction is made between consumption experiences that have entirely altruistic motivations and those experiences that, in addition, have a less selfless aspect. Illustrations of ethics as a customer value are provided, including the consumption of charity services and participation in consumer boycotts. Suggestions are made for research that may benefit from the integration provided by the framework.

INTRODUCTION

The typology of value (Holbrook 1994a, 1994b) proposes ethics as one of eight kinds of value in the consumption experience. By way of illustration, Holbrook suggests that the consumption of charity services, such as donating one's blood to the Red Cross, provides this kind of customer value; it "constitutes an ethically virtuous action if one pursues helping others purely for its own sake" (1994b: 54). As well as ethics (or morality), the typology proposes that efficiency, play, excellence, aesthetics, status (or politics), esteem, and spirituality are different kinds of value that consumers may obtain through consumption. The different types of customer value are categorized according to three dimensions; whether the value is extrinsic or intrinsic, self- or other-oriented, and active or reactive.

The purpose of this paper is to examine ethics as a customer value and its fit within the typology. First, I comment on the merits of the customer value framework, confirming its "value" to consumer researchers. Second, I examine ethics as a customer value, providing illustrations of when this type of value may be obtained. Next I examine the conceptualization of ethics within the framework and suggest an alternative conceptualization; I note that it is particularly important to differentiate between ethics and altruism. Finally, I conclude with some suggestions for future research.

HOLBROOK'S TYPOLOGY OF CUSTOMER VALUE

Recognizing that exchange is central to the marketing concept and that marketing transactions involve exchanges of value, Holbrook (1994a: 134) highlights the importance of understanding the nature and types of value customers obtain in the consumption experience. In other words, he asks: what form does the value take that customers hope to receive when they hand over their hard-earned cash? Such a question clearly should be at the core of consumer research.

In providing an answer to this question, Holbrook (1994b: 26-39) identifies, or at least hypothesizes, four key characteristics of customer value. He defines value as "an interactive relativistic preference experience" (1994b: 27). First, it is *interactive* because value can only be obtained through an interaction between the customer and the product; while a product may have many qualities, they only come to represent customer value when they are appreciated by customers within the context of a marketplace exchange. With respect to art, for example, this suggests a distinction between artistic value and customer value; a work of art appreciated by the artist alone may have artistic value but not customer value.

Second, value is *relativistic* because it can never be absolute when it is the result of customers, who differ amongst themselves, making comparisons between alternative possible sources of value in a multitude of different situations. Fashion clothing marketers know too well, for example, that customer tastes differ and may change over time or in response to the arrival of new styles. Hence, the third characteristic that value is a judgement of *preference*.

Finally, value is found in the *experience* of consumption of the product, rather than in its purchase. Typically, the act of purchase is not an end in itself but the means of obtaining experiences derived from the product. It is a marketing axiom that people do not buy products, they buy the services that products provide; as Levitt (1995: 13) put it: "people actually do not buy gasoline... what they buy is the right to continue driving their cars." However, we might recognize that for some products and markets the act of purchase is a part of the consumption experience; I may choose to shop at an expensive delicatessen in preference to a conventional supermarket because this is more enjoyable and, arguably, this is part of the consumption experience derived from the goods purchased.

As well as fleshing out the nature of customer value, Holbrook (1994b: 44-55) also proposes a framework or typology, classifying customer value by three dimensions: 1) extrinsic versus intrinsic, 2) self- versus other-oriented, and 3) active versus reactive (see Table 1 for the complete typology in its most recent form). Esteem, for example, is a value that might be obtained in the purchase of a luxury automobile. It is extrinsic, because the esteem value is instrumentally derived rather than through the act of consumption as an end in itself (compare with the intrinsic value of play). It is other-oriented, because the esteem value is derived from the reaction of others to the customer's ownership of the car, rather than his or her reaction to it (compare with the self-oriented value of excellence that might be derived from product quality). It is reactive, because the esteem value comes from what the car does for the customer rather than what he or she does to it (compare with the active value of efficiency resulting from the functional use of a product).

Types of value are not mutually exclusive. It follows from the earlier discussion of the nature of customer value that a luxury automobile may provide different types of value to different customers. For another customer, the same luxury automobile may provide the extrinsic, self-oriented, and reactive value of excellence. Indeed, for the same customer, the same luxury automobile may provide a combination of values, perhaps play and excellence in addition to esteem. As Holbrook (1994a: 138) notes: "*any* or *all* of the value types distinguished earlier may and often do *occur simultaneously* to *varying degrees* in any given consumption experience." Accordingly, as further discussed below, the framework suggests that ethics is a value that customers may obtain *in addition* to other types of value.

Holbrook's conception of the nature and types of customer value is a useful contribution to consumer research and marketing practice. Its merits for consumer researchers lie in the recognition or assertion that: 1) customer value lies in the consumption experience, not the product; 2) different types of value may be obtained; 3) these types of value may occur simultaneously and to varying degrees in any consumption experience; 4) there is an interrelationship between the different types of value that arise in

TABLE 1
Holbrook's Typology of Value in the Consumption Experience

		Extrinsic	Intrinsic
Self-Oriented	Active	EFFICIENCY (O/I, Convenience)	PLAY (Fun)
	Reactive	EXCELLENCE (Quality)	AESTHETICS (Beauty)
Other-Oriented	Active	STATUS (Success, Impression Management)	ETHICS (Justice, Virtue, Morality)
	Reactive	ESTEEM (Reputation, Materialism, Possessions)	SPIRITUALITY (Faith, Ecstasy, Sacredness)

Source: Holbrook, Morris B. (1995), "Customer Value—A Framework for Analysis and Research." Proposal for Special Topic Session: Association for Consumer Research, 1995, p. 5.

---

consumption; and 5) the types of value may be subject to a higher-order classification (such as the dimensions proposed in Holbrook's typology). Marketing managers would likely find Holbrook's conception of customer value and the typology both accessible and intuitively appealing. It provides scope for improved understanding of the benefits sought by consumers and hence the scope for increased customer satisfaction. More specifically, it might suggest alternative approaches to organizing data in marketing research, concept testing in new product development, and message strategy in advertising.

However, this is not to suggest that researchers or managers should embrace the framework in its entirety. The conception of customer value, including the recognition that there are different types of value, is well-argued by Holbrook (1994a, 1994b). The detail within the framework is more subject to question. It is beyond the scope of this paper to examine the dimensions of the typology and all the different types of value proposed. However, it can be noted that there is uncertainty about the antecedents and consequences of the dimensions.[1] What is the theoretical basis for the three dimension chosen? Holbrook (1994: 39-44) briefly discusses the literature supporting the dimensions chosen, but not alternative dimensions. For example, perhaps there is an affective dimension of the consumption experience—whether the consumer has positive or negative feelings. Do positive or negative feelings influence the type of value consumers obtain? Is this adequately captured in the existing framework? Likewise, is there an economic dimension of value[2] or a tangible/intangible or a physical/mental dimension? Moreover, Holbrook (1994a: 137) has noted the "disappearance of the self-other dichotomy" when faith becomes a state of ecstasy.

The classification of the types of value identified also may be questioned. Perhaps, as indicated above, faith may be classified as self-oriented as well as or instead of other-oriented. Further, is the framework sufficiently inclusive, does it capture all key types of value in consumption? Holbrook (1994b: 58) is correct to observe that some types of value identified in the framework have received little attention from consumer researchers, including ethics or morality in consumption. Yet are some important types of value missing, such as the intellectual value that may be obtained from a subscription to a current affairs magazine or the purchase of an encyclopedia? Indeed, this line of analysis soon suggests more careful limits may need to be imposed on the domain of the framework if it is to avoid the impossible task of attempting to include virtually all types of human behavior. Moreover, are those values that are included adequately delimited and accurately defined? Finally, if value is found in consumption, we might consider whether Holbrook's framework is more accurately about consumer value; it is not primarily as a customer that the value is obtained, indeed, one may not have been the customer and yet still obtain the (consumer) value Holbrook describes.

Concerns about the dimensions of the framework and the types of value identified are addressed throughout the papers in the special session. The primary focus of this paper is on ethics as a type of customer value and how it is classified within the framework.

ETHICS AS A CUSTOMER VALUE
Holbrook's (1994a: 139; 1994b: 45) typology refers to "morality" and, parenthetically, to "virtue or ethical acts". Holbrook

---

[1]This point has also been made by an anonymous reviewer of the special session proposal.

[2]Suggested by another anonymous reviewer of the special session proposal. Arguably, the economic components of value are only means to the end of alternative types of value already captured in the framework.

(1994a: 137) refers to a "pursuit" of morality (hence its classification as active on the active/reactive dimension), that aims at "virtue sought for its own sake as its own reward." He continues by referring to "deontological value" and the concept of duty or obligation to others. Noting that such obligations "often appear in the form of socially accepted rules of conduct or conventions that dictate proper behavior," Holbrook illustrates morality as a customer value by reference to wearing a white dress at one's wedding or a tuxedo to the prom. He adds that ethics is viewed as intrinsically motivated (hence its classification as intrinsic on the extrinsic/intrinsic dimension). Aside from references to charitable contributions, other illustrations of morality as a customer value in Holbrook (1994a), are somewhat whimsical ("Holbrookian"?) in keeping with the lighter tone of this paper.

Holbrook (1994b: 52-54) gives more detailed attention to moral philosophy, yet the essence of his perspective on ethics as a customer value remains the same: "Ethical action involves doing something for the sake of others—with concern for how it will affect them or how they will react to it" (p. 52). The motivation for such action is intrinsic because "virtue is its own reward" (pp. 53, 54). More controversially, he suggests that "the moment we stop pursuing some ethical action as an end in itself and begin pursuing it as a means to some ulterior purpose, it stops being ethical and partakes of some other sort of value" (p. 53). This perspective on ethics requires some examination, as will follow below. In addition, the use of the terms "ethics", "virtue", "morality" and (in Table 1) "justice" interchangeably, is also problematic. Nonetheless, it is clear that Holbrook (1994b) is referring to ethics as a customer value where it reflects doing good for its own sake and as a result of a sense of moral obligation or duty.

By way of illustration, Holbrook (1994b: 54) "defends" the consumption of charity services "on the moral grounds that it is 'right' to behave generously without offering any further reason or objective;" for example, donating money to the United Way, one's blood to the Red Cross, and one's time to a soup kitchen. However, such behaviors only constitute "an ethically virtuous action [i.e., ethics as a customer value] if one pursues helping others purely for its own sake." Indeed, Holbrook (1994b: 54) rejects any self-interested motivations of such behaviors: "If, by contrast, one were to invoke the aim of benefiting from tax deductions, earning gratitude, or improving the neighborhood by reducing the number of street people, the relevant type of value would become political [or status, to use the term adopted in Table 1] rather than moral." As I explain in more detail below, this is a narrow perspective on ethical conduct and I will argue in favor of a broader and more widely accepted view. Holbrook (1994b) raises a conundrum in moral philosophy that has troubled philosophers for centuries: can an act ever be entirely without self-interest? Moreover, from an empirical standpoint, can we ever know? It is generally accepted that doing good has a multitude of motivations, some of which may be self-interested.

While it will be argued that the role of ethics in the typology of customer value needs to be carefully delineated, Holbrook's notion of ethics as a customer value is not in principle disputed. Indeed, I have elsewhere (Smith 1987a, 1987b, 1990; Burke, Milberg and Smith 1993) examined "ethical purchase behavior", as Holbrook (1994b: 58) acknowledges. The consumption of charity services and (arguably) the wearing of appropriate attire in formal settings have been used to illustrate ethics as a customer value. In the next section, ethics as a customer value is further illustrated by consumer boycotts, providing an inductive basis for specifying the meaning of ethics as a customer value.

Consumer Boycotts as an Illustration of Ethics as a Customer Value

Boycotts can take many forms and have been used for centuries (Smith 1990: 134-166). Early examples include boycotts of British goods by American colonists in the Revolutionary War, boycotts of slave-made goods by abolitionists, and, as early as 1327, a boycott of the monks of Christ's Church by the citizens of Canterbury, England in an agreement not to "buy, sell or exchange drinks or victuals with the monastery" (Laidler 1968: 27-30). Laidler (1968: 27) defines boycotting as "an organized effort to withdraw and induce others to withdraw from social or business relations with another." More specifically, the consumer boycott may be defined as "the organized exercising of consumer sovereignty by abstaining from purchase of an offering in order to exert influence on a matter of concern to the customer and over the institution making the offering" (Smith 1990: 140). It is clear from the instrumental purpose evident in these definitions that a consumer boycott often would not qualify as an "ethically virtuous action" under Holbrook's (1994b: 54) conception of ethics. Indeed, Smith (1990: 278-282) argues that consumer boycotts should be viewed as a tool for achieving the social control of business.[3]

However, Smith (1990: 8-9) suggests consumer boycotts (especially where organized by pressure groups) are only the most clearly identifiable and deliberate form of a broader phenomenon, described as ethical purchase behavior, which occurs "where people are influenced in purchase by ethical concerns" (1990: 8). The ethical content of participation in a consumer boycott and ethical purchase behavior generally, notwithstanding possible instrumental motivations, may be illustrated by research on specific boycotts. Consider the following examples (Smith 1990: 233-255):

- An editorial in the *Financial Times*, headed 'Moral Pressure in the Market,' attributed the withdrawal from South Africa by Barclays Bank to a consumer boycott and concluded that this was effective because of the ethical concern of consumers: "ordinary people, revolted by what they have learned about the [apartheid] system from the news media... have proved they can bring effective pressure to bear on commercial organizations... Moral pressure of this kind—whether against apartheid, whaling, the fur trade, vivisection or even the defence industry—is an increasingly important fact of business life" (*Financial Times*, 25 November, 1986).

- The moral opprobrium associated with Nestle's marketing of infant formula in developing countries is well captured in this letter from a supporter of the consumer boycott of Nestle: "My children love Nestle Quik. My husband and I are virtually addicted to Nescafe. But we will no longer be buying these or your other products. We have learned about the suffering your advertising of infant formula

---

[3]With consumer boycott defined as "abstaining from purchase" one might be tempted to argue that there is no exchange and hence no customer value obtained. This is disputed on two grounds: 1) there is still an experience related to the domain of human behavior broadly characterized by Holbrook as consumption, as in research on possessions (Belk 1991); and 2) a boycott typically involves abstaining from the purchase of a given supplier's product with a substitute purchased instead, as Holbrook notes, customer value is a preference experience.

causes... our outrage joins with that of many others and together we will boycott Nestle products until you change" (Smith 1990: 249).

- Middle-class urban America supported the successful, 1965-70 grape boycott, because of concern about the treatment of farm workers and issues of poverty, pesticide misuse, and civil rights. In a union pamphlet entitled *Why We Boycott*, Cesar Chavez later wrote, "The boycott is the way we take our cause to the public. For surely if we cannot find *justice* in the courts of rural California, we will find support with our brothers and sisters throughout the nation (emphasis added)."

- During the boycott of Douwe Egberts coffee, over its sourcing of coffee from Angola (when Angola was seeking independence from Portugal), a Douwe Egberts sales director made the following comment on instructions given to the sales force (Hofstede 1980): "We told them that the company could not take a political position. On the other hand, they know that they should follow the customer—the customer is always right. This was OK as long as the customer was only interested in the taste of coffee. Now, for the first time, the customer expressed an opinion about something very different."

Smith (1990: 260) highlights the importance of moral outrage in consumer boycott effectiveness and success. He notes (1990: 258) that boycotts have expressive as well as instrumental functions: "The boycott is a moral act; an expression by the consumer of disapproval of the firm's activities and disassociation from them." This desire on the part of the consumer to have "clean hands" may mean, as Smith continues, that it is inappropriate to refer to objectives or effectiveness in reference to consumer participation in a boycott; no instrumental motivation may be present, at least for some consumers. This is illustrated by "many consumers' refusal to purchase South African goods, [because of] the wish to avoid tainted (and being tainted by) products of apartheid" (Smith 1990: 158).

More broadly, Smith (1990: 178) defines ethical purchase behavior as "an expression of the individual's moral judgement in his or her purchase behavior." While this definition may be flawed because it can be argued that moral judgement is almost always present in any human behavior—there is a moral burden as a consequence of the human condition—it recognizes the possibility of ethics as a customer value. As well as abstaining from purchase for ethical reasons, in consumer boycotts or perhaps as a vegetarian, Smith (1990: 2-3) also recognizes more affirmative forms of ethical purchase behavior, where products of a particular supplier are sought, as in buying domestically produced goods because it is "the right thing to do." Also noteworthy here is the literature on socially responsible consumption (Smith 1990: 178-181). For example, Engel and Blackwell (1982: 610) refer to socially conscious consumers as "those persons who not only are concerned with their own personal satisfactions, but also buy with some consideration of the social and environmental well-being of others." More broadly still, in a variety of spheres, scholars such as Etzioni (1988: 51-66) have recognized the moral dimension of economics and provided many examples of people apparently acting unselfishly in their economic behavior. In short, there is ample evidence in consumer boycotts and elsewhere to support a role for ethical concern in consumer behavior and the possibility of ethics as a customer value.

AN ALTERNATIVE CONCEPTUALIZATION OF ETHICS AS A CUSTOMER VALUE

While ethical concerns may be recognized as an influence on purchase behavior, can ethics be viewed as a value sought by consumers? There is something troubling about the concept of ethics as a customer value to be obtained in marketplace exchanges. It might be argued that ethics is not appropriately conceived as one of a number of possible values customers might seek, that it is in some way above consideration alongside quality or fun, or that it is beyond the reach of commercial consideration. (Similarly, one might argue that spirituality, at least in relation to religious behavior, is also above comparison with the more earthly types of value.) However, the apparent contradiction of a form of value obtained as ethics, is largely dependent upon a conception of ethics as selfless behavior. If ethics is for its own sake, it is difficult to argue that this can provide "value" to the customer; clearly, value is not sought. Holbrook (1994b: 22) refers to exchange by way of an explanation of customer value, noting that exchange is a transaction involving two agents in which each agent gives up something of value in return for something of greater value. It would seem that if customer value is a form of utility obtained by the customer, then it cannot be obtained for selfless reasons. There is a way of resolving this issue. It requires a broader and more widely accepted perspective on ethics and an understanding of altruism. First, however, let us consider the multiple motivations for participation in a consumer boycott.

In choosing to boycott Barclays Bank, a consumer may have strongly believed that apartheid was wrong and that Barclays' presence as the largest bank in South Africa supported apartheid and was therefore wrong as a consequence. Participation in the boycott may have been motivated by: a) the belief that support of the boycott could help the people of South Africa by forcing Barclays' withdrawal and speeding the downfall of the apartheid regime, an instrumental motivation; b) a desire not be associated with a company that directly or indirectly benefits from apartheid, a 'clean hands' motivation; or c) a reluctance to be seen patronizing the 'apartheid bank', an avoidance of unseemly conspicuous consumption. Although instrumental, the first motivation could qualify as an ethically virtuous action under Holbrook's definition. The second motivation of a clean conscience may also qualify. The third motivation is more problematic, not wishing to be embarrassed or having to brave protesters when visiting a Barclays Bank outlet, reflects self-interest. Given that it is conceivable that all three motivations might be present for any one consumer, would this mean that ethics is not a customer value obtained in participation in the Barclays boycott? Likewise, a vegetarian may be concerned about the treatment of animals and dislike the taste of meat, or working in a soup kitchen may be motivated by a desire to help the homeless and to be seen as a caring individual. In short, there may be ethically virtuous (as defined by Holbrook) and less selfless motivations to some consumption experiences and yet we might still wish to characterize them as consumers obtaining ethics as a customer value.

The concept of altruism provides clarification here. Altruism may be defined (Becker and Becker 1992: 35) in terms of an action intentionally aimed at helping others and involving some other-directed motivation, a regard for the well-being of others for its own sake. In addition, some restrict the term to the placing of the interests of others ahead of those of oneself. Holbrook's conceptualization of ethics as a customer value may more accurately be described as altruism. This presents three problems for consumer researchers attempting to use the typology: 1) truly altruistic acts are rare and some would say never occur or are impossible to identify with certainty; 2) altruism does not include many behaviors we might wish to characterize as ethical; and 3) a broader conceptualization of ethics as a customer value that goes beyond altruism may violate the framework dimensions. The third problem—particularly in terms of whether ethics as a customer value is other-oriented, self-oriented, or both—is addressed in the next section. Below, I argue against a narrow conceptualization of ethics (i.e., altruism) as a customer value in favor of a broader view that can encompass the motivations described in consumer boycott participation and other consumption experiences where ethical concerns are involved but with self-interest present too.

Clearly, to advance this argument, ethics needs to be defined in a way that includes altruism yet also permits less selfless motivations. A consumption experience that provides value or utility because it is ethical is the result of a consumer judgement of how he or she ought to behave, in accord with moral principles or, more simply, a belief about what is the right or good thing to do. Clearly such value could not be obtained by unethical behaviors; for example, by drinking and driving when it is known that driving under the influence of alcohol is wrong because it impairs driving ability and may result in harm to others.

To differentiate between consumption behaviors that are not unethical in the sense of not being wrong and behaviors that deliberately seek to do good, we need to introduce the role of values. (It is also useful to thereby distinguish between moral values and customer value.) An affirmative act of "goodness", promotes what may be conceived as the currency of ethics, namely fundamental human values such as rights, freedom and well-being. These values are "what philosophers call 'prescriptive' or 'action guiding' because they provide standards for directing human choice" (Donaldson 1989: 11). Accordingly, ethics as a customer value results from an affirmative act of goodness that promotes one or more moral values of the individual. Hence, I may participate in a consumer boycott to promote the welfare of blacks in apartheid South Africa, or contribute to a charity to prevent harm to children.[4]

Unresolved, however, is whether such behaviors are truly selfless. As earlier discussed, the notion that a consumption experience may provide utility because it is ethical suggests the behavior is also self-interested. While ethical egoism[5] is rarely advocated by moral philosophers, the arguments of psychological egoists have presented serious challenges to the concept of purely selfless behavior. Psychological egoism discounts as selfless even acts of great personal sacrifice (that would clearly be in keeping with the more restricted definition of altruism, above). As Beauchamp explains (1982: 58): "The psychological egoist does not contend that people always behave in an *outwardly* selfish manner. No matter how self-sacrificing a person's behavior may be at times... the desire behind the action is always selfish; one is ultimately out for oneself—whether in the long or the short run." Philosophical interest in psychological egoism may be traced back to Plato. However, resolution of the issues it raises for philosophers may only lie in a greater understanding of the psychology of human motivation, including unconscious motives (Beauchamp 1982: 61-

62). Nonetheless, it cannot be argued with any certainty that an affirmative act of goodness that promotes moral values of the individual is ever ultimately without self-interest.

Donaldson (1989: 10-11) notes that "values possess legitimacy beyond the boundaries of simple self-interest" and suggests the possible role of "enlightened self-interest". Hence, to conclude this initial conceptualization, ethics as a customer value may be said to arise in a consumption experience when the individual engages in an affirmative act of goodness, promoting one or more moral values for the well-being of others and for reasons of enlightened self-interest.

ETHICS WITHIN THE TYPOLOGY OF CUSTOMER VALUE

The broader, alternative conceptualization of ethics as a customer value (above) is more accommodating of a greater variety of consumption experiences that include ethical concern as a motivating factor, such as those 'acts of charity' that Holbrook would exclude. However, this presents problems when we attempt to return to the framework. Holbrook (1994b: 53) acknowledges that "an ethical egoist... pursues a self-oriented perspective that is clearly inconsistent with the present typology." Yet a self-oriented perspective is conceivably a component within acts that are ostensibly or largely other-oriented. To maintain the integrity of the existing framework, it must be argued that only altruistic value is other-oriented (and active and intrinsic). Any self-interest in otherwise altruistic consumer experiences must be accounted for elsewhere in the framework. This suggests future research to consider the possibility of expanding the framework by sub-dividing ethics as a customer value, differentiating between consumption experiences that have largely altruistic motivations and those experiences that, in addition, have a less selfless aspect. Alternatively, a more parsimonious typology might exclude the self-/other-oriented dimension, especially if its antecedents are uncertain or if it proves problematic when other types of value are more closely examined.

These concerns about the fit of ethics within the typology should be seen as a call for fine-tuning and not dismissive of the framework. The framework has definite merit and highlights interesting conceptual and empirical issues. Indeed, the scope for future research using this typology is considerable, especially research that adopts an integrative approach to customer value. By way of illustration, consider consumer trade-offs between different types of value such as play and ethics in the consumption of alcohol (here it is suggested that ethics is a value obtained by moderating consumption). Research on play and ethics as potentially conflicting types of value obtained in the consumption of alcohol would inform understanding of consumer behavior and, from an industry standpoint, indicate possible approaches to more socially responsible forms of advertising. It might also identify more effective public policy interventions.

Holbrook's perspective on the consumption experience improves our understanding of consumer behavior and points to hypotheses for consumer researchers both directly, in work to develop the framework, and indirectly, in studies across the field that might benefit from a more integrative framework. Indeed, the framework may even have the potential to serve as a paradigm for some consumer researchers.

---

[4]This use of values is preferred to Holbrook's (1994b: 53) use of virtue ("regarded as pursuing the moral end just defined") in part because of the more specialized meaning of virtue found within virtue ethics. Holbrook's reference to justice (see Table 1) is also presumably in regard to a moral end that may be realized when ethics is a customer value. In both cases, the realization of moral values may be considered to be more encompassing.

---

[5]Defined as "the theory that the only valid moral standard is the obligation to promote one's own well-being above everyone else's" (Beauchamp 1982: 57).

REFERENCES

Beauchamp, Tom L. (1982), *Philosophical Ethics: An Introduction to Moral Philosophy* (New York: McGraw-Hill).

Becker, Lawrence C. and Charlotte C. Becker (1992), *Encyclopedia of Ethics* (New York: Garland Publishing).

Belk, Russell W. (1991), "Possessions and the Sense of Past," in Russell W. Belk (ed.) *Highways and Buyways: Naturalistic Research from the Consumer Behavior Odyssey* (Provo, UT: Association for Consumer Research), pp. 114-130.

Burke, Sandra J., Sandra J. Milberg, and N. Craig Smith (1993), "The Role of Ethical Concerns in Consumer Purchase Behavior: Understanding Alternative Processes," in *Advances in Consumer Research*, Vol. XX, Leigh McAlister and Michael L. Rothschild (ed.) (Provo, UT: Association for Consumer Research), pp. 119-22.

Donaldson, Thomas (1989), *The Ethics of International Business* (New York: Oxford University Press).

Engel, James F. and Roger D. Blackwell (1982), *Consumer Behavior* (New York: The Dryden Press).

Etzioni, Amitai (1988), *The Moral Dimension: Toward a New Economics* (New York: Free Press).

Hofstede, Geert (1980), "Angola Coffee—or the Confrontation of an Organization with Changing Values in Its Environment," *Organization Studies* 1:1.

Holbrook, Morris B. (1994a), "Axiology, Aesthetics, And Apparel: Some Reflections on the Old School Tie," in Marilyn Revell DeLong and Ann Marie Fiore (ed.) *Aesthetics of Textiles and Clothing: Advancing Multi-Disciplinary Perspectives* (Monument, CO: International Textile and Apparel Association), pp. 131-141.

Holbrook, Morris B. (1994b), "The Nature of Customer Value: An Axiology of Services in the Consumption Experience," in Roland T. Rust and Richard L. Oliver (ed.) *Service Quality: New Directions in Theory and Practice* (Thousand Oaks, CA: Sage), pp. 21-71.

Laidler, Harry W. (1968), *Boycotts and the Labor Struggle: Economic and Legal Aspects* (New York: Russell and Russell) (reissued, first published 1913).

Levitt, Theodore (1995), "Marketing Myopia" in Ben M. Enis, Keith K. Cox, and Michael P. Mokwa (ed.) *Marketing Classics* (Englewood Cliffs, NJ: Prentice Hall), pp. 3-21 (first published in *Harvard Business Review*, July-August 1960).

Smith, N. Craig (1987a), "Ethical Purchase Behavior," in *Understanding Economic Behavior*, Vol. III, Proceedings of the International Association for Research in Economic Psychology (Aarhus, Denmark: Aarhus School of Business), pp. 949-64.

Smith, N. Craig (1987b), "Consumer Boycotts and Consumer Sovereignty," *European Journal of Marketing*, Vol. 21, No. 5 (1987), pp. 7-19.

Smith, N. Craig (1990) *Morality and the Market: Consumer Pressure for Corporate Accountability* (London: Routledge).

Moderators of Consumer Response to Promotions
Stephen M. Nowlis, Washington State University

Sales promotions have become a ubiquitous element of the consumer's purchase environment. Much of the research on price promotions has relied on scanner data or panel data to measure the effect of price promotions on sales and market share (e.g., Blattberg and Neslin 1990). However, we know less about the underlying process by which consumers are affected by price promotions and the factors which moderate a consumer's response. This session tried to address this issue by examining how the decision process involving promoted products is tempered by various factors. For instance, two of the papers in the session suggested that the decision context, or set of alternatives under consideration, might moderate the consumer's response to promoted products, while the third paper attempted to show how certain situational variables and consumer-specific characteristics moderate the effect of promotions. We believe that this approach led to a richer understanding of the consumer's response to promotions, as it attempted to show how aspects of the decision environment would influence the preference for promoted products.

The first paper, by Jennifer Gregan-Paxton and Linda G. Schneider Stone, considered how the promotion intensity by a given option may affect the preference for both the promoted option and for the options in the set which do not promote. They reported findings from a computer-based experiment which indicated that, under certain circumstances, preferences actually increased for the brand that did not promote when its competition did promote. In this sense, they suggested that the actions of the promoted brand, or context, may have a systematic effect on the preferences for the nonpromoted brands in the set.

The second paper, by Stephen M. Nowlis and Itamar Simonson, examined the role of the choice set composition in moderating the effect of price promotions. For instance, an important finding is that high-tier (high quality, high price) brands tend to gain more share from price promotions than do low-tier brands (e.g., Blattberg and Wisniewski 1989). However, a question that naturally arises is: How general is this asymmetric effect, and what factors moderate its magnitude? In their paper, the authors examined how the choice context moderates the impact of price promotions, focusing on the above finding, by affecting how consumers switch between brands in the set. The results of four experiments were reported that supported the hypotheses.

The third paper examined the process by which point-of-purchase (P-O-P) advertising and promotions affect consumer choice behavior. J. Jeffrey Inman and Russell S. Winer developed and tested a theoretical model of P-O-P advertising effects. The model consisted of three conditional stages incorporating factors influencing exposure to P-O-P advertising, choice of the advertised product category, and choice of the advertised brand. Their model was tested in a large-scale field intercept study of 2000 consumers and provided the basis for better understanding the underlying process of P-O-P advertising's effect on choice behavior and assessed the relative impact of situational variables and consumer-specific characteristics on choice.

The discussion leader, Barbara Kahn, engaged the audience in a general discussion of the issues raised in this session.

REFERENCES

Blattberg, Robert C. and Scott A. Neslin (1990), *Sales Promotion: Concepts, Methods, and Strategies*, Englewood Cliffs, NJ: Prentice-Hall.

Blattberg, Robert C. and Kenneth J. Wisniewski (1989), "Price-Induced Patterns of Competition," *Marketing Science*, 8 (Fall), 291-309.

Cognitive Aging in Consumer Contexts
Carolyn Yoon, University of Toronto

SESSION PARTICIPANTS

"Circadian Arousal and Cognitive Functioning"
Cynthia P. May, University of Arizona
Lynn Hasher, Duke University

"Age Differences in Consumers' Processing Strategies and Implications for Persuasion"
Carolyn Yoon, University of Toronto
Lynn Hasher, Duke University

"Are Aging Consumers More Vulnerable to the Belief Enhancing Effects of Repetition?"
Sharmistha Law, University of Toronto
Fergus I. M. Craik, University of Toronto

Discussion leader
Catherine Cole, University of Iowa

Amongst the most significant trends shaping North American demography is the aging of the baby boomer generation. With birth rates declining and life expectancies increasing, the elderly segment is expected to continue on its path of disproportionate growth for several decades to come. This phenomenon has recently garnered a good deal of media attention and, consequently, many marketers have started to identify and develop products and services that would appeal to this segment. But while there appears to be widespread agreement about the importance of more effectively targeting and communicating to the senior market, relatively little theory-based research exists in the consumer behavior literature to guide marketers in addressing these issues (see Cole and Houston, 1987 for an exception). This is somewhat surprising in light of the enormous volume of theoretical and empirical research that has been generated by gerontologists and cognitive aging psychologists in the last decade.

Although knowledge about cognitive aging is far from complete, a general finding in the literature is that older adults have memory deficiencies when compared to young adults (Kausler, 1990; Salthouse, 1991). A number of theoretical explanations have been advanced by cognitive aging researchers to explain such age-related impairments in memory. Two of the most widely accepted theoretical approaches for conceptualizing decrements in cognitive performance in older adults are reduced processing resources (Craik, 1983; Craik and Byrd, 1982; Hasher and Zacks, 1979; Zacks and Hasher, 1988) and deficient inhibitory functioning (Hasher and Zacks, 1988). This session brought together three papers that served to demonstrate how these theoretical accounts of cognitive aging can be applied to settings that improve our understanding of information processing by older consumers.

The first paper by May and Hasher adopted the inhibition view to account for age differences in cognitive functioning. Based on two studies, they presented evidence that changes in inhibitory functioning may be responsible for the synchrony between an individual's peak in circadian arousal and the time of testing in both young and older adults. Different tasks were used to assess individuals' ability to inhibit or prevent strong, well-learned responses that were inappropriate for the particular context. Results across the studies indicated three consistent findings: (1) generally speaking, older adults are less efficient at inhibiting unwanted responses; (2) both younger and older adults demonstrate deficits in inhibitory functioning at their off-peak times of day; (3) the magnitude of age differences in inhibitory functioning depends critically on the time of day at which individuals are tested. In the morning, when older adults are at their peak but the young adults are not, age differences in inhibition are attenuated and in some instances eliminated. In the evening, however, when young but not old are at their peak, age differences are robust and potentially exaggerated. Implications of these results for marketing to the elderly market were discussed.

The second paper by Yoon and Hasher employed the limited capacity framework to study age-related processing differences and investigated how age differences may be reduced by time of day and message incongruity. They found that during optimal time of day when greater resource capacity is available, older consumers are more sensitive to changes in message incongruity and are able to engage in levels of detailed processing that are equivalent to those of young adults. During non-optimal time of day, however, older people were found to rely on schema-based processing regardless of the level of cue incongruity. Finally, implications for persuasibility of the elderly in consumer contexts were discussed.

The final paper by Law and Craik investigated how mere repetition of statements results in an inflated rating of their validity ("truth effect") and how memory is an important mediator of this effect. Since normal aging is associated with declines in memory performance, the overall purpose of this research was to examine whether older adults are particularly vulnerable to the negative effects of repetition, and whether conditions exist under which these age-related differences can be "remedied." In two separate experiments, the elderly were shown to be more susceptible to the truth inflating effect of repetition and that task conditions exist which eliminate this age-related difference.

The discussion led by Cole emphasized the importance of accounting for various subject-related and task factors in studying age differences in cognitive functioning in consumer and applied contexts.

REFERENCES

Cole, C. A., & Houston, M. J. (1987). Encoding and Media Effects on Consumer Learning Deficiencies in the Elderly. *Journal of Consumer Research*, 24, 55-63.

Craik, F. I. M. (1983). On the Transfer of Information from Temporary to Permanent Storage. *Philosophical Transactions of the Royal Society of London, Series B*, 302, 341-359.

Craik, F. I. M., & Byrd, M. (1982). Aging and Cognitive Deficits: The Role of Attentional Resources. In F. I. M. Craik & S. Trehub (Eds.), *Aging and Cognitive Processes: Advances in the Study of Communication and Affect* (pp. 191-211). New York: Plenum Press.

Hasher, L., & Zacks, R. T. (1979). Automatic and Effortful Processes in Memory. *Journal of Experimental Psychology: General*, 108, 356-388.

Hasher, L. & Zacks, R. T. (1988). Working Memory, Comprehension, and Aging: A Review and a New view. In G. H. Bower (Ed.), *The Psychology of Learning and Motivation: Advances in Research and Theory*, Vol. 22. San Diego: Academic Press.

Kausler, D. H. (1990). Motivation, Human Aging, and Cognitive Performance. In J. E. Birren & K. W. Schaie (Eds.), *Handbook of the Psychology of Aging* (pp. 171-182). San Diego: Academic Press.

Salthouse, T. A. (1991). *Theoretical Perspectives on Cognitive Aging*. Hillsdale, NJ: Lawrence Erlbaum Associates.

Zacks, R. T., & Hasher, L. (1988). Capacity Theory and the Processing of Inferences. In L. L. Light & D. M. Burke (Eds.), *Language, Memory and Aging* (pp. 154-170). New York, NY: Cambridge University Press.

The Role of Role in Consumers' Responses to Advertising, Sales, and Service Interactions

Margaret C. Campbell, University of California-Los Angeles

Jennifer L. Aaker, University of California-Los Angeles

A considerable amount of research in consumer behavior focuses on interactions between the marketer and the consumer. Much of this research conceptualizes a consumer-marketer interaction in terms of the attributes of the action. For example, the consumer's processing and evaluation is typically considered in terms of whether or not the salesperson is efficient, the ad is humorous, or the service provider is competent. However, recent work on the Persuasion Knowledge Model (Friedstad and Wright 1994; Wright 1986) indicates that the consumer's thoughts about the marketer's thoughts can be a component of the consumer's processing and that these "schemer schema" (Wright 1986) exercise an important influence on the evaluation of the marketing interaction.

The purpose of this special topic session was to explore how perceived roles can influence the inferences that a consumer makes about the interaction. All three papers proposed and explored ways in which the consumer's role perceptions influence his or her interpretation of the marketer's thinking and how the consumer's interpretations affect the consumer-marketer interaction. While the three papers were all concerned with role and consumers' inferences about the marketer's thinking, each paper explored these issues with different contexts, roles, and dependent variables.

Campbell presented a paper proposing that consumers can either be "active observers" (e.g., asking for assistance or making a purchase) or "passive observers" (e.g., browsing or waiting in line) of a marketer. An active observer is the target of the marketer's attention and both interacts with and observes the marketer. A passive observer observes the interaction between the marketer and the active observer without interacting with the marketer. This research hypothesized that role influences inferences about the marketer and evaluation of the interaction. A between-subject experiment testing the effects of role in a sales encounter context indicated that, compared to an active observer, a passive observer was more likely to consider the salesperson as an active persuader, inferring greater persuasive influence of the salesperson. The data showed that passive observers had more negative and fewer positive thoughts about the salesperson and were less satisfied with the interaction.

The second paper, by McGill, Drolet, and Anand Keller, proposed that a service provider can play both the role of seller, and is thus to be evaluated by the consumer, and the role of referent group member, and thus evaluates the consumer. This research hypothesized that some consumers may care about what the service provider thinks of them and that such a "self-conscious" consumer's inferences about the service provider's opinion influence the consumer's evaluation. The results of an experiment showed that for self-conscious consumers, satisfaction is a function of their feelings towards the service provider more than their beliefs regarding the service provider or other service characteristics. For consumers who are not self-consciously looking to the service provider for an evaluation of their own knowledge, performance, etc., beliefs regarding functional service characteristics have a greater influence on satisfaction than do their feelings toward the service provider.

The paper by Aaker, Brumbaugh and Grier explored consumers as members of an advertisers' target market versus non-target market (defined as those who perceive themselves to *not* be the target of an advertisement). By examining consumers' processing strategies and evaluations when in both roles, the authors hypothesized and showed that negative effects can occur when consumers perceive themselves to be in the non-target market. Further, the results of the experiment showed that target market status affects the processing of the advertisement. While target market members tend to process the advertisement more centrally, non-target market members process the advertisement more peripherally; an effect that is mediated by subject "distinctiveness". The theoretical and practical implications of this research were discussed.

Peter Wright, as discussant, provided direction for the discussion by framing the papers in terms of consumers' thoughts about the "marketing game." He encouraged comment on ways to conceptualize the interaction between consumer and marketer that emphasize the two-sided nature of the interaction and the strategic qualities of consumers' thinking.

Special Session Summary
Let's Talk Shop: Multiple Interpretive Perspectives on Studying Consumer Shopping Behavior

Michelle R. Nelson, University of Illinois at Urbana-Champaign

INTRODUCTION

"Shop 'till you drop" seems to represent the sentiments and behaviors of the American consumer. Indeed, over $1.5 trillion are exchanged annually in the retail setting—in more than 2.4 million retail stores in this country (*Census of Retail Trade*, 1990).

Because of its pervasiveness, shopping has also captured the interest of consumer researchers attempting to understand the motivations and behaviors behind this avocation (Belk, Sherry and Wallendorf 1988; Rook 1987; Sherry and McGrath 1989). Because shopping is a *process* and has many meanings, it is especially ripe for study by interpretive researchers. Gainer and Fischer (1991) suggested that "interpretive methods are particularly useful in probing socio-cultural factors involved in shopping which may be impossible to capture through the use of more typical instruments of marketing research" (p. 597).

As such, this session was designed to offer perspectives from multiple interpretive methodologies to examine the shared consumer experience of *shopping*. In the first paper, McGrath and Stoughton-Underwood employed projective techniques *and* shopping with consumers in a study of shopping behaviors at a midwestern outlet mall. Next, Compeau and Nicholson discussed the advantages of method offered from a first-person, phenomenological point of view, using text from in-depth interviews. Finally, the paper by Nelson et al. focused on the benefits of "shopping with consumers" as a unique form of participant observation.

By asking "what is gained?" and "what is lost?" when using these methods, we generated a lively discussion which blossomed into questions and concerns about the ontology and epistemology within the interpretive paradigm.

SESSION DISCUSSION

To facilitate audience participation, Nancy Ridgway (University of Colorado) offered some questions to consider. "How do you know which methods (and how many) to use?" prompted debate among presenters and audience members and lead to discussion of related issues.

In considering the methodologies advanced by these three papers and the interpretive paradigm in consumer research overall, it was concluded that qualitative research is inherently multimethod in focus (Brewer and Hunter 1989). In answering the "how many" question, it was suggested that convergence of interpretations obtained from multiple methods and/or multiple researchers offers a way to enhance validity and reliability, but it was also noted that the criteria for judging qualitative data differed from those of quantitative data. According to Denzin and Lincoln (1994), "the use of multiple methods, or triangulation, reflects an attempt to secure an in-depth understanding of the phenomenon in question" (p.2).

Issues such as representation (i.e., "the problems of showing the realities of lived experiences of the observed setting" - Altheide and Johnson 1994) and reporting (and editing) of verbatims were also deliberated. It was suggested that limits on manuscript length often forced researchers to edit informants' verbatims, creating a greater authority on the author's interpretations. Offering complete transcripts was suggested as one way to combat such problems.

In asking which method(s) are most appropriate for consumer shopping, we might look to the *Handbook of Qualitative Research* whose editors advance, "Qualitative research, as a set of interpretive practices, privileges no single methodology over any other" (Denzin and Lincoln 1994, p.3). As such, it was generally agreed among those present at the session that the choice of research methodology depended upon the specific questions that were asked and the situation. "All of these research practices can provide important insights and knowledge" (Nelson, C. et al. 1992).

REFERENCES

Altheide, David L. and John M. Johnson (1994), "Criteria for Assessing Interpretive Validity in Qualitative Research," in Norman K. Denzin and Yvonna S. Lincoln, (Eds.) *Handbook of Qualitative Research*, Thousand Oaks, CA: Sage Publications, 485-499.

Belk, Russell, John Sherry, and Melanie Wallendorf (1988), "A Naturalistic Inquiry into Buyer and Seller Behavior at a Swap Meet," *Journal of Consumer Research*, 14 (4): 449-470.

Brewer, J. and A. Hunter (1989). *Multimethod Research: A Synthesis of Styles*. Newbury Park, CA: Sage.

Census of Retail Trade. Nonemployer Statistics Series — Northeast, U.S. Bureau of the Census, Washington, D.C. 1990, 1-3.

Denzin, Norman K. and Yvonna S. Lincoln (1994), "Introduction: Entering the Field of Qualitative Research," in Norman K. Denzin and Yvonna S. Lincoln, (Eds.) *Handbook of Qualitative Research*, Thousand Oaks, CA: Sage Publications, 1-18.

Gainer, Brenda and Eileen Fischer (1991), "To Buy or Not to Buy? That is Not the Question: Female Ritual in Home Shopping Parties," in Rebecca H. Holman and Michael R. Solomon, (Eds.) *Advances in Consumer Research*, Vol. 18, Provo, Utah: Association for Consumer Research, 597-602.

Nelson, C., P.A. Treichler, and L. Grossberg (1992), "Cultural Studies," In L. Grossberg, C. Nelson and P.A. Treichler (Eds.), *Cultural Studies*, New York: Routledge, 1-16.

Rook, Dennis (1987), "The Buying Impulse," *Journal of Consumer Research*, 14(2), 189-199.

Sherry, John, Jr. and Mary Ann McGrath (1989), "Unpacking the Holiday Presence: A Comparative Ethnography of Two Gift Stores." In Elizabeth Hirschman (ed.), *Interpretive Consumer Research*, Provo, UT: Association for Consumer Research, 148-167.

PAPER ABSTRACTS

Experiential Descriptions versus Objective Descriptions: The Power of a First-Person View of Shopping

Larry D. Compeau and Carolyn Y. Nicholson
Clarkson University

Today, since consumers are generally relegated to acquiring goods rather than producing them, shopping has a special significance in consumers' lives. Shopping is a complex personal and social event; several different levels of meaning exist simultaneously for the consumer. Thus, a method that allows the personal significance of the psychological, social, and cultural meanings of shopping to emerge is required.

This significance is embedded in the consumer's life world context, and researchers must come to know shopping experiences *as they were lived*, i.e., as the consumer experienced them. In this way, we move beyond a view of shopping as an object-like behavior that can be examined and reported on by a detached third person (the researcher) and gain access to the experience as it was lived by the consumer in its specific context (Thompson, Locander, and Polio 1989). Although other methods are available (e.g., think aloud method, analysis of written statements), perhaps the most powerful technique available to access another's experiences is the existential phenomenological in-depth interview (Kvale 1983). This paper presents a brief introduction to the existential phenomenological method, but quickly moves to a critical examination of the *output* of existential phenomenological in-depth interviews.

Third person research approaches (e.g., surveys, experiments, and observation) restrict understanding of shopping. They have an externally imposed narrative structure which constrains the experience to the structure, i.e., shoppers can only relate their experiences relative to what the researcher's structure allows. More importantly, these methods undervalue the mutually defining nature of the shopping context and the shopping experience itself.

The existential phenomenological interview approach acknowledges shopping as more than just behavior—shopping is considered a meaningful lived experience that is part of the consumer's world. Thus, consumers are not viewed as objects whose experiences can be observed; instead they are considered inseparable from their worlds, which must also be grasped to understand the experience. The consumer and his or her world co-constitute one another, and it is through understanding this world that the meaning of shopping emerges. One implication of this perspective is that the interview must capture detailed characteristics of the consumer's life-world beyond shopping behavior.

The existential phenomenological interview produces a verbatim transcript wherein the consumer provides rich, detailed descriptions of shopping experiences as he or she lived them. This first-person view provides access to the consumer's experiences, including details regarding his or her life world. Thus, researchers immerse themselves in a consumer's experiences in order to get as close as possible to having lived those experiences as that consumer lived them (Wertz 1983). Through this immersion process, the researcher is able to grasp the meaning of each shopping experience and develop an essential structure of shopping for that consumer. The meaning does not emerge solely from consumers' descriptions of their behaviors, nor from their description of their life-world, but from both as one contextualizes the other.

This process is brought to life via a detailed case study, illustrating both the power and the limitations of this first-person view of shopping. Stacey (a pseudonym), similar to other shoppers we've interviewed, has no trouble describing, in detail, a wide variety of shopping experiences. Through immersion into Stacey's shopping experience in the context of *her* lived world, we come to know the meaning of shopping for Stacey. This meaning, presented, in the form of a phenomenological description and essential structure of shopping for Stacey, illustrates the distinct contribution of the first person approach to the study of shopping.

The existential phenomenology interview method is considered here as a complement to, not a replacement for, other methods. We view this method as shedding "light where the other sees only shadow" (Valle and King 1978). Thus, existential phenomenology

as both perspective and method is valuable for developing a richer understanding of shopping.

REFERENCES

Kvale, Steinar (1983), "The Qualitative Research Interview: A Phenomenological and a Hermeneutical Mode of Understanding," *Journal of Phenomenological Psychology, 14* (Fall), 171-96.

Thompson, Craig J., William B. Locander, and Howard R. Pollio (1989), "Putting Consumer Experience Back into Consumer Research: The Philosophy and Method of Existential-Phenomenology," *Journal of Consumer Research, 16* (September), 133-46.

Valle, Ronald and Mark King (1978), "An Introduction to Existential-Phenomenological Thought in Psychology," in Ronald Valle and Mark King, (Eds.), *Existential-Phenomenological Alternatives for Psychology*, New York, NY: Oxford University Press, 6-17.

Wertz, Frederick J. (1983), "From Everyday to Psychological Description: Analyzing the Moments of Qualitative Data Analysis," *Journal of Phenomenological Research*, 14 (Fall), 197-242.

Dream On: Projections of Ideal Shopping
Mary Ann McGrath and Anne Stoughton-Underwood
Loyola University Chicago

The realms of the popular press and consumer myth have presented polarized and stereotyped images of male and female shoppers. Men and women are portrayed as living (and shopping) in separate worlds. Several comic strips, such as *Cathy* or *For Better or For Worse*, play on this scenario, while a popular book proclaims that *Men Are From Mars; Women Are From Venus* (Gray 1992). While female shoppers have proven to be a group yielding rich insights on shopping (Otnes, Kim and Lowrey 1992; Sherry and McGrath 1989; Otnes, McGrath and Lowrey 1995), there has been restrained research interest both on male shopping behavior and on the differentiation of gendered behaviors in the retail context.

The study presented here had a three-fold objective. First, it sought to identify components of ideal shopping behavior for men and women. Second, its goal was to understand the perception of male and female shopping behaviors from the perspective of each gender. Third, the study sought to gain insight into how male and female shopping behaviors are differentiated in both reality and in the ideal. To this end, two forms of projective methodologies were employed with a sample of male and female shoppers contacted in a mall-intercept situation.

McGrath, Sherry and Levy (1993) detail both the theory and analysis of such projective methods. Findings of this study indicate that both similarities and differences exist between male and female shopping behaviors. When either gender is in a store that is characterized as "ideal," shoppers linger, browse, and enjoy touching and "playing" with merchandise, and savor visual and aural atmospherics. Males appear to gravitate toward simpler, less-busy settings, while women envision a myriad of merchandise and attributes that can meet their specific or personalized needs.

REFERENCES

Gray, John (1992). *Men Are From Mars; Women Are From Venus*, New York: Harper Collins.

McGrath, Mary Ann, John F. Sherry, Jr. and Sidney J. Levy (1993), "Giving Voice to the Gift: The Use of Projective Methods to Recover Lost Meanings," *Journal of Consumer Psychology*, 2(2), 171-191.

Otnes, Cele, Young Kim, and Tina M. Lowrey (1992), "Christmas Shopping for 'Easy' and 'Difficult' Recipients: A Social Roles Interpretation," *Journal of Consumer Research*, 15(3), 422-433.

Otnes, Cele, Mary Ann McGrath and Tina M. Lowrey (1995), "Shopping With Consumers: Usage as Past, Present and Future Research Technique," *Journal of Retailing and Consumer Services*, 2(2), 97-110.

Sherry, John, Jr. and Mary Ann McGrath (1989), "Unpacking the Holiday Presence: A Comparative Ethnography of Two Gift Stores." In Elizabeth Hirschman (ed.), *Interpretive Consumer Research*, Provo, UT: Association for Consumer Research, p. 148-167.

Shopping with Consumers: Retrospective and Prospective Methodological Applications

Michelle R. Nelson, University of Illinois
Cele Otnes, University of Illinois
Mary Ann McGrath, Loyola University
Tina M. Lowrey, Rider University

To discern what "shopping with consumers" can offer as a viable methodology in the future, we reflected on its past uses in consumer research, through a census review, tracing studies from 1960 until the present. From this census, we show that seven hundred sixty-four cited articles in four journals specifically examined some aspect of consumer prepurchase and purchase activity (Otnes, McGrath and Lowrey 1995).

Of the 812 total methods used, only *five* used shopping with consumers as a means of studying prepurchase or purchase behavior and only 23 used in-store observation for examining shopping. Indeed, past research has often focused upon the information-processing approach and has manipulated variables in simulated shopping settings (Bettman 1970; Bettman and Zins 1977; Iyer 1989; Park et al, 1989). Thus, we argue that although there has been limited usage in the past, shopping with consumers has potential as a means for richer, more "naturalistic" data collection and text generation.

Using data collected during the 1994 Christmas season, we showed how active interaction between researcher and informant can help explicate consumer shopping behaviors and motivations. Shopping allows the researcher the following advantages: (1) observing consumer shopping as it unfolds; (2) allowing greater proximity to the consumer; (3) providing access to informants' shopping agendas; and (4) building trust and empathy for future interactions.

We compared shopping with consumers to other interpretive methodologies, particularly the post-hoc interview and passive observation. For those interested in gaining insight into consumer shopping strategies or processes, we show that the active participation of the researcher can allow for "the best of both worlds." Specifically by combining the interview and participant observation, we claim a more accurate and thorough record of the behavior while it is happening, rather than a post-hoc recollection from the shopper in an interview setting or a "guessing strategy" employed by a researcher from an observation post.

By actively participating while observing the shopper, the researcher also gains virtually unrestricted proximity to the informant. In this way, s/he can interact and converse freely with the informant while shopping and also "in transit" to and from the research sites. This allows the researcher to request clarification or verification about observed behavior while still in the field. The intense interaction between informant and researcher also enables them to quickly and easily build a more trusting relationship, with ripe potential for future interactions.

REFERENCES

Bettman, J.R. (1970), "Information Processing Models of Consumer Behavior," *Journal of Marketing Research*, 7 (August), 370-376.

Bettman, J.R. and M.A. Zins (1977), "Constructive Processes in Consumer Choice," *Journal of Consumer Research*, 4 (September), 75-85.

Iyer, E.S. (1989), "Unplanned Purchasing: Knowledge of Shopping Environment and Time Pressure," *Journal of Retailing*, 64 (Spring), 40-57.

Otnes, Cele, Mary Ann McGrath and Tina M. Lowrey, (1995), "Shopping With Consumers: Usage as Past, Present and Future Research Technique," *Journal of Retailing and Consumer Services*, 2(2), 97-110.

Park, C.W., E.S. Iyer, and D.C. Smith (1989), "The Effects of Situational Factors on In-store Grocery Shopping Behavior: The Role of Store Environment and Time Available for Shopping," *Journal of Consumer Research*, 15 (March), 422-433.

Virtual Community: A Sociocognitive Analysis

Neil A. Granitz, Arizona State University
James C. Ward, Arizona State University

The internet is a new forum for consumer behavior, a forum that is rapidly expanding, but has been the focus of little published research in marketing outlets. Since 1988, the number of individuals with access to the internet appears to have almost doubled each year, growing to a conservative estimate of 27 million people worldwide in 1994 (Merit 1994). Many consumer and industrial marketers, now have a presence on the internet, or plan to, often on the World Wide Web, whose graphical interface facilitates promotional efforts. The mass media, consumer marketers, and advertising agencies seem to be in the midst of internet discovery and exploitation (Wells 1994, Fawcett 1994, Donaton 1994). Despite the apparent paucity of research about how consumers will behave in computer-mediated communications environments, sweeping speculations are being made about how the information superhighway will change marketing.

Practitioners and academics alike have speculated that as consumer decisions move on-line, the cognitive and social context of decision-making will change in ways that are as yet only partially understood (Benjamin and Wigand 1995). For example, at the individual cognitive level, the increasing availability of extensive, easily retrievable, and easily stored databases relevant to product/service purchases may lower the cost of information search for the typical on-line consumer, perhaps decreasing the proportion of consumers that engage in what some researchers consider a suboptimal degree of search.

However, the sociocultural, not the cognitive, aspects of internet participation have prompted the most discussion and interest in the media, and have significant implications for consumer behavior on-line. In particular, the idea that virtual communities, novel sociocultural environments, exist in cyberspace, has been widely remarked upon and debated (Barlow 1995, Jones 1995). For students of consumer behavior, the possibility of virtual community raises the issue of whether consumers are turning to the internet for "w.o.m." (word-of-mouth) advice about their purchase decisions.

One of the strongest and most established ideas about the transmission of marketplace information is the importance of interpersonal communication. Extremely consistent research has demonstrated the significance of interpersonal sources in influencing marketplace choice (Price and Feick 1984). Research has shown that interpersonal communication affects preference and choices (Arndt 1967) and that interpersonal communication is often the most important source of information (Katona and Mueller 1955).

Traditionally, many consumers seeking expert, unbiased advice about a purchase have turned to their circle of social ties — family members, co-workers, neighbors, and friends. But in an America increasingly characterized by social disintegration (single parent households, only children, the break-up of the extended family, the increasing rate of career changes and moves), many consumers' circle of ties may be limited and include no one with expertise about their interest. Consumers may be turning to the internet to not just examine ads and order, but to interact with others who share their "consuming passions" in discussion groups such as those in the rec. and alt. areas of the usenet, a part of the internet devoted to news groups whose members communicate with one another by e-mailing messages to a common bulletin board. Many of these groups are devoted to the discussion of products, services, or sources of entertainment.

The reality of virtual community is controversial. Some commentators have documented, in a largely anecdotal sense, their own experience with communities of others on the net (Rheingold 1995, MacKinnon 1995). By some accounts, many have found their internet friends far closer, and more influential in major and minor decisions (including consumer decisions) than friends, co-workers, or even family.

Others have questioned the existence of virtual community by pointing out that participants rarely have any on-going commitment to computer-mediated social relations and often feel no sense of responsibility for the consequences or accuracy of what they say (Kadi 1995). They point out that participants in discussion groups are usually anonymous, physically distant, and not involved in the on-going exchanges of favor for favor that characterize many social relations in the "real" world. Thus, some maintain that the "social ties" that exist are hardly worthy of the name, or are at least of a different character than social ties in face-to-face communities.

Students of consumer behavior have so far been largely absent from the debate about virtual community. However, the social and technical environment may have wide-ranging influence on the interpersonal aspects of on-line consumer behavior. Marketers have long known the critical role of interpersonal ties in a variety of phenomena studied under headings such as word-of-mouth, reference group influence, group decision-making, and opinion leadership/diffusion of innovations. If interactive computer-mediated discussion groups represent a new technical and perhaps cultural context for social relations, the study of community on the net, and its influence on the content, patterns, and structure of interchange, is vitally important for consumer researchers to understand.

Face-to-face communities include, minimally, social actors, social ties, and communications among the actors, channelled by the pattern of ties among them. Each of these, and their interrelations, should be studied in the context of consumption-related communications in computer-mediated groups. The possible differences that may exist between face-to-face and cyberspace groups are illustrated by the differences between w.o.m. (word-of-mouth) and w.o.l. (word-on-line). In an internet discussion forum, anyone, even a complete stranger, can break into the discussion of the community at any time. Such behavior is not considered unusual, forward, or impolite as it might be in face to face groups. In fact, many "netizens" would consider saying something as better than merely "lurking." Furthermore, a questioner often addresses the group as a whole, or whoever is on-line, not just one target individual. Everyone is empowered to reply, although a significant question is how many do, and in particular who really does much of the question answering, explaining, and advice giving in usenet groups. The replies to a question create a conversational "thread," a record of the discussion, perhaps spanning several days, about a topic. Here again is a significant difference of w.o.l. from w.o.m. W.O.M. is said and expires, except perhaps in the memory of the listener. W.-O.-L. becomes part of a public record, that may influence hundreds or thousands more "listeners" than the original target of the comment. W.O.L. and other sociocultural aspects of internet discussion groups seem sufficiently novel phenomena to deserve further study.

The nature of communication is one aspect of consumer behavior in discussion groups, but it is created by individuals and channelled by their social ties. Thus, another important issue to understand in the context of computer-mediated discussion groups is the character of the participants and how their individual differences (e.g., in expertise about the topic) interact with social ties and structure.

Ward and Reingen (1990) have emphasized the importance of studying how social and cognitive processes interact on group decision-making. An attempt to relate individual differences, social structure, and communication flows, would seem to offer a useful approach for the study of virtual community on the internet. If virtual communities exist in computer-mediated discussion groups, they represent a novel context for social relations and the relation of individual differences to the content and structure of these relations. Social actors on the usenet create roles for themselves in a decontextualized environment. This freedom from the usual indicants of role and status (e.g., wealth, appearance) may increase the salience of other social resources, such as expertise about the focal topic, as an indicant of status. A sociocognitive approach suggests a focus on the relation of individual status indicants on the net, such as expertise, to social structure, and the flow and content of communication.

In the present study, we explored the nature of virtual community on a usenet discussion group and its relation to the flow of consumption-relevant communication. The usenet refers to a set of approximately 7500 discussion groups distributed world-wide across the internet. Under a variety of headings, users can discuss issues ranging from medical ethics to Melrose place. The usenet is only a small part of the internet, but it is representative of the rapidly growing parts of the net that provide forums for individuals to discuss topics of interest. These forums exist on not only the usenet, but on commercial services such as American Online, local bulletin board systems (e.g., the San Francisco bay area's Well), and on other parts of the net. These forums have been the focus of discussions about virtual community, and are relevant to marketers because of their popularity, and their frequent devotion to products and services.

We approached our study with several specific research questions, influenced by an interest in the relation between social and individual processes in human communities. First, we expected to find at least some evidence of community in a usenet group, as shown by ongoing communications defining a social structure consisting of a pattern of ties among the participants. Second, we expected cognitive and social structures to be related. Since the purpose of a usenet group devoted to a product or service is information exchange about the focal topic, knowledge should translate into social power. Celsi et. al. (1993) noted this when they found that within-group status increased as one gained experience and formed interpersonal relationships. Given the uneven distribution of knowledge likely about even a low-tech product or service, we expected more expert participants to be at the center of the group's social structure. Similar to the findings of Schouten and McAlexander (1995) regarding novice Harley-Davidson bikers and "experienced" Harley-Davidson bikers, we expected novices to direct questions towards experts and to accept their comments about a variety of issues. In accordance with Raven (1965), we expected expert power to confer the status to arbitrate opinion on the net. We also expected to find that sociocognitive structures would channel the content of communication. That is, we expected experts to be the actors most likely to correct and critique other users' opinions, and novices to be most likely to ask questions. Finally, although we anticipated finding virtual community on the usenet, we expected that only a small minority of participants in even a special interest group would be involved in extensive interaction with one another. Our speculation about this last issue was based upon exploratory observation of usenet groups.

METHODS

The Rec.Food.Drink.Coffee group (a group devoted to the discussion of coffee consumption) was chosen for study because it met several criteria. First, the group focused on consumption. Second, the group had been in existence for some time (several years), so patterns of social structure had a chance to emerge. Third, the group was currently active, with well over one hundred members contributing. Finally, the group concerned a commonly purchased product, coffee. We felt that study of a group focused on more esoteric or technical issues might be prone to exaggerate the role of expertise or social ties in channelling communication.

We examined the complete record of discussion for two separate two week periods in early February and early March. In total, 204 people contributed to the usenet discussion group in the periods studied. The choice of two separate periods not too widely separated in time kept the data to a manageable size and provided a more longitudinal perspective while not sacrificing the continuity of the group. The sample had to be cleansed of discussions that began prior to the start of data collection, because without a complete record, we found it hard to identify the participants and often the topic of the string. However, whether a string was answered or not answered - if it began in one of the periods, it was included in the analysis. This lead to a total number of 24 strings studied in period 1 and 31 strings studied in period 2. Usenet members may post messages directly to one another's E-mail addresses. These communications could not be captured for our study.

Transcript Analysis

Usenet discussions are not "real-time." Users send mail to one another which is posted in the discussion groups' file. Participants may address the group as a whole, perhaps by asking a question, or may specifically "talk" to another participant by incorporating his or her name, or often a portion of some previous message being commented upon. Participants seemed careful to identify the conversation they were contributing to, a habit that facilitated analysis of the data. The order and hierarchical structure of the report, along with dates, names, and addresses on the messages themselves, helped organize the conversation for analysis. Two types of analysis was performed on the data - content analysis and social network analysis.

(i) Content Analysis

The content analysis had several objectives. The first was to determine the type of consumption related comment. We classified comments into the following categories: questions (how do I make espresso?), product recommendations (buy the Acme espresso machine), advice about how to do something related to coffee (this is how you make good espresso), explanation of how something works (here's how the Acme espresso machine works), comments (adding to a conversation — you should also consider this when buying an espresso machine), disagreements (you are wrong about how the Acme espresso machine works), announcements (Acme has a new machine available), and what we classified as assorted replies. The total length in number of words of individual contributions by category was also estimated and recorded.

The second objective of the content analysis was to measure the number of different aspects of coffee consumption that a particular individual mentioned in his or her total volume of comments. The number of different attributes in a person's cognitive structure for a product is one measure of his or her expertise about the product. After a thorough preliminary study of the transcripts, we developed a list of 34 different coffee-related concepts that we scored all the transcripts for. We then computed the total number of comments in each category for each individual under study, and labelled the variable "aspects".

TABLE 1
Content Analysis of Usenet Communications

Content Category	Expert (n=10)			Novice (n=194)			All (n=204)	
	#	col %	row %	#	col %	row %	#	col %
Question	10	-	.01	2197	.19	.99	2207	.13
Reply	115	.02	.18	510	.04	.82	625	.04
Product Recommend	1238	.24	.35	2272	.20	.65	3510	.21
How-to Advice	994	.19	.30	2350	.20	.70	3344	.20
Explanation	736	.14	.20	2911	.25	.80	3647	.22
Disagreement	695	.14	.67	335	.03	.33	1030	.06
Comment	632	.12	.47	714	.06	.53	1346	.08
Announcement	710	.14	.74	248	.02	.26	958	.06
Total	5130	-	.31	11537	-	.69	16667	-

(ii) Social Network Analysis

The social network analysis began by creating a participant by participant interaction matrix. Each message was coded for its originator and its target (the message it referred to). Messages with no particular reference were coded as being directed to the group as a whole. We then counted the number of times each individual contributed messages concerning each other individual's messages. To fit the requirements for network analysis, the data matrix was dichotomized and symmetrized, and then analyses of actor centrality and clique membership were performed using the Ucinet social network analysis software.

Analysis

The data resulting from the content analysis and the individual level data from the network analysis (individual centrality scores) were entered into a person (204) by variable data file and further analyzed by *spss*. For relevant analyses, experts were distinguished from novices by a score of four or more on the aspects of coffee noted (complexity) measure. This quantitative measure of "expert" was qualitatively checked by one of the researchers who is an "expert" on coffee and who was familiar with virtually all the on-line experts' arguments. The resultant list of experts matched his subjective judgement of who was expert very well.

RESULTS

Little data has been reported on the content of what is said on usenet discussion groups, particularly as it relates to consumption. Table 1 shows the results of a content analysis.

The column aggregating both expert and novice communications shows that over 20 percent of the total words were devoted to product recommendations, and another 20 percent were devoted to discussions of how to use a product (e.g., how to use an espresso machine). The other categories (e.g., explanations) include passages indirectly concerning consumption (e.g., why world coffee prices increased), and other passages more relevant to purchase decisions (e.g., why inexpensive coffee grinders do not work well). Overall, the majority of talk in the group was highly relevant to product or service purchase decisions.

The influence of social and cognitive factors on the content of communication is evident when we contrast the distribution of type of comment by expert *vs.* novice. Novices asked virtually all the questions. Experts rarely violated their social role as experts by

asking a question. Instead, the ten experts (selected by the complexity of their cognitive structure for coffee) contributed over one third of the words devoted to product recommendations, almost half the comments about others' remarks, and about two-thirds of the remarks that explicitly disagreed with others. These data strongly suggest that the more expert participants in the group played the role of arbiters of group opinion. They, more than anyone else, decided if some remark about coffee was "wrong", and these evaluations were rarely challenged by less expert participants. Overall, experts contributed about one third of the group's content. Thus, we observe an individual cognitive difference (expertise) related to a social role (arbiter of group opinion) channelling communication (the direction of questions) and its content (critical of others or not). The reluctance of experts to ask questions of the group seems at first somewhat surprising, but when we consider that in an on-line environment, the only way to establish and reinforce one's role is through communication, we might be less surprised about the expert's refusal to step out of role in their postings.

We next created a correlation matrix of the communication scores of each actor, the expertise scores of each, and the social network centrality scores of each. The matrix of pearson correlations is shown in Table 2. All significance tests are two-tailed, based on a null hypothesis of zero correlation. The correlations show the strong relation of social structure to the flow of communication in the usenet group. Higher network centrality was significantly correlated with total length of remarks (r=.46), virtually every specific category of remark, and especially disagreement (r=.40). The one exception is asking questions, which shows no significant correlation with network centrality.

Overall, the clique analysis identified 93 cliques of 3 or more actors in the usenet group. Of the 204 participants, 98 were in a clique and the rest were in dyads or isolates. Thus, about half of the participants were connected to a "group." All the expert participants were in one or more cliques. The participant with the highest expertise (aspects) score (20) was also a participant in the most number of cliques (19), or about 20 percent of the total. This actor also had the highest centrality score of any of the experts.

Table 2 also shows the strong positive relationship between expertise and social network centrality (r=.63). Experts in this usenet group, perhaps because of the social value of their knowledge, enjoy privileged network positions with many incoming links. The correlation of disagreement with centrality (r=.40), and

TABLE 2
Pearson Correlation Coefficients
(two tailed significance/n=204)

	(1)	(2)	(3)	(4)	(5)	(6)	(7)	(8)	(9)	(10)	(11)
(1) Central	1.00										
(2) Aspects	.63 **	1.00									
(3) Question	.03	.01	1.00								
(4) Disagreement	.40 **	.73 **	-.04	1.00							
(5) Comment	.35 **	.39 **	-.05	.19 *	1.00						
(6) Explanation	.12	.33 **	-.03	.31 **	.04	1.00					
(7) How-to	.37 **	.35 **	-.04	.11	.17 *	.05	1.00				
(8) Misc. Reply	.28 **	.30 **	-.02	.15 *	.13 **	.09	.14	1.00			
(9) Announcement	.18 *	.24 **	-.05	-.01	.21 *	-.03	.18 *	.02	1.00		
(10) Length	.46 **	.68 **	.18 *	.50 **	.40 **	.74 **	.52 **	.28 **	.29 **	1.00	
(11) Prod. Rec.	.40 **	.63 **	-.03	.60 **	.25 **	.12	.17 *	.27 **	-.02	.36 **	

* P<.05
**P<.001

the expertise measure (r=.73), provides some support to the validity of the expertise measure. Despite the high correlation between network centrality and expertise, the latter was much more strongly correlated (p<.05) to disagreement, perhaps because evaluation is usually a social function of experts.

We performed t-tests of expert *vs.* novice mean difference scores across the communication content and network centrality measures. The tests show a pattern of significant communication differences between experts and novices. Experts had higher mean network centrality (15.9 vs. 3.1, t=3.5, p=.01) than novices, and of course, higher aspect (# of coffee attributes employed) scores (7.2 vs. .5, t=9.0, p=.01). Novices asked significantly more questions than experts (11.3 for novices vs. 1.0 for experts, t=3.6, p<.01), but experts had higher mean scores for disagreements (69.5 vs. 1.7, t=2.1, p=.07), comments (63.2 vs. 3.7, t=2.2, p=.05), product recommendations (123.8 vs. 11.7, t=1.9, p=.09), and explanations (73.6 vs. 15.0, t=1.9, p=.06). Experts also had a marginally higher mean for how-to advice (99.4 vs. 12.1, t=1.8, p=.10). The small sample size of experts (n=10), and high variances resulted in significance levels less than one might expect given the magnitude of the mean differences. These expert versus novice differences were re-tested defining expert participants mentioning three "aspects" of coffee instead of four. The results were the same for 7 out of 8 tests. A chi-square test (p<.05) also confirmed that content categories vary across the expert and novice distinctions. Overall, experts were clearly influential sources of W.O.L. in the group examined.

DISCUSSION

We began our project with the objective of exploring how individual characteristics, in particular expertise, related to the social structure of a usenet discussion group, and how the individual and social dimensions of the group related to the pattern of consumption-relevant communication within the group. Our sample of interactions strongly confirmed our expectations. Social and cognitive structure were closely related on the usenet. More central network actors seemed to be more expert about coffee, as measured by the complexity of their knowledge structures about coffee. These more central, expert actors appeared to function as informational resources and arbiters of opinion on the net. However, our suggestion about the apparent influence of experts is an inference drawn from the structure of the discourse, not a conclusion based on any measure of actual influence.

Sociocognitive structure channelled communication and its content. Less socially central participants were more likely than more central participants to ask questions of the group. The more central actors were less likely to do so, perhaps because asking a question of the group would have undermined their role as experts who knew all the answers, and thus had little need of asking questions. Central actors were much more involved than most participants in answering questions. These answers included product recommendations (XYZ is a good firm to mail order coffee from), how-to advice (e.g., how to modify a particular brand of coffee grinder so it works better), and explanations (e.g., why a fine grind is needed for Turkish coffee). The asymmetrical structure of discourse in these groups suggests that central actors were exercising expert power (French and Raven 1959), and had real influence on other participants. Whether advice was followed is an issue that could be followed up in future research.

One implication of these findings for marketers is that a relatively small number of participants on usenet groups may strongly influence the opinions of hundreds of other participants, and perhaps thousands of "lurkers" who peruse the group discussion without contributing.

More central actors enjoyed "prestige" mainly because of their expertise. In our sample of strings, the central actors made little of such indicators of status as occupation, income, or place of residence that may influence whose opinion is respected in face-to-face groups. Also, obviously, the appearance (attractiveness, height, dress) of these actors could not influence other's reliance upon them. Although more research is necessary, these observations suggest that opinion leaders in computer-mediated groups like the usenet may rely on differently weighted bases of social power than those found in face-to-face groups.

Earlier we raised the issue of the nature and extent of "virtual community" in usenet groups and similar forums on the internet. Our data provide some insight into this debate. We found cliques within the usenet that often centered around expert participants. Thus, interaction had social structure, perhaps one sign of community. Although the data entered into our network analysis reflected only the presence or absence of a tie, our initial tabulation of interactions among actors found that most of the participants in cliques were interacting many times over a period of several weeks. Thus, social ties influenced communication, another sign of community. Finally, we noted that only a small number of the participants had any degree of social centrality. A slight majority were not in cliques, and only contributed a few lines of comment. Thus, virtual communities that influence consumption decisions appear to exist on the internet, but the percent of users involved to any extent in such groups may be small.

RESEARCH OPPORTUNITIES

Marketers, more than academics, have taken the initiative in calling for research on internet consumer behavior. However, available wisdom appears sketchy, and is more often based upon opinion or personal experience than systematic research. The explosion of computer-mediated consumption behavior is an opportunity for consumer researchers to do timely, much needed studies that could be of considerable theoretical interest because of the unique character of interaction on the net.

The consumption phenomena on the internet that seem high priorities for exploration include W.O.L. (word on-line), referral networks, opinion leadership, diffusion of innovations, information search (and retention), involvement with interactive ads, the character of discourse, attitudes toward marketing, characteristics of users, expert-novice differences, the character of community, and the extent to which participants rely on one another for consumer advice, to name only a few of the most obvious potential issues.

The computer-mediated discussion groups have enduring characteristics as social and cultural environments that justify re-exploring issues previously studied in more conventional environments. Discussion groups such as the one we investigated communicate to one another in a way different in many respects from face-to-face discussion. First, the communication is written, not spoken. Contributors to the discourse have the opportunity to carefully ponder and craft their remarks. Furthermore, they do so with a complete record of the comments they are responding to at their disposal. They need not pause, interrupt themselves, or limit the length of their remarks to give another speaker his or her turn, as would be expected in conversational discourse. Finally, contributors are no doubt conscious that their remarks become part of a public record, that hundreds, if not thousands may access or respond to.

Additionally, the participants interact in a social environment that is different in more than just a physical sense. They are separated from the social and cultural contexts that influence the character of face-to-face exchanges. This raises fascinating issues about the interaction between the individual and the group in the creation of identities and roles. In most social contexts, the individual's choice of identity and role is highly constrained by the circumstances of their background, appearance, status, neighborhood and workplace. On the internet, the individual is free to choose the groups he or she wishes to identify with, and create a role as "expert" divorced of prior social disqualifications from such roles. Confronted with this opportunity, do consumers merely re-enact their daily roles, or create new and different ones?.

The social and technical environment of the internet may be uniquely facilitative for the pursuit of consumer research. For example, Ward and Reingen (1990) have emphasized the importance of studying how social and cognitive processes interact in group decision-making. Unfortunately, access to a precise sequential history of interactions, and their content, is difficult in most field settings except computer-mediated communication environments such as usenet groups. The precise record of discussion groups could facilitate analysis of communications focusing on more than their content. Discourse analysis is the study of the structure of conversation — the structure of who speaks, in what way, and how much. Consumer researchers could employ discourse analysis to better understand such issues as opinion leadership.

Furthermore, researchers need not be limited to passive analysis of the products of interaction on the usenet. Participants could easily be interviewed via E-mail. The possibility exists of asking participants to come to the researchers' own internet site, where they might be asked to interact with software there. Either approach would allow the collection of questionnaire measures of influence, opinion leadership, social structure, etc. The internet presents some difficult sampling issues, and some real sampling opportunities. At present, internet users are not "representative." They are likely to be male, higher in socioeconomic status, and more computer-literate than average. Furthermore, identification of group participants is often difficult since some contribute only periodically and others are perpetual "lurkers" who monitor but do not contribute to the conversation. Longitudinal data collection seems a necessity. The sampling opportunity represented by the internet is the almost unprecedented access offered to narrowly defined groups of consumers from around the world. A sample of consumers with even the most rare or bizarre interest is now but a mouse click away.

REFERENCES

Barlow, John Perry (1995), "Is There a There in Cyberspace?" *Utne Reader*, No. 68 (March-April), 53-59.

Benjamin, Robert and Rolf Wigand (1995), "Electronic Markets and Virtual Value Chains on the Information Superhighway," *Sloan Management Review*, (Winter), 62-72.

Celsi, Richard L., Randall L. Rose, and Thomas W. Leigh (1993), "An Exploration of High Risk Leisure Consumption through Skydiving," *Journal of Consumer Research*, 20 (June), 1-23.

Donaton, Scott (1994), "OK to put Ads on Internet, but Mind your Netiquette," *Advertising Age*, Vol.65 No.18 (April), 3.

Fawcett, Adrienne Ward (1994) "Interactive Awareness Growing," *Advertising Age*, Vol. 65 No. 42, 30.

French, John R.P. jr. and Bertram H. Raven (1959), "The Bases of Social Power," in *Studies in Social Power*. ed. Dorwin Cartwright, Ann Arbor: University Michigan Press, 150-167.

Jones, Steven G. (1995), "Understanding Community in the Information Age," in *Cybersociety: Computer-Mediated Communication and Community*, ed. Steven G. Jones, Thousand Oaks, California: Sage Publications, 10-35.

Kadi, M.(1995), "Welcome to Cyberia," *Utne Reader*, Vol. 68, 57-59.

Katona, George and Eva Mueller (1955), "A Study of Purchase Decisions, " in *The Dynamics of Consumer Reaction*, ed. Lincoln H. Clark, New York: New York University Press, 30-87.

MacEvoy, Bruce and Linton Freeman (1987), *UCINET: A Microcomputer Package for Network Analysis*. Irvine, Ca: University of California, School of Social Sciences, Mathematical Science Group.

MacKinnon, Richard C. (1995), "Searching for the Leviathan in Usenet," in *Cybersociety: Computer-Mediated Communication and Community*, ed. Steven G. Jones, Thousand Oaks, California: Sage Publications, 112-137.

Merit Network, Inc. (1994), "Internet Growth Statistics." URL:ftp://nic.merit.edu/nsfnet/statistics.

Price, Linda and Lawrence Feick (1984), "The Role of Interpersonal Sources in External Search: An Informational Perspective," in *Advances in Consumer Research IX* , ed. Thomas C. Kinnear, Ann Arbor Mi: Association for Consumer Research, 250-253.

Raven, Bertram H. (1965), "Social Influence and power, " in *Current Studies in Social Psychology*, ed. I.D. Steiner and M. Fishbein, New York: Holt Rinehart and Winston, Inc. 371-378.

Rheingold, Howard (1995), "The Virtual Community," *Utne Reader*, No. 68 (March-April), 60-65.

Schouten, John W. and James H. McAlexander (1995), "Subcultures of Consumption: An Ethnography of the New Bikers," *The Journal of Consumer Research*, 22 (June), 43-61.

Ward, James C. and Peter H. Reingen (1990), "Sociocognitive Analysis of Group Decision Making among Consumers," *The Journal of Consumer Research*, 17 (December), 245-262.

Wells, Melanie (1994), "Desperately Seeking the Superhighway," *Advertising Age*, Vol. 65 No. 43, 14.

The Bolo Game: Exploration of a High-Tech Virtual Community

Eric G. Moore, University of Michigan
Sanal K. Mazvancheryl, University of Michigan
Lopo L. Rego, University of Michigan

INTRODUCTION

The popularity of computer and video games has made it possible for millions of people to encounter these games on a regular or occasional basis. Some people play computer/video games only once, while others are instantly and completely absorbed by it and make them a large part of their lives. The purpose of our study is to use qualitative methodology to investigate experienced computer game players and to try and understand both the motives for playing these games and the effects of games on players lives. We focus on one *"community"* that we find has been created around a computer game called Bolo. The qualitative research methods used in this study include in-depth interviews of experienced game players, participant-observation of Bolo game sessions, and non-traditional sources such as Usenet postings and material from World Wide Web pages. These sources are combined into an interpretation of the issues and themes which surround a computer-based community at aggregate and individual levels.

LITERATURE REVIEW

From the introduction of Pong by Atari over fifteen years ago to today's high-tech animations from Nintendo and Sega, the rapid pace of technological developments have made electronic games increasingly accessible. This ease of access created a demand for a variety of games to satisfy the heterogenous tastes of players. Computer and video games can be found on a wide variety of topics, but much of the media attention about games is focused on the huge popularity of games with a high level of violent content such as Mortal Kombat and Doom. Despite the violent nature of some games, the overall field of computer and video games has experienced a spectacular increase both in number and variety of games, and these games are popular across a wide spectrum of users. Such popularity is reflected on the immense success of companies such as Nintendo and Sega (which compete in a huge $7 billion market), as well as through the approximately 40% of all U.S. families who now own PC's.

Games are believed to provide positive experiences, including pleasure, amusement, self-fulfillment through successfully completing the game, and the communal feelings associated with participating with other players. One of the key features of such games is that they abstract from reality and allow the players to experience new worlds and present novel challenges to explore and overcome. The experiences provided by games can be so enthralling to some people that games become an essential part of the players lives and are a significant outlet for leisure consumption.

In order to explore the different dimensions that might be involved with leisure consumption (we are implicitly assuming game playing as a leisure activity), we now turn to the Celsi, Rose and Leigh (1993) framework. According to this theory, the forces that drive leisure consumption are based on a dramatic world view that is inherent to the development of modern Western societies. This dramatic world view is based on the interaction of conflicting social forces which lead to the build up of both physical and psychic

tensions in the individual. These tensions threaten the individual's control and place within the society with the final outcome of inducing a loss of autonomy and diminishing the individual's sense of self. These opposing macro social forces can have a dual nature where some are protagonist and others antagonistic, with possible examples such as good vs. evil and life vs. death. These conflicting forces build up physical and psychological stress which must eventually be released in order to resolve the conflict and this is done through the choice of leisure activities.

A similar approach was taken by Lyng (1990), who builds on the Marx-Mead synthesis (see Mead, 1934a) and introduces the concept of *edgeworking*. Lyng believes that the synthesis provides a social psychological explanation for risky leisure consumption. Again, the development of modern Western societies is the starting point and members of society fail to develop the social self as a consequence of the social divisions and class separations introduced by the industrial revolution and labor specialization. Consequently, the ego does not develop because there is no notion of group and belonging within this fragmented society. This situation is often characterized as *"oversocialization"*, where societal needs and priorities overcome individual necessities and wants. Under these particular conditions, and according to Batuik and Sacks (1981), the social world becomes obscure, both in terms of understanding as well as in terms of actions to the individual. This is a consequence of the fact that individuals no longer feel responsible for their own destiny, and truly believe that their own life is just one of many within the society.

As a consequence of these societal changes and transformations, the individual feels alienated from society and this induces a search for the self outside the typical social groups of family, religion and the local community. Cushman (1990) has argued that this has led to the formation of the empty self, in a world that is lacking in community and tradition. It is therefore not surprising that the individual feels a deep sense of disconnectedness. He or she then seeks to address these shortcomings by reshaping their political, cultural and social forms and relationships. Such an individual therefore has an incentive to try and forge new groups where he or she feels a sense of belonging, an integration function that used to be performed by the groups in conventional society. One particular setting that is said to provide the development of the self is leisure consumption. This can be seen as the reason for the proliferation of special interest/activities groups which then become social communities.

In addition to the macro forces driving the search for the self in outside groups, Celsi et al. (1993) introduce complementary internal variables to explain the individual motivations behind leisure consumption. These variables represent inter- and intra-personal motives, ranging from normative motives to self-efficacy motives and hedonistic motives. Celsi et. al (1993) trace a path of motivations starting with normative motives which lead to trial and stress the ideals of thrill and survival. Later, the motives move to self-efficacy, which stresses pleasure and achievement and lead to group identity. Finally, hedonistic motives introduce a sense of community and stress personal identity and *flow* (Csikszentmihalyi, 1985). Flow is usually interpreted as a state of mind in which the individual is extremely concentrated on a small set of stimuli. One important consequence of flow is the distorted notion of time and

---

[1]The authors would like to thank Prof. Aaron Ahuvia, for his guidance and comments, without which this paper would not have been possible.

space experienced. The concept of flow is seen as very important to the success of leisure consumption through the sense of absorption within the experience.

Several studies have explored risky leisure consumption activities (skydiving, Celsi et al. (1993); river rafting, Arnould and Price (1993); drug and alcohol abuse, Thompson (1974)) and the findings seem to provide support for the dramatic world view and oversocialization in modern Western societies. Additionally, supporting evidence was also found for the individual's search for a sense of belonging and self-fulfillment and the formation of groups of individuals in non-traditional settings. The members of a river rafting expedition (Arnould et al, 1993) form a *"communitas"* (a sense of community that transcends typical social norms and conventions) with their own set of norms, rites of passages and emotional attachments. Similarly, the skydivers in Celsi et al's (1993) group did share such a sense of communitas, most evident from their reaction to the unfortunate death of a member of their group. In a related context, Ong (1971) argues that in the postmodern world, the pervasiveness of various forms of media has made reproducible the community of orality. Members of celebrity fan clubs also talk about how important being with other members of the community is to them (O'Guinn, 1991). These groups or communities, and more particularly its members, are often characterized as exhibiting certain characteristics and behaviors such as flow. These findings suggests that leisure consumption could eventually give rise to the formation of communities (Celsi, 1993; Arnould, 1993), with specific and purposeful rules and behavior. These communities, though unconventional in a sense, are also very real and based on some tangible shared real life experiences. In that sense such a group is not radically different from say a group of friends who share common interests and do things together. To understand what such a community might be and what it might represent, it is essential to try and comprehend the reason for its' existence.

Ray Oldenburg proposes in his 1989 book, *The Great Good Place*, there are three essential places in people's lives : the place we live; the place we work; the places we gather for conviviality. He called the last of the above, "third places", which he described as follows:

" Third places exist on neutral ground and serve to level their guests to a condition of social equality.. they are taken for granted and have a low profile...The character of a third place is determined most of all by its regular clientele and is marked by a playful mood, which contrasts with people's more serious involvement in other spheres."

He further argues that the decline in the informal public life in America means that lifestyles are affluent, yet are plagued by boredom, loneliness and a sense of alienation.

In his book, *The Virtual Community*, Howard Rheingold (1993) takes an interesting look at such subcommunities. He feels that cyberspace is one of the ways in which people can find others with similar interests through discussion groups and personal interactions on-line and perhaps choose to later meet them in real life. In a phenomenon paralleling our actions in a traditional community, where we search through our pool of neighbors and professional colleagues, of acquaintances and even acquaintances of acquaintances, in order to find people who share our values and interests, virtual communities exchange information about one another, disclose and discuss our mutual interests, and sometimes become friends. One difference is that in a virtual community one can first directly go to the place where our favorite subjects are

being discussed and then get acquainted with people who share our likes and dislikes. In this sense, the topic is the address. One cannot, in real life, walk up to strangers and look for people who like avant-garde Finnish film makers or who have two kids and live in Sacramento; you can however join a bulletin board on these topics. Because we cannot see one another in cyberspace, physical appearances are less important in such communities, (probably the first human community where this holds true), and people can choose who they want to be. Ironically though, people often end up revealing themselves much more intimately on cyberspace than they would be inclined to without the mediation of screens and pseudonyms and the importance of this shared sense of trust.

Our research will investigate a community of game players to explore the macro issues of the sense of community and the individual level search for the self and for flow experiences in the group of computer gamers who choose to play Bolo. This area of exploration was a logical avenue for us, as the literature on leisure consumption and the literature on computer games have not addressed such issues together before.

METHODOLOGY

Bolo is a multi-player tank game, developed by Stuart Cheshire, that is typically played over a network or through the Internet. The goal of the game is to capture various strategic targets such as pill boxes and supply bases and to prevent the opposition from obtaining these strategic targets. Each game takes place on a battlefield or "map", composed of water, ground, trees and pavement. There are only a few simple actions that can be performed by the tank in the game (such as move, shoot, and build structures), but they are flexible enough to allow an extremely varied game play.

The game of Bolo was chosen for this study because it is a multi-player game and is very interactive. In addition, there is real-time conversation capability that plays an important role in the game and there is an existing group of dedicated, experienced gamers who play regularly. Bolo was also a convenient game to research due to the ease of access to players and the availability of Internet-based resources for data collection purposes. The flexibility of the game environment and the large amount of communication between players in the game makes Bolo an excellent game for our study. One of the researchers had extensive previous experience with Bolo and was accepted as a fellow player/observer rather than only as a researcher. From this position as a participant-observer, data was collected in an unobtrusive manner about player attitudes toward the game and issues involving the game.

DATA COLLECTION METHODS

The exploratory nature of the study provided an opportunity to collect information from a variety of sources to build a theory about experienced computer game players. The approach used, called grounded theory, is based on the idea that the process of data collection and data analysis should serve to reveal the relationships and major issues involved (Glaser and Strauss, 1967). The data gathering process was carefully designed to utilize multiple sources, which were then combined in the interpretation. These sources included in-depth interviews of experienced game players, Internet postings, and participant observation of direct player-to-player communication while interacting in game settings.

IN-DEPTH INTERVIEWS

The initial investigation was a set of individual interviews conducted with three experienced male computer gamers. The average age of respondents was 25, and they had an average of 12 years of computer game experience. All of the respondents had completed an undergraduate education and each was pursuing an advanced degree. Each was familiar with many games, including having played Bolo extensively. The subjects were informed of the goals of this research project and each was asked to discuss their experiences of playing games over their lifetime. The interviews were designed to reduce the impact of any preconceptions that would influence or distort the interviewing and analysis processes by using relatively unstructured interviews and letting the respondent shape the discussion. The interviews lasted 45 min. to 60 min. Each interview was taped and then transcribed. Both of these were done by the authors themselves, ensuring maximal involvement. An initial interpretation of the responses from these individual interviews led to the exploration at the aggregate level from additional sources.

ADDITIONAL DATA SOURCES

There are several sources that we accessed to gather more information about the community of Bolo players. There are three main sources. First, the various archives on the Internet such as / umich.edu/game/war/bolo contain the files to run the game, map files created by other players that allow different battlegrounds, and additional software and text files to help the players. Second, the Usenet newsgroup rec.games.bolo is a central location for the players to communicate with each other, to post notices about upcoming Bolo tournaments, and to discuss topics of interest to the community. A new World Wide Web site http://student-www.uchicago.edu/users/vboguta/bolo/bolo.html, contains links to the software archives, data files explaining strategy techniques and game advice, and screen shots of interesting game events. These sources of information are important to the game players for a variety of purposes including getting the latest game programs, disseminating information about game tactics, discussing various current controversies about the programs or player behavior and in particular about commenting on particular events from recent games.

RESULTS AND DISCUSSIONS

The three separate methodologies illuminated interesting aspects of the issues in a manner similar to observing a subject/consumer in many different settings. The challenge then is to critically interpret the data in a manner that gives us insights into the research issues. We have handled this by considering the results at both an individual level and at the aggregate level. Another way of thinking about this is that at the aggregate level we observe the macro behavior and at the individual level we try to build a set of explanations and identify emergent themes in the light of our observations and existing theories. As mentioned earlier, the data analytic method used is the grounded theory of Glaser et al, 1967.

THE BOLO COMMUNITY: A PROFILE

The demographics of the people we interviewed seems to roughly correspond with the sources of postings on the Internet newsgroups. The Bolo community consists mainly of male (few women are active players) players who tend to be students, research professionals or academics, with ages ranging from 18 to 40. The source computer of the game player is identified for the other players when they are all connected to a game and they can range from university computers to NASA and government installations.

From the postings on the Internet, and for reasons we shall soon outline, it was clear to the researchers that there existed a sense of community among the members of this group. This is not surprising, as the group members shared common passions and had similar demographics and certain psychographics. Some of the more enthusiastic members have planned tournaments where the players can get together for games with as many as 16 players in a single game. Due to connection restrictions that cause games to run very slowly, games are usually practically limited to only six players. Consequently, the tournaments allow for very different styles of games and are very enjoyable for the participants. In addition, they provide an opportunity to meet opponents (who are really other members of their community) face to face.

COMMUNITY ISSUES

One of the most important issues to the community is the influx of new players. One person recently posted a thread (a internet colloquialism for a thought or an idea) to the Usenet that new players were possibly being discouraged due to excessive annihilation by more experienced opponents. This was a concern for the community because it depends on having a constant source of players available as older players graduate or lose interest. To address this question, the members of the community created a lengthy discussion on the role of competition in the Bolo community. This discussion provoked many responses and the general conclusion was that competition is essential to the Bolo community. This is an interesting development, which reinforces the fact that such a collection of players is indeed a community. This community has clearly delineated *insiders* (the existing players) and *outsiders* (players trying to enter), *boundaries* and *concepts of authority* (do we let them in?). Further, it is a functioning community able to discuss issues and more importantly come to a *consensus*. Amazing really, if you consider that no two people in the community have ever met each other. Such communities were called *Real-Time Tribes* by Rheingold (1993). He identifies three fundamental elements that allowed such virtual communities to construct themselves: artificial but stable identities, quick wit, and the use of words to construct an imagined shared context for communications. As we discuss throughout the paper, we do find that such issues are indeed important in our Bolo community.

GAME ETIQUETTE

During the game play, there are informal matters of etiquette that are generally followed by the players. Players who do not follow these conventions are bombarded with sanctions in the form of messages from the other players to correct or change their behavior. One of the most important conventions is that once a game begins, another player should not connect to the game. The entry of the new player often delays the network connection and slows the game play or stops it entirely. Other conventions are to minimize the number of invisible mines laid randomly in the game and to stop playing when one player calls "hold", which is usually when a boss or faculty member enters the room. The last accepted rule of etiquette is to graciously concede a game when you are about to lose. The players could always simply quit and leave the game, but this behavior is considered rude and is often followed by a stream of derogatory messages about the player who left without conceding. Informal conversation before and after the game is viewed by the players as one of the benefits of internet games. This informal advice passed between the players is important for creating connections between the members of the community, as well as providing the less experienced players helpful tips to increase their skill levels. Once again , we find that the Bolo players function as a virtual community in cyberspace.

INDIVIDUAL LEVEL: FLOW / POSITIVE BENEFITS OF GAMES

As referred previously, flow involves extreme concentration on a relatively small set of stimuli and induces time and space distortions on the individuals who experience it. Flow is also seen as being a rewarding experience. We found that all respondents referred to experiencing benefits while playing games with statements such as *"It is fun and I check the finder* (a program that displays all the current Bolo games on the Internet*) and the newsgroups all the time to see what is going on"*. The thrill of competition is an integral component of playing Bolo. One posting echoes this, *"I think that it is fun to really stomp on someone once in a while"*. The thrill of achieving goals against real-time opponents is seen as both challenging and fun.

In addition, the sense of absorption characteristic of flow was clearly important because all the interview respondents reported intense involvement and distorted notions of time and space. One quote about this sense is, *"When you get very involved with a game, the real world frame completely disappears. It happens all the time, especially if the game is new and very intense"*. One respondent indicated that the sensation is so intense that, *" I would play up to ten hours a day on a new game and only take minimal breaks and then go back to the computer"*.

This sense of flow and time-distortion provided by Bolo and other games is a positive benefit for many individuals. In addition, many players reported that they felt a thrill or rush of excitement while playing games: *"I recognize that there is an adrenaline response to some of the games and in aggressive games as Bolo, there is a situation where I feel an adrenaline rush or tension"*, and *"I remember when I used to participate in sports...I got the same kind of adrenaline rush"*. Thus, beyond simple pleasure derived from playing games, membership in the Bolo community also serves to develop other personal attributes. This is similar to the experiences of other leisure groups examines in the literature (skydiving (Celsi et. al., 1993); river rafting (Arnould and Price, 1993)) and also congruent with extant literature (Csikszentmihalyi, 1985).

SEARCH FOR SELF

One of the most important reasons for becoming a member of a community is to be identified as a member of that community. One of the first tasks as a new player of Bolo is to choose a name or *"handle"*. This tag appears on the computer screen during the game play and identifies the otherwise identical tanks. A player can change his or her handle at any time, but the importance of a handle to a player goes beyond simply identifying the tank in the game. This handle from the game extends to his or her persona in the Bolo community. The most advanced players are instantly recognized, with such divers and exotic handles as Black Lightning, MegaWatt, Wintermute, Santa, Hillbilly Bob, Montezuma's Revenge and Pooh. The stability of these nick names is one of the few formal structured requirements of net space. The handle of a player can be changed at any time, but it is considered a breach of netiquette to play under more than three different names. In addition, there is a great deal of status and prestige in a handle that is important to the players. The process of building name recognition takes time and as the player's skill levels increases so does his or her social standing. One person reported that, *"I know that there will always be room to improve my Bolo skills as long as I play the game"*. The different levels of skill give the less experienced players something to aspire to achieve. There have been several attempts to formally rank the players, but at the highest level of skill it is difficult to differentiate between the best players. An important feature of a Bolo game is to have evenly matched players, and the identities and past histories that are embedded in a long-time handle are important in setting up games of players with balanced skill levels. This is seen in the quote, *"The best games I've played are the tough ones with very evenly matched teams"*.

The importance of player skill is a crucial mechanism for gaining recognition in the community. However, there are several other ways to get recognition: building game maps, programming computer *"brains"* to control the tank and filming movies of exciting moments of game play. The game maps serve as the playing field for Bolo and new variations are constantly being developed. A second area is designing computer programs called "brains" or *"bots"* that control the tank during the game. Brains can be used for solitary play or to automate certain parts of the game functions to aid the player. A third method involves a brain program called *"Spielborg"*. Spielborg is able to capture the images on the screen as the game is occurring and to play back "movies" of the game action at a later time. These movies allow the individuals to gain greater attention by demonstrating their playing skill or to display interesting or unique game situations.

The above issues of (i) a search for an identity and (ii) gaining recognition and acceptance confirm our expectations based on the literature. In particular, the hypothesis that, in advanced industrialized Western societies, due to a fragmentation of existing social groups (Mead, 1934a; Lyng, 1990; Batuik and Sacks, 1981)and consequent feeling of an empty self (Cushman, 1990), people will search for the self in newer and different settings. While there is no reason why such communities cannot form in a varied set of contexts, most of the extant literature reveals that leisure groups are the ones most frequently observed. These groups then develop into communities (Celsi, 1993), in our case, the Bolo virtual community.

THE ROLE OF CHANCE

The role of personal skill is important to level of status in the community, but Bolo games certainly have elements of chance which can significantly influence the outcome of the game. However, players tend to downplay its importance and attribute the success to superior player skills. For example, *"Almost of the times you play with someone who is better than you, you always lose"*. While some subjects reported that luck can play an important role in the game outcome, (*"When you are playing someone who is better than you, the key is luck"*), they still recognize that skills are the most important factor in establishing hierarchy. However, every member of the community is aware that people occasionally have bad days and the importance is skill demonstrated over time. This aspect of such community needs to be investigated further. While Bolo can be thought of as a low simulated perceived risk (leisure) consumption experience, this did not come out strongly in the data analysis. Whether this is a function of the research limitations, the type of game or confounding effects like edgeworking (Lyng, 1990) is a matter to be resolved in future work.

CONCLUSIONS AND FUTURE DIRECTIONS

We are witnessing an important shift in the concept of the self and the nature of interpersonal relationships that define our communities. More conventional social orders and boundaries are fast disappearing, to be replaced by newer and sometimes not so obvious forms of social organizations. Specialization of tasks and advances in technology are some of the contributing factors towards these hidden developments. We have, however, used this very technological change to develop the innovative research tool of Internet searches of posting, newsgroups and bulletin boards. This research tool is both powerful and unobtrusive in nature. These public access resources let us observe the subjects in the most natural environment providing us with rich data and information. While it does not right now have the capability to be used as a stand alone research technique, when used in combination with conventional techniques like in-depth interviews and participant observations it proved to be a powerful tool. In the future with the explosion of data sources on the network we think that this method should be used more often to gain insights that would otherwise be hard to obtain. This methodological innovation is one of the major contributions of our paper.

The identification of a *"virtual"* community is also, we believe, a key contribution of this paper, perhaps the first time that such a community has been identified in the academic literature in consumer behavior. Our research techniques and analysis have helped us begin to answer such key questions (Rheingold, 1993) about virtual communities as : What are the minimum elements of communication neccesary for a group of people to cocreate a sense of community? What types of groups can and do emerge from such interactions? What kinds of cultures emerge when you remove from human interactions all cultural artifacts except the written word and electronic pictures?

While the above are important contributions, more work needs to be done in this ever changing area. It would be interesting to track the Bolo community as it evolves with new patterns of behavior and possibly subcultures. Already there are different groups of players who learned to play using different versions of the game and have different preferred styles for attacking and defending in the play. A typology of the players would be an useful exercise. Further, we presume that many such virtual communities are being formed around the "world" with varying common denominators and the implication of these communities on the development of alternative societal forms will be extremely interesting. Further research should look at these issues and maybe some possible generalizations across cyber communities.

REFERENCES

Arnould, Eric J. and Linda L. Price, (1993), "River Magic: Extraordinary Experience and the Extended Service Encounter", Vol 20, *Journal of Consumer Research.*

Batuik, M. E. and H. L. Sacks, (1981), "George Herbert Mead and Karl Marx: Exploring Consciousness and Community", *Symbolic Interaction.*

Celsi, Richard L., Randall L. Rose and Thomas W. Leigh (1993), "An Exploration of High-Risk Leisure Consumption Through Skydiving", Vol 20, *Journal of Consumer Research.*

Csikszentmihalyi, M. (1985), "Reflections on Enjoyment", Vol 28, *Perspectives in Biology and Medicine.*

Cushman, Phillip, (1990). "Why the Self is Empty: Toward a Historically Situated Psychology", *American Psychologist,* 45 (May) 599-611.

Delk, J. L. (1980), "High-Risk Sports as Indirect self-destructive Behavior", *The Many Faces of Suicide,* Simon & Schuster.

Glaser, B. and Anselm Strauss (1967), *The discovery of grounded theory.* Chicago: Aldine.

Langer, E. J. (1975), "The Illusion of Control", Vol 32, *Journal of Personality and Social Psychology.*

Lofland, John and Lyn H. Lofland, (1984), *Analyzing Social Settings,* Wadsworth Publishing Company.

Lyng, Stephen (1990), "Edgework: A Social Psychological Analysis of Voluntary Risk Taking", Vol 95, *American Journal of Sociology.*

McCracken, Grant (1988), *The Long Interview,* SAGE Publications, Inc.

Mead, G. H. (1934a) 1950. *Mind, Self, and Society,* edited by C. W. Morris. Chicago: University of Chicago Press.

Mead, G. H. (1934b) 1964. *George Herbert Mead on Social Psychology,* edited by A. Strauss. Chicago: University of Chicago Press.

O'Guinn, Thomas C., (1991). "Touching Greatness: The Central Midwest Barry Manilow Fan Club", *Highways and Buyways,* Association for Consumer Research.

Ong, W.J., (1971). *Rhetoric, romance, and technology.* Ithaca, NY: Cornell University Press.

Rheingold, Howard, (1993). *The Virtual Community.* Addison-Wesley Inc., MA.

Thompson, H. (1974). *Playboy Interview: Hunter Thompson.* November, pp. 75-90, 245-46.

Life On The Net: The Reconstruction of Self And Community

Siok Kuan Tambyah, University of Wisconsin-Madison

ABSTRACT

This paper depicts life on the Internet as an unique consumer behavior phenomenon that reveals important issues in the reconstruction of self and community. It is argued that the Internet embodies a technological revolution of the 1990s with its radical dimensions of time, space, social roles and situations, boundaries and communities. The Internet provides anonymity or enacted liminality for its users, which leads to the emergence of the Net Self and Net Communitas. Anonymity further plays out into the dialectics of freedom versus control, and security versus vulnerability. Future research ideas are suggested.

INTRODUCTION

Ever since the term "information superhighway" was coined in 1992, it has become a byword in our vernacular, and enjoyed a growing presence in the media (Freedom Forum Media Studies Center 1995). The computer industry leaders, Microsoft, Novell Inc. and Intel Corp., envision that the computer is about to become indistinguishable from the TV set. Linking networks of such computers to cable TV boxes will finally lay the groundwork for the information superhighway. An important component of the information superhighway are the existing networks that connect millions of computer users around the globe. Among these networks, the Internet (or the Net) is undoubtedly the most well-known and extensive.

The purpose of this paper is to analyze the consumer behavior facets of the Net as it penetrates the ideological, social and psychological fabric of our modern society. Specifically, this analysis focuses on the reconstruction of self and community, and two dialectics that emerge from the concept of anonymity on the Net: freedom versus control, and security versus vulnerability. Although the Net has been a pervasive phenomenon for a number of years, its consumer behavior aspects have not been fully explored. This paper seeks to address this timely issue as the Net has clearly transcended its basic function as a computer network.

First, I will provide a brief overview of the Net and the services it offers. Second, I describe some key dimensions of the times we live in which form the backdrop for the emergence of the Net as a unique social and consumer behavior phenomenon. Third, I present the Net as a rich tapestry of consumer behavior processes using a framework of rites of passage, liminality, and communitas. These three concepts will then be linked in a systematic way. In this approach, a key Net characteristic of anonymity will be shown to result in a liminal state that can lead to: (1) the reconstruction of self, where the individual takes on the Net Self, and (2) the reconstruction of community, where Net Communitas emerges in a virtual community resulting in a sense of kinship. The presence of both the Net Self and Net Communitas then set the stage for two key dialectics to emerge: (1) freedom versus control, and (2) security versus vulnerability. Their influence on the reconstruction of self and community is discussed. Finally, I suggest some avenues for future research to enhance our understanding and appreciation of life on the Net.

WHAT IS THE INTERNET?

The Net is a "network of networks, tens of thousands of computers connected in a web, talking to one another through a common communications protocol" (Ayre 1994). The Internet Society claims that there are 20 to 30 million active Net users and that the number is growing by about 160,000 users per month

(Ubois 1995). The three most common Internet services used are electronic mail, information databases and bulletin boards. Electronic mail enables Net users to send messages to one another electronically. Information databases offer opportunities for learning, business, research and entertainment in many spheres of influence (FARNET 1994). Bulletin board systems (BBSs) are customized online systems where Net users congregate around a modem that allows them to post messages (putting a message on a bulletin board). They began as informal communities but now many bulletin boards have been started by entrepreneurs for business and personal interests. Usenet (User network), a popular segment of the Net, is a public network made up of thousands of *newsgroups* and organized by topic. A *newsgroup* is a bulletin board-like forum or conference area where you can post messages on a specified topic. Newsgroups exist for a huge range of subjects, for example, hobbies, social concerns, and so on.

Apart from information sources, the Net also offers many popular culture activities. For example, the Rolling Stones broadcast twenty minutes of live audio and video from a performance at the Cotton Bowl in Dallas (Strauss 1994). Often, Net users interact to collaborate on creative projects, such as writing music (Fiedler 1994), creating art (Bellafante 1995), and playing fantasy role-playing games in multi-user dungeons or MUDs (Ayre 1994).

THE NET AS EMBODIMENT OF TECHNOLOGICAL REVOLUTION

In this section, the Net is shown to be a reflection of the times we live in. Specifically, the Net embodies the compression of time and space (Ellul 1964; Gergen 1991; McLuhan 1964) and fluid social situations, which contributes to the feeling of "no sense of place" (McLuhan 1964; Meyrowitz 1985). These two dimensions make it possible for Net users to interact in an unstructured way at all hours of the day and night, and even preserve a record in the form of hard copy (Roszak 1986). In addition, the Net clearly illustrates the blurring of traditional boundaries, and challenges our established notions of communities. This has an important impact on the way Net users interact on an anonymous basis which results in the reconstruction of self and community. These dimensions will each be discussed.

Time-Space Compression

"We have extended our central nervous system itself in a global embrace, abolishing both space and time as far as our planet is concerned" (McLuhan 1964, p.19).

Time-space compression refers to processes that revolutionize the objective qualities of space and time which force us to alter how we represent the world to ourselves (Harvey 1989, p.240). As the time taken to transverse space (that is, to get from one place to another) diminishes through innovations in transportation and telecommunications (Ellul 1964; McLuhan 1964), time itself ceases to be a measure of space. A natural consequence is that "distance no longer exists and man has vanquished space" (Ellul 1964, p.328). As an embodiment of time-space compression, the Net provides "instant travel" and "real time". The Net enables people from different parts from the world to communicate and exchange ideas immediately with one another without being physically present in the same place.

No Sense of Place

Nothing can be further from the spirit of the new technology than "a place for everything and everything in its place" (McLuhan 1964).

Goffman (1959) describes social life as a multi-staged drama in which we each act out different roles in different social arenas, depending on the nature of the situation, our particular role in it, and the makeup of the audience. Meyrowitz (1985, p.39) suggests that when we find ourselves in a given setting, we often unconsciously ask "Who can see me, who can hear me?" and "Who can I see, who can I hear?" The answers to these questions help us decide on appropriate behaviors. However, Gergen (1991) proposes that technological change has exposed us to such an "enormous barrage of social stimulation" that we are moved to a stage of saturation which substantially changes our experiences of self and other.

Thus it seems that people no longer seem to "know their place" because they no longer have a place in the traditional sense of a set of behaviors matched to physical locations and the audiences found in them (Meyrowitz 1985). Rather than physical settings, social situations can now be conceptualized as "information settings" that are created by electronic media (Meyrowitz 1985). This phenomenon of *no sense of place* is widespread on the Net where users are enmeshed in myriad information settings. Net users cannot be seen or heard by other Net users. This anonymity enables them to take on new and/or multiple roles and selves. This phenomenon will be explored in more detail in the sections on enacted liminality and the Net Self.

Blurred Boundaries and Transformed Communities

Boundaries, as in the traditional sense, set limits (how far you can go), define the area of contention, and provide some form of enclosure. The word community is derived from the word "common"; the first syllable meaning "together" or "next to" and the second having to do with barter or exchange (Sanders 1994). Communities have been conventionally defined by social markers such as race and income, and usually occupied a bounded, geographical space. Therefore, to belong to a certain community typically involves engaging in a web of relationships and embracing its shared values and goals (Sanders 1994).

However, boundaries in our time-and-space compressed world and on the Net are getting increasingly indeterminate and the traditional, bounded community has deteriorated. Take the example of Robert and Carleen Thomas, a Californian couple, who were charged and drew jail sentences for sending pornographic images via a computer bulletin board system. Their prosecution is the first obscenity case in which operators of a computer bulletin board were charged in the place where the material was received rather than where it originated. Their defense lawyer's appeal focuses on the U.S. Supreme Court's 1973 ruling that defines obscenity by local community standards. He maintains that with the advent of computer networks which have no boundaries, the meaning of "local communities" is debatable (Chicago Tribune, 3 December 1994). New radical forms of community such as symbolic communities (Gergen 1991) and virtual communities (Rheingold 1993), have surfaced. These *transformed communities* are not geographically bounded and are usually characterized by the capacity of their members for symbolic exchange—of words, images, information—mostly through electronic means (Gergen 1991). An excellent example is the Well (the Whole Earth 'Lectronic Link), where the sense of oneness in the virtual community also permeates their real lives when Net users attend one another's real-

life parties, weddings and funerals (Rheingold 1993). The concept of transformed communities will be further highlighted in the section on Net Communitas.

CONSUMER BEHAVIOR PROCESSES ON THE NET

Although Net users extensively utilize information resources on the Net, their relationship with the Net surmounts rational considerations. Net users interact with the Net in more personal and symbolic ways. Therefore, my analysis does not focus on information processing, the search for and use of information on the Net, and/or the adoption of technological products, although these are important research issues as well. Instead this paper focuses on the relatively more experiential aspects of Net users' consumer behavior (Hirschman and Holbrook 1982, Holbrook and Hirschman 1982), especially pertaining to the reconstruction of self and community. In this respect, this paper adopts the framework of rites of passage, liminality (van Gennep 1960) and communitas (Turner 1974b) as a guide to understanding consumer behavior processes on the Net. Specifically, it is contended that Net users enact a state of liminality during which they engage in deeply symbolic processes related to the reconstruction of self and the creation of Net Communitas.

Rites of Passage, Liminality and Communitas

Van Gennep (1960) describes *rites de passage* as comprising three phases: (1) separation, in which the individual symbolically detaches him/herself from his/her position in the social structure, (2) margin or transition, in which the individual is in an ambiguous state, free from classification, and (3) reaggregation or incorporation, in which the individual reenters the social structure, often but not always at a higher status level. The intervening phase of margin or transition is also known as liminality. *Liminality* has been viewed as a state of no-place and no-time where social structure disappears or is simplified and generalized (Turner 1974b). In primal cultures, liminality is a collective experience mediated by culturally prescribed rituals that gave individuals an experience of communitas or shared psychological support through major status passages (van Gennep 1960). However, in our world of technological complexity and fragmented social relationships, modern commentators have argued that people experience a different, more isolated form of liminality (Turner 1974a).

Turner (1974b) argues that it is in liminality that *communitas* emerges, either in the form of a spontaneous expression of sociability or in a cultural and normative form, emphasizing equality and comradeship as norms. Communitas bonds people with "feelings of linkage, of belonging, (and) of group devotion to a transcendent goal" (Arnould and Price 1993). The creation of communitas typically begins with minimization or elimination of the outward marks of rank and status (Turner 1969; van Gennep 1960). Then through a shared sacred experience (Belk, Wallendorf and Sherry 1989), such as river rafting (Arnould and Price 1993) and skydiving (Celsi, Rose and Leigh 1993), communitas emerges and bonds individuals together. Communitas is often placed in opposition to structure, which is defined as "the patterned arrangements of role-sets, status-sets and status-sequences" consciously recognized and regularly operative in a given society (Turner 1974b). Structure is the notion of society as a differentiated segmented system of structural positions. In contrast, communitas is the perception of society as a homogeneous, undifferentiated whole. This distinction is important in understanding the dialectic of freedom versus control discussed in a later section.

Anonymity as Enacted Liminality

Many online forums on the Net, for example hobbyist BBSs and some sensitive newsgroups grant anonymity to their users (Godwin 1995). People use handles for their real names and develop personae to go with those handles. Crucial aspects of one's identity which would be involuntarily revealed in a face-to-face meeting can be masked on the Net unless one chooses to reveal them. Net users are judged primarily not by who they are but by their ideas and what they write (Garrison 1994; Seabrook 1994). The impersonality and immateriality of the online experience has a liberating and leveling effect; it blanks out race, age, gender, looks, timidity, and handicaps. It encourages frankness and removes caution (Roszak 1986, p.169; Garrison 1994). The result is that the Net is a community where "information is the true currency of democracy" (Ralph Nader quoted in Long 1994, p.66).

An important implication of anonymity on the Net is that it enables users to enact a state of liminality. Net users when interacting on an anonymous basis are symbolically stripped of their status trappings. They are liberated from their role expectations and social constraints. The interaction between and among individuals is thus democratic, vibrant and fluid. It is argued in this paper that enacted liminality can produce two significant processes and outcomes: (1) the reconstruction of self, in which the user recreates his/her identity and personality, and (2) emergence of Net Communitas, in which the user feels a certain oneness with other Net users.

THE NET SELF

Net users do not view the Net as a passive personal computer or a node of a computer network. The Net provides more than an extension of a person's work, hobbies and/or social circle. However, Net users do not merely relate to the technologies on the Net as servomechanisms or are compelled to "serve these objects, these extensions of ourselves, as gods or minor religions" (McLuhan 1964, p.55). Instead they are more purposefully and actively involved in embracing the technologies of the Net, and using its redefining power in constructing their identities. One Net user even described himself as having "mutated into a new life-form" (Romenesko 1994).

Self-extension and self-reconstruction have been well documented in many spheres of consumer research (e.g. Belk 1988; Wallendorf and Arnould 1988). In addition, the re-construction of self has been found to be important in periods of role transitions like immigration (Mehta and Belk 1991) and major life events (Schouten 1991). To these situations, this paper adds the liminoid state induced by the anonymity provided by technologies available on the Net. Net users often refer to their identity on the Net as the "Net Self", as opposed to IRL (in real life). In their liminoid states, Net users assume various and/or multiple roles and personalities, live in virtual worlds and maintain virtual relationships (Garrison 1994). It is argued that this Net Self, by virtue of its emergence during enacted liminality, is also *relational, democratic and experiential* in nature.

The Net Self is a *relational* self because it is constructed through relationships, and immersed interdependence (Gergen 1991), as Net users interact with one another on common ground. Net users are acutely aware of their connectedness with other users and how that constitutes a crucial element of their Net Self (Rheingold 1993). In addition, the Net Self is *democratic* because the technologies of the Net and the anonymity it provides erode specific gender roles (Gergen 1991; Meyrowitz 1985), and abolish distinctions of class and race. On the Net, women, the elderly, the young, the handicapped and other minorities, can be evaluated and respected for their ideas and contributions, and not for their physical attributes. Finally, the Net Self is an *experiential* self that flirts with fantasy and make-believe. Although Net users do use Net resources for research, education and such, they also indulge in more hedonistic exploits ((Hirschman and Holbrook 1982; Holbrook and Hirschman 1982) such as fantasy games, and the creation of art and music. This is consistent with Turner (1974a) who views liminality as involving the "antistructural element of play, the freedom to experiment with new categories of meaning".

NET COMMUNITAS

Net Communitas or social interrelatedness refers to how an individual Net user bonds with other Net users, and experiences a sense of common, shared destiny. In enacted liminality, users devoid of their social rank and status become freer to connect with other users on a common basis. As a result, Net communitas surfaces. Many Net users testify to the exceptional bonds they feel with the people they interact with on the Net (Rheingold 1993). John Perry Barlow, co-founder of the WELL, found comfort from his WELL community in coping with the death of a loved one. He said, "Those strangers, who had no arms to put around my shoulders, no eyes to weep with mine, nevertheless saw me through. As neighbours do" (Barlow 1995, p.56).

Apart from warm, sociable feelings, Net Communitas also reveals itself in the ways in which basic human needs for community, engagement and dependence are met (Slater 1979). Even many human rights abuses are curtailed because of actions set in motion through the Net. For example, a Russian dissident was released from jail after Net users wrote to the Russian government expressing concern over his arrest (Long 1994). In another touching scenario, a suicial man was saved when Net users spotted his suicide message on the bulletin board, tracked him down in Miami County, Indiana, and notified police to reach him before he killed himself (Boston Globe, 24 October 1994).

Criticism has constantly been levelled at the unfeeling nature of machines and technology, and their undesirable effects on social relationships and values (Ellul 1964). Roszak (1972) suggests that our technological achievements "leave ungratified that dimension of the self which reaches out into the world for enduring purpose, undying value." There are skeptics who feel that virtual communities do not exhibit the qualities of true communities because they lack human contact, and that computers and networks isolate people from one another (Stoll 1995). On the Net, however, it is the cold, isolating, mechanical technology that does enable the birth of Net Communitas (Herz 1994; Susan Brownmiller quoted in Long 1994). Barlow (1995) suggests that the traditional community as we know it is "largely a wraith of nostalgia", and that it is possible to create a community in cyberspace with the human spirit and the basic desire to connect.

Like real-life communities, virtual communities face certain threats to their cohesion and harmony. Despite Net users' willingness to build and sustain community, the Net faces tensions that threaten to break up communities and break down individuals. These tensions are discussed in the following section.

DIALECTICS ON THE NET

Two main dialectics emanate from the phenomenon of anonymity or enacted liminality on the Net. Dialectics refer to "the juxtaposition or interaction of conflicting ideas or forces" (Random House Webster's College Dictionary 1992, p. 372). Anonymity propagates the fundamental consequence of freedom, which in turn plays out into the dialectics of (1) Freedom versus Control, and (2) Security versus Vulnerability.

Freedom versus Control

The dialectic of Freedom versus Control is an issue in all forms of democracy. This tension has also been noted in consumer research on life themes (Mick and Buhl 1992; Thompson, Locander and Pollio 1990). Freedom has been described as "being free of restriction (having the freedom to make the choices one wants)" (Thompson, Locander and Pollio 1990, p.353) and as being free to explore the opportunities and take the risks life has to offer (Mick and Buhl 1992). In the context of the Net, where an information democracy is purported to exist, anonymity gives Net users freedom to express their views, and simultaneously savor a diversity of opinions and ideas. However, there is also concern regarding the limits to freedom of expression. Debates rage on whether "flaming" (sending online insulting messages), hate mail, viruses, pornography, profanity and defamation, are legitimate forms of free speech (Seabrook 1994; Siegel 1994). In one instance, a college student asserted that it was within his rights to post messages on the Internet about torturing and murdering a female classmate (Chicago Tribune, 10 February 1995; Levy 1995). In another scenario, artists are enthusiastic about the freedom and possibilities of experimenting in a new medium, but are concerned that they would lose control of their works once recordings, texts or pictures are converted to digital form (Wallich 1995).

There has always been considerable difficulty in deciding on the form and extent of control in any democracy, for example, in the realm of consumer policies (Moorman and Price 1989). In the context of the Net, these difficulties are compounded because the Net operates in an environment where conventional notions of speech, property and place take on profoundly new forms (Rothfeder 1994). For example, a new definition of copyright law in cyberspace proposed by the Working Group on Intellectual Property Rights would make using almost everything anyone creates in cyberspace illegal (Wallich 1995).

In response to these tensions, Net users have always maintained that the Net is essentially set up and run as a self-regulating body (Adam Curry as quoted in Long 1994). There is some general agreement that undesirable forms of digital speech are hurting the Net, but there is reluctance to enforce policies that discourage anonymity and curb freedom. Net users contend that censorship and control could be disastrous to what may be the last place where genuine liberty thrives (Garrison 1994). Also, the task of monitoring thousands of networks and bulletin boards is simply unworkable (Godwin 1995; Levy 1995). On a more crucial note, if anonymity is abolished on the Net, enacted liminality is suspended and the reconstruction of the Net Self would be destroyed. It would not be possible for a democratic Net Self to emerge because Net users would be identified and trapped by their social status. Control, by imposing structure on Net interaction, also impairs the formation of Net Communitas. This is because structure differentiates individuals by their status, whereas communitas disregards status and bonds individuals together (Turner 1974b). The Net Self and Net Communitas both require the freedom afforded by anonymity to flourish.

Security versus Vulnerability

The second dialectic of Security versus Vulnerability reflects tensions on the Net when freedom results in users taking advantage of one another or harming one another, and in doing so, destroying Net Communitas. This dialectic reflects a common occurrence in democracies and has been documented more recently among the many problems associated with information technologies (Bloom, Milne and Adler 1994, Morris and Pharr 1992). This dialectic arises because in the Net setting, anonymity affords privacy to Net users, but it also lends a cloak of secrecy to those who abuse the rights of others. Net users, individuals and organizations alike, take risks whenever they interact on the Net. They are vulnerable, for example, to having their accounts "fingered", "spoofing" (having someone electronically impersonating them), vicious pranks, and terrorist-like attacks by hackers. Victims can suffer the dissemination of misleading information, damage to personal reputation, and criminal activity (Godwin 1995). Recent cybercrime cases such as the hacker gang headed by "Phiber Optik" (Slatalla and Quittner 1994) and the exploits of Kevin Mitnick, a notorious hacker from North Carolina, who hacked the WELL's electronic mail accounts, and used the WELL as a screen to launch anonymous attacks on networks throughout the Net (Hafner 1995; McGrath 1995), have clearly exposed the fragility of the Net that accompanies its prevailing freedoms.

These freedoms have also exposed the underlying fragilities of many democracies. Specifically while the underlying freedoms expressed in democracies like the Net insure equal access and equal liberties, the system is, in fact, not without its sources of systematic discrimination. For example, Net users who identify themselves as women, and/or use handles/names that are obviously female, are especially vulnerable to online animosity and sexual harrassment from men (Kantrowitz 1994, Tannen 1994). Net users react to this vulnerability in many different ways. For instance, many women hide on the Net by simply reading messages others have posted and not posting any of their own ("lurkers") or when they do talk, use male pseudonyms (Herz 1994). Women also select Net sites they are more comfortable in, such as East Coast Hangout (ECHO) (Herz 1994) and Women's Wire (Online Access January 1995).

In response to the threats to security, the government has devised the Clipper Chip which encrypts messages as they leave Net users' computers (Levy 1995). However, the Clipper Clip met with resistance from Net users who view the device as an intrusive surveillance attempt of the government. Also, groups like pedophiles, cults and pornography clubs can use the device to avoid detection and conceal crime (Levy 1995; Seabrook 1994). So, despite the vulnerabilities Net users are exposed to, they appear to place a premium on their freedom that far outstrips the perceived benefits security measures can offer. Moreover, like democracies, distinct mechanisms for protecting vulnerable subsegments have evolved that allow them to participate in a marginalized manner. At the same time, this participation has spawned the development of distinct and well functioning subcommunities.

FUTURE RESEARCH AND CONCLUSION

Apart from the issues raised in this paper, there are additional research areas which would be fruitful to pursue. First, in line with the call for consumer research that is sensitive to the feminine voice (Bristor and Fisher 1993; Hirschman 1993), research on gender issues on the Net should consider how the reconstruction of self differs for women on the Net. It is suggested that women tend to look at the usefulness of technology, and they want machines that meet people's needs (Kantrowitz 1994). In contrast, men tend to be obsessive about the technology itself, and view machines as extensions of their physical power. However, there may also be a softer male side emerging on the Net as men find it easier to open up on electronic mail (Tannen 1994). Second, the intricate interplay of power and democracy should be studied as they impact who gains access to the Net. Researchers should contemplate how the Net can avoid becoming elitist and hegemonic, and how the Net can be made available to all consumers without discrimination (Kadi 1995; Ratan 1995; Stuart 1995). Especially valuable would be research on power and authority structures within cyberspace communities and how they influence access to and control over the creation and communication of information. Also, studying the impact of emerging Net technologies on countries with varying stages of development would yield useful insights in this area of research. Third, the juxtaposition of reality and virtuality presents itself as an interesting arena of consumer behavior. There has been debate on whether virtual communities dilute the meaning of real communities (Smolowe 1995), and how Net users commute between and manage the two (Stoll 1995). Moral linkages among people, and ethical issues at personal and communal levels are potential areas of research.

The research issues outlined above are a fraction of the many challenges facing consumer researchers studying the Net. Despite the difficulties of making the Net safer and more available to all consumers, its ideals of liberty, equality and fraternity strike intensely responsive chords in modern humankind. As the Net commands a growing presence in consumers' lives, it will undoubtedly continue to forge deep consumption meanings for Net users and communities. However, as it does that, like all democracies, it must also find a way to balance the delicate trade-offs associated with freedom that all communities must grapple with.

REFERENCES

Arnould, Eric J., and Linda L. Price (1993), "River Magic: Extraordinary Experience and the Extended Service Encounter," *Journal of Consumer Research*, 20 (June), 24-45.

Ayre, Rick (1994), "Making the Internet Connection," *PC Magazine*, 11 October, 118-139.

Barlow, John Perry (1995), "Is There a There in Cyberspace?" *Utne Reader*, March-April 1995, 53-56.

Belk, Russell W. (1988), "Possessions and the Extended Self," *Journal of Consumer Research*, 15 (September), 139-168.

_____, Melanie Wallendorf and John F. Sherry, Jr. (1989), "The Sacred and Profane in Consumer Behavior: Theodicy on the Odyssey," *Journal of Consumer Research*, 16 (June), 1-38.

Bellafante, Ginia (1995), "Strange Sounds and Sights," *Time*, Spring, 14-16.

Bloom, Paul N., George R. Milne and Robert Adler (1994), "Avoiding Misuse of New Information Technologies: Legal and Societal Considerations," *Journal of Marketing*, 58 (January), 98-110.

Boston Globe, 24 October 1994, "Computer message helps stop a suicide," *Washington Post*.

Bristor, Julia M. and Eileen Fischer (1993), "Feminist Thought: Implications for Consumer Research," *Journal of Consumer Research*, 19 (March), 518-536.

Chicago Tribune, 3 December 1994, "Sending of Computer Porn Draws Jail Terms For California Couple," Associated Press, 16.

Chicago Tribune, 11 February 1995, "Man Arrested for Rape Message on Internet," Associated Press, 16.

Celsi, Richard L., Randall L. Rose and Thomas W. Leigh (1993), "An Exploration of High-Risk Leisure Consumption through Skydiving," *Journal of Consumer Research*, 20 (June), 1-23.

Ellul, Jacques (1964), *The Technological Society,* New York: Vintage.

FARNET (1994), *51 Reasons / How We Use the Internet and What It Says About the Information Superhighway,* eds. Martha Stone-Martin and Laura Breeden, Lexington MA: FARNET Inc.

Fiedler, David (1994), "Oh, the Places You'll Go," *Netguide*, December, 18-20.

Freedom Forum Media Studies Center (1995), "How Do They Call It? Let Us Count the Ways," *Scientific American*, February, 30.

Garrison, Peter (1994), "Liberty, Equality and Fraternity," *Netguide*, December, 50-53.

Gergen, Kenneth J. (1991), *The Saturated Self: Dilemmas of Identity in Contemporary Life*, New York: BasicBooks.

Godwin, Mike (1995), "Who Was That Masked Man?" *Interworld*, January, 22-25.

Goffman, Erving (1959), *The Representation of Self in Everyday Life*, Garden City, New York: Doubleday.

Hafner, Katie (1995), "A Superhacker Meets His Match," *Newsweek*, 27 February, 61, 63.

Harvey, David (1989), *The Condition of Postmodernity: An Enquiry Into the Origins of Cultural Change*, New York: Blackwell.

Herz, J.C. (1994), "Pigs in (Cyber)Space," *GQ*, October, 156-162.

Hirschman, Elizabeth C. (1993), "Ideology in Consumer Research, 1980 and 1990: A Marxist and Feminist Critique," *Journal of Consumer Research*, 19 (March), 537-555.

_____ and Morris B. Holbrook (1982), "Hedonic Consumption: Emerging Concepts, Methods and Propositions," *Journal of Marketing*, 46 (Summer), 92-101.

Holbrook, Morris B. and Elizabeth C. Hirschman (1982), "The Experiential Aspects of Consumption: Consumer Fantasies, Feelings and Fun," *Journal of Consumer Research*, 9 (September), 132-140.

Kadi, M. (1995), "Welcome to Cyberia," *Utne Reader*, March-April, 57-59.

Kantrowitz, Barbara (1994), "Men, Women and Computers," *Newsweek*, 16 May, 36-43.

Levy, Steven (1995), "Technomania," *Newsweek*, 27 February, 25-29.

Long, Marion (1994), "We Are the World," *Netguide*, December, 55-66.

McLuhan, Marshall (1964), *Understanding Media: The Extensions of Man,* New York: McGraw Hill.

McGrath, Peter (1995), "Info Snooper-Highway," *Newsweek*, 27 Febraury, 60-61.

Mehta, Raj and & Rusell W. Belk (1991), "Artifacts, Identity, and Transition: Favorite Possessions of Indians and Indian Immigrants to the United States," *Journal of Consumer Research*, 17 (March), 398-410.

Meyrowitz, Joshua (1985), *No Sense of Place: The Impact of Electronic Media on Social Behavior,* New York: Oxford University Press.

Mick, David Glen, and Claus Buhl (1992), "A Meaning-based Model of Advertising Experiences," *Journal of Consumer Research*, 19 (December), 317-337.

Moorman, Christine and Linda L. Price (1989), "Consumer Policy Remedies and Consumer Segment Interactions," in *Journal of Public Policy and Marketing*, 8, 181-203.

Morris, Linda and Steven Pharr (1992), "Invasion of Privacy: A Dilemma for Marketing Research and Database Technology," *Journal of Systems Management*, 10-11, 30-31, 42-44.

Online Access (1995), "1995: Smaller Services On the Rise," January, 47.

Random House Webster's College Dictionary (1992), New York: Random House.

Ratan, Suneel (1995), "A New Divide Between Haves and Have-Nots?" *Time*, Spring, 25-26.

Rheingold, Howard (1993), *The Virtual Community: Home-steading on the Electronic Frontier*, New York: Addison Wesley.

Romenesko, Jim (1995), "Internet Insider: For Better of For Worse: How Cyberspace Has Changed Lives," *Online Access*, January, 32.

Roszak, Theodore (1972), *Where the Wasteland Ends*, Garden City, New York: Doubleday.

_____ (1986), *Cult of Information: The Folklore of Computers and the True Art of Thinking*, New York: Pantheon.

Rothfeder, Jeffrey (1994), "The People's (Virtual) Courts," *Netguide*, December, 91-94.

Sanders, Scott Russell (1994), "The Web of Life," *Utne Reader*, March-April, 69.

Schouten, John W. (1991), "Selves in Transition: Symbolic Consumption in Personal Rites of Passage and Identity Reconstruction," *Journal of Consumer Research*, 17 (March), 412-425.

Seabrook, John (1994), "My First Flame," in *The New Yorker*, 23 March, 70-79.

Siegel, Martha S. (1994), "Computer Anarchy," *Chicago Tribune*, 12 December 1994, 15.

Slatall, Michelle and Joshua Quittner (1995), *Masters of Deception: The Gang that Ruled Cyberspace*, HarperCollins.

Slater, Philip E. (1976), *The Pursuit of Loneliness*, Boston: Beacon Press.

Smolowe, Jill (1995), "Intimate Strangers," *Time*, Spring, 20-24.

Strauss, Neil (1994), "Stones Toss Hats Online," in *Chicago Tribune*, 25 November, New York Times Service.

Stoll, Clifford (1995), "The Internet? Bah!" *Newsweek*, 27 February 1995, 41.

Stuart, Reginald (1994), "High-tech Redlining," *Utne Reader*, March-April, 73.

Tannen, Deborah (1994), "Gender Gap in Cyberspace," *Newsweek*, 16 May 1994, 40-41.

Thompson, Craig, William Locander and Howard Pollio (1990), "The Lived Meaning of Free Choice: An Existential-Phenomenological Description of Everyday Consumer Experiences of Contemporary Married Women," *Journal of Consumer Research*, 17 (December), 346-361.

Turner, Victor (1969), *The Ritual Process: Structure and Anti-Structure*, Chicago: Aldine.

_____ (1974a), "Liminal to Liminoid in Play, Flow and Ritual: An Essay in Comparative Sociology," Rice University Studies, 60 (3), 53-92.

_____ (1974b), *Drama, Fields and Metaphors: Symbolic Action in Human Society*, Ithaca, New York: Cornell University Press.

Ubois, Jeff (1995), "Ruling Class," *Internet World*, January, 60-65.

van Gennep, Arnold (1960), *The Rites of Passage*, trans. M. B. Vizedom and G. L. Caffee, Chicago: University of Chicago Press.

Wallendorf, Melanie and Eric J. Arnould (1989), "My Favorite Things: A Cross-Cultural Inquiry into Object Attachment, Possessions and Social Linkages", *Journal of Consumer Research*, 14 (March), 531-547.

Wallich, Paul (1995), "The Chilling Wind of Copyright Law?" *Scientific American*, February, 30.

Creating or Escaping Community?: An Exploratory Study of Internet Consumers' Behaviors

Eileen Fischer, York University
Julia Bristor, University of Houston
Brenda Gainer, York University

ABSTRACT

What, if any, kind of community can be formed through consumption? This paper offers a preliminary exploration of the types of communities formed around and through the consumption of one particular commodity, and internet news group. After identifying some of the most generic aspects of traditional communities, and reviewing some ideas in the popular literature on "virtual communities," it undertakes a hermeneutic analysis of texts formed by the users (and producers) of a particular newsgroup. It concludes with implications for research on consumption communities and some preliminary thoughts regarding social policy development.

Can consumption create communities? And if so, how do they compare with "traditional" communities such as neighborhoods? Many have argued that the individualistic pursuit of goods, promoted by marketing in general and advertising in particular, is partially responsible for the breakdown of traditional communities (e.g. Campbell 1987; Lasch 1979, 1991, 1994). Others have suggested that as traditional communities disintegrate, commonalities in consumption leads to the formation of certain types of communities (e.g. Boorstin 1973).

Understanding the types of communities formed through consumption is important given the many social commentators who argue that community is a vital human phenomenon that must be consciously preserved, promoted or protected in the contemporary world (e.g. Drucker 1994; Etzioni 1993; Lasch 1994).

To begin an exploration of this area, we have undertaken a preliminary study of the consumption of a commodity which has, in itself, attracted enormous attention: the internet. One of the primary reasons that we have chosen to study the consumption of internet services is that there is considerable interest, not only among consumer researchers, but also among the general public, about whether networks of people linked by computers are or are not *real* communities. One example is a recent issue of the *Utne Reader*, most of which was devoted to contrasting "cyberhoods" with neighborhoods. Another comes from the posthumously published work of Christopher Lasch (1994), where he argues that the information highway should be abandoned because it is splintering neighborhoods. A third comes from a volume by Howard Rheingold (1993) who asserts that the use of computer networks can help restore the community that has been lost in modern life.

A secondary reason we have chosen this particular consumption phenomenon for investigation is that it appears to involve multiple "layers" of consumer behaviors. That is, in studying the consumption of internet services, we will invariably study consumer behaviors related to an array of other (perhaps more tangible) consumer goods, since the internet is increasingly a marketplace where virtually anything could be virtually bought or sold. Thus, the internet is not merely a commodity around which consumption communities may form; it is also a means through which consumption communities centered on other goods and services may be established and developed.

To delimit the focus of this study, we wish to emphasize that we will focus here solely on a community maintained through the consumption of one particular aspect of the internet — a specific news group. The consumer behavior of interest is use of or participation in this newsgroup. We will not address the ways that traditional face-to-face communities (e.g. a network of friends) may affect or be affected by consumer behaviors or motivations. Thus we will not investigate directly the possibility that traditional communities are destroyed by individuals' materialistic pursuit of goods, or the equal possibility that such communities are fostered and maintained in part through consumption.

To frame and inform our study of the types of communities formed through the internet, we first review the literature on the nature of communities. We articulate, based on this review and our own experience, our prior expectations concerning the nature of internet communities. We then describe our empirical study. Next we present and interpret some of our findings. We conclude by linking these findings back to the broader questions regarding the ways that consumption may create or destroy communities, and discuss the implications for future research and for social policy development.

WHAT IS A COMMUNITY?

Much of the rhetoric regarding the loss of, need for, and virtues of community is unconcerned with defining the central construct of interest. Yet the term is susceptible to a wide variety of meanings in common parlance. For instance, one contemporary dictionary includes the following definitions (and *many* more): 1) a body of individuals organized into a unit or manifesting awareness of some unifying trait 2) the people living in a space or region and usually linked by common interests; 3) an interacting population of different kinds of individuals; 4) a group of people marked by a common characteristic but living within a larger society that does not share that same characteristic; 5) any group sharing interests or pursuits; 6) shared activity: social intercourse: fellowship, communion, especially social activity marked by a feeling of unity but also individual participation completely willing and not forced or coerced and without loss of individuality; (Webster's Unabridged Third New International Dictionary). Some scholars whose main area of study is community comment with frustration on the myriad common usages of the term; they complain that this causes "confusion" and "a lack of conceptual rigor" (Poplin 1979, p. 4). However, even scholars of community vary widely in their assumptions about what the core elements of community may be.

One key element of debate is the nature of the bond between community members. The early twentieth century scholars of community (e.g. Park 1926/1979) stressed common geographic locality as the starting point for defining community. Hillery (1955) reviewed diverse definitions of community and found that no author denied that the area in which people reside *could* be an element of what defines their community. But some sociologists try to inject scientific precision by insisting that an *essential* feature of community is that it refer to people in units of territorial or geographic organization (e.g. Parsons 1959).

Among those who focus on geography as the defining bond among members of a community, there has been a tendency to assume as an ideal type geographic communities which are small, homogenous, and have a strong sense of group solidarity, manifesting Tonnies' (1957) ideal type of *gemeinschaft*, i.e. relations of emotion, continuity and fulfillment (see, e.g., Redfield 1947). This characterization, however, is commonly regarded as the product of nostalgic wishful thinking and "blinker-like . . . fieldwork" (Bell and Newby 1971). Geographic communities of whatever size are just as likely to have strong elements of what Tonnies characterized as *gesellschaft* — impersonal, contractual, rational relationships — and to manifest considerable heterogeneity, individualism, and alienation (Pahl 1968; Wild 1981). Thus, although studies of spatially linked groups are still conducted, there is considerable agreement that "any attempt to tie particular patterns of social relationships to specific geographic milieux is a singularly fruitless exercise" (Pahl 1968: 293).

In response to the limitations of notions of community circumscribed by geography, many scholars have come to regard communities instead as sets of social relations among people (Hillery 1955). Social relationships may run the gamut from casual acquaintance to close friend to extended family, but are usually assumed to involve some degree of personal knowledge about those with whom one has a relationship. People embedded in social relations are assumed to feel some sense of belonging (Wild 1981).

Network analysts in particular have argued that communities must be perceived as sets of relationships to other people, whether these relationships exist within or beyond specified geographic or institutional boundaries (e.g. Wellman 1982). Relationships are viewed as critical because they are the sources of emotional support, social companionship and supportive resources that are believed to be at the heart of communities. An important variant feature of communities bound by social relationships is whether or to what extent the ties between community members are strong or weak (Wellman 1982). Granovetter's (1974, 1985) work has heightened awareness that the types of resources provided through weak ties tend to differ considerably from those provided through strong ties. Strong ties may provide greater emotional and material support, but weak ties may act as bridges for ideas or information to be transferred from one group to another (see also Frenzen and Nakamoto 1994; Ward and Reingen 1990).

Some scholars of community do not assume that the bonds between people within a community need even be as strong as weak ties. They argue that the bond may be an experience, idea or thing which people have in common, whether or not they know specific others in their community, have actual social relationships with them, or live in the same geographic region. Common bonds may provide for members of a community of this kind a sense of shared identity, but such bonds are unlikely to entail the emotion or provide a level of social and tangible resources comparable to that which flows across social relationships with known others. For instance, some anthropologists have referred to and studied as a community those people whose common bond was that they had attended or identified with the rock music festival held in Woodstock, New York in 1968 (e.g Myerhoff 1975). Such communities may be planned and intentional (like a kibbutz or a club) or relatively unplanned (like an academic community) (Falk Moore and Myerhoff 1975), but in either case are expected to provide the members with a sense of identification within a larger collectively similar to Belk's (1988) notion of the "community level of self."

This review suggests that communities may be characterized as groups linked by social relationships and a sense of belonging, or by common bonds and a sense of shared identity (the difference may be more one of degree than of kind). The former kind of community would seem to be most likely to occur when members of the community can interact on a face-to-face basis over an extended period of time and in diverse situations. The latter kind of community does not, by definition, require face-to-face interaction and would seem likely to occur under a wide variety of situations.

WHAT ARE SOME COMMON PREJUDGMENTS AND PERCEPTIONS OF INTERNET CONSUMPTION COMMUNITIES?

As noted above, many ideas have appeared in the popular press regarding internet communities. Before we attempt to summarize them, we will briefly describe the types of services available on the internet through or around which consumption communities may form. Note that we regard the internet as a set of services to be consumed, and that we consider users of these services consumers; thus we speak of communities formed on or supported by the internet as consumption communities. One type of service that consumers with internet access can use is electronic mail (e-mail), a facility well known to most academics. This service allows individuals to communicate with others who also have e-mail accounts by sending them a private mail message. It also allows the user to send the same message to a group of other users specified on a "mailing list." A related but distinct service is provided by "discussion groups." Individuals with an e-mail account can "join" or "subscribe to" discussion groups purportedly focused on particular topics. As the name implies, these are groups of individuals who believe they share an interest in the particular topic area which defines the discussion group. Messages sent by any member of the discussion group are received by all members of the group, who can decide whether or not to read them and/or reply to them. Distinct again from these are "newsgroups," which are also referred to as bulletin boards. Any individual with full internet access can browse through the postings or post a message to the newsgroup (without joining, as in the case of a discussion group; note however, that users without full internet access may elect to join specific new groups by dialling in specifically to them). Other services available on the internet include access to the information stored in the "pages" of the World Wide Web (WWW). Many of these WWW "pages" are promotional materials posted by corporations; others are the products of individual — or community — initiatives. Another major category of service is file transfer protocols which enable an internet user to move a copy of some "shareware" (free software) or other information from a remote computer to the user's local computer.

There is no consensus in the popular press regarding internet communities. Some believe that the consumers of internet newsgroups and discussion groups may derive both knowledge and communion from one another, though they acknowledge that internet groups also entail the conflict, factionalism, gossip, and envy that characterize human interactions in most contexts (e.g. Barlow 1995; Rheingold 1993; Smith 1992). Others argue that computer networks are not real communities because they are formed based on choice rather than on necessity, because they tend to consist of demographically similar and privileged members, and because they can easily be exited (e.g. Kadi 1995; Sanders 1995). While we do not dismiss these observations as incorrect, a reading of the academic literature on community reveals that the same observations can be and have been made of other groups considered to be communities. Based, then, on our own initial perceptions, and the review of the literatures on both communities and the internet, we developed a number of expectations prior to our empirical study. First, we anticipated that links exhibited between members of an internet group would vary considerably, ranging from common bond through to strong tie. Second, we anticipated that the resources shared would include both information and emotional support. Third we believed that there would be some evidence that members shared a sense of identity with and/or belonging to others who participated in the group.

METHODOLOGY

Since this is a very preliminary examination, we limited our empirical study to an hermeneutic analysis (Arnold and Fischer 1994) of the listing and interchanges which occurred on a single newsgroup service over a one month period. We selected<bit.listserv.down-syn>, a group focused on Down's Syndrome, for three reasons. First, we believed that this would have the possibility for sharing a range of types of bonds. Second, we believed that this group would have certain "consumption interests" in common in addition to their principal concern and that we might learn about consumption communities in two ways through examining the text created by this group. That is, we would learn about the community made possible through internet consumption for people interested in the topic of Down's Syndrome *and* we would learn about the potential community among consumers of particular products (e.g. vitamins and drugs taken by people with Down's Syndrome) and services (e.g medical services for people with Down's Syndrome). Finally, one member of the research team had recently become interested in the topic area of Down's Syndrome because of the birth of a nephew with this condition.

As outlined by Arnold and Fischer (1994), to conduct our analysis, we began by specifying the "problem" of interest, which is described above. To try to identify our own preunderstandings, the research team spent considerable time identifying the communities of which they felt themselves to be members and their perceptions of what those communities were and did. We then compared those perceptions with what we thought we might encounter in internet newsgroups, which none of us had accessed prior to the commencement of this study (one of us was an active member of a discussion group prior to beginning the study, and all of us were steady users of e-mail for several years). We supplemented our initial understandings with our review of the academic literature on community and the popular literature on internet- based communities, and formulated these understandings as the "prior expectations" listed above. We then undertook a semiotic-structural analysis of the texts, resolving contradictions among elements of the texts through the process of hermeneutic circling. Below we describe the observations and the (self and other-related) understandings we developed and provide some textual evidence to support these understandings.

SELECTED TEXT AND INTERPRETATIONS

We begin by quoting excerpts from perhaps the most striking piece of text we encountered:

I got a request from someone on the list to tell you a little more about my son. I thought I would post it here [accessible to everyone] instead of e-mailing privately in case anyone is curious, because I have seen a lot of new names here since I started following this newsgroup last fall. My son, Karl was born last February 13. . . . It was quite a shock to all of us when he . . . turned out to have Down Syndrome and a severe heart defect! After letting me hold him for a few minutes, they whisked him off to the NICU. . . . He was born at eleven p.m. and about midnight they told me they thought he had DS and a tetralogy . . . . [F]inally at 3:00 a.m. . . . I asked if I could go hold him again. I held my sweet, peaceful baby with an oxygen tube stretched to his nose and decided that he was such a beautiful sweet baby that it was going to O.K. It turned out that my son had AV Canal . . . and Hirschsprung's Disease

also, which is a bowel defect. He had to have a colostomy done . . . . As you can see my son's life was filled with an awful lot of medical problems. As though to compensate for them though, he had a real zest for life, and all of his therapists commented on how alert he was. . . . At five months of age, he had his open heart surgery. . . . [H]e didn't do as well as expected . . . and when we were finally able to take him home it was with oxygen, a feeding tube, and with pulmonary hypertension. [After that] things settled down, and except for his eating he was acting like a pretty normal kid. He learned to roll over, played with toys, babbled . . . he just hated to eat. In December we had the bowel surgery and when he fell asleep in the hospital, his heart was really slow and there were a few other complications but we weren't that worried . . . . [J]ust a few weeks after his surgery he started to act really sick, and I was in the car to take him to an appointment . . . when he fell asleep and went into cardiac arrest. They tried for half an hour to resuscitate him. . . . [I]t was a real shock for us. I was really looking forward to watching Karl grow, and learn to eat, and sit alone, and talk, and do the things that babies and kids do. . . . Karl was 11 months old when he died. . . . I'm sorry if' I've taken up too much space. If there is anything else anyone would like to know, I'm always happy to talk about the little boy I was privileged to have, even for so short a time.

Some of the responses to this text included the following:

(1) "You did not take up too much space. You are a very brave and kindred woman to have told us about your son Karl. Thank you for reminding us how precious and short life is.

(2) Please accept my condolences on the death of your son. As I recall Karl left to live with God the same week that [another user's] baby did. I'm sure they are best friends in heaven. God bless you for having the strength to stay with the group and still be interested in our kids. You will always be a part of this group. If you ever get [near me] I'd love to share [my son] with you for a while.

One reply from the first writer was: "I got a lot of wonderful, very touching e-mail regarding my post about my son Karl. Thanks guys. This is a great group." A second revealed even more strikingly the personal nature of the contacts she had made with other members of the news group:

I'm not ready to have more kids yet, but I will certainly love any other ones I have, DS or no, and I've thought about adopting a disabled baby someday too. It's too bad that it takes something like having one of these babies yourself to realize that all people are wonderful, disabled or not.

This interchange seems to indicate reasonably strong ties, emotional sharing and a sense of belonging among these members of an internet community. Examples of seemingly less close bonds and of more purely informational sharing were also abundant. For example, one topic which attracted many postings was vitamins and nutritional supplements. One writer asked about the link between deficiency of some essential nutrient and dry skin, and for advice regarding a pending appointment with a paediatrician for metabolic testing. Another replied:

Vitamin A deficiency. . . can cause dry skin. Problems with the metabolism and/or absorption of essential fatty acids could also be contributing factors. . . . You may want to do some basic nutritional assessments of tissue vitamin levels, tissue trace mineral levels, and oxidation stress tests. . . . But there are a few issues that you may need to know in dealing with your doctor. First, vitamins and minerals need to be measured at the tissue level. Blood tests are not ideal. Doctors may not know about recent advances in testing tissue vitamin levels and may try to tell you that vitamin tests are a waste of money. Maybe blood tests are, but measuring cellular nutritional reserves are a very accurate assessment of biological nutritional deficiencies. . . . Bottom line, don't let your doctor steam roll you into not doing these state-of-the-art tests for your children. Stick to your guns and insist that they order the tests. If they refuse and won't discuss the matter, fire them and find a new doctor.

As our framing of this study indicates, we did not anticipate labelling internet based communities as "false." We believed that they could and would manifest the theoretical properties of communities: links between members ranging from common bonds to strong ties, sharing of information and emotional support resources, and an evident sense of shared identity or belonging. This consumption community, at least, seems as "real" (and as varied) as face-to-face communities may be. Perhaps a more difficult question is how this consumption community might be distinct from face-to-face communities. We address this below.

One observation we had not anticipated stemmed from our own experience as "voyeurs" or "eaves-droppers" of the conversations in the newsgroup (please note, though, that permission was obtained from those quoted in this paper). Anyone with access to internet service can monitor the newsgroup and take whatever information they seek without revealing themselves, or reciprocating with either information or emotional support. Though greater benefits may stem from fuller participation, the possibility for deriving benefits without contributing is large because of the public nature of the resources.

A second, related observation concerns the public posting of letters such as that excerpted above. The contents of this letter might be regarded as highly intimate, and in face-to-face communities might be shared only with the closest of friends and family. At the same time, in face-to-face communities, the potential is greatest for deriving emotional support from those who are closest. In this newsgroup, the relationship between the strength of a tie and the resources which might be derived from it appears modest. Relative strangers can share intense emotions.

A third observation relates to not infrequent comments about well-meaning but unhelpful friends and relatives (presumably members of the writers' face-to-face networks). For example, one writer noted that her son didn't cry much as a newborn. She then states:

> My husband and I were comfortable with his behavior but sometimes our relatives made us nervous with repeated comments about lack of crying. Believe me, when you are trying to cope with the news of DS AND falling in love with your baby it doesn't help to have people point out the differences between your baby and "normal" kids.

---

[1]This is not to say that consumption can only help to create self-selected, easily entered and exited communities. There is evidence that consumer behaviors such as gift giving are essential to establishment and reinforcement of "traditional" communities which are less self-selected and which are very difficult to enter and exit (e.g. Cheal 1988; Stack 1974).

Taking these three observations together, we formed an understanding of internet communities as liberating, in that they freed people from the obligations and the constraints that are often part of face-to-face networks. In internet communities, users are free not to talk, they are free to be emotional with those they do not know well, and they are free to distance themselves momentarily from those they normally have great allegiance to. It is almost as though internet communities can provide a relief from face-to-face communities. This does not mean that users will transfer allegiances away from one to the other, but rather that they may derive benefit from the opposing properties of each.

A second observation concerning the potentially unique nature of internet communities relates to the way that power or control may be redistributed through the copious, immediate, and easy sharing of information they facilitate. In particular, the community of consumers of particular commodities — for instance, the medical services referred to in the second interchange above — acquire power by recognizing their common interests and sharing information regarding products and services. Many of the exchanges regarding products and services of mutual interest to the users of this newsgroup had a tone of defiance of authority. The quote above regarding "sticking to your guns" with doctors is typical. Another example is the following advice regarding obtaining services from local recreation facilities: "Do not supplicate. Your child has a right to be there, and the rec department has a legal obligation to accommodate. Don't ask for favors; assert your rights." Based on this observation, we developed an understanding of internet-based consumption communities as distinctively empowering, not simply because of they access to information they provide but because of the sense of collective identity forged with other consumers.

CONCLUSIONS

If there seems any main message to be drawn from this preliminary empirical investigation of the use of the internet, it is that communities *may be* created through consumption of this technology, and that they may be uniquely liberating and empowering. At the same time, they are (as critics complain) self-selective, voluntary in nature, and easy to enter and exit. It is hazardous to generalize, but it is possible that some of the communities which might be built around or through the common consumption of other offerings might share similar properties.[1] Consider, for example, the community which Arnould and Price (1993) discovered emerging among co-consumers of a river-rafting service. Like the internet users we "observed," these consumers self selected the opportunity to enter the community and could voluntarily opt out of it. Also like the internet community, consumers of the river rafting service tended to find the experience liberating and empowering. Much more research on consumption communities is needed before we will understand more completely their nature and variety.

If, however, communities built around the common consumption of a good or service tend to share the properties suggested above what might the implications be? Bell and Newby (1974) have noted that sociologists tend to confuse what community *is* and what community *should be*. The same appears to hold true for contemporary critics of the community derived from internet use in particular and (perhaps) consumption in general. It is a falsely nostalgic ideal to expect communities of any kind to conform completely to Tonnies' ideal *gemeinschaft* type wherein relations are characterized by emotion, continuity and fulfillment. Internet consumption can lead to the formation and maintenance of many diverse forms of community. Some, but not all, of these will inevitably be closer to Tonnies' alternate *geselleschaft* . Still it would appear that communities founded upon the common bond of interest in a particular topic — or product — *can* evolve into communities that provide the resources that we might (often vainly) seek from geographically local or face-to-face communities.[2]

One social policy implication of this work would appear to be that providing wider access to the consumption communities formed around and through the internet could be beneficial. At present, access to the internet is largely restricted to those who can afford the service, though efforts to provide wide-spread access through "free-net" links is underway in some centers. Even if the barrier of income is reduced, however, there are likely to be remaining obstacles of a more socially constructed nature. Internet critics and enthusiasts alike (e.g. Barlow 1995; Lasch 1994) fear that users tend to be disproportionately privileged and highly educated. It seems likely that there are systemic factors that discourage access to internet-based communities for those who are most in need of the resources such communities might provide. In summary we believe that consumption communities, particularly internet-based communities, should be neither sanctified or demonized: however, to increase whatever value they may offer, we believe that attention must be paid to increasing access to such communities among those groups systematically less likely to enter them. At present — and perhaps inevitably — internet communities may reinforce existing power and privilege structures.

REFERENCES

Arnould, Eric and Linda Price (1993), "River Magic: Extraordinary Experience and the Extended Service Encounter," *Journal of Consumer Research*, 20, 1 (June), 24-45.

Belk, Russell (1988), "Possessions and the Extended Self," *Journal of Consumer Research*, 15, 2 (September), 139-168.

Barlow, John Perry (1995), "Is There a There in Cyberspace?" *Utne Reader*, 68 (March-April), 53-56.

Bell, C. and H. Newby (1971), *Community Studies*, London: Allen and Unwin.

Boorstin, Daniel (1973) *Americans: The Democratic Experience*, New York: Random House.

Campbell, Colin (1987), *The Romantic Ethic and The Spirit of Modern Capitalism*, Oxford, England: Basil Blackwell.

Cheal, David (1988) *The Gift Economy*, London: Routledge

Drucker, Peter (1994), "The Age of Social Transformation," *The Atlantic Monthly*, November, 53-80.

Falk Moore, Sally and Barbara Myerhoff (1975), "Prologue" in *Symbol and Politics in Communal Ideology*, eds. Sally Falk Moore and Barbara Myerhoff, Ithaca: Cornell University Press, pp. 13-23.

Frenzen, Jonathan and Kent Nakamoto (1993), "Structure, Cooperation and the Flow of Market Information," Journal of Consumer Research, 20, 3 (December), 360-375.

Granovetter, Mark (1973), "The Strength of Weak Ties," *American Journal of Sociology*, Vol. 78 (6), 1360-1380.

_____ (1985), "Economic Action and Social Structure: The Problem of Embeddedness," *American Journal of Sociology*, 91(3), 481-510.

Gove, Philip (ed.) (1981), *Webster's Unabridged Third New International Dictionary*, Springfield, MA: Merrian Webster Inc.

Hillery, George (1955), "Definitions of Community: Areas of Agreement," *Rural Sociology*, 20, 194-204.

Kadi, M. (1995), "Welcome to Cyberia," *Utne Reader*, 68 (March-April), 57-59.

Lasch, Christopher (1978), *The Culture of Narcissism: American Life in the Age of Diminishing Expectations*, New York: Norton.

_____ (1991), *The True and Only Heaven*, New York: Norton.

_____ (1994), *The Revolt of the Elites and the Betrayal of Democracy*, New York: Norton.

Loughlin, Thomas (1993), "Virtual Relationships: The Solitary World of CMC," *Interpersonal Computing and Technology: An Electronic Journal for the 21st Century*, 1 (1) (no page numbers).

Myerhoff, Barbara (1975), "Organization and Ecstasy: Deliberate and Accidental Communitas among Huichol Indians and American Youth," *Symbol and Politics in Communal Ideology*, eds. Sally Falk Moore and Barbara Myerhoff, Ithaca: Cornell University Press, pp. 34-67.

Pahl, R. (1968), "The Urban-Rural Continuum" in *Readings in Urban Sociology*, ed. R. Pahl, Oxford: Pergamon Press.

Parsons, Talcott (1959), "The Principal Structures of Community," in *Community*, ed. C. Friedrich, New York: Liberal Arts Press.

Park, Robert (1926/1979), "The Urban Community as a Spatial Pattern and a Moral Order," reprinted in *Urban Social Segregatation*, ed. C. Peach, London: Longman, 21-31.

Poplin, Dennis (1979), *Communities: A Survey of Theories and Methods of Research* (second edition), New York: MacMillan Publishing Co.

Redfield, Robert (1947), "The Folk Society," *American Journal of Sociology*, 52 (3), 293-308.

Rheingold, Howard (1993), *The Virtual Community*, Reading MA: Addison-Wesley.

Sanders, Scott (1994), "The Web of Life," *Utne Reader*, 68 (March-April), 69-71.

Smith, Marc (1992) "Voices from the WELL: The Logic of the Virtual Commons," Masters Thesis, Department of Sociology, UCLA.

Stack, Carol (1974), *All Our Kin: Strategies for Survival in a Black Community*, Toronto: Fitzhenry & Whiteside.

Talbot, Stephen (1994), "Countercultural Computing," *Interpersonal Computing: An Electronic Journal for the 21st Century*," 2 (2), 74-87.

Tonnies, Ferdinand (1957) *Community and Association*, London: Routledge and Kegan Paul.

Ward, James and Peter Reingen (1990), "Sociocognitive Analysis of Group Decision Making among Consumers," *Journal of Consumer Research*, 17, 3 (December), 245-262.

Wellman, Barry (1982), "Studying Personal Communities," *Social Structure and Network Analysis*, eds. Peter Marsden and Nan Lin, Beverly Hills CA,: Sage.

Wild, Ronald (1981), *Australian Community Studies and Beyond*, Sydney: George Allen and Unwin.2

---

[2] We acknowledge, of course, that such the internet technology like any other can be used in diverse ways for quite opposite ends, and that it is possible that internet use will ultimately be dominantly isolationist and antithetical to community (cf Loughlin 1993; Talbot 1994).

The Relationship Between Environmental Issue Involvement and Environmentally-Conscious Behavior: An Exploratory Study

Linda R. Stanley, Colorado State University
Karen M. Lasonde, Colorado State University

ABSTRACT

The effect of environmental issue involvement on both overall and specific types of environmentally-conscious behavior, including consumer behavior, is examined. Where information is easily gathered and there is not an initial capital investment, involvement and behavior are significantly correlated. On the other hand, involvement is not significantly correlated to behavior when that behavior results in private benefits to the individual. Finally, where there are initial capital costs and specialized knowledge required, the behavior is performed fairly infrequently by all groups but somewhat more frequently by high involvement groups.

The 1990s are being called the decade of the environment, and consumer interest in the environment appears to be high. According to Wasik (1992), most open-ended surveys find that 70-90% of consumers are willing to do their part for the environment; 50% have claimed they would make green purchases. Producers of consumer goods are responding to this demand. The Marketing Intelligence Service reports that between 1985 and 1990, over 700 "green" products were introduced—a rate 20 times higher than all other regular product introductions, and 20% of all new household items in 1990 boasted they were environmentally friendly (Schorsch 1990).

Although environmental issues are just now becoming an important aspect in business decision making, environmental issues have appeared in the marketing literature since the early 1970s. The literature during that time included examining concern for the causes of air pollution (Kassarjian 1971), the use of non-phosphate detergents (Kinnear and Taylor 1973), and consumption activities (Webster 1975).[1] During the early 1980s, conservation behaviors of consumers became a focus. Research during this time covered such areas as the motivations for everyday conservation behaviors (De Young 1985-1986), the personal satisfactions derived from conservation activities (De Young 1986), the determinants of ecologically responsible consumption patterns (Balderjahn 1988), the characteristics of participants engaged in conservation behaviors (Granzin and Olsen 1991), and the types of conservation behaviors in which consumers can engage (Ritchie and McDougall 1985).

Research interest in environmental consumption behavior seemed to wane especially in the mid to late 1980s, but a resurgence of marketing and consumer behavior interest in environmental issues has recently occurred. The *Journal of Public Policy and Marketing* devoted a special issue in Fall 1991 to environmental issues with a broad variety of topics explored. Additional research in the 1990s on environmental marketing issues includes measuring environmental consciousness (Burnett, Bacon, and Hutton 1993, Troy 1993), measuring the effects of moderating variables on environmental buying behavior (Moore 1993) and scale development to measure such things as consumers' attitudes toward the environment (Rolston and di Benedetto 1994) and the "green gap" between an ideal green product and what is available (Michael and Smith 1993).

ENVIRONMENTAL BEHAVIOR

Overall, the environmental marketing literature has not provided either consistent results concerning relationships between variables or effective segmentation schemes. Little is still known about who engages in what types of environmental behavior and for what reasons. One reason why this might be true is because many of these studies have researched particular types of environmental behaviors, such as purchasing laundry detergents, recycling, disposing of garbage, and voting. Even where more general measures of environmental consciousness have been developed and used, the research still focused on product buying behavior of individuals.

However, there are many environmental behaviors that an individual may choose to engage in; buying environmentally is only one of them. Some individuals will choose to engage in as many environmental behaviors as they have the opportunity to; some will choose several behaviors to perform, one possibly being "green" buying; others will choose to perform no environmental behaviors. Most environmental behaviors take some investment at least initially in time, money and/or physical and mental effort. For example, buying "green" products may cost more; recycling takes time; and in general, most environmental behaviors are at least perceived to be more expensive and to take more time. Therefore, even individuals who appear to have positive attitudes toward the environment or environmental behaviors may not engage in specific environmental behaviors since they may be choosing a portfolio of behaviors based on perceived benefits and costs. This suggests that it may be appropriate to study a broad range of environmental behaviors to gain further understanding into these behaviors. If individuals choose from a portfolio of environmental behaviors, then different types of environmental behaviors will show different relationships to variables that are likely to impact individuals' ability and motivation to evaluate the costs and benefits and actually perform the behavior.

In this paper, we develop a broad scale of environmental behavior that encompasses many different types of behaviors, including purchase, consumption, and disposal. We then test whether the types of behaviors measured by the scale are differentially related to a variable that is likely to impact the evaluation of costs and benefits. We chose involvement in environmental issues as this variable. First, we would expect that an overall measure of environmental behavior would be positively related to involvement in environmental issues.[2] But more importantly involvement is likely to impact individual's perceptions of the costs and benefits of behaving in an environmentally-conscious manner because of the key role that information plays in evaluating and performing environmental behavior.

---

[1] For a more complete list of environmental marketing references see Lasonde (1994).

[2] Although a clear consensus has yet to be reached in completely defining the meaning of the involvement construct, most researchers agree that the level of involvement can be understood by the degree of personal relevance or importance that a decision or issue holds in the mind of the consumer (Park and Young 1986, Celsi and Olson 1988). Therefore, it can be expected that high issue related relevance should lead to formation of beliefs and then attitudes which are more likely to be acted upon than low issue related relevance.

An evaluation of perceived benefits and costs will be, in part, dependent upon an individual's knowledge about the true costs and benefits of the behavior. Through information processing individuals learn about opportunities to behave environmentally and then evaluate these opportunities. Those more involved with environmental issues may be more likely to evaluate the true merits of any particular behavior, and therefore, may engage in a different set of environmental behaviors than those who are less involved in environmental issues.

Actually performing a behavior often requires that an individual at least initially invest in information search and processing to gain the task knowledge necessary to carry through the intention. Those who are more highly involved in environmental issues may be more likely to engage in those behaviors that require some sort of specialized knowledge or where barriers to action are information based. An individual may have an attitude that recycling is good, but if they do not believe that environmental issues are important or personally relevant then they are less likely to seek the information that will be required in order to engage in recycling.[3]

METHODOLOGY

Because this study is exploratory in nature, a convenience sample of approximately 400 Principles of Marketing students was used. Nonprobability sampling of college students produced a relatively homogenous sample that allows exploratory research to reveal a more general theoretical understanding (Calder, Phillips, and Tybout 1981).

Survey Instrument

The first section utilized the 20-item Personal Involvement Inventory (PII) developed by Zaichkowsky (1985). Respondents' levels of involvement in environmental issues were measured by asking them "to judge concern for environmental issues such as solid waste, resource depletion, air/water pollution, chemical additives and harm to nature". These five environmental issues were taken from Troy (1993) as the five dimensions that define the construct of consumer environmental consciousness. Much research on environmental consciousness has focused on very specific environmental concerns, such as packaging and recycling, but this study required a comprehensive definition of consumer environmental consciousness such as that proposed by Troy (1993). In order to measure respondents' involvement with the construct of environmental consciousness, the five issues were listed on the top of the involvement scale to ensure that each respondent was rating their involvement based on the same definition.[4]

The purpose of the second section of the survey was to measure a broad range of respondents' environmental behaviors. We did not find an already developed scale because available scales were either borrowed from other disciplines, outdated in comparison to environmental behavior today, or focused on environmental products or on a specific environmental behavior.

To develop a scale to measure environmental behavior, Churchill's (1979) paradigm for developing better measures was used. A list of 46 questions was developed and pretested. Table 1

lists the environmental behaviors (in shortened form). The questions came from the five areas that define environmental consciousness, as well as three dimensions of behavior—purchase, consumption and disposal. A workbook, *A Global Action Workbook*, that describes a comprehensive action plan for households wishing to behave environmentally was also used to ensure that the set of environmental behavior items was exhaustive. The questions, placed on a 7-point Likert scale, asked respondents how often they perform a variety of environmental behaviors. Respondents were given benchmarks for each number on the scale, e.g. 1=never, 2=almost never, 3=occasionally, 4=half the time, ... 7=always.[5]

RESULTS

The final survey yielded 301 usable responses. Responses were considered unusable is they were incomplete. Summary statistics and frequency distributions were calculated for each of the 20 items on the involvement scale. Items were scored 1 for low involvement and 7 for high involvement. Means for the 20 items range between 4.53 and 6.16, and standard deviations are all less than 1.60. Reliability analysis on the involvement scale yielded a Cronbach's alpha of .95. This is consistent with Zaichkowsky's (1985) alphas of .95 to .97 for the same scale measuring involvement with four products.

An overall distribution of respondents' involvement with environmental issues was tabulated by summing each respondent's answers for the 20 items into a new variable called INVOLVE. Totaling the 20 items gives a score that can range from 20 to 140. The actual sample range was 23 to 140; 14 respondents had scores of 140. The frequency distribution for INVOLVE is skewed to the right with a mean of 111, showing that the respondents are highly involved with environmental issues.

---

[3]The importance of information is seen in a study by De Young (1989) that examined the difference between recyclers and non-recyclers. His results suggested that recyclers and non-recyclers were similar in their pro-recycling attitudes, extrinsic motivation, and the degree to which they viewed recycling as a trivial activity. They differed significantly, however, in the degree to which they required additional information about recycling.

[4]This section of the survey was pretested in two different forms. One form listed the five environmental issues at the top of a single involvement scale. The second form had five individual involvement scales with a single environmental issue at the top of each scale. The pretest showed that the "high profile" environmental issues, such as air/water pollution, were highly skewed towards high involvement. This shows that the individual involvement scales were capturing small elements of involvement with certain environmental issues. However, for this study, a more general measure of involvement with environmental consciousness, as defined by all five issues together, was needed.

[5]The environmental behavior scale was pretested on a sample of 87. Reliability analysis produced a coefficient alpha of .86, which shows good internal consistency (Churchill 1979). Many of the questions were edited further because of questions raised by respondents while the survey was being given. The frequency distributions from the pretest statistics showed that answers to some questions were skewed to one side of the scale or the other, while others were more normally distributed. This reveals that the questions ask about a variety of environmental behaviors ranging from those that are commonly performed to those that are only performed by a few. Also included among the environmental behavior questions were three social desirability questions. A common problem often mentioned in the environmental literature is respondents over-reporting their environmental behavior because acting environmentally is the socially desirable thing to do (Crowne and Marlowe 1964). If survey respondents in this study demonstrate a social-desirability response set it may not be possible to conclude anything from their survey responses because they are not true responses.

TABLE 1

Means, Correlations to INVOLVE, and Factor Loadings of Items in the Survey

	Mean	Correlation to INVOLVE	Factor Loading
Factor 1 PURCHASE			
buy biodegradable laundry soap	3.16	.311*	.658
buy recyclable products	3.98	.423*	.647
buy natural hygiene products	2.70	.189*	.617
reduce overall consumption	3.33	.334*	.603
buy organic	3.01	.175*	.598
buy products in recycled packages	3.97	.393*	.593
buy local products	3.75	.124*	.545
buy alternative cleaners	2.52	.133*	.522
flush toilet less	3.07	.251*	.504
buy food in bulk	3.27	.139*	.496
buy products in reusable containers	3.73	.208*	.439
Factor 2 RECYCLE			
recycle plastics	3.32	.291*	.799
recycle glass	3.33	.275*	.773
recycle newspaper	4.72	.193*	.738
recycle tin cans	3.16	.247*	.707
recycle aluminum	4.96	.238*	.677
recycle magazines	2.57	.103	.630
recycle grocery bags	4.42	.284*	.610
recycle white paper	4.25	.238*	.521
Factor 3 MAINTAIN			
keep tires inflated	5.17	.066	.722
keep engine tuned	4.51	.115	.680
add/replace weatherstripping	2.94	.025	.497
recycle motor oil	3.34	.033	.460
Factor 4 CURTAIL			
turn air conditioning down	5.32	.236*	.548
turn heat down	4.25	.118*	.532
conserve bathroom water	4.80	.202*	.531
fuel efficient car	5.17	.212*	.442
conserve tap water	3.72	.238*	.436
thermostat setting	3.38	.243*	.417
Factor 5 TRANSPORT			
avoid driving	3.31	.257*	.721
walk or bike	4.08	.156*	.702
use public transportation	2.68	.039	.472
car pool	2.77	.188*	.457
Factor 6 EFFICIENT			
install toilet dams	1.57	.001	.509
replace light bulbs	1.94	.224*	.454
buy water saving devices	2.14	.126*	.450
turn temperature down on water heater	2.56	.147*	.365
Items on Survey Not in Above Factors			
avoid aerosol containers	4.92	.350*	
avoid burning wood for heat	5.25	.111	
conserve water in shower	1.82	.133*	
pour oil, paint, toxics down drain	6.00	.154*	
compost kitchen and organic waste	1.89	.050	
bring own grocery bags to store	1.58	.228*	
plant trees to help environment	2.65	-.051	
eat less animal products	2.74	.320*	
avoid disposable products	4.76	.118*	

*correlation is significantly different at .05 level

TABLE 2
Mean Responses of Behavior Variables and Correlations With INVOLVE

	Mean Response[a]	Standard Deviation	Correlation With INVOLVE
BEHAVE37	3.51	.87	.394*
BEHAVE46	3.53	.83	.420*
PURCHASE	3.29	1.07	.376*
RECYCLE	3.85	1.44	.325*
MAINTAIN	3.95	1.51	.096
CURTAIL	4.42	1.23	.315*
TRANSPORT	3.32	1.38	.253*
EFFICIENT	1.99	1.23	.148*

[a]The rating scale ranged from 1=never to 7=always.
*Is significantly different from zero at .05 level.

Environmental Behavior Scale

Means and standard deviations for each of the 46 items on the environmental behavior scale are presented in Table 1. The 7-point Likert scale was coded 1 for a response of "Never" and 7 for a response of "Always". The means for the environmental behavior questions ranged from 1.57 for installing toilet dams to 6.00 for avoiding pouring oil and toxics down the drain. These means suggest that the scale includes a diversity of behaviors that range from those that are rarely performed to those that are frequently performed.[6] The results of the reliability analysis on the environmental behavior scale yielded a Cronbach's alpha of .90, showing high internal consistency of the scale. Deletion of any of the items did not alter the alpha by more than .01.

The environmental behavior items were factor analyzed using principal components analysis, varimax rotation for factor extraction and mean substitution for missing values. To obtain a reasonable and interpretable number of factors, factor solutions were attempted by forcing a specified number of factors to be extracted. A six-factor solution was determined to best fit the data because of the factors' interpretability and the summary statistics.

The exploratory nature of this study enables us to retain items that may provide good information, even though the statistics do not look as strong as would be desired. However, items were eliminated for the following reasons: a factor loading less than .35, low item to total correlation, or poor fit logically into a factor. This reduced the original number of 46 environmental behavior items by 9 and left 37 items.[7] The Eigenvalues ranged from 10.20 to 1.49, and 41.7 percent of the variance in the data was explained by the six factors. The six factors, with their corresponding items and the items' factor loadings are presented in column 3 of Table 1.

---

[6]The statistics for the social desirability questions showed no evidence of social desirability bias.

[7]Turning down the thermostat on your water heater, was moved from factor 1, purchase behaviors, to factor 6, efficiency behaviors, because it loaded greater than .36 on both factors, but was a more logical fit into factor 6. Because this research is exploratory, it is more useful to try to determine the causes for multiple loadings, rather than eliminate items that contribute information.

In creating the questions for the environmental behavior section of the survey, the activities of purchase, consumption, and disposal were used as the basis to define environmental behavior. Factor 1 reflects purchase behaviors; factor 2 reflects recycle/disposal behaviors. Factors 3 through 6 reflect consumption behaviors similar to those used by Ritchie and McDougall (1985), which they called curtailment, maintenance, and efficiency. Factor 3, maintenance behaviors, are behaviors that ensure equipment is working properly, such as keeping the tires on your car inflated and keeping your engine tuned. Factor 4, curtailment behaviors, are behaviors that show reduced living patterns, such as using less heat, air conditioning, and water. Factor 5, transportation/curtailment behaviors, shows changes in transportation use, such as avoiding driving on high pollution days. And finally, factor 6, efficiency behaviors, are one-time, structural modifications that consumers are engaging in, such as installing toilet dams.

The environmental behavior items were then summed in three ways: (1) the 37 remaining items were summed for each respondent into a variable called BEHAVE37, (2) all 46 environmental behavior items were summed for each respondent into a variable called BEHAVE46, and (3) the items in each of the six factors were summed for each respondent into variables called PURCHASE, RECYCLE, MAINTAIN, CURTAIL, TRANSPORT, and EFFICIENT. Summary statistics for these new variables are in columns 1 and 2 of Table 2. Note that the mean responses for all but one of the summed behavior variables are less than 4.42, suggesting that the mean respondent performs these behaviors less than half the time.

Correlations

INVOLVE was correlated with each of the summed behavior variables. These correlations appear in column 3 of Table 2. The correlations of INVOLVE with the overall behavioral variables, BEHAVE37 and BEHAVE46, are .39 and .42, respectively. These are significantly different from zero at r<.000 and relatively high, especially for the early stages of research. The correlations of INVOLVE with each of the six variables representing the different factors range from .10 to .38. The factor, PURCHASE, had the highest correlation with INVOLVE (.376); RECYCLE had the next highest correlation (.325); CURTAIL had the third highest correlation (.315). The only correlation (.096) not significantly different from zero was for the factor, MAINTAIN.

TABLE 3
Behavior Means for Different Levels of Involvement

	Involvement Levels		
Behavior[a]	Low	Medium	High
PURCHASE	2.79*	3.26**	3.91
RECYCLE	3.19*	3.86**	4.58
MAINTAIN	3.84	3.80**	4.40
CURTAIL	3.81*	4.49**	4.94
TRANSPORT	2.83*	3.36	3.78
EFFICIENT	1.77	1.97	2.32
BEHAVE37	3.05*	3.49**	4.05
BEHAVE46	3.05*	3.52**	4.06

[a]The rating scale ranged from 1=never to 7=always.
*Is significantly different from behavior mean for medium involvement level.
**Is significantly different from behavior mean for high involvement level.

Respondents were categorized into three involvement groups, indicative of low involvement, medium involvement, and high involvement according to Zaichkowsky (1985).[8] Behavior means were calculated for each involvement group across all behavior variables. These results are in Table 3. Analyses of variance showed a significant difference among the behavior means at the three different levels of involvement for each behavior variable. T-tests were used to compare the behavior mean for one level of involvement with the behavior mean for another level of involvement. It was found that the means for different levels of involvement were significantly different except for TRANSPORT at medium and high involvement (r<.06), EFFICIENT at medium and high involvement (r<.11), EFFICIENT at low and medium involvement (r<.19), and MAINTAIN at low and medium involvement (r<.866). The largest percentage difference between behavior means at low and high involvement were for RECYCLE (30.4%) and PURCHASE (28.6%) while the smallest percentage difference was for MAINTAIN (12.7%).

DISCUSSION

The distribution of respondents' scores of their involvement with environmental issues shows that most individuals in this sample are relatively highly involved. This is probably to be expected since this is a student group. University students tend to more aware of environmental issues because they are more exposed to them. For example, the student newspaper often carries articles of an environmental nature, there are environmental student groups that hand out information on campus, and students are required to take a pre-approved environmental course before graduating. This finding is also consistent with research that has found younger persons hold greater attitudinal concern for environmental issues (for example, see Buttel and Flinn 1978).

On the other hand, the mean responses for all but one of the summed behavior variables were less than the midpoint of the scale,

[8]Subjects whose involvement scores fell into the bottom 25 percent of the overall distribution were classified as having low involvement with the product. Subjects whose scores fell into the middle 50 percent were classified as having medium involvement, and subjects whose involvement scores were in the top 25 percent were classified as having high involvement.

suggesting that the mean respondent only performs these sets of behaviors less than half of the time. The highest mean response was for the factor, CURTAIL; the mean respondent performed these behaviors over half of the time. This may reflect, in part, the cost savings that immediately accrue to an individual who performs these behaviors. The mean respondent also performed the sets of behaviors in RECYCLE and MAINTAIN about half the time. The survey city has a city-wide curbside recycling program and the university has recycling bins for newspaper and aluminum all over campus and recycling bins for other items at the student center, making these behaviors relatively easy. On the other hand, some of the behaviors in MAINTAIN are done not just for environmental reasons, but to save money in the long-run, for example, keeping a car tuned up or installing weatherstripping. These things may help explain the relatively high mean response for MAINTAIN. The mean respondent performed the sets of behaviors in PURCHASE and TRANSPORT occasionally (less than half of the time), which may indicate their relative inconvenience, often higher cost, and lack of availability. Finally, the set of behaviors in EFFICIENT was performed, on average, almost never. These behaviors represent investments by the individual and some are likely to be difficult for renters, 83.8% of the sample.

The correlations show that involvement with environmental issues is significantly related to overall environmental behaviors. In addition, it is correlated to some but not all individual sets of behaviors. These results are also borne out by the significant differences between the behavior means at the three different levels of involvement. Involvement with environmental issues appears to have the greatest effect on purchase behaviors and recycle behaviors and minimal effect on maintenance behaviors. For the overall behavior variables, BEHAVE37 and BEHAVE46, the difference between the high involvement group's and the low involvement group's behavioral means is 1, which although is a significant difference is not overwhelmingly large.

The variables with the greatest difference in behavioral means between high and low involvement individuals, RECYCLE and PURCHASE, are both variables that have little economic benefit in performing them (and may actually have an economic cost). In addition, they do require some information about how to perform them. This information often comes in the guise of what can be done to benefit the environment and is often fairly accessible. On the other hand, the variable with the least difference, MAINTAIN, is likely to have economic and other private benefits in performing the behaviors associated with it. In addition, the information required to perform these behaviors is often not associated with environmental issues at all. EFFICIENT also had a relatively low correlation with involvement and relatively low means across the three involvement levels. Behaviors within this factor often require very specialized knowledge to perform and an initial expenditure that respondents may be unwilling to pay (in exchange for costs savings that will accrue over time). This would be especially true for this sample because of the large number of renters.

CONCLUSION

Where information is more easily gathered and is associated with environmental issues and where there is not an initial capital investment associated with the behavior, involvement and behavior appear to be significantly correlated. On the other hand, involvement does not appear to be significantly correlated to behavior when that behavior results in significant private benefits to the individual. Finally, where there are initial capital costs and specialized knowledge required, the behavior is performed fairly infrequently by all groups but somewhat more frequently by high involvement groups.

If information is a key variable in the performance of environmental behaviors, then how the consumer attends to this information will be relevant to understanding how and why a consumer makes environmental behavior decisions. Some have argued that many consumer decisions do not involve extensive search for information or a comprehensive evaluation of choice alternatives (Olshavsky and Granbois 1979). That is, low involvement decisions are made differently than those that are higher in involvement. Others have suggested that high involvement with consumer decisions will lead the consumer to search for more information and spend more time and effort making an appropriate choice (Clarke and Belk 1978). If this is the case, an appraisal of the consumer's level of involvement with environmental issues may tell us what sort of search and evaluation patterns we can expect from consumers with different levels of involvement.

REFERENCES

Balderjahn, I., (1988), "Personality Variables and Environmental Attitudes as Predictors of Ecologically Responsible Consumption Patterns," *Journal of Business Research*, (17), 51-56.

Burnett, John J., Bacon, Donald R., and Hutton, R. Bruce (1993), "Profiling Levels of Environmental Consciousness: A Cluster Analytic Approach," *Combined Proceedings of the American Marketing Association*, (Summer), 117-118.

Buttel, Frederick H. & William L. Flinn (1978), "Social Class and Mass Environmental Beliefs: A Reconsideration," *Environment and Behavior*, 10 (September), 433-450.

Calder, Bobby J., Lynn Phillips, and Alice M. Tybout (1981), "Designing Research for Application," *Journal of Consumer Research*, 8 (September), 197-207.

Celsi, Richard L. and Jerry C. Olson (1988), "The Role of Involvement in Attention and Comprehension Processes," *Journal of Consumer Research*, 15 (September), 210-224.

Churchill, Gilbert A. (1979), "A Paradigm for Developing Better Measures of Marketing Constructs," *Journal of Marketing Research*, 16 (February), 54-73.

Clarke, Keith and Russell W. Belk (1978), "The Effects of Product Involvement and Task Definition on Anticipated Consumer Effort," in *Advances in Consumer Research*, Vol. 5, ed. H. Keith Hunt, Ann Arbor, MI: Association for Consumer Research, 313-318.

De Young, Raymond (1985-86), "Encouraging Environmentally Appropriate Behavior: The Role of Intrinsic Motivation," *Journal of Environmental Systems*, 15 (4), 281-291.

_____ (1986), "Some Psychological Aspects of Recycling: The Structure of Conservation Satisfactions," *Environment and Behavior*, 18 (July), 435-449.

_____ (1988-89), "Exploring the Difference Between Recyclers and Non-recyclers: The Role of Information," *Journal of Environmental Systems*, 18 (4), 341-351.

Granzin, Kent L. and Olsen, Janeen E. (1991), "Characterizing Participants in Activities Protecting the Environment," *Journal of Public Policy and Marketing*, 10 (Fall), 1-27.

Kassarjian, Harold H. (1971), "Incorporating Ecology Into Marketing Strategy: The Case of Air Pollution," *Journal of Marketing*, 35 (July), 61-65.

Kinnear, Thomas C. and Taylor, James R. (1973), "The Effect of Ecological Concern on Brand Perceptions," *Journal of Marketing Research*, 10 (May), 191-197.

Lasonde, Karen M. (1994), *The Relationship Between Environmental Issue Involvement and Environmentally Conscious Behavior: An Exploratory Study*, Master Thesis, Colorado State University.

Michael, Judd H. and Smith, Paul M. (1993), "The "Green Gap" in Proenvironmental Attitudes and Product Availability: Parental Tradeoffs in Diapering Decision-Making," *Proceedings of the 1993 Marketing and Public Policy Conference*, Mary Jane Sheffet, ed., 92-108.

Moore, Karl James (1993), "Emerging Themes in Environmental Consumer Behavior," *Proceedings of the 1993 Marketing and Public Policy Conference*, Mary Jane Sheffet, ed., 109-122.

Olshavsky, Richard W. and Donald H. Granbois (1979), "Consumer Decision Making—Fact or Fiction?" *Journal of Consumer Research*, 6 (September), 93-100.

Park, C. Whan and S. Mark Young (1986), "Consumer Response to Television Commercials: The Impact of Involvement and Background Music on Brand Attitude Formation," *Journal of Marketing Research*, 23 (February), 11-24.

Ritchie, J.R. and McDougall, G.H.G. (1985), "Designing and Marketing Consumer Energy Conservation Policies and Programs: Implications From a Decade of Research," *Journal of Public Policy and Marketing*, 4, 14-32.

Rolston, Clyde P. and di Benedetto, C. Anthony (1994), "Developing a Greenness Scale: An Exploration of Behavior Versus Attitude," *Combined Proceedings of the American Marketing Association*, (Winter), 335-340.

Schorsch, Jonathan (1990), "Are Corporations Playing Clean With Green?", *Business and Society Review*, (Fall), 6-9.

Troy, Lisa Collins (1993), "Consumer Environmental Consciousness: A Conceptual Framework and Exploratory Investigation," *Combined Proceedings of the American Marketing Association*, (Summer), 106-114.

Webster, Frederick E. (1975), "Determining the Characteristics of the Socially Conscious Consumer," *Journal of Consumer Research*, 2 (December), 188-196.

Zaichkowsky, Judith Lynn (1985), "Measuring the Involvement Construct," *Journal of Consumer Research*, 12 (December), 341-352.

Ecological Information Receptivity of Hispanic and Anglo Americans

Linda L. Golden, University of Texas at Austin
Judy K. Frels, University of Texas at Austin
Vern C. Vincent, University of Texas-Pan American
Gilberto de los Santos, University of Texas-Pan American

As the enactment of NAFTA increases trade across the United States and Mexico border, the dissemination of ecological information to consumers in this area will increase in importance. The purpose of this study is to explore receptivity to information between Hispanic and Anglo Americans in the context of dissonance theory and selective exposure to information. It explores the following questions: What factors influence receptivity to ecological information, and are there differences between Hispanic and Anglo Americans on these factors? Dissonance theory suggests that those individuals who currently exhibit ecologically-conscious attitudes and behaviors will be most receptive to ecological information.

No previous research was identified that investigated differences in information receptivity between Hispanic and Anglo Americans. However, there has been recently a considerable amount of attention directed toward the study of Hispanic consumer behavior which is summarized below.

PREVIOUS RESEARCH ON HISPANIC CONSUMER BEHAVIOR

Over the last decade a great deal of research has investigated different aspects of consumer behavior for various subcultures in the United States, including Hispanics. The need for research on Hispanic markets specifically is often discussed in conjunction with figures which state that in the near future Hispanics will overtake African Americans as the largest minority group in the United States (Exeter 1987). In addition, the need for additional research on Hispanics is supported by surveys of various industry groups, such as packaged goods manufacturers (Albonetti and Dominguez 1989). Clearly, the Hispanic subculture in the United States has been identified as an important group of individuals with respect to the dollar impact of their consumption behavior.

The published research conducted thus far on Hispanic consumers has focused on three broad areas: levels of cultural assimilation of Hispanics living in the United States, segmentation of the Hispanic market, and comparison of Hispanic and Anglo consumer behaviors, with many studies combining two of these areas.

Cultural Assimilation Studies

Studies of cultural assimilation or acculturation have typically focused on changes in the behavior patterns of Hispanics in areas such as language, food, dress, information search, and consumption patterns. The Hispanic acculturation research has suggested that Hispanics' consumption patterns cannot be viewed as a simple median between their culture of origin and the dominant culture in the United States. Instead, it is proposed that these patterns represent a unique combination of elements from the culture of origin and ideas about the dominant culture which may be outdated by several years (Wallendorf and Reilly 1983; Penaloza 1994). Other studies have presented contrary findings, suggesting that Hispanics' consumption patterns fall on a continuum between the two cultures, depending on the level of acculturation of the sample (Faber, O'Guinn, and McCarty 1987).

Webster (1992) found that level of cultural identification can significantly influence the types of information search undertaken. High-Hispanic identifiers, or those Hispanics who more frequently use the Spanish language, are more influenced by radio advertisements, billboards, family members, coworkers, coupons and point-of-purchase displays, while Hispanics who more frequently use English are more influenced by magazine advertisements, brochure advertisements, Yellow Pages, sources such as *Consumer Reports*, window shopping, and product labels (Webster 1992). Donthu and Cherian (1994) found that High-Hispanic identifiers are more likely to seek Hispanic vendors, to be loyal to brands used by family and friends, and to be influenced by targeted media than Low-Hispanic identifiers. However, High-Hispanic identifiers are also less concerned about economic value (Donthu and Cherian 1994).

Use of Spanish-language media has been studied and found to be more frequently used by strong rather than weak Hispanic identifiers (Deshpande, Hoyer, and Donthu 1986). The preference for Spanish-language media over more mainstream media was also given as a reason for lower coupon usage among strong Hispanic identifiers (Donthu and Cherian 1992). O'Guinn and Meyer (1983) found that very real and significant differences exist between those Hispanics who prefer Spanish-language radio and those who do not. Those who prefer Spanish-language radio are more likely to be older, married, less educated, and speak Spanish at home. In addition, they tend to spend more on records and soft drinks than do Hispanics who do not prefer Spanish-language radio.

MARKET SEGMENTATION STUDIES

A related but smaller stream of research has focused on strategies for reaching the Hispanic market more efficiently through segmentation. Segal and Sosa (1983) gave an overview of the characteristics of the Hispanic ethnic group, its buying behaviors, and its media preferences. This information was then used to make suggestions for developing a strategy for segmenting the Hispanic market. O'Guinn and Meyer (1984) suggested that the Hispanic market can be segmented based on the language preferred when listening to the radio.

COMPARATIVE STUDIES OF HISPANIC AND ANGLO CONSUMERS

A third stream of research has focused on uncovering specific consumer behavior differences between Hispanic and Anglo consumers. There have been conflicting results regarding brand loyalty and coupon usage. Some studies found Hispanics to be more brand loyal than Anglo Americans (Deshpande, Hoyer, and Donthu 1986; Donthu and Cherian 1992) and less prone to use coupons (Donthu and Cherian 1992). Other studies found no differences (Saegert, Hoover, and Hilger 1985; Wilkes and Valencia 1986; Mulhern and Williams 1994). Kaufman and Hernandez (1990) suggested that lower coupon usage among Hispanics may be due to lack of support for coupons throughout the channel in Hispanic markets.

One study found no difference in price responsiveness between Hispanic and Anglo Americans (Mulhern and Williams 1994), although another found cost or availability of credit to be a major discriminating variable between Anglos and high and low acculturation Hispanics (Faber, O'Guinn, and McCarty, 1987). Hispanic and Anglo Americans have not been shown to differ in their purchase of generic products (Wilkes and Valencia 1985,

Advances in Consumer Research
Volume 23, © 1996

1986), but Hispanics do appear to be more likely than Anglos to buy the brand that their parents bought, prestigious brands, and brands advertised to their ethnic groups (Hoyer and Deshpande, 1982). In much of this research, income factors were controlled.

Research also suggests that because of family structure factors such as size, age, and language, Hispanics tend to spend more on consumer items and food, have different product needs, spend more on high status items, have higher brand loyalty, and use coupons less frequently (Alaniz and Gilly 1986). In addition, Webster (1994) found a positive relationship between husband dominance in the purchase decision and Hispanic ethnic identification: Wives from more acculturated couples have more equality in decision making but have not supplanted their husbands as the primary decision maker.

Significant differences have been found between the value orientations of Anglo and Hispanic Americans, but no statistically significant differences were found among various Hispanic subcultures (Valencia 1989). Compared to Anglos, Hispanics value imagination, independence, a comfortable life, pleasure, cheerfulness, politeness, and self-control more than Anglos (Valencia 1989); however, the methodology of this research has been questioned (Wood and Howell 1991).

In sum, the literature does suggest that there are distinct differences between Hispanic and Anglo American consumers. However, the nature of those differences appears to vary by domain. Since our research focuses on the ecological area, we next review that literature.

PREVIOUS RESEARCH ON ECOLOGICAL BEHAVIOR IN SUBCULTURES

Since at least 1971 (Kassarjian) numerous studies have investigated ecological attitudes and/or behaviors. Many studies were published in the 1970s (e.g., Henion 1972; Mazis, Settle, and Leslie 1973; Kinnear and Taylor 1973; Kinnear, Taylor, and Ahmed 1974; Webster 1975; Fisk 1975; Maloney, Ward, and Braucht 1975; Brooker 1976; Reizenstein and Barnaby 1976; Murphy 1976; Henion and Wilson 1976; Belch 1979; Antil and Bennett 1979; Murphy, Laczniak, and Robinson 1979). Research activity subsided during the 1980s, as relatively few studies were conducted (e.g., Durand and Ferguson 1982; Robin 1984; DeYoung 1986; Gill, Crosby, and Taylor 1988; Balderjahn 1988; DeYoung 1989). In the 1990s, however, research on ecological attitudes and behaviors resumed more prominently (e.g., Newhouse 1990; Diamond and Loewy 1991; Kangun, Grove, and Kilbourne 1991; Kangun, Carlson, and Grove 1991; Granzin and Olsen 1991; Ellen, Wiener, and Cobb-Walgren 1991; Dickerson, Thibodeau, Aronson and Miller 1992; Alwitt and Berger 1993; Iyer and Banerjee 1993; Howenstine 1993; McCarty and Shrum 1993; Hackett 1993; Shamdasani, Chon-Lin, and Richmond 1993; Jackson, Olsen, Granzin, and Burns 1993; Banerjee and McKeage 1994; Joy and Auchinachie 1994).

A small percentage of ecological research has looked at cross-cultural or subcultural considerations. Several of these studies have focused on differences in ecological responsiveness between Anglos and African Americans (Murphy, Kangun, and Locander 1978; Caron 1989; Cornwell and Schwepker 1992) with even fewer investigating Hispanic ecological behavior (Noe and Snow 1990; Howenstine 1993).

In a study employing the "New Environmental Paradigm" (NEP) scale, Noe and Snow (1990) found that Hispanics sampled from national park visitors held a more pro-NEP (i.e., pro-environmental) attitude than did Hispanics from the general population. When Hispanics and Anglos were compared, attitudes of Hispanics who were park visitors were more similar to Anglos (park visitors and general population) than to Hispanics who did not use the park.

In a study of recycling behavior and obstacles to recycling, Howenstine (1993) found that Anglo Americans, African Americans, Asian Americans, and Hispanic Americans differ in their recycling behavior. Hispanics have the lowest reported incidence of recycling, yet unlike other ethnic groups, the reasons Hispanics give for not recycling do not differ significantly from non-Hispanics who do not recycle.

While the research is currently limited, there are empirical indications that Hispanics and Anglos do differ in their ecological orientations and behaviors. How this translates regarding ecological information receptivity has not been previously researched, but cognitive dissonance theory and selective exposure do give guidance on general predictions of influences on ecological information receptivity.

COGNITIVE DISSONANCE THEORY AND SELECTIVE EXPOSURE TO INFORMATION

Cognitive dissonance, one of several cognitive consistency theories, is defined as an inconsistency between two or more cognitions held by a person (Festinger 1957). Cognitions can include such things as knowledge, opinions, or beliefs about oneself, about one's behavior, or about issues such as ecology. Dissonance theory states that people seek to reduce dissonance by eliminating or reducing these inconsistencies through two methods: 1) avoiding information that contradicts existing attitudes, choices, or behaviors, and 2) seeking out information supportive of existing attitudes, behaviors, and choices (Festinger 1957; Tan 1981).

Selective exposure to information is one of the main derivations of this theory of cognitive consistency. It states that the search for information on a topic does not stop after a decision has been made or an attitude has been formed, but continues as the person weighs the advantages and disadvantages of the various alternatives. The most general case states that people will be more receptive to information which is consistent with their decisions, beliefs, and attitudes and will avoid information which is dissonant (Frey 1986).

Thus, people who engage in a particular behavior or who hold positive attitudes about a topic will be more receptive to information that supports those attitudes and behaviors. This can be measured as one's receptivity to information. In addition, selective exposure also suggests that receptivity will also be biased by certain factors activated in the decision-making or attitude formation process, such as freedom of choice in developing the decision or the belief, the level of dissonance, the level of commitment to the cognition, and the reversibility of the decision (Frey 1986; Festinger 1964).

Since its introduction in 1957 (Festinger), the popularized conceptualization of dissonance theory has narrowed greatly, and it is now often framed as a post-decision phenomenon, with the consumer seeking to alleviate discomfort after a decision (particularly a purchase) about which uncertainty exists. While this study relies more on the original, more encompassing definition of dissonance theory, it is still consistent with those versions of the theory which state that a decision must be made for dissonance to occur. In the case of ecologically-conscious behaviors, consumers are faced several times each day with the decision whether or not to behave in an ecologically-conscious manner. Shopping for groceries, disposing of household garbage, and consuming scarce resources (such as water when showering [Dickerson, Thibodeau, Aronson, and Miller 1992] or energy when driving to work) all involve a decision to behave ecologically or not. These decisions, while easily revisable when next confronted, are all capable of creating dissonance within the consumer.

HYPOTHESES

Dissonance theory and the derived concept of selective exposure to information suggest that receptivity to information will be a function of ecological attitudes and prior behaviors such that consumers whose attitudes, intentions and behaviors are more ecologically-oriented will have higher receptivity to future ecological information. This leads to the following hypotheses.

H_1: Receptivity to ecological information will be significantly influenced by ecological concern such that consumers with the highest ecological concern will have the highest receptivity to ecological information.

H_2: Receptivity to ecological information will be significantly influenced by ecological self-perceptions such that consumers with the highest ecological self-perceptions will be the most receptive to ecological information.

H_3: Receptivity to ecological information will be significantly influenced by the responses to ecologically-friendly packaging such that consumers with the highest intentions to purchase products with ecologically-friendly packaging will be most receptive to ecological information.

H_4: Receptivity to ecological information will be significantly influenced by prior ecological buying behaviors such that consumers who are most ecologically-oriented in their buying behaviors will be the most receptive to ecological information.

H_5: Receptivity to ecological information will be significantly influenced by prior recycling behaviors such that consumers who recycle the most frequently will be the most receptive to ecological information.

In addition, as previously discussed, prior research on Hispanic and Anglo consumers has shown both differences and similarities between the groups depending on the phenomenon being studied. In this research we are testing the following null hypothesis for Hispanic and Anglo consumers:

H_0: There will be no difference between Hispanic and Anglo consumers with respect to the influences on receptivity to ecological information.

METHOD

A self-administered questionnaire was developed after an extensive review of the literature. Schwepker and Cornwell's (1991) work provided items for ecological packaging response measurement and several other attitudinal questions. Other studies provided inspiration for questions on ecological concern (Ellen, Wiener, and Cobb-Walgren 1991) and recycling behavior indices (Jackson, Olsen, Granzin, and Burns 1993). In sum, six ecological indices were included in the instrument, each incorporating multiple measures (see Table 1 for final indices).

After initial construction, the questionnaire was submitted to a focus group of six regional environmental experts, four from the United States and two from Mexico, for critique concerning content, relevancy, wording, and any possible misinformation. Members of the focus group represented five different environmental groups or agencies, as well as county and city officials. Focus group suggestions were incorporated into the development of the questionnaire prior to pre-testing which resulted in minor changes.

The questionnaire was constructed in both Spanish and English. In constructing the Spanish version of the questionnaire, the questionnaire was translated into Spanish by one translator and "back-translated" into English by a second translator. Any ambiguities were reconciled by a third translator. Both the English and Spanish versions of the questionnaire were pre-tested twice with the different subcultural groups. More than two hundred respondents participated in the pre-testing procedure.

Sample

Two hundred Mexican Americans and two hundred Anglo Americans completed the consumer environmental behavior survey during a two-week period in the spring of 1994 in the Lower Rio Grande Valley of South Texas. Local Mexican American residents were surveyed randomly during their visit to the largest shopping mall in the area, with every Mexican American surveyed having the option of responding to an English or Spanish version of the questionnaire. The two hundred "winter Texans," predominantly retired Anglo Americans from mid-eastern states, were contacted in the shopping mall and in recreational vehicle and mobile home (RV/MH) parks to insure an adequate sample size, as the shopping mall consumers in the area are heavily Hispanic. The number of refusals to participate was slightly less than three percent, but two percent of the final surveys were discarded due to lack of sufficient information for processing.

ANALYSES AND RESULTS

The ecological indices were refined using exploratory and confirmatory factor analysis. The final ecological attitude, intention, and behavioral indices resulting from those analyses are listed in Table 1, which provides a complete description of the questions comprising the six ecological indices. All factor loadings were +.56 or greater, and the confirmatory factor analysis' goodness of fit measures met current standards for acceptable fit ($c^2/df=1.88$, LISREL's Goodness of Fit Index=.92 and Adjusted Goodness of Fit=.88 [Jöreskog and Sörbom 1988]).

Relationships between Receptivity to Information and the Ecological Indices

Separate regression analyses were run for each group with the Receptivity to Information Index (RII) as the dependent variable and the other ecological indices as independent variables. As shown in Table 2, the adjusted R^2 value for Anglo Americans is .25 and for Mexican Americans is .39. A statistically significant amount of the variance in RII is explained by the other attitudinal and behavioral ecological indices.

The Ecological Concern Index (ECI) is significantly associated with information receptivity for both Anglo and Mexican Americans (Table 2). Hypothesis 1 predicted that there will be a statistically significant relationship between receptivity to information (RII) and ecological concern (ECI) such that persons with the highest ecological concern will be most receptive to ecological information. Thus, this hypothesis is supported for both Anglo and Mexican Americans.

TABLE 1
Ecological Indices and Receptivity to Information Index

RII: Receptivity to Information Index (alpha=.77)
        I wish I knew more about environmental issues.
        I want more information on environmental issues.
        I wish I had more information on how to recycle.

ECI: Ecological Concern Index (alpha=.75)
        I am concerned about the thickness of the ozone.
        I am concerned about the reduction of the rain forests.
        I am concerned about pollution in the Rio Grande River.

ESPI: Ecological Self-Perception Index (alpha=.85)
        How environmentally aware do you consider yourself to be?
        In general, how environmentally-concerned do you consider your behavior to be?
        I regard myself as someone who thinks environmentally.

EPRI: Ecological Packaging Response Index (alpha=.83)
        I would purchase a product in a biodegradable package before purchasing a similar product in a package that is not recyclable.
        I would purchase a product in a recyclable package before purchasing a similar product in a package that is not recyclable.
        I would be willing to purchase some products (now bought in smaller sizes) in larger packages with less frequency.
        I would purchase a product with an untraditional package design (for example, round where most are square) if it meant creating less solid waste.

EBBI: Ecological Buying Behavior Index (alpha=.82)
        How often does the environmental impact of a product's packaging influence your buying behavior?
        How often does a firm's environmental practices influence your buying behavior?
        How often do you read package labels for environmental information?

RBI: Recycling Behavior Index [a] (alpha=.77)
        How frequently do you recycle, return to the store, or otherwise reuse empty containers or bottles?
        How frequently do you recycle or reuse paper, newspapers, or cardboard containers?
        I recycle whenever possible.

[a]On each scale 1="Disagree," "Never," or "Not at all," and 7="Strongly agree," "Always," or "Very much," as appropriate for the wording.

The Ecological Self-Perception Index (ESPI) is not significantly associated with information receptivity for either Anglo or Mexican Americans; thus hypothesis 2, predicting a statistically significant relationship is not supported for either subcultural group. Hypothesis 3 predicted that there will be a statistically significant relationship between receptivity to information and ecological packaging response (EPRI) such that persons most responsive to ecological packaging will have the highest receptivity to information. This hypothesis is supported for Mexican Americans but not for Anglo Americans. Likewise, hypothesis 4 which predicted a statistically significant relationship between receptivity to information and ecological buying behavior (EBBI) is only supported for Mexican Americans. Since recycling behavior is not significantly associated with receptivity to information, hypothesis 5 is not supported for either group.

The null hypothesis, H_0, stated that there would be no difference between the two groups on the factors that influence their receptivity to information. The null hypothesis is not supported, as different variables statistically influence information receptivity for Mexican and Anglo Americans. As mentioned above, only ECI is statistically significant for both groups. No other ecological index is statistically associated with receptivity to information for Anglo Americans, but the Mexican American receptivity to information is statistically associated with ECI, EPRI, and EBBI.

Differences Between Subcultural Groups on Ecological Indices

It is interesting to note the differences between subcultural groups with respect to their receptivity to information and scores on the ecological indices. ANOVA results and Scheffé tests for each index between subcultural groups are shown in Table 3. All indices were composed of three questions and, hence, had a maximum possible mean score of 21 except for EPRI which was composed of four questions and had a maximum score of 28.

Mexican Americans and Anglo Americans do not differ significantly from each other on their information receptivity (RII), ecological concern (ECI), or ecological buying behavior (EBBI), but do differ in terms of their ecological self-perceptions (ESPI), ecological packaging response (EPRI), and recycling behaviors (RBI). The Anglo Americans are more ecologically-oriented in their response to packaging, perceive themselves as being significantly more ecologically-oriented, and report higher levels of recycling behavior than do the Mexican Americans. Not only are different scales influential in terms of receptivity to information between Anglo and Mexican Americans, but the two groups exhibit

TABLE 2

Regression Analyses for Receptivity to Information Index and Ecological Indices

Sample	Index	Beta	t	p	Mean	Adjusted R^2
Anglo Americans	ECI	.36	4.95	.01	17.32	.25[a]
	ESPI	.02	.24	.81	14.71	
	EPRI	.14	1.68	.09	21.41	
	EBBI	.14	1.66	.10	11.01	
	RBI	.08	.91	.36	15.03	
	Constant		3.21	.01		
Mexican Americans	ECI	.34	4.61	.01	16.54	.39[b]
	ESPI	-.01	-.12	.91	11.90	
	EPRI	.36	4.76	.01	19.31	
	EBBI	.22	2.58	.01	9.88	
	RBI	-.16	-1.76	.08	9.95	
	Constant		3.50	.01		

[a]MS=139.18, F=11.47, p<.01 with 5, 155 df, MSerror=12.13.
[b]MS=283.39, F=22.03, p<.01 with 5, 162 df, MSerror=12.86.

TABLE 3

Analysis of Variance and Scheffé Results for Cultural Groups of Receptivity to Information Index

Cultural Group	Means[ab]					
	RII	ECI	ESPI[c]	EPRI[c]	EBBI	RBI[c]
Anglo Americans	16.16	17.25	14.79	21.51	11.11	14.95
Mexican Americans	15.80	16.62	12.02	19.04	10.07	10.23

[a] RII mean square=12.01, F=.64, df=1, 382, p<.50.
ECI mean square=39.08, F=2.52, df=1, 386, p<.20.
ESPI mean square=754.14, F=30.66, df=1, 391, p<.01.
EPRI mean square=592.26, F=15.07, df=1, 387, p<.01.
EBBI mean square=103.16, F=3.69, df=1, 381, p<.10.
RBI mean square=2141.24, F=74.99, df=1, 381, p<.01.

[b] Means are from a total possible score of 21 on all indices except EPRI, where the highest possible score is 28.

[c] Statistically different means for this index between Mexican Americans and Anglo Americans, p<.05.

differences in their ecological orientations via self-perceptions and behavior.

DISCUSSION AND CONCLUSIONS

The conclusions that can be drawn from this research are restricted to the sample characteristics and methodology used. Neither of the samples can be considered a cross-section of their respective subcultures. Nonetheless, relevant insights into differences between Anglo and Mexican Americans can be obtained from this research.

The results suggest that the stronger the ecological concern, the higher the receptivity to information for both Mexican and Anglo Americans. This supports dissonance theory and selection exposure perspectives. However, receptivity to ecological information is more complicated than this, as the influences upon ecological receptivity do appear to vary by ethnic group.

More of the ecological attitudes and behaviors examined in this research are associated with information receptivity for Mexican Americans than for Anglo Americans, and these attitudes and behaviors explain much more of the variance for Mexican Americans. For Anglo Americans, ecological concern (ECI) is the only significant predictor for information receptivity. Behavior and other attitudes are not related. Conversely, for Mexican Americans, a complex of attitudes, intentions, and behaviors are important influences on information receptivity: ecological concern (ECI), ecological packaging response (EPRI), and ecological buying behavior (EBBI). The results point out that the receptivity to information of Anglo Americans and Mexican Americans is not influenced by the same factors. Neither group's information receptivity is influenced by prior recycling behavior or ecological self-perception, according to this study.

The relationships between the independent and dependent variables could also be driven by involvement theory. Involvement theory would suggest that the more personally relevant an issue is to a person, the more attention a person will give to information on that issue (Celsi and Olson 1988). Therefore, the more one is involved with ecological issues, either situationally or enduringly, the more likely one is to give attention to ecological information.

Another aspect of selective exposure to information suggests that people may choose to be exposed to dissonant information when they believe that they may have the chance to revise their decision in the near future or when future similar decisions are anticipated (Frey 1986). Buying behavior, particularly for non-durables, is a decision that is "revisable" at the next time of purchase, and in most cases, future similar decisions are antici-pated. Receptivity to information of Mexican Americans, who exhibit lower ecological buying behavior than Anglo Americans, is influenced by previous ecological buying behavior. This may be relevant for the practical use of increasing ecological buying practices in the future.

Recycling behavior suggests a similar situation. As described above, when a behavior is to be repeated and hence can be modified, receptivity to dissonance-creating information may increase if that information can be used to alter behavior. Therefore, one might expect recycling behavior to be negatively related to information receptivity: those who do not recycle now may wish to know more, while those who already recycle may not need to know more. In fact, this may be the situation for Mexican Americans, who have a low mean for recycling but for whom the recycling behavior index had a negative influence ($p < .10$) on receptivity to information.

Marketers who wish to position their products as ecologically beneficial will reach the most receptive Anglo American audience by targeting those Anglo Americans who already exhibit ecological concern. Other than the ecological concern index, no other index was associated with the receptivity of Anglo Americans. However, for Mexican Americans, ecological buying behavior and ecological packaging response was associated with receptivity to information, suggesting that the Mexican American audience can also be reached via information on product labels, ecologically-friendly packaging, and ecologically-conscious practices on the part of the firm.

REFERENCES

Alaniz, Lisa Penaloza and Mary C. Gilly (1986), "The Hispanic Family—Consumer Research Issues," *Psychology and Marketing*, 3 (Winter), 291-304.

Albonetti, Joseph G. and Luis V. Dominguez (1989), "Major Influences on Consumer-Goods Marketers' Decision to Target U.S. Hispanics," *Journal of Advertising Research*, 29 (February/March), 9-21.

Alwitt, Linda F. and Ida E. Berger (1993), "Understanding the Link Between Environmental Attitudes and Consumer Product Usage: Measuring the Moderating Role of Attitude Strength," in *Advances in Consumer Research*, Vol. 20, eds. Leigh McAlister and Michael Rothchild, Provo, UT: Association for Consumer Research, 189-194.

Antil, John H. and Peter D. Bennett (1979), "Construction and Validation of a Scale to Measure Socially Responsible Consumption Behavior," in Karl E. Henion and Thomas C. Kinnear (eds.), *The Conserver Society,* Chicago: AMA, 1979.

Balderjahn, Ingo (1988), "Personality Variables and Environ-mental Attitudes as Predictors of Ecologically Responsible Consumption Patterns," *Journal of Business Research*, 17, 51-56.

Banerjee, Bobby and Kim McKeage (1994), "How Green is My Value: Exploring the Relationship Between Environmental-ism and Materialism," in *Advances in Consumer Research*, Vol. 21, eds. Chris T. Allen and Deborah Roedderjohn, Provo, UT: Association for Consumer Research, 147-152.

Belch, Michael A. (1979), "Identifying the Socially and Ecologically Concerned Segment Through Life-Style Research: Initial Findings," in Karl E. Henion and Thomas C. Kinnear (eds.), *The Conserver Society*, Chicago: AMA, 1979.

Brooker, George (1976) "The Self-Actualizing Socially Conscious Consumer," *Journal of Consumer Research*, 3 (September), 107-112.

Caron, Judi Anne (1989), "Environmental Perspectives of Blacks: Acceptance of the 'New Environmental Paradigm,'" *Journal of Environmental Education*, 20 (3), 21 - 26.

Celsi, Richard L. and Jerry C. Olson (1988), "The Role of Involvement in Attention and Comprehension Processes," *Journal of Consumer Research*, 15 (September), 210-224.

Cornwell, T. Bettina and Charles H. Schwepker Jr. (1992), "Attitudes and Intentions Regarding Ecologically Packaged Products: Subcultural Variations," in *Proceedings of the 1992 Conference of The American Academy of Advertising*, ed. Leonard N. Reid, 119-121.

Deshpande, Rohit, Wayne D. Hoyer, and Naveen Donthu (1986), "The Intensity of Ethnic Affiliation: A Study of the Sociology of Hispanic Consumption," *Journal of Consumer Research*, 13 (September), 214-220.

DeYoung, Raymond (1986), "Encouraging Environmentally Appropriate Behavior: The Role of Intrinsic Motivation," *Journal of Environmental Systems*, 15 (4), 281-292.

_____ (1989), "Exploring the Difference Between Recyclers and Non-Recyclers: The Role of Information," *Journal of Environmental Systems*, 18 (4), 341-351.

Diamond, William D. and Ben Z. Loewy (1991), "Effects of Probabilistic Rewards on Recycling Attitudes and Behavior," *Journal of Applied Social Psychology*, 21 (19) 1590-1607.

Dickerson, Chris Ann, Ruth Thibodeau, Elliot Aronson, and Dayna Miller (1992) "Using Cognitive Dissonance to Encourage Water Conservation," *Journal of Applied Social Psychology*, 22 (11), 841-854.

Donthu, Naveen and Joseph Cherian (1992), "Hispanic Coupon Usage: The Impact of Strong and Weak Ethnic Identifica-tion," *Psychology and Marketing*, 9 (November/December), 501-510.

_____ and _____ (1994), "Impact of Strength of Ethnic Identification on Hispanic Shopping Behavior," *Journal of Retailing*, 70 (4) 383-393.

Durand, Richard M., and Carl E. Ferguson, Jr. (1982), "The Environmentally Concerned Citizen: Demographic, Social-Psychological, and Energy Related Correlates," in *Marketing Theory: Philosophy of Science Perspectives*, eds. Ronald F. Bush and Shelby D. Hunt, 211-214.

Ellen, Pam Scholder, Joshua Lyle Wiener, and Cathy Cobb-Walgren (1991), "The Role of Perceived Consumer Effec-tiveness in Motivating Environmentally Conscious Behav-iors," *Journal of Public Policy and Marketing*, 10 (2), 102-117.

Exeter, Thomas (1987), "How Many Hispanics?" *American Demographics*, 9 (May), 36-39.

Faber, Ronald J., Thomas C. O'Guinn, and John A. McCarty (1987), "Ethnicity, Acculturation, and the Importance of Product Attributes," *Psychology and Marketing*, 4 (Summer), 121-134.

Festinger, Leon (1957), *A Theory of Cognitive Dissonance*, Stanford, CA: Stanford University Press.

_____ (1964), *Conflict, Decision, and Dissonance*, Stanford, CA: Stanford University Press.

Fisk, George (1973), "Criteria for a Theory of Responsible Consumption," *Journal of Marketing*, 37 (April), 24-31.

Frey, Dieter (1986), "Recent research on selective exposure to information," in *Advances in Experimental Social Psychology*, ed. L. Berkowitz, Orlando, FL: Academic Press, 41-80.

Gill, James D., Lawrence A. Crosby, and James R. Taylor (1986), "Ecological Concern, Attitudes, and Social Norms in Voting Behavior," *Public Opinion Quarterly*, 50, 537-554.

Granzin, Kent L., and Janeen E. Olsen (1991), "Characterizing Participants in Activities Protecting the Environment: A Focus on Donating, Recycling, and Conservation Behaviors," *Journal of Public Policy and Marketing*, 10 (2), 1-27.

Hackett, Paul M. (1993), "Consumers' Environmental Concern Values: Understanding the Structure of Contemporary Green Worldviews," in *European Advances in Consumer Research*, Vol 1, ed. Gary J. Bamossy and W. Fred van Raaij, Provo, UT: Association for Consumer Research, 416-427

Henion, Karl E., II (1972), "The Effect of Ecologically Relevant Information on Detergent Sales," *Journal of Marketing Research*, 9 (February), 10-14.

Henion, Karl E., II, and William H. Wilson (1976), "The Ecologically Concerned Consumer and Locus of Control," in Karl E. Henion and Thomas C. Kinnear (eds.) *Ecological Marketing*. Chicago: AMA, 1976.

Howenstine, Erick (1993), "Market Segmentation for Recycling," *Environment and Behavior*, 25 (1), 86-102.

Hoyer, Wayne D. and Rohit Deshpande (1982), "Cross Cultural Influences on Buyer Behavior: The Impact of Hispanic Ethnicity," in *Proceedings of the AMA Educators' Conference*, ed., Bruce J. Walker et al., Chicago: American Marketing Association, 89-92.

Iyer, Easwar and Bobby Banerjee (1993), "Anatomy of Green Advertising," in *Advances in Consumer Research*, Vol 20, ed. Leigh McAlister and Michael Rothchild, Provo, UT: Association for Consumer Research, 494-501.

Jackson, Anita L., Janeen E. Olsen, Kent L. Granzin, and Alvin C. Burns (1993), "An Investigation of Determinants of Recycling Consumer Behavior," in *Advances in Consumer Research*, Vol 20, ed. Leigh McAlister and Michael Rothchild, Provo, UT: Association for Consumer Research, 481-487.

Jöreskog, Karl G. and Dag Sörbom (1988), *LISREL 7: A Guide to the Program and Applications*, Chicago: SPSS Inc.

Joy, Annamma and Lisa Auchinachie (1994), "Paradigms of the Self and the Environment in Consumer Behavior and Marketing," in *Advances in Consumer Research*, Vol 21, ed. Chris T. Allen and Deborah Roedderjohn, Provo, UT: Association for Consumer Research, 153-157.

Kangun, Norman, Les Carlson, and Stephen J. Grove (1991), "Environmental Advertising Claims: A Preliminary Investigation," *Journal of Public Policy and Marketing*, 10 (2), 47-58.

_____, Stephen J. Grove, and Williams E. Kilbourne (1991), "The Green Alternative: A Prognosis for Further Development and Its Marketplace Impact," in *Proceedings of the AMA Educators' Conference*, ed. Terry L. Childers et al., Chicago: American Marketing Association, 233-236.

Kassarjian, Harold H. (1971), "Incorporating Ecology into Marketing Strategy: The Case of Air Pollution," *Journal of Marketing*, 35 (July), 61-65.

Kaufman, Carol J. and Sigfredo A. Hernandez (1990), "Barriers to Coupon Use: A View From the Bodega," *Journal of Advertising Research*, 30 (5), 18-25.

Kinnear, Thomas C. and James R. Taylor (1973), "The Effect of Ecological Concern on Brand Perceptions," *Journal of Marketing Research*, 10 (May), 191-197.

_____, _____, and Sadrudin A. Ahmed (1974), "Ecologically Concerned Consumers: Who Are They?" *Journal of Marketing*, 38 (April), 20-24.

Maloney, Michael P., Michael P. Ward, and G. Nicholas Braucht (1975), "A Revised Scale for the Measurement of Ecological Attitudes and Knowledge," *American Psychologist*, VOL 30 (July) 787-790.

Mazis, Michael, Robert B. Settle, and Dennis C. Leslie (1973), "Elimination of Phosphate Detergents and Psychological Reactance," *Journal of Marketing Research*, 10 (November), 390-395.

McCarty, John A. and L. J. Shrum (1993), "A Structural Equation Analysis of the Relationships of Personal Values, Attitudes and Beliefs About Recycling, and the Recycling of Solid Waste Products," in *Advances in Consumer Research*, Vol 20, ed. Leigh McAlister and Michael Rothchild, Provo, UT: Association for Consumer Research, 641-646.

The Influence of Culture on Pro-Environmental Knowledge, Attitudes, and Behavior:
A Canadian Perspective

Michel Laroche, Concordia University
Roy Toffoli, Concordia University
Chankon Kim, Concordia University
Thomas E. Muller, Griffith University[1]

ABSTRACT

The influence of culture on pro-environmental behavior was examined. Results indicate that francophones have *lower* scores on eco-literacy and concern for *local* environmental issues than Ontario anglophones. No significant differences were found between the two groups on pro-environmental attitudes and the purchase of ecologically-unfriendly products. The French showed a greater concern for *global* environmental issues than Ontario consumers. Quebec anglophones revealed attitudes and behavior consistent with acculturation. These disparities may arise from cultural differences in the weights assigned to the two components of the Fishbein model, and from the way habitual behavior overrides attitudes and intentions.

Concern and research about the environment over the last 25 years has experienced cyclical changes. A flurry of initial interest in the 70s was followed by rapid decline. In fact, not much academic research has been done since that time. However, the present decade is witnessing a renewed interest in ecological issues. The National Anxiety Center reports that among the issues making up its top ten worry list are five dealing with the environment (Schlossberg 1990). The present wave of interest, however, appears to be much more pervasive and centered in the consumer marketplace (Berger 1991).

There is evidence that knowledge of environmental issues, attitudes toward the environment, and environmentally-friendly behavior vary across cultures (Ahmed, deCamprieu and Hope 1981). Given the current interest in the ecology and new emphasis on the marketplace, it would seem fitting to examine the impact of culture on environmental awareness and behavior in a Canadian context. More specifically, the "Strong English" viewpoint as represented by Ontario residents, the "French" viewpoint of francophone Quebec residents, and the "Acculturated English" viewpoint of Quebec anglophone residents will be examined in terms of their respective ecological knowledge or eco-literacy, concerns toward local and global environmental issues, and environmentally-friendly behavior. This study also explores a particularly important aspect of pro-environmental consumer behavior: the interaction between culture and the knowledge-attitude-behavior relationship.

THE ROLE OF CONSUMERS IN GREEN MARKETING

The role of consumption in environmental solutions has been underestimated. Today, marketers are told to heed consumers before the big brother (government) steps in (Schlossberg 1992). Recent polls show that a growing number of consumers are recognizing their own responsibilities and contributions to green marketing (see Berger 1991). Faced with the new challenge from socially

or environmentally concerned consumers, the business world is adopting the societal dimensions of marketing (Kotler and Turner 1993) in an active manner. Lever Brothers in late 1989 launched a $20 million campaign to reduce and eventually eliminate any adverse impact its products may have on the environment; seeing the environment as being a consumer need, Procter & Gamble has already reduced the thickness of plastic in its disposable diapers and is trying to find compatible materials to replace the plastic backsheet (Welds 1991). Similarly, Loblaw's Inc., Canada's largest food retailer, introduced a new product line in 1989, called the G.R.E.E.N. line (Goldberg 1989) in response to the increasing consumer demand for environmentally friendly products. Although these are not purely voluntary efforts initiated by businesses, the environmental dimension in consumer demand does seem to play an important role in driving consumer product manufacturers to become more environmentally conscious. To some extent, what were once "macro" corporate issues, to be managed through government lobbying, have become "micro" consumer issues that require attention, understanding and dialogue at the level of the consumer (Berger 1991).

Unfortunately, the majority of consumers do not yet realize that they can make a substantial impact on environmental problems. What most consumers feel they can contribute to are merely the reduction of litter, indoor air pollution, and solid waste (Miller 1991). Despite the large number of consumers who express their concerns about the environment, few people are willing to act at personal expenses, such as paying premiums for environmentally friendly products and making a sacrifice in their present lifestyles (Maclean's 1990; Welds 1991; Miller 1991). In Canada, the paradox between what consumers say and what they do is exhibited clearly in the studies that show that Canadians are the second-ranked country in the world for per capita emissions of carbon dioxide, one of the main causes of the greenhouse effect and global warming, and are first-ranked among countries for the per capita production of garbage, ahead even of their American neighbors (Mittelstaedt 1991). Moreover, consumers often misperceive environmental issues and lack the knowledge to make environmentally responsible consumption decisions. Rothe and Benson's (1974) notion of "intelligent consumption" and Fisk's (1973) concept of "ecological imperatives" reflect the need to educate the consumer to become aware of environmental problems and their relation to his/her consumption patterns.

FRENCH AND ENGLISH QUEBECERS VS ONTARIO

There have been many studies that compare consumption and lifestyle patterns between French and English Canadians (Mallen 1977; Tigert 1973; Schaninger, Bourgeois, and Buss 1985; Hui et al. 1993). Most of these studies have shown that differences exist. Using these findings, some researchers have proposed "theories" about the characteristic traits of French Canadians vis-à-vis those of English Canadians. According to Mallen (1977), French Canadians exhibit a more hedonistic consumption attitude and behavior than their English Canadian counterparts. The expression *joie-de-vivre* is often used to characterize the French-Canadian attitude of

[1]The authors gratefully acknowledge the financial support of the Fonds FCAR, the comments of anonymous reviewers, and the assistance of Isabelle Miodek.

196

Advances in Consumer Research
Volume 23, © 1996

looking for the good things in life. They are also characterized as more conservative in their attitudes and less willing to take risks. This is supported by the past empirical findings indicating that French Canadians tend to be more brand loyal than English Canadians, and that, in many cases, the leading brand among French Canadians has a much higher share than the leading brand among English Canadians (Kindra, Laroche, and Muller 1994). Closely related to these traits, according to Mallen, is French Canadians' non-price cognitive trait. That is, if a product is liked by French Canadians, it will be bought regularly and price will unlikely be an obstacle to purchase. In view of their stronger tendency to engage in self-indulgent consumption, it is expected that, compared to English Canadians, French Canadians will exhibit less concern for those environmental problems which require their personal sacrifice. The study by Ahmed, deCamprieu, and Hope (1981) which compared the attitudes of French Canadians and English Canadians toward energy and related environmental concern supports this view. They found that French Canadians have a negative image of energy and ecology concern and are less concerned about the ecological impact of energy sources. A further basis for this contention is that the environmental conservation movement has been largely an upper middle class phenomenon. Given the strong rural root of French Canadians (Bouchard 1980) and their historically lower social status, one might expect the same (Ahmed, deCamprieu, and Hope 1981).

Arbuthnot and Lingg (1975) compared the environmental knowledge, attitudes, and behavior of the French (in France) and Americans. They found the French to be more preoccupied with their personal economic gain or loss when faced with environmental questions, and to be less concerned with the future consequences of present behavior. Overall, the authors found the Americans' environmental attitudes to be more pro-ecological than their French counterparts. Several other findings have a bearing on the present study. First of all, the researchers observed that the five environmental attitude scales were much more internally consistent for the Americans than the French. They believe that this may demonstrate "that the French are characterized by rather more specific and independent attitudes toward environmental issues than are the Americans" (1975:278). Second, they found that the five attitudinal scales were predictive of recycling behavior for the Americans, but not for the French. For the latter, the comparable correlations did not differ significantly from zero. Third, for the Americans, it was found that the degree of informativeness predicts recycling; for the French, on the other hand, the two are independent. Thus, a difference also exists in the relationship between environmental knowledge and recycling behavior. The relationship between the affective component of ecological concern and the cognitive component was found to be mixed for both samples. The authors conclude by suggesting that knowledge may act as a mediating variable between attitudes and behavior.

In contrast to Quebec, Ontario's economy has been based more on the manufacturing sector, and the latter is also in closer physical proximity to the heartland of American heavy industry. These factors, coupled with the greater influence of American media and values on Ontario consumers than on francophone Quebecers, means that information, attitudes, and behavior may have coalesced faster in the former than in the latter.

Anglophone Quebecers are greatly influenced by American media and values. However, due to the forces of assimilation, brought on by the increasing use of French in the schools and in the workplace, the behavior of this group will tend to be modified by the values and norms of the majority population (Schaninger, Bourgeois, and Buss 1985; Ryan 1972).

Comparing Ontario and Quebec

The intent of the study was to explore differences in eco-literacy and pro-environmental attitudes and behavior between members of Canada's major sub-cultures. Most important, was the desire to probe for a possible cultural effect on the failure of consumers' beliefs and environmental attitudes to translate themselves into environmentally-friendly actions. To help guide the research, and in the interest of clarity, a series of research questions are proposed.

On the basis of the previous review, it was expected that Ontario consumers would be more knowledgeable about environmental issues than their French counterparts in Quebec. Also, given the stronger manufacturing base of the Ontario economy, consumers from this province, in contrast to French consumers, would probably show greater concern for *local* environmental problems which call for immediate personal efforts than for *global* environmental problems such as ozone depletion and the "greenhouse effect." This greater knowledge and concern would, in turn, translate themselves into more environmentally friendly attitudes and purchase behaviors than their French Canadian counterparts.

Previous findings had also revealed a discrepancy between consumers' beliefs and verbal commitments about the environment and their actions. Hence, the "causal" linkages between these variables were not predicted to be very strong. However, for the reasons described earlier, it was anticipated that the linkage between pro-environmental attitudes and behavior for the French would not differ significantly from zero; that is, the disparity between attitudes and behavior would be more acute for the French than for the Ontario consumers.

Lastly, in keeping with an acculturation model (Ryan 1972), it was expected that the scores of Anglophone Quebecers on awareness, attitudes, and pro-environmental behavior would be intermediate between those of the French and Ontario consumers

RESEARCH METHODOLOGY

The data used were collected using personally administered questionnaires in the Montreal (Quebec) and Hamilton (Ontario) areas. The interviews were of approximately 20 minute duration. In both regions, using an area sampling method, five census tracts were first selected randomly from 1986 Canadian Census maps. Residential streets were then chosen from these districts, and efforts were made to contact as many residents on these streets as possible. The survey collected 187 and 180 completed questionnaires from the Hamilton and the Montreal region respectively.

Dependent Variables

Eco-literacy. This was measured by testing the respondents' ability to identify or define a number of ecologically related symbols (e.g., the recycling symbol), concepts (e.g., the three R's of environmentally responsible behavior), behavior (e.g., the simplest way to reduce car fuel consumption), etc.

Some items were open ended, whereas others were in a multiple choice format. In measuring the respondent's concern for local and global environmental issues, an open-ended question was used, prior to any other environment-related question, which asked for the respondent's choice of "the single greatest environmental concern facing us today."

Attitudes toward the environment. Fourteen statements (1-10 agreement scale) tapped the respondents' feelings about a broad spectrum of issues ranging from legislation (e.g., "There should be tougher anti-pollution laws...") to "junk-mail" (e.g., "I feel that newspapers...and so-called "junk-mail" are the greatest contributors to pollution").

TABLE 1
Comparisons Among the Three Subcultural Groups

	Ontario (N=185)	Anglophones (N=126)	Francophones (N=46)	F-test
Eco-Literacy Score (Max. score=100)	**48.1** [50.1]	47.6 [45.4]	41.7 [39.8]	5.52^a
Greatest Concern	%	%	%	
Pollution	48	51	**61**	$\chi^2 = 29^a$
Recycling/garbage	**27**	11	11	
Ozone depletion	7	5	4	
Global warming	3	2	0	
Others	11	28	17	
Don't know	3	4	7	
E-Factors	(Means)	(Means)	(Means)	
E-Activism	**6.65**	6.24	6.24	1.27
Solid waste	**6.87** [6.82]	6.02 [6.09]	5.99 [5.94]	4.67^b
Unconcerned	4.34	**4.49**	3.79	2.25
Scepticism	5.15	**5.18**	4.86	0.56
Bought (past year)	%	%	%	
Spray-on deodorant	**18**	10	9	$\chi^2 = 5.3^c$
Air freshener	**38**	22	28	$\chi^2 = 9.9^a$
Organically grown	**21**	13	7	$\chi^2 = 7.4^b$
Insect spray	**36**	18	*11*	$\chi^2 = 19.3^a$
	(Means)	(Means)	(Means)	
Unfriendly Behavior	4.04 [3.98]	3.67 [3.74]	4.15 [4.20]	0.319
Pay more - gas	$0.76 [0.78]	**$0.88 [0.86]**	$0.78 [0.77]	2.96^c
Lower heat	43%	29%	26%	$\chi^2 = 9^a$
Behavior - Transp.	%	%	%	
Public transit	*11*	**28**	25	
Car well-tuned	**46**	40	33	$\chi^2 = 19^b$
Car pool	16	6	**19**	
Tire pressure	6	6	6	
More slowly	21	21	17	

Notes: Analyses of covariance controlled for age, education, marital status and presence of children. ^{a} $p < 0.01$; ^{b} $p < 0.05$; ^{c} $p < 0.10$; [ ] = adjusted means.

Behavior toward the environment. This was assessed using four sets of questions:

1 The highest price per litre of gasoline that the respondent would be willing to pay at the pump, knowing that every cent above 65 cents would represent an air pollution tax to help defray the cost of cutting air pollution.
2 Willingness to engage in 7 environmentally-friendly behaviors, for example: turning-off lights, using a clothesline, turning down the heat, etc.
3 Purchase of 12 environmentally-unfriendly products (over the past year): disposable diapers; plastic knives, forks, or spoons; spray-on deodorants; non organically grown fruits and vegetables, etc. An index of *unfriendly purchasing behavior* was also obtained by summing the responses to these twelve questions.
4 Resolutions made with respect to driving: 1) use of public transportation; 2) better tuning of vehicle; 3) car

pooling; 4) ensuring proper inflation pressure in tires; and 5) driving at reduced speed.

Independent Variables

Ontario residents operationalized the "Strong English" viewpoint, francophone Quebec residents represented the "French" viewpoint, and the Quebec anglophones operationalized the "Acculturated English" viewpoint.

RESULTS

In order to test the difference in the levels of environmental knowledge (*Eco-Literacy*) acquired by the "Strong English" and "French" groups, the average scores obtained by each group were computed and subjected to analysis of covariance (ANCOVA), controlling for the effects of age, education, marital status, and the presence of children. As shown in Table 1, the overall F-test was found to be significant (F=5.52, p<.01). Post-hoc comparisons were then carried out using the Scheffé test to control for family wise error. The only significant contrast found was that between the French and Ontario samples (F=9.926; df=2/356; p<.05), thus showing a higher level of *Eco-Literacy* on the part of the Ontario respondents.

To examine for possible differences in the groups' levels of concern vis-à-vis local and global issues, responses to the open-ended question asking for "the single greatest environmental concern facing us today" were first grouped into six categories: 1. pollution (includes air, water, and general pollution); 2. recycling/garbage concerns; 3. ozone depletion; 4. global warming/greenhouse effect; 5. others (a mixed bag including acid rain, deforestation, toxic wastes, vanishing wildlife, etc.); and 6. did not know.

A cross-tabulation was subsequently performed using the five categories of concern and cultural group (Ontario consumers, French Quebecers, English Quebecers) as two variables (see Table 1). The chi-square test indicated a significant relationship between these two variables (χ^2=29, p<.01). An examination of the column percentage figures in Table 1 shows that more than twice as many Ontario consumers as Quebec consumers, 27% versus 11%, cited the *local issues* of garbage and/or recycling as the single greatest concern facing us today. On the *global environmental issues* relating to ozone depletion and global warming, there do not appear to be any great difference in the levels of concern between the two groups. However, the scores on the "pollution" and "others" category, which represent mainly global issues, now show a marked reversal with the previous findings, with the francophones now demonstrating greater concern. Thus, it would appear that Ontario consumers show greater concern for *local environmental issues* which require immediate personal efforts.

The test for attitudinal differences followed. To obtain the dependent variables, the 14 attitudinal questions mentioned earlier were first factor analyzed. This produced four factors which explained 47% of the variance. The first factor, *E-Activism*, represents a pro-active stance via à vis the reduction of excess packaging, re-utilizing shopping bags, belief in tougher anti-pollution laws, etc.; the second factor, *Solid Waste Orientation*, captures negative attitudes toward junk mail and excess packaging; the third factor, *Unconcerned Attitudes*, reflects an attitude that pollution problems are greatly exaggerated; while the last factor, *Sceptical Attitudes*, captures a sense of powerlessness to rectify ecological problems, and scepticism with respect to various claims made by manufacturers. Index scores of these attitudinal variables were then obtained by taking the means of each set of items loading on the attitudinal factors. An ANCOVA, controlling for the effects of age, education, marital status, and the presence of children, was then carried out with the index scores as dependent variables and the subcultural groups as independent variables (Table 1). The only significant effect was for *Solid Waste Orientation* (F=4.67, p<.05). Post hoc comparisons using a Scheffé adjustment only revealed a significant difference between the means of the Ontario and Quebec anglophone subjects (F=7.159; df=2/350; p<.05). In sum, it appears that Ontario consumers and French Canadians hold fairly similar attitudes vis-à-vis the environment.

In order to assess the subcultural differences with regards to the purchase of environmentally unfriendly products, an ANCOVA was carried out on the *Unfriendly Behavior* index described earlier, partialling out the four covariates. No significant differences between the groups were found. In terms of energy conservation, differences were observed between the groups: French Canadians demonstrated a greater propensity to use public transit and car pools, although they are still not as responsive as their Ontario counterparts when it comes to lowering the heat, keeping their car well-tuned, and driving more slowly.

Scores on environmental knowledge, concern for local and global issues, attitudes, and behavior for the anglophone Quebecers were then compared to those of their francophone and Ontario counterparts. No consistent pattern appears. For instance, there was no significant difference between the Quebec anglophones' scores on *Eco-Literacy* and those from Ontario-as expected. On the other hand, when examining the four environmental concern factors, a significant difference appeared on the *Solid Waste* factor, showing that their attitude was closer to their francophone counterparts. For the *Unconcerned* factor, on the other hand, Quebec anglophones seem to be closer to the Ontario subjects than to the French. We can conclude that Quebec anglophones appear to have developed a very distinctive set of attitudes and behaviors. This set of attitudes and behaviours may have evolved from their acculturation as a means to allow them to better integrate into two communities whose *general* attitudes differ from each other (Ryan 1972).

One aim of this study was to better understand the relationships which may exist between environmental knowledge, attitude, and pro-ecological behavior, as well as the moderating effects of culture on these "causal" linkages. This was motivated by the desire to see whether the cultural differences between the "Strong English" from Ontario and the French Canadians revealed the same patterns of relationships as were found in the study by Arbuthnot and Lingg (1975) between the U.S. subjects and the European French.

One way of assessing the relationships between the various attitudinal components and the possible moderating effects of culture, is to test a *causal model* incorporating the causal paths and interaction effects[2]. The model tested in the present study is shown in Figure 1. In this model, the culture variable represents the two principal cultural groups, the French and "Strong English," dummy coded as 1 and 0, respectively; while the other variables are as defined earlier. *E-Activism* was selected as the attitudinal variable since it was the most reliable of the four attitudinal indices, and since it had the best face validity.

Multi-stage regressions (Cohen and Cohen 1983) were used to estimate the path coefficients. Four covariates, namely, age, education, marital status, and the presence of children were first entered into the equations to partial out their effects. The values of the path coefficients found to be significant or marginally significant are shown on the diagram.

Three interactions were tested: (1) a *Culture* x *Eco-Literacy* interaction effect on *E-Activism* (Attitude); (2) a *Culture* x *E-Activism* interaction effect on *Unfriendly Behavior*; and (3) a *Culture* x *Eco-Literacy* interaction effect on *Unfriendly Behavior*. None of these reached significance; leading us to conclude that the two sub-cultures tested do not appear to have a differential effect on the knowledge —>attitude—>behavior relationships. Thus, although culture was found to influence the level of *Eco-Literacy* between the French and Ontario English, it had no influence on the other path coefficients.

Those causal pathways that were found to be significant were of relatively low magnitude. Additional support for the relationships shown in Figure 1 comes from examining the patterns of association between the above variables. Table 2 presents the partial correlations obtained between *Eco-Literacy*, *E-Activism*, and *Unfriendly Behavior*. Again, the correlations obtained for the

---

[2]The authors wish to thank an anonymous reviewer for the suggestion of using this approach. In the interest of clarity, the interactions are not indicated on the diagram.

FIGURE 1
Casual Diagram with Interactions

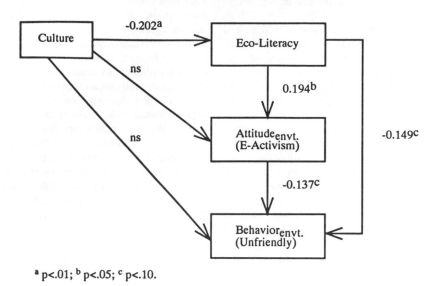

^{a} p<.01; ^{b} p<.05; ^{c} p<.10.

TABLE 2
Partial Correlations for the Three Sub-Cultures: Eco-Literacy by Attitudes and Behavior, E-Activism by Behavior

	Ontario	Anglophones	Francophones
Attitudes	Eco-Literacy	Eco-Literacy	Eco-Literacy
E- Activism	0.20^a	0.30^a	0.27^b
Solid Waste	0.04	0.08	0.05
Unconcerned	0.02	-0.14^c	-0.37^a
Sceptical	-0.15^b	-0.10	-0.11
Unfriendly Behavior			
Eco-Literacy	-0.17^b	-0.23^a	-0.25^c
E-Activism	-0.15^b	-0.30^a	-0.22^c

Note: Partial correlations were calculated to control for age, education, marital status and presence of children.
^{a} p < 0.01; ^{b} p < 0.05; ^{c} p < 0.10.

Ontario and Francophone samples are significant, but weak. These weak relationships could be due to either the inadequacy of the model, poor operationalization of the variables, or to measurement error.

DISCUSSION AND CONCLUSIONS

These findings contrast with those of the Arbuthnot and Lingg (1975) study. Whereas they found equal levels of environmental knowledge between the two groups, the present findings reveal a significant effect of culture on this cognitive component: French Canadians were found to have a significantly lower level of environmental knowledge than their Ontario counterparts. This may be due to the lesser influence of American media on francophones.

Contrasting findings also appear with respect to the relationships between knowledge, attitudes, and behavior. Whereas in the earlier study environmental knowledge and attitudes both predicted recycling behavior for Americans and not for the European French, in the present study, no cultural interactions were found: the relationships were weak, but essentially the same. It should be kept in mind that the Arbuthnot and Lingg study was carried out in 1975

when the environmental movement was still relatively young. The intervening twenty years of industrial activity and concomitant environmental degradation which has occurred in Europe may have given rise, in the words of Arbuthnot and Lingg to "a growing coalescence of information, attitudes, and actions on the part of the [European] French." (1975:281). One may predict that the relationship between environmental knowledge, attitudes, and environmentally friendly behavior for the European French should be more consistent than what it was in the earlier study. This would certainly merit a new study comparing the original groups to each other and to the French Canadians.

This study did confirm an important effect originally found by Arbuthnot and Lingg: namely, the direct mediational effect of environmental knowledge on behavior. This has important theoretical and practical value. From a theoretical perspective, it points to a variable other than intentions as being able to influence pro-environmental behavior. Thus, *Eco-Literacy* can influence behavior either directly, or through the standard Fishbein and Ajzen pathway (Fishbein and Ajzen 1975; Ajzen and Fishbein 1980). Although there is considerable evidence showing the applicability of the Fishbein-Ajzen behavioral intention model to pro-environmental behavior (Bowman and Fishbein 1978; Kantola, Syme, and Campbell 1982; Stutzman and Green 1982), there is also a growing literature which found direct effects of external variables on various forms of behavior (Fisher 1984; Bagozzi 1981; Bentler and Speckart 1979; Kantola et al. 1982). As Fisher (1984:119) states: "Taking these findings together, it can be speculated that the theory of reasoned action is a generally useful predictor, across behavioral domains, but that inclusions of external variables that are relevant in a specific behavioral domain may improve prediction of that type of behavior."

This is also echoed by Stutzman and Green (1982) who noted that Fishbein and Ajzen's model is appropriate for simple behaviors, analogous to a single act criterion. For multiple act criteria and more complex behaviors such as energy consumption one needs to take a more complex view of the model by including other variables which have been directly linked to energy consumption. They examined the predictive ability of consumers' conservation *knowledge* and *income*, in addition to the normal Fishbein and Ajzen variables. They found knowledge to predict energy usage relatively accurately. Although they had also predicted that a change in knowledge should also directly affect the belief system and, in turn, intentions and behavior, their results failed to substantiate this correlation. By contrast, in this study, *Eco-Literacy* is also exerting an influence on the belief system of the subjects.

In conclusion, knowledge about the environment plays a multi-faceted role in influencing behavior: It provides the subject with knowledge about action strategies; it provides knowledge of issues; and, it helps shape attitudes and intentions through the belief system. This leads to the practical aspects of the knowledge variable: It points to important leverage points whereby marketers and agencies can influence pro-environmental behavior.

Cultural Interactions with Subjective Norm and Past Eco-Friendly Habits

Two important variables which may also help explain the reason why the Quebec French display the same level of pro-environmental consumption as their Ontario counterparts, despite their lower level of environmental knowledgeability, are the Subjective Norm (SN) and past eco-friendly habits. According to the Fishbein and Ajzen model, there are two antecedents of behavioral intentions: a personal attitude component (A_{act}), and a societal attitude or subjective norm component (SN). It is believed that culture may exercise its effect by influencing the relative weight placed on the A_{act} and SN components in the formation of intentions to purchase ecologically friendly products. Kantola et al. (1982), for instance, applied the Fishbein model to explain behavioral intentions to conserve water. Both SN and A_{act} were found to be correlated with BI, with the former having the strongest relationship ($r=.42$ and $r=.27$, respectively). Support was also found in the area of energy conservation (Stutzman and Green 1982; Olsen 1981; Midden and Ritsema 1983).

There is also evidence that the cultural dimension of Individualism/Collectivism (Triandis 1989) influences the relative weight placed on these two variables. According to Triandis (1993:174-175), "When predicting social behavior, collectivists pay more attention to norms than to attitudes, whereas individualists pay more attention to attitudes than to norms." As evidence for this, he cited two studies (Bontempo and Rivera 1992; Kashima et al. 1992). Similar findings were obtained in consumer behavior by Lee and Green (1990).

That French Canadians tend to be more collectivistic than their English counterparts has been shown before (Lortie-Lussier and Fellers 1991; Lortie-Lussier, Fellers and Kleinplatz 1986; Punnett 1991; Major et al. 1994). This sub-culture appears to have better defined and stronger beliefs about the expectations of important others (NB) and would have greater motivation to comply with these referents (MC) than would their English counterparts. Consequently, the behavioral intentions of French Canadians should reflect a greater contribution of the SN component of the Fishbein model than would the English. A strong positive SN component could compensate for a low or negative A_{act} component, with the result that the French could have a greater propensity to behave in a pro-environmental manner, even though they might demonstrate weak (personal) beliefs toward the issues.

Another factor which may explain the differential effects of environmental knowledge on eco-friendly consumption, is past behavior. Past habits may override the attitudinal (A_{act}) and subjective norm (SN) components, and affect behavior directly in the case of a number of products, especially the low involvement kind used in the present study (Bentler and Speckart 1979; Landis, Triandis, and Adamopoulos 1978). Other situational effects could also intercede between attitudes and actual pro-environmental behaviors, for instance, the availability of "green" products, recycling facilities, and the personal cost of recycling.

Confirmation of these conjectures would have important implications for environmental education and consumer communication. It could help explain the "paradox" between what people profess, and their actions. It could also point to the need for a different behavioral influence strategy for French Quebecers. For this sub-culture, an optimal strategy would probably require altering beliefs about referent expectations, the identification or creation of opinion leaders, the simulation of word-of-mouth communication, and a greater emphasis on referent power in advertisements.

The findings on the greater propensity of French Canadians to use public transit and car pools seems to indicate that the campaigns sponsored by the provincial and municipal governments over the last fifteen years to encourage people to make greater use of public transit, and cutting down on the use of personal automobiles may be paying off. The image that the French have of energy and the ecological impact of energy generation may be evolving in a positive direction. This may also be the result of the almost daily reminders of the tremendous costs, both financial and ecological, of developing hydroelectric generating stations in the far northern regions of Quebec.

An apparent weakness of this study is that environmentally oriented behaviors were narrowly measured, using only the respondent's past purchases of products that are harmful to the environment. Employment of a much wider range of behavior indicators should produce more reliable findings.

Results of this study suggest that there is much work to be done modifying the behavior of the Canadian public with respect to profligate consumption and established consumer habits. If Canadian consumers are to make environmentally-sound product and lifestyle choices, they will need to be better informed about how their current behavior is affecting the natural environment. Further, marketers, policy-makers, and consumer advocates need to take into greater account cultural disparities in developing campaigns aimed at stemming and reversing environmental degradation.

REFERENCES

Ahmed, S.A., R. deCamprieu, and P. Hope (1981), "A Comparison of English and French Canadian Attitudes Toward Energy and the Environment," in *Marketing,* vol. 2, ed. R. Wyckham, Montreal: Administrative Sciences Association of Canada, 1-10.

Ajzen, I. and M. Fishbein (1980), *Understanding Attitudes and Predicting Social Behavior*, Englewood Cliffs, N.J.: Prentice Hall.

Arbuthnot, J. and S. Lingg (1975), "A Comparison of French and American Environmental Behaviors, Knowledge, and Attitudes," *International Journal of Psychology*, 4, 10, 275-281.

Bagozzi, R. P. (1981), "Attitudes, Intentions and Behavior: A Test of Some Key Hypotheses," *Journal of Personality and Social Psychology*, 41, 607-627.

Bentler, P.M. and G. Speckart (1979), "Models of Attitude-Behavior Relations," *Psychological Review*, 86, 452-464.

Berger, I.E. (1991), "A Framework for Understanding the Relationship Between Environmental Attitudes and Market Behaviours," Working Paper, University of Toronto.

Bontempo, R. and J.C. Rivera (1992, August), *Cultural Variation in Cognition: The Role of Self-Concept in the Attitude-Behavior Link*. Paper presented at the meeting of the Academy of Management, Las Vega, NV.

Bouchard, J. (1980), *Differences*, Montreal: Heritage.

Bowman, C.H. and M. Fishbein (1978), "Understanding Public Reaction to Energy Proposals: An Application of the Fishbein Model," *Journal of Applied Social Psychology*, 8, 319-340.

Cohen, J. and P. Cohen (1983), *Applied Multiple Regression/Correlation Analysis for the Behavioral Sciences*, 2nd Edition. Hillsdale, N.J.: Lawrence Erlbaum Associates.

Fishbein, M. and I. Ajzen (1975), *Belief, Attitude, Intention, and Behavior: An Introduction to Theory and Research*. Reading, Mass: Addison-Wesley.

Fisher, W.A. (1984), "Predicting Contraceptive Behavior Among University Men: The Role of Emotions and Behavioral Intentions," *Journal of Applied Social Psychology*, 14(2), 104-123.

Fisk, G. (1973), "Criteria for a Theory of Responsible Consumption," *Journal of Marketing*, 37 (2), 24-31.

Goldberg, R. (1989), "Loblaw Companies Ltd.: President's Choice G.R.E.E.N.: Something Can Be Done," Harvard Business School Case #9-590-051, Harvard Business School.

Hui, M., M. Laroche, C. Kim, and A. Joy (1993), "Equivalence of Lifestyle Dimensions Across Four Major Subcultures in Canada," *International Journal of Consumer Marketing*, 5 (3), 15-35.

Kantola, J.J., G.J. Syme and N.A. Campbell (1982), "The Role of Individual Differences and External Variables in a Test of the Sufficiency of Fishbein's Model to Explain Behavioral Intentions to Conserve Water," *Journal of Applied Social Psychology*, 12(1), 70-83.

Kashima, Y., Siegel, M., Tanaka, K., and E.S. Kashima (1992), "Do People Believe that Attitudes Cause Behavior? Toward a Cultural Psychology of Attribution Processes," *British Journal of Social Psychology*, 31, 111-124.

Kindra, G.S., M. Laroche, and T.E. Muller (1994), *Consumer Behaviour: The Canadian Perspective*, Second Edition, Scarborough, ON: Nelson Canada.

Kotler, P. and R.J. Turner (1993), *Marketing Management: Analysis Planning, Implementation and Control*, Canadian 7th edition, Scarborough, ON: Prentice-Hall Canada.

Landis, D., H.C. Triandis, and J. Adamopoulos (1978) "Habit and Behavioral Intentions as Predictors of Social Behavior," *Journal of Social Psychology*, 106, 227-237.

Lee, C. and R.T. Green (1990), "Cross-Cultural Examination of the Fishbein Behavioral Intentions Model," *Journal of International Business Studies*, 289-305.

Lortie-Lussier, M. and G.L. Fellers (1991), "Self-Ingroup Relationships - Their Variations Among Canadian Pre-Adolescents of English, French, and Italian Origin," *Journal of Cross-Cultural Psychology*, 22:4, December, 458-471.

Lortie-Lussier, M., G.L. Fellers, and P.J. Kleinplatz (1986), "Value Orientations of English, French, and Italian Canadian Children - Continuity of the Ethnic Mosaic?" *Journal of Cross-Cultural Psychology*, 17:3, September, 283-299.

Maclean's (1990), "Hopes and Fears: People are Prepared to Change," September 17, 50-51.

Major, M., McCarrey, M., Mercier, P., and Y. Gasse (1994), "The Meanings of Work and Personal Values of Canadian Anglophone and Francophone Middle Managers," *Canadian Journal of Administrative Sciences*, 11(3), (September), 251-263.

Mallen, B. (1977), *French Canadian Consumer Behavior: Comparative Lessons From the Published Literature and Private Corporate Marketing Studies*, Montreal: Advertising and Sales Executives Club of Montreal.

Midden, C.J. and B.S. Ritsema (1983), "The Meaning of Normative Processes for Energy Conservation," *Journal of Economic Psychology*, 4(1-2), (October), 37-55.

Miller, T.A.W. (1991), "Green Marketing: What's Happening to Environmentalism?," Speech at the American Demographics Consumer Outlook Conference, June.

Mittelstaedt, M. (1991), "All the Worry Over Ecology Fails to Stem Consumption," *Globe and Mail*, June 4, C1-C2.

Olsen, M.E. (1981), "Consumers' Attitudes Toward Energy Conservation," *Journal of Social Issues*, 37(2), 108-131.

Punnett, B.J. (1991), "Language, Cultural Values and Preferred Leadership Style: A Comparison of Anglophones and Francophones in Ottawa," *Canadian Journal of Behavioral Science*, 23(2), 241-244.

Rothe, J.T. and L. Benson (1974), "Intelligent Consumption: An Attractive Alternative to the Marketing Concept," *MSU Business Topics*, Winter, 29-34.

Ryan, M.G. (1972), "Bilingual Attitudes Towards Authority: A Canadian Study," Reprint of a paper presented to the International & Intercultural Division, Speech Communication Association, Chicago, Illinois, December 27-30, 14.

Schaninger, C.M., J.C. Bourgeois, and W.C. Buss (1985), "French-English Canadian Subcultural Consumption Differences," *Journal of Marketing*, 49 (Spring), 82-92.

Schlossberg, H. (1992), "Marketers Told to Heed Consumers Before Big Brother Steps In," *Marketing News*, April 27, 10.

Stutzman, T.M. and S.B. Green (1982), "Factors Affecting Energy Consumption: Two Field Tests of the Fishbein-Ajzen Model," *The Journal of Social Psychology*, 117, 183-201.

Tigert, D.J. (1973), "Can a Separate Marketing Strategy for French Canada Be Justified: Profiling English-French Markets Through Lifestyle Analysis," in *Canadian Marketing: Problems and Prospects*, eds. Donald N. Thompson and David S. Leighton, Toronto, ON: Wiley of Canada, 113-147.

Triandis, H.C. (1989), "Cross-Cultural Studies of Individualism and Collectivism," in *Nebraska Symposium on Motivation 1989: Cross-Cultural Perspectives*, 37, ed. J.J. Berman, Lincoln: University of Nebraska Press, 41-133.

Triandis, H.C. (1993), "Collectivism and Individualism as Cultural Syndromes," *Cross-Cultural Research: The Journal of Comparative Social Science*, Vol. 27 (3-4), 155-180.

Welds, K. (1991), "Unwrapping the Environment," *Canadian Grocer*, June, 18-23, 41.

Searching for Dominance: The Effect of Similarity on Brand Choice

Alex Chernev, Duke University

This paper examines the effects of similarity on brand choice and how dominance relationships between choice options moderate these effects. Presented research is based on the notion that consumers restructure choice problems in an attempt to minimize tradeoffs between choice options. Particularly, it is proposed that when consumers have a primary reason to choose an asymmetrically dominant alternative, increasing brand similarity on non-primary attributes is likely to increase the choice share of this option. It is argued that the tradeoff difficulty moderates the above effect and that more pronounced similarity effects are associated with more difficult tradeoffs.

Communities and Consumption: Research on Consumer Strategies for Constructing Communal Relationships in a Postmodern World

Craig J. Thompson, University of Wisconsin
Douglas B. Holt, Penn State University

PAPERS & PRESENTERS

Poverty, Consumption, and Community: Exploring Community Formation Among Those Excluded from Membership in a Consumer Society
Douglas B. Holt, Penn St University

Consumption, Community, and the Trans-Cultural Experiences of Sojourners
Siok Tambyah & Craig J. Thompson, University of Wisconsin - Madison

Immigrant Consumers: Fantasies, Realities, and the Transition of the Self
Lisa Penaloza, University of Colorado
Ronald Paul Hill, Villanova University

In fields ranging from moral philosophy (Etzioni 1988) to social psychology (Gergen 1991) to women's studies (Gilligan et al 1990; Radway 1984), the Cartesian focus on individual level experiences is being broadened to address the communal nature of human existence and meaning. One prominent manifestation of this trend is the increasing theoretical attention now being directed to the influences that the desire for communal ties and feelings of interpersonal connectedness exerts upon consumption behaviors (Fischer and Arnould 1990; Fischer and Gainer 1995; Holt 1995a,b; Mehta and Belk 1991; Schouten and McAlexander 1995; Penaloza 1994; Thompson 1996). The papers in this session provide a more focused consideration of the relationships between communal desires and consumption oriented behaviors and meanings. This focus has implication for a broader stream of consumer research that explores the dialectical relationship between individual level consumer decisions/actions and the shared meanings embedded in patterns of social interaction and cultural belief systems.

Social scientists have longed viewed consumption activities as potent, symbolically charged practices that play a central role in the development and maintenance of community. For example, rituals of eating (Douglas 1971), immersion in the spectacle of "sport" (Elias and Dunning 1986), collecting (Belk et al 1991), celebrity fan clubs (O'Guinn 1991) are but a few of the consumption activities that create affiliative bonds and a sense of shared purpose among people. As Western consumer cultures enter the postmodern age, it is likely that the interplay between community and consumption will become more significant to the fabric of everyday life. Specifically, key characteristics of the "postmodern condition" are that 1) social relations and self-identity are centered on consumption rather than production; and 2) consumption increasingly provides a locus of community relationships (Baudrillard 1988; Firat and Venkatesh 1993).

In the consumer research literature, community has typically been conceptualized in the traditional Durkheimian form, that emphasizes sustained social interaction and the experience of "communitas." For example, Arnould and Price (1993) describe how a diverse group of individuals foster a sense of community over the course of a river rafting trip. Holt (1995a) explains communal processes in relation to the sense of affiliation that emerges from the shared (and ritualized) experience of attending and watching professional baseball games. Schouten and McAlexander (1995) discuss the communal bonds formed through joint participation in a subculture of consumption (e.g. Harley-Davidson bike riders).

A limitation of these Durkheimian formulations, however, is that they are not well-attuned to the cultural transformations characteristic of postmodern (or late capitalist) society and the consequent challenges posed to more traditional forms of community affiliation (see Jameson 1989). The postmodern social trajectory is toward increasingly privatized consumer lifestyles — with the phenomenon of "cocooning" being widely noted manifestation — that are marked by fragmented social identities and increasingly transitory populations. Many of these changes can be traced to the unabated expansion of the urban landscape and, second, to the globalization of the world economy which necessitates geographic mobility among both professionals and laboring classes. A number of other postmodern transformations — including the proliferation of consumer lifestyle "options," the increasingly narrowed focus of niche marketing, and the ethos of expressing individuality via consumption symbols — have been posited to undermine the formation of enduring communal ties (Firat 1995). In this fragmented, privatized, and nomadic cultural milieu, the quest for community is rendered more as an ideal than a practical reality (Gergen 1991) and attaining some semblance of this ideal demands ever more creative solutions.

The three presentations in this session speak to these postmodern conditions by exploring how community is constructed through consumption. To better highlight these postmodern issues each paper addresses a social context in which community formation is particularly problematic for the research informants. These respective analyses provide a more nuanced understanding of strategies for forming a sense of community through consumption and, in so doing, develops important implications for understanding the symbolic dimensions of consumer behavior.

Holt provides a sociological analysis of how two lower class men use consumption to construct an alternative form of community in a college town. The experiences of these informants provide rich insights into the process of inclusion and exclusion that underlie communal experiences. Tambyah and Thompson offer a phenomenological account of the consumer experiences of transnational professionals; a class of global sojourners whose nomadic lifestyles exemplifies the state of postmodern transience. Hill and Penaloza present an ethnography of the consumer experiences of Mexican immigrants who have relocated to the United States to escape harsh economic circumstances. Their research places particular emphasis on the question of how Mexican immigrants balance between their ties to previous communities and the need to form a new community (and to some extent social identity) in the United States. This analysis extends previous studies on immigrant consumers by exploring how these perceptions of community affiliation shape their informants' consumption preferences, conceptions of the "good life," and the meanings of their consumer experiences and special possessions. The session discussant David Mick provides a semiotic perspective on the symbolic processes that consumers may use to construct a sense of community from ostensibly privatized consumer activities.

REFERENCES

Arnould, Eric J. and Linda L. Price (1993), "'River Magic': Extraordinary Experience and the Service Encounter," *Journal of Consumer Research* 20 (June), 24-46.

Baudrillard, Jean (1988), *Selected Writings*, ed. Mark Poster, Stanford, CA: Stanford University Press.

Belk, Russell W., Melanie Wallendorf, John F. Sherry, and Morris B. Holbrook (1991), "Collecting in a Consumer Culture," in *Highways and Buyways: Naturalistic Research from the Consumer Behavior Odyssey*, ed. Russell W. Belk, Provo, UT: Association for Consumer Research, 178-215.

Benhabib, Seyla (1992), *Situating the Self: Gender, Community, and Postmodernism in Contemporary Ethics*, New York: Routledge.

Douglas, Mary (1971), "Deciphering a Meal," *Daedalus*, Winter, 61-82.

Durkheim, Emile (1915), *The Elementary Forms of Religious Life*, New York: Free Press.

_____ (1933), *The Division of Labor in Society*, New York: Free Press.

Elias, Norbert and Eric Dunning (1986), *Quest for Excitement: Sport and Leisure in the Civilizing Process*, Oxford: Basil Blackwell.

Etzioni, Amitai (1988), *The Moral Dimension: Toward A New Economics*, New York: The Free Press.

Firat, A. Fuat (1995), "Consumer Culture or Culture Consumed?" in *Marketing in a Multicultural World*, eds. Janeen Costa Arnold and Gary J. Bamossy, Thousand Oaks, CA: Sage, 105-125.

_____ and Alladi Venkatesh (1993), "Postmodernity: The Age of Marketing" *International Journal of Research in Marketing*, 10 (August), 227-251.

Fischer, Eileen and Stephen J. Arnould (1990), "More Than a Labor of Love: Gender Roles and Christmas Gift Shopping," *Journal of Consumer Research*, 17 (December), 333-345.

Fischer, Eileen and Brenda Gainer (1995), "Masculinity and the Consumption of Sport," *Gender and Consumption*, ed. Janeen Arnold Costa, Thousand Oaks: Sage, 84-103.

Gergen, Kenneth J. (1991), *The Saturated Self: Dilemmas of Identity in Contemporary Life*, New York, NY: Basic Books.

Gilligan, Carol, Nona Lyons, and Trudy Hamner eds. (1990), *Making Connections*, Cambridge, MA: Harvard University Press.

Hirschman, Elizabeth C. (1988), "Upper Class Wasps As Consumers: A Humanist Inquiry," *Research in Consumer Behavior, Vol. 3*, ed. Jagdish N. Sheth and Elizabeth C. Hirschman, New York: JAI Press, 102-110.

_____ and Morris B. Holbrook (1992), *Postmodern Consumer Research: The Study of Consumption as Text*, Newbury Park, CA: Sage.

Holt, Douglas B. (1995a), "How Consumers Consume: A Taxonomy of Baseball Spectator's Consumption Practices," *Journal of Consumer Research*, 22 (June), .

_____ (1995b) "Consumers Cultural Differences as Local Systems of Taste: A Critique of the Personality/Values Approach and An Alternative Framework," in *Advances in Consumer Research, Vol.1*, ed. Joseph Cote, Provo, UT: Association for Consumer Research.

Jameson, Frederic (1990), *Postmodernism, or the Cultural Logic of Late Capitalism*, Duke: Duke University Press.

Mehta, Raj and Russell W. Belk (1991), "Artifacts, Identity, and Transition" Favorite Possessions of Indians and Indian Immigrants to the United States," *Journal of Consumer Research*, 17 (March), 398-411.

O'Guinn, Thomas C. (1991), "Touching Greatness: The Central Midwest Barry Manilow Fan Club," in *Highways and Buyways: Naturalistic Research from the Consumer Behavior Odyssey*, ed. Russell W. Belk, Provo, UT: Association for Consumer Research, 102-111.

Penaloza, Lisa (1994), "Atravasando Fronteras\Border Crossings: A Critical Ethnographic Examination of the Consumer Acculturation of Mexican Immigrants," *Journal of Consumer Research*, 21 (June), 32-54.

Radway, Janice (1984), *Reading the Romance: Women, Patriarchy and Popular Literature*, Chapel Hill, NC: The University of North Carolina Press.

Schouten, John and James McAlexander (1995),"Subcultures of Consumption," *Journal of Consumer Research*, 22 (June) 43-61.

Thompson, Craig J. (1996), "Caring Consumers: Gendered Consumption Meanings and the Juggling Lifestyle," *Journal of Consumer Research*, 22 (March), forthcoming.

Immigrant Consumers and Community Bonds: Fantasies, Realities, and the Transition of Self-Identity

Ronald Paul Hill, Villanova University
Liz Somin, Villanova University

ABSTRACT

Recent research in the *Journal of Consumer Research* has investigated the impact of immigration on consumer behavior. This study extends previous work through long interviews with recently arrived immigrants who came to the United States to join relatives. Our focus is on their "consumption" images of the U.S. and the sources of these images as well as the roles previous and new possessions play in the development of their post-immigration identities. Three themes serve to summarize our findings.

INTRODUCTION

He is an American, who leaving behind him all his ancient prejudices and manners, receives new ones from the new mode of life he has embraced, the new government he obeys, and the new rank he holds. The American is a new man, who acts upon new principles.

Hector St. John de Crevecouer, 1782

The issue of immigration has, once again, captured the attention of the United States population. Popular press reports show that Americans are intolerant of the flow of people into this country regardless of their status. As Yang (1995, p. 35) states: "Americans are fed up not only with illegal immigrants but with legal ones, too....They [reformers] want to cut down on the number of newcomers to the U.S. on family-unification visas by creating a point system that measures applicants' potential for contributing to the economy. The criteria: education, job skills, and English-language abilities." Yet, as the *Atlantic Monthly* (Connelly and Kennedy 1994) notes, whether this concern has "realistic" or racist origins is inconsequential; as the population continues to rise in countries steeped in poverty and political repression, the poor of these regions will continue to migrate to the so-called "western paradise."

Consistent with recent research by Penaloza (1994), this study extends previous work through long interviews with recently-arrived immigrants who came to the United States in order to join relatives. We explore their images of this country compared to their home countries before their arrival, with an emphasis on material images (e.g., houses, cars, clothing, foods, etc.) and their sources (e.g., TV, movies, music, etc.). We then examine the possessions brought to this country in their relocation and their meanings within the context of their previous and new identities. Finally, we investigate the possessions they have acquired since their arrival, and focus our attention on the ones that remind them of home as well as those that were purchased for the first time.

The findings from this study can be summarized in three themes: 1) Material fantasies versus material realities among these immigrants as well as changing expectations and their sources; 2) The role of possessions in the maintenance of aspects of the pre-immigration self; and 3) The role of possessions in the transformation of the post-immigration self.

THE STUDY

Once the general thesis of this investigation was established, an interviewers' guide was developed. This guide, presented in the Table, was designed to determine the informants' backgrounds, reasons for immigrating, and images of our consumer culture as well as the importance of possessions to them. Please see the Table for more details.

In order to locate newly arrived immigrants, we contacted the Philadelphia office of the Department of Immigration and Naturalization. Individuals in this office suggested we contact one of the numerous religious-affiliated groups in our community established to provide assistance to newly arrived immigrants. The Incarnate Heart of Mary (IHM) Literacy Center in Philadelphia was particularly accommodating, and we conducted long interviews with ten adult students from Mexico, South Vietnam, Columbia, Pakistan, El Salvador, Laos, Haiti, and Ecuador.

Interviews were conducted on a voluntary basis, with staff support to help us find willing informants. Interviews were conducted in English, but informants were encouraged to respond in their native languages if they preferred. In these circumstances, a translator from the center was utilized to explain the questions as well as the responses. Because of the concerns of our informants, all recordings of the interviews were destroyed after transcription and no attempt was made to associate information with informants' real names.

THE RESULTS

The first set of questions asked informants' their rationales for coming to the U.S. While the simple answer was to reunite with their loved ones who preceded them here, the underlying reasons were more complex. Primarily, they can be categorized as "freedom" and "opportunity." The former implicates many of the dominant institutions in any society, the latter involves the economic system. Thus, freedom from persecution was part of the motivation for these individuals:

One woman from Laos simply stated "Because my country is a communist."

A Pakistani woman explained "Pakistan hard. My religion Jesus Christ. Difficult Pakistan. Murder."

Opportunity, on the other hand, was for education, especially for children (a Vietnamese woman stated "My family come here children ah go to school. I think America very good."), or for economic advancement here or in their home countries (a Mexican man responded "Economic conditions are fair in Mexico, and only reason when I went to work in computers I was told on several occasions that if I was bilingual the opportunities for getting a job were much greater.").

The next set of questions examined their images of the U.S. as well as their lives here following immigration. While all believed that their lives would improve in a variety of ways once they arrived, their expectations differed depending upon their country of origin. For example, the informants from Laos, Cambodia, and Vietnam had little or no prior experience with western media and products, relying on a limited number of books and word of mouth for their impressions. On the other hand, the informants from Mexico and South America had first hand experience with U.S. industry icons, including McDonalds, Tops, Jack in the Box, Denny's, WalMart, Sam's, Kmart, Target, Sears, and Clover, allowing them to form more fully their impressions and expectations of this country.

206

TABLE
Interviewers' Guide
New Immigrants

1) Tell me a little bit about yourself. (Probe for age, [note sex and race], education, country of origin, family relationships, occupation, and current profession.) Are you the first one in your family to come to the US? If not, who was here before you?

2) Tell me why you came to the United States? (Probe for the American [material] dream; Did you come with a plan for living here in mind?)

3) What was your image of the United States before you came? (Probe for material images—houses, cars, clothing, foods, etc.) How did you come by the image? (TV, movies, music—ask for specifics.)

4) What was your life like before you came here? (Probe for American products purchased in their home country.) What is your life like now that you are here? (Probe for material life—housing, clothing, food, cars, etc.) How is it the same and how is it different from your picture of America before arriving?

5) What did you bring from your home country? (Probe for a variety of possessions—especially "sacred" items such as pictures, mementos, etc.) Why did you bring these items? (Probe for its cultural meaning particularly in relation to the self—is it self defining?) Do you still have these item? Do they still have the same value?

6) What do you buy in this country that reminds you of home? (Probe for whether these products make them feel "at-home.") Where do you buy these items? (Probe for similar shopping patterns and outlets to their home country versus adopting the American approach.)

7) What do you buy in this country that is different than your home? (Probe for new products that help them redefine themselves as Americans—search for the meaning behind these purchases.)

Further, advertisements as well as movies helped exacerbate these images, and *Terminator*, *Delta Force*, *Beauty and the Beast*, and a variety of children's cartoons were mentioned.

Unfortunately, virtually all of our informants were dissatisfied with their lives and current situations, especially with regard to the "quality" of Americans, their material existence, job opportunities, and the conditions of cities. The images of freedom and opportunity that gave them the courage to make this difficult transition were unrealized. Consider the following comments by a Mexican man that summarizes their frustrations well:

> Two images [I] have...of the U.S. One is good and the other is bad. One is that it is a capitalist nation, and they paint a very rosy picture for us through movies. [But] when you come to the U.S., it is much harder to work to earn money to be in society from the image they paint. I thought the people here would be of a higher quality, they would also be smarter, but it turned out that they were not as smart as they are painted both through the movies and the general consensus of Hispanics.

When asked about the possessions that they brought from their previous homes, the answers were surprisingly curt and the list was very short. Virtually all of the informants discussed clothing, concentrating on their attempts to bring items that were suitable to their (expected) new lives in the U.S. However, informants also indicated the difficulties they had acquiring in advance or bringing these goods to their new homes. Reasons ranged from their relative poverty to political concerns stemming from their desire *not* to alert the authorities to the permanent status of their "visit" to the U.S.

Other items that were brought from their previous homes tended to be "sacred" possessions (see Belk et al. 1989; Hill 1991). The most common property mentioned had little innate cultural significance but was symbolic of their previous lives and families—

photographs or videos. For example, a Haitian woman told us that she brought the video tape of her wedding as well as her wedding album. A Mexican man provided more insight into the role of family photos in his life when he noted that they served as motivation and a reminder of "why he is here." Thus, these items served to ground our informants in their previous "worlds" and social identities.

Finally, regarding the meanings of and experience with products from this country since their arrival, two general categories seem particularly germane. The first deals with the acquisition and preparation of food. Informants felt that the customs of this country involving the processing and preservation of foods was inadequate to their needs, bordering on repugnant (a Columbian man stated that "The meat is cold here. In Columbia no. The meat is fresh.), and they believed that the preparation of food has much less significance in this country. As one response, our informants preferred to create a sense of continuity with their previous lives and cultures by growing their own food when possible (a Laotian woman stated "Here summertime I plant it.) and frequenting small shops that cater to their nationalities (a Pakistani woman).

The second category, admittedly an atypical "product," is the English language. The informants uniformly believe that their family's abilities or inabilities with this new and often strange sounding language was their key to long-term successful acculturation into U.S. society and economic success. Whether this is in fact the case, is a different empirical question.

CONCLUDING COMMENTS

As noted earlier, the findings from this study can be summarized in three themes. First, the material fantasies that existed among these immigrants before coming to the U.S. failed to become material realities, due, in part, to limited job opportunities. In the end, virtually all of our informants had substantially modified (and lowered) their expectations in this regard. Second, relatively few possessions were brought from their home countries, but these sparse items, as well as customs such as food preparation, played an important role in the maintenance of the pre-immigration self. Third, "atypical" possessions such as "acquiring" the English language were seen as integral in the transformation of the post-immigration self into an individual capable of successfully maneuvering within our society.

As mentioned earlier, the informants in this study, like many of the immigrants who came to this country as a result of the family reunification principle of the Immigration and Nationality Act Amendments of 1965, were fleeing the poverty and violence of the Third World (see Mills 1994). Noonan (1994, p. 177) notes:

> In many ways, immigrants know what Americanism is better than we do. They've paid us the profoundest compliment by leaving the land of their birth to come and spend their lives with us. And they didn't come here to join nothing, they came to join something—us at our best, us as they imagined us after a million movies and books and reports from relatives. They wanted to be part of our raucous drama, and they wanted the three m's—money, mobility, meritocracy.

Unfortunately, when they arrived they often experienced profound disappointment at the lack of opportunity and overt or covert racism. National debate, of course, will continue to concentrate on the ethnocentric issue of *how many*, but a humane society also must consider the quality of life of these individuals once they exist with our borders.

REFERENCES

Belk, Russell W., Melanie Wallendorf, and John F. Sherry, Jr. (1989), "The Sacred and the Profane in Consumer Behavior: Theodicy on the Odyssey," *Journal of Consumer Research*, 16 (June), 1-38.

Connelly, Matthew and Paul Kennedy (1995), "Must It Be the Rest Against the West?" *Atlantic Monthly*, 274 (December), 61-84.

Hill, Ronald Paul (1991), "Homeless Women, Special Possessions, and the Meaning of 'Home': An Ethnographic Case Study," *Journal of Consumer Research*, 18 (December), 298-310.

Mills, Nicolaus (1994), "Introduction: The Era of the Golden Venture," in *Arguing Immigration*, ed. Nicolaus Mills, New York, NY: Touchstone, 11-27.

Noonan, Peggy (1994), "Why the World Comes Here," in *Arguing Immigration*, ed. Nicolaus Mills, New York, NY: Touchstone, 176-180.

Penaloza, Lisa (1994), "Atravesando Fronteras/Border Crossings: A Critical Ethnographic Exploration of the Consumer Acculturation of Mexican Immigrants," *Journal of Consumer Research*, 21 (June), 32-54.

Yang, Catherine (1995), "Immigration: You Can't Test For Drive and Ambition," *Business Week*, May 29, 35.

Building Brand Equity Through Packaging: A Multi-Methodological Perspective

Robert Underwood, Virginia Polytechnic Institute and State University

SPECIAL SESSION OVERVIEW

A review of the consumer behavior literature reveals little theoretical development in the area of packaging and its communicative effects. This gap is problematic because macro-market trends have increased the importance of packaging in consumer decision making and in the development of brands. The objectives of this session were: 1) to explore the role of packaging in the building of brand equity, 2) to expand theoretical development in the area of packaging's influence on consumer behavior, and 3) to report substantive findings about the relationship of package design to individual choice and brand equity.

In keeping with the conference theme, these papers used diverse methodologies: qualitative research, analysis of an innovative market database, and a field experiment using a virtual reality simulation. The three papers also illustrated a range of research objectives with respect to packaging and brand equity: theory generation, theory testing, and establishing substantive relationships between packaging and brand equity.

SESSION SUMMARY

Ozanne and Underwood sought to expand the conceptual development in the area through a qualitative examination of packaging's influence on customer-based brand knowledge. Utilizing McCracken's (1988) long interview technique, interviews (over 300 subject-product interactions) were conducted with a heterogeneous sample in a grocery store walkthrough format, affording the researchers the opportunity to identify emerging themes which tap the entire range of packaging's influence. In addition to the expected themes of package/product utilities (e.g., functional, aesthetic, symbolic, etc.), one unexpected theme which was evident across all informants was the theme of the duplicity of packaging communication. This theme highlights the need for manufacturers to give greater attention to this point of communication and avoid the perceived deception which often adversely affects consumers' brand equity. Ozanne offered Habermas's theory of communicative competence as a set of useful norms (i.e., norm of comprehensibility, norm of sincerity, norm of legitimacy, norm of truthfulness) that must occur for "authentic" communication (i.e., communication that is free from distortion) to take place. She suggested that this offers a useful benchmark against which manufacturers can judge their communication (i.e., packaging) and seek to improve their level of distortion-free communication. It was also argued that it is in both the interest of the manufacturer (in increasing brand equity) and the consumer to do so.

Susan Nelson, director of research for Landor Associates, Inc. presented the second paper in the session, an analysis of the Young & Rubicam/Landor Associates BrandAssetx Valuator (BAV) database that explored how three generalized packaging design approaches correlate with four key measures of brand building: differentiation, relevance, esteem, and knowledge. The three generalized package design approaches were:

1. Image/positioning graphics dominant (no product vignette/illustration)
2. Image/positioning graphics dominant (with product vignette/illustration)
3. Copy/typography dominant

The analyses did not support the hypothesis that packaging graphics approach, in and of itself, is associated with brand strength and vitality. She suggested that brands which have attained national distribution stature are so thoroughly a composite of multiple marketing variables that no one variable (in this case, packaging graphics approach) can have a significant impact on brand strength. Nelson suggested that more insight may be gained via a sub-analysis by product category (e.g., sauces vs. snack foods vs. beverages).

The final paper (Underwood, Klein, and Burke) tested theoretical propositions about how a specific package design element, incorporating a picture of the product on the package, affects consumer attention, brand evaluations, and product choice. Propositions derived from theories about visual/verbal information and cue utilization suggest that design effects will differ for (1) national versus private label brands, and (2) brands that differ significantly in terms of the degree of experiential benefits provided. The research was conducted in two experiments, one of which utilized a virtual reality simulated shopping system called *Visionary Shopper*. Preliminary results indicated a significant picture effect for highly experiential private label products in terms of attention and choice. This finding supports the hypotheses that picture effects should be stronger for private label brands and more experiential products.

Special Session Summary
New Developments in Mental Accounting: Implications for Consumer Choice

Ravi Dhar, Yale University

A wide body of research indicates that decisions are affected by how outcomes are framed. Mental accounting is a type of framing in which individuals are hypothesized to form psychological accounts for the outcomes. While the anecdotal examples are widely known, the mechanisms underlying the phenomena are still not well understood (Thaler 1993). The present symposium hopes to provide insights into several choice anomalies that are better understood as mental accounts.

Despite having different objectives, the four papers investigating mental accounting processes have certain commonalties. The general theme is that mental accounting induces people to behave in a fashion that violates normative behavior in systematic ways. The present papers also share common elements in terms of the process underlying principle of mental accounting. In doing so, the papers examine the link between mental accounts and theories of categorization. In particular, principles of categorization can be used to understand the causes, effects, and the processes of mental accounting.

The study of mental accounts has important implications for the role and definition of consumer behavior and marketing. By treating normatively equivalent procedures for providing information as unequal, mental accounts helps to understand the motives underlying such behavior. While sharing a common theme, the researchers address different surface problems (e.g., savings, pricing, bundling) using different methodologies (laboratory experiments, process measures, and field research.) The first paper (Greenleaf, Morwitz, and Johnson) examines the practice of "divided pricing" by which many firms divide the price for a product or service into at least two parts rather than charging a single, all inclusive price. Standard economic theory suggests that consumers will be indifferent between an all-inclusive price and divided prices that add to the same amount. The authors conduct a series of experiments which demonstrate that using divided prices can increase consumers' demand and expenditure, and reduce their perceptions of the price of a product.

The second paper (Prelec and Loewenstein) explores attitudes to borrowing and saving decisions, and presents relevant survey data. The authors show how the preferences for borrowing and saving programs depend on the degree to which the cash flows are psychologically coupled to specific products. For savings programs, they find a preference for a highly coupled arrangement, such as savings for college tuition, rather than more loosely coupled ones, such as savings for some general category of expenditure. The theoretical part of the paper translates these findings into a formal mental accounting model.

The third paper (Dhar and Simonson) studies how consumers make spending decisions in a number of related categories. According to classical choice theory, the choice for each component should depend only on individuals preferences and the set of available alternatives in each component. The authors propose that people's choices in each component of the bundle may be influenced by choices and outcomes of other components in the same mental category. Such a viewpoint broadens the set of outcomes that may serve as complements in a consumption situation. The results are inconsistent with the notion of mental budgeting and a number of other existing explanations.

The fourth paper (Heath and Fennema) examines the intuitive rules that people use in determining whether they are "getting their money's worth" by performing a kind of "mental depreciation" or "amortization." Not surprisingly, people feel that items depreciate over times and uses. People feel that they get their money's worth faster if an item is used for special occasions. In a field study, the authors examine student's behavior for a dorm meal plan that has a high up-front membership fee, but very low marginal costs.

Given the diversity of the papers, the direction of the discussion was to arrive at a unifying force rather than a session summary. Ratneshwar, the discussant helped to highlight some of the promising avenues that are emerging in this area of decision research as well as make suggestions for future research based on the findings in the categorization literature.

The Effect of Information Presentation Format and Decision Frame on Choice in an Organizational Buying Context

James E. Stoddard, University of New Hampshire
Edward F. Fern, Virginia Polytechnic Institute and State University[1]

ABSTRACT

We conducted a series of experiments in order to explain anomalous findings from a previous set of experiments. In our previous work, we expected individual organizational buying decisions that were framed as gains to lead to cautious supplier choices and individual organizational buying decisions that were framed as losses to lead to risky supplier choices. We found the opposite. Namely, gain frames led to risky choices. Subsequent experiments suggested that the information presentation format had an effect on subjects' choices. We found that subjects in our experiments used the information as presented and did little information transformation. It seems that adjusting the information presentation format led to changes in the choices that subjects made when decisions were framed as gains or losses. These results support the "concreteness" principle (Slovic 1972) which suggests that individuals use information as presented and do little, if any, information transformation before making decisions.

Prospect theory has been used by researchers to explain the effect of decision frames on organizational buying behavior. Findings from much of this research support the theory's predictions. At the individual buyer level, organizational buying decisions framed as gains tend to lead to cautious supplier choices and those framed as losses tend to lead to risky supplier choices (e.g., Puto 1985, 1987; Qualls and Puto 1989).

In our own work we have attempted to replicate and extend these findings to buying groups. First, we expected that individual buying decisions that were framed as gains would lead to cautious choices and those framed as losses would lead to risky choices. Second, we wished to extend the gain/loss frame effect to the group buying context, hypothesizing that buying group interaction would increase the magnitude of these decision frame effects (McGuire, Kiesler, and Siegel 1987; Neale et al. 1986).

Initially, we conducted two replication experiments to test prospect theory predictions at the individual buyer level. However, contrary to previous research in the area we found that individual organizational buying decisions framed as gains led subjects to choose the risky supplier and those decisions framed as losses led subjects to choose the cautious supplier.

Prospect theory suggests that the individual choice process consists of two phases, editing and evaluation (Kahneman and Tversky 1979). During the initial editing phase the choice options are hypothetically reformated in order to simplify subsequent evaluation and choice. During the editing phase actual choice outcomes are coded into gains and losses relative to some psychologically determined reference point. The determination of the reference point and subsequent coding of choice outcomes into either gains or losses is proposed to be affected by the formulation of the offered prospects (Kahneman and Tversky 1979, p. 274).

The present paper describes and demonstrates the effect of several information presentation format factors. Our work suggests that subjects do little editing to simplify choice alternatives. Rather, subjects used only explicitly displayed information in the form in which it was displayed, supporting the concreteness principle advanced by Slovic (1972).

BACKGROUND

Research in organizational buying demonstrates that framing affects the individual buyer's choices as prescribed by prospect theory (Kahneman and Tversky 1979). Accordingly, a buyer's preference for a supplier is partially determined by the way the purchasing decision is framed. Should a buyer be faced with a decision between two suppliers, one whose outcome is known with certainty and another whose outcome is probabilistic, the buyer will tend to choose the cautious supplier when the decision is framed as a gain and the risky supplier when the decision is framed as a loss.

This framing effect is explained by the value function in prospect theory. The value function represents the relation between objectively determined gains and losses and the subjective value a person places on these gains and losses (Whyte 1989). When faced with a choice between a cautious supplier and a risky supplier, the buyer's reference point shifts to that of the cautious supplier. The buyer compares the subjective value associated with the risky supplier's possible outcomes to the subjective value associated with the certain outcome of the cautious supplier. Since the value function is concave for gains, the difference between the subjective value associated with the risky supplier's more positive objective outcome and the subjective value of the cautious supplier's objective outcome is less than the difference between the subjective value of the risky supplier's less positive objective outcome and the subjective value of the cautious supplier's objective outcome (assuming that the expected value of the certain and the risky suppliers' offers are the same). From this new reference point (i.e., the subjective value of the cautious supplier), it appears that the buyer will gain little and faces the possibility of losing a lot by choosing the risky supplier. Therefore, the buyer will choose the cautious supplier.

When decisions are framed as losses, the buyer should choose the risky supplier. When faced with this type of decision the buyer's reference point once again shifts to the subjective value associated with the cautious supplier. However, since the value function is convex for losses, the difference between the subjective value associated with the risky supplier's less negative outcome and the subjective value of the cautious supplier's outcome is greater than the difference between the risky supplier's more negative outcome and the cautious supplier's outcome. From this new perspective it appears that the buyer's gain may be great with little to lose by choosing the risky supplier over the cautious supplier.

Empirical research has found support for these framing effects in the organizational buying context. Puto (1985, 1987) found that an easy-to-attain reference point (i.e., high budget, gain frame condition) tended to cause buyers to choose a supplier which offered a guaranteed outcome while a difficult-to-attain reference point (i.e., low budget, loss frame condition) tended to cause buyers to choose a supplier which offered two possible outcomes (i.e., the risky supplier). Schurr (1987) has demonstrated similar effects in a negotiation and bargaining setting. He found that bargaining teams thinking "a gain is at stake" made less risky bargaining agreements than teams thinking "a loss reduction is at stake."

[1]This research was partially funded by a grant from The R.B. Pamplin College of Business.

TABLE 1
Framing Results for Goods and Services

Supplier Choice Frequency for Goods				
	Order of Stimulus Presentation			
	Gain Frame First		Loss Frame First	
Choice/Decision Frame	Gain Frame	Loss Frame	Gain Frame	Loss Frame
Cautious Supplier	A 47 (73.4%)	C 36 (56.3%)	A 28 (43.7%)	C 45 (70.3%)
Risky Supplier	B 17 (26.6%)	D 28 (43.7%)	A 36 (56.3%)	D 19 (29.7%)
Total Subjects	64	64	64	64
Supplier Choice Frequency for Services				
	Order of Stimulus Presentation			
	Gain Frame First		Loss Frame First	
Choice/Decision Frame	Gain Frame	Loss Frame	Gain Frame	Loss Frame
Cautious Supplier	A 32 (50.0%)	C 47 (73.4%)	A 28 (43.8%)	C 37 (57.8%)
Risky Supplier	B 32 (50.0%)	D 17 (26.6%)	B 36 (56.2%)	D 27 (42.2%)
Total Subjects	64	64	64	64

Qualls and Puto (1989) examined hypotheses relating certain factors to the initial reference point, decision frame, and subsequent choice of buyers. They found that the procurement budget was related to the initial reference point, the initial reference point was related to the decision frame, and the decision frame was related to subsequent choice. Buyers who framed alternatives as gains tended to choose the certain (a sure thing) alternative, and buyers who framed the alternatives as losses tended to choose the risky (probabilistic) alternative.

EXPERIMENTAL RESULTS

We attempted to replicate the results of this previous research before extending the theoretical notions to buying groups. We constructed four organizational buying procurement scenarios within which were embedded our experimental manipulations (see a sample in Appendix 1). Of the four scenarios, two were goods-based and two were service-based. Since the subjects were students, we designed the purchasing scenarios to look like typical case studies that are frequently used in business courses. The subjects were told that the experimenters were testing the cases for possible inclusion in an industrial marketing course.

We conducted two separate experiments to test the effect of decision frame on supplier choice, one goods-based experiment and one service-based. Each experiment was a within-subjects design where subjects were either exposed to a gain (loss) frame scenario first and then a loss (gain) frame scenario. In all, two-hundred and fifty-six undergraduate business student subjects from a major southeastern university responded to the experimental stimuli.

As can be seen in Table 1, subjects made choices opposite to those predicted by prospect theory a majority of the time. In these experiments subjects tended to choose the risky supplier when the decision was framed as a gain and the cautious supplier when the decision was framed as a loss.

DISCUSSION

In this section we will discuss plausible theoretical explanations for the results of experiment one. We believed that the primary explanation for our inconsistent results was that the operationalization of gain and loss frames was somehow different from that of previous work in the area. We addressed this issue by examining break-even effects, the effect of wording, and the effect of probabilities associated with the risky supplier.

Recent research by Thaler and Johnson (1990) and Ross (1991) suggests that decisions framed as losses do not always cause individuals to choose the risky alternative. Specifically, they propose that the way in which a gain or loss frame is operationalized can affect the choices people make. There are at least two different ways in which a gain or loss frame can be operationalized while maintaining equal expected value between a cautious and risky prospect. In one method, one of the possible risky outcomes equals the original reference point. In the other method neither risky outcome equals the original reference point.

Thaler and Johnson (1990) and Ross (1991) provide evidence to suggest that when decisions are framed as losses and neither risky outcome allows the individual to reach the original reference point, the individual may choose the cautious alternative. In addition, they propose the opposite result in the gain frame condition. That is, if both risky outcomes are above the initial reference point the individual may choose the risky as opposed to the cautious alternative. Thaler and Johnson (1990) call this the "break-even effect."

One theoretical notion that could explain this "break-even effect" has do with perceived risk. Perceived risk has been conceptualized as a multiplicative function of decision-related uncertainty and the aversive consequences associated with the decision (Webster and Wind 1972, Sheth 1973). This formulation of perceived risk implies that if either: (1) decision-related uncertainty regarding a possible supplier is low, or (2) the aversive consequence associated

TABLE 2
Results from the Break-Even Effect

Choice/Frame	Experiment 3		Experiment 4 (MBA's)	
	Gain Frame	Loss Frame	Gain Frame	Loss Frame
Cautious Supplier	A 16 (57.1%)	C 18 (64.3%)	A 8 (66.7%)	C 7 (58.3%)
Risky Supplier	B 12 (42.9%)	D 10 (35.7%)	B 4 (33.3%)	D 5 (41.7%)
Total Subjects	28	28	12	12

with selecting a supplier is low, then the perceived risk associated with selecting that supplier would be low. Presumably, in choosing between suppliers, buyers would select the supplier with the lowest level of associated perceived risk.

In the situation where a buyer has identical information about each of two suppliers in a choice set, the buyer is likely to evaluate the perceived risk of choosing a supplier solely on the two suppliers' outcomes. This could be the case since an equal amount of information about each supplier implies an equal level of uncertainty regarding each supplier's offer. Therefore, the only pieces of information left for the buyer to use in differentiating between the two suppliers' offers are their respective outcomes.

When a buying decision is framed as a gain and the uncertainty between two suppliers is the same, it is unlikely that the buyer would feel decision making risk because the aversive consequences associated with a choice between gains is likely to be low. The buyer is in a no-lose situation. This could cause a buyer to select a risky supplier over a cautious supplier because there is little to lose and there is an even greater possible gain associated with choosing the risky supplier.

Conversely, when a buying decision is framed as a loss and the uncertainty between the two suppliers is the same, it is likely that the buyer will feel a high level of decision making risk because the aversive consequence associated with a choice between losses is likely to be high. Here, the buyer would lose no matter which choice the buyer makes. Rather than risk even greater losses, the buyer might choose the cautious supplier to minimize down side risk.

We decided to explore whether the lack of an opportunity for the subjects in our first two studies to "break-even" was an explanation for our inconsistent results. Also, we thought that the use of a within-subjects design may have exacerbated the opposite choice effect by forcing subjects to make opposite choices when exposed to a different frame after they were first exposed to an initial decision frame and made an initial choice. To test for the break-even effect and for the effect of our experimental design, we conducted a third experiment. In this experiment we changed the outcomes associated with the risky supplier's offer so that one of the outcomes met the procurement budget (a reference point) in both the gain and loss conditions. In addition, we utilized a between-subjects design rather than a within-subjects design. Subjects were 56 undergraduate business majors at a major northeastern university (see Table 2).

As can be seen in Table 2, subjects exposed to the gain frame tended to choose the cautious supplier when one of the risky supplier's possible outcomes equaled the reference point (i.e., budget). However, those in the loss frame also tended to choose the

cautious supplier. Our results were consistent with predictions of prospect theory for the gain frame condition when there existed a possibility to break-even, and opposite to the predictions of prospect theory in the loss frame condition. Tests for differences in proportions for cells A through D for experiments one versus three and two versus three were conducted at the .10 level of significance (i.e., $z_{crit}=1.28$). No differences were found.

We thought that the nature of the sample could be influencing our results. Perhaps the organizational buying scenarios which we had constructed were too complex for subjects that had no experience in making such decisions. Therefore, we decided to readminister the experimental stimuli developed for the third experiment using a sample of MBA students, assuming that MBA students would have more experience with making these type of complex organizational buying decisions. The forth experiment was also a between-subjects design with a sample of twenty-four MBA students from a major northeastern university (see Table 2). Tests for differences in proportions were not significant.

The results of experiment four were consistent with those of the third experiment. Namely, decisions that were framed as gains tended to elicit cautious supplier choices when one of the risky supplier's possible outcomes equaled the reference point (i.e., budget). However, decisions framed as losses also led to cautious supplier choices. Therefore, differences in the sample did not seem to account for the results that we obtained..

We conducted post experimental interviews with the sample of MBA's so that we could determine how their decisions were being made. During these interviews we asked the subjects to make a choice between the following two prospects:

A: 50% chance to win $1000   B: Win $500 for sure
   50% chance to win $0

and also the following two prospects:

A: 50% chance to lose $1000   B: Lose $500 for sure
   50% chance to lose $0

Consistent with findings from previous research (e.g., Kahneman and Tversky 1979), an overwhelming majority of subjects chose the cautious prospect in the first instance and the risky prospect in the second.

We reworded our decision frame manipulations to be more consistent with the manipulations found in Kahneman and Tversky (1979). Specifically, we included a table within each scenario that summarized the decision to be made, in terms of the gains and losses

TABLE 3
Scenarios with Summary Tables

Choice/Frame	Experiment 5 - Equal Probabilities		Experiment 6 - Unequal Probabilities	
	Decision Frame			
	Gain Frame	Loss Frame	Gain Frame	Loss Frame
Cautious Supplier	A 15 (75.0%)	C 11 (55.0%)	A 17 (94.4%)	C 6 (31.6%)
Risky Supplier	B 5 (25.0%)	D 9 (45.0%)	B 1 (5.6%)	D 13 (68.4%)
Total Subjects	20	20	18	19

TABLE 4
Results of Significance Tests for Differences in Proportions Between Experiments Five and Six

Cell	Hypothesis	Z score	Result
A	$P_{5A} < P_{6A}$	-1.6376	Supported
B	$P_{5B} > P_{6B}$	1.6376	Supported
C	$P_{5C} > P_{6C}$	1.4730	Supported
D	$P_{5D} < P_{6D}$	-1.4730	Supported

that would accrue from each choice. In addition, the wording of the scenarios was simplified and they were administered in a between-subjects design with a sample of forty undergraduate business students.

The addition of the summary table delineating the actual gains and losses associated with the two supplier choice alternatives enabled us to approximate the results achieved in earlier research in the area (see experiment five results in Table 3). Specifically, subjects in the gain frame condition chose the cautious supplier significantly more than those in the loss frame condition (t=-1.32, df=38, p<.10). However, a majority of subjects in the loss frame condition still chose the cautious supplier. In addition, tests for differences in proportions for cells A through D between experiments four and five were not significant. Finally, we altered the probabilities associated with the outcomes of the risky supplier while maintaining the condition of equal expected value between the cautious and risky suppliers' offers. The revised stimuli were administered in a sixth between-subjects experiment to a sample of thirty-seven undergraduate business students (see Appendix 2 and Table 3). The results in reported in Table 3, experiment six, are consistent with previous research. A majority of subjects in the gain frame condition chose the cautious supplier and a majority of subjects in the loss frame condition chose the risky supplier (t=-5.03, df=35, p<.01). Furthermore, tests for differences in proportions in cells A through D between experiments five and six were significant (see Table 4). We readministered the same stimuli to another sample of thirty-seven undergraduate business students in a seventh experiment to insure that our results from experiment six did not capitalize on chance (see Table 5). These results replicate those from the sixth experiment. A majority of subjects in the gain frame condition selected the cautious supplier and a majority of subjects in the loss frame condition selected the risky supplier (t=-1.99, df=35, p<.05).

SUMMARY

In our experiments we found several effects of information presentation format on choice. Initially, we will provide an overview of the results obtained in the experiments. Subsequently we will discuss their theoretical relevance.

First, individuals tended to choose the risky supplier under the gain frame and the cautious supplier under the loss frame when there existed no possibility for one of the risky supplier's potential outcomes to equal the initial reference point.

Second, including the possibility for one of the risky supplier's outcomes to break-even resulted in a shift in choice for decisions framed as gains. When the risky supplier was offered the opportunity to break-even, choices framed as gains caused subjects to choose the cautious supplier.

Third, the inclusion of the break-even possibility under the loss frame condition did not appreciably change subjects' choices. They continued to choose the cautious supplier. This effect did not seem to be caused by the sample that was used in the experiment.

Fourth, inclusion of a summary table in the scenarios that specified the actual gains and losses that would accrue as a result of each decision tended to make choices under the gain frame condition more extreme. In experiment three under the gain frame condition, 57% of subjects chose the cautious supplier and in experiment four 67% of subjects chose the cautious supplier. The addition of the summary table in experiment five resulted in 75% of subjects choosing the cautious supplier.

Fifth, the inclusion of the summary table specifying the gains and losses that would accrue as a result of each decision tended to cause a larger proportion of subjects to choose the risky supplier although this effect was not large. In experiment three 38% of subjects chose the risky supplier and in experiment four 42% of subjects chose the risky supplier under the loss frame condition.

TABLE 5
Replication of Experiment 6 Results

Choice/Frame	Decision Frame	
	Gain Frame	Loss Frame
Cautious Supplier	13 (76.5%)	9 (45.0%)
Risky Supplier	4 (23.5%)	11 (55.0%)
Total Subjects	17	20

The addition of the summary table in experiment five resulted in 45% of subjects choosing the risky supplier.

Sixth, altering the probabilities associated with the risky supplier's outcomes while maintaining equal expected value between the risky and cautious suppliers' offers appeared to have had the greatest effect on choices made under the loss decision frame condition. In experiment five (equal probabilities for each possible risky supplier outcome), 45% of subjects chose the risky supplier under the loss frame. In experiment six, 68% chose the risky supplier and in experiment seven 55% chose the risky supplier. It appears that individuals prefer to be risk seeking under the loss frame condition when there is a small probability of a large loss and a high probability of no loss, even though the expected value of the risky supplier's offer equals that of the cautious supplier. Only when we altered the probabilities of the risky supplier's outcomes did we notice a majority of our subjects making the risky supplier choice under the loss frame. Now we will discuss the relevance of our research to prospect theory.

THEORETICAL RELEVANCE

Prospect theory proposes that an individual's choice process consists of two-stages, an initial editing stage and a subsequent evaluation stage (Kahneman and Tversky 1979). In the first stage, individuals engage in a preliminary analysis of the choice alternatives. In the second stage, the edited choice alternatives are evaluated and the alternative with the highest value is chosen. We would like to present our research results within the context of this two-stage choice process.

During the editing phase of a decision, individuals are posited to organize and reformulate the choice alternatives in order to simplify the choice. One of the major editing operations that individuals engage in during this phase is hypothesized to be the coding of objective outcomes as gains or losses relative to some subjectively determined reference point (Kahneman and Tversky 1979).

Thaler and Johnson (1990) have presented several editing rules that individuals might use to simplify and encode choice alternatives. One of the proposed editing rules is based on the concreteness principle, originally suggested by Slovic (1972). According to Slovic (1972), concreteness is the notion that individuals tend "to use only the information that is explicitly displayed in the stimulus object and will use it only in the form in which it is displayed (p. 14)." This suggests that subjects do no active editing, but simply make decisions based on the information as it is actually presented to them (Thaler and Johnson 1990).

Although Thaler and Johnson (1990) ruled out concreteness as a possible explanation for their results, our studies lend support for concreteness. Specifically, given no break-even possibility, subjects in the gain frame chose the risky supplier and those in the loss frame chose the cautious supplier. Including the possibility to break-even led subjects in the gain frame to choose the cautious supplier but had little effect on choices in the loss frame condition. The addition of a summary table delineating the amount saved or lost and the probabilities of occurrence associated with each choice alternative resulted in a larger proportion of subjects making a cautious supplier choice under the gain frame and a larger proportion choosing the risky supplier under the loss frame. Finally, altering the probabilities associated with the risky supplier yet maintaining the equal expected value condition between the cautious and risky supplier's offers resulted in a larger proportion of subjects making a cautious supplier choice under the gain frame and a larger proportion of subjects choosing the risky supplier under the loss frame.

In summary, we have found that the effect of a gain or loss decision frame on the choice between a cautious and risky supplier is sensitive to how the information is presented to subjects. In each scenario, the expected value of the cautious supplier whose outcome was known with certainty was equal to the expected value of the risky supplier with probabilistic outcomes.

In the gain frame condition, three factors caused the buyers' choices to vary (1) the "break-even effect," (2) inclusion of a summary table, and (3) altering the probabilities associated with the risky supplier's offer. It appears that the greatest effect on choices under the gain frame was the ability of subjects to break-even. If neither of the risky supplier's outcomes equaled the initial reference point, the overall value of its offer appeared to be greater than that of the cautious supplier. However, if one of the risky supplier's outcomes afforded the possibility of reaching the initial reference point, its overall value was less attractive than that of the cautious supplier.

Under the loss frame condition, choices varied as a result of summarizing information (in terms of gains and losses with associated probabilities) and by altering the probabilities associated with the outcomes of the risky supplier. The greatest effect on choices under the loss frame seemed to be the altering of the probabilities associated with the outcomes of the risky supplier. Shifting from equal to unequal probabilities for each outcome tended to make the risky supplier's offer more attractive to subjects. A small possibility of a large loss was outweighed by a large possibility of a small loss (or no loss) and resulted in a majority of subjects choosing the risky supplier over the cautious supplier.

More generally, under a gain frame, choices may vary from cautious to risky and under a loss frame choices may vary from cautious to risky. It seems that the way information is presented to subjects affects their choices. These results lend support to the notion that decision makers tend to use information that is explicitly displayed, and only in the form in which it is displayed. Information that must be inferred or transformed seems to be discounted or ignored (Slovic 1972).

APPENDIX 1
Sample Organizational Buying Scenario

R.B. Pamplin College of Business
Virginia Polytechnic Institute and
State University

Rev. 1/93

Audio-Visual Purchase (A)

The Media Services Division of Virginia Tech has recently requested software projector panels so that computer graphics can be displayed on existing overhead machines. The Purchasing Department issued requests for proposals for software projector panels to several manufacturers. Only two software projector panel manufacturers met bid specifications.

As the buyer for audio-visual products for Virginia Tech you must select one company to provide the thirty-two software projector panels. *The LCD panel budget has been set at $370,000.*

One manufacturer, A-V Equipment and Supplies, will provide the panels for what is considered to be a certain bid price of $450,000. A second manufacturer, Boxlight, will provide the same quality projector panels for what is considered to be an uncertain bid price of $410,000.

You have contacted some of Boxlight's previous customers. Half of the previous customers said that Boxlight had no trouble meeting delivery deadlines, and the other half said there may be some trouble. If deadlines are not met, it could result in a cost of $490,000.

As you can see, the cost to the university will be over the budget of $370,000 resulting in a budget deficit. Depending on the supplier chosen, the cost to the university could be either:

1) A-V Equipment and Supplies - $450,000 certain bid.
2) Boxlight - Either $410,000 or $490,000 depending on Boxlight's performance.

CONCLUSION

The purpose of this paper was to demonstrate that the way in which information is presented to subjects affects their choices given a gain or loss decision frame. The empirical results that we obtained in seven experiments demonstrate that choices within a decision frame vary based on break-even effects, information presentation effects, and probability effects. The magnitude of choice variation under a gain frame was greatest for inclusion or exclusion of break-even opportunities. The magnitude of choice variation under a loss frame was greatest for changes in the probabilities associated with the risky alternative's possible outcomes. These results support the notion that individuals tend to use information in the format in which it is presented, and do little information transformation.

REFERENCES

Kahneman, Daniel and Amos Tversky (1979), "Prospect Theory: An Analysis of Decision Under Risk," *Econometrica*, 47 (March), 263-90.

McGuire, Timothy W., Sara Keisler, and Jane Seigel (1987), "Group and Computer-Mediated Discussion Effects in Risk Decision Making," *Journal of Personality and Social Psychology*, 52 (5), 917-30.

Neale, Margaret A., Max H. Bazerman, Gregory B. Northcraft, and Carol Alperson (1986), "Choice Shift Effects in Group Decisions: A Decision Bias Perspective," *International Journal of Small Group Research*, March, 33-42.

Puto, Christopher P. (1985), "The Framing of Industrial Buying Decisions," unpublished doctoral dissertation, Duke University.

_____ (1987), "The Framing of Buying Decisions," *Journal of Consumer Research*, 14 (December), 301-15.

Qualls, William J. and Christopher P. Puto (1989), "Organizational Climate and Decision framing: An Integrated Approach to Analyzing Industrial Buying Decisions," *Journal of Marketing Research*, 26 (May), 179-92.

Ross (1991), "Performance Against Quota and the Call Selection Decision," *Journal of Marketing Research*, 28 (August), 296-306.

Schurr, Paul H. (1987), "Effects of Gain and Loss Decision Frames on Risky Purchase Negotiations," *Journal of Applied Psychology*, 72 (3), 351-358.

Sheth, Jagdish N. (1973), "A Model of Industrial Buyer Behavior," *Journal of Marketing*, 37 (October), 50-56.

Slovic, Paul, (1972), "From Shakespeare to Simon: Speculations-And Some Evidence-About Man's Ability to Process Information," *Oregon Research Institute Bulletin*, Vol. 12, No. 2 (April), 1-28.

Thaler, Richard H. and Eric J. Johnson (1990), "Gambling With the House Money and Trying to Break Even: The Effects of Prior Outcomes on Risky Choice," *Management Science*, 36 (6) (June), 643-60.

Webster, Fredrick E. Jr. and Yoram Wind (1972), *Organizational Buying Behavior, Foundations of Marketing Series*, Eugene J. Kelley, ed., Englewood Cliffs, NJ: Prentice-Hall.

Whyte, Glen (1989), "Groupthink Reconsidered," *Academy of Management Review*, 14 (January), 40-56.

APPENDIX 2
Revised Organizational Buying Scenario—Unequal Probabilities

R. B. Pamplin College of Business
Virginia Polytechnic Institute and State University
Blacksburg, VA

ZF350A

Rev. 9/94

Audio-Visual Purchase (A)

Imagine that you are the buyer for a company. Your job requires you to make purchases for the company at the lowest possible cost. The purchasing budget is set by your boss, the purchasing manager.

Imagine further that you must purchase an overhead machine to show transparencies. The purchasing manager has set the purchasing budget for the machine at $350.00.

Finally, imagine that there are only two suppliers of overhead machines that you can choose from for this purchase. One supplier, A-V Equipment, has quoted a price of $430.00. The second supplier, Boxlight, has quoted a price of $350.00 for the same overhead machine.

One concern you have is delivery time. If either supplier can not deliver the overhead machine within two weeks you must purchase the machine from a local retail store at a cost of $590.00.

You have contacted six of A-V Equipment's previous customers and none had a problem with delivery time. You have also contacted six of Boxlight's previous customers. Two said they did have a problem with delivery time and four said that Boxlight had no problem with delivery time.

You have summarized the purchase of the overhead machine in the following way:

Overhead machine purchasing budget:	$350.00
A-V Equipment's bid:	$430.00 (lose $80.00 for sure)
or	
Boxlight's bid:	2/6 chance of $590.00 (33% chance of losing $240) or 4/6 chance of $350.00 (67% chance of losing $0) depending on delivery time.

Decision Processes of the Attraction Effect: A Theoretical Analysis and Some Preliminary Evidence

Lianxi Zhou, Concordia University
Chankon Kim, Concordia University
Michel Laroche, Concordia University

ABSTRACT

Drawing from theories of adaptive behavior and reasons in choice, this study proposes two decision processes leading to the attraction effect. First, an attribute-based process suggests that this effect results from consumers' evaluations, comparisons, or other computations on attribute values. Second, a reason-based process implies that this effect results from consumers' reliance on a dominance and/or a compromise relationship contained in the choice task. Retrospective protocols obtained from a pilot study provide support for the reason-based process but not for the attribute-based process. In addition, theoretical and marketing implications of this study are briefly discussed.

INTRODUCTION

There is much evidence showing the existence of the attraction effect (e.g., Huber, Payne, and Puto 1982; Huber and Puto 1983; Ratneshwar, Shocker, and Stewart 1987; Simonson 1989; Pan and Lehmann 1993; Pan, O'Curry, and Pitts 1995). This effect describes the phenomenon that a new alternative, when added to a choice set, increases the preference and choice probability of an existing alternative. Major findings reported in this area indicate that the attraction effect occurs when the choice set consists of an asymmetrically dominated, a relatively inferior, or a compromise alternative. There is also evidence showing that the attraction effect is influenced by the ambiguity of the information presented about the attribute values of the alternatives. It has been shown that the attraction effect is greater when there is information ambiguity in the choice task than when there is not (Ratneshwar, Shocker, and Stewart 1987; Mishra, Umesh, and Stem 1993). Ambiguity of attribute information may arise from the consumer's lack of knowledge with the product category or when the attribute is fuzzy or less meaningful (Mishra, Umesh, and Stem 1993). Accountability is another construct which has been examined for its impact on the occurrence of the attraction effect. Simonson (1989) reports that the attraction effect was stronger when consumers expected to justify their choices to others.

A number of explanations for the attraction effect have been proposed, including the use of choice rules or strategies, perceptual framing of the decision problem, need for justification, changes in attribute importance, changes in subjective brand evaluations, and consideration set memberships. Past research provides mixed results for these explanations, suggesting the need for further study in this area.

Most of the previous studies investigating the attraction effect used aggregate choices as the dependent variable. As a result, much remains to be known as to the basic processes leading to the attraction phenomenon. The use of process tracing methods such as verbal protocols (Ericsson and Simon 1980) would be potentially useful in gaining direct insights into the reasons for the occurrence of the attraction effect. Against this background, the present study attempts to improve our understanding of the decision processes or mechanisms that underlie the attraction effect. We first present a theoretical analysis of the attraction process and then report preliminary empirical evidence.

THEORETICAL FOUNDATIONS

Adaptive Decision Making

Numerous empirical findings of decision research support the notion that the decision process is governed by a number of rules or strategies (Abelson and Levi 1985). Decision strategies are adaptive to a particular choice task (Payne 1982). Adaptation may occur in two contrasting modes: top-down process and bottom-up process (Payne, Bettman, and Johnson 1992). The cost/benefit framework for strategy selection implicitly assumes a top-down adaptation, whereas the constructive view of decision making reflects a bottom-up adaptation.

There is much evidence showing the adaptive use of heuristics in a more bottom-up fashion (Payne, Bettman, and Johnson 1988; 1992; Klein and Yadav 1989). Support for such adaptive decision making comes from the fact that decision makers tend to use multiple strategies in arriving at a final choice (Payne 1976; Lussier and Olshavsky 1979; Gertzen 1992). The use of hybrid strategies or phased heuristics in decision making implies that people adapt on-line during the decision. Specifically, individuals adapt to changing environments and use combinations of different strategies, often constructing a strategy as they proceed (Bettman and Zins 1977). Of particular importance is the finding that an elimination strategy, such as elimination by aspects, is often used to reduce the choice set to a manageable size and the remaining alternatives are then processed in a more compensatory manner (Johnson and Puto 1987).

The choice set typically used in the past studies has been relatively simple, consisting of two or three alternatives and two attribute dimensions per alternative. According to the view of adaptive decision making, consumers in such a simple decision situation are more likely to use attribute-based strategies, taking into account comparative characteristics of the alternatives when making a final decision. This process may account for the occurrence of the attraction phenomenon.

Recently, Wernerfelt (1995) suggested that the attraction phenomenon can be seen as an outcome of consumers' rational inferences about utilities from market offerings. In fact, some of the other previously proposed theoretical explanations for the attraction effect, such as the consumer's reliance on relative attribute comparisons (Huber and Puto 1983) and tradeoff contrast (Simonson and Tversky 1992), also imply the role of attribute comprehension and inferences in producing the attraction phenomenon. Thus, we put forward the following hypothesis:

H1: The attraction effect results from consumers' evaluations, comparisons, or any other computations on attribute values - namely, the attribute-based process.

Search for Reasons in Decision Making

A number of researchers have proposed a view that in certain situations decision makers tend to make their choices on the basis of available reasons and justifications (Simonson 1989). An example of the reason-based choice can be seen in Slovic's (1975)

Advances in Consumer Research
Volume 23, © 1996

study. He reported that when faced with a choice between two equally valued alternatives, decision makers tend to prefer the one that is better on the more important attribute. According to the author, such an approach to problem solving is likely to occur because the chosen option can be easily justified for oneself and others as being the best decision.

The current theorizing on reason-based decision making has advanced the idea that the decision process involves the search for a dominance structure - a cognitive representation in which one alternative can be perceived as dominant over the others (Montgomery 1983, 1989). The search for a dominance structure in decision making is an appealing process because it provides a ground for justifying the final choice (Montgomery 1983). It permits decision making be based on clear reasons without a reliance on relative weights, attribute tradeoffs, or other effortful computations, thus easing the demands on the decision maker's limited information processing capacity. In this sense, the desire to search for a dominant structure is compatible with the characterization of consumers as limited information processors (Montgomery 1989). As Montgomery further argues, decision makers have the tendency to protect their choices from the competing alternatives, thus the construction of a dominance structure is a desirable goal for decision makers.

In the context of brand decisions, the dominance-search model suggests that brand preference and choice is a function of the dominance structure in the choice set. In most cases, however, a dominance structure may not exist in its pure sense. Therefore, the decision maker needs to restructure the given information in such a way that a dominance structure can be obtained. Montgomery (1989) proposed a number of operations that can be used to achieve this. For example, the decision maker may *de-emphasize* a given disadvantage of the promising alternative and/or *bolster* the disadvantages of non-promising alternatives. According to Montgomery, these operations may result in a fully developed dominance structure in which the preferred alternative is better than the other alternatives on all of the attributes under consideration, or the disadvantages of the preferred choice are completely eliminated, neutralized or counterbalanced.

Unfortunately, little empirical evidence has been reported thus far to support the depiction of decision making as a search for dominance. In studying the effect of the dominance relationship on adaptive decision making, Klein and Yadav (1989) have recently shown that increasing the number of dominated alternatives significantly improve choice accuracy and reduced choice effort. These findings clearly indicate that decision behavior is affected by the dominance structure encountered (or constructed) in the decision process.

In addition to the dominance structure, Simonson (1989) indicated that decision behavior may also be accounted for by the compromise structure - a cognitive representation in which one alternative is seen as a compromise choice (or a middle option) in terms of its attribute values between the existing alternatives. Drawing from the notion of loss aversion (Tversky and Kahneman 1991), Simonson and Tversky (1992) argued that decision makers tend to avoid the selection of extreme alternatives. The construction of a compromise structure is likely to make decision makers feel safe or less risky about their decisions (Huber and Puto 1983; Simonson 1989). It implies that a compromise relationship found among decision alternatives may serve as another good basis for justifying a choice. As in the case of searching for a dominance structure, this decision process similarly involves less considerations of attribute values.

In short, decision making has been described as a process of searching for contextual factors that may provide reasons or justifications for the final choice. Two of these factors are the dominance and compromise relationships among the alternatives in the choice set. The view of reason-based decision making implies that little information integration is required for making a decision. Rather, the main decision task is to establish a dominance and/or a compromise relationship among the alternatives, which in turn can lead to the final choice.

The perspective of reason-based decision making provides an alternative explanation for the occurrence of the attraction effect. As mentioned earlier, decision contexts used in the past studies of the attraction effect incorporated dominance (or near-dominance) and/or compromise relationships. According to the reason-based theory of decision making, these characteristics of the decision context are likely to be used as bases for justification when consumers make their decisions. Therefore, we postulate our second hypothesis as follows:

H2: The attraction effect results from consumers' reliance on a dominance and/or a compromise relationship contained in the choice task - namely, the reason-based process.

It should be noted that Simonson (1989) attempted to examine the reason-based process in explaining the attraction effect. In one of his experiments, Simonson collected think aloud protocols from subjects. However, because the attraction effect was measured only at the aggregate level, the obtained cognitive thoughts could not be used to explain the individual subject's decision process leading to the attraction effect. This lack of an individual level analysis of the decision process renders the author's explanation for the attraction effect less conclusive.

RESEARCH METHODOLOGY

Subjects and Stimuli
Subjects for this preliminary study were twenty university students. Each subject was paid $5 for their participation. Three product categories were used: cars, calculators, and orange juice. They were employed as product stimuli for their relevance to the subject population as well as their representation of different risk and consumer involvement levels (Mishra, Umesh, and Stem 1993).

The attributes used in this study, together with their levels, are similar to those used in previous studies: city mileage per gallon and ride quality rating for cars (Ratneshwar, Shocker, and Stewart 1987), number of functions and probability of repair in the first two years for calculators (Simonson 1989), and price and quality ratings for orange juice (Huber, Payne, and Puto 1982).

Study Design and Procedure
The study was conducted on a within-subject basis to compare the preference pattern found in the core set consisting of two non-dominating brands A and B to that found in the three-alternative set including the original two brands (labelled as X and Y, respectively, to reduce the demand effects) and a new brand (Z). We manipulated the new entrant to be relatively inferior to brand Y. Structurally, the addition of such a new brand will objectively establish not only a dominance (or near-dominance) relationship but also a compromise relationship as well for a given choice task. These characteristics enable us to test the proposed hypotheses (i.e., effects of the

TABLE 1
The Choice Tasks Used in the Study

Attributes	Attribute levels and alternatives		
	X	Y	Z
Cars			
City mileage (MPG)	19	32	34
Ride quality rating	80	60	30
Calculators			
Number of functions (Range: 6-98 functions)	32	24	16
Probability of need for repair in first two years (Range: 0.5% - 15%)	7%	4%	3%
Orange Juice			
Price for 64 fluid ounces	$2.00	$1.20	$1.10
Quality rating	70	50	30

Note: Brands X and Y were labelled as A and B, respectively, in the core choice sets so as to reduce the demand effects. Brand X is the competitor, brand Y is the target, and brand Z is the new entrant.

attribute-based and reason-based processes). Table 1 gives the details of the choice tasks used in this study.

As a within-subject design, this experiment requires choice tasks to be completed by each respondent. Consequently, we can estimate the attraction effect for each respondent. Individual-level estimates of the attraction effect are essential to the understanding of the underlying decision processes.

Subjects were first presented with the core choice set (X and Y of Table 1), and asked to choose the brand they would buy and provide preference ratings on a 0-100 constant sum scale (Mishra, Umesh, and Stem 1993). Next, they repeated this set of tasks for the other two product categories. After taking a ten minute break, they were given the three-alternative set consisting of the two original brands and a new brand (Z) in each product category, and then asked to respond to similar questions to those used in the core choice tasks. Finally, participants were required to complete a set of demographic questions.

Following previous practices, the options were presented in an alternative (row) by attribute (column) matrix format. The order in which the new brand and product category were presented was counterbalanced across subjects.

To provide direct evidence of the attraction effect, retrospective verbal protocols (Ericsson and Simon 1984) were collected from respondents. Subjects were asked to describe how they arrived at the decision immediately after the completion of each choice task involving the three-alternative set. They were instructed to state everything that went on in their minds while they made the choice, as in Ratneshwar, Shocker, and Stewart (1987).

Measures

Attribute-based and Reason-based Processes. Subjects' protocols were separated into individual thoughts, and then coded by two independent judges into categories for attribute-oriented thoughts and reason-oriented thoughts. Thoughts relating to the search for the dominance and/or compromise structure provided in the choice tasks were construed as reason-based, whereas thoughts relating to evaluations, comparisons, or any other computations on attribute values, which do not reflect subjects' focus on the choice set structure, as attribute-based. The number of thoughts was used as an indicator of the extensiveness of the decision process. This measure is similar to that used by Sujan (1985) in his study of category-based and piecemeal processes underlying brand evaluations. Table 2 presents the details of the coding procedure for the two-way decision process.

The criteria for determining the reason-based process were largely based on the operations proposed by Montgomery (1989) for establishing a dominance relationship. Given the purpose of this research, the operations were modified in such a way that the criteria covered dominance as well as compromise relationships objectively contained in the decision context. The criteria used in delineating the attribute-based thoughts come from the elementary information processes proposed by Johnson and Payne (1985). A count of the total number of elementary information processes (EIPs) used for decision making provides a measure of the effort associated with the use of a certain decision strategy (Payne, Bettman, and Johnson 1988; 1992). This study is particularly concerned with consumers' evaluations, comparisons, or any other types of computations on attribute values that would indicate a construction of the overall worth of a specific alternative from the pieces of attribute information provided.

A caution should be taken in interpreting the coding scheme. For example, de-emphasizing and bolstering, criteria for reason-oriented thoughts, appear to be similar to comparing, a criterion for attribute-oriented thoughts. The distinction between them lies in

TABLE 2
Coding Scheme for Responses

Reason-oriented Thoughts
1. Search for Dominance Relationship
2. Search for Compromise Relationship

a) *De-emphasizing* a given disadvantage of the near-dominating alternative or a given advantage of the nearly dominated alternative.

   Example: Brand Y (the near-dominating alternative) and brand Z (the nearly dominated alternative) have a similar city mileage per gallon (32 vs. 34 MPG).

b) *Bolstering* a given advantage of the near-dominating alternative or a given disadvantage of the nearly dominated alternative.

   Example: Brand Y has a much higher ride quality rating than Brand Z (60 vs. 30).

c) *Cancelling* a given disadvantage of the near-dominating alternative by relating it to a disadvantage of the nearly dominated alternative.

   Example: The mileage per gallon of brand Y is not as good as that of brand Z, but brand Y offers a much higher comfort than brand Z - a big deal.

d) *Compromising* the disadvantages of an alternative by relating it to the disadvantages of the other alternatives.

   Example: Brand Y provides a fair compromise between mileage per gallon and ride comfort, and the other two brands (X and Z) tend to stretch to extremes.

Attribute-oriented Thoughts
Cognitive responses which do not reflect the search for
dominance and/or compromise relationships available in the tasks

a) *Comparing* two non-dominated alternatives on an attribute.

   Example: Brand X is very low in fuel efficiency, compared to brand Y (19 vs. 32).

b) *Evaluating* an alternative along a particular attribute dimension.

   Example: The ride quality of brand Y itself is acceptable.

c) *Calculating* the size of the difference of two alternatives for an attribute.

   Example: The quality rating of brand X exceeds that of brand Y by 20 points.

d) *Assessing* the size of the difference of two alternatives for an attribute.

   Example: The 20 point difference in quality rating between brand X and brand Y is not significant for me.

---

that de-emphasizing and bolstering primarily focus on the comparisons of brands between which there is a dominance relationship. Any thoughts related to comparisons between the dominating and the dominated brands (such as, brands Y and Z in Table 2) are deemed to be indications of searching for the dominance relationship contained in the choice task. If comparisons occur between non-dominating brands (such as, brands X and Y), the related thoughts were classified as attribute-based as they do not involve the search for the dominance structure contained in the choice task. *Attraction Effect.* The attraction effect measure used in this study was adopted from Mishra, Umesh, and Stem (1993). It computes the difference between the observed preference share of the target brand and the estimated share of the target derived from the principle of proportionality (Luce 1959). A positive difference found upon addition of the new brand into the choice set signifies the occurrence of the attraction effect. Here, the attraction effect is defined as the net change in market share of the target brand after an adjustment is made for the expected proportional loss based on the constant ratio model. A better understanding of this definition can be seen from the following example given by Mishra, Umesh, and Stem (1993). Consider a core set share of 60 for the target brand Y and 40 for the competitor X. If the decoy Z captures a share of 20, the expected shares of brands Y and X will decline proportionately to 48 (=60-20 x .6) and 32 (=40-20 x .4), respectively. The attraction effect will exist if the observed share of brand Y (target) is greater than 48.

RESULTS

Distinguishing Reason-based Process from Attribute-based Process

The research hypotheses in this study focus on a two-way decision process in producing the attraction effect: (1) the search for a dominance and/or a compromise relationship contained in the choice task (reason-based processing), and (2) the inferences of the values of alternatives from the available attribute information (attribute-based processing).

Subjects' responses were separated into individual thoughts and coded by two judges. The judges were blind to the hypotheses. The interjudge agreement was 87 percent. Disagreements were resolved through discussion, so that all responses were coded. A sample of the attribute-oriented thoughts and the reason-oriented thoughts coded by the two judges is found in table 3, for the choice task involving cars.

Note that the reason-oriented thoughts differ from the attribute-oriented thoughts in the way that they explicitly reflect subjects' consideration of the dominance and/or compromise relationship provided in the choice task. The sample responses suggest that the target brand (Y) can be benefited not only from the choice set structure such as a dominance relationship but from inferences of attribute values as well.

TABLE 3

Choice Task - Cars	Brand X (competitor)	Brand Y (target)	Brand Z (decoy)
City mileage per gallon	19	32	34
Ride quality rating	80	60	30

Notes: a) Structurally, brand Z is nearly dominated by brand Y but not by brand X. In other words, the dominance relationship exists between brands Y and Z; b) Brand Y is also a compromise or middle option in the three-alternative choice set.

1. **Attribute-based Process**
   Subject 2 (chose brand Y)
   • The poor ride quality in brand Z is unacceptable (*Evaluating*).
   • Although the ride quality of brand Y is not as good as brand X (*Comparing*), the difference is not significant compared to the difference between the two brands in gas consumption (*Assessing*).
   Subject 10 (chose brand Y)
   • The quality in driving shouldn't be so bad as in brand X (*Evaluating*).
   • The car which has an acceptable MPG (*Evaluating*) and a quite good ride quality (*Evaluating*) is brand Y.

2. **Reason-based Process**
   Subject 11 (chose brand Y): Brand Y provides a fair equilibrium between gas mileage and ride quality, and the others tend to stretch to extremes (*Compromising*).
   Subject 17 (chose brand Y): I would be more likely to choose brand Y because the mileage per gallon is almost as much as brand Z - just 2 miles less (*De-emphasizing*) but the ride quality rating of brand Z is much lower (*Bolstering*).

3. **Combination of Attribute-based and Reason-based Processes**
   Subject 7 (chose brand Y)
   • Brand Y and brand Z have a similar gas mileage (*De-emphasizing*) but Y has a much higher quality rating (*Bolstering*).
   • Brand Y does over 10 MPG more than brand X (*Calculating*), which is a considerable amount (*Assessing*).
   • Even though the quality rating of brand X exceeds that of brand Y by 20 points (*Calculating*), the ride quality of Y itself is acceptable (*Evaluating*).
   • So, the great difference in MPG between brands Y and X becomes the determining factor (*Assessing*).
   Subject 15 (chose brand Y)
   • Forget brand X as its MPG is too low (*Evaluating*).
   • The mileage per gallon of brand Y is good (*Evaluating*).
   • While not as good as brand Z's MPG, brand Y offers a far more better ride quality (*Cancelling*).

Correlation Analysis

A simple correlation analysis was performed to examine the relative impact of the two-way decision process on the attraction effect. Because the results regarding the amount and pattern of the attribute-oriented and reason-oriented thoughts obtained for the other two product categories were similar to those for cars, the analysis was done only for the choice task involving cars. We were interested in how the attraction effect is related to both the attribute-based process and the reason-based process. Noting that decision behavior is likely to consist of multiple systems that interact in various ways (Payne 1982), we expected that the two processes explaining the occurrence of the attraction effect are more complementary than competitive. A significant relationship was found between the attraction effect and the reason-based process (r=.48; p<.01). But, the relationship between the attraction effect and the attribute-based process was not significant. Consequently, the empirical results reject the hypothesis 1, and provide support for the hypothesis 2.

DISCUSSION AND CONCLUSION

The substantive point of this study is that a dominance and/or a compromise structure contained in a choice task can lead to the attraction effect through two conceptually different decision processes, namely, attribute-based processing and reason-based processing. The attribute-based processing reflects the theory of adaptive decision behavior. This decision process suggests that the attraction effect can be seen as a manifestation of consumers' using other alternatives to infer the values of a specific option in the choice set. Such a conceptualization of the rationales underlying the attraction effect is consistent with the theoretical arguments made by Wernerfelt (1995). Using a number of examples, Wernerfelt describes the attraction phenomenon as an outcome of consumers' rational inferences about utilities from market offerings.

The reason-based processing reflects the theory of the search for reasons in choice. This mechanism suggests that consumers can choose on the basis of the relationships of the alternatives in the choice set rather than the comprehension of the attribute values of alternatives. The attraction phenomenon constructed through the dominance/compromise search can be seen as a manifestation of deviations from rationality in choice. In fact, a number of researchers (e.g., Simonson and Tversky 1993; Pan, O'Curry, and Pitts 1995) have indicated that certain normative assumptions of consumer choice models such as value maximization are inadequate for understanding of the attraction effect and need to be relaxed in order to account for context effects.

While the attribute-based process and the reason-based process represent different construction of the attraction effect, they are more complementary than competitive. Under certain situations, both decision processes may produce the attraction effect simultaneously. There are also situations in which either decision process may operate. The relative impact of the two decision processes on the attraction effect are likely to be affected by a number of individual and task factors. Two noteworthy variables are accountability and information ambiguity.

The retrospective protocols obtained in the present study provide preliminary support for the reason-based process but not for the attribute-based process. The findings could be due to the ambiguity in attribute information. Given the ambiguity of choice alternatives, subjects may feel uncertain about the choices based on attribute values. As a result, they tend to rely on the available dominance structure when making choice decisions. Further research may examine this speculation by manipulating information ambiguity. In addition, the influence of other individual and task variables such as accountability on the attraction process also deserves researchers' attention.

In practice, the focus on the roles of attribute values and choice set structure in consumer decision making would have important implications for competitive strategies. If our conceptualization about context effects in choice is sound, it may suggest that brand competition is both a race to meet customer needs at attribute values and a battle to add distinctive cues such as a dominance relationship over the structure of customer's choice set (Taylor and Fiske 1978). Hence, marketers should devote resources not just to satisfy consumers better than competitors but to create value for consumers by shaping the context of preferences and thus competition (Carpenter, Glazer, and Nakamoto 1994).

Of course, there are several limitations to this preliminary investigation. First, the small size of the sample employed in this study makes our findings tentative. A large sample is certainly needed for further examination of the two-way decision process leading to the attraction effect. Second, the method of data analysis is very simple. Strong conclusions can only be made when other advanced methods are applied here. Yet in spite of these obvious weaknesses, this paper provides encouraging insights into the reasons for the observed attraction effect, and should be followed by more rigorous investigations.

REFERENCES

Abelson, R.P., and Levi, A. (1985), "Decision Making and Decision Theory," In *the Handbook of Social Psychology*, eds., G. Lindzey and E. Aronson, Vol. 1, New York: Random House, 231-309.

Bettman, James R. and Michel A. Zins (1977), "Constructive Processes in Consumer Choice," *Journal of Consumer Research*, 4(September), 75-85.

Boush, David M. and Barbara Loken (1991), "A Process-Tracing Study of Brand Extension Evaluation," *Journal of Marketing Research*, Vol. XXVIII (February), 16-28.

Carpenter, G.S., R. Glazer, and K. Nakamoto (1994), "Meaningful Brands From Meaningless Differentiation: The Dependence on Irrelevant Attributes," *Journal of Marketing Research*, Vol. XXXI (August), 339-350.

Ericsson, K. Anders and Herbert A. Simon (1980), "Verbal Reports as Data," *Psychological Review*, 87 (3), 215-251.

Gertzen, H. (1992), "Component Processes of Phased Decision Strategies," *Acta Psychologica*, 80, 229-246.

Huber, Joel, John W. Payne, and Christopher Puto (1982), "Adding Asymmetrically Dominated Alternatives: Violations of Regularity and the Similarity Hypothesis," *Journal of Consumer Research*, 9, 90-98.

Huber, Joel and Christopher Puto (1983), "Market Boundaries and Product Choice: Illustrating Attraction and Substitution Effects," *Journal of Consumer Research*, 10, 31-44.

Johnson, Michael D. and Christopher Puto (1987), "A Review of Consumer Judgment and Choice," in *Review of Marketing*, ed., Michael J. Houston (Chicago, IL: American Marketing Association), 236-292.

Klein, N.M. and M.S. Yadav (1989), "Context Effects on Efforts and Accuracy in Choice: An Enquiry into Adaptive Decision Making," *Journal of Consumer Research*, 15(March), 411-421.

Lehmann, Donald R. and Yigang Pan (1994), "Context Effects, New Brand Entry, and Consideration Sets," *Journal of Marketing Research*, Vol. XXXI, August, 364-374.

Luce, R. Duncan (1959), *Individual Choice Behavior*, New York: John Wiley.

Lussier, D. A. and R. W. Olshavsky (1979), "Task Complexity and Contingent Processing in Brand Choice," *Journal of Consumer Research*, 6 (September), 154-165.

Mishra, Sanjay, U.N. Umesh, and Donald E. Stem, Jr. (1993), "Antecedents of the Attraction Effect: An Information-Processing Approach," *Journal of Marketing Research*, Vol. XXX (August), 331-349.

Montgomery, Henry (1983), "Decision Rules and the Search for a Dominance Structure: Towards a Process Model of Decision Making," in *Analyzing and Aiding Decision Processes*, eds., P. Humphreys, O. Svenson, and A. Vari, North-Holland and Hungarian Academic Press, Amsterdam/Budapest, 343-369.

Montgomery, Henry (1989), "From Cognition to Action: the Search for Dominance in Decision Making," in *Process and Structure in Human Decision Making*, eds., H. Montgomery and O. Svenson, John Wiley & Sons Ltd. 23-49.

Olshavsky, R. W. (1979), "Task Complexity and Contingent Processing in Decision Making: A Replication and Extension," *Organizational Behavior and Human Performance*, 24, 300-316.

Pan, Yigang and Donald R. Lehmann (1993), "The Influence of New Brand Entry on Subjective Brand Judgments," *Journal of Consumer Research*, 20 (June), 76-86.

Pan, Yigang, S. O'Curry, and R. Pitts (1995), "The Attraction Effect and Political Choice in Two Elections," *Journal of Consumer Psychology*, 4(1), 85-101.

Payne, John W. (1976), "Task Complexity and Contingent Processing in Decision Making: An Information Search and Protocol Analysis," *Organizational Behavior and Human Performance*, 16, 366-387.

Payne, John W. (1982), "Contingent Decision Behavior," *Psychological Bulletin*, Vol.92, No.2, 382-402.

Payne, John W., James R. Bettman, and Eric J. Johnson (1988), "Adaptive Strategy Selection in Decision Making," *Journal of Experimental Psychology: Human Learning, Memory and Cognition*.

Payne, John W., James R. Bettman, and Eric J. Johnson (1992), "Behavioral Decision Research: A Constructive Processing Perspective," *Annual Review of Psychology*, 43

Ratneshwar, S., A.D. Shocker, and D.W. Stewart (1987), "Toward Understanding the Attraction Effect: The Implications of Product Stimulus Meaningfulness and Familiarity," *Journal of Consumer Research*, 13 (March), 520-533.

Simonson, Itamar (1989), "Choice Based on Reasons: The Case of Attraction and Compromise Effects," *Journal of Consumer Research*, 16 (September), 158-174.

Simonson, Itamar and Amos Tversky (1992), "Choice in Context: Tradeoff Contrast and Extremeness Aversion," *Journal of Marketing Research*, Vol. XXIX (August), 281-295.

Slovic, Paul (1975), "Choice Between Equally-Valued Alternatives," *Journal of Experimental Psychology: Human Perception and Performance*, 1 (3), 280-287.

Sujan, Mita (1985), "Consumer Knowledge: Effects on Evaluation Strategies Mediating Consumer Judgments," *Journal of Consumer Research*, 12(June), 31-46.

Taylor, S.E. and S.T. Fiske (1978), "Salience, Attention, and Attributions: Top of the Head Phenomena," in *Advances in Experimental Social Psychology*, Vol. 11, ed. L. Berkowitz, New York: Academic Press.

Tversky, Amos and Daniel Kahneman (1991), "Loss Aversion in Riskless Choice: A Reference Dependent Model," *Quarterly Journal of Economics*, 106(November), 1040-1061.

Wernerfelt, Birger (1995), "A Rational Reconstruction of the Compromise Effect: Using Market Data to Infer Utilities," *Journal of Consumer Research*, 21(March), 627-633.

Information Processability And Restructuring: Consumer Strategies for Managing Difficult Decisions

Eloise Coupey, Virginia Polytechnic Institute and State University
Carol W. DeMoranville, Northern Illinois University

ABSTRACT

Our research is focused on consumer decision making when the available information is difficult to process. To better understand what constitutes processability, we proceed as follows: 1) examine consumers' strategies for managing decisions that are difficult because information is not easily comparable, and 2) assess the effect of display processability on aspects of consumer decision making, including outcome quality, recall, restructuring, and perceptions of the decision. The results of a study provide support for hypotheses about the effects of processability due to information comparability on the processes and outcomes of consumers' choices and judgments.

Consumers are often faced with decisions that are difficult. Unclear preferences, too little (or too much) product information, and complex available information are characteristic examples of person, task and context factors that may increase decision difficulty (Payne, Bettman, and Johnson 1993). There is an abundance of research designed to further our understanding of the effects of these factors on consumer decision making. Most of this research, however, has focused upon the evaluative processes (e.g., choice heuristics) that consumers use to process presented information. In addition, the stimuli characteristic of this research are brand-attribute matrices in which the pieces of information are well-organized and comparable in form (Ford, et al. 1989). Less attention has been focused upon display characteristics that make decisions difficult, or on the processes by which consumers construct or alter displays to make difficult decisions easier (Coupey 1994). The explosion of information available to consumers in new media (e.g., interactive technologies, such as the Internet) emphasizes the need to understand how consumers manage decisions when information from marketers is readily available but is presented in different formats. For instance, if certain forms of information are easier to process than others, then search for similar information may receive disproportionate attention, weight, and processing. We examine consumers' use of information displays when decision making is difficult because characteristics of the information available in a display decrease the processability of that information.

In many real-life decisions consumers collect information from several sources about several brands. When they try to use the gathered information, they may find that not all brands are described in the same manner (e.g., warranty in weeks, months, or years), thus reducing the ability to compare brands attribute by attribute, a process often used for making choices (Biehal and Chakravarti 1982). Decision making can be further complicated if the product under consideration is unfamiliar to the consumer or if the available information is complex and hard to understand. Our research provides insights into the processes by which consumers attempt to make displays processable, and the effects of these processes on outcomes (e.g., preference judgments and choices), perceptions of the decision, and memory for decision information.

Understanding how the processability of information affects decision making is important for consumers, marketers, and public policy makers. Perceptions of difficulty due to low processability may influence the type and amount of information consumers use, as well as the manner in which they use it. By affecting the amount of effort consumers are willing to invest in decision making, processability may also influence the quality of the decisions and the amount, type, and organization of information stored in memory.

Marketers can use knowledge of systematic responses by consumers to variations in display processability to develop product information (e.g., brochures, product displays, packaging, and on-line displays). Public policy makers, working to maintain an equitable balance between consumers and marketers, can use knowledge obtained from basic research on adaptive display construction and use to maximize the benefits of information presentation for consumers.

PROCESSABILITY AND DECISION DIFFICULTY

Why Is Processability Desired?

Information that is easily processable, such as a list of unit prices, can help consumers make better decisions (Russo 1977). Processability can reduce the costs, such as cognitive effort, of acquiring and using information. It may also increase the benefits of consumer decisions, such as saving money or making choices of better quality.

An effort/accuracy framework has often been used to explain how processability affects information use and other aspects of decision behavior such as outcome quality (e.g., Kleinmuntz and Schkade 1993). An effort/accuracy rationale for the appeal of processable displays suggests that because processable information requires fewer operations to transform information to make comparisons, cognitive resources are saved in the acquisition and preparation of information. These resources could simply be conserved or they could be reallocated to another part of the decision process. For example, reallocation may be done to keep available a larger amount of information for further processing or to employ an evaluative strategy that offers greater outcome quality.

Two seemingly contradictory processes for information use have been proposed by decision researchers: 1) concreteness, the tendency to use information as presented (Slovic 1972), and 2) restructuring, the tendency to alter a display (Coupey 1994). These different explanations of behavior can be reconciled within an effort/accuracy framework in which task goals (e.g., judgments or choices) emphasize different levels of processability.

Dimensions of Processability

Russo, Krieser and Miyashita (1975) proposed that information must be both available and processable in order to receive maximum usage by consumers. Russo (1977) demonstrated that providing consumers with lists of brands and their unit prices increased consumers' use of unit price information and their savings. This research suggests that one dimension on which processability is effected is the comparability of information, such as the availability of cost in unit prices for all brands on a list. Consider the following scenario:

Early one morning while you are not yet fully awake, you turn on the shower as the first step in your pre-eight o'clock-class ablution. You drag yourself into the shower only to hop out hastily as the water temperature seems barely above freezing. You are now fully awake, so only a cursory check is needed to confirm your suspicion that the water heater died quietly in the night and a new one must be purchased.

You evaluate several water heaters, but because you have far more experience with the function of a water heater than with its features, you are not sure of the meaning of information on the yellow labels on the water heaters. The salesperson tells you that lower numbers are better, so you choose the water heater with the lowest numbers on the yellow label.

As you skim through *Consumer Reports* the next week, you notice that water heaters are reviewed. You are pleased to learn that the model you selected is the one favored by *Consumer Reports*, although you are still not sure what the numbers on the yellow labels mean.

This example illustrates the idea that it is possible for consumers to make optimal choices without understanding the information used as the basis for comparison. In other words, a consumer could be very confident that he or she has chosen the best brand, but have no idea of why it is good, or how it works.

Another dimension of processability is suggested by Bettman, Johnson and Payne (1991). They state that information use increases when the displays are well-organized and appropriately formatted. "Appropriately formatted' can be construed to include several conditions, such as the similarity of attribute value information, the availability of similar attribute information across brands, and/or the match between the organization of information in a display and how information is stored in memory.

That information use can be influenced by memorial information underscores another facet of processability: the degree to which it can be comprehended. As Russo's (1977) results indicate, merely making information readily comparable may often be a sufficient condition for an optimal choice. However, if the consumer must understand what the information means in order to successfully complete a task, then the concept of processability must be expanded to include characteristics of the decision maker, as well as the information. Suppose the consumer in the above example is now purchasing an automobile. The information on the sticker, such as mpg, may be more processable than that of the water heater because the consumer understands what the numbers mean. This suggests that processability may be influenced by both comparability and understandability.

While the two dimensions of processability may have similar effects on restructuring, decision outcomes, and perceptions of the decision, we limit our investigation in this paper to the effects of varying levels of comparability under conditions of low understandability. This constraint is imposed because we are interested in the effects of restructuring on memory for displayed information. Thus, we wish to avoid confounding subjects' current knowledge structures with information comparability effects. Future research should investigate the effects of varying levels of understandability and any interactions between the two dimensions of processability.

We suggest that although greater processability is preferred to lesser processability, the extent to which consumers are motivated to alter information displays to make information more processable, as well as the processes by which they do so, depends strongly upon the goal for which the information is used (e.g., choice versus judgment).

Judgment and Choice Effects on Restructuring

Consumers often make product decisions that take one of two forms: choices or judgments. While a choice is merely the selection of one brand, there are several types of judgments. For example, consumers may rank brands in order of desirability, rate brands to reflect their desirability or similarity, or provide attribute values to equate brands. Judgment and choice tasks lead to an often-replicated result; strategies for processing display information typically differ as a function of the task goal (Biehal and Chakravarti 1982). Process tracing data tend to suggest that consumers use within-attribute strategies for evaluating display information to make brand choices, but within-brand strategies for making judgments (Billings and Scherer 1988; Schkade and Johnson 1989).

We suggest that task goal not only influences processing strategies, but that it also affects the level of processability desired by consumers. As a result, consumers' actions to modify or restructure an information display are predicted to differ as a function of the task. As in the water heater example, choices can be made with information that is complex and hard to understand — *provided the information is displayed in a form that promotes comparisons of brands on an attribute-by-attribute basis.* Therefore, restructuring a complex display is expected to take the form of making attribute information more comparable. In contrast, in judgment tasks when complex information must be comprehended and retained, mere comparability of attribute information may not suffice. To engender feelings of confidence, consumers may have to perform additional restructuring operations on the display to implement processing strategies that maximize information use or effective storage (i.e., ready accessibility) of brand information into memory for future decisions. In this case, restructuring is expected to take a form of making brands comparable on a more abstract level, as by ranking displayed brands to reflect their relative overall performance, thus increasing processability.

Effects of Processability on Recall and Perceptions

The processability of display information may affect more than just the immediate decision (i.e., restructuring behaviors and outcomes). Information used in the decision may be stored in memory in different cognitive structures, depending upon display processability, and may be more or less accessible. In addition, consumers' perceptions of how difficult it was to use the display information, the effort they felt their decisions required, and their confidence in their decisions may vary with processability and the operations needed to improve processability.

Marketers would like consumers to remember the information they provide about their products. The strength of a memory trace, or what can be recalled, may depend upon the amount of processing and the type of processing carried out to encode and store information (Craik and Lockhart 1972). Because processing to make a choice makes comparability more important than understandability, lower levels of recall are expected for a choice task than for a judgment task. In addition to the task goal, the use of restructuring to increase processability, either by making information more comparable or by decreasing inherent difficulty, is expected to influence memory for presented information. If consumers restructure information to make a choice, memory for that restructured information is expected to be better than that for non-restructured information. Therefore, brand information presented in a form that must be restructured should be more available in memory than information that does not have to be restructured. In judgment tasks, however, we predict more brand-based evaluations and less restructuring for attribute comparability, relative to choice tasks. As a result, the difference in the amount of product information recalled between consumers who make judgments with information that is easy to compare and consumers who make judgments with information that is hard to compare may be smaller, in general, than the difference in recall between consumers who make choices with the same types of information displays.

TABLE 1

Brand	Matrix 1 (EASY)	Matrix 2 (T1)	Matrix 3 (T2)	Matrix 4 (T1T2)
Dominant (Target 1)	Comparable	Noncomparable	Comparable	Noncomparable
Average (Target 2)	Comparable	Comparable	Noncomparable	Noncomparable
Average	Comparable	Comparable	Comparable	Comparable
Inferior	Comparable	Comparable	Comparable	Comparable

Differences in consumers' perceptions of the difficulty of decisions and of effort and confidence in making these decisions, may be affected by the processability of available information. Because choices are often made with attribute-based strategies, decreased processability may lead to higher ratings of decision difficulty and lower ratings of confidence than when information is presented in comparable forms. Even though a decision may be difficult because the information is inherently difficult, effort perceptions are expected to increase only when consumers who make choices attempt to restructure information into a more comparable format.

When consumers make judgments, the use of overall brand evaluations is expected to decrease the impact of low processability due to lack of comparability between brands, relative to that expected for choices among brands. Consumers may feel that making judgments when information is low in comparability is more difficult, but because it does not inhibit use of a brand-based evaluation strategy, this form is not expected to result in significantly different perceptions of effort. If consumers restructure to make information comparable, confidence may be higher than for decisions made when the same information is not restructured.

METHOD

Subjects and Procedure

Forty-one subjects participated in the experiment, which took, on average, twenty-one minutes to complete. The subjects were undergraduates enrolled in an introductory marketing course at a southeastern university. For their participation, subjects received extra credit in the course and a meal of pizza and soft drinks. Each subject received a booklet with the stimuli, instructions, and scales. In the task, subjects indicated their familiarity with eighteen products, and completed four choice [judgment] decisions and related scales, and a recall task.

Stimuli

The stimuli used to elicit subjects' choices and judgments were four brand/attribute matrices, one for each of four products. The products were water softeners, binoculars, sergers, and health insurance policies. These products were selected on the basis of pretests which indicated that similar subject populations were unfamiliar with these products. Unfamiliarity reduced the likelihood that subjects would use information other than that presented in the stimuli booklet to make their decisions. The use of extraneous information could have reduced our ability to gauge the effect of display comparability on outcome quality and other behaviors.

The stimuli were structured so that the quality of choices or judgments could be assessed with respect to display comparability. Each product matrix consisted of four brands and four attributes. One brand was constructed to dominate the other brands on all attributes. Two brands were midrange in quality. A fourth brand was inferior to the other brands on all attributes. Subjects were not asked to restructure the display information. They were told,

however, that they could write in the booklets if they wished. In this respect, restructuring was essentially spontaneous.

Independent Variables

To examine the effects of display processability on decision making, we manipulated two factors: task goal and information comparability. Task goal was manipulated between subjects, so that twenty subjects chose one brand from each product matrix, while twenty-one subjects rated the quality of each brand in each product matrix.

Information comparability was manipulated within subjects. We held the amount of information constant within each matrix display and manipulated the comparability of the display information to create four matrix types for each brand. In one matrix type, all brands were comparable in display form; that is, all attribute values were in the same units. In two matrices, the units that described the attribute values for one brand differed from those used to describe the other three brands in the matrix. In one of these matrices, the dominating brand (Target 1) was different (matrix 2); in the other, one of the average brands (Target 2) was different (Matrix 3). In the fourth matrix, both of the target brands (dominant and average) had attribute units that differed from the other two brands (Matrix 4). Table 1 contains the schema.

This schema enabled us to present all four products to each subject, using each type of matrix one time. Although matrix type was linked to a particular product for each subject, the link was varied across subjects by counterbalancing both the product order and the matrix type.

Dependent Variables

The dependent variables consisted of outcome, processing, and perceptual measures. Outcome variables included decision quality and recall. In the choice task, we measured decision quality by determining whether the subject chose the dominant brand. In the judgment task, we measured decision quality by determining whether the subject gave the highest rating to the dominant brand and the lowest rating to the inferior brand. Recall was assessed by counting the amount of information recalled for the water softener and whether the recalled information was accurate. Dependent variables for processing consisted of the amount and type of restructuring. We measured the amount of restructuring by counting the number of transformations the subject had written in the stimulus booklet. Those transformations were then coded as either standardizing to increase attribute comparability or relabeling to increase brand comparability (Coupey 1994), or some other type of restructuring. For example, changing a brand attribute value to match other attribute values is standardizing (e.g., writing '1.5 hours' next to '2 cycles' or '3 sq. ft.' next to '342 sq. in.'). Writing rankings by attribute values is relabeling (e.g., '1' next to '484 gms,' '2' next to '539 gms,' and '3' next to '681 gms'). The type of restructuring was coded whether or not the information was changed correctly. The perceptual measures consisted of four seven-point Likert items which assessed the difficulty to compare information, difficulty to understand information, effort to make a decision, and confidence in the decision.

RESULTS

Overview

Our results indicate that subjects have different strategies for managing contextually driven decision difficulty, and that the selection of strategies for handling display information is contingent upon the task required of subjects. Subjects' behaviors can be explained as the result of effort/accuracy tradeoffs, in which subjects use different amounts of restructuring operations to achieve different goals suggested by the different tasks. We find that subjects tend to restructure more when doing judgment tasks than when making choices. Contrary to our expectations, however, subjects tend to do relatively more standardizing than relabeling for judgments. However, this finding makes sense when it is interpreted from an effort/accuracy perspective and is consistent with previous research (e.g., Montgomery 1983).

Decision quality and perceptions of the decision are influenced by the amount of restructuring that must be done to make the displays processable. Recall is also affected, although not as strongly.

Manipulation Checks and Other Nuisances

The average rating of familiarity with the eighteen products we assessed was 3.38 on a seven-point scale, where 1 indicated high familiarity and 7 indicated low familiarity. Each of the four products we used in our matrices was significantly less familiar to subjects than the average of the eighteen products (water softener: mean=5.85, p<.0001; binoculars: mean=3.72, p<.04; insurance: mean=4.11, p<.0001; sergers: mean=6.01, p<.0001). The selection of products used in the stimuli was deemed acceptable.

To avoid misinterpretation of the data due to procedural biases, we examined the effect of product and order of problem presentation on the primary dependent measures. There was no significant effect of product or problem order on accuracy (product: (2=3.06, p<.38; problem order: (2=1.72, p<.63). The order of presentation also had no significant effect on perceptions (ANOVA: difficult to compare, p<.51; easy to understand, p<.65; effort, p<.88; confidence, p<.66), recall (ANOVA, p<.62), or restructuring (ANOVA, p<.91). As expected, the product did affect perceptions of how easy the information was to understand (ANOVA, p<.003) and the effort the decision required (ANOVA, p<.04), but Duncan's multiple range tests indicated that the only significant differences were between sergers and binoculars. Sergers were seen as harder to understand and more effortful than binoculars.

In addition, there were significantly more accurate answers than inaccurate ones (125 versus 39: (2=45.10, p<.0001). This suggests that subjects did take the study seriously.

Hypotheses Tests

Outcome Variables. We examined the effect of information comparability on decision quality and recall. For decision quality, the effect of matrix types on accuracy was significant ((2=13.28, p<.0041). Subjects were less likely to be accurate when the dominant brand information was in a different form from the other brands in the matrix. The percentages of accurate responses were: all comparable matrix (EASY): 93%; dominant different (T1): 63%; average different (T2): 83%; both targets different (T1T2): 66%. The task also affected outcome quality ((2=4.89, p<.02). Subjects who made choices were more accurate (84% correct) than subjects who made judgments about the brands (69% correct), but

this may be a function of the more stringent criteria for assessing judgment accuracy[1].

Contrary to expectations, the amount of recall was not affected by the matrix type or by the task. This non-effect may indicate a floor effect; subjects were asked to recall twenty pieces of information, but the median amount correctly recalled was three items.[2]

Process Variables. To assess the effect of task and matrix type on the amount of restructuring, we used a count of all restructuring operations done by each subject on each problem as the dependent measure. The amount of restructuring (all types) was influenced by the task (ANOVA: p<.0001). As expected, subjects did more restructuring for judgments than for choices (judgment: mean=8.82; choice: mean=3.89). Matrix type exerted no significant influence on the total amount of restructuring, but it did affect the types of restructuring.

Types of restructuring were significantly influenced by both of the independent variables. Matrix type influenced the number of standardizing operations (ANOVA: p<.0001). Subjects only standardized information when brands were not in comparable units. Matrix type did not affect the number of relabeling operations (ANOVA: p<.99). Subjects tended to relabel information by ranking attribute value information for each brand. This type of operation was equally effective for choice and judgment decisions. Subjects used both relabeling and standardizing operations more frequently for judgment tasks than for choice tasks (relabeling mean: judgment=4.4, choice=2.5; standardizing mean: judgment=3.1, choice=1.3). The number of other operations, such as summarizing brands, or adding attribute information to the display, also differed by task (ANOVA: p<.01; means: judgment=1.4, choice=.1).

We constructed a relative measure of restructuring to directly observe the differences in amounts and types of restructuring [(RELABEL - STANDARDIZE) / (RELABEL + STANDARDIZE)]. Main effects were found for task and matrix type (both significant at p<.0001). In the choice task, subjects tended to relabel more than standardize. In the judgment task, subjects tended to standardize more than relabel (index means: choice=.35; judgment=-.15). In the EASY matrix, subjects did relatively more relabeling than they did in any of the other three matrix types.

We examined the effects of restructuring on outcome quality and recall. Several effects were notable. When the target brand was comparable, (EASY, T2) less restructuring was done than when the target brand was not comparable (ANOVA, p<.02). As expected, a similar effect was observed for the number of standardizing operations (ANOVA: p<.0003) and the relative amount of standardization (ANOVA: p<.003). To examine the effect of restructuring on outcome quality, we recoded restructuring as a dichoto-

---

[1]Recall that accuracy in choice was reflected by selection of the dominant brand, while in judgment it was reflected by determining the best and worst brands. Although the measure is arguably not comparable across tasks, the alternative measures would have obviated the task manipulation. For example, we could have asked choice subjects to list the best and worst brands; this essentially turns the choice task into a judgment task, thus limiting our ability to observe process differences when they exist.

[2]The failure to observe a task effect on recall may be due to the type of judgment we requested. As noted in the discussion of process variables, the evaluations we elicited in the judgment task appear to have caused subjects to restructure the display by ranking the performance of brands on each attribute. As a result, the attribute value information receives little attention after the display is restructured.

mous variable (i.e., presence or absence of restructuring). We used a dichotomous variable to determine whether restructuring at all — regardless of the amount or type — affected outcome quality. Subjects who made evaluations and who restructured rated the dominant brand more highly than did subjects who did not restructure (ANOVA: p<.04; mean without restructuring=2.83, mean with restructuring=1.4, where lower values indicate better brand ratings). The effect of restructuring on choice quality was not significant.

We had predicted that recall for brand information would differ as a function of the type of restructuring, which itself was proposed to differ depending upon task. The relative amount of different types of restructuring (i.e., standardizing or relabeling) did have a marginal effect on recall (linear regression: p<.07). The more standardizing subjects did, compared with relabeling, the more information they recalled.

Perceptual Variables. An ANOVA to assess the effect of matrix type on: 1) perceptions of difficulty to compare display information, 2) ease of understanding display information, 3) effort to complete a decision, and 4) confidence in a decision was completed. For each scale the matrix with all brands comparable (EASY) differed significantly from the other three matrices, with all p-values less than .007. Subjects uniformly perceived the EASY matrix as less difficult, easier to understand, and less effortful. They were most confident with the EASY matrix.

Analyses of variance also revealed significant effects of the task on all four perceptual measures. Information in the choice task, compared to the judgment task, was deemed less difficult to compare (p<.001) and easier to understand (p<.02). Subjects who made choices were also more confident about their responses (p<.0002) and felt that their decisions required less effort (p<.001) than subjects who evaluated all brands.

We had expected that restructuring would affect subjects' perceptions of the decisions, so that completing task-appropriate operations, such as relabeling for judgment and standardizing for choice would increase confidence and decrease difficulty. Perceptions of effort were only expected to differ if subjects restructured noncomparable displays. Contrary to our expectations, confidence was influenced by restructuring so that the more relabeling subjects did, the less confident they became (linear regression, beta=-.37, p<.002). Confidence was not affected by the amount of standardizing. The amount of restructuring also had no effect on perceptions of difficulty to compare information, ease of understanding information, or effort to decide.

To examine the joint influence of task difficulty and restructuring on confidence in greater detail, we completed two linear regressions. Controlling for the effect of task difficulty (i.e., matrix type), we observed a marginally significant effect of restructuring on confidence (p<.06). With the perception of difficulty as a covariate, a regression revealed a significant effect of restructuring on confidence (p<.02).

DISCUSSION

Our research accomplished three objectives: 1) we examined the proposition that what constitutes a processable display can differ as a function of the task (e.g., choice vs. judgment), 2) we explored the types of restructuring subjects used to make displays more processable in different tasks, and 3) we assessed the effects of varying amounts of comparability and of restructuring on outcome quality, recall and perceptions. Our results indicate that decision difficulty is influenced by display comparability and by task. Subjects not only made better decisions, but felt more confident about their decisions when information was presented in a comparable form. These results were more pronounced for choice than for judgment.

Restructuring was often done to make displays more processable. We demonstrated that subjects adapt their restructuring to demands of the display, allocating more effort to restructure superior brands than inferior brands. This result is consistent with Coupey's (1994) finding of adaptive restructuring. In addition, our research indicates that the strategic use of restructuring operations changed contingent upon the task. Subjects appear to complete multiple display revisions when evaluating brands; they typically standardize all of the available information and then relabel it to reflect relative quality differences. Subjects who make choices tend to restructure only until one brand clearly dominates the others. In this type of task they tend to do more relabeling than standardizing, because relabeling is necessary to determine the best brand on each attribute. Standardization is used when the dominant brand is not in comparable units.

The relationship between restructuring and perceptions of decision difficulty and effort is provocative. We found the amount of restructuring done to a display had little effect on subjects' perceptions of difficulty and effort. Although this result was unexpected, we conclude that the lack of significant differences may indicate that being able to restructure makes difficult decisions less effortful, perhaps by simplifying evaluative aspects of the task.

The effects of display comparability on outcome quality can be explained in terms of effort/accuracy tradeoffs. In addition, differences in choice quality can be related to the difference in processing behaviors that occurs when subjects use information as-is, as suggested by the concreteness principle (Slovic 1972), and when subjects restructure the display (Coupey 1994). Because subjects attempt to maximize outcome quality and minimize decision effort, they process the displayed information opportunistically. If one brand clearly dominates most of the other brands, they choose it — even if another, noncomparable brand remains unexamined. This finding is consistent with the results of research by Slovic and MacPhillamy (1974), who observed that subjects often discard noncommensurate information from a decision.

We suggest that the desire to make good decisions limits the amount of information subjects are willing to eliminate from the decision, and that this elimination process is contingent upon the quality and amount of comparable options. When the only brand that differed was the dominant brand, subjects faced a situation in which two of the remaining brands were very close in overall quality. To make a choice, they restructured the fourth brand. In addition, when the dominant brand and one average brand were different, subjects faced a situation in which using information as is would have reduced the choice set to two brands, thus reducing the expected outcome quality below acceptable levels. To increase their options, they restructured the display.

The effort/accuracy interpretation of display processability effects also provides a plausible explanation for the differences in outcome quality between tasks. Recall that choice subjects only had to choose one brand from a display, while judgment subjects had to rate each brand. This suggests that when it is harder to determine which brand dominates (i.e., in the T1 matrix and the T1T2 matrix), choice subjects lose their advantage; they must restructure to make the target brand comparable and detectable. When a dominant brand can be readily identified (i.e., in the EASY matrix and T2 matrix), choice subjects can make choices more easily than judgment subjects can rate all brands. This interpretation is supported by the absence of significant differences in outcome quality between tasks for matrices in which the dominant brand was different (T1, T1T2), and by the significant difference between tasks when a dominant brand could be detected without altering the display (EASY, T2) ((x^2= 4.02, df=1, p<.04, choice more accurate).

We have focused solely upon how consumers manage decisions made difficult by external factors, such as the task and the processability of the display. Further research is needed to examine the link between relevant information in memory, such as a reference brand, and the strategies used to increase display processability. Because the extent to which consumers are willing to restructure displays may depend heavily upon the structure and accessibility of prior knowledge about a product category, research to investigate the effects of understanding presented information on processability is also needed.

REFERENCES

Bettman, James R. (1979), A Functional Analysis of the Role of Overall Evaluations of Alternatives in Choice Processes, *Advances in Consumer Research, Vol. 7*, Provo, UT: Association for Consumer Research.

Biehal, G., and D. Chakravarti (1982), Information-Presentation Format and Learning Goals as Determinants of Consumers' Memory Retrieval and Choice Processes, *Journal of Consumer Research, 8* (March), 431-441.

Billings, R. S., and Scherer, L. M. (1988), The effects of response mode and importance in decision making strategies: Judgment versus choice. *Organizational Behavior and Human Decision Processes, 49*, 258-281.

Coupey, Eloise (1994), Restructuring: Constructive Processing of Information Displays in Consumer Choice, *Journal of Consumer Research, 21*, 83-99.

Craik, Fergus I. M., and Lockhart, Robert S. (1972), Levels of Processing: A framework for memory research, *Journal of Verbal Learning and Verbal Behavior*, December, 671-684.

Ford, J. Kevin, Neal Schmitt, Susan L Schechtman, Brian Hults, and Mary L. Doherty (1989), Process Tracing Methods: Contributions, Problems, and Neglected Research Questions, *Organizational Behavior and Human Decision Processes, 43*, 75-117.

Kleinmuntz, Don N., and David A. Schkade (1993), Information Displays and Decision Processes, Psychological Science 4 (4) July, 221-227..

Montgomery, Henry (1983), Decision rules and search for a dominance structure: Towards a process model of decision making. In P. C. Humphreys, O. Svenson, and A. Vari (Eds.), *Analyzing and aiding decision processes*, 343 - 369. North Holland: Amsterdam.

Payne, John. W., James. R. Bettman, and Eric. J. Johnson (1993), *The Adaptive Decision Maker*. Cambridge University Press: Cambridge.

Russo, Jay Edward (1977), The Value of Unit Price Information, *Journal of Marketing Research, XIV(May)*, 193-201.

Russo, Jay Edward, G. Krieser, and S. Miyashita (1975), An Effective Display of Unit Price Information, *Journal of Marketing, 39* (April), 11-19.

Schkade, David A., and Johnson, Eric J. (1989), Cognitive processess in preference reversals. *Organizational Behavior and Human Decision Processes, 44*, 203-231.

Slovic, Paul (1972), From Shakespeare to Simon: Speculation - and some evidence - about man's ability to process information. *Oregon Research Institute Bulletin*, 12 (3).

Slovic, Paul, and Douglas MacPhillamy (1974), Dimensional Commensurability and Cue Utilization in Comparative Judgment, *Organizational Behavior and Human Performance, 11*(April), 172-194.

Advertising Effects Under Different Combinations of Motivation, Capacity, and Opportunity to Process Information

Theo B.C. Poiesz, Tilburg University, the Netherlands
Henry S.J. Robben, Delft University of Technology, Delft, the Netherlands

ABSTRACT

Like the Elaboration Likelihood Model (Petty and Cacioppo 1986), the MOA (Motivation, Opportunity, and Ability) framework (Batra and Ray, 1986; MacInnis and Jaworski, 1989) refers to motivation and ability as general determinants of advertising processing. It differs from the ELM by its explicit distinction between ability and opportunity. A study is reported in which the effect of the three factors on advertising processing and effect measures is assessed. Results provide partial support for the hypotheses and for the relevance of a distinct opportunity factor. Implications for future advertising studies are discussed.

INTRODUCTION

Commercial communication is becoming increasingly important as the result of general market, marketing, and product developments. Possible reasons relate to (perceptions of) the lack of market transparancy and to diminishing interbrand differences within many product categories (see, e.g., Foxman, Muehling, and Berger 1990; Foxman, Berger, and Cote 1992). These developments negatively affect brand differentiation possibilities.

In principle, a variety of marketing instruments may be used to distinguish a brand from its competitors. Marketers tend to be reluctant, however, to differentiate brands on the basis of price, and often lack the possibility to differentiate on the basis of distribution. This contrast between differentiation needs and limitations boosts the importance of the role of communication, which is reflected in the growing number and variety of media, messages, and commu nication attempts (Poiesz and Robben 1994).

The suggested developments directly affect three parties in the area of advertising. The growing number of advertising exposures require consumers, as the first group, to be increasingly selective, which limits or even prevents message processing. The second group, advertisers, are faced with the combination of increasing advertising costs and decreasing advertising effects. This problem needs to be solved by the third party, the producers of advertising - the media suppliers and advertising agencies. (By consequence, the latter party confronts a new phenomenon: 'accountability', referring to advertising performance justifications *before* rather than *after* media expenditures).

Academic and commercial advertising researchers form the party that is indirectly affected by these developments. The stronger call for accountability may be equated with a stronger need for 1. an adequate and applicable consumer behavior basis for advertising decisions, and 2. reliable and valid diagnostic instruments for the assessment of advertising quality. However, while the need for a behavioral foundation of advertising effectiveness seems to be increasing, the present body of knowledge often cannot be readily applied. There appears to be no single, generally applicable theoretical and methodological framework that may be easily applied to the diagnosis of the quality of a *particular* advertising message prior to exposure. The empirical evidence reported in the academic literature is not very helpful either. The evidence is acquired in individual studies that tend to address single aspects of advertising messages, styles of execution, media characteristics, or exposure situations. In sharp contrast, advertising decisions cannot relate to these isolated aspects, but need to refer to their particular, complex interactions.

In summary, market and marketing developments seem to result in the convergence of the interests of advertising practitioners and advertising researchers. Both parties are faced with the issue of accountability, and with the issue of validity as its academic counterpart. There is a need for a single and parsimonious approach for the judgment of the communication potential of individual advertising messages. Even though such an approach does not seem to be avaible, we will elaborate upon two general approaches that seem to provide a useful starting point.

SELECTING A GENERAL FRAMEWORK

In recent years several attempts have been made to introduce an overall theoretical framework for the explanation of advertising processing. The best known approach is that of the Elaboration Likelihood Model (ELM) by Petty and Cacioppo (1983, 1986), which specifies motivation and ability as the primary conditions for advertising processing and persuasion. If these conditions are favorable, argument-based processing is expected to take place. If either one or both of these conditions is/are unfavorable, processing is based on message execution aspects at best. While the ELM focuses upon motivation and ability, other approaches explicitly distinguish between motivation, ability, and *opportunity* to process an advertising message (the so-called MOA-framework, Andrews, 1988; Batra and Ray 1986; Curry and Moutinho 1993; MacInnis and Jaworski 1989; MacInnis et al. 1991). In the ELM, the concept of opportunity is subsumed under that of ability.

If we were to discard of opportunity-related elements in the ability concept, and would distinguish opportunity from ability, the latter concept would acquire a meaning that is more exclusively related to personal capacity, capability, or proficiency. With this conceptualization of ability, opportunity may be defined as the extent to which external conditions, unrelated to personal factors or characteristics, are favorable or unfavorable for message processing to take place.

There seem to be no *a priori* theoretical or meta-theoretical reasons why the two-factor approach (motivation/ ability) is more or less desirable than an approach employing three factors (motivation/ ability/ opportunity). Which would imply that the choice between the two approaches is basically a matter of emphasis by the individual researcher. Yet, we will present several arguments that seem to favor the explicit inclusion of a distinct opportunity factor next to motivation and ability.

The reasons why we prefer to use the three factor approach are the following:

- A distinct opportunity factor requires the researcher to focus upon differences between laboratory and actual advertising exposure situations. In the introduction it was argued that actual advertising exposure conditions are becoming increasingly unfavorable (also in terms of opportunity). The exposure conditions in research settings tend to be relatively favorable, however;
- The specification of a separate opportunity factor provides a better possibility for the distinction between person related and situation related influences;
- For advertising practitioners it is useful to know whether (suboptimal) message processing should be attributed to

the recipient, to the message, and/or to the exposure situation. Depending upon the diagnosis, there is a substantial difference between the necessary correction measures. Explicit identification of possible determinants (e.g., ability vs. opportunity) is crucial for adequate diagnosis and intervention decisions.

In order to avoid confusion between ELM and MOA interpretations of the concept of ability, we will refer, in the following, to *capacity* (cf. Robben and Poiesz 1993). The conceptual and semantic meaning of capacity is more associated with personal rather than environmental characteristics.

Motivation, capacity, and opportunity may be interpreted in either an objective or subjective way. This is tantamount to saying that all three factors may be both externally manipulated (by advertisers or researchers) and subjectively assessed (by consumers or research participants). We assume that the inclination to process an advertising message is more dependent upon *subjective* assessments of motivation, capacity, and opportunity, than upon its objective counterparts. For example, even though the amount of time available for processing a particular ad can be judged as amply sufficient on 'objective grounds', processing may not take place if the consumer perceives the time as insufficient.

With regard to the operationalizations (manipulations and multi-item measurement scales) of the three general factors several observations may be made:

Generally, the emphasis is on motivation and ability/capacity only; to our knowledge, the concept of subjective or perceived opportunity is generally ignored. Several possible reasons may be mentioned:
- Depending upon the level of the opportunity factor, its role may be trivial in the sense that common sense does not assume any effect if opportunity is absent or very low;
- Conceptually, opportunity has not been elaborated. Its dimensions are not clear, but are likely to include time, distance, and external distraction;
- To the extent that the role of opportunity is not trivial (when we speak of, for example, limited, sufficient, or ample time), it is not clear how it interacts with the other two main factors motivation and ability;
- At high levels of motivation, limitations with regard to opportunity may possibly be overcome by increasing capacity (e.g. attention);
- A possible reason why opportunity is relatively neglected is that it is easier to acquire data for publication purposes if research participants are provided with more opportunity to react to the stimulus. In this sense there may be a systematic bias in the methodology of advertising research in that the exposure conditions tend to be favorable relative to those in actual circumstances.

In summary, there are several reasons why the operationalization of opportunity lagged behind those of motivation and ability/capacity. At the same time we must note that opportunity is a potentially important factor. Ad processing results that have been observed in the literature may be related to a particular (sufficient) level of opportunity only. The effects of motivation and ability/capacity may differ depending on the level of available opportunity.

Another observation with regard to the operationalization of the three factors is that in some advertising studies, these factors are operationalized or manipulated merely in terms of *some* of its aspects or antecedents. For example, motivation has a tendency to be operationalized as product involvement or personal relevance (see, for instance, Zaichkowsky, 1985), ability/capacity is often operationalized in terms of product knowledge or experience; and opportunity (if operationalized at all) is operationalized in terms of exposure time. Obviously, motivation as a general factor may not be dependent upon involvement or personal relevance only, but may depend upon the combination of executional and media characteristics as well. Similarly, the operationalization of ability/capacity should not reflect product knowledge only, as knowledge is merely an aspect or antecedent, next to other possible aspects or antecedents (such as product and message familiarity, message comprehensibility, recipient intelligence, memory capacity, etc.). Finally, even though time to process is *an* aspect of opportunity, the overall concept and operationalization of opportunity should not limit itself to processing time, but should include, for example, external distractions and distance to the stimulus as well.

For the present purposes it does not suffice to identify *some* operationalization of motivation, capacity, and opportunity and to establish the effect of that operationalization on processing. Rather, we need operationalizations that may be assumed to *fully* cover the conceptual meanings of motivation, capacity, and opportunity to process. In the case of a particular advertising message we may simply not know which particular aspects of motivation, ability/capacity or opportunity are at play. Then, more general operationalizations are preferred. In the present study we will attempt 1. To explicitly introduce opportunity as one of the factors to be considered; and 2. To use operationalizations of the three factors that are of a general nature so as to avoid the suggestion of an emphasis on a particular aspect or determinant.

The following hypotheses overlap with and partly add to the theoretical notions put forward by the ELM (Petty and Cacioppo 1983; 1986) and the MOA-framework (as elaborated by MacInnis and Jaworski 1989; MacInnis et al. 1991):

H1: Motivation, capacity, and opportunity are positively related to the advertising processing related measures: ad recognition (REC_{AD}) and recall (RCL_{AD}), and brand recognition (REC_B) and recall (REC_B);

H2a: Ad recognition and ad recall are positively related to the attitude toward the ad (A_{AD});

H2b: Brand recognition and brand recall are positively related to attitude toward the brand (A_B);

H3: Attitude toward the ad is positively related to attitude toward the brand (A_B);

H4a: Attitude toward the ad is positively related to Intention to act (I_{ACT})

H4b: Attitude toward the brand is positively related to Intention to act (I_{ACT}).

These hypotheses can be summarized in the Figure 1:

METHOD

Subjects and design

Hundred-and-twenty six female members of the Product Evaluation Laboratory Research Panel of Delft University of Technology participated in the study. Age varied between 25 and 83, with a median of 50 years. The data of four participants were not used in subsequent analyses because the presentation of one stimulus was flawed. All received a small monetary compensation for their efforts (about $6.00) and a small gift. Subjects were randomly assigned to one of the eight experimental cells. The design was a 2*2*2 factorial design with two levels ('high' and 'low') for each

FIGURE 1
Proposed model

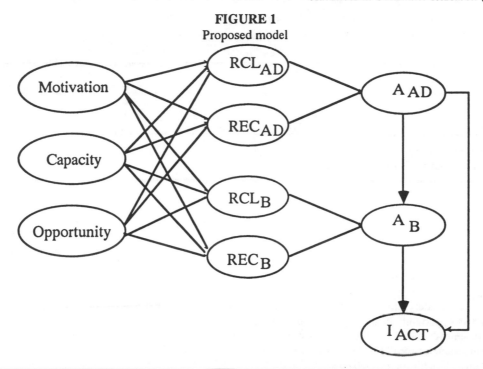

of the between-subjects factors motivation, capacity, and opportunity.

Stimuli

The stimuli were slides of mock-up car advertisements. The top half of the slide showed the car, the bottom half presented the body copy and the brand name, 'Tewikan.' This is a nonexistent brand name, for which it was established in a separate pilot study that it does not carry any negative or positive connotations in the Dutch language.

Independent variables

Opportunity to process the information contained in the ad was either low (slide presentation of 12 seconds) or high (20 seconds). A separate pilot study indicated that 12 seconds was barely enough to see the picture and read the text in the ad. Capacity to process the information was either facilitated by presenting the body copy in everyday language (high), or impeded by presenting the copy in technical jargon (low). Motivation was either enhanced by presenting a full-color picture with a relevant headline ('For your safety') (high) or diminished by presenting a black-and-white picture without the headline (low).

Dependent Measures

Six measures were included that represented early ad-processing effects in the hierarchy of advertising effects (affective, cognitive) and later effects (intentions to act).

Attitude toward the Ad (A_{AD}). Three semantic differential-type items assessed subjects' evaluation of the ad on 7-point scales ($\alpha=.94$). The anchor points were "very negative-very positive," "very unfavorable-very favorable," and "very bad-very good."

Attitude toward the Brand (A_B). Similarly, subjects' evaluation of the brand was assessed ($\alpha=.97$).

Brand Name Recall (RCL_B). Subjects wrote down the name of the brand as they recalled it. This response was classified on a 3-point scale (incorrect, partially correct, fully correct).

Advertisement Recall (RCL_{AD}). Subjects answered on a 7-point scale whether they could recall the advertisement very badly (1) or very well (7).

Brand Recognition (REC_B). On a separate page, using a single 7-point scale ("Not sure at all-Very sure"), subjects indicated how sure they were that "TEWIKAN" was the brand name identified on the ad.

Advertisement Theme Recognition (REC_{AD}). Similarly, they indicated whether safety was the product attribute stressed by the ad.

Intention to Act. On two separate 7-point scales (totally disagree-totally agree), subjects indicated the extent to which they wanted more information on the advertised car, and their wish for a test drive. The significant and positive correlation between both measures ($r=.76$, $p<.0001$) warranted the construction of a single intention to act measure, I_{ACT}.

Procedure

The present study was embedded in a larger investigation involving different experiments by several investigators. This multistudy setting was familiar to the subjects as they all had cooperated previously with the research panel. The total investigation was presented as a set of product evaluation tests. All separate studies involved an evaluation of durable or fast-moving consumer goods.

For the present experiment, subjects sat in front of a projection screen. A research associate read the instructions aloud while the subjects read them simultaneously. A slide projector with an accurate timing device presented the advertisements for either 12 or

TABLE 1

Subjective appraisals of motivation, capacity, and opportunity
Mean factor scores and mean scale scores (italics)

Factor Score Coefficient of	Experimental Condition		t-Value	p-Value
	Low	High		
Motivation	-.20 *2.12*	.21 *2.76*	2.05 *2.67*	.022 *.010*
Capacity	-.42 *3.39*	.36 *4.61*	4.13 *4.18*	.001 *.001*
Opportunity	-.39 *4.05*	.37 *5.29*	4.01 *3.87*	.001 *.001*

Notes. -p values are one-tailed.
-Scales range from 1 - 7; 7 most positive.

20 seconds. Immediately after the projection, subjects completed a scale assessing their subjectively experienced motivation, capacity, and opportunity to process the commercial information. They completed 16 motivation items (e.g., "This advertisement does not appeal to me" and "This advertisement captures my attention"), 12 capacity items (e.g., "I have trouble understanding this advertisement" and "It was immediately clear what this advertisement wanted to say"), and 14 opportunity items (e.g., "You need more time for this advertisement" and "I think the circumstances for watching this advertisement are ideal"). All responses were given on 7-point scales with a "1" indicating "totally disagree" and a "7" indicating "totally agree."

The items for the scales were obtained through qualitative and quantitative pretest studies. In one qualitative pretest, conducted by a professional market research agency, four group discussions involving six persons at a time, each produced statements on 38 different ads. Subsequently, these statements were evaluated with regard to two different ads (a transformational ad on beer and one informational ad on insurance) in survey with 686 respondents by the same agency.

RESULTS

Appropriateness of the Stimuli. To assess the extent to which the subjects typically avoid ads like the one shown in the study, they answered this statement on a 7-point scale (from "totally disagree" to "totally agree"). The mean score (X=5.79, SD=1.81) suggested that the subjects could relate to the ads in the experiment.

Principal Components Analysis. An initial principal components analysis of the items designed to measure the motivation, the capacity, and the opportunity to process the ad, yielded 13 factors accounting for 74.3% of the variance. Inspection of this solution showed that the large majority of these factors contained only items designed to measure either the motivation, the capacity, or the opportunity to process information. Therefore, in line with the theoretical model underlying this study, a three-factor solution was forced, yielding six items for each theoretically defined factor with factor loadings and communalities of .50 or greater, accounting for about 63% of the variance. The factor scores for each factor were used to represent subjective appraisals of the motivation, the capacity, and the opportunity to process the information contained in the experimental stimuli.

Manipulation Checks. The (regression-method) factor scores of the motivation, capacity, and opportunity factors were subjected to t-tests to estimate the extent to which they varied systematically given the respective manipulations. Table 1 presents the results of these tests. The results show that the independent variables induced the hypothesized subjective experiences in the subjects, i.e., that the manipulations worked as intended.

Test of the conceptual model.

Using LISREL 8 (Jöreskog and Sörbom 1993) the conceptual model specified in Figure 1 was subjected to path analysis. The results showed that the specified covariance structure (see Figure 1) fitted the data poorly (χ^2=123.32, df=23, p=.000; goodness of fit index=.83). Inspection of the modification indices suggested several unexpected but theoretically interesting additional paths: from motivation to A_{AD} and from capacity to A_{AD} and A_B. Also, an error covariance was suggested between REC_{AD} and REC_B.

Reestimation of the path model including these new paths resulted in a significant improvement over the first model although the final fit indices remained unsatisfactory (χ^2=51.43, df=20, p=.000; goodness of fit index=.92; $\Delta\chi^2$=80.89, Δdf=3, p < .001).

The path analyses highlighted several aspects. First, that motivation, capacity, and opportunity have independent effects on a subset of the processing variables REC_{AD}, RCL_{AD}, REC_B, and RCL_B. Second, motivation and capacity also have independent and direct effects on the affective outcome variables A_{AD} and A_B. Third, the role of opportunity is limited to influencing the cognitive processing variables, and it does not affect processing outcomes later in the information processing hierarchy.

The intention to act upon the information contained in the advertisement either through asking for additional information or by wanting a test drive is marginally positively influenced through A_{AD}; A_{AD} also influenced A_B. These relationships are consistent with general research on the role of A_{AD} in advertising research although we also expected a positive influence of A_B on I_{ACT} (see, e.g., Brown and Stayman 1992).

The results reported in Table 2 provide only partial support for the hypotheses. Motivation, capacity, and opportunity are not consistently related to advertising processing effects and more general advertising effects. Yet, individual relationships suggests that each one of these factors does have a function in the explanation of the variance in the dependent measures.

DISCUSSION

The main goal of the present study was to assess the relevance of the explicit distinction of an opportunity factor apart from motivation and capacity factors. Opportunity was found to have a significant impact on brand name recall and on brand name recognition. However, it did not affect the recall and the recognition of the advertisement.

Several characteristics of the present study may account for the observed findings. First of all, it should be noted that there are no well developed and standardized measurement scales for motivation, capacity, and opportunity. Second, the opportunity manipulation may have suffered from the complexities discussed in the introduction. Opportunity was manipulated by varying exposure

TABLE 2
Standard Path Coefficients (Initial and after modification)

	Init.	Mod.		Init.	Mod.
Motivation - RCL_{AD}	-.46*	-.46*	Capacity - RCL_{AD}	.38*	.38*
Motivation - REC_{AD}	-.21	-.21	Capacity - REC_{AD}	-.11	-.11
Motivation - RCL_B	.04	.04	Capacity - RCL_B	.08	.08
Motivation - REC_B	.07	.07	Capacity - REC_B	-.18	-.18
Motivation - A_{AD}		.45*	Capacity - A_{AD}	.06	
			Capacity - A_B	.43*	
Opport. - RCL_{AD}	-.08	-.08			
Opport. - REC_{AD}	.15	.15			
Opport. - RCL_B	.43*	.43*			
Opport. - REC_B	.37*	.37*			
$RCLAD - A_{AD}$	.06	.09	$A_{AD} - A_B$	.44*	.28*
$REC_{AD} - A_{AD}$	.13	.22*	$A_{AD} - I_{ACT}$	.23*	.23*
$RCL_B - A_B$	.30*	.10	$A_B - I_{ACT}$	.20	-.20
$REC_B - A_B$	-.17*	-.07			

chi square	init.	123.32 (df 23)	mod.		51.43 (df 20)
GFI		.83			.92
p		.000			.000

* indicates significance level of less than .05 (two-tailed test)

time, and exposure times were set at 'barely enough to see the picture and read the text' and 'amply sufficient' (almost twice as much exposure time). This manipulation may have been experienced by subjects as being sufficient and more than sufficient. In other words, opportunity may have been manipulated in a positive region of the opportunity dimension, and may not have created opportunity differences as intended by the authors. The effect of opportunity on brand name related measures warrants more systematic attention to the opportunity variable in future studies. Here we want to repeat the suggestion that advertising research may be biased toward favorable opportunity or exposure time conditions.

Another characteristic of this study that may have affected the nature of its outcomes is the quality of the advertising stimuli. The stimuli were non-professional mock-up ads which led to relatively low evaluations by the subjects. As a result, the high motivation stimuli received in fact a neutral score on the evaluation dimension, and the low motivation stimuli received a very low score. This may imply a deviation from the types of advertising messages used in main stream advertising studies, and may provide an explanation for the unexpected negative (significant) relationship is observed between Motivation and RCL_{AD}: -.46 (t=3.28, p<.01). A *post hoc* interpretation of this result is that remarkably unattractive ads were remembered better than the more professional looking ones.

It would be premature to point here at managerial implications of the results obtained with this study. However, some general observations can be made that point to the relevance of the present discussion for advertising practice. One of the most notable differences between advertising exposure in laboratory conditions and in real life is that in the former, the opportunity to process a message tends to be relatively favorable. Actual advertising situations, media characteristics or environmental factors strongly affect the opportunity to process a message. Actual exposure conditions rarely come close to the ideal viewing situation: either processing time is insufficient (fast ads, MTV-like productions) or

distraction is too high (crying children in the living room). Although ads may have been perfectly executed to capture consumers' attention, to touch them personally, and talk to them at the correct level of understanding, consumers need the opportunity to process these. To put it differently, the effects of motivation and capacity may very much depend upon the availability of sufficient opportunity to process. In future studies, effects of motivation and capacity should be studied under diffent opportunity conditions to approach external validity and contribute to the question of accountability.

REFERENCES

Andrews, J. Craig (1988), "Motivation, ability, and opportunity to process information: Conceptual and experimental manipulation issues," *Advances in Consumer Research*, 15, 219-225.

Batra, Rajeev and Ray, Michael L. (1986), "Situational effects of advertising repetition: The moderating influence of motivation, ability, and opportunity to respond," *Journal of Consumer Research*, 12, 432-445.

Brown, Stephen and Stayman, Douglas M. (1992), "Antecedents and consequences of attitude toward the ad. *Journal of Consumer Research*, 19, 34-51.

Curry, Bruce and Moutinho, Luiz (1993), "Neural networks in marketing: Modelling consumer responses to advertising stimuli," *European Journal of Marketing*, 27, 5-20.

Foxman, E.R., P.W. Berger and J.A. Cote (1992), "Consumer brand confusion: A conceptual framework," *Psychology and Marketing*, 9, 123-141.

Foxman, E.R., Muehling, D.D. and Berger, P.W. (1990), "An investigation of factors contributing to consumer brand confusion," *Journal of Consumer Affairs*, 24, 170-189.

Jöreskog, Karl G. and Sörbom, Dag (1993), LISREL 8. Chicago, Ill. Scientific Software International, Inc.

MacInnis, Deborah J. and Bernard J. Jaworski (1989), "Information processing from advertisements: Toward an integrative framework," *Journal of Marketing, 53*, 1-23.

MacInnis, Deborah J., Christine Moorman, and Bernard J. Jaworski (1991), "Enhancing and measuring consumers' motivation, opportunity, and ability to process brand information from ads," *Journal of Marketing*, 55, 32-53.

Petty, Richard E. and John T. Cacioppo (1983), "Central and peripheral routes to persuasion: application to advertising," in *Advertising and Consumer Psychology*, eds. Larry Percy and Arch G. Woodside. Lexington, MA: Lexington Books, 3-23.

Petty, Richard E. and John T. Cacioppo (1986), *Central and Peripheral Routes to Attitude Change,* New York: Springer-Verlag.

Poiesz, Theo B.C. and Henry S.J. Robben (1994), "Individual reactions to advertising; theoretical and methodological developments," *International Journal of Advertising*, 13, 25-53.

Robben, Henry S.J. and Theo B.C. Poiesz (1993), "The operationalization of motivation, capacity and opportunity to process an advertising message," *European Advances in Consumer Research*, 1, 160-167.

Zaichkowsky, Judith L. (1985), "Measuring the Involvement Construct," *Journal of Consumer Research,* 12, 341-352.

Truth in the Meaning of Advertisements

K. Patrick Meline, University of Wisconsin-Madison

ABSTRACT

A review of the literature suggests that consumer research has not fully investigated the nature of various consumer meaning processes. This paper suggests that meaning is a simultaneous, two-stage process involving meaning construction (termed the nature of meaning) and an assessment of meaning validity (termed the truth in meaning). Contributions from traditional information processing and postpositivist perspectives are integrated in developing this perspective. The nature of meaning is explored and propositions are offered addressing the role of consumer goals and knowledge in the development of meaning. Finally, implications for consumer research are offered.

INTRODUCTION

Advertisements often weave a complex tale incorporating elements of fiction such as metaphor, drama and tropes (Scott 1994) which extend beyond that of simple cues used by marketers to provide product information. Consumer researchers, however, have traditionally focused on the motivational elements of ads which relate to brand information and have treated other ad elements as distractions to processing which presumably have a limited impact on ad effectiveness (see e.g., Goodstein 1993). However, as advertisers push the creative boundary, it would seem reasonable to suggest that consumer researchers must strive to develop theory which will embrace consumer responses to both creative and informational components of ads. Toward this goal, postpositivistic researchers have begun to investigate the meanings of advertisements via literary theory (Scott 1994), semiotics (Mick and Buhl 1992) and cultural consumption (McCracken 1988).

This stream of literature has offered many insights about consumer response to ads, but has yet to integrate these findings with the traditional information approach characterized by a focus on product-specific cues (e.g., Batra and Ray 1986; Meyers-Levy 1991). This neglect is likely due to the difference in orientation of researchers. The information processing perspective has investigated consumer motivations, but results have appeared to view an ad as nothing more than a conglomeration of adjustable cues (MacInnis, Moorman and Jaworski 1991; Petty, Cacioppo and Schumann 1983) suggesting that ads predominantly act upon passive consumers. The meaning perspective has also focused on consumer motivations with results commonly identifying the situation of the consumer in terms of life themes (Mick and Buhl 1992) or social context (Scott 1994), conversely suggesting that intelligent, active consumers act upon ads. While this may be an oversimplified comparison, the current debate over these issues in the consumer research domain has been the impetus for the current work and others (see e.g., Friestad and Wright 1994; Scott 1994).

This paper suggests that these two perspectives may be successfully integrated by establishing meaning as the central process by which consumers make inferences about advertisements. Meaning is conceptualized as both the recognizable, personally-relevant representations which consumers ascribe to ads and also judgements of the perceived accuracy of these representations in relation to one's knowledge and goals. The former will be referred to as the *nature of meaning* and the latter will be called the *truth in meaning*. This simultaneous, yet two-stage, meaning construct is consistent with other conceptualizations of meaning (Lakoff 1987), but extends current work in the consumer research domain by offering an explicit definition of meaning which incorporates the consumer's natural quest for veridicality (Lakoff and Johnson 1980).

This approach to meaning highlights the contribution of both advertising text and personal beliefs and experiences in the development of meaning. The importance of this combination of text and person has been recognized by both information processing (Wright 1973) and postpositivist researchers (Scott 1994). However, relating these factors to the correspondence between meanings, goals and knowledge (i.e., truth in meaning) in a comprehensive fashion requires an integration of these two streams of research. In so doing, current definitions of consumer goals must be expanded to encompass both life thematic goals characteristic of postpositivistic research (e.g., Mick and Buhl 1992) and brand related goals characteristic of information processing research (e.g., Huffman and Houston 1993; MacInnis et al. 1991).

Another value of this conceptualization of meaning is the recognition that meanings of ads are directly compared to consumer goals and knowledge in order to form an accuracy judgement. This account of truth is inherent in meaning (Lakoff 1987) and is supported by research which suggests that a high correspondence between consumer goals or knowledge and consumer meanings for advertisements may result in enhanced motivation and deeper levels of processing (Markus and Nurius 1986; Mick and Buhl 1992; cf. Alba and Hutchinson 1987; Johnson and Russo 1984).

TWO VIEWS OF CONSUMER RESPONSES TO ADVERTISEMENTS[1]

The Information Approach

The traditional information processing perspective has construed ads as essentially composed of adjustable product-related cues which act upon passive consumers (McCracken 1987). Typical empirical investigations of advertising effectiveness measure recall of brand names and/or product features and most independent and dependent variables are operationalized at the product or brand level (e.g., MacInnis et al. 1991; Petty et al. 1983). According to this perspective, the primary goal of consumers is to gather product-related information which is subsequently used for the purpose of judging brands. Any non-product related information contained in ads is considered peripheral to the consumer's focus. Further, consumers are seen to be easily influenced by the adjustment of cues which direct the flow of information via limited persuasion routes (Mick and Buhl 1992).

Common constructs utilized in the information processing perspective include prior knowledge (Hoch and Deighton 1989), motivation, opportunity and ability (MacInnis et al. 1991). These factors have commonly been associated with the level of ad processing undertaken by the consumer (e.g., Goodstein 1993; MacInnis et al. 1991). Wright (1986b) skeptically evaluates the widely accepted attitude toward the ad (Aad) construct by questioning a global assessment of an ad's impact as an accurate measure of an individual's reactions to an ad's content. Wright proclaims that the "original interest in attitude toward the ad arose from these ideas: (1) ads contain stimuli *other* than those assertions and

---

[1] To facilitate comparison and integration of ideas from both the information and meaning perspectives, this section intentionally presents a polarized view of these perspectives. The author acknowledges that not all studies in the domain are adequately characterized by this cut and dry view.

pictures that convey information about the advertised product, and (2) people might have affective or emotional reactions to those "other" stimuli that, through some process, modify their global evaluation of the advertised product per se" (p. 108).

Wright (1986b) concludes that Aad does not achieve the goal of investigating peripheral content in ads and it leaves us wondering how respondents interpret its items with respect to multiple ad-related reactions. As suggested by Wright (1986a), although consumers may understand the intended message of an ad and evaluate it as good and highly entertaining, no particular correspondence between ad meanings and the individual's goals and knowledge would necessarily result in that evaluation since it is unclear what particular meanings global evaluations are measuring. This paper asserts that a focus on the meaning process will address these concerns.

The Meaning Approach

Although the information approach is prevalent in consumer research, some researchers have begun to move away from the advertising as information perspective and have instead examined advertising as meaning. Mick (1986) has eloquently asserted that researchers should ask the question "What do people do *with* advertising?" instead of asking "What does advertising do *to* people?" The focus suggested by these researchers and others (e.g., McCracken 1988; Scott 1994) is on the meaning of advertisements construed by the individual. This emerging stream of research has emphasized that a consumer actively assigns meaning to advertising cues rather than simply drawing information from the ad (see McCracken 1987 for a detailed discussion).

This emphasis on meaning explicitly acknowledges its subjective nature. Interpretations of ads can vary on an intra and inter-individual basis because of the socioeconomic background, cultural and personal experiences or complex motives of the consumer (Hirschman 1980; Mick and Buhl 1992). This is not to say, however, that each individual will construct completely unique meanings for ads. On the contrary, it is because of common life experiences that meanings may be shared among individuals (Scott 1994; Thompson, Pollio and Locander 1994).

The meaning approach has also emphasized the multidimensionality of meaning. In this view, consumers construct multiple meanings for advertisements. Meaning is viewed as a constructive, dynamic process (Mick and Buhl 1992) by which meaning can be constructed for multiple elements of a stimulus. In this respect, as consumers continue to process an ad new meanings are likely to be developed, some meanings may be more important than others (Wright 1973) and changes in meaning may occur (Friestad and Wright 1994).

A TWO-STAGE MEANING PROCESS

A synergy between the information and meaning perspectives is suggested to result in a simultaneous, two-stage meaning process by which consumers may construct multiple meanings for informational and non-informational elements of an ad. Concurrently, this paper suggests that a validity assessment of meaning (termed the truth in meaning) is constructed through comparison of constructed meanings to an individual's goals and knowledge.

The Nature of Meaning

This paper asserts that meaning is the central process by which consumers make inferences about advertisements. An encompassing view of the meaning process must take into account both the meanings assigned to informational components of an ad related to the product or brand and the meanings consumers ascribe to the creative elements of an ad. This view has several important

assumptions.

First, this view assumes that the consumer of ads actively assigns meaning to both informational and non-informational components of ads. The product-level approach to meaning characteristic of the information perspective and the life-thematic approach to meaning, characteristic of the meaning perspective, are integrated by taking this view of a consumer. Second, this view assumes that the nature of meaning is inherently subjective. Specifically, it recognizes that the intended meanings of ads as conceived by the advertiser are not necessarily the meanings constructed by the individual[2]. Concurrently, this view recognizes that ascribed meanings are individually constructed, but bounded by one's social context.

Third, this view assumes that the nature of meaning is multi-dimensional. Because of the multiple responses consumers will make and the dynamic nature of meaning we must consider the possibility that conflicting meanings will be constructed and ascribed to an ad, some of which may be more or less important than others and therefore given more or less weight by the individual. A full explication of the meaning process must address how a consumer will cope with conflicting, weighted meanings.

Truth In Meaning

The element of meaning proposed to most directly affect a consumer's motivation to process is the truth in meaning. In this context, truth[3] is meant to represent the correspondence or fit between one's nature of meaning and the goals and knowledge of the individual. For example, a consumer watching a commercial for an exercise machine which shows an extremely fit model working out may form the intended meaning of "This machine will help me get in shape like that person." Assuming that getting in shape is a goal of this consumer, the correspondence between meaning and goal would be high.

However, the same consumer may also construct the unintended meaning of "This ad is trying to mislead me by using sex appeal." The fit between this meaning and the individual's knowledge of appropriate marketing tactics would be low since deception is not a desirable characteristic of advertisers for most consumers. This view is highly compatible with recent information processing research which regards consumers of advertising (and persuasion attempts, in general) as actively involved with assessing the motives of advertisers based on an individual's knowledge of marketing tactics (Friestad and Wright 1994).

Similar notions of correspondence have been examined in the consumer research domain. Meyers-Levy and Tybout (1989) investigates the level of congruity between a product and its corresponding product category schema. Their findings suggest that moderate incongruity will lead to the most favorable product evaluations. Goodstein (1993) extends their work by demonstrating that ad typicality, brand goals and prior category affect influence ad processing. Mick and Buhl (1992) also demonstrates the importance of fit between meaning and goals upon an individual's desire to process an ad.

---

[2]This is simply the encoding/decoding process recognized by most models of the communication process.

[3]As noted by one reviewer, the word truth may involve "nasty ontological and epistemological connotations." In the current context, however, every effort was made to emphasize the individual construction and subjective nature of ascribed meanings bounded by a social construction of reality.

FIGURE 1
A Two-Stage Meaning Process

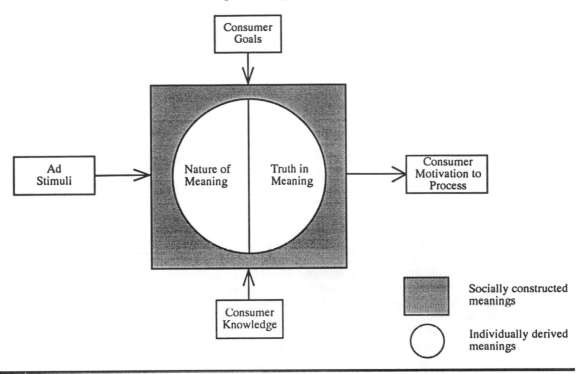

Scott (1994) suggests that the passive consumer stereotype prevalent in consumer research (see e.g., Petty et al. 1983) has been the result of misinterpretations of Wright's (1973, 1975, 1986a) stream of research with respect to cognitive responses and schemer schema. Scott (1994) calls for the replacement of this stereotype with that of an active, skeptical consumer by refocusing on reader resistance to ads and recognizing ads as truth-telling fictions. By investigating the multiple meanings of ads defined in this manner we can better appreciate how consumers may interpret and understand advertising without necessarily believing it.

PROPOSITIONS

Figure 1 illustrates the meaning process proposed by this paper. The diagram indicates the important role multi-level goals and knowledge play in the meaning process. A common assumption in the consumer research literature is integrated into the process and emphasizes that meanings are individually derived and socially shared meanings may be constructed. An assessment of truth in meaning is proposed to influence consumer motivation to process the ad. The following proposition results:

P1: Consumers assess an advertisement via a process of comparing constructed meanings ascribed to the ad with the individual's relevant goals and knowledge, resulting in an assessment of the truth in meaning.

The Effect of Consumer Goals and Knowledge on Meaning Processes

Previous research has restricted consumer goals to product-related information (e.g., Huffman and Houston 1993; MacInnis et al. 1991). This approach provides an easier means of assessment, but does not take advantage of research which has investigated consumer goals from a more holistic approach (e.g., Mick and Buhl 1992). To facilitate the integration of these perspectives, consumer

goals are defined here as a hierarchial set of inter-related acquisition, consumption, or disposition motives which a consumer maintains through a continual process of redefinition. This view of consumer goals is drawn from a wide base of consumer research and other relevant literature which suggests such a consumer goal hierarchy (see e.g., Huffman and Houston 1993; McGuire 1974; Mick and Buhl 1992). Product benefits can be the means through which consumer goals are momentarily sufficed (Huffman and Houston 1993). Likewise, the processing of information contained in an ad can be a means by which consumer goals are satisfied. However, the concept of consumer goals is expanded here to encompass both basic wants and higher-order goals.

Current research highlights the importance of consumer goals in direct relation to meaning. Mick and Buhl (1992) developed a meaning-based model of advertising experiences by identifying life themes and life projects (life themes representing profound existential meanings and life projects representing meanings related to the self and extended self) as goals used to make sense of an advertisement. In effect, Mick and Buhl (1992) found that these consumer goals are a driving force behind the actualized meanings an individual ascribes to an ad.

Huffman and Houston (1993) investigated lower-level consumer goals defined at the level of the product class and presented subjects with a common goal in a task-oriented experiment. While their objective was to investigate the role of consumer goals in the learning process, a major contribution of the article was to demonstrate that knowledge is organized according to the goals of the individual. Thus, the interpretation of information (and therefore meaning) is inherently affected by the goal orientation of the consumer.

Consumer goals are hierarchial in that some goals will have a more pervasive and enduring impact upon a person's life. This type of life goal will influence an individual's daily goals in a top-down processing fashion (Mick and Buhl 1992). This view of consumer goals is necessary to accurately describe meaning construction. For the most part, humans do not merely process information in relation to a goal of gathering information. Rather, consumers selectively receive and process information in relation to the relevant goals of their life at a particular point in time (i.e., in a particular context or situation). Thus, the same information will likely have a different meaning if it were to be processed in relation to a different goal or set of goals. The following proposition results:

P2: The nature of meaning is influenced by the hierarchial set of goals which a consumer brings to any given persuasion attempt,

As stated by Friestad and Wright (1994), "One of the consumer's primary tasks is to interpret and cope with marketers' sales presentations and advertising. Over time consumers develop personal knowledge about the tactics used in these persuasion attempts. This knowledge helps them identify how, when, and why marketers try to influence them. It also helps them adaptively respond to these persuasion attempts so as to achieve their own goals." This type of knowledge is considered by Friestad and Wright to be hovering in the consumer's mental framework, ready to be used in the interpretation, evaluation and response to persuasion attempts.

The Persuasion Knowledge Model incorporates product-related knowledge (topic knowledge) with knowledge about a marketer's goals (agent knowledge) and inference-type knowledge of a marketer's tactics (persuasion knowledge) (Friestad and Wright 1994). Consider, for example, a consumer who is highly skeptical about an ad. The individual may point to various tactics utilized by a spokesperson or perhaps to creative elements of the ad which seem misleading. These may be viewed as meanings ascribed by the consumer using agent or persuasion knowledge, respectively. Tactical knowledge of persuasion attempts can readily be seen as distinct from product-related knowledge and agent knowledge, but the relative importance among these knowledge domains with relation to the meanings ascribed to an ad will vary from situation to situation. The following proposition results:

P3: The nature of meaning is influenced by the multiple knowledge structures utilized by a consumer in any given persuasion attempt.

Although consumer knowledge plays an important role in meaning[4], recent evidence suggests that consumer goals are a more basic, driving force behind the construction of meaning (Huffman and Houston 1993; Mick and Buhl 1992). The following proposition results:

P4: Meanings congruent with goals of the individual will be more relevant to the individual than meanings congruent with the knowledge of the individual.

DISCUSSION

Mick (1986) in his seminal piece introducing semiotics to the consumer research domain notes, "And yet consumer researchers,

---

[4]The conventional distinction between objective and subjective knowledge (Brucks 1985; Park Mothersbaugh and Feick 1994) could prove to be enlightening with respect to the construction of meaning, but it is sufficient here to note that both types of knowledge will have an impact.

with few exceptions, have characteristically avoided detailed and systematic inquiry into meaning processes. Perhaps this reflects the shortcomings of current theory and methodologies in consumer research. Or perhaps the role of meaning appears obvious, but also ineffable or intractable" (p. 201). As Levy (1986) suggests, however, it may be unfair to say that consumer researchers (information processing researchers, in particular) have not investigated meaning. An argument could be made that research on attitudes, perceptions, values, involvement and even cross-cultural factors implicitly deals with consumer meanings for products and brands. By not dealing with meaning explicitly, however, these research streams and the few positivistic studies which have dealt specifically with meaning (e.g., Gutman and Reynolds 1986) leave one with the impression of "seven blind men exploring an unfamiliar elephant" (Levy 1986, p.275).

By drawing on research from both traditional information processing and postpositivist traditions, a two-stage process of meaning construction has been developed and propositions addressing the role of goals and knowledge in the construction of meaning have been offered. Because of different researcher orientations, it should not be surprising that only certain aspects of consumers processes have been highlighted in previous research; much like looking at different sides of the same coin. By integrating the meaning and higher-order goals streams of research characteristic of postpositivistic research (e.g., Mick 1986; Mick and Buhl 1992) and the lower-order goals and motivation research characteristic of information processing research (e.g., Huffman and Houston 1993; MacInnis et al. 1991) a richer explanation of consumer responses to ads results.

By identifying the meanings ascribed to ads and the truth inherent in those meanings, the advertising researcher has the ability to delineate multiple responses to ads in terms of various consumer goals and knowledge structures. Free-response recording as utilized in Wright (1973) and the categorization and interpretation methods used by postpositivistic researchers may bring to light ascribed meanings which impact advertising effectiveness and cannot be construed from the global indicators often relied upon. Further, identification of culturally shared meanings of the audience would provide advertisers with powerful tools to capture an audience's attention (Scott 1994). However, advertisers must be mindful of the idiosyncracies of an ad which will influence consumer responses (Wright 1986a).

Future research into the nature of meaning should explicitly attempt to investigate the multiple meanings which consumers ascribe to advertisements. Change in meaning over time has been addressed by relatively few researchers (Olson 1986; see e.g., Belk 1986; Friestad and Wright 1994; Levy 1986) and could have important implications for studying the effectiveness of advertising campaigns. Changes in meaning could also occur as a result of changes in an individual's concept of self, but explicit research in this area has been neglected with few exceptions (Olson 1986; see e.g., Gutman and Reynolds 1986; Mick and Buhl 1992).

Finally, future research should investigate how various levels of what has been termed in this paper *truth in meaning* will affect an individual's motivation to process, the level of comprehension and attention achieved and the route (i.e., central or peripheral) through which persuasion may occur. It may be fruitful to investigate situations in which multiple meanings are ascribed to an ad and how the correspondence between these meanings, goals and knowledge provides conflicting signals to the consumer. Exploration of situations in which the truth in meaning is extremely low may also prove interesting.

REFERENCES

Alba, Joseph W. and J. Wesley Hutchinson (1987), "Dimensions of Consumer Expertise," *Journal of Consumer Research*, 14 (June), 411-454.

Batra, Rajeev and Michael L. Ray (1986), "Situational Effects of Advertising Repetition: The Moderating Influence of Motivation, Ability, and Opportunity to Respond," *Journal of Consumer Research*, 12 (March), 432-445.

Belk, Russell W. (1986), "Generational Differences in the Meaning of Things, Products, and Activities," in *Advertising and Consumer Psychology*, Vol. 3, eds. Jerry Olson and Keith Sentis, New York: Praeger Publishers, 199-213.

Brucks, Merrie (1985), "The Effects of Product Class Knowledge on Information Search Behavior," *Journal of Consumer Research*, 12 (June), 1-16.

Friestad, Marian and Peter Wright (1994), "The Persuasion Knowledge Model: How People Cope With Persuasion Attempts," *Journal of Consumer Research*, 21 (June), 1-31.

Goodstein, Ronald C. (1993), "Category-based Applications and Extensions in Advertising: Motivating More Extensive Ad Processing," *Journal of Consumer Research*, 20 (June), 87-99.

Gutman, Jonathon and Thomas J. Reynolds (1986), "Coordinating Assessment to Strategy Development: An Advertising Paradigm Based on the MECCAS Model," in *Advertising and Consumer Psychology*, Vol. 3, eds. Jerry Olson and Keith Sentis, New York: Praeger Publishers, 242-258.

Hirschman, Elizabeth C. (1980), "Attributes of Attributes and Layers of Meaning," in *Advances in Consumer Research*, Vol. 7, ed. Jerry C. Olson, Ann Arbor, MI: Association for Consumer Research, 7-12.

Hoch, Stephen J. and John Deighton (1989), "Managing What Consumers Learn from Experience," *Journal of Consumer Research*, 53 (April), 1-20.

Huffman, Cynthia and Michael J. Houston (1993), "Goal-oriented Experiences and the Development of Knowledge," *Journal of Consumer Research*, 20 (September), 190-207.

Johnson, Eric and J. Edward Russo (1984), "Product Familiarity and Learning New Information," *Journal of Consumer Research*, 11 (June), 542-550.

Lakoff, George (1987), *Women, Fire, and Dangerous Things*, Chicago, IL: University of Chicago Press.

_____ and Mark Johnson (1980), *Metaphors We Live By*, Chicago, IL: University of Chicago Press.

Levy, Sidney (1986), "Meanings in Advertising Stimuli," in *Advertising and Consumer Psychology*, Vol. 3, eds. Jerry Olson and Keith Sentis, New York: Praeger Publishers, 214-226.

MacInnis, Deborah J., Christine Moorman, and Bernard J. Jaworski (1991), "Enhancing and Measuring Consumers' Motivation, Opportunity, and Ability to Process Brand Information from Ads," *Journal of Marketing*, 55 (October), 32-53.

Markus, Hazel and Paula Nurius (1986), "Possible Selves," *American Psychologist*, 41 (September), 954-969.

McCracken, Grant (1987), "Advertising: Meaning or Information," in *Advances in Consumer Research*, Vol. 14, eds. Melanie Wallendorf and Paul F. Anderson, Provo, UT: Association for Consumer Research, 121-124.

_____ (1988), *Culture and Consumption*, Bloomington, IN: Indiana University Press.

McGuire, William J. (1974), "Psychological Motives and Communication Gratification," in *The Uses of Mass Communications: Current Perspectives on Gratifications Research*, eds. J. G. Blumler and E. Katz, Beverly Hills, CA: Sage Publications, 167-196.

Meyers-Levy, Joan (1991), "Elaborating on Elaboration: The Distinction between Relational and Item-specific Elaboration," *Journal of Consumer Research*, 18 (December), 358-367.

_____ and Alice M. Tybout (1989), "Schema Congruity as a Basis for Product Evaluation," *Journal of Consumer Research*, 16 (June), 39-54.

Mick, David Glen (1986), "Consumer Research and Semiotics: Exploring the Morphology of Signs, Symbols and Significance," *Journal of Consumer Research*, 13 (September), 196-213.

_____ and Claus Buhl (1992), "A Meaning-based Model of Advertising Experiences," *Journal of Consumer Research*, 19 (December), 317-338.

Olson, Jerry (1986), "Meaning Analysis in Advertising Research," in *Advertising and Consumer Psychology*, Vol. 3, eds. Jerry Olson and Keith Sentis, New York: Praeger Publishers, 275-283.

Park, C. Whan, David L. Mothersbaugh and Lawrence Feick (1994), "Consumer Knowledge Assessment," *Journal of Consumer Research*, 21 (June), 71-82.

Petty Richard E., John T. Cacioppo, and David Schumann (1983), "Central and Peripheral Routes to Advertising Effectiveness: The Moderating Role of Involvement," *Journal of Consumer Research*, 10 (September), 135-146.

Scott, Linda M. (1994), "The Bridge from Text to Mind: Adapting Reader-Response Theory to Consumer Research," *Journal of Consumer Research*, 21 (December), 461-480.

Thompson, Craig J., Howard R. Pollio and William B. Locander (1994), "The Spoken and Unspoken: A Hermeneutic Approach to Understanding the Cultural Viewpoints that Underlie Consumers' Expressed Meanings," *Journal of Consumer Research*, 21 (December), 432-452.

Wright, Peter L. (1973), "The Cognitive Processes Mediating Acceptance of Advertising," *Journal of Marketing Research*, 10 (February), 53-62.

_____ (1975), "Factors Affecting Cognitive Resistance to Advertising," *Journal of Consumer Research*, 2 (June), 1-9.

_____ (1986a), "Reactions to an Ad's Contents versus Judgements of the Ad's Impact," in *Advertising and Consumer Psychology*, Vol. 3, eds. Jerry Olson and Keith Sentis, New York: Praeger Publishers, 108-117.

_____ (1986b), "Schemer Schema: Consumers' Intuitive Theories About Marketers' Influence Tactics," in *Advances in Consumer Research*, Vol. 13, ed. Rich Lutz, Provo, UT; Association for Consumer Research, 1-3.

Visual Attention to Advertising: The Impact of Motivation and Repetition

Rik G.M. Pieters, Tilburg University, The Netherlands
Edward Rosbergen, University of Groningen, The Netherlands
Michel Hartog, Analyse, The Netherlands[1]

ABSTRACT

Using eye-tracking data, we examine the impact of motivation and repetition on visual attention to advertisements differing in argument quality. Our analyses indicate that repetition leads to an overall decrease in the amount of attention. However, while at first high motivation subjects attend to the ad for a longer time than low motivation subjects, this effect of motivation disappears after two exposures. More specifically, our results suggest that the second exposure counts most. In contrast, the order in which the ad elements are attended to is unaffected by repetition and motivation. Yet, the number of ad elements that are skipped becomes larger as the number of exposures increases. Implications of our results for theories of advertising repetition are formulated.

INTRODUCTION

In 1972, Britt, Adams, and Miller demonstrated that consumers were, on average, exposed to between 300 and 600 advertisements per day, which made it impossible for them to attend to all those ads. As competition for the limited attention of consumers is even more a key issue in today's crowded markets and media, it is important to understand how and when consumers devote attention to commercial stimuli, and what determines their attentional strategies. However, "... despite the tremendous amount of money spent on buying consumer attention, little to no research is done on consumer attention" (Janiszewski and Bickart 1994, p. 329). Instead, with some exceptions (e.g., Celsi and Olson 1988; Janiszewski 1993; MacKenzie 1986; Moore, Hausknecht, and Thamodaran 1986; Morrison and Dainoff 1972), the main focus of consumer research has been on information processing and on the effects of advertising on attitude change. In such research, relevant characteristics of the stimuli are considered to be (the quality of) arguments and cues. Arguments and cues are defined in ways that implicitly assume that some level of information processing has already taken place, because the receiver must combine physical characteristics of the stimuli and comprehend their meaning to know whether these characteristics are arguments or cues.

To date, little is known about processes of attention, in particular of visual attention to advertising. We agree with Van der Heijden (1992) that theories of visual attention should take into account both a bottom-up, world-driven approach and a top-down, subject-driven approach by acknowledging exogenous as well as endogenous factors impacting on visual attention. In this study, we examine the impact of an important endogenous factor, consumers' motivation to process information, and an important exogenous factor, the opportunity to process information, as represented by advertising repetition. More specifically, we examine the effects of motivation and repetition on visual attention to advertisements that contain either strong or weak arguments. Visual attention is measured by recording subjects' eye movements. We focus on the

amount of attention that is paid to the elements within the ad, and on the order in which the elements are attended to.

CONCEPTUAL BACKGROUND

Visual attention is generally conceptualized as "... a brain operation producing a localized priority in information processing—an attentional 'window' or 'spotlight' that locally improves the speed and reduces the threshold for processing events" (Deubel and Schneider 1993, p. 575). Eye movements are commonly treated as an operational definition of visual attention. Although there is not a complete one-to-one correspondence between eye position and attention (Van der Heijden 1992), it is generally assumed that "where the eyes go, so goes attention" (Christianson et al. 1991, p. 699).

Generally, people search stimuli for meaning and not for specific targets (Gould 1976). Kahneman (1973) argued that in free-viewing or undirected attention tasks, in which they control the time they spend attending to a series of pictures, subjects who are given no specific instructions behave similarly to those instructed to linger on "interesting" stimuli, and quite differently from those who follow a "pleasingness" set. This suggests that the eyes tend to be guided to areas which are "... ecologically likely to be most informative" (Kahneman 1973, p. 56). Mackworth and Morandi (1967) found that informative areas are identified very early in the observations.

Cognitive theories of persuasion provide indications of the effects of motivation, repetition, and argument quality on attention. Here it is important to distinguish (a) attention to physical characteristics of the elements of an advertisement, such as the location, the size and the mode, text or pictorial, of the elements, from (b) comprehension and interpretation of the content of the elements, i.e., the content perceived as arguments or as cues. In research, it is frequently assumed (e.g., Petty, Cacioppo, and Schumann 1983) that arguments are part of the textual elements of the ad, while cues reside in the pictorials. Miniard et al. (1991) showed, however, that product-relevant pictures are more likely to be perceived as arguments than as cues, whereas pictures devoid of product relevant information are perceived as cues. In our study, we specifically investigate the visual attention of subjects for pictures and text, under different levels of argument quality (high vs. low).

Several studies have examined the effects of repeated exposure to an advertisement on the number of cognitive responses elicited as well as on the attitudes formed (e.g., Calder and Sternthal 1980; Haugtvedt et al. 1994). Most results support some variant of the two-factor theory (e.g., Cacioppo and Petty 1985; Calder and Sternthal 1980). According to the theory, repeated presentations of a message provide recipients with a greater opportunity to consider the implications of the content of the message in a relatively objective manner. Once a consumer has considered the implications of the message, however, tedium and/or reactance are elicited by the excessive exposure, which results in more counterarguing. The two-factor theory was developed to account for the results of repeated exposure under conditions of external pacing, where consumers do not control the exposure duration themselves. However, in real life, consumers often do control the exposure duration, such as when they are confronted with magazine or newspaper ads. In such situations, it is not obvious what the effect of repeated

[1]The research on which this paper is based was funded by Melvo Beheer, Hilversum. Participation of the second author was made possible by a grant of the Economic Research Foundation, which is part of the Netherlands Organization for Scientific Research (NWO). We gratefully acknowledge the support and help of Dominique Claessens throughout the research.

exposures to the ad will be. A likely overall effect is that learning about the ad will lead to a decrease in the time consumers attend to each subsequent exposure of the advertisement. Furthermore, across exposures a larger reduction in exposure time is likely to occur for low motivation consumers than for high motivation consumers, because the latter consumers are more motivated to attend intensively to all ad elements. In summary,

H1a: Duration of visual attention to an ad decreases under repeated exposures, irrespective of consumers' motivation and argument quality.

H1b: Across repeated exposures, duration of visual attention to an ad decreases more rapidly for low motivation consumers than for high motivation consumers, irrespective of argument quality.

Research further shows that high motivation consumers devote more attention to an ad, and that a larger part of their attention is devoted to ad elements containing arguments (Celsi and Olson 1988). However, it is not known whether strong arguments attract more or less attention than weak arguments. It might well be that the amount of time devoted to strong vs. weak arguments is the same, but that only the content and intensity of the ensuing information processing differs. On the other hand, it might be that weak arguments receive less attention than strong arguments. Research indicates that under conditions of low involvement, some 65% of the total fixation time is devoted to pictures, because they lead to higher activation and are cognitively less taxing to process than text (Kroeber-Riel 1993).

In addition, since opportunity to attend and, hence, elaboration likelihood increases as the number of exposures increases, differences between high and low motivation conditions are likely to disappear under repeated exposure. Based on this analysis, we offer the following hypotheses:

H2a: Under high motivation conditions, a larger portion of the exposure time is devoted to the textual elements of an advertisement, whereas under low motivation conditions a larger portion is devoted to the pictorial elements, irrespective of argument quality.

H2b: Differences in the distribution of visual attention across ad elements between high and low motivation conditions disappear as the number of exposures increases.

Two different patterns of visual attention for specific ad elements across repeated exposures are conceivable. First, it might be that during the first exposure(s), consumers have insufficient opportunity to attend to all the elements of the ad. If this happens, they may attend to the "missed" elements during subsequent exposures. This could be called the sequential attention effect of repeated exposures as elements are attended to one-by-one (Loftus 1983). Second, it might also be that during the first exposure(s) consumers attend to all elements of the ad in a global manner to obtain an overall impression of its informative value, and that they use subsequent exposures to attend more intensively to the elements until some level of sufficiency is reached. This could be called the hierarchical attention effect as subsequent exposures stimulate "deeper" levels of engagement in the ad (Craik and Lockhart 1972). In real life, a combination of both processes is likely to occur depending on factors such as the control consumers have over the exposure, the duration of the exposure, the complexity and novelty of the ad, the motivation of the consumers, and so forth (Cacioppo and Petty 1985). Increasing familiarity with the advertisement need not only lead to decreasing amounts of time consumers attend to

message elements (H1a), but may ultimately lead to consumers skipping ad elements altogether, because a glimpse of some elements makes them realize that they already know the content of the other elements. Hence, we expect that when consumers control their exposure to advertising, the sequential effect of repetition will prevail; or,

H3: The number of ad elements attended to decreases across exposures, irrespective of consumers' motivation and argument quality.

Regarding the specific order in which ad elements are attended to, a rule of thumb in advertising is that the top-left corner is the probable entry point for visual attention and has the highest communication value, while the bottom-right corner has the lowest communication value (Janiszewski 1990). The dominant architecture for print ads is to have a headline on the top, a pictorial in the middle, and text below, with a packshot in the bottom-right corner. In view of the research showing that consumers have schemas about marketing and advertising tactics that are used (Friestad and Wright 1994; Kirmani 1990), it is likely, although research is scarce (cf. Gould 1976), that consumers have ideas about the dominant architecture of advertising as well. Since we use ads that have this dominant architecture, we expect consumers to attend first to the headline, then to the pictorial followed by the text, and finally to the packshot, and we expect this order to be constant across exposures, motivational conditions, and argument quality. Besides, we do not expect that skipping of ad elements affects the order in which the remaining elements are attended to.

H4: The order in which ad elements are attended to remains constant across exposures, irrespective of consumers' motivation and argument quality, and the order is: headline followed by pictorial followed by text followed by packshot.

METHOD

Subjects. Forty-eight female and twenty male consumers ranging in age from 19 to 52 years were invited to participate in a study by a market research company. The study lasted approximately half an hour, and subjects were paid the equivalent of twenty dollars for their participation.

Design. A 2X2X3 (motivation X argument quality X repetition) design was used, with motivation and argument quality as between-subjects factors and repetition as a within-subjects factor. A strong and a weak version of an advertisement for an unknown brand of shampoo, Aquavital, were specially designed by an advertising agency. Both versions contained a headline (10% of the ad's size), a pictorial (37%), a packshot (9.5%), and five arguments in favor of the product (11%). The strong version listed five strong arguments; e.g., "The sea extracts in Aquavital provide natural materials that are essential to the strength and the vitality of your hair." An example of the five arguments that were used in the weak version of the ad is "It is suited to everyone's hair." The arguments were selected on the basis of the results of a pilot study, in which ten subjects evaluated a list of arguments on their believability, comprehensibility, originality, and strength. The headline was adjusted to the type of arguments that was used and the combination of headline and arguments was tested on its persuasive force.

To manipulate subjects' motivation to process the Aquavital ad, a procedure was followed that is similar to the procedure used by Petty, Cacioppo, and Schumann (1983). Subjects in the high motivation condition were instructed to watch all ads carefully. They were explained that the study's purpose was to gain insight

TABLE 1
Results of the manipulation checks

Measures	Low motivation		High motivation		ANOVA[1] ($F_{1,64}$-values)		
	Weak	Strong	Weak	Strong	M	A	MxA
Argument quality	-0.18	0.69	-0.46	0.48	0.57	7.56 [b]	0.02
Motivation to evaluate	-0.47	-1.07	0.36	-0.50	4.04 [a]	2.27	0.20
Involvement	0.99	1.80	1.81	2.01	4.86 [a]	4.67 [a]	1.67

[1] M = Motivation; A = Argument quality;
[a] $p < 0.10$; [b] $p < 0.05$

into the way information is used to form judgments about the products advertised. In addition, subjects in the high motivation condition were promised a choice of shampoo from several brands at the end of the session. Subjects in the low motivation condition were told that the study's purpose was to develop a new method for testing "draft versions" of ads. They were instructed to evaluate the ads themselves.

All subjects were exposed to the Aquavital ad three times. The target ads were embedded in a sequence of thirteen ads, which promoted eight different products: shampoo (shown three times), soup (three times), rice (twice), salad-dressing, sunburn lotion, sports shoes, garden furniture, and a vacuum cleaner. The Aquavital ads were in the second, the fourth, and the ninth position of the sequence. In this paper, only results with respect to the Aquavital ads are presented.

Procedure. Upon entering the experimental room, subjects received a booklet containing the instructions regarding the experiment. They were informed that their eye movements would be recorded while they were attending to slides of "draft versions" of ads. In addition, the purpose of the study was explained. After subjects finished reading, the instructions were verbally provided once more. Next, subjects were seated in front of a screen, on which the slides were projected from the back, and were instructed to place their chin on a small chinrest. Eye movements were recorded by an infrared camera located at the subjects' left side, such as not to interfere with the subjects' normal viewing behavior. The camera was trained on the subjects' right eye. Eye positions (fovea) were recorded fifty times a second.

Before the slides with the ads were shown, subjects were instructed to press a button in front of them to go through the ads at their own pace. Ads were shown to the subjects for twenty seconds at most. After attending to the ads, subjects performed a calibration task. Next, they completed a questionnaire containing questions about their motivation to process the ad, and their evaluation of the quality of the arguments in the ad.

Measures. Motivation to process the ad was measured in two separate ways. First, subjects were asked to rate on a seven-point scale (completely agree—completely disagree) their motivation to evaluate the arguments listed in the ad. Second, involvement in shampoo was measured using the following six items (seven-points, strongly agree—strongly disagree) of the Consumer Involvement Profile (Kapferer and Laurent 1985): (1) "When you purchase a brand of shampoo, it's not a big deal if you make a mistake," (2) "It is really annoying to purchase a shampoo that is not suitable," (3) "A poor choice of shampoo would be upsetting," (4)

"I am indifferent to the shampoo I use," (5) "I attach a great importance to shampoo," and (6) "I have a strong interest in shampoo." Scores on the six items were averaged (coefficient alpha=0.76).

Evaluation of argument quality was assessed by having subjects rate the arguments on three seven-point items anchored by very convincing—not at all convincing, very weak—very strong, and not at all believable—very believable (coefficient alpha=0.91). Scores on the three items were averaged.

RESULTS

Manipulation checks. Evaluation of argument quality is compared for the two argument conditions using ANOVA. As expected, strong arguments are perceived to be stronger than weak arguments, whereas evaluations by high vs. low motivation subjects do not differ (see Table 1, first row).

ANOVAs further indicate that manipulations of motivation was successful as well. The level of motivation significantly influences both motivation to evaluate arguments and involvement, with high motivation subjects having higher scores than low motivation subjects (Table 1).

Tests of hypotheses. Since the reliability of eye-tracking data may suffer from factors such as blinking of the eye and tearfluid in the eye, several checks were conducted which indicate that for sixteen subjects the reliability of the data was too low to use them in further analysis. These subjects were divided equally between the four between-subjects conditions. The remaining 52 subjects are divided between the four conditions in the following way: 23 subjects belong to the high motivation group, twelve were exposed to strong and eleven to weak arguments; 29 belong to the low motivation group, fifteen were exposed to strong and fourteen to weak arguments. For each subject, the eye-tracking data were transformed into variables representing (1) the total time subjects attended to each ad element and to the total ad (i.e., gaze duration); and (2) the exact moment subjects attended to an ad element for the first time (from the start of a particular exposure).

Multivariate analysis of variance (MANOVA) with repeated measures indicates that hypothesis 1a is supported (Table 2, fifth and eighth row, fourth column); i.e., overall gaze duration decreases significantly from the first to the second as well as from the second to the third exposure (see Table 3).

In line with past research, overall gaze duration is longer for high motivation subjects than for low motivation subjects, but this difference only holds for the first and second exposure, and not for the third exposure (Table 3). Figure 1 indicates that the drop in

TABLE 2
MANOVAs for total gaze duration and proportion of total gaze duration per ad element within and between exposures

	Between-subjects effects $(F_{1,48})$[1]			Within-subjects effects $(F_{2,96}$ and $F_{1,48})$[2]			
	M	A	MxA	R	RxM	RxA	RxMxA
Headline	0.81	0.35	0.00	2.56 [a]	0.09	0.51	0.63
Pictorial	5.41 [b]	0.00	2.11	5.00 [c]	2.27	1.05	0.46
Text	2.72	0.37	1.39	13.95 [c]	2.48 [a]	0.08	0.42
Packshot	0.70	3.53 [a]	0.00	5.55 [c]	0.66	0.28	0.02
Overall	4.86 [b]	2.96 [a]	0.00	74.03 [c]	2.27	1.12	0.10
Diff pictorial [3]	0.09	0.17	0.91	1.20	4.06 [b]	1.77	0.08
Diff text	0.09	0.05	0.01	0.71	6.04 [b]	0.14	1.03
Diff overall	1.23	0.90	0.11	3.32 [a]	1.37	0.90	0.09
Kendall's tau	0.27	1.41	0.90	2.46	2.08	2.08	0.73

[1] M = Motivation; A = Argument quality; R = Repetition.
[2] d.f. = 2,96 for the first five rows, and 1,48 for the last four rows.
[3] Diff refers to the difference in values between two successive exposures.
[a] $p < 0.10$; [b] $p < 0.05$; [c] $p < 0.01$

overall gaze duration between the first and second exposure is larger for low than for high motivation subjects, although this difference is not significant (Table 3). From the second to the third exposure, however, overall gaze duration drops significantly stronger for high than for low motivation subjects. Hence, partial support for hypothesis 1b is found. Argument quality, finally, has a marginal effect on overall gaze duration, where only for the second exposure overall gaze duration is longer for ads containing weak rather than strong arguments.

With respect to the various ad elements, we find that motivation only affects the proportion of overall gaze duration that is devoted to the pictorial significantly (Table 2). In support for hypothesis 2a, Table 3 reveals that this proportion is larger for low than for high motivation subjects, although the difference is significant for the second exposure only. Since for text elements no differences between levels of motivation are found, hypothesis 2a is not fully supported. However, the significant interaction-effect between repetition and motivation (Table 2) indicates that differences between high and low motivation subjects in the proportion of overall gaze duration devoted to text actually exist, but that these differences are not constant across exposures. In fact, this difference is only significant for the second exposure, during which high motivation subjects devote a larger part of their attention to text than low motivation subjects (Table 3). For low motivation subjects, the part of overall gaze duration devoted to the text decreases and the part devoted to the pictorial increases mainly from the first to the second exposure, whereas the same changes occur for high motivation subjects mainly from the second to the third exposure (see Table 2). Hence, hypothesis 2b is supported; i.e., differences in the distribution of visual attention across ad elements disappear as the number of exposures increases, albeit that no differences existed for the first exposure either.

Except for the packshot, no significant effect of argument quality on the distribution of visual attention across ad elements is found (Table 2), which supports hypothesis 2a. Table 3 shows that only during the first exposure a larger part of the visual attention was devoted to the packshot for ads containing strong rather than weak arguments.

Analyses further reveal that the total number of ad elements skipped during the third exposure (54 out of 208=52X4) is significantly larger than the number of elements skipped during the first exposure (10; $\chi_2^2 = 24.802$, p<0.001), which supports hypothesis 3. Except for low motivation subjects exposed to weak arguments, the number of elements skipped increases significantly across exposures for all between-subjects conditions.

Finally, the order in which the ad elements are attended to for the first time is the same for most subjects. Subjects first attend to the headline and then to the pictorial, which supports hypothesis 4. Only the ranking of text and packshot show differences due to the fact that these elements are skipped most. Rank correlations of the orders in which the ad elements are attended to during successive exposures (Kendall's tau) all significantly differ from zero, which indicates that this order hardly changes across exposures. ANOVAs reveal no differences due to subjects' motivation, but the consistency in the orders for the first and second exposure is higher for weak than for strong arguments (i.e., Kendall's tau is higher).

DISCUSSION AND IMPLICATIONS

While in past research, effects of advertising characteristics on cognitive responses and attitudes have been studied frequently, only few studies have dealt with the effects on visual attention. In this study, we examined the effects of motivation, argument quality and repetition on two aspects of visual attention, gaze duration and gaze sequence. Overall, the results confirmed our hypotheses, but

FIGURE 1

Effect of repeated exposures on gaze duration

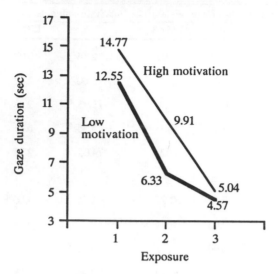

TABLE 3

ANOVAs for total gaze duration and proportion of total gaze duration per ad element within and between exposures[1]

| | Low motivation | | High motivation | | ANOVA $(F_{1,48})$[2] | | |
	Weak	Strong	Weak	Strong	M	A	MXA
Exposure 1							
Headline	19%	15%	18%	21%	0.23	0.01	0.46
Pictorial	16%	14%	8%	13%	2.65	0.06	1.47
Text	49%	55%	57%	49%	0.04	0.00	1.61
Packshot	9%	14%	10%	14%	0.03	4.82b	0.00
Overall	12.61	12.49	15.21	14.37	3.05a	0.12	0.08
Exposure 2							
Headline	22%	23%	20%	22%	0.44	3.27a	1.28
Pictorial	30%	22%	11%	12%	7.03b	0.69	0.64
Text	37%	33%	56%	50%	6.51b	0.38	0.03
Packshot	11%	15%	8%	13%	0.78	1.70	0.04
Overall	7.74	4.82	11.14	8.78	6.79b	3.62a	0.04
Exposure 3							
Headline	23%	23%	28%	29%	0.51	0.00	0.01
Pictorial	25%	20%	12%	22%	1.33	0.17	2.37
Text	26%	31%	38%	27%	0.30	0.09	1.33
Packshot	17%	24%	12%	19%	0.75	1.77	0.00
Overall	5.57	3.49	5.96	4.19	0.21	2.75	0.02
Exp. 2 vs. Exp. 1							
Pictorial	+14%	+8%	+3%	-1%	4.23b	1.18	0.24
Text	-12%	-21%	-1%	+2%	4.63b	0.27	0.57
Overall	-4.87	-7.67	-4.07	-5.59	0.77	1.86	0.15
Kendall's tau[3]	0.38	0.31	0.70	0.29	1.35	3.18a	1.79
Exp. 3 vs. Exp. 2							
Pictorial	-5%	-1%	0%	+10%	2.42	1.50	0.43
Text	-11%	-2%	-18%	-23%	3.52a	0.09	0.82
Overall	-2.16	-1.34	-5.18	-4.59	6.75a	0.36	0.01
Kendall's tau	0.29	0.32	0.27	0.25	0.10	0.00	0.03

[1] Proportions do not necessarily sum to 1, because the ad elements as they are defined do not cover the full page.

[2] M = Motivation; A = Argument quality.

[3] Kendall's tau measures the rank correlation between the order in which the ad elements are attended to for the first time during two successive exposures.

[a] p < 0.10;   [b] p < 0.05

they also showed that the effects of consumers' motivation and argument quality differ across exposures.

Quite surprisingly, our results support Krugman's (1972) three-exposure hypothesis of the effect of repetition on advertising effectiveness. He argued that the first exposure leads to an identification reaction, since the consumer tries to understand what the stimulus and its content are about. The second exposure leads to an evaluation reaction in which the consumer tries to determine whether the advertised product is important, relevant or new. The third and subsequent exposures then lead to recognition reactions since the consumer realizes that he/she has been exposed to the ad before. Although the three-exposures hypothesis is evidently too simple to account for the effects of repeated exposure to advertising, it does stress the crucial role of the second exposure, as in this exposure consumers actually interact with the ad. In the present study, for the first exposure no differences were found between conditions with respect to the attention devoted to ad elements. In the second exposure, clear, significant differences between high versus low motivation consumers were observed for attention devoted to the pictorial and the text. In the third exposure, these differences disappeared again. The results indicate that during the second exposure, low motivation consumers devote a larger proportion of their time to the pictorial, while the high involvement consumers devote over 50% of their time to the text. The fact that the largest differences in the focus of attention occurred during the second exposure is suggestive of its importance. Although all exposures may play their role in advertising effectiveness, it may be that the "second exposure counts" (SEC). Future research may explore the validity of the SEC effect across exposure situations, advertising stimuli and subjects.

In addition, advertising repetition may have at least two effects on visual attention that mirror results found in decision making (Payne, Bettman, and Johnson 1988), where, under time constraints, consumers have been found to either "filter" (i.e., do different things) or to "accelerate" (i.e., do the same things faster) processing. Of course, applying a time constraint means limiting the opportunity to process, while repetition means increasing the opportunity to process. Hence, it might be that under repeated exposure consumers just pay more attention to all ad elements, without changing the proportion of attention spend to the specific ad elements, which could be called "deepening" and may be seen as the reverse of acceleration. On the other hand, under repeated exposure consumers may also pay attention to different ad elements, which could be called "highlighting" as the reverse of filtering. If highlighting occurs, the proportion of time spend across exposures changes significantly. Our results which reveal changing proportions across exposures and increased skipping of elements are suggestive for a highlighting effect to occur. However, it is not clear whether this effect also occurs when consumers have more stringent time constraints (shorter exposure durations) than was the case in this study.

Finally, although previous research has shown that pictorials may contain (strong) arguments and body texts may contain peripheral cues (Unnava and Burnkrant 1991), and that for such situations the standard ELM predictions are confirmed, it may not always be recommendable to use such an advertisement structure. Our results indicate that, overall, high motivation subjects tend to pay more attention to the text than to the pictorial, whereas low motivation subjects tend to pay more attention to the pictorial than to the text. Since it is assumed that cues are most effective for low motivation consumers, and arguments for high motivation consumers, it may, in general, be more effective to place arguments in the text, and cues in the pictorial.

REFERENCES

Batra, Rajeev and Michael L. Ray (1985), "How Advertising Works at Contact," in *Psychological Processes and Advertising Effects*, ed. Linda F. Alwitt and Andrew A. Mitchell, Hillsdale, N.J.: Lawrence Erlbaum Associates, 13-44.

Britt, Steuart H., Stephen C. Adams, and Allan S. Miller (1972), "How Many Advertising Exposures Per Day?" *Journal of Advertising Research*, 12 (December), 3-9.

Cacioppo, John T. and Richard E. Petty (1985), "Central and Peripheral Routes to Persuasion: The Role of Message Repetition," in *Psychological Processes and Advertising Effects*, ed. Linda F. Alwitt and Andrew A. Mitchell, Hillsdale, N.J.: Lawrence Erlbaum Associates, 91-111.

Calder, Bobby J. and Brian Sternthal (1980), "Television Commercial Wearout: An Information Processing View," *Journal of Marketing Research*, 17 (May), 173-186.

Celsi, Richard L. and Jerry C. Olson (1988), "The Role of Involvement in Attention and Comprehension Processes," *Journal of Consumer Research*, 15 (September), 210-224.

Christianson, S.A., E.F. Loftus, H. Hoffman, and G.R. Loftus (1991), "Eye Fixations and Memory for Emotional Events," *Journal of Experimental Psychology: Learning, Memory, and Cognition*, 17, 693-701.

Craik, F.T.M. and R.S. Lockhart (1972), "Levels of Processing: A Framework for Memory Research," *Journal of Verbal Learning and Visual Attention*, 11, 671-684.

Deubel, H. and W.X. Schneider (1993), "There is No Expressway to a Comprehensive Theory of the Coordination of Vision, Eye Movements and Visual Attention," *Behavioral and Brain Sciences*, 16 (3), 575-576.

Friestad, Marian and Peter Wright (1994), "The Persuasion Knowledge Model: How People Cope with Persuasion Attempts," *Journal of Consumer Research*, 21 (June), 1-31.

Gould, John D. (1976), "Looking at Pictures," in *Eye Movements and Psychological Processes*, ed. Richard A. Monty and John W. Senders, Hillsdale, NJ: Lawrence Erlbaum Associates, 323-345.

Haugtvedt, Curtis P., David W. Schumann, Wendy L. Schneier and Wendy L. Warren (1994), "Advertising Repetition and Variation Strategies: Implications for Understanding Attitude Strength," *Journal of Consumer Research*, 21 (Jun), 176-189.

Janiszewski, Chris (1990), "The Influence of Print Advertisement Organization on Affect Toward a Brand Name," *Journal of Consumer Research*, 17 (Jun), 53-65.

Janiszewski, Chris (1993), "Preattentive Mere Exposure Effects," *Journal of Consumer Research*, 20 (Dec), 376-392.

Janiszewski, Chris and Barbara Bickart (1994), "Managing Attention," in *Advances in Consumer Research*, 21, 329.

Kahneman, Daniel (1973), *Attention and Effort*, Englewood Cliffs, N.J.: Prentice Hall.

Kapferer, Jean-Noël and Gilles Laurent (1985), "Consumer Involvement Profiles: A New Practical Approach to Consumer Involvement," *Journal of Advertising Research*, 25 (December), 48-56.

Kirmani, Amna (1990), "The Effect of Perceived Advertising Costs on Brand Perceptions," *Journal of Consumer Research*, 17 (September), 160-171.

Kroeber-Riel, Werner (1993), *Bild Kommunikation: Imagerystrategien für die Werbung*, München: Verlag Franz Vahlen.

Krugman, Harold E. (1972), "Why Three Exposures May Be Enough," *Journal of Advertising Research*, 12, 3-9.

Loftus, Geoffrey R. (1983), "Eye Fixations on Text and Scenes," in *Eye Movements in Reading: Perceptual and Language Processes*, ed. Keith Rayner, New York: Academic Press, 359-376.

MacKenzie, Scott B. (1986), "The Role of Attention in Mediating the Effect of Advertising on Attribute Importance," *Journal of Consumer Research*, 13 (September), 174-195.

Mackworth, N.H., and A.J. Morandi (1967), "The Gaze Selects Informative Details Within Pictures," *Perception and Psychophysics*, 2, 547-552.

Miniard, Paul W., Sunil Bhatla, Kenneth R. Lord, Peter R. Dickson, and H. Rao Unnava (1991), "Picture-based Persuasion Processes and the Moderating Role of Involvement," *Journal of Consumer Research*, 18 (June), 92-107.

Moore, Danny L., Douglas Hausknecht, and Kanchana Thamodaran (1986), "Time Compression, Response Opportunity, and Persuasion," *Journal of Consumer Research*, 13 (June), 85-99.

Morrison, Bruce John and Marvin J. Dainoff (1972), "Advertisement Complexity and Looking Time," *Journal of Marketing Research*, 9 (November), 396-400.

Payne, John W., Jim R. Bettman, and Eric J. Johnson (1988), "Adaptive Strategy Selection in Decision Making," *Journal of Experimental Psychology: Learning, Memory and Cognition*, 14, 534-552.

Petty, Richard E., John T. Cacioppo, and David W. Schumann (1983), "Central and Peripheral Routes to Advertising Effectiveness: The Moderating Role of Involvement," *Journal of Consumer Research*, 10 (September), 135-146.

Unnava, H. Rao and Robert E. Burkrant (1991), "An Imagery-Processing View of the Role of Pictures in Print Advertisements," *Journal of Marketing Research*, 28 (May) 226-231.

Van der Heijden, A.H.C. (1992), *Selective Attention in Vision*, New York: Routhledge.

Yarbus, A.L. (1967), *Eye Movements and Vision* (translated by B. Haigh), New York: Plenum Press.

An "Importance" Subscale for the Consumer Involvement Profile

Kenneth C. Schneider, St. Cloud State University
William C. Rodgers, St. Cloud State University

ABSTRACT

After reviewing the structure (dimensionality) of two scales that have been proffered as measures of the involvement construct, Zaichkowsky's Personal Involvement Inventory (PII), and Laurent and Kapferer's Consumer Involvement Profile (CIP), the authors propose and provide initial support for a new subscale for the CIP; one designed to measure Importance, a construct not now encompassed by that scale. The relationship between Importance and the remaining CIP subscales designed to measure various involvement antecedents (ie., Interest-Pleasure, Sign, Risk Probability and Risk Importance) is then discussed.

INTRODUCTION

While the specific wording still changes from one author to the next, most consumer researchers would probably not argue with a characterization of *product involvement* as a consumer's "heightened motivational state" (Mittal 1989a, p. 697) toward some product or service category that derives from its relevance or importance to the consumer. As such, product involvement can be distinguished from involvement with other objects, including the purchase process (Slama and Tashchian 1985, Mittal 1989), advertising messages (Andrews and Durvasula 1991), and so on. This so-called relevance or importance, in turn, results from one or another personal or situational conditioners, referred to as involvement antecedents.

Consumer researchers have made considerable progress toward developing a scale to measure the product involvement construct in the past ten years or so. To date, however, attendant research has proceeded along two parallel, non-intersecting lines of inquiry. As a consequence, researchers now have available two rather disparate involvement scales, the Personal Involvement Inventory and the Consumer Involvement Profile.

The next section presents a brief discussion of the structure or dimensionality of these two scales. After that discussion, an extension which adds an "Importance" subscale to the Consumer Involvement Profile is proposed and analyzed. It is intended that the new subscale will allow the Consumer Involvement Profile to more fully measure the involvement construct.

COMPARING THE STRUCTURE OF TWO INVOLVEMENT SCALES

Personal Involvement Inventory. The twenty item, semantic differential scaled Personal Involvement Inventory (PII) was originally proposed and analyzed by Zaichkowsky (1985). This scale, conceived as a unidimensional scale to identify the personal relevance of a particular product to the consumer, has been further analyzed and refined by Celuch and Evans (1989), Flynn and Goldsmith (1993), Jain and Srinivasan (1990), McQuarrie and Munson (1987, 1992), Mittal (1989a), and Zaichkowsky (1986).

Of particular concern here, several authors have addressed the dimensionality of the PII. After strenuously arguing for a restrictive, unidimensional definition of product involvement, Mittal (1989a) suggested that the original PII contained at least three constructs. These include (1) product involvement itself (six scale items that measure the importance, relevance and significance of the product, plus "of concern," "matters" and "means a lot" to me), (2) a hedonic antecedent of product involvement (four scale items that measure interest in, fascination with, appeal of, and excitement generated by the product), and (3) an amalgam of scale items that probably measure something more akin to attitude than involvement.

Indeed, McQuarrie and Munson (1992) have recently presented a new version of the PII, more or less revised along these lines. Those authors suggest organizing the PII into (1) an Importance dimension of the product involvement construct using five items from the PII (Mittal's "involvement itself"), (2) an Interest dimension of the product involvement construct using three items from the PII and two new items (Mittal's hedonic antecedent), and (3) remaining items from the PII to be discarded (Mittal's "attitude-like" items, plus a potpourri of items (e.g., mundane, nonessential) thought to be complexly worded).

Consumer Involvement Profile. In an independent line of inquiry, Laurent and Kapferer (1985) proposed a quite different scale; the sixteen item, Likert scaled Consumer Involvement Profile (CIP). Unlike Zaichkowsky's unidimensional scale, the CIP is actually a series of subscales, each designed to measure an antecedent of product involvement. When using the CIP, level of involvement must be inferred from observed measurements on these antecedents. The five antecedents proposed by Kapferer and Laurent include Interest, Pleasure, Sign, Risk Probability and Risk Importance.

The CIP has also been further analyzed and refined by Celuch and Evans (1989), Jain and Srinivasan (1990), Kapferer and Laurent (1985a, 1985b, 1993), Mittal (1989a), Mittal and Lee (1988), and Rodgers and Schneider (1993). Of particular concern here is that two of Laurent and Kapferer's antecedents, Interest and Pleasure, seem to merge into a single factor in studies using American consumers, a conclusion that was reached independently by Jain and Srinivasan (1990), and by Rodgers and Schneider (1993). Thus, in U.S. domestic use anyway, the CIP seems to contain four dimensions, (1) Interest-Pleasure (Mittal's hedonic antecedent), (2) Sign, (3) Risk Probability, and (4) Risk Importance. Indeed, in their most recent set of replication studies, Kapferer and Laurent (1993) often found a similar merging of the Interest and Pleasure factors in studies using French consumers.

Comparing the Scales' Structures. Consequently, two separate lines of scale development research have led to scales with only one overlapping dimension; level of interest in or pleasure derived from the product. In motivating their Interest subscale, McQuarrie and Munson (1992) refer to it variously as emotional involvement (see, also, Park and Mittal 1985, Vaughn 1986, and Zaichkowsky 1987) and as a measure of the enjoyment derived from a product. Indeed, the two new items added to the PII and included in the Interest subscale—fun, and neat (as opposed to dull)—are direct measures of pleasure. Thus, the Interest component of McQuarrie and Munson's revised version of Zaichkowsky's PII and the merged Interest-Pleasure antecedent subscale in the CIP should readily converge. (In fact, Celuch and Evans (1989) have already found fairly large correlations between the original PII and the original Interest and Pleasure subscales in the CIP.)

Whether this Interest-Pleasure subscale found to reside in the CIP (or, equivalently, this new Interest subscale in the revised PII) constitutes a second dimension of involvement or an involvement antecedent will be a matter of considerable debate for some time yet to come. The authors here are inclined to support Mittal's characterization of Interest-Pleasure as a hedonic antecedent of involvement, for several reasons. First, like all constructs, product involvement can be as narrowly or broadly conceived as a researcher chooses; it is hoped that continued research and discussion eventually leads to definitional convergence. Whenever possible, however, parsimony suggests that several rather narrowly defined constructs are preferable to few rather broadly defined ones. As noted earlier, the core of product involvement concerns the importance or relevance that a product assumes for a given consumer. Everything else can be just as easily considered as either leading to, paralleling, or flowing from the *importance* that is involvement.

Thus, like Mittal (1989a), the authors here contend that product involvement itself should be narrowly conceived, encompassing only the importance or centrality of the product to the consumer. Other facets, including the extent to which a consumer finds a product or service category interesting or pleasurable, can be linked to involvement without necessarily being involvement.

Indeed, in a temporal context, the authors strongly believe that Interest-Pleasure is more properly considered a hedonic antecedent of involvement (as in the CIP) than as a dimension of involvement (as in the PII). Certain products (e.g., hobbies, many participative sports) come to mind as ones that are relevant and important to the consumer precisely because of the pleasure they bring. It is difficult to imagine, for example, the model railroader's or the amateur golfer's intense concern for their respective associated products as being primarily derived from anything but the sheer enjoyment of the activity (though it is stipulated that there may be contributory symbolic value or risk related antecedents at work as well). For some product categories and some consumers, then, importance or personal relevance is driven primarily by the pleasure or interest inherently found in the product. For such products, Interest-Pleasure is, indeed, an antecedent.

Also, certain other products (e.g., "life's little indulgences," some leisure activities) can be thought of as being a source of interest or pleasure yet not particularly important to many consumers. It is difficult to imagine, for example, that the consumption of a candy bar or a VCR rental, while admittedly a source of at least temporary pleasure or interest, would have any great relevance to the individual. In such situations, even a relatively high level of perceived interest or pleasure does not result in the sorts of behavioral outcomes normally associated with high involvement products. For instance, one rarely sees more than a modicum of information seeking attendant to the purchase of a chocolate bar or the latest video release. Thus, not all interesting or pleasurable products seem to be involving, as would be the case if Interest-Pleasure were classified as a second dimension of the product involvement construct.

In general, then, a compelling case can be argued for thinking of Interest-Pleasure as an antecedent that can (but, not always must) lead to product involvement, and for thinking of product involvement itself as a unidimensional concept that signifies the importance or relevance of the product to the individual.

What is clear is that current versions of both the PII and the CIP are incompletely structured. Specifically, the PII measures personal relevance or importance (ie., product involvement itself), and one of several antecedents (ie., Interest-Pleasure). On the other hand, the CIP measures a richer array of antecedents (ie., Interest-Pleasure, Risk Importance, Risk Probability and Sign), but has no direct measure of personal relevance or importance (ie., product involvement itself).

One acceptable solution for the researcher intent on measuring both product involvement and its antecedents is to utilize a combination of the PII and CIP scales. In doing so, one need only recognize that the two scales employ different response formats; the PII uses a semantic differential format and the CIP uses a Likert format. A second solution entails expanding either scale so that both product involvement and its possible triggering antecedents can be measured under the same format. The next section sets forth a proposed new subscale for the CIP; one designed to measure product importance itself.

AN IMPORTANCE SUBSCALE FOR THE CIP

Exhibit 1 presents a seven item importance subscale that was crafted as a potential addition to the CIP. These seven items were derived from several sources. One (IMP02) is an item reassigned from the five item merged Interest-Pleasure subscale that resulted from U.S. applications of the CIP (see Rodgers and Schneider 1993). (While IMP02, an item from the original CIP Interest subscale, consistently loaded with four other items measuring interest taken in or pleasure derived from a product, its wording ("I attach great importance to selecting a —") is such that it should be realigned with other items purporting to directly measure product importance instead of those that measure Interest-Pleasure.) One item (IMP04) is an adaptation of an item that appeared in an Importance subscale in an early version of the CIP (see Laurent and Kapferer 1985). Three items (IMP03, IMP06, and IMP07) are unabashed Likert scaled versions of items from the Importance subscale in the revised PII (see McQuarrie and Munson 1992). Finally, two items (IMP01 and IMP05) are especially written for this new CIP subscale. As with other items in the CIP, each of the seven items in the proposed Importance subscale is measured with a five-point Likert scale.

The dimensionality and reliability of the proposed Importance subscale for the CIP were investigated in two separate studies. Results from both studies appear in Exhibit 2.

Study 1: Health Care Clinic. Study 1 was conducted in conjunction with a survey of customers and noncustomers of a major health care clinic in a mid-sized, upper midwest MSA. Responses to the seven item Importance subscale only were obtained from 514 adult participants in the survey. Interviews were conducted by telephone, and queried participants as to the importance attached to selecting a "health care clinic". Specific responses (and associated numerical scores) were "totally agree" (1), "somewhat agree" (2), "neither agree nor disagree" (3), "somewhat disagree" (4), and "totally disagree" (5).

According to Exhibit 2(A), a factor analysis led to a one factor solution (with Eigenvalue of 3.860) that explained 55.2% of the response variance. (Note that the factor analytic routine did not prespecify a one factor solution; using a criterion minimum Eigenvalue of 1.0, only one emerged.) An internal consistency analysis led to an alpha of .846. Note, however, that IMP07 might be superfluous to the scale. Its factor loading and item to total correlation were both lower than for the remaining six items.

Study 2: Financial Institution. Study 2 was conducted in conjunction with a survey of customers and noncustomers of a financial institution serving a tri-county, nonurbanized, upper midwest area. Responses to the seven item Importance subscale, and to the four CIP antecedent subscales, were obtained from 267 adult participants in the survey. Responses were obtained through a mailed questionnaire follow-up to a preliminary telephone interview, and queried participants as to issues concerning the selection of a "financial institution". Specific responses (and associated numerical scores) were "totally disagree" (1), "disagree" (2), "neither agree nor disagree" (3), "agree" (4), and "totally agree" (5).

According to Exhibit 2(B), results for Study 2 were virtually identical to those of Study 1. A single factor solution again emerged from the analysis (with Eigenvalue of 3.654), and the full seven item subscale's alpha was .847.

EXHIBIT 1

Proposed "Importance" Items for CIP Scale

IMP01	Choosing a ------ is a big decision in one's life.
IMP02	I attach great importance to selecting a ------.
IMP03	I don't usually get overly concerned about selecting a ------. (Reverse Scored)
IMP04	Which ------ I choose doesn't really matter to me. (Reverse Scored)
IMP05	Choosing a ------ takes a lot of careful thought.
IMP06	Decisions about selecting a ------ are serious, important decisions.
IMP07	It means a lot to me to have a ------ to use.

EXHIBIT 2

Psychometric Evaluation of the CIP "Importance" Subscale

(A) Study 1: Health Care Clinic					
Item Number	Factor Loadings	Item Mean	Item Std Dev	Item to Total Correlation	Alpha if Item Deleted
IMP01	0.817	1.47	0.73	0.629	0.824
IMP02	0.791	1.51	0.76	0.706	0.813
IMP03	0.779	2.14	1.31	0.658	0.828
IMP04	0.752	1.73	1.15	0.635	0.824
IMP05	0.740	1.62	0.94	0.689	0.811
IMP06	0.719	1.38	0.69	0.656	0.822
IMP07	0.578	1.20	0.51	0.436	0.848
3.860 = Eigenvalue 55.2% = Variance Explained			Alpha for Scale = 0.846		
(B) Study 2: Financial Institution					
Item Number	Factor Loadings	Item Mean	Item Std Dev	Item to Total Correlation	Alpha if Item Deleted
IMP01	0.753	3.94	0.92	0.640	0.820
IMP02	0.785	3.84	0.92	0.682	0.813
IMP03	0.692	3.15	1.07	0.584	0.833
IMP04	0.651	3.87	0.84	0.551	0.834
IMP05	0.781	3.68	0.78	0.667	0.818
IMP06	0.724	3.82	0.74	0.613	0.826
IMP07	0.658	3.97	0.73	0.535	0.836
3.654 = Eigenvalue 52.2% = Variance Explained			Alpha for Scale = 0.847		

Overall, then, this new Importance subscale for the CIP does appear to be unidimensional with reasonable internal consistency. (In the interest of succinctness, IMP07 can probably be deleted from the subscale; it adds little to the psychometric properties of the subscale.) In addition, the respective item means suggest that far more consumers agree than disagree that decisions about financial institutions are important ones, and even more agree than disagree that decisions about medical clinics are important ones. While far from even a minimally acceptable assessment of the Importance subscale's validity, these results conform with what a reasonable person would have expected a priori, and do at least tentatively establish that the subscale is measuring what it purports to measure; perceived importance attached to a product, or in this case, a service.

THE RELATIONSHIP BETWEEN IMPORTANCE AND ITS ANTECEDENTS

As previously noted, Laurent and Kapferer originally intended to include an Importance subscale in the CIP. Ultimately, they gave up that goal, presumably because the Importance subscale could not be isolated from other subscales in the CIP. But, if Importance flows from one or another antecedent (or a combination thereof), one would expect such a relationship to its antecedents to exist. Indeed, Importance is more properly considered a dependent variable to the set of independent variable antecedents. This would, of course, suggest searching for a regression relationship involving Importance rather than attempting to isolate an independent Importance factor.

Exhibit 3 presents the results of such a regression analysis using the full set of CIP data from Study 2 (with IMP07 deleted from the new Importance subscale). The complete model was highly significant (F= 56.6; p < .001), with R-Squared of 53.6%.

There are significant relationships between Importance and each of the four CIP antecedents in the model. Three of those relationships are linear. Consequently, it was concluded that, at least so far as the choice of a financial institution is concerned, product importance is linearly related to Interest-Pleasure, to Sign and to Risk Importance. Among the three linear relations, that to

EXHIBIT 3
Regression Results for Six Item CIP Importance Subscale Versus Four Involvement Antecedents
Study 2: Financial Institutions

Antecedent	Coefficient	T-Ratio	P-Value
Interest/Pleasure	0.251	3.78	<.001
Sign	0.183	4.37	<.001
Risk Importance	0.447	8.81	<.001
Risk Probability:			
Linear Coefficient	-0.750	-3.77	<.001
Quadratic Coefficient	0.100	3.01	<.010
Constant	1.954		

Risk Importance was especially strong. Based on the regression coefficients (which can be directly compared here because all data was input as arithmetic "means" of five point scales), product importance is particularly responsive to increases in risk importance. The choice of a financial institution tends to become especially involving as, from one consumer to another, the perceived consequences of a poor decision increase.

The fourth relationship, that between Importance and Risk Probability, is particularly intriguing. The preliminary linear regression model resulted in a significant negative coefficient being assigned to Risk Probability. Because such an inverse relationship would have been counter to the expected linkage between perceived risk and involvement, further analysis was undertaken. Indeed, the scatterplot reproduced in Exhibit 4 suggested a quadratic relationship involving the Risk Probability antecedent. So, squared terms for Risk Probability, and for each of the other three antecedents as well, were constructed and allowed to enter the regression model. Only the quadratic term for Risk Probability did so.

Apparently, then, there is a curvilinear relationship between the importance attached to financial institutions and the perceived chance of making a poor decision. Consumers who are quite confident of their ability to make a good choice, and those who are not at all confident of their ability, tend to be more involved in the selection of a financial institution than are consumers between these extremes.

Among the several plausible, if speculative, explanations for such a curvilinear relationship, the authors offer the following. What if Exhibit 4 depicts a "point in time" view of a dynamic process that includes, as an intervening variable, information acquisition over time? That is, suppose consumers who perceive a given product or service category as fraught with considerable potential for making purchase errors also devote themselves to acquiring information and, ultimately, expertise, about that product over time.

The extremes in Exhibit 4, then, might represent consumers at different points in the acquisition of that expertise. Some consumers—perhaps younger ones—who think of a product category as particularly risky in terms of the chance of making a poor choice, become very involved with those choices, including acquiring some level of expertise about the product. Over time, these consumers, who maintain a consistent if not growing level of involvement, nonetheless find themselves eventually with considerable self-confidence in their decision making ability.

Meanwhile, other consumers, who perceive only a moderate level of risk probability attendant to the decision, do not tend to become as involved and, hence, do not tend to acquire information and expertise about the product. Consequently, their beliefs about risk probability would tend to remain the same over time.

It is true that the acquisition of product expertise would also tend to characterize consumers who become involved with a product via other antecedents; Interest-Pleasure, Risk Importance or Sign. However, is it likely that product expertise would alter neither the extent to which those consumers find the product category inherently interesting, pleasurable or self-expressive, nor the perceived magnitude of external negative consequences of a poor choice. Thus, the linear relationship between involvement and these antecedents would be preserved, the acquisition of product expertise notwithstanding.

At any rate, all of this is currently little more than pure speculation, except that product importance remains curvilinearly related to the perceived risk probability attendant to choosing a financial institution. Interesting extensions of this study might include (a) determining whether the nature of this relationship holds across other product and service categories, and (b) testing, perhaps in a structural equations environment, the possibility that information acquisition serves, over time, as an intervening variable between product importance and risk probability.

CONCLUDING OBSERVATIONS

The research reported herein attempted to "complete" the CIP scale developed by Kapferer and Laurent by adding a subscale designed to measure the personal relevance or importance of a product to the consumer. While in need of additional psychometric evaluation, especially with respect to tests of validity, the CIP is now capable of measuring product involvement itself (through this new Importance subscale), as well as four crucial antecedents to such involvement.

The study also presented preliminary evidence that three of the antecedents (Interest-Pleasure, Sign and Risk Importance) are linearly related to involvement, with Risk Importance the most strongly related. The fourth antecedent, Risk Probability, appears to be related to involvement in a curvilinear fashion. But, considerably more research needs to be undertaken to replicate those relationships with other populations, and to extend them to product and service categories other than financial institutions.

EXHIBIT 4
Means Plot — Importance Subscale Versus Risk Probability

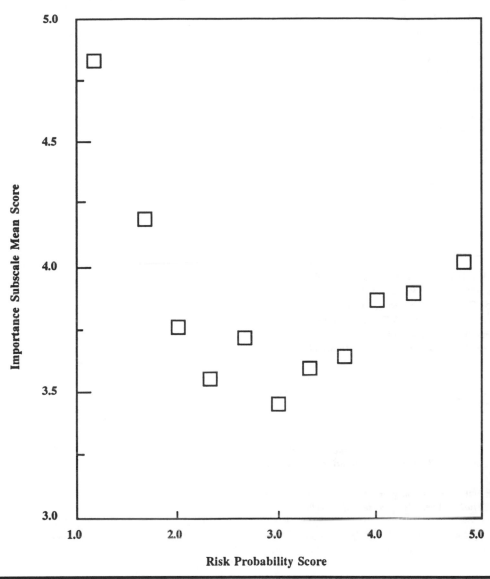

Finally, it appears as if researchers are inching ever closer to a generally accepted involvement measurement scale. With the PII now expanded to encompass Interest-Pleasure (and perhaps, eventually, other involvement antecedents as well), it and the CIP move nearer and nearer to one another's dimensionality. Indeed, it is hoped that at some point there is little to differentiate the two scales save for their response formats. It was the authors intent here to encourage such a convergence.

REFERENCES

Andres, J. C. and S. Durvasula (1991), "Suggestions for Manipulating and Measuring Involvement in Advertising Message Content," in R. H. Holman and M. S. Solomon, eds., *Advances in Consumer Research*, 18, Association for Consumer Research, 194-201.

Celuch, K. and R. Evans (1989), "An Analysis of the Convergent and Discriminant Validity of the Personal Involvement Inventory and the Consumer Involvement Profile," *Psychological Reports*, 65, 1291-1297.

Flynn, L. R. and R. E. Goldsmith (1993), "Application of the Personal Involvement Inventory in Marketing," *Psychology & Marketing*, 10 (July-August), 357-366.

Jain, K. and N. Srinivasan (1990), "An Empirical Assessment of Multiple Operationalizations in Involvement," in M. E. Goldberg G. Gorn and R. W. Pollay, eds., *Advances in Consumer Research*, 17, Provo, UT, Association for Consumer Research, 594-602.

Kapferer, J. N. and G. Laurent (1985a), "Consumer's Involvement Profile: New Empirical Results," in E. Hirschman and M. Holbrook, eds., *Advances in Consumer Research*, 12, Provo, UT, Association for Consumer Research, 290-295.

Kapferer, J. N. and G. Laurent (1985b), "Consumer Involvement Profiles: A New Practical Approach to Consumer Involvement," *Journal of Advertising Research*, 25 (December-January), 48-56.

Kapferer, J. N. and G. Laurent (1993), "Further Evidence on the Consumer Involvement Profile: Five Antecedents of Involvement," *Psychology & Marketing*, 10 (July-August), 347-355.

Laurent, G. and J. N. Kapferer (1985), "Measuring Consumer Involvement Profiles," *Journal of Marketing Research*, 22 (February), 41-53.

McQuarrie, E. F. and J. M. Munson (1987), "The Zaichkowsky Personal Involvement Inventory: Modification and Extension," in P. Anderson and M. Wallendorf, eds, *Advances in Consumer Research*, 14, Provo, UT, Association for Consumer Research, 36-40.

McQuarrie, E. F. and J. M. Munson (1992), "A Revised Product Involvement Inventory: Improved Usability and Validity," in J. F. Sherry and B. Sternthal, eds, *Advances in Consumer Research*, 19, Provo, UT, Association for Consumer Research, 108-115.

Mittal, B. (1989a), "A Theoretical Analysis of Two Recent Measures of Involvement," in T. K. Srull, ed., *Advances in Consumer Research*, 16, Provo, UT, Association for Consumer Research, 697-702.

Mittal, B. (1989b), "Measuring Purchase-Decision Involvement," *Psychology and Marketing*, 6 (Summer), 147-162.

Mittal, B. and M. Lee (1988), "Separating Brand-Choice Involvement from Product Involvement Via Consumer Profiles," in M. J. Houston, M. Wallendorf and P. Anderson, eds, *Advances in Consumer Research*, 15, Provo, UT, Association for Consumer Research, 43-49.

Park, W. C. and B. Mittal (1985), "A Theory of Involvement in Consumer Behavior: Problems and Issues," in J. N. Sheth, ed., *Research in Consumer Behavior*, JAI Press, Greenwich, CT, 201-231.

Rodgers, W. C. and K. C. Schneider (1993), "An Experimental Evaluation of the Kapferer-Laurent Consumer Involvement Profile Scale," *Psychology & Marketing*, 10 (July-August), 333-345.

Slama, M. E. and A. Tashchian (1985), "Selected Socioeconomic and Demographic Characteristics Associated with Purchasing Involvement," *Journal of Marketing*, 49 (Winter), 72-82.

Vaugn, R. (1986), "How Advertising Works: A Planning Model Revisited," *Journal of Advertising Research*, 26 (February-March), 57-66.

Zaichkowsky, J. L. (1985), "Measuring the Involvement Construct," *Journal of Consumer Research*, 12 (December), 341-352.

Zaichkowsky, J. L. (1986), "Conceptualizing Involvement," *Journal of Advertising*, 15 (2), 4-14.

Zaichkowsky, J. L. (1987), "The Emotional Aspect of Product Involvement," in P. Anderson and M. Wallendorf, eds., *Advances in Consumer Research*, 14, Provo, UT, Association for Consumer Research, 32-35.

The Determinants of Satisfaction: An Experimental Verification of the Moderating Role of Ambiguity

Prashanth U. Nyer, Chapman University

ABSTRACT

This study extends the findings of Yi (1993) in which he finds that performance ambiguity plays a moderating role in the way consumer satisfaction is determined. This study investigates the role of both performance ambiguity and the ambiguity of expectations in the consumer satisfaction process using an experiment. When perceived performance is ambiguous, the effect of expectations on satisfaction is increased, while the effect of perceived performance on satisfaction is decreased. When expectations are ambiguous, the effect of expectations on satisfaction decreases while the effect of performance on satisfaction increases. The implications of these findings are discussed.

The importance of consumer satisfaction (CS) as a subject of research lies in it's ability to influence various consumer phenomena such as repurchase, brand loyalty, word-of-mouth and complaint behavior. The expectancy-disconfirmation model of consumer satisfaction (Oliver, 1980) has received much attention in the past decade and a half. According to this model CS is determined by prior expectation, perceived performance and by the disconfirmation of expectation - the subjective difference between perceived performance and expectation.

Various studies have investigated the robustness of the model under differing conditions. The direct effect of perceived performance on CS has been confirmed by many studies including those by Churchill and Suprenant (1982), Oliver and DeSarbo (1988) and Tse and Wilton (1988). According to Tse and Wilton (1988), perceived performance was the single most important determinant of CS. Perceived performance was also shown to have an indirect effect on CS by influencing disconfirmation. However, studies conducted by Cadotte, Woodruff and Jenkins (1987) and Oliver (1980) do not report a significant effect of perceived performance on CS.

The effect of disconfirmation on CS has also been verified by many studies. Oliver and DeSarbo (1988) found disconfirmation to be the most significant predictor of CS. What is of more relevance to this paper is the effect of expectation on CS. While some studies have found a significant direct effect of expectation on CS (Bearden and Teel 1983; Swan and Trawick 1981, Tse and Wilton 1988, Westbrook and Reilly, 1983), others have not reported a direct effect of expectation on CS (Cadotte, Woodruff and Jenkins 1987, Oliver and Bearden 1983).

Clearly the effects of expectation and perceived performance on CS is not constant under all circumstances. Under certain conditions expectation fails to have a significant direct effect on CS, while under other circumstances perceived performance may have no significant direct effect on CS. These findings point to the moderating influence of an external variable.

Yi (1993) suggests that the ambiguity with which product performance is evaluated is capable of moderating the effects of both expectation and perceived performance on CS. Consumers may be unable to unambiguously evaluate the performance of some products. For example a light bulb may be advertised as having an extra long life of 3000 hours, causing consumer expectation to be formed with little ambiguity. On the other hand very few consumers bother to measure the actual life of their light bulbs, leading to a great deal of ambiguity as far as the product performance is concerned. In such a situation, expectation will play a bigger role in determining CS while perceived performance will take on a

diminished role. Performance ambiguity can be high when the performance is being judged mostly on subjective criteria (e.g., most fashion products, music, or art) or when there is difficulty in measuring the performance as in the example above. Yi (1993) draws upon the research by Hoch and Deighton (1989) and Hoch and Ha (1986) and upon the self perception theory to find theoretical support for such a phenomenon.

As discussed earlier, the expectancy disconfirmation model of CS has two primary antecedents for satisfaction - prior expectation and perceived performance. The third predictor of satisfaction - disconfirmation of expectation - is the subjective difference between perceived performance and expectation. Since Yi (1993) has shown that performance ambiguity moderates the effect of expectation and performance on CS, the next step then is to investigate whether expectation ambiguity has a similar moderating effect on the role of expectation and performance on CS.

The expectancy disconfirmation model of CS can be seen as a form of information integration, where two sets of information - prior expectations and perceived performance - are integrated to form satisfaction judgments. The two information integration models that have received much attention are the adding model and the averaging model (Anderson 1981). The averaging model posits that an attribute's importance or weight will change as the importance of other attributes change. With the adding model, the weights of attributes are independent of each other. Various studies including those by Anderson and Lopes (1974) and Birnbaum and Stegner (1979) have tested these two models and found support for the averaging model. Under an averaging model scenario, it is easy to see how ambiguous information (information capable of multiple interpretations) is weighted less, leading to a greater emphasis on unambiguous information.

Consumers may have difficulty forming unambiguous prior expectations under many circumstances. Lack of information, complex information or inability to understand the information, are all factors that could lead to high expectation ambiguity. Thus products using new and complex technology may present a challenge to the naive consumer trying to form expectations. Thus when expectations are ambiguous, it could be hypothesized that the role of expectations in determining CS will be diminished while effect of perceived performance on CS will be enhanced.

Since disconfirmation is a function of expectation and perceived performance, and since the focus of this paper is on these two variables, this paper's initial focus is on the total effects of expectation and perceived performance on CS. The total effect of expectation on CS would include not only the direct effect of expectation on CS, but also the indirect effect of expectation on CS through disconfirmation. While the first set of analyses examine the total effects of expectation and perceived performance on CS, the second set of analyses (using a multiplicative regression model) examine the direct effects of expectation, perceived performance and disconfirmation on CS.

The following hypotheses are proposed:

H1. When performance is ambiguous and when expectation is unambiguous, expectation will have a stronger total effect and performance will have a weaker total effect on CS, compared to the situation in which both expectation and performance are unambiguous.

H2. When performance is unambiguous and when expectation is ambiguous, expectation will have a weaker total effect and performance will have a stronger total effect on CS, compared to the situation in which both expectation and performance are unambiguous.

METHOD

A full factorial experiment was designed in which two factors, performance ambiguity (high and low) and expectation ambiguity (high and low) were manipulated. Subjects consisted of 132 undergraduate students enrolled in an introductory marketing course at a large mid-western university. The subjects were randomly assigned to the four experimental conditions. Subjects were informed that they were about to evaluate one of the many test formulations of a new stain remover, and that other subjects would be evaluating different formulations.

Each of the 132 subjects were provided with coded plastic containers containing the stain remover. In reality all subjects received the identical stain remover, which was a diluted solution of a popular chlorine based bleach mixed with some perfume to mask it's smell.

The subjects were provided with an instruction sheet that contained the manipulation for expectation ambiguity. Subjects in the low expectation ambiguity condition read the following statement:

The formulation that you have been given was tested by an independent product testing laboratory and was rated as good on the following 5 point scale.

Excellent, Good, Average, Fair, Inferior.

The subjects in the high expectation ambiguity condition read the following:

The formulation that you have been given was tested by an independent product testing laboratory and was rated as follows:

"The cleansing power of the test sample was estimated using the Modified Photometric Test (MPT) using refracted light at 3457Å. The difference between the reflectiveness of a stained cellulose medium before and after administration of the test sample was measured. This sample obtained a differential score of 2.37 Lumens."

The instruction sheet also included measures of expectation and the manipulation check for expectation ambiguity.

Subjects were then provided with detailed instructions on testing the stain remover. Each subject was provided with a piece of stained cloth. Subjects in the low performance ambiguity condition received a piece of cloth whose smooth white surface made it relatively easy for subjects to evaluate the effectiveness of the stain remover. Subjects in the high performance ambiguity condition received a lightly colored cloth with an irregular pattern and a relatively rough texture which made it difficult for them to evaluate the effectiveness of the stain remover.

These manipulations of expectation and performance ambiguities were selected on the basis of a pilot study. They were shown to have significant effects on the variable being manipulated (expectation ambiguity or performance ambiguity) while having no significant effect on other variables (expectation and performance).

After treating the stained cloth with the stain remover for a specified amount of time, subjects were instructed to inspect the cloth for traces of the stain, and to complete the next questionnaire which included measures of perceived performance, performance ambiguity and satisfaction.

Multiple measures were used to assess all the concepts. All ambiguity concepts were measured using three variables. These included a measure of the difficulty of evaluation, a measure of the confidence in the evaluation and a measure of how sure the respondent was with his or her evaluation. The first two measures were based on those used by Yi (1993). The latter two scales were reverse coded to reflect the ambiguity with which the evaluations were being made.

Perceived performance was measured using three 7 point bipolar scales (very low - very high performance, inferior - superior performance, bad - good performance). Similarly expectations and satisfaction were measured with three scales each while disconfirmation was assessed using two measures. The lowest Chronbach was 0.77 for the disconfirmation construct. All other constructs attained s well above 0.8 thereby demonstrating high levels of reliability.

Comparison of regression coefficients using dummy variables was used to test the hypotheses that the relative importance of expectations and performance in determining CS will be different under different levels of expectation ambiguity and performance ambiguity. This methodology permits a direct comparison of the regression coefficients for two regression models. Hypothesis 1 can be tested by comparing the regression model under conditions of unambiguous expectation and unambiguous performance to the regression model under conditions of unambiguous expectation and ambiguous performance.

Similarly hypothesis 2 can be tested by comparing the regression model under conditions of unambiguous expectation and unambiguous performance to the regression model under conditions of ambiguous expectation and unambiguous performance.

Two dummy variables (D1, D2) were added to the data set to represent the three situations being investigated - both performance and expectation being unambiguous (0,0), ambiguous performance, unambiguous expectation (1,0) and unambiguous performance, ambiguous expectation (0,1).

RESULTS

Manipulation checks showed that the manipulations of the two factors were successful. The mean values of expectation ambiguity in the high and low expectation ambiguity conditions were 5.11 and 3.16 ($F=118.64_{130,1}$ $p=0.00$). Similarly the mean value of performance ambiguity in the high and low performance ambiguity conditions were 5.04 and 3.03 ($F=87.02_{130,1}$ $p=0.00$).

An ANOVA was conducted to ensure that the manipulations of expectation ambiguity and performance ambiguity did not affect the levels of expectation and perceived performance. As the pilot study had indicated earlier, neither manipulation had a significant effect on the levels of expectation or perceived performance. This is important since a significant effect of the manipulations of the ambiguity variables on expectation or performance would have caused confounding, leading to a less than rigorous testing of the hypotheses.

To test hypothesis 1, a dummy variable regression was conducted using dummy variable D1 and observations where expectation ambiguity was low. D1 took the value of 0 where neither performance nor expectation were ambiguous, and was 1 when performance alone was ambiguous. A regression model was run in

TABLE 1

Dependent Variable: Satisfaction
Multiple R=0.75,
Adjusted R Square=0.53,
$F_{61,5}$=15.86

R Square=0.57,
Std Error=0.66
p= 0.00

Variable	B	SE B	T	Sig. T
Expectation	0.17	0.16	1.12	0.27
Performance	0.78	0.12	6.75	0.00
D1*Exp	0.40	0.21	1.92	0.06
D1*Perf	-0.27	0.17	-1.57	0.12
D1	0.03	0.16	0.17	0.87
Constant	0.86	0.77	1.12	0.27

TABLE 2

Dependent Variable: Satisfaction
Multiple R=0.84,
Adjusted R Square=0.68,
$F_{59,5}$=28.48

R Square=0.71,
Std Error=0.78
p= 0.00

Variable	B	SE B	T	Sig. T
Expectation	0.17	0.19	0.94	0.35
Performance	0.78	0.14	5.71	0.00
D2*Exp	-0.69	0.24	-2.83	0.01
D2*Perf	0.41	0.18	2.21	0.03
D2	0.04	0.20	0.20	0.84
Constant	0.86	0.91	0.95	0.35

which the predictor variables were Expectation, Performance, D1*Expectation, D1*Performance and D1. The dependent variable was CS. The result of the regression is depicted in Table 1.

The coefficients of Expectation and Performance represent the baseline model (where both performance and expectation are unambiguous) while the variables including the term D1 denote the adjustments made to reach the model in which performance alone is ambiguous. If hypothesis 1 were true, D1*Expectation should be positive and significant (i.e. expectation should exert a stronger influence on CS), and D1*Performance should be negative and significant (i.e. perceived performance should have a weaker influence on CS).

An examination of the coefficients in Table 1 shows that as hypothesized D1*Expectation is positive and significant (at the 0.10 level). Thus as performance ambiguity goes from low to high, the effect of expectation on CS increases (B=0.40). The coefficient of D1*Performance was hypothesized to be negative and significant. Table 1 shows that though D1*Performance is not significant, it is close to attaining significance and is of the correct polarity.

To test hypothesis 2, a dummy variable regression was conducted using dummy variable D2 and observations for which performance ambiguity was low. D2 took the value of 0 where neither performance nor expectation were ambiguous, and was 1 when expectation alone was ambiguous. A regression model was run in which the predictor variables were Expectation, Performance, D2*Expectation, D2*Performance and D2. The dependent variable was CS. The results of the regression are depicted in Table 2.

As before, the coefficients of Expectation and Performance represent the baseline model (where both performance and expectation are unambiguous) while the coefficients beginning with D2 denote the adjustments made to reach the model in which expectation alone is ambiguous. If hypothesis 2 is true, D2*Expectations should be negative and significant (i.e. expectation should exert a weaker influence on CS), and D2*Performance should be positive and significant (i.e. perceived performance should have a stronger influence on CS).

An examination of the coefficients in Table 2 shows that as hypothesized D2*Expectation is negative and significant. Thus as expectation ambiguity goes from low to high, the effect of expectation on CS decreases (B=-0.69). As hypothesized, the coefficient of D2*Performance is positive and significant. As expectation ambiguity goes from low to high, the effect of performance on CS increases (B=0.41).

The above analysis has provided some evidence for the moderating role of performance ambiguity and expectation ambiguity in influencing the effects of perceived performance and expectation on CS.

The CS model which is typically expressed as shown in equation 1, can now be expressed as shown in equation 2 below.

$$CS=f (Exp, Per, Dis) \qquad (1)$$
$$CS=f (Exp, Per, Dis, APPer, APExp, AEPer, AEExp) \qquad (2)$$

where Exp refers to expectation, Per refers to perceived performance, Dis refers to disconfirmation of expectation, AP

TABLE 3

Dependent Variable: Satisfaction
Multiple R=0.76   R Square=0.58
Adjusted R Square=0.57   Std Error=0.79
$F_{128,3}$=59.50   p=0.00

Variable	B	SE B	T	Sig. T
Expectation	0.24	0.12	2.08	0.04
Performance	0.69	0.13	5.24	0.00
Disconfirmation	0.31	0.15	2.07	0.04
Constant	4.19	0.07	60.97	0.00

TABLE 4

Dependent Variable: Satisfaction
Multiple R=0.87   R Square=0.75
Adjusted R Square=0.74   Std Error=0.62
$F_{124,7}$=54.32   p= 0.00

Variable	B	SE B	T	Sig. T
Expectation	0.27	0.09	2.97	0.00
Performance	0.62	0.10	6.04	0.00
Disconfirmation	0.25	0.12	2.12	0.04
APPer	-0.17	0.04	-4.59	0.00
APExp	0.22	0.05	4.82	0.00
AEPer	0.22	0.04	5.85	0.00
AEExp	-0.10	0.06	-1.75	0.08
Constant	4.21	0.05	77.36	0.00

---

refers to the performance ambiguity, AE refers to expectation ambiguity, and terms such as APPer refer to the product of AP and Per. The multiplicative terms in eq. 2 represent the moderating effect of the ambiguity variables.

As suggested by Yi (1989), the regression model using multiplicative terms was analyzed using mean-centered independent variables. This reduces the effects of multi-collinearity which are sure to be present in such models.

Table 3 represents the analysis of the model of CS represented by eq. 1

Table 4 shows the analysis of the multiplicative model represented by eq. 2.

All the variables in the multiplicative model in Table 4 are significant (one barely so) and in the right direction. The negative coefficient for APPer denotes that as performance ambiguity (AP) increases, the effect of perceived performance (Per) on CS reduces. Similarly the negative coefficient of AEExp implies that as the expectation ambiguity (AE) increases, the effect of expectation on CS decreases. The positive coefficients of APExp and AEPer can also be interpreted in a similar manner.

An F test was used to test whether the model indicated by eq. 1 (R square=0.58) is significantly inferior to the model indicated by eq. 2 (R square=0.75) in predicting CS. The resulting F statistic ($F_{4,128}$=2.79) was significant at the 0.05 level, indicating that the multiplicative model is significantly superior to the expectancy disconfirmation model in predicting CS.

DISCUSSION

This study demonstrates that the ambiguity with which expectation and performance are evaluated have a significant impact on the influence of prior expectation and perceived performance on CS. As the ambiguity of expectation increases, the influence of expectations on CS decreases, while the influence of perceived performance on CS increases. Conversely as the ambiguity of performance increases, the influence of perceived performance on CS decreases while the impact of prior expectation on CS increases.

Marketers of products with high performance ambiguity should focus on creating very high and unambiguous expectation since CS will be strongly influenced by expectation. Similarly, marketers of products with high expectation ambiguity should focus on achieving very high and unambiguous performance evaluations since CS in such situations will be determined mostly by perceived performance.

This paper extends the research done by Yi (1993) by studying the ambiguity of expectation in addition to the ambiguity of performance. It also uses an experimental design rather than Yi's survey methodology.

This study has limitations. While data was collected from subjects exposed to both high performance ambiguity and high expectation ambiguity, this data has not been used in the analyses reported here. This was because there was no theoretical basis to form hypotheses for this condition. How do consumers who are subject to both ambiguous expectations and ambiguous performance judge satisfaction? This question has not been answered in this paper.

REFERENCE

Anderson, Norman H. (1981), *Foundations of Information Integration Theory*, New York: Academic Press.

_____ and Lola Lopes (1974), "Some Psycholinguistic Aspects of Person Perception," *Memory and Cognition*, 2 (January), 67-74.

Bearden, William O. and J. E. Teel (1983), "Selected Determinants of Consumer Satisfaction and Complaint Reports," *Journal of Marketing Research*, 20 (February), 21-28.

Birnbaum, Michael H. and Steven E. Stegner (1979), "Source Credibility in Social Judgment: Bias, Expertise, and the Judge's Point of View," *Journal of Personality and Social Psychology*, 37 (January), 48-74.

Cadotte, Ernest R., R. B. Woodruff, R. L. Jenkins (1987), "Expectations and Norms in Models of Consumer Satisfaction," *Journal of Marketing Research*, 24 (August), 305-314.

Churchill, Gilbert A., Jr. and C. Suprenant (1982), "An Investigation into the Determinants of Customer Satisfaction," *Journal of Marketing Research*, 19 (November), 491-504.

Hoch, Stephen J. and J. Deighton (1989), "Managing What Consumers Learn from Experience," *Journal of Marketing*, 53 (April), 1-20.

_____ and Y. Ha (1986), "Consumer Learning: Advertising and the Ambiguity of Product Experience," *Journal of Consumer Research*, 13 (September), 221-233.

Oliver, Richard L. (1980), "A Cognitive Model of the Antecedents and Consequences of Satisfaction Decisions," *Journal of Marketing Research*, 17 (September), 46-49.

_____ and W. O. Bearden (1983), "The Role of Involvement in Satisfaction Processes," in *Advances in Consumer Research*, Ann Arbor, MI: Association of Consumer Research.

_____ and W. S. DeSarbo (1988), "Response Determinants in Satisfaction Judgments," *Journal of Consumer Research*, 14 (March), 495-507.

Swan, John E. and F. I. Trawick (1981), "Disconfirmation of Expectations and Satisfaction with a Retail Service," *Journal of Retailing*, 57 (Fall), 49-67.

Tse, David K. and P. C. Wilton (1988), "Models of Consumer Satisfaction: An Extension," *Journal of Marketing Research*, 25 (May), 204-211.

Westbrook, Robert and M. D. Reilly (1983), "Value-Percept Disparity: An Alternative to the Disconfirmation of Expectations Theory of Consumer Satisfaction," in *Advances in Consumer Research*, Ann Arbor, MI: Association for Consumer Research.

Yi, Youjae (1989), "On the Evaluation of Main Effects in Multiplicative Regression Models," *Journal of Marketing Research Society*, 31 (January), 133-138.

_____ (1990), "A Critical Review of Consumer Satisfaction," in Review of Marketing 1990, ed. Valerie A. Zeithaml, Chicago: American Marketing Association, 68-123.

_____ (1993), "The Determinants of Consumer Satisfaction: The Moderating Role of Ambiguity," in *Advances in Consumer Research*.

The Five Factor Model and Market Mavenism

Todd A. Mooradian, The College of William and Mary

ABSTRACT

Personality research has recently approached an important consensus regarding the broadest structure of individual differences, converging on five robust factors. These global traits organize diverse findings and networks of theory on individual differences. Meanwhile, consumer researchers have profited from the inclusion of narrow, domain-specific traits. One such focused trait is Market Mavenism, the *propensity to provide marketplace and shopping information*. This research relates Market Mavenism to the Five Factor Model, initiating integration of consumption-relevant traits with that recent consensus and clarifying the content and meaning of Market Mavenism by identifying relationships with both social and conscientious dispositions.

Personality psychology has recently approached consensus regarding the fundamental structure of individual differences, recognizing five global traits which are "real, pervasive, universal and biologically based" (Costa and McCrae 1992a) and which explain much of the variance across the literally thousands of traits and taxonomies proposed in the discipline's extended history (see, e.g., McCrae and John 1992). One of the most important values of this consensus is its potential to serve as an integrative framework organizing the diverse and often disconnected findings and theory on human differences. McCrae and John assert that "Instead of the interminable disputes among competing systems that so long paralyzed the field [of personality psychology], we could see cooperative research and cumulative findings... And instead of the lost insights that a haphazard selection of personality variables is likely to produce, we could see a complete and systematic pursuit of personality correlates" (1992, p. 177). It is important that focused, domain-specific *consumer* differences and *marketing* relevant traits be included in such a synthesis. It will also inform our understandings of those narrow and focused traits to relate them to the higher-order global traits. This note relates one significant consumer difference, the Market Maven trait, with the "Five Factor Model."

PERSONALITY, CONSUMER RESEARCH AND FOCUSED TRAITS

Although early efforts to relate enduring personality differences with consumer behavior were generally disappointing and the findings "equivocal" (e.g., Kassarjian and Sheffet 1991), recent research has been more encouraging (see, e.g., Haugtvedt, Petty and Cacioppo 1992; Foxall and Goldsmith 1988). Much of the progress in this area may be attributed to improved theoretical and methodological precision. One important shift has been toward the identification and adoption of narrower, domain-specific individual differences. Kassarjian and Sheffet criticized the use of "gross personality characteristics such as sociability, emotional stability, introversion, or neuroticism" to predict specific consumer behaviors and asserted that "...if unequivocal results are to emerge, consumer behavior researchers must develop their own definitions and design their own instruments to measure the personality variables that go into the purchase decision..." (Kassarjian and Sheffet 1991, page 292). These concerns have a corollary in the `principle of compatibility' in attitude theory (e.g., Ajzen and Fishbein 1977): just as broad attitudes are poor predictors of specific, narrowly defined and measured behaviors, broad personality traits cannot be expected to directly predict specific consumer behaviors. Over the past several decades personality psychology shared a corresponding concentration on narrow and even "esoteric" traits (see, e.g.,

Funder 1991), but has more recently begun to reexamine global traits and broader patterns of behavior (see discussion of the Five Factor Model, below).

The adoption of focused, domain-specific traits has improved the recognition of and the understanding of individual differences in consumer behavior. Researchers have, for example, recognized enduring differences in information processing (i.e., the Need for Cognition; Cacioppo and Petty 1982; Haugtvedt, Petty and Cacioppo 1992), in the tendency to reference attitudes and actions to social and situational cues (i.e., Self-Monitoring; e.g., Snyder and DeBono 1985; Foxall and Goldsmith 1988), and in the belief that goods and their possession are means to happiness (i.e., materialism; e.g, Richins and Dawson 1992). One important focused individual difference in the area of interpersonal influence is the *propensity to provide marketplace and shopping information*, which distinguishes "market mavens" from other consumers (Feick and Price 1987).

Market Mavens

Market mavens are "individuals who have information about many kinds of products, places to shop, and other facets of markets, and initiate discussions with consumers and respond to requests from consumers for market information" (Feick and Price 1987, p. 85). In specifying the Market Maven construct, Feick and Price emphasize at least two possible motives for developing such general market knowledge. It is useful, particularly in the context of this research, to explicitly distinguish these two elements of the construct: Market mavens may be responding to *felt obligations* to be knowledgeable about product- and shopping-relevant information (i.e., to be `good shoppers') and they may be anticipating that such knowledge will serve to facilitate *social exchanges* and conversations (see Feick and Price 1987, p. 85).

Feick and Price (1987) developed the Market Maven Scale, a unidimensional, six-item Likert-type measure. Although usually referred to by the label for the high pole ("market mavens"), this construct and its measure are, in fact, *continuous* (therefore, perhaps better labeled "Market Mavenism;" e.g., Lichtenstein and Burton 1990). Most studies have trichotomized consumer samples into low, medium and high market maven categories but some analyses have included scale scores as continuous variables in correlation and regression analyses (e.g., Feick and Price 1987; Price, Feick and Guskey-Federouch 1988). Feick and Price demonstrated discriminant validity between Market Mavenism and two other influencer traits, Opinion Leadership and Innovativeness, and related Market Mavenism with awareness of new products, interpersonal information provision (word-of-mouth), general market information seeking (including readership of *Consumer Reports* and the use of diverse sources of market information) and general market interest (including enjoyment of shopping, attention to advertising, and coupon usage; Feick and Price 1987). Slama and Williams showed that these effects generalize across a wide variety of goods, services and marketplace characteristics (1990). In a robust and growing body of literature, Market Mavenism has been linked to: budgeting of groceries, planning of shopping (i.e., the use of lists) and coupon usage (i.e., percentage of trips using coupons, number of coupons used and value of coupons used; Price, Feick and Guskey-Federouch 1988); brand categorization (e.g., the number of brands held in salient, aware, trial and hold sets; Elliott and Warfield 1993); and, attitudes toward direct mail information (Schreiber and Rodgers 1993). The more managerial literature has also noted the importance of Market Mavens: "By targeting market mavens, communicators can diffuse information about marketing changes, messages spanning multiple-product classes and messages about products that may not have much inherent consumer interest. ...[Market mavens] are an important but previously unknown influencer group that needs to be taken into account when new product communication is planned" (*Public Relations Journal* 1988, p. 18-19).

The Five Factor Model
    At the same time that psychology and consumer researchers have profited from the use of *narrow* and *specific* traits, an important consensus has emerged in personality psychology regarding the *broadest* structure of personality. Five fundamental traits have consistently been found to underlie myriad personality taxonomies and questionnaires and have emerged in factor analyses of comprehensive natural language trait lexicons (John 1990; Goldberg 1993). Those traits include (with brief descriptions from Costa and McCrae 1992b, p 14-16):

   Neuroticism. "The general tendency to experience negative affects such as fear, sadness, embarrassment, anger, guilt, and disgust..."
   Extraversion. "In addition to liking people and preferring large groups and gatherings, Extroverts are also assertive, active and talkative. They like excitement and stimulation and tend to be cheerful in disposition. They are upbeat, energetic, and optimistic."
   Openness to Experience. "...active imagination, aesthetic sensitivity, attentiveness to inner feelings, preference for variety, intellectual curiosity, and independence of judgment..."
   Conscientiousness. "...a more active process of planning, organizing, and carrying out tasks... The conscientious individual is purposeful, strong-willed, and determined... scrupulous, punctual, and reliable."
   Agreeableness. "...primarily a dimension of interpersonal tendencies. The agreeable person is fundamentally altruistic ...sympathetic to others and eager to help them, and believes that others will be equally helpful in return."

    These global traits are stable across extended time periods of as long as thirty years (see, e.g., McCrae 1993). They have been related to diverse behavioral, cognitive and affective processes (see, e.g., Digman 1990; John 1990), to genetic determination (e.g., Bergeman, et al. 1993; Heath, Cloninger and Martin 1994) and to underlying physiological systems (e.g., Bullock and Gilliiland 1993; Gray 1987). It is important to note that the recent consensus is not without exception; Cloninger has proposed a three dimensional model of personality based on underlying biological and genetic systems (see, e.g., Heath, Cloninger and Martin 1994). See Digman (1990), John (1990) and Goldberg (1993) for reviews of this Five Factor Model and its background. See Block (1995) for a thorough review of criticisms of the five factor model.
    As noted, one of the important values of the identification of this fundamental model is its capacity to integrate a discipline formerly handicapped by multiple labels for the same constructs (and similar labels for different constructs), disconnected findings and competing theories:

   "One of the central goals of scientific taxonomies is the definition of overarching domains within which large numbers of specific instances can be understood in a simplified way. In personality psychology, a taxonomy would permit

researchers to study specified domains of personality characteristics, instead of examining separately the thousands of particular attributes that make human beings individual and unique" (John 1990, p. 66).

    The recognition of these global 'domains' does not reduce the importance of understanding narrow, focused traits. Personality may be organized within a hierarchy in which the five global traits, or domains are made up of combinations of more specific traits, or 'facets,' which reflect combinations of discrete behaviors (Costa and McCrae 1995, 1992). Such facets, including enduring consumer traits, increase precision and clarify the richness of individual differences. Goldberg noted that "When thus viewed hierarchically, it should be clear that proponents of the five-factor model have never intended to reduce the rich tapestry of personality to a mere five traits. Rather, they seek to provide a scientifically compelling framework in which to organize the myriad individual differences that characterize humankind" (1993, p. 27). Although this integrative capacity has been well recognized, no reported research has connected narrow consumer differences to the Five Factor Model.

RESEARCH PROPOSITIONS
    As noted, market mavens may be influenced by both a responsiveness to feelings of *obligation* or responsibility and an anticipation of *social exchanges* or interactions. These underlying aspects of Market Mavenism suggest relationships with two of the global traits from the Five Factor Model. Extraversion, essentially a positive social trait, should be related directly with *the inclination to anticipate and seek social interactions*. Conscientiousness, the tendency to be responsible, dependable and organized, should relate to *responsiveness to perceived obligations*. Accordingly, it is proposed that both Extraversion and Conscientiousness will be directly related with Market Maven Scale scores (Market Mavenism).

STUDY
    Subjects were 294 undergraduates at two major American universities. All materials were administered and collected in single class or special session periods. The Five Factor Model was measured with the NEO-FFI, a 60-item inventory comprised of five twelve-item scales for each of the factors or traits (Costa and McCrae 1992a; Widiger 1992). Market Mavenism was measured with the six-item Market Maven Scale (Feick and Price 1987). Cronbach's alphas and correlations are presented in the Table. As shown in the Table, for this sample the Five Factor Model demonstrated considerable inter-trait correlations (cf. Costa and McCrae 1992b, p. 100). As anticipated, the Market Maven Scale correlated significantly with both Extraversion and Openness and was not related with the three other domains. (Although Market Mavenism has usually been operationalized as a categorical variable [i.e., low, medium and high], these market maven scores are distributed normally, supporting these analyses of Market Mavenism scores as a *continuous* variable [skewness=-.18, standard error of skewness=.14, therefore, skewness z-score=1.29; see, e.g., Tabachnick and Fidell 1983, p. 79]). Regression analysis showed that Extraversion (β=.19; Significance of T=.001) and Conscientiousness (β=.11; Significance of T=.058) predicted Market Maven scores with an adjusted R^2 of .054.

CONCLUSIONS AND FUTURE RESEARCH
    As suggested by the social and the 'good-shopper' aspects of the Market Maven trait, this study identified relationships between it and both Extraversion and Conscientiousness. Both of these

TABLE 1
Correlations of the Five Factor Model and the Market Maven Scale

	1	2	3	4	5	6
1. Neuroticism	(.85)					
2. Extraversion	-.49**	(.82)				
3. Openness	.27**	-.06	(.74)			
4. Agreeableness	-.13	.43**	.16*	(.80)		
5. Conscientiousness	-.26**	.23**	-.01	.27**	(.85)	
6. Market Maven Scale	-.03	.22††	.01	.03	.15†	(.91)

Note: n=294; Cronbach's alphas are on the diagonal in parentheses.
* p<.01; ** p<.001, two-tailed test.
† p<.01, †† p<.001, one-tailed test.

higher-order global traits have been linked to theory and networks of personality findings via the recent five factor consensus. For example, Extraversion has been closely linked with underlying physiological arousal systems (e.g., Bullock and Gilliiland 1993) and as much as 60 percent of variance in Extraversion (Heath, Cloninger and Martin 1994, p. 773) and 29 percent of variance in Conscientiousness (Bergeman, et al. 1993) has been linked to genetics and heritability.

The identified relationships were, however, not as strong as anticipated, explaining only about five percent of the variance in Market Mavenism. Apparently, this domain-specific characteristic, which has been strongly linked with interpersonal communication and other marketplace behaviors, captures unique differences across consumers. Market Mavenism may be more *environmentally* determined than the global traits in the Five Factor Model. Nonetheless, this study does contribute to the body of knowledge emerging around the Five Factor Model by linking it to narrow traits in the area of consumer psychology and by identifying differences apparently *not* well explained by its five broad domains. These findings also clarify the content of Market Mavenism by supporting the proposition that it is determined in part by at least two underlying characteristics, preference for social interaction (in this case related to products and markets) and responsiveness to obligations (in this case toward responsible and informed consumption). Future research may extend these findings to broader populations and should, especially, extend the integration of consumption-specific individual differences to other traits, including, for example, the Need for Cognition, Self-Monitoring, and Materialism.

REFERENCES

Ajzen, Icek and Fishbein, Martin (1977), "Attitude-Behavior Relations: A Theoretical Analysis and Review of Empirical Research," *Psychological Bulletin*, 84, 888-918.

Bergeman, C. S., Heather M. Chipuer, Robert Plomin, Nancy L. Pedersen, G. E. McClearn, John R. Nesselroade, Paul T. Costa, Jr., and Robert R. McCrae (1993), "Genetic and Environmental Effects on Openness to Experience, Agreeableness, and Conscientiousness: An Adoption/Twin Study" *Journal of Personality*, 61, 2 (June), 159-179.

Block, Jack (1995), "A Contrarian View of the Five-Factor Model Approach to Personality Description," *Psychological Bulletin, 117*, 187-215.

Bullock, Wesley A. and Kirby Gilliiland (1993), "Eysenck's Arousal Theory of Intraversion-Extraversion: A Converging Measures Investigation," *Journal of Personality and Social Psychology*, 64, 1, 113-123.

Cacioppo, John T. and Richard E. Petty (1982), "The Need for Cognition," *Journal of Personality and Social Psychology*, 42, 1, 116-131.

Costa, Paul T. Jr. and Robert R. McCrae (1992a), "Four Ways Five Factors are Basic," *Personality and Individual Differences*, 13 (6), 653-665.

_____and _____(1992b), *Revised NEO Personality Inventory and NEO Five-Factor Inventory Professional Manual*, Odessa, FL: Psychological Assessment Resources.

_____and _____(1995), "Domains and Facets: Hierarchical Personality Assessment Using the Revised NEO Personality Inventory," *Journal of Personality Assessment*, 64, 1, 21-50.

Digman, John M. (1990), "Personality Structure: Emergence of the Five-Factor Model," in *Annual Review of Psychology*, Volume 41, ed. Mark R. Rosenzweig and Lyman W. Porter, Palo Alto, CA: Annual Reviews Inc., 417-440.

Elliott, Michael T. and Anne E. Warfield (1993), "Do Market Mavens Categorize Brands Differently?" in *Advances in Consumer Research*, Vol. 20, Leigh McAlister and Michael Rothschild, eds., Provo UT: Association for Consumer Research, 202-208.

Feick, Lawrence and Linda Price (1987), "The Market Maven: A Diffuser of Marketplace Information," *Journal of Marketing*, 51 (January), 83-87.

Foxall, Gordon R. and Ronald E. Goldsmith (1988), "Personality and Consumer Research: Another Look," *Journal of the Marketing Research Society*, 30 (2), 111-125.

Funder, David C. (1991), "Global Traits: A Neo-Allportian Approach to Personality," *Psycholgical Science*, 2, 1(January), 31-39.

Goldberg, Lewis R. (1993), The Structure of Phenotypic Personality Traits," *American Psychologist*, 48 (1), 26-34.

Gray, J. A. (1987), Perspectives on Anxiety and Impulsivity: A Commentary," *Journal of Research in Personality*, 21, 493-509.

Haugtvedt, Curtis R., Richard E. Petty and John T. Cacioppo (1992), "Need for Cognition and Advertising: Understanding the Role of Personality Variables in Consumer Behavior," *Journal of Consumer Psychology*, 1, 3, 239-260.

Heath, A. C., C. R. Cloninger and N. G. Martin (1994), "Testing a Model for the Genetic Structure of Personality: A Comparison of the Personality Systems of Cloninger and Eysenck," *Journal of Personality and Social Psychology*, 66, 4, 762-775.

John, Oliver P. (1990), "The `Big Five' Factor Taxonomy: Dimensions of Personality in the Natural Language and in Questionnaires," in *Handbook of Personality: Theory and Research*, L. A. Pervin ed., New York: Guildford Press, 66-100.

Kassarjian, Harold H. and Mary Jane Sheffet (1991), "Personality and Consumer Behavior: An Update," in *Perspectives on Consumer Behavoir*, Harold H. Kassarjian and Thomas S. Robertson (eds.), Edglewood Cliffs, NJ: Prentice Hall, 281-303.

Lichtenstein, Donald R. and Scot Burton (1990), "An Assessment of the Moderating Effects of Market Mavenism and Value Consciousness on Price-Quality Perception Accuracy," in *Advances in Consumer Research*, Vol. 17, Marvin E. Goldberg, Gerald Gorn and Richard W. Pollay, eds., Provo UT: Association for Consumer Research, 53-59.

McCrae, Robert R. (1993), "Moderated Analyses of Longitudinal Personality Stability," *Journal of Personality and Social Psychology*, 65, 3(September), 577-585.

_____and Oliver P. John (1992), "An Introduction to the Five-Factor Model and Its Applications," *Journal of Personality*, 60, 2 (June), 175-215.

Price, Linda L. Lawrence F. Feick and Audrey Guskey-Federouch (1988), "Couponing Behaviors of the Market Maven: Profile of a Super Couponer," in *Advances in Consumer Research*, Vol. 15, Michael J. Houston, ed., Provo UT: Association for Consumer Research, 354-359.

Public Relations Journal (1988), 44 (February), 18-19.

Richins, Marsha L. and Scott Dawson (1992), "A Consumer Values Orientation for Materialism and its Measurement: Scale Development and Validation," *Journal of Consumer Research*, 19, 3 (December), 303-316.

Schnieder, Kenneth C. and William C. Rodgers (1993), "Generalized Marketplace Influencers' (Market Mavens') Attitudes Toward Direct Mail as a Source of Information," *Journal of Direct Marketing*, 7 (Autumn), 20-28.

Slama, Mark E. and Terrell G. Williams (1990), "Generalization of the Market Maven's Information Provision Tendency Across Product Categories," in *Advances in Consumer Research*, Vol. 17, Marvin E. Goldberg, Gerald Gorn and Richard W. Pollay, eds., Provo UT: Association for Consumer Research, 48-52.

Snyder, Mark and Denneth G. DeBono (1985), "Appeals to Image and Claims About Quality: Understanding the Psychology of Advertising," *Journal of Personality and Social Psychology*, 49, 3, 586-597.

Widiger, T. A. (1992), "Review #258 [Review of the NEO Personality Inventory]," in *The Eleventh Mental Measurements Yearbook*, J. C. Conoley and J.J. Kramer, eds., Lincoln, NE: The Buros Institute, 603-606.

Special Session Summary
Does Economics Have Anything to Say About Consumer Behavior?

Russell S. Winer, University of California-Berkeley

Although the American Economics Association is one of the sponsoring organizations of the *Journal of Consumer Research*, very few papers using economic theory are published in the journal or presented at ACR. In addition, given most consumer behavior researchers' knowledge of economics does not go far beyond the classical utility maximization framework, there may be some question about what economics can even offer to the field of consumer behavior. The purpose of this session was to "market" economics as an alternative to psychology as a viable modeling framework for better understanding consumer behavior and to "bridge" diverse ACR constituents.

What Do Consumer Behavior and Economics Have to Say About Extensions?
Mary Sullivan, University of Chicago
Byung-Do Kim, Carnegie-Mellon University

Brand extensions have been studied from both consumer behavior and economics perspectives. Consumer behavior researchers and economists have differed in their theoretical approaches in that the former have examined how an extension has influenced cognitive processes while the latter have studied how the extension provides information as an aid to the purchase decision. Differences between the two kinds of researchers extend to the empirical approaches: consumer behavior researchers use experimental methods while economists tend to use secondary data. Two examples of these different approaches to research in the brand extension area studies looking at the "fit" of the extension to the existing brand and the effects of familiarity and expertise on the acceptability of extensions. An example of the consumer behavior research on fit is the use of categorization theory to predict how affect associated with the product category will generalize to the extension. Alternatively, an economic approach to fit assumes that extensions are experience goods and the position of the parent brand's established product provides information about the position of the extension in the market. With respect to familiarity, consumer behavior researchers have posited that affect is more likely to be transferred to an extension by "experts" in a product category when perceived similarity to an existing brand is high. An economic or marketing science approach attempts to measure familiarity using scanner panel data by defining experience by past purchasing behavior of the parent brand. A brand choice model is then estimated linking probability of choice of the extension to this past purchasing variable. In conclusion, both consumer behavior and economics have made important contributions to understanding how extensions work.

Rational, but Non-obvious, Models of Consumer Behavior
Birger Wernerfelt, MIT

Much of the behavioral research in choice is involved with the design of experiments in which actual choice behavior violates fundamental axioms of choice. Some researchers are looking for any behavior which cannot be explained by any rational (e.g. economic) choice model. In this presentation, it is shown that some behavior which has been argued to be non-rational such as the extensive literature on context effects is, in fact, consistent with rational behavior. To do this, ways in which subjects can draw choice-relevant inferences from the set of products available in the market are described and measured. These inferences are assessed in a series of experiments, using the basic attraction and compro-

mise designs from the literature, supplemented by direct measures of inferred product "addresses" (inferred locations of available products on a price-quality one-dimensional Hotelling line) and personal "taste addresses" (ideal points on the line). The change in choice share of a product produced by context is decomposed into three components: (1) a product address shift, (2) a taste address shift, and (3) a residual shift. What have been typically argued as violations of rational choice are instead shown to be the sum of these three effects which are based on rational, i.e. economic, assumptions.

The Economics and Psychology of Consumer Behavior
Sridhar Moorthy, University of Rochester

In many cases, the criticisms of behavioral researchers that economic models of consumers are unrealistic are unjustified. Economic modelers have made considerable progress in reconciling seemingly irrational consumer behavior with rational models. Several examples of where economic models "do well," i.e. explain consumer behavior, are the following. One example is low involvement behavior where economists can model this as a situation where the costs of involvement (e.g. information processing) exceeds the benefits. A second example is the recent work (see presentation #2) which shows that attraction and compromise effects are actually consistent with rational economic behavior as opposed to being violations of rationality as had been previously claimed. However, there are also areas of research where economics has a problem explaining behavior. One example is preference reversals. A second example is the difficulty in explaining the frequency distribution of price endings, most of which end in either 9 or 0. A third area is advertising effects where economic explanations of advertising as having only information content. In summary, behavioral researchers need to understand what is truly psychological and what can be explained by more parsimonious economic models.

Discounting and its Impact on Durables Buying Decisions
Russell S. Winer, University of California at Berkeley

The economic concepts of discounting and discount rates refer to how agents (i.e. consumers) prefer outcomes such as receipt of money sooner rather than later. Comparing discount rates between consumers allows us to infer their relative rates of "time preference" for money. For example, a consumer with a discount rate of 10% would have much greater use for the money today and value it less in the future than the consumer with the 5% rate. The concept of discounting and time preferences can also be applied to a durable goods, multiattribute context. Consumers can be conceptualized to have discount rates for attributes in that they have different rates of "impatience" for product improvements on the attributes. Thus, one can hypothesize a two-dimensional concept of attribute importance: a static concept as is usually measured by attribute importance weights, and a dynamic concept which captures consumer time preferences for the attributes. For example, in the context of laptop computers, a consumer might value the quality of the screen greater than the weight in time t (the present time), but is more impatient for improvements in weight, i.e. weight has a greater discount rate. Other relevant questions on discount rates are how they vary over product categories as well as attributes, how to model differences between consumers, and how they affect purchase incidence of different durable good categories.

Communities of Consumption: A Central Metaphor for Diverse Research

Christine Wright-Isak, Young & Rubicam Advertising

SESSION SUMMARY

There has been a long tradition of community research in sociology. While its implications are extremely relevant to understanding consumer behavior, it has yet to be incorporated into consumer research, although initial discussion has been offered at recent ACR meetings. The purpose of this session was to bring together researchers whose work centers on the concept of *community as more than a metaphor*, and through an active interchange accomplish two main objectives. The first was to demonstrate the value of this concept for consumer research. The second was to show how varied theoretical and methodological orientations contribute to the concept of community and its value in studying consumer behavior. Perhaps most important, the papers presented offered a variety of diverse examples of the concept's use substantively and methodologically. They shared the common theoretical identification of community as a social construction of reality.

Muniz and O'Guinn presented their theory of how consumers form community around consumption of a brand, using the example of the recently introduced Zima beverage brand. Their research synthesizes classic sociology, sociological reader response, and accommodation theory from mass communication to investigate the symbolic and interactive nature of brand significance. Those who buy Zima form and develop a community of fellow consumers. O'Guinn and Muniz argue that central to understanding the phenomenon of a brand's long term value in the marketplace is the community process of social construction in which individuals arrive at shared understandings of meaning. They suggest that any brand comes to stand for a certain shared style of human association, a community of consumers, that attracts new members who want to participate in the norms and satisfactions shared by the other members.

This presentation set the stage for the second paper in which Arthur Kover described the relationship between the sociological clustering of brands and the individual consumer's preference formation. Kover argues that the world of traditional meanings has been breaking up and that new understandings are being socially reconstructed. In this situation consumers look for security and stability. Clusters of brands that have been personalized by means of advertising and consumer experience fit together, and are perceived to be brand communities. To some extent these brand communities offer an alternative form of community to consumers who participate in membership by buying and owning them. The shared meanings invested in these brands, and their collective significance, is another form of the social construction of reality.

Wright-Isak presented the third paper which reviewed the definition of the concept of community, distinguishing its use as a metaphor from its value as a scientific construct. Like the other presentations, this one argued that community is a social construction maintained and subscribed to by its members. The characteristic that defines a given type of community is its ethos, which is a complex of values, attitudes, beliefs along with the social behaviors expected to enact them. Wright-Isak demonstrated that, even though data collection employs familiar consumer research methods, community analysis focuses on aggregate community patterns of belief or behavior rather than on individual variations. She offered the research example of the value of triangulating methods to study a small town. Triangulation revealed that the imagery of belonging inherent in the nature of small town life influenced home purchase decisions in a large metropolitan area.

Stern used Stanley Fish's concept of interpretive community as a central metaphor to discuss the research presentations. She emphasized that community oriented research must be "read" in light of different reading strategies and different research agendas. To provoke discussion, she proposed alternative readings for dented cans of food. To the research audience the cents-off on damaged cans signifies undesirability. However, to impoverished consumers damaged cans are so desirable as "bargains" that consumers roam supermarkets to dent cans so that they can get a reduction in price. From the perspective of diversity, the validity of any interpretation depends on the assumptions that an interpretive community shares. Audience controversy provided a lively discussion of communal strategy as a process of meaning creation that revealed the process of social negotiation among attendees.

PAPER ABSTRACTS

Brand Community and the Sociology of Brands
Albert M. Muniz Jr, and Thomas C. O'Guinn

Brands and related concepts are currently receiving significant research attention. With few exceptions, this work has examined brands from an information-processing perspective. While this has provided valuable insight, a significant domain of inquiry has been relatively ignored, that is, the *sociology of brands*. This lack of epistemological diversity amounts to a major limitation in our knowledge of this core concept, and it points to the field's failure to examine the important social forces that act upon these undeniably social creations. Our proposed theory will draw upon sociological work in community, sociological reader response theory, and accommodation theory. Into this theoretical synthesis, we introduce and situate our concept of *brand communities*, or the core construct of our theory.

The Community of Brands
Arthur J. Kover

The idea underlying this paper is that brands form communities for the consumers who buy them. This expansion of the concept of brand personality supplements the work on meaning of consumer goods as it has been developed primarily by Russell Belk. We will report on the first step in a long-term project on brand communities. People most sensitive to the dynamics of brands will carry out this step as a sample of 25 advertising executives will be asked to describe their own communities of brands as well as sets of brands that might constitute communities for others.

These data are analyzed to examine the extent to which brand communities are idiosyncratic or have commonly understood meaning, falling into defined sets with specific characteristics. They will also provide insight into how meanings of brands are drawn from their sociocultural milieu and focussed or refined by the messages crafted about them. This reality forming process will shed light on the sociological aspects of consumer choice making.

Triangulating Methods to Study Community Phenomena
Christine Wright-Isak

There has been a long and important tradition of community research in sociology. While it has relevant implications for students of consumption, it has yet to be incorporated into consumer behavior research. The value of the concept community to marketers is that it concerns group processes of creating, maintaining, or collectively acting within meanings influence consumption motivations and choices. There is a sense in consumer behavior discussions that community as a concept refers to something more than simply the addition of all the individual psychological factors, but the concept itself is not well understood beyond its metaphorical appeal.

This paper considers the concept of community in its human literal sense and defines it culturally in terms of social processes organized within an ethos of beliefs that are translated into social actions. A brief theoretical review provides background for appropriate ways of measuring community phenomena. Then research findings about small towns demonstrates triangulation. Several methods of gathering data and synthesizing the results address a specific consumption question. The persistence of small town community which was hypothesized to be extinct by the end of the century has occurred because the imagery of its form of community shapes consumers decisions in purchasing a home. Examples of how small town imagery is perpetuated and extended in advertising campaigns, cinema and television are offered.

Emerging Research on US and Canadian Policies Toward Cigarette and Anti-Smoking Advertising and Product Packaging: Effects on Youths and Adults

Cornelia (Connie) Pechmann, University of California, Irvine

OVERVIEW OF SESSION

This session brought together several researchers who have been very active in conducting policy research on tobacco consumption and marketing influences. The researchers were afforded the opportunity to disseminate findings from their most recent studies. The findings consistently showed that tobacco advertising and packaging creates favorable beliefs about smoking. Beliefs about smoking are a prime, often leading, indicator of tobacco consumption. Youths who take up (vs. do not take up) smoking have significantly more favorable beliefs about smoking, as do adult smokers who switch to lower tar—but still harmful—cigarettes rather than quitting.

The session was very well attended, and policy officials from the US Food and Drug Administration (FDA) and the US Federal Trade Commission (FTC) were present. At the ACR lunch talk that followed the session, FDA policy official Bill Schultz stated that his agency's foremost concern was to understand how tobacco marketing may affect smoking by underage youths.

Two Experiments Assessing the Visual and Semantic Images Associated with Current and Plain (Generic) Cigarette Packaging

Authors

The paper was jointly presented by Judith Madill-Marshall of Carleton University in Canada, and Marvin W. Goldberg of Pennsylvania State University. Co-authors are Gerald J. Gorn (University of British Columbia), John Liefeld (Guelph University), and Harrie Vredenburg (University of Calgary).

Objectives

This research was commissioned by the Canadian government to examine the possible promotional effects of current (image-oriented) vs. plain white (generic) cigarette packaging on youth. The presentation reported on two related experiments which represented a part of a national survey administered to 1200 Canadian teens who smoked or were interested in smoking.

Method

The experiments examined teens' visual and semantic images of individuals who smoke different cigarette brands (e.g., feminine brands), in either the brands' current or plain packages. In the Visual Image Study, subjects were asked to indicate, on a five point scale, whether each brand "was right or wrong" for different types of smokers. In the Semantic Image Study, subjects were asked to rate teens who smoked various brands on 15 semantic differentials (e.g., "secure-insecure," "cool- uncool").

Hypotheses

A key hypothesis was that, for a smoker whose attributes were consistent with the package image (e.g., feminine), the white or generic package would be viewed as significantly less appropriate than the current package. This outcome would indicate that it could be useful to remove brand markings (except the name) to reduce the desirable brand images conveyed by cigarette packages.

Findings

The researchers found support for their central hypothesis: By stripping the cigarette package of its unique characteristics (except for brand name in uniform font), the package's self-definitional and "badge" value to teens was significantly reduced. To the extent that youths smoke cigarettes to define and enhance their self image, the expectation would be that the rate of teen smoking would be reduced if plain packaging were the rule.

Cigarette Ads, Anti-Smoking Ads and Peers: Why Do Underage Youths Start Smoking Cigarettes?

Authors

The paper was presented by Cornelia (Connie) Pechmann of the University of California, Irvine. The co-author is Susan J. Knight of the University of California, Irvine. The research was funded by the California's Tobacco-Related Disease Research Program.

Objectives

This experiment tested two competing explanations of why youths smoke: (1) cigarette ads glamorize smoking, and (2) peers who smoke promote the activity. This experiment appears to be the first to compare the two purported causes of underage smoking. The study also examined whether 1 anti-smoking ad can offset the effects of 3 cigarette ads. Massachusetts spends roughly $2.30/capita on anti-smoking ads and activities while the tobacco industry spends about three times as much, or $6.70/capita ($3.50 on ads alone, plus $3.20 on specialty items and events). Will Massachusetts' anti-smoking ads pay off?

Method

Subjects were 675 CA 9th graders. None were regular smokers and all rated smokers as less desirable than nonsmokers, so they conceivably could have been immune to pro-smoking influences. Subjects viewed the ads and peer smoking on videotape, to enhance realism. The 12 minute videos showed four teens (mixed in race and gender) filming ads in their neighborhood for a class project and then (in some tapes) smoking.

Eight videotapes were created, that were identical except for the smoking ads included (either 4 cigarette ads, 4 anti-smoking ads, 1 anti plus 3 cigarette ads, or 4 unrelated-to-smoking, i.e., control ads) and peer smoking (either present or absent). Each ad appeared for an identical length of time, and the total spent on smoking ads matched the time spent showing peer smoking (1 minute), to avoid confounds. The cigarette ads that were used scored highest in pretests with 9th graders, and promoted Camel, Kool, Newport and Capri. The anti-smoking ads also scored highest in pretests and were obtained from the California and Washington State Health Departments, and the American Cancer Society.

After seeing the tapes, subjects were asked how teen smokers look to them (using 21 semantic differentials), and their intent to smoke. Subjects' thoughts about the videotapes (ads and smokers) were also measured. Subjects' initial intent to smoke and smoking behaviors had been assessed unobtrusively two weeks in advance.

Hypotheses

It was hypothesized that cigarette ads, when combined with peer smoking, would increase youths' intent to smoke by making teen smokers look more glamorous. Showing just one anti-smoking ad along with the cigarette ads would nullify such effects.

Prior research (Pechmann and Ratneshwar 1994)[1] had suggested that, when youths have negative prior beliefs about smokers, cigarette ads are so contrary to such beliefs that the ads tend to be discounted. However, when youths see cigarette ads and then see reasonably attractive teens smoking, the ads could become potent or virulent. Peer smoking could personalize the cigarette ad images, making glamorous and youthful ad images seem relevant and believable, as the US Surgeon General contends.[2]

Findings

As predicted, the cigarette (vs. control) ads, when shown with peer smoking, increased subjects' intent to smoke. Likewise, the cigarette ads combined with peer smoking enhanced subjects' perceptions of a teen smoker's social acceptability (likability and sex appeal), life path (intelligence and success), physical state (health, fitness, and cleanliness), and weight (slimness). The cigarette ads did not affect perceptions of a teen smoker's internal welfare (confidence) but the ads chosen did not focus on those attributes.

Including just one anti-smoking ad along with the cigarette ads eliminated (nullified) the cigarette ad effects. The peer smoking only condition had no effects. Overall, the findings indicate that policies to prevent youths from seeing image-oriented cigarette advertising, and/or ensure youths are exposed to adequate anti-smoking ads (e.g., 1 anti ad for every 3 cigarette ads), should reduce smoking rates among underage youths.

Health Policy Implications of Advertised Tar Numbers

Authors

The paper was presented by Joel Cohen of the University of Florida, the sole author.

Objectives

This paper examined the health policy implications of providing smokers with numerical tar ratings in cigarette ads (e.g., "5 mg tar", "10 mg tar"). Such ratings have been included in all cigarette ads since 1970, due to a voluntary agreement among cigarette companies, and the FTC endorses the method used to produce the ratings.

The FTC has recently expressed concern regarding whether smokers might misinterpret tar numbers and thus continue to smoke rather than quit. Lower tar numbers seem to imply less harm and, indeed, ultra low tar cigarettes (1-5 mg) had achieved almost a 13% market share by 1992. Low tar cigarettes (15 mg of tar or less) went from essentially 0% share in 1960 to over 68% share in 1992. Cigarettes with reduced tar slightly lower cancer risk, but do not reduce the risk of heart attack, stroke or other lung disease.

Method

Smokers were contacted via a US national probability telephone survey. They were asked about their awareness, interpretation and use of numerical tar and nicotine ratings.

Hypotheses

The survey questions were designed to determine if smokers were confused about (1) the tar ratings of their brands, (2) how tar ratings affect health risks, and (3) whether decreases in tar ratings lead to directly proportional decreases in tar yields (consumption).

Findings

Few smokers knew the tar ratings for their own cigarettes, except the very low tar (1-5 mg) cigarette smokers. A majority could not correctly judge the relative tar levels of cigarettes. Smokers were unsure about whether switching to lower tar cigarettes would reduce risks. Finally, many smokers incorrectly relied on absolute tar ratings to calculate reduced tar yields. The paper recommends revisions in tar ratings to make them more useful and a required statement on cigarette packages to relate tar levels to risks more explicitly.

---

[1]Pechmann, C. and S. Ratneshwar (1994), "The Effects of Anti-Smoking and Cigarette Advertising on Young Adolescents' Perceptions of Peers Who Smoke," *Journal of Consumer Research*, 21 (September), 236-251.

[2]Executive Summary of Surgeon General's Report on Preventing Tobacco Use Among Young People (1994), Oncology, 8 (May), 16, 19, 46.

SPECIAL SESSION SUMMARY
Marketing Tactics, Search, and Choice

David L. Mothersbaugh, University of Alabama
Timothy B. Heath, University of Pittsburgh
Lawrence F. Feick, University of Pittsburgh[1]

SESSION OVERVIEW

Marketers utilize a variety of tactics designed to persuade consumers to choose one brand over another (e.g., advertising, point-of-purchase displays, etc.). However, little experimental research has examined the effects of such tactics on search and choice (exceptions include Heath, McCarthy, and Mothersbaugh 1994; Miniard, Sirdeshmukh, and Innis 1992; Mitra and Lynch 1995; Simonson, Nowlis, and Lemon 1993; Wright and Rip 1980). For example, advertising research and search and decision process research evidence little overlap. Research on advertising effects generally focuses on brand attitudes but not search and choice outcomes. Research on search and decision processes generally focuses on factors such as choice-set composition rather than on marketer-controlled factors such as advertising. This session attempted to bridge these separate research streams by presenting three empirical studies testing the effects of various marketing tactics on search and choice.

The papers in the session examined a diverse set of marketing variables (e.g., advertising frames, celebrity endorsers, retail displays) in various decision contexts (e.g., high involvement versus low involvement, in-store shopping versus on-line shopping) using divergent methodological approaches (e.g., lab experiments versus field experiments). Three themes emerged from this session. First was the ability of marketing tactics to affect brand choice by altering consumers' decision processes. Mothersbaugh, Heath, and Feick found that advertising features such as celebrity endorsers affected brand choice by influencing which brands consumers searched. Duhan, Areni, and Kiecker found that retail display formats affected brand choice by influencing which attributes consumers used to screen brands early in the decision process. A second theme was the differential processes mediating attitude and choice that can moderate the effects of marketing tactics. Shiv, Edell, and Payne tested the effects of positive and negative advertising frames on attitudes and choice under low involvement. The authors found that negative frames damaged ad and brand attitudes while simultaneously bolstering choice probabilities because the negative ad evaluations accessed during attitude formation were not accessed during choice. A third theme was the potential for non-product-related tactics to have dramatic effects on search and choice. Shiv, Edell, and Payne found that advertising frames can affect choice in low-involvement markets. Mothersbaugh, Heath, and Feick found that positive but vacuous advertising features (i.e., pictures and endorsers) can affect search and choice in high-involvement markets. Duhan, Areni, and Kiecker found that the way in which information is organized in retail displays can affect brand sales.

Detailed abstracts of the individual papers follow.

[1]The authors gratefully acknowledge the insightful comments provided by our discussant, Frank Kardes.

SUMMARIES OF THE INDIVIDUAL PAPERS

The Effects of Message Framing on Aad, Ab, and Brand Choice: When is What You Dislike, What You Choose?
Baba Shiv, Julie A. Edell, and John W. Payne, Duke University

Studies that have examined the effects of framing on persuasion suggest that negative framing is less effective than positive framing under conditions of low elaboration. These findings are consistent with the ELM model according to which peripheral cues such as the valence of ad messages are likely to affect ad and brand evaluations, and hence purchase intentions under conditions of low elaboration. The results from three experiments suggest that the effects of these peripheral cues (valence of ad messages) on brand choice is contingent on the nature of the intervening processing. In Experiment 1 where ad exposure was followed immediately by brand choice, different patterns of results were obtained with conventional ad and brand evaluation measures and with the choice measure - while results on ad and brand evaluations suggested that negative framing was less effective than positive framing (consistent with the ELM model predictions), results on choice suggest the contrary. A 2 x 2 design was used in Experiment 2 with framing as one of the factors and the nature of the intervening processing as the second factor (cognitive responses intervening between ad exposure and brand choice or not). When brand choice was not preceded by cognitive responses, the results in Experiment 1 were replicated. Only when cognitive responses intervened between ad exposure and brand choice were the pattern of results on ad and brand evaluations and those on choice consistent with one another. Experiment 3 used a different product category and the findings were consistent with those obtained in Experiment 2. Investigation of the reasons for these findings suggests that subjects' prior evaluations toward negative ads were not accessed and hence not used in choice when ad exposure was followed immediately by brand choice. Only when respondents thought about their reactions to the ad did these negative evaluations get accessed and in turn used in choice. Whether or not respondents reported their cognitive responses prior to their brand and ad evaluations did not affect these evaluations, suggesting that the measures, by themselves, made prior evaluations toward negative ads accessible.

Advertising as Search Heuristic: Implications for Brand Consideration and Choice
David L. Mothersbaugh, University of Alabama
Timothy B. Heath and Lawrence F. Feick, University of Pittsburgh

Research shows that people often use heuristics to simplify decisions (e.g., Payne, Bettman, and Johnson 1988). Little research, however, has examined consumers' use of advertising as a heuristic in the search process. Our study examines the effects of nonsubstantive advertising features (e.g., attractive pictures) on search and choice in competitive markets with search costs. Prevailing theory suggests that nonsubstantive features have little effect on attitudes when consumers engage in issue-relevant thinking (e.g., Petty and Cacioppo 1986). We propose and demonstrate that despite issue-relevant thinking, nonsubstantive ad features are critical determinants of choice through their influence on search, especially when search costs are high.

Hypotheses were tested using search and choice measures derived from a computer-based marketplace called CompuSearch. The experimental market consisted of nine fictitious brands. Subjects (N=252) first viewed positive but vacuous ads for the brands and then searched for attribute information from CompuSearch. Ad features were manipulated on one brand's ads (the target brand) in a 2 (no picture, attractive picture) X 2 (no endorser, famous endorser) between-subjects design. Advertising for the other brands was held constant across conditions. Search costs were manipulated by charging for information (5 vs. 50 cents per brand) and by delaying information access (1 vs. 60 second delay).

Despite issue-relevant thinking, adding nonsubstantive features to a brand's ads increased the likelihood of that brand being (1) searched, (2) searched earlier in the process, and (3) chosen. In addition, adding a credible celebrity to a brand's ads reduced search of other brands, whereas adding an attractive picture did not. These effects tended to be more pronounced when search costs were higher than when search costs were lower.

This study is relevant to both theory and practice. It shows that despite issue-relevant thinking, relatively trivial advertising features have dramatic and varied effects in the marketplace (e.g., moving brands into consumer consideration sets). Such findings suggest that seemingly trivial advertising features can be critical tactical tools in high involvement markets. They also suggest the need to extend prevailing persuasion theory (e.g., the Elaboration Likelihood Model) to competitive markets involving search costs.

The Impact of Retail Display Format on Product Choice
Dale F. Duhan and Charles S. Areni, Texas Tech University
Pamela L. Kiecker, Virginia Commonwealth University

Research has shown that in order to reduce the amount of in-store information that is considered prior to purchase, consumers eliminate many brands from consideration early in the decision process using simple screening criteria (e.g., "I don't like vanilla," or "private label brands aren't very good"). The manner in which products are organized on store shelves or in special displays is one of many factors that influences the screening criteria used by consumers. Specifically, displaying products according to levels of a specific attribute increases the extent to which the featured attribute is the basis for screening alternatives. This magnifies differences in choice likelihood between alternatives having favorable and unfavorable values on that attribute, but only when that attribute is otherwise not salient. Further, the impact on choice should be most pronounced for brands having strong competitive positions, because some of these brands are eliminated early in the decision on the basis of the display attribute. Thus, strong brands that are eliminated suffer substantial sales declines, and strong brands that survive experience increases in sales.

The general hypothesis described above was tested by combining the results of a mail survey with those of a field experiment. Nine hundred and twenty-eight wine consumers provided information regarding attributes used to compare and select wines via a mail survey. The questionnaire contained items concerning: 1) the importance weights assigned to various wine attributes, 2) whether selection criteria associated with each attribute were stored in memory versus constructed while shopping, and 3) the importance of each attribute in determining "strong" versus "weak" alternatives. The results of the survey were used to construct alternative formats for displaying wines in several stores in a major southeastern, U.S. market. Specifically, the retail displays organized products according to either *region of origin*, a low salience attribute, or *wine variety*, an attribute high in salience.

The results of the experiment revealed that display format had a significant impact on sales levels by region of origin. Sales of products from unfavorably evaluated regions were lower when products were organized by region rather than by variety. However, the corresponding sales increase for products from favorably evaluated regions did not occur. This may, in part, be due to the ratio of products from favorably and unfavorably evaluated regions in each store. As expected, the sales decline was more pronounced for wines having high versus low awareness scores and high versus low brand attitude ratings. By contrast, display format had little or no effect on sales by wine variety. These results suggest that the organization of products in special retail displays alters the criteria used for screening alternatives early in the process by increasing the salience of certain attributes. Although this explanation is consistent with the results of the field experiment, more research is needed to confirm the processes described and to rule out rival hypotheses.

REFERENCES

Heath, Timothy B., Michael S. McCarthy, and David L. Mothersbaugh (1994), "Spokesperson Fame and Vividness Effects in the Context of Issue-relevant Thinking: The Moderating Role of Competitive Setting," *Journal of Consumer Research*, 20 (March), 520-534.

Miniard, Paul W., Deepak Sirdeshmukh, and Daniel E. Innis (1992), "Peripheral Persuasion and Brand Choice," *Journal of Consumer Research*, 19 (September), 226-239.

Mitra, Anusree and John G. Lynch, Jr. (1995), "Toward a Reconciliation of Market Power and Information Theories of Advertising Effects on Price Elasticity," *Journal of Consumer Research*, 21 (March), 644-659.

Payne, John W., James R. Bettman, and Eric J. Johnson (1988), "Adaptive Strategy Selection in Decision Making," *Journal of Experimental Psychology: Learning, Memory, and Cognition*, 14 (3), 534-552.

Petty, Richard E. and John T. Cacioppo (1986), *Communication and Persuasion: Central and Peripheral Routes to Attitude Change*, New York: Springer-Verlag.

Simonson, Itamar, Stephen Nowlis, and Katherine Lemon (1993), "The Effect of Local Consideration Sets on Global Choice Between Lower Price and Higher Quality," *Marketing Science*, 12 (Fall), 357-377.

Wright, Peter and Peter D. Rip (1980), "Product Class Advertising Effects on First-Time Buyers' Strategies," *Journal of Consumer Research*, 7 (September), 176-188.

New Insights Into Variety Seeking

Michal Strahilevitz, University of Illinois at Urbana-Champaign
Daniel Read, University of Illinois at Urbana-Champaign

This session offered a diverse range of papers focusing on the contexts in which variety seeking will be more likely as well as some of the possible underlying mechanisms responsible for people's preferences with regards to thedegree of variety they would find optimal.

The first paper, by Cynthia Huffman and Barbara Kahn, examines the implications to marketers of the fact that individuals are motivated to maintain an optimal stimulation level (OSL). The authors suggest that when marketers offer too much variety, consumers may become so frustrated that they will be unwilling to try new products. The research explores the ways that marketers can present their arrays of options so that the consumer being targeted will be more satisfied by the variety of alternatives available, rather than more confused. The results indicate that the optimal level of variety may depend on the degree customers are aware of their own preferences. The findings also demonstrate that if marketers unobtrusively elicit their customer's preferences, and then offer them the alternatives that they really want, these customers will be much more willing to consume variety.

The second paper, by Michal Strahilevitz, explores the possibility that similar to "sensory specific satiation," individuals may exhibit "cause specific satiation." Both hypothetical contribution decisions and real choices involving real money were used. The results indicate that, even in the absence of information seeking and uncertainty regarding future tastes, individuals still tend to seek variety. The results also demonstrate that both the amount of money available and the time elapsed between contributions can affect allocation preferences when choosing among multiple charities. Also presented were results which suggest that in selecting a "portfolio" of causes to contribute to, many individuals will look for variety with a theme (i.e., sponsoring only females, but from a variety of ethnic backgrounds). As a whole, the results suggest that there may be some sort of intrinsic pay-off from simply *choosing* variety as opposed to *consuming* variety.

The final paper, by Daniel Read, Shobana Kalyanaraman, and George Loewenstein, explores various motives underlying variety seeking behavior. The main motives investigated were information seeking, diversification and what they refer to as "virtuous" variety seeking. The authors demonstrate that "choice bracketing," or the making of choices in combination or separately, can determine which motives will operate when choices are made. Their results indicate that people are more likely to consider the virtues of a diverse portfolio when choices are bracketed together. They also demonstrated that individuals are also more likely to experiment in order to find out what other alternatives might be available when choices are bracketed together. Finally, their results indicate that individuals are more likely to select a virtuous but less enjoyable alternative (e.g., Renting *Schindler's List* as opposed to *Speed*) when choices were bracketed together.

At the closing of the session, Leigh McAlister skillfully led a stimulating discussion where many captivating ideas for future research were raised. The audience departed appearing content that they had selected this session amongst the variety of other attractive alternatives available.

An Introduction to Embodied Cognition: Implications for Consumer Research

Alan J. Malter, University of Wisconsin-Madison

ABSTRACT

This paper introduces the basic features of the newly emerging theory of embodied cognition and examines some possible implications for consumer research. The standard view of memory and information processing is critically reviewed and embodied cognition is proposed as a possible alternative theoretical basis for studying cognitive processes. Areas of consumer research which could potentially benefit from adopting an embodied view of cognition include decision making, information search behavior, and categorization. A brief concluding discussion examines embodied cognition as an alternative explanation for the phenomenon of impulse purchase behavior.

INTRODUCTION

Memory has long been recognized as central to all phases of consumers' processing and interpretation of information (Bettman 1979). Though usually not the focus of consumer researchers, assumptions about the structure and operation of the human memory system underlie most of the core research areas of consumer behavior, including but not limited to: attention and perception, decision making, information search behavior, categorization and concept formation, and consumer expertise. Yet Alba, Hutchinson and Lynch (1991) note the unfortunate fact that "most traditional decision research has treated memory as an annoyance ... rather than as a target for investigation." Since our assumptions about how memory works shape our research designs, hypotheses and, ultimately, our understanding of consumer behavior, they are of critical importance and deserve both careful consideration and periodic reexamination.

Since memory and cognition issues were first introduced in the consumer research literature (Bettman 1975; McGuire 1976), a general consensus has emerged among consumer researchers in adopting the standard memory paradigms, which have often been referred to in the cognitive psychology literature as the "modal view." Most consumer researchers investigating memory and cognition consistently follow a core of authors regarding the fundamental issues of short and long-term memory (e.g., Waugh and Norman 1965; Atkinson and Shiffrin 1968), semantic and episodic memory (e.g., Tulving 1972), and the organization of memory in an associative spreading activation network (e.g., Anderson 1983; Collins and Loftus 1975). While a few consumer researchers (e.g., Alba and Hutchinson 1987; Cohen and Basu 1987) have reviewed some alternatives to these theories, they have either not pursued these ideas further or dismissed them due to various limitations. Though these latter authors exhibit a general sense that the standard memory paradigms are inadequate, they have been reluctant to abandon them for lack of a better theory.

Numerous consumer researchers have reported findings which cannot be easily accounted for by the standard paradigms, such as limited external search for information and non-choice "decisions" (Olshavsky and Granbois 1979), extremely rapid and apparently holistic purchase decisions (e.g., Hoyer 1984), failure to engage in an external search for information in cases of extreme incongruity in a categorization task (Ozanne, Brucks and Grewel 1992), the influence of positive affect on cognitive processes and decision making (Isen 1989); and the apparent suspension of normal cognitive processes in impulse purchase situations (Rook 1987; Thompson, Locander and Pollio 1990).

Meanwhile, following developments in cognitive linguistics (e.g., Lakoff 1987; Talmy 1988), a number of psychologists have recently proposed new theories of how memory works, which offer an alternative explanation for these and other perplexing types of consumer behaviors. While these new memory theories (e.g., Barsalou 1993; Barsalou et al. 1993; Glenberg, in press) are still in the early stages of development and testing and are called various names by their authors, they are part of a new paradigm which can generally be referred to as "embodied cognition." In general, the embodied view of cognition denies the core assumptions of the modal view; instead, it postulates a unitary cognitive system composed of "embodied" (i.e., perceptual, or non-linguistic) concepts. Systems of this type feature the necessary flexibility and sensitivity to context to account for complex analytical and non-analytical consumer behaviors.

The aim of this paper is to introduce some of the basic features of the new models of embodied cognition and to examine some possible implications for consumer research. Specifically, this paper will: (1) briefly review the principal features of the modal view of memory as used in consumer research; (2) describe some of the general limitations of the modal view and review some problematic findings in the consumer research literature; (3) briefly explain the central features of two recent models of embodied cognition (Barsalou 1993; Barsalou et al. 1993; Glenberg, in press); and (4) discuss some areas of consumer research which could potentially benefit from the adoption of an embodied view of cognition.

THE MODAL VIEW OF MEMORY IN CONSUMER RESEARCH

A Summary of Its Basic Features

The standard memory paradigms which have come to be known as the "modal view" in psychology were first discussed in the consumer research literature by Bettman (1975) and McGuire (1976). In a greatly expanded treatment of memory issues, Bettman (1979) further defined and solidified the modal view in consumer research. Central features of many models associated with this view include: (1) the multiple-store approach (e.g., Waugh and Norman 1965; Atkinson and Shiffrin 1968), proposing separate stores or, at least, separate functions and properties for short-term and long-term memory; (2) the multiple systems approach (e.g., Tulving 1972) characterized by distinct systems for semantic memory and episodic memory; and (3) the associative network approach (e.g., Anderson 1983; Collins and Loftus 1975), in which semantic knowledge is organized in a network of nodes linked by propositions and is retrieved through a process of spreading activation.

Subsequently, the modal view of memory in consumer research has been cited, with occasional expansion and elaboration, in countless journal articles and marketing textbooks. Many authors specifically note that Collins and colleagues' (e.g., Collins and Loftus 1975) or Anderson's (1983) spreading activation network serves as the basis for their models of such topics as consumer consideration sets (Nedungadi 1990), consumer learning (Huffman and Houston 1993), mood states (Gardner 1985) and memory for advertising (Burke and Srull 1988).

Limitations of the Modal View

Though the modal view has served as the dominant paradigm in consumer research as well as in cognitive psychology during the past few decades, many of its core elements have been questioned

Advances in Consumer Research
Volume 23, © 1996

by subsequent research. For example, though the notion of a separate short-term memory store was initially supported in the 1960's and 1970's by findings of "recency effects" in free-recall tasks (in which the last few items on a list are remembered better than mid-list items), it was substantially weakened by later findings of such phenomena as long-term recency effects (Glenberg et al. 1983). Evidence showing rapid forgetting of simple information under conditions of distraction (Brown 1958; Peterson and Peterson 1959) also appeared to support the multiple-store approach, but the Brown-Peterson task was found to be critically flawed by proactive interference (see Glenberg, in press, and Greene 1992, for a review of this literature). Furthermore, the debate since the early 1970's over Tulving's (1972) proposal of distinct systems for semantic memory (i.e., general knowledge) and episodic memory (i.e., personal experience/autobiographical knowledge) was largely settled by the evidence presented by McKoon, Ratcliff and Dell (1986), which showed the inseparability of the two. Meanwhile, alternative models of cognition, including some based on exemplars (e.g., Hintzman 1986) and some based on embodied representations (e.g., Glenberg, in press), have shown that a single memory system with a single cognitive process may be capable of handling all types of information (i.e., both semantic and episodic information).

Given such shortcomings of the modal view, it is not surprising that the consumer research literature contains numerous reports of consumer behavior phenomena and experimental results for which the modal view does not provide a satisfactory explanation. Alba et al. (1991) argue that the nature of consumers' decision process is so complex and variable that traditional memory paradigms may be of limited value. They conclude that a "broader conceptualization of memory is necessary," as is a reconsideration of the paradigms we use to examine consumer decision making.

Other authors have directly addressed problems which might arise from the assumption that memory is based on an associative network with spreading activation. For instance, in her discussion of the influences of affect on cognitive processes, Isen (1989) points out that it would be problematic if a positive-affect advertisement for any specific brand of "soft drink" were to also serve as a retrieval cue for positive feelings toward Coke, Pepsi, and every other soft drink (or even other related products, such as beer)! Data on affect show that a person's ability to interpret incoming information, which is neglected in the modal view, is important in circumventing the likelihood that affect from one product will necessarily spread to all other associated products. Isen (1989, pp.111-112) states explicitly that spreading activation models of associative propositions do not account for all the data, noting that "the finding that positive affect influences (broadens) cognitive organization and interpretation of material seems unanticipated by associationist models."

One implication of the modal view of information processing as applied to categorization research is that a major determinant of product typicality should be attribute structure. Loken and Ward (1990) employed attribute structure as a key measure to study the degree to which the salient, goal-related attributes (as determined by an open-ended pretest of subjects) of a category member would be related to its perceived typicality. Though attribute structure was found to be one of six variables significantly related to typicality, it performed much more poorly than expected and yielded results which were inconsistent with Barsalou's (1983) data on ad-hoc categories. In another case, the design of categorization experiments by Ozanne et al. (1992) forced subjects to evaluate products on the basis of attribute information only, thus discouraging the use of holistic processing even in cases of high-discrepancy stimuli. These kinds of results seem to indicate that the standard attribute-based approaches to studying typicality judgments are not sufficiently flexible to reflect the true variability with which consumers classify products. Finally, in their review of alternative models of categorization, Cohen and Basu (1987) noted a growing disenchantment with the "overly cognitive approaches" of the modal view and its mechanistic and computer-like assumptions. Their article provides a rare example of questioning the fundamental assumptions of the modal view; they emphasize the flexible and context-dependent character of information processing and urge consumer researchers to consider alternative approaches.

ALTERNATIVES TO THE MODAL VIEW: MODELS OF EMBODIED COGNITION

So how might memory be structured and operate if it were not an associative semantic network? What other type of memory system might provide a better account of the broad range of consumer behaviors which the modal view has so much difficulty explaining? This paper introduces some of the basic features of two leading models of the newly emerging theory of embodied cognition and proposes that consumer researchers consider embodied cognition as a possible alternative to the modal view[1].

Recently developed models of embodied cognition represent a whole new class of alternative memory theories which propose a completely different basis for the structure and operation of the cognitive system. The theorists who have created these models have been motivated by the most basic questions in cognitive science, which until very recently had been neglected by most scholars in the field. For example, Glenberg (in press) urges the reconsideration of the purpose of the memory system and Barsalou (1993) seeks an account of the core concepts in memory that would be sufficient to explain human task performance. Each has posed a slightly different question based on his own specific research area, leading to some variation in their theories and in the terminology employed in describing them.

Despite these differences, models of embodied cognition subscribe to a number of core principles which together constitute a clear departure from the modal view and establish a new paradigm for studying human cognition and related issues. First, embodied cognition theorists (e.g., Barsalou 1993; Barsalou et al. 1993; Glenberg, in press) explicitly reject a cognitive system based on associated amodal symbols (linguistic labels linked by propositions) in favor of a system based on a more fundamental cognitive unit - perceptual elements - whose meanings are nonpropositional and are derived from being directly grounded in the external environment (for a discussion of the symbol grounding problem, see Harnad 1990). Second, embodied cognition models criticize feature lists (commonly found in psychological models, including the modal view) as inadequate depictions of concepts and, instead, place great emphasis on the structural aspect of mental representations. Third, compositional mechanisms ensure that embodied cognition systems are productive and thus able to account for novel conceptual combinations and creative thought. Fourth, as a result of all of the above characteristics, embodied cognition systems are extremely flexible and highly sensitive to context. Finally, models of embodied cognition propose a single conceptual system with a single process for all types of information. Some theorists (e.g.,

---

[1]Though there have been many other alternative theories of cognition, including, among others, exemplar models and connectionist models, it is beyond the scope of the present paper to review them here or to present a detailed comparison between the modal view and these alternatives.

Glenberg, in press) explicitly deny any structural or functional distinction between either short-term and long-term memory or between semantic and episodic memory.

Since the following two models of embodied cognition involve many complex issues and are still in the early stages of development, a brief introduction of their basic elements will necessarily appear somewhat dense. However, a closer examination of these two models[2] will illustrate their potential to contribute to our understanding of many perplexing consumer behavior phenomena.

Barsalou's Compositional System of Perceptual Symbols

Barsalou's (1993; Barsalou et al. 1993) theory of embodied cognition is based on a new view of concepts, conceptualizations and categories. Barsalou defines a conceptualization as a "temporary construction in working memory, derived from a larger body of knowledge in long-term memory to represent a category," which, in turn, is "a related set of entities from any ontological type (e.g., robins, sweaters, weddings, mountains, plans, anxieties)." A person's conceptualization of a particular category is extremely flexible and may change across contexts. Such categories may not be objectively correct or even accurate; they are simply a person's cognitive representation (perhaps largely unconscious) on a given occasion. In this view of cognition, Barsalou seeks to find a solution to the "ills of amodal symbol systems" by focusing on "the information in concepts that allows people to classify exemplars during perception, to process words semantically during language use, and to reason about categories in induction, problem solving, decision making and other forms of thought" (Barsalou 1993, p.30).

In order to develop a notion of the cognitive mechanisms which could produce such conceptualizations, Barsalou (1993) focused on three of their central properties: (1) Flexibility - conceptualizations can vary widely across individuals - due to individual differences in knowledge - and within individuals - due to the differential retrieval of this knowledge on any given occasion; (2) Structure - a conceptualization is a hierarchical relational structure, containing recursive properties, attribute-value sets, and structural invariants, and is constrained by context; and (3) Linguistic Vagary - verbal descriptions of conceptual content are inherently unprincipled, haphazard, and incomplete (rather than coherent, consistent and complete, as assumed in the modal view). The core concepts, or building blocks, in the cognitive architecture which Barsalou proposes and which can account for these three properties are *perceptual symbols*. This perceptual approach is a dramatic departure from the reliance on linguistic symbols and amodal propositions, which Barsalou notes is central to nearly every psychological theory (other than connectionism) for representing human knowledge.

A key aspect of Barsalou's (1993) system of embodied cognition is its constructive nature: "Selective attention extracts perceptual symbols from experience and ... compositional mechanisms integrate them productively during conceptual combination, imagery, and comprehension." Barsalou describes this mechanism in terms of frame theory, which accounts for the hierarchical relational structure of conceptualizations while allowing for the necessary degree of flexibility in cognition. In such a system, perceptual symbols constitute a "vocabulary of compositional elements" which can be combined (very rapidly) into novel representations in the form of "frames." Two kinds of frame structure represent knowledge of categories in this architecture: a perceptual frame and a

linguistic frame. The perceptual frame "represents the perceptual symbols generally shared by the exemplars (or instances) of a category, as well as the spatial and temporal relations between them," while the linguistic frame consists of an organization of linguistic symbols grounded in the perceptual frame. The process of composing such frames into temporary conceptualizations allows a person to follow the unfolding of perceived events, produce imagined events, and comprehend language.

The structure of conceptualizations and their component frames is a stark contrast to the feature lists which represent knowledge in a wide variety of cognitive models, including most exemplar and prototype models, episodic memory theories, and connectionist models. Since there is no structure relating the various elements in a feature list, such lists contain only independent fragments of a concept's content and thus "provide grossly inadequate representations of concepts" (Barsalou 1993). Moreover, representations must be able to capture the recursive nature of conceptual knowledge, i.e., the "process by which the content of a concept can be continually decomposed." In Barsalou's view, concepts contain multiple levels of hierarchical structure. Knowledge, then, can be viewed as "frames all the way down, with every component of a frame potentially decomposing recursively into a more specific frame"; the content of a frame will depend on the level of analysis. Such a system results in mental representations which are necessarily "dense, complex, and messy," but Barsalou believes that any realistic assessment of the content of human knowledge will take this form. While some cognitive production systems based on propositional networks, e.g., Anderson's (1983) ACT*, can potentially offer a viable processing account of frames, Barsalou contends that ACT* and other such models have not been developed to produce the flexibility and structure of human conceptual knowledge.

Glenberg's Meshed Patterns of Action

Glenberg (in press) urges cognitive scientists to reconsider the basic purpose of the human memory system and to adopt a new approach in theorizing about its possible structure and operation. Glenberg proposes a compositional system of embodied cognition which is similar to Barsalou's (1993), but places greater emphasis on automatic processes and the continuous interaction between properties of the external environment and an individual's physical capabilities. In Glenberg's view, memory exists to serve perception and action in a three-dimensional world and, therefore, mental representations must "support real, physical actions involving your body and the environment." Given this purpose, he finds the associations used in standard memory paradigms (i.e., the modal view) to be "theoretically empty" and proposes that they be replaced with the new concept of *mesh*. More specifically, "mesh" refers to the automatic combination of the spatial-functional patterns of the projectable properties of the environment with encoded patterns of action and the non-projectable properties of previous experience, stored as embodied representations in memory. Such spatial-functional (i.e., embodied) representations of patterns of action are similar to the previously described notion of frames (Barsalou 1993).

In Glenberg's (in press) model of embodied cognition, a conceptualization is a meshed set of patterns which satisfies spatial-functional constraints (not propositional constraints) imposed by the structure of the external environment, the structure of our bodies, and memory. As the environment changes, one conceptualization flows into the next; a particular meshed conceptualization will necessarily be constrained by the previous conceptualization, as in coarticulation in speech production when the pronunciation of a particular vowel is constrained by the

---

[2]A review of other models of embodied cognition and a comparison of their features is beyond the scope of the present paper.

previous consonant. In other words, patterns of action mutually constrain and modify one another. Concepts can become associated only if their separate patterns of action can be combined, or "meshed," given the above constraints; related concepts will mesh easily. Such a cognitive system is extremely sensitive to context and many concepts may exhibit only "temporary compatibility" with one another. The property which allows diverse concepts to mesh together and is the common denominator of meaning is that all concepts are based on coherent patterns of possible bodily movement, represented internally by analogical structures that literally fit together.

In Glenberg's (in press) view, memory has two modes of operation: automatic and effortful. The primary mode involves the automatic meshing of patterns of action and is driven by the environment, which ensures that cognition remains largely reality-based. Alternatively, memory can guide conceptualization by the conscious and effortful suppression of the overriding contribution of the environment. Such suppression is necessary in order for the individual to engage in thinking beyond the immediate situation, e.g., to consciously recollect from memory, to predict and plan future actions, and to comprehend language. Anecdotal evidence supporting the notion of conscious suppression of the environment is the common phenomenon of a person literally blocking out the environment (e.g., by closing or covering their eyes, looking up or away, etc.) when engaging in a difficult mental task.

In contrast to the modal view of memory, Glenberg's (in press) model of embodied cognition proposes a single, embodied, conceptual system of spatial-functional patterns of action which specifically denies distinctions between short-term and long-term memory and semantic and episodic memory. Though Glenberg acknowledges that a type of working memory does exist in the form of the currently active conceptualization of mesh between the environment and embodied representations, he argues that this does not constitute a separate system of short-term memory and does not involve any different functions or processes. The "illusion" of short-term memory is created by constant changes in conceptualization in response to action and is enhanced by the limits on coherent conceptualization at any given moment.

IMPLICATIONS FOR CONSUMER RESEARCH

This concluding section aims to show how embodied cognition principles may offer a viable explanation of many heretofore perplexing consumer behavior phenomena and will highlight some cases in which these principles have been discussed previously in the consumer research literature in the context of other theoretical paradigms. In particular, this section will focus on the potential contribution of embodied cognition to the following two areas of consumer research: (1) very rapid purchase decisions with limited external search for information; and (2) the case of impulse purchases.

Quick Decision Making with Limited Search for Information

Many consumer researchers (e.g., Hoyer 1984; Olshavsky and Granbois 1979) have observed that, contrary to the assumptions of economists and decision theorists, consumers typically make very fast purchase decisions, engage in very limited (if any) search for information and evaluate very few (if any) alternatives. It has been suggested (e.g., Alba et al. 1991) that such consumer behavior may be due to the use of memory-based strategies, which may give consumers the sense that they already have enough information to make a rational decision. The constructive aspect of embodied cognition extends this view by providing a more complete cognitive explanation for this type of behavior. In Glenberg's (in press) model, the constraints of a given situation would lead consumers to mesh limited contextual information with existing elements of knowledge stored in memory to construct a coherent conceptualization. If the current environment and conceptualization were to dominate thoughts of possible alternatives, consumers would feel they have sufficient information to make a rational decision. Only if the stakes were extremely high and time and resources allowed, might consumers feel a need to postpone the decision and pursue an external search for additional information.

Impulse Purchases

A related persistent riddle in consumer research has been the prevalence of what appears to be highly irrational impulse purchase behavior, in which consumers make spontaneous and seemingly choiceless decisions. Consumer researchers (Rook 1987; Thompson et al. 1990) have found that impulse situations are charged with affective feelings, produce an instant sense of rightness to consumers, and stimulate a desire to act immediately. The new models of embodied cognition may provide a reasonable explanation of this phenomenon and complement the many phenomenological descriptions of impulse purchase behavior reported in the consumer research literature. For example, a major theme in Thompson et al.'s (1990) analysis of shopping behavior is the notion of being captivated, which is described as "a perceptually oriented and embodied form of consumer experience... (in which) ... experiencing a product's charm takes priority over analytically evaluating its attributes" (p.356). In captivating situations, objects in the environment seem to dominate conceptualization; products are described by some consumers as not only "catching their eye," but also "jumping out," "striking," and "really hitting" them. In another study (Rook 1987, pp.193-194), consumers reported that impulse-purchase items "stood out from the rest" or formed a persistent visual image in their mind which would not go away until the item was purchased. Alba et al. (1991) have noted that the ease with which certain products will "catch one's eye" will be influenced by memory factors, which is consistent with models of embodied cognition.

A common impression (e.g., Thompson et al. 1990) is that in impulse situations consumers abandon their usually deliberate consideration of a purchase and ordinary behavioral constraints. However, the embodied view of cognition would argue that the usual and natural mode of processing is automatic, in which the current conceptualization is dominated by the external environment (especially by the target object). At that moment, projectable properties from the environment mesh perfectly with patterns of action from memory, producing an extremely coherent (i.e., seemingly "rational") conceptualization, strong positive affect for the product, and the feeling of captivation. The current environmentally dominated conceptualization creates constraints whereby the only compatible subsequent conceptualization will involve a decision to experience the item. In contrast, in order to deliberately evaluate an item, consumers must consciously suppress the contribution of the external environment by effortfully constructing counterarguments regarding such abstract concepts as the affordability and practicality of the item and the future consequences of purchasing it.

REFERENCES

Alba, Joseph W. and J. Wesley Hutchinson (1987), "Dimensions of Consumer Expertise," *Journal of Consumer Research,* 13 (March), 411-454.

_____, J. Wesley Hutchinson, and John G. Lynch, Jr. (1991), "Memory and Decision Making," in *Handbook of Consumer Behavior,* eds. Thomas S. Robertson and Harold H.

Kassarjian, Englewood Cliffs, NJ: Prentice Hall, 1-49.

Anderson, John R. (1983), *The Architecture of Cognition,* Cambridge, MA: Harvard University Press.

Atkinson, Richard C. and Richard M. Shiffrin (1968), "Human Memory: A Proposed System and Its Control Processes," in *The Psychology of Learning and Motivation* (Vol. 2), eds. K.W. Spence and J.T. Spence, New York: Academic Press, 89-105.

Barsalou, Lawrence W. (1983), "Ad-Hoc Categories," *Memory and Cognition,* 11 (3), 211-227.

_____ (1993), "Flexibility, Structure, and Linguistic Vagary in Concepts: Manifestations of a Compositional System of Perceptual Symbols," in *Theories of Memory,* eds. A.F. Collins, S.E. Gathercole, M.A. Conway, and P.E. Morris, Hillsdale, NJ: Erlbaum, 29-101.

_____, Wenchi Yeh, Barbara J. Luka, Karen L. Olseth, Kelly S. Mix, Ling-Ling Wu (1993), "Concepts and Meaning," in *Chicago Linguistics Society 29: Papers from the Parasession on Conceptual Representations,* eds. Katherine Beals, Gina Cooke, David Kathman, Sotaro Kita, Karl-Erik McCullough, and David Testen, Chicago: Chicago Linguistics Society, 23-61.

Bettman, James R. (1975), "Issues in Designing Consumer Information Environments," *Journal of Consumer Research,* 2 (December), 169-177.

_____ (1979), *An Information Processing Theory of Consumer Choice,* Reading, MA: Addison-Wesley.

Brown, J. (1958), "Some Tests of the Decay Theory of Immediate Memory," *Quarterly Journal of Experimental Psychology,* 10, 12-21.

Burke, Raymond R. and Thomas K. Srull (1988), "Competitive Interference and Consumer Memory for Advertising," *Journal of Consumer Research,* 15 (June), 55-68.

Cohen, Joel B. and Kunal Basu (1987), "Alternative Models of Categorization: Toward a Contingent Processing Framework," *Journal of Consumer Research,* 13 (March), 455-472.

Collins, Allan M. and Elizabeth A. Loftus (1975), "A Spreading-Activation Theory of Semantic Processing," *Psychological Review,* 82 (6), 407-428.

Gardner, Meryl Paula (1985), "Mood States and Consumer Behavior: A Critical Review," *Journal of Consumer Research,* 12 (December), 281-300.

Glenberg, Arthur M. (in press), "What is Memory For," *Behavioral and Brain Sciences.*

_____, M.M. Bradley, T.A. Kraus, and G.T. Renzaglia (1983), "Studies of the Long-Term Recency Effect: Support for a Contextually Guided Retrieval Hypothesis," *Journal of Experimental Psychology: Learning, Memory, and Cognition,* 9, 231-255.

Greene, Robert L. (1992), *Human Memory: Paradigms and Paradoxes,* Hillsdale, NJ: Erlbaum.

Harnad, Stevan (1990), "The Symbol Grounding Problem," *Physica D,* 42, 335-346.

Hintzman, Douglas L. (1986), "'Schema Abstraction' in a Multiple-Trace Memory Model," *Psychological Review,* 93 (4), 411-428.

Hoyer, Wayne D. (1984), "An Examination of Consumer Decision Making for a Common Repeat Purchase Product," *Journal of Consumer Research,* 11 (December), 822-829.

Huffman, Cynthia and Michael J. Houston (1993), "Goal-oriented Experience and the Development of Knowledge," *Journal of Consumer Research,* 20 (September), 190-207.

Isen, Alice M. (1989), "Some Ways in Which Affect Influences Cognitive Processes: Implications for Advertising and Consumer Behavior," in *Cognitive and Affective Responses to Advertising,* eds. P. Cafferata and A. Tybout, New York: Lexington.

Lakoff, George (1987), *Women, Fire, and Dangerous Things: What Categories Reveal About the Mind,* Chicago: University of Chicago Press.

Loken, Barbara and James Ward (1990), "Alternative Approaches to Understanding the Determinants of Typicality," *Journal of Consumer Research,* 17 (September), 111-126.

McGuire, William J. (1976), "Some Internal Psychological Factors Influencing Consumer Choice," *Journal of Consumer Research,* 2 (March), 302-318.

McKoon, Gail, Roger Ratcliff, and Gary S. Dell (1986), "A Critical Evaluation of the Semantic-Episodic Distinction," *Journal of Experimental Psychology: Learning, Memory, and Cognition,* 12 (2), 295-306.

Nedungadi, Prakash (1990), "Recall and Consumer Consideration Sets: Influencing Choice without Altering Brand Evaluations," *Journal of Consumer Research,* 17 (December), 263-276.

Olshavsky, Richard W. and Donald H. Granbois (1979), "Consumer Decision Making - Fact or Fiction?" *Journal of Consumer Research,* 6 (September), 93-100.

Ozanne, Julie L., Merrie Brucks and Dhruv Grewel (1992), "A Study of Information Search Behavior During the Categorization of New Products," *Journal of Consumer Research,* 18 (March), 452-463.

Peterson, L.R. and M.R. Peterson (1959), "Short-Term Retention of Individual Verbal Items," *Journal of Experimental Psychology,* 58, 193-198.

Rook, Dennis W. (1987), "The Buying Impulse," *Journal of Consumer Research,* 14 (September), 189-199.

Talmy, Leonard (1988), "Force Dynamics in Language and Cognition," *Cognitive Science,* 12, 49-100.

Thompson, Craig J., William B. Locander, and Howard R. Pollio (1990), "The Lived Meaning of Free Choice: An Existential-Phenomenological Description of Everyday Consumer Experiences of Contemporary Married Women," *Journal of Consumer Research,* 17 (December), 346-361.

Tulving, Endel (1972), "Episodic and Semantic Memory," in *Organization of Memory,* eds. Endel Tulving and Wayne Donaldson, New York: Academic Press.

Waugh, N.C., and D.A. Norman (1965), "Primary Memory," *Psychological Review,* 72, 89-104.

A Comparison of the Usage of Numerical Versus Verbal Nutrition Information by Consumers

Madhubalan Viswanathan, University of Illinois

ABSTRACT

The objective of this paper is to compare verbal versus numerical presentations in facilitating the usage of nutrition information by consumers. Verbal nutrition information, due to its descriptive nature, is argued to be used to a greater degree than numerical nutrition information, which requires a reference point in order to be interpreted. Hypotheses are developed and tested to evaluate this proposition. The results of an experiment suggest that verbal information may have several advantages in terms of weight given to brand information in making judgments of healthiness, accuracy of subsequent ratings of brands based on attribute information, and accuracy of recall of brand information. These advantages appear to persist even when numerical information is presented with summary information to facilitate its interpretation. This research demonstrates several advantages for verbal when compared to numerical nutrition information. Implications for consumer research on nutrition information in particular and product information in general are discussed.

Understanding how consumers use nutrition information is an important area in consumer research. Consumer researchers have examined how consumers use nutrition information presented on packages. In light of the new labeling requirements, several formats for presenting nutrition information have been tested including verbal presentations of nutrition information, and the presentation of nutrition information per serving of a brand along with the Daily Value (cf., Levy et al. 1991). The objective of this paper is to compare the usage of numerical versus verbal nutrition information. Hypotheses based on the proposition that verbal information is likely to be used to a greater extent than numerical information were tested in an experiment. The rest of the paper is organized as follows. Past research of relevance is briefly reviewed in the next section followed by a description of the hypotheses. The details of an experiment conducted to test the hypotheses are then presented followed by a discussion of the implications of this research.

REVIEW OF PAST RESEARCH AND HYPOTHESES

Review of Past Research

Numerical versus verbal presentations of information are of importance in the area of nutrition information as suggested by past research on these two types of information (cf., Scammon 1977; Levy et al. 1991). Past research on nutrition information has focused on the use of different formats, different types of reference information (i.e., U.S. RDA), or preprocessed information such as verbal information in facilitating the interpretation of nutrition information. Researchers have studied the use of different nutritional programs and different presentation formats in order to simplify processing of nutrition information by consumers (cf., Russo et al. 1986; Muller 1985; Levy et al. 1985). Some past research has focused on the effect of reference information and summary information. Moorman (1990) showed that the presentation of nutrition information with reference information in the form of percent of U.S. RDA increased ability to process and accuracy of comprehension. Levy et al. (1991) compared different formats for presenting Daily Reference Values. Viswanathan (1994) showed that summary information such as an average or a range can facilitate the interpretation of numerical nutrition information.

Research in consumer behavior on the processing and use of numerical and verbal product information has direct bearing on research on nutrition information. Venkatesan et al. (1986) suggested that numerical information derives its meaning in comparison with other numerical information and does not have any meaning by itself. On the other hand, verbal information has been argued to be more descriptive in nature (cf., Scammon 1977; Huber 1980; Viswanathan and Childers 1992). Huber (1980) argued and found that evaluations were made more frequently with verbal when compared to numerical information, due to the evaluative nature of verbal information. Viswanathan and Childers (1992) argued that verbal information is more descriptive than numerical information in that it conveys the relative location of a brand on an attribute in terms of highness or lowness.

Past consumer research suggests that some comparison process has to occur in order to interpret numerical information and understand its meaning whereas verbal information can be interpreted directly because of its descriptive nature. By directly conveying the relative location of a brand along an attribute, verbal nutrition information may be easier to use than numerical nutrition information. Therefore, in a setting where nutrition information is presented verbally on some attributes and numerically on other attributes, consumers may tend to use verbal information to a greater degree than numerical information because of the ease of using such information.

Some past consumer research has examined numerical and verbal presentations of nutrition information. Scammon (1977) compared nutrition information presented as verbal adjectives versus percent of U.S. RDA (e.g., "good" versus "35" percent of U.S.RDA on, say, the attribute protein content). The author found that the most nutritious brand was identified more accurately with verbal when compared to percentage information. The author argued that verbal information is relatively preprocessed due to its evaluative nature. Therefore it requires less processing when compared to percentage information which is relatively unprocessed. Viswanathan (1994), in a study that showed that summary information such as an average or a range can facilitate the interpretation of numerical nutrition information, also examined verbal presentations of information. Verbal versus numerical presentations with or without summary information were manipulated between groups of subjects. Verbal information appeared to have several advantages when compared to numerical information without summary information in terms of weight given to information in healthiness judgments, recall and recognition of brand information, and time spent on information. Such a pattern was not found for differences between verbal information, and numerical information with summary information.

The objective of this study is to directly compare the usage of numerical versus verbal nutrition information when information on some attributes of a brand is presented verbally and information on other attributes is presented numerically. Such a manipulation of numerical versus verbal presentations within subjects offers a way of directly comparing whether consumers use one form of information to a greater degree than the other. Direct comparison of the relative usage of verbal versus numerical information within subjects has important implications for consumer research. Situations arise commonly where nutrition information is available in numerical form on some attributes, such as on packages, and in verbal form on some attributes, such as in advertising or in a magazine like

Consumer Reports. In such situations, consumers may, in effect, weigh information in a particular form more heavily than information in some other form. Relative usage of one form of information versus another may best be captured using a within subjects rather than a between subjects approach. In a within subjects approach where consumers are presented with information in different forms such as both numerical and verbal forms, as opposed to a between subject approach, these two forms of information would be in direct competition. Therefore, these two forms of information could be directly compared in terms of the degree to which consumers use one form of information more than the other. Moreover, a within subjects approach is also realistic in representing many situations where information is available to consumers in both forms from a variety of sources.

The basic proposition tested here is that, when information on some attributes of a brand is presented verbally and information on other attributes is presented numerically, consumers may tend to use the verbal nutrition information to a greater degree than the numerical nutrition information. This proposition was evaluated by generating and testing several hypotheses.

Hypotheses

Several hypotheses were generated and tested to investigate whether verbal nutrition information is used to a greater degree than numerical nutrition information. Using a setting where subjects are exposed to nutrition information on several attributes for several brands and then complete several tasks, hypotheses about the weight given to nutrition information in judgments of healthiness of brands, accuracy of recall of nutrition information, and accuracy of brand ratings along attributes were developed and tested.

The first hypothesis was based on the rationale that, if verbal information is used to a greater extent than numerical information, greater weight would be given to such information in judgments of healthiness of brands.

H1: Nutrition information will be given greater weight in judgments of healthiness when it is presented verbally rather than numerically.

The next hypothesis was based on the rationale that, if verbal nutrition information is used to a greater degree than numerical nutrition information, such usage would be reflected in more accurate subsequent recall of verbal when compared to numerical information. Therefore, greater usage of verbal nutrition information was expected to lead to more accurate subsequent recall of such information.

H2: Recall of nutrition information will be more accurate when it is presented verbally rather than numerically.

Similarly, greater usage of verbal information was also expected to lead to more accurate subsequent ratings of brands along attributes, the basis for H3.

H3: Ratings of attributes based on nutrition information will be more accurate when it is presented verbally rather than numerically.

These hypotheses were tested in an experiment described below.

EXPERIMENT

Overview of Design

The procedures were similar to those used by Viswanathan (1994) in terms of the overall design and stimulus materials with a key exception. The experiment manipulated numerical versus verbal information within subjects in order to directly compare usage of these two types of information by individual respondents. Therefore, nutrition information was presented verbally on some attributes and numerically on other attributes. Subjects were exposed to nutrition information on several fictitious brands along several attributes for a product category with instructions to rate the healthiness of each brand. This was followed by judgments of healthiness of each brand (to test H1), and then ratings of brands along attributes followed by recall of brand information (to test H2 & H3). Furthermore, three groups of subjects were used; a group with no summary information for numerical information (the 'no-summary' condition), a group where the median of values or magnitudes of all available brands on an attribute was provided with numerical information (the 'average' condition), and a group where the maximum and minimum values of all available brands on an attribute was provided with numerical information (the 'range' condition). Viswanathan (1994) used a similar design and showed that summary information in the form of a range or an average facilitate the usage of numerical nutrition information. Such a design was used to compare verbal information to numerical information provided with summary information that has been shown to facilitate its interpretation.

Stimulus Materials

The product category, breakfast cereals, with four attributes (calorie content, sodium content, fiber content, and sugar content) was chosen from Consumer Reports (1990). This product category has several attributes that have implications for healthiness judgments, and has been used in past research (cf., Levy et al. 1991). The brand information presented to subjects is shown in Figure 1. Information on cereals was presented numerically for two attributes (i.e., calorie content and sodium content) and verbally for the other two attributes (i.e., fiber content and sugar content). Therefore, the mode of presented information was manipulated within subjects in order to provide comparisons between numerical and verbal information. Four fictitious brands were used. The highest value, lowest value, 75th percentile value, and 25th percentile value of all brands listed in Consumer Reports (1990) were chosen and assigned to each brand for each attribute presented numerically. This was in order to cover the range of possible values on each attribute and employ an equal number of brands that were above or below the median value of all brands in the market place. The labels 'very low', 'low', 'high', and 'very high' were used for the attributes presented verbally.

H1 predicts that greater weight would be given to verbal information when compared to numerical information. To test H1, the relative healthiness of brand information presented in numerical (versus verbal) form was manipulated between brands to assess the weight given to numerical (versus verbal) information in making judgments of healthiness of brands. Relative healthiness was manipulated by providing information on each attribute that was either above or below the median value for brands along that attribute based on Consumer Reports (1990). Moreover, above and below median values for healthiness were decided on the basis that lower fat content, lower sugar content, lower sodium content, and higher fiber content were desirable for healthiness similar to past research (cf., Levy et al. 1991). These relationships were also

FIGURE 1
Nutrition Information Presented in Experiment

Brands of Cereal

Attributes	Numerically Healthy (Verbally Unhealthy)		Verbally Healthy (Numerically Unhealthy)	
	Brand A	Brand B	Brand C	Brand D
Calorie content (in calories)	96	53	125	110
Sodium content (in mg.)	2	79	230	320
Fiber content	Very low	Low	High	Very high
Sugar content	High	Very high	Very low	Low

suggested to subjects in the instructions. The assignment of specific magnitudes or values to brands of breakfast cereals were such that, on two attributes presented numerically (calorie content and sodium content), two brands were below the median on healthiness (see Figure 1 where Brands C & D, referred to as 'verbally healthy' (i.e., 'numerically unhealthy'), had above median calorie content and above median sodium content) and two brands were above the median on healthiness (see Brands A & B in Figure 1, referred to as 'numerically healthy' (i.e., 'verbally unhealthy')). However, on the two attributes that were presented verbally (fiber content and sugar content), the assignment was reversed so that two brands that were above the median on healthiness on numerical attributes were below the median on healthiness on verbal attributes (i.e., below median fiber content and above median sugar content) and vice versa. Therefore, ratings of healthiness of verbally healthy (i.e., numerically unhealthy) versus numerically healthy (i.e., verbally unhealthy) brands were used as indicators of the weight given to numerical versus verbal information. Following the presentation of nutrition information for each brand, judgments of healthiness of brands were collected to test H1. H2 and H3 relate to the accuracy of recall and the accuracy of brand ratings along attributes, respectively. A rating task was used where respondents were asked to rate each of the four brands along each attribute. Subjects also completed a recall task where they were asked to write down brand information that they remembered.

Procedures

90 students at a midwestern university participated in the experiment with 30 students being assigned to each of the conditions based on the type of summary information. The experiment was administered using a questionnaire. Subjects were familiarized with the product category of breakfast cereals, and informed about the attributes on which information would be presented and how information would be conveyed along those attributes. Subjects were also informed that the information presented was based on Consumer Reports and had a high degree of accuracy, in order to minimize discounting of information due to factors such as credibility. They were also instructed that "high fiber content, low sugar content, low sodium content and low calorie content are generally considered as being good for health" and familiarized with the fictitious brand names. Additional instructions describing these two types of summary information were provided for the groups in the 'average' and 'range' conditions, using gas mileage of automobiles as an example.

Subjects were exposed to information on a brand of breakfast cereal on the four attributes mentioned above and then asked to rate the brand on several scales which were presented at the bottom of the same page of the questionnaire. Subjects completed four 5 point scales for each brand relating to the healthiness (5 point scale end-anchored not at all healthy - very healthy), nutrition content (5 point scale end-anchored not at all nutritious- very nutritious), liking (5 point scale end-anchored not at all - very much), and likelihood of purchase (5 point scale end-anchored very low - very high) of the brand. This was followed by a similar procedure for the other three brands, each presented on a different page. At the bottom of each page, subjects were instructed not to turn to a previous page in order to prevent direct comparisons across brands. Next, subjects completed five point rating scales labeled Very low - Very high where they rated each brand on calorie content, fiber content, sugar content, and sodium content. Next, subjects performed a free recall task where they were instructed to write down the information they remembered (i.e., brand name, attribute name, and value), and to write the value in any form in which it came to mind (i.e., in numerical or in verbal form). Finally, importance ratings for each attribute were collected using 7 point scales labeled Not at all important - Very important.

Results

Results of Ratings of Healthiness - H1. Mean healthiness ratings were computed for each subject for the two numerically healthy (i.e., verbally unhealthy) brands and also for the two verbally healthy (i.e, numerically unhealthy) brands. Responses to the scale on healthiness of brands (5 point scale end-anchored not at all healthy - very healthy) were used for this analysis. A 3 (type of summary information; no-summary, average, and range; between subjects) by 2 (numerically healthy (i.e., verbally unhealthy) versus verbally healthy (i.e., numerically unhealthy) brands; within subjects) ANOVA was performed on these mean healthiness ratings. A significant main effect of numerically healthy versus verbally healthy brands was obtained ($F (1,87)=54.26$; $p<.001$). Verbally healthy brands had higher healthiness ratings than numerically healthy brands (3.73 versus 2.74 on a 5 point scale). Stated differently, verbally unhealthy brands had lower healthiness ratings than numerically unhealthy brands. The pattern of results provide support for H1. A non-significant interaction was obtained between type of summary information and numerically healthy versus verbally healthy brands suggesting that the advantage for verbal information persists even when numerical information is presented with summary information to facilitate its interpretation.

Results of Recall - H2. Subjects in the recall task were instructed to recall information in any form they preferred leading to numerical and verbal recall of information that was numerical at presentation, and verbal and numerical recall of information that was verbal at presentation. The proportion of accurately recalled items for each of these forms of recall was computed for each subject. Accurate recall was computed separately using two different criteria; a lenient criterion and a strict criterion. Using the lenient criterion, recall was considered accurate when a recalled item was within one scale-point on either side of the original item based on a five point scale of the 0th, 25th, 50th, 75th, and 100th percentile value on an attribute (e.g., recall of "low" sugar content for a brand as "very low" or "neither low nor high" was considered as being accurate; recall of "125" calories for a brand (i.e., the highest value) as "very high" or "high" was considered as being accurate). Such a criterion for accuracy was used to allow for individual differences in the manner in which subjects translate numerical labels and also to allow for approximate rather than exact recall. Accurate recall using the strict criterion required a recalled item to be identical to the original item based on a five point scale of the 0th, 25th, 50th, 75th, and 100th percentile value on an attribute (e.g., recall of calorie content for a brand of "125" calories (i.e., the highest value) as "very high", i.e., the verbal equivalent on the five point scale described above, was considered as being accurate). The recall data was examined to identify accurately recalled items separately using each criterion and scores were assigned to each subject based on the proportion of all items that were accurately recalled.

A 3 (type of summary information; no-summary, average, and range) by 2 (mode at exposure; numerical versus verbal) by 2 (mode at recall; numerical versus verbal) factorial ANOVA was run on the proportion of accurate recall using the lenient criterion. A significant main effect was obtained for the mode of information at exposure (F $(1, 76)=14.02$; $p<.001$) with higher accuracy for verbal information (.69 versus .58 for verbal versus numerical information). The pattern of results provides support for H2. The interaction between mode at exposure and type of summary information was non-significant suggesting that the advantage for verbal information occurred even when numerical information was presented with summary information to facilitate its interpretation.

A 3 (type of summary information; no-summary, average, and range) by 2 (mode at exposure; numerical versus verbal) by 2 (mode at recall; numerical versus verbal) factorial ANOVA was run on the proportion of accurate recall using the strict criterion. A significant main effect was obtained for the mode of information at exposure (F $(1, 76)=17.51$; $p<.001$) with higher accuracy for verbal information (.36 versus .26 for verbal versus numerical information). Again, the pattern of results provides support for H2. The interaction between mode at exposure and type of summary information was non-significant as with analyses using the lenient criterion.

Results of Ratings along Attributes - H3. Accuracy of brand ratings along attributes used to test H3 were also computed separately using two different criteria; a lenient criterion and a strict criterion. Accurate rating using the lenient criterion required a rating on the five point scale to be within one scale-point on either side of the original item based on a five point scale of the 0th, 25th, 50th, 75th, and 100th percentile value on an attribute. Accurate rating using the strict criterion required a rating to be identical to the original item based on a five point scale of the 0th, 25th, 50th, 75th, and 100th percentile value on an attribute. The data was examined to identify accurately rated items separately using each criterion and scores were assigned to each subject based on the proportion of all items that were accurately rated.

A 3 (type of summary information; no-summary, average, and range) by 2 (mode at exposure; numerical versus verbal) factorial ANOVA was run on the proportion of accurate ratings using the lenient criterion. A significant main effect was obtained for the mode of information at exposure (F $(1, 87)=7.52$; $p<.01$) with a higher accuracy for verbal information (.85 versus .79 for verbal versus numerical information). The pattern of results provides support for H3. The interaction between mode at exposure and type of summary information was non-significant suggesting that the advantage for verbal information occurred even when numerical information was presented with summary information to facilitate its interpretation.

A 3 (type of summary information; no-summary, average, and range) by 2 (mode at exposure; numerical versus verbal) factorial ANOVA was run on the proportion of accurate ratings using the strict criterion. A significant main effect was obtained for the mode of information at exposure (F $(1, 87)=7.64$; $p<.01$) with a higher accuracy for verbal information (.40 versus .34 for verbal versus numerical information). The pattern of results provides support for H3. The interaction between mode at exposure and type of summary information was non-significant as with the analyses based on the lenient criterion.

Discussion of Results

All the hypotheses were supported by the findings. The pattern of results suggest that the provision of nutrition information in a verbal form when compared to a numerical form leads to several advantages in terms of weight given to brand information in making judgments of healthiness, accuracy of subsequent ratings of brands based on attribute information, and accuracy of recall of brand information. These advantages appear to persist even when numerical information is presented with summary information to facilitate its interpretation.

An alternate explanation of the findings in light of the design is that the two attributes presented verbally were more important than the two attributes presented numerically, hence the greater usage of verbal nutrition information. However, in choosing attributes for the study, attributes that were of relevance in making judgments of healthiness were chosen, therefore, all four attributes were likely to be of comparable importance. Importance ratings for each attribute were collected at the end of the study using 7 point scales labeled Not at all important - Very important. These ratings were examined to explore the alternate explanation and appeared to be comparable for the four attributes; 4.02 for calorie content (presented numerically), 5.08 for sugar content (presented numerically), 5.16 for sodium content (presented verbally), and 5.34 for fiber content (presented verbally). A possible exception here is calorie content (presented numerically) which has a somewhat lower rating. However, it is unlikely that this difference in attribute importance in itself influenced the results in terms of a consistent advantage for verbal information across several variables.

GENERAL DISCUSSION

The primary objective of this paper was to compare verbal versus numerical presentations in facilitating the usage of nutrition information. Verbal nutrition information, due to its descriptive nature, was argued to be used to a greater degree than numerical nutrition information, which requires a reference point in order to be interpreted. Hypotheses were developed and tested to evaluate this proposition. The results of an experiment suggest that verbal information may have several advantages in terms of weight given to brand information in making judgments of healthiness, accuracy of subsequent ratings of brands based on attribute information, and accuracy of recall of brand information. These advantages appear to persist even when numerical information is presented with summary information to facilitate its interpretation. This research demonstrates several advantages for verbal when compared to numerical nutrition information.

Limitations of this study include the artificial nature of the experiment. In more realistic settings, nutrition information may be available to consumers on a larger number of attributes than were used in the experiment. Furthermore, additional variables such as comparisons between brands on nutrients need to be studied. The assignment of certain attributes to numerical versus verbal conditions is a potential weakness of this design, although the importance of the attributes appeared to be comparable. The composition of the sample also restricts the generalizability of the findings.

In interpreting the findings of this research, the conditions under which an advantage for verbal information were obtained need to be examined. In the experiment described here, all information on an attribute was either verbal or numerical. Furthermore, judgments of healthiness of brands were made while subjects were exposed information. Although not limitations in a strict sense, these conditions should be noted in interpreting the results of this study. An understanding of the conditions under which there is an advantage for one form of information versus another could provide insight into the processing of these two forms of information. Different results may be obtained if, say, all information on an attribute is not of the same form, or if the task at exposure to information is different.

The limitations described above notwithstanding, this study has important implications for consumer research, both in the area of nutrition information and more generally in the area of product information. This research supplements past consumer research (Scammon 1977; Viswanathan 1994) that has shown advantages for verbal when compared to numerical information. This study also directly compares the use of numerical versus verbal information by manipulating the form of information within subjects. Verbal nutrition information, due to its descriptive nature, appears to be used to a greater degree than numerical nutrition information. Therefore, a key characteristic of product information that appears to facilitate its usage is the degree to which it directly conveys or describes the location of a brand along an attribute. This dimension of descriptiveness could be used to understand the processing of different forms of information by consumers. For example, numerical ratings on a generic scale, such as those used in Consumer Reports, are more descriptive than numerical information on a unit of measurement, such as calories. Such ratings convey the location of a brand more directly because they can be easily interpreted using the end points of the scale. On the other hand, % of Daily Value is similar to numerical information on a unit of measurement because the relative location of a brand on an attribute is not directly conveyed by this form of information.

For practitioners, this study suggests several advantages in the use of verbal information. From the perspective of public policy makers, the use of verbal labels to describe product attributes would require a high degree of preprocessing to develop judgments about highness and lowness on product attributes that could otherwise be made by individual consumers. It may be easier to provide numerical information along with summary information that facilitates its interpretation. Nevertheless, the use of verbal information to supplement numerical information may facilitate the processing of nutrition information by consumers (cf., Levy et al. 1991). Furthermore, the evidence suggesting that verbal information may be used to a larger degree than numerical information highlights the importance of norms for the use of specific verbal labels such as "light" and "green" by manufacturers. For marketers, this research suggests that consumers may tend to give greater weight to verbal when compared to numerical information under certain conditions.

Several lines of future research are suggested by this study. One line of future research should focus on the processes involved in using numerical versus verbal information. The conditions that lead to greater use of one form of information versus the other need to be studied. Such research may provide insight into the processing of these two forms of information. Further research is needed to understand how verbal versus numerical information is used in decision making, and how learning and memory is influenced by these two forms of information. Field studies using verbal versus numerical nutrition information would also provide insight into the effects of variables that exist in realistic settings. In conclusion, the study of verbal versus numerical presentations of nutrition information provides promising avenues for future consumer research both in the specific area of nutrition information and in the more general area of product information.

REFERENCES

Consumer Reports (1990), v. 55, No. 12, 1991 Buying Guide Issue.

Huber, Oswald (1980), "The Influence of Some Task Variables on Cognitive Operations in an Information-Processing Decision Model," *Acta Psychologica*, 45, 187-196.

Levy, Alan S., Odonna Mathews, Marilyn Stephenson, Janet E. Tenney, and Raymond E. Schucker (1985), "The Impact of a Nutrition Information Program on Food Purchases," *Journal of Public Policy and Marketing*, 4, 1-13.

Levy, Alan S., Sara B. Fein, and Raymond E. Schucker (1991), "Nutrition Labeling Formats: Performance and Preference," *Food Technology*, July, 116-121.

Moorman, Christie (1990), "The Effects of Stimulus and Consumer Characteristics on the Utilization of Nutrition Information," *Journal of Consumer Research*, 17 (3), 362-374.

Muller, Thomas E. (1985), "Structural Information Factors which Stimulate the Use of Nutrition Information: A Field Experiment," *Journal of Marketing Research*, 22, 143-157.

Russo, J. Edward, Richard Staelin, Catherine A. Nolan, Gary J. Russell, and Barbara L. Metcalf (1986), "Nutrition Information in the Supermarket," *Journal of Consumer Research*, 13, 48-70.

Scammon, Debra L. (1977), "'Information Load' and Consumers," *Journal of Consumer Research*, 4 (December), 148-155.

Venkatesan, M., Wade Lancaster and Kenneth W. Kendall (1986), "An Empirical Study of Alternate Formats for Nutritional Information Disclosure in Advertising," *Journal of Public Policy and Marketing*, 5, 29-43.

Viswanathan, Madhubalan, "The Influence of Summary Information on the Usage of Nutrition Information," *Journal of Public Policy and Marketing*, 13 (1), 48-60.

Viswanathan, Madhubalan, and Terry Childers (1992). *The Encoding and Utilization of Magnitudes along Product Attributes: An Investigation Using Numerical and Verbal Information*, Unpublished Manuscript.

Reliable and Valid Measurement of Memory Content and Structure as a Function of Brand Usage Patterns

Karen Finlay, University of Guelph

ABSTRACT

The measurement of product knowledge has been examined by a number of researchers using a variety of methods. Differences in usage patterns of consumers may provide an explanation for low overall measurement reliability in past research. This study examines the content and structure of loyal and non-loyal consumers' memory for information about soft drinks using a test-retest procedure. For loyal brand users in a category, cognitive structure is found to be unidimensional. The recall of brands and brand information is focused on the loyal brand, resulting in greater consistency of measurement between occasions. Conversely, the cognitive structure of non-loyals is multidimensional. Information that is most accessible in memory varies to a greater extent between occasions, moderating measurement reliability.

The content and structure of product category information in memory is a topic of growing interest to researchers (Brucks 1986, Gutman 1980, Hirschman and Douglas 1981, Kanwar, Olson and Sims 1980, Mitchell and Dacin 1995). Knowledge content refers to the amount and type of information stored in memory. Knowledge structure refers to the organizational properties of information in memory - properties describing the configuration of nodes representing concepts in memory and the links connecting these nodes. Analysis of knowledge content and structure attempts to delineate the concepts stored in memory about a domain and the way these concepts are configured or organized in memory. The content and structural properties of stored information may affect how consumers search for information and how they process and store new information.

Although several approaches have been used to measure memory content and structure, few attempts have been made to assess the reliability of methods used to measure constructs, convergent validity using the same or different methods, or the discriminant validity of constructs conceived to be distinct. Typical constructs involved in the measurement of memory may not be stable overtime, since new knowledge may be acquired. Nevertheless conceptual variables can be identified and are expected to be constant within a short time horizon, facilitating the worthwhile examination of the reliability and validity of methods used in the literature to measure constructs.

The few studies that have examined reliability and validity issues (Kanwar, Olson and Sims 1980, Olson and Muderrisoglu 1979) did not find strong evidence of measurement reliability or construct validity. Researchers have argued that the probabilistic process of information retrieval from memory and problems of information interference inhibit the potential for strong results. It may be, however, that additional factors moderate reliability and validity. The present research seeks to: identify reliable methods of measuring memory content and structure; examine construct validity of measures of content and structure; and explore the systematic impact of product usage history in limiting the potential for methods to reliably measure constructs.

The reliability and validity of three methods are tested in this study: card sorting (Gutman 1980, Hirschman and Douglas 1980, Marks 1985), free elicitation (Kanwar, Olson and Sims 1980, Mitchell and Dacin 1995, Olson and Muderrisoglu 1979) and category membership elicitation (Rosch and Mervis 1975). These methodologies will be described in detail in the procedures for the study. Table 1 describes the set of seven properties of the content and structure of knowledge measured in this research. Measures were chosen which quantify the size of the knowledge structure, measure the fragmented versus unified nature of it organization, and measure the extent to which information within the structure is categorized or grouped. It was judged these measures would be useful in identifying optimal communication strategies and positionings for brands within the domain. A discussion of which specific properties are of conceptual interest to the study of knowledge content and structure, however, is beyond the scope of this paper. These seven constructs include structural properties examined previously by Scott, Osgood and Peterson (1979). The reliability of the three methodologies is tested using the seven proposed measures of knowledge content and structure for the product class of soft drinks.

It is argued that the reliability and validity of measurement of the content and structure of product consumer product knowledge depends partially on whether a consumer is a loyal brand user (defined in this study similarly to Jacoby and Chestnut's (1978) "hard-core criterion", i.e. use 1 brand 80% or more of occasions) or a non-loyal brand user. An individual may use a variety of brands of soft drinks and hence, may be more receptive to perceiving and processing information about product alternatives and integrating it with information stored in existing knowledge structures. Consequently, the cognitive structure of such an individual may be rich and diverse. The likelihood that a non-loyal user will access the same product information from one occasion to the next is anticipated to be low, however, thereby negatively impacting measurement reliability for all methods and the validity of constructs measured by the same or alternate methods.

A loyal user of a single brand, on the other hand, may have learned overtime to tune out information unrelated to the habitually-used brand. A loyal user may therefore have limited knowledge of the category, stored in a more unidimensional, rigid structure. From one retrieval occasion to the next, a loyal user should be more likely to access the same product information, enhancing measurement reliability and validity. In this study, undergraduate commerce students provided measures of cognitive content and structure using a test-retest design. Differences in reliability, and the convergent and discriminant validity of constructs measured using the same and different methods are hypothesized and assessed separately for both loyal and non-loyal brand users.

METHOD

Choice of the soft drink category for the study was driven by the following considerations: i) the category must be familiar to an undergraduate university sample; ii) the category must be divisible into a variety of sub-categories; iii) a number of different brands must be available within the category; and iv) subsamples of brand loyal and non-loyal consumers should be available.

A considerable amount of time and effort was required to obtain all the measures necessary to assess each subject's knowledge content and structure in two separate sessions (combined duration: 2 hours). Consequently, the number of subjects in the study was necessarily small, consistent with sample sizes employed

Advances in Consumer Research
Volume 23, © 1996

by other researchers in the paradigm (Kanwar Olson and Sims 1980, Mitchell and Dacin 1995). Twenty individuals attending an undergraduate business course at a large, urban, university participated for course credit. Two sessions were held two weeks apart within a classroom situation. The two-week interval was chosen to allow subjects' memory of first session responses to dissipate, while limiting the amount of new information that might be naturally acquired about the product class as a result of advertising exposure or product usage. Subjects were aware that a second research session was required, but were told that this research was unrelated to that of the first session.

Procedures

The following set of procedures were used to measure the seven content and structure constructs using the three methodologies. At the first session subjects were given one-and-a-half minutes to "list all the brands of soft drinks they could think of". They were then given a set of blank cards and asked to write one of the brands they recalled on each card. Subjects were asked to sort the cards into broad natural groupings and to list the brands from each group on a sheet along with an indication of why brands were grouped together (card sorting). Subjects were then asked to re-shuffle the cards and form different groupings.

Following the card sorting, free elicitation was taken for four of the recalled brands - the first two brands the individual had recalled and the last two brands recalled. Subjects were asked to write the name of these brands at the top of a sheet and then write everything that came to mind when they thought of the brand. Free elicitation was administered after card sorting as it was feared that memory associations recalled about brands using elicitation might influence the number of natural brand groupings formed.

The second session was exactly the same as the first session until the point of the free brand elicitation. For the second session, the elicitation task was broadened in two respects: 1) the elicitation task was performed for all brands recalled by the subject ("everything that comes to mind when you think of the brand")[1], and 2) after free elicitation for all brands, category membership for each brand was elicited. The subjects were told that the bottom of the free elicitation page contained five lines and they were asked to write the name of a category to which the brand belonged on each line. The following example was provided: "For example, if the brand were Cheer laundry detergent, you might write laundry detergents, lower-priced detergents, and detergents that can be used in cold water". They were told to write categories to which the brand naturally belonged and not to be concerned with filling all five lines. After all elicitations, subjects were asked to use a 7-point scale to indicate how typical or good an example the various brands were of the various categories of soft drinks they had formed at the first session (questionnaires individualized for each subject). This provided a measure of brand typicality, hypothesized to be unrelated to measures of knowledge content and structure, for use in tests of discriminant validity of knowledge measures. A given brand may be judged a more or less typical instance of a brand grouping within a domain. Perceived typicality of a specific brand should be unrelated to the amount of information contained in a domain or how all brands within the domain are organized. The session concluded by asking usage and demographic information. On the basis of usage data, subjects were classified as loyal users if they used the same brand more than 80% of usage occasions; otherwise they were non-loyal users in the current study.

Hypotheses and Results

Measurement Reliability. It was hypothesized that reliability coefficients would be higher among loyal users than among non-loyal users for all methods employed in a test-retest procedure for all measures. Since loyal users are hypothesized to store less information in memory, the likelihood that paths to the same memory items will be activated between occasions should be higher for loyal users. Furthermore, information most accessible at any given point in time should be related to the loyal brand. Consequently, the probability that the same information will be recalled between occasions is anticipated to be greater for loyal than for non-loyal users, enhancing consistency of measurement.

Loyal and non-loyal users were equally reliable in the number of brands accessed or elicited between sessions as indicated by correlation coefficients (.774 loyals, .879 non-loyals versus, difference p<.23, Table 2). Loyal users, however, tended to recall more of the same brands between sessions (87.0% versus 74.5% same brands recalled for non-loyals, T=-1.91, p<.07). Brands accessed by loyal users tended to come from categories to which the loyal brand also belonged (54.4% of all brands for loyal users versus only 37.9% for non-loyal users, based on brand used most often, T=3.03, p<.01). Loyal users appear more focused in their recall of brands. The loyal brand was the first brand accessed 66.7% of the time and the first or second brand 83.3% of the time. Taken together, these results provide support for the hypothesis that the retrieval of brands by loyal users is cued by the loyal brand or influenced by the categories to which the loyal brand belongs, resulting in greater consistency in brands recalled between sessions.

The reliability of the free elicitation method was assessed based on memory item elicitation cued by the first two and the last two brands recalled by respondents at both sessions. For loyal users, it was anticipated that reliability in terms of the number of elicited memory items and the consistency with which items were elicited would be greater for the first two brands recalled than for the last two brands recalled. The loyal brand, with which the loyal user is highly familiar, was expected to be one of the first two brands recalled in both of the sessions. Consequently, memory items elicited in response to brand names recalled should be relatively consistent between the two sessions for the first two brands recalled. On the other hand, brands recalled in the last two positions by a loyal user were expected to vary to a greater extent between sessions. Consequently, lower consistency of items elicited about the last two brands between sessions should result for loyal users. Since brands recalled by non-loyal users in either the first two or the last two positions were expected to be equally random, no difference in the reliability of memory items elicited in response to the first two brand names versus the last two brand names was expected.

Overall, the free elicitation method appears to be a reliable instrument to measure the quantity of items stored in memory among both loyal and non-loyal users (.689 correlation coefficient among loyals, .745 correlation coefficient among non-loyals). Although loyal and non-loyal users were similarly consistent in the number of memory items elicited for the first two brands recalled (.799 correlation loyals versus .762 non-loyals, p<.42), loyal users demonstrated lower reliability in the number of memory items elicited per brand for the last two brands recalled than they did for

---

[1]Due to time constraints, free elicitation was not taken for all brands in both sessions. Instead, priority was given to obtaining elicitation for the first 2 and last 2 brands in an effort to determine whether measurement was more consistent for brands that were more versus less accessible in memory.

TABLE 1
Measures of Memory Content and Structure

Number of Accessible Brands
* number of brands recalled (unaided) in response to an overall product class cue

Number of Categories
* number of brand groupings that exist in an individual's memory for a product class

Average Number of Brands per Category
* the average number of brands in each of the categories formed by an individual

Number of Memory Items
* the number of memory associations recalled by an individual for the product class
* can include any of the following: overall brand evaluations, brand attributes, attribute evaluations, categorical references, advertising information, episodic brand information

Unity
* degree to which all brands in the product class are linked to similar memory items, ie. the extent to which the structure is unidimensional
* calculated as follows:

$$\frac{\sum_{i=1}^{m} c_i}{m.b}$$

where c_i is the number of brands linked to the *ith* memory item, m is the number of memory items, and b is the number of brands in the product class; a higher value indicates that all brands tend to be linked to a greater extent to similar memory items

Domain Dimensionality
* number of combinations of memory items which an individual uses to describe brands in the domain; calculated according to Scott, Osgood and Peterson (1979):

$$\text{Domain Dimensionality} = \log_2 b - \frac{1}{b} \sum_{i=1}^{cc} n_i \log_2 n_i$$

where b is the total number of brands recalled, n_i is the number of brands that are members of a given combination of categories, and cc is the number of combinations of categories

Image Comparability

* the tendency to store all brands in the domain linked to the same large set of memory items
* calculated according to Scott et al:

$$\text{Image Comparability} = \frac{b \sum_{i=1}^{m} p_i - m}{(b-1)(m+1)}$$

where m is the number of memory items recalled, b is the number of brands recalled, p_j is the proportion of the b brands recalled that are linked to the same *jth* memory item, and the score is adjusted so that subjects who recall more memory items receive higher scores

---

the first two brands recalled (.421 versus .799 respectively, p<.05), as hypothesized.

Loyal users additionally recalled fewer of the same memory items for the last two accessed brands between sessions than they did for the first two brands accessed (35.8% versus 61.5% respectively, T=2.18, p<.04, Table 2). Although loyal users appear highly consistent in the recall of memory items for the first two brands recalled, outside of items relating to the loyal brand, loyal users appear less stable in number and consistency of memory items recalled. The examination of recall for the first two versus the last two brands recalled supports the hypothesis that high relative accessibility of the loyal brand (recalled in first or second position at least four out of five times) heavily influences the extent to which the same items are recalled overall between sessions among loyal users.

The reliability of the card sorting method was assessed for the following measures: number of categories, average number of brands per category, number of memory items recalled, unity, domain dimensionality and image comparability. Reliability, when assessed in terms of the correlation in these measures between card sorting sessions was generally lower among non-loyal users for several measures, particularly number of categories (.681 loyals, .158 non-loyals, difference: p<.05), number of memory items (.648 loyals, .186 non-loyals, difference: p<.08), unity (.607 loyals, .099 non-loyals, difference: p<.05) and image comparability (.506 loyals, .016 non-loyals, difference: p<.05, Table 2). The assessment of the reliability of the card sorting method using reliability coefficients also confirmed generally stronger reliability of measurement among loyal versus non-loyal users. Among loyal users, the reliability coefficients for 3 out of 7 measures of memory content and structure were above the .7 level, while only 1 measure out of 7 was above this level for non-loyal users (Table 3).

Overall, measurement reliability using card sorting is stronger for loyal users but below acceptable levels for some measures

TABLE 2

Reliability Results and Means by Subsegments

	Correlation C-S 1 vs C-S 2				Mean Performance		T-Test Loyal/vs. Non-Loyal	
	Total	Loyal	Non-Loyal		Loyal	Non-loyal	t value	p
Measures of Content and Structure:								
# categories	.458*	.681*b	.158b		7.16	6.95	.03	.80
Avg.# brands/category	.307	.315	.325		2.93	3.58	-2.70	.02
% same categories					44.2	61.6	1.79	.11
# memory items	.516*	.648*	.186		7.74	8.60	-1.78	.09
% same					38.4	44.3	- .67	.40
Unity	.401	.607*b	.099b		0.301	0.280	.47	.32
Domain Dimensionality	.475*	.182	.431		2.335	2.902	-2.91	.01
Image Comparability	.264	.506**b	.016b		0.183	0.135	1.79	.05
Free Brand Elicitation								
# brands accessed	.795*	.774*	.879*		11.10	12.50	-3.24	.00
% same					87.0	74.5	-1.91	.07
Unity	n/a	n/a	n/a		0.155	0.122	2.00	.03
Domain Dimensionality	n/a	n/a	n/a		2.576	3.074	-3.08	.00
Image Comparability	n/a	n/a	n/a		0.072	0.040	1.78	.05

	Total	Loyals	Non-Loyals	T-Test	
% same memory items					
First 2 brands	64.7	61.5	69.3	- .56	.58
Last 2 brands	48.7	35.8	55.0	-1.28	.22
Correlation E1 vs E2 - all brands	.704*	.689*	.745*		
- first 2 brands	.780*	.799*c	.762*c		
- last 2 brands	.479*	.421 c	.645**c		

Note. C-S 1 and C-S 2 are results from the card sorting at the first and second sessions respectively
E1 and E2 are results from the free elicitation at the first and second sessions respectively
* significantly different from zero at $\alpha < .05$, two-tailed test
** significantly different from zero at $\alpha < .05$, one-tailed test
b-b difference significant loyal versus non-loyal at $\alpha < .10$
c-c difference significant between elicitation for first two versus last two brands at $\alpha < .05$

(particularly domain dimensionality and image comparability), even among this group. Reliability of measure using card sorting is alarmingly low for non-loyal users for several measures (reliability coefficients: number of categories .22, number of memory items .39, unity .13 and image comparability .07. Future research should consider limitations in measurement reliability using card sorting.

Free elicitation, on the other hand, did produce acceptable reliability results overall among both loyal and non-loyal users, as discussed earlier, for the two measures of memory content tested (# of brands accessed and memory item elicitation). Free elicitation, therefore, appears a strong method for measuring information content stored in memory. Future research should confirm if its strength extends to the reliable measurement of properties of memory structure.

Convergent Validity. It was hypothesized that strong convergence would result for variables measured by different methods among loyal users. Values in the validity diagonal (same variables measured by different methods) of the multitrait-multimethod matrices in Table 3 confirmed that reasonable convergence (.56 to .75 inter-item correlations) between methods was obtained among loyal users for all but two measures, domain dimensionality (.24) and image comparability (.14). Domain dimensionality and image comparability had been the two measures not reliably measured among loyal users using the card sorting method. Low reliability of measurement for one method would explain low convergence results between methods.

Further evidence of convergent validity would be provided if inter-item correlations obtained between the same variable mea-

TABLE 3
Multitrait-Multimethod Matrix

Card Sorting	Card Sorting						
	AB Elic. only	CAT	BR/CAT	MI	UN	DD	IC
CAT	n/a	P:R .62 / .81 .22					
BR/CAT	n/a	P:NP .31 / .48 -.00	P:R .45 / .48 .42				
MI	n/a	P:PC .75 / .80 .68	P:NP .54 / .59 .46	P:R .68 / .80 .39			
UN	n/a	P:NP .35 / .49 .06	P:NP .35 / .40 .32	P:NP .43 / .51 .24	P:R .51 / .70 .13		
DD	n/a	P:PC .67 / .70 .64	P:NP .40 / .34 .45	P:PC .62 / .62 .64	P:NC .18 / .00 .23	P:R .52 / .44 .54	
IC	n/a	P:NP .27 / .44 .09	P:NP .38 / .36 .38	P:NP .44 / .52 .24	P:PC .67 / .73 .58	P:NC .20 / .11 .27	P:R .05 / .32 .07
BT	n/a	P:NP .55 / .66 .33	P:NP .45 / .52 .40	P:NP .50 / .54 .45	P:I .04 / .05 .04	P:I .44 / -.13 .63	P:I .09 / .09 .09
Elicitation							
AB	P:R .84 / .84 .94						
CAT	P:NP .60 / .63 .53	P:PC .14 / .67 -.66					
BR/CAT	P:NP .68 / .66 .77	P:NP .20 / .62 -.39	P:PC .35 / .56 -.01				
MI	P:NP .60 / .60 .58	P:PC .56 / .65 .39	P:NP .39 / .51 .19	P:PC .44 / .59 .11			
UN	P:NP .62 / .62 .70	P:NP .08 / .50 -.54	P:NP .29 / .47 -.04	P:NP .35 / .48 .08	P:PC .55 / .67 .19		
DD	P:NP .68 / .66 .75	P:PC .33 / .62 -.28	P:NP .49 / .55 .44	P:PC .43 / .52 .24	P:NC .35 / -.46 .37	P:PC .58 / .24 .59	
IC	P:NP .63 / .62 .70	P:NP -.13 / .33 -.53	P:NP .30 / .44 .06	P:NP .40 / .47 .16	P:PC .66 / .76 .36	P:NC .33 / .05 .40	P:PC .04 / .14 -.47
BT	P:NP .62 / .60 .71	P:NP -.01 / .67 -.24	P:NP .48 / .77 -.53	P:NP .04 / .04 .02	P:I .00 / .08 -.08	P:I -.01 / -.59 .28	P:I .04 / .11 -.05

Note. The first information displayed in the cell is the prediction, to the right of which is results for the sample overall; the second line of the cell first displays results for loyal users and then non-loyal users; AB = # of brands accessed; CAT = # of categories; BR/CAT = average number of brands per category; MI = number of memory items; UN = unity; DD = domain dimensionality; IC = image comparability; BT = brand typicality. P: indicates the prediction for the cell. All predictions are for loyal users only. R indicates a prediction of reliability of measurement; PC indicates positive convergence; NC indicates negative convergence; I of indicates a prediction of independence or no convergence and NP indicates no prediction for that cell.

---

sured by different methods were higher than the inter-item correlations between that variable and any other variable measured by the same method or by a different method. For loyal users, values in the validity diagonal (same variables measured by different methods) tended to be higher than values in adjacent columns or rows (i.e. when compared to a different variable measured by a different method), and higher than correlations between different variables using the same method. These results provide further evidence of convergent validity among loyal users. Among non-loyal users, similar analyses do not provide evidence of convergent validity. Because reliability of measurement was so low for this group, however, it is impossible to know whether lack of convergence actually exists or is a by-product of low reliability.

Additional evidence of convergent validity can be found by examining results for specific measures expected to positively and negatively converge. Positive convergence had been expected among measures describing the number of categories of brands reported, the number of memory items and domain dimensionality. As more categories are formed in a domain, more memory associations should be stored which describe or rationalize the basis for categorization. Similarly, as the number of categories and the number of memory items in a domain increase, so should domain dimensionality, or the number of combinations of memory items used to describe a domain. Among loyal users, strong positive convergence resulted among these 3 measures, with an average inter-item correlation of .70 (.62 to .80 range) when the same method was used and an average inter-item correlation of .61 (.52 to .66 range) when different methods were used (Table 3). Comparable average correlations were much lower for non-loyal users (.61 same method; .12 different methods).

It was hypothesized that negative convergence would result between domain dimensionality and unity and between domain dimensionality and image comparability, particularly among loyal users. Unity and image comparability describe the unidimensionality of cognitive structure, while domain dimensionality describes its fragmentation. Using the same method, inter-item correlations among loyal users between domain dimensionality and unity and domain dimensionality and image comparability were .00 and .11 respectively, while using different methods they were -.46 and .05. While not providing strong evidence of an inverse relationship between variables, evidence of lack of convergence is encouraging.

Discriminant Validity. Evidence of discriminant validity was expected in the form lack of strong positive or strong negative intercorrelations between mean brand typicality and each of three properties of memory structure - unity, domain dimensionality and image comparability, when measured by the same or different method. Brand typicality was therefore expected to be unrelated to measures of knowledge structure. Inter-item correlations of brand typicality with these three properties of cognitive structure among loyal users were .05 -.13 and .09 when the same method was used, and .08, -.59 and .11 when different methods were used (Table 3). Evidence of independence is therefore found in five out of six cases.

CONCLUSIONS AND IMPLICATIONS

Several conclusions can be drawn from the reliability and validity analysis performed on data from this study. First, it appears, that loyal users can be more reliably measured than non-loyal users using either card sorting or elicitation methods. Based on the measures analyzed using free elicitation in this study, this method more reliably measures constructs than does card sorting. The reliability of the card sorting method was unacceptably low for some measures, even among loyal users.

Card sorting, as executed by researchers previously in the literature and in this study, does not appear to be a reliable or valid method to measure knowledge content and structure, particularly among users of a variety of brands in a category. The card sorting method, where all brands are sorted into exclusive groupings may force subjects to form categories that may not naturally exist within their cognitive structure, thereby inhibiting the potential for reliable measurement. A more natural brand grouping task for respondents may be one where a group of brands can be chosen from the pool of accessed brands without the need to group and label all remaining brands in the pool each time a group is chosen. This finding is also of relevance for market researchers in the field who frequently use card sorting as a facilitating technique in qualitative research.

Despite the fact that measurement reliability using card sorting was limited, convergence between card sorting and elicitation methods was found among loyal users for measures expected to be positively related. Preliminary discriminant validity results were also promising among loyal users. Taken together, the pattern of convergent and discriminant validity establishes support for construct validity, at least among loyal users. Contributions of this research fall in two areas. First, it has provided a better understanding of how individual usage differences can affect the reliability of measurement of memory content and structure constructs. Non-loyal users appear to less consistently retrieve the same information and the same amount of information between occasions than do loyal users. If an individual uses multiple brands in a category, the probability that information about the same brand will have been most recently activated in memory between occasions will be reduced. When asked to recall information about a category, the entry point into the network of stored information is likely to be the most recently used brand or the brand for which an ad was most recently seen and processed. Activation will spread to adjacent items in memory from the first activated brand into the stored

structure of information. If the most recently activated brand is different between occasions for non-loyal users, the subset of information recalled from the domain is more likely to differ.

Loyal users, on the other hand, will be more likely to have recently activated the same brand between occasions. The most recently activated brand will tend to be the loyal brand and loyal users may have been less likely to attend to, process, or recently activate information in memory about an alternate brand between occasions.

The second contribution of this research is the identification of methods of measurement that more reliably measure memory content and structure. When both loyal and non-loyal users are sampled, free elicitation appears to perform better than card sorting. Card sorting, as executed in this study with respect to the soft drink category, appears to be a less reliable method, especially among non-loyal users.

FUTURE RESEARCH

This study began the process of identifying reliable and valid methods of measuring knowledge content and structure. As with previous studies in this area, sample size was relatively low and this should be addressed in future research. Nevertheless, it appears that the loyal/non-loyal user dichotomy appears important to the determination of differences in knowledge content and structure for the soft drink category. More finite subsegments of category users should be examined in future research to obtain a better understanding of the potential influence of usage patterns on reliable construct measurement. It can be hypothesized, for example, that several homogenous subsegments of consumers exist for the soft drink category. Consumers loyal to a particular brand may be knowledgeable about a variety of other brands, but choose one brand on the basis of conscious preference. Alternatively, the loyalty of a second segment may be based purely on habit, with little awareness and knowledge of alternative brands in a product class. Non-loyal users may consciously choose from a preferred set of brands, or their choice may be random, based on little category knowledge. Finally, a subset of users might technically be classified as non-loyal, but subcategory loyal (regularly use brands from only one subcategory, e.g. diet colas). This latter group could be hypothesized to store information unidimensionally, similar to loyal users of a single brand. Identification of subsets of consumers with homogenous cognitive content and structure for a product class would aid in the refinement of communication strategies and further the examination of the moderating effect of usage patterns on reliability and validity of measurement.

REFERENCES

Brucks, Merrie (1986), "A Typology of Consumer Knowledge Content", *Advances in Consumer Research*, 13, 58-63.

Gutman, Jonathan (1980), "A Means-End Model for Facilitating Analyses of Product Markets Based on Consumer Judgements), *Advances in Consumer Research*, 8, 116-121.

Hirschman, Elizabeth C. and Susan P. Douglas (1981), "Hierarchical Cognitive Content: Towards A Measurement Methodology", *Advances in Consumer Research*, 8, 100-105.

Jacoby, Jacob and Robert W. Chestnut (1978), *Brand Loyalty Measurement and Management*, New York, NY: John Wiley and Sons.

Kanwar, Rajesh, Jerry Olson, and Laura Sims (1980), "Toward Conceptualizing and Measuring Cognitive Structure", *Advances in Consumer Research*, 8, 122-127.

Mitchell, Andrew A. and Peter A. Dacin (1995), "Differences by Expertise in the

Content and Organization of Knowledge for a Product Class", Working paper, Faculty of Management Studies, University of Toronto.

Olson, Jerry C. and Aydin Muderrisoglu (1979), "The Stability of Response Obtained by Free Elicitation: Implications for Measuring Attribute Salience and Memory Structure", *Advances in Consumer Research*, 6, 269-275.

Rosch, Eleanor and Carolyn B. Mervis (1975), "Family Resemblances: Studies in the Internal Structure of Categories", *Cognitive Psychology*, 1, 573-605.

Scott, William A., D. Wayne Osgood, and Christopher Peterson (1979), *Cognitive Structure*. Washington, D.C.: V.H. Winston & Sons.

Consumer Evaluations of Line Extensions: A Conjoint Approach

Moonkyu Lee, Yonsei University
Jonathan Lee, University of Pittsburgh
Wagner A. Kamakura, University of Pittsburgh

ABSTRACT

Line extensions have been a basis for strategic growth for many firms during the past decade. The viability of line extensions largely depends on how consumers perceive the new features of the extensions. This study examined how consumers differ in their evaluations of original products and line extensions in terms of behavioral characteristics, using an individual-level conjoint analysis. Of particular interest was to compare and contrast the effects of consumer characteristics on evaluations of line extensions with those of brand extensions. A within-subjects conjoint experiment was conducted which involved rankings of full profiles of original products and line extensions. The results showed that subjects' evaluations of the new features of line extensions were influenced by three behavioral factors: perceived brand strength, perceived typicality, and product usage. Theoretical and managerial implications of the results are discussed.

INTRODUCTION

Launching a new product is a risky endeavor because of the high costs of introduction and the low probability of success. One increasingly popular strategy for lowering the costs and improving the odds is to extend a well-known brand name to a new product. The use of existing brand names involves at least two strategic options: line and brand extensions (Aaker and Keller 1990; Farquhar 1989; Tauber 1981). Line extensions occur when the original brand name is extended by modifying features (such as flavors, sizes, or varieties) within the existing product category (e.g., *Diet Pepsi* or *Liquid Tide*), whereas brand extensions take place when the brand name is used to enter a completely different product category (e.g., *Clorox* laundry detergent or *Zenith* computers). Thus, these two strategies, although conceptually related, are quite different from each other and are expected to work in different ways.

Line extensions, the focus of the present study, are prevalent in the marketplace. According to *Gorman's New Product News*, 6,125 new products were accepted by groceries in the first five months of 1991. Of these, 89% were line extensions, 6% were brand extensions, and only 5% bore new brand names (Dornblaser 1992). From a company's point of view, it may be less risky and costly to use an existing brand name in introducing a new product with relatively minor changes. Although intuitively appealing and widely used, this line extension strategy does not necessarily guarantee success. Another study conducted by the *Association of National Advertisers* reports that 27% of line extensions fail (*ANA* 1984). As an example, in 1993, *PepsiCo.* introduced *Crystal Pepsi*, a clear cola with the impression of purity, to tap into a New Age mentality among young consumers. But the sales figures of this product have not been encouraging thus far (*Business Week* 1994). Industry analysts speculate that the company failed to impress consumers with any real benefits of the product other than the pure and natural image (*Marketing News* 1994). Then what determines the success or failure of a line extension? The *Crystal Pepsi* example provides insights into this question. It suggests that critical to the success of a line extension is whether or not consumers value the newly added features of the extension. If so, a question remains as to what makes consumers appreciate or reject those features.

This study investigates how consumers evaluate original brands and their line extensions using an individual-level conjoint analysis. Two brands and their extensions are examined. The objectives are: (a) to trace the changes in attribute importance from original products to line extensions, (b) to determine the importance weights of the new features of line extensions, and (c) to assess the relative influence of several consumer behavioral characteristics on the importance weights of those new features. These individual characteristics include (a) consumers' perception of similarity between the original and extended brand, (b) brand attitude, (c) brand knowledge, (d) product experience, and (e) product usage.

THEORETICAL BACKGROUND

Consumer Evaluations of Brand and Line Extensions

Recent research attention has predominantly focused on consumer responses to brand extensions. It has been shown that consumers engage in a categorization process when evaluating a brand extension, and that they use their affect associated with the original brand when they find a good "fit" or similarity between the parent brand and the extension (Aaker and Keller 1990; Boush and Loken 1991; Roux and Lorange 1993). However, as mentioned earlier, the distinction between line and brand extensions is a matter of type, not a matter of degree. A line extension typically involves modification of an attribute(s) of a current product. Therefore, it creates at most a slight or moderate level of inconsistency from its parent brand. From the standpoint of the categorization framework, such a level of inconsistency is likely to be filtered or ignored (Neisser 1976), and thus, the line extension is perceived to be "typical" of the original brand and triggers affect transfer from the original to the extended brand. If so, according to the categorization model, all line extensions should be successful. In reality, however, this is not the case as there are numerous examples of failure in the market. Thus, consumer evaluations of line extensions should be considered from a different perspective.

The Schema Pointer Plus Tag Model

The schema pointer plus tag (SP+T) model provides a useful framework for understanding how consumers evaluate line extensions. The SP+T model makes specific predictions about how information is encoded, comprehended, and recalled (Graesser 1981; Graesser, Gordon, and Sawyer 1979; Woll and Graesser 1982). It suggests that information that is congruent with schematic expectations is stored in memory along with a "pointer" to the generic schema that best matches the information. On the other hand, schema-incongruent information is encoded in a separate memory location and marked with a unique "tag." The model predicts that schema-incongruent information is particularly well recognized and better recalled in comparison with congruent information, since it occupies a unique space in memory.

Line extensions generally share most attributes in common with parent brands, with the exception of one or more features. Thus, from the standpoint of the SP+T model, these common attributes are encoded within the original brand schema with new, modified features tagged with them. It is expected that consumers pay more attention to and remember the new features better, and

TABLE 1
Description of Conjoint Design

Product Category	Original Product and Line extension	Attributes	Number of Levels
Laundry Detergent	Tide	Price	3
		Brightness	3
		Whiteness	3
		Stain Removal	3
	Tide with Bleach	Price	3
		Brightness	3
		Whiteness	3
		Stain Removal	3
		Extra Bleach	3
Soft Drink	Coke	Price	3
		Fizziness	3
		Sweetness	3
		Thirst Quenching	3
	Coke Clear	Price	3
		Fizziness	3
		Sweetness	3
		Thirst Quenching	3
		Color	2

thus, when they are asked to make their evaluations of a line extension, they rely more heavily on these features than on their affect associated with the original brand. These features become a focal point of the evaluations of the line extension. Therefore, the success of a line extension hinges on whether these new features are perceived as important and appealing.

The Effects of Consumer Characteristics on Evaluations of Line Extensions

Little research to date has dealt with consumer characteristics as potential determinants of line extension success. Research on brand extensions offers some insights into how individual characteristics affect the way consumers react to extended brands in general.

First, as mentioned earlier, many studies found that the "fit" or similarity between the parent and extended product has a positive impact on consumer evaluations of extensions (Aaker and Keller 1990; Boush and Loken 1991; Park, Milberg, and Lawson 1991). Second, Smith and Park (1992) empirically demonstrated that the strength of the parent brand is related positively to the market share of the brand extension. Brand strength or the equity built up in the name of an existing brand is operationalized by consumer attitude toward the brand (Aaker and Keller 1990; *Marketing Science Institute* 1988) or brand familiarity (Keller 1993). These two factors are also examined as potential determinants of line extension success. Finally, it has been indicated that consumer knowledge about the original and new product categories positively influences consumer evaluations because experts, compared to novices, tend to use more elaborate inferences to find a fit between the two categories (Muthukrishnan and Weitz 1991).

Two knowledge constructs have been conceptualized: subjective and objective knowledge (Brucks 1985; Park and Lessig 1981;

Park, Mothersbaugh, and Feick 1994). In the present research, in addition to consumers' self-assessed knowledge, product usage is included as an objective measure of knowledge.

METHOD

An individual-level conjoint analysis was used in this study to estimate partworths of each attribute level across respondents using rank-ordered data obtained from multiple conjoint tasks. The experiment examined two product categories, laundry detergents and soft drinks, where line extensions are commonly found. A brand was selected for each category: *Tide* for laundry detergents and *Coke* for soft drinks. Then, line extensions were chosen or created for each brand; the extension for *Tide* was *Tide with Bleach*, an existing extension, while the extension for *Coke* was *Coke Clear*, a hypothetical case. Finally, based on *Consumer Reports* (1992), several relevant attributes from each product category were selected for the conjoint task.

An orthogonal fractional-factorial design was used in the study. For each product category, the experimental task involved the ranking of two sets of full profiles, that is, 12 profiles for each original product and line extension. Therefore, each subject completed four conjoint tasks, which resulted in two sets of within-subjects rankings. In addition to the conjoint data, subjects provided information about their individual characteristics which were mentioned earlier. The profiles of the line extensions included marginal or additional attributes which were not present in those of the original products. Subjects for this study were 188 undergraduate and graduate students at a major state university. They were offered an incentive of four dollars to complete the questionnaire. Table 1 shows the design of the conjoint experiment for the two product categories described above.

TABLE 2
Partworth Estimates of *Coke* and *Coke Clear*

Attributes	Original Product *Coke* Average Partworth	Original Product *Coke* Attribute Importance	Line Extension *Coke Clear* Average Partworth	Line Extension *Coke Clear* Attribute Importance	Overall Changes in Attribute Importance
Price	0.279	0.729	0.011	0.011	-0.718
Fizziness (Moderate)	0.145	3.918	-0.072	4.685	0.767
Fizziness (Strong)	0.097		0.054		
Sweetness (Moderate)	0.198	3.271	0.080	4.379	1.108
Sweetness (Strong)	-0.148		-0.088		
Thirst Quenching (Moderate)	-0.256	4.655	-0.214	5.064	0.410
Thirst Quenching (Strong)	1.09		0.404		
Color (Clear)			-0.024	6.159	6.159

DATA ANALYSIS AND RESULTS

Based on the rank-ordered data obtained from the conjoint experiment, the following procedure was used to test the effects of behavioral factors on the changes in attribute importance. First, individual-level conjoint models were fit separately to the rankings of the full profiles of the original products and line extensions. With rankings transformed into ratings, which then were rescaled as deviations from the mean, a model was estimated by ordinary least squares (OLS). The model yielded unbiased estimates of individual-level parameters. Individual-level estimation allows arbitrary heterogeneity in the coefficients across respondents (Elrod, Louviere, and Davey 1992). Therefore, for each subject i within each choice set, the individual-level regression model of preference ratings, R_{ij}, of the alternatives j was given as:

$$(1) \quad R_{ij}^o = \sum_k \sum_l \beta_{il(k)}^o \xi_{jl(k)}^o$$

$$R_{ij}^e = \sum_k \sum_l \beta_{il(k)}^e \xi_{jl(k)}^e$$

where
- k = number of attributes
- $l(k)$ = number of levels in attribute k
- $\xi_{jl(k)}$ = vector of conjoint variables associated with l th level of attribute k in profile j
- $\beta_{il(k)}$ = vector of response parameters of subject i for l th level of attribute k

and $\sum_{l(k)} \beta_{il(k)}^o = 0$ for all k.

For both product categories, the effect of price was assumed to be linear and modeled based on a single variable, while the effects of other variables were assumed to be non-linear and modeled based on two effect-type dummy variables.

Second, the importance of each attribute, I_{ik}, was computed using partworths of different attribute levels. Then, the changes in attribute importance from original products to line extensions, DI_{ik}, were obtained from the differences between them for each individual. That is, for each attribute in both the original products and line extensions, the importance of attributes for subject i was obtained by:

$$(2) \quad I_{ik}^o = \max(\beta_{il(k)}^o) - \min(\beta_{il(k)}^o)$$

$$I_{ik}^e = \max(\beta_{il(k)}^e) - \min(\beta_{il(k)}^e)$$

And the changes in attribute importance between the original products and line extensions were given as:

$$(3) \quad DI_{ik}^e = I_{ik}^e - I_{ik}^o$$

The changes in attribute importance obtained from equation (3) served as dependent variables in testing the effects of behavioral factors. Table 2 shows the partworth estimates and importance of each attribute obtained by averaging estimates over all subjects for *Coke* and *Coke Clear* respectively; Table 3 reports those for *Tide* and *Tide with Bleach*.

TABLE 3
Partworth Estimates of *Tide* and *Tide with Bleach*

| Attributes | Original Product | | Line Extension | | Overall |
| | *Tide* | | *Tide with Bleach* | | |
	Average Partworth	Attribute Importance	Average Partworth	Attribute Importance	Changes in Attribute Importance
Price	2.262	2.262	3.558	3.558	1.297
Brightness (Moderate)	0.003	4.168	0.134	5.641	1.473
Brightness (Strong)	-0.309		-0.778		
Whiteness (Moderate)	0.168	3.729	0.540	5.309	1.579
Whiteness (Strong)	-0.518		-0.977		
Stain Removal (Moderate)	0.172	4.346	0.120	5.711	1.365
Stain Removal (Strong)	-1.202		-1.417		
Extra Bleach (Moderate)			-0.176	4.985	4.985
Extra Bleach (Strong)			0.556		

Finally, five individual difference variables were measured: (a) perceived similarity between the parent and extended brands, (b) brand attitude, (c) brand knowledge, (d) product experience, and (e) product usage. Except for product usage, all variables were measured with multi-item scales. Measurement items used in this study were excerpted from the previous research on brand extensions mentioned earlier.

Several principal components were identified based on the behavioral variables. The results of the factor analysis in Table 4 and Table 5 show that four rotated factors provided a good summary of the data, accounting for 96 percent of the standardized variance. The first component in both product categories was a measure of brand familiarity since it showed approximately equal loadings on brand knowledge and product experience. Product usage and perceived typicality were based on single items, while perceived brand strength was a combination of brand attitude, knowledge, and product experience.

Then, the regressions of DI_{ik} were run on the rotated factor scores of those principal components to examine the influence of the behavioral factors on any changes in preferences *between* the original products and line extensions. For both product categories,

four common factors were found: (a) brand familiarity, (b) perceived brand strength, (c) perceived typicality and (d) product usage. Table 4 present the results of the factor analyses for the soft drink and for the laundry detergent categories, respectively. Based on the factor scores of each individual, S_{iF}, the regression model was given as:

$$(4) \qquad DI_{ik} = \sum_{F=1}^{4} S_{IF}$$

Pooled regressions were run across subjects with changes in attribute importance as dependent variables and four behavioral factors as independent variables.

Table 5 reports the results of the regression based on equation (4) for *Coke* and *Coke Clear*. Analysis of Variance (ANOVA) results show that the importance changes in fizziness and color were significant. Furthermore, in both regressions, perceived brand strength and perceived typicality were significant in evaluating those attributes. However, it should be noted that the direction of the main effects was negative (cf. Aaker and Keller 1990; Boush and Loken 1991; Smith and Park 1992).

TABLE 4
Consumer Behavioral Variables and Factor Pattern

Rotated Factor Pattern (*Coke*)

	Factor 1 (Brand Familiarity)	Factor 2 (Perceived Brand Strength)	Factor 3 (Usage)	Factor 4 (Perceived Typicality)
Similarity	0.003	-0.012	-0.042	0.998
Satisfaction	0.395	0.913	0.017	-0.020
Knowledge	0.948	0.188	0.056	-0.034
Experience	0.841	0.413	0.106	0.051
Usage	0.090	0.022	0.995	-0.042
Cumulative Proportion	48.2%	69.4%	87.6%	96.3%

Rotated Factor Pattern (*Tide*)

	Factor 1 (Brand Familiarity)	Factor 2 (Usage)	Factor 3 (Perceived Typicality)	Factor 4 (Perceived Brand Strength)
Similarity	-0.015	0.032	0.999	0.016
Satisfaction	0.338	0.009	0.019	0.941
Knowledge	0.923	0.011	0.017	0.231
Experience	0.927	-0.051	-0.039	0.210
Usage	-0.025	0.998	0.032	0.007
Cumulative Proportion	44.9%	66.4%	85.1%	96.2%

TABLE 5
Regression Results (*Coke*)
Influence of Consumer Behavioral Factors upon Changes in Attribute Importance

Changes in Attribute Importance	Behavioral Factors				Analysis of Variance (F / Prob>F)
	Brand Familiarity	Perceived Brand Strength	Perceived Typicality	Usage	
^Price	0.475 (0.565)	0.736 (0.365)	0.865 (0.405)	0.542 (0.462)	0.65 / 0.62
^Fizziness	-0.030 (0.883)	-0.368b (0.069)	-0.60a (0.005)	0.125 (0.493)	2.65 / 0.03
^Sweetness	-0.005 (0.982)	-0.186 (0.372)	0.116 (0.601)	0.240 (0.205)	0.68 / 0.60
^Thirst Quenching	-0.442a (0.039)	0.023 (0.913)	-0.249 (0.265)	0.105 (0.581)	1.42 / 0.22
Color	-0.319 (0.512)	-0.859b (0.074)	-0.879b (0.086)	0.659 (0.131)	1.99 / 0.09

(.)   p-values
^   Attribute Importance (extension)—Attribute Importance (original)
a   Significant at the 5% significance level
b   Significant at the 10% significance level

TABLE 6
Regression Results (*Tide*)
Influence of Consumer Behavioral Factors upon Changes in Attribute Importance

Changes in Attribute Importance	Behavioral Factors				Analysis of Variance (F / Prob>F)
	Brand Familiarity	Perceived Brand Strength	Perceived Typicality	Usage	
^Price	-0.906 (0.251)	-0.571 (0.495)	2.033a (0.017)	0.931 (0.223)	2.18 / 0.07
^Brightness	0.101 (0.707)	0.134 (0.641)	-0.045 (0.877)	0.009 (0.971)	0.09 / 0.98
^Whiteness	-0.117 (0.662)	-0.375 (0.190)	0.359 (0.216)	0.228 (0.382)	1.01 / 0.39
^Stain Removal	0.182 (0.522)	0.134 (0.657)	-0.047 (0.877)	0.372 (0.178)	0.64 / 0.63
Extra Bleach	-0.352 (0.377)	-0.075 (0.860)	0.423 (0.326)	0.946a (0.014)	1.86 / 0.12

(.)   p-values
^   Attribute Importance (extension) - Attribute Importance (original)
a   Significant at the 5% significance level

Table 6 shows the regression results for *Tide* and *Tide with Bleach*. The effect of perceived typicality was significant for changes in price importance. For the other attributes, there were no significant effects of the behavioral factors which were common to the original product and the line extension. Unlike the soft drink category, neither perceived brand strength nor perceived typicality was found to be a significant behavioral factor in evaluating the marginal attribute, extra bleach. Only product usage was significant. ANOVA results show that the significant effects of the behavioral factors were found only for changes in price importance between *Tide* and *Tide with Bleach*.

DISCUSSION

The results of this study generally support the intriguing notion that the additional features of line extensions are not always valued by consumers, that is, they are valued or ignored depending on several behavioral factors. For *Coke Clear*, it was found that two factors had a negative influence on the valuation of the "clear" color: perceived brand strength and perceived typicality. This is somewhat counter-intuitive and appears to be inconsistent with the results of the previous studies on brand extensions. For instance, Smith and Park (1992) found that brand strength is positively related to the market performance of brand extensions, and Boush and Loken (1991) revealed that perceived fit between parent brands and brand extensions enhances consumer evaluations of extensions. Although these studies are not directly comparable to the present research due to differences in methodology and dependent measures, the results of this study imply that the consumer evaluation process for line extensions might be quite different from that for brand extensions. For *Tide with Bleach*, product usage had a positive impact on the valuation of the added attribute, "extra

bleach." The results from the two extension conditions, considered in combination, suggest that there are brand differences in consumer valuations of new features of line extensions. Thus, marketing managers should first understand how their brands are perceived by consumers when planning on a line extension rather than simply relying on the strength of the reputation of their brands.

Although the additional features of the line extensions were not selected on the basis of any theoretical taxonomy, some interpretations are possible by understanding the basic characteristics of those features. For many consumers, the clearness of cola, although not very meaningful or relevant, has a unique, pure, and natural image. The results of this study, however, indicate that such an attribute is not valued even by consumers who have a favorable impression about the brand name, *Coke*, and those who perceive the extension, *Coke Clear*, to be consistent with the image of original *Coke*. It is speculated that since *Coca Cola* has been in the market for a long time, consumers seem to have built up a strong emotional attachment or inertia about the brand, that is, they do not like to see any change in it. This is why *Coca Cola* company had to abandon its *New Coke* line and introduce *Coca Cola Classic* years ago. Consumers liked the taste of *New Coke* but did not consider it important (McCarthy and Pereault 1993). Carpenter, Glazer, and Nakamoto (1994) found in their experiments that consumers often value distinguishable, unique, but irrelevant attributes. However, specific brand names were not given in their studies. Their results might have been different if subjects were given brand names.

The bleach content of laundry detergent is a utilitarian or functional feature. It is also valuable and relevant to creating an actual benefit for consumers who use the product. Therefore, it is quite natural that this attribute is more valued by those who use more laundry detergent. The name *Tide* seems to be associated with function and performance, rather than any symbolic values. The results of this study are consistent with Park *et al.* (1991) and Broniarczyk and Alba (1994) in the sense that these studies underscore the importance of brand-specific images and associations for the successful introduction of brand extensions. Marketing practitioners planning on line extensions should make sure they add to or modify the feature(s) that match the image of their current brand. More importantly, they should keep in mind that the strength of a brand name does not always guarantee the success of a line extension since the evaluation of the extended product is determined primarily by consumer perceptions of the new feature(s).

From a modeling point of view, it should be pointed out that the estimation method used in this research does not allow the test of statistical significance of the changes in attribute importance. Thus, an immediate extension of the current study would be to develop a latent class model of line extension evaluations that can infer schema characteristics from the significant changes in attribute importance using multiple choice sets and associate the schema pointer plus tag model with consumer behavioral factors.

REFERENCES

Aaker, David A. and Kevin L. Keller (1990), "Consumer Evaluations of Brand Extensions," *Journal of Marketing*, 54, 27-41.

Association of National Advertisers, Inc. (1984), *Prescription for New Product Success*, New York.

Broniarczyk, Susan M. and Joseph W. Alba (1994), "The Importance of the Brand in Brand Extension," *Journal of Marketing Research*, 31 (May), 214-228.

Boush, David M. and Barbara Loken (1991), "A Process-Tracing Study of Brand Extension Evaluation," *Journal of Marketing Research*, 28, 16-28.

Brucks, Marrie (1985), "The Effects of Product Class Knowledge on Information Search Behavior," *Journal of Consumer Research*, 12 (June), 1-16.

Business Week (1994), "Does Pepsi Have Too Many Products?" February 14, p.64.

Carpenter, Gregory S., Rashi Glazer, and Kent Nakamoto (1994), "Meaningful Brands from Meaningless Differentiation: The Dependence on Irrelevant Attributes," *Journal of Marketing Research*, 31 (August), 339-350.

Consumer Reports (1992), Buying Guide Issue, 56, 12, New York: Consumers Union of United Sates, Inc.

Dornblaser, L. (1992), "New Product Totals for 1991 Soar Past 16,000 Level," *New Product News*, Gorman Publishing Co.

Elrod, Terry, Jordan J. Louviere, and Krishnakumar S. Davey (1992), "An Empirical Comparison of Ratings-Based and Choice-Based Conjoint Models," *Journal of Marketing Research*, 29 (August), 368-377

Farquhar, Peter H. (1989), "Managing Brand Equity," *Marketing Research*, 1, 24-35.

Graesser, Arthur C. (1981), *Prose Comprehension Beyond the Word*, New York: Springer-Verlag.

_____, Sallie E. Gordon, and John D. Sawyer (1979), "Recognition Memory for Typical and Atypical Actions in Scripted Activities: Tests of a Script Pointer + Tag Hypothesis," *Journal of Verbal Learning and Verbal Behavior*, 18, 319-332.

Green, Paul E. and Abba M. Krieger (1987), "A Consumer-Based Approach to Designing Product Line Extensions," *Journal of Product Innovation Management*, 4, 21-32.

Keller, Kevin L. (1993), "Conceptualizing, Measuring, and Managing Customer-Based Brand Equity," *Journal of Marketing*, 57 (January), 1-22.

McCarthy, E. Jerome and William D. Perreault (1993), *Basic Marketing*, 11th ed., Homewood, IL: Irwin.

Muthukrishnan, A. V. and Barton A. Weitz (1991), "Role of Product Knowledge in Evaluation of Brand Extensions," in *Advances in Consumer Research*, ed. Rebecca H. Holman and Michael R. Solomon, Provo, UT: Association for Consumer Research, Vol. 18, 407-413.

Reddy, Srinivas K., Susan L. Holak, and Subodh Bhat (1994), "To Extend or Not to Extend: Success Determinants of Line Extensions," *Journal of Marketing Research*, 31 (May), 243-262.

Roux, Elyette and Frederic Lorange (1993), "Brand Extension Research: A Review," in *European Advances in Consumer Research*, ed. W. Fred Van Raaij and Gary J. Bamossy, Provo, UT: Association for Consumer Research, Vol. 1, 492-500.

Marketing News (1994), "Consumers Show Little Taste for Clear Beverages," 28, 11 (May 23), p.1.

Marketing Science Institute (1988), Research Topics 1988-1990, Cambridge, MA.

Neisser, U. (1976), *Cognition and Reality: Principles and Implications of Cognitive Psychology*, San Francisco: W. H. Freeman.

Park, C. Whan and V. Parker Lessig (1981), "Familiarity and Its Impact Consumer Decision Biases and Heuristics," *Journal of Consumer Research*, 8 (September), 223-230.

_____, Sandra Milberg, and Robert Lawson (1991), "Evaluation of Brand Extensions: The Role of Product Feature Similarity and Brand Concept Consistency," *Journal of Consumer Research*, 18, 185-193.

_____, David L. Motherbaugh, and Lawrence Feick (1994), "Consumer Knowledge Assessment," *Journal of Consumer Research*, 21, 1, 83-99.

Smith, Daniel C. and C. Whan Park (1992), "The Effects of Brand Extensions on Market Share and Advertising Efficiency," *Journal of Marketing Research*, 29 (August), 296-313.

Tauber, Edward M. (1981), "Brand Franchise Extension: New Product Benefits from Existing Brand Names," *Business Horizons*, 24, 36-41.

Woll, Stanley B. and Arthur C. Graesser (1982), "Memory Discrimination for Information Typical or Atypical of Person Schemata," *Social Cognition*, 1, 4, 287-310.

Theoretical and Empirical Linkages Between Consumers' Responses to Different Branding Strategies

Aron M. Levin, University of Kentucky
J. Charlene Davis, University of Kentucky
Irwin Levin, University of Iowa

Different marketing concepts and branding strategies revolve around the image a brand has and its role in settings such as brand extensions (Aaker and Keller 1990; Broniarczyk and Alba 1994) and product bundling (Gaeth, Levin, Chakraborty and Levin 1990; Venkatesh and Mahajan 1993). Recently, marketers have begun using new branding strategies such as dual branding and co-branding in which two brands are combined on a single product. Because of their very recent status, these strategies have not been explored in the academic literature. This paper will describe how central concepts such as brand image and brand equity affect and are affected by the various branding strategies. In addition, we will develop experimental designs and analytic procedures to uncover the common and distinct processes in consumer evaluations of these different strategies. Finally, a demonstration study is included which serves as an initial exploration of one of the experimental designs.

Although each of the above strategies has unique characteristics, they all share a common thread. Specifically, they require consumers to make an overall product evaluation based on two potentially inconsistent evaluations. In addition, it is possible that consumers' attitudes toward one brand will impact their evaluations of the brand that it is paired with. Thus, our primary interest lies in exploring both how consumers integrate impressions of two different brands to make a purchase decision, and how one brand's image impacts the other's image. Our conceptualization of brand image is consistent with Keller's (1993) definition of "perceptions about a brand as reflected by the brand associations held in consumer memory" (p. 3).

OVERVIEW OF BRANDING STRATEGIES

Product Bundling

Product bundling is a strategy in which two or more different products are sold together for one price. A bundle typically includes a primary product and a less expensive tie-in product. Some examples are a cellular phone "free" with the purchase of a television set and a computer that comes complete with a printer. Although bundling has been studied primarily from a pricing perspective (Guiltinan 1987), it can also be considered a branding phenomenon. In some instances, both components of the bundle are the same brand (a Panasonic phone bundled with a Panasonic television), while in others the components of the bundle are different brands, such as a bundle that includes a Packard Bell computer and an Epson printer. Interestingly, past research has found that despite the fact that the primary product is usually worth considerably more than the tie-in product, consumers may place equal weight on each part of the bundle in forming evaluations of the overall package (Gaeth et al. 1990).

One implication of such findings is that a negative evaluation of one brand may have serious effects on the other brand's equity. Briefly, brand equity is the perceived added value that a brand name brings to a product (Farquhar 1989; Keller 1993). For example, when a low quality tie-in brand is bundled with a high quality primary product, the consumer's negative evaluation of the low-quality brand may be transferred to the higher quality brand (Gaeth et. al 1990).

Brand Extensions

Companies have long recognized that by capitalizing on their well-known brand names, the tremendous cost and risk of launching a new product can be reduced. By extending brands, a firm hopes to capitalize on one of its most important assets, specifically, its brand name (Aaker 1991). A brand extension strategy uses an existing brand name as part of a brand for a new product. Some recent brand extensions are: Ocean Spray candy, Reeses Peanut Butter Cup Cereal and Colgate toothbrushes.

Research on brand extensions has suggested that brand equity can become "diluted" when consumers are unfavorable toward the extension (Loken and Roedder John 1993). Interestingly, most studies in this area have found that unsuccessful extensions tainted consumers' beliefs about the overall brand only when the extension was *similar* to other products under the particular brand (Keller and Aaker 1992; Loken and Roedder John 1993; Romeo 1990). It is possible that comparable effects exist when consumers evaluate co-branded products, dual brands or product bundles.

Dual Branding

As a relatively new concept, dual branding has yet to be clearly defined. The term is commonly used to denote hybridized retailers utilizing a single location site (Nation's Restaurant News 1994). This strategy is increasingly popular in the fast-food industry, where a number of franchised chains have recently joined alliances with each other and created dual brands. For example, it is now possible to buy Arby's and Long John Silvers products in the same building. Dual branding may appeal to franchise owners because it extends their menus and gives the customer more selection. It is particularly convenient for families or co-workers who dine out, but cannot agree on where to go (Benezra 1994). In addition, this strategy may be an effective counter to strong competition by sharing costs and acquiring a more desirable location (McDowell 1994; Nation's Restaurant News 1994).

We foresee dual branding research developing parallel to our study of co-branding; assessing the impact that one brand's image has on the other in a dual brand situation. A recent example highlights the potential risks and benefits of such alliances. Earlier this year, the *Wall Street Journal* reported an agreement between Sears and Jiffy Lube in which the two companies would share space at Sears auto-service centers. The agreement allows Jiffy Lube to expand its current operations by 456 locations, and offers Sears an opportunity to shore up its reputation in light of consumer fraud scandals that rocked the company in 1992 (Patterson 1995). As with other branding strategies, the possibility exists that Sears' tarnished brand image may have negative effects on Jiffy Lube's image. Conversely, the possibility exists that if Jiffy Lube's brand image is sufficiently strong, it may enhance consumers' perceptions of Sears auto-service centers.

Co-Branding

As with dual branding, the recent emergence of the co-branding strategy leaves it loosely defined. Co-branding is the use of two distinct brand names on one product. The strategy has become very popular with credit cards (the Ford Visa card, for example) and food products (Betty Crocker cake mix with Sunkist lemon flavor) as a way of enhancing brand equity (Carpenter 1994). Similar to product bundles, co-brands typically include one component of the product that is more prominent than the other. Hereafter, we refer to these as *base* and *supplemental* products. For example, Ben and Jerry's Heath Bar Crunch includes a base product (Ben and Jerry's ice cream) and a supplemental one (Heath candy bar pieces). Similar to product bundling (and unlike dual branding), the consumer cannot choose between the two brands.

THEORETICAL FOUNDATION

A primary purpose of this paper is to consider the processes by which consumers evaluate brands used in various branding strategies. For example, in co-branding, we are interested in how consumers reconcile their attitudes toward two brand name products that are packaged and sold as a single unit. In the case of dual branding and product bundling, consumers may partake of one brand name product and avoid consumption of the other branded product. For co-branding, however, the branded products are virtually inseparable. In spite of differences with respect to separability and consumption of the two brand name products, we contend that all three strategies share common elements in that each relies on a brand's image to attract consumers and each features the introduction of additional information (and attitude objects) for the consumer to process and evaluate.

Our interest lies in whether consumers tend to *contrast* or *assimilate* attitudes toward two separate brands when they are combined in a marketing strategy. A contrast effect occurs when the evaluation of an object is moving away from a point of reference, while a judgment of an object that tends to move toward a contextual anchoring point is known as assimilation (Meyers-Levy and Sternthal 1993; Sherif and Hovland 1961). In this case, a contrast effect would occur if an unknown brand enhances consumers' reactions to a known brand *or* if a known brand diminishes evaluations of an unknown brand when they are part of the same marketing strategy. Conversely, assimilation would occur if a well known brand enhances evaluations of an unknown brand *or* if an unknown brand diminishes evaluations of a known brand. Research on brand extensions (Loken and Roedder John 1993) and product bundling (Gaeth et. al 1990) suggests that when consumers evaluate such marketing strategies, they often assimilate information. That is, a consumer's affect toward one element may be transferred to the other element. It is possible that consumer evaluations of co-brands and dual brands will parallel these findings.

A number of theories attempt to explain whether people will tend to contrast or assimilate pieces of information or attitudes (Martin and Tesser 1992). One theory that predicts assimilation between attitudes is known as balance theory (Heider 1945). We suggest that balance theory provides a reasonable explanation of the phenomena of interest, and predicts how consumers' separate attitudes toward brand names are reconciled in evaluating the combined brand package.

Heider's balance theory (1945) is one of a set of concepts known as cognitive consistency theories (Schewe 1973). Congruity theory and cognitive dissonance also belong to this set of concepts. All three theories hold that individuals seek to maintain consistency or internal harmony among their attitudes, values and opinions (Festinger 1957; Heider 1945, 1958; McCaul, Ployhart, Hinsz, and McCaul 1995; Okechuku and Wang 1988; Osgood and Tannenbaum 1955; Schewe 1973; Tellis 1988). In the branding strategies previously described, the potential for disharmony between attitudes toward the two brands is a significant consideration.

A cursory reading of the popular business press illuminates the importance of preserving a brand's equity. Companies are battling the value conscious consumer of the 90's by combining two brands in an effort to create the perception of increased worth of the product (Carpenter 1994). Pairing two brands creates the potential for linking a brand that has positive affect with one that has less positive - or even negative - affect. In the present context, balance theory would predict assimilation; if an unknown or less preferred brand is paired with a well known brand, the consumer's evaluation of the unknown brand may be enhanced. Conversely, and consistent with balance theory, we argue that it is also possible for the evaluation of a well known brand to be diminished when it is paired with an unknown or less preferred brand.

Because balance theory is concerned with the direction of attitude change, it is possible to predict outcomes of combining positive, neutral, and negative brand names (Heider 1945, 1958). These varying combinations can lead to different evaluations of the separate brand names as well as the resulting overall evaluation. Balance theory will help us interpret results of the studies designed to address the research questions enumerated in the next section.

RESEARCH QUESTIONS AND HYPOTHESES

We will describe procedures for addressing basic research questions such as the following:

1) How important is brand name as part of the mix of elements present in a particular marketing strategy? Is the presence of an established brand name the most important element?
2) How are various elements of a branding strategy combined in determining consumers' reactions to the strategy?
3) How does the overall evaluation of the strategy impact the subsequent image of the brand?
4) How do each of the above, particularly #3, differ across particular branding strategies? For example, is a brand's image apt to be impacted more by using it as part of a brand extension, dual branding, product bundling, or co-branding strategy?

Research questions 2 and 3 represent perhaps the key issues to marketers. Balance theory provides the basis for specific hypotheses. If a branding strategy includes addition of a brand that is evaluated unfavorably, then that brand will bring down the consumer's reaction to the strategy and will also damage the image of the brand that it is paired with. Conversely, if the added brand is evaluated favorably, then it will raise the consumer's evaluation of the strategy and will enhance the image of the original brand. Thus, we state the following hypotheses:

H_1: Evaluation of a co-branded product will be an average of the evaluation of the individual brands.

H_2: A brand's equity will be enhanced by the addition of a brand that raises the evaluation of the strategy; a brand's equity will be diminished by the addition of a brand that lowers the evaluation of the strategy.

The following is an illustration of how such research questions and hypotheses may be addressed for a particular branding strategy. Later, we discuss applications to the other branding strategies of interest.

TABLE 1

Mean Ratings of Brownie-Chocolate Chip Co-Brands and Component Brands

Mean ratings of co-brand

		chip brand	
		unknown	well-known
brownie brand	well-known	6.94 (n=17)	8.02 (n=17)
	unknown	6.72 (n=20)	7.88 (n=16)

Mean ratings of brownie

		chip brand	
		unknown	well-known
brownie brand	well-known	7.10	7.73
	unknown	6.52	7.58

Mean ratings of chips

		chip brand	
		unknown	well-known
brownie brand	well-known	5.88	8.00
	unknown	5.97	7.17

DEMONSTRATION PROJECT ON CO-BRANDING

To illustrate how the ideas expressed here may be operationalized and tested, a demonstration study of co-branding was conducted. Subjects were given a sample of brownie with chocolate chips to taste and asked first to rate the combination and then the separate component products. All subjects were given the same combination of Martha White brownies with Nestle's chocolate chips. Although co-brands exist in this product category with *two* well-known brands (Betty Crocker brownies with Nestle's chips, for example), an off-brand was chosen to minimize the possibility of a ceiling effect. Next, different subjects were provided different labels for the co-brand: Betty Crocker brownies with Nestle's chocolate chips, Betty Crocker brownies with Rich's chocolate chips (a fictitious brand), Mrs. Bakewell's brownies (a fictitious brand) with Nestle's chocolate chips, and Mrs. Bakewell's brownies with Rich's chocolate chips. In other words, we employed a 2 X 2 factorial design to manipulate whether the base product was designated as a well-known brand or as a fictitious brand and whether the supplemental product was designated as a well-known brand or as a fictitious brand. This design was intended to determine how each component brand affects the evaluations of the co-brand and, further, how variations of one brand affect evaluations of the other brand. For example, if ratings of the brownies are higher when a well-known brand of chocolate chips is added than when an unknown brand is added, this would be a demonstration of assimilation effects.

Procedure

Seventy students from two Marketing classes at a large Southeastern university were told they were part of a taste-test study. Each student was given a 2-inch by 2-inch sample of the brownies with chips to taste and was asked to fill out a response booklet. In the booklet, the co-product was labeled as one of the four combinations described above. The booklets with the different labels were given out in random order. Participants were asked, first, to rate the taste, quality, and likelihood of purchase of the combined product. Each rating was on a scale of 1 to 10 (The three scales were highly correlated and were thus combined for analysis with MANOVA). Subjects were then asked to rate only the brownie component and then only the chocolate chip component on each of the three scales. It was stressed that these component ratings were designed to obtain their evaluations of the single products separate from their evaluations of the combined product (co-brand).

Results and Discussion

Table 1 shows the mean composite ratings from the MANOVA (also on a scale of 1 to 10) for each combination of product label and each type of judgment. The overall MANOVA model was significant (F=2.3, Wilks' (=.748, p<.03). Ratings of the composite co-brand (top of Table 1) show that the labeling of the supplemental product (chocolate chips) actually had a larger effect than the labeling of the base product (brownie mix). In fact, only the supplemental product label had a statistically significant effect on the ratings of the composite co-brand, F(1, 66)=4.40, p<.05.

Ratings of the base product, interestingly enough, were also affected more by the labeling of the supplemental product than by the labeling of the base product itself. Substituting a fictitious brand name for the supplemental product apparently affected the evaluations of the base product. The effect of the supplemental product label, in this case, was of borderline statistical significance, F(1,66)=2.75, p=.10. Finally, as seen at the bottom of Table 1, ratings of the supplemental product were greatly affected by its labeling and this effect was statistically significant, F(1,66)=6.75, p<.01.

It is important to note here that these effects were demonstrated with relatively modest sample size and, more importantly, *without varying the actual product experience*. Participants in the different conditions tasted the same co-branded product; only the brand names were varied. These labeling effects are reminiscent of the framing effect found by Levin and Gaeth (1988) where ground beef labeled as "75% lean" was evaluated more favorably than ground beef labeled as "25% fat", despite the fact that all subjects tasted the same ground beef.

Even larger effects would be expected if, for example, the actual quality of the supplemental product was varied. More important than showing that labels affect evaluations of the composite co-branded product was showing that *one brand's label affects evaluations of its co-brand*. It is an empirical question as to whether other supplemental brands will have the same effect as chocolate chips in brownies. Future research should also include a control group who evaluates the separate products without experiencing them in combination. Nevertheless, this demonstration showed that brand image can be affected by the co-branding strategy in a manner consistent with balance theory; when one brand (chocolate chips) was thought to be inferior, it brought down both the evaluations of the composite product and the evaluations of the other brand (brownie mix). Recall that studies of product bundling found that even an inexpensive tie-in product can have a disproportionate influence on evaluations of the bundle (Gaeth et al., 1990). Given the similarity of the present findings to earlier studies of product bundling, an empirical link seems to be established between bundling and co-branding. In general, however, studies of product bundling have not included measures of the impact on the image of the primary product. Future studies should include such measures.

RESEARCH EXTENSIONS

The basic features of the demonstration project on co-branding were: 1) factorially manipulating some characteristic of both brands; 2) asking subjects to rate the combined product; and 3) asking subjects to rate each component product separately. These basic design and measurement features can be extended to assess consumers' reactions to other branding strategies.

For dual branding, consider a pizza parlor and an ice cream/frozen yogurt shop housed together. The pizza parlor could be identified by any of several brands varying in familiarity and/or perceived quality; Likewise for the ice cream/frozen yogurt shop. Pilot work would be necessary to identify distinct instances of each category. Subjects would then be asked to consider the various hypothetical combinations formed by factorially manipulating these two categories. Some of the combinations would be compatible in terms of brand recognition. For instance, a familiar and highly regarded ice cream company could be paired with a familiar and highly regarded pizza parlor. Others would be incompatible, high in one case and low in the other. An additional independent variable of interest might be the distance saved in making a single trip to the joint location as compared to separate trips for pizza and ice cream. And, of course, by broadening the categories one could examine the importance of complementarity of the dual brands: how does a pizza-ice cream parlor combination compare to a pizza-cookie shop combination?

As with the co-branding illustration, a variety of scales could be used to assess the attractiveness and convenience of each dual brand. Most basic, however, would be the consumer's judged likelihood of patronage. ANOVA (or MANOVA) could then be used to decompose these judgments into the contribution of each type of brand on the overall judgment (Anderson 1982).

Finally, in order to assess whether brand image was affected by the dual branding strategy, each brand would be rated on scales such as quality and prestige after consumers reacted to that brand as part of a dual brand. These ratings could then be compared to those obtained from a control group not exposed to the dual brands. Is the image of Pizza Hut enhanced by associating it with Ben and Jerry's? What about Ben and Jerry's image?

While interesting research has already been done on product bundling and brand extensions, gaps in this research are revealed by applying the present conceptual framework. Within this framework, research can simultaneously address the following issues: 1) how brand names contribute to consumers' perceptions of a branding strategy; and 2) how brand image is affected by a brand's inclusion in the new marketing strategy.

Research addressing both issues simultaneously can be accomplished as readily with product bundling and brand extensions as with co-branding and dual branding. In each case the key is to include evaluations of the brand or brands separate from evaluations of the entire package (the product bundle or the new product with the established brand name). To investigate brand extensions, for example, the following two-part procedure could be used: 1) compare consumers' evaluations of the brand extension when the actual brand name is given vs. a fictitious name; 2) after collecting ratings of the brand extension, ask the consumers to rate the brand name on a series of bipolar scales such as trustworthy-untrustworthy, high quality-low quality and reliable-unreliable and compare these to ratings obtained from consumers who were not exposed to the brand extension.

SUMMARY AND IMPLICATIONS

This paper describes a common framework for addressing consumer reactions to several different branding strategies. The strategies of co-branding, dual branding, product bundling and brand extensions all involve positioning an established brand name in a new context. We suggest that simple, straightforward experimental designs can simultaneously address two important issues common to each branding strategy: how the brand name contributes to the evaluation of the new marketing strategy and how the brand's image is ultimately affected. A general scheme for dealing with the first issue is to manipulate whether the well-known brand name or a fictitious name is identified in the new marketing strategy. The second issue can be addressed by comparing evaluations of the brand name between those consumers who were exposed to the new marketing strategy and those who were not.

Results from the demonstration project on co-branding lead us to predict that consumer responses to each branding strategy will reveal both an effect of brand equity on the acceptance of the branding strategy and an effect on the brand's subsequent image. There is also ample theoretical justification for such predictions. According to balance theory (and more generally, theories that predict assimilation between attitudes), judgments of a new marketing strategy will be based on balancing the impressions of each element in the mix (see also N. H. Anderson's 1982 averaging theory) and the impression of each individual element (e.g., brand name) will be adjusted to fit the evaluation of the entire mix. It is a question for future research to compare the magnitude of these effects across the various branding strategies.

For consumer researchers it is important to discover the extent to which common processes are involved in reactions to different marketing strategies. For marketers it is important to develop tools for measuring consumer reactions to various strategies and the potential impact on the image of their brand by including it in a new marketing strategy. In this paper we attempt to provide some simple but effective tools.

REFERENCES

Aaker, David A. (1991), *Managing Brand Equity*, 1st ed. New York: The Free Press.

_____ and Kevin Lane Keller (1990), "Consumer Evaluations of Brand Extensions," *Journal of Marketing*, 54 (January), 27-41.

Anderson, Norman H. (1982), *Methods of Information Integration Theory*. New York: Academic Press.

Benezra, Karen (1994), "Working on the Chain Gang," *Brandweek*, 36 (36), 44-51.

Broniarczyk, Susan M. and Joseph Alba (1994), "The Importance of the Brand in Brand Extension," *Journal of Marketing Research*, 31 (May), 214-228.

Carpenter, Phil (1994), "Some cobranding caveats to obey," *Marketing News*, 28 (23), 4.

Farquhar, Peter H. (1989), "Managing Brand Equity," *Marketing Research*, 1 (September), 24-33.

Festinger, Leon (1957), *A Theory of Cognitive Dissonance*. Evanston, Ill.: Row, Peterson and Company.

Gaeth, Gary J., Irwin P. Levin, Goutam Chakraborty, and Aron M. Levin (1990), "Consumer Evaluation of Multi-Product Bundles: An Information Integration Analysis," *Marketing Letters*, 2 (January), 47-58.

Guiltinan, Joseph P. (1987), "The Price Bundling of Services: A Normative Framework," *Journal of Marketing*, 51 (April), 74-85.

Heider, Fritz (1958), *The Psychology of Interpersonal Relations*. New York: John Wiley and Sons.

_____(1945), "Attitude and Cognitive Organization," *Journal of Psychology*, 21, 107-112.

Keller, Kevin Lane (1993), "Conceptualizing, Measuring, and Managing Customer-Based Brand Equity," *Journal of Marketing*, 57 (January, 1-22.

_____and David A. Aaker (1992), "The Effects of Sequential Introduction of Brand Extensions," *Journal of Marketing Research*, 29 (February), 35-50.

Levin, Irwin P. and Gary Gaeth (1988), "How Consumers Are Affected by the Framing of Attribute Information Before and After Consuming the Product," *Journal of Consumer Research*, 15 (December), 374-378.

Loken, Barbara and Deborah Roedder John (1993), "Diluting Brand Beliefs: When Do Brand Extensions Have a Negative Impact?" *Journal of Marketing*, 57 (July), 71-84.

Martin, Leonard, and Abraham Tesser (1992), *The Construction of Social Judgments*. Hillsdale, N.J.: Lawrence Erlbaum Associates, Inc.

McCaul, Kevin D., Rob E. Ployhart, Berln B. Hinsz, and Harriette S. McCaul (1995), "Appraisals of a Consistent Versus a Similar Politician: Voter Preferences and Intuitive Judgments," *Journal of Personality and Social Psychology*, 68 (February), 292-299.

McDowell, Bill (1994), "Branded," *Restaurants and Institutions*, 104 (October 1), 18-20.

Meyers-Levy, Joan and Brian Sternthal (1993), "A Two-Factor Explanation of Assimilation and Contrast Effects," *Journal of Marketing Research*, 30 (August), 359-368.

Nation's Restaurant News (1994), "Seeing Double: Sharpening the Focus on Future of Dual-Branding," 28 (September 5), 39.

Okechuku, Chike and Gongrong Wang (1988), "The Effectiveness of Chinese Print Advertisements in North America," *Journal of Advertising Research*, 28 (October/November), 25-34.

Osgood, Charles E., and Percy H. Tannenbaum (1955), "The Principle of Congruity in the Prediction of Attitude Change," *The Psychological Review*, 62 (January), 42-55.

Patterson, Gregory A. (1995), "Sears Picks Jiffy Lube to Oil Auto-Service Operations," *Wall Street Journal*, March 23, B6.

Romeo, Jean B. (1990), "The Effect of Negative Information on the Evaluation of Brand Extensions and the Family Brand," in *Advances in Consumer Research*, Vol. 18, Rebecca H. Holman and Michael R. Solomon, eds. Provo, UT: Association for Consumer Research, 399-406.

Schewe, Charles D. (1973), "Selected Social Psychological Models for Analyzing Buyers," *Journal of Marketing*, 37 (July), 31-39.

Tellis, Gerard J. (1988), "Advertising Exposure, Loyalty, and Brand Purchase: A Two-Stage Model of Choice," *Journal of Marketing Research*, 25 (May), 134-144.

Venkatesh, R. and Vijay Mahajan (1993), "A Probabilistic Approach to Pricing a Bundle of Products or Services," *Journal of Marketing Research*, 30 (November), 494-508.

Consumer Heuristics: The Tradeoff Between Processing Effort and Value in Brand Choice

Carter A. Mandrik, Virginia Polytechnic Institute and State University

ABSTRACT

This paper proposes a conceptual framework for studying consumers' choice between national and private label brands. The purpose is to understand consumers' use of simplifying heuristics in making quality judgments between the two. The focus is on the apparent tradeoff being made by consumers between information processing effort minimization and value (objective quality/price) maximization. To lay the groundwork for future validation of the model, two scales are developed to measure consumers' *convenience orientation* and *brand name-quality schematism*. Correlational analysis of the data provides some tentative support for this conceptualization. Implications for brand equity are discussed and directions suggested for future research.

INTRODUCTION

Consumer decision making has been studied with regard to processing ability, as a function of both individual differences and situational constraints (e.g., Capon and Kuhn 1982; Henry 1980; Jacoby, Speller, and Berning 1974; Park, Iyer, and Smith 1989) and motivation to expend processing effort and effort reduction strategies (e.g., Bettman, Johnson, and Payne 1991; Hoyer 1984; Hoyer and Brown 1990). A common thread running through these studies is that consumers must strike a balance between their desire for judgmental accuracy and their desire to minimize effort expenditure. One way to achieve this balance is for consumers to use cognitive heuristics (rules of inference) to simplify decision making, minimize effort and at the same time deliver an adequate level of confidence that the judgment is correct (Chaiken, Liberman, and Eagly 1989). This paper attempts to add insight into consumers' use of heuristics in quality judgments and how these relate to the processing goals of effort reduction and value maximization.

The focus here will be on quality judgments made between a manufacturer's (name) brand and a private label (store) brand for grocery products. This decision is an important one to study because of the recent brand equity losses suffered by brand marketers through competition from private labels (Hoch and Banerji 1993; Kim 1993). Furthermore, as prototypes, these two classes of brands have historically existed opposite each other on dimensions related to the quality judgment (e.g., price cues, amount of advertising, social status). Thus, in addition to making this a salient distinction for consumers, the contrast between them allows easier exposition of the conceptualization used here. I use as a conceptual framework Chaiken's (1980, 1987) Heuristic-Systematic model, an information processing model widely used in persuasion. The aim in this paper is to propose the model and develop scales for future use in model validation. The data provided in scale development are analyzed for an exploratory investigation of several hypothesized relationships between consumers' use of heuristics and motivation-related traits. Finally, implications for brand equity are discussed and further research avenues suggested.

CONCEPTUAL DEVELOPMENT

The Heuristic-Systematic model (H-S) is conceptually similar to the Elaboration Likelihood Model of persuasion (ELM, Petty and Cacioppo 1986), which more marketing scholars may find familiar. Systematic and heuristic processing in the H-S are analogous to

central and peripheral routes in the ELM. Systematic processing is prototypically viewed as a "comprehensive, analytic orientation in which perceivers access and scrutinize all informational input for its relevance and importance to their judgment task"; alternatively, individuals processing heuristically "focus on the subset of available information that enables them to use simple inferential rules, schemata, or cognitive heuristics to formulate their judgments and decisions" (Chaiken, Liberman and Eagly 1989, p.212-213). Systematic processing requires higher levels of cognitive effort and capacity than heuristic processing. Because people prefer less effortful to more effortful modes of information processing, individuals must be more highly motivated to process systematically. It is necessary to state a few assumptions and define terms before applying the model to the brand choice context.

Assumptions and Definitions

As used here, the model assumes that the products under consideration are identical in "objective" quality, differing only along extrinsic attributes (e.g., brand name, price, and packaging). Objective quality refers to the inherent technical superiority of a product based in its physical attributes, as opposed to "perceived" quality which is influenced by other, peripheral aspects, such as "image" (Zeithaml 1988).[1] A second assumption is that consumers generally seek to maximize the value of their purchases. "Value" here refers to the ratio of objective quality to the price paid (Zeithaml 1988). This definition of value, though restrictive, follows from the first assumption of identical objective quality, thus allowing hypothetical comparisons of consumers' ability to make quality judgments between product choices (similar to Pechmann and Ratneshwar (1992)). It is central to the arguments made in this paper—especially those concerning brand equity: sometimes consumers take "the easy way out" and use a heuristic (which may or may not be reliable) to infer higher objective quality for name brand products than for private labels. Several conditions under which a consumer is most likely to do this are outlined below.

The inferential rules termed here "consumer heuristics" are somewhat different than the "choice heuristics" (e.g., "Elimination by Aspects" or "Equal Weight" heuristics) discussed in Bettman, Johnson, and Payne (1991), which are more procedural decision rules. These may require considerable cognitive effort and knowledge, especially if used to optimize the decision (Hoyer 1984). The consumer heuristics discussed here are much simpler, similar to the "tactical" heuristics discussed by Hoyer (1984). They are used to make quality judgments (central to value maximization) and depend on extrinsic attributes like brand name and price or other heuristic cues (e.g., promotion signals, amount and content of advertising), which are controlled by the marketer. Examples of these heuristics are "high price implies high quality," "name brand products are higher quality," or "heavily advertised brands are higher quality". The brand associations formed through advertising efforts may also serve as heuristic cues: "doctors recommend..." or "more hospitals use X brand..." invokes the "experts can be trusted" and "consensus implies correctness" heuristics, respectively, to connote high quality.

The H-S proposes three motivational concerns, or processing goals. The *accuracy motivation*, which reflects a desire to achieve informationally valid opinions or judgments, is assumed to be primary. When applied to the consumer context, the accuracy motivation translates to "value maximization". Acting under this motivational concern, the consumer's overriding goal is to get the

---

[1] For discussions of the concept, see Zeithaml (1988) and Lichtenstein and Burton (1990).

TABLE 1
Factors Affecting Processing of Product Information.

1. Accuracy Motivation	2. Impression Motivation	3. Defense Motivation
a. Value consciousness +(+)	a. Social importance + (?)	a. Dogmatism + (-)
b. Convenience orientation - (-)	b. Publicly consumed	b. Innovativeness - (?)
c. Need for cognition + (+)	product + (?)	c. High perceived
d. Disposable income - (-)	c. Self-monitoring, ATSCI,	switching costs + (-)
e. Product related knowledge ? (∩)	Prestige sensitivity,	
f. Processing ability ? (-)	CSII + (?)	
g. Time pressure ? (-)		
h. Availability/diagnosticity		
of information ? (-)		
i. Price-quality schematism ? (-)		
j. Brand-quality schematism ? (-)		

Key: "+"=positive relationship   "?"=uncertain relationship
          "-"=negative relationship   "∩"=inverted "U" relationship
      Symbols denote relationship between factor and motivational concern.
      Symbols inside parentheses denote relationship between factor and systematic processing.

highest product quality at the lowest price. As in the original H-S model, it is assumed here to be the primary motivation underlying brand choice. *Impression motivation* refers to "the desire to express attitudes that are socially acceptable" (Eagly and Chaiken 1993, p. 340). This motivation may be aroused when "the identities of significant audiences (real or imagined) are salient to the individual, when social relationships are important, or when people must communicate their attitudes to potential evaluators" (Chaiken, Liberman, and Eagly 1989, p. 236). *Defense motivation* refers to the individuals desire to defend particular attitudes. In the consumption setting this would be roughly analogous to brand loyalty. Individuals who process within the defense motivation are more closed minded, selective, and biased in their information processing, attending to information that supports their opinions and ignoring (or derogating) that which does not (Eagly and Chaiken 1993). Systematic processing of attribute information is curtailed, and the consumer is likely to employ one of the simplest effort- and risk-reducing rules: the habitual heuristic, "choose what one chose last time" (Bettman, Payne, and Johnson 1994).

Several factors associated with each motivational concern and the processing mode used to reach quality judgments are listed in Table 1. Some traits predisposing consumers to be motivated to impress others through the brands they choose are the traits *self-monitoring* (Becherer and Richard 1978; Snyder 1987), *consumer susceptibility to interpersonal influence* (Bearden, Netemeyer, and Teel 1989), *attention to social comparison information* (Bearden and Rose 1990) and *prestige sensitivity* (Lichtenstein, Ridgway, and Netemeyer 1993). Situational factors would be *social importance* (Leary and Kowalski 1990)[2] and whether or not it is a *publicly consumed* product (Bearden and Etzel 1982). Traits related to the defense motivation might be *dogmatism* (Rokeach 1960) and *innovativeness* (Leavitt and Walton 1975), while a situational factor would be *high perceived switching costs* (Kerin, Varadarajan, and

Peterson (1992) (see Table 1). Because the present interest is in understanding how processing differences (systematic versus heuristic) interact with the value maximizing motive, further discussion focuses on the accuracy motivation.

Accuracy Motivation

Consumers must be *motivated* and *able* to process systematically. Processing systematically they would, for example, use unit pricing information, read labels, compare intrinsic attributes between brands, and make trial purchases. To the extent that systematic processing yields accurate judgments, a consumer so doing would choose the private label because it offers the same quality at a lower price. Consumers *not* sufficiently motivated or able to process systematically may process the judgment using heuristics. They would then focus on available heuristic cues (e.g., extrinsic attributes or advertising cues) and make an inference of higher quality for the name brand product. Consumers that employ these heuristics are more likely to choose the national brand.

Influences on Motivation to Process Systematically

Several factors contribute to the level of motivation experienced in each purchase situation (see Table 1). The consumer trait, *value consciousness*, the "concern for price paid relative to quality received" (Lichtenstein, Netemeyer, and Burton 1990), should increase the individual's motivation to process systematically in order to obtain the best value. Monroe and Mazumdar (1988) suggest another trait related to motivation when they note that "shoppers who are not price-conscious are presumed to be convenience-oriented" (p. 371). *Convenience orientation* is defined here as the tendency to prefer comfort and ease in shopping behavior and a willingness to pay higher prices for it. It represents a general motivational deficit in the consumption setting and should therefore decrease systematic processing of quality judgments. *Need for cognition* (NFC, Cacioppo and Petty 1982) is related to the motivation to obtain judgmental confidence through systematic processing. Low NFC individuals may employ heuristics chronically (Eagly, Liberman, and Chaiken 1989) and make more incorrect inferences based on extrinsic cues like promotion signals that do not signify a real reduction in price (Inman, McAlister, and Hoyer 1990). *Low income* or high *budget constraints* should increase consumers' motivation to devote processing effort to judgments that affect value maximization.

---

[2]In a recent integrative review of the impression management (a.k.a., self-presentation) literature by Leary and Kowalski (1990), the authors present a model in which they describe three antecedents to impression motivation. The scope of this paper prohibits detailed presentation of these factors to the summary concept of "social importance".

Strength of heuristics. If a heuristic is perceived to be reliable (i.e., lead to valid judgments), it may be employed more often because the individual is able to attain a sufficient level of confidence while reducing effort (Chaiken, Eagly, and Liberman 1989). This aspect is known as the "strength" of a heuristic, and individual differences exist for particular ones. *Price-quality schema* refers to a consumer's "generalized belief across product categories that the level of the price cue is related positively to the quality level of the product" (Lichtenstein, Ridgway, and Netemeyer 1993). This trait reflects the strength of the heuristic "price reflects quality". High P-Q schematics should process quality judgments using this heuristic, and therefore be more likely to choose the higher priced name brand. A related concept is what I term here *brand-quality schematism*[3], the generalized belief that the brand name cue (national brand or private label) is a useful indicator of product quality in decisions between manufacturer and private label grocery products. It reflects the strength and chronicity of use of the "name brands are high quality" heuristic.

Constraints on Ability to Process Systematically

Consumers motivated to process quality judgments systematically may at times lack the ability. Systematic processing "is adversely affected by situational variables and individual differences that constrain people's capacities for in-depth information processing (e.g., time pressures, lack of domain-specific expertise" (Chaiken, Liberman, and Eagly 1989, p.212). Constraints on systematic processing in the consumer setting are listed in Table 1.

Two individual constraints on systematic processing would be low *product-related knowledge* (Park and Lessig 1981; Rao and Monroe 1988) and low *processing ability* (Capon and Kuhn 1982; Henry 1980). If consumers have low product knowledge, it is more difficult for them to process attribute information systematically. They are more likely than experts to rely on some heuristic cue (e.g., a non-diagnostic extrinsic attribute) to make quality inferences (Rao and Monroe 1988). For inexperienced consumers presented with a brand-selection task, the brand awareness heuristic ("buy the best known brand") served as the dominant choice rule (Hoyer and Brown 1990). Several situational constraints are identified. *Time pressures* limit ability to process systematically (Park, Iyer, and Smith 1981). The *availability/diagnosticity of product information* is important, because if information is unavailable or nondiagnostic before the decision is made the consumer must rely on whatever cues are available (e.g., heavy advertising (Kirmani 1990)) to make judgments. Supporting this is the finding that the "price-quality" relationship is stronger the less information is available (Lichtenstein and Burton 1989; Rao and Monroe 1989; Zeithaml 1988).

EMPIRICAL INVESTIGATION

Of the factors identified that may affect consumers' use of heuristics, I now explore the relationship among four traits. Two of them, value consciousness and convenience orientation, are directly related to motivation in a consumption setting. The other two, price-quality schematism and brand name-quality schematism, are related to the strength or chronic accessibility of consumer heuristics. Although convenience orientation does not directly implicate product quality judgments, it should be positively related to use of consumer heuristics because of the underlying motiva-

tional deficit. Value consciousness reflects high motivation to obtain value, and thus should be negatively related to use of consumer heuristics to reach quality judgments.

Research Hypotheses

Consumers high in value consciousness should have higher motivation to process quality judgments systematically, reducing the tendency to simply rely on the brand name and price as a heuristic to infer quality. Therefore,

H1a: Value Consciousness is negatively related to brand name-quality schematism.

H1b: Value Consciousness is negatively related to price-quality schematism.

Highly convenience-oriented consumers should be more likely to reduce effort by relying on heuristics to infer quality. This suggests the following relationships:

H2a: Convenience orientation is positively related to brand name-quality schematism.

H2b: Convenience orientation is positively related to price-quality schematism.

Chronic use of heuristics in general may reflect underlying individual differences in processing orientations (Chaiken, Liberman, and Eagly 1989). Additionally, consumers who are highly P-Q schematic should be more likely to associate high quality with the more expensive name brands. Therefore the two heuristic trait measures should be related:

H3: Price-quality schematism is positively related to brand name-quality schematism.

METHOD

Scales for value consciousness (VC) and price-quality schematism (P-Q) were available (Lichtenstein, Ridgway, and Netemeyer 1993). The scales for convenience orientation (CO) and brand name-quality schematism (BN-Q) were developed here.

Scale Development. Two focus groups (n=8, 12) were conducted to explore the meaning of convenience when shopping and of reliance on brand name in product choice. From these discussions and consultation with professional colleagues, conceptual definitions of CO and of BN-Q were composed (see Conceptual Development above). Next, a pool of approximately 30 items was generated based on these definitions. To help establish face validity, this set of items was judged for consistency with each conceptual definition by a marketing faculty member and two marketing PhD students, which resulted in the addition and rewording of several items, and the deletion of several judged to be inadequate. Seven items for the CO scale and 12 for the BN-Q scale were retained. These items were interspersed with items from the value consciousness and price-quality schematism scales (Lichtenstein, Ridgway, and Netemeyer 1993) and responses were obtained from a convenience sample of 83 undergraduate business students at a large Southeastern university.

Exploratory factor analysis and internal consistency reliability analysis in the statistical package SPSS were used to select indicators for each scale. Maximum likelihood was used to extract the factors. In line with the expectation of measuring four distinct constructs, a clear four-factor structure emerged (based on eigen values greater than one). An oblique rotation (p=.5) was used to extract the maximum amount of variance, because it was assumed

---

[3]The construct is named "price-quality schema" in Lichtenstein, Ridgway, and Netemeyer (1993), but for grammatical consistency I use "schematism" to refer to the schema-related constructs.

TABLE 2
Bivariate Correlation Results (n=83)

	bn-q schema	conven	p-q schema	valucons
bn-q schema	1.0 (—)	.452 (.000)	.458 (.000)	-.478 (.000)
conven		1.0 (—)	.399 (.000)	-.379 (.000)
p-q shema			1.0 (—)	-.160 (.147)
valucons				1.0 (—)

(p-values in parentheses)
bn-q schema=brand name-quality schematism
conven=convenience orientation
p-q schema=price-quality schematism
valucons=value consciousness

a priori that the factors would be correlated[4]. For the CO and BN-Q scales, only items that loaded on the factor above .4 and did not have high cross-loadings were retained for the internal consistency reliability analysis (Saxe and Wietz 1982), leaving five and nine items for each scale, respectively. Reliability analysis resulted in the deletion of one item from the BN-Q scale. Coefficient alphas were .84 for the five-item CO scale and .88 for the eight-item BN-Q scale. Scales appear in the Appendix.

Hypothesis testing. After finding that the scales displayed adequate unidimensionality and internal consistency, correlation analysis was used to test the hypotheses. The following results were obtained.

RESULTS

Correlation Analysis. Table 2 lists the results of the correlation analysis. All correlations are in the predicted directions, and all but one (between price-quality schema and value consciousness) are significant at p<.001. Thus, all hypotheses were supported, except H1b which received only directional support (see Table 2).

DISCUSSION

Research Implications

Before proceeding it is necessary to state the limitations of the study. First, the correlation analysis is seriously limited by using the same sample to develop the scales and test the hypothesized relationships. Also, the sample used is one of convenience, constraining any attempts to generalize. Another issue is that the correlations may be attributable to shared method variance, as well as "self-generated validity" (Feldman and Lynch 1988). It would therefore be unwise to draw strong conclusions based on this exploratory investigation. With these caveats in mind, it is interesting to note the strong correlations between the variables, indicating

some degree of association between the two motivational traits and the use of the two consumer heuristics. Thus there is tentative support that the consumer heuristics represented by price-quality schema and brand name-quality schema may be more likely to be used by consumers who are not motivated to make systematic comparisons(i.e., they are not highly value conscious), or who prefer convenience when shopping. The model's ability to integrate prior research coupled with the mild support offered here suggests its usefulness as a framework for studying consumer choice behavior.

In the work of Lichtenstein, Netemeyer, and Burton (1990), value consciousness is established as a trait and contrasted against coupon proneness in its effect on shopping behavioral variables (e.g., coupon use, *Consumer Reports* use, price knowledge) or other consumer orientations (e.g., involvement, shopping competitiveness). However, as a motivation, it has not been well defined in terms of possible antecedent factors. The theoretical framework used here suggests several factors, for example income or budget constraints, and need for cognition. The level of disposable income should affect both a consumer's value consciousness and convenience orientation. Peripheral support for this comes from the finding that consumers switch from national brands to private labels in worse economies (Hoch and Banerji 1993). NFC reflects a motivation to devote effort to processing, and should therefore be associated with both value consciousness and with convenience orientation. Applied to the consumption setting, the model seems useful for explicating these relationships and others that are involved in quality judgments and brand choice.

Market Implications

In order to maximize value (as price/objective quality) consumers must be able to make accurate judgments of quality for between-brand value comparisons. Because judgments based on heuristics may be less accurate or prone to bias (Tversky and Kahneman 1974), their use may compromise the consumer's goal of value maximization. Furthermore, the reliability of the heuristics studied here may be considerably lower than in years past as private label products continue to narrow the quality gap (Hoch and Banerji 1993). Of course, we can easily expand the concept of value to

---

[4]Structure and pattern matrices, communality estimates, and correlations among the reference axes are available from the author upon request.

APPENDIX
Brand name/Quality Schematism and Convenience Orientation Scales

Brand name/Quality Schematism	Strongly Agree					Strongly Disagree	
1. Brand name is not that important to me when I am deciding on which product to buy.	1	2	3	4	5	6	7
2. I rely heavily on brand name when shopping.	1	2	3	4	5	6	7
3. I only buy manufacturer brands.	1	2	3	4	5	6	7
4. *Store brands are generally similar in quality to manufacturer brands.	1	2	3	4	5	6	7
5. *I regularly purchase store brands.	1	2	3	4	5	6	7
6. I trust manufacturer brands more than store brands.	1	2	3	4	5	6	7
7. It's risky to buy a store's own brand for most products.	1	2	3	4	5	6	7
8. *Store brands are of comparable quality to manufacturer brands.	1	2	3	4	5	6	7

Convenience Orientation	Strongly Agree					Strongly Disagree	
1. Convenience is more important to me than low prices.	1	2	3	4	5	6	7
2. Anything that adds convenience to my life is worth paying a little extra for.	1	2	3	4	5	6	7
3. I will pay more to avoid waiting in line.	1	2	3	4	5	6	7
4. I am willing to pay higher prices for convenience.	1	2	3	4	5	6	7
5. *I don't mind waiting in line if it means I will get lower prices.	1	2	3	4	5	6	7

*Reverse coded.

include not only the time and effort savings associated with relying on consumer heuristics in brand choice, but the symbolic value of the brand name to the consumer. Then the tradeoff between processing effort and judgmental accuracy would seem to be a moot point. However, while this broader concept of value is relevant, it does not render irrelevant the more restricted one when we take into account the consumer's goals for the purchase situation. For the consumer whose goal is to obtain the highest objective quality at the lowest price (value maximization as used here), the other aspects of value associated with the brand name or price may be unimportant. In this circumstance, whether the consumer believes the extrinsic cue to be diagnostic of product quality becomes a relevant question.

Implicit in this framework is the concept of brand equity. Definitions of brand equity view it as a financial asset measured in increased market share or profit margins or, from the consumer's perspective as a set of favorable associations, both of which are attributable to the brand name's influence on consumers (Aaker 1991; Farquhar 1992; Keller 1993; Srivastava and Shocker 1991). The framework outlined factors that affect consumers reliance on heuristics associated with extrinsic cues like brand name or price. If brand choice depends in part on their use (which reflects processing motivations), then so does brand equity as market share and profit margins (i.e., price premiums). And because novice consumers rely on (non-diagnostic) extrinsic cues to determine a products' quality (Rao and Monroe 1988), it can be said that at least a little

brand equity capitalizes on their lack of ability. Additionally, advertising can influence consumers—especially novices—to make inaccurate assessments of product attributes; these "favorably biased attribute perceptions" are acknowledged as one source of brand equity (Park and Srinivasan 1994). Lichtenstein and Burton (1989) note that "the mere marketplace survival of brands that offer poor quality in relation to their price suggests that consumers are far from perfect in their assessment of price-quality comparisons" (p. 431). This is not to suggest that name brands are not high quality, simply that some consumers may falsely infer they are higher quality than a private label, and that this false inference may contribute to brand equity for the national brand. Consumer heuristics at present favor the brand equity of national brands, but marketers of brands that do not offer noticeable quality differences may be in trouble the more value conscious people become. Private labels should thus encourage systematic comparisons between their products that offer similar quality to the name brands.

Future research

Several other lines of research are suggested by this conceptual framework. One proposition worth exploring is: the less motivated or the less able a consumer is to process systematically, the more potential there exists for brand equity of the national brand versus a private label. Throughout the conceptual development of this paper I have discussed trait factors and situational factors. The importance of situational influences on consumer behavior has been recognized (e.g., Belk 1975), but an explicit "trait-versus-situation" approach (Monson, Hesley, and Chernick 1982) would be useful for exploring the antecedents to each motivation. Causal models that link traits to other variables like income or need for cognition are called for. General attitudes toward private labels, like perceived status and quality compared to name brands, may differ with time or region, which suggests the need for replication of earlier studies on this topic (e.g., Myers 1967). A review of methods for studying consumer decision making can be found in Bettman, Johnson, and Payne (1991).

CONCLUSIONS

The purpose of this paper was to propose a model of consumer choice that shed light on consumers' use of heuristics to simplify the decision process between national and private label brands. This conceptualization suggests that there is a tradeoff between effort minimization and value maximization, if we restrict the meaning of value to the ratio of objective quality to price. It can be argued that a national brand's equity may be maximal for product purchase situations in which consumers are unmotivated or compromised in their ability to accurately determine product quality—and hence, assess value. Consumers may use heuristic cues like price and brand name to infer higher quality for the national brand, when in fact it may be the same as the private label. This is especially true for consumers who lack knowledge and/or processing ability. While the research reported is only in an exploratory stage, the results obtained beckon further efforts.

REFERENCES

Aaker, David A. (1991), *Managing Brand Equity*, New York: The Free Press.

Bearden, William O. and Michael J. Etzel (1982), "Reference Group Influence on Product and Brand Purchase Decisions," *Journal of Consumer Research*, 9 (September), 183-194.

_____, Richard G. Netemeyer, and Jesse E. Teel (1989), "Measurement of Consumer Susceptibility to Interpersonal Influence," *Journal of Consumer Research*, 15 (March), 473-481.

_____, and Randall L. Rose (1990), "Attention to Social Comparison Information: An Individual Difference Factor Affecting Consumer Conformity," *Journal of Consumer Research*, 16 (March), 461-471.

Becherer, Richard C. and Lawrence M. Richard (1978), "Self-Monitoring as a Moderating Variable in Consumer Behavior," *Journal of Consumer Research*, 5 (December), 159-162.

Belk, Russell W. (1975), "Situational Variables and Consumer Behavior," *Journal of Consumer Research*, 2 (December), 157-177.

Bettman, James R., Eric J. Johnson, and John W. Payne (1991), "Consumer Decision Making," in *Handbook of Consumer Behavior*, Thomas S. Robertson and Harold H. Kassarjian (eds.), Englewood Cliffs, NJ: Prentice-Hall, 50-84.

Capon, Noel and Deana Kuhn (1982), "Can Consumers Calculate Best Buys?," *Journal of Consumer Research*, 8 (March), 449-453.

Chaiken, Shelley (1980), "Heuristic Versus Systematic Information Processing and the Use of Source Versus Message Cues in Persuasion," *Journal of Personality and Social Psychology*, 39, 752-766.

Chaiken, Shelley (1987), "The Heuristic Model of Persuasion," in *Social influence: The Ontario symposium*, Vol. 5, M.P. Zanna, J.M. Olson, & C.P. Herman (eds.), Hillsdale, NJ: Erlbaum, 3-39.

_____, Akiva Liberman and Alice H. Eagly (1989), "Heuristic and Systematic Information Processing Within and Beyond the Persuasion Context," in *Unintended Thought*, J.S. Uleman & J.A. Bargh (eds.), NY: Guilford Press, 212-252.

Eagly, Alice H. and Shelley Chaiken (1993). *The Psychology of Attitudes*. Chapter 7 (pp. 305-349). NY: Harcourt Brace Jovanovich.

Farquhar, Peter H. (1992), "Managing Brand Equity," *Journal of Advertising*, RC7-RC12.

Feldman, Jack M. and John G. Lynch (1988), "Self-Generated Validity and Other Effects of Measurement on Belief, Attitude, Intention, and Behavior," *Journal of Applied Psychology*, 73 (3), 421-435.

Henry, Walter A. (1980), "The Effect of Information-Processing Ability on Processing Accuracy," *Journal of Consumer Research*, 7 (June), 42-48.

Hoch, Stephen J. and Shumeet Banerji (1993), "When Do Private Labels Succeed?," *Sloan Management Review*, 34 (Summer), 57-67.

Hoyer, Wayne D. (1984), "An Examination of Consumer Decision Making for a Common Repeat Purchase Product," *Journal of Consumer Research*, 11 (December), 822-829.

_____ and Steven P. Brown (1990), "Effects of Brand Awareness on Choice for a Common, Repeat-Purchase Product," *Journal of Consumer Research*, 17 (September), 141-148.

Inman, J. Jeffrey, Leigh McAlister, and Wayne D. Hoyer (1990), "Promotion Signal: Proxy for a Price Cut?," *Journal of Consumer Research*, 17 (June), 74-81.

Jacoby, Jacob, Donald Speller and Carol Kohn (1974), "Brand Choice Behavior as a Function of Information Load: Replication and Extension," *Journal of Consumer Research*, 1 (June), 33-42.

Keller, Kevin Lane (1993), "Conceptualizing, Measuring, and Managing Customer-Based Brand Equity," *Journal of Marketing*, 57 (January), 1-22.

Kerin, Roger A., P. Rajan Varadarajan, and Robert A. Peterson (1992), "First-Mover Advantage: A Synthesis, Conceptual Framework, and Research Propositions," *Journal of Marketing*, 58 (October), 33-52.

Kim, Peter (1993), "Restore Brand Equity!," *Directors and Boards*, 17 (Summer), 21-29.

Kirmani, Amna (1990), "The Effect of Perceived Advertising Costs on Brand Perceptions," *Journal of Consumer Research*, 17 (September), 160-171.

Leary, Mark R. and Robin M. Kowalski (1990), "Impression Management: A literature Review and Two-Component Model," *Psychological Bulletin*, 107, 34-47.

Leavitt, Clark and John Walton (1975), "Development of a Scale for Innovativeness," in *Advances in Consumer Research*, Vol. 2, Mary Jane Schlinger (ed.), Ann Arbor, MI: Association for Consumer Research, 545-554.

Lichtenstein, Donald R. and Scot Burton (1989), "The Relationship Between Perceived and Objective Price-Quality," *Journal of Marketing Research*, 26 (November), 429-43.

_____, Richard G. Netemeyer, and Scot Burton (1990), "Distinguishing Coupon Proneness from Value Consciousness: An Acquisition-Transaction Utility Theory Perspective. *Journal of Marketing*, 54 (July), 54-67.

_____, Nancy M. Ridgway, and Richard G. Netemeyer (1993), "Price Perceptions and Consumer Shopping Behavior: A Field Study," *Journal of Marketing Research*, 30, 234-245.

Monson, Thomas C., John W. Hesley and Linda Chernick (1982), "Specifying When Personality Traits Can and Cannot Predict Behavior: An Alternative to Abandoning the Attempt to Predict Single-Act Criteria," *Journal of Personality and Social Psychology*, 43 (2), 385-399.

Monroe, Kent B. and Tridib Mazumdar (1988), "Pricing-Decision Models: Recent Developments and Research Opportunities", in *Issues in Pricing: Theory and Research*, Timothy M. Devinney, ed. Lexington, MA: Lexington Books, 361-88.

Myers, John G. (1967), "Derminants of Private Brand Attitudes," *Journal of Marketing Research*, 6 (February), 73-81.

Park, C. Whan and V. Parker Lessig (1981), "Familiarity and Its Impact on Consumer Decision Biases and Heuristics," *Journal of Consumer Research*, 8 (September), 223-230.

_____, Easwar S. Iyer, and Daniel C. Smith (1989), "The Effects of Situational Factors on In-Store Grocery Shopping Behavior: The Role of Store Environment and Time Available for Shopping," *Journal of Consumer Research*, 15 (March), 422-433.

Park, Chan Su and V. Srinivasan (1994), "A Survey-Based Method for Measuring and Understanding Brand Equity and Its Extendability," *Journal of Marketing Research*, 31 (May), 271-288.

Pechmann, Cornelia and S. Ratneshwar (1992), "Consumer Covariation Judgments: Theory or Data Driven?," *Journal of Consumer Research*, 19 (December), 373-386.

Petty, Richard E. and John T. Cacioppo (1986), "The Elaboration Likelihood Model of Persuasion," in *Advances in Experimental Social Psychology*, Vol. 19, L. Berkowitz (ed.), New York: Academic Press.

Rao, Akshay R. and Kent B. Monroe (1988), "The Moderating Effect of Prior Knowledge on Cue Utilization in Product Evaluations," *Journal of Consumer Research*, 15 (September), 253-264.

_____ and Kent B. Monroe (1989), "The Effect of Price, Brand Name, and Store Name on Buyers' Perceptions of Product Quality: An Integrative Review," *Journal of Marketing Research*, 26 (August), 351-7.

Rokeach, Milton (1960), *The Open and Closed Mind*, New York: Basic Books.

Saxe, Robert and Barton A. Weitz (1982), "The SOCO Scale: A Measure of the Customer Orientation of Salespeople," *Journal of Marketing Research*, 19 (August), 343-51.

Sellers, Patricia (1993), "Brands: It's Thrive or Die," *Fortune*, 128 (4), 52-56.

Snyder, Mark (1987), *Public Appearances/Private Realities: The Psychology of Self-Monitoring*. NY: W.H. Freeman and Company.

Srivastava, Rajendra K. and Allan D. Shocker (1991), "Brand Equity: A Perspective on its Meaning and Measurement," Working Paper No. 91-124. Cambridge, MA: Marketing Science Institute.

Tversky, Amos and Daniel Kahneman (1974), "Judgment Under Uncertainty: Heuristics and Biases," *Science* (185), 1124-1131.

Zeithaml, Valarie A. (1988), "Consumer Perceptions of Price, Quality, and Value: A Means-End Model and Synthesis of Evidence," *Journal of Marketing*, 52 (July), 2-22.

Special Session Summary
Something's Missing: Modern Cognitive Approaches to Decision Making with Incomplete Information

Julie R. Irwin, New York University
Robert Meyer, University of Pennsylvania

BACKGROUND

Many purchase decisions involve some degree of uncertainty and reasoning about missing information. The attributes and attribute levels of the goods may be incompletely expressed, the meaning of the attributes and their values may be confusing or unfamiliar, and the complex relationships among attributes may not be well understood. One useful way to conceptualize a purchase decision is as a *problem* to be solved; cognitive psychologists traditionally characterize a problem in terms of three distinct stages/processes: forming a search space (i.e. "consideration set"), developing a problem representation, and then employing reasoning strategies to reach a solution. The three papers in this session sequentially examined consumer decision making at each of these stages, and each of the three papers was rooted in a different influential cognitive approach, allowing the discussant and audience to compare and contrast three theories of how consumers import information into the decision process when full information is not available.

Image Theory and the First Phase: How are Consideration Sets Formed when Information is Missing?
Joydeep Srivastava, Gillian Naylor, Lee Roy Beach
University of Arizona

Two experiments were conducted in a purchase scenario to explore the nature of consumers' responses when they encounter missing information in a pre-choice screening task. The product used for the first experiment was described by four uncorrelated attributes. Thus, subjects could not make inferences regarding the missing attributes from the information that was present. In the second experiment, we used correlated attributes to examine whether subjects infer the value of the missing attribute from the information that was present, and whether they assume missing information implies a negative value on the attribute. The importance of the attributes within subjects was also manipulated to examine whether subjects would be more likely to infer information that is critical to the decision. We found that missing information affected pre-choice screening, but that unacceptable attribute levels had a stronger effect on screening than did missing attribute levels, and missing information was not treated as an indication of a negative attribute level.

When is Constructive Processing Necessary?
Familiarity and Reasoning in Judgment and Choice
Eloise Coupey, V.P.I.
Julie R. Irwin, New York University
John Payne, Duke University

In the absence of information from memory on how or what to choose, a decision maker often must construct a preference from the information at hand. Such on-line construction can lead to preference inconsistencies across mode and context, because contextual information is used to help guide reasoning. In three experiments, we established that a prevalent inconsistency (judgment versus choice) depended on *familiarity* with the products (preferences for unfamiliar products were much less consistent), and that this interaction was explainable by the sorts of simplistic reasoning strategies adopted by decision makers when they lack information on how to weight the product attributes.

Inference Generation and Correction: Cognitive Capacity and the Use of Relevant cues
Gita Venkataramani Johar, Columbia University
Carolyn Simmons, LeHigh University

We hypothesized a two-stage model of product perception such that certain "intuitive" inferences (e.g., correlational inferences such as "high price implies high quality") are made spontaneously without requiring much capacity. However, these inferences are then corrected if there is external information that invalidates the spontaneous inference and consumers have sufficient cognitive capacity. The cognitive capacity manipulation allows the test of the sequence in which the two stages occur. Results from two experiments partially support the hypotheses. In the first experiment, subjects in both high and low capacity conditions gave higher quality ratings to a high priced TV brand compared to a control condition not given price information. However, only subjects in the high capacity condition corrected this inference if they were also given corrective information implying that the high price-high quality inference rule was not diagnostic in this instance. Both low and high capacity subjects encoded the correction as evidenced by equivalent recall of the corrective information in both conditions. Experiment 2 found similar support for the long warranty-high quality inference. Spontaneous inferences are not frequently observed in experiments manipulating product information. However, when such inferences are made, correction appears to be the second step which is more effortful than the step of making spontaneous inferences. Faulty inferences may sometimes be maintained in the face of disconfirming information.

DISCUSSION

Robert Meyer's discussant comments centered on the sources of uncertainty in consumer choice. Consumers can be uncertain about the actual choice options available, or about how to evaluate the choice options (i.e. people may be unsure about what the object is and/or how they feel about it). He also nicely summarized the important findings and unanswered questions in each of the studies. For the screening paper, he emphasized the importance of learning and adapting; for the constructive preferences paper he surmised that the effects might depend on the nature of familiarity/experience with the products; and for the inference-making paper he suggested that the direction of effort (e.g. toward rationalizing the inference instead of correcting it) may make a difference. Discussion among the audience members followed a similar pattern and focused on the nature of familiarity and knowledge.

Another Cup of Coffee: The View from Different Frames

Donald R. Lehmann, Columbia University

J. Edward Russo, Cornell University

The concept of applying different research approaches (paradigm frames) to the same specific problem was the subject of a special session. Inspired by some observations of Johnson and Russo (1994), the session featured six quite different talks about brand loyalty for coffee, a topic chosen because it has been widely studied. Unlike the general debates about method superiority, this "case study" both highlighted strengths and weaknesses and, due to the quality and good spirit of the presenters, produced friendly, useful interchange.

Six quite different approaches were presented. Sunil Gupta and Randy Bucklin presented a measure of brand loyalty based on scanner panel data that combined preference and price sensitivity and, using latent class analysis, segmented consumers based on their loyalty. Eric Johnson and Wes Hutchinson analyzed multiple methods, including brand recall and brand switching, for describing the structure of the mental representation of brands and found remarkable similarity across methods. Susan Fournier and Julie Yao used a structured qualitative procedure similar to Zaltman's Metaphor Elicitation Technique and drew interesting conclusions from eight consumers' brand loyalties and attitudes toward coffee. Jagmohan S. Raju used game theory to develop some consequences of promotional strategy and then demonstrated the results on actual sales data. Bill Wells described his approach to using the behavior of TV show characters to gain insight into behavior (as interpreted by writers) by showing how coffee is used in certain typical ways. Finally, Christine Wright-Isak showed how the role of coffee and ad appeals has changed in response to changes in society as a whole over a 50-year period.

A discussion highlighted the strengths and weaknesses of these methods (a.k.a., highlights and shadows; see Johnson and Russo, 1994). The six approaches were organized along an interpretivist-positivist continuum. Literary analysis anchored the interpretivist end, with clinical psychology and the case study tradition in sociology nearby. Game theory and related techniques from economics resided at the far positivist end with cognitive and social psychology adjacent and quantitative sociology nearby. This continuum was then used to place and contrast four major characteristics of the scientific enterprise (Table 1).

The discussion, both prepared and interactive, combined to yield distinctions in terms of emphasis on (1) causes vs. measurement vs. consequences, (2) use of existing vs. specially-collected data, (3) inferred vs. revealed behavior and attitudes, and (4) focus on individual vs. segment vs. aggregate. Perhaps surprisingly to some, not only did the methods complement each other but the authors from quite different traditions were able to both present and talk to each other in an understandable way. Moreover, some generalizations/consistencies emerged which suggest that, for coffee, loyalty is mainly a category phenomenon (and an addictive one at that). The segment of brand loyals, however, is quite strongly brand loyal.

One other conclusion seems worth preserving in the record of the session. Taking the debate between different paradigm frames down to a specific case was valuable as much for what seems to have been precluded as for the complementarity and convergence of findings that occurred. The focus on a particular problem of applied science, understanding consumers' purchase of brands of coffee,

altered the nature of the sometimes acrimonious debate between advocates of the interpretivist and positivist approaches. When the scope of this debate remains general, there is often a presumed competition between the paradigms that is supported by selected, non-overlapping case illustrations. Focusing on a specific problem emphasized what everyone knows but often forgets in the heat of debate, that different valid methods are complementary. No single approach can claim a monopoly on good science. Finally, the focus on scientific insight and contribution also serves to shift the focus away from a pernicious competition for supremacy based on political power. In stead of which side has more JCR articles or research awards, the basis of discussion was contribution to knowledge. All this said, however, we acknowledge again that this salutary shift of the terms of the debate required not only the focus on a specific problem but also the goodwill of the six presenters.

We think this type of session is important, especially for doctoral students, and hope something like it continues at future meetings.

REFERENCE

Johnson, Eric J. and J. Edward Russo (1994) "Competitive Decision Making: Two and a Half Frames," *Marketing Letters*, 5, July, 289-302.

TABLE 1

Highlighted Elements of the Interpretivist and Positivist Paradigm Frames

Elements	Interpretivist	Positivist
Goals of theory and results	Richness of understanding Insight Case-based value, including value to the participants who are studied	Parsimony Optimality Generality
Data collection	Bottom-up Avoidance of preconceptions Selection of relevant observations after data collection	Top-down Hypothesis/theory-driven Data collections limited to observations preselected as relevant
Results Inference process for results	Interpretation based on full context Atheoretical, especially the avoidance of theoretical lenses	Theory-driven Tests of hypothesis
Observations: Number Duration	 1-10 Measured in minutes to hours	 10-100 and up Measured in seconds to minutes

Consuming Experiences and Experiencing Consumption: It's Not What You Consume But How You Consume It

Ruth Ann Smith, Virginia Polytechnic Institute and State University

The basic premise of this special session was that consumption episodes give rise to experiences that are purposefully sought by consumers. The three presentations focused on research pertaining to experiences deriving from different types of consumption episodes, as summarized below.

The Politics of Pleasure, The Ethics of Experience

Linda Scott, University of Illinois at Champaign-Urbana

Scott's remarks focused on social critics who condemn experience-seeking consumption. Charges that consumption of experience as an end in itself is "meaningless," that pleasure is "obscene," and that abundance is "degrading" have been used to condemn such consumption experiences as the purchase and use of luxuries, recreation, and self-expressive acts like using make-up. Scott contended that these criticisms reflect an ideology based in Puritanism, Christian asceticism, Enlightenment economics, and class and ethnic prejudice.

She challenged this view of "moral" consumption on the grounds that its focus on basic material needs, rather than spiritual needs, devalues the best in what is human. She further contended that legitimate needs for self-expression are limited by this view In which the only acceptable consumption is that necessary for subsistence. Third, she argued that this perspective characterizes as "irrational" and "aberrant" consumer behaviors occurring with such frequency as to suggest that it is the definitions of rationality and aberrance that are inappropriate, rather than the behaviors. Finally, she provided evidence that this view is a moral smoke screen used to oppress marginal groups. She advocated a new view of consumption-as-process, in which consumption is conceptualized as experience-seeking, self expression, and personal development, rather than consumption-as-outcome.

Experiential Diversity in Product Enthusiasm: A Lifecycle Analysis

Peter H. Bloch and John L. Stockmyer, University of Missouri

Product enthusiasm, which represents the highest level of consumer involvement, has traditionally been cast as having an object focus and providing experiences that are sought as an end in themselves. In this investigation of car enthusiasts, Bloch and Stockmyer provide evidence that enthusiasts are not monolithic with respect to their experiences with a product category. Rather, their findings indicate that these experiences differ across enthusiasts and that the experience of an enthusiast changes through time.

Based on a survey of approximately 200 car enthusiasts, Bloch and Stockmyer identified six clusters (aesthetic, nostalgic, status/social, sensational, recreational, and stress-reducing) that differed in terms of the primary experience with cars. In some cases (e.g. the aesthetic cluster), the experiences were sought as an end in themselves, while in others (e.g. the status/social cluster) the experiences were socially instrumental. A comparison of the temporal duration of enthusiasm revealed a lifecycle such that an enthusiast may seek different experiences at various stages of the involvement with the product category.

Experientialism: Conceptualization and Measurement

Ruth Ann Smith, Virginia Polytechnic Institute and State University
Richard J. Lutz, University of Florida

Smith and Lutz proposed that experientialism is the experience-based counterpart to materialism and defined it following Richins and Dawson (1992) as a set of centrally held beliefs about the importance of experiences in one's life, and consisting of the three dimensions of centrality (beliefs that experiences are at the center of one's life), happiness (beliefs that experiences are essential to one's satisfaction and well-being), and success (beliefs that one's own and others' success is judged by the number and quality of experiences).

Two studies resulted in the development of a reliable (minimum subscale ($\alpha = .82$) 18-item measure. A correlation of .53 between the experientialism and materialism happiness subscales suggested that both possessions and experiences are instruments to attaining happiness. Experientialism was also highly correlated with a value on excitement (Kahle 1983). Finally, the happiness subscale exhibited significant negative correlations with life satisfaction (Andrews & Withey 1976), indicating that consumption experiences, like objects, are used to reduce dissatisfaction with life.

REFERENCES

Andrews, Frank M. and Stephen B. Withey (1976), *Social Indicators of Well-Being: American's Perceptions of Life Quality*, New York: Plenum.

Kahle, Lynn R., ed. (1983), *Social Values and Social Change: Adaptation to Life in America*, New York: Praeger.

Richins, Marsha L. and Scott Dawson (1992), "A Consumer Values Orientation for Materialism and Its Measurement: Scale Development and Validation," *Journal of Consumer Research*, 19 (December), 303-316.

Charting a Public Policy Research Agenda
Joel B. Cohen, University of Florida

This conference witnessed somewhat of a return to one of ACR's roots: the involvement of the consumer research community in issues affecting consumers' welfare. I had the privilege of organizing sessions featuring William Schultz, Deputy Commissioner for Policy at the Food and Drug Administration and Joan Bernstein, Director of the Bureau of Consumer Protection at the Federal Trade Commission, with the added and much appreciated participation of former FTC Commissioner Andrew Strenio, Lee Peeler (the Bureau's Associate Director, Division of Advertising Practices) and Bill Wilkie.

Bill is particularly representative of the small number of ACR members who have made substantial and continuing contributions to important public policy issues over the years. Such contributions flow from a willingness to tackle substantial issues that don't always fit snugly within a theoretical framework or research paradigm. One has to be prepared to examine them for their own sake, often from several competing perspectives. Moreover, those of us who have worked on such topics recognize that our well-practiced skills at constructing convenient representations of multifaceted problems can lead to research conclusions that may not be taken seriously by policy makers.

Such conceptual framework issues are hardly unique to public policy research. I frequently advise doctoral students at the problem definition stage to act a bit like a person who has acquired a large, wooded tract of land. Before deciding on the shape and structure of the house you are eager to build, it is a good idea to walk the perimeter of your territory to get a good sense of the lay of the land and how you can best accommodate to it. In plainer language, most important research contributions start with a conceptualization that is broad enough to encompass the most meaningful definition of the "problem space." This is what enables the researcher to make sensible choices about factors to be measured and manipulated over a series of studies.

Unfortunately, this implies formidable startup costs for those thinking about contributing meaningful research on public policy issues. This realization is very likely to have stunted the development of a stronger consumer research presence in areas where we are likely to have something meaningful to contribute. One part of the solution to this dilemma requires a helping hand from policymakers who have the vision to appreciate our field's potential contributions.

The very high level participation of FTC and FDA officials at this conference is intended to signal these agencies' willingness to assist consumer researchers to become more familiar with a variety of issues that these agencies view as important and which are likely to benefit from the various perspectives and research skills we can bring to bear. The immediately following papers by Jodie and Bill are intended to highlight current activities at these agencies, so that consumer researchers who are interested in tackling some of these issues can think further about them and then contact appropriate individuals to help "jump start" such projects. Some of the research topics these agencies would like to see our field address are well-defined and primarily lack good descriptive data. In other cases, consumer researchers can play an important role in helping to contribute to a better understanding of the issues and alternative ways of addressing them. I think you will find many of the research needs highlighted in the accompanying papers to be both meaningful and challenging. Both agencies look forward to inquiries and input from scholars in our field.

Federal Trade Commission Solicits Consumer Research

Joan Z. Bernstein, Federal Trade Commission[1]

Last October, I had a wonderful opportunity to address the ACR annual conference and share with your association my views on the direction of the FTC's consumer protection program effort and how your work can influence our efforts. During the presentation, I emphasized how important accurate information about consumer behavior is to our mission, and I extended to the ACR membership a general invitation to assist the FTC by conducting research that would be of help to our policy determinations.

For those readers who didn't attend the conference, some background information about the FTC may be useful. Most of the FTC's consumer protection activities focus on two fundamental questions: First, what claims are consumers receiving from particular business practices? And, second, are those claims deceptive or "unsubstantiated?" But even after the FTC determines that a law violation has occurred, we will still confront the question of whether the FTC's proposed remedy — which often involves the disclosure of information — helps the situation, or makes it worse. Often, we're reminded of a story about a zookeeper whose kangaroos kept escaping. Each time the kangaroos escaped, the zookeeper would round them up, and make the fence higher. Sitting outside the zoo one day, gazing up at the zookeeper adding yet more fencing, one of the kangaroos asked the other, "How high do you think he'll build the fence?" "I don't know," replied the other. "Maybe to the sky, if he doesn't start locking the gate at night."

The zookeeper story is an apt analogy to the challenge we face when we try to devise the correct responses to deceptive business practices. No one knows better than the consumer research community that assumptions about how consumers will react in certain situations do not always hold true. If our understanding of how consumers will react to certain information is inaccurate, we face the possibility of devising seemingly strong remedies that in real life don't effectively keep deception "fenced-in." This approach can be doubly troublesome. First, it doesn't deter deception; second, it can impose significant costs. Both hurt consumers.

The Commission's need for accurate information about consumer behavior far exceeds its ability to fund the needed studies. That's why it's so important for the FTC to communicate with your association. To the extent that you understand our research needs, you can direct your efforts towards projects that can play an important role in helping develop informed public policy decisions.

Accordingly, the following paragraphs provide examples of current issues we are dealing with where more research would be useful. At the end of each paragraph is the name and phone number of an FTC staff member who is familiar with these issues. If you are considering conducting research in any of these areas, please feel free to call and discuss your ideas: We can update you on current issues, and we always welcome your input. Here are the issues:

1. Disclosures, disclosures and more disclosures.

Advertisers use disclosures to provide additional information; the government mandates them in an effort to correct deception. At the same time, academic literature and FTC case law consistently point out the very limited communication value of many of the disclosures actually used in advertising. Research on several disclosure-related issues would help us better understand what kinds of disclosures are most effective at protecting consumers.

a. Critical disclosures of health or safety information. When FDA authorizes over-the-counter sales of drugs previously available only by prescription, the FTC becomes responsible for ensuring that the new OTC drug's advertising is not deceptive or unfair. When a health or safety claim *must* be conveyed, (*e.g.*, "see your doctor before taking this OTC drug,") how can advertising best accomplish this? What is the maximum amount of information such a message can include before its effectiveness diminishes? How well do clear and conspicuous disclosures correlate with appropriate actions by consumers? *FTC contact: Sue Cohn (202) 326-3053.*

b. Traditional automobile sales and leasing disclosures. Disclosures are included in these ads to facilitate comparison shopping. Yet, you are all familiar with auto sales or leasing ads where the disclosures are hard to understand even if you tape them and then replay them using the pause button. This is an area of current controversy, with the Federal Reserve Board actively considering changes in its regulation. There are many questions to answer. What are the outside limits on how much information a disclosure can effectively convey in television advertising? Where disclosures convey more than a consumer can understand, what is the effect — do the disclosures alert the consumer to the fact that there is something more they need to know, or does the consumer just ignore the fine print? *FTC contact: Carole Reynolds (202) 326-3230.*

c. Alternative leasing disclosures. Congress recently enacted legislation allowing radio ads for consumer leases to disclose basic information, accompanied by a referral to an 800-number or other source where more detailed information is available. We'd be interested in data on the effectiveness of this new, alternative approach to long disclosures. Do consumers respond to this opportunity? How does it affect their awareness of material information? How do the effectiveness of traditional and alternative disclosure mechanisms compare at conveying material information to consumers who participate in lease transactions? *FTC contact: Carole Reynolds (202) 326-3230.*

d. Disclosures in food health advertising. The FTC is committed to following a program of food advertising enforcement that is consistent with FDA's food labelling regulations, keeping in mind differences between labelling and advertising, and between the statutory mandates of the two agencies. A number of researchers have already responded to a prior request for research on subjects pertinent to this commitment, and those studies have been a valuable aid to our harmonization efforts. Additional topics warrant study. For example, if an ad claims that a dairy product containing saturated fat reduces osteoporosis, does that claim imply to consumers that consuming the dairy product will reduce the risk of osteoporosis without increasing the risk of another health related condition? If it does convey a general "good for you" claim, what kind of disclosure best conveys the presence and significance of the risk-increasing nutrient — a numerical disclosure of the percent of daily value of fat contained in each serving, a concise verbalization, or some other disclosure format? *FTC contact: Anne Maher (202) 326-2987.*

---

[1]The views reflected in this article are those of Ms. Bernstein and do not necessarily reflect the opinion of the Federal Trade Commission or any Commissioner.

2. How will the advent of the Internet affect consumers?

We are witnessing an explosion in the use of computers to communicate, shop, and buy. On-line services and the Internet contain substantial advertising, but much of it is in a format that differs from traditional media advertising. Moreover, the on-line environment offers significant ability to disclose additional information. This new environment provides great promise for consumers and significant challenges for consumer protection agencies. How do consumers interpret Internet ads? Do they regard them as more or less credible than more traditional media advertising? How are consumers using this new, information-rich marketing environment to make purchases and what problems are they encountering? Are there special opportunities to provide better consumer protection through consumer education in this environment? Answers to these questions will improve the Commission's ability to protect consumers who use this important medium. *FTC contacts: Lucy Morris (202) 326-3295; Marianne Watts (202) 326-3074.*

3. How is the FTC's new Telemarketing Rule working?

Changes in media are sometimes accompanied by new venues for fraud, as was demonstrated in the last decade with the advent of that free rider on the telemarketing system, telemarketing fraud. The Commission adopted a Telemarketing Sales Rule, effective December 31, 1995, that provides consumers with important protections against high tech highwaymen. It requires a telemarketer, before it commences a sales pitch, to tell the consumers that the call is a sales call, the name of the seller, and what is being sold. If the call is for a prize promotion, the telemarketer must tell the consumer that no purchase or payment is necessary to enter or win. The Rule prohibits telemarketers from misrepresenting any information about their goods or services, about the earnings potential, profitability, or liquidity of an investment, or the nature of a prize. The Commission is interested in follow-up research on the Rule's effectiveness. Are telemarketers complying with the Rule's disclosure requirements? Are these requirements reducing consumer injury? How much is it costing legitimate telemarketers to comply with the new Rule? *FTC contact: Judy Nixon (202) 326-3173.*

4. Just what is "Made In USA?"

This spring we'll be holding a workshop in Washington to consider the Commission's policy regarding "Made In USA" claims. The purpose of the workshop is to evaluate the Commission's historical approach to these claims in light of our increasingly global economy. We need to be sure that our policies protect consumers and enhance competition. This may be an area where consumer expectations are evolving rapidly, and their expectations may depend upon what product is being advertised. Thus, we would be interested in research that evaluates questions such as the following: How do consumers interpret the "Made In USA" claim when made in connection with products of varying complexity, for example, a piece of furniture, a kitchen blender, or a personal computer? If a plastic product is manufactured in the U.S., do consumers care that the raw materials are imported, or in what form? To what extent do consumers recognize that many complex products assembled in the U.S. may contain some imported parts? How can product labels convey such information? *FTC contacts: Elaine Kolish (202) 326-3042; Beth Grossman (202) 326-3019.*

5. Corrective advertising and other information remedies.

When are they warranted and what works best? The Commission is interested in improving the ways that it addresses past deception. Our orders against deceptive advertisers require that they cease disseminating false claims, and some require a monetary remedy. In addition, we are authorized to order corrective advertising in some cases, especially where false advertising played a substantial role in creating or reinforcing in the public's mind a false belief about a product, and the belief is expected to linger on after the false advertising ceases. In assessing the usefulness of this remedy, the Commission could benefit, first, from guidance on how to determine whether advertising creates a lingering misperception. Second, we are interested in research evaluating what kinds of corrective messages are most effective — what kind of language (disclaiming past claims or clarifying specific facts), what format (embedded or free standing), and in what media (direct mailings, product label disclosures, disclosures in subsequent advertisements). *FTC contact: Joel Winston (202) 326-3153.*

6. What is the effect of alcohol advertising on consumer use?

Our enforcement policies generally assume that advertising influences purchase and use decisions for an advertised product. Certainly, when consumers call in to order a product featured on an infomercial while the show is still running, we can be confident that the advertisement influenced the decision to buy. Yet, it is sometimes suggested that some products are in a different category — that consumer decisions are made without reference to advertising, or that such advertising influences brand selection only. The question of the effect of advertising on consumption in a mature market is a very difficult one. While a great deal of work has been done in this area, more would be helpful. *FTC contact: Janet Evans (202) 326-2125.*

7. What do tar and nicotine claims mean?

Cigarette ads and packages may contain representations regarding the product's tar or nicotine yield, either in the form of numerical rating or descriptive terms such as "low tar" and "ultra light." The Commission staff is considering whether to recommend that the method used to determine cigarette tar and nicotine ratings be revised, and also whether certain marketing terms used by the cigarette industry may be misleading. Questions for research include: What do the tar and nicotine ratings convey to consumers when featured on cigarette packages or in cigarette ads? What is the meaning conveyed to consumers by the terms, "ultra light," and "low tar," when contained in a cigarette ad? *FTC contact: Shira Modell (202) 326-3116.*

8. Getting the word out.

Consumer education may be the most important task for consumer protection, and it is vital that we do a better job here. The consumer who has been educated about prevalent scams, what to look for in a lease transaction, and how to interpret a health claim, is substantially less likely to be injured. Consumer education efforts are costly, however, and it is essential that our efforts are effective. What are the best ways for consumer protection law enforcement agencies to use consumer education to advance their mission? What media and what kinds of messages are most likely to reach consumers in a manner that will protect them from future injury? Taking the example of telemarketing fraud, what kind of consumer education would be most effective? *FTC contacts: Carolyn Shanoff (202) 326-3270; Toby Levin (202) 326-3156.*

9. Are we missing something?

The consumer protection issues we address — food health issues, telemarketing prize scams and credit fairness — tend to cut broadly across income levels. Moreover, we make a special effort to target practices that particularly injure the vulnerable, such as fraudulent investment operators who make it their business to feed on the life savings of the elderly. Nonetheless, we would welcome research that evaluated whether there are special consumer protection problems among low-income consumers that the FTC could effectively address under its deception or unfairness jurisdiction. *FTC contact: Lee Peeler (202) 326-3090.*

These are just a few of the many issues the FTC is working on currently. Again, I encourage you to call the FTC contact person in a given area if you have an interest in conducting research in that area. I believe that it is important for us to have a close working relationship with those in your field, and I hope this article will inspire many ACR members to consider conducting research pertinent to the FTC. Your research can assist our agency as we attempt to establish sensible policies to guide commercial practices while protecting American consumers.

Food and Drug Administration's Suggested Consumer Research Ideas

William B. Schultz, Food and Drug Administration

Senior staff at the Food and Drug Administration (FDA) were asked, "In what areas would consumer research be helpful, especially where rulemaking is concerned?" The suggestions that were raised in response to this question fall into a few categories: patient information, food/drug labeling and tobacco. The following is a broad overview of the ideas that were suggested, along with the names of contact people who would be able to provide more detailed information:

1. Patient Information:

The FDA has proposed a program called Medication Guides, a voluntary initiative that would encourage pharmacists to distribute information (a patient information leaflet) about a drug at the time that the patient receives the medication. There are issues that need to be researched regarding this area, including:

- Who is the "average" consumer;
- What sort of format is the best to convey important information to the consumer;
- Which information is absorbed and which is ignored, why, and how can more information be absorbed; and
- If a patient reads information, i.e. dosage instructions and warnings, does having knowledge affect patient behavior (for example, will giving patients the information have the desired effect of improving patient compliance and ability to avoid adverse reactions)?

2. Labels:

Another common theme for consumer research would involve labels—both for food and over-the-counter (OTC) drugs. The FDA has recently implemented the Nutrition Labeling and Education Act, which requires nutrition information on packaged foods. The FDA hopes to assess how consumers use these new "Nutrition Facts" labels. Similarly, FDA is currently developing a labeling initiative for OTC drugs. Also, many cosmetics have labeling that people should read before use. Issues surrounding these intiatives include:

- Comprehension of the labels—FDA has heard complaints from groups such as senior citizens who find the new food label difficult to understand, particularly the "serving size" area, and how it relates to the entire package. What can be done to make this information clearer to all readers;
- Use of sunscreen—there is a rising incidence of skin cancer in the United States; is this due to lack of education about the dangers of being in the sun, or due to failure to use sunscreen/cosmetics with a high enough SPF;
- How often consumers actually read nutrition labels;
- Does having nutrition information affect consumer behavior, i.e. diet or product selection;
- Could a label on OTC drugs increase patient awareness;
- Would improved or revised OTC labeling affect consumer product selection; and
- Will improving OTC drug labeling result in improvements in product use (e.g. avoiding adverse reactions)?

3. Tobacco:

Last August, the FDA published a proposed regulation restricting the access of tobacco for minors. A large part of this regulation dealt with the effect of advertising on underage use of tobacco. A great deal of consumer research was used to support the proposed rule. Some areas where additional consumer research on tobacco may be useful to the agency include:

- How can one best gauge the effect of an educational campaign against tobacco use on underage smoking;
- What would comprise an effective educational campaign;
- What is the best design for anti-smoking messages for youths/teens; and
- How successful would "tombstone" (black-and-white, text-only) advertising be in reducing teen tobacco use?

The above suggestions provide broad ideas. For more detailed discussions regarding these topics, please contact Paul Coppinger in the Office of Planning and Evaluation at (301)443-4230, or one of the following contact people:

Tobacco-related issues: Judy Wilkenfeld, Office of Policy, (301) 827-3350

Patient Information: Lou Morris, Center for Drug Evaluation and Research, (301) 827-2828

Food Labeling: Alan Levy, Center for Food Safety and Nutrition (301) 205-9448

Peak Experiences and Mountain Biking: Incorporating the Bike into the Extended Self

Kimberly J. Dodson, University of Utah

ABSTRACT

Peak experiences are highly intense, significant, and fulfilling experiences for people and are often considered turning points which lead to a change in self-concept and identity. During times of identity modification, objects are often incorporated into the extended self. By examining peak experiences among mountain bike owners, this study shows that there is a correlation between the occurrence of a peak experience and the incorporation of the mountain bike and the activity of mountain biking into the extended self.

INTRODUCTION

What's neat about mountain-bike riding is that you are able to fuse the moment and your intention together ... There's none of this thinking about what you're doing and then doing it. It's an existential dream because you're right there in the moment (Patrick 1988).

Mountain biking, especially in the mountains of the western United States, is an exciting, intense, physically challenging sport in which riders are constantly faced with opportunities for self-discovery through the testing of mental and physical limits. A sense of freedom is often associated with riding—freedom from the hassles and stress of everyday life as you become absorbed in the ride and focus on your bike, the trail, and your body, as well as the freedom which accompanies an activity that demands quick reactions and reflex behaviors. To achieve these periods of "freedom," a rider may endure a grueling ride, push her or his body beyond perceived limits, withstand adverse conditions, or survive a thrilling wreck. Yet even in light of these seemingly negative situations, the ultimate outcome is often feelings of elation and a sense of achievement. These feelings are possibly influenced by exceptional performance, overcoming adversity and skill limitations, reaching the summit, or simply riding surrounded by tremendous scenery and the natural environment. Mountain biking symbolizes virtues of ruggedness and individualism, and for many, the bike becomes an extension of their personality that allows them to exhibit rough riding techniques to bolster confidence and present a certain social image (Patrick 1988).

PEAK EXPERIENCES AND MOUNTAIN BIKING

The sport of mountain biking, like many other intense leisure activities (e.g. river rafting, skydiving, motorcycling), inherently provides opportunities for riders to achieve *peak experiences*. A *peak experience* is characterized as a transformational experience and one that surpasses the usual level of intensity, meaningfulness, and richness (Privette 1983). It leads to feelings of joy and self-fulfillment (e.g. the transcendent sense of awe and achievement upon reaching the summit of a ride) and is bounded in time rather than enduring over time (Csikszentmihalyi 1990; Privette and Bundrick 1991). Such an experience leaves a lasting impression and requires the person to display clear focus, complete absorption, loss of self-awareness, personal integration with the world or object, personal control and mastery, awareness of personal power, heightened emotion, spontaneity, freedom from everyday cares, and a sense of achievement (Arnould and Price 1993; Celsi, Randall, and Thomas 1993; Csikszentmihalyi 1990; Privette 1983; Unger and Kernan 1983; Wuthnow 1978; Yeagle, Privette, and Dunham 1989). Often this experience has such a high emotional content and lasting impact that it is difficult to describe and is characterized by individuals saying, "you have to do it to understand" (Privette 1981; Arnould and Price 1993).

PEAK EXPERIENCES AND THE EXTENDED SELF

A defining characteristic of the peak experience is the renewal of self and a deeper sense of meaning and purpose in life (Arnould and Price 1993; Celsi, Randall, and Thomas 1993; Wuthnow 1978). This intensification of self is often characterized by increased self-confidence, discovery of internal strength, personal growth in attitudes and feelings, a general sensation of learning more about yourself, increased ability to believe in yourself, and an overall feeling of rejuvenation and exhilaration (even when physically exhausted) (Arnould and Price 1993; Privette 1981; Yeagle, Privette, and Dunham 1989; Wuthnow 1978). The experience often works to crystallize and center your sense of self due to the necessity of extreme focus (Arnould and Price 1993; Privette 1981; Wohl 1977).

In many leisure activities, certain pieces of equipment are essential for achieving the desired experience. Examples of such objects are mountain bikes, rafting equipment, parachutes, motorcycles, or off-road vehicles. McAlexander and Schouten (1995) propose that in a peak experience situation, the object intimately involved in the experience will be associated with the feelings evoked by the experience and incorporated in the resulting modified self-concept and social identity. The object involved in the peak experience may itself symbolize the new self-concept because it embodies the sensations of the experience and is a reminder of the self-revelatory incident. This possible association between the emotions and transcendence achieved through a peak experience and the object involved in that experience is also relevant when considering that possessions act to store memories and feelings (Belk 1988). By symbolizing and attaching our selves to our past, objects can act to help us know who we are. Objects associated with peak experiences may not only be a reminder of the experience, but may also become valued for their potential to lead to subsequent peak experiences.

The object associated with the peak experience may also become a symbol that acts to identify the person socially with the characteristics of the chosen leisure activity. According to Haggard and Williams (1992), leisure activities are selected for their ability to construct situations that provide individuals with information that they are who they believe themselves to be, and provide others with information about who they are as well. Participation in leisure activities functions to affirm participants' identities because activities symbolize certain desirable character traits, or identity images. Symbols associated with a particular leisure activity (e.g. mountain bike, running shoes, river raft, parachute) are adopted by a person so that she or he will be identified with the characteristics of the activity (Haggard and Williams, 1992). A peak experience may help a person identify characteristics she or he wishes to display everyday. Therefore, the object associated with the experience will become an important personal and social symbol of those characteristics and desired identity. A mountain bike rider, for example, might have a peak experience which evokes feelings of confidence, mastery, self-control, and achievement. The bike will then become a symbol to both the rider and to others that she or he maintains these qualities.

Studies concerning the concept of the *extended self* have proposed that those objects most closely identified with an individual's sense of self will be valued more highly by that individual and maintain a position of heightened importance within her or his life (Belk 1988; Csikszentmihalyi and Rochberg-Halton 1981). The model of extended self used in this paper is based on Belk's work which presents the extended self as a multi-layered construct including the body of the person, external objects and personal possessions, other persons, places, and group possessions (1988). Objects within the extended self work to help the individual learn, define, and remind her or himself of who she or he is, and can include those objects that best exemplify the individual's identity and are representative of the individual's attitudes and beliefs.

A high emotional attachment to objects within the extended self separates the self-relevant aspects of a possession from the functional, non-self attachment (Belk 1989; McAlexander and Schouten 1987). Consequently, a functional object such as a bike will have more meaning to the individual whose self it is a part of than merely being a means of transportation. The bike will be considered a part of self and if it is stolen or removed, there will be a sense of loss of self (Belk, 1988; Holbrook and Hirschman 1982). In addition, because the individual's identity is expressed through the object, the object will be highly cared for (Belk 1988), and this may be reflected through careful maintenance and the purchase of associated products.

Incorporation of a particular object into a person's extended self generally occurs at a transitional time when a person desires to reconstruct self (Andreasen 1984; Csikszentmihalyi 1981; McAlexander and Schouten 1989; McAlexander et al. 1993; Schouten 1991). Objects associated with the new self are those most closely incorporated into the extended self. Peak experiences are considered turning points that lead to a change in self-concept and identity (Privette and Bundrick 1991), so there is a strong possibility that objects associated with a peak experience will be incorporated into the extended self during the role modifications that occur following a peak experience.

STUDY DESIGN

This study proposes to test the relationship between the occurrence of a peak experience while mountain biking and the incorporation of the mountain bike into the rider's extended self.

Hypothesis: Experiencing a peak experience while mountain biking is positively correlated to the incorporation of the bike into the biker's extended self.

In addition to testing the basic hypothesis that peak experiences are related to a product's incorporation into the extended self, this study will also explore the influence of incorporating the bike into self on purchase activity for bike-related products.

Data Collection

Data were collected using a survey of 66 mountain bike owners. A purposive sampling technique was used for this study, and mountain bike owners were approached at two Western universities in two states and asked to participate. It is important to recognize that this study occurred in the American West, and mountain biking experiences in the West may be different from mountain biking in other parts of the country.

Measures

The survey instrument included a number of items which measured the constructs defining attainment of a peak experience, incorporation of the bike into the extended self, purchase behavior, and personal discovery about the mountain bike or biking as a result of the peak experience.

After initial refinements, peak experience was operationalized through items drawn from the literature rated on six-point agree-disagree scales. The focus was on respondents' most memorable mountain biking experiences. These constructs were intended to measure whether a peak experience was attained. Based on prior research, the peak experience constructs included: self discovery, positive self-feelings, reflection on the experience, experience not easily described, absorption, spontaneity, newness, lasting influence on life, intensity, sense of emotion, and desire for repetition (Csikszentmihalyi 1990; Privette 1982; Privette 1983; Privette 1985a; Privette 1985b; Privette and Sherry 1986; Wuthnow 1978). See Table 1 for the measures of these constructs.

Additional items were created to address the specific focus of this study on the association of an object with the experience. The constructs for this included: reliance on bike, connection to bike, and quintessential application of bike. See Table 1 for the measures of these constructs.

Incorporation into the extended self was similarly measured through the operationalization of items which were rated on six-point agree-disagree scales and six-point important-not-important scales. The extended self constructs were developed based on previous extended self research and included: centrality to identity, attachment, contamination, care, dependence, and disposition (Belk 1988; Belk and Austin 1986; Sivadas and Machleit 1994). Two of the items, "My bike helps me narrow the gap between what I am and what I try to be" and "My bike is central to my identity" are measures taken directly from Sivadas and Machleit (1994). See Table 2 for the items used to measure extended self constructs.

To measure the desire to purchase goods related to mountain biking, four measures were developed that included liking to buy products related to biking, owning things to associate the individual with biking, buying new things specifically for the bike, and the importance of the bike having the latest accessories. See Table 3 for these measures.

A number of items were also created to measure personal discovery and attitude change following the peak experience about the mountain bike and mountain biking. These eight measures are listed in Table 4.

Additionally, an open-ended question was included that requested respondents to recall their most memorable mountain biking experience and describe it. The question preceded the peak experience questions, which it helped to frame. For purposes of this paper, the open-ended question was analyzed to provide qualitative data regarding mountain biking as an activity that may involve peak experiences and incorporation of the bike into the extended self. Finally, demographic data such as number of bikes owned, length of ownership of current bike, number of years riding mountain bikes, most important use of mountain bike, gender, and age were asked of the respondents.

Sample Characteristics

The sample of 66 mountain bike owners had a modal age of 22 years (range of 18 to 46 years) and included 7 female respondents. Respondents reported owning their current bike (the one considered when answering the survey questions) for a mean of 3.3 years, although the mode was 1.0 year and the range from 0.5 to 14 years. Number of mountain bikes ever owned ranged from 1 to 5, and the mode was 1. The number of years involved in mountain biking ranged from less than one year to 14 years, with a mean of 5.2 years and a mode of 8.0 years. Recreation and sport was reported as the most important use of their bike by 42 respondents, as compared to exercise (18 respondents), commuting (4 respondents), or racing (1 respondent).

TABLE 1
Peak Experience Survey Items

Item	Corrected Item-Total Correlation
I was totally absorbed in the experience and lost sense of time.	.7764
The experience caused me to feel differently about myself.	.7684
The experience stands out in my mind because it was so intense.	.7493
The meaning of the experience was so personal it would be hard to describe.	.7440
I discovered new things about myself.	.7427
The experience was emotionally intense.	.7345
I thought about my life and who I want to be.	.7330
The experience had more than the usual level of intensity.	.7263
Only I can fully understand what the experience meant to me.	.7126
My total focus and attention were on the event.	.7122
My bike felt like a part of me during the experience.	.6817
The experience made me reflect on who I am.	.6799
My actions just came out of me during the experience.	.6756
I felt my bike and I had experienced something together.	.6395
My bike and I worked together.	.6203
I felt more positive about myself.	.6117
Now I hope to have another experience like this one.	.6030
The experience was emotionally unlike anything I had felt before.	.5921
I got my bike just so I can have experiences like this one.	.5635
I was thinking of nothing but what was happening at that moment.	.5605
I have confidence in myself that I didn't have before.	.5562
The experience was exactly what my bike was designed for.	.5383
I felt as though I was having the ideal mountain biking adventure.	.5355
My actions were new.	.5318
I felt free and spontaneous.	.5278
I would like to have a similar experience again.	.4973
My bike was more than a tool to accomplish was I wanted.	.4824
I still remember the feelings I felt during the experience.	.4687
I had never had an experience quite like that before.	.3901
Standardized Item Alpha =	.9530

TABLE 2
Extended Self Survey Items

Item	Corrected Item-Total Correlation
My bike holds a special place in my life.	.8656
Biking holds a special place in my life.	.7478
My bike is central to my identity.	.7381
Biking is central to who I am.	.7138
I feel emotionally attached to my bike.	.6745
My Bike helps me narrow the gap between what I am and try to be.	.6708
Biking helps me be who I want to be.	.6708
If my bike was stolen from me I will feel as if part of me is missing.	.6648
If I wasn't able to bike, I would feel as if part of me was missing.	.6565
I would be a different person without my bike.	.6468
I hesitate to loan my bike to others for fear it will be different when it returns.	.5555
I feel betrayed when my bike breaks down.	.5234
It is important to me that my bike be well-maintained.	.4827
I take good care of my bike.	.4801
If I decided to get rid of my bike, it would be important that it go to a good home.	.4779
I like to be identified as a mountain biker.	.4764
I trust my bike.	.4551
Biking is more important to me than any particular bike I have owned.	.4539
Even if I need a new bike, I will still keep my current bike.	.4036
If my bike doesn't work well I feel that it has let me down.	.3472
Standardized Item Alpha =	.9220

TABLE 3
Purchase Behavior Survey Items

Item	Corrected Item-Total Correlation
I like to buy products related to biking.	.7248
It is important that my bike have "cool" accessories.	.7149
I like to buy new things for my bike.	.6448
I like to own things that associate me with biking.	.5669
Standardized Item Alpha =	.8320

TABLE 4
Discovery Survey Items

Item	Corrected Item-Total Correlation
My bike was more important to me after the experience.	.7595
After the experience, my interest in biking increased.	.7258
I discovered new things about my bike.	.7128
I discovered new things about biking that I did not know before.	.7108
The meaning of biking changed in my mind because of the experience.	.6953
Biking became more important to me because of the experience.	.6900
After the experience I felt differently toward my bike.	.6170
I felt more connected to my bike after the experience.	.5629
Standardized Item Alpha =	.8320

Analysis and Results

The experience. The open-ended question provided evidence that mountain biking is a sport which allows for diverse biking opportunities and memorable experiences. Of the sample, 43 respondents reported their most memorable bike memory as one which contained many of the characteristics of a peak experience. The experiences reported ranged from riding around the neighborhood with friends to extreme competitive riding (performance situations). For example, one 24-year-old male described his peak experience:

> Winning a State points race in the expert class. It was at Solitude Ski resort. There were about 60 people in my class. On the last lap I moved from 4th up to 1st. I was riding a Specialized StumpJumper Epic (carbon filter) custom-built. I felt great! I felt like I deserved it! A whole audience of people were there.

Peak riding experiences also focused on communion with nature. According to one 26-year-old male:

> Riding Spider's Rim in Moab ... getting to the cliff edge after 20 or so miles and looking out over the valley floor a mile below. Big sense of accomplishment and experience; humbling that nature is so huge and grand.

Incorporation of Mountain Bike or Mountain Biking. Factor analysis of the Extended Self measures clearly indicated that respondents did not differentiate between incorporation of the bike versus incorporation of biking. The measures loaded on the same factors, and in many cases loaded with exactly the same value.

Thus, respondents did not differentiate between the incorporation of their mountain bike and the incorporation of mountain biking in their extended selves.

Peak Experience and Incorporation into Extended Self. Analysis of the quantitative data was performed by creating summated variables for both *Peak Experience* and *Incorporation into Extended Self.* These variables included measures of the identified constructs, and reliability tests resulted in a Cronbach's alpha for *Peak Experience* at .95 and a Cronbach's alpha for *Extended Self* at .92.

The key correlation, between *Peak Experience* and *Extended Self* was significant at $p<.001$ and had an $R^2=.36$. This indicates that 36% of the variance between having a peak experience and incorporating the bike into the extended self was accounted for through this relationship, and there is a probability less than .001 that this was due to chance. Thus, the hypothesis that having a peak experience is related to the incorporation of the bike into the extended self is supported. The remainder of the paper examines consequences of this association between peak mountain biking experiences and feelings that the bike is a part of self.

Discovery about mountain bike and mountain biking. A scale was also created for the measures of discovery and attitude change following the peak experience about the mountain bike and mountain biking. This *Discovery* variable included eight measures and had a reliability Cronbach's alpha of .90. When correlated to the *Extended Self* variable, the result was an $R^2=.37$ at significance $p<.001$. The results of this correlation indicate that there is a significant relationship between discovery about the mountain bike and mountain biking and incorporating the bike into the extended self; 37% of the variance is accounted for with a very low probability that this is due to chance. Therefore, discovering new things about the bike and what the bike means to the rider, as a result of a peak experience, is related to the incorporation of that bike into the rider's extended self.

Purchase Behavior and Extended Self. The scale for *Purchase Behavior* included four items and had a Cronbach's alpha of .83. A correlation between *Purchase Behavior* and *Extended Self* was significant at p<.001 and had an R^2=.35. This result indicates that there is a relationship between the desire to buy new accessories for the bike and products associated with biking if the bike is incorporated into the extended self. Similarly, a correlation between *Purchase Behavior* and *Peak Experience* was significant at p<.001 and had an R^2=.18. Although the relationship is not as strong as the one found between *Purchase Behavior* and *Extended Self*, this correlation does indicate that there is some relationship between the occurrence of a peak experience while mountain biking and the desire to buy bike-related products.

DISCUSSION

The results reported here support the hypothesis that there is a positive association between peak experience while mountain biking and the incorporation of the mountain bike into the biker's extended self. Unfortunately, from this associational study it is not possible to determine the direction of this relationship. It may be either that a peak experience leads to incorporation of the object into the extended self and/or that having something highly cathected into the self leads to a greater propensity for a peak experience. These two possibilities are captured by excerpts from two memorable accounts:

I was timid yet not hesitant cruising along the ridge on the poison spider trail in Potash. I knew then that I had bonded with my Cannondale.

22-year-old male

I'm just not [yet] that close to my bike to really have a memorable experience.

22-year-old male

Although it is not possible to determine the direction of the relationship between peak experience and cathexis into extended self, the correlation of *Discovery* and *Extended Self* does indicate that greater resultant discovery and attitude change due to a peak experience relates to greater incorporation of the mountain bike and mountain biking into the extended self. Intuitively, the relationship would seem most likely to move from peak experience toward incorporation into the extended self as the mountain bike is recognized as an avenue to fulfillment and self-discovery, and one respondent described this relationship succinctly:

Slick Rock, Moab . . . My first time on Slick Rock . . . Incredible experience with biking. I found a true passion for biking then. I felt free.

The relationships between *Extended Self* and *Purchase Activity* and between *Peak Experience* and *Purchase Activity* have relevance for understanding the consequences of an object becoming incorporated into the self. Belk (1988) describes that when parts of the extended self are highly cathected they are better cared for and maintained. According to the present results, the tendency to care for something within the extended self expands to include the willingness to purchase accessories for the cathected object and devote resources to its care and improvement.

The inability of a factor analysis to separate the measures of incorporation of the mountain bike versus incorporation of the

activity of mountain biking indicates that respondents viewed the two as intertwined. That is, the intrinsic value of the mountain bike and mountain biking are undifferentiated among the respondents. This inability to separate the tangible object with the experiential activity reflects on the proposed importance of the object in achieving a peak experience, as a peak experience while mountain biking is the same as a peak experience with the mountain bike. The relationship between a peak experience and incorporation into extended self would then indicate that a peak experience while mountain biking will result in incorporation of both the mountain bike and the activity of mountain biking into the self.

A final point of discussion is the importance of other people to the attainment of a peak experience. Privette and Bundrick (1991) and Arnould and Price (1993) report that other people are a consideration in a total experience. However, they do not indicate whether people are important or unimportant in the attainment of a peak experience. Further research might explore the impact of other people on a peak experience, and if having others along enhances the tendency to incorporate the object and activity into the extended self or inhibits it. According to one respondent:

My best experience with my current bike was during the summer of 1994 riding downhill at Skibowl. It was a full day of intense terrain with 5 great friends who I've ridden with since we were 11-years-old. I learned a lot about what makes a person a true friend, but I couldn't put it in writing.

21-year-old male

The potential brand loyalty, accessory interests, and word of mouth of individuals who have incorporated an object involved in a peak experience into their extended self provide marketing opportunities unlike those found with consumers who are only minimally self-invested in particular products. Such opportunities include providing means and opportunities for consumers to achieve peak experiences and marketing accessories to a population who has a particular activity-related object highly cathected to self.

At a different level, this study introduces the relationship between peak experiences and incorporation of related objects into the extended self and opens the door for further research into this relationship. Consumers are able to personalize mass-produced products through their unique experiences with these objects. A peak experience is notable for its apparent ability to extend mere personalization of an object to cathexis into extended self.

Exploring the influence of companions on peak experience, determining if extrinsic motivations make a difference, and pursuing the relationships between the type of peak experience, biking experience of the rider, and incorporation into self are examples of potential research to build upon this study.

REFERENCES

Andreasen, A. R. (1984), "Life Status Changes and Changes in Consumer Preferences and Satisfaction," *Journal of Consumer Research*, 11, 784-794.

Arnould, Eric J. and Linda L. Price (1993), "River Magic: Extraordinary Experience and the Extended Service Encounter," *Journal of Consumer Research*, 20 (June), 24-45.

Belk, Russell W. (1988), "Possessions and the Extended Self," *Journal of Consumer Research*, 15 (September), 139-168.

Belk, Russell W. (1989), "Extended Self and Extending Paradigmatic Perspective," *Journal of Consumer Research*, 16 (June), 129-132.

Belk, Russell W. and Mark C. Austin (1986), "Organ Donation Willingness as a Function of Extended Self and Materialism," *Advances in Health Care Research*, 1986 Proceedings, eds. M. Vankatesan and Wade Lancaster, Toledo, OH: Association for Health Care, 84-88.

Celsi, Richard L., Rose L. Randall, and Leigh W. Thomas (1993), "An Exploration of High-Risk Leisure Consumption Through Skydiving," *Journal of Consumer Research*, 20 (June), 1-23.

Csikszentmihalyi, M. and E. Rochberg-Halton (1981), *The Meaning of Things: Domestic Symbols and the self*, Cambridge: Cambridge University Press.

Csikszentmihalyi, M. (1990), *Flow: The Psychology of Optimal Experience*, New York: Harper & Row, Publishers, Inc.

Haggard, Lois M. and Daniel Williams (1992), "Identity Affirmation through Leisure Activities: Leisure Symbols of the Self," *Journal of Leisure Research*, 24: 1-18.

Holbrook, Morris B. and Elizabeth C. Hirschman (1982), "The Experiential Aspects of Consumption: Consumer Fantasies, Feelings, and Fun," *Journal of Consumer Research*, 9 (September), 132-140.

McAlexander, James H. and John W. Schouten (1987), "To Me/For Me and the Extended Self: A Consumer-Experiential Perspective of Services," *American Marketing Association Winter Educator's Conference Marketing Theory*; ed. Belk et al., 56-60.

McAlexander, James H. and John W. Schouten (1989), "Hair Style Changes as Transition Markers," *Sociology and Social Research*, 74 (1), 58-62.

McAlexander, J. H. and J. W. Schouten (1995), "Peak experiences and the biker culture," presentation at the *Society for Consumer Psychology*, Winter conference.

McAlexander, James H., John W. Schouten, and Scott D. Roberts (1993), "Consumer Behavior and Divorce," *Research in Consumer Behavior*, 6, 153-184.

Patrick, Kevin (1988), "Mountain Bikes and the Baby Boomers," *Journal of American Culture*, 17-24.

Privette, Gayle (1981), "The Phenomenology of Peak Performance in Sports," *International Journal of Sport Psychology*, 12, 51-58.

Privette, Gayle (1982), "Peak Performance in Sports: A Factorial Topology," *International Journal of Sport Psychology*, 13, 242-249.

Privette, Gayle (1983), "Peak Experience, Peak Performance, and Flow: A Comparative Analysis of Positive Human Experience," *Journal of Personality and Social Psychology*, 45 (December), 1361-1368.

Privette, Gayle (1985a), "Experience as a Component of Personality Theory," *Psychological Reports*, 56 (February), 263-266.

Privette, Gayle (1985b), "Experience as a Component of Personality Theory: Phenomenological Support," *Psychological Reports*, 57 (October), 558.

Privette, Gayle and Charles M. Bundrick (1991), "Peak Experience, Peak Performance, and Flow: Correspondence of Personal Descriptions and Theoretical Constructs," *Journal of Social Behavior and Personality*, 6, 169-188.

Privette, Gayle and David Sherry (1986), "Reliability and Readability of Questionnaire: Peak Performance and Peak Experience," *Psychological Reports*, 58 (April), 491-494.

Sivadas, Eugene and Karen A. Machleit (1994), "A Scale to Determine the Extent of Object Incorporation in the Extended Self," in *Marketing Theory and Applications*, Vol. 5, C. Whan Park and Daniel C. Smith, ed. Chicago, IL: American Marketing Association.

Schouten, John W. (1991), "Selves in Transition: Symbolic Consumption in Personal Rites of Passage and Identity Reconstruction," *Journal of Consumer Research*, 17 (March), 412-425.

Unger, Lynette S. and Jerome B. Kernon (1983), "On the Meaning of Leisure: An Investigation of Some Determinants of the Subjective Experience," *Journal of Consumer Research*, 9 (March), 381-392.

Wohl, Andrzej (1977), "Sport and the Quality of Life," *International Review of Sport Sociology*, 12, 35-48.

Wuthnow, Robert (1978), "Peak Experiences: Some Empirical Tests," *Journal of Humanistic Psychology*, 18 (Summer), 59-75.

Yeagle, Ellen H., Gayle Privette, and Francis Y. Dunham (1989), "Highest Happiness: An Analysis of Artists' Peak Experience," *Psychological Reports*, 65, 523-530.

I Shop, Therefore I Am: The Role of Possessions for Self Definition

Shay Sayre, California State University, Fullerton
David Horne, California State University, Long Beach

Mute black night,
Sudden fire.
Destruction.

Deng Ming-Dao

Furniture? Gone. Clothing? Gone. Home? Gone. Cherished items? Gone. So reads the personal inventory list of countless victims of natural disasters. On the day before the disaster struck, the same victims had defined themselves, in part, through material objects they had accumulated during their lives. Would the destruction of personal possessions result in a restructuring of values and lifestyles for the victims? If so, how would those changes manifest themselves in the post-disaster purchase behavior of those victims?

In 1992, the insurance industry paid out $23 billion for destruction due to catastrophic loss in the U.S. (Scism, 1994). Media coverage of such disasters describes grief and disclosed astronomical costs from physical damage, but few reporters allocate space or time to the personal reconstruction process. The billions of dollars paid out in claim settlements to policy holders for the replacement of lost items provides an unique opportunity to study post-disaster consumer buying behavior. One important issue for study is the repurchase process. As Belk often suggests, by considering the role of consumption in providing meaning in life, we may develop a stronger vision of the significance of consumer research.

Post-disaster conditions provide a singular opportunity for studying certain aspects of consumption. Unlike normal purchasing patterns that are episodic in nature, post-disaster buying necessitates an overwhelming and pervasive commitment to personal restoration through the acquisition of new furniture, new clothing, new art, and sometimes even a new home in a very short period of time. Whether they realize it or not, disaster victims have the opportunity, through their purchases, to re-define themselves. Understanding the nature of that purchasing process is the objective of this exploratory study. Specifically this research utilized one community, transformed by a natural disaster, to investigate the relationship between material objects and personal identity. Using Babbie's (1989) definition of a proposition, we strive to draw conclusions drawn about the relationships among concepts; specifically, we plan to investigate some general propositions based on the literature of materialism and self-definition. We will utilize exploratory research to derive further insights into the relationship between newly purchased material objects and individual redefinition by victims of natural disaster.

LITERATURE REVIEW

The literature on disaster research, the nature and meaning of possessions, self-gifts, and identity are reviewed here to ground this study.

Disaster Research

Disaster literature emanates from several perspectives: psychologists study the grief and loss brought on by disaster (Gist & Lubin 1989; Bravo, et al 1990); sociologists are interested in group reaction and adaptation to disaster (Fiske & Taylor 1984): and organizations formulate policy to manage disaster relief activities (Wolfenstein 1957).

The use of natural disasters as a setting for the study of consumer behavior is almost absent from the literature. Sayre (1994) examined change in the meanings of possessions lost for victims of a firestorm, but did not explore how shifts in meaning affected post-disaster consumption or repurchasing behavior. Because insurance settlements would enable disaster victims in this sample to repurchase destroyed items[1] , this study embraces Sayre's notion of "absence" (implying temporary separation) of possessions rather than "loss" (denoting permanent separation) of possessions. Although we acknowledge the loss of cherished items or "favorite things," (Mehta & Belk, 1991) this study does not concern itself with irreplaceable objects. The absence notion is useful for conceptualizing the purchasing mindset of disaster victims.

Nature and Meaning of Possessions

The significance of material objects to people has been of interest to consumer behavior researchers since psychological theories of development were used to approach how people attached meaning to objects (Piaget 1957; Erikson 1979) . Possessions have been studied as collections (Stewart 1984), money (Lungren 1980; Furnham and Lewis 1986), pets (Cain 1985), gifts (Cheal 1986), and body parts (Rook 1985).

According to Furby (1978), possessions are multidimensional; she points out that possessions take on meaning from the society in which they are used. Lancaster and Fodly (1988) suggests that the use and control of objects are principal characteristics of ownership. Csikszentimihalyi and Rochberg-Halton (1981) made the psychological connection between objects and personal meaning in their study of ownership which investigated how extensively things shape the identity of the users. These authors, and later Walendorf, Belk and Heisley 's (1988) research from the Consumer Behavior Odyssey, demonstrated that possessions are infused with meaning by those who own them.

Osgood (1952) defines meaning as a bundle of components including experiences, images and feelings in addition to information. Meaning can reside in the object itself or in the mind of the user. Most material objects receive meaning through association with specific use and contexts. Kleine & Kernan (1991), who define meaning as a perception or interpretation of an object, developed a social-psychological paradigm for how individuals ascribe meanings to contextualized objects that embraces symbolic differentiation.

The relationship between material things and individuals is often overshadowed by the concept of property which cannot be separated from the basic relationship between being and having (Sartre 1969), a relationship that purports the importance of goods for self-definition. Miller's (1987) notion of personal property, which assumes a genuinely self-productive relationship between persons and objects, is a manifestation of Sartre's notion that is particularly relevant to this study.

However, since disaster had destroyed the possessions that were vested with significant meanings, victims may decline to make similar emotional reinvestments in their new purchases. In

---

[1]IRS law specifies that insurance settlement proceeds must be spent within two years of the settlement date; unspent funds are taxable as regular income.

Advances in Consumer Research
Volume 23, © 1996

fact, we expect disaster victims to place less significance in the objects they will or have acquired as symbols of self than they had previously placed in personal possessions.

Proposition #1: Objects will be less significant to respondents as symbols of self than they were prior to the disaster.

Self-gifting

Out of necessity, disaster victims become prone to materialism because the main focus of their post-disaster lives is to rebuild and rebuy for themselves and their families. Belk (1979) and Sherry (1983) stress that the roles and meanings of self-gifts (gifts purchased for one's self or family) are context bound. In this instance, the context for gift buying is repurchasing involuntarily disposed goods, an area not covered by research on gift giving.

According to Mick and Demoss (1990), self-gifts can be the result of disappointments, depression and/or having extra money. They proposed a dimension of "specialness" in gifting which, when applied to self-gifts, brings an extra meaningfulness based on the uncommonness or deserving elements. When applied to interpersonal gifts, specialness also implies extra meaningfulness facilitated by qualities of sacredness and deep emotions. The extent to which specialness, deserving, and money figure into the nature of purchasing is of interest to this post-disaster research where one would expect self-gifting to be an integral part of the repurchase process.

Impulse buying, defined by Rook (1987) as the urge to buy immediately, is often associated with sensitive emotional states and may play a role in disaster victim purchasing. Because of the psychological reorientation caused by physical displacement and loss and by the sense of immediaacy, we expect disaster victims to approach repurchasing with a different perspective than had they not experienced disaster. We also expect impulse buying and gifting to play a role in purchasing behavior among disaster victims.

Proposition #2: Respondents are likely to reward themselves for surviving the emotional trauma of disaster with buying behaviors that are untypical of their previous purchase occasions.

Identity and Self-definition

The idea that we regard possessions as extensions of ourselves has been well developed by Belk (1988), whose research indicates that the relationship established by an attachment to an object by its owner is an important source of identity. Hirschman and LaBarbera (1990) define objects for self-identity as being secular (symbols of accomplishment) and sacred (representative of past and personal memories with relationship links; utility items). Wicklund and Gollwitzer (1982) suggest that the construction and preservation of a self-definition depends heavily on a person's use and possession of symbols of completeness, which can be physical entities that signal to others one's self-definitional attainment. The use of owned possessions to develop and maintain self concept has also been studied by Ball and Tasaki (1992) who emphasized the changing character of identity as a factor in attachment to items.

When possessions are lost, the question of what happens to the self may be of great importance to those who study consumer behavior. Consumer research involving the construction or reconstruction of identity (Solomon 1983; Shouten 1991) suggests that consumer behavior is instrumental in the process. McAlexander, Shouten and Roberts (1994) found that people emerging from loss following divorce placed emphasis on acquisitions that symbolized desired or emerging identities.

In the absence of property, disaster victims are forced to replace their possession-based identity with relationship, values and activity-based self definition. After disasters, victims become "have-nots" and are forced to seek other means of personal identity until they are able to repurchase and reconstruct what was lost. Because disaster victims have no existing benchmark for measuring self-definition, purchases have no relationship to context and are made without contextual influences. And because victims lack the normal context as a basis for purchasing, we expect respondents to initiate change through the purchase of objects unrelated to their past identities.

Proposition #3: The nature and style of post-disaster purchases will evidence change or differences in the lives of the respondents.

In her disaster study, Sayre proposed a matrix to conceptualize the relationship between pre- and post-disaster identity based on Sartre's (1943) definition of self as "doing, having and being." In this study the researchers will use respondents' testimony to more accurately characterize the importance of property (having) for self-definition (being). Our three propositions are based on past disaster research as characterized by Sayre.

METHODOLOGY

As suggested by Wells (1993), we began our research "backwards" with a definite objective—to find out about the repurchase process—and worked back through a methodology that was constructed to give us "thick descriptions" (Geertz 1973). However, collecting elaborate voluntary descriptions of complex buyer behavior from a vulnerable respondent makes the task of the researcher a difficult one.

Stewart and Cash (1988) discusses the difficulty of interviewing grieving respondents and suggests extra care be taken to respect their situation. In order to stimulate the process of self-disclosure (Jourard 1964), researchers decided to utilize a hybrid of the photo-elicitation technique, video-elicitation, which would combine words and images together. We felt this technique would address the sensitive privacy issue.

Video-elicitation was chosen as a projective technique ideal for organizing in-depth interviews to guard the privacy of a sensitive sample. A third-person video exposure was used to lead the respondents to their own disclosures. Since daytime talk show hosts entice viewers and studio participants into intimate revelations, perhaps our simulation could create a para-social relationship between disaster victims and the video characters.

For the purpose of this study, buying situations and circumstances were discussed on video by actors playing the role of disaster victims in the process of rebuilding their lives. At intervals during the video, respondents were asked about their behavior in comparison to the people they had just seen. The video was designed to jog their memories about different aspects of buying and simultaneously be sensitive to their privacy needs.

Gaining access to disaster victims also posed a research problem. One of the researchers in this study, however, was also a disaster victim and president of a homeowners association that acted as a front for issues dealing with rebuilding Through this association, he solicited and got ample volunteers for the study. The other author was a member of the planning commission that dealt with rebuilding regulations for the city where the disaster occurred, and as such was acquainted with many disaster victims. Access not readily afforded to an outsider was granted to both researchers, the second of whom was given sanctioned outsider status because of her relationship to the other author and to the governmental body responsible for overseeing home replacement.

Technique

A script was written and pretested for its ability to lead victims through the stages of purchasing furnishings for their new homes. The script contained fourteen vignettes, each of which became a scene of the videotape. An announcer explained the purpose, and then scenes played out as a couple sitting in a living room discussing their behavior as they recalled their buying experiences. At the end of each scene, questions were posed simultaneously on the screen and by the announcer.

The taping was done by a professional crew to insure that respondents would react to the contents of the video and not to the foibles of an amateur home movie. The investigator played the twelve-minute tape on a TV/VCR unit that was taken to each respondent's residence. The tape was stopped after each scene, and the respondents comments were recorded on an audio tape.

Sample

Eighteen video-elicited interviews were conducted with respondents who had suffered complete losses of their homes. All respondents had substantial insurance settlements and were either building replacement homes or had purchased another home that they needed to completely refurnish. Respondents were representative of the demographics of the entire sample of this city's disaster victims. Two interviews were conducted without the videotape to act as a control for comparison purposes. These respondents, who had also lost everything, were asked the same questions and their replies recorded.

RESULTS

Interpretive analysis of respondents' accounts of their rebuilding and repurchasing efforts was undertaken to test our three propositions and to identify other themes related to the reacquisition process. One surprise emerged from the data.

Object Symbolism

Our first Proposition was that objects would be less significant to respondents as symbols of self than they were prior to the disaster. As expected, objects were not significant symbols of self for disaster victims. Past research (McCracken 1987) suggests that repurchased objects serve as 'dramatic props' that help people deal with the transitions to and performances of their new roles. Although we found respondents purchased items that materialized their future roles, these objects were not significant criteria for self-definition. During the absence of their possessions, most victims undertook personal value reassessments. Many respondents reported that "things" no longer assumed a significant role in their lives. Others were determined not to reinvest their emotional energy in material possessions, but to concentrate on relationships and self-actualization. Transcripts yielded the following disclosures:

I had so much love tied up in my things. I can't go through that kind of loss again. What I'm buying now won't be as important to me. [F 50s]

We got a Wolf range instead of a Kenmore, and a Sub-Zero instead of a Hotpoint. Because we had the money. Not because we care what our friends think. We got quality conscious, I guess. [M 40s]

Yea, we got better stuff, but it doesn't mean anything to us. It's just stuff. [M 50s]

Thus, this research indicated that victims were less likely to place emphasis on objects for self-definition than they had prior to the disaster and their testimony provided support for our first proposition.

Self-gifts and Impulse Buying

Our second proposition was that respondents were likely to reward themselves for surviving the trauma of a disaster with buying behaviors untypical of their previous purchasing behavior. As expected, themes of self-gifting and impulse buying were described in several ways among respondents; the most prevalent are discussed here.

Bigger is Better. Expansion of home size was an element of self-gifting revealed in the text of interviews. Any victim who was rebuilding a destroyed home with the same configuration and less than a 10% increase in the square footage had a city guarantee of an expedited review and permitting process. Those who chose to enlarge their homes or make significant architectural changes (move the garage, change the roofline, etc.) were subjected to more rigorous scrutiny and possible delays. In spite of the financial and temporal incentives to rebuild in kind, only two households interviewed chose that option. Reasons for house expansion centered around the opportunity to improve personal lifestyles—a gift to themselves for surviving disaster. One respondent decided to move rather than rebuild; she went into a retirement community after neighbors rebuked her rebuilding efforts of a slightly larger home. The following are some interview transcripts about rebuilding as gifting.

We decided to go for it. After all, we deserve it, going through the fire and all. Bigger will be better. [F 40s]

We always wanted a larger bedroom and maybe an office. So after the fire, we said, 'why not.' After all, we might never get another chance like this. [M 40s]

Hey, our family is growing and the insurance company is paying, so for sure we're building bigger. [F 30s]

Cash and Carry. Another aspect of self-gifting revealed itself as the novelty of purchasing with a full wallet. Depending on insurance policies, many respondents received significant settlement checks earmarked for either rebuilding or repurchasing household contents. The sudden implosion of funds altered some of their buying habits.

I never used to like to shop, but now that we have the money, it's fun! [M 40s]

[After I got the money] my sister came to town and we went down to the store and bought everything at once. We just picked one of this and one of that. Only took us a few hours. [F 80s]

We got so used to buying that our lifestyles had evolved to a new level. We were very nervous about what would happen when the money dried up. Could we go back to living within our salaries? [M40s]

We had the money, so we took trips. We had no house to come home to, so why not? We went to Europe three times in six months, one time for several weeks. Just for the fun of it. [M40s]

We have some buyer's remorse because we went around spending like kids in a candy store. We got some expensive art—in Japan—that just doesn't go with anything else. [M 50s]

Other victims indicated that, while picking out appliances, they acted on their impulses to buy up in price from what they might have otherwise.

We probably don't need one, but the Sub-Zero is a super special fridge . . . we treated ourselves. [F 40s]

A Wolfe range . . . because we had always wanted one and now we could have it. [M 50s]

Gifting and impulse buying were characteristic of most shopping descriptions.
We Deserve It. The aspect of "deserving" appeared at least once in every interview—a clear indication of self-gifting psychology. Respondents felt that the trauma and hardships endured after the loss of their homes and possessions were ample justification for rewarding themselves. Some bought things out of their normal price range; others upgraded their cars and appliances; all victims improved their dwelling space or quality. Here are some of their rationalizations for spending:

. . . . so we decided to splurge. What the hell, we deserve it. [F50s]

After all we've been through, why should we deny ourselves the best? [M40s}

It's a treat for us, for our pain. [F 30s]

We found ample support for proposition 2, and, indeed, previous buying habits *were* discarded in favor of larger homes, more expensive brand sets, and other items previously out of their financial reach.

Change Manifestations
Our third proposition was that the nature and style of purchases would evidence change or difference in victims' lives. As expected, most respondents opted for change when purchasing replacements for their absent belongings. Two manifestations of change appeared in respondents' transcripts.
Different is Desirable. The decision to change architectural styles was common with our respondents. Only one couple rebuilt exactly the same house; two others built similarly with modifications because they had recently remodeled or purchased. Change was the rule rather than the exception: three respondents wanted to create a certain look in keeping with the city's style; the remainder let their architects have free reign. A few architectural renderings submitted to the city planning department departed substantially from tradition, but most of our respondents decided on more modest designs. The following remarks are from victims who wanted their new homes to reflect personal change:

You can't put back or replace what you had. It was too personal—it was customized. Everything should be new. Our jobs have changed, our lives have changed. Our house will be different, too. [F 40s]

I wanted a different house so that the missing items wouldn't seem gone. I couldn't look in a room and see something was not there anymore. [F 60s]

Only one household wanted no change:

We wanted to feel like we did before. We liked our house and our furniture, so we had the same designer do our plans. [M 70s]

Innovation is Imperative. Research indicates (Erikson 1979) that furniture styles change to correspond with different phases of ones' life cycle, and as such are indicative of change in self-definition. However, when rebuying furniture, only three households opted to change their styles completely; two households were replacing lost antiques with other antiques of a similar period; five households were integrating styles to include pieces similar to their former furniture and styles new to them; one couple replaced their household contents exactly. Overall, respondents were happy for the opportunity to change styles.

I want a mix of styles; stuff with a sense of humor. So I hired a low-key decorator and told her to help me choose, then do the rest. I just wanted to get it finished. The new stuff won't have the same history. You can't buy history, it has to get done. I just want whimsy now. [F 60s]

We changed our [furniture] style. The love is gone for what was lost. We won't love the new things like we did the old, but we'll get by. [F40s]

One obvious exception to the rule was a couple who held fast to their past tradition:

We called Plummers [local furniture store] and had them send over the same furniture we had before. It was newer, of course, but we got the same colors and sizes. It's all just like it was. We didn't want better, and we have no regrets. [F 70s]

We expected that victims' purchases would reflect changes, and respondents confirmed our third proposition through the frequent use of words like "different" and "alternative" in their discussions.

SURPRISE
In addition to our propositions, a theme that emerged from the narrative was the nature and enormity of the shopping experience. Transcripts were filled with remarks about the amount of time victims had allocated to the shopping process. All respondents, without exception, described the experience as a "task" that took much of their efforts for the past year. All but one household, however, had no remorse for the way they conducted their repurchases and rebuilding, and were pleased with the outcomes of their endeavors.

Shopping became my full-time job. I quit work just so I could attend to all the details. You just don't realize how much work is involved in getting everything new. From your shoes to the door knobs, everything has to be chosen. [F 40s]

If I have to make another decision I'll scream. I hired a few people to help me, but I could have used a few more. It's too much for one person to do alone. [F 60s]

No, we'd never have a decorator—shopping is too much fun. [F 40s]

We had all antiques, so we're searching for similar ones. They're ten times the price we paid, but looking is fun. We love poking in shops to find just the right piece. [F 40s]

DISCUSSION

Preliminary results from this research suggest that victims of catastrophic events experience several types of changes that are reflected in the way they relate to material possessions. While all three of our propositions were validated by respondents' testimony, the most significant finding is the extent to which reacquisition involves reconstruction of self-identity for disaster victims. Meanings inherent in possessions that were symbolic of accomplishments, events, or relationships were buried with the objects. Some victims wondered, since the tangible expressions of their skills and talents were gone, whether those skills and talents were lost as well. Did the missing trophy erase the championship game? Most victims, reluctant to reinvest part of themselves in new possessions, viewed objects with detachment. No longer symbols of self, objects served to accommodate rather than to delineate.

Self-gifting seemed to play a significant role in the repurchase process. The notion of "deserving" the best resulted in an elevated evoked set of brands for post disaster consumers—victims moved up in their purchase sets, raising their standards of living. None of the respondents reported choosing items costing less than their predecessors. Testimony indicated that price dropped in relative importance as a purchase attribute for most respondents.

Narratives reflected that, in spite of the elevations in lifestyle through larger homes and more expensive durable goods, respondents placed less importance on their possessions than they did before the fire. The porous relationship that existed between being (self) and having (objects) before the fire was transformed into a fixed relationship: possessions took on a finite value and were less important for self-definition after disaster than they had been prior to the catastrophic event. Narratives also suggest that victims were more likely to look to relationships and ideological symbols of completeness for their personal definitions than they had previously. A change in purchase philosophy was reported by most respondents who believed that fewer objects were better; most said that they preferred product quality over quantity.

A significant discovery that emerged from the data suggests that the more time respondents allocated to shopping, the more they expressed attachment to the objects obtained. Respondents indicated that goods purchased in haste or as part of a multiple-purchase effort were without personal significance. Victims' disclosures caused us to suspect that perhaps the time, place and experience of acquisitions are the factors that lend meaning — when faced with having to replace many objects in a short span of time, there may be less meaning associated with those objects than others purchased over extended time periods in a variety of settings. This characteristic seemed true independent of the cost of the items bought. Thus, the temporal aspect of post-disaster shopping may be important for understanding post-disaster purchase behavior.

For many respondents, meaning could be created through the shopping experience. Because meaning is dependent upon a relationship or a history that exists between an object and its owner, objects become symbols of events, people and places. When objects are destroyed and the symbols are removed, their meanings cannot be replaced simply by repurchasing like items. But if the shopping experience had a story, the object was vested with meaning from the experience.

Limitations

This study is limited by the number of interviews and the narrowness of the geographic data set. The similarity of demographics among respondents also restricts generalization to other victims of catastrophic events who are insured and have upper-middle class incomes. However, our research should be of interest to manufactures and retailers who need to understand differences in post-disaster victims as consumers.

Another problem lies with our inability to measure the levels of Sartre's components of identity, having, being and doing, as they relate to our respondents. Lack of measurement resulted in our evaluating the relationship between the victim's *having* and *being* components after the unexpected event; *doing* was not studied.

CONCLUSION

Within the realm of interesting circumstances caused by disaster and with the cooperation of disaster victims, this study found a changing role of possessions and their meaning. The process of post-disaster identity reconstruction may be conceptualized as a huge shopping trip. For most respondents, the experience was utilitarian in nature and seemed like work. However, on occasion, the shopping experience could be fun. Objects purchased by respondents who perceived shopping as work had little impact on self-definition. Conversely, respondents who approached shopping as fun developed an attachment for the purchase-objects, culminating in a meaningful and identity-building experience.

Babin, Darden and Griffin's (1994) model for evaluating the shopping experience as either work or fun directly corresponds to the level of attachment reported between shopper and purchase during disaster reconstruction. This study expands that model by suggesting that, for all victims of catastrophic loss, the shopping experience may be a substitute for product-owner history, and that the nature of that experience very well may shape the process of reacquisition for the assemblage of identity-facilitating symbols.

REFERENCES

Babin, Barry, William Darden and Mitch Griffin (1994), "Work and/or Fun: Measuring Hedonic and Utilitarian Shopping Value," *Journal of Consumer Research* 20 (March), 644-656.

Ball, Dwane and Lori Tasaki (1992), "The Role and Measurement of Attachment in Consumer Behavior," *Journal of Consumer Psychology* 1 (2), 155-172.

Belk, Russell (1975), "Situational Variables and Consumer Behavior," *Journal of Consumer Behavior,* 2 (4), 157-164.

_____(1988), "Possessions and the Extended Self," *Journal of Consumer Research* 15 (September), 139-168.

Bergadaa, Michelle (1990), "The Role of Time in the Action of the Consumer," *Journal of Consumer Research* 17 (December), 289-302.

Babbie, Earl (1989), *The Practice of Social Research,* 5th Edition, Belmont, CA: Wadsworth.

Bravo, Milagros, Martina Rubio-Stipec, Glorisa Canino, Michael Woodbury and Julio Ribera (1990), "The Psychological Sequelae of Disaster Stress Prospectively and Retrospectively Evaluated," *American Journal of Community Psychology* 18 (5), 661-679.

Cain, A. (1985), "Pets as Family Members," in M. B. Susan (ed.) *Pets and the Family.* New York: Haworth, 5-10.

Cheal, D. (1986), "The Social Dimensions of Gift Behavior," *Journal of Social and Personal Relationships* 3, 423-429.

Csikszentmihalyi, Mihaly and Eugene Rochberg-Halton (1991), *The Meaning of Things: Domestic Symbols and the Self,* New York: Cambridge University Press.

Erikson, E. (1979), *Identity and the Life Cycle.* New York: Norton.

Fiske, Susan and Shelly Taylor (1984), *Social Cognition,* Reading MA: Addison Wesley.

Furman, A. and A. Lewis (1986), *The Economic Mind: The Social Psychology of Economic Behavior.* New York: St. Martins.

Furby, Lita (1978), "Possessions: Toward a Theory of Their Meaning and Function Throughout the Life Cycle," in Baltes, P. (ed) *Lifespan Development and Behavior,* New York: Academic Press, 297-336.

Geertz, Clifford (1973), "Thick Description: Toward an Interpretive Theory of Cultures" in C. Geertz (ed.), *The Interpretation of Cultures,* New York: Basic, 231-267.

Gist, Richard and Richard Lubin, eds. (1989), *Psychological Aspects of Disaster,* New York: Wiley and Sons.

Hirshman, Elizabeth and Priscilla LaBarbera (1990), "Dimensions of Possession Importance," *Psychology and Marketing* 7 (3), 215-223.

Jouard, Sidney (1964), *The Transparent Self.* Princeton, NJ: Van Nostrand Reinhold.

Kleine, Robert and Jerome Kernan (1991), "Contextual Influences on the Meanings Ascribed to Ordinary Consumption Objects," *Journal of Consumer Research* 18 (December), 311-324.

Lancaster and Fodly (1988), "Useful Extensions: A Conceptualization," *Journal for the Theory of Social Behavior* 18, 77-94.

Lingren, H. (1980), *Great Propositions: The Psychology of Money.* Los Altos CA: William Kaufman.

McAlexander, James, John Shouten and Scott Roberts (1994), "Consumer Behavior and Divorce," forthcoming, *Research in Consumer Behavior.*

McCracken, Grant (1987), "Culture and Consumption Among the Elderly: Three Research Objectives in an Emerging Field," *Aging and Society* 7, 203-227.

McKeage, Kim K.R. (1992). "Materialism and Self-Indulgence: Themes of Materialism in Self-Gift Giving," in Floyd Rudmin and Marsha Richins (eds), *Meaning, Measure and Morality of Materialism,* Provo UT: Association of Consumer Research, 140-148.

Mehta, Raj and Russell Belk (1991), "Artifacts, Identity and Transition: Favorite Possessions of Indians and Indian Immigrants to the United States," *Journal of Consumer Research* 17, March, 398-411.

Mick, David Glen and Michelle Demoss (1990), "Self-Gifts: Phenomenological Insights from Four Contexts," *Journal of Consumer Research* 17, (December), 322-332.

Miller, Daniel (1987), *Material Culture and Mass Consumption.* New York: Basil Blackwell.

Osgood, C.E. (1952), "The Nature and Measurement of Meaning," *Psychological Bulletin* 49, 197-237.

Piaget, J. (1959), *Six Psychological Studies.* New York: Random House.

Rook, D. (1985), "Body Cathexis and Market Segmentation," in M.R. Solomon (ed.), *The Psychology of Fashion.* Lexington MA: 233-242.

_____(1987), "Buying Impulse," *Journal of Consumer Research* 14, September, 189-99.

Sartre, Jean Paul (1947), *Being and Nothingness,* New York: Philosophical Library.

Sayre, Shay (1994), "Possessions and Identity in Crisis: Meaning and Change for Victims of the Oakland Firestorm," in C. Allen and D. Roedder (eds.), *Advances in Consumer Research* 21, Provo UT: Association for Consumer Research.

Scism, Leslie (1994), "Insured Losses on Catastrophies Reach $7 Billion," *Wall Street Journal,* March 29, 2.

Sherry, John F. (1983), "Gift Giving in Anthropological Perspective," *Journal of Consumer Research* 10 (2), 157-168.

Shouten, John W. (1991), "Selves in Transition: Symbolic Consumption in Personal Rites of Passage an Identity Reconstruction," *Journal of Consumer Research* 17 (March), 412-425.

Solomon, Michael (1983), "The Role of Products as Social Stimuli: A Symbolic Interaction Perspective," *Journal of Consumer Research* 10 (December), 319-329.

Stewart, Charles and William Cash, Jr. (1988), *Interviewing: Principles and Practices,* 5th Edition, Dubuque IA: W.C. Brown, 94.

Stewart, S. (1984), *On Longing: Narratives of the Miniature, the Gigantic, the Collection.* Baltimore MD: Johns Hopkins University Press.

Wallendorf, Melanie, Russell Belk and Deborah Heisley (1988), "Deep Meaning in Possessions: The Paper," in Michael Houston (ed.), *Advances in Consumer Research* 15, Provo UT: Association for Consumer Research.

Wells, William D. (1993), "Discovery-oriented Consumer Research," *Journal of Consumer Research* 19 (March), 489-504.

Wicklund, Robert and Peter Gollwitzer (1992), *Symbolic Self-Completion,* Hillsdale NJ: Lawrence Erlbaum.

Wolfenstein, Martha (1957), *Disaster, A Psychological Essay,* Glencoe IL: The Free Press.

An Ethnography of Mick's Sports Card Show: Preliminary Findings from the Field

Mary C. Martin, University of North Carolina at Charlotte
Stacey Menzel Baker, University of Nebraska-Lincoln

ABSTRACT

This paper reports the preliminary findings of an ongoing ethnography of a sports card show. This is a unique consumption domain that has yet to be explored empirically in the marketing literature, even though the market for sports cards is significant and continually growing. Participant observation and interviews are being used to study the nature of buying, selling, trading, and social interaction that take place at Mick's Sports Card Show. The emerging cultural themes include a unique language, a unique social structure, and collecting cards for economic and/or traditional and symbolic reasons.

INTRODUCTION

Following the invention of baseball by Abner Doubleday in 1839 came the introduction of sports cards. In the 1880s, sepia-toned, cardboard-backed photographs of sports stars began to accompany certain tobacco products (Vernon, Burroughs, and Mueller 1988). Thus began a phenomenon that has escalated in recent years, especially during the 1980s—sports card collecting for fun and/or profit. Along with this craze came a proliferation of sports card shows, major venues for buying, selling, and trading sports cards.

This paper presents the initial results of an ongoing ethnographic study of a sports card show. The purpose of this ethnographic study is to explore the nature of buying, selling, trading, and social interaction that take place at a sports card show. A postpositivist philosophy of science produced the research approach taken here, consistent with other ethnographic studies that have been conducted in marketing with respect to the homeless (Hill and Stamey 1990), homeless women (Hill 1991), a swap meet (Belk, Sherry, and Wallendorf 1988), a gift store (McGrath 1989), a flea market (Sherry 1990), and new bikers (Schouten and McAlexander 1995). As Schouten and McAlexander (1995) argue, studying consumption patterns of subcultures gives us insight into how people define themselves within their culture. We concur and believe that studying the consumption patterns of sports card dealers and patrons offers unique insights into the value of sports card shows.

In this paper, we will first discuss the increasingly popular and tremendous market for sports cards. Second, we review the academic literature on sports cards and related theories and concepts in marketing that will be enhanced by studying the consumption of sports cards. The research approach and why ethnography is appropriate for studying a sports card show is then discussed. Next, data collection and analysis are described which resulted in a set of "working" or emerging cultural themes that are presented. The paper concludes with a discussion briefly summarizing the emerging cultural themes and offers suggestions for future research.

THE BUSINESS OF SPORTS CARDS

Consumption of sports cards represents a major economic activity in the United States. The demand for sports cards has sky rocketed in recent years as more and more people have become interested in collecting them. Sports card mania has hit the United States as billions of dollars are spent each year on sports cards. In 1990, retail sales of all cards was about $1 billion, up from $100 million in 1981 (Tucker 1991). In 1992, retail sales had grown to $1.4 billion annually with as many as 100 companies vying for a piece of the market (Khalaf 1992). As of 1989, it was estimated that more than 3 million people collect baseball cards, with sports card mania hitting about 50,000 new collectors each year (Morse 1989).

The value of sports cards has escalated as well. For example, a Mickey Mantle card produced by Topps Company in 1965 sold for about $40.00. In April 1995, this same card is valued at $350 to $550 (Beckett 1995). Mantle's rookie card (a 1952 Topps card) is valued at a mere $14,000 to $25,000. As of 1991, the highest price ever paid for a card was $410,000 when hockey player Wayne Gretzky and team owner Bruce McNall purchased a 1910 Honus Wagner card at a New York City auction (Jaffe 1991).

A recent example illustrating sports cards mania involves the highly publicized O.J. Simpson case. A hall-of-famer (and now an accused murderer), O.J.'s football cards are worth quite a bit. Before the murders, his rookie card, a 1970 Topps, was worth about $125. Currently, this card is valued at $90 to $175 (Beckett 1995). During the first week after the murders, one card shop owner in the Midwest experimented by putting all of his O.J. cards out for sale at double the value. Within one day, all cards had been sold, no questions asked. While this dealer had been successful at getting double book value, other dealers and collectors are trading O.J. cards at half of book value. O.J. cards are being pulled at both ends of the price spectrum, an unusual phenomenon (Hitt 1994). Simpson himself, however, is only benefiting from the publicity. In jail, he has autographed about 2,500 of his cards under a $100,000 contract with Signature Rookies Trading Cards (Ellis, Benet, Stambler, and Cunneff 1994).

The sports card business has grown to be so significant that SportsNet, a computerized network of card stores and dealers across the country, was developed and has become the final arbiter of going rates for sports cards. SportsNet functions like a commodity exchange in that dealers, after applying and being accepted into the network for a $49 monthly fee, post buy and sell orders. Up to $5 million worth of cards are exchanged daily. Some dealers even hire employees whose sole responsibility is to watch prices and look for deals on SportsNet (Roush 1994). Thus, the business of sports cards is tremendous and increasingly popular.

THE SPORTS CARD LITERATURE

Though the sports card business is significant, we found only a few studies in the academic literature which have specifically looked at sports cards. Dodgen and Rapp (1992), for example, studied the personality differences of baseball card collectors. They used the Myers-Brigg Personality Inventory to determine if personality influences whether a person collects baseball cards for investment or leisure time activities. The authors found that an investor tends to be more of a "thinker"-type personality, whereas a hobbyist is more of a "feeling"-type personality.

Nardinelli and Simon (1990) and Regoli (1991) both looked at racism in baseball card collecting. Nardinelli and Simon (1990) examined whether race directly affects the value of a player in the market for baseball cards. Their results support the contention that consumer discrimination exists in the baseball card market. For example, the cards of nonwhite hitters sell for about 10 percent less than the cards of white hitters of comparable ability. Regoli (1991), however, found that race and the value of a player's rookie card are not related.

SPORTS CARDS AND THE MARKETING LITERATURE

No studies in marketing have specifically addressed sports card consumption. However, a deep understanding of this type of consumption would enhance our understanding of consumer behavior and "how consumer behavior contributes to our broader existence as human beings" (Belk 1988, p. 139). For example, the phenomenon of buying, selling, and trading sports cards has implications for the self. The role possessions play in contributing and reflecting the self is important to understanding consumer behavior. For example, in the marketing literature, Belk (1988) has suggested the notion of an "extended self," the self that is symbolically extended through possessions. The inclusion of the study of sports cards as a means to extend one's self will enhance our understanding of consumer behavior. As an example of the possible special meaning that sports cards have for one's self, Boswell (1992) describes the transition from wanting to *sell* sports cards for profit to wanting to *give* the cards to friends or wanting to *keep* the cards for his son:

> Then something funny happened. I found myself asking friends if they had any favorite old players. And I began giving away cards. My friends' gratitude was instructive. They loved the cards the way baseball cards were meant to be loved. But what really started to heal me was that, card by card, I regained misplaced parts of my childhood—parts I needed more than I knew. Finding the cards, and the cigar box I'd kept them in, help me realize that I had never gone through my parents' house since my mother died. Like most families, we had painful arguments and imperfect reconciliations. But I never understood the degree to which my memories of growing up had been diminished in sweetness by the distance and independence I had gained. Until I found the baseball cards. Through them, I reconnected with the sincerity of my parents' love. Just being around the cards made me feel cared for and appreciated.

Belk (1990) has expanded his notion of the extended self to include the dimension of time. Specifically, he suggests that besides being defined by our immediate circumstances, we are defined by our pasts and our futures. Sports cards offer a unique link to one's past. This link is illustrated by Boswell's (1992) quote above. In addition, Vernon, Burroughs, and Mueller (1988, p. 124) suggest that "baseball cards are part of the experience of millions of Americans. They are the physical embodiment of dreams and thus usually represent a solid and positive part of childhood memories." In his eulogy at Mickey Mantle's funeral, Bob Costas described how Mantle's cards may offer a link to one's past:

> Mickey Mantle was too humble and honest to believe that the whole truth about him could be found on a Wheaties box or a baseball card. But the emotional truths of childhood have a power to transcend objective fact. They stay with us through all the years, withstanding the ambivalence that so often accompanies the experiences of adults. That's why we can still recall the immediate tingle in that instant of recognition when a Mickey Mantle popped up in a pack of Topps bubble gum cards (Associated Press 1995).

Sports cards also offer a link to one's future, through continuing a collection in one's children. For example, Boswell (1992, p. 55) told his son when asked if he was going to sell his cards, "No, I'm going to save all the good ones for you." Tom Mortenson, editor of *Sports Collectors Digest*, suggests that part of the growth in collecting sports cards can be attributed to parents encouraging their children to collect. He says, "By 1980, the first generation of kids that collected baseball cards were approaching middle age. They realized they had lost a small fortune when their mothers threw out their old collections. These men began urging their kids to collect cards as an investment" (Tucker 1991, p. 65).

A related literature has begun to emerge in marketing as well: the phenomenon of collecting (e.g., Baker and Mittelstaedt 1995; Belk et al. 1991; Smith and Lee 1994). Belk et al. (1988) present some initial propositions about collecting derived from qualitative research. For example, the authors found that: 1) collections seldom begin purposefully; 2) addiction and compulsive aspects pervade collecting; 3) collecting legitimizes acquisitiveness as art or science; 4) profane to sacred conversions occur when an item enters a collection; 5) collections serve as extensions of self; 6) collections tend toward specialization; 7) post-mortem distribution problems are significant to collectors and their families; and, 8) there is a simultaneous desire for and fear of completing a collection. Other research in marketing (e.g., Belk et al. 1991; Formanek 1991) has suggested that collectors often have multiple motivations for collection including investment, obsession, preservation, and legitimization of the personal and social self. Given that collecting sports cards is a popular activity for both adults and children, examination of this consumption domain will enhance our overall understanding of collectors and collecting.

ETHNOGRAPHIC RESEARCH APPROACH

Having its roots in cultural anthropology, ethnography is a research approach that allows one to describe an in-tact cultural group or an individual typical of a cultural group (Arnould and Wallendorf 1994; Spradley 1980). Culture, as defined by Arnould and Wallendorf (1994, p. 485), is "learned, socially acquired traditions and the lifestyle of a group of people, including patterned, repetitive ways of thinking, feeling, and acting." The sports card show being studied represents an intact culture with unique rules, customs, language, and social relationships. The site is Mick's Sports Card Show in a large, metropolitan area in the Midwest (the name of the show and the informants have been changed to preserve the informants' anonymity). The show takes place in a banquet room in a hotel and occurs one Sunday a month. It attracts generally the same 25 dealers each time (because dealers are signed up to attend one year in advance) and the same patrons (they are sent postcards one week prior to each show to remind them to attend). These dealers and patrons are somewhat serious about sports cards (versus a sports card show in a mall, for example, where many children, adolescents, and lookers attend), thus the show selected offers a rich context to study.

Because of the lack of literature and theoretical base with respect to sports cards shows, an ethnographic approach is appropriate. This qualitative research design is allowing us to develop a rich, comprehensive understanding of the phenomenon by studying a sports card show in a natural setting and interpreting the meanings associated with buying, selling, and trading cards. Several research questions are guiding our work: What is the nature of buying, selling, trading, and social interaction at this sports card show? What types of people are buyers/sellers/traders at this sports card show? What occurs in a buyer-seller/trader-trader interaction? Why do people go to this sports card show? Why do people buy/sell/trade sports cards? What do sports cards mean to collectors? How/why do people begin collecting sports cards?

These research questions have allowed us to explore several cultural themes (e.g., Winthrop 1991) after two visits to the show and several interviews with dealers and patrons. Specifically, the emerging cultural themes to be described subsequently include:

Language - What unique language characterizes dealers and patrons at Mick's Sports Card Show?

Social Structure - What are the enduring, culturally patterned relations between individuals or groups at Mick's Sports Card Show, including the forms of relationship and characteristics of any groups? What characterizes the different forms of relationships at the show (e.g., what are the exchange processes for short-term business relationships and how are they different from exchange processes which characterize long-term business relationships)?

Economy - How do activities at Mick's Sports Card Show facilitate activity directed at economic ends (i.e., for what economic reasons are sports cards collected, including buying and selling)?

Traditions and Symbolism - How is collecting sports cards transmitted through time and through whom? What do sports cards symbolize to dealers and/or patrons at Mick's Sports Card Show?

DATA COLLECTION METHODS AND ANALYSIS

Consistent with Arnould and Wallendorf's (1994) suggestion, participant observation and interviews are the primary methods of data collection being used in this ethnography. Photographs are supplementing these data sources. Thus far, two visits to the show have resulted in approximately ten hours of observation with the first observation period lasting for six and one-half hours and the second lasting for three and one-half hours.

Participant observation included interaction with dealers and patrons as they bought, sold, and traded sports cards. For example, by sitting behind dealers' tables, their interactions with patrons could be observed. Detailed fieldnotes were taken, recording the activities that occurred during an interaction and verbatim conversations between the dealers and patrons. The fieldnotes also included our personal comments, feelings, and reactions that we experienced during the observations and interviews. After transcription, the fieldnotes were approximately 16 pages in length (single-spaced).

During the first visit to the show, one dealer and two patrons were interviewed. The interviews were conducted using an interview protocol as a guide, with heavy reliance on the use of probes. Given our research questions, the initial interviews with dealers and patrons included questions such as: Did you buy/sell/trade any cards today? Why did you buy/sell/trade this card(s)? What does this card(s) mean to you? What occurred during the interaction between you and the seller/buyer/trader? Do you collect baseball cards? Why do you collect baseball cards? How does it feel when you buy/sell/trade a card? The first set of interviews were tape-recorded and transcribed. Each interview lasted approximately twenty to thirty minutes. After transcription, the interviews were approximately 24 pages in length (single-spaced).

In addition to participant observation and interviews, photographs were taken of the setting and of interactions taking place. The photographs are allowing us to more thoroughly describe the setting (e.g., displays of cards) and the interactions (e.g., how patrons and dealers look at cards and price guides or make an exchange).

Data collection and analysis are being guided by the developmental research sequence described by Spradley (1980). This sequence is a systematic eight-step approach where data collection and analysis occur simultaneously.

A DESCRIPTION OF THE SITE

Mick's Sports Card Show takes place in a banquet room in the basement of a motel in a large, metropolitan area of the Midwest. A large sign above the entrance greets visitors to Mick's Sports Card Show. The wife and daughter of the man who runs the show collect $1.00 admission and offer free coffee and donuts for dealers and patrons.

About 25 dealers attend the show which occurs once a month on a Sunday from 9:00 a.m. to 5:00 p.m. The number of tables each dealer "buys" varies. For example, Dan always has two tables. However, the dealer next to Dan has four tables (the fee is $50.00 per table). The dealers tend to arrive at the show between 8:00 and 9:00 a.m. to set up. For some dealers, setting up their tables is a lengthy, meticulous process. Dan, for example, arrives by 8:00 a.m. and goes through an hour-long process of unloading, placing cases on the table in a particular order, and then placing cards in the cases (certain cards go in certain cases). For Dan, most of his cards are placed in cases according to sport (i.e., football cards in one case, baseball cards in another). Other dealers place their cards in boxes by year.

When all the dealers are set up, the banquet room appears crowded. Table after table is full of sports cards and related sports memorabilia (e.g., autographed baseballs, posters). Cards are displayed in several ways. For example, Dan has special cases which hold hundreds of cards at a time. Other dealers merely place single cards out on a table for display. Some dealers bring backdrops on which to hang cards or memorabilia.

A few minutes before 9:00 a.m., patrons begin coming to the show. At times, the show is busy—there are many patrons gathered at tables and/or strolling around the show. At other times, like during a Sunday afternoon football game, the show is not as busy—the crowd dwindles and dealers take time to visit other dealers' tables or to take breaks.

A DESCRIPTION OF THE DEALERS AND PATRONS

On first glance, we could tell that both dealers and patrons are sports fans—both tend to wear team sports apparel. For example, Trevor, a patron who was interviewed, wore a Kansas City Chiefs cap and tennis shoes. Dave, a dealer, his wife Donna, and their two young sons all wore Kansas City Chiefs sweatsuits. In fact, Donna had a family photo taken with all of the family members wearing Chiefs apparel. Though not team-specific, Dan, a dealer, wears suspenders of sports sketches.

Dealers are usually very knowledgeable about cards and the type of person who can "swing a deal." For example, as the fieldnotes indicate, Ben, a dealer, seems to be quite a salesperson:

> Ben looks like a real salesperson. He is very energetic as he talks—he talks loud and you can hear and see the enthusiasm in his voice, eyes, and action. Though Ben's table is a few yards away, I can hear Ben telling the customer that he (Ben) has some nice cards. Ben tells the customer that if he gets his name and number, he will continue to look for the cards the customer wants. Ben puts a card back for the customer who marks in a notebook something about what the two talked about.

Mick's Sports Card Show is characterized by "serious" card collectors as well. For example, most patrons come to the show with a list of needed cards. This list(s) may be on single sheets of notebook paper, in spiral or three-ring notebooks, or written in to sports card price guides. The very serious collectors carry a briefcase of some kind to hold lists, price guides, and any purchased/traded cards. Some bring boxes or notebooks of cards in hopes to trade cards. Harry is a serious card collector at the show. He talks about his buying of cards: "people go crazy—it's like drugs. I'm upgrading cards that don't need it. It's getting ridiculous." Most of the patrons also have a somewhat vast knowledge of cards. For example, they know what "rookies" or "keys" are and what determines the value of cards.

EMERGING CULTURAL THEMES

Through an ethnographic study of Mick's Sports Card Show, cultural themes are being developed. A cultural theme is any principle recurrent in a number of domains, tacit or explicit, and serving as a relationship among subsystems of cultural meaning (Spradley 1980, p. 141). In this paper, a set of "working" cultural themes is presented. The themes are described by telling a story through rich description. This description relies largely on quotes from the informants (i.e., the informants' language) and excerpts from the fieldnotes.

A Unique Language

The dealers and patrons at Mick's Sports Card Show share a unique language with respect to card collecting. For example, many types of cards exist: commons, rookies, dupes, keys, semi-keys, mint, near-mint, Mantles, Bretts. Many of these terms refer to a quality that determines a card's worth. For example, a *rookie* card is a player's first-year card and is generally worth more than other years. A *key* card is one for a very good or famous player (e.g., a *Brett* is a George Brett card, a *Mantle* is a Mickey Mantle card) and is generally worth more than a *semi-key*, a card for a good or somewhat famous player, or a *common*, a card for player not well-known. A *mint* card is one that has great quality, including good color, corners, and centering, as well as no creases.

Making a deal has a unique language as well. The fieldnotes describe typical interactions between patrons and dealers:

The customer, before he leaves, asks Dan about a '61 card—"what do you got to have for that '61 Mantle?" Dan looks at his Beckett. He usually looks at the Beckett and then looks upward and appears to be doing calculations in his head. After a few seconds, Dan quotes him $225. He says, "$225. Books at $450. That's about what I got in it."

The *Beckett* is the price guide used by almost all card collectors. Beckett provides *low book* and *high book* prices, which represent a range of value. The low book price is generally for cards that are not in mint condition, while high book price is for cards of mint condition. Some dealers and patrons will only pay a percent of Beckett. For example, Pete, a patron at the show, will only pay 15% above the low Beckett value.

A Unique Social Structure

The social structure of Mick's Sports Card Show is characterized by several forms of relationships among and between dealers and patrons. These different forms of relationships can be distinguished from each other based on *who* is a party to the relationship and *the nature and extent of contact* between the parties to the relationship.

First, *dealer-patron* relationships may be *short-term exchange* relationships. These type of relationships involve one-time transactions between a dealer and patron. A typical one-time exchange between a dealer and patron is exemplified in the following excerpts from the fieldnotes:

The customer lets Dan know that he is looking for some "good '62s." The man is with a boy about 13 years old (probably his son), who is looking at a Beckett price guide. The man now looks at a Beckett at '62 prices. The customer looks at a '62 rookie card that Dan has in one of his cases. Dan takes it out of the case for the man. The man takes the card and pulls it out of the hard plastic cover. The customer tells Dan that he is close to completing his set and says to Dan, "Tell me what you want for this." Dan quotes him $75. The customer looks at the card some more and is thinking about it in silence. Then he points out that the back of the card is not so good—the back is not "squared up"—and says, "doggone it." The customer says he will think about it and that he is looking for other '62s as well.

The customer who is looking for good '62s comes back to Dan's table. He is looking through '62 cards that Dan has in his bargain box. The customer takes out a stack of cards and reads the number of each card to the boy who looks on their list to see if they have the card. Their list is in a price guide (not a Beckett price guide, but a smaller book). When they find a card they don't have, the customer lays it out on the table. The customer has a stack of cards out and asks Dan to "see what he can do on this set of cards." He tells Dan that he will come back later to see.

The customer who had picked out a stack of '62s comes back to Dan's table for a quote. The customer is joking with Dan as they try to make a deal. The customer tells Dan to "get to the bottom line" and that he won't pay 50% for one not in good shape. Dan quotes him a price, the customer counter-offers for $5 less. The final price is $90 for the stack and one single card for $40. The customer pays Dan in cash. I notice he has a big wad of $20 bills.

Dealer-patron relationships, however, may also be *long-term exchange* ones. This type of relationship is exemplified by Dan, a dealer, and Harry, a patron. Dan has been attending Mick's Sports Card Show for about two years. Over that two years, he has frequently done business with Harry, a local physician, and hence has developed a long-term exchange relationship with Harry. Dan is always looking out for cards that Harry needs. Harry comes to the show every month and buys cards only from Dan. Harry likes to upgrade his cards. That is, he buys cards of better quality than ones he already has. When Harry arrives at a show, he immediately comes to Dan's tables and makes himself comfortable at a table behind Dan's tables by sitting down and making room to look at Dan's cards. Harry usually brings a list of cards he needs but has occasionally forgotten his list and has to run back home to get it. Dan and Harry chat as Harry looks at cards, but Harry is very focused on studying the cards he is looking at. When Harry has chosen some cards he would like to purchase from Dan, the exchange is very casual, as illustrated in an excerpt from the fieldnotes:

Harry offers Dan $65.00—"Is $65 all right for you?" he asks. Dan replies, "Whatever's fair for you." Harry writes out a check. Harry asks Dan, somewhat embarrassingly it seems, what his last name is and how to spell it. After Dan tells him, he jokingly says, "He asks me this every month." Joan (Dan's wife) remarks that they've "never had one bounce yet." Harry replies, "Not yet."

As contrasted with the typical short-term exchange relationship, long-term relationships are not characterized by extended periods of negotiation over price, offers, and counter-offers. As Harry leaves, he asks Dan to call him ahead of time (i.e., before the next show) if he "gets a bunch of '64s, '60s, or '61s."

Dealer-dealer relationships may also be short-term or long-term exchange ones. Dealers buy/sell and trade from each other quite often on a one-time basis. These dealer-dealer transactions may also not involve sports cards. For example, Joan (Dan's wife) purchased a vacuum cleaner from Dave, a dealer, who owns a vacuum cleaner shop. Long-term exchange relationships are quite common as well. Dan and Ben, for example, have a long-term exchange relationship where they buy/sell and trade from each other quite often. This exchange takes place in a casual manner similar to that between Dan and Harry. For example, after Ben purchased some cards he wanted to sell some of them to Dan. Dan brought the notebook of cards to his table and looked through them. Then, as excerpts from the fieldnotes illustrates, the exchange occurred:

Ben came over to Dan's table. Dan asks him "What percent of Beckett do you want?" Ben jokes and says, "Full book." Dan laughs and hands the notebook back. Ben then says, "Pick out some and we'll make a deal."

Dan goes over to Ben's table. He takes the notebook back and pulls out his wallet to pay Ben for some cards he found. When Dan came back, I asked him what happened. He told me that he paid $20.00 for about twenty football cards. Ben had first asked him how much the cards booked at. Dan told him about $90.00 high Beckett. Dan told Ben he'd give him $20.00. Ben jokingly asked him, "Aren't they worth $40?" Dan said no and bought them for $20.00.

Dealers also tend to have a sense of camaraderie among them. That is, they make efforts to buy, sell, and trade with each other at reasonable prices. They also try not to "out deal" each other. For example, Pete, a patron, not only comes to the show to buy or trade cards, he also comes to sell cards. However, he is careful not to offend the dealers at the show:

I like to carry some stuff in and try to sell to people. Like if somebody comes to Dan and is looking for something and I hear it, I'm not going to hone in on Dan. But as soon as he leaves Dan's table, I'm going to follow him and then I'll take him out in the parking lot. I didn't pay to be in here, so I'm not going to, you know, do a deal with any other... it's a kind of a brotherhood.

Dealer camaraderie is also evident in that dealers help each other to make sales. For example, the fieldnotes illustrate how Ben helped Dan make a sale:

Ben jumps in on the deal Dan is making with this man. Ben says to the man, "He's usually real fair. I do a lot of business with him." He also tells the man that "if I had them, I wouldn't do any less." The man says he'll take them and writes Dan a check. Ben tells the man that that's a good deal.

Besides exchange and dealer camaraderie, relationships at Mick's Sports Card Show are also personal. The dealers, for example, are not only business associates, they are friends (both at the show and outside of the show) as well. For example, Ben talks about some of the other dealers at the show:

The guy that runs the show is one of my best friends. I really like him, he uses our home all the time at the lake and stuff, I wouldn't let him use that if he didn't. And Dan, like family over here, just wouldn't be the same. I love to yell at him about his smoking. Nothing like a reformed drunk and a reformed cigarette smoker.

This type of personal relationship is also evident between dealers and patrons. For example, Harry is concerned about Dan's smoking too. He continually reminds him to stop smoking.

Finally, family relationships are part of the social structure of Mick's Sports Card Show. Many families attend the show together. Father-son(s) relationships are quite common among the patrons. Among the dealers, many couples run tables. For example, Joan comes to the show with Dan every time, though he does the dealing. This situation is similar to that of Dave and Donna, but they also bring their two young children. While Joan appears to enjoy the show, Donna apparently doesn't as she once told Joan that, "this show sucks."

Collecting Cards for Economic Reasons

The cultural theme of economy centers around the question of "how do activities at Mick's Sports Card Show facilitate activity directed at economic ends (i.e., for what economic reasons are sports cards collected, including buying and selling)?" For many dealers and patrons, reasons for buying, selling, and trading are profit- or expense-oriented. That is, dealers and patrons can make quite a bit of money buying, selling, and trading cards. In fact, the profit potential is the reason Ben started collecting cards:

What happened was, in 1984 I went to buy some Christmas presents and I bought a 1933 Babe Ruth card for 100 bucks and a '77 Topps set. My son was born in '77. And I didn't look at it for about two or three years, and the Babe Ruth card went up to about 5,000 bucks, and that usually gets your attention, and then the '77 set's now about $400. So I realized it wasn't only fun, but something I could make some money at too.

The large profit potential is exciting for Ben, as well as "scary":

It's scary, you know, what you can make. I mean, I've made about $10,000 a month, more than once. Two weeks ago I made $3700, and the week before that here I made $1700, so it was almost $6000. That's a pretty nice hobby.

Though primarily evident in dealers, patrons also consider the economy of collecting cards. For example, Trevor talks about what he looks for in cards when considering buying and reselling of cards:

First of all you look at the price of them, that's the most noticeable. If the price is good then you start looking at the card and you start grading it. If the grading's off on it, I'd give them maybe 25% of what the book says, and then I turn around and I sell it for maybe 2 or 3% more than what I bought it for. So that's where you make your profit margin at.

Collecting may also be a means of covering expenses. As Dan once said, "We've got to sell enough to cover our expenses. Then it's worth it." Dan was referring to covering show expenses (e.g., the cost of transportation to the show and the table fee). However, other dealers and patrons also use the money made from card collecting to cover other expenses. For example, Ben talks about sharing his earnings with his family and covering vacation expenses:

> When I make a nice profit I always give some to my wife, give some to the kids, and she doesn't give me any shit at all. I lay the cards around the living room, and the dining room, and I have the whole basement, but there's a direct relationship how much money she gets and how much griping I get. And she's really not too bad about it. Whenever we travel I take cards. And we always pay for expenses just by stopping at card shops and making some money. Once, this guy gave me $1300 for this box of cards—bought the whole box. When I went outside and started divvying it out, I think I wound up with $300 left. Well, after that nobody ever gave me trouble. I could stop anywhere I wanted, Penny pulls out her book and reads, waits for money. Works real well.

Similarly, Trevor talks about buying cards as an investment to be used to cover future expenses:

> It's a hobby, but also I use my sports cards that I put away maybe someday help my son go to college, help my kids go to college, and/or to hand them down to them, let them collect and maybe start their own little collection.

Sometimes, however, the desire to spend money on cards clashes with other economic needs. For example, one patron interested in several high-priced cards (e.g., ranging from $27.00 to $200.00 a piece) from Dan hesitated to purchase the cards because he had a house payment due.

Tradition and Symbolism of Collecting Cards

Collecting sports cards seems to be a tradition for some dealers and patrons. The fact that many fathers and their sons come to Mick's Sports Card Show together seems to illustrate passing on of tradition. For some, collecting cards is done because they did it as children. For example, Trevor talks about how he got interested in sports cards:

> Oh, that's a long story. Way back in '72, mowing yards as a kid, making $.50 a yard mowing them, just going around through the neighborhood convenience store and buying sports cards. Just things that me and my friends used to do when we were kids. You know, we used to trade and swap them, trade them back and forth, things like that. Just been a hobby ever since, since I was a kid.

> When I was a kid I used to trade all the time. Me and my buddies would get together. We'd all get together with our shoe box full of cards and sit around and "Hey, I'll trade you a Willie Mays for a Nolan Ryan. I'll trade you a couple Hank Aarons for a Thurman Munson and a, you know, and this here, you know, or Willie McCovey, yeah, all right, you know." Yeah, we traded all the time.

In addition, Trevor would like to continue the tradition of collecting cards. He wants "to hand them down to them (his children), let them collect and maybe start their own little collection."

For Trevor, sports cards represent a tradition in another way. Trevor likes to buy older cards —"the original baseball cards," for example. For Trevor, the original baseball cards seem to preserve the tradition of baseball as it used to be when he was a child:

> I'd like to have the 1934s because I'd like to have the Lou Gehrig, the Ruth, and all the old players from the days when baseball was, you know, there. You don't have to worry about strikes and things like that. Back then it was, you know, you go out to the ball game, you chew hot dog, and watch Hank, Babe Ruth hit a home run, or Lou Gehrig smack one. Nowadays everyone's talking money. I mean, it's not a game anymore.

> I probably have about 50,000 of them from when I was a kid, back when I was about 6 years old. I look at them today and I'm like, man, I never thought I'd buy so many cards. For baseball cards now you're spending a dollar and a half, two dollars, three dollars a pack. Heck, when I was buying them, you could get them for 15¢. Like I said, it's not a game anymore. It's a dollar situation, everyone wants the money off of it. And it's strange, it really is, how baseball can really turn from being so nice, going out to a park and watching guys hit a ball, and, getting autographs on a baseball card that you paid maybe five cents for. Now there are strikes, where no one wants to play ball unless they get their millions paid to them, and then you got to spend 40 bucks for a card that you have to go and get an autograph on. It's ridiculous. It's a money market any more, it's not just a game. Kind of sad.

Thus, collecting cards seems to represent passing on of a tradition between family members, as well as a means to preserve traditions experienced as a child.

Sports cards also act as symbolism for dealers and/or patrons at Mick's Sports Card Show. Preserving the tradition of baseball that Trevor described above also represents symbolism of the past. Trevor also talked about what his collection of cards means to him:

> It's just a part of my past, you know, to me my cards are a part of my past. I cherish them like crazy, but like I said, it's part of my past. I'm going to be able to leave to my kids when they get older, and that's basically what my cards mean. Moneywise, yeah, I sell a few of them here and there, but just some of the cards that I don't really care about. Other cards that I do care about I leave for my kids. That's what my collection means to me.

Collecting cards also seems to represent being part of the game. For example, Trevor discussed why he thinks sports cards are popular items:

> Since you can't have an autograph for them (the players) or you can't see them in person all the time, or what have you, why not keep them around. A lot of people get sports cards and that's why they have them.

SUMMARY OF EMERGING CULTURAL THEMES

The cultural themes that are emerging through this ethnographic study of Mick's Sports Card Show include a unique language, a unique social structure, economy, and tradition and symbolism. First, the dealers and patrons of Mick's Sports Card Show tend to use a unique language. They buy and sell "keys," "dupes," "rookies," and "near-mint" cards, for example. Second, the social structure is unique in that several forms of relationships exist among dealers and patrons which are characterized by different exchange processes. Third, dealers and patrons are motivated to buy, sell, and trade cards for economic reasons. Dealers, for example, are very profit-oriented; they enjoy making a profit through selling a card or realizing the profit potential when a card has risen in value. Finally, the tradition and symbolism of collecting sports cards are evident. Some patrons buy, sell, and trade sports cards because they are carrying on a tradition experienced as a child while others view the exchange as symbolic of being part of "the" game.

The cultural themes are intertwined in several interesting ways. For example, the primary reason most dealers attend the show is to make money. To do this, they must understand the language used in negotiation. They must also understand why cards appeal to certain people (e.g., some may want a certain card because it represents the year they were born) so that when they are negotiating they do not focus on attributes of the cards which are irrelevant to buyers or traders. The relationships which are established provide an added benefit to these dealers (e.g., they may "share" customers) because they look out for one another and may actually assist in the sales effort. From these findings, one might hypothesize that all dealers attend shows because of the economic potential; however, this is not necessarily the case. For example, Ben, who deals in a much larger volume of sports cards than the other dealers, attends the show primarily to establish contacts. In fact, Ben expects to lose money at the show. Thus, an alternative hypotheses seems to be that for those dealers for whom the primary place for buying, selling, and trading is Mick's Sports Card Show, the economic culture is most important. For dealers who have additional venues of exchange, the social structure seems to be most important.

The cultural themes presented here are "working" ones. That is, while they appear to represent the culture at Mick's Sports Card Show, future visits to the site will be used to verify them as well as to discover other possible cultural themes. Although an ethnographic study which explores the culture of Mick's Sports Card Show is our primary purpose, we also have uncovered areas within each theme that represent potentially rich areas for future research. In the short run, the social structure and the nature of the relationships at the show are particularly compelling. The show offers dealers an opportunity to engage in symbiotic relationships with patrons and other dealers. It appears that Mick's Sports Card Show may be characterized as an embedded market (Frenzen and Davis 1990) in that both the patrons and dealers derive utility from the sports cards as well as from the social capital of the ties between them.

Another fruitful avenue for research derives from the tradition and symbolism of sports cards. Some patrons refuse to buy any of the newer cards (those produced within the last decade) because the number of companies manufacturing sports-related paraphernalia (including cards, pogs, pennants, figurines, etc.) has increased dramatically. These patrons believe that the cards have been "commercialized" to such an extent that the fun and nostalgia derived from collecting cards have been taken away. Because these new cards are no longer sacred, they do not have special meaning and, in turn, they do not fit with these patrons' collections and do not become part of their extended selves.

Some dealers are also bothered by the proliferation of new cards for economic reasons. These dealers believe it is impossible to be knowledgeable about all of the new items. Because they are unable to develop their expertise, they will not deal in new items which are risky and may not prove to be profitable.

Mick's Sports Card Show offers us a unique opportunity to explore an intact cultural group. Consumer desires for collectibles make it likely that venues such as this sports card show will continue to be of importance. Thus, the transferability of our findings to other similar venues (e.g., comic book or depression glass shows) also deserves consideration in future research.

REFERENCES

Arnould, Eric J. and Melanie Wallendorf (1994), "Market-Oriented Ethnography: Interpretation Building and Marketing Strategy Formulation," *Journal of Marketing Research*, 31 (November), 484-504.

Associated Press (1995), "The Eulogy," *The Charlotte Observer*, August 16, 3B.

Baker, Stacey Menzel and Robert M. Mittelstaedt (1995), "The Meaning of the Search, Evaluation, and Selection of 'Yesterday's Cast-Offs': A Phenomenological Study into the Acquisition of the Collection," in *Enhancing Knowledge Development in Marketing*, B. B. Stern and G. M. Zinkhan (Eds.), 152.

Beckett Baseball Card Monthly, April 1995.

Beckett Football Card Monthly, March 1995.

Belk, Russell W. (1988), "Possessions and the Extended Self," *Journal of Consumer Research*, 15 (September), 139-168.

_____ (1990), "The Role of Possessions in Constructing and Maintaining a Sense of Past," in *Advances in Consumer Research*, M.E. Goldberg, G. Gorn, and R.W. Pollay (Eds.), 17, 669-676.

_____, John F. Sherry, Jr., and Melanie Wallendorf (1988), "A Naturalistic Inquiry into Buyer and Seller Behavior at a Swap Meet," *Journal of Consumer Research*, 14 (March), 449-470.

_____, Melanie Wallendorf, John F. Sherry, Jr., Morris B. Holbrook, and Scott Roberts (1988), "Collectors and Collecting," in *Advances in Consumer Research*, M. Houston (Ed.), 15, 548-553.

_____, Melanie Wallendorf, John F. Sherry, Jr., and Morris B. Holbrook (1991), "Collecting in a Consumer Culture," in *Highways and Buyways*, R.W. Belk (Ed.), Provo, UT: Association for Consumer Research, 178-211.

Boswell, Thomas (1992), "The $50,000 Baseball Cards," *Reader's Digest*, May, 51-55.

Dodgen, Lynda and Adrian Rapp (1992), "An Analysis of Personality Differences Between Baseball Card Collectors and Investors Based on the Myers-Briggs Personality Inventory," *Journal of Social Behavior and Personality*, 7 (2), 355-361.

Ellis, David, Lorenzo Benet, Lyndon Stambler, and Tom Cunneff (1994), "Marking Time," *People*, September 26, 77-82.

Formanek, Ruth (1991), "Why They Collect: Collectors Reveal Their Motivations," *Journal of Social Behavior and Personality*, 6 (6), 275-286.

Frenzen, Jonathan K. and Harry L. Davis (1990), "Purchasing Behavior in Embedded Markets," *Journal of Consumer Research*, 17 (June), 1-12.

Hill, Ronald Paul (1991), "Homeless Women, Special Possessions, and the Meaning of 'Home': An Ethnographic Case Study," *Journal of Consumer Research*, 18 (December), 298-310.

_____ and Mark Stamey (1990), "The Homeless in America: An Examination of Possessions and Consumption Behaviors," *Journal of Consumer Research*, 17 (December), 303-321.

Hitt, Dan (1994), "Wait and See," *Beckett Football Card Monthly*, September, 20.

Jaffe, Michael (1991), "For the Record," *Sports Illustrated*, 74 (12, April 1), 84.

Khalaf, Roula (1992), "Card Glut," *Forbes*, December 21, 89.

McGrath, Mary Ann (1989), "An Ethnography of a Gift Store: Trappings, Wrappings, and Rapture," *Journal of Retailing*, 65 (Winter), 421-449.

Morse, R. (1989), "Baseball Card Shows Document Hobby Explosion," *Sports Collectors Digest*, 16 (June), 178-181.

Nardinelli, Clark and Curtis Simon (1990), "Customer Racial Discrimination in the Market for Memorabilia: The Case of Baseball," *The Quarterly Journal of Economics*, 105 (August), 575-595.

Regoli, Bob (1991), "Racism in Baseball Card Collecting: Fact or Fiction?" *Human Relations*, 44 (3), 255-264.

Roush, Chris (1994), "The Wall Street of Trading Cards," *Business Week*, April 11, 58.

Schouten, John W. and James H. McAlexander (1995), "Subcultures of Consumption: An Ethnography of the New Bikers," *Journal of Consumer Research*, 22 (June), 43-61.

Sherry, John F., Jr. (1990), "Dealers and Dealing in a Periodic Market: Informal Retailing in Ethnographic Perspective," *Journal of Retailing*, 66 (Summer), 174-200.

Smith, Ruth Ann and Renee Lee (1994), "Going with the Flow: Collecting as an Optimal Consumer Experience," paper presented at the Annual Conference of the Association for Consumer Research, Boston, MA.

Spradley, James P. (1980), *Participant Observation*, Fort Worth, TX: Holt, Rinehart, and Winston, Inc.

Tucker, William (1991), "Kids will be Collectors," *Forbes*, February 4, 64-66.

Vernon, John, Wynell Burroughs, and Jean Mueller (1988), "Teaching with Documents," *Social Education*, February, 124-126.

Winthrop, Robert H. (1991), *Dictionary of Concepts in Cultural Anthropology*, New York, NY: Greenwood Press.

The Effects of Context-Induced Mood States on Initial and Repeat Product Evaluations: A Preliminary Investigation

John Hadjimarcou, University of Texas–El Paso
John W. Barnes, University of Texas–El Paso
Richard S. Jacobs, University of Texas–El Paso

ABSTRACT

This study examines the effects of context-induced mood states on initial and repeat global product evaluations, attitude toward the object, and purchase intentions. The on-line and memory-based processing paradigms are used to predict and interpret the effects of positive and negative mood states on product evaluations, and purchase intentions measured at two different times. Consistent with prior findings, the results indicate that subjective affective states influenced initial product evaluations. In contrast, repeat product evaluations were not susceptible to mood states. Implications for advertising, media planning, and retailing are discussed and further research suggestions are offered.

INTRODUCTION

Findings in marketing and social psychology provide strong evidence for the existence of mood effects on various aspects of behavior (e.g., Isen 1970), cognition (e.g., Bower 1981; Bower, Gilligan, and Monteiro 1981; Knowles, Grove, and Burroughs 1993), and judgments of familiar and unfamiliar stimuli (e.g., Johnson and Tversky 1983; Gardner 1985; Batra and Stayman 1990). In general, people in positive moods have strong tendencies to provide positive evaluations and act in positive ways, while people in negative moods tend to do the reverse (Clark and Isen 1982; Gardner 1985). However, the study of the impact of mood states on judgment and behavior has thus far focused on the salience of mood states on *initial* product judgments, while their influence on *repeat* judgments remains largely ignored in the literature. Further, in most situations consumers receive product information and may form initial evaluations of a product in the context of a particular mood state (for example, forming an initial judgment of a product advertised in a commercial during a happy or sad TV program). At a later time, they may be called upon to reconsider the advertised product in an actual purchasing encounter in the context of yet another mood state. An intriguing question is whether mood states are salient at *both* stages of this purchasing scenario. Although advertisers keep mood contexts in mind when developing advertising strategies and media plans (Goldberg and Gorn 1987), a limited understanding of mood effects on repeat product evaluations and purchase intentions may result in inappropriate advertising strategies with costly implications. Greater understanding of such effects is thus needed by researchers and practitioners alike.

The purpose of this study is to investigate the influence of subjective affective states on initial as well as repeat product evaluations. Specifically, we will examine the case where subjects in a positive or negative mood receive information about an ostensibly unfamiliar stimulus which they are asked to evaluate immediately following the presentation of information, as well as after a two-day interval. We also argue that the paradigms of on-line and memory-based processing could be used to accurately predict the direction of both initial and repeat measurements involving global product evaluations, attitude toward the object, and purchase intentions. First, we will present a review of the relevant literature and the conceptual foundations of our study. Following the development of the hypotheses, we describe the study methods, processes, and analysis of the data. Finally, we report the results and briefly discuss implications for future research.

PAST RESEARCH AND CONCEPTUAL FOUNDATIONS

Considerable evidence exists to suggest that mood states affect judgments, behavior, and the recall of information in a mood congruent direction. In particular, using mood congruency theory, researchers agree that subjects processing information in a positive mood state rate ambiguous stimuli as more pleasant (Isen and Shalker 1982), concentrate on positive rather than negative self-relevant information (Mischel, Ebbesen, and Zeiss 1973), and reward themselves more generously (Mischel, Coates, and Raskoff 1968) than those in either a neutral or negative mood state. Further, Bower, Gilligan and Monteiro (1981) examined the impact of mood on cognitions and concluded that subjects were more likely to recall information congruent with their mood at encoding. Bless, Mackie, and Schwarz (1992) also reported that subjects had the tendency to reduce cognitive effort while in a positive mood.

In a marketing context, studies have found that subjects processing information in a positive mood are more likely to provide more positive brand attitudes (e.g., Batra and Stayman 1990). Positive mood states have also been linked to higher levels of persuasion, especially with regard to advertising claims (Batra and Stayman 1990). Similarly, Goldberg and Gorn (1987) reported that viewers who watched commercials during a happy television program were more likely to provide positive cognitive responses and perceive the commercials as more effective than those who watched the commercials in the context of a sad program.

While the congruent effects of positive moods have been substantiated in the literature, the influences of negative mood states have been less predictable (Clark and Isen 1982; Gardner 1985). For example, some researchers have found that being in a negative mood state increases one's antisocial behavior (Moore, Underwood and Rosenhan 1973). At the same time, others have reported that some negative feelings increase prosocial behavior (see Clark and Isen (1982) for an excellent review of the various findings).

In summary, past research focusing on mood states and consumer behavior has reinforced the notion that consumer product evaluations and recall of ad and/or product related information are significantly affected by the consumer's subjective mood. In many cases, mood congruency theory accurately predicts the impact of positive and negative mood states upon salient consumer behavior variables. However, past research has concentrated solely on the impact of mood states on initial product judgments, and thus ignored more externally valid marketing situations that include repeat evaluations. Recent studies have further shown that mood states may not have an impact on *memory-based* evaluations as compared to *on-line* evaluations (Srull 1987; Knowles, Grove, and Burroughs 1993). On-line evaluations involve a simultaneous consideration of available information about a stimulus with "...an implicit or explicit objective of making an evaluation..." (Knowles, Grove, and Burroughs 1993, p. 136). Evaluations via memory-based processing involve the retrieval of information already stored in long-term memory.

Srull (1987), for example, observed congruent mood effects on initial evaluations taken 48 hours after product information was presented. In this case, subjects were initially asked to form an evaluation of the product (on-line condition) while in a mood state.

In contrast, later (but initial) evaluations of subjects first instructed to simply "comprehend" the product information (memory-based condition) failed to exhibit a mood-congruent pattern, even though the subjects also experienced different mood states at encoding (Experiment 1). In the same study, the author investigated the impact of mood states on later evaluations when moods were induced at the time product evaluations were measured (at retrieval). In this case, the results suggested that mood states may affect memory-based evaluations provided they are present when evaluations actually occur (Experiment 2). In the same experiment, Srull (1987) further reported that subjects initially instructed to use the information to form a product evaluation (on-line condition) did not exhibit different evaluations, counter to the mood congruency theory. Consistent with these findings, Knowles, Grove, and Burroughs (1993) reported that delayed mood states did not influence brand evaluations in a memory-based condition, but did affect the amount and type of information recalled by the respondents. Neither of these studies, however, has examined the salience of mood states on repeat product evaluations since the measurements were taken only once (either at encoding—Time One or retrieval—Time Two).

Yet, the majority of consumption situations involve a two-stage process (Keller 1991; Knowles, Grove, and Burroughs 1993). Consumers receive information about products via print and electronic media and may form initial product evaluations at that time. Often the information becomes available while watching a mood-inducing happy/sad TV program, or after reading a happy/sad article in a popular magazine. Consumers may later be called upon to re-evaluate the product in an actual purchase encounter (e.g., in a retail establishment) while they are experiencing a similar or a different mood state. It would be interesting then to examine the influence of mood states at *both* stages of this consumption situation.

On-line evaluations are quite common, whereas memory-based evaluations are relatively infrequent (Hastie and Park 1986). The authors suggest that most individuals form initial predispositions toward a stimulus spontaneously when receiving information about it. This occurs regardless of specific instructions designed to prevent the formation of evaluations. Moreover, simulation of a memory-based situation in an experimental setting may prove to be difficult in itself (Hastie and Park 1986). Nonetheless, it may be impossible to determine whether the subjects formed an overall evaluation of the product at encoding (initial evaluation) or retrieval (perhaps, a repeat evaluation). In this study, therefore, subjects were instructed from the outset to form overall evaluations of the stimulus while stimulus-related information was immediately available to them (on-line evaluation). The subjects were then instructed to provide repeat (not memory-based) evaluations of the stimulus at a later time. Unlike previous research, it is interesting to note that different affective states were induced at *both* evaluation stages.

HYPOTHESES

Given the previous discussion on the mood congruency effects, we would expect initial evaluations to be consistent with previous findings. Therefore, we developed the following hypothesis:

H_1:   Subjects in a positive context-induced mood will provide more favorable global evaluations, attitude toward the object, and purchase intentions than subjects in a negative mood state.

Repeat evaluations cannot readily be considered memory-based evaluations since subjects have already formed their overall

product evaluations at an earlier stage. To reiterate, memory-based evaluations are those occurring at a subsequent time, while information for forming these evaluations was received at an earlier time. The basic premise here is that subjects have not supposedly formed an evaluation at the time stimulus information was received. Therefore, it is expected that when subjects are later called upon to make an evaluation they will retrieve the previously stored information for that purpose. In the present study, subjects were specifically instructed to form evaluations on line. Thus, the impact of mood states on repeat evaluations should be minimal (cf. Srull 1987):

H_2:   Subjects in either a positive or negative context-dependent mood state will provide repeat global evaluations, attitude toward the object, and purchase intentions that are similar to initial evaluations.

METHODOLOGY

Design and Procedure

The subjects were 81 undergraduate students enrolled in marketing courses at a major Southwestern university. They were asked to participate in the study on a voluntary basis, and received extra credit in their class for participation. The experiment was conducted during regularly scheduled class periods. The respondents were also told that they would be participating in two unrelated studies conducted over two consecutive class meetings (or stages).

The subjects were informed that their Stage 1 participation would involve two different studies: an "Empathy Study" and a "Product Evaluation Study." Two days later, the subjects were asked to participate in Stage 2 of the experiment. At that time, they were told that "...preliminary examination of the data collected two days ago led us to believe that we need to collect some additional information..." Otherwise, the procedures for Stage 2 were identical to the procedures used in Stage 1.

Consistent with Batra and Stayman (1990) and Gardner (1992), the experiment was conducted using two separate research assistants in an attempt to mask the connection between the two studies. In addition, the two separate survey instruments were printed on different colored paper, using two different font formats. Later debriefing of the subjects revealed that the participants saw no connection between the two studies either in Stage 1 or Stage 2.

Phase I. As mentioned above, each stage of the experiment included two phases. The first phase of Stage 1 involved the manipulation of context induced-mood states. This was coined as the "Empathy Study." During this phase, subjects were randomly assigned to one of two experimental groups. After completing an informed consent form, forty-one subjects were asked to "...take a few minutes to recall a happy event in your life ...and to write down exactly how you felt during that period." This was done to prime the subjects' affective states prior to reading a similarly-valenced (i.e., happy) story. In contrast, forty subjects were asked to recall a sad event in their life as well as to elaborate on their feelings at the time prior to reading a "sad" story.

In the first phase of Stage 2, approximately half of the subjects that read the happy story in Stage 1 were asked to read a happy story, and the remainder to read a sad story. Similarly, half of the subjects that read the sad story in Stage 1 were asked to read a happy story and vice versa. As in Stage 1, assignment to the two mood treatments in Stage 2 was random.

All four stories (two happy, two sad) were selected from a total of 12 stories pretested at an earlier time using 96 subjects similar to the ones participating in this study. The stories were generated from actual stories found in popular magazines such as Reader's Digest. After reading the stories, pretest subjects were asked to respond to the Mood Short Form (MSF) scale (Peterson and Sauber 1983) to assess their mood state. The four stories ultimately chosen were those eliciting the most positive and negative mood states in our pretest subjects. For example, one of the happy stories described how a middle-aged doctor saved the life of his long-lost early childhood friend, suffering from leukemia, without either of the two realizing at first their early childhood ties. The story becomes happy when both become reacquainted. Another story, designed to elicit a negative mood, featured a pregnant woman's battle with cancer. She ultimately gives birth to a healthy baby boy, despite the massive chemotherapy treatments received during her pregnancy. Soon after the birth, she also finds out that her cancer is in full remission. Tragically, both her husband and baby boy are then involved in a deadly automobile accident.

After reading the story, the subjects were asked to record their feelings and thoughts. Consistent with Gardner (1992), this was done to accentuate the story's impact on mood states. The subjects were then asked to respond to the MSF scale.

Phase II. The second phase of the experiment was conducted immediately following completion of the "Empathy Study." Another researcher asked the participants to complete a second informed consent form and briefly explained the purpose of the study. The subjects were first asked to read information about a new digital audio tape player (code named DAT-111) soon to be introduced in the market. Specifically, the subjects were instructed to "... imagine that you are actually in the market to buy the DAT player ... try to get an idea of what it would be like and of its quality ... try to form as clear an impression of the product as you can. Later, we will be asking you to evaluate the DAT player and its features, and also whether you would purchase it..." The instructions were specifically designed to simulate an *on-line processing* situation (cf. Hastie and Park 1986; Srull 1987; Knowles, Grove and Burroughs 1993). The information consisted of a total of 15 attributes describing various features of the DAT (e.g., it comes with many accessories, average sound quality of 6.7 on a scale of 1 to 10). The attribute information was arranged in random order and presented in a format similar to that found in *Consumer Reports.*

All 15 attributes were derived from a total of 30 attributes pretested at an earlier time. Specifically, 96 undergraduate students from the same population in which the main study was conducted were asked to evaluate the 30 attributes in terms of favorableness on a seven-point Likert-type scale (1-Very unfavorable to 7-Very favorable), and importance in a purchase decision (1-Very unimportant to 7-Very important). Based on these results, the attribute information selected was evaluated as relatively neutral in terms of its favorability. In addition, information was chosen that was considered more or less equally important to the subject population. This was done to avoid biasing for or against any discrete attribute information. We wanted each piece of attribute information to be given an approximately equal chance of being considered in product evaluation regardless of mood state. Consequently, the product could not be clearly evaluated as either positive or negative, but was otherwise regarded as *ambiguous* in terms of its overall appeal. This also implies that the ad was strictly "informational" or fact-based.

To ensure that the evaluations did not simply reflect information in short-term working memory, a distractor task was introduced prior to administering the dependent measures in Stage 1. The participants were simply asked to "... list the brand names of cassette players you remember." Immediately following the

distractor task, the subjects completed global evaluation scales. Also, they were asked to evaluate each of 15 attributes, and indicate their beliefs about whether the product actually had the attributes in question. Finally, the subjects were asked to report their purchase intentions.

Both experimental phases took a total of approximately 25 minutes to complete in Stage 1, but only 20 minutes in Stage 2. The shorter length of time in Stage 2 can be attributed to the fact that respondents did not again receive the attribute information about the DAT-111.

Measures

Mood. To assess the success of the manipulation, mood states were measured using the four-item Mood Short Form (MSF) scale (Peterson and Sauber 1983). The subjects were asked to indicate their feelings on the following five-point Likert-type scales (1-Strongly agree to 5-Strongly disagree): "At this moment I feel edgy or irritable," "For some reason, I am not very comfortable right now," "As I answer these questions, I feel very cheerful," and "Currently I am in a good mood." Ratings of the last two items were reverse-coded prior to data analysis. Consistent with the pretest results, subjects who read the stories designed to induce a positive mood were significantly happier for both Stage 1 and Stage 2 (x=4.02 and 4.03) than those who read the sad stories (x=2.68 and 2.49, p's <.001). The Cronbach's alpha coefficient of reliability for this four component measure of mood was .81 for Stage 1 and .84 for Stage 2. Although not initially considered, the intensity of the positive and negative mood states was approximately the same in both stages.

Global Evaluation. Respondents were asked to evaluate the DAT on five seven-point dependent measures (extremely low appeal-extremely high appeal, bad-good, unpleasant-pleasant, unagreeable-agreeable, unsatisfactory-satisfactory; α=.94) representing global evaluation of the DAT. The items used are similar to those used by Marks and Kamins (1988). The average of these five measures was used for data analysis.

Attitude Toward the Object. Attitude toward the object (Ao) was based on the summed set of beliefs (1-Strongly agree to 7-Strongly disagree) about the DAT's 15 attributes weighted by the evaluation (1-Very bad to 7-Very good) of these attributes.

Purchase Intentions. Purchase intentions were measured as an average of two five-point Likert-type scales (1-Definitely will buy to 5-Definitely will not buy; 1-Definitely like to have to 5-Definitely not like to have; Jamieson and Bass 1989). Ratings for the two purchase intentions scales were reverse-coded prior to data analysis.

RESULTS

Stage 1 results were analyzed using one-way multivariate analysis of variance (MANOVA). Three measures of interest (global evaluation, attitude toward the object, and purchase intentions) were analyzed simultaneously as a function of context-induced mood (positive, negative). Specifically, subjects in a positive mood provided different evaluations of the product on the four measures of interest than subjects in a negative mood (Wilks' Λ=.854; p<.007). To further clarify the nature of the results, supplementary analyses for each dependent variable were conducted separately. Not surprisingly, univariate tests confirmed the earlier MANOVA results. Relative to subjects in a negative mood those in a positive mood provided a more favorable global evaluation of the product (x=3.25 vs. 3.89; $F_{(1, 79)}$=6.44, p<.01; eta^2=.08) and a more favorable attitude toward the object (x= 608.34 vs. 506.10; $F_{(1, 79)}$=11.93, p<.001; eta^2=.13). Finally, subjects in a

TABLE
Means of Dependent Measures (Stages 1 & 2)

Stage 1	Positive	Positive	Negative	Negative
n	20	21	22	18
Ao	578.95 (133.97)	636.33 (131.65)	517.5 (109.65)	492.17 (157.49)
Global Evaluation	3.91 (1.190)	3.87 (1.10)	3.44 (1.18)	3.02 (1.06)
Purchase Intentions	2.33 (.67)	2.71 (.86)	2.34 (.61)	1.86 (.74)
Stage 2	**Positive**	**Negative**	**Negative**	**Positive**
n	20	21	22	18
Ao	620.25 (124.56)	639.48 (147.59)	568.82 (133.55)	489.89 (159.54)
Global Evaluation	4.05 (1.17)	3.73 (1.22)	3.59 (1.20)	3.04 (1.06)
Purchase Intentions	2.65 (.75)	2.55 (.88)	2.36 (.60)	1.92 (.71)

Note: Numbers in parentheses are standard deviations.

positive mood provided higher purchase intentions for the product than those in a negative mood (x= 2.52 vs. 2.13; $F_{(1, 79)}=5.75$, $p<.02$; $eta^2=.07$). Hypothesis 1, therefore, was supported.

Unlike previous research in the mood literature, this study also investigated the role of mood states in repeat evaluations. The Table shows the results on all dependent measures for each of the four groups (Positive-Positive, Positive-Negative, Negative-Negative, and Negative-Positive) for both stages. Repeated-measures MANOVA for each group revealed no significant differences in evaluations between Stages 1 and 2 (all *p*'s=n.s.). Further analysis using paired sample t-tests also showed no significant differences for individual dependent measures (all *p*'s=n.s.). The analysis performed here provides support for the hypothesized effects presented in Hypothesis 2.

DISCUSSION AND CONCLUSIONS

This study investigates the influence of context-induced mood states on initial and repeat product evaluations. Considered together, the results of the present study indicate that while mood states have a definite impact on initial product evaluations, repeat evaluations may not be susceptible to an individual's subjective mood state. This can appropriately be explained using the on-line and memory-based evaluation paradigms advanced in the literature.

According to past research, individuals can form evaluations of a stimulus in either of two processing paradigms. Consider first on-line processing. In this case, subjective affective states would influence judgments, since the judgments are being formed while individuals experience an affective subjective state (cf. Srull 1987). Our findings on the impact of affective subjective states on initial evaluations provide support for this. On the other hand, those individuals receiving the stimulus information without a specific objective to initially form an overall evaluation would not provide mood-laden judgments. The latter is true, since those judgments would be formed at a later time (perhaps, in the absence of mood). However, the impact of mood states on memory-based evaluations as described in the literature does not clearly account for our findings on repeat evaluations.

Repeat evaluations are those that follow already formed (or initial) evaluations of a stimulus. Unlike memory-based evaluations, repeat evaluations are, in fact, formed at an earlier stage (on-line) and occur again for a second time. Since individuals are not asked to process incoming attribute information when repeat evaluations take place, it is unlikely that affective states would have any impact on repeat evaluations. Indeed, the findings in this study

provide support for this conceptualization. Unlike Srull's (1987) Experiment 2, in our study mood states were induced at both the encoding (initial) and retrieval (repeat) stages. Our findings are consistent, however, with Srull's results. This suggests that mood states may not be quite as salient in subsequent evaluations.

To put our findings in a proper perspective, some limitations of the study must be considered. First, the use of specific stories to induce the desired mood states does not imply that other contexts, or even other stories, can evoke similar moods. Therefore, evidence across studies using different contexts to manipulate mood may provide results that are either consistent or inconsistent with the findings of this study. Second, different kinds of positive and negative moods should be employed to test the prescribed hypotheses. Third, the study did not examine the information recalled by the respondents. According to earlier findings, the amount and type of information recalled by subjects were consistent with the mood congruency theory. It would be interesting, therefore, to examine whether recall of information in an experimental context (such as the one described in our study) would provide support for earlier findings in the literature. Finally, the study did not involve the manipulation of the affective tone of the ad. Past research has shown that the ad's affective tone may interact with context-induced mood to influence salient dependent measures (Gardner 1992). It would be useful to include such manipulations in future research.

The findings of the study have interesting implications for advertising, media planning, and retailing. Specifically, the results suggest that mood states are very important in forming initial evaluations of products. Therefore, a careful selection of the contexts within which ads and other promotional materials are presented is important. At the same time, the results suggest that attempts to influence mood states at later stages in an effort to change or enhance initial product evaluations (or product perceptions) may be unsuccessful. It would be beneficial, for example, to place major emphasis on the advertising of new products to influence initial, rather than later, judgments via mood states. This may be of particular importance to retail establishments that employ environmental stimuli (e.g., scents, background music) to influence mood states. Our results suggest that it may be costly and ineffective for retailers to influence evaluations of specific products.

REFERENCES

Batra, Rajeev and Douglas M. Stayman (1990), "The Role of Mood in Advertising Effectiveness," *Journal of Consumer Research*, 17(September), 203-214.

Bless, Herbert, Diane M. Mackie, and Norbert Schwarz (1992), "Mood Effects on Attitude Judgments: Independent Effects of Mood Before and After Message Elaboration," *Journal of Presonality and Social Psychology*, 63(4), 585-595.

Bower, Gordon (1981), "Mood and Memory," *American Psychologist*, 36(2), 129-148.

_____, Stephen Gilligan, and Kenneth Monteiro (1981), "Selectivity of Learning Caused by Affective States," *Journal of Experimental Psychology: General*, 110(December), 451-473.

Clark, Margaret and Alice Isen (1982), "Toward Understanding the Relationship Between Feeling States and Social Behavior," in *Cognitive Social Psychology*, eds. Albert Hastorf and Alice Isen, New York: Elsevier/North-Holland, 73-108.

Gardner, Meryl P. (1985), "Mood States and Consumer Behavior: A Critical Review," *Journal of Consumer Research*, 12(December), 281-300.

_____ (1992), "Responses to Emotional and Informational Appeals: the Moderating Role of Context-Induced Mood States," in *Advertising and Consumer Psychology*, eds. E. Clark, T. Brock, and D. Stewart, Hillsdale, N.J.: Lawrence Erlbaum, Inc.

Goldberg, Marvin E. and Gerald J. Gorn (1987), "Happy and Sad TV Programs: How They Affect Reactions to Commercials," *Journal of Consumer Research*, 14(December), 387-403.

Hastie, Reid and Bernadette Park (1986), "The Relationship Between Memory and Judgment Depends on Whether the Judgment task is Memory-Based or On-Line," *Psychological Review*, 93(6), 258-268.

Isen, Alice (1970), "Success, Failure, Attention, and Reaction to Others: The Warm Glow of Success," *Journal of Personality and Social Psychology*, 15(4), 294-301.

_____, and Thomas Shalker (1982), "The Effect of Feeling State on Evaluation of Positive, Neutral, and negative Stimuli: When You 'Accentuate the Positive,' Do You 'Eliminate the Negative'?" *Social Psychology Quarterly*, 45(1), 58-63.

Jamieson, Linda F. and Frank M. Bass (1989), "Adjusting Stated Intention Measures to Predict Trial Purchase of New Products: A Comparison of Models and Methods," *Journal of Marketing Research*, 26(August), 336-345.

Johnson, Eric and Amos Tversky (1983), "Affect Generalization, and the Perception of Risk," *Journal of Personality and Social Psychology*, 45(1), 20-31.

Keller, Kevin L. (1991), "Cue Compatibility and Framing in Advertising," *Journal of Marketing Research*, 28(February), 42-57.

Knowles, Patricia A., Stephen J. Grove, and W. Jeffrey Burroughs (1993), "An Experimental Examination of Mood Effects on Retrieval and Evaluation of Advertisement and Brand Information," *Journal of the Academy of Marketing Science*, 22(2), 135-142.

Marks, Lawrence J., and Michael A. Kamins (1988), "The Use of Product Sampling and Advertising: Effects of Sequence of Exposure and Degree of Advertising Claim Exaggeration on Consumers' Belief Strength, Belief Confidence, and Attitudes," *Journal of Marketing Research*, 25(August), 266-281.

Mischel, W., Brian Coates, and Antonette Raskoff (1968), "Effects of Success and Failure on Self-Gratification," *Journal of Personality and Social Psychology*, 10(4), 381-390.

_____, Ebbesen, E., and A. Zeiss (1973), "Selective Attention to the Self: Situational and Dispositional Determinants," *Journal of Personality and Social Psychology*, 27, 129-142.

Moore, Bert, Bill Underwood, and D.L. Rosenhan (1973), "Affect and Altruism," *Developmental Psychology*, 8(1), 99-104.

Peterson, Robert A., and Matthew Sauber (1983), "A Mood Scale for Survey Research," in *AMA Educators' Proceedings*, eds. Patrick Murphy et al., Chicago, IL: American Marketing Association, 409-414.

Srull, Thomas K. (1987), "Memory, Mood, and Consumer Judgment," in *Advances in Consumer Research*, Vol. 14, eds. Melanie Wallendorf and P. Anderson, Provo, UT: Association for Consumer Research, 404-407.

Consumer Attributions of Product Failures to Channel Members

John R. O'Malley Jr., Virginia Tech

ABSTRACT

We develop and present a conceptual framework of consumer attributions for product failures when multiple channel members are present. This framework is based on the attribution theory principles of Kelley and Weiner and the central and peripheral processing modes from the Elaboration Likelihood Model of Petty and Cacioppo. We use this model to describe the affect of product failure on a range of emotional and behavioral consequences.

INTRODUCTION

The objective of this paper is to increase our understanding of the attribution processes used by consumers in the event of product failures[1]. Most attribution studies on product failures look at whether consumers perceive the product failure to be internal or external to themselves (Folkes 1984). This paper will use attribution theory to build on previous work in product failures and expand it into the area of channel research. Specifically, we will propose a model based on attribution theory and multiple processing paths to explain consumer attributions of product failures regarding channel members. In this framework, we will describe how consumers' determine and respond to product failure in which there are multiple channel members.

In many buying situations, the consumer is aware of more than one channel member. For example, a buyer could go to J.C. Penney to buy Levi's jeans or to a specific automobile dealer to buy a specific make of automobile. In both cases, multiple parties (i.e., the retailer and manufacturer) are responsible for the quality of the product. If there is a product failure, there are two salient parties that the consumer could hold causal; in the above examples, the retailer and the manufacturer.

As another example, a customer can purchase a product from a mail firm, such as Lands End. In this case, the buyer is aware of the retailer, Lands End, and the facilitator that delivers the package (e.g., Federal Express or UPS). If there is a product failure, such as a late delivery, the buyer may attribute causality to either Lands End or the facilitator or both.

This area of research is important to both practitioners and researchers. For practitioners, this research illustrates the potential for channel partners and consumers to perceive different channel members as the cause of a product failure. Knowing which channel partner consumers view as causing the product failure will enable the channel to respond more effectively to customer needs. For academic researchers, the proposed model can extend the limitations of present research on product failures to include multiple members of a channel.

BACKGROUND

Causal Antecedents

Kelley (1973) describes attribution theory as a way to understand how people "answer questions beginning with *why* ." When an individual perceives an outcome as unexpected, negative, or important, the individual begins the attribution process (Weiner 1986). When there is a product failure (i.e., product performance expectations are disconfirmed) the attribution process is initiated (Hunt, Smith, and Kernan 1989).

Past research into product failures has investigated whether the consumer or someone else is held causal[2] for a product failure. Attribution theory suggests, however, that people externalize failures and hold other parties causal for the failure. For example, Folkes and Kostos (1986) found that drivers blamed car mechanics for car breakdowns and car mechanics blamed drivers for breakdowns. Belk, Painter, and Semenik (1981) reported that only 11 out of 359 respondents attributed the cause of the energy crisis to "me and people like me." Thus, consumers are likely to find the cause of a product failure to be external.

Kelley and Michela (1980) have identified three specific causal antecedents: motivation, knowledge (information), and prior belief. Individuals need to be motivated to expend the cognitive effort necessary to determine the cause of behavior, especially when the behavior is expected (Pyszczynski and Greenberg 1981). Additionally, consumers need to have knowledge or information to determine the causes of situations. Somasundaram (1993) found that consumers with more product knowledge made more causal statements than consumers with low product knowledge. For a consumer to determine which channel partner has caused a product failure, the consumer would need to have knowledge of the channel and its structure. Without this knowledge, the consumer would only have one channel member, the one the product was purchased from, to hold causal for a product failure.

Processing Paths

Weiner (1986) reports that there is a "simplicity" to causal thinking. Kelley (1973), on the other hand, describes causal schemas, such as multiple necessary causes and multiple sufficient causes, which imply more than a simple causal attribution process. We propose to reconcile both approaches by suggesting that people use more than one processing path when making attributions. One processing path requires minimal cognitive resources while the second path requires significant cognitive resources.

Both Petty and Cacioppo (1984) and Chaiken, Liberman, and Eagly (1989) develop two paths for information processing that could be used to explain the consumer's cognitive activity during the causal attribution process. While there are differences between the Elaboration Likelihood Model of Petty and Cacioppo and the Heuristic-Systematic Model of Chaiken, Liberman, and Eagly, both describe two separate paths that people use to process information. We will use Petty and Cacioppo's central and peripheral paths, which have been tested with consumer products (Petty, Cacioppo, and Schumann 1983), to describe how consumers make causal attributions. The peripheral path, which requires a low level of cognitive resources, can explain the simplicity described by Weiner (1983). Kelley and Michela (1980) also point to causal attributions that are based on salience and primacy, which imply a more peripheral processing route. The central path, which requires more cognitive resources than the peripheral processing path, is consistent with the "naive scientist" described by Kelley (1973).

The three causal antecedents—motivation, knowledge, and prior belief—appear to affect both the attributions made by consumers and the processing path that consumers use. Depending

---

[1] Product failure is used to describe any situation where a consumer perceives that a product (either goods or services) does not meet their expectations about the product.

[2] Causal is used to indicate that someone perceives a party as the cause of an event. Responsibility is a separate construct and is not used.

FIGURE 1
Consumer Attributions of Product Failure

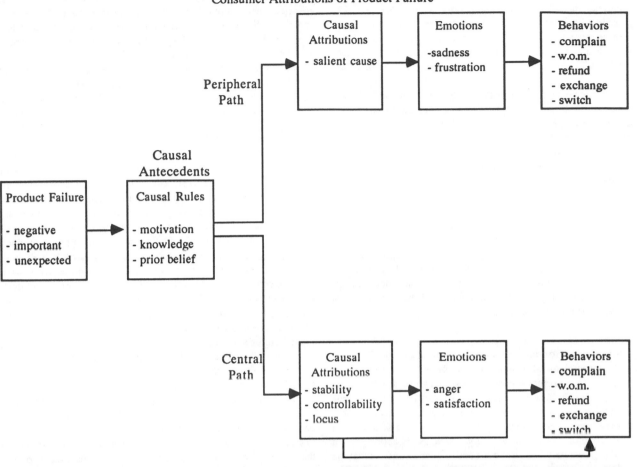

upon the level of knowledge, motivation, and prior belief, the individual will either use a peripheral or central processing path to make attributions. Folkes and Keisler (1991) noted that consumers "often do not have the motivation or ability to collect information" about causes, which suggests that different processing paths may be used by consumers when making causal attributions. According to Petty and Cacioppo, people use the central processing route when motivation and ability are relatively high. When either motivation or ability is low then the peripheral processing route is used. Figure 1 contains a description of the proposed model.

We hypothesize that with a low level of knowledge and a low level of motivation, consumers will use a peripheral path to determine causal attributions. We also hypothesize that if a consumer has a high level of motivation, but a low level of knowledge, or a high level of knowledge, but a low level of motivation, consumers will use the peripheral path. Only when consumers have a high level of knowledge and a high level of motivation will they expend the effort required to use a central processing path to determine causal attributions.

CONCEPTUAL MODEL

Peripheral Path

When using the peripheral path, causal attributions will be based on simple rules such as salience or primacy; that is, the consumer will accept the first adequate explanation (Kelley and Michela 1980). For example, when a consumer receives a package that is delivered late by the U. S. Postal Service, he/she could use a

peripheral path (based on prior beliefs or saliency) that the postal service is the likely cause of the delay.

Central Path

Weiner (1986) identified three causal dimensions—locus of control, stability, and controllability—that are likely to be involved in central processing. Locus of control refers to whether the cause is internal or external to the individual. Stability refers to whether the cause is permanent or temporary (Folkes 1984, Heider 1958). For example, a restaurant meal could be poorly prepared as a result of the cook making a mistake in the recipe (unstable) or as a result of the cook being incompetent (stable). Controllability refers to the volitional nature of the cause. For example, a late shipment could be the result of bad weather (uncontrollable) or the result of poor logistics (controllable).

Research has demonstrated (Folkes 1984, Folkes, Koletsky, and Graham 1987) that consumers' perceptions of the causal dimensions (locus, control, and stability) affect consumer expectations of redress for the product failure, anger at the firm, and intention to repurchase from the firm. Locus of control, however, is unlikely to vary when a product fails because consumers tend to externalize product failures.

Once a consumer has identified the stability and controllability of the event, he/she will then use causal rules to identify which channel member or members are the cause of the product failure. Kelley (1972) has identified a variety of causal rules or schemas that individuals use to determine causation which "reflect the individual's basic notions of reality." "The two basic schemas are

(1) multiple sufficient causes and (2) multiple necessary causes. The first schema, multiple sufficient causes, indicates a condition in which the individual believes that either of two causes individually could cause the outcome. For example, a consumer could determine that a late delivery could result from either the delivery firm being late or the shipper shipping the package late. Either party could individually cause the outcome—the late arrival of the package.

Multiple necessary causes is a condition where the individual believes that both parties are needed to create conditions for the outcome to occur. For example, the consumer could determine that the package arrived so late that both the shipper and the shipping firm must have failed to perform as expected.

As illustrated in the two examples, the more negative (or more extreme) the outcome, the more likely the individual will believe that multiple necessary causes were required. In contrast, when there is a less extreme outcome, individuals are more likely to use a multiple sufficient causal schema (Kelley 1972). This concept also is supported by research (Einhorn and Hogarth 1983) that indicates when an effect (outcome) is large, then people expect the cause to be large. Large could be either one firm failing in a major way or a combination of two firms failing. Additionally, large could also include a particular combination of the dimensions of stability, controllability, and locus.

Emotions

Attributions for product failures generate emotions. For example, research has shown that attributions of control and stability have an effect on emotions, such as—anger and desire to hurt the firm's business (Folkes, Koletsky, and Graham 1987). Consumers who perceive product failures as either unstable or uncontrollable by a firm are less angry with that firm. Bitner (1990) also found that perceived controllability and stability affected satisfaction. When customers perceive that a firm has control over a cause or that the cause is stable, the customer is more dissatisfied than when the firm does not have control or the cause is unstable. We believe these findings will hold whether the customer perceives one or both channel members as the cause for the product failure.

When a product failure occurs, the consumer will experience emotion using either processing path. The type and intensity of emotions, however, may differ between the two paths. When consumers use the central processing path, they are likely to develop intense emotions, such as anger, as more cognitive resources are being used (Weiner 1985). and are likely to be angry with one or more channel partners. When the peripheral processing path is used, consumers are   likely to develop fewer intense emotions, such as frustration and disappointment. Thus, the consumer may experience some negative emotion, but may be unlikely to attribute blame to any channel member.

Based on these different emotional responses, we hypothesize that:

- Consumers who use a central processing path when making attributions will experience more intense emotions and will attribute more causal responsibility to channel members than consumers who use a peripheral processing path.

Behavioral Consequences

Psychological consequences (emotions) often lead to behavioral consequences, such as complaining, word-of-mouth, requesting refunds, exchanging products, and switching suppliers (Folkes 1984; Folkes, Koletsky, and Graham 1987; Boldgett and Granbois 1992). Peripheral processing, with its less intense emotions, should result in consumers having fewer channel specific responses; that is, the consumer may be frustrated or disappointed, but not be able to direct their emotions toward a specific channel member or members. We also would expect that the consumer would be less likely to switch brands or retailers because their emotional response is not directed at a specific channel member. We also would expect these behavioral consequences to be relatively temporary and susceptible to change (Petty and Cacioppo 1984).

Customers who use a central processing path have more intense emotions that are likely to lead to more specific behavioral consequences. For example, higher levels of anger toward a firm are likely to lead to a higher level of complaining behavior and a reduced likelihood of repurchasing from that firm (Folkes, Koletsky, and Graham 1987). More stable attributions and controllability of product failures also are likely to lead to a higher level of complaining behavior, lower levels of intention to repurchase the product, and reduced willingness to use the supplier. When there are multiple channel participants whom the consumer views as both stable and able to control the delivery and quality of their product, we expect consumers will be more likely to switch from both channel parties. If the consumer found just the manufacturer causal, then the consumer would be more likely to switch manufacturers, and not retailers. In a similar vein, if the consumer perceived the retailer to be a stable or controllable cause for the failure, then he/she would be likely to switch retailers, but still purchase the same manufacturer's product.

According to Petty and Cacioppo (1984), central processing results in attitudes that are relatively enduring and resistant to change. We would expect behavioral consequences developed from consumers using the central processing route also to be more enduring and resistant to change. Thus, a customer who uses central processing and decides to switch from one firm to another is likely to stay with the new firm and would be difficult to convert back to the original firm. We also would expect a consumer who uses central processing and who changes channels (e.g., from a retailer-manufacturer channel to a catalog company) would be unlikely to change back to the original channel.

Based on the two information processing paths, we hypothesize the following:

- Customers who use central processing will have more directed behavioral consequences, targeted at specific channel partners, than customers using the peripheral processing path.

- Customers who use central processing will have more enduring changes in their behavioral consequences than customers who use peripheral processing.

Conclusion

We have developed a model of consumer attributions for product failures when two channel members are present. We hypothesize that consumers can follow two information processing routes, which are based on the individual's level of knowledge and motivation, when making attributions. The two different routes, central and peripheral, have different implications on the emotions and behavioral consequences of consumers. Individuals who use central processing use multiple sufficient causes and multiple necessary causes to determine which channel member or members are the cause of a product failure. Individuals who use peripheral processing are likely to follow simple rules such as saliency to determine which channel member or members are the cause of the product failure. Central processing also leads to more intense emotions than peripheral processing. These emotions then lead to behavioral consequences that include complaining, refunds, exchanges, and switching.

The proposed framework has several managerial implications. For example, if managers can determine the causal attributions made by their consumers, then strategies can be developed to reduce the consumer's perception of the cause of the product failure. In addition, if a manager can identify the different emotions that consumers experience because of product failures, he/she will be able to better train service personnel to handle customer complaints. Research (Bitner 1990) has found that customer dissatisfaction can be reduced by appropriately responding to customer complaints.

Finally, the framework suggests a few venues for future research. The proposed model provides a framework to further understand the consumer attribution process in relation to product failures and is applicable in both service and good products. The model implies that service failures, where consumers often have less knowledge of the channel structure, will generally be processed peripherally. The use of this peripheral path may result in more causal attributions for the party most proximal to the consumer, and less for the product manufacturer. Research also is needed to determine which channel member the consumer expects to receive redress from in the event of a product failure.

REFERENCES

Belk, Russell, John Painter, and Richard Semenik (1981), "Preferred Solutions to the Energy Crisis as a Function of Causal Attributions," *Journal of Consumer Research*, 8 (December) 306-312.

Bitner, Mary Jo (1990), "Evaluating Service Encounters: The Effects of Physical Surroundings and Employee Responses," *Journal of Marketing*, 54 (April) 69-82.

Blodgett, Jeffrey G. and Donald H. Granbois (1992), "Toward an Integrated Conceptual Model of Consumer Behavior," *Journal of Consumer Satisfaction, Dissatisfaction, and Complaining Behavior*, 5, 93-103.

Chaiken, Shelly, Akiva Liberman, and Alice Eagly (1989), "Heuristic and Systematic Information Processing within and Beyond the Persuasion Context," in *Unintended Thoughts*, J. S. Uleman and J. A. Bargh, eds. New York:Guilford Press.

Einhorn, Hillel J. and Robin Hogarth (1983), "Diagnostic Inference and Causal Judgment: A Decision Making Framework," *Working Paper*.

Folkes, Valerie S. (1984), "Consumer Reactions to Product Failure: An Attributional Approach," *Journal of Consumer Research*, 10 (March) 398-409.

_____ (1988), "Recent Attribution Research in Consumer Behavior: A Review and New Directions," *Journal of Consumer Research*, 14 (March) 548-565.

_____ and Barbara Kotsos (1986), "Buyers' and Sellers' Explanations for Product Failure: Who Done It?," *Journal of Marketing*, 50 (April) 74-80.

_____, Susan Koletsky, John L. Graham (1987), "A Field Study of Causal Inferences and Consumer Reaction: The View from the Airport," *Journal of Consumer Research*, 13 (March) 534-539.

_____ and Tina Kiesler (1991), "Social Cognition: Consumers' Inferences about the Self and Others," in *The Handbook of Consumer Behavior*, Thomas S. Robertson and Harold S. Kassargin, eds. Englewood Cliffs, N.J: Prentice Hall.

Heider, Fritz (1958), *The Psychology of Interpersonal Relations*. New York:John Wiley & Sons, Inc.

Hunt, James M., Michael F. Smith, and Jerome B. Kernan (1989), "Processing Effects of Expectancy-Discrepant Persuasive Messages," *Psychological Reports*, 65 1359-1376.

Kelley, Harold H. (1972), "Causal Schemata and the Attribution Process," in *Attribution: Perceiving the Causes of Behavior*, Morristown:General Learning Press.

_____ (1973), "The Process of Causal Attribution," *American Psychologist*, (February) 107-128.

_____ and John L. Michela (1980), "Attribution Theory and Research," *Annual Review of Psychology*, 31 457-501.

Petty, Richard E. and John T. Cacioppo (1984), "The Effects of Involvement on Responses to Argument Quantity and Quality: Central and Peripheral Routes to Persuasion," *Journal of Personality and Social Psychology*, 46 (July) 69-81.

_____, John T. Cacioppo, and David Schumann (1983), "Central and Peripheral Routes to Advertising Effectiveness: The Moderating Role of Involvement," *Journal of Consumer Research*, 10 (September) 135-146.

Pyszczynski, Thomas A. and Jeff Greenberg (1981), "Role of Disconfirmed Expectancies in the Instigation of Attributional Processing," *Journal of Personality and Social Psychology*, 40 (July) 31-38.

Somasundaram, T. N. (1993), "Consumers Reaction to Product Failure: Impact of Product Involvement and Knowledge," *Advances in Consumer Research*, 20 215-218.

Weiner, Bernard (1985), "An Attributional Theory of Achievement Motivation and Emotion," *Psychological Review*, 92 (No.4) 548-573.

_____ (1986), *An Attributional Theory of Motivation and Emotion*, New York: Springer-Verlag.

Components of Consumer Reaction to Company-Related Mishaps: A Structural Equation Model Approach

Brian K. Jorgensen, Humboldt State University

ABSTRACT

The study addressed in this paper examines the relationship of the circumstances underlying a company-related mishap and company management's communicated response to the mishap as factors influencing consumer reaction. A structural equation model is run on experimental data to test the interrelationship of cognitive, emotional, and attitudinal components of consumers' reactions. The stated likely cause of an incident is found to have a more profound effect on the consumer than does company response. Consumers' judgments of company responsibility for an incident are shown to combine with consumers' emotional reactions in serving as predictors of attitudes and behavioral intentions.

INTRODUCTION

While most companies are constantly striving to become better known to their customers, some types of publicity are clearly undesirable. When disaster or scandal hits a company, consumers may very well choose to head in another direction. In a June 1993 survey of more than 1,000 Americans conducted by public relations consultants Porter/Novelli, a majority of respondents indicated that wrongdoing by a company is likely to affect their purchase of the companies' products or services. Further, these respondents had good memories for companies involved in crisis situations, even when the crises were several years old. When asked to name specific incidents, 51% mentioned the Exxon Valdez oil spill of 1989, 22% mentioned Sears' auto repair difficulties of 1992, and 11% mentioned the Tylenol product tamperings that took place in 1982.

Although crisis prevention is now an important function for many companies, company-related mishaps of all types continue to happen. In fact, some suggest that the number of serious incidents appears to be growing (Carey 1991; Lerbinger 1986). In recent months or years, we have witnessed allegations of tainted food and beverage, crashes of trains and aircraft, and a major snafu involving the accuracy of a well-known computer chip. The ongoing nature of these types of incidents, the likelihood that they will receive high levels of media attention, and the seriousness of their impact on consumers suggest the need for continuing research on how consumers respond to companies in crisis. The focus of the study presented here is on understanding the interrelationship among consumers' cognitive, attitudinal, and behavioral reactions to a company in crisis and the role that the company's communicated response to the crisis may play in influencing consumers' processing of the incident.

BACKGROUND AND HYPOTHESES

While general treatments of crisis management are varied and abundant, empirical examinations of consumer response to company crisis situations are few and very recent. Since consumer response to company crisis is a fairly new field, no clear consensus has yet been reached as to what might be the most important features of these situations for study. Some suggestions include: the reputation of the firm or brand (Romeo, Weinberger, and Antes 1994; Siomkos and Malliaris 1992), the performance history of the

company with regard to product-related problems (Griffin, Babin, and Attaway 1991), the nature of commentary by external parties (Siomkos and Malliaris 1992), credibility cues relating to the communication of the incident (Griffin, Babin, and Attaway 1991; Romeo, Weinberger, and Antes 1994), and the severity of the incident (Romeo, Weinberger, and Antes 1994). Although at least some support has been found for the relevance of each of these factors, this paper focuses on two other factors that have been found to have substantial impact on consumer reaction, namely, the causal circumstances underlying the company-related incident and the nature of the company's communicated response.

Causal Circumstances Surrounding a Company-Related Crisis

When a company-related crisis, disaster, or mishap takes place, the first question on everyone's mind is "Why?". Investigators comb the site, bodies are examined or autopsied, the "black box" is recovered and scrutinized so that the cause can be understood and future mishaps avoided. Members of the public seek causal information to guide their judgments, feelings, and behavioral reactions toward parties involved in the incidents (Weiner 1986).

Weiner's (1986) research indicates that once a person has attributed a particular cause to an incident, this causal attribution may be expected to have particular consequences based on the attribution's position along three dimensional continua. The three dimensions of causality are locus, controllability, and stability. The locus of an incident is the degree to which the incident, action, or occurrence is internal to or external a person or company. Controllability describes the extent to which the incident is controllable by the target person or company. An incident whose cause is internal to a company, such as a machinery malfunction, may not necessarily be considered completely controllable by the company. In general, however, company-related incidents with external causation are likely to be considered uncontrollable, while incidents with internal causation are more likely to be considered controllable. The third dimension, stability, concerns the extent to which an incident is considered likely to recur. Although issues surrounding the stability of the cause may be important in some company mishap situations, the stability dimension is not examined in the study presented here.

According to Weiner's (1986) theory, the point at which a particular cause lies along each of the causal dimensions gives rise to particular emotions and cognitions. Behavioral intentions flow from these thoughts and feelings. The controllability dimension, which is particularly important to cases of company mishap or wrongdoing, influences judgments of responsibility and emotions of anger and sympathy. Folkes (1984; Folkes, Koletsky, and Graham 1987) found that when product failure was viewed as controllable by the company, consumers expressed more anger than when the failure seen as uncontrollable. Causal attributions and feelings of anger combined to influence consumer intentions to complain about the failure and to repurchase the product.

As part of an experimental study of single versus multiple explanations for negative company-related events, Jorgensen (1994) compared consumer reactions to incidents based on internal/controllable causes and external/uncontrollable causes. The study showed that locus and controllability had a significant effect of judgments of responsibility, feelings of anger, and intentions to

[1]1993 press release.

346

purchase. Griffin, Babin, and Attaway (1991) found a significant effect of what they termed "locus of responsibility" on attitude toward a (fictional) company in an experiment involving a food poisoning incident. They also found that locus of responsibility had a marginal effect on purchase intentions toward the company. Using an experimental factorial survey approach to examine factors influencing consumer response to negative product safety information, Romeo, Weinberger, and Antes (1994) found that the degree to which a company was said to have tested a product before introduction affected all three of their dependent measures: brand opinion, purchase risk, and purchase intention. Although not a manipulation of locus or controllability per se, this examination of company culpability evidences consumers' use of responsibility judgments in responding to companies.

H1: Consumers will find a company more responsible for a negative incident that is viewed as internal to and controllable by the company than for a negative incident that is viewed as external to and uncontrollable by the company.

H2: The more responsible a company is judged to be for a negative incident, the more negative consumer emotions will be toward the company.

Company Communicated Response to a Negative Incident

When a company finds itself involved in a negative incident, it is likely to use impression management to formulate a response (Ginzel, Kramer, and Sutton 1992; Russ 1991). The impression management literature describes five types of "account" that may be used to communicate a response to a difficult situation: confession, excuse, justification, denial, and silence (Schönbach 1980; McLaughlin, Cody, and O'Hair 1983). Of these responses, denial and variations on confession have been most often examined in the company crisis literature. These two extremes on the response scale are also addressed in the study presented here, with the intention of pursuing other forms of response in future research. While confession embodies, at least to some degree, an acceptance of blame, denial is an attempt to shift blame as far from the suspected party as possible (Schlenker 1980). To the extent that the party is indeed not responsible or that the situation is sufficiently ambiguous with respect to responsibility, a denial may be an effective form of reducing blame (Weiner, Graham, Peter, and Zmuidinas 1991).

H3: A company that confesses and apologizes for a negative incident will be judged to be more responsible than a company that denies responsibility for the incident.

Although judgments of company responsibility have generally not been addressed in the consumer behavior literature, attitudinal responses have been addressed (Griffin, Babin, and Attaway 1991; Romeo, Weinberger, and Antes 1994; Siomkos and Malliaris 1992). In the first two of these papers, the authors found that a proactive company response in which product safety problems are redressed has a more positive effect on brand attitudes than a denial or no comment response. Similarly, Siomkos and Malliaris found that voluntary recall of a potentially dangerous product leads to more positive brand attitudes than either denying responsibility or involuntarily recalling product. Impression management studies outside of the crisis management domain have found that confession, including apology and redress, has a softening effect on people's feelings and attitudes (Darby and Schlenker 1982; Weiner, Graham, Peter, and Zmuidinas 1991).

H4: Consumer emotions will be less negative and attitudes will be more positive when a company confesses and apologizes for a negative incident than when a company denies responsibility for the incident.

The crisis management literature recommends that a company's response to a crisis be prompt (Garbett 1988). Although consumer behavior research has not addressed the promptness of company response, the promptness recommendation seems sound in light of real-world experience. Johnson & Johnson was praised for its prompt action following the Tylenol poisonings of 1982, while Exxon received a critical drubbing for its slowness to act following the Valdez oil spill. More generally, Kremer and Stephens (1983) found that following a negative event, mitigating information delivered promptly was more effective in reducing retaliation than the same information delivered after a delay.

H5: Consumer emotions will be less negative and attitudes will be more positive when a company responds immediately to a negative incident than when a company delays its response.

Although the timing of mitigating information is addressed in both Kremer and Stephens (1983) and Weiner, Graham, Peter, and Zmuidinas (1991), the timing of potentially aggravating information, such as a denial of responsibility, is not addressed. While timing of response may have a different impact for denial of responsibility than confession of responsibility, no interaction is hypothesized here. Possible interactions are, however, investigated in the data analysis.

The Effects of Judgments and Feelings on Punitiveness and Behavioral Intentions

Consumer judgments, feelings, and attitudes are most interesting when shown to have an influence on consumer behaviors. While the studies of consumer reaction to company crisis cited above found effects of crisis situation and company response on measures of attitudes, they did not find significant effects on measures of purchase intentions. This failure to find significant results may have been due to the fact that the researchers examined only direct effects. Structural equation modeling allows for the investigation of both direct and indirect effects. The hypotheses in this section address the effects of judgments, feelings, and attitudes on punitiveness toward the company and purchase and investment intentions.

In her work on consumer attributions, Folkes (1984; Folkes, Koletsky, and Graham 1987) found that both attributional dimensions and emotions could have an effect on consumers' behavioral intentions toward a company. In the present study, traditional measures of attitudes, emotions, and intentions are supplemented by a measure of "punitiveness," the extent to which consumers feel that a company should be pardoned and/or punished for a mishap. Punitiveness is viewed here as an attitudinal construct with both affective and cognitive elements to it. Thus, judgments of responsibility along with negativity of emotions and attitudes should influence levels of punitiveness. In turn, the degree of punitiveness, combined with more general emotions and attitudes should impact consumer purchase and investment intentions. In fact, purchase and investment behaviors may be some of the most obvious means by which consumer can punish an errant company.

H6: The more responsible a company is considered to be for a negative incident and the more negative emotions and attitudes are toward the company, the more punitive consumers will feel toward the company.

H7: The more punitive consumers feel toward a company involved in a negative incident and the more negative their emotions and attitudes are toward the company, the lower will be intentions to purchase from or invest in the company.

METHODOLOGY

The data for this analysis were collected experimentally, using a convenience sample of adult consumers who were contacted at their places of employment and various other public places. A total of 129 usable questionnaires were filled out. Average age of the subjects was 36, and 60% of the subjects were female. Each questionnaire consisted of a cover page with instructions and a short vignette describing a company-related mishap. The vignette was followed by two pages of dependent measures, manipulation checks, and sample description questions. Each subject saw only one vignette, so the study design was completely between subject.

To increase external validity, variations on two company-related situations were used for the experimental vignettes. Thus, the study had a 2x2x2x2 design, the four factors being: company situation, causal attribution supplied, company response, and timing of company response. One of the company situations that was used addressed an airline accident in which all passengers and crew had been killed, while the other situation addressed a string of illnesses and deaths resulting from the taking of an over-the-counter drug. The study was designed to be collapsed across scenario if the pattern of results was the same for each scenario. Various scenarios had been pretested to use for the vignettes. The chosen situations had one relatively internal and controllable cause and one relatively external and uncontrollable cause. Causes that were judged as very near the endpoints of the locus and controllability scales were rejected so that some ambiguity with respect to the degree of company responsibility could be preserved. Real-world incidents are generally ambiguous in that while they are generally not intentional, one can always conceive of how by doing more the company might have forestalled the mishap.

Both the airline accident and the drug poisoning vignettes were printed and presented like short newspaper stories. Although subjects were informed that the companies and situations were fictional, they were asked to respond as though the incidents were real. For all vignettes, a description of the incident was followed by a statement to the effect that "investigations into the [incident] indicate that it was most likely caused by [cause]." Internal/controllable airline accident and drug scare causes were, respectively, "serious error made by a poorly trained pilot" and "machinery malfunction resulting in the wrong combination of chemicals." External/uncontrollable causes were "a severe, unpredictable storm that hit the aircraft mid-flight" and "product tampering that took place while the product was on store shelves."

Two elements of company response were examined: the content of the response and the timing of the response. In terms of the timing of response, each vignette reported either that the company had made its response immediately or after a delay of ten days. With respect to the content of the response, each vignette included either a confession condition or a denial condition. The confession condition stated, "We at [company] fully accept our responsibility in this matter. We are very sorry and express our deep-felt apology to the victims and their families. We will do all that we can to compensate them for their loss." The denial condition stated, "We at [company] do not feel that we are responsible for this incident. These kinds of incidents seem to happen periodically regardless of what kinds of precautions are taken."

After reading the vignette, subjects responded to a number of dependent measures and manipulation checks measured on seven-point scales. Multiple questions were asked for each construct with the exception of the behavioral intentions. Two separate question orders were used. The dependent measures addressed the following constructs: judgment of degree of company responsibility ("not at all responsible - very responsible," "very much to blame - not at all to blame," "very controllable - not at all controllable"), anger toward the company ("very annoyed - not at all annoyed," "not at all angry - very angry"), sympathy toward the company ("very sorry - not at all sorry," "not at all sympathetic - very sympathetic"), attitude toward the company ("very favorably - very unfavorably," "very bad - very good"), extent to which the company should be punished ("heavily fined - not fined at all," "no punishment - heavy punishment"), extent to which the company should be forgiven ("not at all forgiving, - fully forgiving," "full pardon, no pardon"), purchase intention ("very unlikely to choose - very likely to choose"), and investment intention ("very likely to invest in - very unlikely to invest in"). Eventually, measures of anger were combined with reverse-scored measures of sympathy to arrive at a measure of negative emotion, and measures of punishment were combined with reverse-scored measures of forgiveness to arrive at a measure of punitiveness. Other multiple measures were also designed to be averaged for the analysis.

The dependent measures were followed by manipulation checks investigating perceptions of the extent to which the company's response was "prompt" versus "delayed" and the extent to which the company accepted "full responsibility" versus "no responsibility." Finally subjects were asked to respond to manipulation checks regarding the locus, controllability, and stability of the likely cause given for the incident. These manipulation check items were anchored by "wholly internal to [company] - wholly external to [company]," "entirely controllable by [company] - entirely uncontrollable by [company]," and "a type of cause that is very likely to occur again" - "a type of cause that is very unlikely to occur again."

RESULTS AND DISCUSSION

Examination of the data using scenario as a factor in analysis of variance (ANOVA) computations showed the pattern of results to be substantially the same across the two company scenarios. Therefore , the results reported here are collapsed across the two companies. Direct relationships between manipulated variables and dependent measures were preliminarily investigated using ANOVA. A structural equation model was then developed, using EQS, so that both direct and indirect relationships among variables could be examined.

Manipulation Checks

Analyses of the manipulation checks using ANOVA showed the checks to all be successful. The response given by the company (confession or denial) had a significant effect on the manipulation check item for how much responsibility the company had accepted $(F(9,123)=498.05, p<.001)$. The timing of management's response significantly effected the promptness manipulation check item $(F(9,124)=89.50, p<.001)$. The causal attribution given had a significant effect on locus $(F(9,121)=130.24, p<.001)$ and controllability $(F(9,121)=103.96, p<.001)$. No manipulation of the stability construct was attempted in the study, and none of the manipulated variables had a significant effect on the item measuring stability.

TABLE

Significant Effects of the Causal Attribution Manipulation

Variable	Cell Means		Significance
	Internal/Controllable	External/Uncontrollable	
Company Responsibility	5.80	3.84	$F_{1,129}$ =77.61, p<.001
Negative Emotion	5.37	4.39	$F_{1,129}$ =20.51, p<.001
Attitude	2.35	3.31	$F_{1,129}$ =22.34, p<.001
Punitiveness	5.62	3.89	$F_{1,129}$ =101.51, p<.001
Purchase Intention	1.76	2.86	$F_{1,129}$ =15.83, p<.001
Investment Intention	1.80	2.47	$F_{1,129}$ =6.92, p<.01

Reliability of Aggregated Measures

Acceptable coefficient alpha scores were found for each of the groups of measures that were aggregated. The score for the responsibility variables was .87, for the negative emotion variables was .80, for the attitude variables was .81, and for the punitiveness variables was .87.

Analysis of Variance Results

Prior to running the structural equation model, ANOVA computations were performed for each of the dependent measures to investigate direct effects and the possibility of interactions. Only one significant interaction was found, as described below. No significant main effects of the timing of company response were found. The likely cause of the incident given in the vignette had a significant impact on each of the dependent variables, as shown in the Table.

Significant main effects for company response were found with respect to the measures of negative emotion (F(1,129)=5.09, p<.05) and attitude (F1,129)=9.10, p<.01). The mean level of negative emotion in the confession conditions was 4.64 and in the denial conditions was 5.13. A significant interaction of company response and timing of the response was found for the attitude measure (F1,129)=5.96, p<.05). While confession led to more positive attitudes than did denial, *delayed* confession led to the most positive attitudes (mean=3.58). The mean attitudes for immediate confession, immediate denial, and delayed denial were 2.70, 2.58, and 2.46 respectively.

Hypotheses

The results of the structural equation model run on the data are summarized in the Figure. Overall, the model has a good fit with a chi-square value of 35.03 based on 27 degrees of freedom. The probability value for this chi-square statistic is 0.138, indicating that the model cannot be rejected at the .05 level. Further, the model has a Bentler-Bonett Normed Fit Index value of 0.946 and a Comparative Fit Index value of 0.987. Fit indices above the .90 level are generally considered as indicators of a good fit (Hu and Bentler 1995).

Each of the significant paths is labeled with its standardized path coefficient. All paths that are shown are significant at the .05 level. Non-significant paths, including paths that had originally been hypothesized, are not shown. Also, because the timing of management response did not have any significant effect, it was dropped from the model. Each of the individual hypotheses is briefly addressed below.

*Hypothesis 1. Because degree of controllability and perceived company respon*sibility are practically synonymous, the strong path between causal attribution given and responsibility is essen-tially a manipulation check. The more internal/controllable the incident, the more responsible a company is considered to be.

Hypothesis 2. As predicted by Weiner's (1986) model, the degree of controllability and responsibility is highly linked to negative emotions. Anger toward a company is higher and sympathy is lower when the company is considered to be highly responsible.

Hypothesis 3. Confessing responsibility for an incident was hypothesized as leading to higher levels of perceived responsibility. Although the path between company response and judgments of responsibility was not significant at the .05 level, and thus does not appear in the Figure, it was marginally significant and in the expected direction. Therefore, confessing responsibility may be a two edged sword, on the one hand leading to higher levels of perceived responsibility while, on the other hand, leading to a softening of negative emotional reactions, as addressed by Hypothesis 4.

Hypothesis 4. It was expected that a company's confessing and apologizing would reduce the level of negative emotions felt toward the company while improving attitudes toward the company. However, the path to emotions was significant, while the path to attitude was not. Still, the path between emotions and attitudes was very strong, suggesting a strong indirect effect of confession and apology on attitudes.

Hypothesis 5. As mentioned above, the paths between timing of company response and emotions and attitudes were not significant.

Hypothesis 6. Punitiveness of consumers toward a company involved in a serious mishap was expected to be affected by judgments of responsibility along with emotions and attitudes. Although responsibility and negative emotions were found to play a role, general attitudes did not have an effect on punitiveness. In fact, as illustrated in the Figure, attitudes proved to be a dead-end variable, with no significant effects on punitiveness, purchase intentions, or investment intentions.

Hypothesis 7. Emotions, attitudes, and punitiveness were hypothesized as influencing consumers' purchase and investment intentions. Although degree of consumer punitiveness did influence purchase and investment intentions, emotions played a direct role only with regard to purchase intentions. As mentioned above, attitudes did not play a major role in either intention measure.

Summary and General Discussion

The results of this structural equation analysis lend credence to the general thrust of Weiner's (1986) attribution theory, which predicts that attributional judgments give rise to feelings and attitudes which, in turn, give rise to behavioral intentions. The research also shows the extreme importance of causal information

FIGURE
Structural Equation with Standardized Path Coefficients for Significant Paths

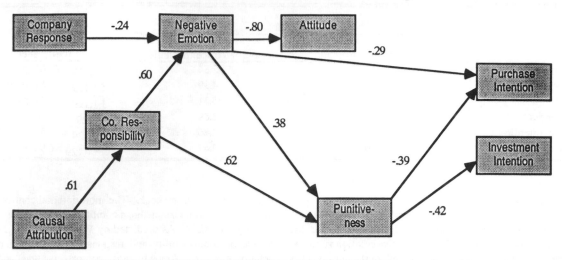

on how consumers react to negative company-related incidents. Even in the face of somewhat ambiguous causal information, widely different company responses played only a minor, secondary role in influencing consumer reactions.

Although timing of a company's response did not play its expected role in this study, one should not necessarily conclude that it is an irrelevant factor. Given the design of the study, the manipulation of response timing was probably the weakest of the manipulated elements. Subjects may have been able to envision a causal scenario with a particular management response, but they may have had a hard time imagining how a delay of response would influence their reactions. Also, in a real-world situation, a delay in response would probably be accompanied by the arrival of various other pieces of information that might influence consumer reaction to a greater extent than the delay.

The failure of the attitude measure to have an impact on the intention measures is initially unsettling to those who expect that feelings should lead to attitudes, which should then lead to intentions. However, the attitude measures here were very general measures of attitude toward the company. The measures of punitiveness that were taken here could be viewed as more specific measures of attitudes and, as such, more predictive of behavioral intentions (Ajzen and Fishbein 1977). Punitiveness was the only variable directly predictive of investment intention. This is understandable, given that an investment is more likely to be based on a rational analysis of a company's value and future than on more visceral concerns for personal safety. A company seems a less attractive investment if it is likely to be punished by regulatory agencies or groups of victimized consumers.

CONCLUSIONS AND FUTURE DIRECTIONS

The circumstances underlying a company-related mishap along with the company's communicated response to the mishap have implications for consumers' feelings, attitudes, and intentions toward the company. Through a structural equation model, the study presented here was able to demonstrate that previous studies' failure to find effects with regard to purchase intentions may have been due to these studies' non-examination of indirect effects. The study presented here was also able to place the relative effects of causal attribution and company response into perspective. Finally,

this study compared the differences in factors influencing purchase intentions versus investment intentions following a negative company-related incident.

The research presented here still leaves a number of questions unanswered. One particular question that suggests the need for continued research is how much more important the role of company response is in situations that are more causally ambiguous. When causation is unclear, to what extent might a company's response be effective in changing consumers' perceptions of locus, causality, and responsibility? Other company responses that were not addressed here, such as excuses and justifications, should also be examined, particularly in light of more ambiguous situations, where blame might be more easily manipulated. Additionally, real crisis situations and real company names should be used to further test the external validity of the findings here.

REFERENCES

Ajzen, Icek and Martin Fishbein (1977), "Attitude-Behavior Relations: A Theoretical Analysis and Review of Empirical Research," *Psychological Bulletin*, 84 (5), 888-918.

Carey, John (1991), "Getting Business to Think about the Unthinkable," *Business Week*, June 24, 104-107.

Darby, Bruce W. and Barry R. Schlenker (1982), "Children's Reactions to Apologies," *Journal of Personality and Social Psychology*, 43 (October), 742-753.

Folkes, Valerie S. (1984), "Consumer Reactions to Product Failure: An Attributional Approach," *Journal of Consumer Research*, 10 (March), 398-409.

_____, Susan Koletsky, and John L. Graham (1987), "A Field Study of Causal Inferences and Consumer Reaction: The View from the Airport," *Journal of Consumer Research*, 13 (March), 534-539.

Garbett, Thomas (1988), *How to Build a Corporation's Identity and Project Its Image*, Lexington, MA: Lexington Books.

Ginzel, Linda E., Roderick M. Kramer, and Robert I. Sutton (1992), "Organizational Impression Management as a Reciprocal Influence Process: The Neglected Role of the Organizational Audience," in *Research in Organizational Behavior, Volume 15*, eds. L. L. Cummings and Barry M. Staw, Greenwich, CT: JAI Press, 227-266.

Griffin, Mitch, Barry J. Babin, and Jill S. Attaway (1991), "An Empirical Investigation of the Impact of Negative Public Publicity on Consumer Attitudes and Intentions," in *Advances in Consumer Research*, Vol. 18, eds. Rebecca H. Holman and Michael R. Solomon, Provo, UT: Association for Consumer Research, 334-341.

Hu, Li-Tze and Peter M. Bentler (1995), "Evaluating Model Fit," in *Structural Equation Modeling: Concepts, Issues, and Applications*, ed. Rick H. Hoyle, Thousand Oaks, CA: Sage, 76-99.

Jorgensen, Brian K. (1994), "Consumer Reaction to Company-Related Disasters: The Effect of Multiple Versus Single Explanations," in *Advances in Consumer Research*, Vol. 21, eds. Chris T. Allen and Deborah Roedder John, Provo, UT: Association for Consumer Research, 348-352.

Kremer, John F. and Laura Stephens (1983), "Attributions and Arousal as Mediators of Mitigation's Effect on Retaliation," *Journal of Personality and Social Psychology*, 45 (August), 335-343.

Lerbinger, Otto (1986), *Managing Corporate Crises: Strategies for Executives*, Boston: Barrington Press.

McLaughlin, Margaret L., Michael J. Cody, and H. Dan O'Hair (1983), "The Management of Failure Events: Some Contextual Determinants of Accounting Behavior," *Human Communication Research*, 9 (Spring), 208-224.

Romeo, Jean, Marc G. Weinberger, and David Antes (1994), "An Investigation of the Communication Cues that Affect Consumers' Responses to Negative Product Safety News," working paper, Research Centre for Consumer Behaviour, The University of Birmingham, England.

Russ, G. S. (1991), "Symbolic Communication and Image Management in Organizations," in *Applied Impression Management: How Image-Making Affects Managerial Decisions*, eds. R. A. Giacalone and P. Rosenfeld, Newbury Park, CA: Sage.

Schlenker, Barry R. (1980), *Impression Management*, Belmont, CA: Wadsworth, Inc.

Schönbach, P. (1980), "A Category System for Account Phrases," *European Journal of Social Psychology*, 10 (April-June), 208-224.

Siomkos, George J. and Peter G. Malliaris (1992), "Consumer Response to Company Communications During a Product Harm Crisis," *Journal of Applied Business Research*, 8 (Fall), 59-65.

Weiner, Bernard (1986), *An Attributional Theory of Motivation and Emotion*, New York: Springer-Verlag.

_____ , Sandra Graham, Orli Peter, and Mary Zmuidinas (1991), "Public Confession and Forgiveness," *Journal of Personality*, 59 (June), 281-312.

SPECIAL SESSION SUMMARY
Customers in the Organizational Context: How Organizations' Decisions Incorporate Customer Information

Prakash Nedungadi, Indiana University
Ajay K. Kohli, The University of Texas at Austin

This session explored the role of customer information in organizational decision making. The first paper *Engineering Customer Experiences* by Lewis P. Carbone described the importance of understanding customers' sensory responses to a variety of environmental triggers. These environmental triggers or clues include "mechanics" or things such as landscapes, thoughtfully placed traffic signs, recorded music and "humanics" or behavior of people (which can be creatively designed in). Next it described a systematic approach for understanding the influence of environmental cues on customers' perceptions and experience quality. Using this information, a service provider may design in specific mechanics and humanics to enhance customer perceptions of the service quality.

The second paper *When the Manager Becomes the Measure: The Use of Personal Information in the Development of Managers' Understanding of Consumers* by Christine Moorman examined the role of factual versus personal information in managerial decision making. Factual information refers to information about customers (e.g., their preferences in a food category), whereas personal information refers to information about a manager in his or her role as a customer (e.g., the manager's preferences in a food category). The paper described a data collection effort focused on product development teams and the rich qualitative data collected on managers' actions over a period of several weeks. Preliminary results obtained from a small sample of the data for illustrative purposes were described. Perhaps the most striking finding was that managers tended to use personal information far more than factual information to guide their decision making.

The two papers sparked a very lively discussion covering a number of themes. Some of the themes explored were as follows: What is the impact of environmental clues in experiments designed to test theories? Do we need to pay explicit attention to "mechanics" and "humanics" in designing such experiments? Is the use of personal information undesirable or desirable? On the one hand it may undesirable because what should count is factual information; on the other hand it may be useful for managers to be able to relate to information in a meaningful way to have confidence in the information. What can be done to increase the use of customer information by managers? For example, one suggestion was to make customer information more vivid by having managers talk with customers face to face, or observe customer focus groups rather than simply read research reports summarizing customer opinions or behavior.

Magic and Consumer Behavior
Cele Otnes, University of Illinois at Urbana-Champaign

Many topics of recent interest to consumer researchers—such as hedonic consumption, the consumption of "sacred" goods and services and ritualistic consumption—imply, but have not directly addressed, the assumption that consumer behavior may possess a magical dimension. The three papers presented in this session, and the comments made by the discussant, explored this issue of magic and consumer behavior.

The first paper presented, "Natural Magic: Packaging the Transformative Power of Nature," was by Eric J. Arnould and Linda L. Price, of the University of South Florida. The authors argue that transformative experiences are increasingly in demand by consumers. However, an issue that is widely overlooked is the resemblance of such activities to magical rites. This presentation offered new research that extends our understanding of "river magic," and contributes to understanding the role of magic in consumer behavior. River magic, like all magic, depends for its effects on three phenomena: 1) the condition of the participants; 2) the conduct of a rite, and 3) a verbal formula. The qualitative research presented shows how river magic effects emotional transformations by evoking the transcendent powers that are immanent in the natural landscape through ritualized performance and rhetoric.

The second paper presented was "The Magic of the Makers: The Witches Behind American Cosmetics Advertising," by Linda M. Scott of The University of Illinois at Urbana-Champaign. Scott began her presentation by observing that most of the famous-name cosmetics in American consumer culture have been produced and marketed by women. These women established successful commercial enterprises on the promise of potions that could transform female consumers into vamps, princesses, celebrities, socialites, or any of a number of other attractive personae. Before modern mass production and advertising, there were conjurers, healers, and voodoo queens who claimed to work magic through products they made themselves. In this presentation, the tradition of the "American witch" was examined in the contexts of contemporary cosmetics marketing and consumption.

The final paper presented was "The Transformative Power of Products," by Cele Otnes, of the University of Illinois at Urbana-Champaign. This presentation examined whether and how consumers experience transformations through product use. Ninety-two undergraduate advertising majors were asked to write about a time a product had "transformed [them] in any significant manner." The directions were purposely vague so that respondents would articulate how they defined the nature of transformative experiences with products. All but four wrote about transformative experiences, and products from 23 different categories were mentioned—ranging from macaroni and cheese to a Rolex watch. In addition, 13 different types of transformations (including physical transformations, confidence, comfort, rite-of-passage, and sexual transformations) were mentioned more than once. Excerpts from the essays reveal that products do indeed have transformative powers that are very real to consumers, and consumers are able to articulate the types of transformations that occur when using various products or services.

The discussant for this session was John F. Sherry Jr. of Northwestern University, who reaffirmed the importance of studying magic in consumer contexts, and who offered salient suggestions for further pursuit of study in this area.

Advertising and the Cultural Meaning of Animals

Barbara J. Phillips, The University of Texas at Austin

ABSTRACT

One explanation for the proliferation of animal trade characters in current advertising practice proposes that they are effective communication tools because they can be used to transfer desirable cultural meanings to products with which they are associated. The first step in examining what messages these animals communicate is to explore the common cultural meanings that they embody. This paper presents a qualitative analysis of the common themes found in the cultural meanings of four animal characters. In addition, it demonstrates a method by which cultural meanings can be elicited. The implications of this method for advertising research and practice are discussed.

ADVERTISING AND THE CULTURAL MEANING OF ANIMALS

American popular culture has quietly become inhabited by all sorts of talking animals and dancing products that are used by advertisers to promote their brands. These creatures, called trade characters, are fictional, animate beings or animated objects that have been created for the promotion of a product, service, or idea (Phillips 1996). Commercials with these characters score above average in their ability to change brand preference (Stewart and Furse 1986). It appears, then, that trade characters can be effective communication tools. However, it is unclear why this is so. Although trade characters are popular with advertisers and consumers, their role in communicating the advertising message has been generally taken for granted without investigation.

It has been hypothesized that there are several reasons why advertisers use trade characters: to attract attention, enhance identification of and memory for a product, and achieve promotional continuity (Phillips 1996). However, one of the most important reasons for the use of trade characters in advertising may be that they can be used to transfer desired meanings to the products with which they are associated. By pairing a trade character with a product, advertisers can link the personality and cultural meaning of the character to the product in the minds of consumers. This creates a desirable image, or meaning, for the product. The first step in supporting this explanation of trade character communication is to show that these characters do embody common cultural meanings that can be linked to products.

Research has shown that *animal* characters are one of the most commonly used trade character types in current advertising practice (Callcott and Lee 1994). Animals have long been viewed as standard symbols of human qualities (Neal 1985; Sax 1988). For example, in American culture, "everyone" knows that a bee symbolizes industriousness, a dove represents peace, and a fox embodies cunning (Robin 1932). It is likely that advertisers use animal characters because consumers understand the animals' cultural meanings and consequently can link these meanings to a product. Therefore, the cultural meaning of animals may lie at the core of the meanings of animal trade characters. This paper describes a method for eliciting character meanings, presents a qualitative analysis of the cultural meanings of four animal characters, and discusses the broader implications that these results have for advertising research and practice. This qualitative study of animal meanings is motivated by several issues. Understanding the cultural meanings that consumers assign to animal characters will assist in developing successful advertising campaigns; practitioners can create characters that embody desired brand meanings while avoiding characters with negative associations. In addition, by highlighting an underutilized research method by which the cultural meaning of characters can be elicited, this paper presents a way for practitioners, researchers, and regulators to understand what messages specific characters are communicating to their audiences. This method may be useful in other types of advertising research as well; researchers have asked for measures of cultural meaning for celebrity endorsers (McCracken 1989) and for symbolic advertising images (Scott 1994). Finally, by showing that animal characters have common cultural meanings, this paper builds support for one of the first empirical explanations of how trade characters "work" in advertising, and creates a foundation for future trade character research.

The next section of the paper will present the theories used to illuminate the research question: *Do there exist shared meanings that consumers associate with specific animal characters? If so, how can these meanings be elicited, and what are their common themes?* The third section will introduce a method by which the cultural meanings of characters can be elicited, and will present the procedures used in this research study. The fourth section will discuss the results of the study, and the last section will draw general conclusions.

Conceptual Development of the Research Question

It has been suggested that advertising functions, in general, by attempting to link a product with an image that elicits desirable emotions and ideas (McCracken 1986). For example, the image of a child may invoke feelings of pleasure, nostalgia, and playfulness. By showing a product next to such an image, advertising encourages consumers to associate the product with the image. Through this association, the product acquires the image's cultural meaning.

Trade characters may be one type of image that advertisers use because these characters possess learned cultural meanings. These meanings are similar to the personalities that consumers associate with characters from other sources such as movies, cartoons, and comic books. For example, Mickey Mouse is viewed as a "nice guy," while Bugs Bunny is seen as clever, but mischievous. Individuals do not invent their own meaning for cultural symbols; they must learn what each symbol means in their culture (Berger 1984) based on their experiences with the character. For example, consumers' ideas about the meaning of "elephant" are shaped by Dumbo movies and African safari TV programs, and colored by news stories about a rampaging elephant that trampled its trainer. Consequently, although each individual brings his or her own experience to the meaning ascription process, consensus of character meaning across individuals is possible through common cultural experience.

In advertising, trade characters' meanings are used to visually represent the product attributes (Zacher 1967) or the advertising message (Kleppner 1966). For example, Mr. Peanut embodies sophistication (Kapnick 1992), the Pillsbury Doughboy symbolizes fun (PR Newswire 1990), and the lonely Maytag repairman stands for reliability (Elliott 1992). However, the consumer must correctly decode the trade character's meaning before it can have an impact (McCracken 1986). Therefore, characters' meanings must be easily understood by consumers if they are to correctly interpret the character's message. As a result, advertisers frequently use animal trade characters (Callcott and Lee 1994), because consumers are thought to have learned the animals' cultural meanings and consequently are likely to correctly decode the advertising message.

The first step in examining the association between animal trade characters and the products they promote is to explore the symbolic meanings conveyed by the animals used in these advertisements. That is, if an advertiser places a bear (e.g., Snuggle) or a dog (e.g., Spuds McKenzie) next to his product, what do these animals represent to the audience? Rather than examine individual animal characters, however, it is necessary to first study an animal's general cultural meaning. This is because the animal category (e.g., bear, dog, etc.) provides the primary, or core meaning of an individual character. Although an advertiser can choose to highlight certain animal meanings over others (e.g., "softness" for Snuggle Bear and "wildness" for Smokey Bear), the core set of animal meanings dictate what is possible for that character to express. Snuggle fabric softener would not find it easy to use a porcupine, pig, or flamingo to express "softness."

In addition, by studying the broad animal category to which the character belongs, it is possible to make generalizations that can help practitioners create and use animal characters effectively. For example, if advertisers know that the animal "cat" shares several positive core meanings, they can create cat characters that capitalize on those meanings. Alternatively, if "cat" meanings contain negative attributes that reflect badly on the associated product, advertisers may want to use a different character.

Method

It is difficult to explore the perceived meaning of a trade character by asking subjects directly, as their responses tend to be superficial and descriptive. "Smokey Bear? Oh, he's brown and wears a hat." Other qualitative methods, such as in-depth interviewing, tend to be time- and labor-intensive — features that advertisers may want to avoid. As an alternative, word association is an easy and efficient method for exploring psychological meaning. It can be administered to a group and can elicit the meanings of more than one animal per session, yet provides rich information regarding cultural meaning. Szalay and Deese (1978) state that because a word association task does not require subjects to communicate their intentions, it decreases subjects' rationalizations, and it taps associations that are difficult to express or explain. Further, word association does not require thoughts to be expressed in a structural manner. Instead, this technique produces expressions of thought that are immediate and spontaneous, and this spontaneity, along with an imposed time constraint, is thought to reduce subjects' self-monitoring and conscious editing of responses. Finally, the method reduces experimenter bias because no organization or categories are imposed on subjects to limit their responses — a primary draw-back of quantitative research.

The word association method is not new; other marketing and advertising researchers have used it to understand how consumers perceive products (Kleine and Kernan 1991) and to determine a product's attributes to aid in product positioning (Friedmann 1986). However, perhaps because it is "old hat," this method has been consistently overlooked and underutilized in consumer behavior research.

In the present study, informants were asked to respond to *verbal* animal names during the word association task (e.g., "bear") rather than to visual images of the animal. Verbal animal names are thought to elicit broad responses that reflect much of the information that an individual has learned to associate with the category, "bear." In contrast, the way an animal is visually portrayed can narrow its meaning (Berger 1984). A realistic picture of a bear may elicit a different part of the core meaning of "bear" than a cartoon bear. Images of actual trade characters, such as Smokey Bear or Snuggle, may elicit even narrower meanings associated only with

those characters. Therefore, verbal animal names were used to generate broad, complete responses. However, it is possible that advertisers could use both verbal and visual animals in a word association task when creating characters. Responses to the verbal animal name would provide core meanings while responses to the visual character would provide a measure of how successfully the particular representation of an animal captured desired meanings. This possibility will be discussed further in the conclusion section of this paper.

The informants for this study were 21 male and 15 female undergraduate students enrolled in an advertising management course at a major state university. Students participated in the study during their regular class time. Of these respondents, 92% were between the ages of 20 and 25. The use of this student sample precludes concluding that the results of this study reflect the "true" cultural meaning of each animal. However, this sample is useful to show that a common cultural meaning for each animal exists in a homogeneous population and can be elicited through research, whether that population is composed of undergraduate students or other target markets of interest to advertisers.

Each informant received a package containing a cover page, an instruction page, and five word association sheets. The instructions for the word association task were read aloud and informants' questions regarding the task were answered. For each word association task, respondents had one minute to write one-word descriptions of whatever came to mind when they thought about the animal listed at the top of the page (Szalay and Deese 1978). Informants were instructed to write these words in the order in which they came to mind and it was stressed that there were no wrong answers. The first animal listed in the package was lobster, which was used as a practice task to familiarize students with the word association method. After completing the practice task, informants' remaining questions about the task were answered. Respondents then completed four more animal word associations, responding to the words: penguin, ant, gorilla, and racoon. The particular animals were chosen to reflect the interests of the author; other animals could illustrate the commonality of animal meanings as well. The order in which the four animals were presented was randomized to control for order effects.

The words generated by informants in response to the animal word association were grouped into categories, or themes that emerged from the data. Each animal was analyzed separately except lobster, the practice task, which was not coded. For each animal, words that were similar in meaning or that had a common theme were grouped together. Each informant's responses were added to the tentative themes discovered in the previous informants' responses, thus supporting those themes or allowing them to be changed (Strauss and Corbin 1990). Guidelines suggested by Szalay and Deese (1978) were followed when identifying common themes.

Words that could not be placed into any category were placed into an "other" category. These words did not have an identifiable association with the animal; they are thought to be associations to words other than the animal (i.e., chain associations) or words that show that the respondent was thinking of something other than the task at hand. There were only 10 to 16 of these words for each animal.

A second researcher re-classified all of the response words into the categories to check the soundness of the themes. There was an initial 86% agreement between researchers; disagreements were resolved through discussion and re-analysis of informant responses. The response words for all of the animals are available from the author.

FIGURE 1

Cognitive Map of Penguin Themes

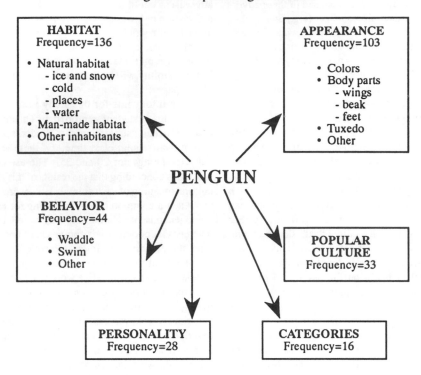

The themes elicited in response to each animal were illustrated using cognitive maps, representing a pictorial overview of each animal's meaning. The cognitive map summarizes the objects and ideas that informants collectively associate with each animal, and organizes these associations into meaningful themes (Coleman 1992). The cognitive map also identifies the number of times each theme was mentioned, giving an idea of the relative importance of each theme to the animal's shared meaning.

RESULTS AND DISCUSSION

General Results

Informants mentioned between 315 and 386 words in response to each animal, or approximately 9 to 11 words per individual. It was surprising that more than 90% of informants' responses could be classified into six or seven main themes for each animal. In addition, informants' words were easily coded into these themes, reflecting a high degree of similarity between respondents. Also, words with the highest frequencies were mentioned by 8 to 25 individuals which suggests a high degree of consistency across individuals' responses. These results support the idea that there exist shared cultural meanings that consumers generally associate with animals, and that these meanings can be elicited through word association.

Interestingly, although it was not the intent at the outset, the themes that emerged from the data were remarkably similar between animals. The primary themes mentioned by informants include: (a) Appearance, (b) Habitat, (c) Personality, (d) Human/animal interaction, (e) Popular culture, and (f) Behavior. These six categories seem to be most salient for consumers, and may offer the greatest help in creating animal characters for use in advertising campaigns. *Appearance* summarizes informants' mental image of the animal — how they expect the animal to look. *Habitat* describes informants' expectations of where these animals live and the

objects that surround them. *Personality* represents the personality traits that informants associate with each animal. *Human/animal interaction* describes how humans coexist and interact with these animals, while *Behavior* describes their typical actions. *Popular culture* highlights cultural references that already exist for each animal, including sources such as television programs, movies, books, and ads. The themes for each animal are given below in greater detail.

Penguin

A cognitive map of the themes associated with "penguin," along with the frequency with which they were mentioned, are shown in Figure 1. The dominant themes that emerge from the data are *Habitat* and *Appearance*. *Habitat* includes a natural habitat made up of the subthemes of: (a) ice and snow, (b) cold, (c) places such as Antarctica and the South Pole, and (d) water. Informants also listed other inhabitants of this environment such as fish, polar bears, and whales. Informants also mentioned *Appearance* as an important penguin theme, focusing on the subthemes of: (a) color, which was mostly black and white, (b) body parts such as wings, beaks, and feet, and (c) the formal tuxedo that penguins seem to be wearing. Tuxedo was the most often mentioned word, with 23 mentions. This strong association seems to have affected other themes, as discussed below.

Both of the dominant themes suggest that a penguin is associated with rich visual imagery. When confronted with the word "penguin," it appears that individuals conjure up an image of a penguin, and describe him (*Appearance*) and his surroundings (*Habitat*). This interpretation is supported by a third theme, *Behavior*, which was mentioned less often. This category includes the subthemes of: (a) waddle, (b) swim, and (c) other actions, which also contribute to visual imagery. *Behavior* was mentioned 44 times, suggesting that respondents frequently visualize the penguin in motion.

FIGURE 2
Cognitive Map of Ant Themes

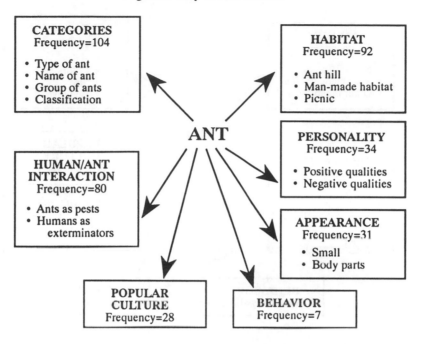

In analyzing the dominant themes, it seems that penguins are viewed as having little interaction with humans. The penguin appears to be isolated from all but a few Eskimos (according to two informants) except when viewed in a man made habitat (e.g., "Sea World"), and even that type of interaction is rarely mentioned (2% of the time). This lack of human/penguin interaction is not surprising given penguins' remote location in the world and the fact that they are removed from informants' daily experiences.

Another theme, *Personality*, is characterized by a duality; for the most part, penguins are personified as silly creatures (e.g., cute, funny, goofy, playful, etc.) but they also can be viewed as formal animals (e.g., distinguished, classy, behaved, mannered, etc.), even by the same individuals. This contradiction may stem from the fact that penguins are strange-looking members of the bird family and waddle comically instead of flying, but also appear to wearing a tuxedo, a cultural symbol of formality and manners.

The remaining penguin themes are *Popular culture* and *Categories*. Penguins are associated with a surprisingly large number of popular culture references including movies, videogames, mascots, and cartoons. *Categories* refers to the hierarchical categorization of objects, in which an object can be placed in a superset (generalization hierarchy) or a subset (part hierarchy) (Anderson 1990). For example, a penguin is a bird (superset), and a type of penguin is an emperor (subset). In the same way, a group of penguins is called a flock, or a herd (at least for one respondent).

Ant

A cognitive map of the "ant" themes is shown in Figure 2. The three dominant ant themes are: *Categories, Habitat,* and *Human/ ant interaction. Categories* includes: (a) type of ant such as red or army, (b) name of ant such as worker or queen, (c) group of ants such as colony, and (d) classification of ant such as insect. The importance of this theme for ant contrasts sharply with that for penguin; *Categories* was mentioned 104 times for ant, but only 16 times for penguin. This suggests that the ant themes are less associated with images, and more associated with verbal or propositional knowl-

edge (Anderson 1990). That is, when asked to respond to the word "ant," it appears that respondents retrieve verbal information that they have learned in the past such as: the head ant is called the queen, the male ant is called the drone; ants live in colonies; etc. This interpretation is supported by another dominant theme, *Habitat*, where the subthemes of: (a) hill, and (b) man-made habitat also appear to contain verbal associations. For example, the most-often mentioned words in each subtheme, "hill" and "farm," could be elicited with a fill-in-the-blank word task (i.e., "ant____"). The same cannot be said for penguin (e.g., "penguin *ice*", "penguin *cold*", etc.).

Some imagery is associated with ant, though, as seen in the *Habitat* subtheme of (c) picnic. For the most part, however, other themes support verbal, non-imagery based associations for ant. For example, the ant's image-based themes, *Appearance* and *Behavior*, contain far fewer words (31 and 7) than do these same categories for penguin (103 and 44). Also, many of the words in *Appearance*, such as antenna, thorax, and abdomen, seem associated with knowledge propositions rather than image. Surprisingly, even the *Popular culture* theme supports a verbal view because many of the responses in this category make use of word play such as "Aunt Bea" and "antichrist."

A dominant theme for ant that did not exist for penguin is *Human/ant interaction.* This focus on interaction is understandable given that ants are usually part of informants' daily environment and experience. In this category, ants interact with humans by annoying them and causing them pain; "bite" was mentioned 19 times by respondents. Humans interact with ants as exterminators; we kill them. It is surprising then, that under the theme *Personality*, ants are personified as having more positive than negative qualities. Words like "strong," "hard-working," and "determined" are used by respondents. Perhaps individuals have learned to associate these positive qualities with ants through stories, songs, and fables such as "The Grasshopper and the Ant," while negative associations such as pest come from informants' own experiences. In the same

FIGURE 3
Cognitive Map of Gorilla Themes

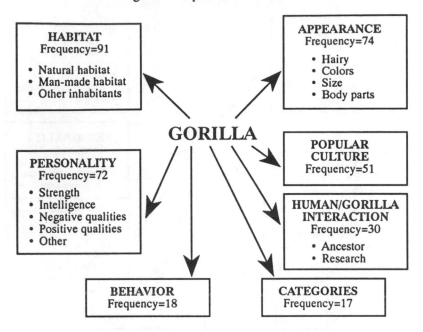

way as with penguin, there is a duality in the ant's perceived personality — industrious and diligent, yet irritating and better off dead. These strongly negative associations may signal advertisers to use caution in utilizing this animal in ads; advertisers must be sure that only desirable characteristics are transferred to the brand.

Gorilla

A cognitive map of "gorilla" themes is presented in Figure 3. The dominant themes that emerge from the data are *Habitat*, *Appearance*, and *Personality*. Gorilla's dominant themes, like those of penguin, are rich in visual imagery and appear to be visually based. For example, *Habitat* contains images of: (a) natural habitats such as the jungle, (b) man-made habitats such as zoos and cages, and (c) other inhabitants, most notably bananas and monkeys. In the same way, *Appearance* is composed of: (a) hairy, (b) colors, (c) size, and (d) body parts like big hands and big teeth.

Gorilla is the first animal in this study to have *Personality* as a dominant theme. As with penguin and ant, gorilla is personified in two different ways—as a fierce monster with negative attributes, and as a gentle giant with positive ones. The theme *Popular culture* gives a possible reason for this duality. "King Kong," the movie(s) that portrays a giant gorilla destroying cities and battling other monsters, received 15 direct and indirect mentions, while "Gorillas in the Mist," the movie that portrays gorillas as human-like, endangered creatures received 12.

Human/gorilla interaction appears as another gorilla theme (as it did for ant) even though the gorilla, like the penguin, is remote and removed from respondents' daily lives. While the interaction between humans and ants was concrete and experience-based, the interaction between humans and gorillas is viewed more symbolically by informants, with the subthemes: (a) ancestor, and (b) research. As our ancestors, gorillas were associated directly with humans through Darwin's theory of evolution. Informants also recognized the research link between gorillas and humans as we study them for their benefit (e.g., "endangered") or for ours (e.g., "sign language").

Racoon

A cognitive map of "racoon" themes is shown in Figure 4. The dominant themes that emerge from the responses are: *Appearance, Habitat,* and *Personality,* suggesting that a racoon's personality is an important part of its collective meaning, in the same way as a gorilla's. The words associated with racoon also appear to be imagery-based like those for penguin and gorilla.

Unlike the observations made for other animals, there is no separate theme of human/racoon interaction. The reason for this is that the idea of interaction is woven throughout each category. For example, informants listed both trees and rooftops, wilderness and drainage ditches as racoon habitats. Food included crawfish and trash, and other inhabitants were likely to be both possums and coon dogs. This suggests that the racoon is not seen as having a separate environment like ant (e.g., "hill") or gorilla (e.g., "jungle") which can sometimes overlap with a human environment. Rather, the racoon shares our habitat in an integrated way.

The theme *Personality* includes: (a) thief, (b) positive qualities like cute and playful, and (c) negative qualities such as sneaky and troublesome. Although informants listed both negative and positive attributes for racoon, its personality does not appear to be a duality, unlike the other animals studied. This is because respondents viewed the racoon as possessing both positive and negative qualities at the same time as part of the same personality role. Racoon is personified most often as a bandit (10 mentions), and also is called a rascal or a scoundrel. It appears that we admire a racoon's intelligence and audacity while deploring the mess they make when the intrude on our property.

CONCLUSION

This study has supported the view that consumers associate shared meanings with animals and has provided a description of the common themes found in the cultural meanings of four specific animals. In addition, the results of this study support the use of the word association method to elicit those cultural meanings.

FIGURE 4
Cognitive Map of Racoon Themes

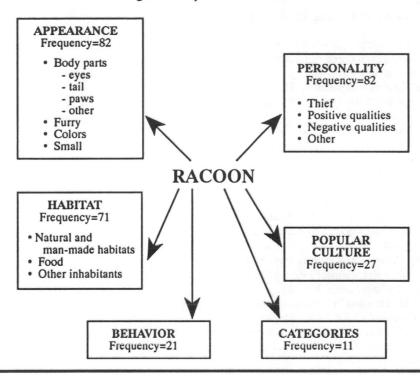

Respondents generated six common themes of interest to advertisers in response to each animal: Appearance, Habitat, Personality, Human/animal interaction, Popular culture, and Behavior. It is clear that these themes have practical applications in advertising. The themes of appearance, habitat, and behavior can help define a "natural" look for an animal and its environment in an ad, while other popular culture references in response to the word association task can warn the advertiser if the animal has already been linked to another product or idea. The most meaningful themes for advertising use, however, are personality and interaction. Through these themes, an advertiser can explore the core meanings consumers associate with a specific animal. If advertisers understand this core meaning, they can appropriate all or part of the animal's meaning for their products. Advertisers can match positive qualities to the product attributes or the advertising message, or avoid using the animal if it elicits negative associations.

The benefit of eliciting core animal meanings is that by using the associations that already exist in our culture, advertisers do not have to educate consumers as to what their animal characters mean. Consequently, an ad's message will be more quickly and easily decoded and understood. Many advertisers intuitively take advantage of shared meanings to create suitable characters; this paper presents a method for explicitly capitalizing on the shared cultural meanings of animals in trade character advertising.

This study has theoretical implications for trade character research as well. By showing that animals have common cultural meanings, the results support the idea that animal-based trade characters also embody these shared meanings. Therefore, it is possible that trade characters can be used to transfer a common meaning to a product. Future trade character research should focus on the transfer process by testing the ability of trade characters to influence product meanings.

In addition, the results of this study suggest interesting avenues for future research regarding *visual* trade character meanings.

How does the core meaning of an animal character (as determined through consumer response to a verbal animal name) relate to the meaning of the character's visual image? For example, a study could compare teens' responses to the word "camel" on a word association task with their responses to an image of Joe Camel. Does Joe retain his "camelness" or are his meanings entirely different? How do Joe's meanings, as an animal, compare to the meanings of the human Marlboro cowboy? The meanings of many existing animal characters could be explored using these methods.

The use of the word association method has applications beyond trade character research. McCracken (1989, p. 319) calls for the creation of an instrument to "detect and survey" the cultural meanings that are present in celebrity endorsers. Scott (1994) states more generally that an exploration of how symbolic advertising images are interpreted in consumer culture is needed to advance consumer behavior research. Given its success in eliciting the cultural meaning of animals, the word association method seems suited to explore the cultural meanings of celebrities and symbolic images in advertising as well.

In conclusion, this study has shown that consumers associate shared cultural meanings with animal characters. These meanings can be elicited through the word association method, and contain common themes that can be used to further advertising theory and practice.

REFERENCES

Anderson, John R. (1990), *Cognitive Psychology and Its Implications*, Third Edition, New York, NY: W.H. Freeman and Company, 123-135.

Berger, Asa (1984), *Signs in Contemporary Culture: An Introduction to Semiotics*, New York: Longman.

Callcott, Margaret F. and Wei-Na Lee (1994), "A Content Analysis of Animation and Animated Spokes-Characters in Television Commercials," *Journal of Advertising*, 23(4): 1-12.

Coleman, Laurence J. (1992), "The Cognitive Map of a Master Teacher Conducting Discussions with Gifted Students," *Exceptionality*, 3: 1-16.

Elliott, Stewart (1992), "Loneliness in a Long-Lasting Pitch," *The New York Times*, May 15, C1.

Friedmann, Roberto (1986), "Psychological Meaning of Products: Identification and Marketing Applications," *Psychology and Marketing*, 3: 1-15.

Kapnick, Sharon (1992), "Commercial Success: These advertising figures have become American icons," *The Austin American-Statesman*, April 25, D1.

Kleine, Robert E. and Jerome B. Kernan (1991), "Contextual Influences on the Meanings Ascribed to Ordinary Consumption Objects," *Journal of Consumer Research*, 18: 311-323.

Kleppner, Otto (1966), *Advertising Procedure*, 5th edition, Englewood Cliffs, NJ: Prentice Hall, Inc.

McCracken, Grant (1986), "Culture and Consumption: A Theoretical Account of the Structure and Movement of the Cultural Meaning of Consumer Goods," *Journal of Consumer Research*, 13: 71-84.

McCracken, Grant (1989), "Who Is the Celebrity Endorser? Cultural Foundations of the Endorsement Process," *Journal of Consumer Research*, 16(December): 310-321.

Neal, Arthur G. (1985), "Animism and Totemism in Popular Culture," *Journal of Popular Culture*, 19(2): 15-24.

Phillips, Barbara J. (1996), "Defining Trade Characters and Their Role in American Popular Culture," *Journal of Popular Culture*, 29(4): forthcoming.

PR Newswire (1990), "Oh Boy! Pillsbury Doughboy Turns 25!" September 20.

Robin, P. Ansell (1932), *Animal Lore in English Literature*, London: John Murray.

Sax, Boria (1988), "Anthromorphism in Animal Encyclopedias of Nineteenth Century America," *New York Folklore*, 14(1-2): 107-122.

Scott, Linda M. (1994), "Images in Advertising: The Need for a Theory of Visual Rhetoric," *Journal of Consumer Research*, 21(September): 252-273.

Stewart, David W. and David H. Furse (1986), *Effective Television Advertising: A Study of 1000 Commercials*, Lexington, MA: Lexington Books.

Strauss, Anselm and Juliet Corbin (1990), *Basics of Qualitative Research: Grounded Theory Procedures and Techniques*, Newbury Park, CA: Sage Publications, Inc.

Szalay, Lorand B. and James Deese (1978), *Subjective Meaning and Culture: An Assessment Through Word Associations*, Hillsdale, NJ: Lawrence Erlbaum Associates.

Zacher, Robert Vincent (1967), *Advertising Techniques and Management*, Homewood, IL: Richard D. Irwin, Inc.

The Disposal of Consumers: An Exploratory Analysis of Death-Related Consumption

Terrance G. Gabel, The University of Memphis
Phylis Mansfield, The University of Memphis
Kevin Westbrook, The University of Memphis

The worlds that man constructs are forever threatened by the forces of chaos, finally by the inevitable fact of death... every human order is a community in the face of death. -Peter L. Berger (1990, p. 80)

Death is a great opportunity for the living... -Michael Bliss (1994, p. 160)

When families got the ashes, there was no way of knowing whether they had their husband or wife or a cocker spaniel... At least 30 percent of the time, the ashes at the service belonged to someone else... -Former crematorium employee quoted in Collier and Kelly (1991)

ABSTRACT

Complementing and extending recent psychological, sociological, and consumer research on death and its impact on consumer decision making, this exploratory study provides both an additional perspective on the issue of consumer vulnerability and a preliminary examination of meaning associated with death-related consumption.

INTRODUCTION

Recently, death and dying research in the fields of psychology and sociology has moved beyond customary consideration of predominantly negative attitudes towards death in the direction of deeper meaning associated with these attitudes. At the same time, at least four important trends have emerged with regard to death and the consumption of death-related products in the United States: 1) the continuing privatization of death, 2) the increasing popularity of goods and services associated in some fashion with death (e.g., angel-related products [see Miller 1994] and prearranged funeral services [see Shermach 1994]), 3) public concerns over alleged unethical marketer behaviors in the funeral-service industry, and 4) forecasted dramatic increases in the numbers of deaths in coming years.

With the exception of the recent work of Gentry (i.e., Gentry et al. 1994 & 1995; Gentry and Goodwin 1995), death-related discussions by marketing and consumer researchers have focused mainly on social marketing efforts aimed at educating consumers about life-threatening behaviors and diseases (e.g., AIDS [see Frankenberger and Sukhdial 1994]). Although Gentry (i.e., Gentry et. al. 1994) deals extensively with the impact of grief associated with the loss of a loved one on post-death consumer decision making, passivity, and subsequent vulnerability and (opportunities for) abuse, relatively little attention has been paid to meanings

ascribed to either post-death or pre-need death-related consumption. In response to this neglect, after providing brief historical and theoretical backgrounds of death-related consumption, this study undertakes both an extension of past discussions of vulnerability associated with the consumption of death-related products (i.e., by considering both post-death and pre-need consumption) as well as an exploratory analysis of consumer meaning with respect to such consumption in the United States.

HISTORICAL BACKGROUND[1]

The historical underpinnings of death-related consumption in the U.S. may be traced to the Puritanical concept of death established around 1630, which depicts death as "deserved for a sinful people" (Burns 1990). Although death-related consumption and exchange (e.g., payment for funeral services and land) no doubt transpired in association with many burials dating back to the arrival of the Pilgrims, the first clear example of the marketing of death-related products appears to have occurred in the late 1740s, when the first known postmortem paintings appeared. In these plague and disease-ridden early years of American history, death-related consumption was undertaken by groups of individuals (i.e., families and entire communities).

Privatization of Death

Community-based death-related consumption and other associated activities found in early American history gradually became more privatized (i.e., individualized and professionalized—isolated within families and hidden from public view). Although the "privatization of death" was not complete until the early years of the 20th century, this practice was greatly facilitated by the fact that insurance benefits had replaced the aid survivors received from the community and extended family by the end of the 18th century (Burns 1990). Additionally, throughout the 1800s, name changes enhanced the image of many death-related goods and services, with the result of increasing public acceptance of the notion that professionals (e.g., furniture manufacturers, undertakers, and insurance companies) were capable of handling all burial arrangements with little family or community participation. For example, the more pleasing "cemetery" replaced "graveyard" or "burial ground" in 1831. "Coffins" were supplanted by "caskets" in 1859, as was "undertaker" by "funeral director" in 1882. Full-service "funeral homes" first appeared in 1885. By 1910, domestic "parlors," formal rooms in the home used for social meetings associated with death and other occasions, had effectively been transferred from the home to professional service provider facilities. By 1930, the "funeral parlor" had become "the center of care for the dead."

Consumer Vulnerability

Following purchases of homes and automobiles, those of death-related products rank as the third largest expenditure for many consumers (Lino 1990). Unlike other major purchases, those for death-related goods and services occur at times of both new consumption roles (e.g., widow, widower, single-parent) and great anxiety and emotional instability (Gentry et al. 1994, 1995). Add to this the fact that markups of up to 900 percent are charged for death-related goods and services (Lubove 1993) and the issue of consumer vulnerability becomes an important concern.

---

[1]This section relies heavily on Burns' (1990) "Death in America: A Chronology." In that the original chronology is presented in appendix form with unnumbered pages, the quotations which appear here do not include page numbers. In order to facilitate reader location of citation content in Burn's chronology, the year(s) of occurrence associated with the text are indicated when applicable.

Unfortunately, there exists a long and rich history of consumer abuse with regard to death-related consumption in the United States. Burns (1990) suggests that the origins of this abuse coincide most directly with the first successful marketing of life insurance in 1830:

> Beneficiaries often receive more money than they had ever had at one time... As a result of large sums of money given to beneficiaries at a psychologically vulnerable time, the funeral industry develops lavish funeral rituals.

Consumer rights were again threatened in the mid 1850s when "Cemetery superintendents, by setting rules for burial and for plot decoration, start to exert a powerful role in the death ritual" (Burns 1990). Over the course of the next fifteen years, further control over death-related consumption was wrested from consumers when the first formal associations of both undertakers and cemetery superintendents were formed. These two associations, the Funeral Directors National Association of the U.S. and the Association of American Cemetery Superintendents, "directed the course of the American funeral during the next 75 years." These developments, in conjunction with the simultaneous discovery and public acceptance of embalming, appear to have permanently established the role and influence of professional service providers as dominant in the burial process. This power was so strong that no investigation of death-related product marketing was conducted until 1926, when it was found that "... funeral directors 'charge what the traffic will bear,' and that the poorest families carried the heaviest burden of cost" (Burns 1990). Further, no other "serious attempt at a general study of funeral costs" was undertaken until the mid 1970s, at which time several published investigations of abuse in the industry (e.g., Mitford 1963) led to the availability of "more simplified, cost-conscious funerals."

Consistent with Burns' (1990) account of the rich history of consumer abuse, and in spite a major Federal Trade Commission investigation in 1978 (see Engel 1984), recent reports suggest that such practice is indeed alive and well. As previously discussed, the sheer cost of death-related goods and services, purchased at times of high anxiety and emotional instability, is sufficient to warrant charges of consumer abuse. Although a complete treatment of this topic is well beyond the scope of this discussion, additional reports of abuse associated with death-related consumption include: 1) incomplete or fraudulent information being provided to consumers (Engel 1984; Good 1994; Hildula 1990), 2) the removal of gold teeth and body parts for sale without proper authorization (Torres 1995), 3) tasteless, fear-based advertising (Good 1994), 4) financial improprieties (Conner 1994; Good 1994; Sinclair 1991; Torres 1995), 5) the switching and mixing of (cremated) human ashes with those of animals (Collier 1991; Collier and Kelly 1991), 6) collusion among "traditional" service providers in an effort to competitively harm innovative, low-cost providers (Engel 1984; Hildula

1990; Salerno 1990), 7) conflicts of interest held by industry commissioners (Barnhart and Saville Hodge 1985; Engel 1984), 8) state funeral service commissions repeatedly ignoring consumer complaints (Engel 1984; Miller 1995), and 9) a general and persistent difficulty in getting meaningful consumer protection legislation enacted (Antitrust and Trade Regulation Report 1989; Cain 1994; Collier and Kelly 1991; Connors 1993; Sinclair 1991).

THEORETICAL BACKGROUND

Literature concerning death and bereavement (i.e., "'consolation literature' written by women and clergymen") rose to popularity beginning in 1830 (Burns 1990). While the importance of death has long been recognized by sociological and psychological researchers, studies have tended to focus primarily on negative attitudes held towards death (Holcomb, Neimeyer, and Moore 1993). Consumer researchers (i.e., Gentry et. al. 1994 & 1995; Gentry and Goodwin 1995) have examined diminished decision making skills, consumer passivity, and resultant vulnerability and abuse in the face of grief resulting from the death of a loved one. Recently, sociological and psychological research has begun to address additional issues relevant to the study of death from a consumer or consumption perspective. Topics of particular importance include both the privatization and meaning of death.

Privatization of Death

From a sociological perspective, Mellor and Shilling (1993) suggest that the ongoing privatization of death has achieved particular significance due to three characteristics of modern society: 1) the growing role played by the reflexive re-ordering of biographical narratives in the construction of self-identity,[2] 2) increased identification of the self with the body, and 3) consistent with the perspective of Belk, Wallendorf, and Sherry (1989), the diminished scope of the sacred. With regard to the first two points, Mellor and Shilling contend that, due to both decreasing requirements for the legitimation of reality and increasing confusion and anxiety, death is increasingly viewed by relatively isolated individuals as a "powerful threat." Pertaining to the diminished scope of the sacred, the authors (p. 416) state that:

> ... with the decline of traditional religious belief, and the attendant desacralisation of death, there was even less of an impulse to keep it in the public domain... The death itself will frequently be greeted with few ritual, religious and communal signs of mourning other than a funeral.

In summary, Mellor and Shilling (1993, p. 417) contend that:

> ... the processes of individualisation and privatisation leave many people uncertain, socially unsupported, and vulnerable when it comes to dealing with death.

From a consumer perspective, vulnerability is increased due to the fact that less (family or communal) thought and planning now go in to death-related consumption decision making. As a consequence, consumers may make quick—if not also rash—decisions.

Meaning of Death

The privatization of death in modern American society suggests that death may no longer be as meaningful as it once was in that rich familial and communal meaning now exists as an isolated phenomenon (Mellor and Shilling 1993). Contrast the following passages, the first documenting the relative shallowness of mean-

---

[2]With regard to this modern phenomenon, Mellor and Shilling (1993, p, 413) state that "... self- identity is now something constructed through continual re-ordering of self-narratives" and provide as an example therapies, life-guides, and self-help movements which "clearly assist large numbers of people in constructing and reconstructing their life narratives in order to establish a reliable 'sense of self' in the context of a seemingly hostile and threatening world."

ings more commonly ascribed to death, and the second describing the more richly detailed meaning of "decoration day" activities still routinely practiced in Blue Ridge Mountain communities:

> Relationships that are lovingly complex during life become reduced to package deals. As a society, we've lost the knowledge of caring for our own dead. People feel that they are unable to do anything for a departed friend except spend money. So they spend as much money as they can, and then, after the event, feel unfulfilled as well as broke (Carlson 1991, p. 80).

> There is hardly a summer Sunday in any area that is not some family's decoration day... On decoration day, the preachers and singers situate themselves in a visible spot and begin to preach and sing as people arrive with baskets of fresh flowers and food. The graves are soon heaped with a blaze of color and care is taken so that no grave is slighted... When I was a child, my favorite decoration day fell in early September when chinquapins were ripe and the late summer days were fading into harvest. We were always invited to the Woody family decoration... the Woody decoration had a beautiful ritual built into the day's structure that was unique (Wiseman Boulton 1991, pp. 81-82).

With the first passage, lack of meaning is directly linked with capitalistic tendencies not only to act in opportunistic fashion—on the part of the marketer—but also to perceive the spending of money as the solution to most, if not all, problems—on the part of the consumer. Here, the meaning of death reduced to the spending of money, possibly in order to symbolically demonstrate how much one cared for the deceased or avoid the stigma associated with a "cheap funeral," has prompted Hyde (1983, p. 45) to suggest that:

> ... For those who believe in transformation (either in this life or another), ideologies of market exchange have become associated with the death that goes nowhere... The parking lots and aisles of discount stores may be where the restless dead of a commodity civilization will tread out their numberless days.

From a more academic perspective, in their extensive content analysis study of free-form response elicitation with regard to the meaning of death, Holcomb, Neimeyer, and Moore (1993) find that the presence or absence of a "personal philosophy of death" is highly instrumental in the perceptual construction of death. The authors find that persons who profess to hold a coherent philosophy view death as more purposeful, expected, and as involving some form of continued existence. On the other hand, findings indicate that those lacking a personal philosophy tend to view death negatively, and exhibit low levels of both death acceptance and understanding. Although Holcomb, Neimeyer, and Moore (1993) do not discuss the meaning of death from a consumer behavior perspective, their findings do indicate that death-related studies in general should assess meanings above and beyond mere negative (or other) attitudes towards death, stating (p. 316) that: "... there is a need to complement... standardized measures with other methods that permit subjects to disclose their perspectives on death in their own words."

RESEARCH METHODOLOGY

Consistent with but in much more exploratory fashion than other consumer researcher efforts to capture and portray consump-

tion-related meaning (e.g., Hirschman 1992; O'Guinn and Faber 1989; Schouten 1991; Thompson et al. 1990), in-depth consumer interviews, ranging in length from one to two hours, were conducted by all members of the three-person research team. Also, a four-hour interview with "Vince," a former industry employee with nearly 20 years of diverse experience, was undertaken to further explicate abuses and vulnerabilities associated with the provision of funeral services in the U.S. The level of interview structure evolved from totally unstructured to semi-structured in nature as data collection and analysis progressed. In accord with Spiggle's (1994) notion of "iterative data collection," this evolution in level of structure was iteratively based, with (structured) questions asked in later interviews being based on issues emerging in earlier (unstructured) interviews. Consumer informants included:

1. "Alice," a white female in her late 50s who had recently been in charge of arranging funeral services for both of her parents,

2. "Bill," a white male in his early 40s recently responsible for the arrangement of funeral services for his late father,

3. "Celeste," a white female in her early 40s in charge of burial arrangements for her father who had died in an automobile accident, and

4. "Robert," a white male in his mid 60s who had, within the last five years, engaged in a variety of death-related consumption activities including the arrangement of funeral services for several relatives, as well as for himself and his wife, the latter in prearranged form.

Three of these four informants engaged in their death-related consumption in two adjoining southern states in mid-sized and larger cities. The final consumer informant's experiences took place in a small Midwestern community. In that our informants discussed experiences relating to both pre-need and post-death (i.e., after the death of a loved one) consumption, our research differs from the work of Gentry (Gentry et al. 1994 & 1995; Gentry and Goodwin 1995), which deals exclusively with post-death phenomenon. As a result, our study seeks to gain a preliminary understanding of death-related consumption experiences not only of consumers making important, unfamiliar decisions under conditions of grief, but also the experiences of consumers trying to avoid such situations.

All consumer interviews were tape-recorded with the expressed permission of individual informants. Analysis was conducted in iterative fashion by all members of the three-person research team. Not only was the initial analysis of each interview iteratively analyzed—to guide both future data collection and analysis—but, in accord with Hirschman (1992) and Thompson et al. (1989, 1990), each interview transcript was reviewed by multiple researchers after the development of global themes based on initial data analysis and interpretation. Consumer meaning in this context was assessed by seeking patterns across: 1) the meanings and experiences of individual informants, and 2) the interpretations—of informant meaning and experience—of individual researchers (see Spiggle 1994). In that Vince requested that his interview not be recorded, his insights were documented via the taking of detailed notes by one researcher which were then transcribed (by the interviewer) and analyzed and interpreted (by all members of the research team).

RESEARCH FINDINGS

Consumer Abuse and Vulnerability

Consumer informants largely echoed those issues discussed in extant reports, with particular emphasis on a lack of consumption alternatives and financial and other transactional improprieties. However, our interview with Vince is most informative in this regard. In a most general sense, Vince views the funeral service industry as characterized by a high level of collusion among large, powerful "traditional" (i.e., high-priced and opportunistic) organizations. He stated that:

This is business, it's not loving and sharing like it's thought to be. Making money is the whole thing... Its merely a religious facade... The funeral directors and prearrangers are set up on a bonus plan to facilitate sales. This drives selling more products and getting the money from the family then and there.

In addition to these general comments, Vince's discussion tended to center around—and add detail to—the following topics previously identified as being exemplary of abuses and vulnerability associated with death-related consumption.

Incomplete or Fraudulent Consumer Information. Vince informed us in great detail of how he perceives there to be a negligent lack of consumer information disclosure. He stated that funeral homes regularly fail to *voluntarily* inform the consumer that neither embalming nor vaults are required under state law. If the consumer is to become knowledgeable in these matters, they must do so of their own initiative, a scenario which our informant described as rare given the consumer's psychological state. With regard to these issues as well as the practice of taking advantage of the time pressures faced by grieving consumers, Vince informed us that:

The funeral home withholds this information because they can pick up an additional $350 for the (embalming) service... Most of the time, the customer does not want to ask or be informed. They don't want to face death nor think about having to face death... We always want to create time pressures... The philosophy is to get them in there and get them out as fast as possible... A lot of family members are tired at the death. They have been up late while the person died at the hospital. The trick is to get them down at the funeral home first thing in the morning to work out all the details. They are more vulnerable and in shock and will make quicker decisions.

One manner in which these highly pressured, "quick decisions" might be avoided is by means of pre-arrangement of burial services. However, Vince's opinions with regard to industry practice here likewise sheds light on consumer abuse and vulnerability. He stated that selling pre-arranged services is particularly effective directly after the death of a family member, partly due to the fact that cognitive dissonance over overpaying has yet to set in:

We know that if we can market to a consumer three weeks after the death of a family member, we got them because death is on their mind... We used to ask people that had funeral services in the past when they would sit down and realize they had spent too much on the service. People usually say about three weeks to a month later... So you hit them quick after the funeral to get them in to make other arrangements...

Industry Collusion. Based on his diverse experience, Vince also described in detail his perceptions of rampant industry collusion leading to restricted consumer choice. Consistent with popular press reports (i.e., Engel 1984; Hildula 1990; Salerno 1990), it is his opinion that funeral directors and industry associations are opposed to the introduction of nontraditional (i.e., low-cost retail) funeral services. Further, he claims that large conglomerate organizations which own many funeral homes and cemeteries across the nation "blackball" discount providers by: 1) directly contacting manufacturers of caskets and threatening them that business from the large organizations will cease if goods are sold to discount retailers, and 2) assessing surcharges on services in which caskets were not purchased at the funeral home. Moreover, he stated that he feels that funeral homes "taint" the business of discount retailers through both slander and outright sabotage.

Exorbitant Pricing. On average, our consumer informants stated that they had spent in the range of $5,000 to $7,000 on the burial of family members, a figure consistent with other reported estimates (e.g., Hildula 1990; Lino 1990). Although Vince's discussion of rapacious pricing in the industry ran the full gamut of goods and services offered—despite marginal differences in quality—two issues of particular importance to our purposes involve high markups on product accessories and discrimination against members of lower socioeconomic classes. Regarding markups, Vince's discussion of casket mattresses is most instructive:

If you look at the mattress, there are two kinds. The more expensive casket (mattress) usually will have some type of spring-like mechanism. People don't realize that the person is dead and it doesn't matter... Of course, they want mamma to be comfortable... I've seen as much as $1,000 to change out the mattress... It only costs me about $10, but the customer is happier.

With respect to members of lower socioeconomic classes being discriminated against, Vince stated that, to his surprise, he has found that discount retailer clientele consists mainly of upper-class individuals more knowledgeable of product alternatives and the marginal nature of product quality differences. Further, he also informed us that minority customers in general tend to pay more for caskets because the features they require for religious and other reasons are not commonly included in standard (U.S.) product designs. As a result, caskets for minority individuals often must be modified or custom-made at significant cost to the consumer.

Meanings of Consumption

The findings and discussions of Belk, Wallendorf, and Sherry (1989), Burns (1990), and Mellor and Shilling (1993) all suggest that meanings associated with death-related consumption in modern American society can be expected to be less rich (e.g., consist of less sacred or community-based content) than in earlier times. Although our cross-sectional study cannot claim to assess this hypothesized shift, it does aspire to provide a preliminary, exploratory analysis of meanings ascribed to death-related consumption.

Overall, while only one of our informants—Bill—discussed his or her experience(s) in predominantly positive and rewarding fashion, our exploratory findings suggest three interrelated categories of consumption meaning.

Peace of Mind. In both pre-need and non-pre-need death-related consumption contexts, feelings regarding attainment of "peace of mind" were expressed by consumer informants. From the pre-need perspective, Robert's security motivations were readily apparent as he told us how he had sought to avoid problems he had witnessed others beset by as a result of waiting to the last minute to make burial arrangements:

> The one (private cemetery) I'd like to go to is the one they have all the problems with. They don't take care of the graves. They sell the whole cemetery to somebody different... and then they got new owners that don't honor the contracts. I went to the (public) city cemetery, which sounded like the best deal, but they can't guarantee where you go; can't guarantee who's going to be buried by you.

Post-death consumption likewise involves security motivations and meanings. For example, two comments made by Alice, the first regarding burial clothing chosen for the deceased and the second with respect to criteria used in casket selection, are instructive:

> ... it was really comforting because during visitation many of the people had said 'Oh your daddy looked so neat in that coat'... So its funny how little things like that can be reassuring to you.

> We had agreed that when mother died that we wanted something appropriate, yet we were not going to get the most deluxe thing. My sister had a phobia about metal caskets that they looked cold to her. So we had selected a wood casket for mother. It had a peach lining in it. We decided we would go with the same thing with daddy. Of course, it had cream lining, which was more appropriate for a man.

Similarly, Celeste expressed her frustrations in her search for peace of mind through death-related product consumption:

> ... my parents had bought cemetery plots several years before.... I do remember the headstone. We didn't get the headstone for like a year or a year and a half. And it was very expensive. My mother wanted to take time to think about it and she did want to shop around a little bit... But you know, the cemetery would only accept certain kinds... and she ended up going through the cemetery... It was kind of strange, because if you went back to visit the gravesite... you had to search for it. The only reason we knew where it was was that there was a little dogwood tree planted close to the site.

Finally, Bill, in discussing not wanting to put his deceased father in "the cheapest casket" available, alluded to latent peace-of-mind consumption meaning when asked what criteria he had used to make the casket purchase:

> Cost mostly, also looks/general appearance. I was interested in costs because my dad did not have very much life insurance and I knew that I was going to be responsible for the remaining bill... I did not buy the cheapest casket, but bought the cheapest casket that looked okay.

Practitioners are well aware of the fact that consumers seek peace of mind through death-related product consumption. Unfortunately, while the majority of product providers cater to this need

in a positive manner, some may view the opportunity differently. According to Vince:

> Men are easiest to sell to. They come and usually are emotional and feel guilty... like they haven't spent enough time or money in the past and they buy expensive caskets for their spouse or mother. Especially if the mother has been in the nursing home and the son hasn't gone and visited there for a long time and he wants the 'best' for mamma... like he's on a guilt trip. Also people who have been in an accident or a young person, the family tends to spend more—like they are compensating for the tragedy... People buy caskets because of what people think. All this is emotional bull. We cater to the emotional satisfaction of people. They need a peace of mind.

The Search for Trust. Consistent with the observations of Gentry et al. (1994), consumers, in their quest for peace of mind via death-related consumption, typically search for individuals upon whom they can depend. In this context, the issue of the product provider being perceived as someone who can be trusted by "helping the consumer" with necessary yet "tedious" activities (e.g., dealing with other intermediary good or service providers) versus taking advantage of this situation arises. Bill, Alice, and Celeste all mentioned that the funeral homes they had dealt with offered to mail in life insurance checks on their behalf, ridding them of the possibly unpleasant task of dealing with the insurance company. Bill spoke of these services in highly positive fashion and as a factor in his choice of service providers. However, as most particularly discussed by Celeste, although the consumer is relieved of this task, it also assures that the funeral home will be paid and further raises the possibility for abuse in that the financial transactions which transpire do so with limited consumer monitoring and control. Further, as she told us, she was distressed by the fact that funeral home personnel knew the amount of their life insurance benefit and seemed determined to get her and her grieving mother to spend the full amount. On this and other issues related to the trust that she was frustrated in finding, Celeste informed us that:

> One thing I remember is that they knew we had an insurance policy for like $15,000 because it was an accidental death and we were almost led to believe, 'Well, you've got that much money...' Whenever I would say anything about price, they would refer to that. They would refer to the fact that we had that much insurance... Because we had the insurance policy, they pretty much knew they were going to get the money—like within 30 days... I do remember in the casket showroom. We went down to the basement and there was a room of probably like 20 caskets and they would go through explaining each one but the prices weren't on them. You had to ask each time and they had to tell you. In a way, that made me kind of upset, because I felt like they could have adjusted the prices depending on how much money they knew you had.

Fear, Avoidance, and Expediency. Consistent with Gentry et al.'s (1994) contention that consumers avoid post-death transactions, and in spite of meanings associated with the search for trust and peace of mind, death-related consumption is to be avoided, with as little time as possible being spent on decision making. Although our informants seemed reluctant to discuss fear, avoidance, and expediency, these feelings were at least briefly alluded to or implied in many of the interviews. Celeste, when asked if she felt a need to end the decision-making process in an expedient manner, stated: "Definitely, as soon as we could... Just get out of there." Similarly, Alice told us that:

I think most people are terrified of death... and it's something you want to shove to the back of your mind and put off... Daddy had died on early Monday morning and we felt that if we could go ahead and have the visitation on Tuesday night and have the service on Wednesday that would be better... Giving everyone time to get there and then to go ahead and get it done... There was not a lot of discussion.

Summary of Consumer Meanings. Consideration of these three areas of consumer meaning, along with individual consumer responses, leads to a final and somewhat troubling observation. Alice, who exhibits the richest, most intense meaning in her consumption experience as expressed in her strong pursuit of both "trust" and "peace of mind," also seems the most willing to rationalize away negative, if not possibly abusive, consumption episodes as either "honest mistakes" or acceptable/normal marketer behavior. For example, in response to the funeral director appearing to have pre-established which services would be provided, while stating that: "More or less he said, 'This is what we will do'," in contrast to other informants faced with similar situations, she expressed no concern whatsoever. Troubling here is the notion that those consumers who derive the richest meaning from death-related consumption may also be the most vulnerable to abuse.

DISCUSSION

Based on Buddhist thought, *The Tibetan Book of the Dead* (Thurman 1994) emphatically proposes that we, as humans, create, and therefore subject ourselves to, the fear of death. However, based on our exploratory findings, in capitalistic U.S. society, marketplace factors appear to create (consumption-related) fear above and beyond that originating and dwelling solely in the human imagination. Whereas Mellor and Shilling (1993, p. 428) contend that "In relation to death... it can be argued that modernity... has emptied tradition, ritual and, increasingly, virtually all overarching normative meaning structures of much of their content," we would add, borrowing from Carlson (1991), that modernity has also effectively emptied the pockets of many consumers to an excessive degree, in large part due to a lack of consumer choice. Further, in similar fashion, whereas Mellor and Shilling (1993, p. 417) state that the "... processes of individualisation and privatisation leave many people uncertain, socially unsupported, and vulnerable when it comes to dealing with death," we submit the following from a consumer research perspective: The processes of individualization, privatization, *and greed* leave many *consumers* uncertain, socially unsupported, vulnerable, *abused and broke* when it comes to dealing with death in contemporary American society. Consumer desires to hasten the death-related acquisition and consumption process often play directly into the opportunistic designs of funeral service providers. Add to our findings the fact that record numbers of U.S. consumers will be both dying and purchasing death-related products in the next twenty to thirty years (Bliss 1994; Kirkland 1994), and the critical need for public policy to address the death-related consumption issues becomes clear.

Public Policy Implications

Although in strong agreement with Gentry et al.'s (1994) public policy discussion and recommendations, our perspective prescribes a more activist and collectivist role for consumers of death-related products. Changing current patterns of consumption and abuse in modern American society demands substantive legal reform and educational programs aimed at altering perceptions of the role of professional death-related goods and services providers. In order to curb consumer abuse and vulnerability associated with

consumption, new laws should be developed, with more active consumer representation and input, which both lessen the likelihood of opportunistic behavior and encourage competition among goods and service providers. However, this alone will not likely be sufficient. In order to still better guard against the continuation of abuse and vulnerability, programs aimed at extensive consumer education with regard to product availability, industry laws, and alternative burial arrangements are called for. Perhaps most importantly, the fostering of greater opportunities for increased familial and communal caring of the dead should be a top priority. One manner in which this goal may be pursued entails programs aimed at creating what Ozanne and Murray (1995) refer to as "reflexively defiant" (i.e., radically critical) consumers who actively question existing economic, political, and social structures. Further, consistent with Alwitt's (1995) call for the formation of small buying groups of poor consumers, it is suggested here that vulnerable consumers of death-related goods and services likewise form interfamily or community-based alliances to ensure themselves greater marketplace power.

Limitations and Future Research

While this study both extends previous consumer research on vulnerability associated with the consumption of death-related goods and services and introduces the notion of consumption meaning in this context, it is *highly exploratory* in at least two respects. First, with regard to our discussion of consumer meaning, our small sample of informants consists exclusively of white, middle-class Americans. As a result, the generalizability of our findings to other consumers, most particularly members of other cultures and subcultures, is restricted. Similarly, although our research differs from the work of Gentry and his colleagues by including a consideration of consumption activities associated with pre-need—rather than exclusively post-death—death-related consumption, our findings are based on a very small sample size. Future research efforts investigating the consumption of death-related products should further these important limitations of the current research.

REFERENCES

Alwitt, Linda F. (1995), "Marketing and the Poor," *American Behavioral Scientist*, 38 (February), 564- 577.

Antitrust and Trade Regulation Report (1989), "Ban on Phone Solicitations for Funeral Services Passes Constitutional Muster," 16 (May 16), 432.

Barnhart, Bill, and Sally Saville Hodge (1985), "Breaking New Ground in the Funeral Business," *Chicago Tribune*, (October 14), 2C.

Belk, Russell W., Melanie Wallendorf, and John F. Sherry (1989), "The Sacred and The Profane In Consumer Behavior: Theodicy on the Odyssey," *Journal of Consumer Research*, 16 (June), 1- 38.

Berger, Peter L. (1990), *The Sacred Canopy: Elements of a Sociological Theory of Religion*. New York: Anchor Books.

Bliss, Michael (1994), "Ashes to Ashes, Gravy from Graves," *Canadian Business*, 67 (June), 160.

Burns, Stanley B. (1990), *Sleeping Beauty: Memorial Photography in America*. Al Tadena, CA: Twelvetrees Press.

Cain, Rita Marie (1994), "Call Up Someone and Just Say 'Buy'," *American Business Law Journal*, 1 (February), 41.

Carlson, Lisa (1991), "Caring for Our Own Dead," *Utne Reader*, 47 (Sept.-Oct.), 79-81.

Collier, Randy (1991), "Widow Sues Over Husband's Ashes," *The Arizona Republic*, (June 18), A1.

_____ and Charles Kelly (1991), "Ashes of Humans, Animals Allegedly Mixed by Mortuary," *The Arizona Republic*, (April 28), A1.

Conner, Charles (1994), "Sued Funeral Home Shapes Action Plan," *(Memphis) Commercial Appeal*, (August 25), 3B.

Connors, Christopher (1993), "New Law Will Protect Privacy of Video Renters," *Gannett News Service*, (December 15).

Engel, Margaret (1984), "Funeral Regulators Hit as Servants of Industry," *Washington Post*, (June 26), A1.

Frankenberger, Kristina D. and Ajay S. Sukhdial (1994), "Segmenting Teens for AIDS Preventive Behaviors with Implications for Marketing Communications," *Journal of Public Policy and Marketing*," 13 (Spring), 133.

Gentry, James W., Patricia F. Kennedy, Katherine Paul, and Ronald Paul Hill (1994), "The Vulnerability of Those Grieving the Death of a Loved One: Implications for Public Policy," *Journal of Public Policy and Marketing*, 13 (Fall), 128-142.

_____, _____, _____, (1995), "Family Transitions During Grief: Discontinuities in Household Consumption Patterns," *Journal of Business Research*, 34 (September), 67-79.

_____ and Cathy Goodwin (1995), "Social Support for Decision Making During Grief Due to Death," *American Behavioral Scientist*, 38 (February), 553-563.

Good, Jeffrey (1994), "Broken Trusts," *St. Petersburg Times*, (September 4), 1D.

Hildula, Scott (1990), "Ghia Offers Low-Cost Coffin Choices," *San Francisco Business Times*, 4 (March 26), 1.

Hill, Ronald P. (1994), "Researching Sensitive Topics in Marketing: The Special Case of Vulnerable Populations," *Journal of Public Policy and Marketing*, 14 (Spring), 143-148.

Hirschman, Elizabeth C. (1992), "The Consciousness of Addiction: Toward a General Theory of Compulsive Consumption," *Journal of Consumer Research*, 19 (September), 155-179.

Holcomb, Laura E., Robert A. Neimeyer, and Marlin K. Moore (1993), "Personal Meanings of Death: A Content Analysis of Free-Response Narratives," *Death Studies*, 17 (July-August), 299-318.

Hyde, Lewis (1983), *The Gift*. New York: Vintage Books.

Kirkland, Richard I., Jr. (1994), "Why We Will Live Longer and What It Will Mean," *Fortune*, (February 21), 66-78.

Lino, Mark (1990), "The $3,800 Funeral," *American Demographics*, 12 (July), 8.

Lubove, Seth (1993), "If You Gotta Go...," *Forbes*, 151 (January 4), 16.

Mellor, Philip A. and Chris Shilling (1993), "Modernity, Self-Identity, and the Sequestration of Death," *Sociology*, 27 (August), 411-432.

Miller, Cyndee (1994), "People Want to Believe in Something," *Marketing News*, 28 (December 5), 1,2.

Miller, Vince (1995), "Death Board's Untidy Demise," *Fresno Bee*, (January 7), B6.

Mitford, Jessica (1963), *The American Way of Death*. New York: Simon & Schuster.

O'Guinn, Thomas C. and Ronald Faber (1989), "Compulsive Buying: A Phenomenological Exploration," *Journal of Consumer Research*, 16 (September), 147-157.

Ozanne, Julie L. and Jeff B. Murray (1995), "Uniting Critical Theory and Public Policy to Create the Reflexively Defiant Consumer," *American Behavioral Scientist*, 38 (February), 516-525.

Salerno, Steve (1990), "Dead Heat: How a Casket K-Mart Kicked Off Orange County's Lively Funeral Wars," *Los Angeles Magazine*, 35 (April), 66.

Schouten, John W. (1991), "Selves in Transition: Symbolic Consumption in Personal Rites of Passage and Identity Reconstruction," *Journal of Consumer Research*, 17 (March), 412-425.

Shermach, Kelly (1994), "Pay Now, Die Later: Consumers Urged Not to Delay That Final Decision," *Marketing News*, 28 (October 24), 1,6.

Sinclair, Norman (1991), "State Cemetery Act Needs Teeth, Regulators Say," *Detroit News*, 117 (January 8), A1.

Spiggle, Susan (1994), "Analysis and Interpretation of Qualitative Data in Consumer Research," *Journal of Consumer Research*, 21 (December), 491-503.

Thompson, Craig J., William B. Locander, and Howard Pollio (1989), "Putting Consumer Experience Back into Consumer Research: The Philosophy and Method of Existential-Phenomenology," *Journal of Consumer Research*, 16 (September), 133-146.

_____, _____, _____, (1990), "The Lived Meaning of Free Choice: An Existential-Phenomenological Description of Everyday Consumer Experiences of Contemporary Married Women," *Journal of Consumer Research*, 17 (December), 346-361.

Thurman, Robert A.F., trans. (1994), *The Tibetan Book of the Dead: Liberation Through Understanding in the Between*. New York: Bantam Books.

Torres, Vicki (1995), "Trial Starts in Mortuary Battle," *Los Angeles Times*, (February 10), B10.

Wiseman Boulton, Doris (1991), "Decoration Day," *Utne Reader*, 47 (Sept.-Oct.), 81-82.

Metaphors of Consumer Desire

Russell W. Belk, University of Utah
Güliz Ger, Bilkent University
Søren Askegaard, Odense University

The human species is not a species of needs but of desires. (J. Duvignaud)

Desire, in the colloquial sense of the word, refers to a strong longing, to something for which a person intensely yearns, or to the process of fervently wishing for something. Consumption is increasingly seen as being based upon desires, not simply upon needs (Baudrillard 1988; Bocock 1993). Yet desires are seldom mentioned in the consumer behavior literature, where similar phenomena are more often downgraded to mere "wants" or else naturalized as "needs." The neglect of desire within consumer research conceals the passionate feelings that we experience in connection with many consumption activities. Philosophical discussions of the mind also show a relative neglect of desire and a substitution of beliefs as the paradigm of the intentional (Marks 1986; Schueler 1995). Yet, a desire without a belief seems as powerless to move us to action as a belief without a desire (Marks 1986, p. 12). Desire, passion, and bliss remind us of our Dionysonian side: motion, intoxication, eroticism, fertility, mania, animal unconsciousness, as well as death and terror, ecstatic frenzy, and the unity of life and death. Desires are ever changing, infinitely renewable wishes inflamed by imagination, fantasy, and a longing for transcendent pleasure. And the pursuit of individual desire is a source of fear and a target for control. For desires involve powerful emotions and fervent passion. Consumer desires, more even than sexual desires, have spawned revolutions, wars, and crimes.

In this paper we explore the ways in which we speak of desire in several different languages (English, French, Danish, and Turkish) and the metaphorical tropes through which desire is described. As Lakoff and Johnson (1980) aptly demonstrate, our understandings are constructed through and highly dependent upon metaphors. By examining the major metaphors through which we express our consumer desires, we believe we learn something about the essence of contemporary consumer motivation. What we discover is something far different from a logical and utilitarian conception of consumer behavior. If the fundamental domains of human existence such as eating, drinking, and mating can evoke strong passions or "desires," what might it mean if we refer to these domains in expressing our longing for other consumption objects? We suggest that the use of such metaphors involves a magical appropriation of deep passions. Furthermore, these metaphors may legitimize desire by allowing us to believe that our wishes are needs; transforming the superfluous into the essential. Hence, such metaphors become excuses for indulging desires by rendering them as uncontrollable, natural, and animalistic needs.

OBJECTS OF DESIRE

Some social philosophers place "desire" in the center of understanding human societies (Kojåve 1947; Radkowski, 1980). Desire, to Radkowski (1980), is not a human attribute — on the most fundamental level humans do not have desires — but it is an expression of the specific form of being in the human species. Campbell (1987) relates consumer desires to a romantic ethic of fantasizing which he sees as the distinct feature the modern individual. The motivation for this fantasizing of "myself as I could be" is that desire is itself pleasurable. More specifically, the hedonism of this modern "generation of longing" is that "the desiring mode constitutes a state of enjoyable discomfort, and that wanting rather

than having is the main focus of pleasure-seeking" (Campbell 1987 p. 86). Since reality cannot live up to the perfect worlds of daydreaming, inspired by advertising as well as by general mythologies of "the good life," the dynamism of the market does not depend on fulfilling desires but rather on their perpetual recreation.

Desire is also culturally constituted and shared (Radkowski 1980; Stewart 1984). Perhaps one of the domains where the link between desire and the social world of objects becomes most visible (or audible), is the language we use to qualify these objects. Words are metaphorical windows to our imaginary world (Williams 1982). While consumer desires are expressed using an array of metaphors including magic, religion, fire, romantic love, dreams, thirst, hunger, sex, and addiction, the last three seem to dominate the languages we consider and we restrict our treatment to these metaphors. Together, they makeup much of what are labeled "appetitive desires" (Davis 1986). Not only is consumer imagination commonly expressed in terms of hungers, sexual longings, and addictions, these desires are also often used interchangeably.

The Eating Metaphor

You are what you eat. This popular phrase indicates the intimate character of eating and its pivotal importance for our being in the biological as well as in the anthropological, sociological, and psychological senses of the word. The domain of eating is of special importance firstly because it refers to a biologically necessary pattern of behavior that has been a fundamental preoccupation for all societies throughout history. Secondly eating implies incorporating foreign elements into our bodies, thus introducing objects into our most intimate sphere — indeed, intimus in Latin is the superlative of interior. Eating is constructing a self, quite literally. Hence, metaphors taken from the domain of eating to describe feelings about objects or experiences other than culinary ones may indicate a high degree of cathexis of this object or experience to the self.

Incorporation, however, is dangerous and may be feared as well as embraced. The short story (and film), 'Babette's Feast' represents a good example of Puritan condemnation of earthly desires. Among the film's 19th century Puritan peasants, no distinction was made between (sinful) bodily appetites such as good food, wine, and sexuality or other bodily "weaknesses." All turn the mind away from the (true) spiritual desire for 'living in Christ'. Thus, when obliged to grant Babette her only wish: to cook the villagers a splendid meal, these villagers fear that it will be "witch's Sabbath". And they take precautions not to get carried away by their sinful behavior. They encourage each other: "Let's pray we don't taste the food" and agree not to praise or even to talk about the food, in order for this ignorance to save their souls from the devilish temptations. Today, however, such ideas do not prevent most people from enjoying earthly pleasures. In Danish, the word for delicious itself ("lækker") can also be applied for consumer goods. Thus, it is perfectly normal to say for instance "a delicious car", "a delicious blouse" or even a "delicious desk". The only requirement seems to be that there must be some aesthetic aspect to the good in question. Knowledge (a central part of self-construction and a special type of consumer good) can be described in several languages as something for which we thirst. And in Danish colloquial speech and slang a whole menu of applicable food metaphors appear. Most important among them probably is

Advances in Consumer Research
Volume 23, © 1996

the adjective "fat." In the past several decades, especially among younger people, it has often been applied to consumed experiences, such as a "fat concert" or a "fat voyage," or directly to consumer goods such as a "fat house", a "fat chair" or even a "fat dog," all without implying any degree of obesity. In the United States hip-hop and youth slang, the word is used similarly, sometimes spelled "phat." This metaphor, although of recent origin, reaches back to times when fat in a Western context was seen as a sin of luxury implying liberation from hunger and need. It is the richness of fat or creamy foods that is transferred to the consumer goods by the use of 'fat' as a metaphor. In several languages "cream" indicates the very top of the product quality range (e.g., in English, "the cream of the crop"). In French we might be so lucky as to get "la creme de la creme" of something.

Recent fat-related slang expressions in Denmark include "broad ymer," (ymer is relatively high fat milk product), replacing the word "fat" with sometime synonym "broad." Since ymer is inherently high in fat content, this creates comic redundancy and suggests an even fatter (and, implicitly, better) product or experience. A Danish hyperbole, used in a very similar way, is the expression "knee-high cress" which, by assuming an unnatural height of this herb, alludes to fantasies and desires of unlimited abundance. Again, a humorous effect is obtained, here by selecting a relatively negligible and unimportant food item as a symbol of abundance. This expression and the previous one, while now out of fashion, were used to describe extraordinary (consumer) experiences such as listening to a favorite record or possessing a fine racing bike. They both allude to the ecstasy of plenty and the feeling of a having a "better than real" experience. A more persistent metaphor of a similar kind is that of the 'cornucopia', which can be used in several languages to designate an abundance of consumer goods or possibilities, but which originally referred to a mythical goat's horn overflowing with food delicacies.

Fat is not the only edible metaphor that connotes "good" consumption objects. Biologically humans are born with a preference for the sweet taste among the four universal types of taste (MacClancy 1992). This innate preference is also reflected in metaphors of consumer desire. In Turkish as well as English, the adjective 'sweet' can be used to qualify both an attractive person and an attractive consumer good. Indeed in all the Germanic languages, different types of consumer goods may qualify as "sweet." This metaphor seems to be used most often in connection with goods that have a feminine linkage, either because they are predominantly used by women, such as female clothing, or because they evoke associations of cuteness, softness, roundness, or other traditional connotations of femininity (Coward 1984).

A final Danish metaphor of consumer desire drawn from the realm of eating is the word "kræs". This word is in its strictest sense a common denominator for something good to eat. The sound of it seems to onomatopoietically connote crispiness. However, it can also be used to qualify something of good quality outside of the domain of food products, with a metaphorical effect similar to "cream." In the expression "kræs for kendere" ("for those who know") it adds a further dimension of connoisseurship, implying that only the discerning can enjoy the sublime consumption experience of a particular object. Just as enjoying a single malt Scotch whisky can be a tough experience for beginners, so can a "difficult" piece of music or a finely crafted technical good be troublesome for laymen to appreciate. Such an object thus becomes "kræs for kendere".

Desires can also involve avoiding negative consumption experiences, in which case negative food metaphors may be applied. A general and internationalized disparagement is that something is "not my cup of tea." Also, a specific consumption experience can be qualified as a "thin cup of tea" in Danish, indicating an unsatisfactory level of pleasure or benefit. In Turkish another expression evoking the same disappointing and dissatisfying consumption experience is, "His/her eyes are hungry/starving [although the stomach is full]". Less obviously, perhaps, desires can be expressed by reference to eliminating food by defecating or urinating. Such desires remind us that from a Freudian perspective any bodily excretion is connected to feelings of lust. Thus, paradoxically, something can be "defecatingly" or "urinatingly" good in Danish and, at the same time, the mere word for "shit" is obscene, just as is the case in English or German (in Danish also "pee" applies). The ambiguity of defecation and urination (relief and disgust) is thus reflected in this way Danes can qualify objects: as something "defecatingly good" (referring to the relieving process) or as shit (referring to the disgusting result/object).

The Sexual Metaphor

We sometimes describe our fervent desire for a consumer good as a lust. We intensely yearn for it, burn for it, and ache with desire. In invoking the hot burning passion associated with sex we borrow a further metaphor (heat) used with sexual desire to describe passion as an elemental, uncontrollable reaction, as in being consumed by flame. Thus when sexual metaphors are enlisted to describe our love of products, they imply being consumed by passion. Sexual metaphors for consumer desire also bespeak an animalistic urge that is basic, sensual, instinctual, and uncontrollable. We are inflamed with a carnal lust to possess and merge with anthropomorhized non-carnal objects. The word luxury comes from the Latin for lust, *luxuria*. As with lust, strong consumer desire pervades our body. Reason, morality, and concern for others are cast aside as every fiber of our being becomes transfixed with an overwhelming and urgent appetite that torments us:

Admit it. You want it. All of us see the stuff — maybe just a slick little red espresso maker, or maybe just a slick little red Saab 900 Turbo — and even though some of us would rather die a horrible disgusting death than admit it, we want it. Some of us want it real bad (Handy 1988, p. 108).

Handy further suggests that advertising like the catalogs of The Sharper Image act as high tech pornography igniting our lust the goods portrayed. We need not accept the Freudian idea of consumer desire as sublimated libidinal desire in order to accept that there is something very akin to the sharp passion of sexual yearning in our intense longing for certain consumer goods.

When we anthropomorphize consumer goods as objects of longing we display a key element of fetishism. Ellen (1988) argues that the sexual fetishism discussed by Freud and the commodity fetishism diagnosed by Marx are in reality a part of a single phenomenon. Fetishistic anthropomorphism is evident in Rook's (1987) finding that impulse purchases are often attributed to the goods that "call out" to us to buy them. It is also apparent in Dreiser's (1981) *Sister Carrie*, when the former farm girl Carrie encounters Chicago department stores:

Fine clothes to her were a vast persuasion; they spoke tenderly and Jesuitically for themselves. When she came within earshot of their pleading, desire in her bent a willing ear. Ah, ah! the voices of the so-called inanimate (p. 98).

Anthropomorphized merchandise in the early department stores is even more clearly seen in Zola's (1958) description of Denise's visits to *Au Bonheur des Dames*, modeled on Bon Marché in Paris:

A crowd was stopped before the shop windows, women pushing and squeezing, devouring the finery with longing, covetous eyes. And the stuffs became animated in this passionate sidewalk atmosphere... awakening new desires in her flesh, an immense temptation to which she would fatally succumb (pp. 17-18).

The sexual metaphor for consumer desire is also seen in Willis' (1991) account of the packaging of certain consumer goods, paralleling the display windows of retail stores:

Of all the attributes of mass-produced commodity packaging today, the most important is the use of plastic. The plastic cover acts as a barrier between the consumer and the product, while at the same time it offers up a naked view of the commodity to the consumer gaze. ... Shaped and naked, but veiled and withheld, the display of commodities is sexualized. Plastic packaging defines a game of câche — câche where sexual desire triggers both masculine and feminine fantasies. Strip-tease or veiled phallus — packaging conflates a want for a particular object with a sexualized form of desire (p. 4).

In consumer desire, as in sexual desire, visual senses dominate with the shopper's gaze replacing the male gaze (Urry 1990). As with sexual desire, fantasy and fantasizing play a key role in fueling this desire. Fantastic consumer desires are stimulated by cinema (Friedberg 1993), books and magazines (Davies 1983), and advertising Lears (1994). Beyond their role in creating consumer desires, these media also legitimize, reinforce, and transform even unconscious consumer wishes into imperative needs (Shabad 1991).

Nevertheless, the sexual metaphor of consumer desire also suggests that the state of wanting itself is simultaneously exciting, pleasurable, and frustrating: an exquisite torture. Ackerman (1994) suggests that the origin of this tendency in courtship was with the medieval model of courtly love. It continued into the Renaissance period when it developed among the bourgeoisie as well, who nearly endlessly teased and flirted, all while delaying the fulfillment of sexual intercourse. While the waiting period may have diminished in the contemporary West, in such rituals as kissing and foreplay we continue to delay sexual consummation and we continue to find the postponement a pleasureable means of protracting the excitement. This is Campbell's (1987) pleasureable frustration or the desire to desire (Doane 1987).

While the sexual metaphor for consumer desire might be applied to both men and women, historically it has been directed more to female consumers. The development of the department store in particular has been characterized as a seduction of women by male store owners (Bowlby 1985, 1993; Reekie 1993; Williams 1982). As Reekie (1993) describes it,

...like courtship, selling entailed a series of negotiations between the sexes premised on the assumption that man was the hunter and woman his legitimate prey. Both selling and courtship scripts of the early twentieth century were structured by clearly demarcated sex roles predicated on the assumption of a man's right of conquest and female passivity. Man was the pursuer, woman the pursued; man the active initiator, woman the pliant respondent (p. xvii).

Through retail display women were tempted and enticed to fondle the merchandise and based on assumed childlike vulnerability to buy or even steal consumer luxuries they could ill-afford (Abelson 1989). Such sex role stereotypes invoke an even older image of women as having uncontrolled and insatiable sexual desires (Halpern 1990), even though this male fear is sometimes repressed by imagining women to be without sexual desire (Jacobus 1990; Kaplan 1983). It is not a long jump from women as insatiable sexual beings to women as insatiable consumers — a long-standing stereotype of the modern age readily seen in Dreiser's Carrie and Zola's Denise. Although department stores were marked as "women's spaces" or "an Adamless Eden" (Benson 1988), department stores and shopping malls have now become de-feminized such that men are no longer marginalized and are increasingly a target of seductive retailers (Reekie 1993).

Laqueur (1992) sees the rise of overt sexuality and the rise of consumer desire as historically interlinked in the creation of consumer culture. Lefebvre (1991, p. 162) extends the sexual metaphor at this more macro level by suggesting that marketers are pimps to our consumer desires, catering to our every whim and weakness. In the marketer-as-pimp sexual metaphor, unlike the department store-as-seducer variant developed by Reekie (1993), the product itself is the attraction and marketers merely tempt us with goods made to appear infinitely desirable. But in both cases, we are impelled as consumers by overwhelming palpable desires that are intensely felt and create longing akin to intense sexual desire. Thus does consumer desire, like sexual desire, continually excite us in an unfulfillable quest.

The Addiction Metaphor

When we refer to our weakness for or dependence upon something we buy repeatedly, we call it addiction, implying both devotion and obsession. Rug collectors in Turkey sometimes refer to themselves as "rug addicts", and praise their devotion, making it seem less negative. Addiction implies a lack of control: "I didn't intend to buy it but I couldn't resist," "I lost myself", "I could not hold myself," "I am hooked", "I have an illness for it" (in Turkish and Danish). Other terms used are duped, seized, captured, enslaved, astounded, dumbfounded, stupefied, bewildered, or mad for something. A true (non-metaphorical) addiction "exists when a person's attachment to a sensation, an object, or another person is such as to lessen his [sic] appreciation of and ability to deal with other things in his environment, or in himself, so that he has become increasingly dependent on that experience as his only source of gratification" (Peele 1985). Addiction, the 'strong appetite', involves devotion, dependence, surrendering control, habit, obsessiveness, and preoccupation with the object to the detriment of well-being (Orford 1985; Peele 1985).

In addition to drugs, stimulant beverages and foods (tea, coffee, chocolate, sugar — luxuries democratized as part of the rise of consumer culture — Mintz 1993, p. 264), gambling, sex and relationships, collecting, and shopping, can also be addictive. If the addiction to drugs is chemical, addiction to "drug foods" is both chemical and social (Mintz 1993), and the social construction of desire attempts to reign in the placebo power of "drug goods".

Many similarities can be detected between the elements of addiction (Orford 1985; West and Kranzler 1990) and the properties of the consumerism, especially among compulsive buyers and some collectors. Consumerism involves desiring more and more goods, having an unquenchable desire for goods, longing for transcendent meanings, and seeking experiences of otherness and unusual states of consciousness (Cross 1993). Compulsive buyers discuss their compulsion using drug analogies: "It's almost like you're on a drunk. You are so intoxicated;...I got this great high. It was like you couldn't have given me more of a rush" (O'Guinn and Faber 1989, p. 153). Like addicts, collectors are comrades, sharing deep ecstatic emotional involvement (Belk, et al. 1991), and forming 'consumption communities' (Boorstin 1968). Among collectors "A sense of longing and desire...is met by adding to the collection. But this is a temporary fix, a staving off of withdrawal, followed by a feeling of emptiness and anxiety that is addressed by searching for more" (Belk, et al. 1991, pp. 202-203). Consumption has been called a disease (Porter 1993). A preoccupation with consumption, such that other important activities are neglected, and the persistent involvement in consumption despite clear evidence that it has become problematic, are observed in the work-and-spend ethic that precludes the luxury of free time in a consumer culture (Cross 1993). Among compulsive buyers, shopping becomes a major leisure activity, possessions are valued over friends and other activities, and there is de facto acceptance of Barbara Kruger's neo-Cartesian creed, "I shop therefore I am" (O'Guinn and Faber 1989). As addicts narrow their repertoire of pleasures to routine drug-taking, so do consumers in engaging in certain ritualistic consumption (Rook 1985), in devoting themselves to their collection, or in buying ten $10 shirts (O'Guinn and Faber 1989).

The relaxation, anesthesia, and sleepy happiness, as well as the arousal and thrill created by drugs, can also be created by goods. Goods and shopping soothe us, thrill us, put us in a better mood, and help us forget our problems. And, although we realize that the thrill of shopping and buying does not last long, after a period of abstinence, shopping binges and splurges return. Despite the sleepy happiness, or power and stimulation found in drugs, their dark side is also common knowledge. Breaking drug dependency starts with acknowledging the power of the drug: the first step in Alcoholics Anonymous (adapted by other groups for other addictions, including Shopaholics and Spendermenders, O'Guinn and Faber 1989) is to admit powerlessness over alcohol. The next steps involve turning to another devotion, to God or a "higher power." The loss of control or freedom is a common aspect of the experience of addiction. For example, from a Western perspective drunkenness has been seen as a form of madness in which the will is overcome by passion (Jacobus 1990) or in which self control and reasoned judgment come to be dominated by the pursuit of pleasure. Likewise, in a consumer society, we may feel we are possessed by our possessions (Maffesoli 1993). This is rationalized as an irresistible compulsion or craving — "I simply have to have this" — especially in impulse buying, compulsive buying, and collecting. This admission of inability to resist parallels the self-attribution of addiction among drug addicts to explain and excuse to society the drug use and to remove it from moral censure and responsibility for behavioral change. With the power seen as external, addicts believe that they cannot resist the temptation. So do collectors (Belk et. al 1991). Besides escaping blame and guilt, perceiving power to reside in things allows us to lose ourselves in appetites for art or music and to derive pleasure from a temporary transcendence, a loss of consciousness (Watney 1983, p. 75) like that experienced with addictive drugs.

While addiction involves craving and loss of control, desire is not an automatic response to antecedent cues or physiological states; it is a dynamic motivational process that involves culturally-based anticipations and expectations of pleasure or pleasurable relief. Several decades ago, groups of young people started to smoke banana skins, which are inert. One-third of the users reported psychedelic experiences and thousands were caught up in the craze. Outcome expectancies involving imagination and fantasy underlie drug effects, as with the expectancy that alcohol is a "magic elixir" capable of transforming emotional states (Marlatt 1987). Hence, addiction is not in the drug but in the user. Ceremonial, restrained, or moderate use of "addictive" drugs also attests to this possibility. Historical and cultural context influence views of

addiction, as seen in 16th century BC Thebean physicians prescribing opium for crying children, just as, millennia later, Victorian babies were dosed with the opiate Godfrey's Cordial by their nurses to keep them quiet. Today candy bars, ice-cream, or chewing gums are used to placate children.

CONCLUDING REMARKS

One consequence of thinking of consumer desire as sexual or addictive, is that especially within Christian cultures, it carries a taint of sin and creates guilt. While this, like guilt from indulgent eating (Bordo 1990; Coward 1984), potentially inhibits spending and consumption, it also serves to make the desire more exciting. As with sex (Parker 1991) and eating (Mintz 1993), the sense of transgression in "sinful" consumer indulgence makes us relish the pleasure all the more. This same pleasure in transgression may help explain the lethal attraction of cigarette smoking which takes on "...poetic qualities of a sacred object or an erotic one, endowed with magical properties and seductive charms, surrounded by taboos and an air of danger — a repository of illicit pleasure, a conduit to the transcendental, and a spur to repression" (Klein 1993, pp. xii-xiii). Like sex, drugs, and smoking, consumer desire relishes transgression and provides only fleeting, but ever-renewable pleasure upon consummation.

The strong acquisitive appetites of collectors (Belk, et al. 1991) and travelers (Cross 1993) have been suggested to involve the power of the objects to magically transform everyday life into a new realm of experience, a fantasy life, and an experience of otherness — other times, places, or people. The drug addict, the collector, and the traveler each pursue an altered state of consciousness. Like drugs, travel and carnival involve experiencing pleasurable differences (Thompson 1983). These differences offer excitation, and the uncertainties and tensions associated with them produce a relaxation of social protocols and taboos. When on holiday or suffering an addiction, normal discipline is relaxed, and restraint gives way to indulgence. Again, pleasure comes from breaking taboos, engaging in the exotic, escaping imposed order, and satisfying suppressed desire for disorder. Parallel arguments suggest that consumer pleasure, as with erotic pleasure, is derived from the knowledge of 'mal', of one's wrongdoing and from transgressive desires (Bataille 1973). Pleasure opposes order as Dionysus opposes the Olympian Gods, especially Apollo. Desire thus pursues the forbidden. Perfumes like Opium, Taboo, and My Sin all appeal to this transgressive aspect of desire.

With sex in particular, but also with pleasures in general, the constructs of sin and evil have also been used in an attempt to control even the most harmless of self-indulgent desires and practices like snacking or masturbation (Foucault 1985; Tiger 1992). We are urged to employ self-control and self-restraint to avoid exercising such desires. Similarly in consumption avoiding giving in to desire is often cast as a battle of will against selfish indulgence (e.g., Bordo 1990; Hoch and Lowenstein 1991). Just as one of the historic opportunities for suspending or subverting control of eating and sex in Western culture has been Carnival (Bakhtin 1968; Parker 1991), Lears (1994) demonstrates that consumer advertising and personal selling are inherently carnivalesque in their appeals for release and indulgence.

But bliss from eating, sex, drugs, or consumption dissipates very quickly. The continued craving and search for renewed bliss may become a pleasureless pursuit of pleasure. Oscillation between bliss and pains of craving and dependency are as much part of consumer culture as is intermittent bliss. If wanting rather than having is the focus of modern pleasure-seeking, and desire is defined in terms of pleasure (Campbell 1987; McCracken 1988), endless desiring turns into a chronic deficiency (Falk 1994). Frustration becomes the permanent state.

REFERENCES

Abelson, Elaine S. (1989), *When Ladies Go A'Thieving: Middle-Class Shoplifters in the Victorian Department Store*, New York: Oxford University Press.

Ackerman, Diane (1994), *A Natural History of Love*, New York: Random House.

Bakhtin, Mikhail (1968), *Rabelais and His World*, trans. Helene Iswolsky, Cambridge, MA: MIT Press.

Bataille, Georges (1973) [1948], *Théorie de la religion*, Paris: Gallimard (coll. tel)

Baudrillard, Jean (1988), *Selected Writings*, Mark Poster, ed., Stanford, CA: Stanford University Press.

Belk, Russell W., Melanie Wallendorf, John F. Sherry, Jr., and Morris B. Holbrook (1991), "Collecting in a Consumer Culture," in Russell W. Belk, ed., *Highways and Buyways: Naturalistic Research from the Consumer Behavior Odyssey*, Provo, UT: Association for Consumer Research, 178-215.

Benson, Susan Porter (1988), *Counter Cultures: Saleswomen, Managers, and Customers in American Department Stores*, Urbana, IL: University of Illinois Press.

Bocock, Robert (1993), *Consumption*, London: Routledge.

Boorstin, Daniel J. (1968), "The Consumption Community," in *The Consuming Public*, Grant S. McClellan, ed., New York: H. W. Wilson, 9-23.

Bordo, Susan (1990), "Reading the Slender Body," in Mary Jacobus, Evelyn Fox Keller, and Sally Shuttleworth, *Body/ Politics: Women and the Discourses of Science*, London: Routledge, 83-112.

Bowlby, Rachel (1985), *Just Looking: Consumer Culture in Dreiser, Gissing, and Zola*, New York: Methuen.

Bowlby, Rachel (1993), *Shopping with Freud*, London: Routledge.

Campbell, Colin (1987), *The Romantic Ethic and the Spirit of Modern Consumerism*, Oxford: Basil Blackwell.

Coward, Rosalind (1984), *Female Desire*, London: Paladin.

Cross, Gary (1993), *Time and Money: The Making of Consumer Culture*, London: Routledge.

Davies, Tony (1983), "Transports of Pleasure: Fiction and Its Audiences in the Later Nineteenth Century," in Frederic Jameson, et al., eds., *Formations of Pleasure*, London: Routledge & Kegan Paul, 46-58.

Davis, Wayne A. (1986), "The Two Senses of Desire," in Joel Marks, ed., *The Ways of Desire: New Essays in Philosophical Psychology on the Concept of Want*, Chicago: Precedent, 63-82.

Doane, Mary Ann (1987), *The Desire to Desire: The Woman's Film of the 1940s*, Bloomington, IN: Indiana University Press.

Dreiser, Theodore (1981), *Sister Carrie*, Harmondsworth: Penguin (original 1900, New York: Doubleday, Page and Company).

Ellen, Roy (1988), "Fetishism," *Man*, 23 (June), 213-235.

Falk, Pasi (1994), *The Consuming Body*, London: Sage.

Foucault, Michel (1985), *The Use of Pleasure: The History of Sexuality*, Volume 2, New York: Random House (original *L'Usage des Plaisirs*, Paris: Editions Gallimard, 1984).

Friedberg, Anne (1993), *Window Shopping: Cinema and the Postmodern*, Berkeley, CA: University of California Press.

Halpern, David M. (1990), "Why is Diotima a Woman? Platonic Eros and the Figuration of Gender," in David M. Halperin, John J. Winkler, and Froma I. Zeitlin, eds., *Before Sexuality: The Construction of Erotic Experience in the Ancient Greek World*, Princeton, NJ: Princeton University Press, 257-308.

Handy, Bruce (1988), "Sweet Savage Teapot: The Rise of Yuppie Porn," *Utne Reader* 26 (March/April), 108-112 (Original in *Spy*, December, 1987).

Hoch, Stephen J. And George F. Lowenstein (1991), "Time inconsistent Preferences and Consumer Self-Control," *Journal of Consumer Research*, 17 (March), 492-507.

Jacobus, Mary (1990), "In Parenthesis: Immaculate Conceptions and Feminine Desire," in Mary Jacobus, Evelyn Fox Keller, and Sally Shuttleworth, eds., *Body/Politics: Women and the Discourses of Science*, New York: Routledge, 11-28.

Kaplan, Cora (1983), "Wild Nights: Pleasure/Sexuality/ Feminism," in Frederic Jameson, et al., eds., *Formations of Pleasure*, London: Routledge & Kegan Paul, 15-35.

Klein, Richard (1993), *Cigarettes are Sublime*, Durham, NC: Duke University Press.

Kojåve, Alexandre (1947), *Introduction ê la lecture de Hegel*, Paris: Gallimard.

Lakoff, George and Mark Johnson (1980), *Metaphors We Live By*, Chicago: University of Chicago Press.

Laqueur, Thomas W. (1992), "Sexual Desire and the Market Economy During the Industrial Revolution," in Domna C. Stanton, ed., *Discourses of Sexuality: From Aristotle to AIDS*, Ann Arbor, MI: University of Michigan Press, 185-215.

Lears, Jackson (1994), *Fables of Abundance: A Cultural History of Advertising in America*, New York: Basic Books.

Lefebvre, Henri (1991), *Critique of Everyday Life*, Volume 1, London: Verso (original *Critique de la Vie Quotidienne* I: Introduction, Paris: L'Arche, 1958).

MacClancy, Jeremy (1992), *Consuming Culture: Why You Eat What You Eat*, New York: Henry Hope.

McCracken, Grant (1988), *Culture and Consumption: New Approaches to the Symbolic Character of Consumer Goods and Activities*, Bloomington, IN: Indiana University Press.

Maffesoli, Michel (1993), *La contemplation du monde: Figures du style communautaire*, Paris: Grasset.

Marks, Joel (1986), "Introduction: On the Need for Theory of Desire," in *The Ways of Desire: New Essays in Philosophical Psychology on the Concept of Wanting*, Joel Marks, ed., Chicago, Il: Precedent Publishing, 1-15

Marlatt, G. Alan (1987), "Alcohol, the Magic Elixir: Stress, Expectancy, and the Transformation of Emotional States" in Edward Gottheil et. al., eds., *Stress and Addiction*, New York: Brunner/Mazel, 302-322.

Mintz, Sidney, W. (1993) "The Changing Roles of Food in the Study of Consumption," in John Brewer and Roy Porter, eds., *Consumption and the World of Goods*, London: Routledge, 261-273.

O'Guinn, Thomas C. and Ronald J. Faber (1989), "Compulsive Buying: A Phenomenological Exploration," *Journal of Consumer Research*, 16 (September), 147-157.

Orford, Jim (1985), *Excessive Appetites: A Psychological View of Addiction*, New York: John Wiley and Sons.

Parker, Richard (1991), *Bodies, Pleasures, and Passions: Sexual Culture in Contemporary Brazil*, Boston: Beacon Press.

Peele, Stanton (1985), *The Meaning of Addiction: Compulsive Experience and Its Interpretation*, Lexington, MA: Lexington Books.

Porter, Roy (1993), "Consumption: Disease of the Consumer Society," in John Brewer and Roy Porter, eds., *Consumption and the World of Goods*, London: Routledge, 58-81.

Radkowski, Georges-Hubert de (1980), *Les jeux du désir: De la technique a l'économie*, Paris: PUF (coll. croisées).

Reekie, Gail (1993), *Temptations: Sex, Selling and the Department Store*, St. Leonards, NSW: Allen & Unwin.

Rook, Dennis (1985), "The Ritual Dimension of Consumer Behavior," *Journal of Consumer Research*, 12 (December), 251-265.

Rook, Dennis (1987), "The Buying Impulse," *Journal of Consumer Research*, 14 (June), 189-199.

Schueler, G. F. (1995), *Desire: Its Role in Practical Reason and the Explanation of Action, Cambridge*, MA: MIT Press.

Shabad, Peter (1993), "Resentment, Indignation, Entitlement: The Transformation of Unconscious Wish into Need," *Psychoanalytic Dialogues*, 3 (4), 481-494.

Stewart, Susan (1984), *On Longing. Narratives of the Miniature, the Gigantic, the Souvenir, the Collection*, Baltimore, MD: The Johns Hopkins University Press.

Thompson, Grahame (1983), "Carnival and the Calculable: Consumption and Play at Blackpool," in Frederic Jameson, et al., eds., *Formations of Pleasure*, London: Routledge & Kegan Paul, 124-137.

Tiger, Lionel (1992), *The Pursuit of Pleasure*, Boston: Little Brown.

Urry, John (1990), *The Tourist Gaze: Leisure and Travel in Contemporary Society*, London: Sage.

Watney, Simon (1983), "The Connoisseur as Gourmet," in Frederic Jameson, et al., eds., *Formations of Pleasure*, London: Routledge & Kegan Paul, 66-83.

West, Robert and Henry J. Kranzler (1990), "Craving for Cigarettes and Psychoactive Drugs," in David M. Warburton, ed., *Addiction Controversies*, Chur, Switzerland: Harwood Academic Publishers, 250-260.

Williams, Rosalind (1982), *Dream Worlds: Mass Consumption in Late Nineteenth-Century France*, Berkeley, CA: University of California Press.

Willis, Susan (1991), *A Primer for Daily Life*, London: Routledge.

Zola, Emile (1958), *Ladies' Delight, April Fitzlyon*, trans., London: Abelard-Schuman (original 1883, *Au Bonheur des Dames*, Paris: Carpentier).

Country of Origin and Ethnocentrism: An Analysis of Canadian and American Preferences Using Social Identity Theory

Garold Lantz, University of Manitoba
Sandra Loeb, University of South Dakota

This study utilizes conjoint analysis in an exploratory analysis to ascertain the value consumers in Canada and the United States place on a product being from their own, or another, country. The resultant utilities are related to a consumer's level of consumer ethnocentrism. It is expected that consumers rating high in consumer ethnocentrism would rate products from their country significantly higher, and products from other countries significantly lower, than those with low levels of consumer ethnocentrism. The results were primarily as surmised, with a few unexpected results.

It is proposed that there is a conceptual difference between the part of the country of origin effect which can be explained by country image and the part explainable by nationalistic tendencies. This paper uses social identity theory to further explicate the role of the nationalistic tendencies in an exploratory empirical study. Our belief is that consumers who are highly ethnocentric (strong national social identity) will behave more favorably toward products from countries viewed similar to theirs than do those who exhibit lower levels of ethnocentricity.

COUNTRY OF ORIGIN EFFECT

The country of origin (COO) effect refers to the preference consumers may express towards a product based upon the country where it was made. Since the first academic study of the subject by Schooler (1965) research in the COO effect has been voluminous. However, there has been little theoretical development (for a review, see Samiee 1994). This paper offers social identity theory to explain one part of the COO effect, the home country bias.

The COO effect has typically been attributed to instances where country of origin is used as a cue for quality, or rather as a surrogate for quality attributes, particularly if other product information is missing (Bilkey and Nes, 1982; Hong and Wyer, 1989). If an objective assessment of the product in question cannot or has not been made, the perceived reputation of the country may be substituted. This is often referred to as "country stereotype" or "country image". Many studies (see for example Papadopolous and Heslop, ed. 1993) have focused on this aspect of the COO effect and in most instances it probably accounts for most of the COO effect.

Additionally, the COO effect involves the issue of loyalty to the home country. While not universal, the home country bias has often been noted (see Samiee 1994 for a review). Exceptions to the home country bias generally involve foreign countries with a particularly good reputation for certain products (Nagashima 1970; Cattin, Jolibert and Lohnes 1982). Despite the exceptions, recent research has made it increasingly apparent that a person may purchase domestic goods solely to favor the domestic economy as an expression of support (Olsen, Granzin and Biswas, 1994). While a large part of the COO effect is explainable by country image, this paper focuses on the home country bias. We seek to make the theoretical connection of the social identity element to the COO model and to begin fleshing out the role of social identity with an empirical study.

Social Identity Theory

Social identity theorists posit that the self-concept is made up of two distinct aspects; the personal identity and the social identity (Tajfel 1978; Turner 1982). The personal identity includes specific attributes of the individual such as competence, talent and sociability. The social identity is defined as "that part of an individual's self-concept which derives from his knowledge of his membership in a social group (or groups) together with the value and emotional significance attached to that membership" (Tajfel 1981, p.225). It is widely agreed that individuals feel a need to maintain a positive self-image or self-esteem (Festinger 1954). Social identity theorists believe that the need to maintain a positive self-esteem includes social identities as well as the personal identity (Luhtenan and Crocker 1992).

The central tenet of social identity theory is that people feel a desire and propensity to build a positive identity for themselves which may be manifested by their identification with various groups (Turner 1982; Tajfel 1981). These groups may include family, friends, the community, race, religion or nation.

There has been a limited amount of work done regarding nationalism in the country of origin context by Shimp and Sharma (1987) and others (Herche 1992; Netemeyer, Durvasula and Lichtenstein 1991). Shimp and Sharma's (1987) concept and the scale they developed to measure it, the Cetscale, concerns the extent to which individuals feel a desire or a duty to support the domestic economy in the face of foreign competition. In terms of social identity theory it can be said that consumers have a national identity. The national identity may be strong in some consumers and weak in other consumers. The Cetscale, which focuses on the purchase of products, measures the economic manifestation of the national identity.

The implications for a COO effect are that individuals seek out ways to distinguish their national social category from others. It is proposed that a portion of the COO effect may be due simply to a desire by people to distinguish their group from others when they are in a purchase situation.

It is hypothesized that this national identification is strong enough in some people to make them willing to show a preference for a domestic product when they could spend less for an imported product, while the national identification is weaker in others, leading them to switch to the lower priced imported product at a lower price differential.

ETHNOCENTRISM

Ethnocentrism is the term which has often been applied to the home country bias portion of the COO effect (Shimp and Sharma 1987). Generally speaking, it is a broad term which may apply to any social group and it mixes neatly with the social identity theory concept of ingroup favoritism. In an effort to explain racist behavior Sumner (1906) coined the term ethnocentrism to refer to the way people identify themselves as group members (ingroups) and distinguish themselves from others (outgroups). The ingroup sees itself in opposition to the outgroup; the ingroup being superior and the outgroup held in contempt. Ethnocentrism has been seen to increase when there is a perceived threat to the group (Campbell 1965). It is likely that the same phenomenon occurs when there is a perceived threat to the economic well being of the nation.

Ethnocentrism is defined in terms of ingroup/outgroup orientation where the ingroup is preferred and is seen in opposition to others. Relating this to the COO effect, the nation is the ingroup of interest and the threat to the group is given in an economic context.

Advances in Consumer Research
Volume 23, © 1996

A person may make a reasoned judgment to support domestic products because it is good for the collective health of the economy of the country or the person may make a moral judgment that it is a duty. Ethnocentrism relates to social identity theory in a similar fashion; the social-identity group of interest is the nation.

EMPIRICAL STUDY

Methodology

It is hypothesized that most respondents have a preference for domestic products when price is equal, but that as the price differential increases, those with lower levels of national social identity will be more likely to choose products based on criteria other than the country of origin, such as price. In order to examine these relationships conjoint analysis will be used to examine the tradeoffs samples of Americans and Canadians are willing to make in evaluating the purchase of products from the United States, Canada and Mexico. Then, the differences in purchase preference between Americans and Canadians who are high and low in national identity, as manifested by their scores on the Cetscale, will be examined. Finally, some differences between Americans and Canadians will be examined.

Subjects

Two groups of subjects were considered in this study, a Canadian group and an American group. The Canadian respondents for this survey were students from two classes of undergraduate marketing courses at a central Canadian university. There were seventy four respondents. The American respondents were students from undergraduate marketing classes at a university in central U.S.. There were one-hundred fourteen U.S. respondents.

Survey Design

This study seeks to isolate the home country bias aspect from the country image stereotype aspect of the COO effect. This will be accomplished in two ways: 1) by using real life samples of a rather mundane product, computer mouse pads, which are observably equal in quality; and, 2) by testing countries both where quality should and should not be an issue.

The product chosen to be tested is very important. Studies focusing on country image have shown that when a product is more complex, the country of origin is of increased importance to consumers (Heslop, Liefeld and Wall 1987). Also, country image is usually used as a surrogate for information to assess the quality of the product. Use of brand name products also have an impact on country image. In order to minimize the effect of country image, computer mouse pads were chosen because they are simple, nondistinctive and virtually generic. Additionally, actual examples of identical Mexican and American made mouse pads, and a very similar (differed in color) Canadian-made mouse pad were located, indicating that the product choice was realistic. Also, the student respondents were likely to have some familiarity with mouse pads.

Assuming that country image has been substantially removed due to the products being observably equal in quality, any COO effect detected should be explainable largely by variations in the respondents' personal characteristics. The characteristic of primary interest, national social identity, will be assessed using the Cetscale (Consumer Ethnocentric Tendency Scale) developed by Shimp and Sharma (1987). The Cetscale has been validated in several studies (Herche 1992; Netemeyer, Durvasula and Lichtenstein 1991).

Products were assessed by the respondents using a main effects conjoint analysis. There are several advantages to the use of conjoint analysis. Realistic product attributes can be assessed without drawing undue attention to any one, such as the country of origin. Conjoint analysis has been found to be an excellent means of segmenting consumers (Green and Krieger 1991). Finally, on other occasions it has been found to be an effective means of eliciting the COO effect without biasing the respondent (Johansson, Douglas and Nonaka 1985).

Canadian Survey

Actual examples of mouse pads illustrating two levels of color (blue and grey) and two levels of style (contoured edge and no contoured edge) were displayed for the respondents. Also, the label of one was read regarding the manufacturer's locations (Canada, the United States, and Mexico) to illustrate that the purported countries of manufacture were realistic. The subjects were not shown pads representing each combination in the conjoint, but rather representative mouse pads. Finally, it was stated that the prices given ($4.25, $4.36 and $4.47 CDN) were similar to the prices at which the mouse pads were actually offered for sale. This was done to assure respondents that they were being asked to make choices which were similar to choices they might actually have to make when selecting a computer mouse pad at a store. For the conjoint students were asked to rank nine products (attribute combinations of country of origin, price, style, and color). The nine combinations were selected using a fractional factorial selection process in the *Conjoint Designer* (Bretton-Clark 1988).

It is worth noting the closeness of the three prices. There is a low price, a medium price which is 2.5% higher and a high price which is 5.0% above the low price. This narrow price range was chosen for the managerial implications which can be drawn from the results, and so that price would not overwhelm the effects of other attributes. When observed in an actual retail setting, computer mouse pads from different countries were priced identically. Managers apparently believe that the country of origin is of little consequence. It is expected that when prices are the same or nearly the same, consumers will differentiate between products by some other means; in this case, by country.

When the conjoint was administered, respondents were presented with the following scenario: "You are in need of a computer mouse pad and have gone to the store to purchase one." Respondents were then asked to rank each combination of product attributes. The respondents then completed the questionnaire consisting of the Cetscale and other items.

American Survey

The survey administered to the 114 American respondents was the same except for two factors. First, the prices were spread farther apart: a base price of $3.06, a price 3.5% higher of $3.17, and a price 7% higher of $3.27. Second, the "style" factor of the Canadian survey was replaced by a "made of recycled materials" or "not made of recycled materials" label on the package. The changes were made to satisfy other research interests. Because of this, the conjoint portion of the studies are not directly comparable.

RESULTS AND DISCUSSION

Results and Discussion of the Canadian Survey

The analysis was done in two parts. First, the overall group utilities were used in the conjoint analysis to establish the relative importance of each of the product attributes. The computer package *Conjoint Analyzer*, by Bretton-Clark was utilized. The sample was then broken down into two groups, those high and low on consumer ethnocentrism according to respondents' score on the Cetscale.

TABLE 1
Canadian Sample
Country of Origin Mean Utilities

Grouping	U.S.A. Utility	Mexican Utility*	Canadian Utility*
Overall	0.1760	-1.3500	1.1918
Low economic nationalism	0.2861 (0.7483)	-1.1490 (0.8750)	0.8679 (0.9413)
High economic nationalism	0.0391 (0.9158)	-1.6333 (1.1406)	1.5943 (1.0456)

Notes. Overall N=74. Low nationalism, N=35. High nationalism, N=39.
Values in parentheses are standard deviations of means.
* significant differences in means of low and high consumer ethnocentrism groups at .05.

Low and High consumer ethnocentrism was determined by looking for a natural split. The resultant segments were close to equal in size. The conjoint analysis for these two groups was compared.

The conjoint analysis yields group utilities which are preference ratings for each attribute at each level, and utilities for individual respondents at each attribute at each level. Group utilities show the relative importance of each attribute in the respondent's choosing a preference. The preference ratings for each level of each attribute show their importance relative to each other.

An examination of the overall group utilities of the conjoint portion of the study show that there is a significant country effect. Surprisingly, the effect for country (34.53%) is even greater than for price (32.03%). Due to the mundane, low involvement nature of the product being tested, it was expected that price would be the product attribute which was most important to consumers with country coming in second (Bruning, Lockshin and Lantz, 1993). This relative positioning is likely due to the narrow range of the prices. The colors and stylistic product attributes had overall utilities of 19.17% and 14.27%, respectively. The strong country effect shows that the COO can be found even under conditions where it should be minimal due to the removal of product quality as an issue.

In order to examine whether national identity would be manifested as home country bias, respondents were divided into two groups: those scoring high or low on Cetscale. Of the seventy four respondents, thirty-five were low and thirty-nine were high. A comparison of the group utilities of respondents high and low on consumer ethnocentrism shows a significant difference in the relative importance of price and country. Respondents low on consumer ethnocentrism rate price as most important (36.16%) while country is lower (24.69%). In fact, country is only slightly more important than color. For respondents high on consumer ethnocentrism, country is much higher (42.75%) while price is much lower (27%). This shows a decreased sensitivity to price for respondents high on consumer ethnocentrism, while respondents low on consumer ethnocentrism are sensitive to small changes in price.

The relative positioning of the Canadian, U.S. and Mexican group utilities, as seen in Table 1, indicate a strong positive utility for the Canadian product and a strongly negative utility for the Mexican product, while the U.S. product had a slightly positive utility. The positive utility for the Canadian product and the negative utility for the Mexican product was expected. This follows the general finding that domestic products are preferred and products from less developed countries are less preferred. There may be some residual stereotype effect despite the equivalent products. The difference between Canadian and U.S. products is more interesting.

Recent research by Heslop and Wall (1993) shows that typically, Canadians evaluate U.S. products as being essentially equal to Canadian products in terms of quality. Assuming that it is generally true, a difference in preference between U.S. and Canadian-made mouse pads must be explained by something other than country image, since country image is a surrogate for quality. An examination of responses of respondents high and low on consumer ethnocentrism may offer some explanation. Respondents low on consumer ethnocentrism have a much narrower range of preference, and in fact, are more positive towards U.S. products than are those which rank high in consumer ethnocentrism. Respondents high on consumer ethnocentrism, conversely, have a much greater preference for Canadian products than do those low in consumer ethnocentrism, and assess U.S. products lower.

Further, an analysis of variance indicates insignificant U.S.A. utility differences between Canadians who rate low and high in consumer ethnocentrism, and significant differences between low and high groups for both the Mexican and Canadian utilities. This analysis tends to support the research of Heslop and Wall (1993) cited above.

Results and Discussion of the American Survey

The survey of American respondents was analyzed similarly. An examination of the overall group utilities of the conjoint portion of the study show that there is, again, a significant country effect (see Table 2). The country effect is significantly higher than the price effect. This is true despite the fact that prices were spread farther apart than in the Canadian survey. A greater spread in prices should have increased the importance of price.

An examination of the frequency distribution of American respondents on the Cetscale showed that the mean was slightly higher. The American sample was divided into high and low respondents on the Cetscale, and the resultant groups were compared using ANOVA (Table 2). This comparison of the group utilities of respondents who were high and low on consumer ethnocentrism shows differences similar to the Canadian sample;

TABLE 2
American Sample
Country of Origin Mean Utilities

Grouping	U.S.A. Utility*	Mexican Utility*	Canadian Utility
Overall	1.5055	-1.3082	-0.1984
Low economic nationalism	1.1575 (1.2720)	-1.0823 (1.1712)	-0.0752 (0.9420)
High economic nationalism	1.8659 (1.2381)	-1.5423 (1.0566)	-0.3236 (0.7904)

Notes. Overall N=114. Low nationalism, N=58. High nationalism, N=56.
Values in parentheses are standard deviations of means.
* significant differences in means of low and high consumer ethnocentrism groups at .05.

insignificant differences between groups low and high in consumer ethnocentrism were found in utility placed on a product being from Canada, while significant differences were found between groups for the Mexican and American utilities.

Additionally, for those high on consumer ethnocentrism the importance of price dropped while the importance of country increased. Conversely, for the respondents who were rated low on consumer ethnocentrism, the importance of price increased while the importance of country decreased. What was surprising, however, was the magnitude of the difference between the American and Canadian respondents. Even among respondents low on consumer ethnocentrism, the importance of country, as reflected by the conjoint utility, remained relatively high. With the Canadian respondents, much of the differences between the groups were tradeoffs were between price and country. With the American respondents, there was less difference between the groups and there was less change in the importance of country.

Still, the differences cannot be explained solely by consumer ethnocentrism. Since there is a significant difference in utilities placed on U.S., Canadian, and Mexican products, neither the American nor the Canadian respondents simply made a distinction between domestic and foreign goods. They had a clear preference for one foreign good over another. The difference cannot be explained by national identification. Two possible explanations are: 1) that respondents did not accept that the products were of equal quality, and 2) that other social influences were active leading respondents to prefer Canadian products (or American products, in the case of the Canadian sample) over Mexican.

While consumer ethnocentrism alone does not explain the preference, social identity theory does offer possible explanations. Due to a considerable history of trade and social relations between Canada and the U.S. which is not present between Canada and Mexico, there is likely to be some shared identity between them. In recognition of this identity, a preference for U.S. over Mexican goods may be expected.

CONCLUSIONS
This study considers the effect of national identity as a means of explaining the portion of the country of origin effect which is not attributable to country image. An empirical test of national identity, as manifested by consumer ethnocentrism, was made to substantiate this concept using respondents from the U.S. and Canada.

The first conclusion is that, when dealing with mundane, low involvement products, undifferentiated by price, the country of origin is an important variable for all respondents. Second, people do appear to have identification with nation which can be expressed by a purchase intention. When dealing with mundane, low involvement products between which there are small differences in price people with greater consumer ethnocentrism are willing to pay a higher price to buy domestic products, while those who are lower in consumer ethnocentrism are willing to switch to imported products.

Managerial Implications
Retailers who believe that Mexican-made goods of equal quality should be priced equal to domestic goods should re-evaluate this view, particularly if there is greater profitability in selling Mexican-made products due to a lower cost of production. Companies which price these goods lower may achieve greater volume; maximizing profitability.

At the very least, consumer ethnocentrism should be considered useful for segmenting. The results indicate that some portion of the consuming public is willing to pay somewhat more for products made domestically. However, it should be reiterated that this result is highly dependent upon the product being a mundane, low involvement product.

REFERENCES
Bilkey, Warren J. and Erik Nes (1982), "Country-of-Origin Effects on Product Evaluation," *Journal of International Business Studies*, 13 (Spring/Summer), 89-99.
Bretton-Clark (1988), *Conjoint Analyzer, Conjoint Designer*.
Bruning, Edward R., Lawrence Lockshin and Gary Lantz (1993), "A Conjoint Analysis of Factors Affecting Intentions of Canadian Consumers to Shop in U.S. Retail Centers," *Administrative Sciences Association of Canada*, 14 (3), 12-21.
Campbell, Donald (1965), "Ethnocentrism and Other Altruistic Motives," in D. Levine, ed., *Nebraska Symposium on Movivation, vol. 1*, Lincoln, Nebraska: University of Nebraska Press.
Cattin, Philippe, Alain Jolibert, and Colleen Lohnes (1982), "A Cross-Cultural Study of "Made In" Concepts," *Journal of International Business Studies*, (Winter), 131-141.

Cattin, Phillippe and Dick R. Wittink (1982), "Commercial Use of Conjoint Analysis: A Survey," *Journal of Marketing*, 46 (Summer), 44-53.

Ettenson, Richard, Janet Wagner and Gary Gaeth (1988), "Evaluating the Effect of Country of Origin and the "Made in the USA" Campaign: A Conjoint Approach," *Journal of Retailing*, 64 (1), 85-100.

Festinger, Leon (1954), "A Theory of Social Comparison Processes," *Human Relations*, 7, 117-140.

Green, Paul and Abba Krieger (1991), "Segmenting Markets with Conjoint Analysis," *Journal of Marketing*, 55 (4), 20-31.

Herche, Joel (1992), "A Note on the Predictive Validity of the CETSCALE," *Journal of the Academy of Marketing Science*, 20 (3), 261-264.

Heslop, Louise and Marjorie Wall (1993), "Through the Looking Glass: Product-Country Images and International Trade Agreements," in *Product-Country Images*, Ed. Nicolas Papadopolous and Louise Heslop, New York: International Business Press.

Heslop, Louise A., John Liefeld and Margorie Wall (1987), "An Experimental Study of the Impact of Country-of-Origin Information," in R.E. Turner (ed.), Marketing, Vol 8, *Proceedings, of the Administrative Sciences Association of Canada*, 179-185.

Hong, Sung-Tai and Robert S. Wyer (1989), "Effects of Country-of-Origin and Product-Attribute Information on Product Evaluation: An Information Processing Perspective," *Journal of Consumer Research*, 16 (September), 175-87.

Johansson, Johny K., Susan P. Douglas and Ikujiro Nonaka (1985), "Assessing the Impact of Country of Origin on Product Evaluations: A New Methodological Perspective," *Journal of Marketing Research*, 22 (November), 338-396.

Levine, R. and D. Campbell (1972), *Ethnocentrism: Theories of Conflict, Ethnic Attitudes, and Group Behavior*, New York: Wiley, 1-21.

Luhtenan, Riia, and Jennifer Crocker (1992), "A Collective Self-Esteem Scale: Self-Evaluation of One's Social Identity," *Personality and Social Psychology Bulletin*, 18 (3), 302-318.

Nagashima, Akira (1970), "A Comparison of U.S. and Japanese Attitudes Toward Foreign Products," *Journal of Marketing*, 34 (January), 68-74.

Netemeyer, Richard G., Srinivas Durvasula and Donald R. Lichtenstein (1991), "A Cross-National Assessment of the Reliability and Validity of the CETSCALE," *Journal of Marketing Research*, 28 (August), 320-327.

Olsen, Janeen E., Kent L. Granzin and Abhijit Biswas (1994), "Influencing Consumers' Selection of Domestic Versus Imported Products: Implications for Marketing Based on a Model of Helping Behavior," *Journal of the Academy of Marketing Sciences*, 21 (4), 307-321.

Papadopolous, Nicolas (1993), "What Product and Country Images Are and Are Not," in *Product-Country Images*, eds. Nicolas Papadopolous and Louise Heslop, New York: International Business Press.

Papadopolous, Nicolas, and Louise Heslop, eds. (1993), *Product-Country Images*, New York: International Business Press.

Samiee, Saeed (1994), "Customer Evaluation of Products in a Global Market," *Journal of International Business Studies*, 25 (3), 579-604.

Schooler, Robert (1965), "Product Bias in Central American Common Market," *Journal of Marketing Research*, 2 (November), 394-397.

Schooler, Robert (1971), "Bias Phenomena Attendant to the Marketing of Foreign Goods in the U.S.," *Journal of International Business Studies*, (Spring), 71-80.

Shimp, Terence A. and Subhash Sharma (1987), "Consumer Ethnocentrism: Construction and Validation of the CETSCALE," *Journal of Marketing Research*, 24 (August), 280-289.

Sumner, W.G. (1906), *Folkways*, New York: Ginn.

Tajfel, Henri (1978), *Differentiation Between Social Groups*, London: Academic Press.

Tajfel, Henri (1981), *Human Groups and Social Categories*, Cambridge, England: Cambridge University Press.

Tajfel, Henri and John C. Turner (1979), "An Integrative Theory of Intergroup Conflict," in *The Social Psychology of Intergroup Relations*, eds. W.G. Austin and S. Worchel, Monterey, California: Brooks/Cole.

Turner, John C. (1982), "Towards a Cognitive Redefinition of the Social Group," in *Social Identity and Intergroup Relations*, ed. Henri Tajfel, Cambridge, Great Britain: Cambridge University Press.

Exploring Consumers' Evaluations of Counterfeits: The Roles of Country of Origin and Ethnocentrism

Goutam Chakraborty, Oklahoma State University
Anthony T. Allred, Oklahoma State University
Terry Bristol, Oklahoma State University

ABSTRACT

Counterfeit products account for up to six percent of all world trade. Theoretical and empirical research on counterfeit products is scarce, particularly research from consumers' perspectives. This paper presents an empirical study that focuses on factors that influence U.S. consumers' perceptions of risk and attitudes about counterfeits. The results indicate that ethnocentrism and country of origin of the original manufacturer jointly influence consumer perceptions of risk and attitudes about counterfeits. Specifically, we found that highly ethnocentric consumers evaluate counterfeits to be of lesser quality when the original is made in the U.S. rather than in Germany. Conversely, low ethnocentric consumers' quality evaluations of counterfeits do not vary whether the original is made in the U.S. or Germany.

The sale of counterfeit products, unauthorized copies sold as legitimate products, has become a serious threat to national economies, the manufacturers of legitimate products, and consumer welfare. The Department of Commerce estimates that counterfeit products cost U.S. business anywhere from $8 billion to $20 billion annually, with estimates for total domestic job loss starting at 130,000 to as high as 750,000 (Harvey 1988). Counterfeit products are also economically devastating to manufacturers of legitimate products, with the Swiss watch industry losing more than $900 million annually; motor parts industry, $200 million; perfume companies, $70 million; and pharmaceutical companies, $50 million (Matthews 1993). In fact, counterfeit merchandise is an estimated $200 billion enterprise worldwide and is growing rapidly, accounting for up to six percent of all world trade (Levine and Rotenier 1993; Matthews 1993). Although most law enforcement officials view it as a victimless crime and therefore do virtually nothing about it, it can also victimize the consumers who purchase counterfeits. For example, fake amphetamines and tranquilizers are believed to have caused deaths, bogus birth control pills have caused internal bleeding, and counterfeit heart pacemakers have been sold to hospitals for implantation into their patients (Harvey 1988). Additionally, counterfeit airplane engine parts have been brokered to the airlines, and a number of fatal auto accidents have been traced to failures of counterfeit auto parts (Dugan 1984; Ott 1993). Thus, across different industries and industrialized countries, counterfeits affect hundreds of thousands of jobs, increase the costs of marketing legitimate products, destroy brand equity and company reputation, and threaten consumer health and safety. Therefore, marketers of legitimate products as well as labor, national economists, and consumer safety advocates are very interested in identifying ways to reduce and, if possible, eliminate counterfeit products.

Counterfeit activities can be reduced by attacking either one of the two sources in the exchange — the supply of counterfeits or the demand for counterfeits. Most research and anti-counterfeiting efforts have focused on how to keep the supply of counterfeits from reaching consumers. A large number of supply-side research have investigated industry, company, channel, government, and independent actions designed to stop counterfeit products (Bush, Bloch, and Dawson, 1989; Harvey, 1988; Higgins and Rubin, 1986; Olsen and Granzin, 1992, 1993). Despite these numerous supply-side

studies and efforts aimed at reducing counterfeiting, the problem continues to grow. It appears that similar to the illicit drug trade, the supply of counterfeits will always exist as long as there is demand for them (Bloch, Bush, and Campbell 1993). Thus, a relatively unexplored alternative to reducing the supply of counterfeits is to reduce consumer demand for counterfeits. The goals of this research are to: (1) present the findings from an exploratory study that examines how the country of manufacturer of the product being imitated and consumer ethnocentrism impact consumers' perceptions of risk in buying counterfeits, evaluations of quality of counterfeits, and post-purchase feelings about their decisions; and (2) discuss how these findings can be used to develop strategies to dissuade consumers from knowingly purchasing counterfeits. As such, we offer an initial investigation into the demand side of the counterfeit issue, with particular focus on the impact on the public at large and on the national economy.

CONCEPTUAL FOUNDATIONS

Deceptive Versus Non-Deceptive Counterfeiting

Before an effective demand side business strategy or academic study can be designed, it is important to differentiate between two separate types of transactions involving counterfeits: deceptive and non-deceptive. Deceptive counterfeits represent situations in which consumers do not know that they are buying a counterfeit product at the time of purchase, i.e., consumers think they have purchased a genuine product when in fact it is a fake (Grossman and Shapiro 1988). However, in many cases, the public is well aware of illegal markets and the availability of bogus products, i.e., the counterfeits are non-deceptive (Grossman and Shapiro 1988). Non-deceptive counterfeits represent situations in which consumers may be fully aware based on price, quality, and the type of outlet from which the product is purchased that they are buying a counterfeit at time of purchase.

Counter measures to combat deceptive counterfeiting have concentrated on the supply-side, because consumers are unaware that they are purchasing counterfeits. Almost all supply-side solutions propose educating both retailers and consumers in spotting fakes. Thus, the solutions assume that consumers are not going to purchase counterfeits knowingly. In other words, supply-side solutions essentially involve transforming a deceptive counterfeit purchase situation into a non-deceptive counterfeit purchase situation. Because all efforts to stem demand ultimately seem to involve non-deceptive counterfeits, we have focused our investigation on this type of counterfeit.

Country of Origin

Country of origin of a product has been found to influence consumers' product evaluations across a variety of product classes and purchase situations (Bilkey and Nes 1982). In the context of a non-deceptive counterfeit purchase, there are two different countries of origin that may influence consumers' evaluations of counterfeits. First, American consumers tend to believe that most counterfeits are manufactured abroad in less-developed or developing countries and imported to the U.S. (Bamossy and Scammon 1985). Thus, the country of origin of the counterfeit (COC) may

Advances in Consumer Research
Volume 23, © 1996

FIGURE 1
Effects of Ethnocentrism and Country of Origin in Non-Deceptive Counterfeits

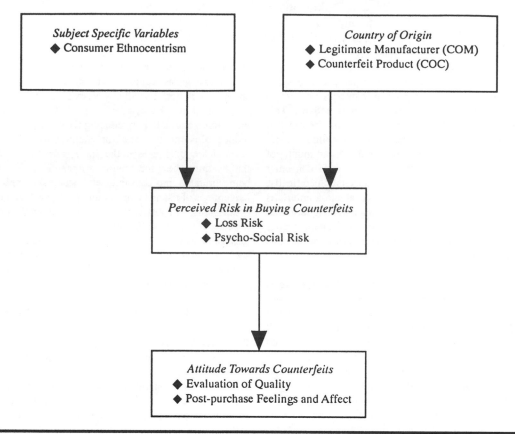

influence consumers' judgments of these products. Second, because evaluating non-deceptive counterfeits necessarily involves comparisons with the legitimate product being imitated, the country of origin of the original manufacturer (COM) may also be important to consumers' evaluations of counterfeits.

Country of origin has also been found to influence consumers' perceived risk of purchase such that consumers perceive more risk in purchasing a foreign-made product than one manufactured in the U.S. (Hampton 1977). Consumers' perceptions of risk may also influence their evaluations of and feelings toward counterfeit products (Allred, Chakraborty, and Sukhdial 1994). There is some risk involved in buying counterfeit products that are perceived to be made abroad. Part of this risk may be derived from the possibility of inferior performance resulting in financial, safety, and time risk. In fact, consumers perceive that such risks exist in purchasing counterfeit products (Bamossy and Scammon 1985).

Additionally, consumers may also perceive other more psychological or social risks in buying counterfeits, some of which may be derived from the purchase of foreign counterfeits in particular. American consumers seem to have a clear idea of the consequences of buying counterfeits made abroad given that the COM is the U.S., e.g., financial losses to U.S. companies and lost U.S. jobs (Bamossy and Scammon 1985). Thus, nationalistic biases, patriotism, and concerns about U.S. companies and jobs are likely to mean that American consumers will perceive foreign-made counterfeits as more risky to their self-image or the image portrayed to others, leading to more negative evaluations of the counterfeit, particularly when the original product is made in the U.S. rather than abroad. In other words, American consumers are more likely to perceive higher risk and feel more negatively toward

a counterfeit if they know that the foreign-made counterfeit is "ripping off" a U.S. brand rather than a foreign brand. However, these effects are probably more likely for highly ethnocentric consumers than those who are low in ethnocentrism.

Consumer Ethnocentrism

Consumer ethnocentrism represents an individual difference characteristic, with American consumers who are highly ethnocentric believing that purchasing imported products is inherently wrong because, from their perspective, it hurts the domestic economy, causes job loss, and is plainly unpatriotic (Shimp and Sharma 1987). Shimp and Sharma (1987) found that ethnocentrism is positively correlated with American consumers' attitudes toward U.S. products and negatively correlated with their attitudes toward foreign-made products, suggesting that judgments by consumers high in ethnocentrism are likely to be biased towards valuing the positive aspects of domestic products and devaluing those aspects of foreign-made products. Thus, highly ethnocentric consumers are likely to perceive foreign-made counterfeits as more risky and of lesser quality when the original is made in the U.S. than when the original is made abroad, while the COM is unlikely to influence the risk perceptions and subsequent evaluations of foreign-made counterfeits by those consumers low in ethnocentrism. These effects are summarized in Figure 1, which is an adaptation of Dowling and Staelin's (1994) model of perceived risk in the context of non-deceptive counterfeit purchase.

We designed an experiment to investigate these ideas. Specifically, we were interested in the effects of consumer ethnocentrism and the COM on consumers' perceptions of risks, their evaluations of counterfeits, and their expected post-purchase feelings. Although the COC may also influence consumers' evaluations of counterfeits, we decided to hold the COC constant because American consumers tend to believe that counterfeits are manufactured mostly in less-developed countries. We expected that highly ethnocentric American consumers would judge foreign-made counterfeit products as more risky and of less quality, leading to higher levels of post-purchase feelings of guilt when imitating a U.S.-made product than when imitating a non-U.S.-made product. Conversely, we expected that the COM would make no difference to low ethnocentric American consumers in their perceptions of risk or assessments of quality in buying counterfeits and in their feelings of guilt.

METHOD

Subjects and Product Selection

One hundred and thirty undergraduate marketing students (all U.S. nationals and 47% male) from a large midwestern university were provided extra credit for participating in our scenario-based quasi-experiment. As mentioned earlier, a wide variety of products is being counterfeited. Based on the results of informal interviews where we asked students to identify products that they believed were most frequently counterfeited, we chose auto parts as the product class for our study. Counterfeit auto parts are frequently mentioned in the literature. The literature is not clear, however, about which specific counterfeit products are purchased knowingly (non-deceptive counterfeiting). The informal interviews suggested that in the student consumer population, counterfeit auto parts are often purchased knowingly. Ninety-six percent of our sample owned a car.

Experimental Design

Subjects were randomly assigned into a 2 X 2 between-subjects factorial design. The first manipulated factor was the COM, with two levels — U.S. and Germany. Pretests indicated that subjects' perceptions of quality of auto parts made in the U.S. or Germany were about equal. Specifically, on a 9-point scale with end-anchors as unfavorable (1) and favorable (9), the mean perceptions of 40 students were 7.65 for U.S. and 7.43 for German-made auto parts ($t(39)=0.61$, $p=.54$). The second factor was derived based on subjects' scores on the shortened version (ten items) of Shimp and Sharma's (1987) CETSCALE measured on a 7-point Likert-type format. In our sample, the range of CETSCALE score was from 10 to 70, with a mean of 44.63 and s.d. of 15.01. These summary statistics are similar (after appropriate conversion from 7 to 5 point format) to those reported by Shimp and Sharma (1987) for testing the shortened version. To create a clear difference between the high and low ethnocentric groups, subjects were classified as low or high ethnocentric based on whether their scores were in the lower 33rd percentile (less than a score of 39) or upper 33rd percentile (a score of 51 or higher) of the CETSCALE scores in our sample. Subjects whose scores fell in the middle third of the distribution of the CETSCALE were not included in the data analysis. This procedure has been used by prior consumer researchers (Inman et al. 1990).

Procedure

The scenarios and questionnaires were distributed to students in two sections of the same class taught by the same instructor and took about fifteen minutes to complete. Participants were told that the study was divided into parts. In the first part they were asked to read a short article from a business publication. This article described the global nature of the counterfeiting problem and the efforts by IACC (an international organization) to stop counterfeit-

ing. The COC was held constant by stating in the article that counterfeits are typically made in developing countries such as Mexico or India. In the pretest, we found subjects' quality perceptions about auto parts made in Mexico and India were about equal (means of 3.22 and 3.24, respectively; $t(39)=0.08$, $p=.98$), but the average ratings of auto parts made in India or Mexico were significantly lower than the average ratings of auto parts made in the U.S. or Germany ($t(39)=12.70$, $p=.0001$). Subjects were first asked to indicate their perceptions about the business article and then to read a scenario describing a purchase situation involving a counterfeit auto part. Subjects were instructed to imagine that they were in the purchase situation. Several pretests were conducted to create scenarios that were realistic and easy to understand.

In the scenarios, the COM was manipulated by designating the manufacturer of the genuine auto part as "a U.S. company" or "a German company" as described below:

"Your car has been giving you problems for last couple of weeks. Sometimes it just won't start. However, if you keep turning the key in the ignition, it eventually starts after several attempts. You take it to a repair facility to have it checked. You are told that you need to replace the part that regulates the flow of gas to the engine.

After checking with a couple of stores, you come to know that the auto part, made by a U.S (German) company, is readily available in many stores and sells for about $350. It comes with a one-year warranty. However, a friend of yours tells you that he has recently purchased a counterfeited copy of a similar auto part for only $75.00 from a small independent store."

Dependent Measures

We were interested in measuring three sets of dependent variables: perceived risk, quality evaluations, and post-purchase feelings of guilt. We conjectured that the COM and consumer ethnocentrism would interact to influence the perceived risk of purchasing a counterfeit. In turn, we thought that this risk would influence both product quality evaluations as well as post-purchase feelings of guilt. Our risk measures included 9-point items designed to tap both overall risk as well as financial, performance, safety, time, social, and psychological risk (Bauer 1960; Cunningham 1967; Jacoby and Kaplan 1972). For instance, "What is the risk that the counterfeit auto part will not perform as expected?" was used for measuring performance risk; and "Considering the expense associated with the purchase of this product, how risky would you say purchasing the counterfeited auto part would be?" was used for measuring financial risk, with anchors "not risky at all" and "very risky." Subjects indicated their quality evaluations on two 9-point items assessing counterfeit quality and value. Subjects' expected post-purchase feelings of guilt were measured on three 7-point Likert-type items, such as "If you bought the counterfeit, you would feel guilty." Finally, subjects responded to a shortened version of the CETSCALE (a 10-item version of the original scale designed to measure consumer ethnocentrism). This scale was administered last in order to avoid the possibility of cueing subjects to the fact that we were examining the role of ethnocentrism in their judgments about counterfeits.

RESULTS

Assessment of Measures

A common factor analysis of the CETSCALE confirmed the unidimensionality of the 10 items. The Cronbach's alpha for these items was .93. The factor analysis of the eight questions related to

TABLE 1

Mean Perceived Risk in Buying Counterfeits

Country of Manufacture (COM) of Legitimate Product	Loss Risk		Psycho-Social Risk	
	Low Ethnocentric	High Ethnocentric	Low Ethnocentric	High Ethnocentric
U.S.	4.80	5.97	2.84	4.52
Germany	5.94	4.79	3.92	2.45

Note: Scales ranged from 1 (not risky at all) to 9 (very risky).

TABLE 2

Mean Quality Evaluations of Counterfeits and Post-Purchase Feelings of Guilt

Country of Manufacture (COM) of Legitimate Product	Quality Evaluations[a]		Post-Purchase Feelings of Guilt[b]	
	Low Ethnocentric	High Ethnocentric	Low Ethnocentric	High Ethnocentric
U.S.	5.35	4.06	5.14	4.46
Germany	5.20	5.74	4.80	5.82

Note: [a] Scales ranged from 1 (low quality) to 9 (high quality). [b] Scale is reverse coded and ranged from 1 (strongly agree) to 7 (strongly disagree) to a statement of feeling guilty after buying counterfeits.

consumers' perceptions of risk in buying counterfeits suggested two orthogonal dimensions, accounting for about 73% of the variance. The first dimension appears to be the "loss" risk (The risk questions pertaining to investment, expense, performance, safety, time, and opportunity had loadings of .74 or more on this dimension.) The second dimension appears to be the "psycho-social" risk. (The risk questions pertaining to self-image and what others may think of you had loadings of .90 or more on this dimension.) The Cronbach's alpha for the two dimensions were .90 and .89, respectively. We used the average scores of the items loading on these two dimensions as measures of perceived risk — loss risk and psycho-social risk.

An index for quality evaluations was created by averaging the two questions pertaining to the ratings of quality and value (r=.93). An index for post-purchase feelings of guilt was also created by averaging the three questions related to feelings of shame and guilt after buying a counterfeit auto part (Cronbach's alpha=.85).

We expected an interaction within the 2 X 2 analysis of variance. Specifically, we expected highly ethnocentric subjects would evaluate the foreign-made counterfeit auto part as more risky and of lower quality and express more expected post-purchase feelings of guilt when the COM was U.S. rather than when the COM was Germany. However, no such effect of COM would occur for those subjects low in ethnocentrism. We tested this hypothesized interaction first on the two perceived risk dimensions, then on quality evaluations and expected post-purchase feelings of guilt, and finally examined the mediating nature of perceived risk on the latter two variables.

Effects of COM and Ethnocentrism on Perceived Risk

We used MANOVA to investigate whether consumers' perceptions of risk in buying counterfeits are influenced by their nationalistic feelings as well as the COM of the original product. The dependent variables are subjects' average scores on the loss risk and the psycho-social risk dimensions. The interaction between COM and ethnocentrism is significant at the multivariate level (Wilk's Lambda=0.873, $F(2,83)$=6.02, p=.003) as well as at the univariate levels ($F(1,84)$=6.49, p=.01 for the loss risk, and $F(1,84)$=9.83, p=.001 for the psycho-social risk). However, the main effects are not significant either at the multivariate or univariate levels. The means for interpreting the interaction effect for the risk dimensions are reported in Table 1.

The pattern of the interaction for both dimensions of risk are consistent, although the effect is more pronounced for the psycho-social risk. The means indicate that when the original is made in the U.S. high ethnocentric consumers perceive more loss and psycho-social risk in buying counterfeits than low ethnocentric consumers. However, the situation is reversed when the original is made in Germany. The high ethnocentric consumers perceived lower loss and image risk in buying counterfeits than low ethnocentric consumers.

Effects of COM and Ethnocentrism on Quality Evaluations and Post-Purchase Feelings of Guilt

We also used MANOVA to check whether the evaluations and post-purchase feelings of low or high ethnocentric subjects are differentially influenced by the COM of the original product. The interaction effect is marginally significant at the multivariate level (Wilk's Lambda=0.943, $F(2,83)$=2.56, p=.09) as well as at the univariate levels ($F(1,84)$=2.99, p=.08 for quality evaluations, and $F(1,84)$=4.63, p=.03 for expected post-purchase feelings of guilt). However, the main effects are not significant either at the multivariate or univariate levels. The means for interpreting the interaction effect of COM and ethnocentrism on consumers' judgments and post-purchase feelings are reported in Table 2.

The pattern of the interaction is very similar between evaluations and post-purchase feelings. The means indicate that high ethnocentric consumers evaluate counterfeits more negatively when the original is made in the U.S. compared to when the original is made in Germany. However, for low ethnocentric consumers, the differences in evaluations of counterfeits are about equal regardless of where the original is made. For post-purchase feelings, the means indicate that high ethnocentric consumers expect to feel more guilty when buying counterfeits knowing that the original is made in the U.S. compared to when the original is made in Germany. However, low ethnocentric consumers expect to feel about the same level of guilt regardless of where the original was made.

Mediating Effects of Perceived Risk

In order to generate some insights about the mediating role of perceived risk on consumers' evaluations of counterfeits, we conducted a MANCOVA using the perceived risk dimensions as the covariates and the consumers' quality evaluations and post-purchase feelings as dependent measures (Mitchell 1986; Petty and Cacioppo, 1977). The results of this analysis indicate that when the effects of perceived risk are controlled for, the COM and ethnocentrism interaction effects on consumers' evaluations of counterfeits and their post-purchase feelings of shame and guilt are eliminated ($F(1,82)=0.97$, $p=.32$ and $F(1,82)=0.01$, $p=.98$, respectively). Thus, perceived risk is necessary to explain the differences in quality evaluations and feelings. To determine whether perceived risk precedes consumers' evaluations and feelings, we also analyzed the data using the latter as covariates with the risk dimensions as the dependent variables. The results of this analysis indicate that the COM-by-ethnocentrism interaction remains significant even after the effects of consumers' evaluations and feelings are partialled out of the risk perceptions (loss risk: $F(1,82)=2.76$, $p=.09$, and psycho-social risk: $F(1,82)=4.85$, $p=.03$). This seems to indicate that perceived risk is acting as a mediator between the COM and ethnocentrism and consumers' evaluations of counterfeits and post-purchase feelings of guilt.

DISCUSSION

We started this research with the belief that any strategy aimed at managing the counterfeit problem should include ways to reduce the demand for counterfeits. In reviewing the consumer behavior literature, we identified at least two constructs, COM and ethnocentrism, that we thought would influence consumers' perceptions of risk in buying counterfeits, which in turn would affect consumers' evaluations of counterfeits. The results of our study support our conjecture.

Our results should be viewed with caution because of the exploratory nature of the study and the relatively small sample size from a rather homogenous population. These limitations notwithstanding, the results provide several interesting insights into how the COM and ethnocentrism impact consumers' evaluations of counterfeits and their post-purchase feelings about their decisions to purchase counterfeits. For instance, we find that when considered in isolation, the COM and ethnocentrism have no effect on consumers' evaluations of counterfeits or their post-purchase feelings. That is, on an average, high or low ethnocentric consumers evaluate the quality of counterfeits to be about equal. Also, on an average, consumers' evaluations of the quality of counterfeits are about equal whether the original is made in the U.S. or Germany. However, we find that high ethnocentric consumers evaluate the counterfeit to be of lesser quality when the original is made in the U.S. rather than in Germany, whereas low ethnocentric consumers evaluations of the quality of counterfeits remain the same whether the original is made in the U.S. or Germany.

Although our results are generally consistent with what we predicted, the increase in perceived risk by low ethnocentric consumers when the COM changed from U.S. to Germany was unexpected. We can offer a post hoc explanation for this result. Although we had pretested subjects' quality expectations for the U.S. and Germany and found them to be approximately equal, perhaps those subjects low in ethnocentrism generally believed German automotive parts to be of higher quality than their U.S. counterparts. Given this possibility, the risk of purchasing a counterfeit originating from a developing country may be greater when the COM is Germany rather than the U.S. We did not measure consumers' ethnocentrism in our pretests; however, Shimp and Sharma's (1987) findings regarding consumer ethnocentrism would seem to support such results.

The managerial implications of our results relate to reducing demands for counterfeits. Our results suggest that U.S. manufacturers may be able to use emotional appeals to tap the nationalistic and patriotic feelings of some consumers by making salient that the counterfeits are made abroad, and thus buying counterfeits essentially hurts the U.S. economy. Specifically, those consumers high in ethnocentrism may be more likely to internalize and act on such appeals. Additionally, perceived risk appears to mediate these effects on consumers' evaluations of counterfeits, at least those pertaining to the COM and consumer ethnocentrism. Thus, communicating the risks of counterfeits may be important for policy-makers concerned about consumer protection against potentially harmful counterfeit products.

The theoretical contribution of this research is in extending the domain of the country of origin research to include counterfeit purchases. The extant research on country of origin effects has focused on the role of country of origin as a cue for evaluation of product quality for a single product. We extended this research first by arguing that in non-deceptive counterfeit purchase situations the country of origin of both legitimate manufacturers (COM) and counterfeiters (COC) would influence consumers' perceptions of risk in buying counterfeits and their evaluations of quality of counterfeits. Thus, while previous research has documented only *direct* effects of country of origin (i.e., influence of country of origin of a product on consumers' evaluation of the same product), we found *indirect* effects of country of origin (that is, the country of origin of the product being imitated had an effect on consumers' evaluations of counterfeits). Second, our results show that rather than being a simple cue for quality, the country of origin has a more complex effect in the sense that it interacts with ethnocentrism, an individual difference variable, in influencing subjects' evaluations of quality of counterfeits.

Limitations and Future Research Directions

One of the limitations of this study is the use of a single product class. This is particularly important because the perceived risk in buying counterfeits may depend on the product class. In this study, the use of auto parts as a product class may have produced identical effects of the COM and ethnocentrism on both loss and psycho-social risk. However, it would be interesting to explore whether the effects are different across product classes where one of the risk dimensions may dominate the others. For instance, psycho-social risk elements may be more salient than risk of loss when consumers consider buying a counterfeit Rolex watch. Similarly, the loss risk may be more salient than psycho-social risk in a counterfeit pharmaceutical drug purchase situation. In such cases, the effects of the COM and ethnocentrism on perceived risk as well as consumers' evaluations may be very different than what we found in this study.

In this study, the countries of the manufacturer of the counterfeit product (COC) were developing countries such as Mexico or India, and this variable was held constant across the experimental cells. However, many counterfeits are also made in developed countries. Thus, it would be interesting to investigate whether the pattern of the COM-by-ethnocentrism interaction remains the same when consumers believe that the counterfeits are manufactured in a developed country.

Our focus in this paper was on the functional characteristics of counterfeits as they influence consumers' perceived risk, which in turn affect their evaluations of counterfeits. Our conceptualization was therefore built on the model of perceived risk. Future research could look into other related literatures concerning authenticity, forgery, brand quintessence, sacralization, and singularity in an effort to enrich the proposed theoretical framework.

Conclusions

Counterfeits constitute a significant portion of world trade, yet very few academic research exists about why consumers purchase counterfeits knowingly. We pointed out at the beginning of this paper that manufacturers of legitimate products are primarily directing their efforts to the channel members to reduce the supply of counterfeits. However, the results from our exploratory study indicate that when highly ethnocentric consumers buy counterfeits knowingly, they feel more guilty when the original is made in the U.S. versus Germany. This suggests that manufacturers of legitimate products may also be able to reduce the demand of counterfeits by using suitable advertising appeals directed to highly ethnocentric consumers' feelings of nationalism and patriotism.

REFERENCES

Allred, Anthony T., Goutam Chakraborty, and Ajay S. Sukhdial (1994), "The Effect of Failure Rate and Country-of-Origin on U.S. Consumers' Attitude Towards Counterfeits: An Exploratory Study," Working Paper, Oklahoma State University, Stillwater, OK 74075.

Bamossy, Gary and Debra L. Scammon (1985), "Product Counterfeiting: Consumers and Manufacturers Beware," in Advances in Consumer Research, Vol. 12, eds. Elizabeth C. Hirschman and Morris B. Holbrook, Provo, UT: Association for Consumer Research, 334-339.

Bauer, R.A. (1960), "Consumer Behavior as Risk Taking," in Dynamic Marketing for a Changing World, ed. R.S. Hancock, Chicago, IL: American Marketing Association, 389-398.

Bilkey, Warren J. and Erik Nes (1982), "Country-of-Origin Effects on Product Evaluations," Journal of International Business Studies, 13 (Spring/Summer), 89-99.

Bush, Ronald F., Peter H. Bloch, and Scott Dawson (1989), "Remedies for Product Counterfeiting, Business Horizons, 32 (January), 59-65.

Bloch, Peter H., Ronald F. Bush, and Leland Campbell (1993), "Consumer 'Accomplices' in Product Counterfeiting: A Demand-Side Investigation," Journal of Consumer Marketing, 10 (4), 27-36.

Cordell, Victor V. (1991), "Competitive Context and Price as Moderators of Country of Origin Preferences," Journal of The Academy of Marketing Science, 19 (Spring), 123-128.

Cunningham, S. M. (1967), "The Major Dimensions of Perceived Risk," in Risk Taking and Information Handling in Consumer Behavior, ed. D.F. Cox, Boston, MA: Harvard University, 82-108.

Dowling, Grahame R. and Richard Staelin (1994), "A Model of Perceived Risk and Intended Risk Handling Activity," Journal of Consumer Research, 21 (June), 119-134.

Dugan, T.M. (1984), "Counterfeit!" Consumers Digest, 23 (September/October), 21-23 and 72-73.

Grossman, Gene M. and Carl Shapiro (1988), "Foreign Counterfeiting of Status Goods," Quarterly Journal of Economics, 103 (February), 79-100.

Hampton, Gerald M. (1977), "Perceived Risk in Buying Products Made Abroad by American Firms," Baylor Business Studies (October), 53-61.

Han, C. Min (1988), "The Role of Consumer Patriotism in the Choice of Domestic Versus Foreign Products," Journal of Advertising Research, 28 (June/July), 25-32.

Harvey, Michael G. (1988), "Industrial Product Counterfeiting: Problems and Proposed Solutions," Journal of Business and Industrial Marketing, 2 (Fall), 5-13.

Higgins, Richard S. and Paul H. Rubin (1986), "Counterfeit Goods," Journal of Law and Economics, 29 (October), 211-230.

Inman Jeffrey J., Leigh McAlister, and Wayne D. Hoyer (1990), "Promotion Signal: Proxy for a Price Cut?" Journal of Consumer Research, 17 (June), 74-81.

Jacoby, J. and L. B. Kaplan (1972), "The Components of Perceived Risk," in Proceedings of the 3rd Annual Conference of the Association for Consumer Research, ed. M. Venkatesan, Chicago, IL: Association for Consumer Research, 382-393.

Levin, Irwin P., J. D. Jasper, John D. Middelstaedt, and Gary J. Gaeth (1993), "Attitudes Toward 'Buy America First' and Preferences for American and Japanese Cars: A Different Role for Country-of-Origin Information," in Advances in Consumer Research, Vol. 20, eds. Leigh McAlister and Michael L. Rothschild, Provo, UT: Association for Consumer Research, 625-630.

Levin, Joshua and Nancy Rotenier (1993), "Seller Beware," Forbes, 15 (October), 170-174.

Matthews, Virginia (1993), "Piracy on the High Street," Marketing Week, 16 (August), 18.

Mitchell, Andrew A. (1986), "The Effect of Verbal and Visual Components of Advertisements on Brand Attitudes and Attitude Toward the Advertisement," Journal of Consumer Research, 13 (June), 12-24.

Nagashima, Akira (1970), "A Comparison of Japanese and U.S. Attitudes Toward Foreign Products," Journal of Marketing, 34 (January), 68-74.

Olsen, Janeen E. and Kent L. Granzin (1992), "Gaining Retailers' Assistance in Fighting Counterfeiting: Conceptualization and Empirical Test of a Helping Model," Journal of Retailing, 68 (Spring), 90-109.

_____ and Kent L. Granzin (1993), "Using Channels Constructs to Explain Dealers' Willingness to Help Manufacturers Combat Counterfeiting," Journal of Business Research, 27 (June), 147-170.

Ott, James (1993), "U.S. Indicts Broker in Alleged Scam," Aviation Week & Space Technology, 138 (April), 36.

Petty, Richard E. and John T. Cacioppo (1977), "Forewarning, Cognitive Responding, and Resistance to Persuasion," Journal of Personality and Social Psychology, 35 (4), 645-655.

Shimp, Terence A and Subhash Sharma (1987), "Consumer Ethnocentrism: Construction and Validation of the CETSCALE," Journal of Marketing Research, 24 (August), 280-289.

Measuring the Effects of Framing Country-of-Origin Information: A Process Tracing Approach

Irwin P. Levin, University of Iowa
J. D. Jasper, University of Iowa
Gary J. Gaeth, University of Iowa

ABSTRACT

One appeal to consumer nationalism is to communicate information about the use of American workers in manufacturing a particular product. Phased narrowing, a newly developed process tracing technique, was used to model how the impact of this information, "framed" differently across experimental conditions, changes over successive decision stages in narrowing down the choice of an automobile. In the presence of other cues, the nationalistic cue had its greatest effect among consumers scoring high on a scale of nationalism and when framed as "% American workers employed" rather than "% non-American workers employed." This framing effect increased in magnitude across successive decision stages. These results have implications for how and when country-of-origin information should be provided.

Country-of-origin information has traditionally been communicated to consumers as simply the nationality of the company manufacturing the product (Bilkey & Nes, 1982; Gaedeke, 1973; Han, 1988; Hong & Wyer, 1989; Obermiller & Spangenberg, 1989). With the advent of multinational or "hybrid" products, however, this simple classification is at best incomplete. Products such as automobiles may have parts made and/or assembled in several different locations. Recent research has thus turned to how people respond to other country-of-origin cues, one of which is the percentage of American workers employed in manufacturing a product. It has been shown, for example, that consumers prefer companies employing a larger rather than a smaller percentage of American workers in manufacturing and assembling automobiles (Levin & Jasper, 1996). It has also been suggested that this particular cue may play its biggest role in the early phases of considering choice options while final choices may be more apt to be governed by price and quality. In other words, it has been suggested that the American consumer as a gesture to supporting the American worker may initially strive to *consider* companies that employ mostly American workers but will ultimately *choose* on the basis of value (Levin, Jasper, Mittelstaedt, & Gaeth, 1993).

Several questions, of course, arise in investigating this issue: 1) What is the most effective way of communicating information about employment of American workers? In this study we compare two ways of "framing" this information: giving the "percentage of American workers" employed in manufacturing a product or the "percentage of non-American workers". 2) How is this information weighted at different stages of the decision process? In this study we use a multi-attribute multi-stage decision task. 3) How do individuals differ in using this information? In this study we use an individual difference measure of consumer nationalism derived from Shimp and Sharma's (1987) ethnocentrism scale. The last two questions were addressed with the aid of a new method that we call "phased narrowing" (Levin & Jasper, 1995). This method is an extension of earlier methods designed to trace the process by which choice options are screened and narrowed down before reaching a final decision (Beach & Potter, 1992; Bettman, 1979; Newell & Simon, 1972; Payne, 1976; Payne, Bettman, & Johnson, 1993). What's unique about phased narrowing is that it requires decision makers to use a series of discrete steps and, with the aid of special analytic tools, it is capable of examining changes in attribute importance across stages and of relating these changes to measurable individual differences.

In our original study (Levin & Jasper, 1995), for example, subjects were given a multiattribute-multioption phased decision making task in which they began with 18 automobile options and were asked in successive stages to narrow them down to 6, then to 3, and finally to 1. These successive stages roughly parallel what researchers studying the formation and use of consideration sets would label as the transition from "awareness set" to "consideration set" to "choice set" to "final choice" (Nedungadi, 1990; Roberts & Lattin, 1991; Shocker, Ben-Akiva, Boccara, & Nedungadi, 1991). One of the attributes used to describe each of the 18 options was "% American workers employed." The major finding was that the importance of this nationalistic cue decreased for most subjects as they approached a final decision. However, for those scoring highest on a scale of consumer nationalism, this tendency reversed. For these subjects, the attribute "% American workers" actually increased in importance as they approached a final decision.

The present study was designed to extend this research by investigating how the processes uncovered in the preliminary study would be impacted by the manner in which the information about the percentage of American workers was presented. In fact, this will be the first study to evaluate whether information framing effects increase or decrease as one approaches a final decision. Previous research using objectively equivalent product information labeled in different terms (e.g., 50% success rate vs. 50% failure rate of a medical treatment, or 80% lean vs. 20% fat ground beef) has shown that more favorable evaluations are produced with labels evoking positive associations than with labels evoking negative associations (Christensen et al., 1991; Davis & Bobko, 1986; Levin & Gaeth, 1988; Marteau, 1989; Wilson et al., 1990). In the present case, identifying a product as employing "50% American workers" should be more apt to call attention to the virtue of keeping Americans employed than identifying a product as employing "50% non-American workers". Therefore, we predict that employment information presented as "% American workers employed" should lead to more favorable product evaluations than equivalent information presented as "% non-American workers employed". In addition, based on previous research and theory, we predict that the importance or weight of the employment factor relative to other factors should be greater for those scoring high on a scale of consumer nationalism or ethnocentrism than for those scoring low and that changes in the importance of this factor over successive decision stages should be different for high and low nationalism consumers; specifically, only high nationalism consumers should show an increasing emphasis on employing American workers as they approach a final choice. Because the issue has never been investigated before, interactions involving the framing variable and decision stage are an open question, as is the issue of whether the effect of information framing on initial impressions and associations is transient or persistent.

FIGURE 1
Stimulus Design for Set of 18 Options

Price ($)   Quality Rating

Price ($)	50	54	58	66	70	74	82	86	90
7250	Y	Z							
8875	X		Z						
10500		X	Y						
12125				Y	Z				
13750				X		Z			
15375					X	Y			
17000							Y	Z	
18625							X		Z
20250								X	Y

% American Workers

X = 80%   Y = 50%   Z = 20%

METHOD

Design and Procedure

Subjects (105 undergraduate students at a large midwestern university) were tested in small groups of size 2 to 12. Subjects in the "% American" condition (N=52) were given the following cover story:

> You will be presented with a number of different choice situations involving cars. Each car will be described by a retail price, a rating of overall quality, and information concerning the percentage of American workers involved in making that particular brand. The overall quality ratings, in each case, are obtained from a leading independent consumer publication (e.g., *Consumer Reports*). The lowest (worst) possible rating is 0 and the highest (best) possible rating is 100. Each rating is derived from a weighted average of all important features associated with cars. Percentages of American workers in this study are based on the number of man-hours required to make and/or assemble each car and its components.

For subjects in the "% non-American" condition (N=53) the phrase "percentage of American workers" was replaced by "percentage of non-American workers." Each subject was then given an envelope containing 18 individual cards, on which each "brand" option (identified by the letters A through R) was described by the percentage of American (or non-American) workers involved in making the product, an overall quality rating, and a retail price.

Choice options were constructed under the assumption that subjects who choose on the basis of price will select options of low price, subjects who choose on the basis of quality will select options of high quality, and subjects who choose on the basis of nationalistic cues will select options manufactured by a high percentage of American workers. The 18 options depicted in Figure 1 have the property that no one option dominates any other option on all three attributes. The "X," "Y," and "Z" designations serve to mark those

options where a high, medium, and low percentage of American workers (or low, medium, and high percentage of non-American workers), respectively, were employed in the manufacturing process. (The equivalent version of 80% American workers, for instance, is 20% non-American workers, and so on.) These placements were designed to make % American workers independent of price and quality which are negatively related.

Parts 1, 2, and 3 (the successive stages task) followed the cover story and appeared on separate pages of the experimental booklet. Each part required subjects to select a smaller number of cards from those cards that they had either been given (Stage 1) or had selected previously (Stages 2 and 3). The critical instructions for each part, respectively, were as follows:

> Please open your envelopes, and take out all of the cards. After examining each of the 18 brands carefully, choose 6 brands that you would be interested in looking at if window shopping for a car. The 6 brands that you select should be brands that you would want, at some point in time, to examine first-hand at a dealership.

> Assume now that you're actually interested in buying a new car. Look over the six cards again that you selected in Part 1. Choose 3 brands from among those six that you would seriously consider buying.

> Again, look over the cards. This time examine the three brands that you selected in Part 2. Which 1 of these three brands do you think you would actually buy?

Finally, subjects were given a 10-item attitude survey designed to measure their nationalism/ethnocentrism. Nine of the 10 items in the survey were taken directly from the CETSCALE developed by Shimp and Sharma (1987). The 9 items chosen correspond to numbers 1, 3, 5, 8, 11, 13, 15, 16, and 17 of that scale.

FIGURE 2
Mean standard scores for the nationalistic cue as a function of frame, decision stage, and nationalism group

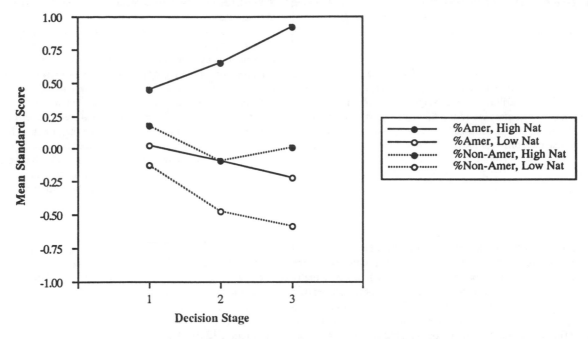

A 10th item, extent of agreement or disagreement with "Buy America first" (used by Levin et al., 1993), was also included in the survey. Responses to each statement were made on a 7-point Likert-type scale where strongly agree=7 and strongly disagree-1. The sum of all 10 items defined our nationalism score. In previous research, this score has been found to be significantly higher for subjects owning American cars than for subjects owning foreign cars.

The nationalism survey was administered last in order to avoid the possibility of cueing subjects to the fact that we were examining the role of nationalism in their choice behavior. Subjects in each framing condition were classified as High Nationalism if their scores were in the top third of scorers on the nationalism scale. Those scoring in the bottom two-thirds on the scale were classified for present purposes as Low Nationalism, because our previous research has consistently shown that those scoring low or medium tend to respond similarly.

RESULTS
The results of primary interest center around the differential influence that country-of-origin information has across stages depending on whether it is labeled as "% American workers" or "% non-American workers." With phased narrowing, the relative influence or impact of an attribute can be tracked across stages by computing the mean value of that attribute for the options selected at each stage. The logic here is that the more important an attribute is in the selection process compared to other attributes, the more likely it will be that the options selected will be favorable on that attribute (and possibly unfavorable on other attributes).

In order to compare different attributes on the same scale, values are converted into standard scores. For each attribute, values are converted by subtracting the middle level of the attribute in the stimulus design and dividing by the standard deviation of the attribute levels. Positive standard scores represent selection of options that are, on average, above the middle level of an attribute;

negative standard scores represent selection of options that are, on average, below the middle level and unfavorable on that attribute. Because options available at one stage depend on selections made at earlier stages, absolute standard score values are not independent across stages. Nevertheless, differences in the mean standard score from one stage to the next represent the marginal incremental influence of the target attribute at that stage. We believe that this way of computing and comparing attribute importance is simpler and more direct than other methods that require inferences from non-choice data.

Figure 2 displays the mean standard scores for the attribute "% American/non-American workers" for options selected at each decision stage and classified on the basis of nationalism group and framing condition. Inspection of Figure 2 reveals the following trends: 1) The mean standard scores for the nationalistic attribute are higher in the "% American" framing condition than in the "% non-American" condition; 2) The mean standard scores are higher for the High Nationalism group than for the Low Nationalism group; 3) The difference between the two nationalism groups and the difference between the two framing conditions (for each nationalism group) increase in magnitude across stages; and 4) In general, scores decrease or remain constant across stages, except for the High Nationalism subjects in the "% American" frame condition, for whom there was actually an increase across stages.

In order to test the reliability of these trends, a 2 X 2 X 3 ANOVA was conducted with two between-subjects factors (2 levels of information frame and 2 levels of subject nationalism) and one within-subject factor (3 levels of decision stage). The following effects were significant at or beyond the .01 level: frame, $F(1, 101)=15.66$; nationalism group, $F(1, 101)=25.18$; decision stage x frame, $F(2, 202)=5.43$; and decision stage x nationalism group, $F(2, 202)=6.73$. The interaction between decision stage and frame shows that the magnitude of the framing effect increases reliably across stages. The interaction between decision stage and nationalism group shows that the difference between High and Low

Nationalism subjects also increases reliably across stages. As a result of the conjunction of these effects, the nationalistic cue had its largest effect in Stage 3 for High Nationalism subjects receiving the information in terms of "% American workers employed" and its smallest effect in Stage 3 for Low Nationalism subjects receiving the same information in terms of "% non-American workers employed".

Although not the primary interest of the present paper, the use of standard scores also permits a comparison of the relative importance of different attributes at each stage. By comparing standard scores across attributes, we found that quality was generally the most important factor, followed by % American/non-American workers, and then price for the particular array of attribute levels in the present study. An interesting exception, however, was that the importance of the nationalistic cue equaled that of quality in Stage 3 for the High Nationalism group in the % American condition.

DISCUSSION

This research extends previous research (Levin et al., 1993; Levin & Jasper, 1996) in showing that the percentage of American workers employed in manufacturing a particular product is a source of information related to country-of-origin which can potentially affect consumers' choices of "hybrid" products, and, like the earlier studies, we found this to be especially true for those consumers who score high on a scale of nationalism or ethnocentrism. An interesting new finding, however, is that those placing the greatest importance on the employment factor were those who scored highest on a scale of nationalism *and* who received the information framed in terms of employing American workers rather than in terms of employing non-American workers. Furthermore, this particular group was the only one for whom the influence of the employment factor actually increased across decision stages.

The observed "framing effect" is of particular interest because the literature appears mixed as to whether "accentuating the positive" or "accentuating the negative" has the greatest effect on attitudes and behavior. Prior work by Levin and Gaeth (1988), however, suggests that when a particular attribute of an object to be judged is labeled in such a way as to produce positive rather than negative associations (e.g., lean beef is healthy whereas fat beef is unhealthy), then more favorable evaluations can be expected. To distinguish this from other types of framing effects, this phenomenon has been called "attribute framing" (Levin, Schneider, Gaeth, & Conlon, 1995). In the present case, if employing American workers is seen as a desirable goal—as it certainly appears to be—then stressing the percentage of American workers employed rather than the percentage of non-American workers employed, makes a product much more attractive.

The specific nature of the interaction between frame and decision stage provides additional new information about attribute framing. In sum, it appears that the focus on positive or negative aspects of choice options produced by positive or negative labels continues to guide decisions and has a cumulative effect that intensifies across stages. An interesting question for future research is whether there is a general tendency for an independent variable like information frame or a subject variable like nationalism that initially focuses attention on a particular factor to have even greater effect in later stages.

Results showing that attribute impact changes over decision stages and across subject characteristics support the use of appropriate process tracing methods, like phased narrowing, to provide further insights into how individual consumers process information. Because of the promise shown by the phased narrowing method, current work is aimed at testing its validity by showing how

choices are influenced by the constraints imposed by forced stages and by assessing consumers' reactions to using this technique. In this test, responses will be compared between phased and unphased decision tasks.

In addition to the theoretical and methodological implications of this study, there are practical implications as well. Recently, information has been made public about where the various parts of a multinational or "hybrid" product (such as many current makes of automobile) are made and assembled. The current study shows that in order to provide the maximum appeal to consumer nationalism, this information should stress the percentage of American workers employed. The use of a phased decision making task, in addition, allowed us to show that in some instances the impact of this form of country-of-origin information may actually increase as one approaches a final decision. For some consumers then, information concerning where parts are made should be particularly relevant if supplied at the point of purchase.

REFERENCES

Beach, L. R., & R. E. Potter (1992). The pre-choice screening of options. *Acta Psychologica, 81,* 115-126.

Bettman, J. (1979). *An information processing theory of consumer choice.* Reading, MA: Addison-Wesley.

Bilkey, W. J., & E. Nes (1982). Country-of-origin effects on product evaluation. *Journal of International Business Studies, 13,* 89-99.

Christensen, C., P. S. Heckerling, M. E. Mackesy, L. M. Bernstein, & A. S. Elstein (1991). Framing bias among expert and novice physicians. *Academic Medicine, 66*(9, Suppl.), 76-78.

Davis, M. A., & P. Bobko (1986). Contextual effects on escalation processes in public sector decision making. *Organizational Behavior and Human Decision Processes, 37,* 121-138.

Gaedeke, R. (1973). Consumer attitudes toward products made in developing countries. *Journal of Retailing, 49,* 13-24.

Han, C. M. (1988). The role of consumer patriotism in the choice of domestic versus foreign products. *Journal of Advertising Research,* 25-32.

Hong, S., & R. S. Wyer (1989). Effects of country-of-origin and product-attribute information on product evaluation: An information processing perspective. *Journal of Consumer Research, 16,* 175-187.

Levin, I. P., & G. J. Gaeth (1988). Framing of attribute information before and after consuming the product. *Journal of Consumer Research, 15,* 374-378.

Levin, I. P., & J. D. Jasper (1995). Phased narrowing: A new process tracing method for decision making. *Organizational Behavior and Human Decision Processes, 64,* 1-8.

Levin, I. P., & J. D. Jasper (1996). An experimental analysis of nationalistic tendencies in consumer decision processes: The case of the multi-national product. *Journal of Experimental Psychology: Applied, 2,* 17-30.

Levin, I. P., J. D. Jasper, J. D. Mittelstaedt, & G. J. Gaeth (1993). Attitudes toward "Buy America first" and preferences for American and Japanese cars: A different role for country-of-origin information. *Advances in Consumer Research, 20,* 625-629.

Levin, I. P., S. L. Schneider, G. J. Gaeth, & A. B. Conlon (1995). All frames are not created equal: A typology of valence framing effects: Working paper. University of Iowa.

Marteau, T. M. (1989). Framing of information: Its influence upon decisions of doctors and patients. *British Journal of Social Psychology, 28,* 89-94.

Nedungadi, P. (1990). Recall and consumer consideration sets: Influencing choices without altering brand evaluations. *Journal of Consumer Research, 17,* 245-253.

Newell, A., & H. A. Simon (1972). *Human problem solving.* Englewood Cliffs, NJ: Prentice-Hall.

Obermiller, C., & E. Spangenberg (1989). Exploring the effects of country of origin labels: An information processing framework. *Advances in Consumer Research, 16,* 454-459.

Payne, J. W. (1976). Task complexity and contingent processing in human decision making: An information search and protocol analysis. *Organizational Behavior and Human Decision Processes, 16,* 366-387.

Payne, J. W., J. R. Bettman, & E. J. Johnson (1993). *The adaptive decision maker.* Cambridge, England: Cambridge University Press.

Roberts, J. H., & J. M. Lattin (1991). Development and testing of a model of consideration set composition. *Journal of Marketing Research, 28,* 429-440.

Shimp, T. A., & S. Sharma (1987). Consumer ethnocentrism: Construction and validation of the CETSCALE. *Journal of Marketing Research, 24,* 280-289.

Shocker, A. D., M. Ben-Akiva, B. Boccara, & P. Nedungadi (1991). Consideration set influences on consumer decision-making and choice: Issues, models, and suggestions. *Marketing Letters, 2,* 181-197.

Wilson, D. K., K. A., Wallston, & J. E. King (1990). Effects of contract framing, motivation to quit, and self-efficacy on smoking reduction. *Journal of Applied Social Psychology, 20,* 531-547.

Real Things: The Social and Symbolic Value of Genuine Products and Brands

Kent Grayson, London Business School

IF ANYONE TELLS YOU THEIR COLA'S THE SAME AS COKE, DON'T BUY IT.
- *full-page Coca-Cola advertisement the London Times April 18, 1994*

On April 18, 1994, Britain's Sainsbury supermarket chain launched a soft drink called Classic Cola. What made Classic Cola different from other store-branded colas was its packaging, which was so similar to Coke's that even a Sainsbury cashier mistook one for the other (The Economist 1994a). This similarity was successful in moving Sainsbury's share of the U.K. cola market from 16% to 25% (Nichol 1994).

Manufacturers of everything from diapers to perfumes have faced comparable incursions by look-alike competitors. Judging from such apocalyptic headlines as "A Farewell to Brands" (Doyle 1993), "No End to March of Private Label" (DeNitto 1993), and "The Death of the Brand Manager" (The Economist 1994b), it is easy to conclude that traditional brands are no longer the valuable assets they once were. On the other hand, the hype about private labels often ignores the fact that most markets continue to be dominated not by knock-offs, but by original brands. For example, when faced with two cans of cola that look and taste almost exactly the same, a majority of U.K. consumers will still choose the more expensive, heavily advertised product over the unadvertised knock-off. The purpose of this special session is to examine some symbolically-oriented explanations for this phenomenon.

To be sure, a partial explanation has already been developed from research on consumer learning and the pioneering advantage (e.g., Alpert, Kamins & Graham 1992; Carpenter & Nakamoto 1989). When a product's ideal attribute combination is ambiguous, consumers learn to associate benefits with the pioneer, and therefore adjust their product category and ideal point accordingly. A later entrant may offer the same benefits, but must generally do so in comparison with the first mover and the adjusted ideal point. Because this comparison will invariably favor the pioneer, it will therefore support the pioneer's prominence as the market leader.

However, while this behavioral-learning explanation is useful, more symbolically oriented consumer researchers can offer a complementary alternative perspective, which may further enrich our understanding of the ways in which consumers value original products versus knock-offs. Ever since Levy (1959) asserted that "people buy things not only for what they can do, but also for what they mean," theorists and practitioners have recognized that consumers gain symbolic and experiential benefits from brands and products (e.g., Belk 1988; Keller 1993; Mick 1986; Solomon 1983). This perspective suggests that—in addition to adjusting category structure in favor of an early entrant—consumers may attach special symbolic value to an original or genuine product.

The symbolic approach also draws focus away from order of entry (which is critical when considering cognitive category development) and toward consumer definitions of originality and genuineness. The key interest is not how consumer cognition changes over time, but rather how consumers make judgments about genuineness (and the related constructs of sincerity, originality and authenticity). Thus, the symbolic perspective is useful in examining not only relatively new markets with true pioneers, but also the more common crowded markets where "the original" is more a matter of perception than of fact.

The special session brings together researchers whose work explores the symbolic value of original products, each from a distinct research perspective. Mason, Lefkoff-Hagius and Lee draw primarily from cognitive psychology; Grayson and Shulman build from theory in symbolic interactionism; and Aaker and Drolet explore the topic using social psychology.

REFERENCES

Alpert, Frank H.; Michael A. Kamins and John L. Graham, "An Examination of Reseller Buyer Attitudes Toward Order of Brand Entry," *Journal of Marketing*, 56 (July), 25-37.

Belk, Russell W. (1988), "Possessions and the Extended Self," *Journal of Consumer Research*, 15 (September), 139-168.

Carpenter, Gregory S. and Kent Nakamoto (1988), "Consumer Preference and Pioneering Advantage," *Journal of Marketing Research*, 26 (August 1989), 285-298.

Doyle, Kevin (1993), "A Farewell to Brands?" *Incentive*, 167 (July), 24-28.

Denitto, Emily (1993), "No End to March of Private Label," *Advertising Age*, 64 (November 1), S-6.

The Economist (1994a), "Unreal," *The Economist*, 331 (May 14), 20.

_____ (1994b), "Death of the Brand Manager," *The Economist* 331 (April 9), 67-68.

Keller, Kevin Lane (1993), "Conceptualizing, Measuring and Managing Customer-Based Brand Equity," *Journal of Marketing*, 57 (January), 1-22.

Levy, Sidney J. (1959), "Symbols for Sale," *Harvard Business Review*, 37 (July/August), 117-124.

Mick, David Glenn (1986), "Consumer Research and Semiotics: Exploring the Morphology of Signs, Symbols, and Significance," *Journal of Consumer Research*, 13 (September), 196-213.

Nichol, David (1994), "Coke Monday: North America's Soft Drink Industry, This Is Your Wake-Up Call," speech given at Hesse Meyers Beverage Digest Conference, Grand Hyatt Hotel, New York, NY (May).

Solomon, Michael R. (1983), "The Role of Products as Social Stimuli: A Symbolic Interactionist Perspective," *Journal of Consumer Research*, 10 (December), 319-329.

Seeing Double?: Consumers' Perceptions of Similarity Between Original Products and Knockoffs

Charlotte Mason, University of North Carolina
Roxanne Lefkoff-Hagius, University of Maryland
Yih Hwai Lee, University of North Carolina

ABSTRACT

Recent years have witnessed a substantial increase in the share of private-label goods across many categories. They currently account for about 20% of all U.S. food and consumer product sales, and some experts predict further increases to 33% (Stern, 1993). This trend, if it continues, is a major concern for manufacturers who have invested heavily in advertising and promotion to build their brands' equity. Of paramount concern is the increasingly aggressive stance of the so-called 'knock-off' or 'look-alike' products - or what private label manufacturers prefer to call 'brand equivalents.' By closely mimicking the packaging and features of popular brands, knock-offs hope to lure consumers with their lower prices. Manufacturers of the original brands feel knock-offs are an infringement designed to feed on the goodwill of their brands and result in confused customers.

Not surprisingly, knock-offs do attract consumers, although their success varies across categories. In many over-the-counter pharmaceuticals, store brands - which often are knock-offs - are the number one or two seller. In the fragrance market there are as many as 27 copycat marketers - some of which even knock-off other knock-offs (Sloan, 1987). Other categories including beer, baby food, and dental products seem relatively impervious to knock-offs. Conventional wisdom holds that some categories are insulated by intangible factors including image, emotional factors, and doubts about quality (Shapiro, 1993).

Although trade publications are full of facts and anecdotes about knock-offs, there is little academic research which has systematically explored consumers' responses to these knock-offs vis-à-vis the original, authentic brands. Using survey-based paired comparisons of visual stimuli, we examine consumers' perceptions of similarity between authentic products and the corresponding knock-offs with respect to several dimensions including physical features, performance, value, quality, and image. We examine which dimensions contribute the most to overall perceived similarity and how the relative weights vary across groupings of product categories. We also explore the relationships between purchase intentions and perceived similarity judgments across category groupings. Drawing both on conventional wisdom as reported in the trade press as well as the theoretical literatures in marketing and psychology, we test two sets of hypotheses. The first set relates to the classification of goods and attributes. For example, using the characteristic-beneficial-image attribute typology suggested by Myers and Shocker (1981) and others, we expect knock-offs to be judged more similar with respect to physical features than either performance or image. Drawing on the functional-symbolic-experiential classification (Park, Jawarski, MacInnis 1986), we expect similarity of performance to be relatively more important for functional products than for symbolic products. The second set of hypotheses link the similarity judgments to consumers' characteristics including attention to social comparison information (Lennox and Wolfe, 1984) and reported brand and category purchase behavior.

REFERENCES

Lennox, Richard D. and Raymond N. Wolfe (1984), Revision of the Self-Monitoring Scale, *Journal of Personality and Social Psychology*, 46(6), 1349-1369.

Myers, James H. and Allen D. Shocker (1981), The Nature of Product-related Attributes, in *Research in Marketing*, Vol. 5, ed. Jagdish N. Sheth, Greenwich, CT: JAI, 211-236.

Park, C. Whan, Bernard J. Jaworski and Deborah J. MacInnis (1986), Strategic Brand Concept-Image Management, *Journal of Marketing*, 50(4), 135-145.

Shapiro, Eben (1993), Price lure of private-label products fails to hook many buyers of baby food, beer, *Wall Street Journal* (May 13), B1.

Simpson, Wayne (1994), Seeing Double: The success of store brands has brought with it an epidemic of packaging knockoffs, *BrandWeek* (October 17), 30-35.

Sloan, Pat (1987), Knock-offs deliver blows to fragrance market. *Advertising Age* (March 2), S-14.

Stern, Gabriella (1993), Cheap Imitation: Perrigo's Knockoffs of Name-Brand Drugs Turn into Big Sellers, *Wall Street Journal* (July 15), A1.

The Genuine Article: Product Authenticity and its Value to Consumers

Kent Grayson, London Business School
David Shulman, Northwestern University

ABSTRACT

Belk (1990) suggests that authentic objects cannot be substituted because they have been "contaminated" by a sacred experience, and that non-contaminated objects therefore "lack sacred power to carry our memories." The purpose of this research was to examine how consumers experience this contamination process, and what it means for one object to carry memories, while another one cannot.

Drawing from previous work on authenticity (e.g., Baudrillard 1983, Lowenthal 1992, Sartre 1956, Trilling 1972) we explored the social value of authenticity through a series of 30 depth interviews. Subjects were asked about favored possessions, and in particular those that could not be replaced by a facsimile. What factors made the object distinct and irreplacable? What, in other words, made the "real" object authentic, while the facsimile would be a "fake"? The data enrich our understanding of authenticity and its role in consumption.

First, the data support a conception of authentic objects as more than just reminders (Belk 1990, Wallendorf and Arnould 1988). A reminder prompts a memory of an experience, but it need not have been part of an experience. For example, when asked if he would be willing to trade his favorite journal for an exact copy, a respondent said that he would not: "I mean you can remember that you wrote up the journal and everything like that . . . And sure, a copy of a journal is nice; but to have the actual thing there means a lot more." Having the actual thing means having something that was actually and physically part of the experience. Thus, in addition to reminding the owner of this experience, the authentic object validates that the owner participated in the experience. Like irrefutable evidence found at a crime scene, authentic objects provide undeniable evidence that the owner was part of the experience, something that a copy (which was not part of the experience) cannot do.

Second, the data challenge the notion that memories are essentially imaginary and hypothetical (Belk 1990). Authenticity cannot be hypothetical; the object was part of the experience or it was not. If it was part of the experience, then the object validates the experience. If it was not part of the experience, then the object can at best only remind. One respondent described a bowtie from a prom as follows: "I guess it's just, like, the fact that, you konw, it came from that actual night, like that's where the meaning comes from. You could try to say, oh, I'll just transplant it. But you know deep down that it's just some bowtie from any store anywhere. It doesn't mean the same thing."

Thirdly, the data highlight the role of authentic objects in supporting their owners' conception of a personal life history. Because time is so ephemeral, it is difficult to concretize. Ricoeur (1984) has argued that this is the main role of the narrative: to make time more concrete. Authentic objects make time more concrete by serving as "narrative storehouses"; unique indices of a life story in which the objects themselves played a part. A woman's ring holds the story of how her grandfather was a singer but had to make ends meet by being a jeweler. A woman's autograph from Disney World holds the story of how Goofy sat next to her on the riverboat ride. For these informants, a replica of the favored object would not serve as a narrative storehouse because it would not be permeated.

Having distinguished materially authentic objects from other kinds of favored objects, we use our framework to describe how symbols such as brands can gain authentic status, particularly through "commemorative marketing." Following from our research results, we suggest that the more a brand is associated with life narratives, the more it becomes materially authentic to the target consumer.

REFERENCES

Baudrillard, Jean (1983), *Simulations*, trans. Paul Foss and Alexander L. Biel, New York, NY: Semiotext(e).

Belk, Russell W. (1990), "The Role of Possessions in Constructing and Maintaining a Sense of the Past," *Advances in Consumer Research*, volume 17, 669-676.

Lowenthal, David (1992), "Counterfeit Art: Authentic Fakes," *International Journal of Cultural Property*, 1.

Ricoeur, Paul (1984), *Time and Narrative*, Kathleen McLaughlin and David Pellauer trans., Chicago, IL: University of Chicago Press.

Sartre, Jean-Paul (1956), *Being and Nothingness*, New York, NY: Washington Square Books.

Trilling, Lionel (1972), *Sincerity and Authenticity*, London: Harvard University Press.

Wallendorf, Melanie and Eric J. Arnould (1988), "'My Favorite Things": A Cross-Cultural Inquiry into Object Attachment, Possessiveness, and Social Linkage," *Journal of Consumer Research*, 14 (March), 531-547.

To Thine Own Self Be True: The Meaning of "Sincerity" In Brands and Its Impact on Consumer Evaluations
Jennifer Aaker (UCLA)
Aimee Drolet (Stanford University)

ABSTRACT

Hallmark cards. Campbell's soup. Hershey's candy bars. One of the common characteristics which describe, drive and differentiate each of these brands is "Sincerity." While many psychologists have discussed the meaning of sincerity in human personality (Norman 1963) and behavior (Schlenker 1981; Swann et al. 1992), the validity and import of this construct in consumer behavior has received considerably less attention. Yet an understanding of what it means for a brand to be sincere or authentic has become increasingly important as the number of brands, particularly me-too brands in many product categories grows (Kotler 1991).

The purpose of this research is to gain insight into the construct "Sincerity" as it applies to brands. First, we address the question, what is the meaning of sincerity, by defining the construct and by identifying what is associated with sincerity in consumers' minds. Second, we explore the antecedents of sincerity, or how brands develop and maintain high levels of sincerity. Third, we examine the consequences, both theoretical and practical, of possessing "Sincerity" as a brand.

To address these three areas, a multi-method approach is taken. First, a large-scale survey was conducted in which consumers were asked to rate 37 brands in multiple product categories on 114 personality traits. Based on an exploratory and confirmatory factor analyses, five brand personality factors resulted. The factor that explained the most variance (27%) was termed "Sincerity," which consisted of four parts: "Simple" (typified by traits such as basic, down-to-earth and family oriented), "Honest" (typified by traits such as sincere, loyal and caring), "Authentic" (typified by traits such as genuine, ageless and traditional), and "Warm" (typified by traits such as cheerful, happy and sentimental). The purpose of this exercise was to determine some of the distinct associations with Sincerity, to identify a sub-sample of "Sincere"

brands for further analysis (see below) and to explore the consequences of having "Sincerity." The latter goal was achieved by conducting a series of regressions where consumer preferences for brands that scored low vs. high on "Sincerity" were compared. The variance explained in preference was significantly higher for brands which scored high (vs. low) on "Sincerity." Moreover, this effect was unique for "Sincerity" (vs. the other four personality factors).

Second, a laboratory experiment was conducted to examine the psychological mechanism by which "Sincerity" operates. We hypothesized that "Sincerity" is an affectively-laden construct which evokes the affective component of attitudes. By juxtaposing "Sincerity" with a second brand personality factor, "competence," as well as manipulating the affective vs. cognitive nature of two advertisements of "Sincere" vs. "Competent" brands, we were able to show that indeed "Sincerity" is more affectively laden while "Competence" is more cognitively laden. Finally the paper conclues by linking these findings with thos in social psychology (e.g., Swann, et. al. 1992), a discussion of the possible negative consequences of having "Sincerity," as well as suggestions for future research.

REFERENCES

Norman, Warren T. (1963), "Toward an Adequate Taxonomy of Personality Attribute: Replicated Factor Structure in Peer Nomination Personality Ratings," *Journal of Abnormal and Social Psychology*, 66, 574-583.

Schlenker, Barry (1981), *Impression Management*, Belmont, CA: Wadsworth.

Swann, William, A. Stein-Seroussi, R.B. Giesler (1992), "Why People Self-Verify," *Journal of Personality and Social Psychology*, 62, 392-401.

Discussant Presentation
Clarifying the Construct: What is Authenticity?
Barbara B. Stern, Rutgers, The State University of New Jersey

Each paper in the session seems to use a different definition of "authenticity," reflecting a larger problem of terminological confusion endemic to the topic. To disentangle this confusion, the discussion will focus on clarifying the construct and making explicit the link between the session papers. Literary criticism is the source of the analysis of "authenticity" as a multi-dimensional construct, different from but related to "sincerity," "genuineness," and "realness." The discussion borrows Lionel Trilling's definition of authenticity and builds on Grayson/Shulman's usage of "narrative storehouse" to signify four different dimensions of authenticity—genuineness, positive valuation, cultural, and personal. The first two dimensions are found in Trilling's definition and the latter two are derived from Grayson/Shulman's. The derivation takes the concept of a "narrative storehouse" to the next level, enabling a distinction between products that reside in a cultural storehouse versus those that reside in a personal one. This distinction permits closer examination of the nature of authenticity and the process of creating it.

To begin with Trilling, authenticity refers to objects that are what they appear to be (genuineness) and that are worth the positive valuation they are accorded in their own sphere (positive valuation). That is, authenticity is defined on two dimensions in terms of two questions: "Is the object what it appears to be?" and "Is it worth the admiration it is being given in its domain?" (see Trilling 1972, p.93). Moving to Grayson/Shulman, authenticity is defined in personal terms, which suggests that it can also be defined in cultural terms.

The Aaker/Drolier and Mason/Lefkoff-Hagius/Lee papers treat "authenticity" as a phenomenon specific to the marketplace based on both dimensions. In Aaker/Drolier, authenticity is one of four factors summing up to "sincerity," a construct, and authentic is defined as the aspect of it that signifies "genuine," "ageless," "traditional." This is a culturally specific definition based on temporality, for a genuine brand is a "pioneer" one that precedes later entries into the product market and is deemed "ageless" because it has been around longest. The advantage of pioneer brands is that consumers learn to associate benefits with them and that the positive association enables pioneers to continue market leadership over time.

A similar cultural time-based definition is used in mason/Lefkoff-Hagius/Lee's paper, where "authenticity" refers to a product that is deemed original because it is the first one and that holds on to consumer loyalty even when later knock-offs emerge. The knock-offs are lower in price and are called "brand equivalents" or "imitations." The paper deals with consumer perceptions of similarity and their attraction for the original authentic brand versus the imitative equivalent. In both papers, the notion of genuineness the product is what it appears to be) is linked to historical precedence—the product was the first of its kind—and to positive evaluation because of its originary status (the product commands loyalty). In this sense, both papers imply that an authentic brand is one whose genuineness and value has enshrined it in the cultural narrative storehouse, "holding" a story significant to the culture and non-substitutable.

In Grayson/Shulman's paper, attention shifts from the cultural to the personal storehouse. Here, authenticity refers to something that the consumer associates with a favored possession—a special object dear to him/her. Trilling's criteria apply, although on a personal rather than on a cultural level. The object is original or genuine in the sense that the consumer defines it that way, and the object is valued because of its role in the consumer's life. That is, the emphasis turns away from historical time (did this object take on meaning in the consumer's life?). A favored possession gains authenticity because it has been permeated by a person or event significant in a consumer's life. The more a brand is associated with life narratives, the more it becomes authentic, and thus meaningful, to a consumer.

Once the construct of authenticity is seen as multi-dimensional rather than monolithic, "genuineness" and "positive valuation" can be seen as components along with "personal" and "cultural." The issue of creating authenticity then becomes one of maximising the capacity of advertising to act as a spearhead endowing products/brands with desired attributes and/or moving them from the personal to the cultural level.

REFERENCES

Trilling, Lionel (1972), *Sincerity and Authenticity*, London: Harvard University Press.

New Perspectives on Brand Differentiation

Alex Chernev, Duke University
Ziv Carmon, Duke University

Decisions regarding a brand's positioning and differentiation are becoming increasingly important and complex in today's cluttered marketplace. This session focuses on recent studies that identify some innovative differentiation strategies and investigate their underlying rationales.

In the first paper, Carpenter, Lehmann, Nakamoto, and Walchli offer a new perspective on the advantages and disadvantages of being a pioneering brand, focusing on how competing brands can successfully differentiate themselves. In the second paper, Chernev examines how similarity can be used to enhance a brand's differentiated positioning in the marketplace. In the third paper, Ariely and Wallsten (1995) investigate dominance relationships between brands and their effect on brand differentiation.

Carpenter et al. examine the role of differentiation in strategic brand positioning. Specifically, their research explores the use of differentiation to successfully attack a market pioneer (Carpenter and Nakamoto 1989). They show that certain differentiation strategies can be easily imitated by the pioneer, leaving competitors without a sustainable advantage. They suggest that an attacker can use a pioneer's positioning to create a competitive advantage for itself by exploiting the pioneer's limited ability to extend its product line.

Chernev examines the effect of attribute similarity on brand differentiation and consumer choice. Building on the reason-based analysis approach (Shafir, Simonson and Tversky 1993) and the dominance search framework (Montgomery 1989), he proposes that consumers view common features as reasons for choosing the brand that is dominant on the most important attribute. Thus, when one of the attributes has primary importance, adding common features will benefit the brand with the best value on that attribute, increasing differentiation and leading to a divergence of brands' choice shares. The data supported the notion that in certain contexts similarity can increase brand differentiation.

Ariely and Wallsten present a theory of preference construction that addresses the issue of differentiation in multiattribute product space. In a series of three studies they investigate how dominance relations between attributes affect consumer preferences and brand choice. Based on the notion that information that helps differentiate among similar items receives greater attention, they propose an original explanation of the asymmetric dominance effect (Huber, Payne and Puto 1982). In particular, they suggest that the observed shifts in the choice shares can be attributed to the dominance relationships between brand attributes.

Ziv Carmon, the discussion leader, concluded the session by integrating the individual presentations into a more general framework, highlighting the role of similarity and dominance relations between the brands on consumer preferences. He noted that while these three papers adopt different approaches, they complement each other in providing a better understanding of the role of brand differentiation in consumer choice.

REFERENCES

Ariely, Dan and Thomas S. Wallsten (1995), "Seeking Subjective Dominance in Multidimensional Space: An Explanation of the Asymmetric Dominance Effect," *Organizational Behavior and Human Decision Processes*, 63 (3), 223-232.

Carpenter, Gregory S. and Kent Nakamoto (1989), "Consumer Preference Formation and Pioneering Advantage," *Journal of Marketing Research*, 26 (August), 285-298.

Huber, Joel, John W. Payne, and Christopher Puto (1982), "Adding Asymmetrically Dominated Alternatives: Violations of Regularity and the Similarity Hypotheses," *Journal of Consumer Research*, 9 (June), 90-98.

Montgomery, Henry (1989), "From Cognition to Action: The Search for Dominance in Decision Making," in H. Montgomery and O. Svenson (Eds.), *Process and Structure in Human Decision Making*, John Wiley & Sons, 23-49.

Shafir, Eldar, Itamar Simonson, and Amos Tversky (1993), "Reason-Based Choice," *Cognition*, 49, 11-36.

Advances in Consumer Research
Volume 23, © 1996

Capturing the Dynamics of Consumption Emotions Experienced During Extended Service Encounters

Laurette Dubé, McGill University
Michael S. Morgan, Cornell University

The session brought together researchers who have used a rich diversity of conceptual frameworks and methodological approaches in their work on dynamic aspects of consumption emotions in extended service encounters. Presenters have developed innovative ways to measure and model the pattern of changes in emotional experience over time, to identify moderators of these in-process trends and their relationship with post-consumption judgments and behaviors.

In the first presentation, Price, Arnould, and Hausman, have used qualitative research methods to unravel the themes that dominate consumption experience in extended service encounters. Their results describe how the nature and intensity of consumption emotions evolve over time during the extended service encounter. They show how emergent relationships between service providers and customers and other key elements such as the physical and social setting moderate emotional responses to the service experience.

In the second presentation, Eliashberg and Sawhney introduce a theory-driven mathematical modeling approach to the dynamics of hedonic consumption experiences and use it for predicting individual differences in the enjoyment of a movie. Their results suggest that consumers' enjoyment may be largely determined by the interaction between individual characteristics and the emotional content of the movie. Based on simulation analyses, they show that individuals presenting different emotional predispositions (e.g., sensation seeking characteristic) express a different pattern of responses in the process of viewing movies, this effect being dependent upon the emotional content of the movie.

The third presenters, Dubé and Morgan, propose that the pattern of changes in consumption emotions during extended service encounters contribute to retrospective global judgments, over and above effects due to specific levels of emotional instances. They also suggest that one's ability and motivation to manage emotions during the service delivery process may influence the strength of trend effects in retrospective judgments. They propose that gender is a primary moderator of trend effects based on the abundance of empirical evidence showing that men and women vary a great deal in how they experience, express and manage emotions. These predictions were supported in two field studies that involve different conceptualizations of emotions and use service settings varying in terms of duration and affective expectations.

Finally, the discussant, Doug Stayman highlights the necessity, for future research, of studying the dynamics of both affective and cognitive aspects of extended service encounters. Service managers and marketers will benefit from a deeper understanding of how both set of factors shape consumption experience. This will help to more precisely segment markets and to more effectively fine-tune service design and communications.

Using Participant Observation to Unravel Emotional Moments of Extended Service Encounters
Linda L. Price, Eric J. Arnould, and Angela Hausman

This research profiles patterns of change in emotional experiences over the course of an extended service encounter. It illustrates a social constructivist approach to emotions, and emphasizes the active role of providers and customers in evoking "feeling rules" that channel the expression of emotion. The research builds on our previous research on extended service encounters, here focusing on the emotional dimension rather than temporal duration or proxemic relationships.

Participant observation (p.o.) provides the primary source of data, supplemented by in-depth interviews, and multi-stage surveys. P.o.'s traditional strengths—access to naturally occurring emotions unfolding in real time, access to multiple participants' experiences and to the interaction of multiple participants—expose the complex emotional and behavioral details of the service encounter, including interactive and relational elements that contribute to the emotional experience. As compared to other techniques for assessing emotional experience, p.o. connects felt emotions with their behavioral expression, and allows felt emotions, including dissonant ones, to be assessed in temporal, physical, and social context.

The research reported here deals with an extended single incident service encounter in a wilderness setting (white water river rafting). Results describe the unfolding of emotional experience and show how emergent relationships between service providers and customers and other key elements such as the physical and social setting moderate emotional responses to the service experience. Findings show that there is a predictable rhythm to the emotional experience: residual stress, confusion, anxiety, and excitement on day one of the trip yielded to relaxation, flow, excitement and affection on day three. Day four emphasizes aesthetic pleasure and feelings of love, warmth and affection. The last day is marked by exhilaration and calm relaxation, but also feelings of sadness, regret and the stress of reentry into everyday life. Throughout we illustrate the social channeling and construction of emotions by both customers and guides.

Findings of the study contribute to the emerging literature on relationship marketing and complement research employing dynamic process models of service quality and service satisfaction by focusing on the temporal enactment and interpretation of emotions.

Dynamic Modeling of Hedonic Consumption Experiences
Jehoshua Eliashberg and Mohanbir S. Sawhney

This research builds upon the experiential view of consumer behavior to develop an innovative modeling approach to studying the dynamics of hedonic consumption. In this paper, we present a conceptual framework as well as a mathematical model for describing and predicting the determinants of individual differences in the enjoyment of hedonic consumption experiences. We apply this framework to the context of movie viewing experience.

The conceptual framework proposes that the enjoyment of the experience is an outcome of the dynamic interaction between stable individual difference factors, temporary moods, and the emotional content of the experience. We model the interaction between the temporary moods of an individual and the emotional content of the movie as a stochastic process. The interaction determines the individual's instantaneous emotional states. We develop analytical expressions for the dynamic evolution of the probability distribution of the levels of achieved emotional stimulation, and, through individual difference factors, the expected enjoyment. All measurements are taken prior to watching the movie. We use these measurements to predict individual differences in the ex-post enjoyment of the movie. We present an empirical test of the model. Encouraging results are found at the individual and segment level. Results show that individuals varying on the personal characteristic of Sensation Seeking manifest a different pattern of emotional responses in the process of viewing movies, and this effect interact with the emotional content of the movie. Methodological and managerial implications are presented. We demonstrate the usefulness of the modeling methodology to formalize, model, measure and predict the dynamics of emotional response during hedonic consumption. Our approach also has the potential for aiding in segmentation and targeting decisions for a new experiential product, by studying the sensitivity of the enjoyment model to different Sensation Seeking segment profiles, and identifying segments that would be most responsive to the product. Future research is discussed.

Trend Effects and Gender Differences in Retrospective Judgments of Consumption Emotions in Extended Service Encounters
Laurette Dubé and Michael S. Morgan

In this research, we propose that the pattern of changes in consumption emotions during extended service encounters contributes to retrospective global judgments over and above effects due to specific levels of emotional instances. We also suggest that one's ability and motivation to manage emotions during the service delivery process may influence the strength of trend effects in retrospective judgments. We propose that gender is a primary moderator of trend effects based on the abundance of empirical evidence showing that men and women vary a great deal in how they experience, express and manage emotions.

We report the results of two field studies that involve different conceptualizations of emotions (basic dimensions of positive and negative emotions, Watson, Clark, and Tellegen 1988; specific consumption emotions, Mano and Oliver 1993) and use service settings varying in terms of duration and affective expectations (hospitals, college meal plans).

In both studies, subjects reported instances of consumption emotions on a daily basis and retrospective global judgments of these emotions. First-day reports and average daily percentage of changes were used as predictors of retrospective judgments of consumption emotions. Retrospective global judgments were a positive function of the increase or decrease of instances of emotions over time. Consistently with predictions based on the literature on gender differences in emotions, men's retrospective judgments of positive emotions were highly sensitive to trend effects, with no trend effect for negative emotions. In contrast, women demonstrated trend effects in judgments of a more diversified set of emotions. Theoretical and managerial implications of the results as well as future research are discussed.

Special Session Summary
A Forum On Health-Related Consumer Behavior

Meryl P. Gardner, University of Delaware
William D. Harris, Quinnipiac College

How consumers make and implement health-related decisions can have literally life and death consequences. Health-related behaviors are conceptually different from the more usual phenomena we study—the decision to eat nutritiously is remade every time you pass Mrs. Field's Cookies. Implementation is often difficult and involves continual tradeoffs. In fact these tradeoffs are often intimately related to life satisfaction. Diverse paradigms have been used to explain these behaviors. But, no one has brought them together. To further complicate the issue—people are studying different parts of the elephant—such as nutrition detection, stress reduction, exercise behavior —which may not involve the same target market, but are all health-related consumer behaviors. This special session was designed to bring together diverse perspectives on consumer health-related behaviors and in so doing enrich our understanding of this complex area of investigation.

The goal of the proposed session was to bring together divergent theoretical and methodological approaches to understanding how consumers make decisions about health-related products. Issues were approached from several theoretical perspectives, including prospect theory, information processing, and systems theory. Methodological issues such as message framing, dynamic behavior modeling, and longitudinal analysis were discussed.

It is hoped that by examining health-related behaviors from these divergent perspectives, we as consumer researchers will be able to move toward a richer understanding of the motivators and structural components behind this important aspect of consumer behavior. By studying health-related behaviors from within a consumer behavior framework, we hope to gain a richer understanding of health-related behavior from the perspective of why people purchase the products they do, and how they act, think, and feel during the process of buying and consuming these products. It's through the act of studying healthy lifestyle decision making along a continuum ranging from goal formulation to purchase and consumption behaviors that distinguishes this form of inquiry from that of investigating health-related behavior in general.

Stephen Hoch led an engaging discussion with the audience on the issues raised in the following papers.

A Model of Consumer Health-Related Behavior
William D. Harris and Meryl P. Gardner

This paper provides a theoretical framework for investigating the role of personal motivators in leading a healthy lifestyle. The focus of the discussion was on a model designed to describe the multi-level linkages of goal directing constructs to behavior. In addition, the model serves as theoretical basis for later empirical tests of hypothesized relationships among the constructs and enables us to see if the same relationships fit across a wide variety of behaviors.

Personal motivators of health-related behavior include demographics, psychographics, social factors, and situational factors. The effects of these four categories of variables on behavior are believed to be mediated by motivation and ability. Support for the motivation and ability linkage to behavior is given by Moorman and Matulich (1993) and Lutz, MacKenzie and Belch (1983).

Three important demographic factors that have been found repeatedly in the health-related behavior literature are age, gender, and income. The psychographic variables of interest are affect intensity, risk adversion, locus of control, and attributional style.

Bolden (1994) and Jacques (1994) attribute social factors such as peer influence to be important determinates of the performance of health-related behaviors. Finally, the situational factors highlighted in the model are affective state, cognitive state, and physical state.

Through the examination of relations found in our model we hope to find answers to the following research questions: How do people decide to start taking better care of themselves? How do people decide whether to actually follow through with these decisions in spite of temptations to do otherwise? What are the characteristics of people who do/don't take care of themselves? Do people who take care of themselves in one way take care of themselves in other ways? In other words, are health-related behaviors compensatory or complementary?

A Quasi-Experiment to Assess the Consumer and Informational Determinants of Nutrition Information Processing Activities: The Case of the Nutrition Labeling and Education Act
Christine Moorman

Research Summary. This paper reports a longitudinal quasi-experiment that uses the implementation of the NLEA to examine the consumer and informational determinants of nutrition information processing activities. Over 1000 consumers from balanced demographic, geographic, and site categories were observed and surveyed within a supermarket setting and across twenty different product categories. Results indicate that consumers acquired and comprehended more nutrition information at the point of sale in the post-NLEA condition than in the pre-NLEA condition. The NLEA did not, however, always influence these outcomes irrespective of individual consumer differences. Specifically, results indicate that the NLEA strengthened the positive relationship between motivation to process and nutrition information acquisition, and transformed a positive relationship between consumer skepticism in food products and nutrition information acquisition into a negative one. In the area of nutrition information comprehension, the NLEA weakened the relationships between motivation to process and nutrition information comprehension as well as diet and label knowledge and nutrition information comprehension while strengthening the relationship between diet-disease knowledge and nutrition information comprehension. Finally, the NLEA reduced differences in nutrition information comprehension for healthy and unhealthy product categories, while slightly widening differences in nutrition information acquisition in favor of unhealthy product categories.

Public Policy Implications. This study provides a set of initial findings of the impact of the Nutrition Labeling and Education Act on consumer processing of nutrition information. Findings suggest that consumers acquire and comprehend more nutrition information following the introduction of the new labels. Therefore, designing more complete, more comprehensible, and less potentially deceptive information across a wider range of food products has increased the level of nutrition information that consumers acquire and comprehend at the point of sale.

A goal that appears to be implicit in the NLEA is to facilitate consumers' use of nutrition information irrespective of their individual processing capabilities. In other words, most consumers should be able to use the new nutrition labels in their food choices.

The results of this study suggest that the NLEA was only partially successful on this issue. Specifically, the new nutrition labels were comprehensible to consumers with varying levels of motivation and most types of nutrition knowledge. However, the new labels seem to widen consumer differences in terms of how much nutrition information was actually acquired — with more motivated consumers and less skeptical consumers acquiring more post-NLEA. If nutrition/health programs strive for greater equity in acquisition, different approaches will apparently need to be adopted in program design. For example, it is not clear that nutrition labels are the appropriate tool to motivate less interested consumers. Fear appeals, on the other hand, may be more effective in drawing attention to the critical information contained on nutrition labels (Moorman 1990). On the other hand, if equity is not a policy goal, the approach taken in the case of the NLEA appears to fulfill other important objectives such as making information available in a comprehensible format.

Of more concern appears to be a group of highly skeptical consumers who remain very pessimistic about the truthfulness of nutrition information and the healthfulness of food products, despite the NLEA, and who, as a result, acquire little to no nutrition information. Future research needs to address the causes of this skepticism. If, for example, this skepticism arises from ignorance or misinformation, education/persuasion programs targeting these consumers may be needed. On the other hand, if this skepticism arises from social structural features such as not feeling integrated into a well-established business/government system, which might come from socioeconomic status or ethnicity, other types of programs may needed that attempt to bridge into communities exhibiting such characteristics.

Finally, consistent with the NLEA's apparent ability to reduce comprehension differences, it narrowed differences across healthy and unhealthy products. However, the NLEA also widened differences in nutrition information acquisition, in favor of unhealthy product categories. We attribute some of these differences to the fact that nutrition information was available for unhealthy products in the post-NLEA period but not in the pre-NLEA period. The gains, however, were very large for unhealthy products, suggesting two important implications. First, there is likely to be a public health benefit associated with this gain. Second, these results suggest that nutrition is likely to increasingly become a basis for competition in unhealthy product categories.

REFERENCES

Moorman, Christine (1990), "The Effects of Stimulus and Consumer Characteristics on the Utilization of Nutrition Information," *Journal of Consumer Research*, 17 (December), 362-374.

Message Framing and Cancer-Related Consumer Behaviors
Peter Salovey and Alexander J. Rothman

Health communications can emphasize either the benefits or the costs associated with a health behavior. Although asking people to consider an issue in terms of associated costs rather than benefits is thought to be an effective way to motivate behavior, empirical work of this kind has produced inconsistent results. The application of message framing to health promotion has been insensitive to important features of health-relevant decisions. The influence of framed information on decision-making rests especially on whether performing a behavior entails a risky or certain outcome. A framework will be presented that demonstrates how perceptions of the health behavior under consideration shape the relative effec-tiveness of loss- and gain-framed messages. In particular, the extent to which a behavior is considered to be illness-detecting versus health-affirming determines the degree to which people are more persuaded by loss- or gain-framed information, respectively. Finally, we suggest that paying greater attention to features of the situation in which health-related decisions are made allows for a richer understanding of how framed information influences judgment and behavior.

Findings from two lines of research are presented. In the first set of studies, we examined the moderating effect of involvement with the health issue and type of target behavior on the influence of message framing on intentions to perform health behaviors relevant to preventing or detecting skin cancer. In our samples, women as compared to men were more concerned about sun tanning and skin cancer and therefore were considered to be more involved with this health issue. In one experiment, exposure to gain- versus loss-framed messages differentially influenced the intentions of female (high involvement) and male (low involvement) subjects to obtain a skin cancer detection examination. In a second experiment, women who read gain-framed pamphlets were more likely than those who read loss-framed pamphlets to request sunscreen with an appropriate sun protection factor.

Our second line of research concerns the promotion of screening mammography for the early detection of breast cancer. A large sample of employed women not adhering to current guidelines for obtaining mammography screening was assigned randomly to view either gain-framed (emphasizing the benefits of obtaining mammography) or loss-framed (emphasizing the risks of not obtaining mammography) persuasive videotapes that were factually equivalent. Consistent with predictions based on prospect theory, women who viewed the loss-framed message were more likely to have obtained a mammogram in the subsequent 12 months following the intervention.

The pattern of results from our laboratory suggests that gain-framed messages have an advantage in promoting low-risk, certain behaviors like most preventive actions, but that loss-framed messages more effectively promote actions that involve greater risk and uncertainty, such as most early detection behaviors. Changes in perceived risk and emotional reactions may mediate these framing effects.

REFERENCES

Bolden (1994), "Perception of Oral Health Needs by Southeast Iowa Non-Dental Care Providers," *Special Care Dentist*, 14 (5), 194-197.

Jacques (1994), "Rates of Bicycle Helmet Use in an Affluent Michigan County," *Public Health Report*, 109 (2), 296-301.

Lutz, MacKenzie and Belch (1983), "Attitude Toward the Ad as a Mediator of Advertising Effectiveness: Determinants and Consequenses, *Advances in Consumer Research*, 10, ed. Richard Bagozzi and Alice Tybout, Ann Arbor: Association for Consumer Research, 532-539.

Moorman and Matulich (1993), "A Model of Consumer's Preventive Health Behaviors: The Role of Health Motivation and Health Ability," *Journal of Consumer Research*, 20 (2), 208-228.

Incorporating Perceived Risk into Models of Consumer Deal Assessment and Purchase Intent

Charles M. Wood, University of Missouri-Columbia
Lisa K. Scheer, University of Missouri-Columbia

ABSTRACT

This paper attempts to integrate two streams of pricing research dealing with perceived risk and assessments of "the deal" within the context of an expanded model based on the Dodds and Monroe (1985) model of perceived value. A sample of 245 consumers recorded their assessments of the value of the deal offered in a print advertisement, the perceived risk associated with the purchase, and their purchase intentions. The results indicate support for the basic expanded model.

INTRODUCTION

The marketing literature on pricing has been developing for over 20 years, beginning with Monroe's (1973) classic piece which established price as an important focus for both marketing practice and research. Since that time, much effort has been put into understanding consumer perceptions and response to pricing in a variety of contexts (e.g. Berkowitz and Walton 1980; Della Bitta, Monroe, and McGinnis 1981; Shimp and Bearden 1982; Burton and Lichtenstein 1988; Urbany, Bearden, and Weilbaker 1988; Mobley, Bearden, and Teel 1988; Lichtenstein, Burton, and Karson 1991; Grewal, Gotlieb, and Marmorstein 1994). This paper integrates two streams of pricing research regarding perceived risk and assessments of "the deal" within the context of the Dodds and Monroe (1985) model of perceived value. It also attempts to bring coherence to the numerous measures currently being used in pricing research. Finally, it offers a model for future testing and research.

THEORY

Model and Relationship to Previous Research

Much effort has been placed in the marketing literature on defining, measuring, and predicting consumer assessment of marketing communications. Dodds and Monroe (1985) propose a model of consumer evaluation of price, perceived quality, and perceived value. They suggest that consumer willingness to buy is affected by perceived value, and that perceived value is affected by both perceived quality and perceived monetary sacrifice. This model can be viewed, however, as including specific examples of broader concepts. We take a broader view in which perceived value results from an assessment of the tradeoff between: 1) the benefits the consumer receives in the deal at hand (one of which is product quality); and 2) the costs the consumer incurs to obtain those benefits (one of which is perceived monetary sacrifice). This perspective of benefits versus costs could potentially encompass many aspects relevant to the consumer evaluation process. Figure 1 depicts a general model of perceived value and purchase intention, an enhancement of the original Dodds and Monroe (1985) model. An examination of previous pricing studies suggests several possible "expected benefits" and "expected costs."

Various potential benefits could be examined, such as perceived quality (Dodds and Monroe 1985). Other benefits previously examined include product features (Wheatly, Walton, and Chiu 1977) and "desirability" (Berkowitz and Walton 1980). All of these benefits are part of the overall product evaluation the consumer makes; in this study we examine overall product evaluation.

There are also a variety of potential costs, both tangible and intangible, that are associated with a product purchase. As for tangible costs, one could adopt the Dodds and Monroe (1985) approach and measure perceived monetary sacrifice, that is, the amount that must be paid to acquire the product. Alternatively, we chose to examine the monetary outlay relative to expectations, that is, the actual selling price minus the expected selling price. Prospect theory (Kahneman and Tversky 1979) argues that consumer evaluation and buying behavior could be impacted greatly by the extent to which the ultimate monetary outlay differs from the expected basis point. In addition, the work on perceived risk in marketing (Shimp and Bearden 1982; Grewal, Gotlieb, and Marmorstein 1994) suggests that a consumer forms perceptions regarding the intangible costs such as "psychic costs" in the form of anxiety, frustration, downtime, etc. as well as the performance and financial risk associated with a given product-price deal. Unlike the price, which is known with certainty and immediately paid, risk represents an uncertain, probabilistic potential future financial outlay. We therefore propose to examine how a broad expected benefit, product evaluation, and three cost factors — the monetary outlay relative to expectations, performance risk, and financial risk — affect consumer evaluation of the deal and likelihood of purchasing the product.

Measures

A variety of measures have addressed aspects regarding the assessment of the deal. However, there seems to be no consensus on the proper measures to use, and some scales appear to be measuring the same underlying construct. Numerous studies have examined how various presentations of price and product information impact consumer assessments of value and attitude toward the deal. For example, scales assessing the *value* of a deal have been used by a number of researchers under a number of names: "Value for the Money" (Berkowitz and Walton 1980); "Value of the Offer" (Della Bitta, Monroe, and McGinnis 1981); "Perceived Value of the Deal" (Burton and Lichtenstein 1988; Lichtenstein, Burton, and Karson 1991); "Perceived Offer Value" (Urbany, Bearden, and Weilbaker 1988; Mobley, Bearden, and Teel 1988). Other measures focusing on consumer *attitude* regarding an advertised offer have also been developed: "Perceived Savings" (Berkowitz and Walton 1980); "Attitude toward the Deal" (Burton and Lichtenstein 1988; Lichtenstein, Burton, and Karson 1991). The measures developed by Burton and Lichtenstein (1988) make a distinction between the cognitive and the affective dimensions of attitude toward the deal. We propose that these various scales all tap the same underlying construct: Overall evaluation of the deal. Thus, we include Evaluation of the deal in our model, and examine its effect on the consumers' reported purchase intention. The selected measures were not intended to encompass the entire set of constructs relevant to deal evaluation, but to build upon prior research and to sift and clarify the predominant measures previously used in pricing research. (See Appendix).

To summarize, our hypothesized model operationalizes specific examples of concepts drawn from the general model of perceived value and purchase intention. It integrates two streams of research in risk and consumer value assessment, incorporating the effects of product evaluation, performance risk, financial risk, and monetary outlay relative to expectations on evaluation of the deal and, ultimately, on purchase intent.

FIGURE 1
General Model of Perceived Value and Purchase Intention

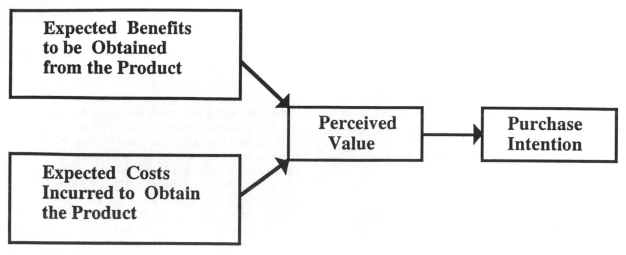

METHOD

Sample

Two hundred and forty-five consumers were recruited in a midwestern community for the study. In an effort to achieve a representative sample, the consumers were selected from several community, civic, and church groups representing a variety of ages, incomes, occupations, and levels of education. Each participant answered a series of questions after viewing a mock print advertisement for a television. Seventeen evaluative measures focussing on evaluation of the deal (items measuring both value assessment and attitude toward the deal), product evaluation, perceived performance risk, perceived financial risk, and purchase intention were drawn from previous scales and used in the questionnaire. (See Appendix for a list of measures used).

Prior to seeing the complete advertisement, participants were shown a picture of the television as it would appear in the advertisement, but without any price information. They were then asked to provide their estimate of the selling price of the television. After they completed this task, they were shown the advertisement with the pricing information and were asked to assess the deal using 17 scaled items. Five items measured "Value of the deal," four assessed "Attitude toward the deal," two concerned performance risk, two measured financial risk, three comprised the product evaluation measure, and one purchase intent item was used. In keeping with the majority of the existing measures, 7-point bipolar scales were used. As discussed earlier, "monetary outlay relative to expectations" was calculated as the difference between the actual selling price and the expected selling price.

Scale Creation

Exploratory factor analysis was performed on all variables in the model except for the single-item Purchase Intention dependent variable in order to examine convergent validity and discriminant validity among the four constructs of product evaluation, performance risk, financial risk, and overall evaluation of the deal. Squared multiple correlations were used as initial communality estimates, an iterated principal components method was used (SAS: Method=Prinit), and oblique rotations were performed due to the probable correlations between the factors. As discussed earlier, our measures were combinations of items from existing scales for the

four constructs. We therefore expected to extract four factors: one related to evaluation of the deal; one reflecting product evaluation; and two others representing perceived performance risk and perceived financial risk. The analysis revealed three factors which were clearly interpretable: Evaluation of the deal; Perceived Risk; and Product evaluation.

We expected an item assessing the attractiveness of the product features to load with the product evaluation measures, but it loaded on the deal evaluation factor. This may have been due to confusion regarding the understanding of the phrasing of the question. Participants may have been thinking of the features of the offer, the advertisement, or the product features. We expected the item "This is a poor value..." to load with the deal evaluation measures, but it loaded most heavily on the product evaluation factor. Participants may have been thinking more about product quality as they assessed the offer considering the money that would have to be spent. Interestingly, an item directly assessing product quality loaded weakly (below 0.4) on all three factors, indicating that it may be measuring a construct distinct from those extracted. In our sample at least, product quality and product desirability appear to be distinct constructs. Product desirability seems to have a more proximal impact on evaluation of the deal as it involves an evaluation of the product based on a numerous contextual factors (e.g. price, quality, motivation) through the prism of the consumer's own orientation. This is consistent with the work of Lichtenstein, Ridgway, and Netemeyer (1993) who demonstrated that individual orientations can affect responses to advertised offers. For example, if a low-price conscious consumer views a high quality product, they are likely to associate it with a high price and view the product as undesirable. On the other hand, a prestige-oriented consumer would find a high price-high quality item as highly desirable. These individual differences in consumer perception of quality and price are also in agreement with the ideas set forth by Monroe and Krishnan (1985). For the above reasons, these three items were deleted from further analysis.

As shown in Table 1, the results of the subsequent factor analysis revealed three factors which represented Deal Evaluation, Perceived Risk, and Product Desirability. As expected, the first factor effectively combined the previous measures of value assessments and attitude toward the deal. The second factor combined the performance and financial risk items. This differs from Grewal,

TABLE 1
Factor Pattern

Item	Deal Evaluation	Perceived Risk	Product Desirability
Worthmon	0.68	-0.04	0.10
Attdeal	0.57	0.21	0.22
Gooddeal	0.82	0.09	-0.13
Pricqual	0.80	0.04	0.04
Savings	0.86	-0.02	-0.17
Pricacce	0.85	-0.22	0.12
Excedeal	0.86	-0.04	0.12
Gooddeci	0.65	0.33	-0.10
Doubtwrk	-0.15	0.77	0.02
Hirepair	-0.07	0.76	0.10
Confperf	0.15	0.49	-0.07
Riskypur	0.23	0.55	0.16
Notdesir	0.18	0.18	0.43
Variance Explained:	75%	16%	2%
Cronbach's Alpha:	0.93	0.78	n/a

Gotlieb, and Marmorstein (1994) who, using a confirmatory factor analysis, established discrimination between the two constructs. We will combine these two risk elements into one scale for our purposes. The results also reveal that a single-item of product desirability discriminates from both the deal evaluation and the perceived risk factors. It also appeared as distinct from the quality measures. The reliability of the multi-item scales was assessed using Cronbach's alpha. The scales, the items that comprise the scales, and their corresponding alphas are reported in Table 1.

RESULTS

Research Model Examined

The factor analyses led us to slightly modify our original constructs to reflect the results and insights. The revised model that we established and set out to test is shown in Figure 2. Measures were developed for each construct based on the factor analyses. Product desirability was represented by a single item, perceived risk was measured by four items, monetary outlay relative to expectations was calculated as discussed earlier, evaluation of the deal was measured with eight items, and purchase intention was measured with a single item (Likelihood to buy).

Model Assessment

In order to demonstrate the mediating effect of Deal Evaluation on Purchase Intention, the procedures described in Baron and Kenny (1986) were followed. The procedure sets forth the following steps to test for mediation: 1) regress the mediator on the independent variable(s); 2) regress the dependent variable on the independent variable(s); and 3) regress the dependent variable on both the independent variable(s) and on the mediator. To establish mediation, the following conditions must hold: the independent variable(s) must affect the mediator in the first equation; the independent variable(s) must be shown to affect the dependent variable in the second equation; and the mediator must affect the dependent variable in the third equation. If these conditions all hold in the predicted direction, then the effect of the independent variable(s) on the dependent variable must be less in the third equation than in the second. Perfect mediation holds if the indepen-

dent variable(s) has no effect when the mediator is controlled. Using the terms of Baron and Kenny, Evaluation of the deal is the hypothesized mediator in our model, Purchase intention is the dependent variable, and Product Desirability, Perceived Risk, and Monetary outlay relative to expectations are independent variables.

Three versions of the model were analyzed by multiple regression and their R-squares compared in order to determine the best model:

(1) Evaluation of the Deal = f (Product Desirability, Perceived Risk, Monetary outlay relative to expectations)
(2) Likely to Buy = f (Product Desirability, Perceived Risk, Monetary outlay relative to expectations)
(3) Likely to Buy = f (Product Desirability, Perceived Risk, Monetary outlay relative to expectations, Evaluation of the Deal)

The results of these analyses are reported in Table 2.

The results reveal that the three conditions set forth for mediation in Baron and Kenny (1986) are met: 1) the independent variables all affect the mediator (Evaluation of the deal) in the first equation; 2) Product desirability and Perceived risk affect Purchase intention in the second equation (Monetary outlay relative to expectations has no effect); and 3) Evaluation of the deal affects the dependent variable in the third equation. For the Product desirability construct, perfect mediation occurs through Evaluation of the deal since its effect on Purchase intention in equation 2 is significant and it is not significant in equation 3. It also appears from a comparison of the coefficients in Table 2 that Perceived risk has a powerful effect on both Evaluation of the deal and Purchase intention. In addition, Monetary outlay relative to expectations has no unique effect on Purchase intention directly or through Evaluation of the deal, but it does have a strong effect on Evaluation of the deal. Purchase intention is apparently driven by the perceived risk associated with the purchase as well as the overall cost/benefit tradeoff represented by Overall deal evaluation. These findings are depicted in Figure 3. This tentative, revised model is presented here for future testing and verification.

FIGURE 2
Specific Research Model Tested

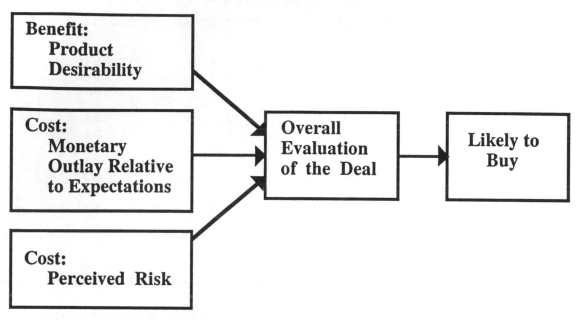

TABLE 2

Equation	Dependent Variable	Independent Variable	Coefficients	P-values	Model R-square
1	Deal Evaluation	Product Desirability	0.25	.0001	.39
		Perceived Risk	0.34	.0001	
		Outlay relative to Expectations	-0.41	.0001	
2	Likely to Buy	Product Desirability	0.28	.002	.28
		Perceived Risk	0.64	.0001	
		Outlay relative to Expectations	-0.14	.20	
3	Likely to Buy	Deal Evaluation	0.63	.0001	.38
		Product Desirability	0.12	.18	
		Perceived Risk	0.43	.0001	
		Outlay relative to Expectations	0.14	.22	

CONTRIBUTIONS, LIMITATIONS, AND FUTURE RESEARCH

The results of the analyses make several important contributions to research in pricing. We offer a general model expanding the framework established by Dodds and Monroe (1985). The perceived risk literature and the value assessment literature are integrated in this model. A more consistent measure of deal evaluation is offered which combines various pricing measures previously examined in a piecemeal manner. Finally, the broadened general model is tested using the measures developed.

This study lends support to the basic framework proposed by Dodds and Monroe (1985), yet provides the basis for a broader conceptualization of the tradeoffs involved in consumer evaluations of deals. This broader, more general model extends the Dodds and Monroe (1985) model by incorporating the tradeoff between costs and benefits inherent in a value assessment. In this case, the risks and monetary outlay relative to expectations associated with a purchase are evaluated alongside the beneficial, desirable qualities of the product.

Future research should keep the following limitations of this study in mind. Although actual consumers were used in the sample, the data were collected in an experimental setting. Other researchers have used field studies to examine consumer price perceptions. Three of our product evaluation variables loaded unexpectedly in the factor analysis, reducing our evaluation of product desirability to a single item. Future research should attempt to develop a multi-item measure of product desirability to encompass perceived quality, consumer motivation, and individual orientations consistent with Lichtenstein, Ridgway, and Netemeyer (1993).

It is also possible that the performance risk and financial risk constructs impact this framework at different points. For example, perceived performance risk may be a determinant of product desirability as well as potential costs, while perceived financial risk may play a more important role in whether or not positive Evaluations of the deal are translated into actual Purchase intentions. Since we did not achieve discrimination between these two constructs, we could not examine these issues; future research could address these possibilities.

FIGURE 3
Depiction of Results

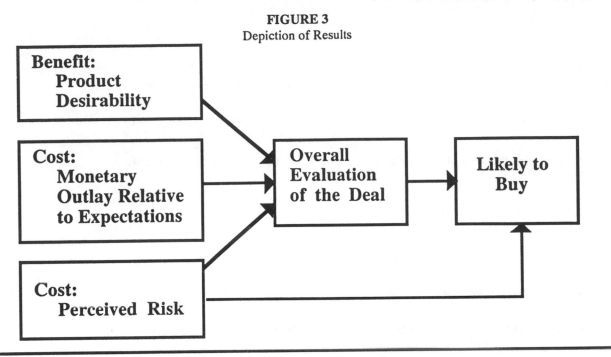

This study also has relevance to practitioners interested in achieving favorable consumer evaluations of advertised offers. By incorporating the notion of perceived risk and demonstrating its importance to consumers not only in the deal evaluation stage, but also in the purchase intention stage, this study offers insight into the importance of communicating information to consumers that allays their concerns about performance risk and financial risk (information about product quality, warranties, and money-back guarantees).

REFERENCES

Baron, Reuben M. and David A. Kenny (1986), "The Moderator-Mediator Variable Distinction in Social Psychological Research: Conceptual, Strategic, and Statistical Considerations," *Journal of Personality and Social Psychology, 51* (December): 1173-1182.

Berkowitz, Eric N. and John R. Walton (1980), "Contextual Influences on Consumer Price Responses: An Experimental Analysis," *Journal of Marketing Research, 17* (August): 349-358.

Burton, Scot and Donald R. Lichtenstein (1988), "The Effect of Ad Claims and Ad Context on Attitude Toward the Advertisement," *Journal of Advertising, 17* (1): 3-11.

Della Bitta, Albert J., Kent B. Monroe, and John M. McGinnis (1981), "Consumer Perceptions of Comparative Price Advertisements," *Journal of Marketing Research, 18* (November): 416-427.

Dodds, William B. and Kent B. Monroe (1984), "The Effect of Brand and Price Information on Subjective Product Evaluations," *Advances in Consumer Research, 12* : 85-90.

Grewal, Dhruv, Jerry Gotlieb, and Howard Marmorstein (1994), "The Moderating Effects of Message Framing and Source Credibility on the Price-perceived Risk Relationship," *Journal of Consumer Research, 21* (June): 145-153.

Kahneman, Daniel and Amos Tversky, "Prospect Theory: An Analysis of Decision Under Risk," *Econometrica, 55* (March): 263-291.

Lichtenstein, Donald R., Scot Burton, and Eric J. Karson (1991), "The Effect of Semantic Cues on Consumer Perception of Reference Price Ads," *Journal of Consumer Research, 18* (December): 380-391.

Lichtenstein, Donald R., Nancy M. Ridgway, and Richard G. Netemeyer (1993), "Price Perceptions and Consumer Shopping Behavior: A Field Study," *Journal of Marketing Research, 30,* (May): 234-245.

Mobley, Mary F., William O. Bearden, and Jesse E. Teel (1988), "An Investigation of Individual Responses to Tensile Price Claims," *Journal of Consumer Research, 15* (September): 273-279.

Monroe, Kent B. (1973), "Buyers' Subjective Perceptions of Price," *Journal of Marketing Research, 10* (February): 70-80.

Monroe, Kent B. and Joseph D. Chapman (1987), "Framing Effects on Buyers' Subjective Product Evaluations," *Advances in Consumer Research, 14* : 193-7.

Monroe, Kent B. and R. Krishnan (1985), "The Effect of Price on Subjective Product Evaluations," in *Perceived Quality: How Consumers View Stores and Merchandise*, Jacob Jacoby and Jerry C. Olson, eds., Lexington, MA:Lexington Books, 209-232.

Shimp, Terrence A. and William O. Bearden (1982), "Warranty and Other Extrinsic Cue Effects on Consumers' Risk Perceptions," *Journal of Consumer Research, 9* (June): 38-46.

Thaler, Richard (1985), "Mental Accounting and Consumer Choice," *Marketing Science, 4* (Summer): 199-214.

Urbany, Joel E., William O. Bearden, and Dan C. Weilbaker (1988), "The Effect of Plausible and Exaggerated Reference Prices on Consumer Perceptions and Price Search," *Journal of Consumer Research, 15* (June): 95-110.

Wheatly, John J., Richard G. Walton, and John S. Y. Chiu (1977), "The Influence of Prior Product Experience, Price and Brand on Quality Perception," *Advance in Consumer Research, 4* : 72-77.

APPENDIX

Value Items Used	*Source(s)*
Worthmon	
"This television is definitely worth the money"	Urbany, Bearden, Weilbaker (1988)
Poorvalu	
"The television is a poor value for the money"	Berkowitz and Walton (1980) Mobley, Bearden, Teel (1988)
Pricqual	
"Considering the price, this TV is of excellent quality for the price"	Della Bitta, Monroe, McGinnis (1981)
Savings	
"If I buy this TV, I will be saving a significant amount of money"	Burton and Lichtenstein (1988)
Gooddeci	
"I'm confident that buying this TV is a good decision"	Lichtenstein, Burton, Karson (1991)

Attitude toward the Deal Items Used	
Attdeal	
"My attitude about this deal is favorable / unfavorable"	Lichtenstein, Burton, Karson (1991)
Gooddeal	
"In my opinion, the deal offered is good / poor"	Burton and Lichtenstein (1988) Lichtenstein, Burton, Karson (1991)
Pricacce	
"This televisions' price is very acceptable"	Della Bitta, Monroe, McGinnis (1981)
Excedeal	
"Considering everything, I think this is an excellent deal"	Lichtenstein, Burton, Karson (1991)

Product Evaluation Items Used	*Source(s)*
Highqual	
"The featured TV is a high quality product"	Della Bitta, Monroe, McGinnis (1981) Dodds and Monroe (1985)
Notdesir	
"This is *not* a very desirable television"	Della Bitta, Monroe, McGinnis (1981)
Featattr	
"This television's features are very attractive"	Della Bitta, Monroe, McGinnis (1981)

Perceived Risk Items Used	*Source(s)*
Doubtwrk	
"I have serious doubts that this TV will work satisfactorily"	Grewal, Gotlieb, Marmorstein (1994)
Riskypur	
"Considering the amount I would have to pay for this TV, purchasing this TV would be risky / not risky"	Grewal, Gotlieb, Marmorstein (1994)
Hirepair	
"If I buy this TV, I probably will have to pay higher maintenance and repair costs in the future"	Grewal, Gotlieb, Marmorstein (1994)
Confperf	
"I am very confident that this TV will perform the functions that were described"	Grewal, Gotlieb, Marmorstein (1994)

Purchase Intention Item Used	*Source(s)*
Likebuy	
"How likely is it that you will buy this TV? (very likely / very unlikely)"	Berkowitz and Walton (1980)

Need Hierarchies in Consumer Judgments of Product Designs: Is It Time to Reconsider Maslow's Theory?

Richard Yalch, University of Washington
Frederic Brunel, University of Washington

ABSTRACT

Although lacking empirical support, a hierarchical need structure (e.g., Maslow's Hierarchy of Needs) remains a common view of human motivation. This paper discusses it as a method to understand consumers' reactions to product design. In two experiments, consumers evaluated different brands of shavers and toothbrushes. The tested products varied in functional and aesthetic features. Evaluative criteria ranged through a need hierarchy from basic needs to self-actualization needs. As expected, consumers perceived the plain functional products to be equivalent to the fancy aesthetic products in satisfying basic needs but inferior for higher level needs. Consumers were willing to pay 30% more for an aesthetic shaver and 22% more for an aesthetic toothbrush compared to functional equivalents.

INTRODUCTION

Although empirical support for a hierarchical consideration of needs is virtually nonexistent in consumer research, this perspective remains popular in consumer textbooks (e.g., Schiffman & Kanuk 1994). More interestingly, research challenging the existence of a need hierarchy (e.g., Kahle, Bousch & Homer 1988) has had no noticeable effect on its popularity. Finding it difficult to believe that a popular concept can be without merit, an effort was undertaken to determine if there were any circumstances for which consumers might evidence a hierarchy when determining the value of satisfying different needs. That is, do consumers place a greater value on satisfying different needs? And, do these values relate to the order proposed by Maslow and other social scientists?

The purpose of this paper is to reconsider the usefulness of need hierarchies for product design. Along with advertising, product design seems to be a natural area of application. Marketers can clearly add or subtract features that would appeal to different needs. For example, providing air bags in automobiles may appeal to the safety need whereas a CD player might appeal to self-actualization. This is not to rule out the possibility that some features such as a cellular telephone might appeal to several needs—safety for emergencies and status for ego needs. As the most common hierarchical perspective, this paper first briefly reviews the major elements of Maslow's Theory of Motivation and relevant research. Next, it presents a model linking need hierarchies to product design considerations. From this, two research studies investigating whether consumers use hierarchical considerations to evaluate how well different products satisfy their different needs are described. Limitations and issues for future research conclude the paper.

NEED HIERARCHIES

Space does not permit a detailed description of the many theories and concepts regarding need hierarchies. Fortunately, most consumer researchers should be familiar with their basic elements. Texts such as Schiffman and Kanuk (1994) provide a more extensive description. The most widely discussed theory is probably Abraham Maslow's Theory of Motivation. Maslow (1954, 1970) postulated that most human needs can be classified into one of five categories: Physiological Needs (e.g., food, water, air, shelter), Safety and Security (protection, stability), Social (affection, friendship and belonging), Ego (prestige, success, self-respect), and Self-actualization (self-fulfillment). Maslow further stated that individuals were first driven to satisfy their most basic needs (e.g., food would take precedence over safety and security if one were hungry and felt unsafe). However, once a lower level need was satisfied, individuals would be driven toward the next higher level need (e.g., safety and protection would take precedence over food for the individual who was not hungry but felt unsafe). After a period of being ignored in the pursuit of higher level needs, the lower level need would eventually build through deprivation. This would ultimately make it the dominant need (when the individual became hungry, food would again become a higher priority).

Maslow's theory of the individual has been applied to countries. Developing societies tend to focus on lower order needs (physiological and safety), whereas prosperous societies concentrate on higher order needs and only occasionally worry about satisfying lower order ones. For example, Plummer (1989) interpreted surveys conducted in the U.S., U.K. and Germany in the 1980's to argue that self-actualization has increased as a result of economic prosperity. Although linking growing self-actualization concerns and behavior with a society's economic well-being is consistent with hierarchical theories, this study does not demonstrate a hierarchical relationship for the other dimensions specified by these theories.

In what appears to be the only direct consumer test of multiple needs, Kahle, Beatty & Homer (1986) used a life style measure (List of Values) to test Maslow's theory of a need hierarchy. They used responses to two national surveys asking individuals to indicate the relative importance of different values in their tests. The large percent of persons indicating a high priority for lower level needs was interpreted as evidence that few individuals reach the highest need levels. Further, their finding that many individuals expressed concern about self-fulfillment was considered inconsistent with the belief that self-actualization was relatively rare because it required satisfaction with the four lower-level dimensions. Secondly, they looked at the mean ages of the persons who expressed the most interest in each value/need. Here, findings that the oldest persons endorsed the dimensions of security and being well-respected whereas the youngest persons endorsed self-fulfillment were also taken as not supporting Maslow's model. The final test involved looking at the primary and secondary categories (values rated most and second most important by each respondent) and observing that these responses did not correspond to Maslow's hierarchy. For example, only 31% of the individuals who selected self-respect as their highest value also highly rated being well-respected by others (two needs at equivalent levels in the need hierarchy). Thus, Kahle et al. (1988) concluded that their interpretation of the responses to the LOV scale did not support Maslow ("It is evident that Maslow's system does not seem especially plausible in the context of these data," p. 14).

Before accepting this conclusion, it should be noted that Kahle et al.'s (1988) failure to support Maslow's hierarchy may reflect some features of the study as well as limitations of the theory. For example, values are not exactly the same as needs. Similarly, although needs probably change in similar ways for most persons as they age, it is likely that there are substantial individual differences. Thus, it is not difficult to imagine some elderly individuals feeling liberated and prepared to fulfill themselves whereas others

Advances in Consumer Research
Volume 23, © 1996

see their lives as an increasing struggle to cope with declining health and income. Similarly, young persons whose parents are providing for their basic needs may be more concerned about higher order needs than basic ones. These issues aside, Kahle et al.'s conclusions suggest that need hierarchies like those proposed by Maslow may not be as prevalent and easily observable as many textbooks imply. Nevertheless, the simplicity and logic of the theory suggest that it should have some relevance to consumer behavior.

It is interesting to speculate why Maslow's Theory remains so popular despite failing to receive empirical support. One possible reason is that it is intuitively plausible that individuals have a variety of needs and prioritize them in a hierarchical order. However, if it is so plausible, why is it so difficult to generate supporting evidence? The choice of testing situations and varying interpretations of the theory may be factors. For example, most tests (e.g., Kahle et al. 1988), consider the theory as it applies to everything individuals do over a long period of time. This aggregation across persons and situations ignores the many other influences on their lives. Further, it is not consistent with the notion that priorities may change as life experiences change. Consumers may shift from a focus on not-yet-satisfied needs to previously satisfied ones that have slipped into a state of deprivation. In contrast, we advocate considering how the individual elements of the marketing mix (product, price, promotion and distribution) may map onto human needs. Also, we consider it useful to evaluate their effect on all needs rather than a few. Our view is that a study focusing on needs addressed by marketing decisions such as product design might better reveal the hierarchical structure associated with needs and show their relationship to consumer judgments.

RELATING A NEED HIERARCHY TO PRODUCT DESIGN EVALUATIONS

The paucity of research investigating consumer reactions to product design parallels the situation for tests of the theory of a need hierarchy. Marketers and consumer researchers stress the importance of product design (e.g., Bloch, 1995; Kotler and Rath 1984) but the journals are devoid of empirical research examining how consumers consider design features. Nevertheless, the public press has clearly identified design as a major competitive weapon (*Business Week* 1988, 1990, 1993). Success stories like the Ford Taurus and Black & Decker's revitalization of GE's small appliance business testify to the selling power of attractive designs. Interestingly, the world of high technology is also witnessing increasing concern with how products look as well as perform (*InfoWorld* 1991). To avoid the bleak prospect of competing in commodity markets featuring a battle for survival among the lowest cost producers, technology firms like Apple Computer are trying to add value through innovative and attractive product designs (e.g., PowerBook) to differentiate their products. Whether and how this adds value is not clearly understood. Do consumers care about the appearance of what are primarily functional products? This paper assesses whether concepts of a need hierarchy might provide a starting point for understanding consumer judgments of the value of product designs.

Unlike some views of the need hierarchy, we do not feel that need considerations are an all or nothing process. Rather, it appears that individuals may try to satisfy a variety of needs at a time (i.e., most products represent a bundle of benefits). Thus, rather than completely sacrificing their safety to acquire food and water, individuals are more likely to prefer a situation where they satisfy both. Often, the issue is one of tradeoffs. What is more valuable, better food or more security? In a society where scarcity is rarely experienced for most things (which is not to say that most things are available in unlimited quantities, just that most persons can get more of something they want if they are willing to give up other things), it is plausible that the supply and demand of products relate to the need hierarchy. Products that satisfy only the lowest level needs (e.g., physiology and safety) should be relatively common, whereas products that satisfy higher order needs such as ego and self-actualization should be more scarce. These differences should translate into prices in such a way that consumers value and expect to pay more for products that appeal to higher order needs than for those appealing only to lower order needs. This is the basic proposition motivating two experiments which consider whether product design features associated with higher order needs result in more favorable product evaluations.

METHOD: STUDY ONE

The fifty participants in the study were college students attending a large state university in the Northwestern part of the United States. The independent variable in the study was a manipulation of the aesthetic quality of an electric shaver. Product design was manipulated by having pictures of two shaving products differing in aesthetic appeal. One had a very boxy and relatively unattractive design, whereas the other had a slick, elongated shape. The dependent measures were a series of seven-point bipolar adjective scales selected to represent different needs that might be satisfied by an electric shaver and a single open-ended question regarding an appropriate price for each product.

The respondents were intercepted on campus, presented with a booklet and asked if they would be willing to evaluate some products as part of a student marketing research project. Each booklet consisted of a cover page followed by two pages of questions. Each page consisted of a picture of an electric shaver, sets of bipolar adjective scales and a question determining the expected price for the pictured product. The order of products was varied from booklet to booklet.

The bipolar adjective scales were developed from several lists of needs as presented in consumer texts (e.g., Engel, Blackwell & Miniard 1993, p. 285) that seemed to capture a range of concerns from utilitarian to hedonic. The set of needs roughly corresponds to Maslow's five levels except that the lowest need level had to be converted to basic performance because Maslow's physiological needs (representing hunger and thirst) did not seem relevant for an electric shaver. In addition, the highest levels were expanded into several scales because aesthetic concerns were thought to be most likely to be manifested at this level. The list of the needs, a brief description and the pairs of bipolar adjectives used to measure each one are presented in Table 1. A factor analysis demonstrated that these groupings had discriminant and convergent validity. The research issue was whether they were considered in a hierarchical order.

HYPOTHESES AND RESULTS: STUDY ONE

There were two hypotheses. The first concerned the effect of product aesthetics. Because the design enhancements affected only the appearance of the item and not its performance, it was predicted that the need hierarchy would be evident in the evaluations of the shavers. Consumers were expected to perceive increasingly greater differences between the products as the need being evaluated represented a higher order concern. That is, the least difference would be for the lowest level need, second least for the next highest level and so on such that the greatest differences would be for the highest level needs. The source of this difference would be increasingly lower ratings for the functional and higher ratings for the aesthetic product as the need level increased.

The second hypothesis concerned price expectations. Even though the design features did not affect the performance of the

TABLE 1
List of Needs, Descriptions & Operationalizations[1]

Needs	Conceptual Definitions	Measures: Study 1	Measures: Study 2
1. Basic function	Ability to perform the primary product function	Easy to maneuver /difficult to maneuver Close shave/unclose shave	Cleans well/cleans poorly Basically effective/ basically ineffective
2. Safety	Reduce concerns over physical safety and harm	Safe/dangerous Comfortable shave/ uncomfortable shave	Gentle/rough Safe/unsafe
3. Affiliation and belongingness	Satisfy the need to be accepted by others	Feel secure giving as a gift/feel insecure giving as a gift Feel comfortable lending to a friend/feel uncomfortable lending to a friend	Likely to be used by my friends/not likely to be used by my friends Popular/not popular
4. Achievement	Satisfy basic desire to demonstrate success	High status/low status Prestigious/not prestigious	High status/low status Prestigious looking/Not prestigious looking
5. Beauty	Satisfy desire to have attractive things in environment	Enjoyable to look at/ unenjoyable to look at Appealing/unappealing	
6. Variety seeking	Maintenance of a preferred level of psychological arousal and stimulation	Unique/common Innovative/not innovative	
7. Self-expression	Need to develop freedom in self expression	Made for me/not made for me Distinctive/plain	Distinctive/plain Innovative design/non-innovative design

[1]List of needs adapted from a table in Engel, Blackwell and Miniard (1993), p. 285.

products, it was expected that consumers would expect to pay a price premium for attractive products. In other words, there are financial rewards to manufacturers who offer aesthetically appealing products because they satisfy higher level needs. Beyond the common observation that consumers may have learned that attractively designed products are luxury items and therefore should cost more, it was expected that the prices would closely reflect the need level. In other words, it was predicted that the correlations between need judgments and price expectations would be higher for higher order need evaluations than for lower order need evaluations.

The mean evaluations of the aesthetically appealing shaver were compared to those for the functional shaver using each set of bipolar adjectives representing the seven need categories and for all fourteen items combined using paired t-tests (Table 2). As expected, the more appealing designed product was judged more favorably than the purely functional one (means 6.42 versus 3.02, p < .001).

As can be seen in Figure 1, the results generally support the hierarchical nature of evaluations. The difference in the evaluations between the aesthetic and functional product become increasingly larger as the level of the need increases. However, counter to expectations, the evaluations of the fancier product did not increase as the need level increased but tended to be uniformly high across the range of attributes. As expected, there is a decided drop-off in evaluations of the plain product as the attributes represent higher

order needs. The only observed exception to these tendencies is for the basic performance dimension where the aesthetic product did much better and the functional product much worse than expected.

The second hypothesis suggested a relationship between favorable evaluations on the higher order attributes and expected prices. Although respondents stated that they expected to pay about $50 for the less aesthetically appealing product and over $65 for the more aesthetically appealing product, correlations between need evaluations and price expectations did not evidence a closer correspondence as the need level increased (see rightmost column in table 1). Thus, it appears that consumers equally weight satisfaction of lower and higher order needs.

STUDY TWO

Experiment one was undertaken to demonstrate that aesthetic improvements are evidenced by more favorable judgments of the product's ability to satisfy higher order needs and that a failure to consider aesthetic appeal results in less favorable judgments. The experiment was only partially successful. There was evidence of a drop-off in evaluations for the low aesthetic appeal product but little gain in evaluations for the high aesthetic product as the need level became higher. This may be merely a measurement issue. Respondents may be more critical in judging products on higher order needs compared to lower order ones. Also, the respondents in experiment one did not have to make a tradeoff between aesthetics

TABLE 2
Product Evaluations by Type of Product Using Hierarchy of Attributes

Attributes	Aesthetic Product	Functional Product	t-value (n = 50)	Correlation with Price Differences *
Basic performance	6.7	4.2	6.1	.46
Safety	6.3	5.3	2.5	.50
Affiliation	6.7	3.5	7.2	.45
Achievement	6.7	2.1	9.5	.49
Visual appeal	7.0	1.7	8.5	.50
Variety-Seeking	7.1	1.7	11.0	.51
Self-Expression	6.5	1.0	12.5	.46

* Last column shows product moment correlations between the difference in need dimension scores between two products and the difference in their prices.

FIGURE 1
Ratings of Functional and Aesthetic Products Using Attributes Based on Hierachy of Needs

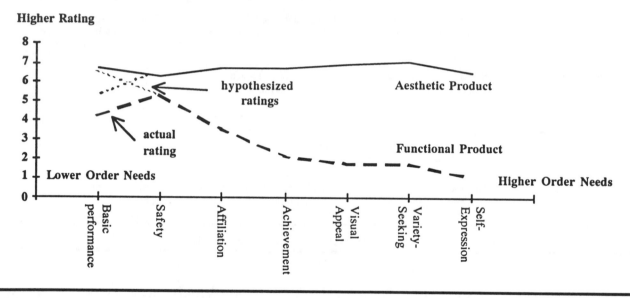

and functionality. The observed pattern of evaluations may merely reflect opinions that the aesthetic shaver was a better shaver. These concerns were addressed in a second experiment that attempted to compare functionality and aesthetics by manipulating both at two levels. In addition, experiment two explored the possibility of individual differences by assessing each respondent's concern with the different need levels.

METHOD: STUDY TWO

Design and Procedure

One hundred and fifty five undergraduate college students attending an introductory marketing course at a large state university participated in an experiment. The two dimensions of product design manipulated were the aesthetic and functionality qualities of a toothbrush. Four toothbrushes were selected from an original set of eight actual marketed products based on pre-test ratings of their level of aesthetic and functional qualities. All were blue to keep color constant.

Each subject evaluated all four products in a random order, resulting in a two by two within subject factorial. Participants examined four toothbrushes glued to a board that was circulated by the experimenter. The dependent measures were a series of bipolar

adjectives scales selected to represent a hierarchy of needs (see Table 1). Measures had been pretested across a sample of 30 students before the final study. Participants were also asked to evaluate the design qualities of each product, using bipolar scales for both the aesthetic dimension (conventional-sophisticated and old-fashioned-futuristic) and the functionality dimension (do a very poor brushing job-do an excellent brushing job and have very poor functional characteristics-have excellent functional characteristics). Finally, respondents indicated the price they would be willing to pay for each brush, using an open-ended question. After evaluating all four products, subjects answered a self-actualization scale (adapted from Brooker, 1975), and other individual characteristics measures.

HYPOTHESES AND RESULTS: STUDY TWO

In study two, it was expected that consumers who confronted a tradeoff between aesthetic and functional features would perceive greater value in the aesthetics. Further, it was expected that the value differences would be related to the perceived satisfaction of higher level needs. The tradeoff between aesthetic and functional designs was tested using the two sets of items discussed above. Repeated measures analysis of variance revealed a significant main effect of the aesthetic manipulation on aesthetic judgments

FIGURE 2
Ratings of Products Varying in Aesthetics and Functionality Using Attributes Based on Need Hierachy

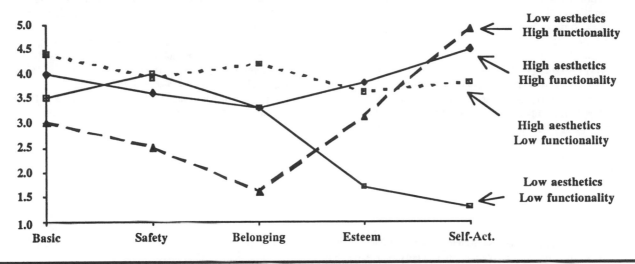

(F(1,147)=577, p<.0001). However, aesthetic judgments were also significantly affected by the functionality manipulation (F(1,147)=88.0, p<.001) and the interaction of aesthetic and functional design (F(1,147)=463.8, p<.0001). The latter two effects may be attributed to an unexpectedly high rating for the high functionality-low design toothbrush. As expected, the functionality judgments were affected by the functionality manipulation (F(1,150)=68.7). They were also affected by the aesthetic manipulation (F(1,150)=3.9, p<.05). The interaction effect was not significant (F < 1).

Figure 2 shows the need satisfaction judgments for the four products. A repeated measures analysis of variance revealed significant main effects of functionality (F(1,143)=177.5, p<.001), need level (F(4,572)=59.8, p<.001), the interaction between functionality and aesthetics (F(1,143)=14.2, p<.001), the interaction of functionality and need level (F(4,572)=18.8, p<.001), aesthetics by need level (F(4,572)=292, p<.001) and the three-way interaction of functionality, aesthetics and need level (F(4,572)=154.5, p<.001). On average, products with high aesthetics received more favorable evaluations than products with low aesthetic appeal as the need level increases. An exception is that the high functionality-low aesthetic product is very favorably evaluated on the higher order needs. This unexpected finding may be attributed to the fact that this product was probably not low in aesthetic appeal. The manipulation check rating of 4.5, while lower than the two high aesthetic products (5.3 and 6.2), was considerably higher than the other low aesthetic product (1.9). The effects of the aesthetic and functionality manipulations on the price estimates for the four toothbrushes were analyzed using a repeated measures analysis of variance. This revealed main effects for aesthetics (F(1,145)=40.7, p < .001) and functionality (F(1,145)=59.5), p<.001) but an insignificant interaction. Thus, the highest expected price was for the high aesthetic-high functionality product (mean price = $2.07) and the lowest was for the low aesthetic - low functionality product (mean price = $1.26). Unexpectedly, there was little price difference between the two compromise products. The mean price of the high aesthetic-low functionality product ($1.74) was only slightly greater than for the low aesthetic-high functionality product ($1.69).

DISCUSSION

The research presented in this paper applied an overlooked psychological concept of a need hierarchy theory (e.g., Maslow's

Theory of Motivation), to a neglected area of marketing, product design. This research is significant because it seminally demonstrates the relationship of a need hierarchy to consumer judgments. In the first experiment, consumers judged two electric shavers to be functionally equivalent but the more appealing appearance of one shaver resulted in expectations that it would better satisfy higher order needs than the less attractive shaver. The "European" styling of the fancy shaver clearly appealed to the consumers' self-actualization needs. Further, consumers equated satisfying this higher order need with a substantial price premium. However, the comparison of a high aesthetic - low functionality product-with a low aesthetic - high functionality product in study two did not demonstrate that aesthetics are preferred to functionality. This may be attributed to the relatively small judged difference in aesthetics compared to the large difference in functionality.

Finding a relationship between product aesthetics and premium prices supports the growing attention paid to product design (cf., *Business Week* 1993). It also contrasts with Quelch's (1987) prescriptions for marketing premium products. His list of success factors included "excellent quality, high priced, selectively distributed through the highest quality channels and advertised parsimoniously." Product quality was defined mostly in terms of functional features not found on the lower priced versions of the product. This research suggests that the appearance of the premium product may be as important as its functional features.

Several limitations of this research should be noted. First and importantly, Maslow's view of needs focused on individual differences as well as societal differences. Although individuals provided information about their self-actualization concerns and the relative importance of various needs, these data did not appear to moderate the relationships reported above. This may be a result of the relatively homogenous student population used in this study. It would be interesting to study how individuals varying more in social class (need importance appears to correlate with social class membership) or cultural background evaluate the aesthetic qualities of products and translate these evaluations to expected prices. For example, do higher income consumers more strongly prefer to satisfy higher needs than lower income consumers?

Additional research is needed exploring the relationship between product design and needs. Several issues remain unanswered. For example, what is the appeal of foreign styling? Or, more broadly, what are the characteristics of products that cause them to be considered aesthetically appealing? How do colors, shapes, and other definable dimensions determine aesthetic appeal? Bell, Holbrook and Solomon (1991) present an interesting model exploring the relationships between product features and design evaluations. A paper by Bloch (1995) published after this research was conducted provides the most comprehensive review of product design research issues.

A very intriguing question is to determine what factors cause consumers sometimes to prefer functional products and other times aspire to aesthetically pleasing products? The functional but unattractive Volkswagen Beetle in the 1950's and 1960's was very successful competing against the less reliable but more stylish American automobiles. Did this reflect tough economic times that resulted in a focus on lower order needs or some other factor? Similarly, fashions sometimes change to favor aesthetically unappealing clothes (e.g., "the grunge look") and other times to stress elegance. Understanding the role of needs in these fashion cycles would be valuable.

Lastly, how does Maslow's Need Hierarchy relate to other aspects of marketing? As mentioned in the introduction, it is straightforward to identify advertising that seems to appeal solely to one of the need levels. The research presented in this paper suggests that price evaluations might be higher when the product's advertising focuses on higher order needs. However, this remains to be demonstrated. Similar research could be done for the other two elements of the marketing mix, price and distribution.

In a recent paper, Herrington (1993) uses Maslow's hierarchy to prescribe how marketers can augment their products to better appeal to consumers. For example, he argues that the core product represents the basic physiological need, reliability and on-time product delivery are equated with safety, customer interaction is related to belongingness, innovations with esteem, and developing a supplier-customer partnership represents self-actualization. Although we might quarrel with some of Herrington's assignments, we agree that Maslow's Theory of a Need Hierarchy offers a promising way to look at how consumers evaluate the Total Product.

REFERENCES

Bell, Stephen, Morris Holbrook and Michael Solomon (1991), "Combining Esthetic and Social Value to Explain Preferences for Product Styles with the Incorporation of Personality and Ensemble Effects," *Journal of Social Behavior & Personality*, 6(6) 243-274.

Bloch, Peter H. (1995), "Seeking the Ideal Form: Product Design and Consumer Response," *Journal of Marketing*, 59 (July), 16-29.

Brooker, George (1976), "The Self-Actualizing Socially Conscious Consumer," *Journal of Consumer Research*, 3 (September), 107-112.

Business Week, "Smart Design," April 11, 1988.

Business Week, "California Design: Funk is In," June 15, 1990.

Business Week, "Hot Products: Smart Design is the Common Thread," June 7, 1993, pp. 54-78..

Engel, James, Roger Blackwell and Paul Miniard (1993), *Consumer Behavior*, Seventh Edition. Chicago: Dryden Press.

Herrington, Mike (1993), "What Does the Customer Want?" *Across the Board*, (April), v.30, p. 33.

InfoWorld, "Innovation by Design," June 3, 1991, 57-58.

Kahle, Lynn, Sharon Beatty and Pamela Homer (1986), "Alternative Measurement Approaches to Consumer Values: The List of Values (LOV) and Values and Life Style (VALS), *Journal of Consumer Research*, 13 (December), 405-409.

Kahle, Lynn, David Bousch and Pamela Homer (1988), "Broken Rungs in Abraham's Ladder: Is Maslow's Hierarchy Hierarchical?" in David Schumann, ed. *Proceedings of the Society for Consumer Psychology*.

Kotler, Philip and Alexander Rath (1984), "Design: A Powerful but Neglected Strategic Tool," *Journal of Business Strategy* (Fall), 16-21.

Maslow, Abraham (1954), *Motivation and Personality*, First Edition. New York: Harper & Row.

Maslow, Abraham (1970), *Motivation and Personality*, Second Edition. New York: Harper & Row

Plummer, Joseph (1989), "Changing Values: The New Emphasis on Self-Actualization," *The Futurist* (January-February), 8-13.

Quelch, John ((1987), "Marketing the Premium Product," *Business Horizons* (May-June), 38-45.

Schiffman, Leon and Leslie Kanuk (1994), *Consumer Behavior*, Fifth Edition, Englewood Cliffs, N.J.: Prentice-Hall.

Measuring Perceived Brand Parity

James A. Muncy, Valdosta State University[1]

ABSTRACT

Perceived brand parity relates to the perception among consumers that all major alternatives in a product class are similar. Though high levels of brand parity greatly concerns many marketing professionals, scant empirical research has been published on the topic. The current paper presents the results of a research project which developed a multi-item scale measuring perceived brand parity for consumer nondurable goods and applied the scale to investigate perceived brand parity's impact on cognitive brand loyalty, price sensitivity, and perceived utility of marketplace information. Implications for marketing theory and practice are discussed.

INTRODUCTION

Kottman (1977) argued that product differentiation is the *"sine qua non* of successful marketing" (p. 146). Within a product category, when such differentiation does not exist (i.e., all brands are very similar), brand parity is said to exist. According to Kottman (1977) brand parity can be very problematic to the marketing managers:

> ...the idea of parity is an anathema in marketing. It is antithetical to the notion of differentiation, and product differentiation is regarded as the lifeblood of successful national brand marketing and advertising. (p. 146)

These feelings have been echoed by several leading marketing and advertising practitioners (see, for example, Giges 1988; Kanter 1981; Sloan 1989).

Is this concern justified? Based on intuition it would seem so. Very often the primary goal of a marketing program is to create a customer base that is cognitively brand loyal and insensitive to price competition. However, such a customer base may be difficult to develop in the absence of perceived differences between major brand alternatives. Few consumers would likely say "I am going to be loyal to a specific brand even though all of the major brands in the product category are just alike." Neither does it seem likely that a customer would be willing to pay a higher price for a particular brand when the major alternatives in a product category are all the same. Even developing a preference for a specific brand may be very difficult when all of the brands in the particular category are seen as being alike.

In a similar way, customers appear to be insensitive to marketplace information in circumstances of high brand parity. Muncy (1990) discusses a research study which found a strong relationship between perceived brand differences and information search. He explained these findings by stating that "it is only when the consumer perceives that differences actually do exist that he or she is motivated to find out information about what these differences are" (p. 146). Others have also argued that consumers are also less receptive to advertising when high parity perceptions exist (Giges 1988). If consumers are less receptive to marketing communications when parity perceptions are high, then they may not even give advertisers the opportunity to present information which could

change such parity perceptions. So battling brand parity may be confounded by its own very existence.

Given all of the difficulties created by high parity perceptions, it is not surprising that Allen Rosenshine, the President and CEO of the Omnicom Group (BBDO's parent company) stated that it is the "very purpose of advertising to differentiate brands in the consumer's mind and to minimize brand parity where it does exist" (Giges 1988, p. 68). What is surprising is that very little empirical research has been published on brand parity. Most of the assertions given above on the relationship between brand parity and brand loyalty, price sensitivity, and receptiveness to market information are based on intuition or slight empirical evidence. No scale with demonstrated psychometric properties even exists for measuring brand parity. The small amount of empirical evidence that does exist is based on single item measures of brand parity or simple laboratory manipulations.

The current paper discusses the results of a research project which was developed to address these two concerns. First, a scale measuring brand parity was developed. Second, the scaled was administered to a national sample of consumers to see if it related as expected to measures of brand loyalty, price sensitivity, and perceived utility of marketplace information. The second part of this research was done both to test the effect of brand parity on key consumer behavior variables which interests advertisers and to investigate the construct validity of the measure developed.

WHAT IS PERCEIVED BRAND PARITY?

Before discussing the empirical investigation, it is important to explore the nature of brand parity. For the current study, *perceived brand parity (PARITY)* will be defined as *the overall perception held by the consumer that the differences between the major brand alternatives in a product category are small.* Thus, when consumers perceive the major brand alternatives as being similar, then PARITY is high. Conversely, when consumers perceive the alternatives as being dissimilar, PARITY is low.

PARITY can be seen as the opposite of product differentiation. When a firm is able to successfully differentiate itself in the consumer's mind, then it is diminishing brand parity. However, though brand differentiation is usually used in reference to a specific brand, parity relates to the whole product class (or at least the major alternatives in the product class). Once any major alternative becomes highly differentiated in the consumer's mind, either horizontally or vertically, then brand parity vanishes for the whole product class. The only possible exceptions could be when a brand becomes vertically differentiated by becoming highly inferior in the consumer's mind or when a brand becomes horizontally differentiated in such a way that the consumer no longer sees himself or herself as in the market for this brand. In both of these cases, the differentiated brand is no longer seen by the consumer as being a major brand alternative (for a discussion of the distinction between horizontal and vertical product differentiation, see Beath and Katsoulacos 1991).

It should also be noted that, as defined, brand parity exists as a perception in the consumer's mind and not necessarily as an intrinsic characteristic of a product class. Thus, it is possible that a consumer would perceive no parity for a product category where the brands are basically alike; conversely, a consumer could have high parity perceptions for a product category where the brands are quite dissimilar. Though one would expect that actual product similari-

[1]The author wishes to thank James B. Wilcox and Roy D. Howell of Texas Tech University for their helpful comments at various stages of this research.

ties or differences have a major impact or the degree of perceived brand parity, it is likely that other marketplace factors (such as advertising) and consumer characteristics (such as experience with the product) also influence perceived parity.

VARIABLES RELATED TO PARITY

Numerous consumer and marketplace variables might potentially be related to PARITY. The current study selected three such variables which are of particular interest to adverting and marketing managers. These three are cognitive brand loyalty (LOYALTY), price sensitivity (PRICE), and perceived utility of marketplace information (INFO). Before discussing the specific hypothesized relationship between these variables and PARITY, it is important to define them.

Cognitive Brand Loyalty (LOYALTY)

Definitions of brand loyalty abound. Jacoby and Chestnut (1978) reviewed over 200 studies which used over fifty different definitions of brand loyalty. They concluded that these conceptualizations can be categorized as defining either behavioral brand loyalty, cognitive brand loyalty, or a combination thereof. The current research studied the narrower of these concepts— *cognitive brand loyalty (LOYALTY)* is studied here and it is defined as *a psychological commitment to a particular brand due to some real or imagined superiority attributed to that brand.*

Price Sensitivity (PRICE)

The only variable that has been empirically related to brand parity in any significant way whatsoever is price sensitivity (Brooker, Wheatley and Chie 1986; Lambert 1972; Leavitt 1954; Obermiller and Wheatley 1984; Obermiller and Wheatley 1985; Tull, Boring and Gonsior 1964). All of these studied the conditions under which brand parity impacts *price sensitivity (PRICE)* which, as defined for this study, refers to *the consumers willingness to select a lower priced alternative if one such alternative exists.*

Perceived Utility of Marketplace Information (INFO)

Newman (1977) concluded that consumer information search will continue until the costs of search outweigh the benefits. As indicated above, information search may be impacted by perceived brand parity because the consumer sees the marketplace information as being less useful when all brands are seen as being the same. Thus, the current research studied the *perceived utility of marketplace information (INFO)* which is defined as *the overall perception in the consumer's mind that the information provided in the marketplace is useful for making brand purchasing decisions.*

HYPOTHESES

The current study tested three main hypotheses and made an assumption about a fourth relationship. These relationships are modeled in Figure 1. Each of these hypotheses will now be discussed.

PARITY and LOYALTY (γ_{11})

Jacoby (1971) conducted a three hour group interview with six housewives. He discussed several consumer nondurable products. From this interview, he concluded the following:

...perhaps the strongest mediator of brand loyalty was whether the housewife perceived quality differences to exist across various brands making up that particular product class. That is... the greater the perceived differences in quality across brands, the more individuals felt it was important to differen-

tiate across these brands, and the greater the likelihood of the individual being brand loyal. (p. 28)

Muncy (1990) reports similar findings. These two authors both provide empirical evidence (though *very limited*) that PARITY may be one of the most (if not the most) significant predictor of brand loyalty. More importantly, the intuitive reasons given for expecting brand loyalty to be related to brand parity seems plausible. However, there is clearly a need for a stronger empirical test of this relationship. Thus, the first hypothesis tested in the current study is as follows:

Hypothesis 1: Higher levels of perceived brand parity (PARITY) will result in lower levels of cognitive brand loyalty (LOYALTY).

PARITY and PRICE (γ_{21})

The one variable that has been systematically related to brand parity is price sensitivity (Brooker, et al. 1986; Lambert 1972; Leavitt 1954; Obermiller and Wheatley 1984; Obermiller and Wheatley 1985; Tull, et al. 1964). The overwhelming evidence is that consumers are less price sensitive when they perceive large differences between alternatives than when they perceive such differences to be small. Most researchers believe, and empirical evidence supports, the assertion that consumers will have a greater tendency to use price as a cue for product quality when parity is low than when parity is high. It may also be that consumers see little benefit of paying a higher price when all brands are seen as being basically alike. In either case, the empirical evidence to date supports the following hypothesis:

Hypothesis 2: Higher levels of perceived brand parity (PARITY) will result in higher levels of price sensitivity (PRICE).

PARITY and INFO (γ_{31})

Very little research exists on the impact of brand parity on specific steps in the consumer decision making process. Muncy (1990) discussed a research project where perceived brand differences had a substantial influence on information search. The explanation given was that if consumers see all brands as being similar, then there is little benefit of information search because the search would not provide useful information which would help differentiate the choice set. This is consistent with Newman's (1977) hypothesis that consumers will engage in information search only if the perceived benefits exceed the costs. If parity decreases the perceived benefits of search, less search should occur.

The current research did not study the impact of brand parity on information search *per se*. Rather, it focused on parity's impact on the perceived utility of marketplace information. First, it was not feasible to study information search since this research studied nondurable purchases and very little if any pre-purchase information search typically precedes such purchases (Deshpande, Hoyer and Jeffries 1982; Hoyer 1984; Wells and LoSciuto 1966). Second, though information search may be of more interest in basic consumer research, it seems that the perceived utility of market information may be of more interest to those in marketing. Thus, the current study tested the following specific hypothesis:

Hypothesis 3: Higher levels of perceived brand parity (PARITY) will result in less perceived utility of marketplace information (INFO).

FIGURE 1
Model for Parity Study*

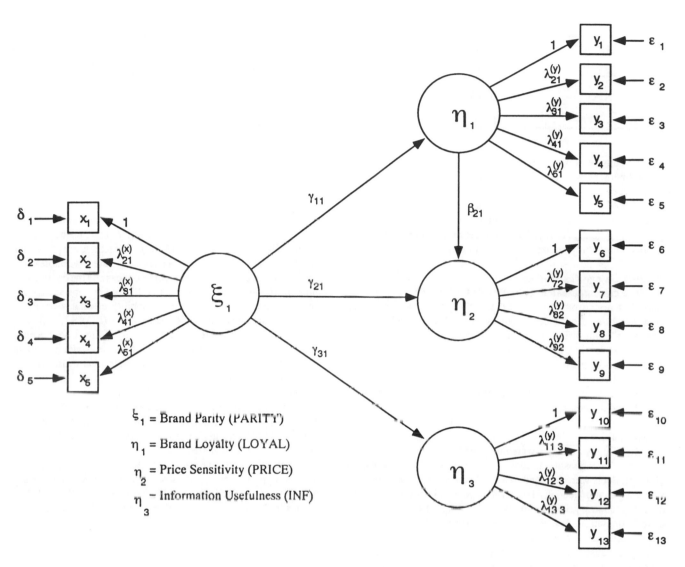

ξ_1 = Brand Parity (PARITY)

η_1 = Brand Loyalty (LOYAL)

η_2 = Price Sensitivity (PRICE)

η_3 = Information Usefulness (INF)

*Consistent with LISREL 7

LOYALTY and PRICE (β_{21})

A fourth relation was assumed though it was not a specific focus of the current study. It was assumed that, as consumers become more cognitively brand loyal, they become less price sensitive. The conceptual link between these two variables is so strong that the first attempt to measure cognitive brand loyalty used a laboratory measure of price sensitivity as an indicant of such commitment (Pessemier 1959). Thus, in the testing of the current hypotheses, it was assumed that LOYALTY would be negatively related to PRICE.

METHODOLOGY

The current study followed the procedure suggested by Churchill (1979) for scale development. Initially, multi-item scales for each construct of interest were developed. The scales were then administered (with appropriate modifications) iteratively to differ-

ent groups of students until they demonstrated adequate inter-item consistency. The four scales were then administered to a national sample of consumers.

Instrument Development

Twenty-nine students enrolled in an undergraduate consumer behavior class at a major southeast university were asked to give statements that described products based on their similarity to other brands. Based on their responses and on previous research (Kanter 1981; Leavitt 1954; Tull, et al. 1964), a set of eight statements were developed to measure PARITY. These statements were given in a questionnaire to 93 students enrolled in an introductory marketing class. Measures of the three other variables of interest in the current study (price sensitivity, cognitive brand loyalty, and perceived utility of marketplace information) were developed in a similar way.

TABLE 1
Coefficient Alpha for All Scales

	Laundry Detergent	Shampoo	Toothpaste	All Data
LOYAL	0.859	0.858	0.866	0.862
PRICE	0.838	0.866	0.858	0.856
INFO	0.701	0.655	0.564	0.644
PARITY	0.905	0.909	0.885	0.900

As suggested by Churchill (1979), an iterative of pretesting and refinement was conducted using various student samples. After three iterations, the result were five item scales for PARITY and LOYALTY and four item scales for INFO and PRICE. All four of the scales demonstrated reliability within the range suggested by Nunnally (1978). The four scales and eighteen items used in the current study are presented in Appendix A.

Product Categories Studied

The current research studied PARITY across a varying set of consumer nondurables. From the initial pretest with students, three nondurable product categories were identified where there were significant differing opinions as to the degree of similarity among brands. The three product categories were laundry detergent, shampoo, and toothpaste. For all of these product categories, there were some respondents who perceived all brands as being similar and there were some respondents who believe there to be large brand differences.

Questionnaire

Three questionnaires were developed—one for each product category. Each questionnaire was identical except that the names of the products were changed. The eighteen statements developed above were embedded in a letter sent to selected consumers asking them to respond, giving them instructions, and thanking them for their participation. Subjects were asked to circle their responses on a five-point scale from SA (strongly agree) to SD (strongly disagree). Because there was a desire to maximize response rate and because the current study simply focused on four key variables, the eighteen statements and only the eighteen statements discussed above were included on the questionnaire. Through doing so, the questionnaire and the solicitation letter could all be printed on the front side of one page (on university stationary). It is believed that this is the reason why the current study obtained a very high response rate (see discussion below).

Sample

The sample consisted of 1,200 heads of households obtained from a large mailing list company (Alvin B. Zeller of New York). The sample was divided into three groups of 400 each with each group receiving a questionnaire pertaining to one of the product categories studied. Two waves were mailed. A surprising 82% response rate was obtained (62% with the first wave and 21% in the second wave). This high response rate was attributed to the shortness of the questionnaire and the ease with which consumers could respond to the survey (see discussion above).

ANALYSIS AND RESULTS

Coefficient α (Cronbach 1951) was computed for each construct and within each product category (see Table 1). These reliability estimates are generally consistent with what was obtained in the pretest except that the reliability estimates for INFO (especially for toothpaste) were slightly lower (ranging from 0.56 to 0.70) and the reliability estimates for PARITY were slightly higher (ranging from 0.86 to 0.91).

The conceptual model presented in Figure 1 was tested through LISREL 7 (Jöreskog and Sörbom 1989). The results are presented in Table 3. The correlations between the latent variables are presented in Table 4. The goodness of fit indices and the completely standardized solutions for the λ_x's and λ_y's are consistent with what one would expect given the reliability estimates obtained through calculating coefficient α. Only $\lambda^y_{5\,1}$ (LOYALTY5) and $\lambda^y_{6\,2}$ (PRICE1) were low (below .65). Though future research may want to reevaluate and possibly reword these two statement, their λ's were not so low that they were likely to significantly impact the overall research findings.

Hypothesis 1 (negative effect of PARITY on LOYALTY) received strong support. The estimates for $\gamma_{1\,1}$ (PARITY $\rightarrow$ LOYALTY) were all negative with absolute magnitude greater than 0.7. This clearly indicates that those who see all brands as being similar have a lower tendency to be cognitively brand loyal.

Hypothesis 2 (positive effect of PARITY on PRICE) received moderate support. Though the absolute correlations between ξ_1 (PARITY) and η_2 (PRICE) were high (ranging from .71 to .77), the estimates for $\gamma_{2\,1}$ (PARITY $\rightarrow$ PRICE) were all between .11 and .21. The reason is clear when one looks at the estimates of $\beta_{2\,1}$ (LOYALTY $\rightarrow$ PRICE), none of which are smaller than .76. Thus, much of the relationship between PARITY and PRICE is accounted for by the strong relationship between PARITY and LOYALTY and the corresponding strong relationship between LOYALTY and PRICE. However, even when these indirect effects are partialed out, there is evidence that PARITY does have a moderate direct influence on PRICE.

Hypothesis 3 (negative effect of PARITY on INFO) received moderate to strong support with $\gamma_{3\,1}$ (PARITY $\rightarrow$ INFO) ranging from -.289 to -.481. Given the lower coefficient α's associated with INFO, it is possible that there was attenuation in the relationship identified and that this relationship would be even stronger if better measures were used.

DISCUSSION AND FUTURE RESEARCH

Is parity "an anathema in marketing?" From the results of the current research, it could certainly be concluded that it is. The consumer with high parity perceptions appears to be less brand loyal, more price sensitive, and less receptive to marketplace information. Thus, it is not surprising that so many in marketing are saying that advertisers must work hard to battle brand parity (Giges 1988; Kanter 1981; Sloan 1989).

Parity should also be of interest to consumer researchers. It is a fairly simple construct to conceptualize and operationalize but its

TABLE 2
Results from Structural Equations Analysis

	Laundry Detergent	Shampoo	Toothpaste	Full Sample
Sample Size	331	327	327	985
Goodness of Fit Index	0.890	0.874	0.900	0.920
Adjusted Goodness of Fit Index	0.857	0.836	0.869	0.896
Root Mean Square Residual	0.072	0.074	0.068	0.061
Completely Standardized Solution				
$\lambda^x_{1\,1}$ (PARITY1)	0.855	0.852	0.848	0.852
$\lambda^x_{2\,1}$ (PARITY2)	0.688	0.726	0.735	0.719
$\lambda^x_{3\,1}$ (PARITY3)	0.677	0.693	0.658	0.675
$\lambda^x_{4\,1}$ (PARITY4)	0.624	0.619	0.670	0.639
$\lambda^x_{5\,1}$ (PARITY5)	0.872	0.817	0.862	0.851
$\lambda^y_{1\,1}$ (LOYALTY1)	0.688	0.736	0.717	0.715
$\lambda^y_{2\,1}$ (LOYALTY2)	0.825	0.847	0.827	0.834
$\lambda^y_{3\,1}$ (LOYALTY3)	0.620	0.674	0.678	0.656
$\lambda^y_{4\,1}$ (LOYALTY4)	0.894	0.908	0.924	0.909
$\lambda^y_{5\,1}$ (LOYALTY5)	0.434	0.474	0.439	0.454
$\lambda^y_{6\,1}$ (PRICE1)	0.606	0.449	0.352	0.462
$\lambda^y_{7\,1}$ (PRICE2)	0.756	0.741	0.603	0.695
$\lambda^y_{8\,1}$ (PRICE3)	0.688	0.672	0.695	0.694
$\lambda^y_{9\,1}$ (PRICE4)	0.776	0.811	0.776	0.789
$\lambda^y_{10\,1}$ (INF1)	0.757	0.757	0.735	0.750
$\lambda^y_{11\,1}$ (INF2)	0.727	0.718	0.660	0.703
$\lambda^y_{12\,1}$ (INF3)	0.888	0.898	0.905	0.897
$\lambda^y_{13\,1}$ (INF4)	0.903	0.896	0.827	0.876
$\gamma_{1\,1}$ (PARITY → LOYALTY)	-0.720	-0.728	-0.697	-0.704
$\gamma_{2\,1}$ (PARITY → PRICE)	0.209	0.187	0.109	0.162
$\gamma_{3\,1}$ (PARITY → INFO)	-0.289	-0.431	-0.481	-0.399
$\beta_{2\,1}$ (LOYALTY → PRICE)	-0.757	-0.800	-0.862	-0.813

impact on consumer decision making may be quite dramatic. The current research provided a measure which can be used in surveys to measure brand parity. It also identified variables that relate to brand parity. However, it did not even begin to explore what may cause brand parity perceptions. To what extent is brand parity related to actual differences between products and to what extent is it related to marketing variables (such as advertising) or consumer variables (such as familiarity with product). These are all interesting questions that would have implications for both consumer behavior theory and marketing practice.

The current paper presented one model of parity's effect on certain key consumer behavior constructs. The current model could be debated. Thought the current empirical findings seemed to indicate that it is a viable model, other models could also be developed and tested. Though this is an adequate model, it does not necessarily mean that it is the best model. Further research is needed to address this question.

Also, the current study related brand parity to a limited set of variables. Other variables should also be investigated. For example, how would parity perceptions impact attitude formation or the choice of a decision heuristic or how might perceived brand parity relate to brand equity? These also deserve future research.

REFERENCES

Beath, John and Yannis Katsoulacos (1991), *The Economic Theory of Product Differentiation*, Cambridge: Cambridge University Press.

Brooker, George, John J. Wheatley and John S. Y. Chie (1986), "The Effects of Sampling and Information on Brand Choice when Beliefs in Quality Differences are Ambiguous", *Advances in Consumer Research*, 13 , 272-276.

Churchill, Gilbert A. (1979), "A Paradigm for Developing Better Measures of Marketing Constructs", *Journal of Marketing Research*, 16 (February), 64-73.

Cronbach, Lee J. (1951), "Coefficient Alpha and the Internal Structure of Tests", *Psychometrica*, 16 (September), 297-334.

Day, George S. (1969), "A Two-Dimensional Concept of Brand Loyalty", *Journal of Advertising Research*, 9 (June), 29-35.

Despande, Rohit, Wayne D. Hoyer and Scot Jeffries (1982), "Low Involvement Decision Making: The Importance of Choice Tactics", in *Marketing Theory: Philosophy of Science Perspectives*, Ronald P. Bush and Shelby D. Hunt (ed), American Marketing Association: Chicago.

Giges, Nancy (1988), "World's Product Parity Perception High", *Advertising Age*, 59 (June 20), 66-68.

Handelsman, Moshe (1987), "Varied Purchase Behaviour as a Result of Purchase History and Perceived Brand Similarity", *Journal of the Marketing Research Society*, 29 , 293-315.

Howard, John A. and Jagdish N. Sheth (1968), *The Theory of Buyer Behavior*, John Wiley and Sons: New York.

Hoyer, Wayne D. (1984), "An Examination of Consumer Decision Making for a Common Repeat Purchase Product", *Journal of Consumer Research*, 11 , 822-829.

TABLE 3
Correlation Matrix of Latent Variables

Laundry Detergent

	LOYAL	PRICE	INFO	PARITY
LOYAL	1.000	-0.907	0.208	-0.720
PRICE	-0.907	1.000	-0.218	0.754
INFO	0.208	-0.218	1.000	-0.289
PARITY	-0.720	0.754	-0.289	1.000

Shampoo

	LOYAL	PRICE	INFO	PARITY
LOYAL	1.000	-0.936	0.314	-0.728
PRICE	-0.936	1.000	-0.332	0.770
INFO	0.314	-0.332	1.000	-0.431
PARITY	-0.728	0.770	-0.431	1.000

Toothpaste

	LOYAL	PRICE	INFO	PARITY
LOYAL	1.000	-0.937	0.336	-0.697
PRICE	-0.937	1.000	-0.341	0.709
INFO	0.336	-0.341	1.000	-0.481
PARITY	-0.697	0.709	-0.481	1.000

All Data Combined

	LOYAL	PRICE	INFO	PARITY
LOYAL	1.000	-0.927	0.281	-0.704
PRICE	-0.927	1.000	-0.293	0.734
INFO	0.281	-0.293	1.000	-0.399
PARITY	-0.704	0.734	-0.399	1.000

Jacoby, Jacob (1971), "A Model of Multi-Brand Loyalty", *Journal of Advertising Research*, 11 (June), 25-31.

Jacoby, Jacob and David B. Kyner (1972), "Brand Loyalty Versus Repeat Purchase Behavior", *Journal of Marketing Research*, 10, 1-9.

Jacoby, Jacob and Robert W. Chestnut (1978), *Brand Loyalty: Measurement and Management*, John Wiley and Sons: New York.

Jarvis, Lance P. and James B. Wilcox (1977), "True Vendor Loyalty or Simple Repeat Purchase Behavior", *Industrial Marketing Management*, 6, 9-14.

Jöreskog, Karl and Dag Sörbom (1989), *LISREL 7 User's Reference Guide*, Scientific Software, Inc.: Mooresville, IN.

Kanter, Donald L. (1981), "It Could Be: Ad Trends Flowing From Europe to U.S.", *Advertising Age*, 52 (February 9), 49-52.

Keller, Maryann (1993), "Choking On Complexity," *Automotive Industries*, 173 (April), 13-13.

Kottman, E. John (1977), "Promoting the Parity Product", *Journal of Consumer Affairs*, 11 (Summer), 145-150.

Lambert, Zarrel V. (1972), "Price and Choice Behavior", *Journal of Marketing Research*, 9 (February), 35-40.

Leavitt, Harold J. (1954), "A Note on Some Experimental Findings About the Meaning of Price", *Journal of Business*, 27 (July), 205-210.

Lefkoff, Roxanne and Charlotte H. Mason (1990), "The Role of Tangible and Intangible Attributes in Similarity and Preference Judgements", *Advances in Consumer Research*, 17, 135-143.

Miniard, Paul W., Deepak Sirdeshmukh and Daniel E. Innis (1992), "Peripheral Persuasion and Brand Choice," *Journal of Consumer Research*, 19 (September), 226-239.

Muncy, James A. (1990), "Involvement and Perceived Brand Similarities/Differences: The Need for Process Oriented Models", *Advances in Consumer Research*, 17, 144-148.

Newman, Joseph W. (1977), "Consumer External Search: Amount and Determinants", in *Consumer and Industrial Buying Behavior*, Arch G. Woodside, Jagdish N. Sheth and Peter D. Bennett (ed), North-Holand Publishing Co.: New York.

Nunnally, Jum C. (1978), *Psychometric Theory*, McGraw-Hill: New York.

Obermiller, Carl and John J. Wheatley (1984), "Price Effects on Choice and Perceptions Under Varying Conditions of Experience, Information, and Beliefs in Quality Differences", *Advances in Consumer Research*, 11, 453-458.

Obermiller, Carl and John J. Wheatley (1985), "Beliefs in Quality Differences and Brand Choice", *Advances in Consumer Research*, 12, 75-78.

Pessemier, Edgar A. (1959), "A New Way to Determine Buying Decisions", *Journal of Marketing*, 24 (January).

APPENDIX 1
Measures Used In Study (Laundry Detergent)*

Five Item Scale Measuring Perceived Brand Parity (PARITY)

PARITY1   I can't think of many differences between the major brands of laundry detergent.
PARITY2   To me, there are big differences between the various brands of laundry detergent.**
PARITY3   The only difference between the major brands of laundry detergent is the price.
PARITY4   Laundry detergent is laundry detergent; most brands are basically the same.
PARITY5   All major brands of laundry detergent are basically alike.

Five Item Scale Measuring Cognitive Brand Loyalty (LOYAL)

LOYAL1   If I went to the store and they were out of my favorite brand of laundry detergent, I would simply purchase another brand.**
LOYAL2   Only under extreme circumstances would I consider purchasing a brand of laundry detergent different from the one I usually buy.
LOYAL3   There are other brands of laundry detergent which are just as good as the one I usually purchase.**
LOYAL4   To me, the brand of laundry detergent I usually purchase is clearly the best brand on the market.
LOYAL5   If the store was out of my favorite brand of laundry detergent, I would go somewhere else or wait until later to buy some.

Four Item Scale Measuring Price Sensitivity (PRICE)

PRICE1   I would be willing to pay more to buy my regular brand of laundry detergent rather than buy another brand.**
PRICE2   If I had a coupon for a brand of laundry detergent other than the one I usually purchase, I would probably use it.
PRICE3   I generally buy the least expensive brand of laundry detergent I can find.
PRICE4   If a brand of laundry detergent other than the one I usually purchase was on sale, I would probably buy it.

Four Item Scale Measuring Perceived Usefulness of Market Information (INFO)

INF1   It can be helpful to read the information on a box of laundry detergent.
INF2   I cannot get any useful information from watching a television advertisement about laundry detergent.**
INF3   Magazine advertisements for laundry detergent contain useful information which can be helpful in identifying the best brand.
INF4   Information about the various brands of laundry detergent is both available and useful.

* Note: All items measured on a five point scale from SD (strongly disagree) to SA (strongly agree)
** Reverse Scored

Sloan, Pat (1989), "Battling Product, Ad Parity: Frost Urges Daring in Creative, Agency Structure", *Advertising Age*, 60 (August 28), 47.

Tull, D. S., R. A. Boring and M. H. Gonsior (1964), "A Note on the Relationship of Price and Imputed Quality", *Journal of Business*, 37 (April), .

Wells, William and Leonard A. LoSciuto (1966), "Direct Observation of Purchasing Behavior", *Journal of Marketing Research*, 3 (August), 227-233.

The Health Care Consumption Patterns of Asian Immigrants: Grounded Theory Implications for Consumer Acculturation Theory

H. Rika Houston, University of California, Irvine
Alladi Venkatesh, University of California, Irvine

ABSTRACT

Since cultural beliefs about the body, health, illness, and social norms do not suddenly disappear when immigrants arrive in a new country or culture, understanding such beliefs is important for anyone attempting to serve their health care needs. The authors of this paper use grounded theory to investigate the health care consumption patterns of recent Asian and Pacific Islander immigrants to the United States. Utilizing participant observation, focus groups, and interdisciplinary secondary data, the authors explore the sociocultural dimensions of health care consumption among such immigrants before and after migration to the United States. Unique consumption patterns are revealed which offer conceptual departures from traditional consumer acculturation theory and its notions of a linear progression towards Anglo-conformity. Recommendations are made for future research on consumer acculturation, health care consumption, ethnicity as a construct in consumer research, and methodological pluralism in cross-cultural consumer research.

I. INTRODUCTION

In the decade between 1980 and 1990, the Asian and Pacific Islander population in the United States experienced a dramatic increase of 107.8%, compared to a total U.S. population increase of only 9.8% (*U.S. Department of Commerce, 1983, 1992*). In spite of this dramatic increase, virtually no scholarly research in marketing or consumer behavior has been conducted on understanding or targeting this important consumer group. This neglect is further accentuated when one considers the burgeoning percentage of immigrants who comprise an increasing proportion of the ethnic groups in this population. For instance, it includes, but is not limited to ethnic groups such as the Chinese, Filipino, Japanese, Asian Indian, Korean, Vietnamese, etc.(*U.S. Department of Commerce, 1992*).

Although this rich cultural and ethnic diversity presents challenges to any group who is attempting to introduce new ideas, products, or practices to these emerging consumers, some groups encounter extraordinary challenges. In particular, the multitude of marketers who deliver health care services to such consumers are among those who face these challenges on a daily basis. In order to design and implement culturally-appropriate health care services, these change agents are charged with the often overwhelming agenda of understanding such emerging consumers when information about their health care consumption patterns is either sparse, superficial, or fragmented. For instance, existing health-related statistics on Asians and Pacific Islanders in the United States disclose significant problems in a number of health-related areas. Lack of awareness in these communities is one of the causes for such reported problems as higher cervical cancer rates, higher hepatitis B rates, and dramatic increases in reported AIDS/HIV cases (*Lin-Fu, 1988; Mo, 1992; Easterlin, 1988*). However, cultural barriers have been shown to contribute much more significantly to the ineffective diffusion of health promotion and health care delivery programs (*Lin-Fu, 1988; Mo, 1992; Easterlin, 1988*).

The specific objective of this study is to explore the sociocultural dimensions of health care consumption among recent Asian and Pacific Islander immigrants in the United States. These sociocultural dimensions are investigated within the context of the consumer acculturation process. Accordingly, this study explores the consumption patterns of such immigrants as they adapt to the cultural framework of the U.S. health care delivery system. The basic research questions that will be investigated are as follows:

1) What cultural influences exist in the health care consumption patterns of Asian immigrant consumers?

2) What indigenous health beliefs are still practiced by Asian immigrants after migration to the U.S.? When and why are they practiced?

3) How do Asian immigrant consumers integrate indigenous health beliefs and practices with mainstream health practices and services?

4) What lessons can consumer researchers learn from the study of marginal populations such as recent Asian immigrants?

II. RESEARCH METHODOLOGY

This study utilizes a grounded theory approach of investigation. This type of approach involves a systematic set of procedures to develop an inductively-derived grounded theory about a phenomenon. The research findings constitute a theoretical formulation of the reality under investigation, rather than consisting of a set of numbers or a group of loosely related themes. The purpose of the grounded theory method is to build theory that is faithful to and illuminates the area under study. As a result, the researcher does not begin with a theory, then proceed to prove it. Instead, the researcher begins with an area of study. In grounded theory, the intent is to explain phenomena in light of the theoretical framework that evolves during the research itself, not to be constrained by theory that has already been developed (*Strauss and Corbin, 1990*).

During the months of July 1993 through February 1994, extensive field work was conducted in cooperation with two leading community-based organizations in southern California. The first organization is a leader in providing culturally and linguistically appropriate primary health care services and health prevention programs to immigrants in the Cambodian, Chinese, Filipino, Japanese, Korean, Laotian, Samoan, Tongan, Thai, and Vietnamese communities. The second organization is a leader in serving the needs of the Southeast Asian immigrant and refugee community in southern California.

The source documents for this study consisted of field notes gathered during the eight months of participant observation conducted from July 1993 through February 1994, interview transcripts from in-depth interviews conducted in the field when possible, translated interview transcripts from a focus group of Vietnamese refugees/immigrants, and relevant interdisciplinary data gathered during the course of the field work and during concurrent secondary research efforts. In order to maintain confidentiality, the real names of informants and participants have not been used.

III. RESEARCH FINDINGS

Informants and participants revealed three major categories of culturally-based or culturally-different health care consumption patterns during the course of the field work. Cultural health beliefs,

418
Advances in Consumer Research
Volume 23, © 1996

FIGURE 1
The Health Care Consumption Patterns of Asian Immigrants

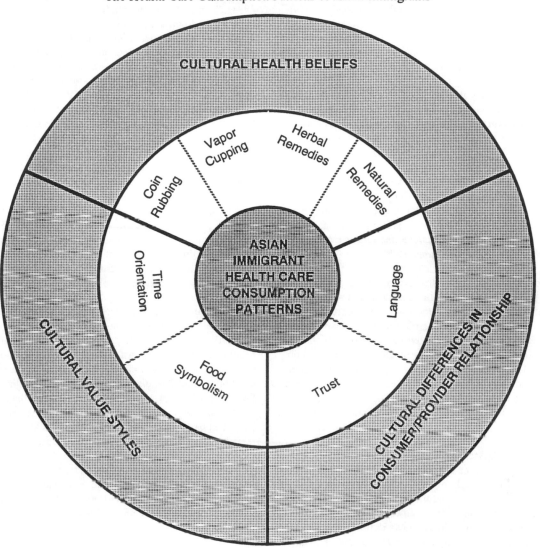

cultural value systems, and cultural differences in the consumer/ provider relationship were all revealed as critical factors in their consumption experiences (*see Figure 1*).

1. Cultural Health Beliefs

Indigenous or native health beliefs, since they are often significant in the health care consumption experiences of many Asian immigrants, can provide tremendous insights into understanding why and how alternative approaches are still practiced after migration to a new country of residence. Informants and participants in the Vietnamese refugee community discussed the use of indigenous health beliefs for various illnesses and ailments, as well as for the ongoing maintenance of good health.

The cultural health beliefs of vapor cupping (*giac hoi*) and coin rubbing (*cao gio*) arose numerous times during a focus group discussion of cultural health beliefs in the Vietnamese refugee community. Thi Cuc, A Vietnamese refugee participant in her late 40s, discussed the use of vapor cupping to "suck out the poisonous air." As a health practice, vapor cupping was deemed more effective than prescription medicine for ailments such as headaches.

...you take a glass tube, put a burning piece of paper in it, and put the cup on the skin. When the skin swells up, it sucks out the poisonous air. In Vietnam, it is called vapor cupping...when we have a headache, we drink medicine but it has no effect. Cupping will help...it is very good. *Vietnamese Immigrant Community, Focus Group Interview, February 1994.*

Participants also discussed the use of coin rubbing (*cao gio*) as a cultural health belief still in practice. This indigenous health practice involves rubbing the skin with a coin to alleviate common symptoms of illness. The back, neck, head, shoulders, and chest are common sites of application (*Yeatman and Dang, 1980*). Nguyen, a Vietnamese informant in his late 40s, agreed that the use of coin rubbing was still prevalent among Vietnamese in the United States.

Headaches need coin rubbing. If we are sick, we drink medicine and we don't get over the sickness. Without coin rubbing, we have the feeling that we are still sick. Even drinking Tylenol again and again the sickness isn't gone. The next day, I had to use coin rubbing then it was gone. *Vietnamese Immigrant Community, Focus Group Interview, February 1994.*

In addition to alternative health practices such as vapor cupping and coin rubbing, participants also discussed the use of alternative health remedies, both of an herbal and non-herbal origin. Tu, a Vietnamese woman in her early 40s, discussed the use of certain herbs to steam out poisonous sweat from a person's body. Several participants described the consumption of urine to maintain or regain strength, especially after childbirth.

In Vietnam, there are all sorts of herbs...mint leaves, lemon grass, lemon tree leaves. We boil a pot of water then put in some salt. We boil the water very carefully, let all of the steam out, and wipe up the poisonous sweat. *Vietnamese Immigrant Community, Focus Group Interview, February 1994.*

(After childbirth) the mother-in-law went and asked for urine from small children...small boys. They put hot pepper in the urine and made their daughter-in-law drink it. It is really good. Urine with saffron in it. Three months later, the daughter was really in good health. *Vietnamese Immigrant Community, Focus Group Interview, February 1994.*

While the consumption of urine, regardless of what spices are used to disguise its apparently bitter taste, may not seem appealing or acceptable to the average American health care provider or consumer who does not practice traditional Vietnamese health beliefs, these comments reveal an obvious trust in the reliability and value of doing so for the purposes of gaining or maintaining a healthy physical condition. From the Vietnamese immigrant or refugee perspective, therefore, this alternative belief system is viewed as being more valid or at least as valid as opposing medical remedies which may be offered by the U.S. biomedical health care system.

2. Cultural Value Systems

Cultural values can be viewed as emotionally-charged priorities which direct the people of any certain culture to selectively attend to some goals while subordinating other ones (*Terpstra and David, 1991*). Such value systems can consist of such concepts as optimism, frugality, and attitudes toward time, change, work, wealth, and achievement (*Terpstra and David, 1991*). They are often rooted in underlying assumptions about power, rank, and often religion (*Terpstra and David, 1991*). During the course of this study, two primary cultural values were revealed by participants. In particular, participants displayed differences in time orientation and food symbolism which could present challenges to the traditional health care delivery system in the United States.

Time Orientation. On a variety of occasions during the course of field work, informants expressed their frustrations in coping with inflexible scheduling within the U.S. health care delivery system. One informant, a Tongan health care professional in her late 20s, expressed great frustration when she attempted to schedule a mobile health outstation on adolescent pregnancy prevention in her community. While such health education programs are implemented routinely with few complications in the mainstream community, trying to schedule them in the Tongan community involves a thorough understanding of the Tongan concept of time.

In the next week or so, she anticipated conducting an outstation in the Tongan community. She did not, however, have a date, place, or time. She was unnecessarily apologetic about this lack of details and expressed her frustration on my behalf that "this is how Tongans live...we don't plan ahead." *Tongan Immigrant Community, Field Notes, August 1993.*

Existing literature strongly supports the existence of this cultural difference in time orientation (*Hall, 1959, 1966, 1976, 1983; Chung, 1992*). People from low context cultures, such as those in the dominant culture of the United States, tend to have a monochronic time orientation (*Hall, 1959*). This orientation towards time includes a preference for controlling time through schedules, evaluating outcomes according to efficiency of time, and attaching a sense of urgency to whatever singular task one is doing at the time (*Hall, 1959, 1966, 1976, 1983; Chung, 1992*).

In direct contrast, as the results of this exploratory study confirm, people from high context cultures such as the majority of Asian and Pacific Islander cultures, tend to have a polychronic orientation towards time. This orientation towards time includes believing that time is a natural cycle that cannot be controlled, evaluating outcomes according to their ability to respect the interpersonal relationships involved, and attaching importance to the long-term process rather than immediate results (*Hall, 1959, 1966, 1976, 1983; Chung, 1992*). With such a sharp contrast in the monochronic time orientation of health care providers and the polychronic time orientation of Asian immigrant health care consumers, it is no wonder that frustration, miscommunication, and low utilization of services often results.

Food Symbolism. During the course of field work, food as an aspect of culture was observed and discussed as an important variable in the health care consumption experience of informants and participants. Community health outstations, regardless of their health care focus, utilized food as a subtle attraction factor and sometimes blatant promotional incentive. Maria, a Filipino informant in her mid 20s, discussed how food symbolized love in the Filipino community. Filipino senior citizens, she conveyed, are somewhat obsessed with the idea of feeding everyone else. Food is a constant part of daily life and it symbolizes love. Therefore, the rejection of it is considered as a personal insult.

We discuss the events of the day and laugh about being "force-fed" by the seniors. Food, she comments, is love in Asian cultures...they all want you to weigh 200 pounds. If you don't you are always too skinny. *Filipino Immigrant Community, Field Notes, August 1993.*

At one mobile health outstation for hypertension screening, food as was used as an incentive to attract target consumers to the private home where the outstation was conducted.

The food is set up on the table...a rich assortment of pork, beef, noodles, salads, and rice provide vivid pictures of dietary concerns...a strange dichotomy to observe the hypertension screening equipment on one table and a roasted pig (*a native delicacy*) on the next table. *Filipino Immigrant Community, Field Notes, August 1993.*

According to Hartog and Hartog (*1983*), food has great symbolic importance. While the symbolic nature of food exists in all cultures to some extent, however, the specific symbolism in each culture or ethnic group within can vary substantially. As these data suggest, health care providers should pay considerable attention to the specific nature of the role food symbolism plays in the both the direct delivery of health care services, as well as the indirect aspects of health care delivery such as the effectiveness of promotion and outreach. Furthermore, food symbolism may have considerable impact on important issues such as compliance with recommended medical treatment and even confidence in the competence of health care providers (*Hartog and Hartog, 1983*).

3. Cultural Differences in the Consumer/Provider Relationship

Cultural differences in the consumer/provider relationship encompass all the culturally-based nuances in the relationship between a health care consumer and a health care provider. In addition to the critical issue of rapport or trust this key relationship may require, cultural differences also address the complexities of the communication process that takes place between a health care consumer and provider.

Trust. During the participant observation phase of this study, informants and participants repeatedly emphasized the need to establish a high level of trust with potential consumers before an effective consumer/provider relationship could be established. Gabriella, a Filipino informant in her late 30s, discussed the difficulty that mainstream health care providers encountered when attempting outreach to ethnic consumers, especially Asian immigrant ones. She said such health care providers were strangers to the community and they were not trusted.

Sala, a Tongan informant and health care provider in her early 30s, described the ease at which she could access consumers in the Tongan community. Everyone already knew her through long-term relationships she had established with members of her church. These church-based relationships were particularly important because the church was and is the center of almost all social activities in the Tongan immigrant community.

The evidence in this study supports this cultural difference in commitment or trust. Informants confirmed that health care providers could not make any progress toward attracting or gaining access to the targeted immigrant communities until they had invested a considerable amount of time and effort in establishing relationships and developing trust.

Language. During the course of the field work, informants and participants frequently expressed concerns for the language barriers they encountered as immigrant consumers in the U.S. health care delivery system. They often viewed the communication process as problematic and as a strong hindrance towards establishing the high level of trust required in the health care consumer/provider relationship. Although interpreters were often utilized to assist with this process, their involvement rarely resolved the communication difficulties.

While aspects of verbal communication and translation alone are overwhelming, few things can test the boundaries of the health care consumer/provider relationship more than the non-verbal communication process. At a permanent clinic site, a nurse was observed in an interaction with a patient. The nurse assumed that the consumer simply did not understand the verbal instructions, when in fact, the nurse was misreading the non-verbal message from the patient.

She (*the Tongan immigrant consumer*) seemed to be attempting to explain that something was wrong. The (*Anglo American*) nurse shook her head and insisted that she had offered the correct course of action. The woman (*consumer*) did not respond. She only looked down at the ground and became silent. Her cues of silence were being misunderstood and ignored by the nurse. Finally, in frustration, the nurse went to find the Tongan (*bilingual, bicultural*) staff person...*Tongan Immigrant Community, Field Notes, July 1993.*

The role of non-verbal communication in high context cultures is an important one. Hall (*1959*) provides excellent, in-depth insights into the nature of "the silent language" of non-verbal communication. In the communication process, significant meaning is attached through non-verbal elements such as phrasing, tone of voice, gestures, posture, social status, history, and social setting (*Hall, 1959; Chung, 1992*). During the course of the field work, informants and participants strongly emphasized the communication process between the health care consumer and the health care provider. It required an understanding of non-verbal communication cues and underlying, alternative cultural values which far exceeded the boundaries of mere bilingual interpretation.

IV. DISCUSSION AND IMPLICATIONS

While prevailing stereotypes may suggest otherwise, the extreme diversity of the Asian and Pacific Islander immigrant population in the United States cannot be overemphasized. These emerging immigrants come from many different countries and each country has its own language(s), culture(s), and experiences. They differ in terms of the historical background in their native countries and in the United States, the number of years of residence in the United States, English language skills, level of urban experience, socioeconomic status, educational achievement, and religious affiliation (*Ross-Sheriff, 1992; Nah, 1993*). In addition, the speed and ease at which they adapt to their new home in the United States varies according to their place of origin, pre-migration occupation and education, traditional values, and socialization experience (*Kessler-Harris and Yans-McLaughlin, 1978*). Without a doubt this complex picture of migration and adaptation creates an emerging population of dynamic, unpredictable American consumers that are hard to understand and even harder to target.

On the topic of health care consumption alone, the challenges seem endless and overwhelming. Recent research on the health status and challenges of Asian and Pacific Islander ethnic groups in the United States, while scarce and inadequate, has established such significant factors as low utilization of health care services, high rates of emergency room usage, lack of prenatal care, and a disproportionately high incidence of disease and socially deviant conditions (*Zane, et.al., 1994; U.S. Commission on Civil Rights, February 1992*). As stated earlier, lack of awareness among Asian and Pacific Islander immigrant consumers of health care services is only one of the causes for such pervasive and continuing problems. In actuality, cultural barriers have been shown to contribute more significantly to the ineffective diffusion of health promotion and health care delivery programs which can help to alleviate or eliminate this disproportionate share of health challenges (*Lin-Fu, 1988; Mo, 1992; Easterlin, 1988*).

Since cultural beliefs about the body, health, illness, and social norms do not suddenly disappear when immigrants arrive in the United States; they can and do create problems in communication, rapport, behavior, and compliance (*Hartog and Hartog, 1983*). Indeed, cultural factors have been shown to influence the way individuals define and evaluate their health problems, seek help for their problems, present their problems to the physician, and respond to treatment (*Zane, et. al., 1994*). It is only through a greatly increased awareness and understanding of these cultural beliefs and differences that health care service providers, as marketers and change agents, can begin the daunting task of affecting these emerging populations in a constructive and effective manner.

The findings of this exploratory investigation have provided important insights into the existence and nature of the role of culture in the health care consumption patterns of recent Asian immigrant consumers. Viewed within the critical context of the consumer acculturation process, these findings point to timely issues regarding the study of consumer subcultures and the consumer acculturation theory which encompasses it. Traditionally, consumer acculturation theory has embraced a linear progression of assimilation by which immigrants change their behavior from that of their culture of origin to that of their culture of residence (*Gordon, 1964; Wallendorf and Reilly, 1983*). Based on research about Europeans who migrated more or less voluntarily to the United States, one of its underlying assumptions is the persistent, overwhelming desire of immigrants to fully assimilate with the dominant, Anglo American culture, especially when such immigrants are members of racially or ethnically subordinate groups (*Gordon, 1964; Feagin and Feagin, 1993*). This assumption is manifested in the popular notion of the American "melting pot" which fosters the idealistic image of diverse racial and ethnic groups blending into a new "American blend" through a mutual adaptation process (*Penaloza, 1994; Venkatesh, 1995*). In reality, however, this notion is more accurately represented by a socialization process of progressive Anglo-conformity by immigrants rather than mutual adaptation among all groups (*Feagin and Feagin, 1993*). Within this challenging context, the idealistic image of the American "melting pot" instead becomes the more realistic one of the American "tossed salad" or "boiling cauldron" (*Venkatesh, 1995*).

The findings of this study confirm the previous conclusions of Wallendorf and Reilly (*1983*), Penaloza (*1994*), and Venkatesh (*1995*). In particular, they draw special attention to the need to expand traditional consumer acculturation theory to reflect unique patterns of consumption that challenge traditional notions of Anglo-conformity. The Asian and Pacific Islander immigrant consumers observed and interviewed in this particular study demonstrated hybrid patterns of health care consumption. These immigrant consumers adapted certain aspects of the mainstream health care system such as the use of over-the-counter medication. However, these same consumers simultaneously maintained many of the cultural health beliefs of their cultures of origin such as coin rubbing, vapor cupping, and herbal remedies for ailments. In spite of the pervasive yet seemingly transparent demands of the monocultural, mainstream health care delivery system, many of the informants and participants displayed ongoing resistance to mainstream health care system requirements such as appointment scheduling, English-language competence, and conformance to the biomedical model of health care itself. Instead, they chose to maintain traditional cultural values concerning time orientation, language, and health practices.

These findings are important ones which present important implications for consumer acculturation theory. The traditional view of acculturation forces immigrant consumption patterns into a process of linear conformity whereby the adoption of consumption patterns belonging to the culture of residence require the gradual surrender of those belonging to the culture of origin. These unique, hybrid patterns of consumption propose a conceptual departure from this process. As revealed by the findings of this study, a linear progression clearly does not take place. In many instances, these immigrant consumers intentionally retain the cultural health beliefs, practices, and expectations of their cultures of origin. In other instances, they adopt new ones learned in their cultures of residence. In a unique way, however, these immigrant consumers often devise hybrid patterns of consumption which are creative reactions to the cultural and social pressures generated by life in a new country. Within this complex social reality, therefore, they hold fast to cultural health beliefs and practices from their original countries, while integrating only those new practices which offer convenience or comfort without threatening the integrity of their cultural traditions.

V. FUTURE RESEARCH

The findings of this study suggest several avenues for future research. Specifically, they suggest the need for future research

which expands consumer acculturation theory, investigates new patterns of consumption in a health care context, further develops ethnicity as a construct in consumer research, and approaches consumer research in a more methodologically pluralistic manner.

Consumer Acculturation Theory. As already mentioned above, the findings of this study suggest the need to expand consumer acculturation theory to appropriately reflect and understand new patterns of consumption among recent immigrants. Future research should further explore the complex, hybrid process of acculturation observed in this study and challenge traditional notions of Anglo-conformity. It should also investigate how and why the acculturation process differs for different groups of immigrant consumers. Finally, it should begin the difficult, but intriguing process of understanding the impact such notions have for marketers who pursue consumers in the ever-changing cultural landscape of the American market place.

Health Care Consumption. In the area of health care consumer research, the results of this study expand existing health care consumption theory to demonstrate how culture influences the health care consumption experiences of immigrant consumers and other marginal populations. Previous theories on health care consumption confirm the role of modifying factors such as age, race, ethnicity, social class, and reference groups in the health care consumption patterns of consumers (*Dawson, 1989; Burns, 1992; Neergaard, 1994*). However, they do not directly or specifically address the influence of culture. They also fail to address the health care consumption patterns of immigrant consumers.

The results of this study also disclose the existence of pluralistic patterns of health care consumption which integrate the traditional, indigenous health beliefs of immigrant consumers with those of the mainstream health care system. Asian immigrant consumers observed and interviewed often practiced traditional healing methods such as coin rubbing and herbal remedies in conjunction with "Western" healing methods prescribed by an American doctor. For instance, some participants discussed the use of coin rubbing for headaches while concurrently using "Western" over-the-counter medication such as Tylenol for the same ailment.

Ethnicity as a Construct in Consumer Research. The findings of this study provide evidence of the important role of culture in general, and ethnicity in particular, in consumption. Future research should continue efforts such as these to increase empirical and conceptual knowledge of these phenomena among Asian immigrant consumers, as well as other emerging and/or marginal consumer populations. When such research focuses on Asian immigrant consumers, it should be expanded to understand the many differences among and between ethnic subgroups, as well as regional differences with respect to the country of origin. Ethnicity, in this sense, should not be viewed simply as a monolithic construct or independent variable (*Venkatesh, 1995*). It should instead be viewed as a complex, cultural condition with profound consequences upon the consumption experiences of immigrants, as well as the members of other subcultural and marginal groups (*Venkatesh, 1995*).

Methodological Pluralism in a Cross-Cultural Consumer Research. The findings of this study demonstrate the benefits of subjective, interpretive approaches to knowledge production, especially when the researcher is investigating emerging consumer populations such as Asian and Pacific Islander immigrants (*Bellenger, et. al., 1976; Jorgensen, 1989; Mo, 1992; Strauss and Corbin, 1990*). Methodologies such as participant observation, for example, are extremely appropriate for the study of certain kinds of human behavior, especially when the social phenomenon in question suggests important differences between the views of outsiders compared to those of insiders (*Jorgensen, 1989*). It can be strongly argued that research methodologies such as these are more appropriate in certain circumstances than more traditional, quantitative ones. One such circumstance occurs when the social phenomenon in question is an emerging one and therefore little or no theory exists as a starting point to suggest either confirmation or departure. A second circumstance occurs when the objective of a study is to gain a deeper understanding of the social phenomenon within the cultural context of the consumer. For instance, Penaloza (*1994*) presents an exemplary ethnographic account of the consumption experiences of Mexican immigrants in the United States. Finally, a third circumstance occurs when the consumer's perspective is important, but quantitative methodologies such as survey research or experimental research are an operational impossibility. Future research should address these important methodological concerns and seek to approach cross-cultural consumer research in a more methodologically pluralistic manner.

VI. BIBLIOGRAPHY

Bellenger, D. N., K. L. Bernhardt, and J. L. Goldstucker (1976), *"Qualitative Research in Marketing,"* American Marketing Association, Chicago, Illinois.

Burns, Alvin C. (1992), "The Expanded Health Belief Model as a Basis for Enlightened Preventive Health Care Practice and Research," *Journal of Health Care Marketing,* 12 (September), 32-45.

Chung, Douglas K. (1992), "Asian Cultural Commonalities: A Comparison With Mainstream American Culture," in Sharlene Maeda Furuto, Renuka Biswas, Douglas K. Chung, Kenji Murase, and Fariyal Ross-Sheriff, Editors, *"Social Work Practice With Asian Americans,"* Sage Publications, Newbury Park, California, 27-44.

Dawson, Scott (1989), "Health Care Consumption and Consumer Social Class: A Different Look at the Patient," *Journal of Health Care Marketing,* 9 (September), 15-25.

Easterlin, L. (1988), "Health of Asian Immigrants, Hepatitis B a Major Concern," *Urban Medicine,* 3.1, 10-12.

Feagin, Joe R. and Clairece Booher Feagin, *"Racial and Ethnic Relations,"* Prentice-Hall, Inc., Englewood Cliffs, New Jersey, 1993.

Gordon, Milton (1964), *"Assimilation in American Life: The Role of Race, Religion, and National Origins,"* Oxford University Press, New York, New York.

Hall, Edward T. (1959, 1981), *"The Silent Language,"* Anchor Books, Doubleday Publishers, New York, New York.

Hall, Edward T. (1966), *"The Hidden Dimension,"* Anchor Books, Doubleday Publishers, New York, New York.

Hall, Edward T. (1976, 1981), *"Beyond Culture,"* Anchor Books, Doubleday Publishers, New York, New York.

Hall, Edward T. (1983), *"The Dance of Life: The Other Dimension of Time,"* Anchor Books, Doubleday Publishers, New York, New York.

Hartog, Joseph and Elizabeth Ann Hartog (1983), "Cultural Aspects of Health and Illness Behavior in Hospitals," *The Western Journal of Medicine,* 139 (December), 910-916.

Jorgensen, Danny L. (1989), *"Participant Observation: A Methodology for Human Studies,"* Sage Publications, Inc., Newbury Park, California.

Kessler-Harris, A. and V. Yans-McLaughlin (1978), "European Ethnic Groups" in T. Sowell, Editor, *"American Ethnic Groups,"* Urban Institute, Washington, D.C., 107-138.

Lin-Fu, Jane S. (1988), "Population Characteristics and Health Care Needs of Asian Pacific Americans," *Public Health Reports,*103.1 (January-February), 22.

Mo, Bertha (1992), "Modesty, Sexuality, and Breast Health in Chinese-American Women," *The Western Journal of Medicine,* 157 (September), 260-264.

Nah, Kyung-Hee (1993), "Perceived Problems and Service Delivery for Korean Immigrants," *Social Work,* 38:3 (May), 289-294.

Neergaard, Keith (1994) "Preventive Health Behaviors in the Family: The Relationship to Health Lifestyle, Consumption Patterns, and Consumer Socialization," Doctoral Dissertation, University of California, Irvine, Graduate School of Management.

Penaloza, Lisa (1994) "Atravesando Fronteras/Border Crossings: A Critical Ethnographic Exploration of the Consumer Acculturation of Mexican Immigrants," *Journal of Consumer Research,* 21 (June), 32-54.

Ross-Sheriff, Fariyal (1992) "Adaptation and Integration Into American Society: Major Issues Affecting Asian Americans" in Sharlene Maeda Furuto, Renuka Biswas, Douglas K. Chung, Kenji Murase, and Fariyal Ross-Sheriff, Editors, *"Social Work Practice With Asian Americans,"* Sage Publications, Newbury Park, California, 45-63.

Strauss, Anselm and Juliet Corbin (1990), *"Basics of Qualitative Research: Grounded Theory Procedures and Techniques,"* Sage Publications, Inc., Newbury Park, California.

Terpstra, Vern and Kenneth David (1991), *"The Cultural Environment of International Business,"* South-Western Publishing Company, Cincinnati, Ohio.

U.S. Commission on Civil Rights (1992), *"Civil Rights Issues Facing Asian Americans in the 1990s,"* Government Printing Office, Washington, D.C., (February).

U.S. Department of Commerce, Bureau of the Census (1983), *"1980 Census of the Population, General Population Characteristics, United States Summary, Race and Hispanic Origin: 1980,"* Government Printing Office, Washington, D.C., (May).

U.S. Department of Commerce, Economics and Statistics Administration, Bureau of the Census (1992), *"1990 Census of the Population, General Population Characteristics, United States Summary, Table 3, Race and Hispanic Origin: 1990,"* Government Printing Office, Washington, D.C., (November).

Venkatesh, Alladi (1995), "Ethnoconsumerism: A New Paradigm to Study Cultural and Cross-Cultural Consumer Behavior" in Gary Bamossy and Janeen Arnold Costa, eds., *"Marketing in a Multicultural World: Ethnicity, Nationalism, and Identity,"* SAGE Publications, 1995.

Wallendorf, Melanie and Michael Reilly (1983), *"Ethnic Migration, Assimilation, and Consumption,"* Journal of Consumer Research, 10 (December), 292-302.

Yeatman, Gentry W. and Viet Van Dang (1980), "Cao Gio (Coin Rubbing): Vietnamese Attitudes Toward Health Care," *Journal of the American Medical Association,* 244:24 (December 19), 2748-2749.

Zane, Nolan, David Takeuchi, and Kathleen Young (1994), *"Confronting Critical Health Issues of Asian and Pacific Islander Americans,"* Sage Publications, Thousand Oaks, California.

Consumer Choice of the Developmentally Disabled

Amy Rummel, Alfred University
Myra Batista, Alfred University
Daneen Schwartz, Alfred University

ABSTRACT

In 1987 the Developmental Disability Bill of Rights and Assistance Act was passed. This doctrine mandates that, as part of social policy, the developmentally disabled have the right of choice and independence. Yet in order to facilitate independence through choice, there must be an understanding of how these individuals make choices. This research provides a preliminary examination of the developmentally disabled consumer choice behavior. Further research recommendations are made.

INTRODUCTION

In 1987 the Developmental Disability Bill of Rights and Assistance Act Amendment was passed. As this amendment states, it's mission is to "...support persons with developmental disabilities to achieve their maximum potential through increased independence, productivity and integration into the community...it is in the national interest to offer persons with developmental disabilities the opportunity, to the maximum extent feasible, to make decisions for themselves and to live in typical homes and communities where they can exercise their full right and responsibilities as citizens" (p. 101 STAT.841).

A critical component to insuring independence for this particular population is their ability to perform autonomous consumer related activities (Conroy & Feinstein, 1988a & b).

The developmentally disabled, by definition, are a population with limited cognitive skills. To date researchers have little information concerning how this population makes consumer related decisions. In reality, many choices of the developmentally disabled have been determined by their care givers such as parents, family member, legal guardian or case worker. Hence, one of the basic benefits of the 1987 Amendment, the ability to make independent choices, has been given to the client's social support system and not to the client. The doctrine of the "maximum extent feasible' has thus taken on a narrow scope of limited participation of the developmentally disabled in their goals and activities. This research is one of the first attempts made to examine how the developmental disabled make consumer related decisions.

Given the exploratory nature of this research, there must be a basic understanding of the three central components: 1) the developmentally disabled, 2) social policy directed at the developmentally disabled, and 3) the role of consumer behavior. Each component will be addressed in part to provide a basis for this line of research.

Mental Retardation Defined

The developmentally disabled is a population which is as heterogeneous as any "normal" population. With this in mind, it is not surprising that to define this population has been difficult and today is still controversial. Yet, some semblance of a definition is needed in order to understand the direction of this research.

A definition used by NARC (National Association of Retarded Citizens) which was borrowed from the American Association of Mental Deficiency, is that "...the mentally retarded person is one who, from childhood, experiences unusual difficulty in learning and is relatively ineffective in applying whatever s/he has learned to the problems of ordinary living" (Schleien & Ray, 1988).

For educational purposes the developmentally disabled were categorized according to IQ level. This was and still is done to some degree to be able to provide the most appropriate type of education or skill training.   Three main categories were applied: (1) the educatable mentally retarded (EMR), individuals with the IQ range of 50-75; (2) the trainable mentally retarded (TMR), who obtained IQ scores from 30-50; and, (3) the severely or dependent mentally retarded, who scored below 30 on the IQ test. These categories eventually identified the type of education a particular individual received ranging from self-help skills (dressing oneself) to learning how to count money etc. This paradigm, found in the educational system, was also utilized in this research.

Educable mentally handicapped (mildly retarded) are usually first identified in the classroom because they are not able to keep up with the other students. Once identified as having an IQ score between 50-75 they are so labeled. They are able to learn the basics of reading, writing, math, etc., but it is not instructed at the normal pace or in as much depth. EMRs are seen as "slow learners" and not necessarily different learners (e.g. learning disabled).

The trainable mentally retarded (moderately retarded) have lower IQ scores (25-50 range) and, hence, their instruction is focused on daily living skills. These might be termed self-help, or social adjustment. The goal is to teach skills which will allow them to function within some type of supervised setting.

The severely mentally handicapped have been institutionalized until recently. Because of their severe intellectual limitations, instruction has been designed towards acquisition of very basic skills. This type of individual usually has a limited verbal capacity. Teaching these individuals alternative methods of communication is critical.

The history involved in educating or merely understanding this population has been long and varied. However, if this population is to be understood from a consumer perspective, a review of the literature regarding efforts towards teaching this population consumer related skills is necessary.

Formation of Social Policy (for the developmentally disabled)

Formal policies which began at defining the relationship between the developmentally disabled and society began around the 1820's. It came in the form of the segregation of this population with the establishment of separate institutions: insane asylums, orphanages, and asylums for the "feeble minded." In 1848 Massachusetts opened the first institution for the mentally retarded. By 1890, fourteen states had followed suit (Davies, 1959, p. 22). As these facilities grew in number the concern became not on training or socialization, but "a conscious attempt to protect society by removing them altogether" (Knoblock, 1987, p. 11). This philosophy soon developed into what is now called "The Eugenics Movement." This movement felt strongly that the mentally handicapped were especially responsible for the spread of moral and social degeneration of society. Such feelings were supported by research of that time (Dugdale, 1910).

While this movement eventually lost its momentum, it played a major role in the formation of social policy today. Still, by 1958, twenty-eight states had sterilization laws for the mentally handicapped (Davies, 1959). However, by 1950, parents began to advocate for the rights of their handicapped children. The National Association for Retarded Citizens was formed at that time and became a platform for advocating quality services. In the 1960's, due, in part, to the efforts of President Kennedy and his family, public attention was focused on the plight of the developmentally disabled. Concurrently, a report published by the Children's Defense Fund estimated that over two million developmentally disabled children were denied access to public education at that time. While there were many public policy advances made during this time of civil rights it was not until 1987 that the Developmental Disability Assistance and Bill of Rights Act (PL 100-146) was passed.

Extant Literature of the Developmentally Disabled Consumer

To date, there has been limited research which examines the adoption of the consumer role by the developmental disabled person. Much of the extant research has focused on such topics as transfer learning (Bachor, 1988; Feuerstein, Rand & Hoffman, 1979), mainstreaming (Myles & Simpson, 1989; Bilken, 1985; Reynolds, Wang & Walberg, 1987), and adaption to independent living (Dattilo & Peters, 1991; Richler, 1984; Schleien & Ray, 1988). There has been some work which looks at the behavior of these individuals in consumer settings (Ferguson & McDonnell, 1991; Westling, Floyd & Carr, 1990; McDonnel, Horner & Williams, 1984). An underlying theme in much of the literature is the concept of adaptive behavior. From this perspective, adaptive behavior is defined in terms of those skills needed to function in society (Macmillan, 1982). Hence, teaching basic skills is viewed as empowering these individuals to obtain access to necessary resources held by the "non-handicapped". This focus on teaching has developed because, by definition, developmentally disabled individuals do not acquire "normal" social skills through the socialization process. The literature indicates that the majority of this particular population does not possess the cognitive ability to decipher and utilize social cues and adopt them into their cognitive or behavioral repertoire. Failure to integrate such cues is then compounded when and if these disabled individuals are excluded from normal family activities in their formative years. Sowers (1982) reported that in fact very few severely handicapped engage in leisure and community activities with their families. A reaction to this situation has been a focus on training behaviors in various structured settings to provide access to societal offerings.

The underpinnings of this extant research is that "training" a behavior or skill such as shopping or buying a cup of coffee may not be enough to enable these individuals to become consumers. To enable this population consumer choice there must be an understanding of how they make choices and how this is related to their ability to adopt the role of consumer.

The purpose of this research is to begin to build an understanding of how and why the developmentally disabled make consumption choices.

METHODOLOGY

Subjects

Two sites, one in Washington, D.C., and another in up-state New York agreed to participate in this study. Thirty-four mentally handicapped were personally interviewed. They ranged in age from 21 to 63 years, with an average age of 33 years. Due to the purpose of the study and the demands of the task, ability to provide verbal responses was the only criteria used for inclusion in this study. Fifteen male and nineteen females were interviewed and of these, 17 were classified as mildly handicapped, 11 were moderately handicapped, and 6 clients were severely developmentally disabled. There was a smaller representation of the severely handicapped due in part to this study's requirement of verbal responses.

Analytic Procedure

Personal interviews were conducted in order to determine those particu   ess   reference to the se
of central im

Each client was solicited to participate in the personal interview. They were told that they were going to be asked about grocery store shopping. Great efforts were taken to assure each client that this was not a test situation. Subjects were brought to the staff lunch room in their work facility. They were then asked their name and basic information about their shopping experiences (i.e., do you go grocery shopping?, With who?). Subjects were then shown 3 to 4 actual products with a particular product category. Physical products were presented because such methodology was found to increase reliability of the responses (Wadsworth & Harper, 1991). They were exposed to a total of 6 product categories. They were: drinks, fruit snacks, bath soap, dish soap, toothpaste and cereal. The purpose of this study was to examine product choice as it might occur in a naturalistic setting. Hence, product categories were selected which these clients might have responsibility for the choice (e.g. packing their lunch for the sheltered workshop), as well as being involved in the product's consumption. A total of 204 response categories were recorded (34 clients x 6 product categories=204). Before the interview began, subjects were asked to verify that they knew what the product category was, and what it was used for. Of the 204 response categories, only in 25 instances did the clients not know the product category. This was due to unfamiliar packaging. This was clarified with all clients before any further questions were asked. During each interview, clients were asked to choose a particular product within each category that they would like to purchase if they were at a store. For each choice, they were asked to explain why they chose that particular one and not the others. All comments were manually recorded. Each interview took anywhere from fifteen minutes to one hour. The client's supervisor provided the level of developmental disability for each client.

RESULTS

Reflective of previous findings, none of the severely handicapped indicated they had been shopping before. Table 1 provides the breakdown.

Table 2 provides a classification of choice. All respondents were asked to explain why they chose the particular product. All reasons were recorded and, hence, there were more reasons given than the actual number of respondents. Examining the pure total of responses, those mildly retarded (EMR) provided a high number of responses than either TMRs or the severely retarded individuals (p<.05).

Examining the content of responses, EMR individuals identify the products' effectiveness more often than the other two populations (30% vs. 12% vs. 10%). This classification, "effectiveness," captured responses such as "best at cleaning dishes," "gets me the cleanest." The number of responses based on sensory information (e.g. color, taste, smell) was highest among the moderate and severely disabled clients compared to the mildly handicapped [49% (TMR) vs. 46% (severely) vs. 35% (EMR).

Another issue that arose which was of interest was the degree of reliance these individuals had on past purchases. Thirty-four percent (34%) of the responses provided by the severely handicapped were "used before" either by self or significant other (e.g. sister, houseparent). This is notable considering only 19% of

TABLE 1
Grocery Shopping Experience by Classification

	Mild	Moderate	Severe
By self	7	0	0
With parents	1	1	0
House parents	1	6	0
Never	2	0	6
Other	6	4	0
Total	**17**	**11**	**6**

responses from the moderately handicapped and 10% of the EMR or mildly handicapped individuals relied on this information for product choice.

QUALITATIVE RESPONSES

Severely Developmentally Disabled

There were notable differences between the three populations. The severely handicapped were more likely to give the same response within and across product categories. For instance, one of the clients, "A," chose Michael Jordan fruit snacks in that product category. When asked why, he responded, "I know him." When asked which fruit snack had the prettiest package or which was healthiest, he again responded Michael Jordan. This perseveration was very typical of respondents who were severely mentally handicapped. When the drink category was placed in front of him, he was very quick to pick out Gatorade and said that he had seen it on T.V. It is highly likely that similar T.V. exposure to Michael Jordan was the basis for the fruit snack choice. The only other basis for choice that was supplied by this client was that it was bought previously by his mother. This was also very typical of the responses provided by this developmentally disabled group.

It is interesting to note that there was little response latency for this group. While no actual timing was recorded, these interviews took less time than did the interviews with the mildly or moderately disabled clients, contrary to what was expected by the researcher. One possible explanation for this is that there were few cues being accessed for choice which decreased response time.

It should also be noted that this particular group of respondents had the most difficult time with providing a rationale for "prettiest package" or "healthiest/most effective product." Often they didn't provide an answer, or repeated a past response.

Moderately Developmentally Disabled

The responses from the moderately disabled clients were more comprehensive compared to the severely developmentally disabled (i.e. more responses and explanation). However, many times the reasons provided for product choice seemed to be based on information obtained from commercials or what were identified from the product box/container. "G" chose Dentalcare for his toothpaste. When asked why, he responded, "Because it's advertised a lot. It has Arm & Hammer in it and that's good." It appeared that often times such choices were not made on these individuals' own thoughts or decision, but on T.V. messages. Through many of these interviews it became very clear that these individuals remember T.V. commercials well and believe advertisements to be absolutely true (no evaluation of commercials). Reason for choice, then, seemed to be a replay of these commercials. For instance, "G" had heard of Arm & Hammer, but was not aware of what it was. He had

actually mistaken a brand name for an ingredient, but knew it was good based on the T.V. ad.

Similar to the severely disabled, there was also a limited use of the word "I" in these interviews. The typical response from these moderately developmentally disabled clients was "because it's advertised a lot" or "it has 100% fruit juice." There were few responses such as "I like it." Similar to the severely developmentally disabled, there was little if any reference to the "self" in these product choices.

Mildly Developmentally Disabled

This population was the most verbal. They were able to provide in-depth reasons for their product choices with little probing. "B" for instance, reported she did most of her own shopping.

Some of the more interesting comments provided were the ones concerning children. "B" was asked to choose the prettiest toothpaste package. After choosing "Slimer," she report that "children would think that Slimer is cool." This response was one of the first to make a distinction between her self and others. Responses such as this identified that she was interpreting the cues provided by the Slimer label and associating them with an appropriate market, i.e. children. Similarly, "D" did not want to choose Lucky Charms cereal because "it's a kid's cereal," and reported "I'm too old for that."

Many of the reasons given for product choice were based on objective criterion such as price (e.g., "It's cheaper in the store") or product packaging (e.g., "the toothpaste pump is much easier to use"). Both of these types of comments indicated that product evaluation had, in fact, taken place.

DISCUSSION

Based on both the quantitative and qualitative results a number of theoretical issues emerge.

Consumption Symbolism

Consumption symbolism has been a long-established tenet of consumer behavior. Even young children are able to decipher consumption symbols and interpret them (Belk, Bahn & Mayer, 1982). However, there appears to be little symbolic meaning of products for the moderate and severe disabled. This was reinforced in the actual interviews when some of the mildly handicapped individuals would reference to "how the product would be perceived: 'that product is for children.'" The question raised is why is there a lack of this interpretation? Is it simply a matter of intelligence or is it a lack of experience?

Cue Utilization

There is a range of difference between the type and amount of product cues utilized among this population. As the quantitative

TABLE 2
Reason for Choice by Classification*

	Mild		Moderate		Severe	
Used Before						
Self	6	(5%)	3	(4%)	1	(3%)
Significant Other			3	(4%)	8	(21%)
Regular Brand	6	(5%)	8	(11%)	4	(10%)
Sensory Info						
Taste	16	(13%)	13	(18%)	2	(5%)
Color	4	(3%)	8	(11%)	8	(21%)
Picture	9	(7%)	8	(11%)	6	(15%)
Smell	11	(9%)	4	(5%)	0	
Packaging	4	(3%)	2	(3%)	2	(5%)
Feel/Softer	0		1	(1%)	0	
Total Sensory Information (6 added together)	44	(35%)	36	(49%)	18	(46%)
Advertising	2	(2%)	5	(7%)	3	(8%)
Easier to use	2	(2%)	0		0	
Price	8	(6%)	3	(4%)	1	(3%)
Effectiveness	38	(30%)	9	(12%)	4	(10%)
Brand name	1	(8%)	0		0	
Size/value for $	5	(4%)	2	(3%)	0	
Ingredients	10	(8%)	4	(5%)	0	
Recyclable	0		1	(1%)	0	
Children like product	3	(2%)	0		0	
Total Responses	**125**		**74**		**39**	

* Number in brackets represent % of responses.
(Total % might not total 100% due to rounding error).

data shows the mildly handicapped individuals access and verbalize more cues and a wider range of cues. A higher proportion of their cues are "rational" such as ingredients and effectiveness. There was evidence in their qualitative responses that they were evaluating their needs and matching these with the product choice. This might be a reflection of their independence. A higher proportion of these individuals reported that they were responsible for their product choice relative to a significant other making those choices for them.

For both the severely and moderately handicapped, product choice often laid in the hands of the significant other. It is possible that this lead to fewer number of cues utilized and a higher reliance on sensory information or information gleaned from advertising. In terms of central vs. peripheral cue utilization, there is a higher incidence of central cues being used by the higher functioning (mildly retarded) than the other two groups. This was reflected in both the types of data obtained.

CONCLUSION

There are many issues raised from this research. Firstly, the developmentally disabled are not one homogeneous population. They differ substantially on how and why they make the consumer choices that they do.

Secondly, this research identifies that the three populations use different cues for the basis of choice. The mildly handicapped, especially, can identify products with some accuracy according to their market positioning (e.g. healthiest product). They use market

information such as commercials to form these opinions. The moderately handicapped show less ability to evaluate commercials and therefore believe such information as truth. This is a similar result found in research done with young children.

Behavior of consumers, to a large degree, is directed by symbolic meaning. In other words, products are consumed because they say something about our "self." Most individuals learn the meaning of consumption through the socialization process. That includes interaction with families, friends and the market place. Results from this study show that these individuals have limited exposure to the market place and/or little personal experience. Does personal experience affect their ability to utilize product cue and to consume symbolically. Certainly, the ability to interpret cue "accurately" is an important issue as these individuals work towards mainstreaming in our society.

Support organizations such as shelter workshops, schools, job training facilities and group homes now have the responsibility for creating choice for this population. There needs to be an understanding of the choices which exist in a client's repertoire and his or her ability to choose. (i.e. Do they understand the outcome of their choices?)

This research represents one of the first efforts to examine the developmentally disabled from a consumer perspective. The findings and their interpretation are limited because of the sample size of respondents and the qualitative nature of the study. More research needs to be done to understand this segment of our population.

REFERENCES

Bachor, Dan. (1988). Do mentally handicapped adults transfer cognitive skills from the instrumental enrichment classrooms to other situations or settings. *The Mental Retardation & Learning Disability Bulletin, 16*(2), 14-28.

Belk, R., Bahn, K., & Mayer R (1982) Developmental recognition of consumption symbolism. *Journal of Consumer Research,* 9, 4-17.

Bilken, D.P. (1985). Mainstreaming: From compliance to quality. *Journal of Learning Disabilities, 18,* 58-61.

Conroy, J., & Feinstein, C. (1988a). *Final draft: Rationale for design of national consumer survey process.* Washington, DC: National Association of Developmental Disabilities Councils.

Conroy, J., & Feinstein, C. (1988b). *Final draft survey instrument: A national survey of consumers of services for individuals with developmental disabilities.* Washington, DC: National Association of Developmental Disabilities Councils.

Dattilo, J., & St. Peter, S. (1991). A model for including leisure education in transition services for young adults with mental retardation. *Education and Training in Mental Retardation* (December), 420-432.

Davidson, P., & Adams, E. (1989). Indicators of impact of services on persons with developmental disabilities: Issues concerning data collection mandates in P.L. 100-146.

Davies, S.P. (1959). *The mentally retarded in society.* New York: Columbia University Press.

Dugdale, R.L. (1910). *The jukes.* New York: Putnam.

Ferguson, B., & McDonnell, J. (1991). A comparison of serial and concurrent sequencing strategies in teaching generalized grocery item location to students with moderate handicaps.

Feuerstein, R., Rand, Y., & Hoffman, M.B. (1979). *The dynamic assessment of retarded performers: The learning potential assessment device, instruments and techniques.* Baltimore: University Park Press.

Knoblock, P. (1987). *Understanding exceptional children and youth.* Boston: Little, Brown & Co.

Langone, J., & Burton, T. (1987). Teaching adaptive behavior skills to moderately and severely handicapped individuals: Best practices for facilitating independent living.

Macmillan, D.L. (1982). *Mental retardation in schools and society* (2nd edition). Boston: Little, Brown.

Mcdonnel, J.J., Horner, R.H., & Williams, J.A. (1984). Comparison of three strategies for teaching generalized grocery purchasing to high school students with severe handicaps. *Journal of the Association for Persons with Severe Handicaps, 9*(2), 123-133.

Myles, B., & Simpson, R. (1989). Regular educator's modification preferences for mainstreaming mildly handicapped children. *The Journal of Special Education, 22*(4), 479-491.

Reynolds, M.C., Wang, M.C., & Walberg, H.J. (1987). The necessary restructuring of special and regular education. *Exceptional Children, 53,* 391-398.

Richler, D. (1984). Access to community resources: The invisible barriers to integration. *Journal of Leisurability, 11*(2), 4-11.

Schleien, S.J., & Ray, M.T. (1988). *Community reaction and persons with disabilities: Strategies for integration.* Baltimore: Paul H. Brookes.

Sowers, J.A. (1982). Validation of the weekly activity interview. Unpublished dissertation, University of Oregon.

Wadsworth, J., & Harper, D. (1991). Increasing the reliability of self report by adults with moderate mental retardation. *JASH, 16,* 228-232.

Westling, D.L., Floyd, J., & Carr, D. (1990). Effect of single setting vs. multiple setting training on learning to shop in a department store. *Journal on Mental Retardation, 94*(6), 616-624.

Brands in Crisis: Consumer Help for Deserving Victims

John Stockmyer, University of Missouri

INTRODUCTION

Product tampering has a devastating impact on consumers and product marketers in the United States. Since the first Tylenol poisoning incident in 1982, reported incidents of tampering have continued; peaking in 1986 when the FDA logged over 1700 complaints about "invasive" tampering (Rosette 1992). According to FDA commissioner Frank Young, more than one billion dollars worth of merchandise was destroyed in 1986 as a result of product tampering emergencies (Stern 1989). Although the number of reported tampering incidents has declined since 1986, tampering complaints have continued at the rate of approximately 500 per year (Rosette 1992). According to FDA forensic research director Fred Fricke, "Every week we get something that's suspected tampering; it never slows down" (Stehlin 1995). The problem is not limited to cases where an actual tampering has occurred. Negative word-of-mouth (Richins 1983) arising from false charges and rumors of tampering are often sufficient to create a market share drop, as demonstrated by the 1993 Pepsi syringe scare (Meyers 1993).

Surprisingly, few marketing studies have addressed consumer response to product tampering. Jackson et al. (1992) examined how demographic factors influence the general level of concern about product tampering. Morgan (1988) reviewed the legal implications of tamper-related issues such as liability and packaging decisions. "Trade" articles focus almost exclusively on the need for better tamper-resistant and tamper-evident packaging. Most of the research on product tampering assumes a crisis management perspective, which focuses on how companies respond to product crises. It is argued here that the crisis management (C/M) approach overlooks consumer reactions, and treats consumer response as a direct function of management response. The objective of this study is to examine consumer response to product crises. Hopefully, this will serve as an impetus for further research on this topic, and provide managers with additional insight into the complicated issues surrounding company crisis response.

The remainder of the paper consists of five sections. The first describes the current crisis management (C/M) approach and its limitations. The second describes helping behavior theory and derives hypotheses regarding consumer response to product tampering. The third presents the experimental methodology used to test the hypotheses. The fourth section describes the results of the experiment. The final section discusses limitations of the study, implications for managerial policy, and directions for future research.

THE CRISIS MANAGEMENT APPROACH AND ITS LIMITATIONS

Interestingly, product tampering has been adopted as a "management" issue. The C/M literature is scattered and largely atheoretical, but it does suggest basic guidelines for handling product crises (Siomkos and Malliaris 1992):

- Get a crisis management team in place before a crisis.
- Quickly (24-72 hours) acknowledge the problem and show concern.
- Voluntarily recall all harmful products if there is a perceived threat.
- Provide direct information regarding harm data to consumers.

The C/M approach is modeled primarily after the successful actions taken by Johnson & Johnson following the Tylenol poisonings in 1982. However, the validity of the C/M approach is increasingly in doubt. The following example demonstrates the poor predictive ability of the C/M approach.

During the Summer 1993 syringe scare, the Pepsi-Cola Co. did not implement a recall, admit there was a problem, or provide timely information to consumers. Their basic strategy was to deny any fault, which led to criticism for reacting inadequately and not being accommodating to the media (Greenberg 1993). However, two weeks after the incident, sales returned to normal levels (Routhier 1993). Pepsi acted inappropriately, yet their market share did not suffer as a result. Clearly, the C/M approach cannot be relied upon as a normative model for company action in a crisis. Siomkos and Kurzbard (1994) express similar concern regarding the acceptance of current practices as laws of general operation. The C/M approach is anecdotal, and it relies on many unstated and untested assumptions.

One unstated assumption is that if the company does not publicly show its concern, consumers will not feel any sympathy for the company, and therefore will not be likely to continue purchasing the company's product. It is quite possible that consumers might feel sympathy for a troubled company even without seeing such a public statement. Also, the link between consumer sympathy and purchase behavior has not been tested.

The C/M approach does not address brand loyalty or perceived company fault, which are important factors influencing purchase intention Another problem with the approach is its associated cost if precisely followed. Many smaller firms could probably not afford a recall, testing and/or replacement of the questionable products.

The C/M approach relies on many untested assumptions, ignores potentially important factors, and is extremely costly to implement. The C/M approach has proven to be ineffective in some cases. Even in situations where the approach seems effective, there is no proof that an alternate approach would not have been equally effective. An examination of how *consumers* respond to product crises is necessary to truly understand the impact of any company strategy on consumer response.

A HELPING BEHAVIOR PERSPECTIVE

This section describes how a reliance on helping behavior literature is applicable in a product crisis context. Some important factors that influence the likelihood of helping are discussed in detail. These factors are then operationalized in a product tampering context, and hypotheses are constructed regarding consumer response to product tampering.

For this study consumer repurchase intention is viewed as a form of helping behavior. The intention to repurchase represents a willingness to assist a victim (the affected company) in distress. Although no prior research could be found in which consumers specifically view companies as victims, this idea has been suggested in previous crisis management research (Kaufmann, Kesner and Hazen 1994). The theory base that guides this study is the norm of justice, which is a rule-based standard that directs people to help those who merit, or deserve assistance (Lerner and Meindl 1981). The critical determination to be made is how one judges when another deserves help. Social psychology literature identifies many factors that influence deservingness and willingness to help. The factors examined in this study are: whether the needy party is trying to help themselves, the relationship between helper and victim, the helper's cost of helping, and the antecedents of helping.

Determination of Self-Help

People feel less empathetic concern for "victims" who are not trying to help themselves, and feel they do not deserve assistance (Betancourt 1990). Self-help is operationalized as the company taking constructive action to "help itself" by recalling products and increasing security following a tampering incident. Company action is viewed as self-help because the primary motivation is to limit its legal liability which would result from additional consumer injuries.

H1: Following a product tampering incident, consumers will rate firms that take constructive action (a) as more deserving of their business, (b) with more sympathy and (c) with higher purchase intentions than firms that do not take constructive action.

The Relationship Between Helper and Victim

Piliavin et al. (1981) reported that people are more likely to be empathetic toward those with whom they have close ties. Clark et al. (1987) and Schoenrade et al. (1986) show that people are more helpful toward those they know and care about than toward superficial acquaintances. The closeness of the relationship is operationalized as the loyalty the consumer has to the brand. This reasoning is consistent with Aaker (1991) who describes brand loyalists as "friends of the brand," because the users generally have an emotional attachment to it. The absence of brand loyalty is viewed as a more superficial relationship.

H2: Following a product tampering incident, consumers who are loyal to the victimized brand will (a) rate the victimized brand as more deserving of their business, (b) feel more sympathy for the victimized brand and (c) report higher continued purchase intentions for the victimized brand than do consumers who are not loyal to the victimized brand.

The Cost of Helping

Another important component of the helping behavior approach is the perceived cost of helping, which is operationalized as the helper's perceived physical risk associated with future consumption of the product. Brand loyalty has proven to be a perceived physical risk reliever for products (Roselius 1971) and services (Mitchell and Greatorex 1993). The following hypothesis extends the concept of risk reduction to a tampering context, where the perceived physical risk can be extreme.

H2d: Following a product tampering incident, consumers who are loyal to the victimized brand will perceive less risk associated with the continued use of the victimized brand than will consumers who are not loyal to the victimized brand.

The Effect of Deservingness, Sympathy and Risk on Purchase Intention

In the tampering context helping is represented by purchase intention. Generally, people are more likely to help others when they feel that the "victim" is deserving of their help (Betancourt 1990; Lerner and Meindl 1981). It has also been shown that helping behavior is directly correlated with empathetic concern (Betancourt 1990). Piliavin et al. (1981) shows that, in general, when the cost of helping increases, the likelihood of helping decreases. A study by Shotland and Straw (1976) found that this relationship holds when the cost of helping is operationalized as the possibility of receiving physical harm.

H3: Following a tampering incident, there is (a) a positive relationship between the perceived deservingness of the victimized brand, (b) a positive relationship between the sympathy for the victimized brand and (c) a negative relationship between the perceived risk of continued use of the victimized brand and purchase intention.

METHODOLOGY

Research Design

The hypotheses were tested in a 2 x 2 between-subjects experiment. The two independent variables were brand loyalty (high/low), and company action (yes/no). The dependent measures assessed four main constructs: deservingness, sympathy, perceived risk and purchase intention (Refer to Appendix 1). Perceived fault was also assessed, because Folkes et al. (1987) and Jorgensen (1994) showed that perceived controllability was inversely related to repurchase intent. Also, Schmidt and Weiner (1988) found that when people attribute difficulties to controllable factors they are usually less willing to help than when they attribute the difficulties to factors beyond the individual's control.

Subjects

Participants in the study were students enrolled in upper-level business courses at a large Midwestern University. Eighty-four subjects participated in pretests. A total of 145 participated in the final experiment. One subject's data was deleted from the analysis due to missing information, leaving a final *n* of 144 (36 per cell). Although the use of a student sample is not ideal, Dipboye and Flanagan (1979) suggest that the use of a homogeneous sample in the early stages of exploratory research may be useful in enhancing the internal validity of the experimental treatments. Also, the tasks required of the subjects were within the domain of their normal experience.

Pretests

Extensive testing was undertaken to make sure the instructions were clear, to check the reliability of the measures, and to gain additional insight into the tampering phenomenon.

Procedures / Stimuli

Students were randomly assigned to the four treatment conditions. A one page (double-sided) "survey" was distributed. Subjects were informed that this was a study about consumer attitudes toward product marketing practices. Participation was voluntary, and subjects were informed that their identities would remain anonymous. Subjects responded to the brand loyalty manipulation, brand loyalty check, and the product tampering scenario on page one. The second page included the dependent measures and company action manipulation check. The entire procedure took less than 15 minutes. The dependent items were randomized to minimize order bias. Half of the subjects received randomized version *A*; the other half received its mirror-image, version *B*.

The initial section included the brand loyalty manipulation. Half of the subjects listed a brand of food or beverage that was one of their favorite products that they purchased on a regular basis (*High brand loyalty condition*). The other half was instructed to imagine a hypothetical brand of food or beverage that they had previously found satisfactory, but was not one of their favorite brands (*Low brand loyalty condition*). The subjects then read the following scenario:

"Now, imagine that your (favorite/hypothetical) brand has been "Tampered" with, and the consumption of this product has resulted in serious injuries to several people. Soon after the injuries were first reported, the "Tamperer" was caught, convicted, and put in jail. As the crisis unfolded, the company decided that:
1) "The tampering incident was beyond their control (Not their fault)."
2) "It was an isolated incident."

The third company statement served as the company action manipulation. The *constructive action* treatment read as follows:

3) "In the best interest of public safety, the company voluntarily removed all of the product from store shelves nation-wide, and made company-wide changes specifically designed to minimize any security threat in the future."

The *no constructive action* treatment read as follows:

3) "Initiating a recall, or changing company procedures was not necessary."

RESULTS AND ANALYSIS

Manipulation Checks
Brand Loyalty. This scale consisted of three items (α=.83) which assessed product liking (really like/really dislike), product seeking (avoid it intentionally/seek it intentionally), and substitutability (anything would be a better substitute/there are NO acceptable substitutes). The results of an ANOVA test indicated that the brand loyalty manipulation was perceived as intended ($F_{1,143}$=256.29, p<.0001), indicating that subjects in the brand loyal group exhibited higher brand loyalty than did those in the non-loyal group (means were 4.34 versus 3.00).
Company Action. The results of an ANOVA test indicated that the company action manipulation was perceived as intended ($F_{1,143}$=38.87, p<.0001), indicating that subjects in the constructive action group perceived greater company action than did those in the non-action group (means were 3.87 versus 2.78).
Fault. Analysis indicated that subjects did not perceive a significant difference in company fault between the brand loyalty conditions (Brand Loyalty $F_{1,143}$=2.14, p=.15). However, subjects did perceive a significant difference (at α=.10) between company action conditions (Action $F_{1,143}$=3.87, p=.051), suggesting that company action reduces company fault in the eyes of consumers (means were 2.72 versus 2.45). Apparently, subjects modified their perceptions of the past event with new information regarding present company behavior. Although unexpected, this result had little influence on the results of the study. The partial correlation between fault and purchase intention (controlling for deservingness, sympathy, and risk) was insignificant (partial r=-.04, p=.309).

Hypotheses Tests
Company Action. The "action" hypotheses were tested using ANOVA. The cell means and critical F-values are reported in Table 1. The results indicate that after a tampering incident, constructive company action is:

- positively associated with deservingness (means: 3.57 vs. 3.84, p=.015)
- positively associated with sympathy (means: 3.40 vs. 3.67, p=.045)
- not significantly associated with risk (means: 2.86 vs. 2.65, p=.13)
- not significantly associated with purchase intention (means: 3.37 vs. 3.56, p=.16)

Hypotheses 1a and 1b are supported; hypothesis 1c was not supported.
Brand Loyalty. The "loyalty" hypotheses were tested using ANOVA. The results indicate that after a tampering incident, brand loyalty is:

- positively associated with deservingness (means: 3.46 vs. 3.95, p<.0001)
- positively associated with sympathy (means: 3.39 vs. 3.67, p=.038)
- negatively associated with risk (means: 2.98 vs. 2.52, p=.001)
- positively associated with purchase intent (means: 3.01 vs. 3.92, p<.0001)

Hypotheses 2a, 2b, 2c and 2d are supported. No significant A X L interactions were found.
Purchase Intention (PI). The following hypotheses were tested using partial correlations (See Table 2). The results indicate that after a tampering incident, there is a:

- positive relationship between deservingness and PI (r=.35, p<.0001),
- non-significant relationship between sympathy and PI (r=.08, p=.167)
- negative relationship between perceived risk and PI (r=-.57, p<.0001).

Hypotheses 3a and 3c are supported; hypothesis 3b is not supported.

DISCUSSION

Company Action
There was no significant link between company action and purchase intention. It appears that the subjects felt more sympathy towards their favorite brands and firms that took action, but that sympathy did not translate into an increased willingness to purchase from (help) the affected company. The fact that sympathy was not significantly related to purchase intent is surprising, because sympathy is thought to be a key factor in regaining market share, and is a major element of the C/M approach. Given the magnitude of the action manipulation, this finding suggests that company action *may not* be a critical factor in an attempt to regain market share. This could be welcome news for affected companies, because it suggests that extensive (costly) action may not be necessary in the wake of a product crisis incident, as was demonstrated in the Pepsi case. However, it would seem unwise to rely upon the results of this single study for directing managerial policy. The subjects' age, and their potentially different risk perceptions (from the average consumer) may have biased the results. It is also possible that consumer purchase intentions may be influenced indirectly through sympathy and deservingness.

TABLE 1

Panel A: Cell Means for Dependent Measures

Company Action	Brand Loyalty	n	Deserve	Sympathy	Risk	Purchase Intent
NO	LOW	36	3.38	3.28	3.14	2.97
NO	HIGH	36	3.77	3.52	2.57	3.77
YES	LOW	36	3.55	3.51	2.82	3.06
YES	HIGH	36	4.13	3.82	2.47	4.06

Panel B:Anova F-Values for Dependent Measures

Source	Deserve	Sympathy	Risk	Purchase Intent
Action (A)	6.11*	4.11*	2.29	1.99
Loyalty (L)	20.74**	4.39*	11.11**	45.14**
A X L	.83	.08	.60	.63

*$p<.05$

**$p<.01$

TABLE 2

Partial Correlations Between Purchase Intention and Brand Loyalty, Deservingness, Sympathy, Risk

Measures	Partial Correlation	Control Variables
Purchase Intent & Loyalty	.34*	Deserve/Sympathy/Risk
Purchase Intent & Deserve	.35*	Loyalty/Sympathy/Risk
Purchase Intent & Sympathy	.08	Loyalty/Deserve/Risk
Purchase Intent & Risk	−.57*	Loyalty/Deserve/Sympathy

*$p<.001$

Brand Loyalty

The most interesting finding is the relationship between brand loyalty and deservingness. Brand equity, or brand loyalty confers many benefits to the firm that owns the brand, such as enhanced profit margins, trade leverage, and higher perceived quality to name but a few (Aaker 1991). However, deservingness of help/patronage has not previously been associated with brand equity. It is known that consumers exhibit strong feelings of commitment toward highly visible products such as cars, clothing, etc., but the results of this study suggest that consumers may feel commitment toward a broader scope of products than was realized. In this study subjects reported strong brand loyalty toward 45 different products ranging from candy bars to fish sticks. Subjects provided both product and brand name specific information.

CONCERNS / LIMITATIONS

Brand loyalty is moderately correlated with deservingness and risk (Loyalty-Risk, $r=-.34$, $p<.001$; Loyalty-Deservingness, $r=.44$, $p<.001$). This might lead one to question whether these constructs are truly independent. It is possible that an underlying factor (such as liking the product) is solely responsible for driving the purchase intention result. This possibility was investigated in two ways. First, a principal components factor analysis with oblique rotation was conducted to assess discriminant validity between the constructs. A five factor solution was chosen on a priori grounds, and the scree test also suggested retention of five factors. The five factors accounted for 79.3% of the variance. The results indicate that, with the exception of purchase intention item 1 double-loading on the deservingness factor, these five constructs appear to demonstrate discriminant validity (Refer to Table 3). Second, a partial correlation analysis was conducted to assess the impact of each variable on purchase intent (Refer to Table 2). The results suggest that deservingness and perceived risk influence purchase intention independently of brand loyalty.

A potential minor problem with the study is the use of the "hypothetical brand." It is not clear whether subjects envisioned these as national brands, store brands, or generic "brands." However, because the subjects were instructed to imagine a product at the "brand" level, there is some confidence that they did not view the hypothetical product as being unbranded, or generic.

A serious threat to the study is the possibility that hypotheses 2 and 3 are not specific to the tampering context. One might suspect

TABLE 3

Factor Solution of Key Measures: Principal Components Analysis with Oblimin Rotation

Measure	Item #	Factor 1	Factor 2	Factor 3	Factor 4	Factor 5
Brand Loyalty	1	.92				
	2	.90				
	3	.75				
Deservingness	1		.95			
	2		.76			
	3		.70			
Sympathy	1			.90		
	2			.93		
	3			.86		
Perceived Risk	1				.44	
	2				.51	
	3				.95	
Purchase Intent	1		.36			.51
	2					.45
	3					.37

Note: Factor loadings below .35 not shown for clarity.

that loyal brands elicit greater sympathy, deservingness, purchase intent, and less physical risk in any context. In order to show that brand loyalty leads to a differential change in any factor because of the tampering, one must compare the end results to "baseline" measures of these factors before the tampering incident. Although this possibility cannot be completely eliminated, there are many reasons why this issue was not considered to be a major concern in this study. First, existing research does not show that brand loyalty ever elicits sympathy or deservingness from consumers. Second, because the study required subjects to select a brand of food or beverage, which must pass strict FDA quality and safety guidelines, it is almost certain that the (normal) level of perceived risk associated with these products approaches zero. It is also assumed that consumers do not normally attribute feelings of sympathy or deservingness to such products. Therefore, because deservingness, sympathy and perceived risk in all likelihood normally approach a similar minimal level across brands, a pre-crisis baseline is "built-in" to the study. Therefore, any significant increase in deservingness, sympathy, or perceived risk associated with brand loyalty must have been elicited by the tampering incident. Third, all hypotheses are directly related to the tampering context, and the items used to test the hypotheses clearly indicate a connection to the tampering incident. Many of the dependent measure items listed in Appendix 1 directly, or indirectly mention the tampering incident. However, because not every item specifically mentions the word tampering, the ANOVAS and correlations were conducted using each individual item of each scale. The results of the individual item runs were essentially identical to the run made with the summated scales. Therefore it can be concluded that all of the items and the hypotheses are specifically tied to a tampering incident.

Crisis Management Implications

Many questions regarding the efficacy of the C/M approach are raised. The results of the study suggest a possible alternative strategy for handling a *no-fault* crisis situation. The current C/M approach suggests placing a heavy emphasis on risk reduction and extensive use of the media to elicit consumers' sympathy. Perhaps a more effective strategy would be to allocate a larger portion of the public relations message towards increasing consumers' awareness of the company's use of manufacturing and distribution processes designed to provide customers with products of the highest possible quality, reliability, and safety. Thus, consumers may be more likely to view the company as one with high integrity, and it therefore does not deserve to be "harmed" by a tamperer. Extreme caution must be taken when developing a crisis management strategy. Reliance on any one approach is probably unwise because of the wide range of factors that influence consumers. While this study does not capture all of the important factors; it does identify a previously unstudied factor (deservingness) and suggests that sympathy may not be a critical determinant of market share rebound. Perceived risk and deservingness appear to be the factors that have significant impact on purchase intent following a product tampering incident. A logical next step is to test the effectiveness of the previously mentioned "integrity appeal" versus the current C/M approach.

Future Research Directions

The deservingness factor needs further research attention. Currently, deservingness is not a recognized component of brand loyalty or brand equity, yet this study suggests that it should be in the future. Additional research is needed to explore other factors that might be influenced by deservingness. Also, research into the origins of company/brand deservingness seems warranted. Is deservingness the result of frequency of use, attributions toward the company/brand, truly liking the product, or something else? Perhaps the helping behavior framework could be used to model the relationship between consumers and retailers. A key question might be to determine what attributes a retailer must have to deserve consumers' patronage. Additional research is needed to investigate this issue. This study suggests that deservingness and sympathy toward brands are elicited by crisis conditions. The possibility that consumers possess substantial initial feelings of sympathy and deservingness toward brands should also be investigated.

REFERENCES

Aaker, David A. (1991), *Managing Brand Equity*, The Free Press, New York.

APPENDIX 1
Selected Measures

Scale	Cronbach's α
Deservingness 1) Even though the tampering incident happened, this co. still deserves my business. 2) The company clearly deserves a second chance. 3) The company does not deserve my continued business. (reverse)	α = .80
Sympathy 1) Because of the tampering incident, I feel sorry for the company. 2) I feel sympathetic toward the company for what happened to it. 3) I do not feel sorry for this company. (reverse)	α = .89
Perceived Risk 1) The use of this brand of product is more risky than the use of some other brand of product that has not been tampered with. 2) It would probably be safer to switch brands. 3) If I buy this brand of product again in the future I'd definitely be taking a risk.	α = .78
Purchase Intention 1) Because of the tampering incident, I'll switch to some other brand. (reverse) 2) The likelihood of my buying this product again is quite high. 3) I will continue to buy this brand of product in the future.	α = .91
Fault 1) The incident was clearly not the company's fault. (reverse) 2) The company is at fault for the tampering incident.	r = .60 [a]
Company Action 1) Company-wide changes were made to make the product safer. 2) The company made significant changes after the tampering incident.	r = .78[a]

Note: All items used 5-point Likert scales (1 = strongly disagree 5 = strongly agree).
[a]Pearson correlation.

Betancourt, Hector (1990), "An Attribution-Empathy Model of Helping Behavior: Behavioral Intentions and Judgements of Help-Giving," *Personality and Social Psychology Bulletin*, 16 (September), 573-591.

Clark, Margaret S., Robert Oullette, Martha C. Powell and Sandra Milberg (1987), "Recipient's Mood, Relationship Type, and Helping," *Journal of Personality and Social Psychology*, 53 (1), 94-103.

Dipboye, Robert and Michael F. Flanagan (1979), "Are Findings in the Field More Generalizable than in the Laboratory?" *American Psychologist*, 34 (February), 141-150.

Folkes, Valerie, Susan Koletsky and John L. Graham (1987), "A Field Study of Causal Inferences and Consumer Reaction: The View from the Airport," *Journal of Consumer Research*, 13 (March), 534-539.

Greenberg, Keith Elliot (1993), "Pepsi's Big Scare," *Public Relations Journal*, 49 (August), 6-7.

Jackson, Gary B., Ralph W. Jackson and Clyde E. Newmiller, Jr. (1992), "Consumer Demographics and Reaction to Product Tampering," *Psychology and Marketing*, 9 (January), 45-57.

Jorgensen, Brian K. (1994), "Consumer Reaction to Company-Related Disasters: The Effect of Multiple Versus Single Explanations," in *Advances in Consumer Research*, Vol. 21, eds. Chris T. Allen, and Deborah Roedder John, Nashville, TN: Association for Consumer Research, 348-352.

Kaufmann, Jeffrey B., Idalene F. Kesner and Thomas Lee Hazen (1994), "The Myth of Full Disclosure: A Look at Organizational Communications During Crises," *Business Horizons*, (July-August), 29-39.

Lerner, Melvin H. and Hames R. Meindl (1981), "Justice and Altruism," in *Altruism and Helping Behavior: Social, Personality and Development Perspectives*," eds. J. Philippe Rushton and Richard M. Sorrentino, Hillsdale, NJ: Lawrence Erlbaum, 137-165.

Morgan, Fred W. (1988), "Tampered Goods: Legal Developments and Marketing Guidelines," *Journal of Marketing*, 52 (April), 86-96.

Meyers, Gerald C. (1993), "Product Tampering and Public Outcry," *Industry Week*, August 2, 41.

Mitchell, V.W. and M. Greatorex (1993), "Risk Perception and Reduction in the Purchase of Consumer Services," *The Service Industries Journal*, 13 (October), 179-200.

Piliavin, Jane A., John F. Dovido, Samuel L. Gaertner and Russell D. Clark, III. (1981), *Emergency Intervention*, New York: Academic Press.

Richins, Marsha L. (1983), "Negative Word-of-Mouth by Dissatisfied Consumers: A Pilot Study," *Journal of Marketing*, 47 (Winter), 68-78.

Roselius, Ted (1971), "Consumer Rankings of Risk Reduction Methods," *Journal of Marketing*, 35 (January), 55-61.

Rosette, Jack L. (1992), "Tamper Evident Packaging: Law Enforcement and the Consumer," *FBI Law Enforcement Bulletin,* (September), 16-19.

Routhier, Rick (1993), "Punching Out A Hoax," *Sales & Marketing Management,* October, 12.

Schmidt, Greg and Bernard Weiner (1988), "An Attribution-Affect-Action Theory of Behavior: Replications of Judgements of Help-Giving," *Personality and Social Psychology Bulletin,* 14 (September), 610-621.

Schoenrade, Patricia A., Daniel C. Batson, Randall J. Brandt and Robert E. Loud, Jr. (1986), "Attachment, Accountability, and Motivation to Benefit Another Not in Distress," *Journal of Personality and Social Psychology,* 51 (3), 557-563.

Shotland, R. Lance and Margaret K. Straw (1976), "Bystander Response to an Assault: When a Man Attacks a Woman," *Journal of Personality and Social Psychology,* 34, 990-999.

Siomkos, George J. and Peter G. Malliaris (1992), "Consumer Response to Company Communications During a Product Harm Crisis," *Journal of Applied Business Research,* 8 (Fall), 59-65.

_____, and Gary Kurzbard (1994), "The Hidden Crisis in Product-Harm Crisis Management," *European Journal of Marketing,* 28(2), 30-41.

Stehlin, Isadora B. (1995), "FDA's Forensic Center: Speedy, Sophisticated Sleuthing," *FDA Consumer,* 29(6), 5-9.

Stern, Walter (1989), "A Common-Sense View," *Packaging,* May, 37-41.

The Roles of Consumer Ethnocentricity and Attitude Toward a Foreign Culture in Processing Foreign Country-of-Origin Advertisements

Byeong-Joon Moon, University of Connecticut

ABSTRACT

This paper focuses on consumers' psychological processing of advertising that pitches a foreign country-of-origin product (brand) in that country's own cultural context, with *no* tailoring of the advertisement to the country where the brand is being promoted and sold. We refer to this type of advertising as *foreign country-of-origin advertising*. The purpose of this paper is to provide a conceptual framework for demonstrating the role of two international setting-specific factors — consumer ethnocentricity (with regard to one's "home" country) and the consumer's attitude toward the foreign culture (depicted in the advertisement) — in the psychological processing of foreign country-of-origin advertising. Specifically, this paper builds upon and contributes to existing advertising effects literature and posits that a consumer's Cad, Aad, Cb, Ab, and PI will differ depending on his/her ethnocentric tendency and attitude toward the foreign culture depicted in the foreign country-of-origin advertising.

INTRODUCTION

An increasing number of firms have created world brands — that are manufactured, packaged and advertised in exactly the same way, regardless of the country in which they are sold. While this unified global marketing strategy is seemingly cost effective because no tailoring of the product or promotion is required, there remains the question as to whether a unified global marketing strategy is the best way of communicating with consumers across borders.

The focus of this paper is on consumers' psychological processing of advertising that pitches a foreign country-of-origin product (brand) in that country's own cultural context, with *no* tailoring of the advertisement to the country where the brand is being promoted and sold. We refer to this type of advertising as *foreign country-of-origin advertising*. An example will help to illustrate foreign country-of-origin advertising: Phillip Morris (a U.S. based multinational organization) has advertised their Marlboro cigarettes with the Marlboro Cowboy as the spokesperson around the world. As another example, General Motors, Unilever, and Parker Pen have also used foreign country-of-origin advertising to promote their brands and services (Schiffman and Kanuk 1994 p.481).

Consumers' psychological processing of foreign country-of-origin advertising is not well understood. Although recent studies on consumer's psychological processing have well established the interrelationships among ad-induced emotional and cognitive responses, attitudes toward advertisements (Aad), brand attitudes (Ab), and purchase intentions (PI) (Burke and Edell 1989; Homer and Yoon 1992; MacKenzie, Lutz and Belch 1986; Park and Young 1986), no research has directly investigated these issues in the context of foreign country-of-origin advertising. Therefore, the purpose of this paper is to provide a conceptual framework for demonstrating the role of two international setting-specific factors —consumer ethnocentricity (with regard to one's "home" country) and the consumer's attitude toward the foreign culture (depicted in the advertisement) — in the psychological processing of foreign country-of-origin advertising. Specifically, this paper builds upon existing advertising effects literature and posits that a consumer's Cad, Aad, Cb, Ab, and PI will differ depending on his/her ethnocentric tendency and attitude toward the foreign culture depicted in the foreign country-of-origin (FCOO) advertising.

A MODEL FOR UNDERSTANDING CONSUMER PROCESSING OF FCOO ADVERTISEMENTS

Recent studies on consumer processing of advertisements have documented a general model of the relationships among cognition about the ad and brand, Aad, Ab, and PI (Burke and Edell 1989; Homer and Yoon 1992; MacKenzie, Lutz and Belch 1986; Park and Young 1986). Specifically, Burke and Edell (1989) provide evidence that

- Emotional responses influence Aad directly and indirectly via Cad.
- Emotional responses influence Cb directly and indirectly via Cad.
- Emotional responses have a direct effect on Ab and an indirect effect via the Cad—>Aad path.

This research provides the starting point from which to introduce our model for understanding consumer processing of foreign country-of-origin advertising.

Our model (Figure 1) builds upon the advertising effects model by integrating two international setting-specific variables— consumer ethnocentricity and consumer's attitude toward a foreign culture. Consumer ethnocentricity and consumer's attitude toward a foreign culture/country are posited as antecedent constructs to foreign country-of-origin ad based cognitive and affective elements.

Because consumer ethnocentricity and a consumer's attitude toward a foreign culture can be considered individual factors such as personality, we believe that they can impact how an individual "sees" and evaluates advertising. With regard to ethnocentrism, patriotic, even xenophobic sentiments wax and wane among Americans and people of other countries. Thus, their personal attitudes and behaviors regarding domestic and foreign products may vary. Similarly, we believe that a consumer's level of ethnocentricity is likely to affect his/her perceptions of a foreign country-of-origin ad.

History and literature indicate that individuals have certain opinions of foreign cultures and/or countries. For example, due to World War II hostilities, some older Americans may have negative attitudes toward Japan and/or Germany. We believe that consumer attitude toward a foreign culture or country may trigger overall affections when they view a foreign country-of-origin ad. We proceed by further defining consumer ethnocentrism and attitude toward a foreign culture and then develop hypotheses about their effects on the ad effects model.

The Role of Consumer Ethnocentricity in Processing FCOO Ad

Ethnocentrism is broadly defined as "the view of things in which one's own group is the center of everything, and all others are scaled and rated with reference to it. Each group nourishes its own pride and vanity, boasts itself superior, exalts its own divinities and looks with contempt on outsiders (Sumner 1906)." Shimp and Sharma (1987) focused on consumer ethnocentricity, defining it as *"the beliefs held by consumers about the appropriateness, indeed morality, of purchasing foreign-made products"* (p. 280).

Sharma et al. (1995) argued that consumer ethnocentricity has the following characteristics (p. 27): "First, consumer ethnocentricity results from the love and concern for one's own country and the fear of losing control of one's own economic interests as the result of the harmful effects that imports may bring to oneself and

FIGURE 1
A Model for Consumer Processing of Foreign Country-of-Origin Advertisements

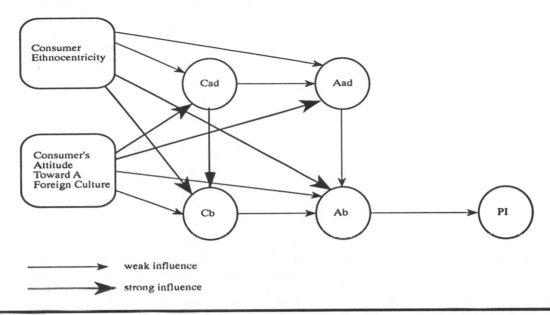

countrymen. Second, it contains the intention or willingness not to purchase foreign products. For highly ethnocentric consumers, buying foreign products is not only an economic issue but also a moral problem. This involvement of morality causes consumers to purchase domestic products even though, in extreme cases, the quality is below that of imports. In the eyes of ethnocentric consumers, not buying foreign imports is good, appropriate, desirable, and patriotic; buying them is bad, inappropriate, undesirable, and irresponsible. Third, it refers to a personal level of prejudice against imports, although it may be assumed that the overall level of consumer ethnocentricity in a social system is the aggregation of individual tendencies."

We argue that the effects of consumer ethnocentricity are stronger on Cb and Ab than Cad and Aad. Because consumer ethnocentricity is conceptualized as consumers' embedded bias to imported products and consumers' beliefs about the morality or appropriateness of purchasing foreign-made products, consumers who have high ethnocentric tendencies will have negative thoughts about and unfavorable attitudes toward foreign-made brands, so consumer ethnocentricity is proposed primarily to affect Cb and Ab in processing foreign country-of-origin ads.

Consumer ethnocentricity is proposed secondarily to affect the perception of the buying proposal of foreign country-of-origin ads. Killough (1978 p.105) argues that "advertising propositions for international transfer consist of two elements which must be considered separately because the reaction to them is different in different countries. The first element—the 'buying proposal' represents the sales points, or those elements of the seller's product judged by the seller to be most persuasive and most relevant to the prospective customer. It is *what* one says. It is the content, not the form. Everything that is not part of the buying proposal is part of *how* one says it. The advertising message is formed when that proposal is developed into a 'creative presentation.' It includes all the visual and verbal elements."

Let's assume an example in which a Japanese consumer who has a high ethnocentric tendency views a foreign country-of-origin ad pitching a U.S. originated brand in an American cultural context. Because s/he has high consumer ethnocentric tendencies, s/he may

worry about losing control of his or her economic interests as the result of the harmful effects that imports may bring to oneself and countrymen. As a result, s/he may show a negative cognitive response and an unfavorable attitude toward the brand itself and the buying proposal of the foreign country-of-origin ad. But the consumer's response to the creative presentation of the ad may be different from that of the buying proposal. S/he may show a positive response and a favorable attitude toward the ad itself independent of Cb and Ab.

Based on previous research on the impact of attitudes on behavior (Chaiken and Eagly 1992; Ajzen 1987; Homer and Yoon 1992), we propose also that Ab influences PI.

Hypothesis 1: Consumer ethnocentricity directly affects Cb and indirectly affects Cb via Cad.

Hypothesis 2: Consumer ethnocentricity directly affects Ab and indirectly affects Ab via Aad or Cb.

Hypothesis 3: Consumer ethnocentricity influences Aad directly and indirectly via Cad.

Hypothesis 4: The impact of consumer ethnocentricity is stronger on Cb and Ab than on Cad and Aad.

The Role of Attitude Toward a Foreign Culture in Processing FCOO Ad

Attitude is defined as "a psychological tendency that is expressed by evaluating a particular entity with some degree of favor or disfavor (Eagly and Chaiken 1993)." A psychological tendency is posited as a state that is internal to the person, and evaluating is cited as all classes of evaluative responding, whether overt or covert, cognitive, affective, or behavioral. Eagly and Chaiken (1993 p.2) proposed "Attitude can be regarded as a type of bias that predisposes the individual toward evaluative responses that are positive or negative. A mental representation of the attitude may be stored in memory and thus can be activated by the presence of the attitude object or cues related to it."

We define consumer attitude toward a foreign culture/country as *"a psychological tendency that is expressed by evaluating the life-styles, values, and customs of a specific foreign culture/country in consumption behavior.*" It is an individual factor in consumer behavior such as consumer ethnocentricity, personality, self-efficacy, and susceptibility to interpersonal influence.

Consumers form attitudes toward a foreign culture through face-to-face activities such as travel, trade, education and, for example, by watching movies or paying attention to world events. Telecommunications has also increased access to the global community. In general, the globalization of the world is accelerating and the peoples of different nations and different cultural zones are becoming more familiar with one another. As a consequence, we can expect people's attitudes about other cultural, ethnic, and religious groups to evolve. We proceed by further discussing a cultural systems perspective of advertising and the rationale of why consumer's attitude toward a foreign culture affects thoughts about and attitude toward foreign country-of-origin ads.

Advertising as a Cultural System. Much of the postmodern research into consumer behavior has focussed on the cultural significance of advertising. Sherry (1991 p.557-563) has reviewed this perspective well: "Sherry (1987) has employed a cultural systems perspective to interpret advertising as a way of knowing, a way of discerning, and a way of creating meaning that structures experience semiotically and semiologically into distinct patterns. McCracken (1986) has advocated a cultural perspective capable of viewing advertising as one conduit in the transfer of meaning from the cultural world to consumer goods. Belk and Pollay (1985) have presented a historical analysis of the ways in which advertising reflects and influences values in the United States, while Sherry and Camargo (1987) have explored the way in which linguistic borrowing creates a promotional patois by which Japanese consumers are able to negotiate cultural continuity and change. Leymore (1975, 1987, 1988) has usefully interpreted advertising as the mythology of consumer culture, and has detailed the rules by which the codes of advertising can be transformed to reveal their culturally significant meanings. Leiss et al. (1986) emphasized the 'real' importance of contemporary advertising as 'the privileged discourse for the circulation of messages and social cues about the interplay between persons and objects.' Carey's (1988 a, b) volumes on the multistranded relationship of culture and communication reveals the dense interpretation of scholarly traditions that has culminated in the recent desire of some consumer researchers to move beyond 'the narrow concern for empirically measuring media effects' to the study of the cultural significance of communication."

This stream of research on advertising suggests that a culture is embedded in an advertisement as a core element. We can infer from this that consumer's attitude toward a foreign culture may affect the thoughts about and attitude toward a foreign country-of-origin ad in that country's own cultural context. So if a consumer has a positive attitude toward the culture of "A" country, s/he may have a favorable attitude toward the advertisement that has the cultural context of "A" country. But if a consumer has a negative attitude toward the culture of "A" country, s/he may have an unfavorable attitude toward the advertisement that has the cultural context of "A" country.

We propose that consumer attitude toward a foreign culture contributes to explaining the variance in advertising effects primarily through the direct route to Cad and Aad or indirectly via the Cad—>Aad path. We propose also that a consumer's attitude toward a foreign culture influences (albeit weaker) Cb and Ab directly or indirectly through Cad—>Cb and Aad—>Ab path.

Hypothesis 5:   Consumer's attitude toward a foreign culture contributes to explaining the variance in foreign country-of-origin ad effects primarily through the direct

route to Cad and Aad and indirectly via the Cad—>Aad path.

Hypothesis 6:   Consumer's attitude toward a foreign culture influences Cb directly and indirectly via the Cad—>Cb path.

Hypothesis 7:   Consumer's attitude toward a foreign culture influences Ab directly and indirectly via Aad—>Ab path and Cb—>Ab path.

Relationship Between Consumer Ethnocentricity and Attitude Toward a Foreign Culture

Consumer ethnocentricity and a consumer's attitude toward a foreign culture have significant communalities in that each is comprised of cultural and individual factors that influence consumer processing of foreign country-of-origin advertisements. They are, however, distinct constructs. Consumer ethnocentricity has an inward focus toward one's own country; a consumer's attitude toward a foreign culture is a predisposition toward a specific foreign culture.

Now we are confronted with a question. Are the two constructs—consumer ethnocentricity and attitude toward a foreign culture—distinguishable? How do these two constructs interact? What happens when a consumer has a high ethnocentric tendency, can s/he still have a favorable attitude toward a foreign culture/country?

Sharma et al. (1995) found a negative correlation between cultural openness and consumer ethnocentrism. Even though consumers who are not familiar with and open to foreign cultures may show a high consumer ethnocentric tendency, they may not necessarily show unfavorable attitudes toward a specific foreign culture. For example, a Japanese woman who has little experience with the people, values, and artifacts of other cultures may have an unfavorable attitude toward importing products. Even though, she has a high ethnocentric tendency in consumption, she may have a favorable attitude toward U.S. or American culture or American life-style. Because consumer ethnocentricity, according to Sharma et al.(1995), is determined not only by openness to foreign culture but also by other social-psychological factors such as the degree of patriotism, conservatism, collectivism/individualism, and demographic factors such as gender, education, and income.

CONCLUSION AND DISCUSSION

This study proposes a conceptual framework permitting the consideration of international setting-specific factors—consumer ethnocentricity and consumer's attitude toward a foreign culture—in consumer processing of foreign country-of-origin advertisements. Both consumer ethnocentricity and consumer's attitude toward a foreign culture are posited as individual factors such as personality, self-efficacy, and susceptibility to interpersonal influences that evoke unique feelings when the consumers view foreign country-of-origin advertisements. But consumer ethnocentricity and attitude toward a foreign culture are different in several perspectives such as the direction (inward vs. outward of one's own country) and nature, so their impacts on consumer processing of foreign country-of-origin advertisements are different.

We suggest that consumer ethnocentricity has a strong effect on Cb and Ab whereas consumer's attitude toward a foreign culture has a strong effect on Cad and Aad because consumer ethnocentricity is believed primarily to evoke negative thoughts about and attitudes toward imported brands but consumer's attitude toward a foreign culture is considered primarily to affect the perception of cultural elements or the creative presentation of the advertising. This argument can be justified by the nature of the two constructs.

Consumer ethnocentricity is a consumer's beliefs about the appropriateness or morality of purchasing foreign-made products and a consumer's embedded bias to imported products, so it is argued primarily to evoke thoughts about and attitude toward foreign-made brands. Consumer attitude toward a foreign culture/country is a psychological tendency that is expressed by evaluating the lifestyles, values, and customs of a specific foreign culture/country in consumption behavior. Culture is embedded in advertising as a core element. We can infer from this that consumer's attitude toward a foreign culture primarily affects the thoughts about and attitude toward a foreign country-of-origin ad in that country's own cultural context.

Understanding consumers' responses to foreign country-of-origin advertisements is important from a variety of perspectives. First, consumer ethnocentricity can activate certain attributes (e.g. beliefs on country-of-origin) in consumers when they view the foreign country-of-origin advertisements, and this may guide their interpretations of product information (e.g. quality) in the ad and thus affect their attitude toward the brand. When consumers view the ads that pitch foreign products, consumer ethnocentricity may arouse negative cognitions or emotions and they may have an unfavorable attitude toward the ad which will affect their brand evaluations. Second, consumers are likely to vary in their attitude toward a specific foreign culture/country and consumers' attitudes may trigger overall affections when they watch a specific foreign culture contextual ad. These overall effects generated by consumers' attitudes toward a culture/country may be transferred to one's attitudes toward the ad, which can subsequently influence brand evaluations and purchase intentions. Also consumer attitudes toward a culture/country may influence Ab directly.

REFERENCES

Ajzen, Icek (1987), "Attitudes, Traits, and Actions: Dispositional Prediction of Behavior in Personality and Social Psychology," *Advances in Experimental Social Psychology*, 1-63.

Belk, Russell, and Richard Pollay (1985), "Images of Ourselves: The Good Life in Twentieth Century Advertising," *Journal of Consumer Research*, 11(4), 887-897.

Burke, Marian C. and Julie A. Edell (1989), "The Impact of Feelings on Ad-Based Affect and Cognition," *Journal of Marketing Research*, 26 (February), 69-83.

Carey, James, Ed. (1988a), *Media, Myths, and Narratives: Television and the Press.* Newbury Park, CA: Sage.

_____ (1988b), *Communication as Culture: Essaya on Media and Society*, Chester, MA: Unwin Hyman.

Chaiken, Shelly and Alice H. Eagly (1992), "The Impact of Attitudes on Behavior," in *The Psychology of Attitudes*, Fort Worth, TX: Harcourt Brace Jovanovich College Publishers.

Eagly, Alice H. and Shelly Chaiken (1993), "The Nature of Attitudes," in *The Psychology of Attitudes*, Fort Worth, TX: Harcourt Brace Jovanovich College Publishers.

Homer, Pamela M. and Sun-Gil Yoon (1992), "Message Framing and Interrelationships Among Ad-Based Feelings, Affect, and Cognition," *Journal of Advertising*, 21(March), 19-33.

Killough, James (1978), "Improved Payoffs From Transnational Advertising," *Harvard Business Review*, 1978, 102-110.

Leiss, William, Stephen Kline, and Sut Jhally (1986), *Social Communication in Advertising: An Essay on the Problem of Needs and Commodities.* Toronto: University of Toronto Press.

Leymore, Varda (1975), *Hidden Myth*, New York: Basic Books.

_____ (1987), "The Structure is the Message—The Case of Advertising," in *Marketing and Semiotics: New Directions in the Study of Signs for Sale*, Ed. Jean Umiker-Sebeok. Berlin: Mouton de Gruyter, 319-331.

_____ (1988), "Inside Information: Structure and Effectivity in Advertising," *International Journal of Research in Marketing*, 4(3), 217-232.

McCracken, Grant (1986), "Culture and Consumption: A Theoretical Account of the Structure and Movement of the Cultural Meaning of Consumer Goods," *Journal of Consumer Research*, 13(1), 71-84.

MacKenzie, Scott B., Richard J. Lutz (1989), "An Empirical Examination of the Structural Antecedents of Attitude Toward the Ad in an Advertising Pretesting Context," *Journal of Marketing,* 53 (April), 48-65.

_____ and George E. Belch (1986), "The Role of Attitude Toward the Ad as a Mediator of Advertising Effectiveness: A Test of Competing Explanations," *Journal of Marketing Research*, 23 (May). 130-143.

Park, C.W. and S. Mark Young (1986), "Consumer Response to Television Commercials: The Impact of Involvement and Background Music on Brand Attitude Formation," *Journal of Marketing Research*, 23 (February), 11-24.

Schiffman, Leon G. and Leslie Lazar Kanuk (1994), *Consumer Behavior*, Fifth Ed. Prentice-Hall, Englewood Cliffs, New Jersey.

Sharma, Subhash, Terence A. Shimp, and Jeongshin Shin (1995), "Consumer Ethnocentrism: A Test of Antecedents and Moderators," *Journal of the Academy of Marketing Science*, 23(1), 26-37.

Sherry, John F., Jr. (1987), "Advertising as a Cultural System," in *Marketing and Semiotics: New Directions in the Study of Signs for Sale*, Ed. Jean Umiker-Sebeok. Berlin: Mouton de Gruyter, 441-461.

_____ (1991), "Postmodern Alternatives: The Interpretive Turn in Consumer Research," in *Handbook of Consumer Behavior*, Ed. Thomas S. Robertson and Harold H. Kassarjian. Prentice-Hall, Inc. Englewood Cliffs, New Jersey, 548-591.

_____ and Eduardo Camargo (1987), "'May Your Life Be Marvelous': English Language Labelling and the Semiotics of Japanese Promotion," *Journal of Consumer Research*, 14(2), 174-188.

Shimp, Terence A. and Subhash Sharma (1987), "Consumer Ethnocentrism: Construction and Validation of the CETSCALE," *Journal of Marketing Research*, 27 (August), 280-289.

Sumner, William G. (1906), *Folkways: The Sociological Importance of Usages, Manners, Customs, Mores, and Morals.* New York: Ginn & Co.

Social Networks: Influence and Information Concerns for Single Divorced Mothers

Myra Jo Bates, University of Nebraska-Lincoln
Patricia F. Kennedy, University of Nebraska-Lincoln

ABSTRACT

The divorce rate in the United States has risen over the years until today there are many households that are headed by single females. Single-parent families' purchase decisions, however, have not been studied in depth in the marketing discipline. This paper examines social network influence in terms of the role of marital status in purchase decisions. Of particular interest is the influence of social network members' input in the purchase decisions of single mothers. Propositions are considered and the implications for marketers, if these propositions prove to be true, are discussed.

INTRODUCTION

This paper begins a search for knowledge regarding the marketplace information provided by members of the social networks of divorced single mothers versus the information provided to married mothers. In marketing, the inputs to purchase decisions of single parent households have not been thoroughly examined. Early family-decision-making studies focused mainly upon the influence of marital partners in joint decision making. With the high divorce rate in the United States, and the corresponding increase in the number of single-parent, female-headed households, the topic is open for investigation. Ahuja and Stinson (1993) found only five articles in the marketing literature that referred to single parents. A subsequent study by Bates and Gentry (1994) did examine single mothers and found that divorced mothers use kinship networks as post divorce family preservation tools. Combining this information with that provided by the work of Iacobucci and Hopkins (1992), which shows that network analysis is suitable for identifying sources and targets of information flow, led to the ideas presented in this paper. The focus of this paper is social network influences, and sources of information from the social network used in purchase decisions by single divorced mothers, and whether influence levels and information sources differ between single divorced mothers and married mothers in intact families. A rising divorce rate in the U.S. increases interest in studying single divorced mothers. This paper provides a definition of a social support network, presents network characteristics, and discusses types of support. Subsequent sections discuss the implications of social network influence and information provided to single mothers in purchase decisions. Propositions are then presented and implications for marketers, if these propositions prove to be true, are discussed.

BACKGROUND

The rising divorce rate in the United States has created an unprecedented number of single parent families. In 1992, close to 1.2 million couples divorced (DeWitt 1992), and it has been projected that nearly two-thirds of first marriages will dissolve (Martin and Bumpass 1989). In any given year approximately 2% of American children experience a divorce, with each divorce now involving just under one child per divorce (DeWitt 1992). In addition, while more fathers are gaining custody of children, 14% in 1990 compared to 10% in 1980, most children of divorce (86%) reside with mothers (Bernstein 1992). Given the continuation of these trends, a majority of American children will spend a portion of their lives in a single parent home, with most of these children living with their mothers.

Questions raised by these trends include: (1) Do single-parents arrive at consumer decisions differently than married parents? (2) Are influences on single parents comparable to those on married parents? (3) Is information gathered in a different fashion by single parents than by married parents? If the answer to these questions is yes, the marketer must ascertain the differences and address the variations to satisfy consumer needs.

The focus of this paper is single-divorced mothers. It becomes important to examine how mothers' social networks affect purchase decisions in terms of influence and information. In addition, it is important to identify any differences between single and married mothers in terms of how they are influenced by their social networks and their use of information garnered from these networks.

DEFINITION

This study investigates social networks and a specific social network, the social support network. No one definition of a social support network exists. Garbarino (1983, p. 5) defines a social support network as "...a set of interconnected relationships among a group of people that provides enduring patterns of nurturance (in any or all forms) and provides contingent reinforcement for efforts to cope with life on a day-to-day basis." The critical dimensions of this definition include the idea of interconnected relationships, the provision by network members of all forms of nurturance, and the idea of contingent reinforcement. For our purpose, social network refers to the aggregation of individuals with whom one is in contact, and support is a network activity from which individuals receive needed assistance. The social support network then includes those social network members providing aid to others. In reviewing the work of other researches in this area, it appears that some of these issues have become confused. For example, House, Umberson, and Landis (1988) note that the related terms social networks, and social support are often used interchangeably. Hughes (1988) adds that authors often do not distinguish between support and social environment which is the social network.

Not all support given by the social network comes from one person (Walker, Wasserman, and Wellman 1993). Relatives, ex-spouses, or parents may provide child care, whereas social needs are more apt to be met by friends or one's children (Kurdek 1988). Garbarino (1983) points out that social support networks often originate from groups, with formal networks arising from professional services and informal networks evolving elsewhere (Richardson and Pfeiffenberger 1983).

Uehara (1990) espouses the idea of exchange within social networks. This exchange is not always dyadic in nature. Uehara's (1990) ideas can be presented as a continuum with one terminal being gift giving, with nothing expected in return, to a direct exchange of resources at the opposite end where one type of resource is traded for another. Midway on this continuum are loans, delayed repayments in kind for support given. Exchange also occurs when support is given to an individual who reciprocates by delivering support to a third person. Comparing married to single mothers in Sweden, Tietjen (1985) found reciprocity important to single mothers because, when able to repay in some way, seeking support is not associated with charity. Leslie and Grady (1988) bolstered this idea when they found that mothers value relationships when they can give as well as receive.

As discussed above, the definition of social networks, provided by Gabarino (1983), embraces several factors: (1) social networks focusing specifically on support exchanged among network members, (2) the social network as an assortment of interacting individuals, and (3) the reciprocal nature of social support must be included in the definition. The last factor is of some importance, especially to those who might have a need to repay others who have helped them. This definition includes the multiple facets of a social network and will constitute the framework for this paper.

SUPPORT

Types of support differ in the literature. Wellman and Wortley (1989) specify emotional aid, companionship, financial aid, and services as dimensions of social support. Hughes (1988) lists categories of help: psychological - a feeling of value; instrumental - provision of goods and services; and informational - sharing advice and knowledge. Divorced mothers feel that child care, financial support, the need for recreational and social activities, an opportunity to discuss feelings, physical intimacy and sexual needs, and discussing divorce-related issues are areas of highest need (Kurdek 1988). Kiecker and Hartman (1994) identify support activities pertaining to purchasing. Functional tasks embody giving information about product features, retail outlets, and prices. Symbolic tasks involve furnishing moral support for the purchase decision, increasing the buyer's confidence when making the decision, and helping determine whether or not the product was appropriate. Whatever terms describe social support activities, all reflect some type of emotional support, such as listening to the recipient, and physical support, like providing material goods and services.

Isaacs and Leon (1986) identify four parental network patterns used to support divorced daughters. These patterns range from emotional and financial aid to child care and offering advice. After divorce, establishing friendships with other divorced individuals is important in that these new acquaintances provide an opportunity to share experiences (McHenry and Price 1991). In Sweden, single mothers receive more network support than married mothers, but single mothers rate their friends and relatives as less supportive than do married mothers (Tietjen 1985). When comparing divorced mothers to married mothers, married mothers rely on neighbors as sources of support whereas divorced mothers depend on friends, especially for instrumental support (Tietjan 1985). However, as one ages, friends become less important than family or kin (Levitt, Weber, and Guacci 1993). Schilling (1987) makes an important point in his assertion that support requirements vary among individuals experiencing the same problems, with no two people having the same level of need.

NETWORK CHARACTERISTICS

One objective of this paper is to create propositions comparing married and single mothers in terms of how influence and information from social networks affect their purchase decisions. Understanding how the general system works will give a foundation for ascertaining how information and influence flow through the network. The propositions stem from understanding the network.

Depth and Density

The first feature of social networks is depth. Fellerman and Debevec (1993, p. 459) define depth in terms of "... the number of generations 'up' or 'down' within a particular relationship in the network. Thus, one generation "down" is children; those of equivalent depth are siblings; and one generation "up" includes parents and their siblings. This definition need not be limited to kin

relationships. Cohorts of one's parents can be considered one generation "up," while one's own non-related cohorts are of equal depth. Intergenerational interaction is not limited to kinship exchange. Support can be obtained from and given to non-related members of the social network. The second feature, density, refers to the extent network members know and interact with each other. The better members know each other, and the more frequent the interaction, the denser the network. Important factors include geographic proximity and frequency of member contacts. Dense kin-filled networks provide mothers with a greater sense of well-being immediately after divorce than less dense or friend-filled networks (Acock and Hurlbert 1993).

Homophily

Schilling (1987) claims that support networks tend to be composed of individuals with common social characteristics. Quinn and Allen (1989) found that some divorced women often look to their church as a safe place for friendship and social activity. These women feel that churches offer a community with similar values and interests. Another area where single women find others of similar interests is in education. Quinn and Allen (1989) found that divorced women who return to school often see their classmates as part of a social network to whom they may turn for support.

Network Stability

The dynamic nature of the social network is another feature needing attention. Following divorce, a woman's network and primary support person changes both immediately and over time (Duffy 1993). For married mothers, husbands are the primary source of support (Levitt, Weber, and Clark 1986), but this source is lost to divorced mothers. Some members, who provided support during the divorce, remain in the network (McHenry and Price, 1991). Others, who feel closer to the former spouse, drop out. In a longitudinal study, Weinraub and Wolf (1983) found that, over the same time period, single mothers name fewer of the same members in their social networks than married mothers. New friends and dating relationships become added sources of support (McHenry and Price 1991). In networks where support is strong for a divorced single mother, members added after the divorce tend to resemble current network members (Leslie and Grady 1985). For divorced single mothers, friends become more important than kin over time (Wagner 1988), although divorced mothers maintain long-term kin relationships (Gerstel 1988; Walker, Wasserman, and Wellman 1993). Studying three generations, Levitt, Weber, and Guacci (1993) found younger women have more friends and older women have more family members in their networks. Children affect the social network (Ishii-Kuntz and Seccombe 1989), with mothers more involved with their social networks than childless women.

Size

Size of networks is another factor. There is no significant difference in size of married mothers' networks when compared to single divorced mothers' networks (Tietjen 1985). There is also no difference in the number of close relationships between married African American mothers and their divorced counterparts (Brown and Gary 1985). However, larger networks offer more opportunity for interaction.

Membership

As stated earlier, the social network changes over time. Members come into or drop from networks as conditions change. By default, the original members of one's social network are relatives, with the most important relationship existing between

FIGURE 1
A Conceptualization of Social Network Influence in Purchase Decisions

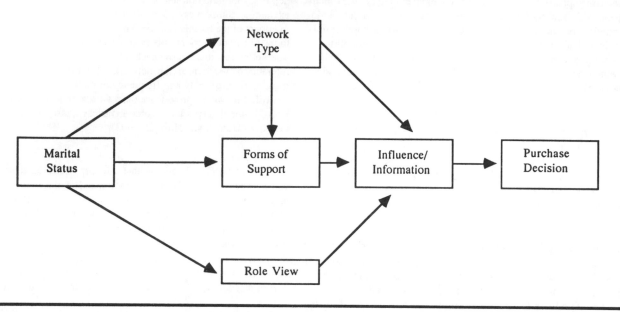

parent and child (Hogan, Eggebeen, and Clogg 1993). Support lasts over the life course and adult children often reciprocate to parents in the latter's declining years. The support of parents given to their divorcing daughters has adjustment-to-the-divorce implications for grandchildren (Isaacs and Leon 1986). Strong relationships between the parents and daughters help a third-generation child adjust more easily to divorce than if weak relationships exist between the older generations.

The relationship between children and their divorcing mothers changes during the divorce process. There is an initial period of disruption and deterioration with gradual establishment of a new relationship (Zastowny and Lewis 1989). Some parenting skills decline in the post-divorce period (Holloway and Machida 1991), with some mothers losing power to their children (Ahuja and Stinson 1993). Single mothers also discuss financial and economic matters with their children more often than married mothers. Economic difficulties are often shared by the single mother with her children (McLoyd and Wilson 1992). With the ongoing relationship between mother and child, each is a member of the other's social network. The children can be providers of support for single mothers (Kurdek 1988).

Social networks range beyond the nuclear and extended families. Zastowny and Lewis (1989) note that community relationships, including friends, reference groups, and other acquaintances are important. McLanahan, Wedemeyer, and Adelberg's (1981) "Conjugal Networks" have a key male member of the social network as the primary source of support for the divorced mother. Within marriage, the spouse is found near the center of the network and is a primary provider of support. Another source of network members is former in-laws (Serovich, Price, and Chapman 1991). Ex-daughters-in-law are more likely to receive support from former in-laws than ex-sons-in-law, but the research is incomplete in this area.

The source of support given divorced, single mothers depends upon the type of support given (Kurdek 1988). Parents give different types of support than do friends, co-workers, or formal support groups. In some cases the ex-spouse was seen as an infrequent source, beyond that of requisite financial payments

(Johnson 1986). This mainly took the form of non-routine child care and was considered more as potential support rather than actual support.

The membership of the social network varies. Family of origin is instinctively included, while old and new friends, acquaintances, former in-laws, and new mates are added or subtracted as the situation warrants. Whatever the form of the network, membership shifts over time. Divorced single mothers employ different people as sources and turn to these various individuals for different types of support. Much of the necessary support is situationally driven as needed by the recipient.

The characteristics of the social network add to our sense of how resources flow among members. It is important to remember that the network consists of different generations, kin and non-kin relationships, and that it is dynamic and changing over time. Life experiences add and subtract members from the system allowing for different types of support from different members.

SOME IMPLICATIONS

As part of day-to-day coping, mothers include purchasing goods and services for themselves and their children. At a minimum, the basic essentials are needed: food, clothing, and shelter. However, purchase decisions are not limited to basics. Mothers make travel decisions, transportation decisions, medical care decisions, gift decisions, insurance decisions, and any number of buying decisions. To make rational decisions they may turn to their social networks for information, or they may be influenced by network members who made similar decisions.

Rather than considering mothers as one homogeneous group, differences between married and single mothers are addressed. The focus of this paper is the provision of information and generation of influence by the social network on the mother's purchasing decisions, and any difference in this process between married mothers and single divorced mothers. The results will have implications for marketing managers.

Figure 1 is a conceptualization of the process whereby the social network affects the purchase decision of mothers, both married and single. The factors that could most affect mothers' decisions include her marital status, type of network with which she is associated, forms of support given by the network, and her views as to what is/are the appropriate role(s) for women in society.

INFLUENCE

In the study of consumer purchase behavior two sources of influence have been examined: dyads and networks. Corfman and Lehmann (1987) and Davis, Hoch, and Ragsdale (1986) looked at dyads in family decision making. These studies concentrated on married couples as the decision making unit. Word-of-mouth communications, encompassing larger clusters of consumers, were studied by Brown and Reingen (1987) and Beardon and Etzel (1982) who looked at reference group influence. These studies looked at the network as influencers in family decisions of intact families. Childers and Rao (1992) added a family type variable to their study of reference group influence on consumer decisions. However, they compared decision making in Thailand, where extended families are more common, to decision making in the United States where nuclear families are more the norm. Recent studies have begun looking at stranger influence. McGrath and Otnes (1995) have identified six overt and five covert interpersonal stranger influencers within a retail setting. Others have looked at the role of children in family decision making. Howard and Madrigal (1990) found that in purchases involving children's use of recreation services the mother was the major source of influence during the information search process, but the child was the predominant influencer at time of purchase.

There is no one source of influence. With children present, it should be expected that they will attempt to exert influence on the parent(s). Mothers in intact families can expect to be the recipients of more attempts to influence than fathers (Ahuja and Stinson 1993; Baranowski 1978; Dornbush, et. al. 1985; Ekstrom, Tansuhaj, and Foxman 1987; Jenkins 1979). When compared to fathers' perceptions, mothers and adolescents reported that adolescents perceived greater influence on purchase decisions for products that were for their use (Foxman, Tansuhaj, and Ekstrom 1989). To extend this idea, children may exert more influence on single parents, especially mothers, than on parents in intact families for several reasons. First, with only one parent present, children can concentrate their efforts on that person. The mother often gives in to the demands of the children as a defense against rejection by the children (Wallerstein and Kelly 1980). Second, single parents are overloaded with daily tasks and responsibilities (Cherlin 1992). Succumbing to a child's influence may be "the easy way out." Finally, single parents may have higher expectations of the child in areas of household chores and personal decisions, and thus, the parent allows more influence (Hetherington 1989). Another factor may be the adolescent's gender. Mother-daughter pairs are more accurate than mother-son pairs in recalling the child's contribution to a purchase decision (Beatty and Talpade 1994).

During the separation and immediately after divorce children's roles change and they begin supporting their mothers by becoming advisors, helpers, or occasional replacements for other adults (Wallerstein and Kelly 1980). The sphere of influence becomes more like that of an adult. In purchase areas where the product is almost exclusively used by the mother, she may be influenced by her children. This leads to the first question: Will children in mother-headed single parent homes exercise more influence on purchase decisions than children in intact families?

Various types of networks exist (McLanahan, Wedemeyer, and Adelberg, 1981). The requirements for support vary and individuals with the same problems do not necessarily require the same level or type of support (Schilling 1987). The type of social

network to which a single mother belongs may have more to do with personality and background than anything else. McLanahan, Wedemeyer, and Adelberg (1981) divided divorced women into stabilizers, who wish to maintain their pre-divorce roles mainly as a wife and mother, and changers, who are trying to establish a new post-divorce identity through a career or new profession. The type of support provided by the network is also related to the attitudes the mother holds concerning the role of women. In McLanahan, Wedemeyer, and Adelberg's (1981) "Family of Origin Network," support by family members tends to be gender related: males give financial aid or perform household repairs and females provide child care and personal advice. The "Extended Network" is composed mainly of new friends, with many divorced individuals as members. This is a more reciprocal type of network with the members exchanging support as needed. McLanahan, Wedemeyer, and Adelberg (1981), also describe a "Conjugal Network" with two subtypes. Both subtypes have a key male member who has a close relationship with the single mother. In Subtype A, other members of the social network resemble those in the Family of Origin Network. In Subtype B, the other network members are similar to an Extended Network.

Advice is a dimension of support (Hughes 1988; Wellman and Wortley 1989). One definition of advice states that advice is a "communication . . . containing information" (Costello 1992, p. 20). Another definition says that advice is "an opinion or recommendation offered as a guide to action, conduct, etc." (Costello 1992, p. 20). This definition, with its reference to opinion, raises the idea of influence or attempted influence, especially if the advice is unsolicited. Fellerman and Debevec (1993) assert that life transition points trigger kinship exchange behavior affecting both parties. Divorce is one of the transition points in life encompassing that period of time from separation to readjustment and acceptance of a new life style. During this time period, the married person starts over as a single person, and when children are involved the parent goes from sharing child-rearing responsibility to being a single or a noncustodial parent.

McLanahan, Wedemeyer, and Adelberg's (1981) "Family of Origin Network" is composed almost exclusively of family members including the woman's parents and her siblings. The support given by this network is usually directed toward the mother with little immediate reciprocation involved. It is assumed that the single mother will repay at a later date to her children, younger siblings, or nieces and nephews. Advice, information, and material services are given to the mother with support being gender oriented (McLanahan, Wedemeyer, and Adelberg 1981). Fathers and brothers offer financial assistance and household repair services; mothers and sisters give child care and advice on personal problems. In Isaacs and Leon's (1986) "Directing Network," advice is both sought by the divorced mother and offered to her by her parents. The unsought advice may be an attempt by the parents to influence the divorced daughter, whereas the sought for advice may be an attempt by the divorced daughter to gather information. This leads to a second question: Will single divorced mothers be given more unsolicited advice about product and service purchases than mothers in intact families?

Mothers' attitudes toward their role as a woman are also a factor. Corfman (1991) discovered that women with non-traditional attitudes toward their roles as females predict more accurately their relative influence in couple decision making. Following divorce, economic necessity forces many homemakers into the workforce (Wallerstein and Kelly 1980). This constitutes a change from the traditional role of stay-at-home wife and mother, and these women reorient their lives to fit into the breadwinner role. Other

TABLE 1
Key Questions for Study

1. Will children in mother-headed single parent homes exercise more influence on purchase decisions than children in intact families?

2. Will single divorced mothers be given more unsolicited advice about product and service purchases than mothers in intact families?.

3a. Are mothers with more traditional views on the role of women more likely to be influenced by their social networks in purchase decisions than mothers with more contemporary views on the role of women?

3b. Are mothers with more traditional views on the role of women less likely to use information from the social network in purchase decisions than women with more contemporary views?

4. Will single divorced mothers have a higher level of influence exchange about products and services with members of their social networks than will mothers in intact families?

5a. Do divorced mothers have more varied sources of information about products and services in their social networks than mothers in intact families?

5b. Do divorced mothers place more importance on the information about products and services that they receive from their social networks than mothers in intact families?

---

mothers, already participating in the workforce, may hold more liberal beliefs on women's roles and will face fewer post-divorce adjustments. Mothers with more traditional attitudes about a woman's role have higher levels of support than do mothers who hold more liberal views on the role of women (Leslie and Grady, 1988). This brings us to a third set of questions. (1) Are mothers with more traditional views on the role of women more likely to be influenced by their social networks in purchase decisions than mothers with more contemporary views on the role of women? (2) Are mothers with more traditional views on the role of women less likely to use information from the social network in purchase decisions than women with more contemporary views? Mothers holding more progressive views on a woman's role may be less influenced by social networks and more likely to rely on their own judgment based on information gathered from the network when making purchase decisions.

Attempted influence can be thought of as reciprocal (Hogan, Eggebeen, and Clogg 1993). The reciprocity factor is valued by single mothers (Leslie and Grady 1988) because it is important in eliminating a feeling of seeking charity when asking for help from their networks (Tietjen 1985). The single mothers' preference for exchange within the network may lead to a greater number of exchanges of influence and information within the social network. This information brings us to a fourth question: Will single divorced mothers have a higher level of influence exchange about products and services with members of their social networks than will mothers in intact families?

INFORMATION

Like people can be found in the network (Leslie and Grady 1988; Quinn and Allen 1989), however, divorced individuals receive more support from diverse networks than from kin-centered networks (Acock and Hurlbert 1993). These diverse networks have members with different backgrounds, interests, etc. This suggests a fifth question: Is the membership of divorced mothers' social networks less homogeneous than the membership of social networks of mothers in intact families?

Information flow through the network is reciprocal. There is no one source, although there may be a main source. The type of information given depends upon the source (Messeri, Silverstein,

and Litwak 1993). It is important to understand that the network is dynamic (Duffy 1993; Gerstal 1988: Walker, Wasserman, and Wellman 1993; Weinraub and Wolf 1983). For married mothers the primary source of support comes from the marital relationship (Levitt, Weber, and Clark 1986). For single mothers the primary support person can change (Duffy 1993). There may be members that are longstanding acquaintances who remain members over the long run but offer little in terms of support. There also may be members who are important in the short run and are out of the network relatively quickly. For single mothers the establishment of new friendships, especially with other divorced mothers, is important because of the opportunity to share like experiences (McHenry and Price 1991), and the single mother is more indebted to her network than the married mother in terms of information exchange (Tietjen 1985). This suggests that, as a consequence, single mothers may establish more potential sources of consumer information than mothers in intact families. The single mother relies on different people for different types of information because she may see the various providers as more knowledgeable in certain areas than in others (Brown and Gary 1985; McHenry and Price 1991). There is some evidence that information seekers rate their knowledge about products below that of those from whom they seek information (Yale and Gilly 1995). We have now arrived at the final set of questions: (1) Do divorced mothers have more varied sources of information about products and services in their social networks than mothers in intact families? (2) Do divorced mothers receive information about more products and services from their social networks than mothers in intact families? (3) Do divorced mothers place more importance on the information about products and services that they receive from their social networks than mothers in intact families? Table 1 summarizes these questions.

CONCLUSION

This paper is a first step in the study of single divorced mothers and how social networks provide information and influence their purchase decisions. The constructs of interest are influence from the network and information flow through the network. A second issue is a comparison between married mothers and single divorced mothers. In studying single divorced mothers and mothers in intact families, areas of special interest include: children's influence, the role of unsolicited advice in purchase decisions, the impact of the mothers' view of women's role on influence and information from the network, the level of information exchange, and the role of variety of and importance placed on information from the network. All of these areas could have implications for marketing managers in strategy formulation, especially in the methods that they employ to communicate with these two groups of consumers.

REFERENCES

Ahuja, Roshan D. and Kandi M. Stinson (1993), "Female-Headed Single Parent Families: An Exploratory Study of Children's Influence in Family Decision Making," in *Advances in Consumer Research,* Vol. 20, eds. Leigh McAlister and Michael L. Rothschild, Provo, UT: Association for Consumer Research, 469-474.

Bates, Myra Jo and James W. Gentry (1994), "Keeping the Family Together: How We Survived the Divorce," in *Advances in Consumer Research*, Vol. 21, eds. Chris T. Allen and Deborah Roedder John, Provo, UT: Association for Consumer Research, 30-34.

Beatty, Sharon E. and Salil Talpade (1994), "Adolescent Influence in Family Decision Making: A Replication with Extension," *Journal of Consumer Research*, 21 (September), 332-341.

Fellerman, Ritha and Kathleen Debevec (1993), "Kinship Exchange Networks and Family Consumption," in *Advances in Consumer Research*, Vol. 20, eds. Leigh McAlister and Michael L. Rothschild, Provo, UT: Association for Consumer Research, 458-462.

Kiecker, Pamela and Cathy L. Hartman (1994), "Predicting Buyers' Selection of Interpersonal Sources: The role of Strong Ties and Weak Ties," in *Advances in Consumer Research*, Vol. 21, eds. Chris T. Allen and Deborah Roedder John, Provo, UT: Association for Consumer Research, 464-469.

McGrath, Mary Ann and Cele Otnes (1995), "Unacquainted Influencers: When Strangers Interact in the Retail Setting," *Journal of Business Research*, 32, 261-272.

Yale, Laura J. and Mary C. Gilly (1995), "Dyadic Perceptions in Personal Source Information Search," *Journal of Business Research*, 32, 225-237.

For a complete list of references please contact the authors at the University of Nebraska-Lincoln.

Group Differences in the Construction of Consumption Sets

Kathleen M. Rassuli, Indiana-Purdue University Fort Wayne
Gilbert D. Harrell, Michigan State University

ABSTRACT

The assortment or set of products a consumer owns has begun to assume an important role in consumer research. This paper proposes a construct, the consumption set, to operationalize sets. Exploratory research presented describes a way to elicit consumption sets from consumers. Interviews were conducted to determine whether consumption sets constructed would differ significantly by occupation group. In addition to significant relationships between occupation and set construction, relationships were found between household life cycle variables and sets. The authors argue, given the group differences found in consumption sets, this construct is a useful theoretical tool to include macro-variables in consumer behavior models.

INTRODUCTION

The marketing literature contains numerous instances of scholars suggesting a shift from research on single products to sets of products (e.g., Wind 1977; Sheth 1979; 1992). There are at least two benefits that can arise from such a shift. First, we know that the products consumers own differ by culture, geographic location, and social class (e.g., Douglas and Isherwood 1978; Hirschman 1986). Yet, these variables are often modeled as exogenous variables. Douglas and Isherwood (1978) contend that there is a code locked in the goods people own; the code relates specific goods to specific cultures. In a similar vein, Hirschman (1986) suggests that common threads run through the lives of one group of consumers she studied. McCracken (1988) and other anthropologists, as well as consumer behaviorists (e.g., Solomon and Assael 1987) have proposed that we must consider the totality of products consumers own — the set. Since set contents are material artifacts of culture (McCracken 1986), sets might provide a mechanism for observing the influence of, heretofore, macro exogenous variables on consumer decisions.

Second, from a marketing standpoint, the set also may shed a new light on consumer decision making. If consumers are creating sets, then consumers may be seeking products for their capacity to initiate or to complete a set. In this set completion mode, a product would be purchased to complement other products in existing sets (Green, Wind and Jain 1972). Choice, then, is not only the output of a discovery and evaluation process, but also an input to the process of building a set. Bandura (1978) believes, "people create and activate environments." Sets of products become part of the consumer's environment (Solomon 1983).

There is a small, but growing, literature that broaches the topic of the influence of sets in consumer behavior (e.g., McCracken 1989; Solomon and Assael 1987; Johnson 1989). In this paper we offer a formal construct for sets and one technique to operationalize the concept. The proposed conceptualization of sets, the *consumption set*, merges the notion of product sets (found in the literature mentioned above) with the standard marketing treatment of products as bundles of attributes. We suggest that attributes might be a common link between goods in a set and with groups of people. Finally, we test whether consumers are able to construct the theorized sets and whether there are group differences in consumption set construction.

PRODUCTS, ATTRIBUTES AND THE THEORETICAL FOUNDATION OF CONSUMPTION SETS

The marketing literature provides a theoretical foundation upon which to build an operational definition of a consumption set. Typically, products are defined as bundles of attributes (Kotler and Armstrong 1991). However, the role of products and their attributes has been expanded by several scholars. McAlister and Pessemier (1982) conceived of products as being stores of attributes. According to the Lancastrian view, products (goods) produce attributes (Lancaster 1966). Thus, one might construe that consumers acquire products for the attributes they store and/or produce.

The idea that products belong to a set implies some type of relationship among them. This relationship suggests an extended role for attributes. To develop this role, one might build on the work of Alderson. He observed that products are not useful in themselves; utility arises in an assortment of complementary goods (Alderson 1957, pp. 198-99). In other words, product purchases are inter-dependent. One might hypothesize that complementary products are those which possess complementary attributes. (Here we would also expect consumption sets to include substitutes and unrelated elements). Furthermore, according to the literature, products can be expected to have both physical (tangible) and perceived (intangible) attributes. Many scholars are in agreement on this point (Wilkie and Pessemier 1973; Lilien and Kotler 1983; Hirschman 1980; Johnson 1988).[1] Therefore, we define a *consumption set* as *the entire assortment or portfolio of complementary, substitute and unrelated attributes and attribute combinations that a consumer holds at a particular time.* A consumption set is the entire universe of products which surrounds a consumer—expressed in attribute form. If, indeed, the attribute composition of consumption sets differs among groups, then perhaps we would be able to use consumption sets to decode consumption messages. Attributes would provide a taxonomical tool for classifying, comparing and evaluating consumption sets.

Consumption sets are created, formed, built and shaped by consumers. Conceivably consumption sets are first created in the consumers mind, and then, take shape in reality. The building process occurs over a period of time. Each choice a consumer makes can be expected to have an impact on the set. Consumption sets can be decomposed into consumption subsets or subgroupings of goods and attributes used together as a system, such as a living room, pantry, wardrobe, laundry, and so forth.[2]

---

[1] For simplicity sake, we only dealt with broad dimensions of attributes. Physical and perceived attributes can be broken down into more elementary components, e.g., brass. Chemicals, compounds, and minerals create brass.

[2] The attribute conceptualization of consumption sets is for operational purposes. The ultimate consumer does not typically enter the market to buy attributes. However, as shown in this study, consumers are aware of the attributes they use to produce consumption sets.

TABLE 1
Physical and Perceived Attributes Appearing in Questionnaire

Physical Attributes			Perceived Attributes			
T1	Wood	S1	Simple	S10	Dramatic
T2	Stone	S2	Futuristic	S11	Rustic
T3	Fabric	S3	Cozy	S12	Tradition
T4	Glass	S4	Natural	S13	Comfort
T5	Brass	S5	Authentic	S14	Practical
T6	Chrome	S6	Understated	S15	Gracious
T7	Leather/Suede	S7	Harmony	S16	Distinctive
T8	Wicker	S8	Classic	S17	Pretty
		S9	Charming	S18	Impeccable

Subjective living room attributes were based on a content analysis of popular magazines, including *Country Home, Architectural Digest, Better Homes and Gardens Home Issue, Traditional Home, Fine Home,* and *Southern Home.*

TESTING FOR GROUP DIFFERENCES IN CONSUMPTION SET CONSTRUCTION

Two macro variables were used to test for group differences in construction of the hypothesized consumption sets. First, to the extent that individuals are members of a group, similarities in consumption sets should be evident. Relying on Hirschman (1986) and Laumann and House (1970), we hypothesized that the consumption sets individuals create—that is, the *attribute profile or composition*—would differ by social strata. Thus,

H₁: *The composition of consumption sets is similar for individuals within a group (e.g., occupation, subculture, culture) and different between groups.*

To test this hypothesis, occupation groups were used.

Household life cycle (HLC) is another important macrovariable. Past research on household life cycles shows that as individuals advance in age, get married, and have children, and as the occupational status of the husband and wife change, household purchases of products (particularly durables) change accordingly. Since we believe that a person's consumption set is created and shaped over time, we expected differences depending upon a subject's stage in the HLC. Given an open-ended task of creating any consumption set, we expected consumers early in the HLC to create a set which resembled their ideal set. Having had time to accumulate a consumption set, we expected persons later in the HLC to create their actual set for the test.

H₂: *Consumers earlier in the household life cycle will create their ideal consumption set, while persons later in the life cycle will reconstruct their actual set.*

METHOD

In order to explore whether it is possible to recover consumption sets and to test for group differences, four groups of consumers were asked to construct a living room set and to complete a lengthy personal questionnaire. A living room consumption subset was chosen for several reasons. We needed to narrow the scope of the test to make the task manageable for subjects. Previous research on living rooms provided some *a priori* expectations about the products and attributes that might be included in living room sets (Csikszentmihalyi and Rochberg-Halton 1981; Laumann and House

1970; McCracken 1989). Living rooms are used for display purposes (Laumann and House 1970), and if, as Douglas and Isherwood (1978) state, people use goods to "signal membership" in groups, living rooms should provide evidence of group membership.

Instrument Subjects responded to a mail questionnaire that had been pre-tested on a sample of 30 subjects. First, respondents were instructed to create a living room set (write out the contents) based on physical and perceived attributes they selected from a list. The second section asked respondents to identify the living room style and to indicate whether the living room that was created was closer to their "actual" living room or an "ideal" living room. Demographic questions were asked at the end.

The main manipulation was a page with seven blank boxes across the top and a list of physical and perceived attributes down the side. Subjects were instructed to fill in each box with any product s/he desired and check off the attributes the product would have. Two stipulations applied: (1) respondents were instructed that the set must be within his/her present income (to prevent outlandish creations that would be out of reach for the subject's occupation group), (2) subject were asked to fill-in at least five of the seven products (to help reduce the number of blank questionnaires). To reduce fatigue, respondents were instructed that they did not have to construct each product in infinite detail. A number of popular magazines were content analyzed to produce a list of physical and perceived attributes shown in Table 1.

Subjects Groups of subjects were chosen from three occupations. Since the purpose of the research is to establish the existence of group differences in the attribute composition of consumption sets, the choice of groups was not essential. Occupation is an important indicator of social status; Hollingshead's two-item index of social status is composed of occupation and education, with occupation weighted more heavily. 443 questionnaires were sent to people employed in various white and blue collar occupations; 246 were returned. Population size (at a particular occupation site)/ sample size/number of questionnaires returned (respectively) are as follows: physicians 270/110/42; college professors 307/200/82; firefighters 400/100/79; and a convenience sample of 43 from a mix of occupations. Ph.D.'s, M.D.'s, and men are over-represented in the sample. Although sample characteristics limit generalizability, they do not affect the major tests regarding differences in consumption set construction across groups.

Partitioning the Data Across the population one should witness heterogeneity in consumption sets composed of attributes, while finding homogeneity within groups. Hierarchical cluster analysis was used to assign each individual to a given cluster. Cluster analysis requires the selection of relatively independent variables, and the choice of a similarity measure, clustering method and the appropriate number of clusters. An examination of the correlation matrix shows that the measurement instrument provided relatively independent attributes. Most correlations were in the single digits with only a few exceptions. The highest correlation, 0.41, is between S5 (authentic) and S8 (classic). Hair, et al. (1987) indicate that attributes which fail to differentiate between or among groups will diminish the quality of the cluster solution. Objective attributes T1 (wood), T3 (fabric), and T5 (brass), as might be expected, were used by 99 percent, 95 percent, and 74 percent, respectively, of all groups. These attributes were not used in the cluster analysis. Square Euclidean distance was chosen for the similarity measure. Punj and Stewart (1983) note that choice of similarity measure "does not appear to be critical...." Ward's minimum variance method was selected as the clustering method. Punj and Stewart (1983) argue that Ward's method is among the better performing, except when outliers are present. We standardized the data in this study to reduce the outlier problem. Finally, a number of methods were employed to ensure the correct number of clusters were chosen. A plot of the coefficients against the number of clusters (scree diagram) yielded four clusters. Using the "mixture model approach" the results of the cluster analysis using Ward's method and the complete linkage method were compared. The cluster analysis was run using 75 percent of the sample, and then the remaining 25 percent were reclustered. This provided a test of the stability of the cluster solution, or evidence of convergence. Discriminant functions were derived, and observations were reclustered on the basis of those functions.

RESULTS

Four clusters emerged from the analysis. Each cluster had a highly unique profile in terms of the mean inclusion of attributes in the consumption sets constructed (Figure 1). A MANOVA routine was performed on the attributes by cluster. The univariate F-tests for each attribute across clusters showed that all perceived attributes were significantly different across clusters at the 0.0001 level, except S18 (impeccable). The only physical attributes that was significant was T8 (wicker).

Cluster Interpretation and Profiling Ten percent of the observations were classified in *Cluster 1* — the "harmonious" cluster. For these individuals, living room sets were characterized by five attributes: simple, practical, natural, understated, harmony. While three of four clusters included the attribute comfort in their sets, Cluster 1 had the highest mean use of this attribute. *Cluster 2* contained 16.9 percent of the respondents — the "distinctives." As Figure 1 shows, individuals in this cluster were characterized by three attributes: distinctive, dramatic, and futuristic. The inclusion of the attribute futuristic is interesting because other clusters avoided it's use. *Cluster 3* contained 43.95 percent of the sample — the "practicalists." The attributes included most in the living room sets created by individuals were: practical, cozy, and comfortable. This cluster also had the largest mean inclusion of rustic. These individuals used fewer attributes per product and also developed fewer products.[3] They are perhaps described better by

attributes they did not include in their set: gracious, understated and futuristic. *Cluster 4* comprised 29.03 percent of the sample — the "classicists." These subjects developed sets composed mainly of three attributes: tradition, classic, and charming. In general, members of this cluster tended to be more expressive when describing the products they created. Figure 1 shows relatively wide use of all attributes. Consumption sets for members of Cluster 4 were not practical or comfortable—attributes used by more frequently by other clusters.

The four clusters were found to be significantly different from one another based on a MANOVA performed on the original clustering attributes. Since clusters were formed using Ward's minimum variance method, the MANOVA provides confirmation of a significant difference in the between, versus within, group variances.[4] Wilk's Lambda was 0.099, with a significance of better than 0.001.

Profiling on variables not used in the clustering procedure. Descriptive statistics for the four clusters for variables other than those used in the clustering procedure are given in Table 2. MANOVA was used to compare the four clusters on income, education and occupation of the household head, and whether this was their actual or ideal set; F-statistics for the first three variables were 6.956, 12.295 and 9.232 (all significant at the .000 level or better). For actual versus ideal, the F-statistic was 2.488 (significant at better than .06). There were no significant differences in style of living room (not shown in Table 2); styles varied a great deal within each cluster.

Demographic Profiles. In *Cluster 1*, sixty percent of the heads of household were employed as professionals. More than two-thirds of these people said they had created their own (actual) living room set. Members of *Cluster 2* were describing their "ideal set" more often than members of other clusters. *Cluster 3* had more non-professionals, fewer college degrees compared to other clusters. More than four-fifths (83%) of *Cluster 4* worked in professional occupations. This cluster had the highest mean income ($65,000+).

Product Use by Cluster. While products were not the focus of this study, some interesting findings appear. The basic products used to create a living room did not differ by cluster: a sofa/couch, a chair or two, an end table, carpet and a fireplace showed no significant differences (Table 3). But, there were significant differences for accessory products. Coffee tables, desks, pianos, televisions, stereos, and paintings were included by some clusters and not by others. For example, Cluster 2 did not include desks, but they did include stereos and paintings. Cluster 3 included televisions, but few pianos. It was in Cluster 4 where pianos were found in living room consumption sets along with paintings.

Internal and external validation. Internal validation was carried out by the split sample validation technique (Punj and Stewart 1983). Seventy-five percent of individuals were reclustered; the same clusters emerged. Then the classification of individuals into clusters was checked to determine whether they were clustered into the same groups as they previously had been. The analysis showed that only 21.7 percent, or 43 out of 198 individuals, were misclassified.[5] This clearly supports the internal validity of the procedure. For external validity, one asks whether the solution is

---

[3] The effect of the heavy use of attributes, by other clusters, would have been minimized by the process of standardization mentioned earlier.

[4] MANOVA was merely used as a check, however, its distinctiveness in profiling variables is somewhat of an overstatement.

[5] Twenty-eight of the 43 (65%) were original members of Cluster 3 who were misclassified into Cluster 2. When we tested the three cluster solution (earlier in the paper), we found that Cluster 2 was combined with Cluster 3. Therefore, this result might be expected.

FIGURE 1
Cluster Profiles on Subjective Attributes

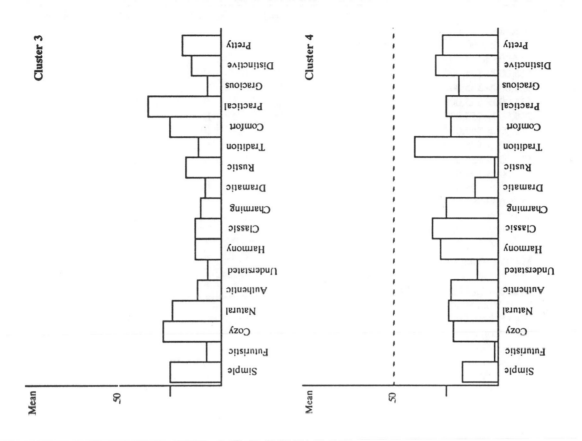

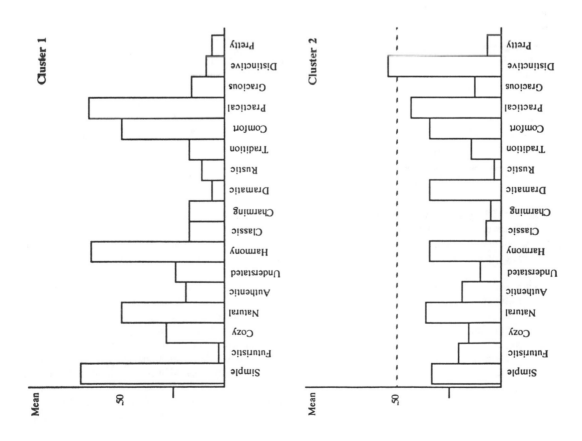

TABLE 2
Percentage Frequencies on Demographic Characteristics by Cluster*

		Clus 1	Clus 2	Clus 3	Clus 4
D7	**Income**				
1	Under $5,000				
2	$5,000> $15,000	4		7	
3	$15,000> $25,000	8	12	19	6
4	$25,000> $35,000	12	12	18	10
5	$35,000> $45,000	20	3	11	18
6	$45,000> $55,000	16	12	13	15
7	$55,000> $65,000	20	10	11	10
8	$65,000> $75,000	8	12	6	4
9	$75,000> $85,000	8	5	3	1
10	$85,000> $95,000		5	2	4
11	$95,000> 105,000	4	19	1	14
12	$105,000> $125,000		2	2	3
13	$125,000> $150,000			2	
14	$150,000> $175,000				4
15	$175,000 and up			3	5
	Missing Value		7	2	6
D10	**Education of Household Head**				
1	Some High School	4		3	1
2	High School Grad	12	12	30	6
3	Some College	12	12	26	14
4	College Grad	16	12	10	11
5	Masters Degree	4	12	2	24
6	Ph.D. or M.D.	52	52	30	46
D8	**Occupation**				
1	Professional	56	62	32	63
2	Semi-Professional	24	5	6	19
3	Skilled Non-Professional	4	14	16	4
4	Non-Skilled Non-Prof.	16	12	40	13
	Missing Value		7	6	1
V2	**Actual vs. Ideal Set?**				
	Actual	68	43	48	62
	Ideal	20	45	40	30
	Both	12	10	3	6
	Other		2	8	3
	Missing Value			1	1

*Percentages on some variables, for some clusters, may sum to more than 100 due to rounding error.

useful (Punj and Stewart 1983, p. 146). An overwhelming majority of respondents (88%) answered in the affirmative to the question of whether they had a picture in mind as they went through the exercise. This is strong support for external validity.

Tests of Hypotheses. Hypothesis 1. We believed that there should be consistency within sets of attributes created by occupation groups of individuals. MANOVA was conducted on a randomized block design, with the physical and perceived attributes as dependent variables and the four original groups as the independent variable. Two blocks of 50 percent of the subjects were chosen at random from the occupational subsamples. The purpose of the blocks was to test for the presence of any effects due to sample stratification. The results of the test show that Wilk's Lambda for the occupation treatment was 0.47; this was significant at better than .001. The blocking variable was insignificant; Wilk's Lambda was .90 with only a 63% level of significance. As part of the output of MANOVA, discriminant weights for the functions that differentiate clusters are produced. (See Table 4, for the standardized discriminant weights and discriminant functions.) Using these weights for classification purposes, a discriminant analysis was performed on a random sample of 90 percent of the total observations. 88.9 percent of grouped cases were correctly classified. All members of the holdout sample were correctly reclassified. Therefore, the results of the test support the belief that, given the opportunity to create a living room consumption set of their choice, individuals within occupational groups will create consumption sets of attributes that were more alike than those across groups. Comparing the cluster results to the original occupation groups, physicians mainly fell into Cluster 2, firefighters mainly into Cluster 3 and professors mainly into Clusters 1 and 4 (Table 2).

TABLE 3
Percentage Creation of Products by Cluster

Var	Product	Clus 1	Clus 2	Clus 3	Clus 4	F	Signif of F
P1	Sofa/Couch	96	93	95	93	.289	.833
P2	Chair 1	84	67	73	74	.609	.610
P3	Chair 2	32	19	25	22	.335	.800
P4	Coffee Table	60	67	46	49	2.446	.065
P5	End Table	40	33	41	42	.347	.791
P6	Desk	12	0	5	11	2.218	.087
P7	Enterain. Center	8	19	17	18	.305	.822
P8	Piano	12	12	6	32	5.845	.001
P9	Fireplace	32	43	29	24	1.519	.210
P10	Television	28	31	53	21	7.024	.000
P11	Stereo*	16	29	26	11	2.502	.060
P12	Lamp	68	45	65	58	2.273	.001
P13	Drapes	12	14	6	11	1.500	.215
P14	Carpet	44	43	33	46	.856	.465
P15	Plant	8	7	7	10	.092	.964
P16	Painting/Picture	20	45	26	49	5.351	.001
P17	Folding Screen	0	5	1	6	1.590	.192
P18	Art Objects	0	5	6	10	1.719	.164
P19	Small Accessories*	8	12	15	24	1.049	.371
P20	Large Accessories*	52	29	39	33	1.321	.260

*The category "stereo" also includes some VCRs. The categories of small and large accessories contain miscellaneous items. In the case of clusters 1 and 4, large accessories included bookshelves; for cluster 3, this category often contained footstools.

Hypothesis 2. The second research question deals with the issue of an actual versus an ideal set. Respondents were asked whether the consumption set they were describing was their actual set, their ideal set, or something else (other). While only those three options were provided, respondents often wrote "both" in the category marked "other." A content analysis of respondents answering "both" reveals that they often said "everything was mine except...," and the exception was "the big screen television" or "the baby grand piano."

Across all clusters, 55 percent of respondents created their own "actual" set. Slightly more than one-third said they had created their ideal. These averages can be broken down by cluster. In Cluster 1, 68 percent created their actual set, 20 percent their ideal. In Cluster 2, 43 percent created their actual set and 45 percent their ideal. For Cluster 3, 48 percent created their actual set and 41 percent their ideal. Sixty-one percent of Cluster 4 created their actual set and 29 percent their ideal. The creation of an actual set may be related to the ability to use more specific attributes (characteristics of Clusters 1 and 4) and/or to Cluster 3's inability to be descriptive.

A second discriminant analysis was performed in an effort to explore the impact of stage in the household life cycle on the creation of an actual, versus an ideal, set. In line with Hypothesis 2, the dependent variable, for the discriminant analysis, was the categorical variable, "actual or ideal," with independent variables — age, marital status, and presence of children 6 years of age and younger, 6–17 years of age, and 18 years of age and older (typical household life cycle variables). All variables had a significant contribution in discriminating between actual sets and ideal sets, except the presence of children under the age of six. The signs of all the variables were as expected. The function correctly discrimi-

nated between actual and ideal sets 60 percent of the time. Wilk's Lambda was 0.9378 (significant at the 0.05 level). The chance of being classified in a group is 50 percent; the model improved on chance to some extent.

LIMITATIONS

The instrument was designed to explore only one part of a consumption set, the living room subset. Given the limited scope, there is room for future refinement. Other subsets may be less prone to group differences than the living room. A limited number of occupation groups were included in the study. Perhaps other occupations would exhibit similar differences. Finally, the sample was over-representative of persons with higher education and of males. One must wonder whether a sample that consisted mostly of females would have developed significantly different living room consumption sets. However, the purpose of the study was not to generalize to other groups, but to show that group differences can be detected in consumption sets and to suggest that perhaps this result can be generalized to other macro influences.

SUMMARY AND IMPLICATIONS

The authors set out to develop a tool sensitive enough to detect group differences in the construction of consumption sets. Such a tool would allow researchers to make comparisons across many types of macro groupings in society.

Taken as a whole the findings suggest that consumption sets specified in attribute form do, indeed, offer such a tool. Different occupational groups did have distinct attribute profiles within the consumption sets they constructed. This research suggests that differences in perceived attributes occur across groups (physical attributes did not). There was no significant difference in the basic

TABLE 4
Standardized Discriminant Coefficients and Discriminant Functions

	Function 1	Function 2	Function 3
S12	-0.41450*	0.16525	0.15812
S9	-0.36554*	0.07370	0.21381
S8	-0.36118*	0.07326	0.18699
S17	-0.30223*	-0.08820	0.02441
S15	-0.22372*	0.21151	0.17913
S5	-0.18695*	0.15884	0.12501
T6	0.11386	0.02948	-0.06341
S16	-0.17541	0.61081*	-0.39134
S10	-0.00701	0.35222*	-0.29995
S11	0.14113	-0.20620*	0.06607
T8	0.11009	-0.13173*	-0.11153
S7	-0.08073	0.38926	0.53362*
S1	0.30622	0.11561	0.43574*
S6	0.08550	0.16039	0.39812*
S2	0.16658	0.17422	-0.34428*
S3	0.02662	-0.11617	0.28293*
S13	0.09555	0.19826	0.26951*
S4	0.14358	0.10986	0.22790*
S14	0.18200	0.12964	0.18414*
T7	0.05035	-0.02275	-0.16505*
T4	0.00273	-0.03477	-0.14850*
S18	-0.07694	0.09044	0.10914*

products included in a consumption set across groups, although some of the accessory products differ. And it is fascinating to note that the overall style of living room consumption sets differed a great deal within a cluster (group). Yet, the attributes used to create these varied styles did not differ. In other words, group members use the same attributes to achieve different styles.

The research reported here implies that attributes might be used to conceptualize the common threads that run through a consumption set (cf., Hirschman 1986). Furthermore, attributes may be a first step in uncracking the group code locked in consumer goods (cf., Douglas and Isherwood 1978). For future research, one might expect the impact of other macro variables to show up in the composition of consumption sets. For example, while basic products composing a consumption set do not differ across groups within the American culture, one might expect them to differ from culture to culture. The product composition of a consumption set may differ due to physiology, geography and/or the unique nature of resource availability. Objective attributes may follow a similar logic. Moreover, some perceived attributes—practicality and comfort—appeared in the consumption sets of all occupation groups under study. The incidence of these attributes in all consumption sets may be the result of a macro influence broader than occupation group, such as culture. Consumers from other cultures might develop different consumption sets of perceived attributes.

CONCLUSIONS

The research is intended to provide a starting point to demonstrate how consumption sets can be recovered from consumer responses and to explore macro differences in consumption set construction. The findings lend credence to the present conceptualization of consumption sets. Given an open-ended task, consumers can create consumption sets consisting of products and attributes. Furthermore, the composition of those consumption sets differs by group membership. Occupation groups were used to test the hypothesis. There were clear differences in the way consumers from different occupation groups combined attributes to create consumption sets. This research is a starting point. The consumption set construct may serve as a conceptual basis for classifying the contents of consumption sets. Once the contents of consumption sets have been inventoried, comparisons could be made across other macro groups — culture, social class, and reference groups. Clear patterns may emerge. A wealth of information may be contained in an analysis of the contents of consumption sets.

REFERENCES

Alderson, Wroe (1957) *Marketing Behavior and Executive Action*, Homewood, IL: Irwin.

Bandura, A. (1978), "The Self System in Reciprocal Determinism," *American Psychologist*, 33 (April), pp. 344-58.

Csikszentmihalyi, M. and E. Rochberg-Halton (1981), *The Meaning of Things: Domestic Symbols and the Self*, Cambridge, England: Cambridge University Press.

Douglas, Mary and Baron Isherwood (1978), *The World of Goods*, Harmondsworth, Middlesex, England: Penguin Books Ltd.

Frank, R. E. and P. E. Green (1968), "Numerical Taxonomies in Marketing Analysis: A Review Article," *Journal of Marketing Research*, Vol. IX (February), 83-98.

Green, Paul E., Yoram Wind, and Arun K. Jain (1972), "Preference Measurement of Item Collections," *Journal of Marketing Research*, Vol. IX (November), 371-77.

Hair, Joseph F., Jr., Rolph E. Anderson, and Ronald L. Tatham (1987), *Multivariate Data Analysis*, New York: Macmillan Publishing Company.

Hirschman, Elizabeth C (1986), "Humanistic Inquiry in Marketing Research: Philosophy, Method, and Criteria," *Journal of Marketing Research*, Vol. XXIII (August), 237-49.

_____ (1980), "Attributes of Attributes and Layers of Meaning," *Advances in Consumer Research*, Vol. 7, ed. Jerry C. Olson, Provo, UT: Association for Consumer Research, 7-12.

Johnson, Michael D. (1989), "The Differential Processing of Product Category and Non-comparable Choice Alternatives," *Journal of Consumer Research*, 16 (December), 300-9.

_____ (1984), "Consumer Choice Strategies for Comparing Non-comparable Alternatives," *Journal of Consumer Research*, Vol. 11 (December), 741-53.

Kotler, Philip and Gary Armstrong (1991), *Principles of Marketing*, Englewood Cliffs, NJ: Prentice-Hall, Inc.

Lancaster, Kelvin J. (1966), "A New Approach to Consumer Theory," *Journal of Political Economy*, Vol. 74, 2, 132-157.

Laumann, Edward O. and James S. House (1970), "Living Room Styles and Social Attributes: The Patterning of Material Artifacts in a Modern Urban Community," *Sociology and Social Research*, 54 (April), p. 326.

Lilien, Gary L. and Philip Kotler (1983), *Marketing Decision Making*, NY: Harper and Row.

McAlister, Leigh and Edgar Pessemier (1982), "Variety Seeking Behavior: An Interdisciplinary Review," *Journal of Consumer Research*, Vol. 9.

McCracken, Grant D. (1989), "Homeyness: A Cultural Account of One Constellation of Consumer Goods and Meanings," In *Interpretive Consumer Research*, ed., Elizabeth C. Hirschman, Provo, UT: Association for Consumer Research, 168-83.

_____ (1988), *Culture and Consumption*, Bloomington: Indiana University Press.

_____ (1986), "Culture of Consumption: A Theoretical Account of the Structure and Movement of the Cultural Meaning of Consumer Goods," *Journal of Consumer Research*, Vol. 13 (June), 71-84.

Morrison, D. G. (1967), "Measurement Problems in Cluster Analysis," *Management Science*, Vol. 13, B-775-80.

Punj, Girish and David W. Stewart (1983), "Cluster Analysis in Marketing Research: Review and Suggestions for Application," *Journal of Marketing Research*, Vol. 20 (May), 134-48.

Sheth, Jagdish N. (1979), "The Surpluses and Shortages in Consumer Behavior," *Journal of the Academy of Marketing Science*, 7 (Fall), 414-26.

_____ (1992), "Acrimony in the Ivory Tower: A Retrospective on Consumer Research," *Journal of the Academy of Marketing Science*, 20 (4), 345-53.

Solomon, Michael R. (1983), "The Role of Products as Social Stimuli: A Symbolic Interaction Perspective," *Journal of Consumer Research*, Vol. 10 (December), 319-29.

_____ and Henry Assael (1987), "The Forest or the Trees?: A Gestalt Approach to Symbolic Consumption," *Marketing and Semiotics: New Directions in the Study of Signs for Sale*, ed. Jean Umiker-Sebeouk, New York: Mouton de Gruyter, 189-217.

Wilkie, William L. and Edgar A. Pessemier (1973), "Issues in Marketing's Use of Multiattribute Attitude Models," *Journal of Marketing Research*, Vol. X (November), 428-41.

Wind, Jerry (1977), "Toward a Change in the Focus of Marketing Analysis: From A Single Brand to an Assortment," *Journal of Marketing*, 41 (October), 12, 143.

Special Session Summary
The Necessity of Metaphorical Reasoning and its Effect on Knowledge Representation and Decision Making

George S. Babbes, University of California at Berkeley

The objective of our session was to discuss the necessity and significance of metaphor in knowledge representation, reasoning and decision-making. The specific goals were to: (1) establish that cognitive structure is often organized metaphorically, and that this structure has significant systematic effects on reasoning and decision-making; and (2) demonstrate how an understanding of metaphor theory can be used to both *create* representations that systematically influence reasoning and decision making, and *uncover* representations that are consciously or unconsciously being utilized in reasoning and decision-making.

The motivation for this session was rooted in the fact that despite widespread use in advertising and consumer research, virtually no research on the cognitive theory of metaphor has been discussed in the marketing literature. This is an effort to augment the literary tradition and recognize metaphor's role as a cognitive instrument.

EMBODIED COGNITION AND METAPHOR ELICITATION

The first paper (Jerry Zaltman) explored the use of visual and other sensory metaphors to elicit the mental models or structure of constructs people have about a product category. The basic premise is that thought is largely created, shaped, and represented by iconic images called metaphors. Further, many of these metaphors are rooted in perceptual and motor systems, and hence, metaphors of physicality are very prominent. The basic idea of embodied cognition reflects the presence of these image-schemata in everyday thought.

Importantly, four basic premises underlie the connection between metaphor and mental models: (1) most human communication is nonverbal, and as such, basic senses have a significant role in learning and communications processes; (2) metaphors are the key windows/mechanisms for viewing a consumer's thoughts and feelings, and for understanding behavior; (3) our senses provide the source for important metaphors, and as such, are potentially important devices for understanding consumers' thoughts and behavior; and (4) consumers have mental models which represent their knowledge and behavior.

Based on these premises, Jerry discussed an approach he developed for uncovering how sensory perceptions map onto abstract thought. This is basically a research tool to recover latent mental models used by consumers. These mental models reveal basic reasoning processes and can provide deep, useful insights about consumers and their emerging needs.

EFFECT OF SENSORY METAPHORS ON PRODUCT EVALUATION

Our second paper (Trudy Kehret-Ward) considered SENSING-IS-EVALUATING metaphors. Examples of these metaphors include: "compare and SEE for yourself," "HEAR the excellence for yourself," "TASTE what all the excitement's about," and "they're MUSIC to your mouth." Trudy's basic research question is: "do these metaphors really help people with the admittedly abstract activity of evaluating products?"

In a past study, Trudy found that SENSING-IS-EVALUATING metaphor headlines created significantly improved product evaluation for product category enthusiasts versus those indifferent to the product category. This was not true of non-metaphor headlines.

This follow-up study, tapping into parallels between metaphor elaboration and vividness, manipulated "imaging" as a mediating variable. Consistent with the vividness literature, "imaging" increased the number of "total" and "product-related" thoughts for enthusiasts, but had no effect on the number of thoughts generated by those indifferent to the category. "Mood" and "task-liking" were also measured, but were unaffected by the "imaging" manipulation.

METAPHOR EFFECTS ON COGNITIVE STRUCTURE, REASONING AND INFERENCE-MAKING

Our third paper (George Babbes & David Aaker) discussed the affect of metaphor on reasoning and inference making. The underlying question was: "if conceptual metaphors do, in fact, structure everyday thinking, to what extent is our reasoning and decision-making affected by a metaphor's conceptual structure?"

The basic hypothesis was that metaphors, like other schemas, enable us to make inferences automatically, unconsciously and with little cognitive effort. If this is the case, it may be difficult to reason independent of metaphor. That is, once a metaphorical mapping is accepted and establishes a cognitive structure, an individual's reasoning and decision making processes may be restricted to a non-arbitrary set of assumptions, operators and outcomes. As a consequence, metaphors can have a powerful effect on reasoning and decision-making.

To test this idea, two experiments were conducted. The first experiment supported the hypothesis that metaphor can create a cognitive structure that: (1) improves memory for brand and product (versus no-metaphor control); and (2) restructures memory to be consistent with metaphorical inferences. The second experiment examined the effect of metaphor on experts versus novices. Findings indicate that novices can be held hostage to reasonable inferences based on metaphor. However, experts are able to reason independent of arbitrary metaphor structures.

DISCUSSION SUMMARY

In the discussion, our discussion leader (Bill Wells) pointed out that we work with metaphors everyday— summary statistics, mathematical models, marketing models, most knowledge structures, etc.— in that we utilize simple, understandable domains to reason about more abstract and complicated ones. Many of the participants relayed similar results and intuitions from their own work complementing results and concepts from the presentations.

Encouragingly, it was clear from the discussion that interest in the cognitive implications of metaphor is strong and gaining momentum. This interest, coupled with progress in other disciplines (e.g. psychology, anthropology, linguistics), portends significant opportunities for productive research in this area.

Special Session Summary
It's News to Me: Framing Effects in New Categories and New Situations

Christina L. Brown, New York University

This session investigated context or framing effects that arise from consumers' attempt to assign a subjective value to a new, unfamiliar, or uncertain case. This issue is of interest because: (1) it addresses an important cause of context effects—the effect of *uncertain values* on evaluation and choice; (2) it sheds light on how a brand's competitive set impacts consumer evaluation of the brand; and (3) it examines how consumers may rely on the frame of reference provided by a category to reduce uncertainty about product values. This session considered such framing effects when a product is new-to-the-world (Dhar and Sawhney), when a product and/or its attributes are unfamiliar to the consumer (Brown and Carpenter), or when a new and different usage situation is proposed for an familiar product (Wansink and Jannsen).

The paper by *Ravi Dhar and Mohanbir Sawhney* demonstrated that consumers evaluate a new-to-the-world product (such as a new communications device) by comparing its attributes to a comparison category (such as cordless phones). In two studies, the authors demonstrated a framing effect in which relative preference for a new-to-the-world product is lowest when the category to which it is compared is superior on the more important attribute. Differences in attribute importance increased the effect of comparative frames, while familiarity with a product category decreased their effect. Explanations based on perceptual associations (i.e., change in perception of attribute importance) did not account for the effects.

The paper by *Christina L. Brown and Gregory S. Carpenter* considered why consumers confronted with an unfamiliar category sometimes treat minor attributes as though they were of major importance. For example, their choice of ground coffee may be affected by the shape of the crystal, which has no objective value. The authors proposed that, although such attributes appear objectively meaningless to researchers, consumers confer subjective value on them by inferring some additional positive or negative benefit to them, in order to solve otherwise intractable choice problems. In situations where a choice problem is easily and appropriately resolved by a more effective strategy, consumers have no motivation to make strongly-valenced inferences about trivial attributes; their choices are less likely to be affected. The authors call this process "strategic inference-making," since consumers will go to the trouble of making such inferences only when strategically necessary to solve a choice problem. An experiment demonstrated that consumers are more likely to choose a brand with a trivial attribute when low variance on more important attributes makes it difficult to discriminate clear superiority among the choice alternatives.

The paper by *Brian Wansink and Paul D. G. Jannsen* examined how changing one's frame of reference can cause changes in the foods one eats. They showed that, when considering a new use for a target product (such as eating mayonnaise with French Fries or drinking Coke in the morning), most people tend to focus on whether the attributes of this product are relevant for the target situation. This often biases consumers against the product's use. This bias can be overcome by redirecting one's frame of reference away the target product. A cross-cultural laboratory study, conducted in the U.S. and the Netherlands, indicated that subjects evaluated the target product more favorably when they did not focus on its specific attributes. This was true regardless of whether they focus instead on situation needs, the attributes of another product, or on something completely unrelated (commuting on the tram).

Our discussant, Eric Johnson, contrasted the various uses of the term "framing" appearing in the three papers and suggested more consistent uses of the term.

Under Siege: How Consumers Respond and Marketers React to Negative Information

Jill G. Klein, Northwestern University

Baba Shiv, Duke University

A well documented finding in the behavioral decision theory and impression formation literatures is the tendency for negative information to be weighted more heavily than positive information (e.g., Fiske 1980; Kanouse and Hanson 1972; Kahneman and Tversky 1979). However, the effects of negative information on consumers are not well understood. Further, our knowledge of how to effectively manage the impact of negative information is limited.

Negative publicity is becoming a major cause for concern among marketing managers as the ability is disseminate such information to large and geographically dispersed consumers is rapidly increasing. While research in social contexts suggests that a number of factors can influence the impact of negative information (Skowronski and Carlston 1989), little work has been done in the context of negative publicity concerning consumer products. This issue was addressed by the authors of the first paper, Jean Romeo, Marc C. Weinberger and David Antes. Their research develops a conceptual model based on risk theory as a framework for integrating and explaining the effects of negative safety information on perceived risk and brand evaluation. A factorial survey (conjoint) analysis was used to asses the importance given to news of potential product hazards. The effectiveness of company response to negative product information was also examined.

The use of "attack" ads by marketers has been growing in popularity both in political (Advertising Age 1987; Devlin 1993) and in consumer product contexts (Business Marketing 1992). However, research findings on the effectiveness of these ads is mixed. On one hand, there is evidence that negative advertising can effectively lower evaluations of the target of the ad (e.g., Homer and Batra 1994). On the other hand, Herstein (1981) and Tinkman and Weaver-Lariscy (1991) suggest that negative advertising can result in a backlash effect against the sponsor.

The second paper, co-authored by Jill Klein and Bridgette Braig, focused on these issues in the context of political advertising. They reported the results of an experiment that examined the relative impact of attacks on an opponent's morality or ability. In addition, their research investigated the effectiveness of positive, negative, and comparative advertisements. Their findings showed that morality attacks were more damaging to the opponent's image than were ability attacks. In addition, comparative advertisements were found to protect the attacking candidate from a backlash effect.

Another issue that we examined in the session was, "If negative advertising has deleterious effects on one's brand, how does the brand manager go about countering these effects?" Baba Shiv presented the results of a series of experiments he conducted with Julie Edell that focus on the effects of negative advertising on brand choice. They first investigated the effects of "attack" advertising on brand choice and found that the effects depend on how elaborate the processing is between ad exposure and choice. They then examined the viability of the "firing back" response (versus a positive non-comparative response) to an attack ad within the context of a "media brawl", such as the current on-air war between MCI and AT&T. Results indicated that a positive response is more effective than a "firing back" response only when the ad directs the consumer's attention to the tactics used by the initiator. Also, the

findings suggested that a "firing back" response actually tarnishes the image of the responding firm.

REFERENCES

Advertising Age (1987), "Negative Spots Likely to Return in Election '88," September 14, 70-78.

Business Marketing (1992), "Mudwrestling: Microsoft's Ads Highlight New Prominence of Negative Marketing in Business, Vol. 77 (September), 28-29, 32.

Devlin, L. Patrick (1993), "Contrasts in Presidential Campaign Commercials of 1992," *American Behavioral Scientist*, Vol. 37, 272 - 290.

Fiske, Susan (1980), "Attention and Weight in Person Perception: The Impact of Negative and Extreme Behavior," *Journal of Personality and Social Psychology*, Vol. 38, 889-906.

Herstein, John A. (1981), "Keeping the Voter's Limits in Mind: A Cognitive Process Analysis of Decision Making in Voting," *Journal of Personality and Social Psychology*, Vol. 40, 843-861.

Homer, Pamela and Rajeev Batra (1994), "Attitudinal Effects of Character-Based Versus Competence-Based Negative Political Communications," *Journal of Consumer Psychology*, Vol. 3. No. 2, 163-185.

Kahneman, Daniel and Amos Tversky (1979), "Prospect Theory: An Analysis of Decision Under Risk," *Econometrica*, Vol. 47 (March), 263-91.

Kanouse, David E., and Reid L. Hanson Jr. (1972), "Negativity in Evaluations," in *Attribution: Perceiving the Causes of Behavior*, Morristown, NJ: General Learning Press, 47-62.

Tinkham, Spencer F. and Ruth Ann Weaver-Lariscy (1991), "Advertising Message Strategy in U.S. Congressional Campaigns: Its Impact on Election Outcome," *Current Issues in Research in Advertising*, Vol. 13, Nos. 1&2, 207-226.

Gay and Lesbian Consumers in the US Marketplace: Historical, Econometric and Advertising Approaches

Lisa Peñaloza, University of Colorado

SESSION SUMMARY

In recent years, marketing and media attention has begun to be directed to gays and lesbians as a distinct consumer subculture. It has been dubbed a "dream market," with estimates of the numbers of gays and lesbians reaching 18.5 million, and estimates of spending power topping 514 billion (Johnson 1993). Businesses targeting gays and lesbians have expanded beyond the initial bars, clubs and bookstores to comprise virtually a full service market that includes media, merchandise catalogues and vacation companies, as well as legal, medical, financial, communications and community support services.

The recent "discovery" of the gay and lesbian market raises a number of important theoretical and practical issues for consumer researchers. With the advent of recognition of the gay/lesbian market, sexuality comes to the fore as a market designator, and it promises to be at least as controversial as gender, race and ethnicity (Peñaloza, in press). This panel brought together scholars from an array of disciplinary affiliations including history, economics, communications and marketing to explore the contours of this emerging consumer culture.

The session began with an overview of key controversies regarding gay/lesbian consumer culture, such as the overlap between the gay/lesbian social movement and gay/lesbian target marketing, the legitimizing effects of marketing efforts targeting gay and lesbian consumers, and the organized resistance to such efforts by other subcultural groups on religious/moral grounds by session chair, Lisa Peñaloza.

Important dimensions affecting the emergence of particular consumer cultures are their economic accommodation in the marketplace and their political incorporation in the larger society, yet the ways in which these two facets of social life interact are underinvestigated research issues. Historian Nan Alamilla Boyd (Women's Studies, University of Colorado, Boulder) discussed her work investigating the role of bar owners and beer distributors in the formation of gay/lesbian consumer culture in San Francisco during the 1960's. The San Francisco Tavern Guild, a loose coalition of gay bar owners, bartenders and beer distributors, united at this time to protect themselves from police harassment and later proved itself very effective in mobilizing and politicizing the gay/lesbian community's spending power

With the increased attention of marketing and advertising practitioners to gay/lesbian consumers, various market statistics have surfaced in recent years, with little agreement regarding their reliability and validity. Economist Sylvia Allegretto (Economics, University of Colorado, Boulder) presented a demographic profile of gay/lesbian households, compiled from the 1990 US Census. The census data was then compared to market statistics released by Simmons Market Research Bureau, Yankelovich Monitor Survey and the Advocate, a major gay publication. Consumer research issues were discussed relating to terminology, data collection and tabulation procedures, and self-selection and social desirability biases.

The third presentation rounded out the session with its focus on a topic of applied consumer research. Communications scholar Peter J. Newman, Jr. (Institute for Communications Research, University of Illinois, Champaign-Urbana) presented research investigating how an individual's perceived risk of HIV exposure and/or direct experience with HIV affected their attitudes towards health maintenance nutrition drink advertising. Currently, it is estimated that one million people are HIV positive. While initially referred to as the "gay disease," HIV is not limited to this segment of the population, and there was some evidence to suggest that gay men were more informed and therefore better able to protect themselves than their heterosexual counterparts. At issue in the study were operationalizations of risk in the field of consumer behavior and identification with a stigmatized group as it affected attitudes toward advertising.

Finally, Dan Wardlow (Marketing, San Francisco State University) commented on the presentations, outlined some issues for further research (Wardlow, in press), and led a spirited discussion that touched on a number of aspects of gay/lesbian consumption phenomena—identity, behavior, reference group influence/membership, community formation and intergroup relations.

REFERENCES

Johnson, Bradley (1993), "The Gay Quandry: Advertising's Most Elusive, Yet Lucrative Target Market Proves Difficult to Measure," *Advertising Age*, 64:18(January 18)29.

Peñaloza, Lisa (in press), "We're Here, We're Queer and We're Going Shopping! A Critical Perspective on the Accommodation of Gays and Lesbians in the US Marketplace," *Journal of Homosexuality*, 31·1/2(Spring 1996)9-41, forthcoming.

Wardlow, Dan, editor (in press), *Gays, Lesbians and Consumer Behavior: Theory, Practice and Research Issues in Marketing*, Binghamton, NY: The Haworth Press, forthcoming.

An Experimental Investigation of Self-Symbolism in Gifts

Mary Finley Wolfinbarger, California State University
Mary C. Gilly, University of California

ABSTRACT

A role playing experiment is employed to investigate the influence of four independent variables on giver- and receiver-congruence. Closeness, similarity, the event being a rite of progression as opposed to a rite of passage, and the giver being female, all resulted in the intention to purchase more receiver-congruent gifts. Closeness also contributed to intentions to choose gifts that were more giver-congruent, an effect opposite to the negative effect anticipated. Surprisingly, sex had no impact on the giver-congruence of the gift. Similarity positively affected giver-congruence of a gift, while the occasion being a rite of passage slightly lessened the giver's intention to purchase a giver-congruent gift.

AN EXPERIMENTAL INVESTIGATION OF SELF-SYMBOLISM IN GIFTS

The ability of gifts to serve as emblems or containers of giver and receiver selves is a major reason for the existence and persistence of gift-giving rituals. From a purely economic standpoint, gift giving behavior is inefficient, as givers imperfectly understand needs and desires of receivers. However, the objects that become gifts transcend their purely economic functions to become representatives and extensions of giver- and receiver-selves, thus allowing the blurring of distinctions between self and other. Arguably, givers are likely to be more or less sensitive to the issue of the gift's ability to be an indicant of self and other; however, empirical research published by Belk (1976; 1979) reveals that in general, self-congruence of the gift with the giver as well as the receiver are important symbolic elements of the gift. As givers, we are familiar with the inclination to purchase self-indicating items through reflection on our own use of self/product language: "It's me" or "It's Kurt (or David or Chris)" is what we commonly exclaim upon finding a gift that matches our, or the receiver's, personality and tastes.

While there exists both empirical evidence and personal experience to suggest that the self-symbolism encoded in gifts is an important element in gift selection, little effort has been directed at understanding the circumstances that might lead to tendencies to encode selves in gifts. With respect to self (or giver)-congruence, both ideal and actual self-concept have been found to be significant predictors of gift choice (Belk 1979). In fact, Belk found that giver-congruence is a better predictor of gift choice than is receiver-congruence. In a qualitative study of gift shops, Sherry and McGrath (1989) found that customers primarily based their gift decisions on their own self image. Belk and Coon (1993) uncovered evidence suggesting that within dating couples, receivers strongly preferred giver-congruent gifts.

Receiver-congruence has also received some research attention. In fact, perhaps the most often discussed rule of gift-giving in both the popular press and scholarly research is the need of a gift selection to demonstrate the giver's familiarity with the receiver's preferences (cf. Caplow 1984). But, why are gifts often receiver-congruent? Giving such gifts situates and validates receivers by allowing their identities to be socially recognized and affirmed. In this sense, gift giving extends Wicklund and Gollwitzer's (1982) notion of "symbolic self completion" to "symbolic other-completion," in that others may choose gifts that create and confirm receivers' identities. Receiver-congruent gifts are generally not conventional gifts, which are "safe," mundane and common; conventional gifts are like commodities. Rather, receiver-congruent gifts are designed to respond to the "yearning for singularization" that exists in a complex society (Kopytoff 1986; McCracken 1986).

In summary, the importance of self-symbolism in gifts has been studied. We contribute to this literature by considering conditions which we believe impact the degree of self-symbolism in gifts: (1) perceived emotional closeness of the giver to the receiver, (2) perceived similarity of the giver with the receiver, (3) occasion for giving and (4) the sex of the giver. We begin with a literature review, followed by a description of the experimental research. The results are presented and discussed.

CLOSENESS, SIMILARITY, OCCASION, AND SEX

Several factors define the context within which gift choices are made. Two of the factors are relational: perceived closeness and similarity of the giver to the receiver. A third factor is the gift-giving occasion. The final factor is the sex of the giver. Each of these factors will be discussed below.

Closeness has been defined as the amount of affection the giver has for the receiver (Belk 1979), a definition which focuses on the emotional content, rather than the structural relationship between the giver and the receiver. Gifts are "tie signs" (Cheal 1988; Goffman 1971) when their primary use is their capacity to represent the nature of the relationship between the receiver and the giver of the gift, especially their emotional closeness. In fact, Hyde (1979) writes that gifts are "false gifts" when they fail to bind people. In general, symbolic tokens are indexical of communicative expressions (Garfinkel 1967). Therefore, the expense and nature of gift symbols tend to vary with the closeness of the relationship (Belk 1979; Caplow 1984; Haas and Deseran 1981; Shurmer 1971).

In addition to the closeness of a relationship, gift symbolism may vary depending on the perceived similarity of the giver to the receiver. While people tend to become closer to those whom they perceive to be similar, closeness and similarity are separate, if related constructs (Brown and Reingen 1987). For instance, a giver may be close to a parent, a sibling, or even a friend or spouse, and not necessarily perceive that they are similar. The impact of similarity on gift giving has only been investigated by Belk (1976) who included it as one element which in combination with the valence of four other factors can impact satisfaction with gift giving.

In addition to the two relationship variables, closeness and similarity, a third variable, the occasion upon which the gift is given, should impact the giver's choice of gift and gift symbolism. Gift-giving occasions are typically ritualistic; Klapp (1969) writes that "ritual is the prime symbolic vehicle for experiencing emotions and mystique together with others...including a sense of one's self as sharing such emotions" (p. 118). The ambiance of ritual ceremonies may heighten the impact of giving and increase the value of the gift (Sherry 1983). Thus we expect that the occasion for giving will impact encoding and decoding of self-symbolism.

Indeed, both Goffman (1967) and much later, Cheal (1988) claimed that the most serious gaps in research on gift giving concerned the lack of comparative information about the variety of occasions upon which gifts may be given. Cheal is helpful in this regard, as he points out that there are two major types of gift-giving occasions: rites of passage (low frequency, large scale events) and rites of progression (high frequency, small scale events).

Several scholars and writers have commented that gift giving is an activity whose main responsibility and interest culturally lies with women (Barnett 1954; Caplow 1982; Cheal 1988; Fischer and Arnold 1990). Fischer and Arnold (1990) refer to giving as "more than a labor of love" and find that more feminine men and women make more effort and buy more gifts at Christmas. Weil and Gould (1991) have specifically studied the interaction of sex of the giver and receiver, finding that men report feeling more expressive (a traditionally feminine characteristic) when giving to women as compared to men, whereas womens' reported expressiveness changes much less between same- and opposite-sex giving. Wolfinbarger and Gilly (1991) found that in terms of general gift-giving attitudes, men are in general less positive and enthusiastic about giving than are women. Given this finding, it is perhaps no surprise that in Otnes et al.'s (1993) qualitative study of gift giving, only one informant who agreed to the study was male.

GIVER-CONGRUENCE OF THE GIFT

Belk (1979) reported that ideal and actual self concept (which are strongly correlated) had larger impacts on choice of gift-giving attributes than did the giver's concept of the receiver. Based on their qualitative research, Sherry and McGrath (1989) would concur, as they reported that customers of gift shops often said that they would like to receive as gifts the objects they were purchasing for others. Givers buy self-congruent gifts to successfully present their self to the receiver, as well as the ease of purchasing such gifts. Occasionally such gifts may be intended to socialize the receiver to be more like the giver.

The idea that the purchase of products is often influenced by congruence with self-image is hardly new and has been supported by past research (cf. Grubb and Hupp 1969; Landon 1974; Sirgy 1982). While Belk and Coon (1993) find that in dating couples, receivers prefer giver-congruent gifts, we expect that this will be less true in other close relationships. First, in longer-term relationships there should be less need to successfully present one's self to a receiver who is already familiar with the giver. Second, the giver should be strongly motivated to please the closer receiver, and thus to choose a gift that is unique to the receiver's, rather than their own, taste. Last, closer givers should have a great deal of information about what receivers desire to get as gifts, thus lessening the tendency of givers to rely on their own tastes in choosing such gifts.

Similarity should have a strong effect on the tendency to buy giver-congruent gifts, as it should result in gifts which simultaneously reflect the giver's and receiver's selves. Such gifts underscore the feeling that givers and receivers live in a shared world, and have common interests and values.

Occasion may impact giver-congruence of the gift as well. Rites of passage, as large-scale social events, tend to have more rules about appropriate gift-giving behavior, leaving a bit less room for the expression of self in giving. Items are commonly given to support the performance of receivers in a newly acquired role. Thus, gifts are likely to be somewhat less giver-congruent on rites of passage as opposed to rites of progression.

Sex of the gift-giver is likely to have an effect on the intentions to choose giver-congruent gifts. In general, women have been found to be more socially sensitive than are men (Chodorow 1978; Gill et al. 1987; Hartsock 1985; Berg and McQuinn 1986). Moreover, women are enculturated to be more enthusiastic about gift giving, and to be more sensitive to the "cultural rules" concerning gift giving (Barnett 1954; Caplow 1982, 1984; Cheal 1988; Hyde 1979). One of these cultural rules is to sacrifice self-presentation motives in order to take into account the needs and desires of the receiver. Therefore, we anticipate that men will be more likely than women to report an intention to buy self-congruent gifts.

Hypothesis 1: Givers will intend to buy more giver-congruent gifts when (a) they perceive the receiver to be more similar. Gifts are less likely to be giver-congruent when (b) the receiver is perceived to be closer (c) the occasion is a rite of progression and (d) the giver is male.

RECEIVER-CONGRUENCE

Gifts to those whom we are close should be more receiver-congruent, as close friends separate themselves from others by showing that they can choose gifts especially for the receiver (Camerer 1988). Additionally, Brown and Reingen (1987) argue that in relationships in which there are strong rather than weak ties, consumers are likely to know more about each other. This is true not just because of the close dyad's direct relationship, but also because of "multiple redundant paths of communication" which are found in strongly tied networks. Because of greater knowledge and motivation, when the giver and receiver are close, gifts are more likely to be receiver-congruent. With respect to similarity, when the giver perceives similarity with the receiver, it is easier to choose receiver-congruent gifts, regardless of closeness. There is also more motivation to please similar receivers, as Krebs (1975) reviews evidence suggesting that people are more empathic to the pain and pleasure of those to whom they believe they are similar.

As for the impact of occasion, rites of progression are personal, and include such events as birthdays, anniversaries, and Mother's Day. The symbolism of gifts given on personal events is more likely to be individual. Consistent with this argument, Belk (1979) discovered that birthday gifts were "uniquely personal" compared to wedding gifts. Similarly, Lowes et al. (1971) discovered that personal gifts predominate on birthdays, anniversaries, and Mother's and Father's Days (all normally rites of progression).

Sex is also anticipated to affect receiver-congruence of the gift. The greater social sensitivity of women, together with their greater culturally-determined involvement in gift occasions, and thus exposure to gift-giving "rules," are likely to result in women choosing gifts which are receiver-congruent (Barnett 1954; Caplow 1982, 1984; Cheal 1988; Chodorow 1978; Gill et al. 1987; Hartsock 1985; Hyde 1979; Berg and McQuinn 1986).

Hypotheses 2: Givers are more likely to intend to give receiver-congruent gifts when (a) the receiver is perceived to be similar (b) the receiver is perceived to be closer and (c) the occasion is a rite of progression. (d) Women are more likely than men to intend to choose receiver-congruent gifts.

RESEARCH METHOD

Scenarios were used to manipulate the closeness, similarity and occasion variables in the experiment. Poe (1977) has suggested the construction of hypothetical role playing situations to study gift giving, and Belk (1979) used 15 gift-giving scenarios in his research. The experimental design is especially appropriate as three of the independent variables, closeness, similarity, and occasion are likely to be moderately or strongly correlated in a non-experimental study. Moreover, actual purchases may not be as good at revealing the "rules" that guide, yet of course, incompletely determine, givers' behavior. Constraints such as time and availability of an appropriate gift are likely to cause diversions from the basic guiding principles and intentions of givers.

The design was a 3X2X2 with experimental manipulations including three levels of closeness which were determined through

TABLE 1

Giver and Receiver-Congruence of Gifts[++]

	Giver-Congruence	*Receiver-Congruence*
OCCASION		
Rite of Passage(153)	2.3[+]	3.0[**]
Rite of Progression(124)	2.6	3.5
CLOSENESS		
Close Friend(108)	2.8[**]	3.5[***]
Friend (70)	2.3	3.4
Acquaintance(99)	2.2	2.8
SIMILARITY		
Similar (142)	3.2[***]	3.4[**]
Dissimilar (135)	1.9	3.0
SEX		
Male (183)	2.4	3.1[**]
Female (94)	2.5	3.5
Multiple R	.50	.41
Squared	.25	.16

[++]No two-way interaction terms were significant, giver and receiver-congruence are measured on a 1 to 5 scale.

[*]$p<.10$

[**]$p<.05$

[***]$p<.001$

[+]$p<.15$

pre-test (close friend, friend, someone you hardly know), two levels of similarity (similar or different with respect to gift-giving preferences) and two occasions (rite of progression — birthday, or rite of passage — wedding). Both of these events were appropriate for the MBA student sample employed, as graduate students are generally old enough to be socialized concerning gift-giving and to be giving gifts for birthdays and weddings. The scenario read as follows:

Imagine you have accepted an invitation to a large [birthday party/wedding] and you will be buying a [birthday/wedding] gift for [a close friend/a friend, but not a close friend/someone you don't know well at all (for instance, a friend of a friend, or a distant relative you rarely see)]. You believe s/he is very [similar to/different from] you with respect to the gifts s/he likes to give and receive.

Each student received three different conditions from the twelve possible. After reading each scenario, subjects were asked to name a particular recipient that would fit the scenario in order to make the task more concrete to them. Manipulation checks revealed that the closeness and similarity conditions were effective ($F=98.7$, $p<.001$ for closeness, $F=117$, $p<.001$ for similarity). At the end of each condition, givers were also asked to name the gift they would choose and to explain why this gift would be chosen.

Self-concepts were measured on a semantic differential scale from "This product is strongly like me [the receiver]," to "This product is strongly unlike me [the receiver]". Sommers (1964), Sirgy (1982), and Landon (1972, 1974) all report that consumers are able to describe themselves and others in terms of products. This procedure also reflects the self/product vocabulary that consumers themselves use, e. g. "It's me," or "It's you."

The sample consisted of 150 MBA students. The third condition completed by each student was removed from consideration, as analysis revealed the presence of an order effect in the third

condition. After removing a few more cases that had incomplete information, the final number of usable cases was 277. Although students can be a less than desirable sample, they are appropriate for studying gift giving in that it is an activity in which students normally participate. The use of students is further justified in this experimental research because (1) theory testing is the primary goal of this research (Calder, Phillips and Tybout 1981) and (2) the use of a relatively homogeneous sample results in control of random sources of error (Cook and Campbell 1979).

RESULTS

Giver-Congruence. As shown in Table 1, hypothesis 1a is not supported; in fact, the directionality suggested by the findings is opposite that anticipated. Closer givers planned to give gifts that were *more*, rather than less, giver-congruent to their very close friends ($p<.05$). Hypothesis 1b is strongly supported, as givers reported they would buy more giver-congruent gifts for more similar receivers ($p<.001$). Hypothesis 1c is only barely suggestive ($p<.15$); givers believed they would give slightly more giver-congruent gifts on rites of progression as compared to rites of passage. Hypothesis 1d is not supported as the sex of the giver had no significant effect on the intended giver-congruence of the gift. No hypotheses were made concerning interaction effects, and no significant effects were found. While no two-way interactions are significant, a three-way interaction between closeness, occasion and sex is suggested by the data ($p<.05$). Women in the sample appeared to make an extra effort to buy more giver-congruent gifts on rites of passage to close friends than to other types of receivers, while mens' strategy did not differ on rites of passage regarding the degree of self-congruence to be encoded in the gift for closer as compared to less close givers.

Receiver-Congruence. The results appear in Table 1. Both hypotheses 2a and 2b are supported, as gifts were intended to be more receiver-congruent when receivers were similar and when they were closer. The impact of occasion on receiver congruence (hypothesis 2c) is also significant (p<.05). In support of hypothesis 2d, women were more likely than men to buy receiver-congruent gifts (p<.05). Once again, no hypotheses were made concerning interaction effects, and in this case, no significant effects were uncovered.

DISCUSSION AND LIMITATIONS

The results of the experiment suggest that there are indeed norms which influence intentions to encode gifts to be either giver- or receiver-congruent. The two conditions of the relationships investigated — closeness and similarity — impacted the intentions of givers to encode gifts to be more or less giver- and receiver-congruent. In fact, greater closeness and similarity both resulted in the desire to make gifts more giver- and receiver-congruent. The result concerning the positive impact of closeness on giver-congruence was unexpected. We predicted that closeness would lead givers to intend to "trade off" giver-congruence to please receivers, and to thus choose *less* giver-congruent gifts. Several reasons can be suggested for the surprising findings. Because of the experimental nature of the task, subjects may have felt that they would be able to choose gifts which simultaneously pleased receivers and successfully presented the giver's self, a task which may have proved more difficult in practice. However, an alternative explanation for the findings should be considered. As did Belk and Coon's (1993) dating partners, the receivers of closer giver's gifts may actually prefer giver-congruent gifts, and givers may be endeavoring to satisfy this desire. Perhaps giver-congruent gifts are perceived to be positive even by dissimilar close receivers because the giver, by giving a gift that represents their self and their interests, is giving of themselves. Thus, rather than "imposing" their self upon that of the receiver, such gifts may often be considered by both the giver and receiver as positive, desirable extensions of the giver. Conceptually, this study suggests that the nature of giver-congruence is such that the construct has both negative and positive dimensions. It may be that giver-congruence is a desired quality by both givers and receivers, as long as such gifts are in some "acceptable range" of receiver-congruence as well. Previous qualitative studies suggested that one source of gift-giving errors is that the disappointing gifts are giver- rather than receiver-congruent (cf. Sherry, McGrath and Levy 1992). Perhaps in reality these unacceptable giver-congruent gifts are less frequent than anticipated.

The impact of perceived similarity with the receiver on self-symbolism, on the other hand, was consistent with our expectations. When the giver perceives similarity with the receiver, then a gift can be purchased that is both giver- and receiver- congruent. In this case, trading off self-presentation motives to buy a gift pleasing to the receiver is unnecessary. Similarity of the giver to the receiver suggests that there is a common understanding within the relationship; this commonality facilitates the expression of sentiments about relationships which Belk (1979) and Scammon et al. (1982) posit to be an important function of gift giving.

Gifts were perhaps slightly more giver-congruent for rites of progression as opposed to rites of passage. The link between the conventional nature of rites of passage and self-symbolism was stronger for the receiver-congruence of gift, which was lessened on rites of passage. Perhaps receiver-congruence requires extra effort as compared to giver-congruence, and givers are less motivated to put forth this extra efforts on rites of passage as compared to rites of progression

Sex did not have an impact on giver-congruence of the gift, a result that may be explained in part by the fact that giver-congruence can be either a desired or undesired characteristic; therefore, the greater social sensitivity of women would not necessarily result in buying less giver-congruent gifts. However, women did intend to buy more receiver-congruent gifts than did men, a finding consistent with womens' greater interest in gift-giving and the domestic sphere of life.

While the experimental design utilized can separate the effects of the independent variables which in practice are correlated, the design nevertheless has limitations. As subjects did not have to actually engage in any search behavior, they could report what they *ideally* would do. Whether or not that goal would be achieved is unclear. In that other studies have suggested that givers do not find gift purchase in general to be a difficult activity (cf. Otnes et al. 1993), it may be that intentions of givers are often carried out. The hypothetical nature of the experiment together with the within subjects design may have resulted in interactions between the independent variables being too subtle to detect (Sawyer 1977). Further research with a different research design is necessary to study the impact of closeness, similarity, occasion and sex on self-symbolism in gifts.

Gift-giving behavior appears to involve an engagement of self and other for many givers. This is especially true for givers buying for receivers they perceive to be both close and similar. Such givers are more likely to feel like receivers are part of their "extended self." While many of us feel obligated to give gifts, and may grumble about the commercialism which promotes this enterprise, giving is nevertheless a meaningful ritual which provides an avenue for the discovery and enlargement of selves.

REFERENCES

Barnett, James (1954), The American Christmas: A Study in National Culture, Ayer Company: Salem, New Hampshire.

Belk, Russell (1976), "It's the Thought that Counts: A Signed Digraph Analysis of Gift Giving," Journal of Consumer Research, 3(December), 155-162.

_____ (1979), "Gift-Giving Behavior," Research in Marketing, Vol. 2, ed. Jagdish Sheth, Greenwich, CT: JAI Press, 95-126.

_____ (1982), "Effects of Gift-Giving Involvement on Gift Selection Strategies," Advances in Consumer Research, Vol. 9, ed. Andrew Mitchell, Ann Arbor MI: Association for Consumer Research, 408-412.

_____ (1988), "Possessions and the Extended Self, " Journal of Consumer Research, 15 (September), 139-168.

_____ and Gregory Coon (1993), "Gift Giving as Agapic Love: An Alternative to the Exchange Paradigm Based on Dating Experiences," Journal of Consumer Research, 20 (December), 393-415.

Berg, John H. and Ronald D. McQuinn (1986), "Attraction and Exchange in Continuing and Noncontinuing Dating Relationships," Journal of Personality and Social Psychology, 50 (5), 942-952.

Brown, Jacqueline Johnson and Peter Reingen (1987), "Social Ties and Word-of-Mouth Referral Behavior," Journal of Consumer Research, 14 (December), 350-362.

Calder, Bobby J., Lynn W. Phillips and Alice M. Tybout (1981), "Designing Research for Applications," Journal of Consumer Research, 8(September), 197-207.

Camerer, Colin (1988), "Gifts as Economic Signals and Social Symbols," American Journal of Sociology, 94, 180-214.

Caplow, Theodore (1982), "Christmas Gifts and Kin Networks," American Sociological Review, 47 (3), 383-392.

_____ (1984), "Rule Enforcement Without Visible Means: Christmas Gift Giving in Middletown," American Journal of Sociology, 89(6), 1306-1323.

Cheal, David (1988), The Gift Economy, New York: Routledge.

Chodorow, Nancy C. M. (1978), The Reproduction of Mothering, Berkeley: University of California Press.

Cook, Thomas D., and Donald T. Campbell (1979), Quasi-Experimentation: Design and Analysis Issues for Field Settings, Chicago: Rand McNally College Publishing Company.

Fischer, Eileen and Stephen J. Arnold (1990), "More Than a Labour of Love: Gender Roles and Christmas Gift Shopping," Journal of Consumer Research, 17 (December), 333-345.

Garfinkel, Harold (1967), Studies in Ethnomethodology, Englewood Cliffs: Prentice-Hall.

Gill, Sandra, Jean Stockard, Miriam Johnson and Suzanne Williams (1987), "Measuring Gender Differences: The Expressive Dimension of the Androgyny Scales," Sex Roles, 17 (7/8), 375-400.

Goffman, Erving (1967), Interaction Ritual, Garden City, Doubelday.

_____ (1971), Relations in Public, New York: Basic.

Grubb, Edward L. and Gregg Hupp (1968), "Perception of Self, Generalized Stereotypes, and Brand Selection," Journal of Marketing Research, 5 (1) 58-63.

Haas, David F. and Forrest A. Deseran (1981), "Trust and Symbolic Exchange," Social Psychology Quarterly, 44(1), 3-13.

Hamm, B. Curtis and Edward W. Cundiff (1969), "Self-Actualization and Product Perception," Journal of Marketing Research, 6 (November), 470-472.

Hartsock, Nancy (1985), "Exchange Theory: Critique From a Feminist Standpoint," Current Perspectives in Social Theory, 6, 57-70.

Katz, Elihu and Paul F. Lazersfeld (1955), Personal Influence, Glencoė, IL: Free Press.

Kopytoff, Igor (1986), "The Cultural Biography of Things: Commoditization as Process," in The Social Life of Things, ed. Arjun Appadurai, Cambridge: Cambridge University Press, 64-91.

Klapp, Orrin E. (1969), Collective Search for Identity, New York: Holt, Rinehart and Winston.

Krebs, Dennis (1975), "Empathy and Altruism," Journal of Personality and Social Psychology, Vol. 32, 1134-1146.

Landon, E. Laird (1974), "Self-Concept, Ideal Self-Concept and Consumer Purchase Intentions," Journal of Consumer Research, 1 (September), 44-51.

Lowes, B., J. Turner, and Gordon Wills (1971), "Patterns of Gift Giving," in Explorations in Marketing Thought, ed. Gordon Wills, London: Bradford University Press, 82-102.

McCracken, Grant (1986), "Culture and Consumption: A Theoretical Account of the Structure and Movement of the Cultural Meaning of Consumer Goods," Journal of Consumer Research, 13 (June), 71-84.

Otnes, Cele, Tina Lowrey and Young Chan Kim (1993), "Christmas Gift Selection for 'Easy' and 'Difficult' Recipients: A Social Roles Interpretation," Journal of Consumer Research, Vol. 20 (2) September, 229-244.

Poe, Donald (1977), "The Giving of Gifts: Anthropological Data and Social Psychological Theory," Cornell Journal of Social Relations, 12 (1), 47-63.

Sawyer, Alan (1977), "The Role of Role Playing In Experiments about Consumer Behavior," in Contemporary Marketing Thought, Vol. 19, Eds., D. Greenberg and D. Bellenger, Chicago: American Marketing Association, 191-194.

Scammon, Debra, Roy Shaw and Gary Bamossy (1982), "Is a Gift Always a Gift? An Investigation of Flower Purchasing Behavior Across Situations," in Advances in Consumer Research, Vol. 9, ed. Andrew Mitchell, Provo, UT: Association for Consumer Research, 408-411.

Sherry, John (1983), "Gift Giving in Anthropological Perspective," Journal of Consumer Research, 10 (September), 157-167.

_____ and Mary Ann McGrath (1989), "Unpacking the Holiday Presence: A Comparative Ethnography of the Gift Store," in Interpretive Consumer Research, ed. Elizabeth Hirschman, Provo, UT: Association for Consumer Research, 148-167.

_____ , _____ and Sidney J. Levy (1992), "The Disposition the Gift and Many Unhappy Returns," Journal of Retailing, 68 (1) Spring, 40-65.

Shurmer, Pamela (1971), "The Gift Game," New Society, 18 (482), 1242-1244.

Sirgy, Joseph (1982), "Self-Concept in Consumer Behavior: A Critical Review," Journal of Consumer Research, 9 (December), 287-300.

Sommers, Montrose S. (1964), "Product Symbolism and the Perception of Social Strata," Proceedings of the American Marketing Association, Vol. 22, 200-216.

Weil, Claudia E. and Stephen J. Gould (1991), Sex Roles, 24 (9/10), 617-637.

Wicklund, Robert A. and Peter M. Gollwitzer (1982), Symbolic Self-Completion, Hillsdale, NJ: Lawrence Erlbaum.

Wolfinbarger, Mary and Mary Gilly (1991), "The Impact of Gender on Gift-Giving Attitudes, or, Are Men Insensitive Clods?," in Gender and Consumer Research, ed. Janeen Costa, Provo, Utah: Association for Consumer Research, pp. 223-230.

Product Symbolism, Self Meaning, and Holistic Matching: The Role of Information Processing in Impulsive Buying

James E. Burroughs, University of Wisconsin-Madison

ABSTRACT

Impulse buying represents an important form of consumer buying experience. Unfortunately, work examining this area has largely failed to consider the potential of a cognitive perspective. To fill this gap, this paper proposes an information processing account of what occurs in an impulsive buying episode. Specifically, it is suggested that much impulsive buying behavior can be characterized as a type of holistic information processing whereby a match is recognized between the symbolic meanings of a particular product and a consumer's self-concept. When such a match is recognized, the resulting urge to purchase the item will be instant, compelling, and affectively charged. So powerful, perhaps, that it overrides any more analytic assessments of the purchasing situation.

INTRODUCTION

Impulse buying is a phenomenon which has long been known to consumer researchers; going back to at least the *DuPont Consumer Buying Studies* initiated in the 1940's (DuPont 1965). Yet, within consumer research, impulsive buying has remained somewhat of an enigma (Rook 1987). The dominant paradigm in consumer research assumes a highly deliberate, analytic, consumer (cf. Bettman 1979; Engel, Blackwell, and Kollat 1978); and as such, has drawn criticism from some researchers who lament that it does a poor job of anticipating this more impulsive type of consumer response (Holbrook and Hirschman 1982; Olshavsky and Granbois 1979; Rook 1987). Meanwhile, specific considerations of impulse buying, have tended to remain at only a taxonomic level (i.e. types of products impulsively bought) (cf. Bellinger et al. 1978); leaving open still the question of the internal mechanisms which must surely drive such behaviors (cf. Rook 1987). It is, after all, "people, not products, who experience consuming impulses" (Rook and Hoch 1985).

Rook's (1987) inquiry provided a notable lift to the study of impulsive buying. In this study Rook utilized methods of phenomenological inquiry to go "inside the consumer," and provide a "thick description" (Geertz 1973) of this type of experience. His study demonstrated impulsive buying to be more than just unplanned purchasing; finding it to be instantly occurring, highly compelling, and hedonically complex. It is as if the consumer is momentarily possessed of forces beyond his/her control (Rook 1987). Such impulsive buying urges have been found to afflict nine out of ten consumers; at least occasionally (Welles 1986).

In complement to Rook's primarily affective account, this paper works to introduce a cognitive account of the impulsive buying experience. Specifically, it will be advanced that such episodes can be characterized by a holistic style of information processing on the part of the individual, which allows him or her to instantly, though perhaps inadvertently, map complex symbolic product meanings onto the self (Belk 1988; McCracken 1986); and in so doing, evoke the types of highly compelling responses described by Rook (1987). In effect, a partial realization of the consumer's deep-seeded, desired-self, is held out in the object in front of them.

Towards this account, this paper briefly reviews the extant literature on impulsive buying, reviews the literature on holistic information processing, and then integrates these perspectives into a unified account. With this as a base, the underlying role of this "self-object meaning-matching" is incorporated into the overall conceptualization. On the whole, it is hoped that this paper helps effect a convergence in the traditional and impulsive perspectives of consumer purchasing. The paper closes with a look at some of the future issues of this convergence.

As a caveat, this discussion is not intended to represent a comprehensive account of all forms of impulsive buying. Piron (1991) distinguishes between experiential impulse buying (the form considered below) and nonexperiential impulse buying. An example of nonexperiential impulse buying might be the spontaneous decision to buy a candy bar in a store checkout line. While certainly unplanned, this latter type of purchase seems an unlikely candidate for the types of complex experiences described by Rook (1987). Also, remembering that you were out of milk upon seeing it on the store shelf, though appearing impulsive, would again fall outside of the scope of the type of impulsive buying considered here.

IMPULSE BUYING: A REVIEW OF THE LITERATURE

As previously discussed, recent work in the area of impulsive buying has been largely informed by Rook's (1987) phenomenological investigation of the topic. Rook found that the requisites of the impulsive buying urge include: (1) a lack of preplanning by the individual whereby (2) a chance encounter with a product (or related stimulus) leads to (3) an immediate and powerful response, which, in turn, creates a state of (4) psychological disequilibrium such that the consumer feels momentarily out of control, and finally (5) this response is hedonically complex (see also Rook and Hoch 1985). To fully appreciate the depth and scope of the impulsive buying experience, this conceptualization is expanded along three lines: antecedents, characteristics, and outcomes.

Impulsive Buying Antecedents. The impulsive buying urge is unplanned. It appears to be set off when an individual incidentally encounters a relevant stimuli (usually the product itself) in the environment (Hoch and Loewenstein 1991; Rook 1987). Though considerable early research attempted to understand which classes of products would lead to such a response (see Bellenger et al. 1978 for a review), Rook (1987) provided that, since virtually any product could be impulsively purchased, the phenomenon was better considered person-centered rather than product-centered. This is not to imply that the product stimuli have not been found to play an important role (Cobb and Hoyer 1986; Hoch and Loewenstein 1991). Hoch and Loewenstein (1991) offer three product conditions which seem conducive to triggering the buying impulse: close physical proximity of the stimulus (e.g. the urge to buy is more likely to be evoked in a shopping mall than in one's office); close temporal proximity of the stimulus (i.e. the positive outcomes of making a purchase are believed to be experienced immediately, as opposed to at some distal point in time); and finally, a high social comparability of the stimulus. That is, an object is more likely to incite an impulsive response if the individual knows that others within his or her social circle already possess such an object.

Impulsive Buying Characteristics. In further describing what the consumer experiences when the impulsive buying urge takes hold, Rook (1987) identifies several themes: the impulsive buying urge appears to arise spontaneously; the impulsive buying urge feels intense; the impulse buying urge reflects animate forces; and the impulsive buying urge is synchronistic. The discussion of the first theme is rather straightforward. After an individual initially encounters a relevant stimulus he/she seems instantly and inexplicably drawn to it (Wolman 1973). What is of relevance is the speed and automaticity with which this appears to occur:

> I was in the Pottery Barn browsing, and saw this crystal candle holder. It came over me instantly. (male-34 in Rook 1987, p. 193)

Coupled with the impulsive urge's swiftness is its intensity. Individuals often report feeling overcome by the need to make a purchase. This need demands satisfaction immediately, and may persist even after the stimulus is removed:

> Once I can see it in my mind, it won't go away until I buy it. If I can see it, that's it. (female-55, describing a piece of jewelry in Rook 1987, p. 193)

Moreover, the need to possess the object often appears, to the individual, to go beyond a merely personal decision; it is as if the object itself comes to have a stake in the purchase:

> The pants were shrieking "buy me," so I knew right then I had better walk away and try and get something else done. (female-35 in Rook and Hoch 1985, p. 25)

Finally, and perhaps most significantly, the consumer perceives an element of synchronicity; that is, the object is perceived to be "meant" for the individual:

> It felt like something that you had been looking for for a long time had appeared before your eyes, and if you don't buy it now you won't have another chance. It is just the right place and time. (female-37, describing a pair of shoes in Rook 1987, p. 194)

As an additional note, the consumer buying episode may be fraught with emotion (Gardner and Rook 1988; Rook 1987; Weinberg and Gottwald 1982). These emotions often appear to be in conflict, though, at least initially, the individual seems enthralled with the possibility of making a purchase.

Impulsive Buying Outcomes. A resonant theme throughout the impulse buying studies is the momentary loss of control that accompanies these encounters. Ultimately there are, of course, two possible outcomes. The consumer may overcome the urge, and forgo the purchase; or, incapable of delaying reward, give in to temptation. When one gives in to the urge, a potpourri of thoughts and emotions may ensue. Rook (1987) reports that occasionally the elation is sustained as the appropriateness of the purchase is confirmed. Or, more likely, there are feelings of remorse as the monetary repercussions (and occasionally more serious issues such as health problems) become apparent (Gardner and Rook 1988; Rook 1987; Wansink 1994).

Finally, from the descriptions provided by Rook, and others, a critical outcome of the impulsive buying episode appears to be a strong bond which is effected between the individual and the product. Yet, Rook stops short of elaborating on exactly how this bond develops or why it is experienced so strongly. This paper attempts to address these gaps, offering a reconceptualization of the impulsive buying experience.

RECONCEPTUALIZING IMPULSE BUYING: THE FUNDAMENTAL ROLE OF HOLISTIC MEANING MATCHING

This paper suggests that one way in which impulse buying can be explained is by conceiving of it as a cognitive process consisting of two components—holistic processing and self-object meaning-matching—whereby the symbolic meanings of objects are holistically matched to salient images of the self. When such a match is effected, the result is a consumer who becomes instantly and powerfully aroused with a desire to possess the object; perhaps to the detriment of any more thorough consideration of the purchase ramifications. It was Thompson et al. (1990) who first proposed combining the perspectives of holistic information processing and self-object meaning-matching into a unified account of impulsive buying. Unfortunately, these researchers only suggested this possibility as an ancillary point in their discussion. A specific consideration of the potential of a holistic self-object meaning-matching account of impulsive buying is for the first time developed here.

Developing this account of impulsive buying presents somewhat of a challenge in that the topics of holistic information processing and of symbolic self-object meaning-matching are actually drawn from two rather different research traditions and, thus, can be most clearly addressed independently. Yet, effecting this separation is not straightforward because comprehending the fundamental role of either topic in this process requires at least a basic grasp of the role of the other topic. In an attempt to get around this dilemma, a brief sketch of the basic tenets of each axiom is offered immediately, after which a more developed discussion of each of these topics, especially as they relate to impulsive buying, is then pursued independently.

Holistic Meaning Matching: Conceptual Overview

It would appear that individuals have at their disposal two general strategies for processing information (Hutchinson and Alba 1991). Of these, the defining feature of holistic information processing is that incoming stimuli are processed as gestalt wholes where the individual determinants of a particular stimulus are collapsed into an overall representation of the object (Foard and Kemler Nelson 1984; Pomerantz 1981). In contrast, in analytic information processing, the processor attends to each individual stimulus characteristic in order to build-up a comprehensive understanding of the object (cf. Bettman 1979; Hutchinson and Alba 1991). Because the stimulus characteristics need not be individually attended to in holistic information processing, it offers the advantages of speed, and reduced cognitive effort (automaticity)(for a review see Kemler 1983; Smith and Kemler Nelson 1988). Holistic processing, characterized by this very undifferentiated style, similarly appears well suited to dealing with very abstract types of information such as object concepts and symbolic meanings of objects (Holbrook and Moore 1981). Conversely, the very deliberate nature of analytic strategies helps to insure comprehension accuracy though this typically comes in lieu of processing speed (Hutchinson and Alba 1991). While consumers' use of holistic information processing strategies has been widely discussed in consumer research (cf. Alba and Hutchinson 1987; Cohen and Basu 1987; Holbrook and Moore 1981; Hutchinson and Alba 1991; MacInnis, Moorman, and Jaworski 1991; MacInnis and Price 1987), it remains the more obscure of the two information processing styles.

Extending the discussion into self-object meaning-matching, the self appears to represent an integral part of information processing regardless of processing strategy used. Combs and Snygg

(1959) summed it up nicely: "As the central point of the perceptual field, the phenomenal self is the point of orientation for the individual's every behavior. It is the frame of reference in terms of which all other perceptions gain their meaning." The self then, represents a semantic filter through which information from the social environment is perceived.

Similarly, the capacity for products to become infused with symbolic meanings, and thus, represent important extensions of the self, has been widely discussed within consumer research (cf. Belk 1988; Mick 1986; Solomon 1983). McCracken (1986) offers that such deep symbolic meanings become embedded in products through a society's institutions, such as fashion and advertising. The individual, in turn, may interpret these meanings as self-relevant, and adopt these products as their own. Though the mechanism McCracken provides to effect this transfer—ritual—is deliberate in nature, considerable evidence suggests that such transfers may also occur holistically (Markus 1977; Markus and Sentis 1982; Sentis and Burnstein 1979).

Whether deliberately or holistically arrived at, when there is a perceived congruence between the symbolic meanings of an object encountered in the environment and one's self-concept, the orientation of the individual towards this object will be intense (Belk 1988; Markus and Sentis 1982). Preliminarily then, the speed of holistic processing, combined with the strength of symbolic self-object meaning-matching appears to provide the explanation missing from Rook's (1987) discussion. To more fully substantiate this conclusion, we now consider each topic more extensively, especially as they tie back to previous understanding of impulsive buying.

Holistic Information Processing: Extended Review

Kemler Nelson (1993) suggests that most individuals appear capable of employing both analytic and holistic styles of processing. So why or when would a holistic information processing strategy be favored (or vice versa)? Based on the literature there appear to be three factors which largely determine the style of processing which will be employed: task characteristics, stimulus characteristics, and individual consumer characteristics.

Task Characteristics. As mentioned, in addition to being much faster, holistic processing is also considered to be less cognitively taxing than analytic processing. Thus, this style of processing will tend to be favored in situations where either the time available to process is quite short, or the amount of information to be processed is quite large (Foard and Kemler Nelson 1984; Kemler Nelson 1984; Ward et al. 1986). In line with this reasoning, Ward et al. (1986) suggest that, because the amount of information incidental in the environment is voluminous, processing commences holistically and then shifts to being more analytic as certain information is judged to merit further consideration. Some, however, have taken issue with making such a blanket statement (Smith and Kemler Nelson 1984).

Stimulus Characteristics. Certain types of stimuli also seem to lend themselves to being processed holistically, despite task characteristics. In general, the more complex the characteristics of the stimulus become the more likely the stimulus is to be processed holistically (Foard and Kemler Nelson 1984; Kemler Nelson 1993, Ward et al. 1986). This complexity may occur due to either the sheer number of characteristics associated with the stimulus or the abstractness of the characteristics associated with this stimulus. When the stimulus is characterized by a large number of tangible attributes, a holistic style of processing creates the potential for errors because important information may not be given adequate

attention, or, conversely, irrelevant information may be given too much weight (Hutchinson and Alba 1991; Smith and Kemler Nelson 1984).

Individual Characteristics. Consumer characteristics also appear to play an important role in the processing strategy evoked. It is important to distinguish here, between processing styles and processing abilities. Processing style simply refers to one's preference for processing in a particular way; though, as mentioned, most adults are capable of switching between styles given sufficient reason (Kemler Nelson 1993; Smith and Baron 1981; see also Childers et al. 1985). Conversely, processing ability, which refers to the competence with which an individual selects and executes a processing strategy given a particular situation (Smith and Baron 1981). Though one's preferred processing style seems to be strictly a matter of individual taste, processing ability appears to be related to intelligence. A study by Smith and Baron (1981) found that less intelligent individuals were generally less capable of recognizing when to switch processing styles and consequently persisted in processing in an inappropriate style given the task and stimulus. Consequently, if the individuals preferred processing style happened to be a holistic one, and the task is better approached analytically, such individuals tended to be more error prone (Smith and Baron 1981).

Holistic Processing: Informing Impulsive Buying

Considering these characteristics of holistic processing, it appears that a case can be made for its role in impulsive purchasing. This section will lay out the basic tenets of this view by considering three central points: (1) holistic processing's role in the antecedents and characteristics of the impulsive buying episode; (2) holistic processing's role in the outcomes of the impulsive buying episode; and finally (3) a special consideration of how holistic processing might provide insight into the individual differences found in people's proclivity to impulsively purchase.

First, consider the antecedents and characteristics of the impulsive buying urge. Recall that the impulsive buying episode appears to be set in motion by information which was initially only incidental in the environment but was also immediately understood as highly self-relevant (Hoch and Loewenstein 1991; Rook 1987). Not only is holistic processing often used to process initially incidental information in the environment, but it also appears particularly adept at handling the highly abstract types of information associated with self-relevant symbolic product meanings. Next, the fact that the impulse buying urge appears to arise spontaneously or automatically further implicates a holistic processing style. It would appear more than chance that this low level of cognitive effort associated with the impulsive buying experience exactly maps to research suggesting that holistic information processing is also characterized by a low level of cognitive effort. Finally, the speed with which the impulse buying urge takes place offers the most compelling evidence that a holistic processing style is operational.

Second, consider the possible outcomes of the impulsive buying urge. The individual may resist the urge to purchase. Perhaps, this type of person is better able to shift processing styles in the manner suggested by Ward et al. (1986) and Smith and Baron (1981); and now more analytically considers the possible consequences of their decision. With this shift they better recognize the merits of deferring purchase and do so. Conversely, Holbrook and Hirschman (1982) and MacInnis and Price (1987) both note that highly self-relevant information will encourage elaborated aspects of fantasy, and possible imagery. Perhaps the salience of this meaning-match has encouraged the individual to become even more steeped in a holistic processing style. This momentary imbalance inhibits any more analytic assessment of the purchase situation and it is only later, when the balance is restored, that the consequences having made the purchase become fully apparent; hence regret.

Third, there is evidence that suggests a correspondence between general processing styles and vulnerability to impulsive buying. Developmental psychologists have found that children, who are notoriously impulsive, also appear largely incapable of processing information analytically (Smith and Kemler Nelson 1988; Zelniker and Jeffrey 1976). More strikingly, this impulsivity-holistic processing link has been similarly found in studies of adults (Smith and Baron 1981; Smith and Kemler Nelson 1984; Ward 1983). Though the amount of empirical evidence is limited, the general conclusion of these researchers seems to be that a holistic processor is predisposed to act only on their initial, gestalt perception, of a purchase situation because this is their principle way of comprehending new information.

Conversely, more analytic processors are more likely to attempt to consider all of the details of a particular situation. Such individuals appear to rotate the situation in mental space in order to try and understand it from numerous angles. By being more reflexive in their assessments, such individuals are more likely to recognize critical, but negative, information in a (purchase) decision (Smith and Kemler Nelson 1984). This finding is consonant with the initial discussion of individual processing styles, from which it can be inferred that, individuals who persisted in processing holistically, tended to set themselves up to making the types of errors typified in an impulsive purchase.

To this point, our extended discussion has considered how holistic processing might provide the mechanism by which impulsive buying is enabled. Yet, in opposition to the character of impulsive buying, it is perfectly plausible for stimuli to be processed holistically and yet not elicit any type of strong response from the individual. Thus, the second half of the equation, self-object meaning-matching, is needed to give impetus to the explanation of impulse buying.

Self-Object Meaning-Matching: Extended Review and Integration

A key part of explaining impulsive purchasing as a holistic matching process involves understanding how symbolic object meanings can become aligned with conceptualizations of the self. To this end, a discussion of self, and then of object meanings is developed and integrated.

The concept of the "self" is perhaps the defining topic of social psychology. Between 1987 and 1993 over 5000 articles on this topic specifically were published (Banaji and Prentice 1994). Basically, the concept of the self refers to the process of reflexivity whereby we are capable of being simultaneously both the subject and the object of our thinking (Gecas and Burke 1995). This reflexivity includes understandings of our attitudes, beliefs, values, identities, and affective states (Gecas and Burke 1995). In effect, our self-concept is who we perceive ourselves to be.

The self-concept is developed through the individual's interaction with the social and physical environments. Over time an understanding of the individual's position within this system becomes internalized as a cognitive schema of the self (Markus 1977; Markus and Sentis 1982). This self-schema or self-concept is believed to provide the fundamental basis against which all future interactions with the environment are evaluated (Markus and Wurf 1987). Moreover, once formed, the core self is believed to be stable but not static (Markus and Wurf 1987). As the individual interacts with the environment, there is an opportunity to refine this self-concept, moving it toward an ideal state. Markus and Nurius (1986) refer to this as the ideal self. It follows that as the self continues to evolve, individuals will seek out objects or relationships which symbolize or reinforce important notions of the self (or ideal self), while avoiding interactions which have equally opposing negative consequences (Markus and Nurius 1986; Sirgy 1982). When such a congruence of meanings is perceived between "the other" and the self, the individual's affinity towards that person or object will, not surprisingly, tend to be intense (Belk 1988; Markus and Sentis 1982; Sirgy 1982).

Approaching the topic from the opposite side of the dyad, a considerable body of literature within consumer research documents the potential of objects to carry symbolic meanings. By meanings, we refer to both the communicative and confirmatory properties of objects to either assert one's individuality within a society or, conversely, to help solidify important social bonds (i.e. symbolize the collective whole) (Solomon 1983). McCracken (1986) suggests that the process by which these symbolic meanings are initially embedded into objects occurs through such social institutions as fashion and advertising. Objects become tools of individual and social definition. As individuals, in turn, interact with their environment they come to understand the social and personal significance of these various object meanings. When these meanings are seen as congruent with important conceptions of the self (or ideal-self), the individual may be motivated to subsequently acquire and incorporate these objects (and their correspondent symbolic meanings) as an important part of his or her self-concept (Belk 1988, McCracken 1986; Mick 1986; Solomon 1983; Rook 1985).

Returning now to a consideration of impulsive buying, it can be suggested that this self-object meaning-matching provides a highly plausible explanation of why the impulsive buying experience is experienced as so compelling. Recall that individuals reported being momentarily driven to possess the object. For instance, these individuals characterized the impulse buying experience, in such ways as "the object came alive," or the "object felt meant for me." These feelings of an intimate bond with the object appear to describe exactly what the individual experiences in self-object meaning-matching. Both are characterized by a strong orientation by the individual towards the object. As a caveat, however, Rook (1985) provides evidence that this self-object meaning-matching process can occur quite deliberately through ritual forms of behavior. Thus, any empirical evidence that self-object meaning-matching also occurs holistically would do much to distinguish this account from Rook's (1985) and strengthen its plausibility as an explanation of impulsive buying instead.

There is a preponderance of evidence to suggest that this self-object meaning-matching process does occur holistically (at least part of the time). Research by Bargh (1984) found that people automatically process self-relevant information; experiencing events with themselves as the central focus. Similarly, work by Markus (1977) found that information which was self-descriptive tended to be processed in greater depth *and* faster than information which was only incidental. Markus suggested that this was possible because one's self schema is kept immediately accessible for information processing while other knowledge schemas must first be activated (this is also known as "top-down" processing; see Smith and Park 1989). Sentis and Burnstein (1979) replicated Markus's findings, and further suggested that such speed and depth was possible because stimuli were chunked or combined into larger, self-relevant units, and so could be processed holistically.

Markus and Sentis (1982) concur, adding that such chunking obviates the need to attend to smaller details, thereby increasing processing efficiency and freeing up cognitive resources for other processes such as elaboration or inferencing (or perhaps fantasies?). As a caveat, of course, such depth of processing occurs with respect to the self, and as such, there is no guarantee that *all* important stimulus information will be considered. As an additional point, the evidence suggests that individuals are capable of assessing the self-relevance of even fairly novel stimuli through a kind of holistic inferencing; whereby understanding is derived from other similar and known stimuli (Markus and Sentis 1982). This suggests that even though the individual may never have seen the object in question (i.e. to be impulsively purchased), he/she is capable of discerning its symbolic meanings by referencing the symbolic meanings of other similar objects.

Summary of the Perspective Offered

To review, I have proposed that consumer research needs a more finely-tuned cognitive account of the impulsive buying phenomenon. Toward this possibility, this paper highlights two gaps in the domain where a cognitive perspective might potentially provide insight. The field has lacked an explanation as to why the impulsive buying urge is experienced with such speed and why it is experienced as so compelling. Toward an explanation, this paper suggests that conceptualizing the cognitive portion of the impulse buying episode in terms of holistic processing, whereby symbolic object meanings are mapped onto important conceptions of the self, provides a plausible explanation for both of these questions. From this discussion it appears reasonable that the strength of self-object meaning-matching and the speed of holistic information processing quite likely represent opposite sides of the same impulsive buying coin. Indeed, to conclude that a holistic self-object meaning-matching process provides a plausible account of the cognitive portion of the impulsive buying experience appears a sage one.

FUTURE DIRECTIONS

To date, a comprehensive empirical study of the cognitive aspects of the impulsive buying experience has not been undertaken. Yet, given that up to 40% of all department store purchases are made impulsively (Bellinger et al. 1978), it is perhaps time to give this issue more empirical attention. However, as with any investigation into cognition, undertaking such a study is complicated by the fact that it is not possible to directly access what is going on in people's minds. Add to this the fact that impulsivity is by nature unpredictable and probably extremely difficult to invoke under laboratory conditions and then the task of empirical investigation becomes even more onerous.

These concerns not withstanding, I would like to speculate (albeit quite tentatively) as to how one might undertake such an investigation. Given the highly complex nature of this topic I suggest a combination of qualitative and quantitative approaches. Basically three issues would need to be addressed. First, determining the nature of a purchase (planned versus impulsive) is needed. Since a laboratory setting does not readily lend itself investigating such a question, perhaps some form of more naturalistic inquiry (such as a mall intercept) could be used; whereby people would be confronted in the mall and, if willing, relate whether a particular purchase had been planned or not (malls are often replete with marketing research facilities so, providing arrangements could be made, this type of approach would seem to have merit). Having determined the nature of the purchase one could also try and determine if indeed the purchase reflected elements of product symbolism and self-meaning (the second issue which would need

to be addressed). Methods of phenomenological interviewing would seem an appropriate technique to shed light on both of these issues. The Thompson et al. (1990) piece is an exemplary use of this type of technique in consumer research.

Finally, one would need to assess, to the extent possible, whether the person had likely utilized holistic information processing at the time of assessing their purchase. Since, in the approach suggested here, each individual is intercepted only after a purchase has been made, the window of opportunity to directly assess this type of information will have passed. Still, one might be able to get information which would serve as a proxy to suggest that, indeed, holistic information processing played a role in impulsive purchasing. Kagen's (1965) Matching Familiar Figures Test (MFFT), is designed to assess levels of impulsivity as well as levels of holistic processing in individuals. If individuals who scored high on the MFFT also reported in their pheonmenological interview making purchases impulsively, this would seem to support the holistic processing-impulsive buying link; rounding out support for a triadic relationship between impulsive purchasing, holistic processing, and self-object meaning-matching. Again, the proposed approach must, at this point, be considered very preliminary.

In providing a comprehensive perspective of impulsive buying, much theoretical work also remains to be done. For instance, a merger of both the cognitive and emotive aspects of impulsive buying likely needs to occur if we are to even hope to approach a full understanding of the complex phenomenon of impulsive buying. Unfortunately, we have barely scratched the surface of the link between cognition and emotion (Hirschman and Holbrook 1982; Isen 1984). Also, as previously noted, Piron (1991) argues that impulsive buying need not occur as the highly compelling experience assumed here; Rook (1987) also describes incidents when the impulsive need to purchase seems to arise spontaneously and is not directed at any particular object. Perhaps it is the act of buying itself which provides such self meaning for these consumers, but this is only speculative. In closing, impulsive buying appears to represent an interesting, multi-dimensional phenomenon which is likely to provide a fertile ground for future research.

REFERENCES

Alba, W. Joseph, and J. Wesley Hutchinson (1987), "Dimensions of Consumer Expertise," *Journal of Consumer Research*, 13 (March), 411-454.
Banaji, Mahzarin R. and Deborah A. Prentice (1994), "The Self in Social Contexts," *Annual Review of Psychology*, 45, 297-332.
Bargh, John A. (1984), "Automatic and Conscious Processing of Social Information," in *Handbook of Social Cognition*, Vol. 3, eds. Robert S. Wyer and Thomas K. Srull, Hillsdale, NJ: Erlbaum, 1-43.
Belk, Russell W. (1988), "Possessions and the Extended Self," *Journal of Consumer Research*, 15 (September), 139-168.
Bellenger, Danny, D. H. Robertson, and Elizabeth C. Hirschman (1978), "Impulse Buying Varies by Product," *Journal of Advertising Research*, 18 (December), 15-18.
Bettman, James (1979), *An Information Processing Theory of Consumer Choice*, Reading, MA: Addison-Wesley.
Childers, Terry L., Michael J. Houston, and Susan E. Heckler (1985), "Measurement of Individual Differences in Visual Versus Verbal Information Processing," *Journal of Consumer Research*, 12 (September), 125-134.
Cobb, Cathy J. and Wayne D. Hoyer (1986), "Planned Versus Impulse Purchase Behavior," *Journal of Retailing*, 62 (Winter), 67-81.

Combs, A. and D. Snygg (1959), *Individual Behavior*, 2nd ed., New York: Harper.

Cohen, Joel, B. and Kunal Basu (1987), "Alternative Models of Categorization: Toward a Contingent Processing Framework," *Journal of Consumer Research*, 13 (March), 455-472.

DuPont DeNemours and Company (1945, 1949, 1954, 1959, 1965), *Consumer Buying Studies*, Wilmington, DE: DuPont DeNemours and Company.

Engel, James F., Roger Blackwell, and David T. Kollat (1978), *Consumer Behavior*, Hinsdale, IL: Dryden Press.

Foard, Christopher F. and Deborah G. Kemler Nelson (1984), "Holistic and Analytic Modes of Processing: The Multiple Determinants of Perceptual Analysis," *Journal of Experimental Psychology: General*, 113 (1), 94-111.

Gardner, Meryl Paula and Dennis W. Rook (1988), "Effects of Impulse Purchases on Consumers' Affective States," in *Advances in Consumer Research*, Vol. 15, ed. Michael J. Houston, Provo UT: Association for Consumer Research, 127-130.

Gecas, Victor and Peter J. Burke (1995), "Self and Identity," in *Sociological Perspectives on Social Psychology*, eds. Karen S. Cook, Gary Alan Fine, and James S. House, Boston: Allyn and Bacon, 41-67.

Geertz, Clifford (1973), "Thick Description: Toward and Interpretive Theory of Culture," in *The Interpretation of Cultures*, ed. Clifford Geertz, New York: Basic Books, 231-267.

Hirschman Elizabeth C. and Morris Holbrook (1982), "Hedonic Consumption: Emerging Concepts, Methods and Propositions," *Journal of Marketing*, 46, 92-101.

Hoch, Stephen J. and George F. Loewenstein (1991), "Time-inconsistent Preferences and Consumer Self-Control," *Journal of Consumer Research*, 17 (March), 492-507.

Holbrook, Morris B. and Elizabeth Hirschman (1982), "The Experiential Aspects of Consumption: Consumer Fantasies, Feelings, and Fun," *Journal of Consumer Research*, 9 (September), 132-140.

_____, and William L. Moore (1981), "Feature Interactions in Consumer Judgments of Verbal Versus Pictorial Representations," *Journal of Consumer Research*, 8 (June), 103-113.

Hutchinson, J. Wesley and Joseph W. Alba (1991), "Ignoring Irrelevant Information: Situational Determinants of Consumer Learning," *Journal of Consumer Research*, 18 (December), 325-345.

Isen, Alice M. (1984), "Toward Understanding the Role of Affect in Cognition," in *Handbook of Social Cognition*, eds. Robert S. Wyer and Thomas K. Srull, Hillsdale, NJ: Erlbaum Publishers, 179-236.

Kagen, J. (1965), "Impulsive and Reflexive Children: Significance of Conceptual Tempo," in *Learning and the Educational Process*, ed. J. Krumboltz, Chicago: Rand McNally, 133-161)

Kemler, Deborah G. (1983), "Exploring and Reexploring Issues of Integrality, Perceptual Sensitivity and Dimensional Salience," *Journal of Experimental Child Psychology*, 36, 365-379.

Kemler Nelson, Deborah G. (1993), "Processing Integral Dimensions: The Whole View," *Journal of Experimental Psychology: Human Perception and Performance*, 19 (5), 1105-1113.

_____ (1984), "The Effect of Intention on What Concepts are Acquired," *Journal of Verbal Learning and Verbal Behavior*, 23, 734-759.

MacInnis, Deborah J., Christine Moormon, and Bernard J. Jaworski (1991), "Enhancing and Measuring Consumers' Motivation, Opportunity, and Ability to Process Brand Information From Ads," *Journal of Marketing*, 53 (October), 32-53.

_____, and Linda L. Price (1987), "The Role of Imagery in Information Processing: Review and Extensions," *Journal of Consumer Research*, 13 (March), 473-491.

Markus, Hazel (1977), "Self-schemata and Processing Information About the Self," *Journal of Personality and Social Psychology*, 35, 63-78.

_____, and Paula Nurius (1986), "Possible Selves," *American Psychologist*, 41 (September), 954-969.

_____, and Keith Sentis (1982), "The Self in Social Information Processing," in *Psychological Perspectives on the Self*, ed. Jerry Suls, Hillsdale NJ: Erlbaum Publishers, 41-70.

_____, and Elissa Wurf (1987), The Dynamic Self-Concept: A Social Psychological Perspective," *Annual Review of Psychology*, 38, 299-337.

McCracken, Grant (1986), "Culture and Consumption: A Theoretical Account of the Structure and Movement of the Cultural Meaning of Consumer Goods," 13 (June), 71-84.

Mick, David Glenn (1986), "Consumer Research and Semiotics: Exploring the Morphology of Signs, Symbols, and Significance," *Journal of Consumer Research,* 13 (September), 196-213.

Olshavsky, Richard W. and Donald H. Granbois (1979), "Consumer Decision Making—Fact or Fiction?" *Journal of Consumer Research*, 6 (September), 93-100.

Piron, Francis (1991), "Defining Impulse Purchasing," in *Advances in Consumer Research,* eds. Rebecca H. Holman and Michael R. Solomon, Provo UT: Association for Consumer Research, 509-514.

Pomerantz, James R. (1981) "Perceptual Organization in Information Processing," in *Perceptual Organization*, eds. Michael Kubovy and James R. Pomerantz, Hillsdale, NJ: Erlbaum, 141-180.

Rook, Dennis W. (1985), "The Ritual Dimension of Consumer Behavior," *Journal of Consumer Research*, 12 (December), 251-264.

_____, (1987), "The Buying Impulse," *Journal of Consumer Research*, 14 (September), 189-199.

_____, and Stephen J. Hoch (1985), "Consuming Impulses," in *Advances in Consumer Research*, Vol. 12, eds. Morris B. Holbrook and Elizabeth C. Hirschman, Provo, UT: Association for Consumer Research, 23-27.

Sentis, Keith P. and Eugene Burnstein (1979), "Remembering Schema-Consistent Information: Effects of a Balance Schema on Recognition Memory," *Journal of Personality and Social Psychology*, 37 (12), 2200-2211.

Sirgy, M. Joseph (1982), "Self-Concept in Consumer Behavior: A Critical Review,: 9 (December), 287-300.

Smith, Daniel C. and C. Whan Park (1989), "Product-Level Choice: A Top-Down or Bottom-Up Process?" *Journal of Consumer Research*, 16, (December), 289-299.

Smith, J. David, and Jonathan Baron (1981), "Individual Differences in the Classification of Stimuli by Dimensions," *Journal of Experimental Psychology: Human Perception and Performance*, 7 (5), 1132-1145.

_____, and Deborah G. Kemler Nelson (1984), "Overall Similarity in Adults' Classification: The Child in All of Us," *Journal of Experimental Psychology* , 113 (1), 137-159.

_____, and _____ (1988), "Is the More Impulsive Child a More Holistic Processor? A Reconsideration," *Child Development,* 59, 719-727.

Solomon, Michael R. (1983), "The Role of Products as Social Stimuli: A Symbolic Interactionist Perspective," *Journal of Consumer Research*, 10 (December), 319-329.

Thompson, Craig J., William B. Locander, and Howard R. Pollio (1990), "The Lived Meaning of Free Choice: An Existential-Phenomenological Description of Everyday Consumer Experiences of Contemporary Married Women," *Journal of Consumer Research,* 17 (December), 346-361.

Wansink, Brian (1994), "The Dark Side of Consumer Behavior: Empirical Examinations of Impulsive and Compulsive Consumption," in *Advances in Consumer Research*, Vol 21, eds. Chris T. Allen and Deborah Roedder-John, Provo UT: Association for Consumer Research, 508.

Ward, Thomas B. (1983), "Response Tempo and Separable to Integral Responding: Evidence for An Integral-to-Separable Processing Sequence in Visual Perception," *Journal of Experimental Psychology: Human Perception and Performance*, 9, 103-112.

_____, Colleen M. Foley and Janet Cole (1986), "Classifying Multidimensional Stimuli: Stimulus, Task, and Observer Factors," *Journal of Experimental Psychology: Human Perception and Performance*, 12 (2), 211-225.

Weinberg, Peter and Wolfgang Gottwald (1982), "Impulsive Consumer Buying as a Result of Emotions," *Journal of Business Research*, 10, 43-57.

Welles, G. (1986), "We're in the Habit of Impulsive Buying," *USA Today*, (May 21), 1.

Wolman, Benjamin (1973), *Dictionary of Behavioral Science*, New York: Van Nostrand Reinhold.

Zelniker, Tamar, and Wendell E. Jeffrey (1976), "Reflective and Impulsive Children: Strategies of Information Processing Underlying Differences in Problem Solving," *Monographs of the Society for Research in Child Development*, 41(5), sn 168.

The Functions of Luxury: A Situational Approach to Excursionism

Bernard Dubois, Groupe HEC
Gilles Laurent, Groupe HEC

ABSTRACT

A large number of persons ("Excursionists") access the luxury product domain only in certain situations. In this paper, we argue that such behavior can be analyzed in terms of the functions played by the products. Each luxury product can fulfill a certain set of functions. Each situation calls for certain functions to be fulfilled. Therefore each luxury product is more appropriate in certain situations than in others. Four situations are designed on the basis of two dichotomies (social vs individual, planned vs impulse). Respondents indicate their behavior in these situations for three products (scarfs, perfumes, diamond rings). A correspondence analysis assesses the strength of the adequacy of each product to each situation.

INTRODUCTION

For many years, consumers were relatively easy to segment in terms of their demand for luxury goods. Two broad clusters could be identified : (i) the Excluded, who had no access to this market but who, in most countries, included a vast majority of the population, and (ii) the "Affluent" (Stanley,1989) who, whether "Old money" (Aldrich; 1988, Hirschman, 1988) or "Nouveaux Riches" (LaBarbera, 1988) had both the desire and the financial ability to make luxury their "art de vivre."

Over the last ten or fifteen years, the market for luxury goods has changed considerably, however, under the influence of two major interrelated factors. On the one hand, many luxury goods companies such as Cartier or Cardin have started to diffuse and "accessorize" their brands, making them accessible to a much wider public than their traditional "élite" clientele. In most cases, the growth achieved by these companies has been spectacular. While, in 1977, the Louis Vuitton company was still a family business with sales under $20 million, its turnover now exceeds $ 1 billion. On the other hand, many consumers who were traditionally excluded from this market expressed a growing desire to acquire luxury items. The idea that everyone had a "right" to access this market got momentum. In their French sample, Dubois and Laurent (1994) found for example that almost 75 % of those who voiced an opinion agreed with the statement: "Today, everyone should have access to luxury goods."

We argue that, under this double influence of supply-led and demand-led factors, a third type of luxury consumers has emerged. We call them "Excursionists" (Dubois et al., 1994) because, in contrast to the Excluded, who have basically no access to luxury goods, and to the Affluent, whose access is more or less permanent, often driven by a quest for secular immortality (Hirschman, 1990), their acquisition and consumption of luxury items is occasional. Excursionists buy and consume luxury goods only in specific circumstances. For them, buying and consuming a luxury item is not an expression of their "art de vivre" but rather an exceptional moment, sharply contrasting with their daily life style.

Even though difficult to estimate, the number of Excursionists seems to have increased in such proportions recently that they would now represent a sizable proportion of the population in industrialized countries. In 1993, Dubois and Duquesne for example reported that, over the last two or three years (depending upon the product category), one European out of two had acquired at least one luxury product, out of a list of fifteen items, but that only one out of twenty consumers had bought five or more of those.

Similarly, Dubois and Laurent (1993) reported that, over the last two years, each European consumer had acquired on average products from two different brands, out of a list containing thirty internationally famous luxury brand names.

Such an evolution of the luxury demand structure probably implies a shift in methods of investigation. Consider the basic problem of customer identification. While Excluded and Affluent consumers can be reasonably well identified on the basis of their level of economic resources (Stanley, 1988) or of their conspicuous behavior (Mason, 1981), Excursionists, given the intermittent nature of their access to luxury goods, are much less easy to profile and to analyze. Since situational factors rather than personal characteristics mediate their journeys into the world of luxury, it would seem that the exploration of the typical circumstances surrounding their acquisition and consumption of luxury items should be given priority. Researching excursionist behavior in luxury requires an understanding of the conditions that make one person an excursionist.

At the same time, the number and diversity of situational factors present a major challenge for researchers who, beyond exploring the behavior of a particular individual vis-à-vis a particular product category (such as perfumes, fashion accessories or jewellery items), have a legitimate wish to analyze consumer behavior across a variety of people and luxury products. Those researchers need a taxonomical instrument, i.e. a measurement tool developed on the basis of a limited number of generic rather than ad hoc situations (Dickson, 1982).

If available, such an instrument could be used in at least two ways. First, one could use it to compare the situational determinants of the consumption of a variety of luxury products and, through an analysis of similarities and differences, have a better understanding of the world of luxury goods and of their functions, as far as consumers are concerned. Provided generic situations are well chosen, a "situational" profile could be developed for each product and used as a basis for comparison. But such an instrument could also be used to assess the propensity of a given person to buy (or to reject) a particular luxury product. Excursionism is not a matter of nature, but a matter of degree. A frequent excursionist is perhaps an individual who purchases or consumes a given product in a wider variety of situations, compared with other people. If, in addition, a given set of situations can be ordered in a sequence according to which fewer and fewer consumers would buy or consume a luxury product as one moves from one situation to the next one, a "situational" scale, i.e. a scale based on situations, can be developed.

The objective of this paper is to report on the development of such an instrument, and to use it in the first way, i.e. to compare the situational determinants of the consumption of several luxury products.

METHOD

In developing our instrument, we faced two major issues. The first one had to do with the selection of specific luxury products, while the second concerned the identification of appropriate situations.

Ideally, in order to fully assess the applicability of our instrument to the world of luxury, we should have selected a rather large variety of luxury items. However, given the constraints on data collection and the pilot nature of this study, we decided, in this first investigation, to focus our attention on only three products: perfume, diamond rings, and designer scarfs. While obviously not completely representative of the world of luxury goods, these products, when considered together, constitute, we think, an interesting sample, at least for illustrative purposes. They were chosen for a variety of reasons. First, and in contrast to other products which could have been chosen (such as cars), all of them have no fundamental utilitarian value, a characteristic generally considered typical of luxury products. As such, in qualitative research, the three products are mentioned very often by consumers invited to provide spontaneous exemplars of the luxury category. Second, they belong to three domains (cosmetics, jewellery and fashion) which, considered jointly, represent (cars excepted) a dominant share of the luxury market (McKinsey, 1990). At the same time, the three products are rather different from each other, in terms of unit price, durability, and anticipated purchase and consumption situations. Diamond rings are generally rather expensive, last "for ever," and are typically bought as gifts, often connected with society rituals such as engagement ceremonies or marriage anniversaries (Rook, 1985). Scarfs are more visible, more sensitive to fashion, and heavily embedded with meanings (Csikszentmihalyi and Rochberg-Halton, 1981) but also less expensive. Finally, perfume is a more intimate product, less durable and it is typically bought more frequently than the other two. At the same time, one should not overemphasize the differences. Even diamond rings, which could be considered as somewhat different from the other two products as least in terms of purchase intentions and price, are not necessarily so. In many countries, jewellery retailers now offer rings with extremely small stones (a few points of a carat) which, while still promoted as "true diamonds", make them no more expensive than certain designer scarfs. At the same time, diamond advertising campaigns, such as those sponsored by De Beers, try to diversify purchase occasions (diamonds for men, marriage anniversaries as opposed to engagement ceremonies, etc.). Although different, diamond rings, perfume and designer scarfs are related (at least in Western cultures) in that they clearly belong to the luxury product domain.

The second problem, that of identifying the nature, number and variety of situations to be included in the instrument was no easy task. Ideally, when analyzing the situational determinants of the acquisition and consumption of luxury products, one would like to develop a list of generic situations which are (i) significantly contrasted from each other so that each additional situation brings a new dimension into the analysis and (ii) collectively representative, or at least illustrative, of the typical buying and/or consumption contexts, so that no essential situational factor is forgotten. Yet, as expressed by Frederiksen (1972) "No prescription can be given to the would-be developer of a taxonomy of attributes of situations with regard to how to proceed," even though this topic has generated considerable debate among situationists both in psychology and consumer research.

Several environmental as well as social psychologists have developed generic taxonomies of situations. For example, Bellows (1963) offered a list of 216 situations characterizing social interactions, while Sells (1963) suggested a detailed outline, containing more than 160 items, "as a preliminary step toward the development of taxonomic dimensions of the stimulus situation in behavior." Similarly, Sherif and Sherif (1956) have argued that it was possible to structure situations involving human beings around four basic dimensions: (i) factors linking the participating individuals (for example antecedent relationships), (ii) factors related to the task or problem to be solved (novelty, complexity), (iii) physical environ-

ment characteristics (space, locations), and (iv) factors connecting the three preceding elements (for example the participants' involvement level in the task). In his seminal article introducing the situational perspective into the consumer behavior literature, Belk (1975a) identified five sets of factors which could be used in categorizing consumer situations: (i) physical surroundings - decor, sounds, lights, (ii) social surroundings - presence or absence of significant others, (iii) temporal perspective - time of the day, time pressure, (iv) task definition - purpose of purchase and (v) antecedent states (mood, physical feelings). Finally, Mehrabian and Russell (1974) have argued that any given situation can be categorized according to its level on each of three dimensions, as perceived by the subject: Pleasure, Arousal, and Dominance.

At the same time, empirical attempts to identify taxonomies of situations that would apply over a variety of product categories have not been extremely successful in consumer research. When comparing, for the same individuals, the factorial structures underlying consumption situations for snacks and for meat products, Belk (1974), for example, found no overlap. The same researcher found only one common dimension when comparing his previous results to situational determinants of the choice of a restaurant (Belk, 1975b). Similarly, when applying to snack consumption three alternative typological schemes for classifiying situations, including the PAD framework, Kakkar and Lutz (1975) found none of them performed spectacularly, nor were any of them closely related to one another.

In this research project, we decided to consider four generic situations, built from a review of the above mentioned literature but also from an analysis of the key characteristics of luxury goods (Dubois and Laurent, 1994). They were contrasted in the following manner. Taking first into account the social environment and the task environment, two key dimensions always present in situational taxonomies, we decided to consider two situations where the consumer would be the only person concerned and therefore would buy for herself and two in which she would be concerned about "significant others." The first two situations were further contrasted in terms of the decision-making process. In the first case, the purchase would be planned, in connection with a personal or professional achievement to be celebrated (situation n° 2 in Table 1), while, in the second, the decision to buy would be made on an emotional, impulse basis (situation n° 4). The two "social" situations were constrated in terms of the nature of the antecedent relationship. In the first one (situation n° 1) and taking into account the fact that our sample only consisted of females, an explicit reference was be made to the "man in your life", while in the second (situation n° 3) explicit reference was made to a social meeting. It should noted that, in the case of diamond rings, the latter situation was described as an engagement ceremony concerning a family member. One could argue that this "social" situation is rather peculiar. The "engagement" situation (for diamond rings) is certainly not the same as the situation in which one has to attend an important meeting, and wishes to make a good impression (for scarfs and perfume). Accordingly, a researcher may be tempted to set aside this "engagement" situation. We would argue that this difference is precisely a good argument not to set it aside. There is a different situation for engagement rings, not because of an arbitrary choice by the authors, but because relevant situations have to be adapted to each product. One cannot offer a scarf or perfume as an engagement present. No one (at least extremely few people) would purchase a diamond ring to make a good impression in an important professional meeting. The situational analysis of a given product cannot be done using situations that are irrelevant to that product. And, conversely, a situation that is relevant for a product

FIGURE 1
The Structural Links Between Situations, Functions and Products

should not be omitted because it is relevant only for that product.

At the same time, this does not imply that there is no general structure in situations. As indicated earlier, we argue that situations can be structured in general terms for luxury products: buying for oneself vs buying for a significant other, planned vs impulse purchase, social relationships vs love relationships, etc. Now, the very nature of the correspondence between luxury products and these situational characteristics explains why all luxury products are not adequate to all situations. Each luxury product can provide a certain set of functions. Each situation requires certain functions. Therefore each luxury product is more appropriate in certain situations than in others. The world of luxury products is not homogeneous. It has a structure that derives from the relationships between situations, functions, and products (Figure 1).

For each situation, each respondent was invited to indicate whether she would have certainly, possibly, or certainly not opted for the luxury item. The sample and data collection procedure have already been described elsewhere (Dubois and Laurent, 1994) and therefore will not be detailed here. Suffice it to say that, although not randomly drawn, the sample consisted of 330 French female consumers (110 for each product, so as to control for respondent idiosyncrasies) selected according to quota set in terms of age and geographical location. Given the nature of the topic under investigation, it was decided to underrepresent lower income categories. All interviews were conducted on a face-to-face basis and the fieldword was carried out by one of the major professional market research companies operating in France. Since, in this research, as in most published situational studies, respondents were invited to put themselves in hypothetical scenarios, situations were investigated as perceived by subjects (Lutz and Kakkar, 1975), rather than "objectively determined" (Belk, 1975b). It should be mentioned that, with the one exception mentioned above concerning diamond rings, all the wordings describing the situations were absolutely identical so that item variability would not contaminate variance observed in the results.

RESULTS

Table 1 presents the results obtained for each situation and each product. It comprises four rows, one for each situation: "Man in your life" ("The man in your life wishes to offer you a gift and asks for your preferences"), "Self-gift" ("You want to celebrate a personal or professional achievement by buying yourself a gift"), "Impulse" ("You see a ... in a shop and you are strongly attracted by it"), and "Social meeting" ("You must attend a meeting in which you want to make a good impression" for perfume and scarfs, "You must buy an engagement ring for one of your children" for a diamond ring). There are nine columns, associated with possible choices in each situation. For each product (scarfs, diamond rings, perfume), interviewees were asked what they would do in each situation. They could provide a positive answer (would certainly buy, or would certainly suggest, denoted +), a moderate answer (would possibly buy, or would possibly suggest, denoted =), or a

negative answer (would certainly not buy, or would certainly not suggest, denoted -). As indicated above, different although comparable samples (in terms of age, income, geographical location, etc.), of size 110 each, were interviewed about scarfs, about diamond rings, and about perfume.

Several comments can be made on the basis of such an table. First, and as expected, significant variability is observed in the results, both in terms of product as well as situations. For each product, the percentage of consumers buying it or suggesting it "certainly" varies, depending upon the situation. For scarfs, it increases from about 5 % to almost 30 %, while the corresponding percentages are 11% vs 26 % for diamond rings and 16 % vs 52% for perfume (respectively). These results demonstrate the danger of profiling the "typical" consumer of a given luxury product and confirm the situational and "excursionist" nature of consumer luxury purchases. While only 5 % of the respondents would suggest to the man in their life to buy them a scarf as a gift, 29% would buy such a product out of impulse (possibly for the same reasons), if confronted with the appropriate product. Similarly, 26 % of the respondents would buy a diamond ring for an engagement ceremony involving their children, but less than half of that number would buy it for themselves. Obviously, those two markets are highly dependent upon short excursions driven by circumstances. It should be noted however that, regardless of which situation is considered, perfume is more readily accepted than scarfs or diamond rings. Its average percentage of rejection is 28 %, to be compared with 53% for diamond rings and 50 % for scarfs. Excursionism in the world of perfume is thus made easier through a wider variety of situations in which this product is judged appropriate. No wonder that perfume is often selected as a prime candidate for brand extension programs implemented by luxury goods companies.

Similarly, it appears that certain products correspond more than others to certain specific situations. For example, diamonds and perfume fit well as gifts offered by the "man in your life," while scarfs seem especially appropriate for impulse purchases. Interestingly enough, the self-gift situation was found to be the least favorable one for all luxury products, a result perhaps reflecting the ambivalence and guilt feelings prevalent in such situations (Sherry et al., 1993).

If confirmed on larger samples, the preceding results would allow one to develop for each product a "situational profile." For example, diamond rings appear, relatively speaking, much more dependent upon social rituals (first choice) than scarfs or perfumes, which are more likely to be purchased without prior planning. At the same time, no product was totally rejected in any scenario. Differences among products about their "situational relevance" are therefore more a matter a degree than of nature. It would therefore appear natural to compute, for each product, a score that would reflect its adequacy to several situations.

In order to establish a global picture of the links between situations and products, and to assess the underlying structure of

TABLE 1
Choices Made for Three Products in Four Situations
(Row percentages)

SITUATIONS	Scarfs			Diamond rings			Perfumes		
	Certainly suggested or bought +	Possibly suggested or bought =	Certainly not suggested or bought -	Certainly suggested or bought +	Possibly suggested or bought =	Certainly not suggested or bought -	Certainly suggested or bought +	Possibly suggested or bought =	Certainly not suggested or bought -
The man in your life wishes to offer you a gift and asks for your preferences.	5.5	44.0	50.5	23.4	31.8	44.9	30.9	42.7	26.4
You want to celebrate a personal or professional achievement by buying yourself a gift.	3.7	33.0	63.3	11.1	21.3	67.6	16.4	44.5	39.1
You must attend a meeting in which you want to make a good impression*.	9.2	36.7	54.1	26.0	33.7	40.4	36.4	31.8	31.8
You see a...........in a shop and you can't resist.	29.4	40.4	30.3	15.0	24.3	60.7	51.8	31.8	16.4

P R O D U C T S

*For diamond rings the situation was reformulated as follows: "You must buy a ring for the engagement ceremony of one of your children."

TABLE 2
Correspondence Between Situations and Luxury Products

	SCARFS			DIAMOND RINGS			PERFUME		
	+	=	−	+	=	−	+	=	−
MAN IN YOUR LIFE	6	48	55	25	34	48	34	47	29
SELF-GIFT	4	36	69	12	23	73	18	49	43
IMPULSE	32	44	33	16	26	65	57	35	18
SOCIAL MEETING	10	40	59	27	35	42	40	35	35

(Numbers represent the number of interviewees chosing each answer, "certainly" (+), "possibly" (=), "certainly not" (−), for each situation and each product.)

FIGURE 2
Correspondence Analysis of Products by Situations

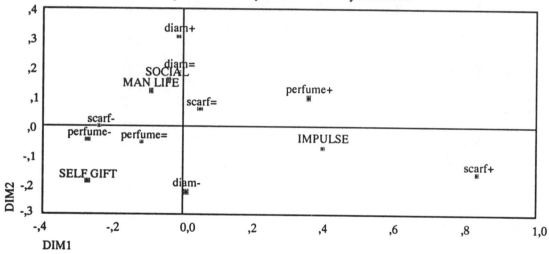

these links, we performed a correspondence analysis (Lebart, Morineau and Warwick, 1984). Correspondence analysis is an appropriate statistical technique here, as we analyze the relationship between two sets of qualitative variables: a set of situations and a set of choices. The data to be analyzed is given in Table 2. They are the raw data underlying Table 1.

The results of the correspondence analysis of this table are given on Figure 2, and in Tables 3 and 4. Two clearly distinct factors appear, with singular values .245 and .142. Together, they explain 96.3% of the variance contained in the respondents' choices. As usual in correspondence analysis, they should be analyzed in terms of both lines (situations) and columns (choices).

The first factor is strongly related to choices related to scarfs and perfume (Table 3). It offers a strong contrast between two situations: impulse buying and self-gifts.

This first dimension can be interpreted, very clearly, in terms of the adaptation of two products (scarfs and perfume) to impulse buying; and of the relative lack of fit between these two products and the situation of a gift you want to make to yourself to celebrate

an achievement. Positive choices on scarfs and perfume, as well as impulse buying, are very strongly associated with the first dimension, and all obtain strongly positive scores. Negative scores on the dimension are associated with a planned self-gift, and with the rejection of scarfs and perfume as appropriate choices. We underline that this first dimension appears almost unrelated to the two other situations ("Man in your life" and "Social meeting"), and unrelated to answers related to diamonds. In other words, the rich and strong interpretation of the first dimension in terms of when scarfs and perfume should and should not be chosen brings no light on the proper use of diamond rings, nor on choices appropriate when others are involved, be it for a social meeting, or when the "other" is a significant one.

Answers to these questions, in fact, are provided by the second dimension (Table 4).

The second dimension is mainly associated with diamond rings. It brings little information on scarfs and perfume. Positive scores are strongly associated with positive answers on the appropriateness of a diamond ring, and on the two situations in which

TABLE 3
Results for the First Dimension

Situation	Contribution of the situation to the dimension	Contribution of the dimension to the inertia of the situation	Score
Man in your life	3.1%	27.6%	-.09
Self-gift	30.5%	68.5%	-.27
Impulse	65.7%	95.7%	.40
Social meeting	0.6%	5.0%	-.04

Choice	Contribution of the choice to the dimension	Contribution of the dimension to the inertia of the choice	Score
Scarf +	45.5%	95.6%	.84
Scarf =	0.5%	20.7%	.05
Scarf -	15.3%	96.4%	-.24
Diamond ring +	0.0%	0.0%	-.01
Diamond ring =	0.0%	0.2%	-.01
Diamond ring -	0.0%	0.0%	.01
Perfume +	24.3%	93.1%	.36
Perfume =	2.9%	58.6%	-.12
Perfume -	11.6%	87.9%	-.27

other persons are involved: the gift by "the man in your life," and the "engagement ring." In contrast, negative scores are associated to negative statements on the appropriateness of a diamond ring, and to situations involving the interviewer alone (impulse buying, and specially the case of a self-gift). Overall, this dimension shows clearly the correspondence of diamond rings with social situations, and its lack of adequation for a self-gift. The second dimension brings very little information related to the appropriate use of scarfs or perfume.

Therefore, this correspondence analysis produces rich, structural information on the appropriateness of different luxury products for different situations, and, therefore, on the functions fulfilled by each product. It is interesting to note, however, that the two dimensions bring separate informations on different sets of situations and products.

There is therefore a double structure underlying situational choices made in relation to luxury products: within products and between products.

The first structure is within products. It explains choices made in different situations for the same product. Here, our conclusion is that one may form a Guttman-like scale on the basis of the different situations. Some situations are more conducive than others to the use of the product. Now, certain persons may want to use the product in all situations, others in no situation. Combined answers to a set of situation-based questions therefore offer a basis for scaling individuals, from the most prone to use this luxury product to the least prone. This individual score may then be related to other individual variables, such as socio-demographics (income) or involvement in the product. In similar research centered on upscale products, we found that such situation-based scales offered more predictive power than income (Dubois and Laurent, 1995).

The second structure is between products. As stated above, each situation requires certain functions related to its characteris-

tics: buying for oneself vs buying for a significant other, planned vs impulse purchase, social relationships vs love relationships, etc. Each luxury product can provide a certain set of functions. Therefore each luxury product is more appropriate for certain situations than for others.

DISCUSSION

The exploratory nature of our study, the first one, to the best of our knowledge, to investigate the situational determinants of luxury good purchases, prevents us from developing too definitive conclusions from our results.

As indicated above, we carefully chose our set of three luxury products (designer scarfs, diamond rings, perfume) so that they would constitute a reasonably illustrative sample of luxury products of interest to women. And similarly for the selection of the four situations. Equally, we used a sample of "real" consumers. Our results should therefore have some external validity. At the same time, we have obviously not performed a final or complete analysis, on a large sample, of all possible luxury products and luxury-related situations. We think therefore that the analysis reported in this paper should be extended in order to obtain a more complete understanding of the adequacy of luxury products to specific situations and, therefore, to specific functions. We advocate surveys dealing with more products (10 or 15, e.g.), and more situations per product (10, e.g.). The domain of content, so to speak, should be more fully sampled in order to obtain a complete analysis of all the functions that can be fulfilled by luxury products. Besides, we suggest that our current analysis may be incomplete, in the sense that it only considers broadly-defined "products," such as "perfume" or "scarfs." It should be interesting to explore these "products" in more detail, either by examining sub-categories (e. g. "eau de toilette" vs "parfum," or different types of jewellery items: rings or bracelets vs earrings, etc.), or brands (an Hermès scarf vs a scarf

TABLE 4
Results for the Second Dimension

Situation	Contribution of the situation to the dimension	Contribution of the dimension to the inertia of the situation	Score
Man in your life	16.6%	47.3%	.12
Self-gift	43.2%	31.3%	-.19
Impulse	9.2%	4.3%	-.09
Social meeting	31.0%	77.6%	.16

Choice	Contribution of the choice to the dimension	Contribution of the dimension to the inertia of the choice	Score
Scarf +	5.5%	3.7%	-.16
Scarf =	2.2%	30.7%	.06
Scarf -	0.0%	0.0%	.00
Diamond ring +	30.2%	99.9%	.31
Diamond ring =	14.2%	99.8%	.18
Diamond ring -	40.6%	99.6%	-.22
Perfume +	5.2%	6.5%	.10
Perfume =	1.5%	9.9%	-.05
Perfume -	0.6%	1.6%	-.04

of a little-known brand, e.g.). It could also be interesting to study luxury-like goods, i. e. products which bear a luxury brand name but do not necessarily command a financial sacrifice.

If confirmed by studies performed on other luxury products, the two-dimensional structure revealed in this research would offer a particularly vivid and yet parsimonious understanding of the dynamics of the luxury market. Since Veblen's first attempts to explain conspicuous consumption (Veblen, 1899), the primary motive ascribed to the acquisition and consumption of luxury goods has been the human desire to impress other people. Recent qualitative research (Cofremca, 1992) has shown, however, that, in line with the general decline of the "status-seeking" motive and the growing self-indulgence trend observed in Western societies, the major force underlying luxury purchases and consumption is shifting from an interpersonal to a personal nature. More and more consumers seem to buy luxury goods more to gratify themselves than to impress others. But all luxury items are not equally perceived as appropriate for that function. By systematically contrasting social and individual situations, our 4-item scale allows one to position products on that dimension. In our study, diamond rings were felt more appropriate "social gifts" than perfumes or scarfs. Of course, one can speculate about the attributes of a product that facilitate or hinder its appropriateness for a given situation. In the case of diamond rings, compared with scarfs and perfumes, price and cultural habits appear as plausible factors. While the price of a product can obviously limit its potential as a self-gift, the marketing strategy used for the product also plays an important role. Diamond rings have for many years been associated by many people with engagement ceremonies and, as a result, at a time when such ceremonies tend to disappear, the diamond jewellery industry has to convince "career women" that diamond products are also appropriate as self-gifts. Equally revealing is the distinction between planned and unplanned purchases. In our study, perfume was

not rejected as a planned self-gift while designer scarfs were. Both products, however, were considered as at least possible impulse purchases. Differences in basic product functions as well as dominant marketing practices could explain such results. Compared to perfume, scarfs are more "products for outside" and also more sensitive to fashion. The almost infinite variety of designs and colors makes it difficult for consumers to plan their purchases and to bypass the shopping stage, which is often conducive to impulse purchases. On the other hand, perfume is a more standardized, more intimate product, and is replaced more often. As a result, it is better suited as a planned self-gift. At the same time, marketing practices can influence the way in which both products are perceived. By increasing the rate of innovation, by relying more systematically on emotional appeals in advertisements, and by using more frequent in-store promotional tactics, perfume manufacturers can facilitate impulse buying. On the other hand, scarf manufacturers can facilitate planned self-purchase by establishing distinctive styles which, reinforced year after year (such as in the Gucci or Hermès collections), reduce the dependence upon fads in favor of enduring symbols of classicism. Through our two individual situations, our scale allows for a monitoring of the perceptions of luxury on that dimension.

There are of course many ways in which our exploratory study could be extended. An obvious first step would be to apply it to a much wider variety of luxury products, so as to better capture the richness of that universe. One could also explore additional situations. Although, at face value, the individual vs social and planned vs impulse dimensions seem the two major dimensions for structuring situations, others such as those linked to the time and physical surroundings dimensions could also be considered.

Finally, one could consider individual differences in associating products to situations, as well as their causes and consequences. While the limited size of our sample prevented us, in this research, from exploring that path, it could very well be the case that not all people equally perceive a given luxury product as adequate for a given type of situation. For example, depending upon consumers' level of financial resources, the luxury product that appears suitable for a social ceremony may vary. Similarly, one could constrast the perception of various socio-demographic segments defined, for example, on the basis of gender, age or cultural background. As suggested by Dickson (1982) such a triangular approach (products, situations and persons) could be very instrumental in better understanding a fascinating but underresearched market.

REFERENCES

Aldrich, Nelson W., Jr, 1988, *Old Money: The Mythology of America's Upper Class*, New York: Alfred A. Knopf

Belk, Russell W., 1974 "An Exploratory Assessment of Situational Effects in Buyer Behavior", *Journal of Marketing Research*, 156-163

Belk, Russell W., 1975a, "Situational Variables in Consumer Behavior", *Journal of Consumer Research*, 2, 157-177

Belk, Russell W., 1975b, "The Objective Situation as a Determinant of Consumer Behavior," in *Advances for Consumer Research*, 2, 427-37

Bellows, R., 1963 "Toward A Taxonomy of Social Situations," in S. B. Sells, ed., *Stimulus Determinants of Behavior*, New York: Ronald Press

Cofremca, 1992, *Etude sur le luxe entreprise à l'initiative du Comité Colbert*. Paris

Csikszentmihalyi, Mihaly and Rochberg-Halton, Eugene, 1981, *The Meaning of Things: Domestic Symbols and the Self*, Cambridge, England: Cambridge University Press

Dickson, Peter R., 1982, "Person - Situation: Segmentation's Missing Link", *Journal of Marketing*, 46 (Fall), 56-64.

Dubois, Bernard and Duquesne, Patrick, 1993 "The Market for Luxury Goods: Income vs Culture", *European Journal of Marketing*, Vol. 1, 35-44

Dubois, Bernard, Enel, Françoise and Laurent, Gilles (1994) "La face cachée du Luxe: Ruses et Excursionnisme," HEC Working Paper

Dubois, Bernard and Laurent, Gilles "Is There a Euroconsumer for Luxury Goods ?," in *European Advances for Consumer Research*, Vol. 1, Fred Van Raaij and Gary Bamossy, eds, 1993, 58-69

Dubois, Bernard and Laurent, Gilles, 1994 "Attitudes towards the Concept of Luxury: An exploratory Analysis," in *Asia-Pacific Advances for Consumer Research*, Vol. 1, Siew Leng Leong and Joe Cote, eds., 273-8

Dubois, Bernard and Laurent, Gilles, 1995, "Upscale Product Proneness: A Situational Approach", in *Proceedings of the 24th Annual Conference of the European Marketing Academy*, Michelle Bergadaà, ed., 1561-6

Frederiksen, N., 1972 "Toward a Taxonomy of Situations," *American Psychologist*, February, 114-123

Hirschman, Elizabeth, 1988, "Upper Class Wasps as Consumers: A Humanistic Inquiry," in *Research in Consumer Behavior*, Vol. 3, Elizabeth C. Hirschman, ed., Greenwich, CT: JAI Press, 115-148

Hirschman, Elizabeth, 1990, "Secular Immortality and the American Ideology of Affluence," *Journal of Consumer Research*, Vol. 17, 31-42

Kakkar Pradeep and Richard Lutz, 1975, "Towards a Taxonomy of Consumption Situations", *AMA Conference Proceedings*, 206-210.

LaBarbera, Priscilla A., 1988, "The Nouveaux Riches: Conspicuous Consumption and the Issue of Self-Fulfillment", in *Research in Consumer Behavior*, Vol. 3, Elisabeth C. Hirschman, ed. Greenwich CT: JAI Press, 179-210

Lutz, Richard J. and Kakkar, Pradeep, 1975 "The Psychological Situation as a Determinant of Consumer Behavior" in M. J. Schlinger,ed., *Advances in Consumer Research*, 2, 439-53

Mason, Roger, 1981, *Conspicuous Consumption*, New York: St Martin's Press

McKinsey, 1990, *L'Industrie du Luxe: Un Atout pour la France*

Mehrabian, A. and Russell, J.A., 1974, *An Approach to Environmental Psychology*, Cambridge: MIT Press

Rook, Dennis, 1985 "The Ritual Dimension of Consumer Behavior", *Journal of Consumer Research*, 12, 251-64

Sells, S.B. 1963. "Dimensions Determinants of Behavior Which Account for Behavior Variance" in S. B. Sells, ed., *Stimulus Determinants of Behavior*, New York: Ronald Press.

Sherif, Muzafer and Sherif, C., 1956, *An Outline of Social Psychology*, Harper and Row

Sherry, John, Jr., Levy, Sidney and McGrath, M.A., 1993 "The Dark Side of the Gift", *Journal of Business Research*

Stanley, Thomas J., 1988, *Marketing to the Affluent*, Homewood, IL: Irwin

Stanley, Thomas J., 1989, *Selling to the Affluent*, Homewood, IL: Irwin

Veblen, Thorsten, 1899, *The Theory of the Leisure Class*, New York: Macmillan

Gender Identity and Gender Salience: A Dual-Path, Person-Situation Approach to Gender Effects in Consumer Research

Stephen J. Gould, Baruch College, The City University of New York

ABSTRACT

Although gender has a major impact on consumer behavior, the detection of its effects in consumer research may be limited by how it is conceived. To provide a fuller theoretical account of gender's impact, this paper examines it in symbolic interactionist terms involving two distinct, but interrelated paths: (1) a person-trait path keyed by gender identity that has been widely studied and (2) a relatively ignored, situational path in which gender becomes salient under certain conditions and which often involves within-person differences. A joint typological model in which both paths interact is also outlined. Finally, research implications are drawn for both paths.

Gender is a broad concept which addresses the perspective one takes on one's own sex as well as incorporating a whole host of psychosocial variables which relate to it in a reciprocal way, i.e., both sex and these other variables interact and change meaning together in terms of self-relevance (Deaux and Major 1987). Two interdependent although different aspects of how gender functions in consumer behavior will be considered in this paper: (1) gender identity and (2) gender salience. *Gender identity* involves one's sense of oneself as a man or woman although in reflecting psychocultural classifications it may also be seen in broader terms to include a third sex (e.g., transsexuals [Herdt 1994]). *Gender salience* concerns one's awareness of one's own gender as it describes oneself at a given time (Cota and Dion 1986). Two people may be equal in gender salience but differ in gender identity (e.g., one person perceives herself to be more feminine than another who nonetheless is equal in gender salience, i.e., both see gender as equally relevant). Likewise, two people may differ in their level of gender salience, but share a common gender identity (e.g., both perceive themselves to be equally feminine, but for one, gender may be more relevant due to differing situational circumstances and/or stronger gender cues). Gender salience may also affect gender identity or aspects of it on a within-person basis (e.g., people feel more masculine or feminine in certain exchanges such as with the opposite sex than in others [cf. Gould and Weil 1991]). This paper examines these two aspects of gender psychology and their implications for consumer research.

A SYMBOLIC INTERACTIONIST PERSPECTIVE

In expressing gendered aspects of consumer behavior, gender identity and gender salience may be seen as reflecting the symbolic interactionist view taken by Solomon (1983) who found that products may be seen either as responses or as stimuli. In the response case, one's self-image is seen as leading to need arousal which leads to product purchase, need satisfaction and impression management (here designated *"Path 1"* and rooted in gender identity, e.g., perceiving oneself as more feminine or masculine) — see Figure 1. In the stimulus case, product symbolism leads to role definition which results in self-attribution, situational self-image, and role performance (here designated as *"Path 2"* and is rooted in gender salience induced by gender cues, such as products which are for one or another sex or use advertising spokespeople of one or another sex). The first path, in Solomon's view, is the one most frequently explored in social science and this appears to remain the case today both in consumer research in general and in gender

research. Also in this perspective, Path 2 adds an experiential dimension in that consumers will make self-attributions based on their experience with products in a way parallel to self-perception theory.

Regarding Path 1, one's *gender identity* as a part of self-concept and manifested in one's self-image, leads to *gender-based need arousal* (i.e., defining one's needs in terms of one's own gender identity) and then to *gendered response* (i.e., product purchase and use congruent with one's gender identity). Path 1 also may be seen to operate in terms of semantic congruency through which according to Burke (1989, p. 161):

> people choose behaviors that have the same meanings as their self-meanings or identities; people with more feminine identities, for example, choose more feminine behaviors, when possible, and avoid more masculine behaviors.

Gender salience, on the other hand, follows Path 2 and emerges situationally. As evoked by product symbolism in the form of products (e.g., Kanungo and Pang 1973) or brand communications or brand names (e.g., Pavia and Costa 1991), it stimulates the construction/emergence of the situational self-concept and/or role identity (cf. Burke and Tully 1977) in terms of *sex role definition* (i.e., a role primes gendered perceptions) which eventually emerges as *gendered self-attribution* (i.e., coming to perceive one's consumption acts in terms of one's own gender — it may also take the form of a situational, gender self-image and/or role performance which is gender oriented). Often Path 2 sequences may occur when attention is called to sex roles rather than being focused on gender-neutral issues or addressing relatively established patterns of gender identity-based, Path 1 consumption (e.g., ads which aim at getting consumers to buy products that run contrary to traditional sex role stereotypes, such as guns for women or household cleaning products for men). Therefore, a consumer may compare his or her situational self-concept to the product image in seeking self-congruence (Solomon 1983). However, while the situational self may enter into consumer decision making, an equally important focus is on changes in the consumer in consumption and post-consumption as reflected in gendered self-attribution. Thus, as Solomon (1983) notes, he or she is actually redefining him or herself in the situation.

While thus far the discussion has focused on the two paths as separate, in reality, as noted by Solomon, the two paths are not isolated from one another. Thus, gender identity may change over time as the sociocultural environment changes (e.g., a woman may change her perceptions of herself as she and others become career women). Gender salience with its situational emphasis may also take on trait properties as some people tend to find gender more relevant in more situations, thus being more gender-conscious than others (Gould and Stern 1989), and/or they develop gender role scripts with respect to a situation which is sufficiently repeated, and/or they draw on a repertoire of gendered selves, actual, possible and ideal which may display varying degrees of stability over time (Markus and Kunda 1986).

In order to more fully explore the impact of these two paths of gender expression on consumer behavior, this paper will consider: (1) gender identity — Path 1, (2) gender salience — Path 2, (3) links

FIGURE 1

The Two Paths of Gendered Consumer Behavior

Path 1: Gender Identity ———> Gender-Based Need Arousal ———> Gendered Response

Path 2: Gender Salience ———> Sex Role Definition ———> Gendered Self-Attribution

Source: Adapted from Solomon (1983)

---

between gender identity and salience, and (4) discussion and implications.

GENDER IDENTITY: PATH 1

Gender identity involves one's sense of oneself as a man or woman. It is also a determinant of product purchase and use and follows Path 1 as consumers seek need satisfaction which is at least partially related to who they are. One's own sex because it is most visible (Deaux and Major 1987) has been viewed as a major component of gender identity. One identifies with one's own sex to varying degrees and includes that identification as a part of one's self-concept. Sex role (gender role) identity, largely based on identifying oneself in terms of masculinity and femininity, also is a key element of gender identity (Storms 1979). Gender identity is also said to be multifactorial in terms of sex role attributes (Spence 1993). Thus, there are a number of aspects of gender identity, including: one's own sex, identity in terms of presenting oneself as masculine or feminine, the degree to which one maintains a stable identity, gender constancy (Frey and Ruble 1992), having a masculine or feminine personality (Deaux and Major 1987), and being involved in everyday consumption and tasks on a gendered basis (Orlofsky and O'Heron 1987).

Between Sex Differences

Differences based on sex have been the subject of a vast amount of research and many have been found (e.g., Gould and Stern 1989). Since one's own sex is such a highly visible component of one's gender identity (i.e., readily identifiable to oneself and the people one interacts with), it becomes a major aspect of the self upon which to hang a great deal of one's thoughts of how others perceive one and of how one perceives others, especially as one infers implicit personality material that is based on gender (e.g., "She is a woman therefore she must be nurturing") [Deaux and Major 1987]). This process suggests that consumers make stereotypic inferences based on sex that carry over into consumption and advertising (e.g., male models being more appropriate for ads for male products and females being used for female products [Kanungo and Pang 1973]).

Sex Roles

While sex accounts for a wide range of differences, these should be seen as "multiply determined" by a whole host of interrelated psychological and sociocultural, as well as biological factors (Deaux 1985). These factors are often framed in terms of sex roles which may be viewed as a major aspect of gender identity. In this regard, a large body of research in this area has stemmed from Bem's (1981) gender schema theory which suggests that there are both sex and non-sex-typed sex roles and people, regardless of biological sex. Thus, gender schema theory operates not so much to explain between sex differences as to look within sex and to suggest that various gendered attributes occur across the sexes. Therefore, Path 1 may be viewed both as a between, as well as a within sex model of gender identity effects. It is especially through

the latter within sex approach that theorists have focused in terms of attempting to frame gender issues in terms of a more socially constructed gender rather than biological sex basis. However, consumer research using such sex role constructs (e.g., the Bem Sex Role Inventory) has been problematic (Gould and Stern 1989). On the other hand, Path 2, gender salience, discussed below offers the possibility of a more potent demonstration of the social construction of gender and its effects on consumer behavior since it focuses on situational and environmental manifestations of and changes in gender expression.

GENDER SALIENCE: PATH 2

Nature of Gender Salience

One of the implications drawn for future research by Deshpande and Stayman (1994) from their study of ethnicity and salience was that sex might function in a similar manner, i.e., sex (or gender) might be more salient in some situations than others, just as they found ethnicity to be. Gender salience as we have noted above concerns the awareness of gender at any given time and is related to Path 2 in which individuals encounter a situation and find gender either to be relevant to it or not. It also reflects within-person differences in that the presence (absence) of gender stimuli (e.g., products, ads) may provoke gender-related (non-gender-related) responses.

Early research concerning gender salience involved groups in which people were distributed differently by sex either on a chronic (McGuire, McGuire and Winton 1979) or temporary (Cota and Dion 1986) basis. It should be noted that while the work of McGuire et al. viewed gender salience in terms of situations which comprise a major structural portion of people's lives (e.g., their living arrangements in which various households may have different gender distributions), the concept has evolved so that situations as we use the term in consumer research (e.g., a particular consumption occasion) may be considered in gender salience terms (Cota and Dion 1986).

Salience research is often seen as consonant with distinctiveness theory which suggests that people will mention traits that are distinct as opposed to common in characterizing themselves (McGuire et al. 1979). Thus, people whose sex was in a minority in a group, a fact which makes them distinct, would more often mention their sex in probing than those who found their sex was in the majority or equal in numbers in the groups they found themselves (McGuire et al. 1979). Based on distinctiveness theory, Deshpande and Stayman (1994) predict that a female spokesperson would be more credible in situations where there is a low proportion of women (she is more distinct) than where there was a higher proportion of women (she is less distinct).

A broader view of gender salience is offered by Deaux and Major (1987, p. 375) who find that any number of primes may activate gender schemata as an aspect of the working self-concept and make gender salient when: (1) gender is a "central, well differentiated component of the self-concept" (e.g., one finds gender to be salient across a wide range of situations), (2) gender schemata have recently or frequently been invoked as a part of one's working self-concept (e.g., one's gender stands out because one is in the minority genderwise in ongoing social settings, such as the home or workplace), (3) situational cues make salient and invoke gender schemata (e.g., the performance of tasks or use of products usually associated with one or another gender; life events such as breast or prostrate cancer), or (4) an outside perceiver causes one to invoke gender schemata (e.g., asking someone for a 'man's' or 'woman's view' may invoke gender schemata where before the person asked, he or she was only thinking in other non-gender-related terms, such as those particularly relevant to the task at hand). Following this approach, many consumer and marketing stimuli likely serve to make gender salient (e.g., the presence of one or the other sex in an ad, the mention or use of a product associated with a specific sex).

The activation of gender schemata in some situations but not in others implies the notion of the working self-concept (Deaux and Major 1987; Markus and Kunda 1986) which is rooted in situational contexts, that is the self-concept activated at the moment. Deaux and Major note that this does not mean that one is likely to change the core sense of one's own gender identity (i.e., its masculinity and/or femininity), but that certain beliefs about one's behaviors or their self-conceptions will change or be modified in a given situation. This perspective underscores the idea of gender salience as having particular impact through its evoking of within-person differences.

Gender Salience in Consumer Research

Only a few consumption-oriented studies have explicitly recognized gender salience. Abrams, Thomas and Hogg (1990) indicated that women placed in mixed groups of males and females (thus making gender salient) found an advertisement less sexist than women in an all-female group (not gender salient). Gould and Weil (1991) found in a study of gift giving that males' Bem Sex Role inventory (BSRI) femininity scores went up while their BSRI masculinity scores went down when they thought about giving a gift to a woman as opposed to a man. Females' masculinity scores went down when they considered giving a gift to a man as opposed to a woman while their femininity scores were not significantly different. Considine and Gould (1991) investigated physician choice and found that the presence of more female doctors made physician gender salient in same-sex terms, men tending to choose male physicians more often than women and women choosing female physicians more often than men. These findings suggest that many consumers' behaviors may be related to fluctuations in their working gender identities. In such cases, one might compare one's situational self-image including its gender aspects with a brand image, much as self-concept theory indicates on a trait basis (Solomon 1983).

While other studies have not recognized gender salience as such, some can be reinterpreted in terms of it. For instance, a gender salience reinterpretation may be applied to the study of radio commercials conducted by Debevec and Iyer (1988). They reported that when a female spokesperson promoted beer (perceived as a male product) and a male promoted dishwashing liquid (perceived as a female product), individuals generally engaged in more self-referencing than when a male served as the spokesperson for beer and a female served as one for dishwashing liquid. Interpreted in gender salience terms, it was the unexpected roles that sparked people to become aware of themselves and presumably their own sex and sex roles although these were not assessed in this study. Subjects hearing commercials with unexpected differences presumably thought about them in terms of comparing their own

gender self-concept with the new standard in the ad and thus more self-referencing was induced. They likely experienced more of a noticeable gender effect, and their gender self-concept and/or gender working self-concept was probably made salient.

Thus, gender salience induced by 'creating new sex roles' may have served to draw more attention to the commercial, thereby stimulating more self-referencing. This view is also consonant with Deaux and Major's (1987) idea that people while unlikely to change their core gender identity may alter gender-related beliefs about themselves if exposed to information which: (1) disconfirms expectations about those beliefs (e.g., people not accustomed to seeing spokespeople opposite in sex to the product image), (2) verifies new beliefs about the self (e.g., people incorporating new information within their self-concept which occurs as they reexamine themselves in terms of the ads), and/or (3) induces people to engage in self-presentation tactics, especially in an experimental setting (e.g., responding favorably to an advertising spokesperson of an unexpected sex).

As another example, consider Richins' (1991) studies of women which relate idealized feminine images (gender salience inducing cues) with changed perceptions of the self, and provide a crucial demonstration of how the salient aspects of the self may affect emotion and self-satisfaction. She found that idealized attractive images could negatively affect a female's satisfaction with herself. From the perspective of Path 2, this process reflects the self-attribution and self-perception which occur when response is made to a salience-inducing stimulus. In this case, women's own degree of physical attractiveness became salient when they saw models who perhaps made them self-conscious. Richins' paper points to the need to conduct research which considers how differences in marketing to the two sexes affects their feelings about themselves. While we have looked at satisfaction largely in Path 1 terms of products as response, we have ignored the effects marketing stimuli have on consumer self-perceptions. Thus, a Path 2, gender salience perspective will focus not only on how much consumers like or dislike, for instance, a particular advertising portrayal of gendered stimuli, but also on how this portrayal makes them feel about themselves, especially in their gendered self-perceptions and attributions.

LINKS BETWEEN GENDER IDENTITY AND SALIENCE

The relationship between gender salience and gender identity is one of dynamic and bi-directional interdependence, i.e., Paths 1 and 2 directly interconnect with each other. On the one hand, situational cues with gender salience-inducing qualities (e.g., the presence of both sexes in an ad) invoke aspects of one's gender identity (e.g., gendered reactions to the presence of both sexes in an ad). On the other hand, one's gender identity in the form of a trait (e.g., gender-consciousness) may cause one to make a situation gender salient (e.g., assessing an ad or product use occasion with gendered meanings). The main link between gender salience and gender identity may be seen to involve person-situation interactions (see Stayman and Deshpande (1989) for a good example of such an interaction in terms of felt ethnicity and situational factors).

Gender aspects of one's self-concept are reflected in trait measures such as the BSRI. However, the expression of one's gender identity is also the product of the context one finds oneself in and involves a person-by-situation interaction (Deaux and Major 1987). Such an interaction, reflecting aspects of both Path 1 and Path 2, may be viewed in terms of the working self-concept. In fact, research has shown that there is an identity salience hierarchy which concerns the probabilities that various identities will be invoked in

FIGURE 2
A Typology of Gendered Attributions and Responses

Gender Salience

		High	Low
Gender Identification	High	High Gender Attribution/Response	Identity-Based Gender Response
	Low	Situation-Based Gender Attribution	Low Gender Attribution/Response

a situation (Serpe 1987). In this regard, some traits which impact on the person-situation interaction may be described as processual schemata or traits in that they describe how people activate other more content-related schemata, such as those related to one's gender identity (Gould and Stern 1993; Ingram et al. 1988). One such processual trait may be defined as one's *"gender identification"* which is the degree to which one generally invokes one's own gender identity across situations. What this means is that one sees (does not see) one's own gender identity as important or standing out among a whole host of identity and role factors that make up one's self-concept (Thoits 1992). Such identification may be said to be high or low but is not necessarily consistently related to other aspects of one's gender identity (e.g., one woman may feel very feminine and another not very feminine but both may possess an equal degree of identification with their gender identities).

Considering the joint person-situation impact of gender identification and gender salience also suggests and points to an interactive typology of gendered (self-related or other) attributions and/or responses (i.e., those which involve and/or are determined by gender, such as being cued by a gender stimulus [e.g., a distinct gendered product] and attributing one's feelings to gender or some aspect of gender). For instance, a female(male) clothing customer might attribute unusual or uncomfortable feelings to being helped by a salesman(woman) and even withdraw from the shopping situation. One's gender identification, reflecting the degree to which one generally invokes one's gender identity, is likely to cause those high in such identification to make more gendered responses across various situations than others. Concerning gender salience, a situation is either more or less likely to invoke gendered attributions.

Taking the two dimensions together as is illustrated in Figure 2, we find four conditions of possible gendered attributions and/or responses: (1) *High Gender Attribution/Response (high-high)* — in which a person with high gender identification placed in a situation of high gender salience would tend to make many gendered attributions and responses, (2) *Identity-Based Gender Response (high-low)* — a person with high gender identification in conditions of low gender salience would still make some gender responses since his or her identity centers on gender, (3) *Situation-Based Gender Attribution (low-high)* — a person with low gender identification placed in a situation of high gender salience would also still make some gender attributions since the situation demands it, and (4) *Low Gender Attribution/Response (low-low)* — a person with low gender identification placed in a situation of low gender salience would make few or no gender attributions or responses. It should be noted that in some cases related to the High Gender Attribution/Response cell, one's gender identification may not emerge or be relevant if there are few or no gender cues (i.e., extremely low gender salience). Not everything is necessarily seen in gendered

terms. Furthermore, this typological model only indicates when there is likely to be a gendered attribution/response, not what its content is. Thus, for example, males might make different gendered attributions/responses in terms of content than females and masculine sex-typed individuals might make different ones from feminine sex-typed individuals.

What is potentially useful about this model is that it tells us not only when gendered responses are likely to occur, but also that it provides a framework for testing when and how gendered responses may be induced. Thus, calibration of gender effects can be done which demonstrates the relative impact of the personal gendering of various consumption issues versus the sociocultural gendering of such issues. While one's personal identity is indeed very much linked with one's sociocultural environment, the concept of gender salience offers a different perspective on the impact of this environment. In this respect, many consumption situations which involve oneself and others may have gender consequences, separate from and/or interacting with one's personal gender identity. They also may symbolize or evoke cultural categories and meanings that one may recognize even though they do not materially affect or alter one's personal identity. Therefore the model suggests considering the more proximal effects of sociocultural variables in priming gender, as well as their more distal effects in determining and forming gender identity. For example, a person may see people acting in gendered ways (e.g., dressing in gender appropriate or distinguishing ways) and while they may be less important to his or her own identity, they nonetheless are important to his or her functioning in the particular situation.

Moreover, the model aims at the heart of vexing contradictions in prior research where various identity measures seemed to work at some times and not at others. For instance, people, low in gender identification may make gendered responses in spite of relatively low gender identification when compared to others (i.e., Situation-Based Gender Attribution). Standard gender measures used as trait measures would be unable to pick up such effects. However, gender identity measures may also be used as change measures in that they may vary across situations as indicated by Gould and Weil (1991) who used the BSRI on a within-subject basis and found that its scores changed across different situations. Thus, many prior studies may have depended on the situation and its cues rather than gender identity per se. Perhaps of most interest in this regard would be this situation-based cell since it represents a pure salience effect and because it suggests the possibility that gender effects may occur even when gender identity effects are low or not determinant of behavior. It is also likely that salience effects override identity effects in many situations. The studies discussed above with respect to gender salience likely reflected this cell's effect. Therefore, consumer researchers should further investigate this cell and recognize that gender identity can be much more flexible and contingent in many of its aspects than has generally been considered. Thus, in many situations, it should be treated as part of the working self-concept (Markus and Kunda 1986) or viewed as interacting with it.

DISCUSSION AND IMPLICATIONS

A bifurcated path model to framing gender effects in consumer behavior has been proposed in this paper. Path 1 which is a person-trait, gender identity approach to them has been more widely researched than Path 2 which is a situational, gender salience approach. A corollary view is to consider three levels of gender effects: (1) between sex differences, a Path 1 route, (2) within-sex differences as suggested by various measures of gender identity, another Path 1 route, and (3) within-person differences as suggested by studies of situations of varying gender salience, a Path 2 route. The model also leads us to consider a typology based on gender identification (Path 1) and gender salience (Path 2) which allows us to examine the important issues of how, when and for whom gender attributions and responses become relevant in consumer behavior. Furthermore, many of the contradictions in Path 1 research regarding gender identity may arise because the situational factors involved in the both model and typology have been overlooked and the idea of a fixed gender identity may have been too rigidly adhered to. Moreover, taking a Path 2 viewpoint allows for the consideration of social and cultural variables in terms of their situational dimensions and influences, especially when it concerns the development of gender effects. Reflecting these perspectives, a number of areas for future research are explored below with an emphasis on Path 2, since so little is known about it.

Gender Salience

What consumer and marketing-related phenomena make gender salient? In this regard, researchers should explore many variables, including consumer characteristics and behaviors, product-services attributes, and promotion stimuli. Regarding consumers, there should be studies of their purchasing and decision making interactions with each other (e.g., in households, work groups, dating) to see when and how different gender mixes and roles make gender salient. With respect to products, researchers should investigate what cues genderize a product, such as user and seller cues and product attributes (e.g., color and shape). With respect to promotion, there should be studies of what cues including the general presence of one or the other sex, presence of one or the other sex in perceived gender-congruent versus gender-incongruent roles, gender meanings, words, images, and odors stimulate gender salience.

Experimental Methodology

The fact that gender may now be seen in more situational terms provides an opportunity for new applications of experimental methodology and removes gender from a strictly trait perspective which limits how it may be studied. In particular, consumer researchers should explore how aware of their own gender consumers are in various gender manipulations. Measures of such awareness might serve as covariates and/or as manipulation checks to see how much of a factor gender is. Trait measures, such as the BSRI, might also be also be used as change measures to reflect differences in the working gender self-concepts evoked (Gould and Weil 1991). In addition, researchers might develop measures which assess how much an individual bases his or her decisions on gender considerations in any given situation and how working (situationally determined) sex roles may be primed. Thus, perhaps various sex-role, self-concept measures will be more predictive when situ-

ational aspects are considered. We need to establish whether this is the case and if so to investigate how and under what conditions. The typology of gender identification and gender salience can provide a framework for such research.

Qualitative Methodology

Various types of qualitative interview methods might be used to explore the nuances and effects of gender identification and salience. The analysis of consumer interviews and stories, pictures they draw, role-playing situations, and the like may provide a thematic overview and theoretic base for further, rich insight into the contents, processes and effects of gendered consumer behavior. For instance in gauging the effects of advertising on self-perceptions (e.g., Richins 1991), researchers could conduct in-depth interview studies of how people react to ads in gendered ways with a particular focus on how ads may evoke and manipulate gender salience.

CONCLUSION

This paper has explored the construction of gender in terms of two interacting paths. Such a dual-path perspective offers a way to address some of the problematic results of prior consumer research involving gender. Path 1, which is relatively known to researchers, concerns gender identity and implies relative stability with respect to consumer behavior. By contrast, Path 2 involves the malleability of gender identity in a given situation due to gender salience. Taking both paths together, researchers may examine how and when consumers are likely to act in a gendered way. We can also see how consumer behavior and related marketing practices may be as much determinants of gendered responses, acting through salience-priming cues, as they are a result of or response to consumers' gender identities. Thus, what we know as "gender" involves more flexibility and more aspects of potential impact than we have previously considered.

REFERENCES

Abrams, Dominic, Joanne Thomas and Michael A. Hogg (1990), "Numerical Distictiveness, Social Identity and Gender Salience," *British Journal of Social Psychology,* 29 (March), 87-92.

Bem, Sandra L. (1981), "Gender Schema Theory: A Cognitive Account of Sex Typing,"*Psychological Review,* 88 (July), 354-364.

Burke, Peter J. (1989), "Gender Identity, Sex, and School Performance," *Social PsychologyQuarterly,* 52 (June), 159-169.

_____ and John C. Tully (1977), "The Measurement of Role Identity," *Social Forces,* 55 (June), 881-897.

Considine, Judith M. and Stephen J. Gould (1991), "The Phenomenon of Choosing a Physician by Gender: The Evidence and Implications," *Journal of Medical Practice Management,* 6 (Spring), 241-243.

Cota, Albert A. and Kenneth L. Dion (1986), "Salience of Gender and Sex Composition of Ad Hoc Groups: An Experimental Test of Distinctiveness Theory," *Journal of Personality and Social Psychology,* 5 (April), 770-776.

Debevec, Kathleen and Easwar Iyer (1988), "Self-Referencing as a Mediator of the Effectiveness of Sex-Role Portrayals in Advertising," *Psychology and Marketing,* 5 (Spring), 71-84.

Deaux, Kay (1985), "Sex and Gender," in *Annual Review of Psychology,* Vol. 36, eds. Mark Rosenzweig and Lyman W. Porter, Palo Alto: Annual Reviews, 49-81.

_____ and Brenda Major (1987), "Putting Gender Into Context: An Interactive Model of Gender-Related Behavior," *Psychological Review*, 94 (July), 369-389.

Deshpande, Rohit and Douglas Stayman (1994), "A Tale of Two Cities: Distinctiveness Theory and Advertising Effectiveness," *Journal of Marketing Research*, 31 (February), 57-64.

Frey, Karin S. and Diane N. Ruble (1992), "Gender Constancy and the "Cost" of Sex-Typed Behavior: A Test of the Conflict Hypothesis," *Developmental Psychology*, 28 (July), 714-721.

Gould, Stephen J. and Barbara B. Stern (1989), "Gender Schema and Fashion Consciousness," *Psychology and Marketing*, 6 (Summer), 129-145.

_____ and _____ (1993), "Gender Consciousness: A Procedural Aspect of Gender-Based Schematic Processing," in *Gender and Consumer Behavior*, ed. Janeen Arnold Costa, Salt Lake City: University of Utah Printing Service, 206-215.

_____ and Claudia E. Weil (1991), "Gift Giving Roles and Gender Self-Concepts," *Sex Roles*, 24 (May), 617-637.

Herdt, Gilbert, ed. (1994), *Third Sex, Third Gender*, New York: Zone Books.

Ingram, Rick E., Debra Cruet, Brenda R. Johnson and Kathleen S. Wisnicki (1988), "Self-Focused Attention, Gender, Gender Role, and Vulnerability to Negative Affect," *Journal of Personality and Social Psychology*, 55 (December), 967-978.

Kanungo, Rabindra N. and Sam Pang (1973), "Effects of Human Models on Perceived Product Quality," *Journal of Applied Psychology*, 57 (April), 172-178.

Markus, Hazel and Ziva Kunda (1986), "Stability and Malleability of the Self-Concept," *Journal of Personality and Social Psychology*, 51 (October), 858-866.

McGuire, William J., Claire V. McGuire and Ward Winton (1979), "Effects of Household Sex Composition in the Spontaneous Self- Concept," *Journal of Experimental Social Psychology*, 15 (January), 77-90.

Pavia, Teresa and Janeen A. Costa (1993), The Winning Number: Consumer Perceptions of Alpha-Numeric Brand Names," *Journal of Marketing*, 57 (July), 85-98.

Orlofsky, Jacob L. and Connie A. O'Heron (1987), "Stereotypic and Nonstereotypic Sex Role Trait and Behavior Orientations:Implications for Personal Adjustment," *Journal of Personality and Social Psychology*, 46 (June), 1034-1042.

Richins, Marsha L. (1991), "Social Comparison and the Idealized Images of Advertising," *Journal of Consumer Research*, 18 (June), 71-83.

Serpe, Richard T. (1987), "Stability and Change in Self: A Structural Symbolic Interactionist Explanation," *Social Psychology Quarterly*, 50 (March), 44-55.

Solomon, Michael R. (1983), "The Role of Products as Social Stimuli: A Symbolic Interactionism Perspective," *Journal of Consumer Research*, 10 (December), 319-329.

Spence, Janet T. (1993), "Gender-Related Traits and Gender Ideology: Evidence for A Multifactorial Theory," *Journal of Personality and Social Psychology*, 64 (April), 624-635.

Stayman, Douglas M. and Rohit Desphpande (1989), "Situational Ethnicity in Consumer Behavior," *Journal of Consumer Research*, 16 (September), 361-371.

Storms, Michael D. (1979), "Sex Role Identity and Its Relationship to Sex Role Attributes and Sex Role Stereotypes," *Journal of Personality and Social Psychology*, 37 (October), 1779-1789.

Thoits, Peggy A. (1992), "Identity Structures and Psychological Well-Being: Gender and Marital Status Comparisons," *Social Psychology Quarterly*, 55 (September), 236-256.

The Role of the Family Environment in the Development of Shared Consumption Values: An Intergenerational Study

Elizabeth S. Moore-Shay, University of Illinois at Urbana-Champaign
Britto M. Berchmans, Salesian Pontifical University

ABSTRACT

Research on the generational transmission of abstract dimensions of consumer behavior such as materialism, perceptions of economic control, and optimism about the future has received limited research attention. This paper focuses on the character and tenor of the home environment as a mediator of intergenerational consensus. Results of a preliminary study are presented in which young adult-parent dyads were asked to report on their own attitudes as well as estimate those of their partner. Examination of the patterns of intergenerational agreement offer tentative insights into the depth of consumer socialization. Implications for future research directions are outlined.

The degree to which parents and their young adult offspring share similar attitudes and values has emerged as a topic of considerable debate among contemporary behavioral scientists. Historically, it has been assumed that children mirror their parents on a variety of social and political values, and that the family is the primary source of cultural transmission in society. Underpinning this perspective is the basic premise that the lessons learned within the family context have an enduring impact on an individual's adult behavior. However, at the same time, debates persist concerning the existence of a generation gap between parents and post-adolescent youth in terms of their social, political, and achievement orientations (e.g., Peterson and Rollins 1987; Whitbeck and Gecas 1988).

Although the term generation gap seems reminiscent of an earlier age, the question of intergenerational continuity and change remains at issue in the 1990's. Unlike generations before them, Generation-X has grown up amidst enormous change both within and outside the home: greater incidence of divorce, more working mothers, an anemic economy, and the threat of disease, including AIDS (Strauss and Howe 1992). They are often characterized as pragmatic, cynical, and uncertain about what the future holds for them. Much of their alleged dissatisfaction is rooted, either directly or indirectly, in personal economic and consumption issues. Concerns about employment opportunities, wealth acquisition, and flexibility in lifestyle choices are perceived to be common. Their expectations about their own economic future and aspirations are purported to be diminished relative to the level of prosperity attained by earlier generations and their parents, in particular (Newman 1993). The picture that is painted is often bleak, even for those who have benefited from good educations and stable family environments.

It was this portrait of a generation, disaffected and cynical that provided the initial impetus for this study. In the broadest sense, we were led to question: (1) the extent to which this portrayal reflects reality, (2) the degree to which parents and children share similar consumption-related values and attitudes, and (3) under what conditions parents influence their children's values. More specifically, this research focuses on how the family context in which children learn mediates intergenerational consensus and change in the realm of deeply-held values like optimism about the future, materialism, and perceptions of control over one's economic destiny. Although these outcomes are far removed from more traditional variables such as product and brand level choice, they affect consumer behavior at a fundamental level. Perceptions of one's

ability to consume, and the value placed on material acquisition influence consumer budget allocation and strategic, potentially life-altering decisions, such as the pursuit of higher education, the purchase of a new home, or even the decision to have children. In his recent review of the status of consumer research, Wells (1993) advocated that researchers attend to the broader, more central dimensions of consumer behavior. It is in that spirit that we focus our attention on the question of what parents teach their children about the pursuit and importance of material goods.

Drawing on the concept of socially-constructed reality, this research focuses on the child's perception of the home environment as a predictor of his(her) personal attitudes as well as the extent to which these attitudes are shared across generations. Of particular interest is the impact of the parent's perceived life-satisfaction, financial management style, and intrafamily conflict on the child's ultimate acceptance or rejection of parental values. This investigation of diagnostic signals within the household extends prior consumer socialization research which has tended to emphasize a parent's general communication orientation or parenting style rather than the specific content of parent-child communications (e.g., Moschis 1985). The research approach is derived from a dyadic model of communication of potential value for understanding intergenerational issues (McLeod and Chaffee 1973).

INTERGENERATIONAL RESEARCH

Consumer researchers have only begun to investigate the skills, attitudes, and behaviors that are transferred intergenerationally. Intergenerational patterns may take a variety of forms ranging from the sharing of specific brand preferences to more abstract consumption-related attitudes and values. One of the first researchers to address intergenerational issues found that a family's ability or inability to attain its financial goals is transmitted from one generation to the next (Hill 1970). In a longitudinal study of three generations, Hill reported intergenerational consistencies in the degree to which family members preplan their financial behaviors and then fulfill those plans. In more recent years, consumer researchers have tended to focus attention on those aspects of consumption which may have the most direct implications for the design of marketing strategy such as store preference, brand loyalty, product category, and brand preferences (e.g., Arndt 1971; Childers and Rao 1992; Moore-Shay and Lutz 1988; Woodson, Childers and Winn 1976). Although there is clear evidence that consumer preferences, skills, and behaviors are transmitted generationally, researchers have not systematically addressed why this occurs.

To begin to address the question of causality, Olsen (1993) utilized ethnographic methods to investigate brand loyalty among several generations within families. Acting as research collaborators, students conducted ethnographies of product use within their own families. The findings were intriguing, indicating that similar loyalties may emerge as an expression of affection and respect, functioning at a very basic level as a reinforcer of familial bonds. Conversely, rejection of a parent's brand and product choices may, in some cases, signify rebellion of a more fundamental nature. Although preliminary, these findings clearly highlight the need for additional investigation of the family context and how it affects the transmission of consumption-related skills, attitudes, and behav-

Advances in Consumer Research
Volume 23, © 1996

iors. Not only is this study suggestive of how goods may convey interpersonal meaning across generational lines, it also demonstrates how little is known about the realities of communication, both explicit and implicit, within the confines of the family. Given the private, intimate nature of this social group, research in this area represents a particular challenge to consumer researchers (Wilkie 1994).

Within the consumer socialization literature, researchers have attempted to address this challenge through the utilization of general communication patterns as predictors of individual family members' consumption-related attitudes and values (e.g., Carlson and Grossbart 1988; Carlson et al. 1994; Moschis and Moore 1979). Family communication patterns have been linked empirically to a variety of socialization outcomes including media use, materialism, and marketplace orientations. In a recent investigation of intergenerational influence processes, Carlson et al. (1994) found that the relationships between these broad parenting orientations and the similarity of mother-child marketplace attitudes and behavior are neither simple nor symmetric. Although prior research has consistently demonstrated the relationship between adolescents' perceptions of the family communication environment and their personal consumption-related beliefs, maternal attitudes bear little relation to particular communication environments. This suggests that any links between the general communication orientation within a family and intergenerational consensus are either tenuous or domain specific.

Collectively, the research findings on intergenerational influence indicate that parents and their adult children share specific preferences, buying styles, and economic management skills. Further research is needed, however, to more completely specify both how and why this occurs. In particular, it is important to consider how the family environment and the child's perception of it influence the degree to which parental views are both understood and ultimately accepted or rejected. Although emanating from divergent conceptual and methodological perspectives, both the Carlson et al. (1994) and Olsen (1993) studies highlight the complexity of the communications that take place within a family context. These communications are both explicit and implicit, with the parents' actions often acting as a signal to the child and vice versa.

Given the complexity of these communications issues, we chose to focus in this exploratory study on a narrowly defined, domain specific set of communication indicators. Rather than concentrating on general patterns of communication (e.g., Carlson et al. 1994), or the frequency of parent-child communication (Moschis and Churchill 1978), a constellation of contextual variables relating to the child's perception of the home environment and the nature of the communications that took place within that environment were investigated. This is based on the assumption that the family is an important mediator of the external environment and the messages an individual confronts. Although the historical context in which this cohort has come of age has been characterized by some potentially disturbing social conditions, how these events are ultimately internalized and reflected in an individual's attitudes and values rests in part upon the family's power to mediate them. In this particular study, we were interested in how children's awareness of and reaction to money-related conflict within the home might affect their likelihood of adopting consumption attitudes, values, and financial management practices that are similar to their parents. If a child grows up in an environment fraught with conflict and in which financial struggle and dissatisfaction exist, rejection of parental values seems likely. Conversely, when children grow up with a perception of financial security, effective management, and parental satisfaction, we might expect to observe significant intergenerational consensus in adulthood. It is noteworthy that there is a substantial body of literature that reports the influence of money-related conflict on the incidence of divorce (e.g., Janus and Janus 1993). However, relatively little is known about how children are affected, either as witnesses or participants, when conflict about financial matters emerges within a family.

Political socialization researchers have shown that the degree of specificity or concreteness of the belief or attitude may influence the extent of agreement across generations (Troll and Bengston 1979). Since consumer researchers have tended to focus on concrete outcomes such as brand and product class preferences in intergenerational research, it is not yet clear whether the more abstract outcomes of interest in the present study such as materialism, perceptions of control over one's economic destiny and general optimism are transmitted generationally (see Carlson et al. 1994, for an exception). The presumed conceptual basis for the limited transfer of abstract attitudes is that children can not accurately read the environment, and as a consequence, have limited insight into the views of their parents. However, even presumably abstract attitudes and values may be successfully communicated from one generation to the next if parental behavior provides appropriate cues to the child. For example, materialism may be communicated through shopping frequency, intensity and related discussion. Similarly, observable conflict within the household about money-related issues may reveal a parent's feeling of economic powerlessness. In the present study, the focus is limited to understanding actual levels of consensus between parent and child, based on the presumption that there are sufficient cues within the household to infer parents' concerns and attitudes about money.

Through the investigation of more abstract dimensions of consumer behavior such as materialism, perceptions of control, and optimism about the future, it becomes possible to enrich our understanding of the levels at which intergenerational influences operate. In conjunction with research efforts that have focused at the level of brand and product preference, investigation of these attitudes and values potentially broadens our understanding of the consumer content that is transferred between generations within the family.

METHOD

A survey was used to investigate intergenerational influences among young adult-parent dyads. This is a particularly interesting population in the study of intergenerational issues because of the eminent transition from dependent to independent financial status. Both parent and child completed questionnaires that asked them to report their own beliefs and attitudes as well as estimates of their partner's. Parent questionnaires were mailed by the researchers and returned within three weeks.

Sample

Sixty-three college students and their parents completed the survey. The students were juniors and seniors enrolled in a marketing communications course at a large midwestern university. The parent-child dyads consisted of the following types: 13 father-son, 15 father-daughter, 27 mother-daughter, and 8 mother-son. The students were predominately from intact families, with 84% reporting that they grew up in households with both original father and mother in residence. The parents were well educated, with 62% of the fathers and 52% the mothers reporting completion of a college degree. The combined parent-child sample was ethnically diverse with 69% white, 16% African-American, 5% Asian, and 5% Latino respondents. Economically, 18% of the families reported household incomes below $40,000, 59% reported annual incomes of between $40,000 and $100,000, and 23% reported incomes in excess of $100,000.

TABLE 1
Summary of Independent and Dependent Measures

Index	No. Items	Scale	Alpha	Source
Independent Variables				
Parent-Child Communication				
General Communication	4	Vo/Vs	.73	Moschis & Churchill (1978)
Conflict about Consumption	4	Vo/Vs	.74	—
Parental Variables				
Parent Financial Management	6	SD	.91	—
Parent General Satisfaction	2	Cs/Cd	.77	Johnston et al. (1989)
Parent-Child Relationship				
Parent Contact	2	Mo/Lo	.50	Campbell et al. (1976)
Closeness	2	—	—	Campbell et al. (1976)
Dependent Variables				
Optimism	1	Vo/Vp	—	—
General Control	2	At/An	.50	Wuthnow (1994)
Monetary Control	3	At/An	.74	Wuthnow (1994)
Parents Owe	1	Ag/No	—	Johnston et al. (1989)
Materialism	14	Sa/Sd	.77	Richins & Dawson (1992)
Personal Satisfaction	4	Cs/Cd	.80	Johnston et al. (1989)

Vo/Vs: Very often = 5, Very Seldom = 1; SD = 7 point semantic differential; Cs/Cd : Completely satisfied = 7, Completely dissatisfied = 1; Mo/Lo: More than once a week = 5, Less often = 1; Vo/Vp : Very optimistic = 5, Very pessimistic = 1; At/An: Almost total control = 5, Almost no control = 1; Ag/No: A great deal = 5, Nothing = 1; Sa/Sd: Strongly agree = 5, Strongly disagree = 1.

Measures

Independent Variables. Four sets of independent variables were examined in this study: demographics (gender and perceived socioeconomic position); parent-child communication (frequency of communication about consumption and communication of conflict); perceptions of parents (parent's financial management skills and parent's life satisfaction); and, parent-child relationship variables (frequency of contact and emotional closeness). An extensive search was conducted for appropriate measures of the constructs of interest. Table 1 provides a summary of the measures used, the sources from which they were obtained, and the reliabilities attained. Two measures were specifically constructed for this study. Conflict about consumption was measured on a 5-point scale (α=.74) based on four items that assess the frequency and tension associated with money-related discussion. For example, "Money was a source of tension between my mother and me." Perceptions of parent financial management skill were measured by asking the children to characterize their parent's behavior on a series of 7-point semantic differential items such as discriminating/naive, wise/foolish, deliberate/impulsive.

Dependent Variables. Table 1 also contains a summary of the dependent measures and their sources. A single 5-point measure was developed to assess optimism. Respondents were asked to specify how they would "characterize their general outlook on life" from 5=very optimistic to 1=very pessimistic. To construct the dyadic measures, euclidean distance measures were constructed based on an item-by-item comparison of parent and child responses for each of the dependent variables.

RESULTS AND DISCUSSION

Two sets of OLS regression analyses were conducted as a means of addressing: (1) the extent to which children's perceptions of their home environment influence their personal economic and consumption-related attitudes (an intraindividual level of analysis), and (2) whether these descriptors of the home environment influence the degree of intergenerational consensus (a dyadic level of analysis). Both are useful in furthering understanding of the consumer socialization process.

Dependent Variable Means

Table 2 presents the means for the individual level scores among the younger generation for each of the dependent variables. Although the popular press suggests that Gen-Xers are pessimistic, that they feel they lack control, and that they are materialistic, this is not true of the respondents in this study. Their overall outlook on life is highly optimistic, they are not particularly materialistic, nor do they report a perceived inability to control their future either economically or in general terms. As a group, they appear to be relatively satisfied with themselves and their prospects for the future.

Factors Influencing Young Adults' Attitudes and Values

Multiple regression was used to assess the extent to which children's perceptions of their home environment affects their optimism about the future, sense of general control over their lives and financial circumstances, expectations of how much their par-

TABLE 2
Children's Means: Dependent Variables

Variable	Mean	SD	Min	Max
Optimism	4.5	.67	2.0	5.0
General control	3.9	.68	2.5	5.0
Money control	4.3	.56	3.0	5.0
Parents owe	3.3	1.11	1.0	5.0
Materialism	3.0	.53	2.1	4.1
Personal satisfaction	5.5	1.06	2.5	7.0

TABLE 3
Children's Individual Analysis: Regression Results

Standardized Beta Coefficients
(Significance Levels)

Independent Variables

Dependent Variables	Gender	Family Positn	Commn Cons	Commn Confl	Parent Fin Man	Parent Satis	Parent Contact	Close	R^2
Optimism	ns	ns	ns	-.38 (.001)	ns	.43 (.01)	ns	.33 (.01)	.30 (.000)
General Control	.23 (.06)	ns	ns	ns	ns	ns	-.35 (.03)	.38 (.02)	.16 (.02)
Money Control	ns	ns	ns	ns	ns	ns	ns	ns	—
Parents Owe	ns	ns	ns	ns	ns	ns	ns	ns	—
Materialism	ns	ns	ns	.26 (.04)	-.28 (.03)	ns	ns	ns	.14 (.02)
Personal Satisfaction	.22 (.06)	ns	ns	ns	ns	.28 (.02)	ns	.33 (.01)	.30 (.001)

Family Positn = Family Socioeconomic Position
Commn Cons = General Communication about Consumption
Commn Confl = Conflict about Consumption
Parent Fin Man = Child's Perception of Parent's Financial Management Skills
Parent Satis = Child's Perception of Parent's General Satisfaction
Parent Contact = Frequency of Visits and Telephone Contact
Close = Emotional Closeness of Parent-Child Relationship

ents owe them financially, materialism, and personal satisfaction. The results of these analyses are reported in Table 3.

Conflict between parents and children about consumption issues emerged as a key indicant of children's materialistic tendencies and optimism. Monetary and spending-related conflict was positively associated with a child's level of materialism (β=.26, p<.04) and negatively associated with their general feeling of optimism (β=-.38, p<.005). However, the frequency or extent of consumption-related communication within the home was not a significant predictor of the attitudes and values children come to hold. Collectively, these patterns suggest that it is the character of communication that transpires between parent and child that shapes attitudes carried into adulthood.

However, direct communication is not the only means through which intergenerational influence occurs. Observational learning also plays an important role in the socialization process. When children perceive their parents as generally satisfied with their lives and skilled financial managers, this has a positive influence on their own general satisfaction and outlook. Perceived parental satisfaction contributes positively to children's optimism (β=.43, p<.001) and feelings of personal satisfaction (β=.28, p<.02). Children's perception of their parents as financial managers emerges as a negative predictor of materialism (β=-.28, p<.03). When parents are viewed as competent financial managers, children seem to develop a greater overall sense of security and stability. Perception of financial incompetence, on the other hand, heightens concerns

TABLE 4
Dyadic Analysis: Regression Results

Standardized Beta Coefficients
(Significance Levels)

Independent Variables

Dependent Variables	Dyad Type	Family Positn	Commn Cons	Commn Confl	Parent Fin Man	Parent Satis	Parent Contact	Close	R^2
Optimism*	ns	ns	ns	-.37 (.01)	ns	.39 (.005)	.24 (.07)	.27 (.04)	.31 (.005)
General Control	ns	ns	ns	ns	.28 (.03)	.36 (.02)	ns	ns	.16 (.02)
Money Control	ns	ns	.23 (.06)	-.43 (.004)	.20 (.09)	.29 (.034)	ns	ns	.34 (.002)
Parents Owe	ns	ns	ns	ns	ns	.31 (.008)	.22 (.034)	-.68 (.000)	.54 (.000)
Materialism	.31 (.02)	ns	ns	ns	ns	ns	ns	ns	.19 (.10)
Child's Mat. Accuracy	ns	ns	ns	ns	ns	ns	ns	ns	—
Parent's Mat. Accuracy	ns	ns	ns	-.37 (.001)	.19 (.11)	ns	ns	ns	.27 (.013)

*For ease of explanation, signs have been reversed so that dyadic measures represent levels of agreement rather than disagreement. Child's Mat. Accuracy = Child's predictive accuracy re: parent's materialism; Parent's Mat. Accuracy=Parent's predictive accuracy re:child's materialism

about monetary matters leading to a greater preoccupation with material goods and their acquisition.

The quality of the relationship between parent and child, defined both in terms of the frequency of contact and affective solidarity, also plays an important role in shaping the optimism, personal satisfaction, and control with which children view their lives. Children who are close to their parents report a greater sense of general control over their lives and future (β=.38, p<.02), greater optimism (β=.33, p<.01), and personal satisfaction (β=.33, p<.01). Frequent contact with parents, on the other hand, contributes negatively to children's sense of general control (β=-.35, p<.03). Given the numerous developmental, social, and financial tasks that adolescents and young adults are called to fulfill (Esman 1990), it is reasonable to expect that those who feel distanced from their parents would experience a certain loss of control and lessening of optimism and personal satisfaction. Although the negative relationship observed between the frequency of parental contact and a child's perception of control seems counterintuitive, it may be that frequent contact may reflect a greater dependence on parents and, as a consequence, a reduced sense of personal agency.

The demographic factors (gender and socioeconomic position) played a more limited role in the prediction of children's attitudes and monetary values. Young men reported greater personal satisfaction than women (β=.22, p<.06) and a stronger sense of general control over external events (β=.23, p=.06). Psychologists have observed a similar pattern, reporting that female adolescents have lower self-esteem and self-satisfaction than their male counterparts (Harter 1990). Economic position, as reported by the child, was not a significant predictor in any of the regression equations. Given the rather surprising nature of this finding, the models were respecified using household income (as provided by

the parent) as a predictor, and again a null result was obtained. Given that the families in the sample reported a broad range of socioeconomic circumstances, it appears that it is the perceptual variables that ultimately influence the attitudes children develop. These findings suggest that it is the character and tenor of the home environment that affect children's economic and consumption outlook rather than the family's actual economic status.

Collectively, the individual level analyses indicate that all three classes of family context variables (communication related, perceptions of parents, and relationship quality) play significant roles in shaping the attitudes and monetary values young adults come to hold. Although this study is limited in its scope, these findings suggest that the child's perception of the home environment affects the content of consumer learning. The discussion now turns to the dyadic analyses that address the question of whether these contextual factors influence the degree of intergenerational consensus. Since communication involves an exchange of information, it is important that researchers adopt an interpersonal unit of analysis and conceptualize variables as interpersonal constructs. The results of these dyadic analyses are reported in Table 4.

Intergenerational Agreement and Accuracy

The dyadic analyses provide additional evidence that children's perceptions of the home environment influence the degree to which they adopt their parents' values and attitudes. Consistent with the individual level analyses, general communication about consumption plays a less pronounced role in consensus building than more specific conversations about money and its use. Parent-child conflict about money and spending choices reduces the extent to which they share optimism about the future (β=-.37, p<.01). It appears that tensions about money lead not only to divergent attitudes but also reduced insight into one another's beliefs. These findings suggest that conflict over financial matters has enduring consequences for the children and the lessons they ultimately internalize.

One of the most important cues within the home appears to be the parent's purported life satisfaction. When children witness high levels of satisfaction, they are more likely to share parental points of view regarding optimism (β=.39, p<.005), general (β=.36, p<.02), and economic control (β=.29, p<.03) as well as parents' presumed financial responsibility (β=.31, p<.008). Parents who exhibit strong financial management skills positively influence the extent to which their children adopt similar outlooks about their capacity to control the future both generally (β=.36, p<.02) and in economic terms (β=.29, p<.034).

Not surprisingly, the quality of the parent-child relationship also significantly influences the degree of intergenerational consensus. More frequent contact leads to similar outlooks about a parent's ongoing financial responsibility to children (β=.22, p<.034). However, children who feel particularly close to their parents tend to overestimate how much their parents currently feel a responsibility to provide for their economic security (β=-.68, p<.000). Although parents seem to feel that their obligation is almost at an end as their children prepare to begin careers, the children appear to retain the view that their parents still feel this responsibility. Perhaps children who are close to their parents are more susceptible to this misperception since they have been well provided for and have not yet adjusted to their changing role as they enter full-fledged adulthood.

For materialism, the analysis was extended to include measures of intergenerational consensus as well as predictive accuracy. By doing so, it was possible to further assess the utility of the dyadic model of communication in the study of intergenerational influence. Developed by McLeod and Chaffee (1973), the coorientational model asserts that it is not only the absolute level of agreement between two individuals that reflects communication effectiveness but their accuracy in predicting one another's point of view. For instance, two people may choose to disagree with respect to an issue yet do so with full knowledge of the other's attitude. Drawing on this approach, both generations were asked to report their own materialism and estimate their partner's. The pattern of findings was quite interesting. As a group, the young adults had great difficulty predicting how materialistic their parents would report themselves to be. The correlation between the children's predictions and parents' actual attitudes was not significant (r=.17, ns). In addition, none of the contextual factors enhanced the children's predictive accuracy. Parents, on the other hand, had much better overall insight into their children's point of view (r=.36, p<.005), although intergenerational conflict negatively affected their predictive ability (β=-.37, p<.0001). The differential accuracy of parent and child lends credence to the claim that measures of accuracy provide additional insight into the consumer socialization process (Moore-Shay and Lutz 1988) beyond that revealed through consensus alone. Through the use of approaches such as the coorientational model, researchers may develop a better understanding of both the content and direction of intergenerational influence.

Consistent with the intraindividual analyses, the demographic factors had little impact on the extent of intergenerational agreement. Household economic status did not predict the level of intergenerational consensus for any of the dependent variables. Future research drawing on a more diverse population is needed to fully understand what, if any, impact a family's socioeconomic status has in the generational transmission of money-related attitudes. However, the results do suggest that the gender composition of the dyad may affect the extent to which parents and children share materialistic views. In particular, sons and mothers were more likely to differ in their views about the role material goods play in their success and happiness (β=.31, p<.02), relative to other dyad types.

Finally, a series of behavioral outcomes regarding savings, debt accumulation, and credit use were assessed. None of these were related to the family context variables of interest, nor were intergenerational relationships detected. This may perhaps best be explained by the life-cycle stage characterizing each of these generations. Given the younger generation's economic constraints, it is not surprising that their financial management behavior bears little relation to that exhibited by their parents. The generational transmission of consumption-related attitudes and values may serve as a kind of latent template for enactment when circumstances later allow. Future research which examines intergenerational issues across different developmental levels may lend additional insight.

CONCLUSIONS AND DIRECTIONS FOR FUTURE RESEARCH

The findings of this exploratory study provide a number of intriguing insights into the generational transmission of deep-seated economic and consumption-related attitudes and values. The character and tenor of the home environment in which children learn has important consequences for the extent to which young adults ultimately come to share their parents' beliefs and values. Although the study sample was limited both in terms of size and diversity, there is at least preliminary evidence that these perceptual factors may, in some cases, override more concrete indicators like socioeconomic status. The child's perception of the parent's life satisfaction and financial skill appear to be important contributors to the development of his(her) own attitudes and willingness to adopt parental views. It may be that the perception of parent satisfaction teaches children that happiness and fulfillment can be achieved across a range of economic circumstances. However, as Olsen (1993) notes, both functional and dysfunctional outcomes are potentially operative. When conflict about money-related matters is evident in the home, children are more pessimistic about their future, more materialistic, and less likely to draw on their parents as consumer role models. Future research is needed to specify more completely the factors within the home environment that either facilitate or inhibit the transmission of these seemingly abstract beliefs and attitudes. Consumption-relevant communications are much more diverse than either this study or existing socialization research seems to allow. An ethnographic approach may be particularly well-suited for furthering our understanding of the form and content of cross-generation communication. Combining this methodology with more traditional survey approaches offers a promising approach for capitalizing on both the richness of qualitative data and the rigor and generalizability of survey methods. Perceptions of control over one's economic future, optimism, materialism, and personal satisfaction are fundamental consumer outcomes. Research on their determinants and consequences in the lives of consumers is important. As such, the conclusions of any single study, particularly one limited in scope and sample, can only be regarded as tentative. Replication and extension across populations and contexts is critical to our understanding of both the content and processes of consumer socialization.

REFERENCES

Arndt, Johan (1971), A Research Note on Intergenerational Overlap of Selected Consumer Variables, *Markeds Kommunikasjon*, 3, 1-8.

Campbell, Angus, Philip E. Converse, and Willard L. Rodgers (1976), *The Quality of American Life: Perceptions, Evaluations and Satisfactions*, New York, NY: Russell Sage.

Carlson, Les and Sanford Grossbart (1988), Parental Style and Consumer Socialization of Children, *Journal of Consumer Research*, 15 (1), 77-94.

Carlson, Les, Ann Walsh, Russell N. Laczniak, and Sanford Grossbart (1994), Family Communication Patterns and Marketplace Motivations, Attitudes, and Behaviors of Children and Mothers, *Journal of Consumer Affairs*, 28 (1), 25-53.

Childers, Terry L. and Akshay R. Rao (1992), The Influence of Familial and Peer-based Reference Groups on Consumer Decisions, *Journal of Consumer Research*, 19 (2), 198-211.

Esman, A. (1990), *Adolescence and Culture*, New York: Columbia University Press.

Harter, Susan (1990), Self and Identity Development, in *At the Threshold: The Developing Adolescent*, S.S. Feldman and G.R. Elliott (eds.), Cambridge, MA: Harvard University Press, 352-387.

Hill, Reuben (1970), *Family Development in Three Generations*, Cambridge, MA: Schenkman.

Janus, Samuel S. and Cynthia L. Janus (1993), *The Janus Report on Sexual Behavior*, New York, NY: John Wiley & Sons, Inc.

Johnston, Lloyd D., Jerald G. Bachman, and Patrick M. O'Malley (1989), *Monitoring the Future: Questionnaire Responses from the Nation's High School Seniors*, Ann Arbor, MI: University of Michigan Institute for Social Research.

McLeod, Jack M. and Steven H. Chaffee (1973), Interpersonal Approaches to Communication Research, *American Behavioral Scientist*, 16 (April), 469-499.

Moore-Shay, Elizabeth S. and Richard J. Lutz (1988), Intergenerational Influences in the Formation of Consumer Attitudes and Beliefs About the Marketplace: Mothers and Daughters, in *Advances in Consumer Research*, Vol. 15, M.J. Houston (ed.), Provo, UT: Association for Consumer Research, 461-467.

Moschis, George P. (1985), The Role of Family Communication in Consumer Socialization of Children and Adolescents, *Journal of Consumer Research*, 11 (March), 898-913.

Moschis, George P. and Gilbert A. Churchill (1978), Consumer Socialization: A Theoretical and Empirical Analysis, *Journal of Marketing Research*, 15 (Nov.), 599-609.

Moschis, George P. and Roy L. Moore (1979), Decision Making Among the Young: A Socialization Perspective, *Journal of Consumer Research*, 6 (2), 101-112.

Newman, Katherine S. (1993), *Declining Fortunes, The Withering of the American Dream*, New York, NY: Basic Books.

Olsen, Barbara (1993), Brand Loyalty and Lineage: Exploring New Dimensions for Research, in *Advances in Consumer Research*, Vol. 20, L. McAlister and M.L. Rothschild (eds.), Provo, UT: Association for Consumer Research, 575-579.

Peterson, Gary W. and Boyd C. Rollins (1987), Parent-Child Socialization, in *Handbook of Marriage and the Family*, New York, NY: Plenum, 471-507.

Richins Marsha L. and Dawson Scott (1992), A Consumer Values Orientation for Materialism and its Measurement: Scale Development and Validation, *Journal of Consumer Research*, 19 (3), 303-316.

Strauss, William and Neil Howe (1992), Thirteenth Generation, Born: 1961-1981, in *Popular Culture: An Introductory Text*, J. Nachbar and K. Lause (eds.), Bowling Green OH: Bowling Green State University Press, 490-504.

Troll, Lillian and Vern Bengston (1979), Generations in the Family, in *Contemporary Theories About the Family*, Vol. 1, W.R. Burr et al. (eds.), New York, NY: The Free Press: 127-161.

Wells, William D. (1993), Discovery-oriented Consumer Research, *Journal of Consumer Research*, 19 (March), 489-504.

Wilkie, William L. (1994), *Consumer Behavior*, 3rd ed., Wiley & Sons.

Whitbeck, Les B. and Viktor Gecas (1988), Value Attributions and Value Transmission between Parents and Children, *Journal of Marriage and the Family*, (Aug.), 829-840.

Woodson, Larry G., Terry L. Childers, and Paul R. Winn (1976), Intergenerational Influences in the Purchase of Auto Insurance, in *Marketing Looking Outward: 1976 Business Proceedings*, W. Locander (ed.), Chicago: American Marketing Association, 43-49.

Wuthnow, Robert (1994), *God and Mammon in America*, New York: The Free Press.

Equity Theory and the Power Structure in a Marital Relationship

Cynthia Webster, Mississippi State University
Samantha Rice, Mississippi State University

ABSTRACT

Marital roles in purchase decision making is explored further by examining power structure shifts from couples' working years to retirement. Specifically, the authors use equity theory to help explain marital role changes as couples make the major life change of retirement. The findings indicate that significant marital power shifts in purchase decision making take place from working to retirement years among the more traditional and unequal-salaried couples, but not among equal-salaried couples. Further, the importance of the product category appears to moderate the relationship between the working/retirement lifestages and marital power in decision making.

INTRODUCTION

The relationship between marital roles and decision making has been of considerable interest to researchers from various disciplines for several decades. The importance of the power structure in a marital relationship has been well documented in the psychological (e.g., Marin et al. 1989; O'Guinn, Imperia, and MacAdams 1987), sociological (e.g., Blood and Wolfe 1960; Kenkel 1961), and economic literature (Ferber 1973). Perhaps most importantly, our understanding of marital roles in decision making has been enhanced greatly by the research done in the marketing field, where we continue to explore the value that marital roles in decision making add to our knowledge of household consumption behavior.

Past related research has focused primarily on changes in marital roles across ethnic identification groups (Webster 1994), demographic and socioeconomic groups (Davis 1976; Green and Cunningham 1975; Munsinger, Weber, and Hansen 1975; Wolgast 1958; Woodside 1975), product attribute decisions (Davis 1970; Hempel 1974; Munsinger, Weber, and Hansen 1975; Woodside and Motes 1979), across different decision phases (Blood and Wolfe 1960; Bonfield 1978; Davis and Rigaux 1974; Hempel 1974; Kenkel 1961; Sharp and Mott 1956), and across the family life cycle (Cox 1975). However, none has concentrated on marital role shifts before and after retirement. In this research, we predict a significant change in relative influence in marital roles once a couple enters retirement and offer equity theory as an explanation of that change. The application of equity theory should depend on the particular economic situation that characterizes a marital relationship (i.e., employment status and money earned by one spouse relative to the other). Thus, the purpose of this study is to determine if the marital roles in decision making change significantly after retirement for three types of couples: the traditional couple (i.e., one where the husband is the "breadwinner" and the wife the "homemaker"), the unequal-salaried couple, and the equal-salaried couple.

Previous Marital Role Research

While marital roles in purchase decision making have received considerable research attention, it is important to note that the majority of the published research is now quite dated. Past research efforts have primarily investigated the influence of individual factors in the decision making process in a marital relationship. For example, the socioeconomic factors studied include income (Davis 1976), job status (Woodside 1975), and education (Munsinger et al. 1975). Findings strongly suggest that as socioeconomic status increases, the power structure within the marital relationship tends to become more syncratic. In a study of Hispanics, Webster (1994) found that a decrease in ethnic identification led to more syncratic decision making. Other factors that have received research attention to determine how they affect marital roles in the purchase decision making include age (Green and Cunningham 1975), family life cycle, and length of marriage (Wolgast 1958). In general, as age and length of marriage increase and as the family life cycle progresses, the marital roles shift from syncratic to autonomic in nature. Yet another factor deemed important in the decision making process within a marital relationship is sex-role orientation (SRO). The SRO research has also shown that a more modern SRO, and hence more egalitarian decision making, is more likely to be present among those with a higher incomes and job status and among those who wait longer to have children (Hazuda, Stern, and Haffner 1988).

Research has shown that with respect to product attributes, men have traditionally been task-oriented leaders, while women have had more influence on emotional and social behavior. Thus, in a marital relationship, purchase decisions dominated by the husband have revolved around relatively "important and functional product attributes" (e.g., price) while the wife has been concerned more with relatively "minor and aesthetic product attributes" (e.g., color) Davis 1970; Hempel 1974; Munsinger et al. 1975; Woodside and Motes 1979).

Yet another area discussed in the literature concerning marital roles in decision making is the relative influence in or input into different decision phases. Traditionally, the husband has dominated in the purchase decisions, especially in what has been considered the more important decision phases. For example, research findings published more than three decades ago show that husbands tended to make the final decision to buy, whereas wives contributed more to the minor phases, such as suggesting the purchase (Blood and Wolfe 1960; Kenkel 1961; Sharp and Mott 1956).

Current Theoretical Orientations

The substantial body of research on marital roles has been mainly guided by three theoretical orientations: resource theory, ideology theory, and involvement. Resource theory argues that "the balance of power will be on the side of that partner who contributes the greatest resources to the marriage" (Blood and Wolfe 1660). Traditionally, husbands have held the majority of the power within the marriage because they have contributed more monetary resources (Davis 1976; Green and Cunningham 1975; Munsinger et al. 1975).

Ideology theory focuses on social norms and culturally determined attitudes (traditionalism/modernity) to predict the role each spouse will play within the marriage (Qualls 1987). In general, the culture into which one is socialized or the one with which one identifies will influence sex-role orientation. Several studies have found a significant relationship between sex-role orientation and relative influence in decision making (Green and Cunningham 1975; Lee 1989; Qualls 1987).

The third concept used to explain marital role power in decision making is involvement. The more highly involved the spouse is in the purchase decision and the more the spouse expresses interest in the product, the more influence that spouse will have in the final purchase decision (Qualls 1987). Traditionally, products have been stereotyped according to which spouse controls the purchase decision. For example, the traditional husband has typically been more involved in product categories such as insurance

Advances in Consumer Research
Volume 23, © 1996

(Bonfield 1978; Davis and Rigaux 1974; Green et al. 1983), automobiles (Davis 1970; Green et al. 1983; Sharp and Mott 1956; Wolgast 1958), and televisions (Woodside and Motes 1979). Conversely, in past years, the wife has been involved more in products associated with the homemaker role, such as appliances (Green et al. 1983; Wolgast 1958), groceries (Bonfield 1978; Davis and Rigaux 1974; Green et al. 1983; Sharp and Mott 1956), and washing machines (Woodside and Motes 1979). (We remind the reader that the literature is quite dated.) In the current research, we borrow equity theory from the social psychology field to determine if it can aid in our understanding of changes in marital roles in purchase decision making as couples proceed through the life cycle.

Equity Theory

This study offers equity theory as another possible explanation of marital power in the decision making process. Equity theory is based on the assumption that individuals are motivated by their desire to be equitably treated in their relationships. The theory holds that one will compare his or her perceived ratio of inputs to outputs to that of a comparative other; inequity will exist if a person perceives his ratio to be lower than another's ratio. Adams' (1965) equity model consists of four essential postulates:

1) Perceived inequity creates tension in an individual.
2) The amount of tension is proportional to the magnitude of the inequity.
3) This created tension motivates the individual to reduce it.
4) The strength of the motivation to reduce the inequity is proportional to the perceived inequity.

Equity theory is a motivation theory that has primarily been used to describe how individuals in organizations react to inequitable compensation compared to other co-workers. Adam's equity model alludes to the fact that an employee who believes to be underrewarded for his or her responsibilities and efforts will strive to create a more equitable balance regarding both monetary and nonmonetary rewards. The application of equity theory can be extended to include other unfair situations, such as an individual who has been allocated a much lighter or heavier work load than a comparative other. Although a quick glance at dysfunctional relationships reveals that steps are not always taken to alter unfair situations, the inequitable relationship is likely to create tension that may be eventually reduced by making the necessary changes in the power base.

The family unit can be viewed as a type of organization in which each of its members expects to be treated fairly. For a couple who has entered the retirement stage of life, resource theory loses much of its applicability since no additional income is supplied by either spouse. However, equity theory states that one or both spouse(s) might feel inequitably treated because he or she is contributing more (or less) to the decision making process. Such a situation is likely to create tension, motivating at least one person to reduce the tension, thereby possibly leading to a more equitable environment.

While somewhat similar, there is a major difference between equity theory and resource theory. Resource theory allows only for the objective comparison of financial assets; on the other hand, equity theory includes comparing individuals on financial assets as well as on other significant factors, such as perceived effort exerted in paid work, housework, child care, financial implementation tasks, etc. Thus, equity theory is subjective in nature as it is based on the perceptions of the individuals involved in the relationship.

This research extends previous spousal decision-making research by primarily focusing on the retirement stage of the life cycle and by testing the applicability of equity theory as an explanation of the shifts in decision-making power as couples move from their working to retirement years. With respect to a couple's financial situation, three types of marital relationships will be considered here: the traditional family, the unequal-salaried family, and the equal-salaried family. The traditional family consists of a husband who is the breadwinner of the family and a wife who performs the role of homemaker. As discussed previously, prior research indicates that this household tends to be husband-dominant before retirement. Once retired, the husband no longer has work responsibilities, but the wife still has her household management responsibilities; thus, she did not retire. However, the husband may feel justified in maintaining the power to which he is accustomed. According to equity theory, the allocation of decision-making power would be out of balance. Hence, the wife is likely to perceive inequity in this relationship and might desire to reduce the tension by moving towards equality in decision making. Therefore, the power in the relationship should shift. For example, the decisions previous research shows as being traditionally controlled by the husband, such as the purchase of automobiles, electrical devices, major furniture items, as well as the decisions concerning the finances and entertainment activities, will be shared more equally between the couple after retirement. Likewise, the decisions concerning the purchase of products associated with the homemaker role will become more eqalitarian.

H1: The traditional family will become less husband-dominant in purchase decision making after retirement.

The second type of family to consider is the unequal-salaried couple. According to equity theory, the lesser-paid spouse will feel unfairly treated if the current decision-making responsibilities remain status quo. Equity theory suggests that an attempt will be made to reduce the perceived injustice by restoring the balance of power in the decision-making process. For example, in the unequal-salaried couple, decisions that once were dominated by the husband, such as finances, family vacations, automobiles, electronic devices, and furniture purchases, will be shared more equally between the couple. The wife would also share more of the routine purchasing decisions with her husband. Thus,

H2: In an unequal-salaried household after retirement, the lesser-paid spouse is likely to view the previous decision-making structure as unfair and attempt to reduce the resulting tension. Therefore, the decision making power will become more equally divided between the two parties.

The third marital situation to consider is the family in which spouses have equivalent salaries. As mentioned previously, resource theory suggests that the spouses will equally share the power before retirement; hence, the division of power in decision making is likely to be perceived as fair by both individuals. Thus, equity theory suggests that no significant changes will occur in decision-making power after retirement.

H3: The couple with equivalent salaries will continue to equally share decision-making power after retirement. Hence, there will be no significant shifts in decision-making power after retirement.

METHOD

Sample

To test the hypotheses set forth in this study, three separate subsamples of married individuals (traditional, unequal-salaried, and equal-salaried) were selected from a major southern metropolitan area. The metropolitan area was sectioned first into nine areas and three of these areas were randomly selected. An analysis of the demographic composition of each area indicated that the three areas should yield a representative sample. Next, four starting points within each area were randomly selected. A systematic sampling technique was then used to select the direction, side of street, starting house, and subsequent households. During a two-month time period, trained field researchers delivered the self-administered questionnaires to couples in their zones. Interviewers were alternated among the three areas to further reduce potential interviewer error.

The interviewers screened the couples, explained the purpose the study, and then secured agreement of the eligible married couple to complete the questionnaire jointly. The couples discussed each product and decided together on a response category. While questioning one spouse has its advantages, many researchers feel that the perceptions of both husband and wife need to be considered in order to explain purchasing behavior (e.g., Rosen and Granbois 1983). To ensure joint participation, the researcher stayed with the couple during questionnaire completion.

The interviewers were instructed to approach couples until they each had a predetermined number of couples who met all of the screening requirements. The screening requirements were: (1) each spouse had to be retired, (2) the couple had to have been married before retirement, (3) the couple must have purchased products in the categories on which this study focused both before and after retirement, and (4) both parties of each couple had to feel that he or she could estimate correctly the relative influence over the years. Since cases in which the wife earned more money than her husband could alter the findings, the unequal-salaried couples had to be comprised of cases where the husband had been the dominant breadwinner. Furthermore, these couples were screened to ensure that the husband had earned at least 25% more than his wife when both were employed. A pilot study indicated that there must be at least a 25% difference in salary for the couple to perceive that they had been an unequal-salaried couple. On the other hand, the pilot study revealed that an equal-salaried couple was one in which the husband made no more than 10% of what his wife had earned. Thus, this additional screening requirement was imposed on the equal-salaried couples.

From 150 eligible couples, 121 agreed to participate, yielding an 80.7% response rate. The 19.3% refusal rate is considered not to be a problem since the examination of the characteristics of the couples who refused showed that they did not significantly differ in terms of demographics from those who agreed to participate. The sample is composed of 41 traditional couples, 46 unequal-salaried couples, and 34 equal-salaried couples. The characteristics of the three subsamples were compared to those of the U.S. population by conducting chi-square tests. All categories were well represented (p>.18) except for socioeconomic status (p=.04). The "traditional" subsample is slightly lower in socioeconomic status than its respective U.S. subpopulation.

Questionnaire

Couples were queried about their relative influence in deciding what to buy and how much to spend with respect to nine product categories. Relying on past research (e.g., Rosen and Granbois 1983; Webster 1994), the product categories were categorized according to purchasing involvement. For each product category, couples were asked to estimate their relative influence during the first part of their working years (or their life together), during the latter half of their working years, and after retirement. Since the product categories of "financial decisions" and "household appliances" might be considered relatively heterogeneous, examples of each were given (e.g., decisions regarding how much money to save and decisions regarding an appliance such as a dishwasher).

The relative influence questions were rated on a validated (Davis 1970) five-point scale. The response categories were 1, "Husband decided"; 2, "Husband more than wife"; 3, "Equal"; 4, "Wife more than husband"; and 5, "Wife decided." Since these five categories refer only to the roles of husband and wife, the response to any given question represents a respondent's perception of the relative influence in the decision. While this well-established scale easily lends itself to comparing means of subgroups (e.g., the higher the mean, the greater the wife dominance), its use prohibits the determination of what "equal influence" actually means (i.e., syncratic or autonomic decision structures).

Analysis

ANOVAs and MANOVAs were used to test the hypotheses. One-tailed t-tests were computed to determine if the change in power structure between the working years and retirement was significantly greater than that between the first and latter parts of the working years.

FINDINGS

The data in Tables 1-3 summarize the changes in marital roles in decision making for the various product categories after couples have moved into the retirement stage of the lifecycle. The first three columns of each table present the group means for couples in the first half of their working years, the latter half of the working years, and after retirement. The last column reveal the F values for a single factor design testing for the effects of working/retirement stage on marital roles in product decision making.

Since both H1 and H2 predicted that marital power would become more egalitarian after retirement, the results of their testing will be presented simultaneously. The overall multivariate results in Tables 1 and 2 indicate that the working/retirement stage has a significant effect on marital roles. For both the traditional couples and the unequal-salaried couples, the working/retirement stage has a significant effect on marital roles for high- and medium-involvement product categories. With respect to both the traditional and unequal-salaried couples, 6 out of 9 of the univariate findings are significant. (The findings for grocery products, however, are the direct opposite of what was hypothesized.) As predicted, the change in marital power in decision making from working to retirement is significantly greater (t>2.07; p<.05) than that from the first half to the latter half of the couples' working years. Thus, H1 and H2 receive support.

An examination of the marital role cell means for the latter half of the working years in Tables 1 and 2 show that the decisions tend to be husband dominant. As predicted by equity theory, however, the power structure shifts towards more equal decision making or—in some cases (i.e., furniture purchases)—towards wife dominance. For both traditional and unequal-salaried couples, there was not a significant shift from husband dominance from the working years to retirement for household appliances, financial implementation decisions, and grocery products. A possible reason for these contradictory findings is that each one of these product categories represents those in which women have been traditionally interested

TABLE 1
Marital Roles[a] Among Traditional Couples (n = 41)

Product Category	First Half of Working Years	Latter Half of Working Years	After Retirement	F
		Stages		
Financial decisions	2.29	2.38	2.86	2.65[b]
Automobiles	2.38	2.60	3.09	3.21[b]
Family vacations	2.50	2.61	2.98	2.25[b]
Wilks's λ				.852[b]
Electronic devices (e.g., tvs, cameras)	1.93	2.22	2.97	4.11[c]
Furniture	2.61	2.84	3.25	3.29[b]
Household appliances	2.91	3.17	3.20	.56
Wilks's λ				.859[b]
Minor entertainment (i.e., movie-restaurant selection)	2.70	2.89	3.21	2.26[b]
Financial implementation	3.43	3.39	3.22	.28
Groceries	4.06	3.90	3.56	1.84
Wilks's λ				.893
Overall Wilks's λ				.871[b]

[a]Marital roles were measured with five-point scales (1=husband decided; 2=husband more than wife; 3=equal; 4=wife more than husband; 5=wife decided).
[b]$p \leq .05$
[c]$p \leq .01$

(Green et al. 1983) and hence wives may not perceive that a significant gain in power would reduce any feelings of inequity. This reasoning is carried further to the changes in marital power with respect to the often routine chore of grocery shopping. This product category is characterized clearly by wife dominance while the husband is employed. Probably perceiving unfairness regarding this tiresome duty, she relinquishes some control after retirement occurs.

Equity theory predicted that there would not a significant change in marital power from the working to retirement years among the equal-salaried couples. Data in Table 3 indicate that none of the univariate or multivariate findings reached significance, thus lending support for H3.

DISCUSSION

Individuals, particularly those in the home environment, would seemingly expect to be treated fairly. If inequity exists, tension and conflict are likely to surface within the relationship and to reduce the conflict, at least one spouse is likely to be motivated to create a more equitable environment. This study focused on this issue by primarily examining how marital roles in purchase decision making change as three types of couples (traditional, unequal-salaried, and equal-salaried) move from working to retirement stages of their life cycle. Equity theory provided a deeper understanding as to why the power structure in both the traditional and the unequal-salaried households shift from husband dominance to greater equality in decision making. Equity theory also explains why the decision-making responsibilities continue to be an equal effort for the equal-salaried couples during the retirement years. While social norms regarding women's role in society have undergone drastic changes in the last three decades, the desire for fairness has always existed.

The present research found that for both the traditional and the unequal-salaried couples, changes in the marital roles for high- and medium-involvement product categories are considerable once retirement commences. This finding, which can be explained by equity theory, indicates that while the wife might have been satisfied with her employed and financially-superior husband dominating in the relatively important decisions, she is likely to perceive unfairness if his purchasing dominance remains intact since his other contributions have been significantly reduced. Another possible explanation for the current finding is that the husband may wish to be relieved from the pressure of making the majority of the important decisions once he is retired. Retirement brings about major life changes that could possibly have an impact on how individuals perceive the fairness of the division of decision-making responsibilities. According the equity theory, the husband who has a greater share of the decision-making responsibilities could possibly perceive this arrangement as inequitable because of the mental effort and time it requires and might wish to relinquish some of the decision-making power to the wife.

This study also found that no significant changes in marital roles occurred across couples of the three financial situations for the low-involvement product categories. Because low-involvement product decisions generally require less problem solving, the spouse who had less power in these decisions before retirement is not likely to perceive that inequity exists if the decision making power remains with him or her after retirement. Similarly, the spouse who had more power regarding products of little personal relevance is not likely to perceive unfairness because of the relatively small amount of decision-making effort required to make such purchases.

TABLE 2
Marital Roles[a] Among Unequal-Salaried Couples (n = 46)

Product Category	Stages			
	First Half of Working Years	Latter Half of Working Years	After Retirement	F
Financial decisions	2.38	2.56	3.04	3.24[b]
Automobiles	2.63	2.72	3.16	2.38[b]
Family vacations	2.67	2.77	3.19	2.31[b]
Wilks's λ				.868[b]
Electronic devices (e.g., tvs, cameras)	2.44	2.60	3.09	3.26[b]
Furniture	2.79	2.88	3.30	2.26[b]
Household appliances	2.86	2.91	3.06	.17
Wilks's λ				.879[b]
Minor entertainment (i.e., movie-restaurant selection)	2.81	2.90	3.10	.65
	3.20	3.21	3.27	.12
Financial implementation	3.91	3.66	3.28	3.03[b]
Groceries				
Wilks's λ				.908
Overall Wilks's λ				.877[b]

[a]Marital roles were measured with five-point scales (1=husband decided; 2=husband more than wife; 3=equal; 4=wife more than husband; 5=wife decided).
[b]$p \leq .05$
[c]$p \leq .01$

TABLE 3
Marital Roles[a] Among Equal-Salaried Couples (n = 34)

Product Category	Stages			
	First Half of Working Years	Latter Half of Working Years	After Retirement	F
Financial decisions	2.83	2.87	3.06	.56
Automobiles	2.90	3.13	3.19	.52
Family vacations	2.84	3.01	3.29	1.43
Wilks's λ				.951
Electronic devices (e.g., tvs, cameras)	2.84	2.89	3.11	.63
Furniture	2.99	3.22	3.18	.49
Household appliances	3.00	3.31	3.20	.80
Wilks's λ				.970
Minor entertainment (i.e., movie-restaurant selection)	2.92	3.09	3.10	.47
Financial implementation	3.11	3.19	3.30	.50
Groceries	3.68	3.25	3.30	1.21
Wilks's λ				.947
Overall Wilks's λ				.954

[a]Marital roles were measured with five-point scales (1=husband decided; 2=husband more than wife; 3=equal; 4=wife more than husband; 5=wife decided).
[b]$p \leq .05$
[c]$p \leq .01$

Although the current study supports equity theory as an explanation of the shift in power structure that occurs in a marital relationship after retirement, there are still several additional questions that need to be addressed in future research. First, the present study found that decision-making power changes are more considerable between the latter working and the retirement stages of the life cycle than between the early working and latter working stages of the life cycle. This pattern was found across all products and across couples representing each of the three financial situations. The larger shift in decision-making power appears as a result of retirement. Future research might concentrate on investigating additional reasons behind the more significant power change occurring after retirement. Second, this study focused only on two major decisions for each product category—what to buy and how much to spend. Future studies might include different types of decision phases, such as those regarding the information search process as well as more minor decisions. Third, an investigation might be made of other theories that can perhaps be used to predict how role structure and comparative influence might change after retirement. For example, time availability and the assumption of different product usage roles might help explain changes in marital roles in purchase decision making. Further, it would be interesting to incorporate different personality types with the concept of equity. For example, using Huseman, Hatfield and Miles, (1987) operationalization, how would a benevolent (those who prefer their outcome/input ratios to be less than the outcome/input ratios of the comparison other), an equity sensitive (those who prefer their outcome/input ratios to equal those of comparison others), and an entitled (those who prefer their outcome/input ratios to exceed the comparison other) react to the presence of inequity in a marital relationship after retirement? Finally, the present study excluded the unequal-salaried couple that consists of a wife who contributes more financial resources to the household than the husband. Since this type of household is becoming more prevalent, future research might include it in an investigation of the nature of relationship between working/retirement years and relative influence in decision making. It would be interesting to discover if the parameters of the relationship are similar to what was discovered in the current study.

REFERENCES

Adams, J.S. (1965), "Inequity in Social Exchange," in L. Berkowitz, ed., *Advances in Experimental Social Psychology*, New York: Academic Press, 267-299.

Blood, Robert O. and Donald M. Wolfe (1960), *Husbands and Wives: The Dynamics of Married Living*, Glencoe, IL: The Free Press.

Bonfield, Edward H. (1978), "Perception of Marital Roles in Decision Processes: Replication and Extension," in *Advances in Consumer Research*, Vol. 5, ed. H. Keith Hunt, Chicago: Association for Consumer Research, 51-62.

Cox, E. P. (1975), "Family Purchase Decision Making and the Process of Adjustment," *Journal of Marketing Research*, 12 (May), 189-195.

Davis, Harry L. (1970), "Dimensions of Marital Roles in Consumer Decision-Making," *Journal of Marketing Research*, 7 (May), 168-177.

_____ (1976), "Decision-Making Within the Household," *Journal of Consumer Research*, 2 (March), 241-260.

Davis, Harry L. and Benny P. Rigaux (1974), "Perception of Marital Roles in Decision Processes," *Journal of Consumer Research*, 1 (June), 51-62.

Ferber, R. (1973), "Family Decision Making and Economic Behavior," in E.B. Sheldon, *Family Economic Behavior: Problems and Prospects.* Philadelphia: J.B. Lippincott Company.

Green, Robert T. and Isabella C.M. Cunningham (1975), "Feminine Role Perception and Family Purchasing Decision," *Journal of Marketing Research*, 12 (August), 325-332.

Green, Robert T, Jean-Paul Leonardi, Jean-Louis Chanson, Isabella C.M. Cunningham, Bronis Verhage, and Alan Strazzieri (1983), "Societal Development and Family Purchasing Roles: A Cross-National Study," *Journal of Consumer Research*, 9 (March), 436-442.

Hazuda, Helen, M.P. Stern, and S.M. Haffner (1988), "Acculturation and Assimilation Among Mexican Americans: Scales and Population-Based Data," *Social Science Quarterly*, 69 (September), 687-706.

Hempel, Donald J. (1974), "Family Buying Decisions: A Cross Cultural Perspective," *Journal of Marketing Research*, 11 (August), 295-302.

Huseman, R.C., J.D. Hatfield, and E.W. Miles (1987), "A New Perspective On Equity Theory: The Equity Sensitivity Construct," *Academy of Management Review*, 12, 222-234.

Kenkel, Williams F. (1961), "Husband-Wife Interaction in Decision Making and Decision Choices," *The Journal of Social Psychology*, 54 (June), 255-262.

Lee, Wei-Na (1989), "The Mass-Mediated Consumption Realities of Three Cultural Groups," in *Advances in Consumer Research*, Vol. 16, ed. Thomas K. Srull, Honolulu, HI: Association for Consumer Research, 771-777.

Marin, Gerardo, Barbara Van Oss Marin, Regina Otero-Sabogal, Fabio Sabogal, and Eliseo J. Perez-Stable (1989), "The Role of Acculturation in the Attitudes, Norms and Expectancies of Hispanic Smokers," *Journal of Cross-Cultural Psychology*, 20 (4), 339-415.

Munsinger, Gary M., Jean E. Weber, and Richard W. Hansen (1975), "Joint Home Purchasing Decisions by Husbands and Wives," *Journal of Consumer Research*, 1 (March), 60-66.

O'Guinn, Thomas C., Giovanna Imperia, and Elizabeth A. MacAdams (1987), "Acculturation and Perceived Family Decision-Making Input Among Mexican American Wives," *Journal of Cross-Cultural Psychology*, 18 (1), 78-92.

Qualls, William J. (1987), "Household Decision Behavior: The Impact of Husbands' and Wives' Sex Role Orientation," *Journal of Consumer Research*, 14 (September), 264-279.

Rosen, Dennis L. and Donald H. Granbois (1983), "Determinants of Role Structure in Family Financial Management," *Journal of Consumer Research*, 10 (September), 253-258.

Sharp, Harry and Paul Mott (1956), "Consumer Decisions in the Metropolitan Family," *Journal of Marketing*, 21 (October), 149-156.

Webster, Cynthia (1994), "Antecedents of Spousal Dominance in Purchase Decision Making," in *Marketing Advances in Theory and Thought*, eds. Brian T. Engelland and Alan J. Bush, Southern Marketing Association, 112-116.

_____ (1994), "Effects of Hispanic Ethnic Identification on Marital Roles in the Purchase Decision Process," *Journal of Consumer Research*, 21 (September), 319-331.

Wolgast, Elizabeth H. (1958), "Do Husbands or Wives Make the Purchasing Decisions?," *Journal of Marketing*, (October), 151-158.

Woodside, Arch G. (1975), "Effects of Prior Decision-Making, Demographics, and Psychographics on Marital Roles for Purchasing Durables," in *Advances in Consumer Behavior Research*, 2, ed. M. Schlinger, Chicago, IL: Association for Consumer Research, 81-91.

_____ and William H. Motes (1979), "Perceptions of Marital Roles in Consumer Decision Processes for Six Products," in *American Marketing Association Proceedings*, eds. Neil Beckwith et al., Chicago, IL: American Marketing Association, 214-219.

Decibels, Disposition, and Duration: The Impact of Musical Loudness and Internal States on Time Perceptions

James J. Kellaris, University of Cincinnati
Susan Powell Mantel, University of Toledo
Moses B. Altsech, Penn State University

ABSTRACT

This study examines the influence of a psychophysical stimulus property of music (loudness) on temporal perceptions, as well as conditions and processes that may govern its effects. Musical volume was manipulated and internal states (affect and arousal) measured in a between-subjects experiment involving 54 female college students. The dependent variables were two dimensions of temporal perception: subjective duration and pace. Results indicate that loudness of music influences both aspects of time perception, that affect moderates the influence of loudness on perceived duration, and that arousal partially mediates the influence of loudness on perceptions of pace. The duration of a time interval seemed shorter to subjects exposed to soft (versus loud) music. This effect was more pronounced among subjects in neutral (versus positive) affective states.

This study seeks to advance psychological time research by exploring the influence of a common environmental stimulus (music) and measured internal states on perceptions of event duration and pace. Music is frequently encountered in commercial environments. It not only shapes the environment, but can influence internal states (Bruner 1990). Thus, music may offer a means by which marketers can influence consumers' temporal perceptions to achieve commercial benefits.

This study examines two key dimensions of temporal perception: duration and pace. Perceived duration refers to how long a time interval seems to last (or, retrospectively, to have lasted). Perceived pace refers to how rapidly the succession of events within a time interval seems to take place. Pace bears a close relation to two other psychophysical variables: informational density and perceived activity (Berlyne 1974). Given a time interval of fixed duration, the sequence of stimulus events (changes) that take place during the interval will seem to happen at a rate which may differ from objective pace.

Perceived duration and perceived pace are conceptually distinct aspects of temporal perception, yet each may play a role in determining the other. Pace perceptions may serve as inferential cues on which time estimates can be based. If changes in the stimulus environment seem to take place in rapid succession, then more stimulus information was encountered. Given that it generally takes longer for more (versus fewer) events to occur, the duration of a time interval filled with more varied stimulation should, in retrospect, seem longer. Conversely, duration estimates may be used to draw inferences about rate of information, i.e., pace. Thus duration estimates and pace perceptions should be positively correlated.

The Influence of Music

Several recent studies have examined effects of music on time perceptions. Kellaris and Kent (1992) found duration estimates to vary as a function of musical modality (key) in a lab study. Keys that facilitated storage and retrieval of information encountered during a time interval produced longer duration estimates than keys that inhibited storage and retrieval. Kellaris and Altsech (1992) found louder (versus softer) music to be judged as longer in duration

by female listeners. The authors attributed this finding to the amount of sensory information to which listeners were exposed and to the greater hearing sensitivities of females. Apparently less (more) seemed to happen during a time interval filled with soft (loud) music. Kellaris and Mantel (1994) found the duration estimates of female subjects to vary as a function of their affective states. Female subjects tended to underestimate lapsed time to a greater extent when they were in less (versus more) positive moods. This finding is consistent with the suggestion that females may tend to store and/or retrieve more information about positively valenced events. In a simulation study of waiting in bank teller lines Chebat et al. (1993) found that the effect of visual stimulation on perceived waiting time depended on the tempo of background music. The "wait" seemed longer to subjects exposed to high (versus low) amounts of visual information when slow music was played, and shorter when fast music was played. Yalch and Spangenberg (1990) found foreground versus background music to influence perceived shopping time in a field study. Younger shoppers reported they had spent more time shopping when exposed to background (softer) music, whereas older shoppers reported longer shopping durations when exposed to foreground (louder) music. Clearly, music can play a role in shaping time perceptions.

The present study focuses on the loudness dimension of music. Because loudness refers to an objective, tangible attribute of sound, it may be considered a psychophysical property (Berlyne 1974). Examination of this property is warranted because it is universally characteristic of auditory stimuli and is easily controlled by marketers in applied settings. Moreover, findings pertaining to musical loudness may generalize to other psychophysical variables.

Loudness is expected to contribute positively to both duration and pace perceptions, because loud (versus soft) music confronts sensory receptors with more salient stimulus information (Kellaris and Altsech 1992). Louder, more salient music should evoke higher levels of attention, processing, and recall of the stimulus event (Dowling and Harwood 1986). As more (versus less) stimulus information is encountered and subsequently recalled from a time interval, listeners should attribute longer durations to the interval (Block 1990; Fraisse 1984; Ornstein 1969).

Loudness should have a similar positive effect on perceived pace because the intensity of a psychophysical stimulus should contribute to arousal and perceived activity (Berlyne 1974). The positive association between arousal and perceived activity may create an illusion of faster pace under conditions of more intense stimulation. The loudness of sounds may also serve as an inferential cue on which judgments of pace can be based. As more (less) stimulus information is encountered and remembered from a time interval, listeners may infer that the succession of events or changes that took place during the interval occurred more quickly (slowly).

The Role of Internal States

Internal states should shape the impact of environmental stimuli on the subjective experience of time (Block 1990). Specifically, when the listener is in a positive (versus neutral) affective state, the effect of musical loudness should be less pronounced. This is expected because when the listener's affect is elevated (positive affect), both cognitive organization and motivation to process are enhanced (Isen 1993). Listeners exposed to soft music while in positive (versus neutral) affective states should therefore process and later recall hearing more auditory information during the time period. As a result, their memory-based time estimates are augmented and should more closely resemble those of listeners exposed to more salient information (louder music).

By contrast, time perceptions of listeners in neutral (versus elevated) affective states should be more prone to effects of musical loudness. Whereas less (versus more) salient information is less (versus more) likely to be attended to and later remembered, memory-based time estimates should be shorter among listeners exposed to soft music and longer among listeners exposed to loud music when affective states do not alter processing strategies.

The influence of musical loudness on temporal perceptions may stem (partly) from the arousal it induces. Arousal has been correlated positively with perceived activity (Holbrook and Anand 1990). Hence arousal is expected to mediate the effect of musical loudness on temporal perceptions, particularly perceptions of pace.

Given that studies have reported effects of positive affect that differ from those resulting from arousal (Isen 1993), affect and arousal are expected to operate independently. In this preliminary study, we attempted to capture the influence of subtle variations in affect and arousal by measuring (rather than manipulating) naturally occurring levels of these internal states. In contrast to past studies, we measure internal states after exposure to the stimulus music. This way, the measures in no way interfere with subjects' duration/pace responses.

METHOD

A factorial between-subjects experiment was conducted to investigate the influence of loudness of music (soft=60dB, loud=90dB), affect (neutral versus positive), and arousal (covariate term) on temporal perceptions. The stimuli consisted of musical excerpts played at varied levels of loudness. Affect and arousal states were measured using multi-item scales. Affect groups were created via median split. Dependent variables were retrospective estimates of the stimulus music's duration and perceived pace. The procedure involved exposing subjects to music over a loudspeaker in small groups, and having them complete a brief questionnaire.

Subjects

Fifty-four (N=54) females were recruited from a subject pool at a midwestern university. Subjects were offered course credit in exchange for participation. Ages ranged from 20 to 27 years, with a median age of 21. Previous research has shown females (versus males) to be generally more sensitive to subjective distortions of time (e.g., Krishnan and Saxena 1984). Hence, a female sample should be more efficient for establishing internal validity. It also avoids potential confounds due to gender differences in responses to music (Lacher 1994).

Stimuli

The stimuli were three-minute excerpts of an original, pop style recording of instrumental music. Whereas the style of the music was generally familiar to our subjects, the specific composition was not. Original music was used to avoid confounding stimulus materials with extraneous associations due to prior exposure.

Loudness was manipulated by adjusting volume controls on the amplifier that controlled the loudspeakers in the listening facility. An average sound level of 60dB was produced under the soft condition and 90dB for the loud condition. These levels were chosen to simulate background and foreground listening conditions respectively (Yalch and Spangenberg 1990). Sound levels were checked using a decibel meter placed at room center, at a distance of five feet from the overhead loudspeaker in each listening booth.

Procedure

Subjects were processed in small groups in a behavioral lab. After assignment to treatment groups, each group was directed to one of the sound-proof listening booths adjacent to the main room of the lab. Stimulus music was piped into each booth via identical equipment from a control room. Subjects were instructed to listen to the music without talking and to complete a self-administered questionnaire after the music stopped playing. Unobtrusive video monitoring during the procedure revealed no violations of the instructions.

Measures

The dependent measures included an open-ended, retrospective duration estimate item and a seven-point perceived pace scale. It is important to note that subjects anticipated answering opinion questions about the music, but could not anticipate the duration estimation task or perceived pace measure. Printed instructions told subjects to provide their best estimate of how long the music had played. A prompt ("I estimate the music I heard lasted for about:") preceded blank spaces labeled "minutes" and "seconds." Such open-ended measures are standard in psychological time research (Block 1990; Fraisse 1984).

The perceived pace measure was a single-item, seven-point semantic differential scale with endpoints labeled "slow(1)" and "fast(7)," preceded by the prompt "The music I heard was." A simple, single-item scale was preferred over more elaborate alternatives because a more complex measure would have imposed greater cognitive demands on subjects. A more demanding task could interfere with the feeling states yet to be measured.

Affect was measured via five-point semantic differential items that were summed and averaged to form a composite scale. The individual items were "good(5)/bad(1), pleasant(5)/unpleasant(1), happy(5)/sad(1), positive(5)/negative(1)." The alpha reliability of the composite scale is .88. To facilitate testing the moderation hypothesis with variance analysis (ANOVA), low and high affect groups were formed via median split (M=3.8). The "low" group (X=3.2), it should be noted, actually represents *neutral* affect rather than negative or dysphoric mood. The "high" group (X=4.4) represents what Isen would label "mildly positive affect," rather than highly euphoric mood. Because affect was measured rather than induced, the range represents the variation that occurs naturally in daily experience. Affect is expected to be independent of musical loudness because affective response to music stems principally from other dimensions, such as pitch or mode (Bruner 1990; Dowling and Harwood 1986).

Arousal was measured on a multi-item adjective checklist adapted from multiple sources (e.g., Hevner 1935; Kellaris and Rice 1993; Nowlis 1965). Printed instructions asked subjects to "Please circle the words that best describe the music," with supplementary instructions to circle as many or as few as apply. Responses were scored as 1 for circled items and 0 for items not circled. A composite arousal score was formed by summing the following items: "arousing, stimulating, boring(*), exciting, vigorous, calm(*)." Items marked (*) were reverse scored. The alpha reliability is .64 for the summed scale. The checklist technique was used to minimize the impact of the measurement process on the responses and to allow internal states to be recorded quickly and easily before they dissipated.

TABLE 1
Overview of Variance Analyses

Independent Variable	Dependent Variable	MANOVA Results				ANOVA Results		
		Wilks' Δ	F	d.f.	$p<$	F	d.f.	$p<$
Loudness of Music	* Duration	.7173	9.65	2,49	.01	12.34	1,53	.01
	* Pace					6.79	1,53	.01
Affective State	* Duration	.9788	.53	2,49	ns	.60	1,53	ns
	* Pace					.29	1,53	ns
Loudness by Affect Interaction	* Duration	.8571	4.08	2,49	.03	8.32	1,53	.01
	* Pace					.31	1,53	ns

A confirmatory factor analysis (CFA) was performed using LISREL VI (Version 6.6) to further assess the validity of the affect and arousal measures. The correlation matrix constructed from the raw data did not differ statistically from the correlation matrix reproduced by the CFA, $\chi^2(34)=32.2$, $p>.50$, thereby indicating that the measurement model fits the data. Consistent with our expectations, affect and arousal are not significantly correlated (Pearson's $r=.14$).

A seven-point loudness scale (1=soft; 7=loud), preceded by the prompt "The music I heard was..." was included to facilitate a check on the manipulation. A final item asked subjects to record their age.

RESULTS

Independent Variable and Confounding Checks

As a check on the integrity of the independent variables, two variance analyses (ANOVAs) were performed. The first analysis examined the impact of musical loudness and affect group on the soft-loud scale described above. As expected, the loudness treatment produced a significant main effect, $F(1,54)=74.34$, $p<.001$, with means in the anticipated direction ($X_{soft}=3.5$, $X_{loud}=5.7$). There were no significant main or interactive effects of low (neutral) versus high (positive) affect group on the loudness check measure. The second analysis examined the impact of musical loudness and affect group on the four-item affect scale. As expected, a significant difference between low ($X=3.2$) and high ($X=4.4$) affect groups was found, $F(1,54)=119.67$, $p<.001$, with no main or interactive effect of loudness on affective state. Thus, each independent variable produced a significant main effect on its corresponding measure, with no unanticipated confounds.

MANOVA

The data support the expectation that perceptions of duration and pace should be intercorrelated (Pearson's $r=.28$, $p<.03$). Because the dependent variables are intercorrelated, a multivariate variance analysis (MANOVA) was performed to avoid Type I error inflation. Results appear in Table 1.

Consistent with expectations, the MANOVA revealed a significant main effect of musical loudness on the combined dependent variables representing temporal perception, Wilks' $\Delta=.72$, $F(2,49)=9.65$, $p<.001$, and a significant loudness by affect interaction, Wilks' $\Delta=.86$, $F(2,49)=4.08$, $p<.03$.

Effects of Musical Loudness

Given the positive MANOVA findings, individual variance analyses (ANOVAs) were performed on each dependent variable. Results appear in Table 1, descriptive data in Table 2.

The analyses show significant, positive main effects of musical loudness on both perceived duration, $F(1,53)=12.34$, $p<.001$, and perceived pace, $F(1,53)=6.79$, $p<.012$, with effect magnitudes of $\omega^2=.16$ and .10 (Keppel 1982) for perceived duration and pace, respectively. Mean duration estimates were shorter (134.3 sec.) under the soft music condition and longer (194.8 sec.) under the loud music condition. Likewise, the pace of the stimulus event seemed slower ($X=5.2$) under the soft music condition and faster ($X=5.8$) under the loud music condition.

The Moderating Role of Affect

A significant loudness by affect interaction was found, $F(1,54)=8.32$, $p<.01$, supporting our expectation that affect moderates the influence of loudness on perceived duration. The estimated magnitude (ω^2) of this effect is .10. The shape of the interaction is illustrated in Figure 1.

The positive effect of musical loudness on perceived duration is more pronounced when subjects are in less positive (i.e., neutral) affective states. Under the low affect condition, duration estimates differ significantly between soft (113.5 sec.) and loud (228.7 sec.) music conditions, $t=3.57$, $p<.002$. No statistical differences between the duration estimates of soft (169.4 sec.) and loud (151.0 sec.) music groups are observed under the high (positive) affect condition, $t=.95$, $p>.10$. The duration estimates of low versus high affect group differ statistically under the loud music condition, $t=2.09$, $p<.05$, but not under the soft music condition, $t=-1.74$, $p=.09$ (two-tailed test). A similar pattern is seen in the group means for pace; however, the interaction is not significant, $F<1$.

The Mediating Role of Arousal

If loudness operates through arousal to influence time perception, several conditions will be observed (Baron and Kenny 1986). First, the independent variable (loudness of music) must produce an effect on the dependent variable(s), i.e., duration and pace, a condition already established above. Second, the independent variable (loudness) must produce an effect on the hypothesized mediator (arousal). To establish this relationship, a variance analysis was performed with loudness as the independent variable and arousal as the dependent variable. Arousal was statistically

TABLE 2
Means and Standard Deviations for Experiment

	Perceived Duration		Perceived Pace	
	Mean	Std. Dev.	Mean	Std. Dev.
Total (N = 54)	165.13	75.17	5.52	.863
Musical Loudness				
* Soft	134.33	57.73	5.22	.892
* Loud	194.82	78.92	5.82	.736
Affective State				
* Low	171.12	97.27	5.43	.896
* High	160.48	53.52	5.58	.848
Low Affect Groups				
* Soft Music	113.50	56.27	5.08	.996
* Loud Music	228.75	96.81	5.82	.603
High Affect Groups				
* Soft Music	151.00	55.06	5.33	.816
* Loud Music	169.37	52.21	5.81	.834

FIGURE 1
Interactive Effect of Loudness of Music and Affect On Perceived Duration of a Time Interval

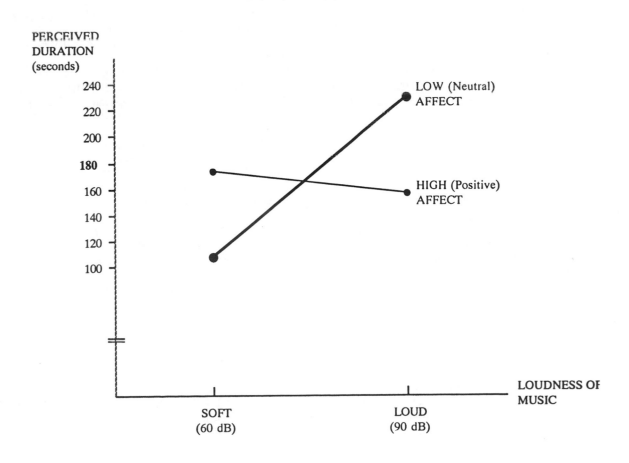

related to loudness, $F(1,54)=4.43$, $p<.04$, with loud music predictably producing greater arousal ($X=4.3$) than soft music ($X=3.4$).

Third, the hypothesized mediator (arousal) must be related to the dependent variable(s). Arousal was found to be statistically related to perceived pace, $r=.23$, $p<.05$, but not to perceived duration, $r=.07$, n.s. Arousal may thus be a mediator of music's effect on perceived pace; but, having failed to meet the third condition, must be disqualified as a potential mediator of music's effect on perceived duration.

The final condition for mediation is that when variation due to the hypothesized mediator (arousal) is removed from the dependent variable (perceived pace), the statistical relationship between the independent variable (loudness of music) and the dependent variable should become non-significant, or at least significantly weaker. An ANCOVA procedure, with perceived pace as the dependent variable, loudness as the independent variable, and arousal as a covariate term, was used to test for this condition. The impact of loudness on perceived pace became slightly weaker ($F=5.1$ and $\omega^2=.07$ with the covariate, versus $F=6.8$ and $\Omega^2=.10$ without the covariate), but the effect was still statistically significant, $p<.03$. We interpret this result as evidence of partial mediation.

DISCUSSION & CONCLUSION

This study has examined the influence of music on aspects of temporal perception among young adult females. The loudness of music was found to contribute positively to both retrospective duration estimates and perceived pace of a stimulus event. Affect was found to moderate the influence of loudness on duration estimates, such that louder (softer) music made a stimulus event seem longer (shorter) to subjects in neutral affective states. Conversely, the time estimates of those subjects in mildly elevated affective states do not appear to be influenced by musical volume. Evidence also suggests that arousal may partially mediate the influence of musical loudness on perceived pace. The positive effect of loudness on pace was somewhat less pronounced when the contribution of arousal was taken into account.

The interactive effect of loudness and affect may provide additional insight into previously reported findings. Yalch and Spangenberg (1990) reported a moderating effect of age of shopper on the influence of background versus foreground music (roughly analogous to soft versus loud music, although different styles of music were used across conditions) on perceived shopping time in a field experiment. Whereas younger (versus older) shoppers reported slightly more positive moods across both conditions, the pattern of the interaction is consistent with the present findings. The internal state (mood) of the shoppers, rather than their age (which was incidentally confounded with positive mood), may have been the actual contingency underlying the observed effect of music.

Concerning our mediation hypothesis, the positive effect of loudness on pace was somewhat less pronounced when the contribution of arousal was taken into account; however, given the relatively small difference measured arousal seems to make, some other process(es) may also intervene between loudness and pace. Future research should explore other potential mediators, particularly cognitive process variables such as attention, storage, and retrieval.

As with any study, certain features of the design (e.g., single sex sample, retrospective paradigm, single item measures) impose limitations to generality, each of which suggests an opportunity for further research. Although the measurement of internal states (affect and arousal) in the current study allows for the analysis of naturally occurring fluctuations, our procedure provides evidence of association, but not causality. In addition to manipulating internal states, future research should use both forced and passive

exposures to environmental stimuli, explore effects of other traits of music and other environmental stimuli, and, of course, replicate and extend the present study using other samples of listeners.

Although the present findings must be considered preliminary, they suggest the intriguing possibility of influencing consumers' time perceptions in commercial settings by manipulating characteristics of the stimulus environment (such as background music). Perhaps sellers and service providers could effect greater customer satisfaction by diminishing the perceived duration of waiting times, by augmenting the perceived duration of rendering individual service, by slowing or increasing the perceived pace of service encounters as appropriate to the situation, etc. For example, the present findings suggest that in situations where consumers are likely to be in neutral affective states, subjective time can be diminished by playing soft music and augmented by playing loud music. In situations where consumers are likely to be in elevated moods, it may not be possible to manage time perceptions by manipulating the loudness of background music. Future research should continue to explore relationships between external stimuli, internal processes, and time-perceptual outcomes, and well as consumptive consequences of time perception.

REFERENCES

Baron, Reuben M. and David A. Kenny. (1986). "The Moderator-Mediator Variable Distinction in Social Psychological Research: Conceptual, Strategic, and Statistical Considerations," *Journal of Personality and Social Psychology* 51, 1173-1182.

Berlyne, D. E. (1974). *Studies in the New Experimental Aesthetics: Steps Toward an Objective Psychology of Aesthetic Appreciation.* Washington, D.C.: Hemisphere Publishing.

Block, Richard A. (ed.). (1990). *Cognitive Models of Psychological Time.* Hillsdale, NJ: Erlbaum.

Bruner, Gordon C., II (1990). "Music, Mood, and Marketing," *Journal of Marketing* 54, 94-104.

Chebat, Jean-Charles, Claire Gelinas-Chebat, and Pierre Filiatrault (1993), "Interactive Effects of Musical and Visual Cues on Time Perception: An Application to Waiting Lines in Banks," *Perceptual and Motor Skills*, 77, 995-1020.

Dowling, W. Jay and Dane L. Harwood. (1986). *Music Cognition.* San Diego, CA: Academic Press.

Fraisse, Paul. (1984). "Perception and Estimation of Time," *Annual Review of Psychology* 35, 1-36.

Hevner, Kate (1935), "Expression in Music: A Discussion of Experimental Studies and Theories," *Psychological Review* 42, 186-204.

Holbrook, Morris B. and Punam Anand (1990), "Effects of Tempo and Situational Arousal on the Listener's Perceptual and Affective Responses to Music," *Psychology of Music* 18, 150-162.

Isen, Alice M. (1993). "Positive Affect and Decision Making." In M. Lewis & J. Haviland (eds.), *Handbook of Emotion.* New York: Guilford, 261-275.

Kellaris, James J. and Moses B. Altsech (1992), "The Experience of Time as a Function of Musical Loudness and Gender of Listener," in J. Sherry and B. Sternthal, eds., *Advances in Consumer Research*, Vol. 19, Provo, UT: Association for Consumer Research, 725-729.

Kellaris, James J. and Robert J. Kent. (1992). "The Influence of Music on Consumers' Temporal Perceptions: Does Time Fly When You're Having Fun?," *Journal of Consumer Psychology* 1, 365-376.

Kellaris, James J. and Susan Powell Mantel (1994), "The Influence of Mood and Gender on Consumers' Time Perceptions," in C. T. Allen and D. Roedder John, eds., *Advances in Consumer Research*, Vol. 21, Provo, UT: Association for Consumer Research, 514-518.

Kellaris, James J. and Ronald C. Rice (1993), "The Influence of Tempo, Loudness, and Gender of Listener on Responses to Music," *Psychology and Marketing* 10, 15-29.

Krishnan, Lila and N. K. Saxena. (1984). "Perceived Time: Its Relationship with Locus of Control, Filled versus Unfilled Time Intervals, and Perceiver's Sex," *Journal of General Psychology* 110, 275-281.

Lacher, Kathleen T. (1994), "An Investigation of the Influence of Gender on the Hedonic Responses Created by Listening to Music," in C. T. Allen and D. Roedder John, eds, *Advances in Consumer Research*, Vol. 21, Provo, UT: Association for Consumer Research, 354-358.

Nowlis, V. (1965), "Research with the Mood Adjective Checklist." In S. S. Tomkins & C. E. Izard, Eds., *Affect, Cognition and Personality* (pp. 352-389). New York: Springer.

Ornstein, Robert E. (1969). *On the Experience of Time*. New York: Penguin.

Yalch, Richard F. and Eric Spangenberg. (1990). "Effects of Store Music on Shopping Behavior," *Journal of Consumer Marketing* 7, 55-63.

Assessing Consumers' Affective Responses to Retail Environments: A Tale of Two Simulation Techniques

Charles S. Areni, Texas Tech University
John R. Sparks, University of Dayton
Patrick Dunne, Texas Tech University

ABSTRACT

Sixty-two student subjects rated either 12 slides of the interiors of various apparel stores (visual stimulus) or 12 in-store background music selections (audio stimulus) using a modified version of the Mehrabian and Russell pleasure/arousal/dominance scale for affective responses. The affect measures were used to predict subjects' perceptions of the visual or the audio stimuli on a number of store image variables (i.e., merchandise selection, prices, service quality, etc.). Results of several multiple regression analyses indicated that the relationships among the affect dimensions and the store image variables depended on whether subjects were in the visual versus the audio stimulus condition. In some cases the signs of the beta coefficients for a given affect dimension were even reversed. Yet, the means and standard deviations for each affect and store image measure did not significantly differ by condition, suggesting the results were due to something other than nonrepresentative samples of audio and visual stimuli.

Much research has been devoted to examining the affective dimensions of a store's image, and their relationships with more specific store perceptions (i.e., prices, merchandise quality, etc.) (see Markin, Lillis, and Narayana 1976; Donovan and Rossiter 1982; Donovan, Rossiter, Marcoolyn, and Nesdale 1995). Consistent with this program of research, Darden and Babin (1994) recently reported systematic relationships among four affect dimensions and perceptions regarding prices, quality, store personnel, and crowding. In particular, they found that higher levels of pleasantness *(unpleasantness)* were associated with: 1) higher (lower) prices, 2) more (less) helpful store personnel, 3) higher (lower) overall quality, and 4) lower (higher) levels of crowding. Further, *activity (sleepiness)* was associated with: 1) more (less) helpful personnel, 2) higher (lower) overall quality, and 3) higher (lower) levels of crowding.

Darden and Babin (1994) relied on a memory-task in which subjects recalled the environments of stores with which they were relatively familiar. The study reported below examines the relationships among affective responses and specific store perceptions using two stimulus-based simulation techniques. Specifically, the retail environments of various apparel stores are simulated via: a) slides of actual store interiors, or b) verbal instructions combined with musical selections. The affect-store image relationships emerging in each condition are compared to one another, and to those obtained by Darden and Babin (1994).

AFFECTIVE RESPONSES AND STORE ATMOSPHERE

The Mehrabian-Russell model describes affective responses to stimuli on three dimensions: pleasure-displeasure, arousal-nonarousal, and dominance-submissiveness (Mehrabian and Russell, 1974; Mehrabian, 1976). Pleasure-displeasure describes happiness or satisfaction with the stimulus; arousal-nonarousal refers to the alertness or excitement evoked by the stimulus; dominance-arousal captures the extent to which the individual controls or is controlled by the stimulus. Donovan and Rossiter (1982) introduced the

pleasure/arousal/dominance (PAD) framework to the study of store atmosphere. They used the PAD model to predict: overall store evaluations, browsing behavior, time spent shopping, affiliation with the store, and the tendency to talk with others while shopping. Although pleasure-displeasure and arousal-nonarousal were useful predictors, dominance-submissiveness exhibited limited explanatory value, due possibly to the questionable internal reliability of the scale. Indeed, many of Mehrabian and Russell's tests of the model revealed questionable predictive validity of the dominance-submissiveness dimension.[1] Owens (1992), in fact, has even recommended that the dominance-submissiveness dimension be dropped in favor of a shopping-specific dimension.

Given that musical selections are used as stimuli in the experiment reported below, it is important to note that studies of musical perceptions also identify pleasure-displeasure and arousal-nonarousal as dimensions on which music is assessed. Wedin (1972), for example, had subjects rate forty music selections from various genres on 125 unipolar adjective scales. The results of a principal components analysis indicated three distinct dimensions labeled: intensity-softness, pleasantness-unpleasantness, and solemnity-triviality. Wedin describes the pleasantness-unpleasantness dimension as corresponding to: "a fundamental quality of emotion that is well-known from several studies" (p. 250). Moreover, the intensity-softness dimension bears a remarkable resemblance to Mehrabian and Russell's arousal-nonarousal continuum. The adjectives most strongly associated with this dimension were: energy, intensity, activity, softness, relaxation, tenderness, and intimacy.[2]

Wedin's third dimension, solemnity-triviality, clearly reflects a departure from the model of Mehrabian and Russell. It was most strongly associated with the adjectives: solemnity, dignity, grandiosity, popularity, and triviality. Consistent with Owen's (1992) recommendation, the research reported below drops the dominance-submissiveness dimension of the PAD model in favor of a distinction more relevant to categorizing apparel stores. Given that

---

[1]Darden and Babin (1994) developed a new scale for measuring affective responses to store environments based on extensive research. Their results indicated that pleasant versus unpleasant and activity versus sleepiness are relatively independent, unipolar dimensions in contrast to the bipolar conceptualization of Donovan and Rossiter (1982). Nevertheless, Darden and Babin's pleasant, unpleasant, activity, sleepiness dimensions are similar enough to Donovan and Rossiter's pleasure-displeasure, arousal-nonarousal dimensions to allow for comparisons.

[2]The last two adjectives, tenderness and intimacy, seem the least consistent with an arousal-nonarousal interpretation. However, research has shown that individuals desire low levels of arousal when interacting with a romantic partner (Butler and Biner, 1987; Biner, Butler, Fischer, and Westergren, 1989; Areni and Kim, 1994). The association of these terms with the others may reflect this preference.

apparel stores can be categorized as featuring: formal attire, business attire, sporting apparel, casual wear, and so on, Wedin's (1972) third dimension seemed ideal for capturing affective responses to the environments of apparel stores.

RESEARCH HYPOTHESES

Eroglu, Ellen, and Machleit (1992) discuss numerous techniques for simulating retail environments ranging in realism from verbal descriptions to actual store interiors, and in the extent to which experimental subjects rely on memories of previous in-store experiences. Researchers using more than one simulation technique have reported generally consistent results across methods (Hui and Bateson, 1990), but many of the simulation methods identified by Eroglu et al. have yet to be compared. Moreover, many dimensions of retail environments are still unexplored. The study reported below examines the relationships among affective responses to the environments of apparel stores and perceptions regarding: 1) the quality of service, 2) merchandise quality, 3) price levels, 4) merchandise selection, 5) the fashion value of merchandise, and 6) the pleasantness of the shopping experience. However, apparel store environments are simulated either by presenting slides of store interiors or by providing verbal instructions and playing musical selections as "background music." There are reasons to suspect that the affect-store image relationships will vary between the two conditions. First, individuals tend to adopt different strategies for processing visual and aural information (Posner, Nissen, and Klein, 1976). Moreover, patrons are likely to rely on different sources of information to form different store perceptions (Mazursky and Jacoby, 1986). Hence, both the null and the alternative hypotheses presented below seem plausible and worthy of examination.

H_0: The relationships among affective responses and store image dimensions do not depend on the method used to simulate retail environments.

H_a: The relationships among affective responses and store image dimensions depend on the method used to simulate retail environments.

An additional research question relevant to the issues presented above is whether the dimensionality of affective responses to retail environments is contingent upon the simulation method. Although no hypotheses are offered, this issue is pursued below.

METHOD

Subjects and Procedure

Sixty-two undergraduate business students were divided into two groups, corresponding to the "store interior" treatment and the "in-store music" treatment. In the store interior treatment, subjects (n=26) viewed twelve slides of the interiors of various apparel stores. The stores were selected so as to be unfamiliar to the subjects. In addition, all references to store names, manufacturers' brands etc. were omitted from the slides. After viewing each slide, subjects responded to the pleasure/arousal/seriousness scale (PAS), adapted from Mehrabian and Russell's (1974) pleasure/arousal/ dominance scale and Wedin's (1972) seriousness/triviality scale. Additionally, subjects rated the stores on six image measures. This procedure was repeated for subjects (n=36) in the in-store music treatment except, instead of slides, subjects listened to twelve two-minute instrumental music selections. Subjects were instructed to imagine themselves shopping for apparel and to base their responses "on the type of clothing store you might associate with the

background music being played." Each subject in both groups provided 12 observations.

Stimuli

The twelve slides of the various retail store interiors were selected from a large pool of slides used in the preparation of a retailing textbook. The primary objective in slide selection was heterogeneity. That is, the final group of twelve slides was intended to represent as heterogeneous a group of retail clothing stores as possible. With a similar objective, music was selected from a large commercial production music library. A variety of musical genre's was included in the final twelve, including pop, rock, country, blues, classical, easy listening, jazz, soul, and so on.

Measures

The performance of the three PAS subscales was assessed using common factor analysis. Items that did not load as predicted or loaded on more than one factor were deleted. The remaining items exhibited satisfactory unidimensionality and internal consistency. The pleasure dimension (α=.92) was composed of three semantic differential items (pleasing/annoying, satisfying/disappointing, hopeful/despairing); the arousal dimension (α=.84) was measured using three items (exciting/calming, frenzied/sluggish, stimulating/relaxing); the seriousness dimension (α=.91) consisted of two items (serious/light-hearted, dramatic/playful). All items were measured on ten-point scales. The twelve pleasure, arousal and seriousness scores obtained from each subject were calculated as the mean of the appropriate scale items. Means and standard deviations for these measures are presented in Table 1.

The six store image items were also measured on ten-point scales. These items were intended to capture a variety of specific impressions (poor service/excellent service, low quality merchandise/high quality merchandise, unpleasant shopping experience/ pleasant shopping experience, low prices/high prices, poor merchandise selection/wide merchandise selection, outdated merchandise/up-to-date merchandise). Means and standard deviations for these items also appear in Table 1. Important for purposes of interpreting the results reported below, there were no significant differences between means or standard deviations for any of the affect or store image variables.

Analysis and Results

Analysis of variance was used to assess whether the relationships among the PAS measures and the store image variables were contingent upon the stimulus condition. Significant (p<.05) arousal by treatment interactions were found for three of the six store image measures (a fourth approached significance; see Table 2). One significant seriousness by treatment interaction also resulted. Overall interaction effects on the six store image items were estimated using multivariate analysis of variance. The results indicated significant (p<.05) overall arousal by treatment and seriousness by treatment interactions.

The specific nature of these significant interactions were investigated further using multiple regression (see Table 2). Responses to the six store image measures were regressed against pleasure, arousal and seriousness scores for the two groups. In general, the models explained a respectable amount of variance and all were significant (p<.01). Consistent with Donovan and Rossiter (1982), the pleasure component of the PAS scale explained most of the variance in the six store image measures. The significant stimulus interactions are more clearly illustrated in the signs and magnitudes of the standardized regression coefficients presented in Table 2. Generally, they are reflected in the significance of the standardized regression coefficient for one group and not the other;

TABLE 1
Means and (Standard Deviations) by Treatment*

	In-Store Music	Store Interior
ST1: Poor/Excellent Service	6.12 (2.29)	5.77 (2.22)
ST2: Low Quality/High Quality Merchandise	6.34 (2.43)	5.71 (2.37)
ST3: Pleasant/Unpleasant Shopping Experience	6.13 (2.46)	5.94 (2.23)
ST4: Low Prices/High Prices	6.41 (2.40)	5.63 (2.34)
ST5: Poor/Wide Merchandise Selection	5.97 (2.22)	6.30 (2.37)
ST6: Outdated/Up-to-date Merchandise	6.59 (2.35)	6.48 (2.41)
Pleasure	4.83 (2.23)	4.87 (2.11)
Arousal	5.45 (2.53)	4.81 (1.97)
Seriousness	6.28 (2.36)	6.22 (2.14)

*None of the means or standard deviations differ by condition at $\alpha = .10$

TABLE 2
Regression Results: Standardized Regression Coefficients

	In-store Music	Store Interior
ST1: Poor/Excellent Service		
Pleasure	-.68*	-.66*
Arousal	.11*	.01
Seriousness	.18*	-.12*
ST2: Low Quality/High Quality Merchandise		
Pleasure	-.66*	-.60*
Arousal º	.13*	-.11*
Seriousness	-.28*	-.27*
ST3: Pleasant/Unpleasant Shopping Experience		
Pleasure	-.79*	-.73*
Arousal º	.13*	-.01
Seriousness	.07*	-.03
ST4: Low Prices/High Prices		
Pleasure	-.53*	-.46*
Arousal º	.02	-.13*
Seriousness	-.33*	-.27*
ST5: Poor/Wide Merchandise Selection		
Pleasure	-.56*	-.52*
Arousal	.05	.01
Seriousness º	.01	-.17*
ST6: Outdated/Up-to-date Merchandise		
Pleasure	-.62*	-.55*
Arousal	-.16*	-.18*
Seriousness	-.13*	-.14*

* Beta estimate for affect dimension significant at $\alpha = .05$

º Treatment x affect dimension interaction significant at $\alpha = .05$

however, in one instance (arousal → ST2), both arousal coefficients are significant but in opposite directions.

Subjects associated higher levels of pleasure with: 1) better service, 2) higher quality merchandise, 3) more pleasant shopping experiences, 4) higher prices, 5) wider selections, and 6) more up-to-date merchandise. Higher levels of seriousness were associated with: 1) better service, 2) higher quality merchandise, 3) higher prices, 4) more up-to-date merchandise, and to a lesser extent, 5) more pleasant shopping experiences and 6) wider selections.

The most interesting results, however, concern the arousal dimension. For subjects in the in-store condition higher levels of arousal were associated with: 1) poorer service, 2) lower quality merchandise, 3) more unpleasant shopping experiences, but surprisingly, 4) more up-to-date merchandise. On the other hand, subjects in the store interior condition associated higher levels of arousal with: 1) higher quality merchandise, 2) higher prices, and 3) more up-to-date merchandise. The discrepancy in the relationship between arousal and merchandise quality is interesting given that the means and standard deviations of the two measures do not differ from one another by stimulus condition at the α=.10 level of significance. Moreover, arousal exhibits consistent relationships with other merchandise perceptions across the two stimulus conditions.

DISCUSSION

Notwithstanding the deliberate selection of stimuli to maximize heterogeneity of impressions, a possible explanation for the reversal of the signs of the beta coefficients between treatments is that the samples of store interiors and background music selections were not representative with respect to the pleasure/arousal/seriousness (PAS) dimensions. Specifically, research has shown an inverted-U relationship between arousal and shopping preferences (Raju, 1980). If the sample of store interiors (background music selections) were systematically below (above) the optimal level of arousal, then one would expect the signs of the beta coefficients to differ. That is, more arousal would be more favorable for the store interior stimuli (i.e., positive betas), whereas more arousal would be less favorable for musical selections (i.e., negative betas).

One strong point against this interpretation is that means and standard deviations for the affect and store image measures were not significantly different by stimulus condition. Moreover, the signs of the betas for each PAS dimension varied across store image variables within each treatment. In other words, for some image dimensions the store interiors were rated as too low in arousal (i.e., positive betas), whereas for others the interiors were too high in arousal (i.e., negative betas). For example, the betas for the arousal dimension were positive for service quality, merchandise quality, and pleasantness of shopping experience, but negative for stylishness of merchandise (see Table 2). This explanation suggests that something other than a biased sampling of stimuli produced the results reported above.

An alternative explanation for these findings is that the *norms* subjects have for background music and store interiors are different with respect to seriousness, and, more importantly, arousal. Although the means and standard deviations for the affect and store image measures did not differ between stimulus conditions, perhaps subjects *expectations* did vary. In particular, retail patrons may expect in-store background music to be somewhat soothing and relaxing relative to the design of store interiors, which they anticipate to be more stimulating. Hence, while actual ratings did not differ between stimulus conditions, ratings relative to expectations did. As a result, the musical selections were seen as generally too arousing, whereas the store interiors were typically not arousing enough.

A second alternative explanation for the findings is that the instructions used in the music treatment were not sufficient for evoking store schema necessary for making meaningful assessments of store image. One additional result supports this contention. In a third experimental condition ("music only"), 53 subjects were asked to rate the same twelve musical selections on the PAS dimensions, but the instructions mentioned nothing about shopping or in-store background music, and the store image items were omitted from the questionnaire. Thus, perceptions of the musical selections in this condition were more stimulus-driven. If the instructions to consider the musical selections in terms of in-store background music and store image were successful in evoking store schema (i.e., "top-down" processing), one might expect results similar to those obtained using the visual stimuli. This, of course, was not the case. If, on the other hand, subjects processing of the "in-store background music" selections was more "bottom-up[3]," then the responses would be more similar to those obtained in the music condition making no mention of a retail context.

A comparison of factor analyses of the PAS dimensions by treatment lends credence to this interpretation. As shown in Table 3, the results were quite similar in the "music-only" and "in-store music" conditions. In both cases, a three factor solution emerged with each item generally loading on the "correct" factor. The factor solution emerging in the visual stimulus ("store interior") condition was considerably different. Although a three factor solution emerged, the loadings of the individual items were markedly distinct. The items regarding arousal-nonarousal and pleasure-displeasure loaded on two factors rather than one; more importantly, these two "distinct" aspects of affective responses loaded on the same two factors! Indeed, this result is probably related to the treatment by arousal interactions reported in Table 3.

It is important to note that the instructions and measures used in this study are not identical to those used by Darden and Babin (1994). Nevertheless, there is a great deal of consistency between their results and the relationships emerging in the visual stimulus condition of the study reported above. If Darden and Babin's pleasant and unpleasant dimensions are comparable to the pleasure dimension discussed above, then pleasure/pleasantness is associated with higher prices, better service, and higher quality in both studies. Moreover, if arousal is equated with Darden and Babin's activity and sleepiness dimensions, then both studies detected an association between higher arousal, and higher prices and higher quality. Thus, the "in-store music" condition seems to produce the most discrepant results. As suggested by the comparison of the results for the "in-store music" and "music only" conditions, the verbal instructions may not have been sufficient for evoking specific mental representations of store interiors.

---

[3]The distinction between "top-down" and "bottom-up" information processing stems from the discovery that perception is influenced by physical characteristics of the perceived stimulus as well as the perceiver's mental representations of the world. Bottom-up processes begin with the sensory input of the stimulus (i.e., musical properties) and proceed to more abstract mental representations, whereas top-down processes begin with mental representations (i.e., store schemas) and proceed to specific sensory input (Glass and Holyoak, 1986). In essence, subjects in the visual stimuli condition may have "matched" each slide to existing store category representations in memory (see Ward, Bitner, and Barnes, 1992). Subjects in the music condition, on the other hand, may have engaged in more detailed processing of stimulus characteristics (i.e., tempo, timbre, modality, etc.) before forming impressions (see Kellaris and Kent, 1992a, 1992b).

TABLE 3
Rotated Factor Pattern: All Items by All Groups

	Store Interior			In-store Music			Music Only		
	F1	F2	F3	F1	F2	F3	F1	F2	F3
Pleasure Items									
pleasing/annoying	.36	.81	.03	.86	-.10	-.03	.83	-.17	.13
satisfying/disappointing	.41	.83	.10	.90	-.04	-.04	.88	-.04	.07
hopeful/despairing	.51	.74	.01	.84	.07	-.08	.77	.15	-.12
Arousal Items									
exciting/calming	.75	.39	-.14	-.11	.85	-.25	-.08	.84	-.18
frenzied/sluggish	.74	.29	-.20	.01	.89	-.15	.13	.78	-.17
stimulating/relaxing	.77	.35	-.05	.05	.83	-.13	.02	.82	-.05
Seriousness Items									
serious/light-hearted	-.13	.05	.77	-.00	-.18	.74	-.03	-.14	.74
dramatic/playful	-.12	-.07	.81	.04	-.34	.76	.00	-.31	.72

CONCLUSION

The research reported above demonstrated that the relationships among affective responses and specific store perceptions depended on whether store environments were simulated via slides or a combination of verbal instructions and musical selections. In general, the musical stimuli were perceived as being too arousing for use as in-store background music, whereas the visual stimuli were typically not arousing enough. Several interpretions of this result are plausible and seem worthy of future research. At a broader level, this research suggests that the multiple bases for simulating in-store environments may not always produce equivalent findings with respect to perceptions and preferences. Although Hui and Bateson (1990) reported similar effects of customer density on perceptions of control and crowding when the former was manipulated via slides versus videotapes, it is not clear that such correspondence will emerge across the simulations methods identified by Eroglu et al. (1992). In particular, a comparison of results obtained using verbal descriptions of store interiors to those based upon more realistic settings (i.e., videotapes and actual stores) would seem a fruitful avenue for future research.

REFERENCES

Areni, Charles S. and David Kim (1994), "The Influence of In-store Lighting on Consumers' Examination of Merchandise in a Wine Store," *International Journal of Research in Marketing*, 11, 117-125.

Biner, Paul M., Darrell L. Butler, Ann R. Fischer, and Amy J.Westergren (1989), "An Arousal Optimization Model of Lighting Level Preferences: An Interaction of Social Situation and Task Demands," *Environment and Behavior*, 21 (1): 3-16.

Butler, Darrell L. and Paul M. Biner (1987), "Preferred LightingLevels: Variability Among Settings, Behaviors, and Individuals," *Environment and Behavior*, 19 (6), 695-721.

Darden, William R. and Barry J. Babin (1994), "Exploring the Concept of Affective Quality: Expanding the Concept of Retail Personality," *Journal of Business Research*, 29, 101-109.

Donovan, Robert J. and John R. Rossiter (1982), "Store Atmosphere:An Environmental Psychology Approach," *Journal of Retailing*, 58(Spring), 34-57.

Donovan, Robert J., John R. Rossiter, Gilan Marcoolyn, and Andrew Nesdale (1995). "Store Atmosphere and Purchasing Behavior," working paper, University of Western Australia.

Eroglu, Sevgin, Pam Scholder Ellen, and Karen A. Machleit (1992), "Environmental Cues in Retailing: Suggestions For a Research Agenda," *Proceedings of the 1991 Symposium on Patronage Behavior and Retail Strategy: Cutting Edge II*, 51-60.

Glass, Arnold L. and Keith J. Holyoak (1986), *Cognition*, New York: Random House.

Hui, Michael K.M. and John E.G. Bateson (1990), "Testing a Theory of Crowding in the Service Environment," in *Advances in Consumer Research*, (eds.) M.E. Goldberg, G. Gorn, and R.W. Pollay, Vol. 17, Provo, UT: Association for Consumer Research, 866-873.

Kellaris, James J. and Robert J. Kent (1992a), "The Influence of Music on Consumers' Temporal Perceptions: Does Time Fly When You're Having Fun?," *Journal of Consumer Psychology*, 1, 365-376.

Kellaris, James J. and Robert J. Kent (1992b), "Consumers' Affective Responses to Music as a Function of Objective Stimulus Properties and Subjective Mediators," working paper, University of Cincinnati.

Markin, Rom J., Charles M. Lillis, and Chem L. Narayana (1976). "Social-Psychological Significance of Store Space," *Journal of Retailing*, 52(1), 43-54.

Mazursky, David and Jacob Jacoby (1986), "Exploring the Developmentof Store Images," *Journal of Retailing*, 62, 145-165.

Mehrabian, Albert (1976), *Public Places and Private Spaces*, New York, Basic Books.

Mehrabian, Albert and James A. Russell (1974), *An Approach to Environmental Psychology*, Cambridge, MA: M.I.T. Press.

Owens, Jan P. (1992), "Store Atmosphere: An Environmental Psychology Approach Revisited," *Proceedings of the 1991 Symposiumon Patronage Behavior and Retail Strategic Planning: Cutting Edge II*, 37-50.

Posner, Michael I., Mary Jo Nissen, and Raymond M. Klein (1976),"Visual Dominance: An Information Processing Account of Its Origins and Significance," *Psychological Review*, 83, 157-171.

Raju, P. S. (1980), "Optimum Stimulation Level: Its Relationship to Personality, Demographics, and Exploratory Behavior," *Journal of Consumer Research*, 7, 272-282.

Ward, James C., Mary Jo Bitner, and John Barnes (1992), "Measuring the Prototypicality and Meaning of Retail Environments," *Journal of Retailing*, 68, 194-220.

Wedin, Lage (1972), "A Multidimensional Study of Perceptual-Emotional Qualities in Music," *Scandinavian Journal of Psychology*, 13, 241-257.

Yalch, Richard and Eric Spangenberg (1990), "Effects of Store Music on Shopping Behavior," *The Journal of Services Marketing*, 4, 31-39.

Fauna, Foraging and Shopping Motives

Derek N. Hassay, University of Manitoba
Malcolm C. Smith, University of Manitoba

INTRODUCTION

In response to criticisms concerning the reliablity and validity of metaphors, projective techniques, and other indirect research methodologies Nash (1963) commented, "[metaphor] has a legitimate place in the development of theory, and undue caution may, in fact, hinder the free exploration of underdeveloped areas of knowledge" (p.336). Alternatively, Holbrook and Hirschman (1982) claimed that the "exploration of consumption as conscious experience must be rigorous and scientific, but the methodology should include introspective reports, rather than relying exclusively on overt behavioral measures" (p.132). Recognizing the potential value of indirect methodologies to marketing theory, a number of researchers have called for a revival of methodological development in this area (Bellenger, Bernhardt and Goldstucker 1976; Dichter 1986; Levy 1985; Zikmund 1982). However, it has been suggested that these methodologies must first be demystified (Levy 1985) and subsequently updated to improve methodological validity and reliability (Bellenger et al. 1976).

This paper addresses both of these recommendations by developing a more theoretically grounded projective technique. In addition, the concurrent validity of this particular methodology will be tested by applying it to the study of shopping styles. The paper begins with overviews of projective techniques and metaphors in marketing. Next, the methodological underpinnings of the Apperceptive Analogue Test are presented followed by an application of this technique to the study of motivation-based shopping styles. Finally, implications for marketers and directions for future research are discussed.

PROJECTIVE TECHNIQUES IN MARKETING

In general, a projective test refers to any indirect methodology in which a subject is presented with an ambiguous stimulus and subsequently asked to "make sense of it" (Haire 1950). Projective techniques are most commonly classified into five categories according to the nature of the response task as follows: association, construction, completion, choice or ordering, and expression (Lindzey and Thorpe 1968). For example, the nature of the stimulus and the response are different for each of these projective instruments: Rohrschach inkblot test, Thematic Apperception Test (TAT), sentence completion and word association tests. However, these techniques are similarly capable of tapping (sub)unconscious aspects of behavior, and eliciting profuse and/or rich responses (Levy 1985, Rook 1988). For example, Rook (1988) suggested that projective methods enable respondents to fantasize and therefore "express both conscious and unconscious wishes and allow their psychological impulses fuller expression" (p. 251).

Dichter (1986) stated that, "marketers are frequently involved in appealing to real or desired self images" (p.160) and that the existence of these self images can be tested with projective tests. Furthermore, Rook (1987) claimed that projective techniques could be used where subjects are "either unable or unwilling to recall or sort out their feelings" (p.197). In addition, the ambiguous stimuli used in projective methods liberate subjects from the confines of bounded, rational, or cooperative responses (Day 1989) thus decreasing the potential for demand artifacts.

Despite the advantages associated with these techniques, they are not without their detractors. For example, Yoell (1974) criticized projectives sugggesting "that they are misunderstood, misapplied, pre-scientific, and the results are often misused" (in Bellenger et al. 1976, p. 38). In general, criticism of projective research has focused on the reliance on subjective interpretation of the projected response.

In marketing, these methods have been criticized because they do not offer managerial prescriptions. However, Haire's (1950) celebrated shopping list study used a projective instrument to uncover latent attitudes towards instant coffee that were found to be an impediment to purchase (i.e., an excuse). Haire (1950), found that the excuses provided valuable clues toward reducing buying resistance, and one need only look to the volume of instant coffee sales to refute the argument that projectives do not offer managerial prescriptions.

Levy (1985), indicated that the use of these techniques has declined since the 1950s and much of this research is of a proprietary nature and, consequently, little is known about the actual techniques used. It is not surprising then that discussions of projective methods in academic literature are predominantly descriptive, with overviews of various forms of projective tests commonplace (Bellenger et al. 1976; Day 1989; Levy 1985). It is believed that what is required is a more rigorous examination of projective techniques such as Rook's (1988) discussion of the TAT.

Similar to Rook (1988), this paper concentrates on one category of projective techniques known as construction techniques. Although cursory the following discussion provides a sufficient introduction to construction methods to provide the conceptual groundwork for subsequent development of the Apperceptive Analogue Test (AAT).

Construction Techniques

In an overview of construction techiques, Lindzey (1961) indicated that, as a group, these methodologies require the subject to "engage in complex, cognitive activities that go far beyond mere association" (p.67). The focus of such techniques is on the response generated by the subject rather than the behavior associated with its production. The most widely recognized construction instrument is the TAT (Murray 1943), which uses a series of picture cards to elicit stories from respondents. It has been suggested that the TAT is the most often used projective technique in market research (Bellenger et. al 1976). However, Rook (1988) cautioned that this assertion may be incorrect since little is known about the use of projectives in contemporary marketing research.

Lindzey (1961), suggested that construction techniques (e.g., the TAT) are most appropriately applied to content issues of personality, and that construction techniques evoke a profusion of responses sensitive to both (un)conscious factors and situational determinants (Lindzey 1961). As a result, construction techniques are especially useful when a holistic research approach is desired; when the relationship of attitudes, behavior and personality to an issue are examined simultaneously.

Despite the benefits associated with construction techniques, they have been criticized because they lack a consistent, objective method of scoring subject responses and are reliant upon the interpretive skills of the researcher. Consequently, their relibility and validity has been questioned along with other projective instruments (Kassarjian 1974). In response to these contentions, Levy (1985) stated:

...projectives make it possible for people to express themselves more fully, more subtly, perhaps even to represent

510
Advances in Consumer Research
Volume 23, © 1996

themselves more fairly. When that happens, the methods do achieve greater validity than methods whose reliability seems more comforting. (p.80)

METAPHORS IN MARKETING

Discovering the similitude between concrete objects and abstract marketing phenomena may partially solve many of the puzzles we have to solve. (Zikmund 1982, p.76)

In an overview of metaphoric thought in psychology, Nash (1963) suggested that metaphors serve various roles in science. First and foremost, metaphor is used to facilitate theory-related communication; by vivifying abstract concepts, metaphor makes theories more palatable and often more parsimonious. Metaphors have also been instrumental in the generation and elaboration of theories. Furthermore, Zikmund (1982) examined the use of metaphor in marketing theory and concluded that metaphors are a legitimate methodology for the development of theory.

Despite the contributions of metaphoric theory, it is widely criticized (Nash 1963; Zikmund 1982). First, metaphors are analogues for phenomena and, as such, are incapable of providing "perfect" explanations for these phenomena and, therefore, the reality of the phenomena being studied must not be lost to the fiction of the metaphor. Secondly, the metaphor must be bounded within a specific context. The architect of the metaphor must delineate those aspects of the phenomena being explained by the metaphor. This contextualization serves to shield the phenomena from over-application of the metaphor and in the process the dilution of its theoretical value.

Metaphors have been used in a variety of contexts in marketing. For example Hunt and Menon (1995) demonstrated the prevalence of warfare, game, organism and marriage metaphors in marketing strategy. In consumer behavior the use of animal metaphors are prolific in both academic literature and common speech. For example, recreational shopping has been characterized as a "hunt" driven by the pursuit of bargains (Bloch, Ridgway and Nelson 1991). Furthermore, Belk (1982) likened the collective behavior of humans to animals storing food for winter, while Rook (1987) described the buying impulse as "animal-like." Alternatively, consumers have been described as "empty-nesters" and their recent focus on home has been described as "burrowing" and "coccooning". The robustness of the animal metaphor is further illustrated by references to the shopping environment as a "zoo," "sea" or "jungle" and consumer behavior at a sale is often likened to a "stampede." A particularly rich application of the animal metaphor is found in Katovich and Diamond's (1986) account of the selling of time-share properties in which the clients are described as "lambs coming into the slaughter."

Research has also demonstrated that consumers use metaphors to animate their purchase behavior. For example, consumers have stated that products "jump out," "strike," "follow," "stare," and "hit" them (Rook 1987; Thompson, Locander, and Pollio 1990). Similarly, marketers use metaphors to create effective sales messages and as Boozer, Wyld and Grant (1991) stated, "listening carefully for evidence of these metaphors provides the basis for 'talking the customer's language" (p. 62). An especially graphic portrayal of the consumer animal is Samsonite's classic advertising campaign featuring a gorilla abusing pieces of their luggage.

Animal metaphors have also been used in marketing research in free association exercises to vivify inanimate objects such as products or companies (Bellenger et al. 1976; Day 1989; Dichter 1986; Levy 1985). The purpose of such exercises is to elicit more apperceptive insights into consumers attitudes towards a brand or organization.

THE APPERCEPTIVE ANALOGUE TEST

The current paper develops a projective-type methodology which has not been previously discussed in marketing literature relevant to projective techniques (e.g., Day 1989; Levy 1985; Rook 1988). In addition, this methodology does not appear to be subsumed by the five traditional classifications of projective techniques (association, construction, completion, choice or ordering, and expressive). This methodology is refered to hereafter as the Apperceptive Analogue Test (AAT), a label which is apropos given its methodological foundations.

In essence, the AAT is rooted in the two aforementioned research methodologies: construction-type projective techniques and metaphor. These two methodologies are similar in that they permit a more phenomenological or holistic interpretation of affect, cognitions, and behavior. The need for such methodologies is expounded by Holbrook and Hirschman (1982) who stated, "the conventional approach to consumer research addresses only a small fraction of the phenomenological data that compose the entire experience of consumption" (p.147). Furthermore, Holbrook and Hirschman proposed that methodological developments in consumer research should focus on the exploration of these phenomenological aspects of consumption.

Specifically, the AAT is a form of projective technique that utilizes a metaphoric projective stimulus. This apperceptive process requires subjects to explore elements of a latent phenomenon by projecting their feelings, emotions, attitudes and behaviors upon this stimulus. What differentiates the AAT from techniques such as free association, is the nature of the projective stimulus which is used to evoke the *apperceptive* response; it is rooted in a metaphor common to the phenomenon being examined. Therefore, both the product of the projective technique (as is the case with construction techniques) and the projective stimulus itself are important. In essence, the subject is being asked to vivify and validate/discredit a metaphoric theory in an indirect manner.

The metaphoric stimulus or *analogue* is an essential element of the AAT because metaphors often provide more parsimonious (not necessarily more accurate, reliable, or valid) descriptions of a given phenomenon. Consequently, it is believed that the analogue provides a more provocative and meaningful stimulus for the subject, thus facilitating the apperceptive process. Consequently, the AAT is appropriate to the holistic study of human behavior in general, and therefore is appropriate to the study of consumer behavior.

MOTIVATION-BASED SHOPPING STYLES: AN APPLICATION OF THE AAT

Most classification attempts are only ways of combating the fear of chaos. Once every respondent and consumer has been neatly pigeon-holed we feel safe. (Dichter 1986, p.162)

The test of any research instrument is its ability to provide either more insightful or more parsimonious explanation to a research question. Therefore, it was necessary to apply the AAT to a well-developed and still active area of research to examine its concurrent validity. Given the fact that projective techniques had there basis in motivation research (Levy 1985) it was decided to apply the AAT to an area of consumer behavior primarily concerned with motives: shopping styles.

It was also necessary to examine an area of research to which metaphoric theories had been applied or for which metaphors were available. Consequently, it was believed that the animal metaphor was sufficiently represented in consumer behavior to provide an appropriate stimulus for the current application. However, it should be noted that while the animal metaphor has been used previously in the study of consumer behavior, this study presents a novel application of the animal metaphor. Specifically, this study uses the animal analogue as the projective stimulus for the AAT in an examination of general shopping motives; whereby individuals liken their shopping behavior to that of animals. Boozer et al. (1991) distinguished metaphor from simile by stating that, "simile makes comparisons explicit by using the words *like* or *as* whereas with metaphor, the comparison is implicit" (p.61). However, as no evidence exists to suggest that individuals react differently to metaphor or simile no such distinction is made in this paper.

Consumer Shopping Typologies

Numerous consumer typologies have been published in marketing journals since Stone's (1954) demarcation of consumer types (for a review see Westbrook and Black 1985). The majority of these studies segment consumers according to lifestyles and, as such, are not specifically focused on shopping (Darden and Ashton 1974; Darden and Reynolds 1971; Moschis 1976). Furthermore, these studies suffer sample and product limitations which hamper generalizability. For example, only Belenger and Korgaonkar (1980) used a gender representative sample in the development of their typology.

With the exception of Tauber (1972), the preponderance of consumer typology studies have adopted a survey methodology with a factor/cluster analytic approach to categorize the consumer types. Yet, the internal consistency of the alpha coefficients reported in many of these studies is unacceptable based on the minimum value of .70 recommended by Nunnally (1978). Furthermore, Durvasula, Lysonski and Andrews (1993) cautioned that these direct research instruments are culturally-bound and require cross-cultural validation.

In his exploratory study, Tauber (1972) found that securing a purchase was not the only motive for shopping, and subsequently identified 11 shopping motives, many of which were not directly related to purchasing. Despite the importance of Tauber's study, its value has not been fully realized by subsequent consumer typology research as only Westbrook and Black (1985) and Sproles and Kendall (1986) have incorporated recreational-based motives for shopping in their typologies.

Researchers have recently begun to examine areas such as: hedonic consumption (Hirschman and Holbrook 1982; Langrehr 1991), shopping as recreation (Bellenger and Korgaonkar 1980; Bloch, Ridgway, and Nelson 1991) and browsing behavior (Bloch and Richins 1983; Jarboe and McDaniel 1987). Researchers have also begun to examine aspects of consumption that are distinct from buying such as possessing and collecting (Belk 1982).

Although, these studies have made significant inroads into specific aspects of the experiential aspects of consumption, they have been conducted in isolation and lack an integrative framework. Metaphorically, we have been unable to experience the forest for the trees. The AAT is believed to be an appropriate methodology for the examination of shopping motives because it offers insights into latent as well as manifest motives. Thus, the AAT should provide a more holistic description of shopping motives one that taps both the hedonic and utilitarian shopping motives. Finally, the AAT offers a more generalizable methodology because it can be easily translated and is not culturally-bound.

Sample

Participants in the study (n=76) were undergraduate business students in a mid-Western Canadian university. However, 11 responses were found to be incomplete and were excluded from subsequent analysis, leaving a sample of 32 males and 33 females. The sample ranged in age from 18-41 yrs, with a mean of 21.8 (s.d.=4.3).

Method

The AAT was self-administered and participants were provided with two pages to construct a written protocol in response to the following:

> We would like you to think of about an animal that best describes you as a consumer. For example, think of the one (1) animal that most closely resembles you (i.e, where, when, and why you shop, who you shop with, etc.) and then in the space provided explain what it is about your behavior that makes this animal an appropriate metaphor.

Results

The AAT was true to its projective foundations as demonstrated by the profusion (response length 17-396 words) and richness of the responses generated by the technique. The following is presented as illustrative of the type of response generated.

> The reason I chose a hawk is basically the speed and grace in which my shopping is done. I glide through the mall and when I see what I want I dive in and 'attack' it. To extend this metaphor the trip to the mall is short and to the point. Just as a hawk swoops down and kills its prey, I see the item and grab it. (M 20)

The first observation made by the authors was the diversity and often disparate behaviors elicited by the same animal stimulus. For example, cats were seen as friendly and easy-going by some and finicky, fussy and antisocial by others. This finding illustrates the degree to which the person's experience influences their stimulus selection, and to some extent revealed respondents knowledge about the animal kingdom. Consequently, no attempt was made to compare various species, or to group respondents according to the selected animal. Additionally, a few respondents failed to identify the particular animal stimulus and yet provided elaborate descriptions of their shopping behaviors, by avoiding species-level analyses these respondents were maintained.

The responses were content-analysed for emergent themes which provided dimensions for the subsequent development of a typology of shopping styles. Although numerous motives, attitudes, and life styles were evident in the responses, these were subsumed by two general themes: purchase timing (Postponed/Delayed Purchase - Immediate Purchase) and shopping impetus (Opportunity Recognition - Need Recognition). The purchase timing dimension emerged from responses relating to the desired/required outcome from the shopping trip. For example, some respondents indicated that they would purchase for immediate consumption regardless of need or product desireability. Alternatively, other respondents reported shopping for future consumption or indicated that they would delay purchase to wait for the "right" product.

The shopping impetus dimension more directly addresses the motivation for the respondents shopping behavior. For example, respondents variously indicated that they were motivated to go shopping because of situational factors such as sales, or more

FIGURE 1
Shopping Styles Typology

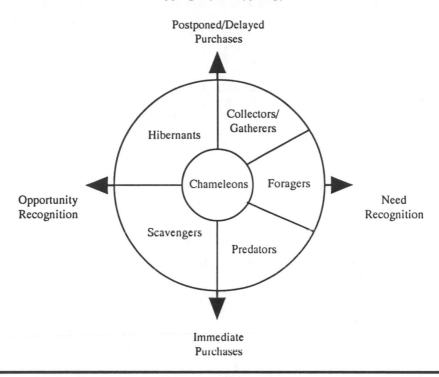

utilitarian motives such as product need. Interestingly, the anchors for this second dimension are similar to those identified by Bloch et al. (1991) as worthy of further study.

Next, these purchase timing and shopping impetus themes were used to categorize subjects into various shopping styles. Initially, the authors separated responses into the four cells of the matrix created by these two dimensions. However, it became apparent that such a categorization was too simplistic and failed to accurately reflect the typology of shopping styles described by the responses. Consequently, the authors were able to collaboratively identify two additional shopping styles. The six shopping styles which emerged and their relationship to the purchase timing and shopping impetus dimensions are illustrated in Figure 1. These six shopping styles are described in the following sections along with the distribution of respondents associated with each shopping style. The styles were labeled in a manner which remains true to the animal metaphor and is intuitively appealing, providing a richness of imagery and description which escapes previous typologies.

Chameleons [10.8%] explicitly indicated that their shopping styles were situation-specific (cougar F 39) or constantly changing (chameleon F 23). For example, one respondent indicated that they have many "moods and personalities" which impact their shopping style (cat F 21). These respondents also suggested that their shopping was dependent on product type (cat F 20), shopping impetus (human M 20), and purchase task (chameleon F 23) suggesting that their behaviors cross the four dimensions illustrated in Figure 1.

Collectors/Gatherers [9.2%] were characterized by their propensity to stock pile needed products (camels M 19, 23; F 21) and were motivated to purchase quantities which would alleviate the need for shopping. However, this stockpiling was apparently driven by two distinct motives: 1) to save money (chipmunk M 20; fox M 22) and 2) a general distaste for shopping (camel M 23). These shoppers also provided detailed accounts of the "sly" techniques they use to insure that they receive the best price such as taking advantage of retailer price guarantees (fox M 22). Finally, a number of these respondents indicated concerns with their susceptibility to marketing efforts. Thus, they may postpone shopping to avoid the sin of temptation.

Foragers [24.6%] are very "particular" (cheetah M 21; raccoon F 23) and pursue a desired product with relentless tenacity (tiger M 20; cat F 20). As Table 2 indicates the foragers bridge the purchase timing dimension as they will delay purchasing to find the "perfect" item. However, they are motivated by the need for a product and thus are motivated only to purchase that item (deer F 20). Due to their unwillingness to satisfice, these respondents also report that they are willing to search extensively and that they are not loyal to any particular retailer (horse F 22). Finally, the single-mindedness of these shoppers was further portrayed by their preference to shop alone (cat F 41).

Hibernants [9.2%] were characterized by their indifference towards shopping. They described themselves as "lazy" (lion, M 36), and "slow" (bear M 21; slug M 19) and were generally disinterested in shopping. However, these individuals indicated they were not frugal and could be quite "aggressive" (bear M 21) with respect to spending money. The hibernants spending patterns are opportunistic rather than need driven, as evidenced by their willingness to forego even required purchases. These shoppers stated that they postponed shopping for financial (squirrel F 20), mood (cat F 18) and fastidious (slug M 19) reasons.

Predators [24.6%] are almost primal in their need to consume. Their shopping is purposive and well-planned to achieve one goal - the attainment of a need satisfying item. Consequently, these respondents all but universally refer to the importance of "speed" in their shopping (cheetah M 19). Subjects explained that pre-shopping planning (snapping turtle M 21) and shopping alone (lioness F 20) facilitated quick hunting trips. These shoppers reported territorial behavior (wolf M 20) and frequent retail establishments where they are assured of success (swan F 28). These hasty trips were a response to a genuine distaste for shopping (Eagle M 19) and consequently some of these shoppers reported to be less discerning (wolf F 24).

Scavengers [21.5%] are motivated by the opportunity to shop rather than a particular product need. Scavengers indicate that they "love" shopping (cat F 22), enjoy "window shopping" (hamster F 19), and are often motivated to shop because of a sale (rabbit F 19). These respondents viewed shopping as a form of "entertainment" (kangaroo F 19), yet indicated a preference for shopping alone to avoid being hurried (panther F 25). The scavengers reported that their purchases were often "impulsive" (tiger F 22) as indicated by statements that they "pounce" (eagle F 19) upon any item that "catches their eye" (eagle M 24). This behavior is rooted in the belief that the item might be unavailable if the purchase is postponed (monkey F 19). Thus, scavengers are opportunists reporting that they are more concerned with an item's style or "uniqueness" (cat F 22) than its price (panther F 25).

DISCUSSION

The typology of consumer shopping styles generated with the AAT mirrors many of the styles identified by previous researchers, thus demonstrating its concurrent validity. For example, the scavengers are similar to Westbrook and Black's (1985) "shopping process-involved" or Sproles and Kendall's (1986) "recreational" consumers. However, the responses generated by the AAT provided insights into shopping behavior that were not addressed by previous research instruments. For example, the two dimensions of shopping motivation: shopping impetus and purchase timing identified were not incorporated in the seven dimensions of shopping motivation identified by Westbrook and Black (1985). However, the puchase timing dimension is particularly interesting in light of McDonald's (1994) research on consumer time perception segments. It is suggested that these two dimensions offer a more parsimonious view of shopping behavior and as such represent a significant contribution to theory development.

Although the generalizability of the shopping typology developed here is hampered by the student sample, it should be noted that this sample is gender representative unlike many of it predecessors. Furthermore, the AAT developed typology offers several advantages over previous typologies. First of all, the AAT is simple to administer and its methodology transcends culture, gender, and age-related boundaries thus facilitating cross-population shopping styles comparisons.

In addition, the shopping styles typology offers a number of managerial and research implications. First of all, marketers should consider the service and atmospheric needs of the various shopping styles and then determine which segments are most attractive to them. Additionally, researchers will find the typology presented here useful as a framework with which to study various elements of consumer behavior. For example, the responses generated by the AAT suggest that these shopping segments will differ in their patronage behaviors, use of retail services, and receptivity to marketing promotions. Future research could focus on testing these assumptions.

To test the generalizability of the typology the authors have begun a program of research using cross-population as well as cross-cultural samples with the AAT. In addition, the authors have begun research into the consistency of shopping styles across different product categories.

Projective techniques are characterized by the profusion and richness of responses they evoke, and the AAT was found to follow this tradition. In addition, the AAT was viewed positively by the respondents many of whom indicated that the exercise was "fun" and "thought-provoking." Lofland (1971), indicated that researchers can be reasonably confident of a constructed typology when respondents are able to recognize themselves in its dimensions. In this regard, our faith in the AAT was buoyed by comments such: "I never knew how well I could be compared to a cat when it comes to shopping" (F 22).

However, every precaution must be made to insure that the selected analogue stimulus does not contaminate or influence the content analysis or subsequent construction of the typology. As previously discussed, metaphors are intuitively appealing and as such can dominate the phenomena they are meant to describe. Consequently, researchers using the AAT must constantly remind themselves that the analogue stimulus is simply an instrument to evoke an apperceptive response and that it has no "life" of its own. To illustrate, identical animal analogues were categorized differently because the motives, attitudes, and/or behaviors elicited were distinct.

Due to its projective nature, the AAT is more likely to uncover subtle culture, gender, and age-related nuances in consumer behavior than more direct methods. The AAT is also flexible as illustrated by the fact that verbal, rather than, written protocols could be used where literacy is a concern. Finally, researchers should find the AAT a useful approach to the study of a variety of holistic/experiential phenomena in marketing, especially in marketing strategy which is ripe with metaphoric content. In this regard we defer to Levy (1985, p.81) who stated:

> Projectives do require the "nerve of interpretation," but the reliability will increase with our willingness to try, and to keep trying until we share the methods as familiar tools among the rest in our research quiver.

REFERENCES

Belk, Russell (1982), "Acquiring, Possessing, and Collecting: Fundamental Processes in Consumer Behaviour," in *Marketing Theory: Philosophy of Science Perspectives*, eds. Ronald F. Bush and Shelby D. Hunt, Chicago: American Marketing Association, 187-190.

Bellenger, Danny N., and Pradeep K. Korgaonkar (1980), "Profiling the Recreational Shopper," *Journal of Retailing*, 56 (3), 77-92.

_____, Kenneth L. Bernhardt, and Jac L. Goldstucker (1976), *Qualitative Research in Marketing*, Chicago: American Marketing Association.

Bloch, Peter H., Nancy M. Ridgway, and James E. Nelson (1991), "Leisure and the Shopping Mall," in *Advances in Consumer Research*, Vol. 18, eds. R. Holman and M. Solomon, Provo, UT: Association for Consumer Research, 445-452.

_____ and Marsh L. Richins (1983), "Shopping Without Purchase: An Investigation of Consumer Browsing Behavior," in *Advances in Consumer Research*, Vol. 10, ed. R. Bagozzi and A. Tybout, Ann Arbor, MI: Association for Consumer Research, 389-393.

Boozer, Robert W., David C. Wyld and James Grant (1991), "Using Metaphor to Create More Effective Sales Messages," *Journal of Consumer Marketing*, 8 (2), 59-67.

Darden, William R. and Dub Ashton (1974), "Psychographic Profiles of Patronage Reference Groups," *Journal of Retailing*, 50 (4), 99-112.

_____ and Fred D. Reynolds (1971), "Shopping Orientations and Product Usage Rates" *Journal of Marketing Research*, 8 (November), 505-508.

Day, Ellen (1989), "Share of Heart: What is it and How can it be Measured?" *Journal of Consumer Marketing*, 6 (1), 5-12.

Dichter, Ernest (1986), "Whose Lifestyle is it Anyway?" *Psychology and Marketing*, 3 (3), 151-163.

Durvasula, Srinivas, Steven Lysonski and J. Craig Andrews (1993), "Cross-Cultural Generalizability of a Scale for Profiling Consumers' Decision-Making Styles," *Journal of Consumer Affairs*, 27 (1), 55-65.

Haire, Mason (1950), "Projective Techniques in Marketing Research," *Journal of Marketing*, 14 (April), 649-656.

Hirschman, Elizabeth C., and Morris B. Holbrook (1982), "Hedonic Consumption: Emerging Concepts, Methods and Propositions," *Journal of Marketing*, 46 (Summer), 92-101.

Holbrook, Morris B., and Elizabeth C. Hirschman (1982), "The Experiential Aspects of Consumption: Consumer Fantasies, Feelings, and Fun," *Journal of Consumer Research*, 9 (September), 132-140.

Hunt, Shelby D. and Anil Menon (1995), "Metaphors and Competitive Advantage: Evaluating the Use of Metaphors in Theories of Competitive Strategy," *Journal of Business Research*, 33 (2), 81-90.

Jarboe, Glen R., and Carl D. McDaniel (1987), "A Profile of Browsers in Regional Shopping Malls," *Journal of the Academy of Marketing Science*, 15 (1), 46-53.

Kassarjian, Harold H. (1974), "Projective Methods," in *Handbook of Marketing Research*, ed. Robert Ferber, New York: McGraw-Hill Book Company, 3/85-3/100.

Katovich, Michael A. and Ron L. Diamond (1986), "Selling Time: Situated Transactions in a Noninstitutional Environment," *The Sociological Quarterly*, 27 (2), 253-271.

Langrehr, Frederick W. (1991), "Retail Shopping Mall Semiotics and Hedonic Consumption," in *Advances in Consumer Research*, Vol. 18, eds. R. Holman and M. Solomon, Provo, UT: Association for Consumer Research, 428-432.

Levy, Sidney J. (1985), "Dreams, Fairy Tales, Animals, and Cars," *Psychology and Marketing*, 2 (2), 67-81.

Lindzey, Gardner (1961), *Projective Techniques and Cross-Cultural Research*, New York: Appleton-Century-Crofts.

_____ and Joseph S. Thorpe (1968), "Projective Techniques," in *International Encyclopedia of the Social Sciences*, Vol. 13, ed. David Sills, New York: MacMillan and Free Press, 561-567.

Lofland, John (1971), *Analyzing Social Settings*. Belmont, CA: Wadsworth.

McDonald, William J. (1994), "Time use in Shopping: The Role of Personal Characteristics," *Journal of Retailing*, 70 (4), 345-365.

Moschis, George P. (1976), "Shopping Orientations and Consumer Uses of Information," *Journal of Retailing*, 52 (2), 61-70, 93.

Murray, H. A. (1943), *Thematic Apperception Test Manual*, Cambridge, MA: Harvard University Press.

Nash, Harvey (1963), "The Role of Metaphor in Psychological Theory," *Behavioral Science*, 8 (October), 336-3455.

Nunnally, Jum (1978), *Psychometric Theory*, New York: McGraw-Hill.

Rook, Dennis W. (1987), "The Buying Impulse," *Journal of Consumer Research*, 14 (September), 189-199. 3

_____ (1988), "Researching Consumer Fantasy," in *Research in Consumer Behavior*, Vol. 3, eds. Elizabeth Hirschman and Jagdish N. Sheth, Greenwich, CT: JAI Press Inc., 247-270.

Sproles, George B., and Elizabeth L. Kendall (1986), "A Methodology for Profiling Consumers' Decision-Making Styles," *Journal of Consumer Affairs*, 20 (2), 189-199.

Stone, Gregory P. (1954), "City Shoppers and Urban Identification: Observations on the Social Psychology of City Life," *American Journal of Sociology*, 60 (July), 36-45.

Tauber, Edward M. (1972), "Why Do People Shop," *Journal of Marketing*, 36 (October), 46-59.

Thompson, Craig J., William B. Locander, and Howard R. Pollio (1990), "The Lived Meaning of Free Choice: An Existential-Phnomenological Description of Everyday Consumer Experiences of Contemporary Married Women," *Journal of Consumer Research*, 17 (December), 346-361.

Westbrook, Robert A., and William C. Black (1985), "A Motivation-Based Shopper Typology," *Journal of Retailing*, 61 (1), 78-103.

Yoell, William A. (1974), "The Fallacy of Projective Techniques," *Journal of Advertising*, 3 (1), 33-36.

Zikmund, William G. (1982), "Metaphors as Methodology," in *Marketing Theory: Philosophy of Science Perspectives*, eds. Ronald F. Bush and Shelby D. Hunt, Chicago: American Marketing Association, 187-190.

AUTHOR INDEX